Lecture Notes in Computer Science 2706

Edited by G. Goos, J. Hartmanis, and J. van Leeuwen

Springer
Berlin
Heidelberg
New York
Hong Kong
London
Milan
Paris
Tokyo

Robert Nieuwenhuis (Ed.)

Rewriting Techniques and Applications

14th International Conference, RTA 2003
Valencia, Spain, June 9-11, 2003
Proceedings

Springer

Series Editors

Gerhard Goos, Karlsruhe University, Germany
Juris Hartmanis, Cornell University, NY, USA
Jan van Leeuwen, Utrecht University, The Netherlands

Volume Editor

Robert Nieuwenhuis
Technical University of Catalonia (UPC)
Dpt. Lenguajes y Sistemas Informáticos (LSI)
Jordi Girona 1, 08034 Barcelona, Spain
E-mail: roberto@lsi.upc.es

Cataloging-in-Publication Data applied for

A catalog record for this book is available from the Library of Congress.

Bibliographic information published by Die Deutsche Bibliothek
Die Deutsche Bibliothek lists this publication in the Deutsche Nationalbibliografie;
detailed bibliographic data is available in the Internet at <http://dnb.ddb.de>.

CR Subject Classification (1998): F.4, F.3.2, D.3, I.2.2-3, I.1

ISSN 0302-9743
ISBN 3-540-40254-3 Springer-Verlag Berlin Heidelberg New York

Springer-Verlag Berlin Heidelberg New York
a member of BertelsmannSpringer Science+Business Media GmbH

http://www.springer.de

© Springer-Verlag Berlin Heidelberg 2003
Printed in Germany

Typesetting: Camera-ready by author, data conversion by Steingräber Satztechnik GmbH, Heidelberg
Printed on acid-free paper   SPIN: 10928714   06/3142   5 4 3 2 1 0

Preface

This volume contains the proceedings of the *14th International Conference on Rewriting Techniques and Applications* (RTA 2003). It was held June 9-11, 2003 in Valencia, Spain, as part of RDP, the *Federated Conference on Rewriting, Deduction and Programming*, together with the International Conference on Typed Lambda Calculi and Applications (TLCA 2003), the International Workshop on First-order Theorem Proving (FTP 2003), the annual meeting of the IFIP Working Group 1.6 on Term Rewriting, the International Workshop on Rule-Based Programming (RULE 2003), the International Workshop on Unification (UNIF 2003), the International Workshop on Functional and (Constraint) Logic Programming (WFLP 2003), the International Workshop on Reduction Strategies in Rewriting and Programming (WRS 2003), and the International Workshop on Termination (WST 2003).

RTA is the major forum for the presentation of research on all aspects of rewriting. Previous RTA conferences were held in Dijon (1985), Bordeaux (1987), Chapel Hill (1989), Como (1991), Montreal (1993), Kaiserslautern (1995), New Brunswick, NJ (1996), Sitges, Barcelona (1997), Tsukuba (1998), Trento (1999), Norwich (2000), Utrecht (2001), and Copenhagen (2002).

This year, there were 61 submissions of which 57 regular research papers and 4 system descriptions, with authors from institutions in France (19.6 authors of submitted papers, of which 11.3 were accepted), USA (6.5 of 9), UK (3.5 of 4.5), Japan (3 of 6), Germany (2.5 of 4), The Netherlands (2.2 of 5.2), Spain (1.5 of 4), Austria (1 of 1), Israel (0.5 of 2.5), Portugal (0 of 1), Algeria (0 of 1), Denmark (0 of 1), Canada (0 of 1), Brazil (0 of 0.6), and Poland (0 of 0.5).

Each submission was assigned to at least four program committee members, who carefully reviewed the papers, in many cases with the help of one or more of a total number of 95 external referees. The merits of the submissions were discussed by the program committee during one week through the Internet by means of the *PC Expert* system. Finally, the program committee selected for publication 26 regular research papers and 6 system descriptions (where 3 of the latter ones had been submitted as regular research papers).

The program committee decided to award the 1000 Euro best paper prize as follows. One half was awarded to two research papers (250 Euro each): *On the Complexity of Higher-Order Matching in the Linear λ-Calculus*, by Sylvain Salvati and Philippe de Groote, and *XML Schema, Tree Logic and Sheaves Automata*, by Silvano Dal Zilio and Denis Lugiez. The other half, 500 Euro, was awarded to Nao Hirokawa and Aart Middeldorp, for their system description *Tsukuba Termination Tool*, a new automated termination prover for rewrite systems.

In addition, at RTA 2003 there were invited talks by David McAllester, *A Logical Algorithm for ML Type Inference* (a joint invited talk with TLCA), Pat

Lincoln, *Symbolic Systems Biology*, and Jean-Louis Giavitto, *Topological Collections, Transformations and their Application to the Modeling and the Simulation of Dynamical Systems*.

Many people helped to make RTA 2003 a success. I am of course grateful to the members of the program committee and to the external reviewers, as well as to the local organizers and the sponsors.

Special thanks go to Andrei Voronkov, who included into his *PC Expert* software (in real time) many new features which improved the quality of the reviewing process, like the extremely good interface for discussion, or the complete hiding of information to PC members with conflicts of interest; for me, it also eliminated most administrative work related to paper assignment, author notification, automated creation of lists of referees, etc.

Finally, I thank the organizers of all co-located events at RDP 2003, which made RTA 2003 even more interesting and attractive to a larger audience, and among them, of course, Salva Lucas: when I suggested hosting RTA in Valencia, his enthusiasm was such that he ended up organizing a major event like RDP.

April 2003   Robert Nieuwenhuis

Program Chair

Robert Nieuwenhuis   *Tech. Univ. Catalonia, Barcelona*

Organizing Chair

Salvador Lucas   *Tech. Univ. Valencia*

Program Committee

Harald Ganzinger	*Max-Planck-Institut*
Claude Kirchner	*Nancy*
Salvador Lucas	*Valencia*
Chris Lynch	*Clarkson*
José Meseguer	*Urbana*
Robert Nieuwenhuis	*Barcelona, Chair*
Tobias Nipkow	*Munich*
Vincent van Oostrom	*Utrecht*
Christine Paulin	*Paris-sud*
Frank Pfenning	*Carnegie Mellon*
Mario Rodríguez-Artalejo	*Madrid*
Sophie Tison	*Lille*
Ashish Tiwari	*SRI*
Andrei Voronkov	*Manchester*
Uwe Waldmann	*Max-Planck-Institut*
Hantao Zhang	*Iowa*

RTA Steering Committee

Leo Bachmair	*Stony Brook*
Hélène Kirchner	*Nancy*
Franz Baader	*Aachen*
Pierre Lescanne	*Lyon*
Aart Middeldorp	*Tsukuba, Chair*
Femke van Raamsdonk	*Amsterdam, Publicity Chair*

Sponsors

Departamento de Sistemas Informáticos y Computación,
Universidad Politécnica de Valencia
European Association for Theoretical Computer Science
European Association for Programming Languages and Systems
CologNET: A Network of Excellence in Computational Logic
Autonomous Government of Valencia (Generalitat Valenciana)
Spanish Ministry of Science and Technology

List of Referees

María Alpuente
Zena M. Ariola
Clara Bertolissi
Stefan Blom
Maria Paola Bonacina
Eduardo Bonelli
H. J. Sander Bruggink
Wilfried Buchholz
Anne-Cécile Caron
Horatiu Cirstea
Manuel Clavel
Mireille Clerbout
Evelyne Contejean
Judicael Courant
David Deharbe
Nachum Dershowitz
Philippe Devienne
Santiago Escobar
Maribel Fernandez
Jean-Christophe Filliatre
Olivier Fissore
Julien Forest
Anthony Fox
David de Frutos
Juergen Giesl
S.J.A. van Gisbergen
Isabelle Gnaedig
Bernhard Gramlich
Terese Hardin
Josś Hernández-Orallo
Thomas Hillenbrand
Ralf Hinze
Alexander Hulpke

Ullrich Hustadt
Jarkko Kari
Yevgeny Kazakov
Delia Kesner
Zurab Khasidashvili
Gerwin Klein
Konstantin Korovin
Orna Kupferman
Pierre Lescanne
Jordi Levy
Kai Lin
Sylvain Lippi
Luigi Liquori
Francisco López-Fraguas
Denis Lugiez
Patrick Maier
Claude Marché
Jerzy Marcinkowski
Narciso Marti-Oliet
Yuri Matiyasevich
Ralph Matthes
William McCune
Aart Middeldorp
Pierre-Etienne Moreau
Anders Møller
Manuel Núñez
Gopalan Nadathur
Huy Nguyen
Hitoshi Ohsaki
Javier Oliver
Fernando Orejas
Peter Ölveczky
Vincent Padovani

Miguel Palomino
Urso Pascal
Michel Petitot
Ricardo Peña
Femke van Raamsdonk
María José Ramírez
Pierre Rety
Alexandre Riazanov
Christophe Ringeissen
Yves Roos
Albert Rubio
Fernando Rubio
Harald Ruess
Isabelle Ryl
Christelle Scharff
Renate Schmidt
Manfred Schmidt-Schauss
Carsten Schuermann
Mark-Oliver Stehr
Gabriele Taentzer
Jean-Marc Talbot
Prasanna Thati
Cesare Tinelli
Marc Tommasi
Ralf Treinen
Xavier Urbain
Germán Vidal
Fer-Jan de Vries
Julie Vuotto
Benjamin Wack
Yevgeny Kazakov
Hans Zantema

Table of Contents

Symbolic Systems Biology

Patrick Lincoln

SRI International
Computer Science Laboratory

Technological breakthroughs have enabled complete genomic sequencing and proteomic study of many species, fueling exponential growth in the available biological data relevant to important biological functions. The computational analysis of these datasets has been hampered by many structural and scientific barriers. The application of symbolic toolsets borrowed from the term rewriting and formal methods communities may help accelerate biologists understanding of network effects in complex biochemical systems of interest.

Unlike traditional biology that has focussed on single genes or proteins in isolation, systems biology is concerned with the study of complex interactions of DNA, RNA, proteins, information pathways, to understand how they work together to achieve some effect. Most systems biology research has focussed on stochastic or differential equation models of biological systems, but lack of knowledge of crucial rate constants reduces the utility of these approaches.

Symbolic Systems Biology, the application of highly automated symbolic tools such as multiset rewriting engines, model checkers, decision procedures, and SAT solvers to systems biology, attempts to leverage what is already known about biochemical systems to accelerate biological understanding. We have developed a toolset called Pathway Logic based on Maude and other symbolic tools, and applied it to signaling and metabolic pathway analysis. Pathway Logic builds on efficient pathway interaction data curation, and enables animation of complex pathway interactions, and in-silico gene knockout experiments. We have also developed methods to automatically analyze "inherently continuous" or hybrid continuous- discrete systems, creating completely symbolic representations which enable extremely efficient analysis of certain types of questions. By constructing an algebra and logic of signaling pathways and creating biologically plausible abstractions, the goal of Symbolic Systems Biology is to provide the foundation for the application of high-powered tools which can facilitate human understanding of complex biological signaling networks, such as multi-cellular signaling, bacterial metabolism and spore formation, mammalian cell cycle control, and synthetic biological circuits.

These tools will be connected to publicly available datasources and toolsets including the BioSPICE platform (available through biospice.org) which provides an interoperable service architecture for integrating model builders, simulators, experimental data repositories, and various analyzers.

R. Nieuwenhuis (Ed.): RTA 2003, LNCS 2706, p. 1, 2003.
© Springer-Verlag Berlin Heidelberg 2003

Confluence as a Cut Elimination Property

Gilles Dowek

École polytechnique and INRIA
LIX, École polytechnique, 91128 Palaiseau Cedex, France.
Gilles.Dowek@polytechnique.fr
http://www.lix.polytechnique.fr/~dowek

Abstract. The goal of this note is to compare two notions, one coming from the theory of rewrite systems and the other from proof theory: confluence and cut elimination. We show that to each rewrite system on terms, we can associate a logical system: *asymmetric deduction modulo this rewrite system* and that the confluence property of the rewrite system is equivalent to the cut elimination property of the associated logical system. This equivalence, however, does not extend to rewrite systems directly rewriting atomic propositions.

The goal of this note is to compare two notions, one coming from the theory of rewrite systems and the other from proof theory: confluence and cut elimination.

The confluence a rewrite system permits to reduce the search space when we want to establish that two terms are convertible. Similarly, the cut elimination property of a logical system permits to reduce the search space, when we want to establish that some proposition is provable.

Moreover, both properties can be used to prove the decidability of convertibility or provability, when this reduction yields a finite search space. Finally, both properties can be used to prove independence results (i.e. that two terms are not convertible or that a proposition is not provable), and in particular consistency results, when this reduction yields an empty search space.

The goal of this note is to show that this similarity between confluence and cut elimination can be seen as a consequence of the fact that to each rewrite system $\mathcal{R}$ rewriting terms, we can associate a logical system: *asymmetric deduction modulo $\mathcal{R}$*, a variant of deduction modulo introduced in [5], and that the confluence property of the rewrite system is equivalent to the cut elimination property of the associated logical system. More precisely, we establish a parallel between

- an equality $t = u$ and a sequent $P(t) \vdash P(u)$,
- the notion of conversion sequence and that of proof,
- the notion of peak and that of cut, and
- the notion of valley sequence and that of cut free proof.

Both valley sequences and cut free proofs may be called *analytic* as they exploit the information present in their conclusion and its sub-parts but no other information.

R. Nieuwenhuis (Ed.): RTA 2003, LNCS 2706, pp. 2–13, 2003.

Finally, we relate a method used to prove cut elimination by defining an algorithm transforming proofs step by step until all cuts are removed (see, for instance, [8]) and a method used to prove confluence by defining an algorithm transforming rewrite sequences step by step until all peaks are removed (see, for instance, [2,9,1]). As an example, we reformulate Newman's confluence theorem [9] as a cut elimination theorem.

Asymmetric deduction modulo can be extended by allowing not only rules rewriting terms in propositions, but also directly atomic propositions. With such rules, confluence and cut elimination do not coincide anymore and confluence is not a sufficient analyticity condition: it must be replaced by cut elimination.

1   Asymmetric Deduction Modulo

In deduction modulo [5], the notions of language, term and proposition are that of first-order predicate logic. But a theory is formed with a set of axioms Γ *and a congruence* $\equiv$ defined on propositions. Deduction rules are modified to take this congruence into account. For instance, the right rule of conjunction is not stated as usual

$$\frac{\Gamma \vdash A, \Delta \quad \Gamma \vdash B, \Delta}{\Gamma \vdash A \wedge B, \Delta}$$

as the conclusion need not be exactly $A \wedge B$ but may be only convertible to this proposition, hence it is stated

$$\frac{\Gamma \vdash A, \Delta \quad \Gamma \vdash B, \Delta}{\Gamma \vdash C, \Delta} \text{ if } C \equiv A \wedge B$$

All rules of sequent calculus, or natural deduction, may be defined in a similar way.

In this note, we consider only congruences defined by a rewrite system on terms. A *rewrite rule* is a pair of terms $\langle l, r \rangle$, written $l \to r$, such that l is not a variable. A *rewrite system* is a set of rules. Given such a system, the relation $\to^1$ is the smallest relation defined on terms and on propositions compatible with the structure of terms and propositions such that for all substitutions θ and all rewrite rules $l \to r$ of the rewrite system $\theta l \to^1 \theta r$. The relation $\to^+$ is the transitive closure of $\to^1$, the relation $\to^*$ is its reflexive-transitive closure and the relation $\equiv$ its reflexive-symmetric-transitive closure. Notice that rewriting does not change the logical structure of a proposition, in particular an atomic proposition only rewrites to an atomic proposition.

A *conversion sequence* is a finite sequence of terms or propositions $C_1, ..., C_n$ such that for each i either $C_i \to^1 C_{i+1}$ or $C_i \leftarrow^1 C_{i+1}$. Obviously two terms or two propositions A and B are convertible if there is a conversion sequence whose first element is A and last element is B. A *peak* in such a sequence is an index i such that $C_{i-1} \leftarrow^1 C_i \to^1 C_{i+1}$. A sequence is called a *valley sequence* if it contains no peak, i.e. if it has the form $A \to^1 ... \to^1 \leftarrow^1 ... \leftarrow^1 B$.

For example, in arithmetic, we can define a congruence with the following rules

$$0 + y \to y$$

$$S(x) + y \to S(x + y)$$

$$0 \times y \to 0$$

$$S(x) \times y \to x \times y + y$$

In the theory formed with the axiom $\forall x \; x = x$ and this congruence, we can prove, in sequent calculus modulo, that the number 4 is even

$$\cfrac{\cfrac{\cfrac{}{4 = 4 \vdash 2 \times 2 = 4} \text{ Axiom}}{\forall x \; x = x \vdash 2 \times 2 = 4} (x, x = x, 4) \text{ } \forall\text{-left}}{\forall x \; x = x \vdash \exists x \; 2 \times x = 4} (x, 2 \times x = 4, 2) \text{ } \exists\text{-right}$$

The sequent $4 = 4 \vdash 2 \times 2 = 4$, that requires a tedious proof in usual formulations of arithmetic, can simply be proved with the axiom rule here, as $(4 = 4) \equiv (2 \times 2 = 4)$.

Deduction modulo a congruence defined by a rewrite system on terms uses this rewrite system only through the congruence it generates. The way these congruences are established is not taken into consideration. Thus, cut free proofs are analytic in the sense that they do not use the cut rule but not in the sense they establish congruences with valley sequences. Hence, we introduce a weaker system, *asymmetric deduction modulo*, where propositions can only be reduced. The rules of asymmetric sequent calculus modulo are given in figure 1.

2   Cut Elimination in Atomic Symmetric Deduction Modulo

We first consider a fragment of symmetric deduction modulo where all propositions are atomic. This system contains only the axiom rule, the cut rule and the structural rules (weakening and contraction).

To relate proofs in atomic deduction modulo and rewrite sequences, we prove that the sequent $P(t) \vdash P(u)$ is provable in atomic deduction modulo if and only if $t \equiv u$. This is a direct consequence of the following proposition.

Proposition 1. *In atomic deduction modulo, the sequent $\Gamma \vdash \Delta$ is provable if and only if Γ contains a proposition A and Δ a proposition B such that $A \equiv B$.*

Proof. If Γ contains a proposition A and Δ a proposition B such that $A \equiv B$, then the sequent $\Gamma \vdash \Delta$ can be proved with the axiom rule.

Conversely, we prove by induction over proof structure that if the sequent $\Gamma \vdash \Delta$ is provable, then Γ contains a proposition A and Δ a proposition B such that $A \equiv B$.

This is obvious if the last rule of the proof is the axiom rule. If the last rule is a structural rule, we simply apply the induction hypothesis. Finally, if the last rule is the cut rule, then the proof has the form

$$\cfrac{\cfrac{\pi_1}{\Gamma \vdash C_1, \Delta} \quad \cfrac{\pi_2}{\Gamma, C_2 \vdash \Delta}}{\Gamma \vdash \Delta} \text{ Cut}$$

$$\frac{}{\Gamma, A_1 \vdash A_2, \Delta} \; (A) \text{ Axiom if } A_1 \rightarrow^* A \leftarrow^* A_2$$

$$\frac{\Gamma \vdash C_1, \Delta \quad \Gamma, C_2 \vdash \Delta}{\Gamma \vdash \Delta} \; (C) \text{ Cut if } C_1 \leftarrow^* C \rightarrow^* C_2$$

$$\frac{\Gamma, A_1, A_2 \vdash \Delta}{\Gamma, A \vdash \Delta} \text{ contr-left if } A_1 \leftarrow^* A \rightarrow^* A_2$$

$$\frac{\Gamma \vdash A_1, A_2, \Delta}{\Gamma \vdash A, \Delta} \text{ contr-right if } A_1 \leftarrow^* A \rightarrow^* A_2$$

$$\frac{\Gamma \vdash \Delta}{\Gamma, A \vdash \Delta} \text{ weak-left}$$

$$\frac{\Gamma \vdash \Delta}{\Gamma \vdash A, \Delta} \text{ weak-right}$$

$$\frac{\Gamma \vdash A, \Delta \quad \Gamma, B \vdash \Delta}{\Gamma, C \vdash \Delta} \Rightarrow\text{-left if } C \rightarrow^* (A \Rightarrow B)$$

$$\frac{\Gamma, A \vdash B, \Delta}{\Gamma \vdash C, \Delta} \Rightarrow\text{-right if } C \rightarrow^* (A \Rightarrow B)$$

$$\frac{\Gamma, A, B \vdash \Delta}{\Gamma, C \vdash \Delta} \wedge\text{-left if } C \rightarrow^* (A \wedge B)$$

$$\frac{\Gamma \vdash A, \Delta \quad \Gamma \vdash B, \Delta}{\Gamma \vdash C, \Delta} \wedge\text{-right if } C \rightarrow^* (A \wedge B)$$

$$\frac{\Gamma, A \vdash \Delta \quad \Gamma, B \vdash \Delta}{\Gamma, C \vdash \Delta} \vee\text{-left if } C \rightarrow^* (A \vee B)$$

$$\frac{\Gamma \vdash A, B, \Delta}{\Gamma \vdash C, \Delta} \vee\text{-right if } C \rightarrow^* (A \vee B)$$

$$\frac{}{\Gamma, A \vdash \Delta} \perp\text{-left if } A \rightarrow^* \perp$$

$$\frac{\Gamma, [t/x]A \vdash \Delta}{\Gamma, B \vdash \Delta} \; (x, A, t) \; \forall\text{-left if } B \rightarrow^* \forall x \; A$$

$$\frac{\Gamma' \vdash A, \Delta}{\Gamma \vdash B, \Delta} \; (x, A) \; \forall\text{-right if } B \rightarrow^* \forall x \; A \text{ and } x \notin FV(\Gamma'\Delta)$$

$$\frac{\Gamma, A \vdash \Delta}{\Gamma, B \vdash \Delta} \; (x, A) \; \exists\text{-left if } B \rightarrow^* \exists x \; A \text{ and } x \notin FV(\Gamma\Delta)$$

$$\frac{\Gamma \vdash [t/x]A, \Delta}{\Gamma \vdash B, \Delta} \; (x, A, t) \; \exists\text{-right if } B \rightarrow^* \exists x \; A$$

Fig. 1. Asymmetric sequent calculus modulo

With $C_1 \equiv C_2$. By induction hypothesis

- Γ and Δ contain two convertible propositions or Γ contains a proposition convertible to C_1,
- Γ and Δ contain two convertible propositions or Δ contains a proposition convertible to C_2.

Thus, in all cases, Γ and Δ contain two convertible propositions.

The next proposition shows that atomic deduction modulo has the cut elimination property, i.e. that all provable sequents have a cut free proof. It is known, in general, that deduction modulo a congruence defined by a rewrite system on terms has the cut elimination property [6], but for the case of atomic deduction modulo, this is a direct consequence of proposition 1.

Proposition 2. *In atomic deduction modulo, all provable sequents have a cut free proof.*

Proof. If a sequent $\Gamma \vdash \Delta$ is provable then, by proposition 1, Γ and Δ contain two convertible propositions and thus the sequent $\Gamma \vdash \Delta$ can be proved with the axiom rule.

We can also define a proof reduction algorithm that reduces cuts step by step.

Definition 1 (Proof reduction).
Consider a proof of the form

$$\frac{\dfrac{\pi_1}{\Gamma \vdash C_1, \Delta} \qquad \dfrac{\pi_2}{\Gamma, C_2 \vdash \Delta}}{\Gamma \vdash \Delta} \; Cut$$

where π_1 and π_2 are cut free proofs.

The multisets Γ and C_1, Δ contain two convertible propositions. Similarly, Γ, C_2 and Δ contain two convertible propositions. Thus,

- *Γ and Δ contain two convertible propositions or Γ contains a proposition convertible to C_1,*
- *Γ and Δ contain two convertible propositions or Δ contains a proposition convertible to C_2.*

Thus, as $C_1 \equiv C_2$, Γ and Δ contain two convertible propositions in all cases and this proof reduces to

$$\frac{}{\Gamma \vdash \Delta} \; Axiom$$

When a proof contains a cut, the proofs of the premises of the highest cut are obviously cut free and this proof reduction algorithm applies. It terminates because it removes a cut at each step. Thus, it produces a cut free proof after a finite number of steps.

3   Cut Elimination in Atomic Asymmetric Deduction Modulo

Let us now turn to asymmetric deduction modulo, still in the atomic case. We prove that in asymmetric atomic deduction modulo, a sequent $P(t) \vdash P(u)$ is provable if and only if $t \equiv u$ and that this sequent has a cut free proof if and only if t and u have a common reduct. Thus, proofs in asymmetric deduction modulo correspond to rewrite sequences and cut free proofs to valley sequences.

Proposition 3. *In asymmetric atomic deduction modulo, the sequent $\Gamma \vdash \Delta$ is provable if and only if Γ contains a proposition A and Δ a proposition B such that $A \equiv B$.*

Proof. Obviously, if the sequent $\Gamma \vdash \Delta$ is provable in asymmetric deduction modulo, then it is provable in symmetric deduction modulo and Γ and Δ contain two convertible propositions.

The converse is slightly more difficult than in the symmetric case because the axiom rule does not apply directly. Assume there are propositions A in Γ and B in Δ such that $A \equiv B$. Then there is a rewrite sequence $A = C_1, ..., C_n = B$ joining A and B. We prove, by induction on the number of peaks in this sequence that the sequent $\Gamma \vdash \Delta$ is provable.

If the sequence contains no peak, then A and B have a common reduct and the sequent $\Gamma \vdash \Delta$ can be proved with the axiom rule. Otherwise, there is a peak i in this sequence. The sequences $C_1, ..., C_i$ and $C_i, ..., C_n$ contain fewer peaks than $C_1, ..., C_n$, thus, by induction hypothesis, the sequents $\Gamma \vdash C_i, \Delta$ and $\Gamma, C_i \vdash \Delta$ have proofs π_1 and π_2. We build the proof

$$\frac{\overset{\pi_1}{\Gamma \vdash C_i, \Delta} \quad \overset{\pi_2}{\Gamma, C_i \vdash \Delta}}{\Gamma \vdash \Delta} \; (C_i) \; \text{Cut}$$

Proposition 4. *In asymmetric deduction modulo, the sequent $\Gamma \vdash \Delta$ has a cut free proof if and only Γ contains a proposition A and Δ a proposition B such that A and B have a common reduct.*

Proof. If Γ contains a proposition A and Δ a proposition B such that A and B have a common reduct, then the sequent $\Gamma \vdash \Delta$ can be proved with the axiom rule. Conversely, if the sequent $\Gamma \vdash \Delta$ has a cut free proof, we prove, by induction over proof structure, that Γ contains a proposition A and Δ a proposition B such that A and B have a common reduct. This is obvious if the last rule is an axiom rule. If the last rule is a structural rule, we apply the induction hypothesis.

We can now state our main proposition that relates confluence and cut elimination.

Proposition 5 (Main proposition). *The cut rule is redundant in asymmetric atomic deduction modulo a rewrite system if and only if this rewrite system is confluent.*

Proof. Assume that the rewrite system is confluent. If the sequent $\Gamma \vdash \Delta$ is provable then, by proposition 3, Γ and Δ contain two convertible propositions. By confluence, they have a common reduct and thus, by proposition 4, the sequent $\Gamma \vdash \Delta$ has a cut free proof.

Conversely, assume that the cut rule is redundant. If $A \equiv B$ (resp. $t \equiv u$) then by proposition 3, the sequent $A \vdash B$ (resp. $P(t) \vdash P(u)$) is provable, thus it has a cut free proof and, by proposition 4, A and B (resp. t and u) have a common reduct.

4   Proof Reduction

Like in the symmetric case (definition 1) we want to design an algorithm reducing proofs and eliminating cuts step by step. In the asymmetric case however this algorithm is a little more involved as it needs to perform shorter steps to reconstruct reductions instead of conversions. This algorithm is a reformulation in sequent calculus of Newman's algorithm that reduces rewrite sequences eliminating peaks, step by step. To define it, we need to use the local confluence of the rewrite system and, to prove its termination, the termination of the system.

Definition 2 (Proof reduction). *Consider a proof of the form*

$$\cfrac{\cfrac{\pi_1}{\Gamma \vdash C_1, \Delta} \qquad \cfrac{\pi_2}{\Gamma, C_2 \vdash \Delta}}{\Gamma \vdash \Delta} \,(C)\ Cut$$

where π_1 and π_2 are cut free proofs.

As π_1 is cut free, Γ, C_1 and Δ contain two propositions that have a common reduct. Similarly, Γ and C_2, Δ contain two propositions that have a common reduct.

If Γ and Δ contain two propositions that have a common reduct C', then this proof reduces to

$$\cfrac{}{\Gamma \vdash \Delta}\,(C')\ Axiom$$

Otherwise, Γ contains a proposition A that has a common reduct B with C_1 and Δ contains a proposition E that has a common reduct D with C_2. Let us write $\Gamma = \Gamma', A$ and $\Delta = E, \Delta'$. We have

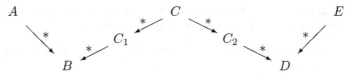

If $B = C$ or $C = D$ then either D or B is a common reduct of A and E and this proof reduces to

$$\cfrac{}{\Gamma \vdash \Delta}\,(D)\ Axiom$$

or to

$$\cfrac{}{\Gamma \vdash \Delta}\,(B)\ Axiom$$

Otherwise we have $B \leftarrow^+ C \rightarrow^+ D$ and there are propositions C_1' and C_2' such that

If there is a proposition C' such that $C'_1 \to^* C' \leftarrow^* C'_2$, then we have

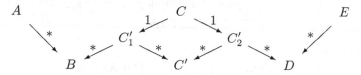

and this proof reduces to

$$\cfrac{\cfrac{\overline{\Gamma',A \vdash C'_1,C'_2,E,\Delta'}\ (B)\ Axiom \quad \overline{\Gamma',A,C'_1 \vdash C'_2,E,\Delta'}\ (C')\ Axiom}{\Gamma',A \vdash C'_2,E,\Delta'}\ (C'_1)\ Cut \quad \overline{\Gamma',A,C'_2 \vdash E,\Delta'}\ (D)\ Axiom}{\Gamma',A \vdash E,\Delta'}\ (C'_2)\ Cut$$

otherwise this proof cannot be reduced.

Example 1. This proof reduction algorithm may fail. Consider the rewrite system

$$a \to b \quad a \to b'$$

There is no way to reduce the proof

$$\cfrac{\overline{P(b) \vdash P(a), P(b')}\ (P(b))\ \text{Axiom} \quad \overline{P(b), P(a) \vdash P(b')}\ (P(b'))\ \text{Axiom}}{P(b) \vdash P(b')}\ (P(a))\ \text{Cut}$$

But this situation cannot occur if the rewrite system is locally confluent.

Proposition 6. *If the rewrite system is locally confluent, then the proof reduction algorithm of definition 2 does not fail.*

Proof. If $C'_1 \leftarrow^1 C \to^1 C'_2$ then, by local confluence, there is a proposition C' such that $C'_1 \to^* C' \leftarrow^* C'_2$.

Example 2. The proof reduction algorithm of definition 2 may loop. Consider the rewrite system

$$a \to b \quad a \to c \quad b \to a \quad b \to d$$

Let A be the proposition $P(a)$, B be the proposition $P(b)$, C be the proposition $P(c)$ and D be the proposition $P(d)$. We write D^n for the proposition D repeated n times. The proof

$$\cfrac{\overline{C \vdash A, D, D^n}\ (C)\ \text{Axiom} \quad \overline{C, A \vdash D, D^n}\ (D)\ \text{Axiom}}{C \vdash D, D^n}\ (A)\ \text{Cut}$$

reduces to

$$\cfrac{\cfrac{\overline{C \vdash C, B, D, D^n}\ (C)\ \text{Axiom} \quad \overline{C, C \vdash B, D, D^n}\ (C)\ \text{Axiom}}{C \vdash B, D, D^n}\ (C)\ \text{Cut} \quad \overline{C, B \vdash D, D^n}\ (D)\ \text{Axiom}}{C \vdash D, D^n}\ (B)\ \text{Cut}$$

that reduces to

$$\cfrac{\overline{C \vdash B, D, D^n}\ (C)\ \text{Axiom} \quad \overline{C, B \vdash D, D^n}\ (D)\ \text{Axiom}}{C \vdash D, D^n}\ (B)\ \text{Cut}$$

that reduces to

$$\cfrac{\cfrac{\overline{C \vdash A, D, D, D^n}\ (C)\ \text{Axiom} \quad \overline{C, A \vdash D, D, D^n}\ (D)\ \text{Axiom}}{C \vdash D, D, D^n}\ (A)\ \text{Cut} \quad \overline{C, D \vdash D, D^n}\ (D)\ \text{Axiom}}{C \vdash D, D^n}\ (D)\ \text{Cut}$$

that contains the initial proof (for $n + 1$) as a sub-proof. The proof reduction algorithm loops on this proof, replacing a cut on the proposition A by one on the proposition B and vice versa.

But this situation cannot occur if the rewrite system is terminating.

Proposition 7. *If the rewrite system is terminating then the proof reduction algorithm of definition 2 is terminating.*

Proof. As the rewrite system is terminating, its reduction ordering is well-founded and thus so is the multiset extension of this ordering.

At each step, the algorithm of definition 2 replaces a cut with the cut proposition C by two cuts with the cut propositions C_1' and C_2' where $C \rightarrow^1 C_1'$ and $C \rightarrow^1 C_2'$. Thus, the multiset of cut propositions in the proof decreases for the multiset extension of the reduction ordering of the rewrite system. Therefore, the proof reduction algorithm terminates.

Corollary 1. *If a rewrite system is locally confluent and terminating then the proof reduction algorithm of definition 2 always succeeds.*

Corollary 2. *If a rewrite system is locally confluent and terminating then asymmetric deduction modulo this rewrite system has the cut elimination property.*

Corollary 3 (Newman's theorem [9]). *If a rewrite system is locally confluent and terminating then it is confluent.*

Remark 1. We have seen that confluence is equivalent to cut elimination and that local confluence and termination imply normalization (i.e. termination of the proof reduction algorithm) and hence cut elimination. But notice that confluence alone does not imply normalization. Indeed, if we add to the rewrite system of example 2 the rules $c \rightarrow e$ and $d \rightarrow e$, we obtain confluence and thus cut elimination, but the counterexample to normalization still holds. We obtain this way an example of system that has the cut elimination property, but not the normalization property. Hence, in asymmetric deduction modulo, normalization is a stronger property than cut elimination.

In [9], Newman proves more than confluence (cut elimination) for terminating locally confluent rewrite systems, as he proves normalization, i.e. the termination of an algorithm that reduces peaks step by step in conversion sequences.

5   Cut Elimination in Full Asymmetric Deduction Modulo

We consider now full asymmetric deduction modulo, and we prove that cut elimination is still equivalent to the confluence of the rewrite system.

Proposition 8. *The cut rule is redundant in asymmetric deduction modulo a rewrite system if and only if this rewrite system is confluent.*

Proof. The fact that cut elimination implies confluence is easy as cut elimination implies cut elimination for the atomic case and hence confluence.

To prove that confluence implies cut elimination, we have to extend the proof of proposition 5 to the non atomic case.

Without loss of generality, we can restrict to proofs where the axiom rule is used on atomic propositions only.

We follow the cut elimination proof of [8]. When we have a proof containing a cut

$$\frac{\begin{array}{cc} \pi_1 & \pi_2 \\ \Gamma, C_1 \vdash \Delta & \Gamma \vdash C_2, \Delta \end{array}}{\Gamma \vdash \Delta} (C) \text{ Cut } C_1 \leftarrow^* C \rightarrow^* C_2$$

then we show that from π_1 and π_2, we can reconstruct a proof of $\Gamma \vdash \Delta$ introducing cuts on smaller propositions than C (i.e. propositions with fewer connectors and quantifiers).

More generally, we prove, by induction on the structure of π_1 and π_2, that from a proof π_1 of $\Gamma, \overline{C}_1 \vdash \Delta$ and π_2 of $\Gamma \vdash \overline{C}_2, \Delta$, where $\overline{C}_1$ and $\overline{C}_2$ are multisets of reducts of some proposition C, we can reconstruct a proof $\Gamma \vdash \Delta$. Notice that, as the rewrite system rewrites terms only, rewriting does not change the logical structure of a proposition (i.e. an atomic proposition only rewrites to an atomic proposition, a conjunction to a conjunction, ...)

There are several cases to consider.

- If the last rule of π_1 or the last rule of π_2 is a structural rule, then we apply the induction hypothesis.
- If the last rule of π_1 or the last rule of π_2 is a logical rule on a proposition in Γ or Δ, then we apply the induction hypothesis.
- If the last rule of π_1 or the last rule of π_2 is an axiom rule on propositions in Γ and Δ, then Γ and Δ contain two propositions that have a common reduct C and we take the proof

$$\frac{}{\Gamma \vdash \Delta} (C) \text{ Axiom}$$

- The key case in the proof of [8] is when both π_1 and π_2 end with a logical rule on a proposition in $\overline{C}_1$ and $\overline{C}_2$. For instance, if C has the form $A \wedge B$, $A_1 \wedge B_1 \leftarrow^* A \wedge B \rightarrow^* A_2 \wedge B_2$ and the proofs π_1 and π_2 have the form

$$\frac{\begin{array}{c} \rho_1 \\ \Gamma, A_1', B_1' \vdash \Delta \end{array}}{\Gamma, A_1 \wedge B_1 \vdash \Delta} \wedge\text{-left}$$

with $A_1 \wedge B_1 \rightarrow^* A_1' \wedge B_1'$ and

$$\frac{\rho_2 \qquad\qquad \rho_3}{\dfrac{\Gamma \vdash A_2', \Delta \qquad \Gamma \vdash B_2', \Delta}{\Gamma \vdash A_2 \wedge B_2, \Delta}} \wedge\text{-right}$$

with $A_2 \wedge B_2 \rightarrow^* A_2' \wedge B_2'$.

In this case, we have $A_1' \wedge B_1' \leftarrow^* A_1 \wedge B_1 \leftarrow^* A \wedge B \rightarrow^* A_2 \wedge B_2 \rightarrow^* A_2' \wedge B_2'$, thus $A_1' \leftarrow^* A \rightarrow^* A_2'$ and $B_1' \leftarrow^* B \rightarrow^* B_2'$ and we reconstruct the proof

$$\frac{\dfrac{\rho_1 \qquad\qquad \dfrac{\dfrac{\rho_2}{\Gamma \vdash A_2', \Delta}}{\Gamma, B_1' \vdash A_2', \Delta}\text{ weak-left}}{\dfrac{\Gamma, B_1', A_1' \vdash \Delta \qquad \Gamma, B_1' \vdash A_2', \Delta}{\Gamma, B_1' \vdash \Delta}(A)\text{ Cut}} \qquad \dfrac{\rho_3}{\Gamma \vdash B_2', \Delta}}{\Gamma \vdash \Delta}(B)\text{ Cut}$$

The case of the other connectors and quantifiers is similar.

- The new case in asymmetric deduction modulo is when the last rule of both proofs is an axiom rule involving a proposition in $\overline{C}_1$ and $\overline{C}_2$. Notice that the proposition C is atomic in this case, as we have restricted the Axiom rule to apply on atomic propositions only. Thus, Γ contains a proposition A that has a common reduct B with C_1 in $\overline{C}_1$ and Δ contains a proposition E that has a common reduct D with C_2 in $\overline{C}_2$. We have

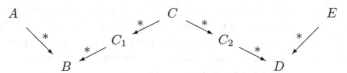

This is the case where we use confluence to obtain that A and E have a common reduct C' and we take the proof

$$\frac{}{\Gamma \vdash \Delta}(C')\text{ Axiom}$$

Remark 2. This proof suggests a cut elimination algorithm that integrates the cut elimination algorithm of sequent calculus and Newman's algorithm: it behaves like the latter for atomic cuts and like the former for non atomic ones. Again, we need the termination of the rewrite system to prove the termination of this cut elimination algorithm.

Remark 3. If we consider now rules directly rewriting atomic propositions to non atomic ones: for instance a rule like $A \rightarrow B \wedge \neg A$ then confluence [3,6], and even confluence and termination [7], do not imply cut elimination anymore. Some propositions have proofs using the cut rule but no cut free proof.

In this case, confluence is not a sufficient analyticity condition anymore. As a consequence, with term rewrite systems, confluence is a sufficient condition for the completeness of proof search methods, such as equational resolution (i.e. resolution where some equational axioms are dropped and unification is replaced by equational unification), but with proposition rewrite systems, confluence is not a sufficient condition for the completeness of resolution modulo and this condition must be replaced by cut elimination (see [4] for a discussion on this point).

Conclusion

When a congruence is defined by a term rewrite system, the confluence of this rewrite system and the cut elimination property for asymmetric deduction modulo this system coincide and analyticity can be defined either using one property of the other.

When the rewrite system is also terminating, then asymmetric deduction modulo not only verifies cut elimination, but also normalization.

But when a congruence is defined by rules directly rewriting atomic propositions, confluence is not a sufficient analyticity condition anymore and must be replaced by cut elimination.

Acknowledgments

I want to thank Thérèse Hardin, Claude Kirchner and Benjamin Werner for comments on a draft of this paper and for many discussions about deduction modulo, confluence, termination and cut elimination.

References

1. L. Bachmair and N. Dershowitz, Equational Inference, Canonical Proofs, and Proof Orderings. *Journal of the ACM* 41(2), 1994, pp. 236-276
2. A. Church and J.B. Rosser, Some properties of conversion. *Transactions of the American Mathematical Society*, 39, 1936, pp. 472-482.
3. M. Crabbé. Non-normalisation de ZF. *Manuscript*, 1974.
4. G. Dowek, Axioms vs. rewrite rules: from completeness to cut elimination. H. Kirchner and Ch. Ringeissen (Eds.) *Frontiers of Combining Systems*, Lecture Notes in Artificial Intelligence 1794, Springer-Verlag, 2000, pp. 62-72.
5. G. Dowek, Th. Hardin, and C. Kirchner. Theorem proving modulo. Rapport de Recherche 3400, Institut National de Recherche en Informatique et en Automatique, 1998. *Journal of Automated Reasoning* (to appear).
6. G. Dowek and B. Werner. Proof normalization modulo. In *Types for proofs and programs 98*, Lecture Notes in Computer Science 1657, Springer-Verlag, 1999, pp. 62-77.
7. G. Dowek and B. Werner. An inconsistent theory modulo defined by a confluent and terminating rewrite system. *Manuscript*, 2000.
8. J.-Y. Girard, Y. Lafont, and P. Taylor. *Proofs and Types*. Cambridge University Press, 1989.
9. M.H.A. Newman, On theories with a combinatorial definition of "equivalence". *Annals of Mathematics*, 43, 2, 1942, pp. 223-243.

Associative-Commutative Rewriting
on Large Terms

Steven Eker

Computer Science Laboratory, SRI International,
Menlo Park, CA 94025, USA
eker@csl.sri.com

Abstract. We introduce a novel representation for associative-commutative (AC) terms which, for certain important classes of rewrite rules, allows both the AC matching and the AC renormalization steps to be accomplished using time and space that is logarithmic in the size of the flattened AC argument lists involved. This novel representation can be cumbersome for other, more general algorithms and manipulations. Hence, we describe machine efficient techniques for converting to and from a more conventional representation together with a heuristic for deciding at runtime when to convert a term to the new representation. We sketch how our approach can be generalized to order-sorted AC rewriting and to other equational theories. We also present some experimental results using the Maude 2 interpreter.

1 Introduction

Rewriting modulo associative and commutative theories, otherwise known as AC rewriting, is a key operation in a number of languages [8,4,5,14] and theorem provers [12,21] employing term rewriting. In general, AC congruence classes are too large to be represented explicitly and so unique representatives, called *AC normal forms* or *AC canonical forms* are used. These are typically generated by replacing nested occurrences of the same AC operator by a *flattened* argument list under a variadic symbol, sorting these arguments under some linear ordering and combining equal arguments using multiplicity superscripts. For example the congruence class containing

$$f(f(\alpha, f(\beta, \alpha)), f(f(\gamma, \beta), \beta))$$

where f is an AC symbol and subterms α, β and γ belong to alien theories might represented by

$$f^*(\alpha^2, \beta^3, \gamma)$$

where f^* is a variadic symbol that replaces nested occurrences of f. A more formal account of this transformation is given in [9]. Of course the linear ordering on terms used to sort the argument list must be extended to these AC normal forms. The multiset ordering has pleasant theoretical properties and is often

R. Nieuwenhuis (Ed.): RTA 2003, LNCS 2706, pp. 14–29, 2003.
© Springer-Verlag Berlin Heidelberg 2003

used for this purpose, though as we will see later, it is seldom the best ordering for a practical implementation.

AC rewriting proceeds by using a special form of matching called *AC matching* on these AC normal forms (with some handling of extension, should an AC operator occur on top of the subterm being rewritten). Following the replacement step, the resulting term is generally not in AC normal form and must be renormalized before another AC rewrite step can be performed.

The problem of deciding whether an AC match exists is known to be NP-complete [3] and remains NP-complete even in the elementary case [11] where there is only a single AC operator with variables and constants. Nevertheless, instances that occur in practice tend not to be pathological and a variety of practical matching algorithms have been designed. There are really two cases that algorithms are designed for.

The first is the general case where arbitrary nonlinearity is allowed. This case tends to arise in theorem proving applications. Algorithms are generally search based, and use several techniques to collapse the search space, such as constraint propagation on nonlinear variables [15], recursive decomposition into subproblems via bipartite graphs [9], ordering matching subproblems based on constraint propagation considerations [10] and Diophantine techniques [11].

The second case is where there is little or no nonlinearity and the pattern falls into one of several forms for which efficient algorithms can be designed. This situation tends to arise when programming with AC rewrite rules. Examples are the depth-bounded patterns in the many-to-one matching algorithm used by ELAN [22,20] and the greedy matching techniques adopted in Maude. Here a full AC matching algorithm of the first kind is needed as a fallback for when the specialized approaches fail to apply.

In recent years these has been much progress in improving the performance of AC rewriting implementations as evidenced by the CafeOBJ/Brute [17], ELAN [4] and Maude [5] systems. Nevertheless, even in the best case, all published algorithms for AC matching (supposing a successful match) and AC renormalization require the examination of all of the arguments in the flattened AC argument lists involved. Thus processing the elements of a set or multiset using AC rewriting will require at least quadratic time as each rewrite step will need at least linear time. This fact is a major hurdle in achieving the goal stated in [20] of promoting AC rewriting to a general purpose programming construct.

In this paper we introduce a new representation for terms in AC normal form and identify a broad class of AC patterns for which a single matching substitution can be computed in time logarithmic in the size of the AC argument list. Furthermore we identify an important class of righthand side replacement terms for which the AC renormalization step can also be accomplished in time logarithmic in the size of the AC argument list. Thus with some care about reduction strategy and the maintenance of *reduced flags* there is a very useful class of AC rewrite rules that can be executed in logarithmic time. We also examine a number of refinements to improve the performance of the basic method and sketch how it can be generalized to handle order-sorted rewriting. We also sketch how our general approach can be adapted to other equational theories. Because our novel AC representation can be cumbersome for more general algorithms and manipulations we discuss machine efficient techniques for converting between representations. To demonstrate the practicality of our approach we give the results of some initial experiments performed using various versions of the Maude 2 interpreter.

1.1   A Motivating Example

Maps, or associative arrays as they are sometimes called in programming, are a very useful data structure that generalize arrays. Consider the Maude 2 specification of the map data type shown in Figure 1. A more elegant specification could be given using an order-sorted signature and an identity but for clarity of exposition we will confine our discussion to the most basic language features.

The data type `Map` is formed from three constructors, one of which is declared to be AC. There are two defined operations, one of which creates a new map by inserting a new domain-range pair into an existing map and the other which looks for a domain-range pair having a given domain value in an existing map and returns the range value or the constant `undefined` if no such pair exists. Note that the last defining equation for each of these operations has the `owise` attribute, indicating that the equation should only be used if no regular equation applies.

Consider the equations defining the insert operation. The first two are for the basis cases, contain only free function symbols and could reasonably be expected to execute in constant time on any modern implementation of term rewriting. The same cannot be said for the third equation. In the case that a match is found, the substitution for M will consist of all but one of the domain-range pairs underneath the variadic AC symbol. Using a traditional representation of AC argument lists, construction of this substitution will take linear time. A similar situation occurs with the second defining equation for the look-up operation. This contrasts with the $O(\log(n))$ time insert and look-up operations of the `map` class template in the C++ Standard Template Library or the `TreeMap` class in Java.

2   Basic Approach

We just consider the simple case of matching where we have a pattern term p containing variables and a subject term s which is ground. We wish to decide if there is a *matching substitution* σ such that $p\sigma = s$, and if there is, compute a single such σ. We do not consider the generation of multiple substitutions, as would be needed to handle conditional equations.

We make the assumption that the same pattern p will be used many times and so we allow arbitrary preprocessing and analysis to be done on p before using it for matching.

Matching is inherently recursive and is performed by recursive decomposition into matching subproblems between the subterms of p and the subterms of s.

```
fmod MAP is
  sorts Domain Range Map .
  op undefined : -> Range .
  op empty : -> Map .
  op _|->_ : Domain Range -> Map .
  op _,_ : Map Map -> Map [assoc comm] .
  var D : Domain . vars R R' : Range . var M : Map .

*** insertion
  op insert : Domain Range Map -> Map .
  eq insert(D, R, empty) = (D |-> R) .
  eq insert(D, R, D |-> R') = (D |-> R) .
  eq insert(D, R, (M, D |-> R')) = (M, D |-> R) .
  eq insert(D, R, M) = (M, D |-> R) [owise].

*** look-up
  op _[_] : Map Domain -> Range .
  eq (D |-> R)[D] = R .
  eq (M, D |-> R)[D] = R .
  eq M[D] = undefined [owise] .
endfm
```

Fig. 1. Maude 2 specification for the map data type.

Solving matching subproblems where the subterms are headed by the same free function symbol is straightforward. We focus on solving matching subproblems where the subterms are headed by the same AC function symbol f^*.

2.1 Returning "Undecided"

The idea is that our fast algorithm will solve the easy problem instances efficiently while leaving harder problem instances to a slower general purpose matching algorithm. Ideally we would be able to make the decision which algorithm to use before runtime, simply from an analysis of the pattern.

Unfortunately, if we adopt this approach, the class of patterns we can handle using the fast algorithm will be quite restricted. Our experience with the greedy matching algorithms used in the Maude 1 interpreter is that it is beneficial to handle a larger class of patterns with a fast algorithm, where the fast algorithm has the option of returning "undecided" if the matching problem turns out to be too hard (generally because of bindings to nonlinear variables that were unknown at analysis time) when the matching is attempted. When this happens, the time spent in the fast matching algorithm is wasted, and the slower general purpose algorithm must be run.

Of course we must be careful in selecting the class of patterns we will handle in the fast algorithm, to ensure that the "undecided" case is atypical, and that the time wasted in the fast algorithm when it does occur is small compared to the cost of running the slow algorithm.

2.2   Stripper-Collector Matching

We now describe our main algorithm, which we refer to as *stripper-collector matching*. Consider an AC matching subproblem

$$f^*(p_1^{k_1}, \ldots, p_n^{k_n}) \leq_{AC}^? f^*(s_1^{q_1}, \ldots, s_m^{q_m})$$

where subject subterms $s_1, \ldots, s_m$ are ground. Since this is a subproblem we assume that matching may have taken place above and that some set of variables B has already been bound, yielding a partial substitution ϕ. The goal of AC matching is to divide up the subject subterms s_j among the pattern subterms p_i and compute a substitution σ consistent with ϕ such that if p_i is assigned a single subject subterm s_j then $p_i\sigma = s_j$ and if p_i is assigned multiple subject subterms $s_{u_1}^{r_1}, \ldots, s_{u_k}^{r_k}$ then $p_i\sigma = f^*(s_{u_1}^{r_1}, \ldots, s_{u_k}^{r_k})$.

Our key idea is to represent the subject argument list $s_1^{q_1}, \ldots, s_m^{q_m}$ using an efficient set data structure. Then we restrict the subpatterns p_i that we will handle in such a way that we can compute a solution with $p_1, \ldots, p_{n-1}$ getting one subject each, while everything else is given to p_n. We refer to $p_1, \ldots, p_{n-1}$ as *strippers* since they have the effect of stripping single arguments from the argument list while we refer to p_n as the *collector* since is collects all the leftover arguments.

Finding the assignments for each of the strippers, $p_1, \ldots, p_{n-1}$, is done using $O(\log(m))$ time searches of the set data structure while the assignment to the collector, p_n is computed using $(n-1)$ $O(\log(m))$ deletes from the set data structure. It is important that we choose assignments to strippers in such a way that should we fail at some stripper we know that there is no match and we do not have to backtrack and consider different assignments for earlier strippers. This leads to further restrictions on the subterms allowed for strippers and the order in which they must be handled. Pattern subterms with $n > 2$ tend to be fairly rare in programming applications so the in the most common case we will have $n = 2$ and we will need to do a single search followed by a single delete operation to compute a matching substitution.

In practice, terms will be represented by directed acyclic graphs, otherwise rewrites with nonlinear righthand sides become unreasonably expensive since variable bindings would need to be copied rather than shared. Thus we cannot do destructive updates on our set data structures since in general they will be shared with other subterms. What we need in fact, is a data structure for *persistent dynamic sets*.

2.3   Persistent Dynamic Sets

Dynamic sets are usually implemented using one of several balanced binary tree data structures [2,1,24]. Insertion and deletion operations can be made persistent by not storing back pointers, allocating new nodes rather than modifying existing nodes and rebuilding the path from a modification back up to the root.

For simplicity we use red-black trees with the particularly elegant persistent insertion algorithm due to Okasaki [23]. Deletion is a rather intricate operation which closely follows the regular red-black tree deletion algorithm given in [7, Chapter 14]. One difference is that, because we are creating new nodes rather than manipulating existing nodes, it pays to combine multiple rotations and avoid creating nodes that are then immediately discarded by the next rotation. Expanding out the four rebalancing cases given in [7, Chapter 14] we arrive at six cases together with their left-right reflections.

2.4   Augmenting the Data Structure

We use the terms in the AC argument list as the keys in our red-black trees. In each node we also maintain the multiplicity of the argument, along with another data item called *maximum multiplicity*. For a given node N, this value is the maximum multiplicity of any node in the subtree rooted at N and can be computed incrementally in constant time. For a given multiplicity k, it allows us to decide in constant time whether a node with multiplicity greater or equal to k exists, and if it does, to locate such a node in logarithmic time.

Insertion and deletion operations take a term and a multiplicity. In the case of an insertion of a term that already exists, rather than do a red-black tree insertion, we create a new node with an increased multiplicity and rebuild the path to the root. In the case of a deletion which does not remove all the multiplicity of the victim, rather than do a red-black tree deletion, we create a new node with a decreased multiplicity and rebuild the path to the root. Thus we are really simulating a multiset.

2.5   Partial Comparison

The existing linear ordering on terms is fine for efficiently locating a given ground term in a red-black tree, and the maximum multiplicity field allows us to efficiently find a ground term with a multiplicity greater or equal to a given value. For efficiently locating potential matches for nonground terms we need another tool. For simplicity we assume that all symbols are either AC or free. A *partial comparison function pc* takes a partial substitution ϕ, a nonvariable, nonground term t and a ground term s and returns a result from the four element set $\{eq, lt, gt, \uparrow\}$ such that the following properties hold.

- $pc(\phi, t, s) = eq$ implies that for every substitution σ consistent with ϕ, $t\sigma = s$.
- $pc(\phi, t, s) = gt$ implies that for every substitution σ consistent with ϕ, $t\sigma > s$.
- $pc(\phi, t, s) = lt$ implies that for every substitution σ consistent with ϕ, $t\sigma < s$.

Note that a partial comparison function is allowed to return $\uparrow$ everywhere.

A partial comparison function pc is *reasonable* if whenever the top symbol of t differs from that of s, $pc(\phi, t, s)$ is either gt or lt. If t and s share the same free top symbol, and we use lexicographic ordering on arguments to linearly order terms with free symbols on top, we can do better. For example when ϕ contains assignments for variables $X_1, \ldots, X_n$, and g is a free function symbol $pc(\phi, g(X_1, \ldots, X_n), g(s_1, , \ldots, s_m))$ should never need to return $\uparrow$.

Let pc be a partial comparison function. Let t be a nonvariable, nonground term and let B be a set of variables. The pair (t, B) is said to be *pc-complete* iff for every partial substitution ϕ that defines exactly the variables in B and every ground term s, $pc(\phi, t, s) = \ \uparrow$ implies that there is a substitution σ compatible with ϕ such that $t\sigma = s$. For example if pc is reasonable, $t = f^*(X, Y)$ and $\{X, Y\} \cap B = \emptyset$ then the pair (t, B) is pc-complete since t will match any term with an f^* on top.

Constructing a good partial comparison function depends on the term ordering chosen. From now on we will assume the existence of a reasonable partial comparison function pc.

2.6   Allowable Subpatterns

We now consider what class of subpatterns can actually be handled in the manner described above. For the collector we require that it be a linear variable; i.e. it must have multiplicity 1 and may not occur elsewhere in the term. For a stripper, there are a number of possibilities.

ground subterm: Here we allow any multiplicity. Since a ground term must match an identical term in the argument list we can just search for that term in the red-black tree, and do a deletion operation. Of course if the term does not occur in the subject argument list with sufficient multiplicity we can return *failure*.

bound variable: Here we also allow any multiplicity. During the analysis phase, when we decide on the order for matching subterms, we will know for each matching subproblem what nonlinear variables will already be bound. If the variable is bound to a term headed by a symbol other than f^* we can treat it as a ground subterm. Otherwise we return "undecided".

nonvariable, nonground subterm: Here we limit multiplicity to 1. Any variables occurring in the nonground term p_i must either be bound or must not occur outside of p_i. Furthermore if there are multiple nonground strippers $p_{v_1}, \ldots, p_{v_k}$ they must have the property that for $c < d$, either p_{v_c} is not unifiable with p_{v_d} (no possible conflict over subject subterms) or p_{v_d} matches p_{v_c} (p_{v_d} is at least as general as p_{v_c}). This restriction ensures that an earlier stripper will not take a subject subterm needed by a later one. We can find a first candidate subject term for assignment to p_i by using our reasonable partial comparison function pc to find the leftmost subject term s_j such that $pc(\phi, p_i, s_j)$ is *eq* or $\uparrow$. If we want to ensure that p_i matches s_j we need also enforce the restriction that (p_i, B) is pc-complete. Since this is quite strict, a practical alternative is to just use s_j as a starting point for a match for p_i, and keep searching, left to right, until we get a match or we reach an s_k such that $pc(\phi, p_i, s_j) = lt$ in which case we can return fail. Of course once we start searching we require linear time in the worst case. Another alternative is to return "undecided" if p_i fails to match s_j. A stripper of this form must be handled after strippers of the first two forms to avoid "using up" a subterm needed by them.

high multiplicity unbound variable: We allow at most one of these and only if there are no nonvariable, nonground strippers. Also the variable must not occur anywhere else in the term (i.e. it is *almost linear* in the sense of [20]). We can find a subject subterm with adequate multiplicity to assign to it in $O(\log(m))$ time if such a subterm exists by following the maximum multiplicity fields in the red-black tree. A stripper of this form must be handled after strippers of the first two forms to avoid "using up" a subterm needed by them.

linear variable: Since linear variables can take anything we can just assign to them anything leftover after the other strippers have been dealt with. This form of stripper is alway handled last.

2.7   A Concrete Example

Consider the matching problem

$$h(f^*(g(D, R), M), D) \leq^?_{AC} h(f^*(g(1, 1), g(2, 4), \dots, g(100, 10000)), 42)$$

where h and g are free binary function symbols and D, R and M are variables. Matching the subterms under the free function symbol h results in a partial substitution ϕ such that $\phi(D) = 42$, and a matching subproblem

$$f^*(g(D, R), M) \leq^?_{AC} f^*(g(1, 1), g(2, 4), \dots, g(100, 10000)) \ .$$

Now assume we use lexicographic ordering on arguments to linearly order terms with free function symbols on top, and the usual ordering on integer constants. We can design a partial comparison function pc such that $pc(\phi, g(D, R), g(i, j))$ returns $\uparrow$ when $i = 42$ and either lt or gt otherwise. Furthermore, $(g(D, R), \{D\})$ will be pc-complete. Thus we can use pc to efficiently locate a subject subterm to match against $g(D, R)$ if one exists.

2.8   Comparison with Many-to-One AC Matching

There are similarities between the class of AC patterns we handle and those handled by the many-to-one AC matching used in ELAN [22,20]. There are two key differences however.

1. We have the restrictions on nonvariable, nonground terms and variables with high multiplicity in order to avoid the need for backtracking.
2. We handle nonlinear variables, as long as they have already been bound by the time the AC matching takes place.

One possible weakness of many-to-one AC matching with large AC terms can be illustrated by the following argument. Suppose we have k patterns each with n subterms under an AC symbol and we have a subject with m subterms under an AC symbol. We consider the worst case: there are no common subpatterns so the many-to-one AC matching algorithm must consider $k.n.m$ combinations of pattern and subject subterms; also, all but the last pattern fails to match so any sequential algorithm must attempt all k patterns. If the sequential algorithm can detect failure quickly for some of the failing patterns it can avoid considering many of the $k.n.m$ combinations of pattern and subject subterms. In the Maude 1 interpreter, some of the special case greedy AC matching algorithms can detect failure in $O(log(m))$ time via binary search even though computing a matching substitution takes linear time. This appears to be the main reason why the Maude 1 interpreter can hold its own against the ELAN compiler, at least for for unconditional AC rewriting [20]. Failing fast is important! The key advantage of our new algorithm over that used in Maude 1 is that not only can we often detect failure in $O(log(m))$ time, but also, in the success case, we can often compute a matching substitution in $O(log(m))$ time.

2.9   AC Renormalization

Following a successful match and replacement, we need to convert the resulting term back into AC normal form. We assume that subterms are already in AC normal form, either because of bottom-up renormalization or because they were assignments to variables. The case we can deal with efficiently is of the form

$$f^*(t_1^{k_1}, \ldots, t_n^{k_n})$$

where for some i, t_i is an AC normal form with top symbol f^*, $k_i = 1$ and for $j \neq i$, t_j has a top symbol different from f^*. In this case we can compute the AC normal form by doing $n - 1$ insertions into the argument list of t_i.

A useful heuristic for deciding when to convert to red-black tree representation in the first place is to set some threshold, T. When we arrive at a renormalization situation of the above form, but t_i currently has its argument list stored in a more conventional representation such as a vector or list, we convert the argument list to a red-black tree if the length of this vector or list exceeds T.

3   Refinements and Generalizations

We now sketch some refinements and generalizations of our basic approach.

3.1   Choice of Ordering on AC Normal Forms

Linear term orderings typically start with some ordering on function symbols and are then built up inductively. In the free theory, lexicographic ordering on arguments is often used. When we come to compare a pair of AC normal forms

$$\alpha = f^*(\alpha_1^{k_1}, \ldots, \alpha_n^{k_n}) \text{ and } \beta = f^*(\beta_1^{j_1}, \ldots, \beta_m^{j_m})$$

with the same top function symbol we need to choose some linear ordering on their argument lists. Although the choice of ordering will in general affect the order in which matching substitutions are found and can therefore affect the efficiency of reduction, it seems hard to predict what effect a given ordering will have on an arbitrary AC term rewriting system. Instead we seek a linear ordering that can be computed quickly in the average case. Typically multiplicity comparisons require several machine instructions while term comparisons involve a recursive call. Thus we would like to minimize the number of subterm comparisons when $\alpha \neq \beta$. One technique is to first compare n and m. If they are equal we then do lexicographic comparison on the sequences of multiplicities, $k_1, \ldots, k_n$ and $j_1, \ldots, j_m$. Only if these sequences are equal do we finally do a lexicographic comparison on the sequences of subterms themselves. One drawback of of this method is that it requires two passes over the argument lists and in the common case that all the multiplicities are 1 the first pass is a waste of time. An alternative in the case that $n = m$ is to do a single pass lexicographic comparison on the sequences $k_1, \alpha_1, \ldots, k_n, \alpha_n$ and $j_1, \beta_1, \ldots, j_m, \beta_m$ of interleaved multiplicities and subterms. This is the ordering adopted in Maude.

3.2   Order-Sorted Rewriting

Order-sorted rewriting is a convenient extension of many sorted rewriting [13]. It complicates our basic algorithm in two ways. Firstly we need to maintain a sort for each reduced subterm. Secondly matching can fail because of sort considerations. Let $s_{f^*} : Sort \times Sort \to Sort$ be the sort function for f^*; it is necessarily associative and commutative. We avoid linear time sort computations by maintaining a sort in each red-black tree node. By adding an artificial identity to s_{f^*} we can calculate the sort of $f^*(t^k)$ in $O(\log(k))$ time using the classical monoid powering by squaring algorithm. When matching fails because of sort considerations, we have to return "undecided"; we minimize the risk of this by always choosing the linear variable of largest sort as the collector.

3.3   Other Equational Theories

Our basic approach of treating AC-matching as one or more deletions and AC renormalization as one or more insertions in a suitable persistent data structure can be generalized to other equational theories. We briefly sketch a couple of important cases.

Suppose we add an identity to an AC function symbol to get an ACU function symbol (the U stands for *Unit*). ACU normalization is very similar to AC normalization except that we do not include identity elements; this means that before doing an insert operation into an ACU argument list we check if the element to be inserted is the identity and do not insert it in that case. ACU matching is complicated by the possibility of collapses that bring alien nonground arguments into their parents theory. But these situations are atypical and can be detected by pattern analysis, in which case a slow general purpose matching algorithm can be used. Collapses also complicate the definition of partial comparison. The other distinctive feature of ACU matching is that variables under an ACU symbol might be assigned the identity element; possibly causing the collapse in the ACU pattern itself. This is just another case to be checked for in the fast algorithm where the matching process would otherwise fail.

A more interesting situation arises when we remove the commutative axiom to get a purely associative function symbol. The case has practical importance because it corresponds to lists. We can get an associative normal form by flattening nested function symbol occurrences without sorting the arguments. A fast matching associative algorithm proceeds by stripping arguments from one or both ends of the subjects associative argument list. Until we encounter a variable subpattern, the correspondence between subpatterns and subject arguments is forced, and there is no restriction on nonvariable subpatterns in this case.

An appropriate data structure for representing associative argument lists is the *Persistent Catenable Deque* of Kaplan and Tarjan [19] or its amortized time simplification [18]. This remarkable if highly intricate data structure supports persistent insertions and deletions from both ends of list together with persistent concatenation, all in constant time. The constant time persistent concatenation, in particular, allows unrestricted associative renormalization, and also allows the construction (by self concatenation) of terms whose explicit representation would be exponential.

Using this data structure to represent associative normal forms, a broad class of associative rewrite rules could be executed in constant time; i.e. with the same complexity as syntactic rewriting.

4   Practical Considerations

We now discuss some of techniques needed for a machine efficient implementation of our approach.

4.1   Iterators

The first thing we need is an efficient way of making an in-order traversal of the argument list under an AC operator without the inconvenience of using recursion. Because of the need for persistence, the nodes in our red-black trees cannot hold back pointers to their parents. Thus we need to hold the path from the root to the current node on an explicit stack. The number of possible red-black tree nodes is bounded by the address space of the machine and the height of the largest red-black tree is bounded by twice the logarithm of this number. Thus we can use small fixed size stacks for iterators. By using fixed size C/C++ arrays to hold these stacks and machine pointers to the top elements, each of the usual stack operations can be implemented in a couple of machine instructions.

An iterator is initialized by stacking the path to the leftmost node in the red-black tree. To find the next node following an in-order traversal we consider two cases:

1. If our current node has a right child we stack this right child together with the path to it's leftmost descendant; otherwise,

$make\_tree(vec, first, size, is\_red)$
 if $size = 0$ **then**
  return nil
 else
  $left\_size := \lfloor size/2 \rfloor;$
  $right\_size := size - 1 - left\_size;$
  $left\_tree := make\_tree(vec, first, left\_size,$
           $left\_size > right\_size$ **and** $pow2min1(left\_size));$
  $right\_tree := make\_tree(vec, first + left\_size + 1, right\_size, \textbf{false});$
  return $new\_node(vec[first + left\_size], left\_tree, right\_tree, is\_red)$
 fi

Fig. 2. Algorithm for constructing a red-black tree from a vector.

2. we pop the stack until the top of the stack refers to a node whose right child is not the node we just popped; if we end up with an empty stack we have completed the traversal.

Thus our implementation becomes a pair of tight loops - one for descending leftmost paths and one for ascending rightmost paths.

For a number of applications, most notably converting a red-black tree to a sequence when we wish a more conventional term representation, it is not important to have the full path to the current node stored on the stack. In this situation we can optimize the traversal algorithm by unstacking the parent node when taking a right branch. Then in case 2 above, we need only pop a single element of the stack. This technique can be viewed as the explicit stack equivalent of the well known tail recursion elimination optimization.

4.2 Red-Black Tree Construction

In order to convert from a conventional term representation to our new representation we need an algorithm for constructing red-black trees from a given ordered sequence. A detailed analysis of this problem together with linear time solutions is given by Hinze [16]. However in the case that our sequence is actually stored as a vector we can use the simpler recursive algorithm shown in Figure 2. The idea is that, at each stage we chose the middle element, preferring the rightmost element in the case of a tie. We then create a node with this element and execute the algorithm recursively on the left and right subarrays to generate the left and right subtrees. It is easy to see that the resulting binary tree will be balanced; the subtle point is to generate node colors that preserve the red-black property. The idea is that if the left subtree is larger than the right subtree there will need to be red nodes in the left subtree to reduce the black height of at least some of its leaves. Furthermore, if the left subtree contains exactly $2^n - 1$ nodes for some n (tested for by the $pow2min1$ function) then we have a complete binary subtree and we can color its root red, reducing the black height of all of its leaves.

It may not be immediately obvious how to efficiently test if some positive integer k is of the form $2^n - 1$, but in fact the $pow2min1$ function can be implemented with 3 or 4 machine instructions using the following C/C++ bit twiddling trick: ((k + 1) & k) == 0. We have presented the red-black tree construction algorithm in recursive form for clarity of exposition but for a real implementation it can be made nonrecursive using an explicit fixed size stack.

4.3 Memory Usage

A vector based representation of AC arguments lists typically uses two machine words per argument, to hold a pointer to the argument and its multiplicity. A linked list representation requires one or two additional machine words per argument depending on whether it is singly or doubly linked.

Our persistent red-black tree representation requires four additional machine words per argument over the vector based representation, to hold the maximum multiplicity, the left and right subtree pointers, and the node color. In the order-sorted generalization, the sort information can share a machine word with the color flag. However unlike the vector and linked list approaches where only subterms are shared, with the red-black tree representation, large parts of the argument lists can be shared between different AC subterms. Depending on the term rewriting system, this can more than compensate for the increase in the per argument cost of storing the argument lists.

5 Experimental Results

To demonstrate the feasibility of our approach we added a red-black tree implementation of AC argument lists and the associated matching and renormalization algorithms to the Maude 2 interpreter [6]. The Maude 2 rewrite engine is otherwise an incremental improvement over that in Maude 1, which already has very competitive AC rewriting performance [20]. The highly modular design of the rewrite engine makes it ideal for this kind of experiment since all rewriting theories plug into an abstract theory interface which provides generic term manipulation primitives. It is therefore easy to support multiple term representations and matching algorithms for a given theory with no effect on the rest of the system.

Consider the following recursively defined function on the natural numbers:

$$f(0) = 0$$

$$f(n + 1) = f(\lfloor n/2 \rfloor) + f(\lfloor n/4 \rfloor)$$

This definition is somewhat reminiscent of the famous Fibonacci function. Indeed the only reason we do not use the Fibonacci function is that rapid growth in the size of the numbers involved obscures the performance of the non-numerical rewriting. In particular, we need two recursive calls and thus will end up using exponential time unless we use some kind of memoization or dynamic programming technique. While Maude has built-in support for memoization, we will keep an explicit memoization table using the map data type defined earlier in

```
fmod MAP-TEST is including MAP .   protecting NAT .
  subsort Nat < Domain Range .
  var N : Nat .  vars M M' : Map .
  op f : Nat Map -> Map .
  eq f(s N, M) = insert(s N,
                       ((f(N, M))[N quo 2]) + ((f(N, M))[N quo 4]),
                       f(N, M)) .
  eq f(0, M) = insert(0, 1, M) .
endfm


red f(100, empty)[50] .
red f(1000, empty)[500] .
red f(10000, empty)[5000] .
red f(100000, empty)[50000] .
red f(1000000, empty)[500000] .
```

Fig. 3. Benchmark problem for map specification.

Table 1. Performance in seconds, rewrites/second and megabytes used.

Size	Rewrites	Vector/legacy			Vector/SC			Red-black tree/SC		
		seconds	rw/sec	MBs	seconds	rw/sec	MBs	seconds	rw/sec	MBs
100	703	0.02	35150	5.2	0.01	70300	5.7	0.01	70300	5.7
1000	7003	0.71	9863	6.0	0.32	21884	6.6	0.11	63663	6.6
10000	70003	158.82	440	20	71.74	975	20	1.61	43480	19
100000	700003	17496.59	40	187	8766.46	79	187	20.73	33767	138
1000000	7000003	-	-	-	-	-	-	306.48	22839	1373

Figure 1, in order to test the speed of the AC rewriting. The Maude code is shown in Figure 3. The function computes a map rather than a single value, and in order to have a concise output, we simply evaluate it near the middle of the range. Note that the subexpression $f(N, M)$ occurs three times in the right hand side of the first equation, but it is only evaluated once because Maude combines common subexpressions.

The results for three versions of Maude 2 running on a 550MHz Ultra-SPARC IIi with 1.5GB of RAM are shown in Table 1. The first version (Vector/legacy) uses the matching algorithms and vector based AC argument list representation inherited from Maude 1, which includes a primitive version of the stripper-collector matching algorithm that does not use partial comparison. The second version (Vector/SC) uses the full stripper-collector matching algorithm presented here but retains the vector based AC argument list representation. The third version (Red-black tree/SC) uses the full red-black tree based stripper-collector matching and renormalization algorithms. The two vector based versions failed to terminate after a cpu-day while attempting the last reduction. Here the runtime grows slightly worse than quadratic while rewriting speed falls off slightly worse than linearly with the full stripper-collector version about twice as fast as the legacy version. With the red-black tree representation, the runtime growth is approximately $n \log(n)$ while rewriting speed falls off approximately logarithmically. All versions show a somewhat bigger than expected slowdown going from size 1000 to size 10000, probably due to L2 cache effects.

6   Concluding Remarks

Our method is somewhat intricate and much care is required in the implementation to avoid linear time algorithms for other parts of the execution process such as term traversal and sort computation. Nevertheless we have shown that our method can provide an approximately $n/\log(n)$ speed up over the already fast algorithms used in Maude 1 for large AC terms and simple AC rewrite rules. We plan to implement persistent data structure based rewriting algorithms for other equational theories in Maude 2 in the near future.

Acknowledgements

This work was partly funded by DARPA through Air Force Research Laboratory Contract F30602-02-C-0130. I thank Pat Lincoln, José Meseguer, Carolyn Talcott and the anonymous referees for their comments on earlier drafts.

References

1. G. M. Adel'son-Vel'skiĭ and E. M. Landis. An algorithm for the organization of information. *Soviet Mathematics Doklady*, 3:1259–1263, 1962.
2. R. Bayer. Symmetric binary B-trees: Data structure and maintenance algorithms. *Acta Informatica*, 1:290–306, 1972.
3. Dan Benanav, Deepak Kapur, and Paliath Narendran. Complexity of matching problems. *Journal of Symbolic Computation*, 3(1–2):203–216, February 1987.
4. Peter Borovanský, Claude Kirchner, Helèné Kirchner, and Pierre-Etienne Moreau. ELAN from a rewriting logic point of view. *Journal of Theoretical Computer Science*, 285(2):155–185, August 2002.
5. M. Clavel, F. Durán, S. Eker, P. Lincoln, N. Martí-Oliet, J. Meseguer, and J.F. Quesada. Maude: specification and programming in rewriting logic. *Journal of Theoretical Computer Science*, 285(2):187–243, August 2002.
6. M. Clavel, F. Durán, S. Eker, P. Lincoln, N. Martí-Oliet, J. Meseguer, and C. Talcott. The Maude 2.0 system. This volume.
7. Thomas H. Cormen, Charles E. Leierson, and Ronald L. Rivest. *Introduction to Algorithms*. MIT Press and McGraw-Hill, 1990.
8. Răzvan Diaconescu and Kokichi Futatsugi. Logical foundations of CafeOBJ. *Journal of Theoretical Computer Science*, 285(2):289–318, August 2002.
9. S. M. Eker. Associative-commutative matching via bipartite graph matching. *Computer Journal*, 38(5):381–399, 1995.
10. Steven Eker. Fast matching in combinations of regular equational theories. In J. Meseguer, editor, *Proceedings of the First International Workshop on Rewriting Logic and its Applications*, volume 4 of *Electronic Notes in Theoretical Computer Science*. Elsevier, 1996.

11. Steven Eker. Single elementary associative-commutative matching. *Journal of Automated Reasoning*, 28(1):35–51, January 2002.
12. S. J. Garland and J. V. Guttag. An overview of LP, the Larch Prover. In N. Dershowitz, editor, *Proceedings of 3rd International Conference on Rewriting Techniques and Applications (RTA '89)*, number 355 in Lecture Notes in Computer Science, pages 137–151. Springer-Verlag, April 1989.
13. J. Goguen and J. Meseguer. Order sorted algebra I: equational deduction for multiple inheritance, overloading, exceptions and partial operations. *Theoretical Computer Science*, 105(2):217–273, November 1992.
14. J. A. Goguen, T. Winkler, J. Meseguer, K. Futatsugi, and J.-P. Jouannaud. Introducing OBJ3. Technical Report SRI-CSL-92-03, Computer Science Laboratory, SRI International, March 1992.
15. Bernhard Gramlich and Jörg Denzinger. Efficient AC-matching using constraint propagation. Technical report, FB Informatik, Universität Kaiserslautern, Pf. 3049, D-6750, Kaiserslautern, Germany, 1988.
16. Ralf Hinze. Constructing red-black trees. In Chris Okasaki, editor, *Proceedings of the Workshop on Algorithmic Aspects of Advanced Programming Languages (WAAAPL '99)*, volume CUCS-023-99 of *Computer Science Technical Reports*, pages 89–99. Columbia University, September 1999.
17. M. Ishisone and T. Sawada. Brute: brute force rewriting engine. In *Proceedings of the CafeOBJ Symposium '98, Numazu, Japan*. CafeOBJ Project, April 1998.
18. Haim Kaplan, Chris Okasaki, and Robert E. Tarjan. Simple confluently persistent catenable lists. *SIAM Journal on Computing*, 30(3):965–977, 2000.
19. Haim Kaplan and Robert E. Tarjan. Persistent lists with catenation via recursive slowdown. In *Proceedings of the 27th Annual ACM Symposium on the Theory of Computing (STOC '95)*, pages 93–102. ACM Press, May 1995.
20. Helèné Kirchner and Pierre-Etienne Moreau. Promoting rewriting to a programming language: A compiler for non-deterministic rewrite programs in associative-commutative theories. *Journal of Functional Programming*, 11(2):207–251, March 2001.
21. William McCune. Solution of the Robbins problem. *Journal of Automated Reasoning*, 19(3):263–276, December 1997.
22. Pierre-Etienne Moreau and Helèné Kirchner. A compiler for rewrite programs in associative-commutative theories. In C. Palamidessi, H. Glaser, and K. Meinke, editors, *Principles of Declarative Programming (PLILP/ALP '98)*, number 1490 in Lecture Notes in Computer Science, pages 230–249. Springer-Verlag, September 1998.
23. Chris Okasaki. Functional pearl: Red-black trees in a functional setting. *Journal of Functional Programming*, 9(4):471–477, July 1999.
24. Salvador Roura. A new method for balancing binary search trees. In Fernando Orejas, Paul G. Spirakis, and Jan van Leeuwen, editors, *Proceedings of the 28th International Colloquium on Automata, Languages and Programming (ICALP 2001)*, number 2076 in Lecture Notes in Computer Science, pages 469–480. Springer-Verlag, July 2001.

A Rule-Based Approach for Automated
Generation of Kinetic Chemical Mechanisms

Olivier Bournez[1], Guy-Marie Côme[2], Valérie Conraud[2],
Hélène Kirchner[1], and Liliana Ibănescu[1] *

[1] LORIA & INRIA Lorraine
615, rue du Jardin Botanique, BP 101
F-54602 Villers-lès-Nancy Cedex, France
{Olivier.Bournez, Helene.Kirchner, Mariana-Liliana.Ibanescu}@loria.fr
[2] Département de Chimie Physique des Réactions (DCPR), INPL-ENSIC
1, rue Grandville, BP 451,
F-54001, Nancy, France
{Guy-Marie.Come, Valerie.Conraud}@ensic.inpl-nancy.fr

Abstract. Several software systems have been developed recently for
the automated generation of combustion reactions kinetic mechanisms
using different representations of species and reactions and different generation algorithms. In parallel, several software systems based on rewriting have been developed for the easy modeling and prototyping of systems using rules controlled by strategies. This paper presents our current
experience in using the rewrite system ELAN for the automated generation of the combustion reactions mechanisms previously implemented
in the EXGAS kinetic mechanism generator system. We emphasize the
benefits of using rewriting and rule-based programming controlled by
strategies for the generation of kinetic mechanisms.

1   Introduction

Combustion reactions are widely present in our everyday life, taking place in engines, burners and industrial chemical reactors, to produce mechanical or thermal
energy, and also to incinerate pollutants or to manufacture chemical substances.
The optimal design and operation of efficient, safe and clean chemical reactors,
engines, burners, incinerators is highly desirable.

The design of combustion processes has mainly been carried out by using
rather empirical models, while fundamental design, based on scientific principles, becomes more and more the main research goal (see e.g. [7,16]). However,
the generation of detailed fundamental kinetic mechanisms for the combustion
of a mixture of organic compounds in a large temperature field requires to consider several hundred chemical species and several thousands of elementary reactions [7]. An automated procedure is the only convenient and rigorous way to
write such large mechanisms.

---

* Work supported by Peugeot Citroén Automobiles.

R. Nieuwenhuis (Ed.): RTA 2003, LNCS 2706, pp. 30–45, 2003.
© Springer-Verlag Berlin Heidelberg 2003

A number of software systems have been developed for this purpose. A non exhaustive list of software systems for automatic generation of detailed kinetic combustion mechanisms is the following: MAMOX [19], NetGen [20], EXGAS [7,22], COMGEN [17]. These systems are[1] implemented using traditional imperative programming, using rather ad hoc data-structures and procedures for the representation and transformations of molecules (e.g. boolean adjacency matrices and matrices transformations). Flexibility is often absent or limited to menu systems, whereas the actual use of these systems, during validation of generated mechanisms by chemists, as well as during their final use for conception of industrial chemical processes, requires modifications, activations or deactivations of involved rules according to new experimental data, reactor conditions, or chemist expertise. Furthermore, existing systems, are limited, sometimes by their technology based on ad hoc structures, to acyclic species, or mono-cyclic species, whereas combustion mechanisms often involve aromatic species, i.e. polycyclic species.

We present in this paper an alternative approach based on rule-based programming and strategies. Rule-based systems have gained considerable interest with the development of efficient compilers. Now, systems like ASF+SDF [13], Maude [5,6], Cafe-OBJ [9], or ELAN [3,4] are used for various applications like constraint solving, protocol verification, modeling of biological systems, and more. This paper presents a system, named GasEl, based on ELAN system, that generates kinetic mechanisms of fuel combustion. This is one of the objectives of a research project that involves two teams from Nancy, France: one team of computer scientists from LORIA[2] and a team of chemists from DCPR[3] that developed the kinetic mechanism generator system EXGAS [7,22].

ELAN has some good properties for the generation of kinetic mechanisms: chemical reactions are naturally expressed using conditional rules, themselves easily understood by chemists; ELAN matching power allows for retrieving patterns in chemical species, thanks to the capability of handling multiset structures through the use of associative and commutative functions; ELAN provides a strategy language and strategy constructors to define control on rules, which appears as essential for designing generation mechanisms in a flexible way; thanks to its efficient compiler, ELAN can handle a large number of rules application (several thousands per second) and is thus well-suited to the computational complexity of the modeling.

Of course, some technical difficulties remain. One of them is that cyclic molecules are easily represented by graphs whereas ELAN can only do term rewriting. Another one is elimination of redundancies that requires intelligent search in huge data sets. The paper presents the solutions that we adopted.

The idea that rewriting techniques can be applied to chemistry is not new. Actually, even the chemical metaphor has been exploited to define computational

---

[1] as far as literature says

[2] LORIA is the Lorraine Laboratory for Research into Information Technology and its Applications

[3] DCPR is the Department of Physical Chemistry of Reactions

models [2]. Indeed, kinetic elementary mechanisms looks like graph rewriting rules. However, at least in this context, existing rewriting softwares are not used in practice for the automatic generation of kinetic combustion mechanisms. One reason is that pure graph rewriting is not sufficient: one needs for example to rewrite not only graphs, but associative commutative forests of graphs, with an explicit possibility of controlling rule applications, as their order is sometimes really important or dependent of external conditions such as temperature. Furthermore, the type of involved rules is particular, in the sense that chemical rules obey to external properties such as conservation laws. We hope this paper is providing some hints to help understand the kind of rewriting which is needed in this type of industrial applications.

The paper is organized as follows: in Section 2, we position the problem of generation of kinetic mechanisms in the whole context of its use by chemists and industrial partners, and we give a brief description of the chemical problem complexity. In Section 3 we give an example of what a detailed kinetic mechanism is for a specific molecule and we give the general procedure for its generation. Section 4 presents a description of the problems and the corresponding solutions we adopted in GasEl. Conclusions and discussions are presented in Section 5.

2   Chemical Problem Description

In this section we give a short presentation of the chemists' challenges in the generation of detailed kinetic mechanisms [7,16].

Mastering the combustion reactions necessitates the elaboration and the validation of a *reaction model*; the description of the whole process is given in Figure 1:

1. The *experimental sequence* produces the experimental results for a given molecule of hydrocarbon, and consists of two phases:
    (a) *experiments* done in laboratory reactors;
    (b) *acquisition and treatment of physical chemical data.*
2. The *modeling sequence* has as input a model of the same molecule of hydrocarbon and gives simulation results obtained after two steps:

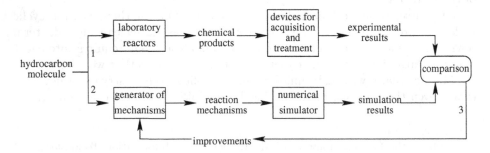

Fig. 1. Elaboration and validation process for a reaction mechanisms model

(a) *generation of reaction mechanisms* by a generator of mechanisms (e.g. EXGAS);

(b) *numerical simulation* by a numerical simulator (e.g. CHEMKIN II [12]).

3. The *analysis and adjustment process* consists of:

(a) *comparison* between the experimental results and the simulation results;

(b) *improvement of mechanisms generator* by introducing new generic reactions or/and fitting generic parameters.

Our system, GasEl, is intended to be a tool in the modeling sequence, a generator of detailed kinetic mechanisms for a specific area: the oxidation and combustion of fuels (e.g. Diesel fuels, petrols).

From a chemistry point of view, the complexity of the problem is induced by the composition of the following aspects:

- The *structural complexity* of hydrocarbon molecules, that can correspond to rather general graphs (planar graphs, trees and also 3D graphs) with many symmetries to be considered.
- The *complex composition of fuels or petrols*. For example, a fuel for a racing car is composed by a mixture of 98 different molecules, and the order of magnitude for the fuel of a normal petrol car is 300 different molecules, and for Diesel fuels is 3000 different molecules.
- The *combinatorial explosion* in the number of chemical species and elementary reactions modeling kinetic mechanisms. For example, 479,206 reactions and 19,052 species are considered in the simulation of tetradecane pyrolysis reported in [8], and there are 1,527 reactions and 404 species in the combustion reaction model generated with EXGAS for the n-heptane [10].
- The *duration of the validation process*. Usually, in 2–3 year, a chemical kinetic experimental PhD thesis validates experimental results for only a few molecules (1 to 2), in a couple of reactors. In the same amount of time, a PhD thesis related to modeling usually validates reaction mechanisms for only 2 or 3 molecules using and requiring several (5 to 10) previously validated experimental results for those molecules.
- The *complexity of numerical simulation*, based on partial derivative equations.
- The *multidisciplinary research* needed, including expertise from thermodynamics, quantum mechanics, transport phenomena, fluid mechanics, chemical reactors, numerical methods, experimental techniques, etc. See for example [7] for a presentation of the variety of mechanisms involved in the modeling of combustion of petrols.

3   Automated Generation of Mechanisms: Primary Mechanism

The purpose of an automated generator of detailed kinetic mechanisms is to take as input one or more hydrocarbon molecules and the reaction conditions and to

```
REACTION MECHANISMS FOR C C C C
Unimolecular Initiations
   C C C C -----> C e + C(e)C C
   C(C)C C -----> C(e)C + C(e)C
Bimolecular Initiations
   C C C C + O=O -----> C(e)(C C C) + O(e)O
   C(C)C C + O=O -----> C(e)C C + O(e)O
Oxidation reactions
   C(e)C + O=O -----> C=C + O(e)O
```

Fig. 2. Fragment of the GasEl output for n-butane: e denote a free electron and molecules with free electrons are free radicals

give as output the list of elementary reactions applied and the corresponding thermodynamic and kinetic data.

For example, for the combustion of the n-butane, C_4H_{10}, 778 reactions are generated by EXGAS, and 164 new species are obtained. A fragment of the GasEl corresponding output is given in Figure 2.

For every reaction, a module, not discussed in this paper, needs to calculate using specific rules associated kinetic parameters (usually encoded by 3 real numbers) and, for every species associated thermodynamic parameters (14 coefficients of some polynoms in EXGAS) [7].

The generated detailed kinetic mechanisms can be the result of several phases: the "primary mechanism" can be followed by the "secondary mechanism", usually based on lumping techniques not considered in this paper, to get even more complete descriptions of the involved mechanisms [7].

In the primary mechanism a set of ten reaction patterns should be applied to an initial mixture of molecules. A complete description of the involved reactions patterns is out of the scope of this paper, but the chemistry-like presentation from Figure 3 gives the flavor of the transformations needed to be encoded.

We mention that every reaction pattern is actually also guarded by "chemical filters", i.e. chemical conditions of applications, not mentioned here, even if several of them are currently implemented: they include considerations on the number of atoms in involved molecules or free radicals, the type of radicals or the type of bonds, etc. Some of them are discussed in [7].

From a computer science point of view, primary mechanism can be seen as the result of several phases (see Figure 4):

1. The initiation phase: *unimolecular* and *bimolecular initiation* reactions (reaction patterns 1 and 2 in Figure 3) are applied to initial reactants, i.e. to the initial mixture of molecules. Let RS_1 be the set of all free radicals that can be obtained.

2. The propagation phase: a set of generic patterns of reactions (reaction patterns 3–8 in Figure 3) are applied to all free radicals in RS_i to obtain a new set RS_{i+1} of free radicals. RS_{i+1} consists in all free radicals of RS_i plus those that can be obtained by these reactions.
   This is iterated until no new free radical is generated.

1	unimolecular initiation (ui)	A—B ⟶ •A + •B
2	bimolecular initiation (bi)	A=B + S—T ⟶ •A—B—T + •S
3	addition of free radicals to oxygen (ad)	O=O + •R ⟶ •O—O—R
4	isomerisation of free radicals (is)	•A—B—TH ⟶ AH—B—T•
5	unimolecular decomposition of free radicals by beta-scission (bs)	•A—B—T ⟶ A=B + •T
6	unimolecular decomposition of hydroperoxy-alkyl free radicals to cyclic ethers (cy)	•A—B—O—OH ⟶ A—B + •OH \ / O
7	oxidation of free radicals (ox)	O=O +•A—BH ⟶ A=B +•O—OH
8	metathesis (me)	•R + A—H ⟶ R—H + •A
9	combination of free radicals (co)	•R + •S ⟶ R—S
10	disproportionation of free radicals (di)	•A—B—T + •R ⟶ A=B + R—T

Fig. 3. Reaction patterns of primary mechanism given by emphasizing patterns like a simple (—) or double(=) bond, a free radical (•A), a specific atom (O, H). Symbols different from atom symbols (C, O, H) are variables and can be instantiated by any radical

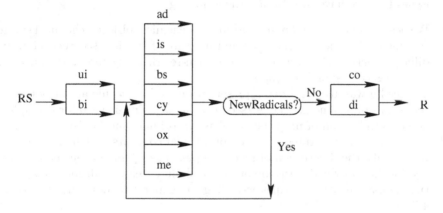

Fig. 4. The Primary Mechanism

3. The termination phase: *combination* and *disproportionation* reactions (reaction patterns 9 and 10 in Figure 3) are applied to free radicals of $\bigcup_i RS_i$ to get a set R of molecules.

4   GasEl — System Description

According to Tomlin et al. [21], a mechanism generation program should have the following features:

- generated chemical species should be stored in a form that can be easily manipulated and its notation must be unique and non-ambiguous (canonical);
- it should generate a given species of reaction only once;

— it should be able to filter out those reactions which are obviously unimportant.

The classical techniques which are known in literature to solve these issues and which are actually used in current existing softwares are the following: molecules are represented by graphs, mostly restricted to the acyclic case, or at least to the mono-cyclic case, and internally represented by their adjacency matrices, i.e. boolean square matrices. One system uses something different here: in EXGAS system, molecules are represented as tree-like structures, i.e special symmetry-factorized trees with maximal sharing, for which some theoretical canonical representation results have been established, but only for acyclic-species [22]. For adjacency matrices, procedures to detect equalities between different graph representations of a same molecule are based on Morgan algorithm [14], or extensions (see for e.g. [11,24]), sometimes using topological indices [18]. With respect to existing systems, the solutions implemented in GasEl are original in several aspects, described in this paper.

Taking advantage from the experience of the team that developed EXGAS, the issues that we have to solve are the following:

1. We need a good *internal representation* for chemical objects: chemical species (i.e. molecules and free radicals) and mixture of species (see Section 4.1): a difficulty here is that we are using a term-rewriting system and that cyclic molecules correspond to graphs.
2. We need a way to *test* if two representations of a molecule are or not representations of a same molecules (see Section 4.3). This is vital for example to detect termination of propagation phase in primary mechanism.
3. We need a way to express into computational concepts various *chemists expertise*, like the description of reactions pattern of primary mechanisms (see Section 4.4), or the description of chemical filters (e.g. conditions on application/non-applications of rules according to temperature domain) (see Section 4.7).
4. We need to allow *flexibility and ease of modification* of the rules that are used for the generation of mechanisms, according to chemist expertise or according to new experimental data (see Section 4.7).

The rest of this paper is devoted to describe how GasEl fulfills in a original way all these requirements.

4.1 Representation of Species

We need a way to represent molecules and free-radicals. We need a priori to fix an external representation for inputs/outputs of the system, as well as a representation for the internal computations. Unlike what is classically done in existing software systems [1], we propose to use the same notation for both.

As ELAN is a term rewriting system, we use the linear notation called SMILES presented in [23]. This notation is compact and well-suited because acyclic graphs are represented as trees. We briefly recall the principles of this representation:

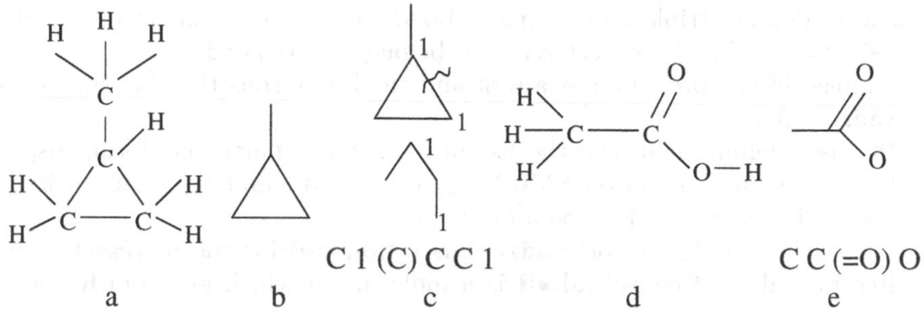

Fig. 5. Representations of molecules: a. molecular graph of methylcyclopropane; b. corresponding hydrogen-depleted molecular graph; c. corresponding SMILES notation; d. molecular graph of Acetic acid; e. corresponding hydrogen-depleted molecular graph and SMILES notation

1. Molecules are represented as hydrogen-suppressed molecular graphs.
2. If the hydrogen-suppressed molecular graph has cycles, we transform it into a tree applying the following rule to every cycle: choose one fresh digit and one single or aromatic bond of the cycle, break the bond and label the 2 atoms with the same digit.
3. Choose a root of the tree, and represent it like a concatenation of the root and the list of its sons.

For example, the term C 1 (C) C C 1 represents methylcyclopropane and the term C C (= O)O represents acetic acid: see Figure 5.

In Figure 6 we give the signature of our notation:

- atoms are represented by their atomic symbols;
- the sort symbol is extended to the concatenation of the sort symbol and int in order to code cycles;

```
C, c, O, o, H   : symbol;      /* Atom specification */
@ @     : (symbol int) symbol;/* Labels for cycle closure specification*/

 -, =, #, ':'    : bond;        /* Bond specification */

e          : radical;
@          : (symbol) radical;    /* Molecules and radicals specification */
@ @        : (symbol radical_list) radical;

@          : (radical) radical_list;    /* List of radicals specification */
@ @        : (bond radical) radical_list;
(@)        : (radical_list) radical_list;
(@) @      : (radical_list radical_list) radical_list (AC);
```

Fig. 6. GasEl signature of molecules and free radicals notation

- single, double, triple and aromatic bonds are represented by the symbols "-", "=", "#", ":", respectively and belong to sort **bond**;
- a molecule is represented as a root and the list of sons that belongs to sort **radical_list**;
- the user definition of the the list of sons has a particular form, inspired by the chemical notation SMILES (see e.g. [23]) and is defined using an associative-commutative operator;
- a special symbol **e** of sort **radical** is introduced for the representation of free radicals (a free radical •R is a molecule in which an atom has a free electron).

4.2   Representation of Mixtures of Species

We need a way to represent mixtures of molecules and free radicals. We propose to benefit here from the Associative Commutative matching possibilities of ELAN: in ELAN, a mixture has the sort **reactif** using the following signature

```
@        : (radical) reactif;
@ + @    : (reactif reactif) reactif (AC);
```

For example, C C C C + O=O + C C (= O)O is a term that represents a mixture of n-butane, oxygen and acetic acid.

4.3   Equality Test for Species

As pointed out by Tomlin et al. in [21], chemical species should be stored in a mechanism generation program in a canonical form: i.e. a unique and non-ambiguous form. Classical canonicity algorithms in this context are either based on transformations applied to the adjacency matrices of the molecule [11,14,24], or restricted to the acyclic case when considering other ad hoc data structures [22].

In our term-based representation, a molecule is a tree. Different choices of the root induce different trees representing the same molecule. We call these trees the *visions* of the molecule: see Figure 7.

Testing if two terms represent the same molecule is done in 2 steps:

1. An operator **AllVis** generates all the visions of a molecule by choosing every node of the tree representing the molecule to be the root.
2. Two terms M_1 and M_2 are equivalent if M_1 and M_2 have the same number of atoms and if M_1 is a vision of M_2:

$$\text{is\_eq}(M_1, M_2) \Rightarrow \text{true if } \text{no\_at}(M_1) = \text{no\_at}(M_2) \text{ and}$$
$$M_1 \in \text{AllVis}(M_2)$$

Our algorithm is exponential. However, recall that no polynomial algorithm is known for the graph isomorphism testing problem. The problem is proved to be **NP** but the question if it is complete or polynomial is a well known open problem [15].

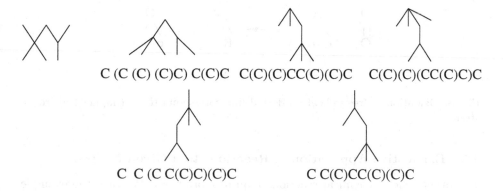

C (C (C) (C)C) C(C)C   C(C)(C)CC(C)(C)C   C(C)(C)(CC(C)C)C

C C (C C(C)C)(C)C   C C(C)CC(C)(C)C

Fig. 7. Visions of ISO-octane: all the distinct visions modulo commutativity

The current version is clearly not optimal. Improvements are currently investigated, in particular classical chemical techniques based on topological indices [18] can be considered.

4.4   Encoding Chemical Reactions

Generic elementary reactions are transformations applied to a mixture of molecules and free radicals.

We need to express the ten elementary reactions of Figure 3. *Addition of free radicals to oxygen, oxidation of free radicals, combination of free radicals and disproportionation of free radicals* are expressed directly as rewrite rules: the generic reaction, expressed as a graph transformation is encoded directly into a term rewrite rule.

For example, the generic reaction of oxidation of free radicals is the following:

$$O=O + \bullet A\text{---}BH \longrightarrow A=B + \bullet O\text{---}OH$$

This means, chemically-speaking, that a molecule of oxygen, O=O, abstracts an H atom in the β position with respect to the radical point, with the formation of the free radical $\bullet$O—OH and an unsaturated molecule (a molecule with a double bond).

This corresponds, in other words, to the graph transformation given in Figure 8 and is coded directly by the following ELAN rewrite rule:

```
[ox] O=O + A(e)(-B x) y => A (=B x) y + O(e)O
        if no_H(B x) >= 1
        end
```

where A and B are variables of sort **symbol**, x and y are variables of sort **radical_list** and the function **no_H(R)** returns the number of implicit hydrogen atoms in the root of R.

$$
\begin{array}{ccc}
\text{O} & \text{A} & \text{A} \quad\quad \text{O} \\
\| \;+\; /\backslash\backslash & \longrightarrow & /\!/\;\backslash \;+\; /\backslash \\
\text{O} \quad \text{e B} \quad \text{y} & & \text{B} \quad \text{y} \quad \text{e} \quad \text{O} \\
| & & | \\
\text{x} \quad \text{H} & & \text{x} \qquad\qquad \text{H}
\end{array}
$$

Fig. 8. Oxidation of free radicals: a dotted line correspond to an (implicit) hydrogen atom

4.5   Exhaustive Application of Reactions to a Given Molecule

The other generic chemical reactions require more work. We take the example of *unimolecular initiation*. An unimolecular initiation consists in breaking a single bond of a molecule and is represented, in the acyclic case, as the following reaction pattern:

$$A\!-\!B \longrightarrow \bullet A + \bullet B$$

Breaking a C—C bond which does not belong to a cycle corresponds to the graph transformation given in Figure 9.

$$
\begin{array}{ccc}
\text{X} & \text{X} & \\
/\backslash & \longrightarrow \quad /\backslash & + \text{ molec2rad(Rad)} \\
\text{Rad} \quad \text{x} & \text{e} \quad \text{x} &
\end{array}
$$

Fig. 9. Unimolecular initiation

Similarly to Section 4.4, we obtain the following ELAN rewrite rule:

```
[ui] X (Rad) x => X(e) x + molec2rad(Rad) end
```

where X is a variable of sort `symbol`, Rad is a variable of sort `radical` and x is a variable of sort `radical_list`. The operator `molec2rad( )` transforms its argument into a free radical and is defined by two ELAN rewrite rules:

```
[] molec2rad(X Rad)     => X (e) Rad   end
[] molec2rad(X (Rad) x) => X (e) (Rad) x   end
```

The power of the associative-commutative matching of ELAN allows us to give generic ELAN rewrite rule [ui] for the unimolecular initiation that will be applied to all sons of root X.

The previous rewrite rules have to be applied everywhere inside the terms and based on the semantics of the strategy language of ELAN, to apply a named rewriting rule (e.g. [ui]) to all sub-terms we adopted the following technique:

1. Apply the operator `AllVis` to the molecule X (Rad) x.
2. Apply the generic ELAN rewrite rules for unimolecular initiation to every vision of the molecule given by the `AllVis` operator.

For cyclic molecules, we have to simulate (a restricted type of) graph-rewriting using term-rewriting.

To deal with cyclic molecules in the *unimolecular initiation*, we need first to test if the bond to be broken is on a cycle or not; in the affirmative case one single free radical is generated by the fusion operator; if the bond to be broken is not on a cycle, the rewrite rule is similar to the acyclic case. Therefore, we need to add the following rule:

```
[ui_cycle] X (Rad) x =>  fusion(X(e) x, molec2rad(Rad))
        where labels_1 := () get_cycle_label (X x)
        where labels_2 := () get_cycle_label (Rad)
        if common(labels_1,labels_2)
        end
```

and to change previous rule [ui] in

```
[ui_CC] X (Rad) x => X(e) x +  molec2rad(Rad)
        where labels_1 := () get_cycle_label (X x)
        where labels_2 := () get_cycle_label (Rad)
        if not(common(labels_1,labels_2))
        end
```

4.6   Encoding the Primary Mechanism

Using the power of strategies of ELAN, the primary mechanism is defined in a natural way. This corresponds to the concatenation of three strategies corresponding to each phase, tryInit for the initiation phase, tryPropag for the propagation phase and tryTermin for the termination phase:

```
[] mec_prim     => tryInit; tryPropag; tryTermin end
```

The user defined strategies tryInit and tryTermin are easily expressed using the ELAN choice strategy operator **dk** applied to the strategies (the ELAN rewrite rule) defining the generic reactions. The **dk** operator (*dont know choose*) takes all strategies given as arguments and returns, for each of them the set of all its results.

```
[] tryInit      => dk(ui, bi) end
```

The output of the initiation phase applied to ISO-octane is illustrated in Figure 10.

Strategy tryPropag is defined as the iteration of one step of propagation using the ELAN strategy iterator **repeat***:

```
[] tryPropag => repeat*(propagOne) end
```

Strategy **repeat** iterates the strategy until it fails and returns the terms resulting from the last unfailing call of the strategy. Strategy propagOne is defined in a similar way as tryInit using a **dk** operator applied to the generic reactions of the propagation phase.

```
Unimolecular Initiations
  C C(C)C C(C)(C)C -----> C e + C(C)(C C(C)(C)C)e
  C C(C)(C)C C(C)C -----> C e + C(C)(C)(C C C(C)C)e
  C(C(C)C)C(C)(C)C -----> C(C(C)C)e + C(C)(C)(C)e
  C(C(C)C)C(C)(C)C -----> C(C(C)(C)C)e + C(C)(C)e
Bimolecular Initiations
  O=O + C(C)(C)C C(C)(C)C  -----> C(C)(C)(C C(C)(C)C)e + O(e)O
  O=O + C C(C)C C(C)(C)C  -----> C(C(C)C C(C)(C)C)e + O(e)O
  O=O + C C(C)(C)C C(C)C  -----> C(C(C)(C)C C(C)C)e + O(e)O
  O=O + C(C(C)C)C(C)(C)C  -----> C(C(C)C)(C(C)(C)C)e + O(e)O
```

Fig. 10. Initiation reactions of ISO-octane combustion

4.7 Flexibility and Control of Application of Elementary Reactions

The previous techniques allows a great flexibility through the power of matching and of the strategy language of ELAN: for examples

- Chemical filters, such as testing if a free radical is β, $\beta\mu$, μ, or Y is easily encoded by matching against corresponding patterns.
- Modifying the set of applied generic chemical reactions in primary mechanism correspond to a direct and natural modification of the corresponding strategy.
- Activating/Deactivating application of generic chemical reactions to cycles corresponds to a simple modification of strategy: replace for example dk(ui_cycle,ui_CC) by dk(ui_CC).

5 Conclusions and Discussions

In this paper, we describe our experience in building a system, named GasEl, based on system ELAN, for the automatic generation of chemical kinetic combustion mechanisms.

The main innovative feature of our system, compared to the existing ones(MAMOX [19], NetGen [20], EXGAS [7,22]), is that it can handle polycyclic molecules.

Compared to EXGAS, GasEl is much more flexible thanks to a modular design, to the rule-based formalism and to the ELAN strategies language.

The outcomes of the GasEl project, that involve chemists from the team that developed EXGAS system, and computer scientists from the team that developed ELAN, are twofold:

Chemists got a new system that extends the generation of combustion mechanisms to (poly)cyclic species. The fact that GasEl is now considered to be the successor of EXGAS shows that they understand the benefits from the presented approach. Further work is to provide them with a friendly interface, allowing to visualize cyclic molecules, to easily introduce new rules and design new strategies, or to connect this tools more directly with existing computer softwares, in order for example to get automatic association of thermodynamic and kinetic parameters to reactions and reactants.

Computer scientists got in modeling of the generation of detailed kinetic mechanisms a real challenge for testing the benefit from using rewriting and rule-based programming controlled by strategies. This experience teaches several things. First, that existing chemical software, at least in the context of automatic generation of chemical kinetic combustion mechanisms, do not use really rewriting techniques, but rather ad hoc structures and techniques. Second, that one reason that explains this fact is that the type of things involved is not pure term-rewriting, nor pure graph-rewriting, nor something directly already present in existing software: as the paper shows, we want "easily-controllable molecule transformations", with the always present needs of testing if a given generated molecule or radical is already obtained. As molecules can be cyclic, and hence correspond to rather general graphs, what we need corresponds to a kind of associative and commutative forest of graphs rewriting controlled by strategies. Since, no existing rewriting software is currently able to deal directly with this kind of features, and taking the advantage from our experience on the ELAN system, we actually developed the application using ELAN, i.e. associative and commutative term rewriting controlled by strategies.

Of course this approach has drawbacks: for e.g. the techniques that are used to emulate graph rewriting can clearly be improved in efficiency. However, as the discussion shows, when repositioning this system in chemist world (see for e.g. the number of processes that can be validated in a PhD) this computer-scientist efficiency issue may not be such an important drawback.

Moreover our approach revealed three further interesting points. First, the time for the development of the tool (two years now) can be compared to the time required for the development of similar features in EXGAS system, even if of course we are using their experience. Second, even if we can not rewrite graphs in ELAN , we have associative and commutative matching and strategies, and hence, we have almost all the required features. And third, and this is the main point, we believe this work has given hints about what is really required to address this type of industrial motivated applications.

Future work includes significant computer tests and chemists validation and, of course offering all the features of EXGAS system, providing a friendly interface, or connecting GasEl with other computer systems, but also to better understand this latter point. For example, this is clear that chemical rules always obey some conservation laws. Can we characterize abstractly chemical rules? Can we characterize the associated rewriting theory?

References

1. John M. Barnard. Structure representation. In Paul von Rague Schleyer, editor, *The Encyclopedia of Computational Chemistry*, pages 2818–2826. John Wiley & Son Ltd, 1998.
2. Gérard Berry and Gérard Boudol. The Chemical Abstract Machine. In *Proceedings of POPL'90*, pages 81–94. ACM, 1990. Also as research report INRIA 1133.

3. Peter Borovanský, Horaţiu Cîrstea, Hubert Dubois, Claude Kirchner, Hélène Kirchner, Pierre-Etienne Moreau, Quang-Huy Nguyen, Christophe Ringeissen, and Marian Vittek. ELAN *V 3.6 User Manual.* LORIA, Nancy (France), september 2002.

4. Peter Borovanský, Hélène Kirchner, Pierre-Etienne Moreau, and Christophe Ringeissen.   An overview of ELAN.   In Claude Kirchner and Hélène Kirchner, editors, *Second Workshop on Rewriting Logic and its Applications WRLA'98*, volume 15 of *Electronic Notes in Theoretical Computer Science*, Pont-à-Mousson (France), 2000. Elsevier Science Publishers.   URL: http://www.elsevier.nl/locate/entcs/volume15.html.

5. M. Clavel, F. Durán, S. Eker, P. Lincoln, N. Martì-Oliet, J. Meseguer, and J.F. Quesada. Towards Maude 2.0. In Kokichi Futatsugi, editor, *WRLA 2000, the 3rd International Workshop on Rewriting Logic and its Applications, September 2000, Kanazawa, Japon.* Electronic Notes in Theoretical Computer Science, 2000.

6. Manuel Clavel, Steven Eker, Patrick Lincoln, and José Meseguer. Principles of Maude. In José Meseguer, editor, *Proceedings of the first international workshop on rewriting logic*, volume 4, Asilomar (California), September 1996. Electronic Notes in Theoretical Computer Science.

7. Guy-Marie Côme. *Gas-Phase Thermal Reactions. Chemical Engineering Kinetics.* Kluwer Academic Publishers, 2001.

8. M.J. De Witt, D.J. Dooling, and Linda J. Broadbelt. Computer generation of reaction mechanisms using quantitative rate information: Application to long-chain hydrocarbon pyrolysis. *Ind. Eng. Chem. Res.*, 39(7):2228–2237, 2000.

9. K. Futatsugi and A. Nakagawa. An overview of CAFE specification environment – an algebraic approach for creating, verifying, and maintaining formal specifications over networks. In *Proceedings of the 1st IEEE Int. Conference on Formal Engineering Methods*, 1997.

10. Pierre-Alexandre Glaude.   *Construction automatique et validation de modèles cinétiques de combustion d'alcanes et d'éthers.* PhD thesis, Institut National Polytechnique de Lorraine - ENSIC - Nancy, France, 1999.

11. Ovidiu Ivanciuc. Canonical numbering and constitutional symmetry. In Paul von Rague Schleyer, editor, *The Encyclopedia of Computational Chemistry*, pages 167–182. John Wiley & Son Ltd, 1998.

12. R. J. Kee, F. M. Rupley, and J. A. Miller. CHEMKIN II. Technical Report SAND89-8009B, Sandia National Laboratories, Livermore, 1993.

13. Paul Klint. A meta-environment for generating programming environments. *ACM Transactions on Software Engineering and Methodology (TOSEM)*, 2(2):176–201, 1993.

14. H.L. Morgan. The generation of a unique machine description for chemical structures - a technique developed at Chemical Abstracts Service. *J. Chem. Doc.*, 5:107–113, 1965.

15. Christos H. Papadimitriou. *Computational Complexity.* Addison-Wesley, 1994.

16. M.J. Pilling, editor. *Low-temperature Combustion and Auto-ignition*, volume 35 of *Comprehensive Chemical Kinetics.* Elsevier, Amsterdam, 1997.

17. Artur Rakiewicz and Thanh N. Truong. Application of chemical graph theory for automated mechanism generation. *accepted for publication*, 2002.

18. Milan Randić. Topological indices. In Paul von Rague Schleyer, editor, *The Encyclopedia of Computational Chemistry*, pages 3018–3032. John Wiley & Son Ltd, 1998.

19. E. Ranzi, T. Faravelli, P. Gaffuri, and A. Sogaro. Low-temperature combustion: automatic generation of primary oxydation reaction and lumping procedures. *Combustion and Flame*, 102:179, 1995.

20. Roberta G. Susnow, Anthony M. Dean, William H. Green, P.Peczak, and Linda J. Broadbelt. Rate-based construction of kinetic models for complex systems. *The Journal of Physical Chemistry A*, 101:3731–3740, 1997.
21. Alison S. Tomlin, Tamás Turányi, and Michael J. Pilling. *Low-temperature Combustion and Autoignition*, volume 35 of *Comprehensive Chemical Kinetics*, chapter 4. Mathematical tools for the construction, investigation and reduction of combustion mechanisms, pages 293–437. Elsevier, Amsterdam, 1997.
22. Valérie Warth, Frédérique Battin-Leclerc, René Fournet, Pierre-Alexandre Glaude, Guy-Marie Côme, and Gérard Scacchi. Computer based generation of reaction mechanisms for gas-phase oxidation. *Computers and Chemistry*, 24:541–560, 2000.
23. David Weininger. SMILES, a chemical language and information system. 1. Introduction to methodology and encoding rules. *Journal of Chemical Information and Computer Science*, 28:31–36, 1988.
24. David Weininger, Arthur Weininger, and Joseph L. Weininger. SMILES. 2. Algorithm for generation of unique SMILES notation. *Journal of Chemical Information and Computer Science*, 29:97–101, 1989.

Efficient Reductions with Director Strings

François-Régis Sinot[1,2], Maribel Fernández[1], and Ian Mackie[1]

[1] Department of Computer Science, King's College London
Strand, London WC2R 2LS, UK
[2] LIX, École Polytechnique, 91128 Palaiseau, France
{francois,maribel,ian}@dcs.kcl.ac.uk

Abstract. We present a name free λ-calculus with explicit substitutions based on a generalized notion of director strings: we annotate a term with information about how each substitution should be propagated through the term. We first present a calculus where we can simulate arbitrary β-reduction steps, and then simplify the rules to model the evaluation of functional programs (reduction to weak head normal form). We also show that we can derive the closed reduction strategy (a weak strategy which, in contrast with standard weak strategies allows certain reductions to take place inside λ-abstractions thus offering more sharing). Our experimental results confirm that, for large combinator based terms, our weak evaluation strategies out-perform standard evaluators. Moreover, we derive two abstract machines for strong reduction which inherit the efficiency of the weak evaluators.

1 Introduction

Over the last few years a whole range of explicit substitution calculi have been proposed, starting from the $\lambda\sigma$-calculus [1]. Although there are many different applications of such calculi, one of the main advantages that we see in describing the substitution process at the same level of β-reduction is that it allows us to control the substitution process, with an emphasis on implementation.

In [7] we introduced a named calculus with explicit substitution, copy and erasing. This calculus implements a *closed reduction* strategy defined by a conditional set of rules and characterized by the fact that substitutions must be closed before they can be propagated. For this reason, although this calculus uses names, α-conversion is not needed. At the end of [7] we also hinted at an alternative presentation of the calculus using *director strings*, which on one hand internalizes the conditions on the reduction rules, and on the other hand offers a simpler, name-free syntax (this version of the calculus was presented in [8]). The purpose of this present paper is to explore the properties of the more general calculi that arise from the new syntax. These calculi then naturally give rise to abstract machines (strategies) suitable for reduction to weak head normal form. Furthermore, we resolve one of the open problems of [7], and derive, from a further generalization of director strings, ways to reduce to full normal form. We consider this important for several reasons:

R. Nieuwenhuis (Ed.): RTA 2003, LNCS 2706, pp. 46–60, 2003.

- Part of the culture of explicit substitutions is name free. Our syntax offers an alternative to de Bruijn indices [6], which has become the standard name-free syntax for such calculi.
- We provide a generalization of director strings, which were introduced in [11] for combinator reduction. In our generalized director strings, reduction under abstractions is allowed and we can simulate arbitrary β-reductions.
- Our notation is natural from an operational point of view in an explicit substitutions calculus: we annotate terms to indicate what they should do with a substitution. Closed reduction can then be seen as a natural restriction that leads to a simple rewrite system for weak reduction.

We thus see the calculi presented in this paper both as an alternative syntax for explicit substitutions and a basis for more efficient implementations of the λ-calculus.

Standard weak explicit substitution calculi avoid α-conversion by allowing neither reduction under abstraction nor propagation of substitution through an abstraction (see for instance [5]). In contrast, our calculi allow certain reductions under, and propagation of substitutions through, abstractions. In this way more reductions can be shared. Moreover we may use the explicit information given by directors to avoid copying a substitution which contains a free variable, avoiding the duplication of potential redexes.

We have implemented a family of abstract machines for weak and strong reduction based on the director strings calculi, and the benchmarks (given in Section 7) show that the level of sharing obtained is close to optimal reduction [12,9,3] with considerably less overheads. Immediate applications of this work include, on one hand λ-calculus/functional language evaluators (where weak reduction is needed), and on the other hand, partial evaluation (also called program specialization) and proof assistants based on powerful type theories (where strong reduction is needed).

Related work. Our work is clearly related to the general work on explicit substitution calculi (starting from the $\lambda\sigma$-calculus [1]). However, it is much more in line with the use of explicit substitutions for controlling the substitution process in implementations of the λ-calculus [2,15,10,13]. Director strings were used in [11] for combinatory reduction, and in [8] for closed reduction, which is the starting point for this present work.

Overview. The rest of this paper is structured as follows. In the following section we provide the background material, specifically we define the syntax of director strings. In Section 3 we present a general calculus where we can simulate arbitrary β-reduction steps. Section 4 presents the simplified local open calculus, and the closed reduction system. We then use these calculi to define several abstract machines: weak (Section 5) and strong ones (Section 6), which we experimentally compare (Section 7). Finally, we conclude the paper in Section 8.

2   Director Strings

We briefly recall the basic ideas of director strings, which were introduced in [11] for combinatory reduction. As an example, consider a term with two free variables f and x, and substitutions for both f and x : $((f(fx))[F/f])[X/x]$. The best way to perform these substitutions is to propagate them *only* to the place in the syntactic tree where they are required. Figure 1(a) shows the *paths* which the substitutions should follow in the tree.

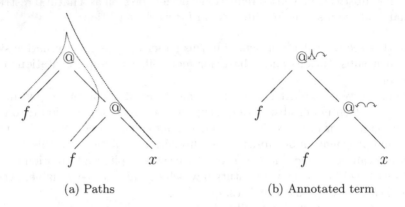

(a) Paths   (b) Annotated term

Fig. 1. Substitution paths and director strings

A natural way to guide the substitutions to their correct destination is given in Figure 1(b) by director strings, which annotate each node in the graph with information about where the substitution must go. When the substitution for f passes the root of this term, a copy of F is sent to both subterms, and the λ director is erased. The second substitution can then pass the root, where it is directed uniquely to the right branch by the director $\curvearrowright$. Note that substitutions are copied only when they need to be: if there is just one occurrence of a variable in a term, then no duplication is performed.

This simple idea works well when the substitution is closed (does not contain free variables). Otherwise, as each open substitution passes a given node we must add the additional directors for each free variable in the substitution.

Definition 1 (λ-calculus with director strings). *We define three syntactic categories:*

Directors: *We use four special symbols, called directors, denoted by α,γ,δ:*

    1. $\curvearrowright$ indicates that the substitution should be propagated only to the right branch of a binary construct (application or substitution, as given below).

    2. $\curvearrowleft$ indicates that the substitution should be propagated only to the left branch of a binary construct.

    3. λ indicates that the substitution should be propagated to both branches of a binary construct.

4. $\downarrow$ indicates that the substitution should traverse a unary construct (abstraction and variables, see below).

Strings: A director string is either empty, denoted by ϵ, or built from the above symbols (as usual we omit the constructor and simply write $\alpha_1\alpha_2\ldots\alpha_n$). We use Greek letters such as $\rho,\sigma\ldots$ to range over strings. The length of a string σ is denoted by $|\sigma|$. If α is a director, then α^n denotes a string of α's of length n. If σ is a director string of length n and $1 \le i \le j \le n$, σ_i denotes the ith director of σ and $\sigma_{\backslash i} = \sigma_1\ldots\sigma_{i-1}\sigma_{i+1}\ldots\sigma_n$ is σ where the ith director has been removed. $\sigma_{i..j} = \sigma_i\ldots\sigma_j$ is our notation for substrings. $|\sigma|_l$ denotes the number of $\curvearrowleft$ and $\curlywedge$ occurring in σ, and $|\sigma|_r$ the number of $\curvearrowright$ and $\curlywedge$.

Annotated Terms: Let σ range over strings, k be a natural number and t, u range over annotated terms, then the following are valid terms:

$$t ::= \square \mid (\lambda t)^\sigma \mid (\lambda^- t)^\sigma \mid (t\, u)^\sigma \mid (t[k/u])^\sigma$$

where $\square$ represents variables (a place holder), $(\lambda t)^\sigma$ is an abstraction where the bound variable occurs in the term t, whereas $(\lambda^- t)^\sigma$ is an abstraction where no new variables are bound. $(t\, u)^\sigma$ is an application, and finally $(t[k/u])^\sigma$ is our notation for explicit substitution, meaning that the variable corresponding to the kth director in t's string is to be replaced by u. We will often write $(t[u])^\sigma$ instead of $(t[1/u])^\sigma$ when the substitution binds the first variable.

The name of the variable is of no interest since the director strings give the path that the substitution must follow through the term to ensure that it gets to the right place, all we need is a place holder. Also, we omit the director for variables since it is always $\downarrow$.

In contrast with other explicit substitutions syntax, ours has explicit information about copying ($\curlywedge$) and erasing (λ^-). This is inspired by linear logic, and will allow us a finer control on substitutions. There is an alternative presentation which adds a director '$-$' to indicate that the substitution should be erased (i.e. the variable to be substituted does not occur in the term). For practical reasons we have chosen a syntax that combines the erasing with the abstraction: we erase terms as soon as possible. Similarly, we will postpone duplication of a term as much as possible. We will discuss this choice again in Section 3.3.

As with most λ-calculi, we will adopt several syntactic conventions: we will drop parentheses whenever we can, and omit the empty string ϵ unless it is essential.

Remark 1. Our use of this calculus is rather as an object language: the image of a translation of correctly formed λ-terms, thus we shall not enter here into a possible set of conditions on when an annotated term is a valid one (such a criterion may be found in [14]). We use a function $[\![\cdot]\!]$ to compile a λ-term into our syntax, and another $(\!|\cdot|\!)$ to read it back. The definitions are straightforward and omitted, we just need to know the order in which directors are generated: in our compilation the *last* director in a string corresponds to the variable bound by the *innermost* λ (see the examples below).

Example 1. We show the compilation of some λ-terms:

$$
\begin{aligned}
I &= [\![\lambda x.x]\!] & &= (\lambda\square)^\epsilon \\
K &= [\![\lambda x.\lambda y.x]\!] & &= (\lambda(\lambda^- \square)^{\downarrow})^\epsilon \\
S &= [\![\lambda x.\lambda y.\lambda z.(xz)(yz)]\!] & &= (\lambda(\lambda(\lambda((\square\square)^{\frown\frown}(\square\square)^{\frown\frown})^{\frown\frown\lambda})^{\downarrow\downarrow})^{\downarrow})^\epsilon \\
2 &= [\![\lambda f.\lambda x.f(fx)]\!] & &= (\lambda(\lambda(\square(\square\square)^{\frown\frown})^{\lambda\frown})^{\downarrow})^\epsilon
\end{aligned}
$$

Lemma 1 (Length of Strings). *Let* $\mathsf{fv}(t)$ *denote the set of free variables of the λ-term t (under Barendregt's convention).*

$$
|\mathsf{fv}(t)| = n \iff [\![t]\!] = u^\sigma \text{ where } |\sigma| = n
$$

In particular, a closed term will always have an empty director string (ϵ).

3 The Open Calculus

We will now give the reduction rules on the above defined terms that will allow us to fully simulate the λ-calculus. This calculus is called *open* (λ_o) in contrast with the calculus for closed reduction (λ_c) defined in Section 4.2, which is simpler but does not fully simulate β-reduction.

3.1 The *Beta* Rule

We need a *Beta* rule to eliminate β-redexes and introduce an explicit substitution instead. In a compiled term $(\lambda t^\nu)^\rho$ the variable bound by the abstraction is determined by the *last* director in ν, and $|\nu| = |\rho| + 1$ (by Lemma 1). The *Beta* rule will therefore create an explicit substitution for $|\rho| + 1$.

$$
\boxed{Beta \mid ((\lambda t)^\rho\ u)^\sigma \rightsquigarrow (t[|\rho|+1\,/\,u])^\sigma}
$$

Remark 2. If the function is closed, then the substitution binds the first (and only) variable of t (the first director): $((\lambda t)^\epsilon\ u)^\sigma \rightsquigarrow (t[u])^\sigma$.

3.2 Propagation Rules

We need rules to propagate the substitutions created by the *Beta* rule. The directors indicate the path that the substitution should follow: we will need a rule per term construct and possible director.

To understand how the rules for the propagation of substitutions are defined, consider a simple case: an application $(t\ u)^{\frown\rho}$ with a substitution, which should be propagated to the left branch of the application node as the director $\frown$ indicates. Assume the substitution concerns the first variable, i.e. we have $((t\ u)^{\frown\rho}[v])^\sigma$. We need a rule of the form:

$$
(App_1) \qquad ((t\ u)^{\frown\rho}[v])^\sigma \rightsquigarrow ((t[v])^{\rho'}\ u)^{\sigma'}
$$

Let's try to find ρ' and σ'. Suppose that a (closed) substitution is applied to the left and right hand-sides of the above equation. If, for example, $\sigma = \rho = \curvearrowright$, then the substitution is for t on the left, so we must have $\sigma' = \rho' = \curvearrowright$ to ensure that the substitution is also guided towards t on the right. If $\sigma = \curvearrowright$ and $\rho = \curvearrowleft$, then it is to be directed towards u, and we must have $\sigma' = \curvearrowleft$ and ρ' is not concerned (say $\rho' = \epsilon$ here). Finally, if $\sigma = \curvearrowleft$, the substitution is for v, and we write $\sigma' = \curvearrowright$ and $\rho' = \curvearrowleft$.

We obtain most of the propagation rules in the same way. Notice that not every combination of directors is to be considered, as some of them do not correspond to valid terms.

Name	Reduction		Cond.
Var	$(\square[v])^{\sigma}$	$\rightsquigarrow \quad v$	
App_1	$((t\ u)^{\rho}[i/v])^{\sigma}$	$\rightsquigarrow \quad ((t[j/v])^{\upsilon}\ u)^{\tau}$	$\rho_i = \curvearrowleft$
	where $\upsilon = \phi_l(\sigma, \rho_{\backslash i}), \tau = \psi_1(\sigma, \rho_{\backslash i}), j = |\rho_{1..i}|_l$		
App_2	$((t\ u)^{\rho}[i/v])^{\sigma}$	$\rightsquigarrow \quad (t\ (u[k/v])^{\omega})^{\tau}$	$\rho_i = \curvearrowright$
	where $\omega = \phi_r(\sigma, \rho_{\backslash i}), \tau = \psi_2(\sigma, \rho_{\backslash i}), k = |\rho_{1..i}|_r$		
App_3	$((t\ u)^{\rho}[i/v])^{\sigma}$	$\rightsquigarrow \quad ((t[j/v])^{\upsilon}\ (u[k/v])^{\omega})^{\tau}$	$\rho_i = \curlywedge$
where $\upsilon = \phi_l(\sigma, \rho_{\backslash i}), \omega = \phi_r(\sigma, \rho_{\backslash i}), \tau = \psi_3(\sigma, \rho_{\backslash i}), j = |\rho_{1..i}|_l, k = |\rho_{1..i}|_r$			
Lam	$((\lambda t)^{\rho}[i/v])^{\sigma}$	$\rightsquigarrow \quad (\lambda(t[i/v])^{\sigma \cdot \curvearrowright})^{\downarrow^{|\sigma|}}$	$\rho_i = \downarrow$
$LamE$	$((\lambda^- t)^{\rho}[i/v])^{\sigma}$	$\rightsquigarrow \quad (\lambda^-(t[i/v])^{\sigma})^{\downarrow^{|\sigma|}}$	$\rho_i = \downarrow$
$Comp$	$((t[j/u])^{\rho}[i/v])^{\sigma}$	$\rightsquigarrow \quad (t[j/(u[k/v])^{\omega}])^{\tau}$	$\rho_i = \curvearrowright$
	where $\omega = \phi_r(\sigma, \rho_{\backslash i}), \tau = \psi_2(\sigma, \rho_{\backslash i}), k = |\rho_{1..i}|_r$		

The various functions ϕ and ψ just compute the *ad hoc* director strings. The details of the functions are not essential and omitted, but they are generated recursively in the same way as above from the table below (left):

σ_1	ρ_1	ϕ_l	ϕ_r	ψ_1	ψ_2	ψ_3
$\curvearrowright$	ϵ	$\curvearrowright$	$\curvearrowright$	$\curvearrowright$	$\curvearrowright$	$\curlywedge$
$\curvearrowleft$	$\curvearrowright$	ϵ	$\curvearrowleft$	$\curvearrowright$	$\curvearrowright$	$\curvearrowright$
$\curvearrowleft$	$\curvearrowleft$	$\curvearrowleft$	ϵ	$\curvearrowleft$	$\curvearrowleft$	$\curvearrowleft$

So for instance :

$$\phi_l(\curvearrowright \sigma, \quad \rho) = \curvearrowright \phi_l(\sigma, \rho)$$
$$\phi_l(\curvearrowleft \sigma, \curvearrowright \rho) = \quad \phi_l(\sigma, \rho)$$
$$\phi_l(\curvearrowleft \sigma, \curvearrowleft \rho) = \curvearrowleft \phi_l(\sigma, \rho)$$

These rules deserve some explanations:

- The Var rule is the simplest. When the substitution reaches such a place holder, we know that it is indeed the right variable (because the substitution has been guided there earlier). Notice that here $\sigma = \curvearrowright^n$ for some n, and all the information we need is in the directors of v (we discard σ).
- The rules for application are the main rules here. Depending on ρ_i, the substitution is guided to the left or right, or copied in App_3 only when there is more than one occurrence of the given variable. The new director strings are computed by *ad hoc* functions from σ and ρ (omitting the ith director of the last one).

- Surprisingly enough, the rules that allow an open substitution to pass through an abstraction (*Lam* and *LamE*) are very simple. This is a quite remarkable property, as this is especially difficult in usual calculi. For example, it requires α-conversion in a calculus with names.
- The *Comp* rule is almost identical to App_2, except that the application is replaced by a substitution. We could have written composition rules for substitutions similar to App_1 and App_3, but the substitutions would then be allowed to *overtake* (i.e. their order would not be preserved), which means that the system would trivially fail to preserve strong normalization.
- We have a small number of propagation rules in comparison with standard explicit substitution calculi. However, our rules require non-trivial syntactical computations on director strings when we consider arbitrary substitutions. The system can be drastically simplified if we impose some restrictions on the substitutions, as we will see in the next section. Note that the condition on ρ_i has been externalized only to improve readability and is of course a simple pattern-matching.

Example 2. We show a reduction sequence using this calculus. Consider the λ-term $\lambda x.(\lambda y.y)x$ which contains a single redex:

$$[\![\lambda x.(\lambda y.y)x]\!] = (\lambda((\lambda\Box)^{\epsilon}\Box)^{\frown})^{\epsilon} \rightsquigarrow (\lambda(\Box[\Box])^{\frown})^{\epsilon} \rightsquigarrow (\lambda\Box)^{\epsilon} = [\![\lambda x.x]\!]$$

Note that an encoding into combinators, using director strings as presented in [11], would not allow this redex to be contracted, and thus if used as an argument could potentially be duplicated. In this sense, our calculus offers a generalization of the director strings of [11].

3.3 Erasing

To write a *BetaE* rule we need a new director '−' meaning that we erase the substitution it concerns. This director may appear anywhere in a string (in the general open rules), so is a director on its own. Moreover, it may appear on binary, as well as unary symbols, so may be mixed with either $\frown, \frown, \lambda$ or $\downarrow$. If we do add this director, we can then write:

$$\boxed{BetaE \Big| ((\lambda^{-}t^{\rho})^{\nu}\, u)^{\sigma} \rightsquigarrow t^{\rho'} \,\Big|\, \rho' = f(\sigma, \rho)}$$

where f is a recursive function that computes the new director string as follows:

$$\boxed{\begin{aligned} f(\frown \sigma, \quad \rho) &= -\, f(\sigma, \rho) \\ f(\frown \sigma, \alpha\, \rho) &= \alpha\, f(\sigma, \rho) \\ f(\lambda\, \sigma, \alpha\, \rho) &= \alpha\, f(\sigma, \rho) \end{aligned}}$$

Obviously, every rule in the system has to be rewritten to take into account the new director. These changes are straightforward and we omit them due to space constraints.

3.4 Properties

The aim of this paper is not to study the properties of the above system as a rewriting system, but rather to use it to implement efficient reduction strategies. However it is worth briefly stating several important properties, omitting the proofs. First, arbitrary β-reductions can be simulated in the following sense: if $t \to_\beta u$ in the λ-calculus, then $[\![t]\!] \leadsto^* [\![u]\!]$ in λ_o. Additionally, λ_o is (ground) confluent and preserves strong normalization.

4   Simplification

We now have a general framework to simulate the λ-calculus with a director strings notation. However, our aim is to search for new efficient reduction strategies, so we may give up completeness if we can gain some efficiency and simplicity, provided that we are still able at least to reduce closed terms to weak head normal form, which is the widely accepted minimal requirement for a λ-evaluator, such as found in functional compilers and interpreters.

4.1   The Local Open Calculus

Let's have a second look at the above defined calculus. From an algorithmic point of view, the rewrite rules cannot be clearly considered as constant time operations, because we have to access directors at arbitrary positions in strings, and the computation of the new director strings looks *a priori* linear in the size of the original ones.

   If we now have a closer look at the *Beta* rule, we may notice that for a redex where the function is closed, we generate a substitution for the first (and only) variable of the function body (which was bound by the abstraction). Moreover, we know from [8] that restricting β-reduction to closed functions still allows to reach weak head normal form, for closed terms. In this section we will thus describe the calculus resulting from this restriction which greatly simplifies the rules. This calculus will be called *local open* (λ_l) because it still allows open substitutions to propagate, even inside abstractions. This does not need global rewrite steps if we restrict the syntax to allow substitutions for the first director only.

Definition 2 (λ_l-calculus). *Below are shown the reduction rules for the local open calculus.*

Name	Reduction		
Beta	$((\lambda t)^\epsilon\ u)^\sigma$	$\rightsquigarrow$	$(t[u])^\sigma$
BetaE	$((\lambda^- t)^\epsilon\ u^\epsilon)^\epsilon$	$\rightsquigarrow$	t
Var	$(\Box[v])^\sigma$	$\rightsquigarrow$	v
App_1	$((t\ u)^{\frown\rho}[v])^{\frown^m \cdot \frown^n}$	$\rightsquigarrow$	$((t[v])^{\frown^m \cdot \frown^{\mid\rho\mid_l}}\ u)^{\frown^m \cdot \rho}$
App_2	$((t\ u)^{\frown\rho}[v])^{\frown^m \cdot \frown^n}$	$\rightsquigarrow$	$(t\ (u[v])^{\frown^m \cdot \frown^{\mid\rho\mid_r}})^{\frown^m \cdot \rho}$
App_3	$((t\ u)^{\lambda\rho}[v])^{\frown^m \cdot \frown^n}$	$\rightsquigarrow$	$((t[v])^{\frown^m \cdot \frown^{\mid\rho\mid_l}}\ (u[v])^{\frown^m \cdot \frown^{\mid\rho\mid_r}})^{\lambda^m \cdot \rho}$
Lam	$((\lambda t)^{\downarrow\rho}[v])^\sigma$	$\rightsquigarrow$	$(\lambda(t[v])^{\sigma \cdot \frown})^{\downarrow^{\mid\sigma\mid}}$
$LamE$	$((\lambda^- t)^{\downarrow\rho}[v])^\sigma$	$\rightsquigarrow$	$(\lambda^- (t[v])^\sigma)^{\downarrow^{\mid\sigma\mid}}$
$Comp$	$((t[w])^{\frown^{n+1} \cdot \frown^m}[v])^{\frown^p \cdot \frown^q}$	$\rightsquigarrow$	$(t[(w[v])^{\frown^p \cdot \frown^n}])^{\frown^{p+n} \cdot \frown^m}$

Even though the rules in this system apply to terms with director strings of a particular pattern, the system is still suitable to reduce general terms, thanks to the following property.

Lemma 2 (Completeness of the reduction). *In any reduct of a closed compiled term, any subterm of the form $(t[v])^\sigma$ has a director string $\sigma = \frown^m \cdot \frown^n$ for some natural numbers m, n.*

Proof. It is sufficient to notice that the rules for propagation only generate substitutions of this form, and that the *Beta* rule does as well: if the term $((\lambda t)^\epsilon\ u)^\sigma$ is well-formed (and it is by induction) then σ is of the form $\frown^n$. □

We remark that, in this calculus, we allow even open substitutions to pass through abstractions, without any global reduction step. This is of course one of the greatest strengths of this calculus, compared to those based on names or de Bruijn indices.

Proposition 1 (Properties of λ_l). *The calculus is correct, adequate for reduction to weak head normal form, confluent, and preserves strong normalization.*

Proof. The proofs are easily adapted from those for λ_c found in [8] and [7]. □

4.2   The Closed Calculus

The notion of closed reduction was introduced in [7] using a calculus of explicit substitutions with names where β-reductions are performed when the function part is closed (as above) and substitutions are propagated through abstractions only if they are closed, which is crucial to avoid α-conversion in a named setting. These restrictions are expressed by rewrite rules with external conditions on free variables, and the internalization of these conditions was the main motivation for the introduction of director strings in [8].

Here we can easily derive a calculus for closed reduction (λ_c) from the table above: *Beta*, *BetaE*, *Var* are the same; in every other rule we force v to be closed, that is, to have an empty string (ϵ). Moreover, in $App_{1,2,3}$, $m = 0$, and in $Comp$, $m = p = 0$ and $n = q$. This thus leads to a very simple rewriting system for weak reduction with several advantages:

- closed substitutions can be propagated through abstractions, which permits more sharing of work than in standard weak calculi,
- we forbid copying open terms, which ensures that we never duplicate a potential redex,
- the usual properties still hold [7,8]:

Proposition 2 (Properties of λ_c). *The calculus is correct, adequate for reduction to weak head normal form, confluent, and preserves strong normalization.*

5 An Abstract Machine for Evaluation

In this section we will exhibit a strategy which makes use of the explicit information carried by director strings to efficiently reduce closed terms to weak head normal form. Efficiency is measured with respect to the total number of rewriting steps (not just β-steps) and we will give experimental comparisons in Section 7.

Notice that the syntax of director strings allows us to identify the moment when we have to copy a term, and we can reduce it before copying. In particular, we may want to use the most general rules, in order to be able to reduce a term to be copied to its full normal form, thus avoiding to copy any redex. However, if we do so, then open substitutions are allowed in App_3 as well, which means that terms with free variables, i.e. potential redexes, might be copied. Our experimental tests confirmed that restricting just that rule to the closed case, we obtain a strategy very similar to closed reduction. This is because the propagation of an open substitution is very likely to be blocked by this restriction. Thus, the best strategy we found is based on the closed calculus, which is quite a good news since it is also the simplest.

We cannot expect to reduce to full normal form with the closed rules, but some open terms can still be reduced. Thus, our strategy to compute the weak head normal form of a term t can be summarized as follows: we use the closed calculus, which allows some extra reductions under abstractions, but we stop the reduction as soon as we reach a weak head normal form of t. The extra reductions are done only when we reduce a subterm to be copied, to share more work than in usual strategies.

To formally specify this strategy we will interleave one strategy which reduces under λ's and one which does not. We thus define three relations: $\rightarrow_w$, $\rightarrow_f$ and $\rightarrow$. The last one will be the strategy we want to exhibit. Below we give the operational semantics of the closed abstract machine:

$$\frac{t \to_w (\lambda r)^\epsilon \quad (r[u])^\sigma \to_w v}{(t\ u)^\sigma \to_w v} \text{ (Beta)} \qquad \frac{t \to_w (\lambda^- v)^\epsilon}{(t\ u)^\epsilon \to_w v} \text{ (BetaE)}$$

$$\frac{t \to_w v \quad v \neq (\lambda r)^\epsilon \wedge (v \neq (\lambda^- r)^\epsilon \vee \rho \neq \epsilon)}{(t\ u^\rho)^\sigma \to_w (v\ u^\rho)^\sigma} \text{ (Arg)}$$

$$\frac{((t[v^\epsilon])^{\frown |\rho|_l}\ u)^\rho \to_w w}{((t\ u)^{\frown \rho}[v^\epsilon])^\sigma \to_w w} \text{ (App1)} \qquad \frac{(t\ (u[v^\epsilon])^{\frown |\rho|_r})^\rho \to_w w}{((t\ u)^{\frown \rho}[v^\epsilon])^\sigma \to_w w} \text{ (App2)}$$

$$\frac{v^\epsilon \to_f v' \quad ((t[v'])^{\frown |\rho|_l}\ (u[v'])^{\frown |\rho|_r})^\rho \to_w w}{((t\ u)^{\lambda \rho}[v^\epsilon])^\sigma \to_w w} \text{ (App3)}$$

$$\frac{(\lambda(t[u^\epsilon])^{\frown |\rho|+1})^\rho \to_w v}{((\lambda t)^{\downarrow \rho}[u^\epsilon])^\sigma \to_w v} \text{ (Lam)} \qquad \frac{(\lambda^-(t[u^\epsilon])^{\frown |\rho|})^\rho \to_w v}{((\lambda^- t)^{\downarrow \rho}[u^\epsilon])^\sigma \to_w v} \text{ (LamE)}$$

$$\frac{v \to_w w}{(\square[v])^\sigma \to_w w} \text{ (Var)} \qquad \frac{(t[(u[v^\epsilon])^{\frown |\rho|}])^\rho \to_w w}{((t[u])^{\frown \rho}[v^\epsilon])^\sigma \to_w w} \text{ (Comp)}$$

$$\frac{t \to_w u \quad (u[v^\rho])^\sigma \to_w w \quad \rho \neq \epsilon}{(t[v^\rho])^\sigma \to_w w} \text{ (Subst)}$$

The reduction relation $\to_w$ is used as a tool to define the other two and should not be interpreted on its own, as it does not treat the case of an abstraction. Notice that the App_3 rule calls the stronger reduction $\to_f$, which is defined by:

$$\frac{t \to_w v}{t \to_f v} \qquad \frac{t \to_f v}{(\lambda t)^\sigma \to_f (\lambda v)^\sigma} \qquad \frac{t \to_f v}{(\lambda^- t)^\sigma \to_f (\lambda^- v)^\sigma}$$

$\to_f$ is the relation which reduces under λ's (but not to full normal form).

$$\frac{t \to_w v}{t \to v} \qquad \frac{}{(\lambda t)^\sigma \to (\lambda t)^\sigma} \qquad \frac{}{(\lambda^- t)^\sigma \to (\lambda^- t)^\sigma}$$

Finally, $\to$ is the combination of the two other relations: we reduce to weak head normal form, but we reduce more the subterms that will be copied.

It may seem that the machine returns terms which are not head normal forms (cf. *(Arg)* rule). In fact, the theory ensures that this is not the case: starting from a closed term, the closed rules allow us to reach a weak head normal form (see Proposition 2). Nevertheless, the *(Arg)* rule may be applied in a reduction of a term to be copied, so it is indispensable.

The *(Subst)* and *(Comp)* rules call for a comment: the restriction on *(Subst)* (v open) forces *(Comp)* to be used as much as possible before reducing to the left of a closed substitution. Both intuition and experimentation confirm that this is indeed the good choice.

6   Reduction to Full Normal Form

We have presented so far a rather complex system to fully simulate β-reduction and simpler systems to reach only weak head normal form. If we were however interested in computing full normal forms, which is the case for many applications (e.g. partial evaluation or proof assistants), then we could of course use the general setting. But this is not really satisfactory because of the complexity and inefficiency of this system. Moreover, it does not provide any guidance towards an efficient strategy. On the other hand, we have an efficient strategy to reduce closed terms to weak head normal form. The idea then naturally arises to use our efficient weak evaluator to reach full normal form, in a way similar to [4].

The idea is to reduce a closed term to weak head normal form, then to distinguish the variable bound by the outermost abstraction in some way (to "freeze" it), so that we can still consider the term under the λ as closed, and recursively apply the same process to this subterm. There are several ways to distinguish those variables in the syntax. Below we present two natural alternatives.

With names. If we choose to represent the frozen variables with names, we can avoid any complex manipulation of the director strings to keep track of the paths to these variables. As a result, we obtain a rather simple system because we can use the usual rules (for example the closed ones), where the frozen variables are just considered as constants and do not need any extra rule. Moreover readback into named λ-calculus is then performed at the same time.

Formally, we extend the syntax of terms in the following way, where σ ranges over strings, and x ranges over variable names:

$$t, u ::= \square \mid (\lambda t)^\sigma \mid (\lambda^- t)^\sigma \mid (t\ u)^\sigma \mid (t[u])^\sigma \mid x \mid \lambda' x.t$$

that is, we add named variables, whose implicit director string is ϵ, and named abstraction binding written as $\lambda' x.t$. We do not write any director string for this abstraction, since we will always consider closed terms of this form.

Using a weak evaluation relation $\Downarrow_w$, we can then define reduction to full normal form $\Downarrow_f$.

$$\frac{t \Downarrow_w (\lambda t')^\epsilon \qquad (t'[x])^\epsilon \Downarrow_f t'' \qquad x \text{ fresh}}{t \Downarrow_f \lambda' x.t''}$$

$$\frac{t \Downarrow_w (\lambda^- t')^\epsilon \qquad t' \Downarrow_f t'' \qquad x \text{ fresh}}{t \Downarrow_f \lambda' x.t''}$$

$$\frac{t \Downarrow_w x \qquad (x \text{ variable})}{t \Downarrow_f x}$$

$$\frac{t \Downarrow_w (u\ v)^\epsilon \qquad u \Downarrow_f u' \qquad v \Downarrow_f v'}{t \Downarrow_f (u'\ v')^\epsilon}$$

Notice that the last rule is used since we are now in a calculus with constants (the named variables), and the weak head normal form of a term may be an application (e.g. $(x\ t)^\epsilon$ where x is a named variable).

If we want to reduce an open term, say with n free variables, we first take n fresh variable names $x_1, \ldots, x_n$ and start the reduction from:

$$((\ldots ((t[x_1])^{\frown^{n-1}} [x_2])^{\frown^{n-2}} \ldots [x_{n-1}])^\frown [x_n])^\epsilon$$

The reduction to normal form follows exactly the same strategy as the corresponding weak reduction. Thus, for terms for which full and weak head normal forms are the same, the two processes need the same numbers of β and total steps. In particular, this strategy is much more efficient than the usual naive one.

Although we now have to deal with names and fresh variables during reduction (which was not the case for reduction to weak head normal form), we still do not have to deal with name capture and α-conversion. Also, the readback is now simplified.

With directors. The previous strategy performs readback at the same time as computation of the normal form, which may, or may not, be wished. We can however implement a similar idea using only directors, obtaining a result in this syntax. We just need a way to distinguish between usual variables, and frozen ones, which correspond to an abstraction outside of the term we actually want to reduce to weak head normal form. This can be done in a quite obvious way: by introducing a new kind of directors corresponding to these frozen variables. However, the frozen part of director strings may be of any form, so we need to use the general rules on this part. From an algorithmic point of view, this means that the cost of a reduction step may be at most linear in the depth of λ-abstractions in the resulting normal form, which still seems reasonable.

7   Experimental Results

Our work has always been motivated by efficiency, so it was essential to implement our machines and compare them experimentally to existing machines. However it is difficult, if not impossible, to find a relevant measure to compare machines implemented in different frameworks. The following benchmarks should thus be taken with great care. It is not intended for direct comparisons between strategies (as the algorithmic cost of a single step may vary) but to illustrate their respective asymptotic behaviours.

We chose our examples in λI (i.e. terms without erasing) in order to isolate the problem of erasing, which is quite orthogonal to the problem of efficiency on λI-terms. The Church numerals are an excellent means to produce a panel of large λ-terms. We recall that Church numerals are of the form $n = \lambda f.\lambda x.f^n x$ and that application corresponds to exponentiation: $n\,m \equiv m^n$. We apply Church numerals in our examples to $I\,I$, where $I = \lambda x.x$, which is sufficient to force reduction to full normal form, and allows comparisons between weak and full reducers.

We compare our machines with a standard call-by-value evaluator (which is always better than call-by-name on these examples), and in addition to the optimal interpreter of Asperti et al. (BOHM [3]). The latter result provides a comparison with the best known evaluator for such terms. We show the total number of steps of these evaluators (including stack manipulations). For BOHM we give the total number of reduction steps. We show the number of β-reductions between round brackets, thus the number shown for BOHM is the minimum number of β-reductions possible. The results for the machines that reduce to full normal form are not shown, as they are the same as those of the underlying weak strategies on these examples.

Term	closed	weak closed	CBV	BOHM
2 2 I I	61 (9)	71 (11)	82 (11)	40 (9)
2 2 2 I I	140 (19)	361 (47)	302 (42)	100 (16)
3 2 2 I I	248 (33)	5842 (705)	3508 (531)	184 (21)
5 5 I I	217 (33)	28161 (4065)	26669 (3913)	229 (33)
4 2 2 I I	448 (59)	1524963 (179395)	852306 (131108)	342 (26)
5 2 2 I I	832 (109)	–	–	847 (31)
2 2 2 2 2 I I	1507714 (196655)	–	–	1074037060 (61)

It is not easy to find a relevant measure for comparison with abstract machines found in wide-spread evaluators. However, to put some of these results into perspective, we remark that the actual time taken to compute, for example, 5 2 2 I I using OCaml is around 5 minutes, and around 3 minutes using Standard ML. The results for both closed reduction and BOHM are essentially instantaneous.

The main point that we want to make with the above table is that closed reduction, a simple implementation of the λ-calculus, clearly out performs traditional strategies, such as call-by-value, and moreover is a serious competitor to highly sophisticated implementations, such as BOHM.

The interesting point is the comparison on large terms. The results show that our machine is able to reduce larger terms than the other machines, and the larger the term, the better is our machine compared to the others. This hints that it allows for a high degree of sharing (because the larger the term, the more possible sharing). The last line of the table shows that our machine eventually explodes in terms of number of β-reductions compared to the optimal one but outperforms BOHM in total number of steps, which is our notion of efficiency.

We also compared our machine to a so-called "weak closed" one, which is the same but forbidding reductions under abstraction. This is to emphasize that allowing such reductions, which is especially easy with director strings compared to usual calculi, is crucial for both sharing and efficiency.

8 Conclusion

We have presented a name-free syntax to represent terms of the λ-calculus with explicit substitutions, in a way that follows the usual intuitions about the operational semantics of the propagation of substitutions. We have given a general calculus on director strings which can fully simulate the λ-calculus, with rather complicated rules. We then described an intermediate calculus, the local open calculus, with very simple rules and still allowing open substitutions to traverse abstractions without global rewriting. Finally, we derived the closed reduction calculus of [8], which internalizes the conditions on the original system [7].

These calculi were used as a basis to describe and implement abstract machines for weak and strong reduction (the latter was an open problem for director strings). Efficiency was our main motivation and guided every one of our choices. We found on practical examples that these machines are quite efficient on large terms and allow for a high degree of sharing. In particular, they quite favourably compare to standard evaluators, which suggests that more efficient implementations of functional languages and λ-calculus based proof assistants are still possible.

References

1. M. Abadi, L. Cardelli, P.-L. Curien, and J.-J. Lévy. Explicit substitutions. *Journal of Functional Programming*, 1(4):375–416, 1991.
2. Z. M. Ariola, M. Felleisen, J. Maraist, M. Odersky, and P. Wadler. A call-by-need lambda calculus. In *Proc. of the 22nd ACM Symposium on Principles of Programming Languages (POPL'95)*, pages 233–246. ACM Press, 1995.
3. A. Asperti, C. Giovanetti, and A. Naletto. The bologna optimal higher-order machine. *Journal of Functional Programming*, 6(6):763–810, 1996.
4. U. Berger, M. Eberl, and H. Schwichtenberg. Normalization by evaluation, 1998.
5. P.-L. Curien, T. Hardin, and J.-J. Lévy. Confluence properties of weak and strong calculi of explicit substitutions. *Journal of the ACM*, 43(2):362–397, 1996.
6. N. G. de Bruijn. Lambda calculus notation with nameless dummies. *Indagationes Mathematicae*, 34:381–392, 1972.
7. M. Fernández and I. Mackie. Closed reductions in the λ-calculus. In J. Flum and M. Rodríguez-Artalejo, editors, *Proc. of Computer Science Logic (CSL'99)*, number 1683 in Lecture Notes in Computer Sciences. Springer, 1999.
8. M. Fernández and I. Mackie. Director strings and explicit substitutions. WEST-APP'01, Utrecht, 2001.
9. G. Gonthier, M. Abadi, and J.-J. Lévy. The geometry of optimal lambda reduction. In *Conference Record of the 19th Annual ACM SIGPLAN-SIGACT Symposium on Principles of Programming Languages*, 1992.
10. T. Hardin, L. Maranget, and B. Pagano. Functional runtime systems within the lambda-sigma calculus. *Journal of Functional Programming*, 8(2):131–176, 1998.
11. J. Kennaway and M. Sleep. Director strings as combinators. *ACM Transactions on Programming Languages and Systems*, 10(4):602–626, 1988.
12. J. Lamping. An algorithm for optimal lambda calculus reductions. In *Proc. 17th ACM Symposium on Principles of Programmining Languages*, 1990.
13. F. Lang. *Modèles de la β-réduction pour les implantations*. PhD thesis, École Normale Supérieure de Lyon, 1998.
14. F.-R. Sinot. Calculs avec chaînes directrices : Implémentation efficace du λ-calcul, 2002. Master's Thesis (Mémoire de DEA), École Normale Supérieure, http://www.dcs.kcl.ac.uk/pg/francois/DEA/.
15. N. Yoshida. Optimal reduction in weak lambda-calculus with shared environments. *Journal of Computer Software*, 11(6):3–18, 1994.

Rewriting Logic and Probabilities

Olivier Bournez[1] and Mathieu Hoyrup[2]

[1] LORIA/INRIA, 615 Rue du Jardin Botanique
54602 Villers lès Nancy Cedex, France
[2] ENS-Lyon, 46 Allée d'Italie
69364 Lyon Cedex 07, France

Abstract. Rewriting Logic has shown to provide a general and elegant framework for unifying a wide variety of models, including concurrency models and deduction systems. In order to extend the modeling capabilities of rule based languages, it is natural to consider that the firing of rules can be subject to some probabilistic laws. Considering rewrite rules subject to probabilities leads to numerous questions about the underlying notions and results. In this paper, we discuss whether there exists a notion of probabilistic rewrite system with an associated notion of probabilistic rewriting logic.

1 Introduction

Rewriting Logic [19] is known to provide a very elegant and powerful framework for unifying a wide variety of models, including concurrency models and deduction systems. Indeed, the basic axioms of this logic, which are rewrite rules of the form $t \to t'$, where t and t' are terms over a given signature, can be read in two dual ways: *computationally*, $t \to t'$ can be read as the local transition of a concurrent system or *logically*, $t \to t'$ can be read as the inference rule of some logic [19]. Several computer systems, including MAUDE [11] and ELAN [7], are based on this framework and have been intensively used in the last decade for the prototyping of various kinds of logics and systems: see survey [18].

In order to extend the modeling capabilities of rule based languages, it seems natural to extend the framework with probabilities: for example, the modeling of concurrent systems requires often to consider that the local transitions $t \to t'$ can be subject to some probabilistic laws [8]. This leads to numerous questions about the underlying theories and results.

In a previous RTA paper [8], *strategies* were shown to provide a nice setting for expressing probabilistic choices in rule based languages. *Probabilistic abstract reduction systems* and notions like *almost-sure termination* or *probabilistic confluence* were introduced and related to the classical notions.

This paper is devoted to a next step: understand whether there exists a valid and useful notion of rewrite system and rewriting logic in presence of probabilities.

In classical (non-probabilistic) rewriting theory each rewrite system induces a reduction relation which defines the relation of an abstract reduction system

R. Nieuwenhuis (Ed.): RTA 2003, LNCS 2706, pp. 61–75, 2003.

over the terms: see e.g. [2]. When considering systems with probabilistic firing of rules, the analog of abstract reduction systems seems to be the notion of probabilistic abstract reduction systems introduced in [8]. Can we build a valid and nice notion of probabilistic rewrite system, that would induce probabilistic abstract reduction systems over terms in a natural way?

A first natural idea seems to consider the following notion: define a probabilistic rewrite system as a classical rewrite system, i.e. a set of rewrite rules, plus associated probabilities (or weights see discussions later): i.e. a probability (or a weight) for each rule.

In the classical setting, the reflexive transitive closure of the relation induced by some rewrite system can be proved to correspond to the smallest reflexive transitive relation that contains the identities involved by the rewrite system and which is closed by substitutions and Σ-operations: see e.g. [2]. That means in particular that one can build a sound and complete proof system that decides if two terms are in relation by the reflexive transitive closure of the reduction relation of a given rewrite system. This proof system corresponds to the deduction rules of Rewriting Logic [19]. Does that work in the probabilistic settings?

We prove in this paper that there is no hope to build a sound and complete proof system that would prove whether two terms are in relation by the reflexive transitive closure of the reduction relation of a given rewrite system with associated probabilities in the general case. Does there exist however a notion of probabilistic rewriting logic?

We propose a notion of probabilistic rewriting logic. One main difference between the proposed setting and the classical rewriting logic setting is that proof terms become now mandatory, in order to have completeness results: we prove that when proof terms are present, probabilistic rewriting logic is sound and complete.

One main interest of rewriting logic lies in its modeling capabilities [18,19]. We show that the proposed probabilistic rewriting logic extends the modeling capabilities of classical rewriting logic.

This paper is organized as follows: classical non-probabilistic theory is recalled in Section 2. Probabilistic abstract reduction systems are recalled in Section 3. Several computability theory results which show that this is not way to have sound and complete proof systems that deal correctly with transitivity are proved in Section 4. The proposed notion of probabilistic rewrite system with its associated semantic is introduced in Section 5. The associated sound and complete probabilistic rewriting logic is discussed in Section 6. The modeling capabilities of probabilistic rewriting logic are exemplified in Section 7. Section 8 discusses related and future work.

2   Rewriting Logic

We need first to recall some classical notions and results (we follow the notations and terminology from [2]): $T(\Sigma, X)$ denotes the set of terms over signature Σ and disjoint set of variables X. When $t \in T(\Sigma, X)$ is a term, let $Pos(t)$ be the set of its positions. For $\rho \in Pos(t)$, let $t|_\rho$ be the subterm of t at position ρ, and let $t[s]_\rho$ denote the replacement of the subterm at position ρ in t by s. The set of all substitutions is denoted by Sub.

Definition 1 (Labeled rewrite system). *A labeled rewrite system* $(\mathcal{R}, \mathcal{L})$ *consists of a set* $\mathcal{R} \subseteq T(\Sigma, X) \times T(\Sigma, X)$ *of rules and a set* $\mathcal{L}$ *of labels, such that each rule in* $\mathcal{R}$ *is bijectively associated to a label in* $\mathcal{L}$*. We write* $g \to d \in \mathcal{R}$ *for* $(g, d) \in \mathcal{R}$ *and* $(l : g \to d)$ *when* $l \in \mathcal{L}$ *is associated to* $g \to d \in \mathcal{R}$*.*

Definition 2 (Abstract Reduction System). *An abstract reduction system* $(A, \to)$ *consists of a set* A *and a binary relation* $\to$ *on* A*, called reduction relation. We write* $a \to b$ *for* $(a, b) \in \to$*, and we write* $\to^*$ *for the reflexive transitive closure of* $\to$*.*

Definition 3 (Reduction relation). *Let* $\mathcal{R}$ *be a rewrite system. The associated reduction relation* $\to_\mathcal{R} \subseteq T(\Sigma, X) \times T(\Sigma, X)$*, also denoted by* $\to$ *when* $\mathcal{R}$ *is clear, is defined by* $t \to_\mathcal{R} t'$ *iff* $\exists (g \to d) \in \mathcal{R}, p \in Pos(t), \sigma \in Sub$*, such that* $t|_p = \sigma(g)$ *and* $t' = t[\sigma(d)]_p$*.*

A rule $g \to d \in \mathcal{R}$ *will be said to be* applicable at the root of term t *if position* p *can be chosen as the root position: i.e. there is a substitution* $\sigma \in Sub$ *with* $t = \sigma(g)$*. In that case,* $\sigma(d)$ *is the the result of its application.*

The idea of rewriting logic is, for a given rewrite system $\mathcal{R}$, to consider $\to_\mathcal{R}$ as the description of a transition system over terms.

Definition 4. *The* executional semantic *of a given rewrite system* $\mathcal{R}$ *is the abstract reduction system* $\mathcal{S}_\mathcal{R} = (T(\Sigma, X), \to_\mathcal{R})$*.*

The derivations of this abstract reduction system correspond to the provable sequents of a logic, called *rewriting logic*. This logic talks about sentences of the form $t \to t'$, meaning that t can evolve toward t' in $\mathcal{S}_\mathcal{R}$ [19].

Proposition 1. *[There exists a sound and complete proof system for* $\to^*$ *[19]] Suppose rewrite system* $\mathcal{R}$ *is fixed. Two terms* $s, t \in T(\Sigma, X)$ *are related by* $\to^*$ *iff* $t \to t'$ *can be established starting with axioms* $l \to r$ *for each rule* $l \to r \in \mathcal{R}$ *by the following proof system:*

Reflexivity: *if* $t \in T(\Sigma, X)$*,*

$$\overline{t \to t}$$

Congruence: *if* $f \in \Sigma_n$*,*

$$\frac{t_1 \to t'_1 \quad \cdots \quad t_n \to t'_n}{f(t_1, \ldots, t_n) \to f(t'_1, \ldots, t'_n)}$$

Replacement: *if* $l : g(x_1, ..., x_n) \to d(x_1, ..., x_n) \in \mathcal{R}$*,*

$$\frac{t_1 \to t'_1 \quad \cdots \quad t_n \to t'_n}{g(t_1, \ldots, t_n) \to d(t'_1, \ldots, t'_n)}$$

Transitivity:

$$\frac{t_1 \to t_2 \qquad t_2 \to t_3}{t_1 \to t_3}$$

Remark 1. Rewriting logic is generally defined considering *rewriting modulo*: sequents correspond to quotient set $T(\Sigma, X)/_E$ where E is a given set of identities [19]. In this paper, we will not consider terms modulo a congruence class. Furthermore, we will not allow conditional rules. We believe this restricted framework to be enough interesting by itself for the following discussions.

Remark 2. In order to represent both a reduction and the proof tree that induces this reduction, *proof terms* can also be considered: the set $\mathcal{PT}$ of proof terms is defined as the set $T(\Sigma \cup \mathcal{L} \cup \{;\}, X)$ of terms on the signature Σ extended with the labels of $\mathcal{L}$ and the binary concatenation operator ";" [10]. Rewriting logic deduction rules can then be adapted to derive sentences of the form $\pi : t \to t'$ meaning that t evolves toward t' in $\mathcal{S}_\mathcal{R}$ using path encoded by proof term π': see [10,19]. But, as shown by previous proposition, unless one wants to define the notion of model [19], or the notion of strategy [10], proof terms are not mandatory.

3 Probabilistic Abstract Reduction Systems

Let S be a countable finite or infinite set. A *stochastic sequence* $(X_n)_{n \geq 0}$ on S is a family of random variables from some fixed probability space to S.

Definition 5 (Homogeneous Markovian Stochastic Sequence). *A stochastic sequence* $(X_n)_{n \geq 0}$ *is Markovian if its conditional distribution function satisfies* $\forall n \geq 1, i_0, \ldots, i_n \in S$, $p(X_n = i_n | X_{n-1} = i_{n-1}, \ldots, X_0 = i_0) = p(X_n = i_n | X_{n-1} = i_{n-1})$. *It is said to be* homogeneous *if furthermore this probability is independent of* n.

In other words, Markov property means that the system evolution does not depend on past, but only on present state. The homogeneity property means that the dynamic is independent of time.

In that case, $P = (p_{i,j})_{i,j \in S}$ defined by $p_{i,j} = p(X_n = j | X_{n-1} = i)$ is a *stochastic matrix on* S: i.e. it satisfies for all $i, j \in S$, $p_{ij} \in [0,1]$ and for all i, $\sum_j p_{ij} = 1$. It is called a matrix even when S is infinite. Homogeneous Markovian stochastic sequences (HMSS) and stochastic matrices are in correspondence, since conversely to any stochastic matrix $P = (p_{i,j})_{i,j \in S}$ corresponds a homogeneous Markovian stochastic sequence: if at time n the system state is $i \in S$, choose at time $(n+1)$ system state j with probability $p_{i,j}$.

In [8], we suggested to extend abstract reduction systems in a homogeneous Markovian way:

Definition 6 (PARS). *A Probabilistic Abstract Reduction System* $\mathcal{A} = (A, \rightsquigarrow)$ *consists of a countable (finite or infinite) set* A *and a mapping* $\rightsquigarrow$ *from* $A \times A$ *to* $[0,1]$ *such that for all* $s \in A$, $\sum_{t \in A} s \rightsquigarrow t = 0$ *or* 1.

A PARS $\mathcal{A}$ is like a HMSS on A whose stochastic matrix is $P = (s \leadsto t)_{s,t}$. However contrary to a HMSS, a state can be *irreducible*, that is such that $\sum_{t \in A} s \leadsto t = 0$. Actually, a PARS can be transformed into a stochastic matrix by adding a new state $\perp$ and reducing irreducible states to $\perp$: let $S = A \cup \{\perp\}$ the extension of A with $\perp$. Extend $\leadsto$ on $S \times S$ by

$$s \leadsto \perp = 1 \quad \text{if s} \in A \text{ is irreducible}$$
$$s \leadsto \perp = 0 \quad \text{if s} \in A \text{ is reducible}$$
$$\perp \leadsto t = 0 \quad \text{for all t} \in A$$
$$\perp \leadsto \perp = 1$$

Definition 7 (Derivation). *A derivation of $\mathcal{A}$ is a corresponding HMSS on S.*

PARS correspond to the extension of Abstract Reduction Systems (ARS) with probabilities. Indeed, to a PARS $\mathcal{A} = (A, \leadsto)$ can be associated a unique ARS $(A, \rightarrow)$, called its *projection,* obtained by forgetting probabilities: $s \rightarrow t$ if and only if $s \leadsto t > 0$. Conversely, to any ARS can be associated several PARS by distributing probabilities over the possible derivations: the projection of these PARS will be the original ARS: see [8] for a full discussion.

4 Probabilities and Transitivity

We now come to the main object of this paper, that is to discuss whether there exists a notion of *probabilistic rewrite system* with some *executional semantic* for which there exists some associated notion of *probabilistic rewriting logic*.

We have not yet defined what *probabilistic rewrite systems* are, but one may expect a *probabilistic rewrite system* to correspond to a classical rewrite system with somehow the addition of probabilities. One may also expect its *executional semantic* to be defined as a probabilistic abstract reduction system over terms. In other words, one would expect to define *probabilistic rewrite systems* and their *executional semantics* by distributing in some manner the probabilities over the executional semantic of classical rewrite systems.

The point is to get something "nice": one may in particular want to have results in the spirit of Proposition 1: there is some associated sound and complete proof system that could derive whether two terms are related in the corresponding *executional semantic*. If it were so, guided by classical theory, we would then call this complete proof system *probabilistic rewriting logic*.

However, we prove in this section that there is no hope to get such a sound and complete proof system.

We start by a computability theory result about homogeneous Markovian stochastic sequences: observe that, when P is a stochastic matrix, and n is an integer, P^n is a stochastic matrix whose entries $(P^n)_{i,j}$ give the probability of going from i to j in n steps [9]. We show that even two steps transitions, that is P^2, is not computable in the general case: a stochastic matrix $P = (P_{i,j})_{i,j}$ is said *recursive* if all its entries are rational and there exists a Turing machine that given i, j outputs $P_{i,j}$. Such a matrix can be represented by an index of a corresponding Turing Machine.

Theorem 1. *The decision problem "given a stochastic matrix P, and some rational q, decide if top-left entry of P^2 is q" is not recursively enumerable.*

Proof. The halting problem "given integer w, decide if Turing machine number w accepts input w" is recursively enumerable non-recursive, and hence, its complement $Co - Halt$ can not be recursively enumerable. We only need to prove that problem $Co - Halt$ reduces to our problem.

Given an input w of $Co - Halt$, consider the matrix $P = (P_{i,j})_{i,j}$ where $P_{1,j} = \frac{1}{2^j}$ for all j, $P_{i,j} = 0$ for all $j > 2$, $P_{i,1} = 0$ (respectively: $P_{i,2} = 1$) if Turing machine number w over input w halts in less than i steps, $\frac{1}{2^i}$ otherwise (resp. $1 - \frac{1}{2^i}$ otherwise). P is a recursive stochastic matrix: all its entries are computable rationals of $[0,1]$, and for $i = 1$, we have $\sum_{j \geq 1} p_{1j} = \sum_{j \geq 1} \frac{1}{2^j} = 1$, and for $i > 1$, $\sum_{j \geq 1} p_{ij}$ is $p_{i1} + p_{i2} = 0 + 1$ or $\frac{1}{2^i} + (1 - \frac{1}{2^i}) = 1$ according to whether Turing machine number w stops on input w in less than i steps or not.

Assume that Turing machine number w does not accept input w. For all $i > 1$ we have $p_{i1} = \frac{1}{2^i}$ and $p_{i2} = 1 - \frac{1}{2^i}$. The top-left entry of P^2 is given by $\sum_{k \geq 1} p_{1k} p_{k1} = \sum_{k \geq 1} \left(\frac{1}{2^k}\right)^2 = \frac{1}{3}$.

Assume that Turing machine number w accepts input w at time i_0. We have $p_{i1} = \frac{1}{2^i}$ and $p_{i2} = 1 - \frac{1}{2^i}$ for all $i \leq i_0$ and $p_{i1} = 0$ and $p_{i2} = 1$ for all $i > i_0$. After a certain row, the first column elements of matrix P are 0 and the second column elements are 1. The top-left entry of P^2 is given by $\sum_{k \geq 1} p_{1k} p_{k1} = \sum_{k=1}^{i_0} \left(\frac{1}{2^k}\right)^2 = \frac{1}{3}\left(1 - \frac{1}{4^{i_0}}\right) < \frac{1}{3}$.

Hence, problem $Co - Halt$ reduces to our problem considering matrix P and rational $q = 1/3$.

Remark 3. The previous proof also shows that the problem of determining if the top-left entry of P^2 is $\geq q$ is not recursively enumerable. The problem of determining whether it is $> q$ can be shown to be recursively enumerable but non recursive.

We now come back to rewriting and probabilities. A point is that one expects the notion of *probabilistic rewrite system* to cover at least homogeneous Markovian stochastic sequences: indeed, any stochastic matrix $P = (p_{i,j})_{i,j}$ on set of states S can be considered as a rewrite system with probabilities: take a constant for each element $i \in S$ and write a rule $i \rightarrow j$ with associated probability $p_{i,j}$ for each i, j.

Suppose there were a sound and complete proof system that could derive whether two terms are related in the *executional semantic* of a given *probabilistic rewrite system*. It is rather natural to expect this proof system not only to talk about whether there is a path between two terms in the executional semantic but also to talk about the probability of this path: otherwise it would have nothing to do with probabilities. In other words, it is natural to expect such a proof system to derive sentences of type $t \leadsto_p^* t'$ (or $t \leadsto_p^n t'$) meaning "term t can evolve to term t' with probability p (respectively in n steps).

We show this is impossible (observe that you can fix $n = 2$ in what follows):

Theorem 2 (There is no sound and complete proof system for $\rightsquigarrow^n$).
There is no way to conceive a sound and complete proof system (axioms + deduction rules) that could derive in the general case for all terms s,t and integer n the probability $s \rightsquigarrow^n t$ of going from s to t in n steps.

Proof. Assume there were a finite (or even a recursively enumerable) set of axioms and a finite (or even recursively enumerable) set of deductions rules that would allow to give probabilities $s \rightsquigarrow^n t$ for all s,t,n. By enumerating recursively axioms and proofs we could enumerate all the possible proofs. Hence, the problem "given some probabilistic rewrite system, some terms s,t and some rational q, decide if $q = s \rightsquigarrow^n t$" would be recursively enumerable. This is in contradiction with Theorem 1 considering systems describing a homogeneous Markovian stochastic sequence.

One may argue that the previous arguments relies on systems with a non-finite set of rules, or that we do not talk about reachability in any number of steps. Actually, we prove:

Theorem 3. *The decision problem "given a PARS represented by a finite set of rewrite rules with probabilities, some states s,t, decide if the probability $s \rightsquigarrow^* t$ of going from s to t in any number of steps is q" is not recursively enumerable.*

Proof. We only need to reduce non-recursively enumerable decision problem $Co - Halt$ to our problem. Let $E \subseteq \mathbb{N}^2$ be the set of couples (w,t) such that Turing Machine number w halts on input w in less than t steps. E is a recursive set. By Bergstra-Tucker theorem [6], there exists a confluent rewriting system on a signature $\Sigma \supset \{0, s, In\}$, where 0 is a constant symbol, s is an unary (successor) function symbol, and In is a binary function symbol, such that for all $x, t \geq 0$,

$$In(s^x(0), s^t(0)) \rightarrow^* \quad 0 \quad \text{if } (x,t) \in E$$
$$\rightarrow^* s(0) \quad \text{if } (x,t) \notin E$$

Consider signature $\Sigma' = \Sigma \cup \{F, Run\}$, where F is binary, Run unary (and these symbols are not in Σ). Consider the rewrite system $\mathcal{R}$ composed of the rules of the rewriting system associated to E plus the rules:

$$Run(x) \rightarrow F(x, 0)$$
$$F(x,t) \rightarrow F(x, s(t))$$
$$F(x,t) \rightarrow In(x,t)$$

Build a PARS on $T(\Sigma', X)$ by assigning probabilities to the reductions of $\mathcal{R}$: put probability $1/2$ on the reductions $F(x,t) \rightarrow F(x, s(t))$ and $F(x,t) \rightarrow In(x,t)$, and probability 1 on all other reductions.

By construction, the probability $p(w)$ that $Run(s^w(0))$ reduces to $s(0)$ is

$$\sum_{n \,|\, (w,n) \notin E} \frac{1}{2^{n+1}}.$$

Indeed, a reduction that leads to $s(0)$ can be written as

$$F(s^w(0), 0) \to \cdots \to F(s^w(0), s^n(0)) \to In(s^w(0), s^n(0)) \to \cdots \to s(0)$$

and the probability of such a reduction is $\frac{1}{2^{n+1}}$.

Observing definition of E, probability $p(w)$ is 1 iff $w \in Co - Halt$, and is < 1 otherwise. Hence, problem $Co - Halt$ reduces to our problem.

Remark 4. The previous proof also shows that the problem of deciding whether $s \rightsquigarrow^* t$ is $\geq q$ is non-recursively enumerable. Deciding whether it is $> q$ can be shown to be recursively enumerable but non recursive.

Using similar arguments to those used to establish Theorem 2, we get.

Theorem 4 (There is no sound and complete proof system for $\rightsquigarrow^*$).
Even when restricting to systems described by a finite set of rewriting rules, there is no way to conceive a proof system that could derive in the general case for all terms s,t the probability $s \rightsquigarrow^* t$ of going from s to t.

5   Probabilistic Rewrite Systems

We now present the notion of *probabilistic rewrite system* with the associated notion of *executional semantic* that we propose.

The rules that can be applied on some term t depend on t. For example for the following rewrite system

$$\mathcal{R} \begin{cases} l_1 : f(a, x) \to x \\ l_2 : f(x, b) \to c \end{cases}$$

over signature $\Sigma = \{f, a, b, c\}$, on term $f(a, b)$ both rules l_1 and l_2 apply, but on term $f(a, a)$ only rule l_1 applies.

Furthermore, on a given term t, one may have the choice to apply a rule at the root of the term, that is to use *replacement* rule, or to rewrite concurrently only (one or several) subterms, that is to use *congruence* rule.

We would like to distribute probabilities over the possibilities: a first difficulty is that we can not hardwire directly probabilities: if we wanted to put probability p_i to rule l_i, for $i = 1, 2$, on term $f(a, b)$ we would expect $p_1 + p_2 = 1$, on term $f(a, a)$ we would expect $p_1 = 1$. This is impossible unless p_2 is 0, i.e. l_2 never applies.

Our proposition is to consider that we do not assign probabilities but *weights*: a weight is some positive real number. The following strategy is then proposed: on a term t, choose some applicable possibility (that is to say a rule that applies at the root of t or *congruence* rule for symbol f if term t is of type $t = f(t_1, \ldots, t_n)$ and some of the t_i is reducible) selecting possibility i of weight w_i with probability $\frac{w_i}{w}$, where w is the sum of the weights of applicable possibilities.

This strategy, even if often considered to avoid problems (see e.g. [14]), which requires to normalize weights to have true probabilities, and then choosing an applicable solution accordingly, may seem artificial.

However, we claim that this is equivalent to a more natural strategy: since the previous strategy is unchanged if all weights are multiplied by some real positive constant, assume that weights w_i are chosen such that $\sum_i w_i = 1$. It can then be also obtained as follows: on a term t, choose *any* possibility selecting possibility i with probability w_i. As long as the chosen possibility can not be applied to t, repeat. When one succeeds to get one that applies to t, apply it.

This is indeed a restatement of following easy observation.

Proposition 2. *Suppose that we have n alternatives that can be partitioned into "bad ones" and "good ones". Suppose that weights $w_1, \ldots, w_n$ (i.e. positive real numbers) are assigned to the alternatives in such a way that $\sum_i w_i = 1$.*
Then the following algorithm:
1. Choose $l \in \{1, \ldots, n\}$ selecting i with probability w_i.
2. If alternative number l is a bad one, then repeat: i.e. goto 1.
3. Answer "alternative number l".

never stops if there is no good alternative, returns with probability 1 some good one otherwise, returning alternative number i with probability $\dfrac{w_i}{\sum_{j \, good \, alternative} w_j}$.

The following problem remains: suppose $t = f(t_1, \ldots, t_n)$ and *congruence* is chosen. In the spirit of classical rewriting logic, we want to allow concurrent rewriting, that is to allow several of the t_i to be rewritten simultaneously. How should we distribute probabilities? We propose to choose the subterms in an independent way. Indeed, n probabilities $q_1^f, \ldots, q_n^f$ (i.e. n real numbers of $[0, 1]$) are associated to each function symbol of the signature of arity n: in an application of *congruence* rule, subterm t_i will be chosen to be rewritten with probability q_i^f. One technical point is that we assume that always at least one subterm is rewritten, and hence the probabilities are probabilities conditioned by this fact.

In a same spirit, we want to allow concurrent rewriting of subterms in application of *replacement* rule. We assume that all the variables in the right member of a rule $l : g \to r$ of the rewrite system appear in the left member. Every rule can then be written as $l : g(x_1, \ldots, x_n, \ldots, x_{n+k}) \to r(x_1, \ldots, x_n)$ where variables $x_1, \ldots, x_n$ are in both members and variables $x_{n+1}, \ldots, x_{n+k}$ are only in left member. We then suppose that to every such rule are associated n probabilities $q_1^l, \ldots, q_n^l$: in an application of *replacement* rule subterm t_i will be chosen to be rewritten with probability q_i^l. Since replacement involves at least one rewrite, we do not expect that at least one subterm is rewritten.

We have now all the ingredients.

Definition 8 (Probabilistic Rewrite System). *A probabilistic rewrite system $(\mathcal{R}, \mathcal{L}, \mathcal{W})$ is given by a labeled rewrite system $(\mathcal{R}, \mathcal{L})$, where all variables in a right member of a rule of $\mathcal{R}$ appears in the left member, with the addition of the following:*

1) a weight (positive real number) w_l for each rule $l \in \mathcal{R}$,
2) a weight w_f for each function symbol of the signature,
3) n reals $q_1^f, \ldots, q_n^f$ of $[0, 1]$ for each function symbol f of arity n,
4) n reals $q_1^l, \ldots, q_n^l$ of $[0, 1]$ for each rule $l : g(x_1, \ldots, x_n, \ldots, x_{n+k}) \to r(x_1, \ldots, x_n)$ of $\mathcal{R}$.
The weights are assumed to be chosen such that $\sum_f w_f + \sum_l w_l = 1$.

We can then introduce the following reduction algorithm:

Definition 9. *Given some probabilistic rewrite system, Reduction is the following recursive algorithm:*
   Input: a reducible term t.
   Output: a term t'.
   Algorithm:
   1. Choose either a rule $l \in \mathcal{R}$ or a symbol f of the signature, according to the probability distribution given by the weights.
   2. If a rule $l : g(x_1, \ldots, x_n, \ldots, x_{n+k}) \to r(x_1, \ldots, x_n)$ was chosen then
   2.1 If $\nexists \sigma \in Sub$ with $\sigma(g) = t$ then repeat: i.e. goto 1.
   / From now on, $t = g(t_1, \ldots, t_{n+k})$ for some $t_1, \ldots, t_{n+k}$ */*
   2.2 Choose $X_1, \ldots, X_n \in \{0, 1\}$ with probability$(X_i = 1) = q_i^l$.
   2.3 For $i = 1, \ldots, n$, let t_i' be the result of the recursive call of algorithm Reduction on t_i when $X_i = 1$ and t_i reducible and let $t_i' = t_i$ otherwise.
   2.4 Return $r(t_1', \ldots, t_n')$.
   3. If a symbol f was chosen
   3.1 If t is not $f(t_1, \ldots, t_n)$ for some $t_1, \ldots, t_n$ then repeat: i.e. goto 1.
   / From now on, $t = f(t_1, \ldots, t_n)$ for some $t_1, \ldots, t_n$ */*
   3.2 Choose $X_1, \ldots, X_n \in \{0, 1\}$ with probability$(X_i = 1) = q_i^f$.
   3.3 If $X_i = 0$ for all i with t_i reducible then repeat: i.e. goto 1.
   3.4 For $i = 1, \ldots, n$, let t_i' be the result of the recursive call of algorithm Reduction on t_i when $X_i = 1$ and t_i reducible and let $t_i' = t_i$ otherwise.
   3.5 Return $f(t_1', \ldots, t_n')$.

Remark 5. This algorithm terminates with probability 1 when given some reducible t. If given some non-reducible t it runs for ever: this is a consequence of Proposition 2.
   We can then define:

Definition 10. *The* executional semantic *of a given probabilistic rewrite system $(\mathcal{R}, \mathcal{L}, \mathcal{W})$ is the corresponding probabilistic abstract reduction system on terms: it is defined as $\mathcal{S}_{\mathcal{R}} = (T(\Sigma, X), \rightsquigarrow)$ where for all s, t, $s \rightsquigarrow p$ is 0 if s is not reducible, and the probability that algorithm Reduction returns t on input s if s is reducible.*

When $(\mathcal{R}, \mathcal{L}, \mathcal{W})$ is a probabilistic rewrite system, call $(\mathcal{R}, \mathcal{L})$ its projection: that is, the classical rewrite system obtained by forgetting probabilities. We have from definitions:

Theorem 5. *The projection of the executional semantic of any probabilistic rewrite system is the executional semantic of its projection.*

6 Probabilistic Rewriting Logic

We now show that there is a sound and complete proof system if proof terms are explicit, i.e. if paths between terms are given.

We propose a logic that works with sequents of type $\pi : t \to_p t'$: when p is a positive real number and $t' \neq \bot$, such a sequent means that term t can evolve to term t' in the executional semantic using the path given by proof term π and that the probability of this path is p. The logic consists of three rules: *reflexivity, congruence, replacement*. Transitivity is not here because of results of Section 4.

A sequent deduced from reflexivity in classical rewriting logic does not correspond to a reduction of the rewriting reduction relation. We suggest to distinguish such a sequent from the others with the use of a new symbol replacing the probability: $\bullet$.

Reflexivity: for all reducible constant a,

$$\mathbf{Ref} : \frac{}{a : a \to_\bullet a}$$

We need a way to express that a term is non-reducible: we propose to use symbol $\bot$. We assume that rules have been added to the rewrite system so that we have the rule $\{\bot_a : a \to \bot\}$ for every non-reducible constant a. When t is a term, we denote by $R(t)$ the set of rewrite rules that can be applied at its root. In particular, we assume $R(a) = \{\bot_a : a \to \bot\}$ for every non-reducible constant a. A sentence of type $\pi : t \to_p \bot$ will mean that t is non-reducible.

Congruence: for all $f \in \Sigma_n$,

$$\mathbf{C} : \frac{\pi_1 : t_1 \to_{p_1} t'_1 \quad \cdots \quad \pi_n : t_n \to_{p_n} t'_n}{f(\pi_1, \ldots, \pi_n) : f(t_1, \ldots, t_n) \to_p f(t''_1, \ldots, t''_n)}$$

with $p = \theta_f^I$, $I = \{i \in \{1, \ldots, n\} | t'_i \neq \bot\}$, $t''_i = \begin{cases} t'_i \text{ if } i \in I \\ t_i \text{ if } i \notin I \end{cases}$

$$\theta_f^I = \begin{cases} \bullet \text{ if } \forall i, \, p_i = \bullet \\ \left(\frac{w_f}{w_f + \sum_{R(t)} w_l}\right) \left(\frac{1}{1 - \prod_{i \in I}(1 - q_i^f)}\right) \left(\prod_{\substack{i \in I \\ p_i \neq \bullet}} q_i^f p_i\right) \left(\prod_{\substack{i \in I \\ p_i = \bullet}} (1 - q_i^f)\right) \\ \qquad\qquad\qquad\qquad\qquad\qquad\qquad\qquad\qquad\qquad otherwise \end{cases}$$

$t = f(t_1, \ldots, t_n)$.

Here, I is the set of subterms that can be reduced. The rule is valid if $I \neq \emptyset$. If $I = \emptyset$, since $f(t_1, \ldots, t_n)$ is non-reducible, the rule becomes

$$\frac{\bot_{t_1} : t_1 \to_1 \bot \quad \cdots \quad \bot_{t_n} : t_n \to_1 \bot}{\bot_{f(t_1, \ldots, t_n)} : f(t_1, \ldots, t_n) \to_1 \bot}$$

Replacement: for all $l : g(x_1, \ldots, x_{n+k}) \to d(x_1, \ldots, x_n) \in \mathcal{R}$,

$$\text{Rep} : \frac{\pi_1 : t_1 \to_{p_1} t_1' \quad \cdots \quad \pi_n : t_n \to_{p_n} t_n'}{l(\pi_1, \ldots, \pi_n, t_{n+1}, \ldots, t_{n+k}) : g(t_1, \ldots, t_n, \ldots, t_{n+k}) \to_p d(t_1'', \ldots, t_n'')}$$

with $p = \theta_l^I$, $I = \{i \in \{1, \ldots, n\} | t_i' \neq \perp\}$, $t_i'' = \begin{cases} t_i' & \text{if } i \in I \\ t_i & \text{if } i \notin I \end{cases}$

and $\theta_l^I = \begin{cases} \bullet \text{ if } \forall i, \ p_i = \bullet \\ \left(\frac{w_l}{w_f + \sum_{R(t)} w_{l'}}\right) \left(\prod_{i \in I | p_i \neq \bullet} q_i^l p_i\right) \left(\prod_{i \in I | p_i = \bullet} (1 - q_i^l)\right) \ otherwise \end{cases}$

$t = g(t_1, \ldots, t_{n+k})$.

Here the rule is correct even when $I = \emptyset$.

The previous rules distribute correctly probabilities onto rewrite rules (the proof can be found in [17]).

Proposition 3. *Let t be a reducible term. Let $S(t)$ be the set of sequents π : $t \to_p t'$ deductible from the rules [Reflexivity, Congruence, Replacement], and such that $p \neq \bullet$. Then $\sum_{S(t)} p = 1$.*

The main property of this proof system is given by following result (the proof, based on repeated applications of Proposition 2, can be found in [17]).

Theorem 6 (The above logic provides a sound and complete proof systems for sequents with proof terms). *Suppose probabilistic rewrite system $\mathcal{R}$ is fixed. For all $t, t' \in T(\Sigma, X)$, there is a path encoded by π between t and t' in the executional semantic of $\mathcal{R}$ of positive probability p iff $\pi : t \to_p t'$ with a positive p is provable using the previous three rules.*

7 Modeling Randomized Systems

In order to argue that our notions of probabilistic rewrite systems, executional semantic and associated logic are natural, we now show how some systems can easily be modeled. We write $l : g \to_p d$ when weight p is associated to rule $l : g \to d$.

Example 1 (Coin flipping). We use constant symbols *head* and *tail* and the following system.

$$\mathcal{R} \begin{cases} h : x \to_{1/2} head \\ t : x \to_{1/2} tail \end{cases}$$

Example 2 (Two players games). Each player has n euros at beginning. At each run, a coin is flipped. If it falls on *head* player 1 wins 1 euro from player 2. If it falls on *tail*, player 2 wins 2 euros from player 1. Game stops when one player is ruined.

Current amount of a player is encoded using constant 0 and unary function s (successor). Binary function *game* is used to group both players, and two constants W_1 and W_2 are used to mean that player 1 or 2 wins. Weight 0 is assigned to function symbol *game*. The game is modeled by the derivations starting from $game(s^n(0), s^n(0))$.

$$\mathcal{R} \begin{cases} h_1 : game(n_1, s(s(n_2))) \rightarrow_{1/2} game(s(n_1), s(n_2)) \\ h_2 : game(n_1, s(0)) \rightarrow_{1/2} W_1 \\ t_1 : game(s(s(s(n_1))), n_2) \rightarrow_{1/2} game(s(n_1), s(s(n_2))) \\ t_2 : game(s(s(0)), n_2) \rightarrow_{1/2} W_2 \end{cases}$$

Example 3 (Two players with two urns). Two players can not see one another and have each an urn. At beginning there are n balls in each urn. At each round they can choose between taking a ball in their urn or doing nothing. With probability p urns are exchanged at each run by some external person. A player with an empty urn loses.

We do as before with constant 0, W_1, W_2 and functions s and *game*. We put weight 0 to functions *game* and s. If the probability that player i takes a ball is q_i, we set $q_1^{ech} = q_1^l = q_1$ and $q_2^{ech} = q_y^l = q_2$.

$$\mathcal{R} \begin{cases} choose : s(x) \rightarrow_1 x \\ ech : game(s(x), s(y)) \rightarrow_p game(s(y), s(x)) \\ l : game(s(x), s(y)) \rightarrow_{(1-p)} game(s(x), s(y)) \\ g_1 : game(0, s(y)) \rightarrow_1 W_1 \\ g_2 : game(s(x), 0) \rightarrow_1 W_2 \\ n : game(0, 0) \rightarrow_1 Tie \end{cases}$$

8   Related Works, Discussions

In this paper, we discussed the existence of a notion of rewriting logic in presence of probabilities. We proved that, unlike what happens for classical theory, accessibility can not be effectively axiomatized, and thus that there is no hope to get a sound and complete logic that would cover transitivity. When transitivity is avoided, in particular when proof terms are explicit and mandatory, we proved that one can define a natural notion of probabilistic rewrite system with some associated semantic, and an associated sound and complete probabilistic rewriting logic.

First-order logics have been proposed to deal with probabilities: see e.g. [3,15]. The impossibility of effective axiomatizations of several first-order logics with probabilities has been proved [1,15], but our results do not seem to follow directly.

The idea of considering rewriting rules with probabilities has already been proposed and illustrated on several examples in [8,14,20], where it is observed that the probabilities cannot be hardwired directly to rules. Paper [8] proposes to avoid the problem by considering the notion of strategy. Papers [14,20] propose a solution similar to the one adopted here considering weights instead of probabilities. Observe that this trick has similarities with classical techniques used to extract a discrete time Markov chain from a continuous one [9], and hence is sometime implicitly or explicitly used for high level modeling of continuous time Markovian systems (see e.g. [13]).

Probabilistic rewriting logic provides a high-level tool for modeling probabilistic systems. Low level models include Markov chains [9] and Markov decision processes if non-determinism is allowed [22]. Other high-level models include models based on Petri nets (cf survey [4]), on process algebra (cf survey [16]), or on automata (cf e.g. [5,13,21,23]). According to the classification [24], our proposition falls into the "generative" case. Observe that our proposition for defining congruence and replacement is similar to (covers) what [12] proposes for the semantic of parallel composition.

The benefits of using a given approach for describing probabilistic systems, compared to another one, depend on the preferred way of describing world, but we believe that our setting is a rather natural and expressive setting, as classical rewriting logic is a rather natural and expressive setting for describing non-probabilistic reactive systems: see survey [18].

Future work includes investigating more deeply the expressive power of the logic. Considering rewriting with congruence classes may constitute a future work direction. Allowing conditional rewriting is another possibility. Another important direction seems also to understand model theory of these systems: Definition 10 reads like the notion of canonical model associated to some given probabilistic rewrite system. What is the notion of model of a given probabilistic rewrite theory? Which results of classical theory (see for e.g. the results in [18,19]) do generalize in this context?

Acknowledgments

The authors would like to thank Claude Kirchner for many helpful discussions and comments about this work.

References

1. Martín Abadi and Joseph Y. Halpern. Decidability and expressiveness for first-order logics of probability. *Information and Computation*, 112(1):1–36, July 1994.
2. Franz Baader and Tobias Nipkow. *Term Rewriting and all That*. Cambridge University Press, 1998.
3. F. Bacchus. *Representing and reasoning with probabilistic knowledge*. MIT-Press, 1990.
4. Gianfranco Balbo. Introduction to stochastic Petri nets. *Lecture Notes in Computer Science*, 2090:84, 2001.
5. Benveniste, Levy, Fabre, and Le Guernic. A calculus of stochastic systems for the specification, simulation, and hidden state estimation of mixed stochastic/non-stochastic systems. *TCS: Theoretical Computer Science*, 152, 1995.
6. A. Bergstra and J.V. Tucker. A characterisation of computable data types by means of a finite equational specification method. In Springer Verlag, editor, *Automata Languages and Programming, Seventh Colloquium*, Lecture Notes in Computer Science, pages 76–90, 1980.
7. P. Borovanský, C. Kirchner, H. Kirchner, P.-E. Moreau, and Ch. Ringeissen. An Overview of ELAN. In C. Kirchner and H. Kirchner, editors, *Second Workshop*

on *Rewriting Logic and its Applications WRLA'98*, volume 15 of *Electronic Notes in Theoretical Computer Science*, Pont-à-Mousson (France), 1998. Elsevier Science B. V. URL: http://www.elsevier.nl/locate/entcs/volume15.html.

8. Olivier Bournez and Claude Kirchner. Probabilistic rewrite strategies: Applications to ELAN. In Sophie Tison, editor, *Rewriting Techniques and Applications*, volume 2378 of *Lecture Notes in Computer Science*, pages 252–266. Springer-Verlag, July 22-24 2002.

9. Pierre Brémaud. *Markov Chains*. Springer, 1991.

10. C. Castro. Solving Binary CSP using Computational Systems. In J. Meseguer, editor, *Proceedings of 1st International Workshop on Rewriting Logic*, volume 4, Asilomar (CA, USA), September 1996. Electronic Notes in Theoretical Computer Science.

11. M. Clavel, F. Durán, S. Eker, J. Meseguer P. Lincoln, N. Martí-Oliet, and J.F. Quesada. Towards Maude 2.0. In *3rd International Workshop on Rewriting Logic and its Applications (WRLA'00)*, volume 36 of *Electronic Notes in Theoretical Computer Science*. Elsevier, 2000.

12. Pedro R. D'Argenio, Holger Hermanns, and Joost-Pieter Katoen. On generative parallel composition. In *Electronic Notes In Computer Science*, volume 22, 1999.

13. L. De Alfaro. Stochastic transition systems. *Lecture Notes in Computer Science*, 1466:423, 1998.

14. Thom Frühwirth, Alexandra Di Pierro, and Herbert Wiklicky. Toward probabilistic constraint handling rules. In Slim Abdennadher and Thom Frühwirth, editors, *Proceedings of the third Workshop on Rule-Based Constraint Reasoning and Programming (RCoRP'01)*, Paphos, Cyprus, December 2001. Under the hospice of the International Conferences in Constraint Programming and Logic Programming.

15. Joseph Y. Halpern. *Discourse, Interaction, and Communication*, chapter A logical approach to reasoning about uncertainty: a tutorial, pages 141–55. Kluwer, 1998.

16. H. Hansson. *Time and Probability in Formal Design of Distributed Systems*. Series in Real-Time Safety Critical Systems. Elsevier, 1994.

17. Mathieu Hoyrup. Réécriture en présence de choix probabilistes. Master's thesis, Ecole Normale Supérieure de Lyon, 2002.

18. Narciso Martí-Oliet and José Meseguer. Rewriting logic: Roadmap and bibliography. *Theoretical Computer Science*, 285(2):121–154, 2002.

19. J. Meseguer. Conditional rewriting logic as a unified model of concurrency. *Theoretical Computer Science*, 96(1):73–155, 1992.

20. Alessandra Di Pierro and Herbert Wiklicky. An operational semantics for probabilistic concurrent constraint programming. In *Proceedings of the 1998 International Conference on Computer Languages*, pages 174–183. IEEE Computer Society Press, 1998.

21. B. Plateau and K. Atif. Stochastic automata network for modelling parallel systems. *IEEE Transactions on Software Engineering*, 17:1093–1108, 1991.

22. M.L. Puternam. *Markov Decision Processes - Discrete Stochastic Dynamic Programming*. Wiley series in probability and mathematical statistics. John Wiley & Sons, 1994.

23. R. Segala and N. Lynch. Probabilistic simulations for probabilistic processes. *Lecture Notes in Computer Science*, 836:481, 1994.

24. Rob van Glabbeek, Scott A. Smolka, Bernhard Steffen, and Chris M. N. Tofts. Reactive, generative, and stratified models of probabilistic processes. In *Proceedings, Fifth Annual IEEE Symposium on Logic in Computer Science*, pages 130–141, Philadelphia, Pennsylvania, 4–7 June 1990. IEEE Computer Society Press.

The Maude 2.0 System[*]

Manuel Clavel[1], Francisco Durán[2], Steven Eker[3], Patrick Lincoln[3],
Narciso Martí-Oliet[1], José Meseguer[4], and Carolyn Talcott[3]

[1] Universidad Complutense de Madrid, Spain
[2] Universidad de Málaga, Spain
[3] SRI International, CA, USA
[4] University of Illinois at Urbana-Champaign, IL, USA

Abstract. This paper gives an overview of the Maude 2.0 system. We
emphasize the full generality with which rewriting logic and membership
equational logic are supported, operational semantics issues, the new
built-in modules, the more general Full Maude module algebra, the new
META-LEVEL module, the LTL model checker, and new implementation
techniques yielding substantial performance improvements in rewriting
modulo. We also comment on Maude's formal tool environment and on
applications.

1 Introduction

Rewriting logic has been shown to have good properties as a semantic and logical
framework [20]. The computational and logical meanings of a rewrite $t \to t'$ are
like two sides of the same coin. Computationally, $t \to t'$ means that the state
component t can *evolve* to the component t'. Logically, $t \to t'$ means that from
the formula t one can *deduce* the formula t'. Furthermore, rewriting logic has been
shown to have good properties not only for specification, but also as a declarative
programming paradigm, as demonstrated by the mature implementations of the
ELAN [1], CafeOBJ [15], and Maude [6] languages.

We will focus in this paper on the main new features in Maude 2.0. We refer
the reader to [4,5] for details on previous releases. Given space limitations, not
even all these new features can be discussed here. The Maude system, its doc-
umentation, and related papers and applications are available from the Maude
website http://maude.cs.uiuc.edu.

The Maude 2.0 system supports both equational and rewriting logic computation with high generality and expressiveness, yet without compromising performance. Functional modules are membership equational theories, whereas system
modules are very general rewrite theories whose rules can have equations, memberships, and rewrites in their conditions, and where some operator arguments
can be *frozen* to block undesired rewrites (see Section 2). Furthermore, Full

---

[*] Research supported by DARPA through Air Force Research Laboratory Contract
F30602-02-C-0130, ONR Grant N00014-02-1-0715, NSF grants CCR-9900326, CCR-
0234603 and CCR-0234524, and by CICYT projects TIC 2000–0701–C02–01 and
TIC 2001–2705–C03–02.

R. Nieuwenhuis (Ed.): RTA 2003, LNCS 2706, pp. 76–87, 2003.

Maude 2.0 supports parameterized modules, theories, and views, and object-oriented modules. Besides supporting equational simplification, Maude 2.0 supports several fair rewriting strategies as well as breadth-first search. Reflective capabilities are substantially extended in a new META-LEVEL module. There are also efficient predefined implementations of useful arithmetic and string data types. Since rewrite theories are ideally suited for specifying concurrent systems, Maude 2.0 supports efficient explicit-state model checking of linear temporal logic (LTL) properties satisfied by finite-state rewrite theories. The efficiency of rewriting modulo axioms has also been increased thanks to some novel implementation techniques. Finally, using reflection an environment of formal tools for Maude 2.0, extending earlier tools, is currently under development.

The structure of this document is as follows. Section 2 discusses the semantics of Maude 2.0. Section 3 presents some of the new features in this release. Section 4 is dedicated to the implementation and performance of the system. Section 5 comments on Maude's formal tool environment. Finally, Section 6 draws some concluding remarks.

2   Generalized Logical and Operational Semantics

The close contact with many specification and programming applications has served as a good stimulus for a substantial increase in expressive power of the rewriting logic formalism in general, and of its Maude realization in particular. Specifically, Maude 2.0 supports rewriting logic computation generalized along three key dimensions. A first dimension concerns the generality of the underlying equational logic. Since a rewrite theory is essentially a triple $\mathcal{R} = (\Sigma, E, R)$, with (Σ, E) an equational theory, and R a set of labeled rewrite rules that are applied *modulo* the equations E, the more general the underlying equational logic, the more expressive the rewriting logic. Maude 2.0's underlying equational logic is *membership equational logic* [22], a very expressive many-kinded Horn logic whose atomic formulas are equations $t = t'$ and memberships $t : s$, stating that a term t has sort s. A second dimension concerns the generality of conditions in conditional rewrite rules that can be of the form,

$$(\forall X) \; r\!: t \to t' \text{ if } \bigwedge_{i \in I} p_i = q_i \; \wedge \; \bigwedge_{j \in J} w_j : s_j \; \wedge \; \bigwedge_{l \in L} t_l \to t_l'$$

where r is the rule label, all terms are Σ-terms, and the rule can be made conditional to other equations, memberships, and rewrites being satisfied. A third dimension involves support for declaring certain operator arguments as *frozen*, thus blocking rewriting under them. Therefore, a Maude (system) module is a *generalized rewrite theory*, defined as a 4-tuple $\mathcal{R} = (\Sigma, E, \phi, R)$, where (Σ, E) is a membership equational theory, R is a set of labeled conditional rewrite rules of the general form above, and ϕ is a function assigning to each operator $f : k_1 \ldots k_n \to k$ in Σ the subset $\phi(f) \subseteq \{1, \ldots, n\}$ of its frozen arguments. In Maude, membership equational theories define the equational sublanguage of *functional modules*.

Unfrozen arguments (those not frozen) are for rewrite theories the analog of the arguments specified in *evaluation strategies* [10] used for equational theories in OBJ, CafeOBJ, and Maude to improve efficiency and/or to guarantee the termination of computations, replacing unrestricted equational rewriting by context-sensitive rewriting [19]. Thus, in Maude 2.0 rewriting with both equations E and rules R can be made context-sensitive. The mathematical semantics of generalized rewrite theories, and thus of modules in Maude 2.0, has been recently developed by Bruni and Meseguer [2], who have given generalized rules of deduction, and have shown the existence of initial and free models and the completeness of rewriting logic deduction relative to the generalized model theory.

There is yet another way in which Maude 2.0 supports rewriting logic and its underlying membership equational logic in its fullest possible generality, namely by the way executability issues are dealt with in the language. The point, of course, is that efficient and complete computation by rewriting is not possible for arbitrary equational theories, unless they satisfy good properties such as confluence, sort-decreasingness, and perhaps termination. Similarly, to be efficiently executable, a generalized rewrite theory $\mathcal{R} = (\Sigma, E, \phi, R)$ should first of all have (Σ, E) satisfying the above executability requirements, and should furthermore be *coherent* [27]. Executability is of course what we want for programming; but it is too restrictive for specification, transformation, and reasoning purposes, even when programming is the ultimate goal. For this reason, in Full Maude (as in OBJ) there is a linguistic distinction between *modules*, that are typically used for programming as executable theories, and *theories*, which need not be executable and are used for specification purposes (for example, to specify the semantic requirements of interfaces in *parameterized* modules). Maude 2.0 supports specification of arbitrary membership equational logic theories and of arbitrary rewrite theories, while at the same time keeping a sharp distinction between executable and non-executable statements (i.e., equations, memberships, or rules). This distinction is achieved by means of the `nonexec` attribute, with which such statements can be labeled. In fact, in Maude 2.0 both modules and theories can be either: (1) fully executable, or (2) partially executable (some statements are `nonexec`), or (3) non-executable (all statements are `nonexec`). Fully executable equational and rewrite theories are called *admissible*, and satisfy the above-mentioned executability requirements; however, in keeping with the desired generality of conditions in equations and rules, extra variables can appear in conditions, provided that they are only introduced by patterns in *matching equations* or in the righthand sides of rewrites (see Section 3.2). Nevertheless, executability is a relative matter. In Maude 2.0 all statements are executable at the metalevel, using reflection and the `META-LEVEL` module (see Section 3.5) but non-executable ones will need strategies to guide their metalevel execution. This support for a disciplined coexistence of executable and non-executable statements allows not only a seamless integration of specification and code, but also a seamless integration of Maude with its formal tools (see Section 5).

3 Some New Features in Maude 2.0

Maude 2.0 presents a number of new features with respect to previous releases. In the following sections we shall discuss some of the most relevant ones, namely, the possibility of accessing the kinds, the new form of conditions in conditional statements, a search facility for doing breadth first search with cycle detection, the new built-in modules, the new possibilities for parameterized programming, the new metalevel, and the LTL model checker. Other features not discussed here include: a rule and position fair strategy, on-the-fly declaration of variables, statement attributes (all statements can be given labels for improving tracing, and we can attach an arbitrary string of metadata to a statement for metaprocessing), the possibility of using efficiently huge towers of unary operator symbols, facilities for improving pretty-printing of terms and for identifying possible incompleteness of specifications, new profiling and debugging features, and so on.

3.1 Access to Kinds

A membership equational signature Σ has a set K of *kinds*, and for each $k \in K$ a set S_k of *sorts* of that kind. Maude does automatic kind inference from the sorts declared by the user and their subsort relations, but kinds are not explicitly named; instead, a kind k is identified with the set S_k of its sorts, interpreted as an *equivalence class* modulo the equivalence relation generated by the subsort ordering. Therefore, for any $s \in S_k$, $[s]$ denotes the kind $k = S_k$, understood as the connected component of the poset of sorts to which s belongs.

Let us assume a graph specification with sorts `Node` and `Edge` and operations `source` and `target` giving, respectively, the source and target nodes of each edge, as well as specific edge and node constants. Then, we extend such a specification by declaring a sort `Path` of paths over the graph, together with a *partial* concatenation operator, and appropriate source and target functions over paths as follows, where the subsort declaration states that edges are paths of length one.

```
subsort Edge < Path .
op _;_ : [Path] [Path] -> [Path] .
ops source target : Path -> Node .
```

This illustrates the idea that in Maude sorts are user-defined, while kinds are implicitly associated with connected components of sorts and are considered as "error supersorts." The Maude system also lifts automatically to kinds all the operators involving sorts of the corresponding connected components to form *error expressions*. Such error expressions allow us to give expressions to be evaluated the benefit of the doubt: if, when they are simplified, they have a legal sort, then they are ok; otherwise, the fully simplified error expression is returned as an error message. Rewriting can occur at the kind level, which may be useful for error recovery.

Given variables E and P of sorts `Edge` and `Path`, respectively, we may express the condition defining path concatenation with the conditional membership axiom

```
cmb E ; P : Path if target(E) = source(P) .
```

stating that an edge concatenated with a path is also a path when the target node of the edge coincides with the source node of the path. This has the effect of defining path concatenation as a partial function on paths, although it is total on the kind `[Path]` of "confused paths."

3.2 More Expressive Conditions in Conditional Statements and Searching

Equational conditions in conditional equations and memberships are made up from individual equations $t = t'$ and memberships $t : s$ using a binary conjunction connective $\wedge$ which is assumed associative. Furthermore, equations in conditions have two variants, namely, ordinary equations `t = t'`, and *matching equations* `t := t'`. For example, assuming a variable E of sort `Edge`, and variables P and S of sort `Path`, the source function over paths may be defined by means of matching equations in conditions as follows:

```
ceq source(P) = source(E) if E ; S := P .
```

Matching equations are mathematically interpreted as ordinary equations; however, operationally they are treated in a special way and they must satisfy special requirements. Note that the variables E and S in the above matching equation do not appear in the lefthand sides of the corresponding conditional equation. In the execution of this equation, these new variables become instantiated by *matching* the term E ; S against the subject term bound to the variable P. In order for this match to decide the equality with the ground term bound to P, the term E ; S must be a *pattern* [6].

The satisfaction of the conditions is attempted sequentially from left to right. Since matching takes place *modulo* equational attributes, in general many different matches may have to be tried until a match of all the variables satisfying the condition is found. All conditional equations in a functional module have to satisfy certain *admissibility requirements*, ensuring that all the extra variables will become instantiated by matching (see [6] for details).

Conditional rewrite rules can take the most general possible form in the variant of rewriting logic built on top of membership equational logic, as explained in Section 2, with no restriction on which new variables may appear in the righthand side or the condition. That is, conditions in rules are also formed by an associative conjunction connective $\wedge$, but they generalize conditions in equations and memberships by allowing also rewrite expressions. Of course, in that full generality the execution of a rewrite theory specified as a system module will require *strategies* that control at the metalevel the instantiation of the extra variables in the condition and in the righthand side [3]. However, a quite general class of system modules, called *admissible modules*, are executable by Maude's interpreter using its built-in strategies. A system module M is called *admissible* if its underlying equational theory is confluent, sort decreasing and terminating, its rules are coherent with respect to its equations, and each of its rewrite rules satisfies certain requirements ensuring that all the extra variables will become instantiated [6].

Operationally, we try to satisfy a rewrite condition $u \rightarrow u'$ by reducing the instance $\sigma(u)$ to canonical form v with respect to the equations, and then trying to find a rewrite proof $v \rightarrow w$ with w in canonical form with respect to the equations and such that w is a substitution instance of u'. When executing a conditional rule in an admissible system module, the satisfaction of all its conditions is attempted sequentially from left to right; but notice that now, besides the fact that many matches for the equational conditions may be possible due to the presence of equational axioms, we also have to deal with the fact that solving rewrite conditions requires *search*, including searching for new solutions when previous ones fail to satisfy subsequent conditions.

Searching is also available to the user through the `search` command, which looks for all the rewrites of a given term that match a given pattern satisfying some condition. When a search command terminates, either because there was a finite state graph, or because a limit to the number of solutions was given, the state graph is retained in memory. It is then possible to obtain the whole generated search graph and to interrogate the state graph for the path from the start term to any reachable state.

3.3 Built-in Funtional Modules

Maude 2.0 includes some built-in functional modules providing convenient high-performance functionality within the Maude system. In particular, the built-in modules of integers, natural, rational and floating-point numbers, quoted identifiers, and strings provide a minimal set of efficient operations for Maude programmers.

The built-in natural numbers allow Maude programmers to deal with natural numbers with a C-like performance for simple arithmetic operations on them (using GNU GMP). Built-in natural numbers bridge the gap between clean Peano-like axiomatizations of numbers with an explicit successor function, and rather more efficient binary representations of unbounded natural number arithmetic. This built-in module allows programmers to manipulate numbers as if they were represented with explicit successor notation, and to reflect those numbers up to the metalevel. Integers are constructed from natural numbers using the unary minus operator. Similarly, the rational numbers are constructed from natural numbers using a division operator. The module of floating-point numbers allows Maude users access to the IEEE-754 double precision floating-point arithmetic when this is supported by the underlying hardware platform. Floats are not algebraic term structures; they are treated as a large set of constants.

Maude's built-in strings are based on the SGI rope package which has been optimized for functional programming, where copying with modification is supported efficiently, while arbitrary in-place updates are not. The Maude string package is compatible with the QID built-in module [6] of quoted identifiers, and interoperates with the Maude 2.0 scheme for metarepresenting user constants. A number of conversion functions is also provided.

3.4   Parameterized Modules and Theories

Full Maude is an extension of Maude written in Maude itself that supports an algebra of parameterized modules, views, and module expressions in the Clear/OBJ style as well as object-oriented modules with convenient syntax for object-oriented applications. We distinguish three key entities: *modules*, which are theories with an initial or free extension semantics; *theories*, with a loose semantics, that can be used to specify the parameters of modules and to state formal assertions; and *view s*, which are theory interpretations used to instantiate parameter theories, refine specifications, and assert formal properties. In Maude 2.0, by means of the Full Maude 2.0 module algebra, modules, theories, and views can all be parameterized.

By using parameterized theories and views we can instantiate parameterized theories and modules in an incremental way, gaining in flexibility. The use of parameterized views allow us, for example, to define a view Set(X :: TRIV) from the trivial theory TRIV with only one sort Elt to the parameterized module SET(X :: TRIV) mapping Elt to the sort Set(X). With this kind of views we keep the parameter part of the target module still as a parameter. For example, given the view Nat from TRIV to NAT and the module LIST(X :: TRIV) of lists, we can have the module LIST(Set(Nat)) of lists of sets of natural numbers, or, given a module STACK(X :: TRIV) of stacks and a view Bool from TRIV to the built-in module BOOL, stacks of sets of booleans with STACK(Set(Bool)).

3.5   Reflection and the META-LEVEL Module

Informally, a reflective logic is a logic in which important aspects of its metatheory can be represented at the object level in a consistent way, so that the object-level representation correctly simulates the relevant metatheoretic aspects. In other words, a reflective logic is a logic which can be faithfully represented in itself.

Maude's language design and implementation make systematic use of the fact that rewriting logic is reflective [8]. In Maude, key functionality of a metalevel theory with several metalevel functions has been efficiently implemented in its functional module META-LEVEL. Maude 2.0 includes improvements in the metarepresentations of terms and modules, and in some of the functions already available in Maude 1.0. Moreover, Maude 2.0 also provides some new metalevel functions. Among others, META-LEVEL includes the following functions: (1) the process of reducing a term to normal form is reified by a function metaReduce; (2) the process of applying a rule to a subject term is reified by functions metaApply and metaXapply; (3) the process of rewriting a term is reified by functions metaRewrite and metaFrewrite, which use, respectively, the top-down rule fair and position fair default strategies; (4) the process of matching a pattern t o a subject term is reified by functions `metaMatch` and `metaXmatch`; (5) a function `metaSearch` reifies the process of searching for a particular pattern term; and (6) parsing and pretty printing of a term, as well as key sort operations, are also reified by corresponding metalevel functions. There are also new ascent functions `upMbs`, `upEqs`, and `upRls` for obtaining the metarepresentation of membership axioms, equations, and rules of a given module in the module database.

3.6   The Maude LTL Model Checker

A model checker typically supports two different levels of specification: (1) a system specification level, in which the concurrent system to be analyzed is formalized; and (2) a property specification level, in which the properties to be model checked—for example, temporal logic formulas—are specified. The Maude LTL model checker has been designed with the goal of combining the very expressive and general system specification capabilities of Maude with an LTL model checking engine that benefits from some of the most recent advances in on-the-fly explicit-state model checking techniques.

A Maude module specifies a rewrite theory $\mathcal{R} = (\Sigma, E, \phi, R)$. Fixing a distinguished sort `State`, the initial model $\mathcal{T}_{\mathcal{R}}$ of $\mathcal{R}$ has an underlying Kripke structure $\mathcal{K}(\mathcal{R}, \text{State})$ given by the total binary relation extending its one-step sequential rewrites. To the initial algebra of states $T_{\Sigma/E}$ we can likewise associate equationally-defined computable state predicates as atomic predicates for such a Kripke structure. In this way we obtain a language of LTL properties of the rewrite theory $\mathcal{R}$.

Maude 2.0 supports on-the-fly LTL model checking for initial states $[t]$ of an admissible rewrite theory $\mathcal{R} = (\Sigma, E, \phi, R)$ such that the set $\{[u] \in T_{\Sigma/E} \mid \mathcal{R} \vdash [t] \rightarrow [u]\}$ of all states reachable from $[t]$ is finite. The syntax of the state predicates we wish to use is defined by means of constants and operators of sort `Prop`, a subsort of `Formula` (i.e., LTL formulas), and their semantics is defined by means of equations involving the operator `_|=_ : State Formula -> Result`. These sorts and operator are declared in the `MODEL-CHECKER` module (and its submodules). Given an initial state, of sort `State`, we can model check any LTL formula involving such predicates with two possible results: `true` if the property holds, or a counterexample expressed as a finite path followed by a cycle if it does not.

Maude offers also a LTL satisfiability decision procedure in its predefined functional module `SAT-SOLVER`, which can also be used as a tautology checker.

4   Implementation and Performance

Maude 2.0, like Maude 1.0, is implemented as a hierarchy of C++ class libraries. There are a large number of incremental improvements, but we highlight the major ones.

The Core Rewrite Engine. The most radical change from Maude 1.0 is the use of a novel term representation based on persistent data structures [9] for *E*-rewriting [11]. In some cases, new rewriting algorithms based on this representation can dramatically improve the rewriting speed for large terms. Table 1 compares the performance of Maude with and without this representation for the example in Appendix A on a 2.8GHz, 2GByte Intel Xeon. The example consists in a specification MAP for a map data type together with a test program MAP-TEST that uses it to compute the Fibonacci function modulo 100.

Another improvement in the core rewrite engine is left-to-right sharing, in which subterms that occur in a lefthand side pattern and are repeated in the righthand side can be shared, so that when an instance of the righthand side is constructed, the subterm matched by the lefthand side subterm can be reused. Other improvements include a new discrimination net algorithm for the free theory that takes sort information into account, and the removal of a number of bottlenecks in the full AC/ACU matching algorithm.

The Metalevel. Apart from the new metaterm representation and new metalevel functions, the big change from Maude 1.0 is improved caching to cut the cost of changing levels in common cases. As well as caching metamodules on a least recently used basis, calls to the metalevel functions that take a numeric argument specifying a solution number—such as metaApply, metaXapply, metaSearch, etc.—are also cached, along with the rewriting state. So a subsequent call to find the next solution can compute it incrementally starting from the old state.

The Model Checker. On-the-fly LTL model checking is performed by constructing a Büchi automaton from the negation of the property formula and lazily searching the synchronous product of the Büchi automaton and the system state transition diagram for a reachable accepting cycle. The negated LTL formula is converted to negative normal form and heuristically simplified by a set of Maude equations, mostly derived from the simplification rules in [14,23]. Rather than the classical tableaux construction [17], we use a newer technique proposed in [16] based on very weak alternating automata to which we add some strongly connected component optimizations adapted from those in [23]. Throughout the computation, the pure propositional subformulas labeling the arcs of the various automata are stored as BDDs to allow computation of conjunctions, elimination of contradictions, and combination of parallel arcs by disjunction. We use the

Table 1. Performance in both seconds and rewrites/second with and without the persistent representation for ACU terms.

Problem size	Rewrites	Without		With	
		Seconds	Rews./second	Seconds	Rews./second
1000	5999	0.25	23996	0.02	299950
10000	59999	55.72	1076	0.21	285709
100000	599999	5676.44	105	2.82	212765

double-depth first method of [18] to lazily generate and search the synchronous product.

5   Formal Tools

In addition to the formal methods directly supported by Maude, one can use Maude as a formal metatool to build other formal tools supporting proofs of correctness of highly critical properties. Reflection and the flexible uses of rewriting logic as a logical framework are the key features making it easy to develop such formal tools and their user interfaces. The paper [7] gives a detailed account of a wide range of formal tools that have been defined in Maude by different authors. Among others, we may mention: the inductive theorem prover ITP tool, the coherence checker and the coherence completion tools, the Church-Rosser Checker tool, the termination checker and the Knuth-Bendix completion tools, the Real-Time Maude tool, etc. There are extensions of these tools currently under development, whose implementations will greatly benefit from the new features of Maude 2.0.

6   Concluding Remarks

The advances in Maude 2.0 have been used to good advantage in several recent applications. The Pathway Logic project uses Maude to develop and analyze biological networks [12,13]. Search and model-checking are used to explore possible execution paths, and the new descent functions are used to analyze and visualize model-checking results. The ascent functions are used to transform the Maude model into a Petri net model for further analysis of possible execution paths. Work on CCS [26] and the Pi-Calculus [25] provides additional examples of the usefulness of new features of Maude 2.0, especially frozen arguments, enriched rule conditions, search, and `metaSearch`. Search, model-checking, and rewrites in rule conditions have been used in a project to model and analyze a proposed secure architecture for accessing remote services in Java [24]. Work is in progress by two of the authors and M. Palomino using the metalevel features and formal tools to define and implement abstractions that convert infinite state models into finite state abstractions [21].

Rewriting logic and its realization in Maude allow for very natural modeling of distributed systems. The next major development of Maude will be to provide an extension that supports executable models that interact with their environment. This will build on the support for concurrent objects and object rewriting in core Maude 2.0 and allow communication with external objects using asynchronous message passing. This will provide access to internet sockets, file systems, window systems, and so on.

References

1. P. Borovanský, C. Kirchner, H. Kirchner, and P.-E. Moreau. ELAN from a rewriting logic point of view. *Theoretical Computer Science*, 285:155–185, 2002.
2. R. Bruni and J. Meseguer. Generalized rewrite theories. To appear in *Procs. of ICALP'03*. LNCS. Springer, 2003.
3. M. Clavel. *Reflection in Rewriting Logic: Metalogical Foundations and Metaprogramming Applications*. CSLI Publications, 2000.
4. M. Clavel, F. Durán, S. Eker, P. Lincoln, N. Martí-Oliet, J. Meseguer, and J. Quesada. Maude Manual, 1999. http://maude.cs.uiuc.edu.
5. M. Clavel, F. Durán, S. Eker, P. Lincoln, N. Martí-Oliet, J. Meseguer, and J. Quesada. The Maude system. In *Procs. of RTA'99*. LNCS 1631, pp. 240–243. Springer, 1999.
6. M. Clavel, F. Durán, S. Eker, P. Lincoln, N. Martí-Oliet, J. Meseguer, and J. Quesada. Maude: specification and programming in rewriting logic. *Theoretical Computer Science*, 285:187–243, 2002.
7. M. Clavel, F. Durán, S. Eker, J. Meseguer, and M.-O. Stehr. Maude as a formal meta-tool. In *Procs. of FM'99*. LNCS 1709, pp. 1684–1703. Springer, 1999.
8. M. Clavel and J. Meseguer. Reflection in conditional rewriting logic. *Theoretical Computer Science*, 285:245–288, 2002.
9. J. R. Driscoll, N. Sarnak, D. Sleator, and R. Tarjan. Making data structures persistent. *Journal of Computer and System Science*, 38:86–124, 1989.
10. S. Eker. Term rewriting with operator evaluation strategy. In *Procs. of WRLA'98*. ENTCS 15. Elsevier, 1998.
11. S. Eker. Associative-commutative rewriting on large terms. This volume.
12. S. Eker, M. Knapp, K. Laderoute, P. Lincoln, J. Meseguer, and K. Sonmez. Pathway logic: Symbolic analysis of biological signaling. In *Procs. of the Pacific Symposium on Biocomputing*, pp. 400–412, 2002.
13. S. Eker, M. Knapp, K. Laderoute, P. Lincoln, and C. Talcott. Pathway logic: Executable models of biological networks. In *Procs. of WRLA'02*. ENTCS 71. Elsevier, 2002.
14. K. Etessami and G. J. Holzmann. Optimizing Büchi automata. In *Procs. of CONCUR'00*. LNCS 1877, pp. 153–167. Springer, 2000.
15. K. Futatsugi and R. Diaconescu. *CafeOBJ Report*. World Scientific, AMAST Series, 1998.
16. P. Gastin and D. Oddoux. Fast LTL to Büchi automata translation. In *Procs. of CAV'01*. LNCS 2102, pp. 53–65. Springer, 2001.
17. R. Gerth, D. Peled, M. Vardi, and P. Wolper. Simple on-the-fly automatic verification of linear temporal logic. In *Protocol Specification Testing and Verification*, pp. 3–18. Chapman and Hall, 1995.
18. G.J. Holzmann, D. Peled, and M. Yannakakis. On nested depth first search. *Design: An International Journal*, 13(3):289–307, 1998.
19. S. Lucas. Termination of rewriting with strategy annotations. In *Procs. of LPAR'01*. LNAI 2250, pp. 669–684. Springer, 2001.
20. N. Martí-Oliet and J. Meseguer. Rewriting logic: roadmap and bibliography. *Theoretical Computer Science*, 285:121–154, 2002.
21. J. Meseguer, M. Palomino, and N. Martí-Oliet. Equational abstractions. To appear in *Procs. of CADE'03*. LNCS. Springer, 2003.
22. J. Meseguer. Membership algebra as a logical framework for equational specification. In *Procs. of WADT'97*. LNCS 1376, pp. 18–61. Springer, 1998.

23. F. Somenzi and R. Bloem. Efficient Büchi automata from LTL formulae. In *Procs. of CAV'00*. LNCS 1633, pp. 247–263. Springer, 2000.
24. C. Talcott. To be presented at the DARPA FTN Winter 2003 PI meeting, TX, USA, 2003.
25. P. Thati, K. Sen, and N. Martí-Oliet. An executable specification of asynchronous pi-calculus semantics and may testing in Maude 2.0. In *Procs. of WRLA'02*. ENTCS 71. Elsevier, 2002.
26. A. Verdejo and N. Martí-Oliet. Implementing CCS in Maude 2. In *Procs. of WRLA'02*. ENTCS 71. Elsevier, 2002.
27. P. Viry. Equational rules for rewriting logic. *Theoretical Computer Science*, 285:487–517, 2002.

A   Map Benchmark Example

```
fmod MAP is
  sorts Domain Range Pair Map .
  subsort Pair < Map .
  op _|->_ : Domain Range -> Pair .
  op empty : -> Map .
  op _,_ : Map Map -> Map [assoc comm id: empty] .
  op undefined : -> [Range] .
 var D : Domain . vars R R' : Range . var M : Map .
  op _[_] : Map Domain -> [Range] .
  eq (M, D |-> R)[D] = R .
  eq M[D] = undefined [owise] .
  op insert : Domain Range Map -> Map .
  eq insert(D, R, (M, D |-> R')) = (M, D |-> R) .
  eq insert(D, R, M) = (M, D |-> R) [owise] .
endfm

fmod MAP-TEST is pr MAP . pr NAT .
  subsort Nat < Domain Range .
 var N : Nat .
  op f : Nat -> Map .
  eq f(0) = insert(0, 1, empty) .
  eq f(1) = insert(1, 1, f(0)) .
  eq f(s s N)
    = insert(s s N, ((f(s N)[s N]) + (f(s N)[N])) rem 100, f(s N)) .
endfm
```

Diagrams for Meaning Preservation[*]

Joe B. Wells[1], Detlef Plump[2], and Fairouz Kamareddine[1]

[1] Heriot-Watt University
http://www.cee.hw.ac.uk/ultra/
[2] University of York
http://www.cs.york.ac.uk/~det/

Abstract. This paper presents an abstract framework and multiple diagram-based methods for proving *meaning preservation*, i.e., that all rewrite steps of a rewriting system preserve the meaning given by an operational semantics based on a rewriting strategy. While previous rewriting-based methods have generally needed the treated rewriting system as a whole to have such properties as, e.g., *confluence, standardization*, and/or *termination* or *boundedness* of *developments*, our methods can work when *all* of these conditions fail, and thus can handle more rewriting systems. We isolate the new *lift/project with termination* diagram as the key proof idea and show that previous rewriting-based methods (Plotkin's method based on *confluence* and *standardization* and Machkasova and Turbak's method based on distinct *lift* and *project* properties) implicitly use this diagram. Furthermore, our framework and proof methods help reduce the proof burden substantially by, e.g., supporting separate treatment of partitions of the rewrite steps, needing only *elementary diagrams* for rewrite step interactions, excluding many rewrite step interactions from consideration, needing weaker termination properties, and providing generic support for using developments in combination with any method.

1 Discussion

1.1 Background and Motivation

A programming language is defined as a set of programs and a way to evaluate (or "execute") the programs. It is increasingly popular to define evaluation via program rewriting [25, 9, 10, 11, 3, 19, 12, 26]. In this approach, evaluation rewrite rules are repeatedly applied at particular program positions which are typically specified using *evaluation contexts* [9].

Other kinds of program rewriting than evaluation are also desirable. Potential uses of rewriting-based program transformations include optimizing compilers, partial evaluators, and program simplifiers. These transformations may use the already existing evaluation rules in arbitrary contexts or use additional rewrite

[*] This work was partly supported by NSF grants CCR 9417382, CCR 9988529, and EIA 9806745, EPSRC grants GR/L 36963 and GR/R 41545/01, and Sun Microsystems equipment grant EDUD-7826-990410-US.

R. Nieuwenhuis (Ed.): RTA 2003, LNCS 2706, pp. 88–106, 2003.

rules. Some transformations may involve global reasoning about the entire program, but many are local and a good match for rewriting-based techniques.

It is important to know when program transformations preserve a program's meaning as given by evaluation. There are many non-rewriting based approaches, such as denotational semantics (models), logical relations, applicative bisimulation and coinduction, etc., but they will not be discussed here because this paper focuses on rewriting-based techniques. Plotkin [25] first devised a rewriting-based method to prove meaning preservation for the call-by-name and call-by-value λ-calculus using *confluence* and *standardization*. At the same time, Plotkin proved that evaluation via rewriting was equivalent to evaluation via abstract machine. Subsequently, this approach has been applied to many systems, including systems with imperative features such as assignments and continuations (examples include [10, 11, 21, 3, 19, 12, 26, 17]).

Warning 1.1 (Not Quite Same as Observational Equivalence) What we call *meaning preservation* is related to *observational equivalence* (sometimes called *observational soundness* [18], *operational equivalence*, *consistency* [25], etc.), but is only the same for *contextually closed* rewriting systems. In this paper, terms have the same *meaning* iff evaluating them yields the same result (divergence or the same halted state). Terms t_1 and t_2 are *observationally equivalent*, written $t_1 \simeq t_2$, iff $C[t_1]$ and $C[t_2]$ have the same meaning for every context C where $C[t]$ places t in the hole of the context C. Proving a rewriting relation R to be meaning preserving implies that $R \subseteq \sim$ only when R is contextually closed; see corollary 7.3 for an example. This paper presents an abstract (syntax-free) framework which does not have any features to represent notions like contexts, so we do not discuss observational equivalence except for specific examples.   □

1.2   Summary of Contributions

The existing rewriting-based tools for proving meaning preservation are difficult to use and sometimes completely inapplicable. To address this problem, this paper presents an abstract framework and multiple diagram-based methods for proving meaning preservation. The new knowledge presented here improves on what is already known as follows.

1. Our methods can be used for rewriting systems that as a whole fail to have confluence, standardization, and/or *termination* or *boundedness* of *developments*. While some of our methods ask for confluence or standardization-like properties, they do so only for subsets of all rewrite steps.
2. We isolate the new *lift/project with termination* diagram (LPT in definition 4.1) and show that it is the key proof idea for previous methods for proving meaning preservation (Plotkin's method based on *confluence* and *standardization* and Machkasova and Turbak's method based on *lift* and *project* [17]). We show that the confluence & standardization method is incomparable in proving power with the lift & project method. We present new LPT-based methods that can handle systems that previous methods can not such as systems without standardization.

3. All of the proof methods dealt with in this paper (including the earlier methods of Plotkin and Machkasova & Turbak) are presented abstractly (free of syntax). Because our methods are abstract, there are no restrictions on the kinds of rewrite rules used. Rewrite rules may be non-left-linear, non-orthogonal (overlapping), non-first-order, etc. Also, our approach does not need a notion of closed *programs* as a subset of terms.

4. All our methods support partitioning the rewrite steps into subsets treated separately with different methods. These subsets need only be closed under (an informal and only intuitive notion of) "residuals with respect to evaluation steps". This partitioning also makes proving termination properties easier.

5. Our framework provides generic support for using developments (i.e., contracting only preexisting marked redexes) together with any method, so each method only needs to work for marked rewrite steps. This makes proving termination properties easier. No notion of *residuals* is needed, which is helpful for systems with highly overlapping rules where defining residuals is hard.

6. In addition to a number of high-level diagram-based methods for proving meaning preservation, we also present low-level methods that are easier to use for people who are not researchers in rewriting. We give as many as possible of the details needed for the non-specialist to use and adapt the proof methods. These low-level methods use simple termination properties and diagrams.

   (a) Termination properties are only needed for ordinary rewriting, not for rewriting of rewrite step sequences (perhaps this should be called meta-rewriting?) as in some abstract standardization methods [20]. The different termination properties that each method requires are simple and easy for the non-specialist to understand, ranging over boundedness (Bnd) and *(weak) normalization* (Nrm) and a bound on the number of evaluation steps in any rewrite sequence (BE in definition 5.1).

   (b) For analyzing rewrite step interactions, each method needs only the completion of *elementary diagrams*, i.e., diagrams where the only given edges are two adjacent single rewrite steps. In contrast, some abstract standardization methods require completing *cubes* [13, 20]. The method choice can depend on which elementary diagrams are completable. All of our methods exclude many rewrite step interactions from consideration.

7. To help rewriting researchers, as much as possible we identify intermediate diagrams to make it easier for new diagrams to be added as needed.

8. Our methods use only the simplest notion of standardization, that a rewrite sequence $t_1 \twoheadrightarrow t_2$ can be rearranged into a sequence $t_1 \overset{\mathbb{E}}{\twoheadrightarrow} t_3 \overset{\mathbb{N}}{\twoheadrightarrow} t_2$ where $\mathbb{E}$ and $\mathbb{N}$ indicate respectively evaluation and non-evaluation steps. Standardization in the literature is a rich and interesting notion [20], but other standardization definitions always imply our definition and the extra details are not useful here, so they are omitted.

Due to tight space limits, most proofs are omitted and also some proofs omit many details, but a long version of this paper with full proof details is available from the first author's home page.

1.3   Acknowledgements

An early informal presentation by Elena Machkasova on the *lift* and *project* diagrams gave significant inspiration, although this work then proceeded independently. Stefan Blom, Elena Machkasova, Vincent van Oostrom, and Lyn Turbak carefully read drafts of this paper and pointed out confusing terminology and errors. Zena Ariola is partly responsible for this work by convincing us to use rewrite rules for letrec that are difficult to prove correct.

2   Mathematical Definitions

Let $S \uplus S'$ denote $S \cup S'$ if $S \cap S' = \emptyset$ and otherwise be undefined. In a proof, "IH" means "by the induction hypothesis" and "w/o.l.o.g." means "without loss of generality".

Let R range over binary relations. Let $\xrightarrow{R}$ and $\xrightarrow{}_{R}$ be alternate notations for R which are usable infix, i.e., both $a \xrightarrow{R} b$ and $a \xrightarrow{}_{R} b$ stand for $R(a,b)$ which in turn stands for $(a,b) \in R$.

Define the following operators on binary relations. Let $R; R'$ be the composition of R with R' (i.e., $\{(a,b) \mid \exists c.\ R(a,c) \text{and}\ R'(c,b)\}$). Let $\xrightarrow{R,0} = R^0$ be equality at the type intended for R. Let $\xrightarrow{R,i+1} = R^{i+1} = (R^i; R)$ when $0 \le i$. Let $\xrightarrow{R,\ge k} = R^{\ge k} = \bigcup_{i \ge k} R^i$. Let $\xrightarrow{R,\le k} = R^{\le k} = \bigcup_{i \le k} R^i$. Let $\xrightarrow{R,j,\le k} = R^j \cap R^{\le k}$ (useful in diagrams when j is existentially quantified). Let $\xrightarrow{R} = R^* = R^{\ge 0}$ (the transitive, reflexive closure). Let $\xleftarrow{R} = R^{-1}$ be the inverse of R (i.e., $\{(a,b) \mid R(b,a)\}$). Let $\xleftarrow{R} = (R^{-1})^{\ge 0}$. Let $\xleftrightarrow{R} = (R \cup R^{-1})$ (the symmetric closure). When $R = R^{-1}$ (i.e., R is symmetric), let $\xleftrightarrow{R} = R$. Let $\xleftrightarrow{R,k} = (\xleftrightarrow{R})^k$. Let $\xleftrightarrow{R} = (\xleftrightarrow{R})^{\ge 0}$.

Let an entity a *be* a *R-normal form*, written is-nf(R,a), iff there does not exist some entity b such that $a \xrightarrow{R} b$. Let an entity a *have* a R-normal form, written has-nf(R,a), iff there exists some b such that $a \xrightarrow{R} b$ and is-nf(R,b). Let $\xrightarrow{R,\mathsf{nf}}$ be the relation such that $a \xrightarrow{R,\mathsf{nf}} b$ iff $a \xrightarrow{R} b$ and is-nf(R,b). A relation R is *bounded*, written Bnd(R), iff for every entity a there is some $k \ge 0$ such that there does not exist an entity b such that $R^k(a,b)$. A relation R is *terminating* (a.k.a. *strongly normalizing*), written Trm(R), iff there does not exist any total function f with as domain the natural numbers such that $R(f(i), f(i+1))$ for all $i \ge 0$. A relation R is *(weakly) normalizing*, written Nrm(R), iff for every entity a there is some entity b such that $a \xrightarrow{R,\mathsf{nf}} b$. Note that Bnd$(R) \Rightarrow$ Trm$(R) \Rightarrow$ Nrm(R).

Diagrams make statements about relations where solid and dotted edges indicate quantification. Metavariables already mentioned outside the diagram are unquantified. Other metavariables (e.g., for node names or used in edge labels) are universally quantified if attached to a solid edge and existentially quantified if attached only to dotted edges. As an example, in a context where

R_1 and R_2 have already been given, the following equivalence holds:

$$
\begin{array}{c}
a \xrightarrow{\quad\quad} b \\
R_2 \left[\begin{array}{c} R_1,k \\ \\ R_1,\leq k \end{array} \right] R_1 \\
c \cdots\cdots\cdots\!\!\!\!\to d
\end{array}
\iff \forall a,b,c,k.\ (a \xrightarrow{R_1,k} b \wedge a \xrightarrow{R_2} c) \Rightarrow \exists d.\ c \xrightarrow{R_1,\leq k} d \wedge b \xrightarrow{R_1} d
$$

In proofs, the reason for each diagram polygon will usually be written inside it.

3 Abstract Evaluation Systems

An *abstract evaluation system* (AES) is a tuple

$$(\mathbb{T}, \mathbb{S}, \mathbb{R}, \mathsf{endpoints}, \mathbb{E}, \mathsf{result})$$

satisfying the conditions given below by axioms 3.3 and 3.4 and the immediately following conditions. The carriers of an AES are the sets $\mathbb{T}$, $\mathbb{S}$, and $\mathbb{R}$. The function $\mathsf{endpoints}$ maps $\mathbb{S}$ to $\mathbb{T} \times \mathbb{T}$. The set $\mathbb{E}$ is a subset of $\mathbb{S}$. The function result maps $\mathbb{T}$ to $\mathbb{R}$. Let t range over $\mathbb{T}$, let s range over $\mathbb{S}$, let r range over $\mathbb{R}$, and let $\mathcal{S}$ range over subsets of $\mathbb{S}$.

The intended meaning is as follows. $\mathbb{T}$ should be a set of terms. $\mathbb{S}$ should be a set of rewrite steps. $\mathbb{R}$ should be a set of evaluation results which by axiom 3.4(1) will most likely contain the symbol $\mathsf{diverges}$ and one or more other members, typically symbols such as halt, error, etc. The halt case might be subdivided into possible constant values of final results. If $\mathsf{endpoints}(s) = (t_1, t_2)$, this should mean that step s rewrites term t_1 to term t_2. The members of $\mathbb{E}$ are the rewrite steps used for evaluation. Let $\mathbb{N} = \mathbb{S} \backslash \mathbb{E}$ (where "$\mathbb{N}$" stands for "non-evaluation"). If $\mathsf{result}(t) = r$, this should mean that r is the observable result of evaluating term t, where $\mathsf{diverges}$ is reserved by axiom 3.4(1) for non-halting evaluations.

Convention 3.1 *In this paper, wherever no specific AES is being considered, statements are about every possible AES.*   □

Let rewriting notation be defined as follows. Given a rewrite step set $\mathcal{S}$, let $\underset{\llcorner}{\mathcal{S}}\lrcorner$ be the binary relation $\{ (t, t') \mid \exists s \in \mathcal{S}.\ \mathsf{endpoints}(s) = (t, t') \}$. Thus, $t \xrightarrow{\mathcal{S}} t'$ iff there exists $s \in \mathcal{S}$ such that $\mathsf{endpoints}(s) = (t, t')$. When a rewrite step set $\mathcal{S}$ is used in a context *requiring* a binary relation on $\mathbb{T}$, then let $\mathcal{S}$ implicitly stand for $\underset{\llcorner}{\mathcal{S}}\lrcorner$. Thus, as examples, $t \xrightarrow{\mathcal{S}} t'$ stands for $t \xrightarrow{\underset{\llcorner}{\mathcal{S}}\lrcorner} t'$ and an $\mathcal{S}$-normal form is simply a $\underset{\llcorner}{\mathcal{S}}\lrcorner$-normal form. When used in a position *requiring* a subset of $\mathbb{S}$ or a binary relation on $\mathbb{T}$, let s stand for $\{s\}$ and let $\mathcal{S}, \mathcal{S}'$ stand for $\mathcal{S} \cap \mathcal{S}'$. Thus, as an example, $t \xrightarrow{\mathcal{S},s} t'$ stands for $t \xrightarrow{\underset{\llcorner}{\mathcal{S} \cap \{s\}}\lrcorner} t'$. When a binary relation on $\mathbb{T}$ is *required* and none is supplied, then let the relation $\underset{\llcorner}{\mathbb{S}}\lrcorner$ be implicitly supplied. Thus, as examples, $t \to t'$ stands for $t \xrightarrow{\underset{\llcorner}{\mathbb{S}}\lrcorner} t'$ and $t \xrightarrow{k} t'$ stands for $t \xrightarrow{\underset{\llcorner}{\mathbb{S}},k} t'$.

Definition 3.2 (Rewrite Step Set Properties). *Define the following rewrite step sets and properties of rewrite step sets:*

Standardization:

$$\mathsf{Std}(\mathcal{S}, \mathcal{S}') \iff \begin{array}{c} t_1 \xrightarrow{\ \ \mathcal{S}\ \ } t_2 \\ {\scriptstyle \mathbb{E},\mathcal{S}'} \searrow \ \nearrow {\scriptstyle \mathbb{N},\mathcal{S}'} \\ t_3 \end{array}$$

Confluence:

$$\mathsf{Conf}(\mathcal{S}) \iff \begin{array}{c} t_1 \xleftarrow{\ \ \mathcal{S}\ \ } t_2 \\ {\scriptstyle \mathcal{S}} \searrow \ \swarrow {\scriptstyle \mathcal{S}} \\ t_3 \end{array}$$

Local Confluence:

$$\mathsf{LConf}(\mathcal{S}) \iff \begin{array}{c} t_1 \xrightarrow{\ \mathcal{S}\ } t_4 \\ {\scriptstyle \mathcal{S}} \downarrow \quad {\scriptstyle \mathcal{S}} \downarrow {\scriptstyle \mathcal{S}} \\ t_2 \xrightarrow{\ \mathcal{S}\ } t_3 \end{array}$$

Meaning Preservation:

$$s \in \mathsf{MP} \iff \begin{array}{c} t_1 \xdashrightarrow{\ \text{result}\ } \\ {\scriptstyle s} \downarrow \quad \searrow r \\ t_2 \xrightarrow{\ \text{result}\ } \end{array}$$

Subcommutativity:

$$\mathsf{SubComm}(\mathcal{S}, i, j) \iff \begin{array}{c} t_1 \xrightarrow{\ \mathcal{S},j\ } t_3 \\ {\scriptstyle \mathcal{S},i} \downarrow \quad \downarrow {\scriptstyle \mathcal{S},\leq i} \\ t_2 \xrightarrow{\ \mathcal{S},\leq j\ } t_4 \end{array}$$

Let $\mathsf{Std}(\mathcal{S})$ *abbreviate* $\mathsf{Std}(\mathcal{S}, \mathbb{S})$. *Let* $\mathsf{SubComm}(\mathcal{S})$ *abbreviate* $\mathsf{SubComm}(\mathcal{S}, 1, 1)$. *Traditionally, only* $\mathsf{Std}(\mathbb{S}) = \mathsf{Std}(\mathbb{S}, \mathbb{S})$ *is considered. The simple definition of* MP *is reasonable because axiom 3.4(1) (given below) means* MP *implies preservation of the existence of* $\mathbb{E}$-*normal forms. See also warning 1.1 and convention 3.1 and do not confuse* MP *with observational equivalence.* □

Axiom 3.3 (Subcommutativity of Evaluation) $\mathsf{SubComm}(\mathbb{E})$. □

Non-deterministic evaluation is useful for rewriting systems with non-deterministic syntax, e.g., the system of [17] where the top syntax level is a set with unordered components. Often, it will be simpler to make evaluation deterministic so that $t_2 \xleftarrow{\mathbb{E},s_1} t_1 \xrightarrow{\mathbb{E},s_2} t_3$ implies that $t_2 = t_3$ or even that $s_1 = s_2$.

Axiom 3.3 does not ensure that any strategy for $\xrightarrow{\mathbb{E}}$ will find $\mathbb{E}$-normal forms when they exist. Strengthening axiom 3.3 so that the bottom and right diagram edges have the same length would ensure this, but is not needed otherwise.

Axiom 3.4 (Evaluation Sanity)

1. *"diverges" Means Evaluation Diverges:*
   $\mathsf{result}(t) = \mathsf{diverges} \Leftrightarrow \neg\mathsf{has\text{-}nf}(\mathbb{E}, t)$.
2. **Evaluation Steps Preserve Meaning:**
   $\mathbb{E} \subseteq \mathsf{MP}$.
3. **Non-Evaluation Steps Preserve Evaluation Steps:**

$$\begin{array}{c} t_1 \xrightarrow{\ \mathbb{E}\ } t_3 \\ {\scriptstyle \mathbb{N}} \downarrow \quad \downarrow {\scriptstyle \mathbb{E}} \\ t_2 \xrightarrow{\ \mathbb{E}\ } t_4 \end{array}$$

   Consequently, if $t_1 \xrightarrow{\mathbb{N}} t_2$, *then* $\mathsf{is\text{-}nf}(\mathbb{E}, t_1) \Leftrightarrow \mathsf{is\text{-}nf}(\mathbb{E}, t_2)$.
4. **Non-Evaluation Steps on** $\mathbb{E}$-**Normal Forms Preserve Meaning:**
   If $t \xrightarrow{\mathbb{N}} t'$ *and* $\mathsf{is\text{-}nf}(\mathbb{E}, t)$, *then* $\mathsf{result}(t) = \mathsf{result}(t')$. □

When defining an AES for a rewriting system, it is trivial to satisfy axioms 3.4(1) and 3.4(2) by using an auxiliary function result' which maps $\{\, t \mid \mathsf{is\text{-}nf}(\mathbb{E}, t) \,\}$ to $\mathbb{R} \setminus \{\mathsf{diverges}\}$ and defining result as follows:

$$\mathsf{result}(t) = \begin{cases} \mathsf{diverges} & \text{if } \neg\mathsf{has\text{-}nf}(\mathbb{E}, t), \\ \mathsf{result}'(t') & \text{if } t \xrightarrow{\mathbb{E},\mathsf{nf}} t'. \end{cases}$$

Indeed, the model of how evaluation should be computed expects to work this way. When $\neg\mathsf{is\text{-}nf}(\mathbb{E}, t)$, it is expected that computing $\mathsf{result}(t)$ involves first finding t' such that $t \xrightarrow{\mathbb{E},\mathsf{nf}} t'$, then computing $\mathsf{result}(t')$, and otherwise diverging if no such t' exists. Thus, the value of $\mathsf{result}(t)$ is unimportant if $\neg\mathsf{has\text{-}nf}(\mathbb{E}, t)$. Reserving the value diverges for this case simplifies things.

Satisfying axioms 3.4(3) and 3.4(4) requires more care in the design of the rewriting system and the AES, but is not hard. Anyway, axiom 3.4(3) is a consequence of the properties WL1 and WP1 or WLP1 from definition 5.1 which typically must also be proven. At first glance, the reader might think that axiom 3.4(3) is simpler than what is needed because in its diagram no relationship is required between t_3 and t_4; however this issue is handled by the LPT diagram from definition 4.1 and in any case a relationship between t_3 and t_4 is only needed when $\mathsf{has\text{-}nf}(\mathbb{E}, t_1)$. The condition of axiom 3.4(3) appears in other abstract frameworks as early as [13] and appears in non-abstract form in [25]. The first explicit statement of the condition of axiom 3.4(4) that we are aware of appears in [16], although the condition is partially present in [3].

Lemma 3.5 (Non-Evaluation Steps on Eval-Normal Forms). *If* $t_1 \xleftrightarrow{\mathsf{N}} t_2$ *and* $\mathsf{is\text{-}nf}(\mathbb{E}, t_1)$, *then* $t_1 \xleftrightarrow{\mathsf{MP}} t_2$. $\qquad\square$

4   Lift/Project Diagrams for Meaning Preservation

This section presents properties of rewrite step sets in definition 4.1 and shows how to use them to prove *meaning preservation*, the important connection between arbitrary-strategy rewriting and evaluation. When evaluation is defined by a subset of the rewrite steps (specified in an AES by the set $\mathbb{E}$), it is necessary to show that arbitrary rewriting preserves the evaluation result in order to have confidence that the non-evaluation rewrite steps are at all meaningful. Traditionally, this has been done by proving confluence (Conf) and standardization (Std), the preconditions of Plotkin's approach [25] (presented in lemma 4.5(1,2)).

Needing confluence and standardization is a big weakness, as shown by the non-confluent system in [17] and the $\lambda^{:=,\mathsf{letrec}}$ calculus we mention in section 9 which has neither confluence nor standardization. In contrast, our new method in theorem 4.3 needs only the *lift/project with termination* (LPT) property. By lemma 4.2, LPT can be obtained from the lift (Lift) and project (Proj) properties. Because lift and project do not imply confluence (lemma 4.5(4)), theorem 4.3 does not need confluence. Furthermore, because LPT implies neither lift nor project (lemma 4.2(8,10)) and lift is equivalent to standardization (lemma 4.4(1)), theorem 4.3 does not need standardization when lift is not used.

Theorem 4.3 differs from earlier work of Machkasova and Turbak [17] in several important ways. First, it is abstract (syntax-free). Second, it provides explicit support for separately proving meaning preservation for different subsets of the non-evaluation rewrite steps. This vastly simplifies auxiliary termination proofs (e.g., for properties Bnd or BE as used in definition 5.1) and is vital when a single method fails to cover all $\mathbb{N}$ steps (e.g., section 9). Third, it needs only the weaker LPT property rather than lift and project. This is vital because lift is equivalent to standardization so the Machkasova/Turbak method fails for systems without standardization (e.g., section 9).

Definition 4.1 (Lift, Project, and Related Properties). *Define the following rewrite step sets and properties of rewrite step sets:*

Strong Lift: Lift:

$$\mathsf{SLift}(\mathcal{S}) \iff \begin{array}{c} t_1 \cdots\!\!\twoheadrightarrow t_4 \\ {}_{\mathsf{N},\mathcal{S}}\downarrow\; {}_{\mathrm{E}}\; \vdots {}_{\mathsf{N},\mathcal{S}} \\ t_2 \!\!\rightarrow\! t_3 \end{array} \qquad s \in \mathsf{Lift} \iff \begin{array}{c} t_1 \cdots\!\!\twoheadrightarrow t_4 \\ {}_{s}\downarrow\; {}_{\mathrm{E}}\; \downarrow {}_{\mathsf{N}} \\ t_2 \!\!\rightarrow\! t_3 \end{array}$$

Lift':

$$s \in \mathsf{Lift}' \iff \begin{array}{c} t_1 \cdots\cdots\cdots\!\!\twoheadrightarrow t_4 \\ {}_{s}\downarrow\quad {}_{\mathrm{E}}\quad {}_{\mathrm{E}}\downarrow {}_{\mathsf{N}} \\ t_2 \!\!\rightarrow\! t_3 \cdots\!\!\twoheadrightarrow t_5 \end{array}$$

Strong Project: Project:

$$\mathsf{SProj}(\mathcal{S}) \iff \begin{array}{c} t_1 \!\!\rightarrow\! t_2 \cdots\!\!\twoheadrightarrow t_4 \\ {}_{\mathsf{N},\mathcal{S}}\downarrow\; {}_{\mathrm{E}}\quad {}_{\mathrm{E}}\; \downarrow {}_{\mathsf{N},\mathcal{S}} \\ t_3 \cdots\cdots\!\!\twoheadrightarrow t_5 \end{array} \qquad s \in \mathsf{Proj} \iff \begin{array}{c} t_1 \!\!\rightarrow\! t_2 \cdots\!\!\twoheadrightarrow t_4 \\ {}_{s}\downarrow\; {}_{\mathrm{E}}\quad \downarrow {}_{\mathsf{N}} \\ t_3 \cdots\cdots\!\!\twoheadrightarrow t_5 \end{array}$$

Strong Lift/Project: Lift/Project:

$$\mathsf{SLP}(\mathcal{S}) \iff \begin{array}{c} t_1 \!\!\rightarrow\! t_3 \cdots\!\!\twoheadrightarrow t_5 \\ {}_{\mathsf{N},\mathcal{S}}\uparrow\; {}_{\mathrm{E}}\quad {}_{\mathrm{E}}\uparrow {}_{\mathsf{N},\mathcal{S}} \\ t_2 \cdots\cdots\!\!\twoheadrightarrow t_4 \end{array} \qquad s \in \mathsf{LP} \iff \begin{array}{c} t_1 \!\!\rightarrow\! t_3 \cdots\!\!\twoheadrightarrow t_5 \\ {}_{s}\uparrow\; {}_{\mathrm{E}}\quad \uparrow {}_{\mathsf{N}} \\ t_2 \cdots\cdots\!\!\twoheadrightarrow t_4 \end{array}$$

Lift/Project when Terminating:

$$s \in \mathsf{LPT} \iff \begin{array}{c} t_1 \!\!\longrightarrow\!\! t_3 \\ {}_{s}\uparrow\; {}_{\mathrm{E,nf}}\quad \uparrow {}_{\mathsf{N}} \\ t_2 \cdots\cdots\!\!\twoheadrightarrow t_4 \end{array} \qquad \qquad \square$$

The Lift and Proj properties given here match the properties by the names "Lift" and "Project" in [17], except that there both properties are defined on the entire rewriting system rather than on individual rewrite steps and both properties specify the step on the left diagram edge to be a N step (the latter difference being inessential). Only the weaker Lift' which is symmetrical with Proj is actually needed together with Proj to obtain LPT (lemma 4.2(7,9)). However, Lift' can not replace Lift in the statement of lemma 4.4(1).

Lemma 4.2 (Relationships between Lift and Project Properties).

1. $\mathbb{E} \subseteq \mathsf{Lift} \cap \mathsf{Proj}$.
2. *If* $\mathsf{SLift}(\mathcal{S})$, *then* $\mathcal{S} \subseteq \mathsf{Lift}$.
3. *If* $\mathsf{SProj}(\mathcal{S})$, *then* $\mathcal{S} \subseteq \mathsf{Proj}$.
4. *If* $\mathsf{SLP}(\mathcal{S})$, *then* $\mathcal{S} \subseteq \mathsf{LP}$.
5. $\mathsf{Lift} \subseteq \mathsf{Lift}'$.
6. $\mathsf{Lift}' \subseteq \mathsf{Lift}$ *need not be true.*
7. $\mathsf{Lift}' \cap \mathsf{Proj} \subseteq \mathsf{LP}$.
8. *None of* $\mathsf{LP} \subseteq \mathsf{Lift}' \cap \mathsf{Proj}$, $\mathsf{LP} \subseteq \mathsf{Lift}'$, *and* $\mathsf{LP} \subseteq \mathsf{Proj}$ *need to be true.*
9. $\mathsf{LP} \subseteq \mathsf{LPT}$.
10. $\mathsf{LPT} \subseteq \mathsf{LP}$ *need not be true.* $\square$

Theorem 4.3 (Relationships between Lift, Project, and Meaning Preservation).

1. $\mathsf{LPT} \subseteq \mathsf{MP}$.
2. $\mathsf{MP} \subseteq \mathsf{LPT}$ *need not be true.*   □

Proof.

1. Suppose $s \in \mathsf{LPT}$. Let $t_1 \xrightarrow{s} t_2$. Suppose neither $\mathsf{has\text{-}nf}(\mathbb{E}, t_1)$ nor $\mathsf{has\text{-}nf}(\mathbb{E}, t_2)$. By axiom 3.4(1), it holds that $\mathsf{result}(t_1) = \mathsf{diverges} = \mathsf{result}(t_2)$, so $s \in \mathsf{MP}$. Suppose instead that either $\mathsf{has\text{-}nf}(\mathbb{E}, t_1)$ or $\mathsf{has\text{-}nf}(\mathbb{E}, t_2)$. Suppose $\mathsf{has\text{-}nf}(\mathbb{E}, t_1)$ (w/o.l.o.g. because only $t_1 \xleftrightarrow{s} t_2$ is used). Then $t_1 \xrightarrow{\mathbb{E},\mathsf{nf}} t_3$ for some t_3. By $s \in \mathsf{LPT}$, it holds that $t_3 \xleftrightarrow{\mathsf{N}} t_4 \xleftarrow{\mathbb{E}} t_2$ for some t_4. Because $\mathsf{is\text{-}nf}(\mathbb{E}, t_3)$, by lemma 3.5 it holds that $t_3 \xleftrightarrow{\mathsf{MP}} t_4$. By axiom 3.4(2) and induction on the lengths of rewrite sequences, it holds that $t_1 \xrightarrow{\mathsf{MP}} t_3$ and $t_2 \xrightarrow{\mathsf{MP}} t_4$. Thus, $t_1 \xleftrightarrow{\mathsf{MP}} t_2$. Thus, $s \in \mathsf{MP}$.

2. Consider this 4-term 3-step AES where all results are the same:

$$
\begin{array}{ccc}
t_1 & \xrightarrow{\ \mathbb{E},s_1\ } & t_2 \\
{\scriptstyle \mathsf{N},s_2}\big\downarrow & & \\
t_3 & \xrightarrow[\ \mathbb{E},s_3\ ]{} & t_4
\end{array}
$$

Then $\mathsf{MP} = \mathbb{S}$, but $\mathsf{MP} \setminus \mathsf{LPT} = \{s_2\}$.   □

4.1   Comparison with Traditional Approach

This subsection compares the lift & project method of Machkasova and Turbak and our LPT method with the traditional confluence & standardization method. Plotkin's traditional approach [25] was separated out and presented abstractly by Machkasova [16] in a form similar to the combination of the proofs of lemma 4.5(1), lemma 4.2(9), and theorem 4.3(1). We have reformulated the argument for the AES framework and modified it to work on subsets of $\mathbb{S}$. Furthermore, we have factored the argument to show it goes through LP (lemma 4.5(1)) and LPT before reaching MP. Thus, it appears that the main previously known rewriting-based methods of showing meaning preservation implicitly use the LPT diagram. Interestingly, in lemma 4.5(3,4) it is shown that the confluence & standardization method and the lift & project method are incomparable in their power; each can address problems that the other can not. Section 5 will develop another method ($\mathsf{WB} \setminus \mathsf{Std}$ in definition 5.1) of proving LPT which can address yet more problems, because it does not require standardization.

The following equivalence of Lift and standardization in lemma 4.4(1) appears in [16], although here it has been parameterized on rewrite step sets.

Lemma 4.4 (Lift Equivalent to Standardization).

1. $\mathcal{S} \subseteq \mathsf{Lift}$ *iff* $\mathsf{Std}(\mathcal{S} \cup \mathbb{E})$. *(Consequently,* $\mathsf{Lift} = \mathbb{S}$ *iff* $\mathsf{Std}(\mathbb{S})$.*)*
2. *The above statement need not be true with* Lift *replaced by* Lift'.   □

Proof.

1. $\mathsf{Std}(\mathcal{S} \cup \mathbb{E}) \Rightarrow \mathcal{S} \subseteq \mathsf{Lift}$ is immediate. $\mathcal{S} \subseteq \mathsf{Lift} \Rightarrow \mathsf{Std}(\mathcal{S} \cup \mathbb{E})$ is proven by induction on the length of rewrite sequences.
2. Consider this 7-term 8-step AES where all results are the same:

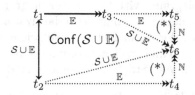

Note that $\mathsf{Lift}' = \mathbb{S}$, but $\mathsf{Lift}' \setminus \mathsf{Lift} = \{s_2\}$. The desired $\mathsf{Std}(\mathbb{S})$ is false, because $t_1 \twoheadrightarrow t_6$ but there is no t such that $t_1 \overset{\mathrm{E}}{\twoheadrightarrow} t \overset{\mathrm{N}}{\twoheadrightarrow} t_6$. $\qquad \square$

Lemma 4.5 (Relationships between Confluence + Standardization and Lift + Project).

1. *If* $\mathsf{Conf}(\mathcal{S} \cup \mathbb{E})$ *and* $\mathsf{Std}(\mathcal{S} \cup \mathbb{E})$, *then* $\mathcal{S} \subseteq \mathsf{LP}$.
2. *Consequently,* $\mathsf{Conf}(\mathcal{S} \cup \mathbb{E})$ *and* $\mathcal{S} \subseteq \mathsf{Lift}$ *imply* $\mathcal{S} \subseteq \mathsf{MP}$.
3. *If* $\mathsf{Conf}(\mathcal{S} \cup \mathbb{E})$ *and* $\mathsf{Std}(\mathcal{S} \cup \mathbb{E})$, *then* $\mathcal{S} \subseteq \mathsf{Proj}$ *need not be true.*
4. $\mathsf{Conf}(\mathsf{Lift} \cap \mathsf{Proj})$ *need not be true.* $\qquad \square$

Proof.

1. Suppose that $\mathsf{Conf}(\mathcal{S} \cup \mathbb{E})$ and (*) $\mathsf{Std}(\mathcal{S} \cup \mathbb{E})$ hold. Using the reason (*) as indicated, the following diagram proves $\mathcal{S} \cup \mathbb{E} \subseteq \mathsf{LP}$ and thus $\mathcal{S} \subseteq \mathsf{LP}$:

2. By lemmas 4.2(9), 4.4, and 4.5(1) and theorem 4.3(1).
3. Consider this 3-term 5-step AES:

Then $\mathsf{Conf}(\mathbb{N} \cup \mathbb{E})$ and $\mathsf{Std}(\mathbb{N} \cup \mathbb{E})$, but $\mathbb{N} \setminus \mathsf{Proj} = \{s_2\}$.
4. Consider this 3-term 2-step AES where all results are the same:

Then $\mathsf{Lift} = \mathsf{Proj} = \mathbb{S}$, but $\neg\mathsf{Conf}(\mathbb{S})$. $\qquad \square$

5   Elementary Diagrams for Strong Lift/Project

According to section 4, one can prove rewrite step sets to have the LPT property in order to prove meaning preservation. Furthermore, LPT can be obtained via stronger properties such as the lift and project properties. However, proving these properties can be very difficult.

To help, this section provides abstract methods for proving strong lift, strong project, and/or strong lift/project for particular rewrite step sets. Definition 5.1 defines that a rewrite step set is *well behaved* when it satisfies either the WB+Std or WB\Std properties. In turn, each of these are conjunctions of a small number of specific properties, one termination property and some *elementary diagrams*, i.e., diagrams where the given edges are two adjacent single rewrite steps. The WB+Std and WB\Std properties are about rewrite step *sets* rather than individual steps because it is necessary to simultaneously treat all the steps in a set that is closed under (an informal and only intuitive notion of) "residuals with respect to evaluation steps". This section's main result (theorem 5.4) is that a well behaved rewrite step set S has either the strong lift and strong project properties or the strong lift/project property.

Each of WB+Std and WB\Std has particular advantages. The termination property of WB+Std requires only a bound on the number of $\mathbb{E}$ steps in a rewrite sequence (BE), not full termination. When used together with the methods of section 6, this is significantly weaker than the *finite developments* property needed by some other proof methods, because it allows infinite developments (and there is no requirement that coinitial developments can be completed to be cofinal). In contrast, WB\Std requires a stronger termination property, but replaces the WL1 and WP1 elementary diagrams with the weaker diagram WLP1. The big advantage of WLP1 is that it does not require standardization. Although WB\Std(S) requires local confluence for S, in fact it is sufficient to have only confluence (lemmas 5.2(3) and 5.3(3)) and the local confluence requirement is only there so that the preconditions of WB\Std(S) are elementary diagrams.

Definition 5.1 (Well Behaved Rewrite Step Sets). *Let* $\mathsf{N}^*\mathsf{EN}^*(S)$ *be the relation* $\xrightarrow{\mathbb{N},S}\!\!\!\!\twoheadrightarrow; \xrightarrow{\mathbb{E},S}; \xrightarrow{\mathbb{N},S}\!\!\!\!\twoheadrightarrow$. *Define the following rewrite step set properties:*

Bounded $\mathbb{E}$*-Steps:* $\mathbb{N}$*-Steps Do Not Create* $\mathbb{E}$*-Steps:*

$$\mathsf{BE}(S) \quad \Longleftrightarrow \quad \mathsf{Bnd}(\mathsf{N}^*\mathsf{EN}^*(S)) \qquad\qquad \mathsf{NE}(S) \quad \Longleftrightarrow \quad \begin{array}{c} t_1 \cdots\!\!\!\twoheadrightarrow t_4 \\ \mathbb{N},S\downarrow \begin{smallmatrix} \mathbb{E},S \\ \vdots \\ \mathbb{E},S \end{smallmatrix} \\ t_2 \longrightarrow t_3 \end{array}$$

Weak Lift 1-Step: *Weak Project 1-Step:*

$$\mathsf{WL1}(S,S') \quad \Longleftrightarrow \quad \begin{array}{c} t_1 \cdots\!\!\!\twoheadrightarrow t_4 \\ \mathbb{N},S\downarrow \begin{smallmatrix} \mathbb{E},S' \\ \mathbb{E},S' \end{smallmatrix} \downarrow S \\ t_2 \longrightarrow t_3 \end{array} \qquad\qquad \mathsf{WP1}(S) \quad \Longleftrightarrow \quad \begin{array}{c} t_1 \longrightarrow t_2 \\ \mathbb{N},S\downarrow \begin{smallmatrix} \mathbb{E} \\ \mathbb{E} \end{smallmatrix} \downarrow S \\ t_3 \cdots\!\!\!\twoheadrightarrow t_4 \end{array}$$

Weak Lift/Project 1-Step: *Standardization to Normal Form:*

$$\mathsf{WLP1}(S) \quad \Longleftrightarrow \quad \begin{array}{c} t_1 \longrightarrow t_4 \\ \mathbb{N},S\downarrow \begin{smallmatrix} \mathbb{E} \\ \mathbb{E} \end{smallmatrix} \updownarrow S \\ t_2 \cdots\!\!\!\twoheadrightarrow t_3 \end{array} \qquad\qquad \mathsf{Std\text{-}nf}(S) \quad \Longleftrightarrow \quad \begin{array}{c} t_1 \xrightarrow{\quad S,\mathsf{nf} \quad}\!\!\!\twoheadrightarrow t_2 \\ \mathbb{E},S,\mathsf{nf} \searrow\quad\nearrow \mathbb{N},S,\mathsf{nf} \\ t_3 \end{array}$$

Well Behaved with Standardization:

$$\text{WB+Std}(\mathcal{S}) \iff \text{BE}(\mathcal{S}) \wedge \text{WL1}(\mathcal{S},\mathcal{S}) \wedge \text{WL1}(\mathcal{S},\mathbb{S}) \wedge \text{WP1}(\mathcal{S})$$

Well Behaved without Standardization:

$$\text{WB}\backslash\text{Std}(\mathcal{S}) \iff \text{Trm}(\mathcal{S}) \wedge \text{LConf}(\mathcal{S}) \wedge \text{NE}(\mathcal{S}) \wedge \text{WLP1}(\mathcal{S}) \qquad \square$$

Lemma 5.2 (Confluence and Standardization-Like Properties).

1. *If* $\text{BE}(\mathcal{S})$ *and* $\text{WL1}(\mathcal{S},\mathcal{S})$, *then* $\text{Std}(\mathcal{S},\mathcal{S})$.
2. *If* $\text{LConf}(\mathcal{S})$ *and* $\text{Trm}(\mathcal{S})$, *then* $\text{Conf}(\mathcal{S})$ *(Newman's Lemma).*
3. *If* $\text{Conf}(\mathcal{S})$, $\text{Trm}(\mathcal{S})$, *and* $\text{NE}(\mathcal{S})$, *then* $\text{Std-nf}(\mathcal{S})$. $\qquad\square$

Lemma 5.3 (Strong Lift and Project Properties).

1. *If* $\text{WL1}(\mathcal{S},\mathbb{S})$ *and* $\text{Std}(\mathcal{S},\mathcal{S})$, *then* $\text{SLift}(\mathcal{S})$.
2. *If* $\text{WP1}(\mathcal{S})$ *and* $\text{Std}(\mathcal{S},\mathcal{S})$, *then* $\text{SProj}(\mathcal{S})$.
3. *If* $\text{Conf}(\mathcal{S})$, $\text{Trm}(\mathcal{S})$, $\text{Std-nf}(\mathcal{S})$, *and* $\text{WLP1}(\mathcal{S})$, *then* $\text{SLP}(\mathcal{S})$. $\qquad\square$

Theorem 5.4 (Well Behaved Rewrite Step Sets).

1. *If* $\text{WB+Std}(\mathcal{S})$, *then* $\text{SLift}(\mathcal{S})$ *and* $\text{SProj}(\mathcal{S})$.
2. *If* $\text{WB}\backslash\text{Std}(\mathcal{S})$, *then* $\text{SLP}(\mathcal{S})$. $\qquad\square$

Proof. By definition 5.1 and lemmas 5.2 and 5.3. $\qquad\square$

6 Marked Rewriting and Developments

Sometimes, a desired termination property (e.g., BE from definition 5.1, Bnd, Trm, or Nrm) fails for a step set $\mathcal{S}$ generated by some rewrite rule(s), but holds for $\mathcal{S} \cap \mathbb{M}$ where $\mathbb{M}$ is a set of *marked* steps. The marks typically force termination by forbidding contracting unmarked redexes and ensuring that "created" redexes are unmarked. To use this method, the desired rewriting system is embedded in a larger marked system with additional marked terms and rewrite steps, so proving the larger system correct also proves the desired system correct.

This section defines conditions on marking and theorem 6.4 proves that when these conditions hold, proving LPT for $\mathcal{S} \cap \mathbb{M}$ (i.e., the marked fragment of the larger marked system) is sufficient to prove LPT for $\mathcal{S}$ (i.e., both the marked and unmarked steps in the larger system). Thus, when any of this paper's methods for proving meaning preservation work for $\mathcal{S} \cap \mathbb{M}$, the methods also work for $\mathcal{S}$. It is worth observing that the style of proof of theorem 6.4 can be repeated for many properties other than LPT, e.g., for Lift (and therefore for standardization).

This section's methods are related to *developments*. A development is a rewrite step sequence starting from a term t where each step contracts a redex which represents work that was already in t and "created" redexes are not contracted. Usually, the notions of "work already present" and "created" are defined using *residuals* of redexes across rewrite steps, sometimes defining residuals using marks. This section's methods do not need any notion of residual.

This is important because there do not seem to be good ways to define residuals for many rewriting systems, e.g., those with highly overlapping rewrite rules.

A *mark structure* for an AES is a tuple

$$(\mathsf{Marks}, \mathsf{markOf}, \mathsf{noMark}, \mathsf{rename})$$

satisfying axiom 6.1 below and the following conditions. The set Marks is non-empty and does not contain $\star$. The function markOf maps $\mathbb{S}$ to $\mathsf{Marks} \cup \{\star\}$. The mark noMark is a member of Marks. The function rename is of type $(\mathsf{Marks} \times \mathsf{Marks}) \to \mathbb{T} \to \mathbb{T}$. Let m range over Marks. Let $\mathbb{M} = \{\, s \in \mathbb{S} \mid \mathsf{markOf}(s) \neq \mathsf{noMark} \,\}$. Let the statement $\mathsf{markOccurs}(m, t)$ hold iff there exist s and t' such that $t \xrightarrow{s} t'$ and $\mathsf{markOf}(s) = m$.

The intended meaning is as follows. The set Marks should contain marks used to track redexes. Each rewrite step s should be marked by the mark $\mathsf{markOf}(s)$. The special mark noMark means "no mark at all". The symbol $\star$ means "can be considered to be any mark because we do not track this kind of rewrite step with marks"; this is a convenience for systems where only some steps have marked versions. The operation $\mathsf{rename}(m_1, m_2)(t)$ should produce a new term t' resulting from renaming all occurrences of the mark m_1 in t to m_2.

Axiom 6.1 (Marking Sanity)

1. **Marked Erasure:**
   For $\mathcal{S} \in \{\mathbb{E}, \mathbb{N}\}$,

   $$\mathsf{rename}(m,m')\downarrow \begin{array}{c} t_1 \xrightarrow{\mathcal{S}} t_2 \\[4pt] \downdownarrows \\[4pt] t_3 \cdots\!\!\rightarrow t_4 \end{array} \uparrow\mathsf{rename}(m,m')$$

2. **$\mathbb{E}$ Marked Unerasure:**

   $$\mathsf{rename}(m,m')\uparrow \begin{array}{c} t_1 \xrightarrow{\mathbb{E}} t_2 \\[4pt] \phantom{\mathbb{E}} \\[4pt] t_3 \cdots\!\!\rightarrow t_4 \end{array} \uparrow\mathsf{rename}(m,m')$$

3. **Erasing Nonexistent Mark:**
   If $\neg\mathsf{markOccurs}(m, t)$, then $\mathsf{rename}(m, m')(t) = t$.

4. **Marks Not Introduced by Rewriting:**
   If $\neg\mathsf{markOccurs}(m, t)$, $m \neq \mathsf{noMark}$, and $t \to t'$, then $\neg\mathsf{markOccurs}(m, t')$.

5. **Fresh Marks:**
   For any term t, there exists a mark $m \neq \mathsf{noMark}$ such that $\neg\mathsf{markOccurs}(m, t)$. $\square$

Convention 6.2 *In this paper, wherever no specific mark structure is being considered, statements are about every possible mark structure.* $\square$

Definition 6.3 (Rewrite Step Set Property for Marks).

$\mathbb{N}$ *Step Can Be Marked:*

$$\mathsf{NM}(\mathcal{S}) \iff \left(\left(\begin{array}{c} m \neq \mathsf{noMark} \\ \wedge\, \neg\mathsf{markOccurs}(m, t_1) \end{array} \right) \Rightarrow \begin{array}{c} t_1 \xrightarrow{\mathbb{N},\mathcal{S}} t_2 \\[4pt] \mathsf{rename}(m,m')\cdots\!\!\nearrow \,\,\searrow\, \mathbb{N},\mathbb{M},\mathcal{S} \\[4pt] t_3 \end{array} \right)$$ $\square$

Theorem 6.4 (Lift/Project when Terminating via Marks). *If $\mathcal{S} \cap \mathbb{M} \subseteq$* LPT *and* NM($\mathcal{S}$), *then* $\mathcal{S} \subseteq$ LPT.   □

Proof. Using axiom 6.1, lemma 4.2(1), and definitions 6.3 and 4.1.   □

7 Example: The Call-by-Name λ-Calculus

This section gives an example of the use of our AES framework and our diagram-based methods for proving meaning preservation. The AES and a mark structure will be defined and then the top-level proof strategy will be presented.

We choose the call-by-name λ-calculus with left-most outermost evaluation to weak head normal forms because it is a small system, needs the mark structure features of section 6, will already be familiar to most readers, and is one of the two systems treated by Plotkin's seminal paper [25]. This system has both confluence and standardization. To illustrate the extra power of our proof methods, we would have preferred to present an example system which does not have these properties, but unfortunately our smallest worked-out example takes many pages in LNCS format to even define and does not need the features of section 6.

Define the AES for the call-by-name λ-calculus as follows. First, define the AES carrier sets $\mathbb{T}$, $\mathbb{S}$, and $\mathbb{R}$ as well as the evaluation step subset $\mathbb{E}$.

$x, y, z \in$ Variable

$\overline{t}$ $\in$ Context $::= \square \mid x \mid (\lambda x \, \overline{t}) \mid (\overline{t_1} \, \overline{t_2}) \mid (\mathsf{let}^n x = \overline{t_2} \mathsf{\ in\ } \overline{t_1})$ $(n \geq 1)$

t $\in \mathbb{T}$ $= \{\overline{t} \mid \overline{t} \text{ has no hole } \square \}$

$\overline{E}$ $\in$ EvalContext $::= \square \mid (\overline{E}\, t)$

R $\in$ Redex $::= (\mathsf{let}^n x = t_2 \mathsf{\ in\ } t_1) \mid ((\lambda x\, t_1)\, t_2)$ $(n \geq 1)$

s $\in \mathbb{S}$ $= \{(\overline{t}, R) \mid \overline{t} \text{ has 1 hole } \square \}$

    $\mathbb{E}$ $::= (\overline{E}, R)$

r $\in \mathbb{R}$ $= \{\mathsf{diverges}, \mathsf{stuck}, \mathsf{halt}\}$

In the term syntax, $(\mathsf{let}^n x = t_2 \mathsf{\ in\ } t_1)$ is used to indicate a *marked* β-redex. Terms and contexts are identified modulo α-conversion as usual. For contexts, α-conversion can not rename bound variables whose scope includes a hole. Substitution of t for x in t', written $t'[x := t]$, is defined as usual. Placing a term or context X in the hole of a one-hole context $\overline{t}$, written $\overline{t}[X]$, is defined as usual.

Now, finish defining the AES by supplying the functions.

$$\mathsf{endpoints}(\overline{t}, (\mathsf{let}^n x = t_2 \mathsf{\ in\ } t_1)) = (\overline{t}[\mathsf{let}^n x = t_2 \mathsf{\ in\ } t_1], \overline{t}[t_1[x := t_2]])$$

$$\mathsf{endpoints}(\overline{t}, (\lambda x\, t_1)\, t_2) = (\overline{t}[(\lambda x\, t_1)\, t_2], \overline{t}[t_1[x := t_2]])$$

$$\mathsf{result}(t) = \begin{cases} \mathsf{diverges} & \text{if } \neg\mathsf{has\text{-}nf}(\mathbb{E}, t) \\ \mathsf{halt} & \text{if } t \xrightarrow{\mathbb{E},\mathsf{nf}} \lambda x\, t' \\ \mathsf{stuck} & \text{if } t \xrightarrow{\mathbb{E},\mathsf{nf}} t' \neq \lambda x\, t'' \end{cases}$$

Define an accompanying mark structure as follows.

Marks $= \{0, 1, 2, \ldots\}$

noMark $= 0$

$\mathsf{markOf}(\overline{t}, (\mathsf{let}^n x = t_2 \mathsf{\ in\ } t_1)) = n$

$$\text{markOf}(\overline{t}, (\lambda x\, t_1) t_2) = 0$$
$$\text{rename}(m_1, m_2) = \theta$$

$$\text{where} \begin{cases} \theta(x) & = x \\ \theta(\lambda x\, t) & = \lambda x\, \theta(t) \\ \theta(t_1\, t_2) & = \theta(t_1)\, \theta(t_2) \\ \theta(\text{let}^{m_1} x = t_2 \text{ in } t_1) = (\text{let}^{m_2} x = \theta(t_2) \text{ in } \theta(t_1)) & \text{if } m_2 \neq 0 \\ \theta(\text{let}^{m_1} x = t_2 \text{ in } t_1) = (\lambda x\, \theta(t_1))\, \theta(t_2) & \text{if } m_2 = 0 \\ \theta(\text{let}^{m} x = t_2 \text{ in } t_1) \ = (\text{let}^{m} x = \theta(t_2) \text{ in } \theta(t_1)) & \text{if } m \neq m_1 \end{cases}$$

Lemma 7.1 (The Framework User's Proof Burden).

1. *Axioms 3.3, 6.1, and 3.4 hold.*
2. WB+Std($\mathbb{M}$).
3. NM($\mathbb{S}$).
4. *If $t_1 \longrightarrow t_2$, then $\overline{t}[t_1] \longrightarrow \overline{t}[t_2]$ for any context $\overline{t}$.*   □

Proof. Many standard proofs by induction which are left to the reader. The only difficult bit is BE($\mathbb{M}$) (part of WB+Std($\mathbb{M}$)). First, Trm($\mathbb{M}$) is proven by a known argument (e.g., see [5]) of rearranging the mark values so that rewriting decreases the multiset of all marks in the term in the multiset extension of $<$. Because the rewriting system is finitely branching, this is equivalent to Bnd($\mathbb{M}$), which in turn implies BE($\mathbb{M}$).   □

Theorem 7.2 (Meaning Preservation). $\mathbb{S} \subseteq \text{MP}$.   □

Proof. Everything implicitly relies on lemma 7.1(1). By lemma 7.1(2) and theorem 5.4(1), SLift($\mathbb{M}$) and SProj($\mathbb{M}$). By lemma 4.2(2,3,5,7,9), $\mathbb{S} \cap \mathbb{M} = \mathbb{M} \subseteq \text{LPT}$. By lemma 7.1(3) and theorem 6.4, $\mathbb{S} \subseteq \text{LPT}$. By theorem 4.3(1), $\mathbb{S} \subseteq \text{MP}$.   □

Corollary 7.3 (Observational Equivalence). *If $t_1 \longrightarrow t_2$, then* result($\overline{t}[t_1]$) = result($\overline{t}[t_2]$).   □

Proof. Suppose $t_1 \longrightarrow t_2$. By lemma 7.1(4), $\overline{t}[t_1] \longrightarrow \overline{t}[t_2]$. By theorem 7.2 and the definition of MP, result($\overline{t}[t_1]$) = result($\overline{t}[t_2]$).   □

8   Related Work

The most closely related work is by Machkasova and Turbak [16, 17, 18]. Their work is discussed throughout this paper, so only a few points will be made here. First, our BE property corresponds to their complicated notion of γ-development [18, sec. 4.5]. The γ-development idea may be implicitly the same as BE [18, p. 193], but the exact relationship is unclear due to the complexity. Second, Machkasova's requirement of γ-confluence on evaluation is incomparable with our requirement of evaluation subcommutativity (axiom 3.3). Because γ-confluence involves the complicated γ-development machinery, we prefer our simpler requirement. Third, our proof diagrams for parts 1 and 2 of lemma 5.3 are similar to some in [18], but are simpler because we do not use γ-developments and we treat marks for developments separately (section 6).

Ariola and Blom [2] define the notion ARSI (ARS (abstract rewriting system) with information content). Using the ordering of an ARSI $\mathcal{A}$, they obtain the *infinite normal form* of a term t from the *information content* of all terms t' such that $t \twoheadrightarrow t'$. They show how to prove $\mathcal{A}$ preserves infinite normal forms by finding a subset $\mapsto \subseteq \rightarrow$ satisfying a diagram roughly like this [2, cor. 4.14]:

$$\begin{array}{c} t_1 \mapsto\!\!\!\!\twoheadrightarrow t_2 \\ \uparrow \quad \vdots \circ \\ t_3 \mapsto\!\!\!\!\twoheadrightarrow t_4 \end{array}$$

The quickest explanation of their $\circ$ relation is to point out that the closest corresponding diagram in our AES framework would be this:

$$s \in \mathsf{GLP} \quad\Longleftrightarrow\quad s \begin{array}{c} t_1 \twoheadrightarrow t_2 \\ {\scriptstyle\mathbb{E}} \uparrow \quad \downarrow {\scriptstyle\mathbb{E}} \\ t_3 \cdots\!\!\twoheadrightarrow t_4 \end{array} \mathsf{SU}(\mathbb{N}^{-1})$$

Key differences between the Ariola/Blom approach and ours are as follows. First, they provide no abstract methods for proving their diagram (corresponding to our elementary diagrams in section 5) but instead prove it individually for each use. Second, the GLP diagram is a stronger requirement than LPT (in fact, $\mathsf{LP} \subseteq \mathsf{GLP} \subseteq \mathsf{LPT}$), so our methods in section 4 are more general. Third, their framework does not provide help in showing the correspondence (needed to prove observational equivalence for the rewriting system) between infinite normal forms (their notion of meaning) and the actual operational semantics, so this burden is left to the user. Fourth, they encourage using a notion of information content which is more complicated than needed for proving meaning preservation (unlike our set $\mathbb{R}$); in fact, their information content seems enough to build a fully abstract model.

Odersky [23] gives conditions proving that a proposed contextually closed transformation $\sim$ is an observational equivalence. One condition is that $\sim$ is *locally stable* [23, p. 2, diagram (2)]:

$$\begin{array}{c} t_1 \rightarrow t_2 \\ {\scriptstyle\sim_1} \big| \quad \simeq \quad \big| {\scriptstyle\sim_1} \\ t_3 \cdots t_4 \end{array}$$

The relation $\sim_1$ is *parallel similarity*, i.e., the use of $\sim$ simultaneously at many different (presumably non-overlapping) positions. Another condition is that $\sim$ *preserves answers*, i.e., $t_1 \sim t_2 \Rightarrow (\mathsf{is\text{-}nf}(\mathbb{E}, t_2) \Rightarrow t_1 \twoheadrightarrow t_2)$.

Odersky's approach is related as follows. Where Odersky uses $\rightarrow$ (normal rewriting) and $\simeq$ (observational equivalence), we would use $\xrightarrow{\mathbb{E}}$ and $\xtwoheadrightarrow{\mathbb{E}}$. Odersky's approach has two versions. In the version shown above, meaning preservation is defined as convertibility in the entire rewriting system with a set of answers ($\mathbb{E}$-normal forms in our setting). The question is then whether more rewrite rules can be safely added. In this case, the diagram must be proven for all rewrite steps. The other version takes an evaluation strategy like we do. In this case, using $\simeq$ on the bottom edge seems more general, but it also seems that in practice this diagram edge would be completed with $\mathbb{E}$ steps. Where Odersky uses $\sim_1$, we would typically use $\xrightarrow{S,M}$ and a combination of one of the well-behavedness conditions of section 5 and the marks of section 6. Odersky's use of parallel (simultaneous) rewriting corresponds to our use of a termination property.

Key differences between Odersky's approach and ours are as follows. Much of Odersky's approach is tied to syntactic extensions of the λ-calculus while our approach is abstract. Odersky does not provide elementary diagrams where each given edge is a single use of a rewrite rule; it seems that one must work with full parallel similarity. Odersky appears to assume standardization is already proven while our approach proves whatever standardization is needed and can work without it. Odersky's approach requires a notion of "preserving evaluation contexts" which we do not fully understand but which we are fairly sure one of our intended applications does not satisfy. Odersky does not distinguish terms that go wrong from those that either diverge or halt normally; thus his framework can not verify that rewriting does not switch between non-wrong and wrong.

9   Future Work

The generalizations of our AES framework and LPT diagrams were developed to handle $\lambda^{:=,\mathsf{letrec}}$, a calculus we are developing for reasoning about call-by-value higher-order programs with mutable reference cells and mutually recursive definitions (i.e., letrec). Evaluation of assignment statements can introduce cycles in the store, so evaluation results may need letrec even if the initial program was letrec-free. A specific evaluation strategy is given for the $\lambda^{:=,\mathsf{letrec}}$ calculus to define the meaning of programs. Calculi for assignments have been done before (e.g., [11]), but $\lambda^{:=,\mathsf{letrec}}$ also includes improvements like very simple evaluation contexts as well as rules for letrec in the style of the work of Ariola and Blom [2]. The only previously known methods for reasoning about the correctness of Ariola/Blom style letrec rules seem more difficult to us.

The development of $\lambda^{:=,\mathsf{letrec}}$ is nearing completion. Because $\lambda^{:=,\mathsf{letrec}}$ is non-confluent (due to using rules for letrec that Ariola and Klop [5] proved non-confluent), we were using the lift & project method to prove meaning preservation. It does not have finite developments, but has a number of rule subsets whose associated rewrite step sets satisfy the BE property. The last barrier to completing the proof of meaning preservation was several critical pairs of a rule named [lift] (name unrelated to the Lift diagram from definition 4.1). One particularly irritating critical pair is only completable as follows:

$$
\begin{array}{ccc}
t_1 & \xrightarrow{\;\mathbb{E},[\mathsf{lift}]\;} & t_3 \\
{\scriptstyle \mathbb{N},[\mathsf{lift}]}\Big\downarrow & & \vdots {\scriptstyle \mathbb{E},[\mathsf{lift}]} \\
& & t_5 \\
\Big\downarrow & & \vdots {\scriptstyle \mathbb{N},[\mathsf{lift}]} \\
t_2 & \xrightarrow[\;\mathbb{E},[\mathsf{lift}]\;]{} & t_4
\end{array}
$$

Unfortunately, this breaks standardization, so the lift & project proof method fails. We considered changing the definition of $\lambda^{:=,\mathsf{letrec}}$, but felt that the changes to "fix" this critical pair would probably break something else. Also, the rules of $\lambda^{:=,\mathsf{letrec}}$ are clearly meaning preserving, so we felt that rather than forcing

$\lambda^{:=,\text{letrec}}$ through awkward contortions to fit a weak proof method, it was the proof method that should be fixed. Fortunately, the WB\Std property can be proven for the [lift] rule steps, so we expect to complete the $\lambda^{:=,\text{letrec}}$ work soon.

After $\lambda^{:=,\text{letrec}}$ is completed, we want to apply our proof methods to equational reasoning for assembly language and maybe also to explicit substitutions.

References

[1] Z. M. Ariola, S. Blom. Cyclic lambda calculi. In *Theoretical Aspects Comput. Softw. : Int'l Conf.*, Berlin, 1997. Springer.

[2] Z. M. Ariola, S. Blom. Skew confluence and the lambda calculus with letrec. *Ann. Pure Appl. Logic*, 117(1–3), 2002.

[3] Z. M. Ariola, M. Felleisen. The call-by-need lambda calculus. *J. Funct. Programming*, 3(7), 1997.

[4] Z. M. Ariola, M. Felleisen, J. Maraist, M. Odersky, P. Wadler. The call-by-need lambda calculus. In *Conf. Rec. 22nd Ann. ACM Symp. Princ. of Prog. Langs.*, 1995.

[5] Z. M. Ariola, J. W. Klop. Lambda calculus with explicit recursion. *Inform. & Comput.*, 139, 1997.

[6] F. Baader, T. Nipkow. *Term Rewriting and All That.* Cambridge University Press, 1998.

[7] H. P. Barendregt. *The Lambda Calculus: Its Syntax and Semantics.* North-Holland, revised edition, 1984.

[8] *Programming Languages & Systems, 9th European Symp. Programming*, vol. 1782 of *LNCS*. Springer-Verlag, 2000.

[9] M. Felleisen, D. Friedman. Control operators, the SECD-machine, and the λ-calculus. In M. Wirsing, ed., *Formal Description of Programming Concepts — III*. North-Holland, 1986.

[10] M. Felleisen, D. P. Friedman. A syntactic theory of sequential state. *Theoret. Comput. Sci.*, 69(3), 1989.

[11] M. Felleisen, R. Hieb. The revised report on the syntactic theories of sequential control and state. *Theoret. Comput. Sci.*, 102, 1992.

[12] K. Fisher, J. Reppy, J. G. Riecke. A calculus for compiling and linking classes. In ESOP '00 [8].

[13] G. Gonthier, J.-J. Lévy, P.-A. Melliès. An abstract standardisation theorem. In *Proc. 7th Ann. IEEE Symp. Logic in Comput. Sci.*, 1992.

[14] D. J. Howe. Equality in lazy computation systems. In *Proc. 4th Ann. Symp. Logic in Comput. Sci.*, Pacific Grove, CA, U.S.A., 1989. IEEE Comput. Soc. Press.

[15] D. J. Howe. Proving congruence of bisimulation in functional programming languages. *Inform. & Comput.*, 124(2), 1996.

[16] E. Machkasova. Techniques for proving observational equivalence. ASCII notes that later turned into [17]. Not sure about year, 1998.

[17] E. Machkasova, F. A. Turbak. A calculus for link-time compilation. In ESOP '00 [8].

[18] E. L. Machkasova. *Computational Soundness of Non-Confluent Calculi with Applications to Modules and Linking.* PhD thesis, Boston Univ., 2002.

[19] J. Maraist, M. Odersky, P. Wadler. The call-by-need lambda calculus. *J. Funct. Programming*, 8(3), 1998.

[20] P.-A. Melliès. Axiomatic Rewriting Theory IV: A diagrammatic standardization theorem. Submitted, 2001.

[21] R. Muller. M-LISP: A representation-independent dialect of LISP with reduction semantics. *ACM Trans. on Prog. Langs. & Systs.*, 14(4), 1992.

[22] M. H. A. Newman. On theories with a combinatorial definition of "equivalence". *Annals of Math.*, 43(2), 1942.

[23] M. Odersky. A syntactic method for proving observational equivalences. Research Report YALEU/DCS/RR-964, Yale Univ., Dept. of Comp. Science, 1993.

[24] A. M. Pitts. Operationally-based theories of program equivalence. In *Semantics and Logics of Computation*, vol. 14 of *Publications of the Newton Institute.* Cambridge University Press, 1997.

[25] G. D. Plotkin. Call-by-name, call-by-value and the lambda calculus. *Theoret. Comput. Sci.*, 1, 1975.

[26] W. Taha. A sound reduction semantics for untyped CBN multi-stage computation: Or, the theory of MetaML is non-trivial. In *Proceedings of the 2000 ACM SIGPLAN Workshop on Evaluation and Semantics-Based Program Manipulation (PEPM-00)*, N.Y., 2000. ACM Press.

Expression Reduction Systems with Patterns

Julien Forest[1] and Delia Kesner[2]

[1] LRI (CNRS UMR 8623), Université Paris-Sud, France, `forest@lri.fr`
[2] PPS (CNRS UMR 7126), Université Paris 7, France, `kesner@pps.jussieu.fr`

Abstract. We introduce a new higher-order rewriting formalism, called *Expression Reduction Systems with Patterns (ERSP)*, where abstraction is not only allowed on variables but also on nested patterns. These patterns are built by combining standard *algebraic* patterns with *choice* constructors used to denote different possible structures allowed for an abstracted argument. In other words, the non deterministic choice between different rewriting rules which is inherent to classical rewriting formalisms can be lifted here to the level of patterns. We show that confluence holds for a reasonable class of systems and terms.

Introduction

Higher-order rewrite systems are able to combine formalisms coming from proof theory, such as λ-calculus, with formalisms arising in algebraic specifications, such as first-order rewrite systems. The main idea behind higher-order rewriting concerns the transformation of terms in the presence of *binding* mechanisms for variables and substitutions. Thus for example, functional and logic programming, equational reasoning, object-oriented programming, concurrent systems and theorem provers may be encoded by higher-order rewrite systems.

Many higher-order rewrite systems exist in the literature starting at the seminal work by J-W. Klop [15]. Many other interesting formalisms [4,13,17,20,22] were introduced later. The theory of higher-order rewriting is considerably more involved than that of first-order rewriting; many articles were devoted to the study of its foundations, applications, semantics and implementation.

In all the higher-order formalisms mentioned before the binding mechanism is only allowed on *variables*. However, most popular functional languages and proof assistants allow definitions by cases via pattern-matching mechanisms. Thus, a natural extension of higher-order rewriting consists in the use of binders for patterns so that a projection function like $\lambda\langle x, y\rangle.x$ would be also acceptable.

The *Pattern-Matching Calculus* [12], proposed as a theoretical framework to study pattern-matching in a *pure functional paradigm*, allows precisely this kind of binding mechanisms. Its evaluation process is given by the following generalization of the standard β-rule to the case of patterns:

$$(\beta_{PM}) \qquad app(\lambda\mathbb{X}.M, N) \longrightarrow M\{\mathbb{X} \text{ by } N\}$$

where $\mathbb{X}$ denotes a pattern and $\{\mathbb{X} \text{ by } N\}$ denotes a substitution resulting from the pattern-matching operation on the pattern $\mathbb{X}$ and the term N.

R. Nieuwenhuis (Ed.): RTA 2003, LNCS 2706, pp. 107–122, 2003.

This calculus was later extended with *explicit operators* [6,5,9]; weak reduction was widely studied in [9]. Another language allowing abstractions on patterns is the ρ-calculus [8], for which typing [14] and explicit operators [7] were defined and analyzed.

In this paper we introduce a new higher-order formalism, called *Expression Reduction Systems with Patterns* (ERSP), where binding mechanisms are allowed on complex patterns. Our calculus constitutes an extension of ERS [13] and SERS [4] to the case of patterns, and a generalization of the Pattern-Matching Calculus to the case of general higher-order rewriting (and not only functional rewriting). ERSP patterns are defined as combinations of standard *algebraic* structures with special *choice* constructors used to denote different possible syntactic forms for any abstracted argument. Thus for example, the function which computes the length of a given list may be specified as the following ERSP term:

$$\lambda\, a\langle nil, cons(x,t)\rangle.a\langle 0, 1 + len(t)\rangle$$

where λ is the classical function binder, a is a special variable used to identify the set of *choice* patterns nil and $cons(x,t)$ with the set of their corresponding continuations 0 and $1 + len(t)$.

We carefully extend all the expected notions of rewriting to our framework, namely, terms, metaterms, rewrite rules, substitutions, reduction, etc. We then identify a class of ERSP, called *orthogonal l-constructor* systems, and a class of terms, called *l-constructor deterministic terms*, for which confluence holds. More precisely, reduction on this class of terms via this class of systems corresponds to reduction on ordinary terms (without patterns) in classical orthogonal higher-order systems [17,20]. Much more, our confluence result turns out to give in particular a confluence result for SERS.

The paper is organized as follows. Sections 1 and 2 introduce the basic ingredients of the syntactic formalism ERSP. In Section 3 we develop an example of reduction in our framework. Section 4 is devoted to study a restriction of the class of ERSP so that confluence will follow (Section 5). We conclude and give many further research directions in Section 6. By lack of space we cannot provide here all the proofs but a complete version of this work can be found in [10].

1   Basic Notions of the ERSP Formalism

We consider a set $\mathcal{UV}$ of *usual variables* denoted $x, y, z, \ldots$, a set $\mathcal{CV}$ of *choice variables* denoted $a, b, c, \ldots$, a set $\mathcal{PV}$ of *pattern metavariables* denoted $\mathbb{X}, \mathbb{Y}, \ldots$, a set $\mathcal{TV}$ of *term metavariables* denoted $M, N, \ldots$, a set $\mathcal{F}$ of *function symbols* equipped with a fixed (possibly zero) arity, denoted $f, g, h, \ldots$, a set $\mathcal{B}$ of *binder symbols* denoted $\lambda, \mu, \nu, \ldots$. We assume all these sets to be denumerable and disjoint. When no special distinction is needed for the previous sets of variables and metavariables will use the symbols $\widehat{x}, \widehat{y}, \widehat{z}, \ldots$.

Metapatterns (p) and metaterms (t) are generated by the grammars:

$p ::= x$	usual variable	$t ::= x$	usual variable
$\mid \ \ X$	pattern metavariable	$\mid \ \ M$	term metavariable
$\mid \ \ f(p,\ldots,p)$	algebraic	$\mid \ \ f(t,\ldots,t)$	algebraic
$\mid \ \ a\langle p,\ldots,p\rangle$	choice	$\mid \ \ a\langle t,\ldots,t\rangle$	case
$\mid \ \ @(p,\ldots,p)$	contraction	$\mid \ \ \mu p.t$	abstraction
$\mid \ \ \_$	wildcard	$\mid \ \ t\{p \ \mathbf{by} \ t\}$	pattern-matching

The constructor $@()$ is varyadic, i.e. it has no fix arity. The constructor $a\langle\ \rangle$ is also varyadic, but with an arity different from 0. We assume that whenever a choice variable a appears inside t, then all its occurrences have the same arity : thus, a term like $\mu a\langle x\rangle.a\langle x,y\rangle$ is not allowed. The symbol $\{$ $\mathbf{by}$ $\}$ is called the pattern-matching constructor. The metaterms $\mu p.t$ and $t\{p \ \mathbf{by} \ t'\}$ define bindings whose scope is t for all the (usual and choice) variables occurring in p.

A metapattern (resp. metaterm) is said to be a *pattern* (resp. *preterm*) if it contains no metavariables. A preterm is said to be a *term* if it contains no pattern-matching constructors.

We denote by $\mathcal{MV}(p)$ (resp. $\mathcal{V}ar(p)$) the set of all the *pattern* metavariables (resp. variables) appearing in a metapattern (resp. pattern) p. We denote by $\mathcal{MV}(t)$ the set of all the *term* metavariables appearing in t.

Definition 1. *A metapattern is called linear if each variable and metavariable appears at most once in it. We use the notation $p \in p'$ to say that the metapattern p appears inside the metapattern p'. A metaterm t is called p-linear iff every metapattern p in t is linear.*

Let us illustrate the use of our syntax by considering the `fibonacci` function specified by the equations `fib(0)=0`, `fib(1)=1` and `fib(x+2)=fib(x)` `+fib(x+1)`.

Using a choice variable a of arity 3 to encode the three different choices given by the previous specification, one possible specification of `fib` in our syntax is:

$$fib(M) \longrightarrow app(\lambda \ a\langle 0, s(0), s(s(x))\rangle.a\langle 0, s(0), app(fib, x) + app(fib, s(x))\rangle, M)$$

where app is the application symbol, λ is the classical function binder, and natural numbers are encoded by $0, s(0), s(s(0)), \ldots$.

A position is a word over the alphabet $\mathbb{N}$; we use ϵ to denote the empty word. The *set of positions* of a metaterm t, denoted $\mathcal{POS}(t)$, is defined as usual [1] except for the term $s\{p \ \mathbf{by} \ u\}$ for which we have $1.1.q \in \mathcal{POS}(s\{p \ \mathbf{by} \ u\})$ if $q \in \mathcal{POS}(s)$ and $2.q \in \mathcal{POS}(s\{p \ \mathbf{by} \ u\})$ if $q \in \mathcal{POS}(u)$ (see also [4] and [10]). The justification of this case comes from the fact that $s\{p \ \mathbf{by} \ u\}$ is informally considered as "$app(\mu p.s, u)$" when reasoning about positions. The *submetaterm* of t at position p is written as $t|_p$. When $t|_p = u$, we will say that p is an *occurrence* of u in t.

The following notion is used to describe the set of variables/metavariables appearing along a given path which will play latter a role of "bound" objects in a terms/metaterms.

Definition 2 (Parameter Path). *Given a metaterm s and $p \in \mathcal{POS}(s)$, we define the parameter path of s at position q, written $\mathcal{PP}(s, q)$, as the following subset of variables and metavariables of s:*

$$
\begin{aligned}
\mathcal{PP}(s, \epsilon) &= \emptyset \\
\mathcal{PP}(f(s_1, \ldots, s_n), i.q) &= \mathcal{PP}(s_i, q), \text{ for } i \in \{1 \ldots n\} \\
\mathcal{PP}(a\langle s_1, \ldots, s_n \rangle, i.q) &= \mathcal{PP}(s_i, q), \text{ for } i \in \{1 \ldots n\} \\
\mathcal{PP}(\mu p.s, 1.q) &= \mathcal{V}ar(p) \cup \mathcal{MV}(p) \cup \mathcal{PP}(s, q) \\
\mathcal{PP}(u\{p \text{ by } v\}, 1.1.q) &= \mathcal{V}ar(p) \cup \mathcal{MV}(p) \cup \mathcal{PP}(u, q) \\
\mathcal{PP}(u\{p \text{ by } v\}, 2.q) &= \mathcal{PP}(v, q)
\end{aligned}
$$

As an example, if $t = M\{g(\mathbb{X}, x) \text{ by } \mu a\langle \mathbb{Y}, s(\mathbb{Y}) \rangle.N\}$, then we have $\mathcal{PP}(t, 2) = \emptyset$, $\mathcal{PP}(t, 1.1) = \{\mathbb{X}, x\}$, and $\mathcal{PP}(t, 2.1) = \{\mathbb{Y}, a\}$.

We assume that different "non parallel" metapatterns appearing on a same path cannot share (meta)variables. Thus for example, $\mu\mathbb{X}.\lambda\mathbb{X}.M$ or $\lambda x.\mu x.M$ are not allowed but the metaterm t given above is allowed. This is just a generalization of what is called "Barendregt's convention on bound variables".

The set of *free (meta)variables* of a metaterm t, written $\mathcal{FV}(t)$, is defined as usual. All the variables appearing in a metaterm t that are not free are called *bound variables*. Without loss of generality we assume the sets of free and bound variables to be disjoint. We work modulo α-conversion on preterms, so that renaming of bound variables is used when necessary to avoid clashes. Thus for example $\mu a\langle x, y, z \rangle.a\langle x, x, v \rangle =_\alpha \mu b\langle x', y', z' \rangle.b\langle x', x', v \rangle$.

Definition 3 (Well-formed metaterm). *A metaterm t is well-formed iff t has no free occurrences of choice/usual variables.*

The metaterms $\mu x.M, \mu\mathbb{X}.M, \mu x.f(M, x)$ and $\mu a\langle x, y \rangle.a\langle x, y \rangle$ are well-formed while $f(a\langle g, g \rangle)$ and $f(x)$ are not.

The following notion is used to talk about the free variables of a term which remain *after* a given choice on a choice variable.

Definition 4 (Localized Free Variables). *Given $a \in \mathcal{CV}$, $i \geq 1$ and a preterm t, the set $\mathcal{FV}_a^i(t)$ of localized free variable of t can be defined as usually done for the set of free variables except for the following case:*

$$
\mathcal{FV}_a^i(a\langle t_1, \ldots, t_n \rangle) = \mathcal{FV}_a^i(t_i) \text{ if } 1 \leq i \leq n
$$

Indeed, $\mathcal{FV}_a^i(b\langle x, y, z \rangle) = \{b, z, x, y\}$ for any i and $\mathcal{FV}_a^1(a\langle x, y, z \rangle) = \{x\}$. Moreover, as we work modulo α-conversion we have $\mathcal{FV}_a^1(\mu a\langle x, y \rangle.a\langle f(x, z), u \rangle) = \mathcal{FV}_a^1(\mu b\langle x, y \rangle.b\langle f(x, z), u \rangle) = \{z, u\}$.

Definition 5 (Acceptable preterms). *Acceptability is the least relation on preterms containing the variables such that:*

- *If $t_1, \ldots, t_n$ are acceptable, then $f(t_1, \ldots, t_n)$ and $a\langle t_1, \ldots, t_n \rangle$ are acceptable for any $f \in \mathcal{F}$ and any $a \in \mathcal{CV}$.*

- If t is acceptable and p is a pattern, then for all $a\langle p_1, \ldots, p_n \rangle \in p$, for all $i \in 1 \ldots n$, and for all $j \neq i$ such that $(\mathcal{FV}_a^j(t) \setminus Var(p_j)) \cap Var(p_i) = \emptyset$, we have that $\mu p.t$ is an acceptable term.
- If $\mu p.t$ and u are acceptable, then $t\{p \text{ by } u\}$ is acceptable.

The role of acceptability is to prevent the creation of new free variables during evaluation. Indeed, the terms $\mu a\langle x, x\rangle.a\langle x, x\rangle$ and $\mu a\langle x, y\rangle.a\langle x, y\rangle$ are acceptable while $\mu a\langle x, y\rangle.b\langle x, y\rangle$ is not since $\mathcal{FV}_a^1(b\langle x, y\rangle) \setminus Var(x) = \{y, b\}$ and $\{y, b\} \cap Var(y) = \{y\}$. The term $\mu a\langle x, y\rangle.a\langle y, x\rangle$ is neither acceptable: if we choose the first branch x in the pattern $a\langle x, y\rangle$ we have then to consequently choose the first branch y in the term $a\langle y, x\rangle$, thus y becomes a *new* free variable.

Precontexts are preterms with one (and only one) occurrence containing a distinguished constant called a "hole" (and denoted $\square$). A *context* is a precontext with no occurrence of the pattern-matching constructor. We remark that the notion of acceptability is not closed by precontexts as for example the preterm $a\langle x, y\rangle$ is acceptable but $\lambda a\langle y, x\rangle.a\langle x, y\rangle$ is not.

Definition 6 (Metasubstitutions/Substitutions). *A metasubstitution θ is a pair (θ_m, θ_v), with θ_m a denumerable set of pairs $\mathbb{X} \triangleright p$ and $M \triangleright t$, and θ_v a denumerable set of pairs $x \triangleright t$ and $a \triangleright i$, where t is a term, i is a natural number and p is a pattern. Application of θ to a (meta)variable $\widehat{x}$ is defined as $\theta\widehat{x} = o$ if $\widehat{x} \triangleright o \in \theta$, and $\theta\widehat{x} = \widehat{x}$, otherwise. We define id as the empty substitution, i.e. $id\widehat{x} = \widehat{x}$ for every $\widehat{x}$. The domain of θ is given by $Dom(\theta) = \{\widehat{x} \mid \widehat{x} \triangleright o \in \theta$ and $o \neq \widehat{x}\}$. A substitution θ is a metasubstitution such that $Dom(\theta_m) = \emptyset$. A metasubstitution $\theta = (\theta_m, \theta_v)$ is said to be well-formed iff $(\bigcup_{M \in Dom(\theta_m)} \mathcal{FV}(\theta_m M)) \cap Dom(\theta_v) = \emptyset$.*

The *union* of two well-formed metasubstitutions θ_1 and θ_2 is denoted by $\theta_1 \sqcup \theta_2$. This union is *only defined* if the resulting metasubstitution is well-formed and if for every (meta)variable $\widehat{x} \in Dom(\theta_1) \cap Dom(\theta_2)$ we have $\theta_1\widehat{x} = \theta_2\widehat{x}$.

We are now ready to define the notion of *pattern-matching*. This operation is not defined in general as a function from patterns and terms to substitutions but from patterns and terms to *sets* of substitutions. We will see latter how to ensure the uniqueness of this result.

Definition 7 (Pattern-matching). *For each pair (p, t), where p is a pattern and t is a term, we associate a set of substitutions as follows:*

$$
\begin{array}{lll}
id & \in \{\!\{ \_ \text{ by } t \}\!\} & \\
\{x \triangleright t\} & \in \{\!\{ x \text{ by } t \}\!\} & \\
\theta_1 \sqcup \ldots \sqcup \theta_n & \in \{\!\{ @(p_1, \ldots, p_n) \text{ by } t \}\!\} & \text{if } \theta_i \in \{\!\{ p_i \text{ by } t \}\!\} \\
\theta_1 \sqcup \ldots \sqcup \theta_n & \in \{\!\{ f(p_1 \ldots p_n) \text{ by } f(t_1 \ldots t_n) \}\!\} & \text{if } \theta_i \in \{\!\{ p_i \text{ by } t_i \}\!\} \\
\{a \triangleright i\} \sqcup \theta_i & \in \{\!\{ a\langle p_1 \ldots p_n \rangle \text{ by } t \}\!\} & \text{if } \theta_i \in \{\!\{ p_i \text{ by } t \}\!\}
\end{array}
$$

We remark that in the last three cases the result of $\{\!\{ p \text{ by } t \}\!\}$ is defined only if $\sqcup$ is defined. Also, all the substitutions in $\{\!\{ p \text{ by } t \}\!\}$ are well-formed since they do not map metavariables. When $\{\!\{ p \text{ by } t \}\!\}$ is a singleton we will make an abuse of notation by writing $\{\!\{ p \text{ by } t \}\!\}$ to denote the only element of this set.

As an example of the previous definition, the pattern-matching $\{\!\{ a\langle 0, x \rangle \text{ by } 0 \}\!\}$ has two solutions: $\{ a \triangleright 1 \}$ and $\{ a \triangleright 2, x \triangleright 0 \}$. This comes from the fact that the pattern $a\langle 0, x \rangle$ contains two "overlapping" subpatterns 0 and x.

Definition 8 (Acceptable/linear metasubstitution). *A metasubstitution* θ *is said to be acceptable (resp. linear) iff for every (meta)variable* $\hat{x} \in Dom(\theta)$, $\theta\hat{x}$ *is acceptable (resp. linear).*

It is time to make the point w.r.t capture of variables in higher-order rewriting.

In CRS [15,16] for example, a metaterm like $\lambda x.M(x)$ allows the (eventual) capture of the variable x while $\lambda x.M$ does not. In this formalism the β-rule has to be written as $app(\lambda x.M(x), N) \longrightarrow M(N)$ which does not correspond to the traditional way to express the β-rule.

In ERS [13] there is a metasubstitution operator which allows to express the β-rule in a more traditional way as $app(\lambda x.M, N) \longrightarrow M\{x/N\}$. The instantiation of the metavariable M may or may not capture the variable x. However, we cannot assume α-conversion on metaterms in this formalism: if we suppose $\lambda x.M =_\alpha \lambda y.M$, then the instantiation of M by x will give two non α-equivalent terms $\lambda x.x \neq_\alpha \lambda y.x$. In order to properly handle α-conversion on terms but not on metaterms two *different* levels of syntax are needed, and this is the approach taken in general in the ERS formalism (see also [4]).

To allow α-conversion on the level of terms but not on that of metaterms a special notion of instantiation is needed, so that application of a metasubstitution $\theta = (\theta_m, \theta_v)$ to a metaterm will be split into two different steps: θ_m is used as *first-order* replacement, so that capture of variables can be provoked, while θ_v is used as *higher-order* substitution, so that no capture of variables is possible.

Definition 9 (Applying a metasubstitution). *Given a metasubstitution* $\theta = (\theta_m, \theta_v)$ *and a metaterm* t, *the application of* θ *to* t *(or instantiation of* t *by* θ*) yields a set of terms, written* $\theta(t)$, *which is computed in two steps:*

1. *First compute the first-order replacement* $\theta_m(t)$ *obtaining a preterm* s *(in the case where* $\theta_m(t)$ *is not still a preterm the application is not defined)*
2. *Then compute the set of terms* $\theta_v(s)$, *where* θ_v *is a higher-order substitution which works modulo* α-conversion *defined as follows:*

$$
\begin{array}{lll}
\theta_v x & \in \theta_v(x) & \text{if } x \in Dom(\theta_v) \\
x & \in \theta_v(x) & \text{if } x \notin Dom(\theta_v) \\
\mu p.t' & \in \theta_v(\mu p.t) & \text{if } t' \in \theta_v(t) \text{ and no capture of variables holds} \\
f(t'_1, \ldots, t'_n) & \in \theta_v(f(t_1, \ldots, t_n)) & \text{if } t'_i \in \theta_v(t_i) \\
t'_i & \in \theta_v(a\langle t_1, \ldots, t_n \rangle) & \text{if } \theta_v a = i \text{ and } t'_i \in \theta_v(t_i)
\end{array}
$$

$$a\langle t'_1,\ldots,t'_n\rangle \in \theta_v(a\langle t_1,\ldots,t_n\rangle) \quad \text{if } t'_i \in \theta_v(t_i) \text{ and } a \notin Dom(\theta_v)$$

$$t' \qquad\qquad \in \theta_v(t\{p \text{ by } u\}) \quad \text{if } u' \in \theta_v(u), \theta'_v \in \{\!\{p \text{ by } u'\}\!\},$$

$$t' \in (\theta'_v \;\sqcup\; \theta_v)(t)$$

and no capture of variables holds

When the metasubstitution θ is a substitution, we may make an abuse of notation by writing $\theta(t)$ instead of $\theta_v(t)$. We also remark that if a metaterm t has no pattern-matching constructor, then, if defined, $\theta(t)$ is a singleton.

Another interesting observation is that even when θ_v of some metasubstitution θ is empty, the second step of the previous procedure must be computed on preterms (which still have pattern-matching constructors to be eliminated).

Let us see how the application of a metasubstitution works on an example. Consider $\theta = (\theta_m, \theta_v)$, where $\theta_m = \{\mathbb{X}/a\langle x, f(z,y)\rangle, M/a\langle g(x,x), z\rangle, N/f(x,x)\}$ and $\theta_v = \emptyset$. In order to compute $\theta(M\{\mathbb{X} \text{ by } N\})$ we first compute $\theta_m(M\{\mathbb{X} \text{ by } N\})$ which gives the preterm $t = a\langle g(x,x), z\rangle\{a\langle x, f(z,y)\rangle \text{ by } f(x,x)\}$.

Now, since α-conversion is allowed on preterms, we obtain

$$t =_\alpha a\langle g(x',x'), z\rangle\{a\langle x', f(z,y)\rangle \text{ by } f(x,x)\} = t'$$

Now, the computation of $\{\!\{a\langle x', f(z,y)\rangle \text{ by } f(x,x)\}\!\}$ gives $\{\rho_1, \rho_2\}$, where $\rho_1 = \{a \rhd 1, x' \rhd f(x,x)\}$ and $\rho_2 = \{a \rhd 2, z \rhd x, y \rhd x\}$, and thus, the second step of the application procedure finally gives a set

$$\theta_v(t') = \{g(f(x,x), f(x,x)), x\}$$

Lemma 1. *If t is acceptable and $\theta \in \{\!\{p \text{ by } t\}\!\}$, then θ is acceptable. Also, if t and θ are acceptable then so is $\theta(t)$.*

2   Rewrite Rules and Reduction Relation

This section introduces the precise syntax used to specify rewrite rules in the ERSP formalism as well as the reduction relation associated to them.

Definition 10. *An Expression Reduction System with Patterns (ERSP) is a set of rewrite rules of the form $l \longrightarrow r$ (written also (l,r)) such that:*

- *l and r are well-formed metaterms,*
- *the first symbol (called head symbol) in l is in $\mathcal{F} \cup \mathcal{B}$,*
- *$\mathcal{MV}(r) \subseteq \mathcal{MV}(l)$,*
- *$\mathcal{FV}(r) \subseteq \mathcal{FV}(l)$, and*
- *l contains no occurrence of the pattern-matching constructor.*

Thus for example, the rule $app(\lambda\mathbb{X}.M, N) \longrightarrow M\{\mathbb{X} \text{ by } N\}$ given in the introduction, which generalizes the classical β-rule to the case of patterns, belongs to our framework.

In order to be able to guarantee that no free variable is "generated" during reduction the following notion will be necessary.

Definition 11 (Path condition). *Let M be a term variable and t be a meta-term. We consider all the occurrences $p_1, \ldots, p_n$ of M in t and their corresponding parameter paths $l_1, \ldots, l_n$. A metasubstitution θ is said to have the path condition property for M in t iff:*

$$\forall \widehat{x} \in \mathcal{FV}(\theta_m M), (\forall 1 \leq i \leq n, \widehat{x} \in \theta_m l_i) \vee (\forall 1 \leq i \leq n, \widehat{x} \notin \theta_m l_i)$$

where the notation $\theta_m l$ denotes the set $\bigcup_{\widehat{x} \in l} \theta_m \widehat{x}$.

This notion is extended to rewrite rules by saying that θ has the path condition for M in (l, r) iff it has the path condition for M in $f(l, r)$, where f is any binary function symbol. This trick is used to consider a rule as a unique "tree".

The classical example of path condition which is not satisfied for a rewrite rule is given by the η-rule of the λ-calculus (see for example [13,4]). Another rule in the same spirit but using patterns is $\lambda f(\mathbb{X}).M \longrightarrow M$. The metasubstitution $\theta = \{\mathbb{X} \rhd x, M \rhd x\}$ does not satisfy the path condition for M in this rule.

We now define the set of "good" substitutions to instantiate rewrite rules. For that we remark that given a rewrite rule $l \longrightarrow r$, the metaterm l does not contain the pattern-matching constructor, so that for any metasubstitution θ the term $\theta(l)$ is a singleton.

Definition 12 (Admissible metasubstitution for metaterms/rules). *A metasubstitution θ is admissible for a metaterm t iff*

- *$\theta(t)$ contains only acceptable terms*
- *θ has the path condition for every term metavariable appearing in t.*

A metasubstitution θ is admissible for a rule (l, r) iff θ is admissible for $f(l, r)$, where f is any binary function symbol.

We remark that this definition implies that given a rule (l, r) both $\theta(l)$ and $\theta(r)$ are defined, so in particular all the pattern/term metavariables in l are also in $Dom(\theta_m)$.

Definition 13 (Admissible reduction relation). *Let $\mathcal{R}$ be a ERSP. We say that s rewrites to t, written $s \longrightarrow_{\mathcal{R}} t$ (or $s \xrightarrow{a}_{\mathcal{R}} t$ when the distinction must be done), iff there exists a rule $(l, r) \in \mathcal{R}$, a well-formed admissible metasubstitution θ for (l, r) and a context C such that $s = C[\theta(l)]$ and $t \in C[\theta(r)]$.*

Even if the relation $\longrightarrow_{\mathcal{R}}$ is defined on any kind of terms, the reduction can only take place on acceptable subterms.

As expected, the relation reduction enjoys good preservation properties.

Lemma 2. *Assume $s \longrightarrow_{\mathcal{R}} t$. Then $\mathcal{FV}_a^i(t) \subseteq \mathcal{FV}_a^i(s)$ (for any a and any i) and $\mathcal{FV}(t) \subseteq \mathcal{FV}(s)$. Also, if s is acceptable, then so is t.*

3   A Complete Example

We consider in this section the well known higher-order function map which takes a function f and a list l and returns the result of applying f to each element of l. This function can be specified as the following Ocaml [18] program:

```
#let rec map(f,l) =   match l with
                      Nil -> Nil
                    | Cons(h,t) -> Cons(f(h),map(f,t));;
```

It can also be specified as the following ERSP rewrite rule:

$$map(\mu \mathbb{X}.F, L) \longrightarrow$$
$$a\langle nil, cons(F\{\mathbb{X} \text{ by } h\}, map(\mu \mathbb{X}.F, t)))\rangle\{a\langle nil, cons(h, t)\rangle \text{ by } L\}$$

Let us see how this implementation of map works on a concrete example. Suppose that we represent natural numbers with constructors 0 and s and let us consider $pred =_{def} \mu b\langle 0, s(n)\rangle.b\langle 0, n\rangle$ in order to denote the predecessor function on natural numbers. Using the metasubstitution $\theta = (\theta_m, \theta_v)$, where $\theta_m = \{\mathbb{X} \triangleright b\langle 0, s(n)\rangle, F \triangleright b\langle 0, n\rangle, L \triangleright cons(0, cons(s(s(0)), nil))\}$ and $\theta_v = \emptyset$ to fire the previous rewrite rule, we can construct the following derivation:

$$t_1 = map(pred, cons(0, cons(s(s(0)), nil))) \longrightarrow$$
$$t_2 = cons(0, map(pred, cons(s(s(0)), nil)))$$

Indeed, the term t_1 is an instance of the left-hand side of the previous rule. In order to obtain t_2 we have to apply θ to the right-hand side of the previous rule. For that, we first instantiate $\{a\langle nil, cons(h, t)\rangle \text{ by } L\}$ with θ_m, then since $\theta_v(\theta_m(L)) = \theta_m(L)$, we can compute the pattern-matching operation $\{\!\{a\langle nil, cons(h, t)\rangle \text{ by } cons(0, cons(s(s(0)), nil))\}\!\}$. We then obtain a substitution $\theta'_v = \{a \triangleright 2, h \triangleright 0, t \triangleright cons(s(s(0)), nil)\}$. Now, we have to instantiate $a\langle nil, cons(F\{\mathbb{X} \text{ by } h\}, map(\mu \mathbb{X}.F, t))\rangle$ with θ_m, then proceed with the application of θ'_v to this last instantiation. The only delicate part is the one concerning the submetaterm $F\{\mathbb{X} \text{ by } h\}$. We have $\theta_m(F\{\mathbb{X} \text{ by } h\}) = b\langle 0, n\rangle\{b\langle 0, s(n)\rangle \text{ by } h\} = t'$ and $\theta'_v(t') = b\langle 0, n\rangle\{\!\{b\langle 0, s(n)\rangle \text{ by } 0\}\!\} = 0$.

The reader may verify that this sequence of operations finally leads to the term t_2. Similarly, we can then continue the reduction till $cons(0, cons(s(0), nil))$.

4   Towards a Subclass of Confluent ERSP

The following two sections are devoted to the study of confluence for a certain class of ERSP which are called the *orthogonal l-constructor* ERSP, and a certain class of terms, which are called *l-constructor deterministic terms*. Intuitively, an orthogonal ERSP is *left-linear* and *not overlapping*. Sufficiency of orthogonality for confluence in first and higher-order rewrite systems is well-known [1]. A constructor ERSP is a system $\mathcal{R}$ where the set of function symbols is partitioned into two different subsets, namely, the set of *constructors*, which cannot be reduced, and the set of *defined symbols*, which cannot be matched. As an example, let us consider the following system which is not a constructor ERSP.

$$\mathcal{R} : \quad a \longrightarrow b, \ app(\mu a.c, M) \longrightarrow c\{a \text{ by } M\}$$

The term $app(\mu a.c, a)$ can be reduced to both $app(\mu a.c, b)$ and c which are not joinable. Thus, $\mathcal{R}$ turns out to be non confluent.

Unfortunately, *orthogonal l-constructor* ERSP do not immediately guarantee confluence as the rule $app(\lambda \mathbb{X}.M, N) \longrightarrow M\{\mathbb{X} \text{ by } N\}$ shows: the term $t = app(\lambda a\langle x, y\rangle.a\langle 0, 1\rangle, 3)$ has two non-joinable reducts 0 and 1 by this unique rule.

The reason is that t contains two "overlapping" patterns x and y inside the choice pattern $a\langle x, y\rangle$. The failure of the confluence property in this case is completely natural since the term t corresponds, informally, to a "non-orthogonal" first-order rewriting system. It is then clear that we have to get rid of this class of terms in order to get a confluence result, this will be done by introducing the notion of *l-constructor deterministic* terms.

We are know ready to give a formal definition of all these notions.

Definition 14 (L-constructor system). $\mathcal{R}$ *is said to be l-constructor iff*

– *The set $\mathcal{F}$ of function symbols can be partitioned into two sets $\mathcal{F}_c$ and $\mathcal{F}_d$, called respectively constructors and defined symbols, such that:*
  • *Each defined symbol is the head of some left-hand side of $\mathcal{R}$.*
  • *All the function symbols in metapatterns of $\mathcal{R}$ are constructors.*
– *For every rule $(l, r) \in \mathcal{R}$, both l and r are p-linear metaterms.*

The system $\mathcal{R}_1 = \{\beta_{PM}\} \cup \{0 + N \longrightarrow N, s(M) + N \longrightarrow s(M + N)\}$ is l-constructor. The system $\mathcal{R}_2 = \{\mu f(\mathbb{X}).M \longrightarrow M, f(0) \longrightarrow 0\}$ is not l-constructor since the function symbol f appears as the head symbol of some rule and inside a metapattern of $\mathcal{R}$. The system $\mathcal{R}_3 = \{\mu f(\mathbb{X}, \mathbb{X}).0 \longrightarrow 0\}$ is not l-constructor since $\mu f(\mathbb{X}, \mathbb{X}).0$ is not p-linear.

Definition 15 (L-constructor objects). *Given a l-constructor system $\mathcal{R}$, we say that a metapattern is l-constructor iff it is linear and all its function symbols are constructors of $\mathcal{R}$. A l-constructor metaterm contains only l-constructor metapatterns. A metasubstitution θ is said to be l-constructor iff $\theta(\widehat{x})$ is l-constructor for any $\widehat{x} \in Dom(\theta)$.*

As an example concerning our previous system $\mathcal{R}_1$, we can observe that the metapattern $s(\mathbb{X})$ is l-constructor but $\mathbb{X} + \mathbb{Y}$ is not since the symbol $+$ is not a constructor function symbol.

We remark that if p is a l-constructor pattern and $\{\!\{p \text{ by } t\}\!\}$ is defined then all its elements are l-constructor substitutions.

Definition 16 (L-constructor reduction relation). *If $\mathcal{R}$ is a l-constructor system, we say that s constructor rewrites to t (written $s \xrightarrow{c}_\mathcal{R} t$) iff there exists a rewrite rule $(l, r) \in \mathcal{R}$, a well-formed l-constructor metasubstitution θ admissible for (l, r) and a context C such that $s = C[\theta(l)]$ and $t \in C[\theta(r)]$.*

As an example, given the previous system $\mathcal{R}_1$, we have $0 + 0 \xrightarrow{c}_{\mathcal{R}_1} 0$ but we do not have $t = app(\lambda(0 + 0).3, 0 + 0) \xrightarrow{c}_{\mathcal{R}_1} 3$ (even if we have $t \xrightarrow{a}_{\mathcal{R}_1} 3$) since the term t is not an l-constructor term.

One can remark that whenever t is a l-constructor preterm and θ is a l-constructor substitution w.r.t. $\mathcal{FV}(t)$, then $\theta(t)$ contains only l-constructor terms. Also as expected, l-constructor terms are preserved during reduction.

Lemma 3 (Preservation of l-constructor terms). *If $\mathcal{R}$ is l-constructor, s is l-constructor and $s \xrightarrow{c}_{\mathcal{R}} t$, then t is l-constructor.*

Definition 17 (Left linear systems). *A rewrite rule $l \longrightarrow r$ is said to be left linear iff l contains at most one occurrence of any term metavariable. A system is left linear if all its rule are left linear.*

As an example, the rule $f(M, M) \longrightarrow 3$ is not left linear while $f(M) \longrightarrow g(M, M)$ and $\mu x.f(x, x) \longrightarrow 0$ are.

Definition 18 (Redexes and overlapping redexes). *A term t is said to be a redex if it is an instance of some left-hand side of rule that is $t = \theta(l)$ for some rule (l, r). A rewrite system is said to be non-overlapping iff*

- *Whenever a redex $\theta(l_j)$ contains another redex $\theta'(l_i)$, then $\theta'(l_i)$ must be contained in $\theta(M)$ for some term metavariable M of l_j.*
- *Likewise whenever a redex $\theta(l)$ properly contains another redex instance $\theta'(l)$ of the same rule.*

Definition 19 (Orthogonal systems). *A rewrite system $\mathcal{R}$ is said to be orthogonal iff $\mathcal{R}$ is left-linear and non-overlapping.*

As an example, the system $\{f(\mu x.x) \longrightarrow 0, \mu \mathbb{X}.y \longrightarrow 1\}$ is overlapping : the redex $f(\mu y.y) = \theta(f(\mu x.x))$ contains the redex $\mu y.y = \theta'(\mu \mathbb{X}.y)$. The system $\{f(\mu \mathbb{X}.M) \longrightarrow 0, \lambda \mathbb{Z}.N \longrightarrow g(2)\}$ is orthogonal.

We now introduce *l-constructor deterministic terms* for which the class of orthogonal l-constructor ERSP will be confluent. Let us start by the following notion.

Definition 20 (Overlapping patterns). *Two patterns p and q are said to be overlapping iff there exists a term t s.t. both $\{\!\{p$ by $t\}\!\}$ and $\{\!\{q$ by $t\}\!\}$ are defined.*

The patterns $f(\_, x)$ and $f(y, g(0))$ are overlapping. Also $a\langle 0, s(x)\rangle$ and $b\langle s(0), s(s(\_))\rangle$ are overlapping.

Definition 21 (Deterministic patterns/terms). *A pattern p is said to be deterministic iff whenever $a\langle p_1, \ldots, p_n\rangle$ appears inside p, then for all $i \neq j$ the patterns p_i and p_j are not overlapping. A term t is said to be a deterministic iff t is acceptable and for every pattern p appearing in t, p is deterministic.*

Thus for example, $b\langle s(0), s(s(\_))\rangle$ is deterministic but $b\langle s(0), s(\_)\rangle$ is not. This definition implies that whenever p is a deterministic pattern, then there exists *at most* one substitution θ belonging to $\{\!\{p$ by $t\}\!\}$.

Definition 22 (Deterministic metasubstitution for metaterms/rules).
A metasubstitution θ is said to be deterministic for a metaterm t iff
- *θ is admissible for t,*
- *$\theta(t)$ contains only one deterministic term,*

Finally, θ is deterministic for a rule (l,r) iff θ is a deterministic for $f(l,r)$, where f is any binary function symbol.

A *metasubstitution θ is deterministic* iff $\theta\widehat{x}$ is deterministic $\forall \widehat{x} \in Dom(\theta)$. Deterministic terms are stable by deterministic substitutions. Also, the substitution obtained by performing a pattern-matching operation on a deterministic pattern p and a deterministic term t turns out to be deterministic.

Definition 23 (Deterministic reduction relation). *Given a system $\mathcal{R}$, we say that s deterministicly rewrites to t (written $s \xrightarrow{d}_\mathcal{R} t$) iff there exists a rewrite rule $(l,r) \in \mathcal{R}$, a well-formed deterministic metasubstitution θ for (l,r) and a context C such that $s = C[\theta(l)]$ and $s = C[\theta(r)]$.*

From now on we use the notation $\xrightarrow{c,d}_\mathcal{R}$ to denote $\xrightarrow{c}_\mathcal{R} \cap \xrightarrow{d}_\mathcal{R}$. As expected, orthogonal systems allows us to preserve deterministic terms.

Lemma 4 (Preservation of deterministic terms). *Given an orthogonal system $\mathcal{R}$, if s is deterministic and $s \xrightarrow{d}_\mathcal{R} t$, then t is deterministic.*

5   The Confluence Proof

This section is dedicated to show that the relation $\xrightarrow{c,d}_\mathcal{R}$ is confluent for orthogonal l-constructor ERSP, that is, orthogonal l-constructor ERSP are confluent on l-constructor deterministic terms. This confluence property can only be proved on the set of acceptable l-constructor deterministic terms. The proof uses a technique due to Tait and Martin-Löf [2] and can be summarized in four steps:
- We define a parallel reduction relation denoted $\ggg_{c,d}$.
- We prove that $\ggg_{c,d}{}^*$ and $\xrightarrow{c,d}{}^*$ are the same relation.
- We show, using Takahashi terms [19], that $\ggg_{c,d}$ has the diamond property on the set of acceptable l-constructor deterministic terms.
- We conclude by the fact that the diamond property implies confluence.

In order to define the $\ggg_{c,d}$ reduction relation, we first need to extend relations on terms to relations on substitutions.

Notation 1 Given any relation $\rightsquigarrow$ between terms and given two metasubstitutions θ and θ', we write $\theta \rightsquigarrow \theta'$ when $Dom(\theta) = Dom(\theta')$, θ and θ' coincide on the sets of choice and pattern variables, and for every $M \in Dom(\theta)$ we have $\theta(M) \rightsquigarrow \theta'(M)$ and $x \in Dom(\theta)$ we have $\theta(x) \rightsquigarrow \theta'(x)$.

In order to relate two sets S and T of metaterms/metasubstitutions via any binary relation $\rightsquigarrow$, we will write $S \rightsquigarrow T$ iff $\forall s \in S, \exists t \in T, s \rightsquigarrow t$ and $\forall t \in T, \exists s \in S, s \rightsquigarrow t$. For any unary relation Φ on metaterms/metasubstitutions, we will write $\Phi(S) = \bigcup_{s \in S} \Phi(s)$.

We can now define the parallel relation as follows:

Definition 24 (The simultaneous relation $\ggg_a$).

- $x \ggg_a x$.
- If $s_1 \ggg_a s'_1, \ldots, s_m \ggg_a s'_m$, then $f(s_1, \ldots, s_m) \ggg_a f(s'_1, \ldots, s'_m)$, $\mu p.s_1 \ggg_a \mu p.s'_1$ and $a\langle s_1, \ldots, s_m \rangle \ggg_a a\langle s'_1, \ldots, s'_m \rangle$.
- If $\theta \ggg_a \rho$, then $\theta(l) \ggg_a \rho(r)$ for any rewrite rule $l \longrightarrow r$ such that θ is admissible for it.

We will denote $s \ggg_c t$ (resp. $s \ggg_d t$) if the metasubstitution θ used in the Definition 24 is not only admissible but also constructor (resp. deterministic). We write $\ggg_{c,d}$ to denote the relation $\ggg_c \cap \ggg_d$.

Given $\ggg \in \{\ggg_a, \ggg_c, \ggg_d\}$, then for every term s we have $s \ggg s$. Also, if $s \ggg s'$ and s is not a redex, then the root symbols of s and s' are the same. Moreover, if also $s = \mathcal{G}(s_1, \ldots, s_m)$, then $s' = \mathcal{G}(s'_1, \ldots, s'_m)$, where $s_i \ggg s'_i$, for $\mathcal{G}$ a function symbol, a case or a binder symbol.

We are now ready to proceed with the second step of Tait and Martin-Löf's technique which consists in showing that the reflexive-transitive closures of $\xrightarrow{c,d}$ and $\ggg_{c,d}$ are the same relation.

We can show by induction on l-constructor patterns that pattern-matching is stable by term reduction.

Lemma 5. *Let $\mathcal{R}$ be a l-constructor ERSP, p a l-constructor pattern and t a term such that $t \xrightarrow{c}{}^*_{\mathcal{R}} t'$. If $\{\!\{p$ by $t\}\!\}$ is defined, then $\{\!\{p$ by $t'\}\!\}$ is also defined and $\{\!\{p$ by $t\}\!\} \xrightarrow{c}{}^*_{\mathcal{R}} \{\!\{p$ by $t'\}\!\}$.*

The previous Lemma does not holds if the pattern p is not l-constructor. Indeed, let $\mathcal{R} = \{a \longrightarrow b\}$ and let us take the non-linear pattern $p_1 = f(x,x)$ and the non-constructor pattern $p_2 = a$. We have that $\{\!\{f(x,x)$ by $f(a,a)\}\!\}$ is defined and $f(a,a) \xrightarrow{c}_{\mathcal{R}} f(a,b)$ but $\{\!\{f(x,x)$ by $f(a,b)\}\!\}$ is not defined. Also, $\{\!\{a$ by $a\}\!\}$ is defined and $a \xrightarrow{c}_{\mathcal{R}} b$ but $\{\!\{a$ by $b\}\!\}$ is not defined.

We can now show by induction on metaterms that reduction of metasubstitutions is stable by application:

Lemma 6. *Let $\mathcal{R}$ be an l-constructor ERSP and θ, ρ two well-formed l-constructor metasubstitutions such that $\theta \xrightarrow{c}{}^*_{\mathcal{R}} \rho$. If for any l-constructor metaterm t such that θ has the path condition for t, $\theta(t)$ is defined and contains only acceptable l-constructor terms, then the same happens for $\rho(t)$ and $\theta(t) \xrightarrow{c}{}^*_{\mathcal{R}} \rho(t)$.*

Lemma 6 allows us to obtain the following fundamental property.

Lemma 7. *Let $\mathcal{R}$ be a l-constructor ERSP. If $\theta \xrightarrow{c}{}^*_{\mathcal{R}} \rho$, and θ is a well-formed l-constructor admissible metasubstitution for (l,r), then $\theta(l) \xrightarrow{c}{}^*_{\mathcal{R}} \rho(r)$ and ρ is admissible for (l,r).*

We are now able to conclude the second step of our confluence proof:

Theorem 1 (Equivalence between $\gg_{c,d}{}^{*}$ and $\xrightarrow{c,d}{}^{*}_{\mathcal{R}}$). *If $\mathcal{R}$ is a l-constructor ERSP, then $s\xrightarrow{c,d} t$ implies $s \gg_{c,d} t$ and $s \gg_{c,d} t$ implies $s\xrightarrow{c,d}{}^{*}_{\mathcal{R}} t$.*

Proof. The first implication holds in a more general case, namely, that $s \longrightarrow s'$ implies $s \gg s'$ for $\longrightarrow \in \{\xrightarrow{a}, \xrightarrow{c}, \xrightarrow{d}\}$ and *any* ERSP $\mathcal{R}$. This can be shown by induction on the definition of $\gg$. The second implication can be shown by induction on the structure of s using Lemma 7.

We are now going to prove the diamond property for the relation $\gg_{c,d}$. For that, we associate a term $\#(s)$ to every term s such that every time $s \gg_{c,d} s'$, for some s', we automatically deduce $s' \gg_{c,d} \#(s)$. Thus, given two different terms s' and s'' such that $s \gg_{c,d} s'$ and $s \gg_{c,d} s''$, we obviously obtain a unique term $\#(s)$ which allows us to close the diagram with $s' \gg_{c,d} \#(s)$ and $s'' \gg_{c,d} \#(s)$. The diamond property will immediately follow.

Definition 25 (Takahashi terms $\#(s)$). *Given a ERSP $\mathcal{R}$ and a term s we define its associated Takahashi term $\#(s)$ by induction as follows:*
- *If $s = x$, then $\#(x) = x$.*
- *If $s = f(s_1, \ldots, s_m)$ (resp. $s = \mu p.s'$ or $a\langle s_1, \ldots, s_m \rangle$) and s is not a deterministic instance of a left-hand side of rule, then $\#(s) = f(\#(s_1), \ldots, \#(s_m))$ (resp. $\#(s) = \mu p.\#(s')$ and $\#(s) = a\langle \#(s_1), \ldots, \#(s_m) \rangle$).*
- *If s is an instance $\theta(l)$ of the left-hand side l of some rule $l \longrightarrow r$, where $\theta = (\theta_m, \theta_v)$ is deterministic for (l, r), then $\#(s) = \#(\theta)(r)$, where $\#(\theta) = (\#(\theta)_m, \#(\theta)_v)$ verifies $\#(\theta)_m(M) = \#(\theta_m(M))$ and $\#(\theta)_v(y) = \#(\theta_v(y))$.*

We can show by induction on terms the following two properties about $\gg$.

Lemma 8. *The term $\#(s)$ is uniquely defined in every orthogonal ERSP.*

Lemma 9. *Let $\mathcal{R}$ be an orthogonal ERSP, let $\gg \in \{\gg_a, \gg_c, \gg_d\}$ and let $s \gg s'$. If $s = \mathcal{G}(s_1, \ldots, s_m)$ and $s' = \mathcal{G}(s'_1, \ldots, s'_m)$ (where $\mathcal{G}$ is a function, binder symbol, case or variable) and $s_i \gg s'_i$, then if s is a redex $\theta(l)$, s' is a also redex $\rho(l)$, for some ρ such that $\theta \gg \rho$.*

Lemma 10. *If $\mathcal{R}$ is l-constructor and orthogonal and $s \gg_{c,d} s'$, then $s' \gg_{c,d} \#(s)$.*

Proof. By induction on the definition of $s \gg_{c,d} s'$ using Lemma 9.

Corollary 1. *If $\mathcal{R}$ is an l-constructor orthogonal ERSP, then the relation $\gg_{c,d}$ is confluent on deterministic constructor acceptable terms.*

Proof. It is well-known that a relation having the diamond property is confluent [1] so that it is sufficient to show that $\gg$ has the diamond property. Let us consider $s \gg s'$ and $s \gg s''$. By Lemma 10 we can close the diagram with $s' \gg \#(s)$ and $s'' \gg \#(s)$.

By Theorem 1 and Corollary 1 we can now conclude with the main result of this section, namely,

Theorem 2. *Let $\mathcal{R}$ be an l-constructor orthogonal ERSP. The relation $\xrightarrow{c,d}_{\mathcal{R}}$ is confluent on acceptable constructor deterministic terms.*

6   Conclusion and Further Work

We have introduced a new *Higher-Order* formalism, called ERSP, in which the abstraction operation is not only allowed on variables but also on more complex patterns. This formalism can be seen as an extension of ERS [13] and SERS [4] to the case of patterns and an extension of [12] to the case of non functional rewriting rules. Many simple notions in the mentioned previous works do not trivially extend in our case: on one hand the complexity of ERSP does not only appear at the level of metaterms but also at the level of terms, on the other hand, binders are not always so simple as in the case of λ-calculus. We carefully extend all the expected notions of rewriting to our framework, namely, terms, metaterms, rewrite rules, substitutions, reduction, etc. The resulting formalism is able to model pattern-matching function/proof definitions.

The more technical part of this work is the identification of a class of ERSP which can be proved to be confluent on an appropriate set of terms. Our confluence result gives in particular a confluence result for SERS.

As mentioned in the introduction, ERSP and ρ-calculus [8] are closely related. The main difference between both formalisms lies in the class of syntactic patterns which are considered: our approach is mainly driven by the set of patterns appearing in functional languages and theorem provers, namely, algebraic patterns with choice constructors, while their approach includes other higher-order patterns (rules in their formalism) not really used in implementation of programming languages.

Many future directions remain to be explored. The first one consists in the definition of implementation languages given by "explicit" versions of this formalism, where both pattern matching and substitution operators are integrated to the syntax. This would result in generalizations of calculi defined in [5,9].

Also, a formal comparison between ERSP and ρ-calculus must be done. In particular, it would be interesting to know if every system in the ρ-calculus can be expressed in a ERSP system and vice-versa. Another interesting question concerns confluence since confluent ρ-systems are characterized via a special *reduction strategy* while confluence is ensured in our case by syntactic restrictions.

Typing is another feature which remains as further work. It is however interesting to remark that the pioneer work on pattern calculi [12] which inspired the definition of ERSP was built, via the Curry-Howard isomorphism, on a computational interpretation of Gentzen sequent calculus for intuitionistic minimal logic. As a consequence, each ERSP pattern constructor comes from the interpretation of some *left* logical rule of Gentzen calculus. It is nevertheless less evident how to associate a Curry-Howard style interpretation to the entire ERSP syntax.

Last but not least, strong normalization of ERSP has to be studied. Indeed, proof techniques to guarantee termination of higher-order formalisms are not straightforward [3,11,21] and they do not extend immediately to our case.

References

1. F. Baader and T. Nipkow. *Term Rewriting and All That*. Cambridge University Press, 1998.
2. H. Barendregt. *The Lambda Calculus: Its Syntax and Semantics*, volume 103 of *Studies in Logic and the Foundations of Mathematics*. North-Holland, 1984. Revised Edition.
3. F. Blanqui, J.-P. Jouannaud, and M. Okada. Inductive-Data-Type Systems. *Theoretical Computer Science*, 277, 2001.
4. E. Bonelli, D. Kesner, and A. Ríos. A de Bruijn notation for higher-order rewriting. In *11th RTA, LNCS* 1833. 2000.
5. S. Cerrito and D. Kesner. Pattern matching as cut elimination. *Theoretical Computer Science*. To appear.
6. S. Cerrito and D. Kesner. Pattern matching as cut elimination. In *14th LICS*. IEEE. 1999.
7. H. Cirstea. *Calcul de réécriture : fondements et applications*. Thèse de doctorat, Université Henri Poincaré - Nancy 1, 2000.
8. H. Cirstea and C. Kirchner. ρ-calculus, the rewriting calculus. In *5th CCL*, 1998.
9. J. Forest. A weak calculus with explicit operators for pattern matching and substitution. In *13th RTA, LNCS* 2378. 2002.
10. J. Forest and D. Kesner. Expression Reduction Systems with Patterns, 2003. Available on `http://www.pps.jussieu.fr/~kesner/papers/`.
11. J.-P. Jouannaud and A. Rubio. The higher-order recursive path ordering. In *14th LICS*. IEEE. 1999.
12. D. Kesner, L. Puel, and V. Tannen. A Typed Pattern Calculus. *Information and Computation*, 124(1), 1996.
13. Z. Khasidashvili. Expression reduction systems. In *Proceedings of IN Vekua Institute of Applied Mathematics*, volume 36, Tbilisi, 1990.
14. C. Kirchner, H. Cirstea and L. Liquori. The Rho Cube. In *FOSSACS'01, LNCS* 2030. 2001.
15. J.-W. Klop. *Combinatory Reduction Systems*, volume 127 of *Mathematical Centre Tracts*. CWI, Amsterdam, 1980. PhD Thesis.
16. J.-W. Klop, V. van Oostrom, and F. van Raamsdonk. Combinatory reduction systems: introduction and survey. *Theoretical Computer Science* 121, 1993.
17. T. Nipkow. Higher-order critical pairs. In *6th LICS*. IEEE. 1991.
18. The Objective Caml language, `http://caml.inria.fr/`.
19. M. Takahashi. Parallel Reductions in lambda-Calculus. *Journal of Symbolic Computation*, 7(2), 1989.
20. V. van Oostrom and F. van Raamsdonk. Weak orthogonality implies confluence: the higher-order case. In *3rd LFCS, LNCS* 813. 1994.
21. F. van Raamsdonk. On termination of higher-order rewriting. In *12th RTA, LNCS* 2051. 2001.
22. D. Wolfram. *The Clausal Theory of Types*, volume 21 of *Cambridge Tracts in Theoretical Computer Science*. Cambridge University Press, 1993.

Residuals in Higher-Order Rewriting

H.J. Sander Bruggink

Department of Philosophy, Utrecht University
bruggink@phil.uu.nl
http://www.phil.uu.nl/~bruggink

Abstract. Residuals have been studied for various forms of rewriting and residual systems have been defined to capture residuals in an abstract setting. In this article we study residuals in orthogonal Pattern Rewriting Systems (PRSs). First, the rewrite relation is defined by means of a higher-order rewriting logic, and proof terms are defined that witness reductions. Then, we have the formal machinery to define a residual operator for PRSs, and we will prove that an orthogonal PRS together with the residual operator mentioned above, is a residual system. As a side-effect, all results of (abstract) residual theory are inherited by orthogonal PRSs, such as confluence, and the notion of permutation equivalence of reductions.

1 Introduction

This paper deals with residual theory: what remains of a reduction after another reduction from the same object has been performed? Let φ and ψ be reductions. Intuitively, the residual of φ after ψ, written φ/ψ, should consist of exactly those steps of φ which were not in ψ. In the literature, residuals have been studied in various degrees of abstraction [2,3,4,6,8,13,14], and for various forms of reduction (e.g. reduction in the λ-calculus, first-order term rewriting, and concurrency theory). In this paper we study residuals in a subclass of Higher-order Rewriting Systems (HRSs), orthogonal Pattern Rewriting Systems (orthogonal PRSs).

Even in first-order term rewriting, calculating residuals is a non-trivial task. Performing a reduction may duplicate the redexes of other reductions, thus potentially increasing the length of their residuals. In the higher-order case, the problems caused by duplication are more severe: now, copies of the same redex may get nested. Consider the orthogonal PRS which consists of the following two rules:

$$\mu : \lambda z.\mathsf{mu}(\lambda x.z(x)) \to \lambda z.z(\mathsf{mu}(\lambda x.z(x)))$$
$$\rho : \qquad \lambda x.f(x) \to \lambda x.h(x,x)$$

Consider the term $s = \mathsf{mu}(\lambda x.f(x))$. The rule μ can be applied to the whole term (because $(\lambda z.\mathsf{mu}(\lambda x.z(x)))(\lambda x.f(x)) =_\beta s$) and the rule ρ can be applied to the subterm $\lambda x.f(x)$, so the following steps exists from s:

$$\varphi : \mathsf{mu}(\lambda x.f(x)) \to f(\mathsf{mu}(\lambda x.f(x)))$$
$$\psi : \mathsf{mu}(\lambda x.f(x)) \to \mathsf{mu}(\lambda x.h(x,x))$$

R. Nieuwenhuis (Ed.): RTA 2003, LNCS 2706, pp. 123–137, 2003.

The residual of ψ after φ is the reduction

$$f(\mathsf{mu}(\lambda x.f(x))) \rightarrow h(\mathsf{mu}(\lambda x.f(x)), \mathsf{mu}(\lambda x.f(x)))$$
$$\rightarrow^* h(\mathsf{mu}(\lambda x.h(x,x)), \mathsf{mu}(\lambda x.h(x,x)))$$

in which we see that one copy of the ρ-redex duplicates another (nested) copy of the ρ-redex.

In this paper we define a projection operator for proof terms, which are witnesses to multistep reductions. The operator projects one proof term over another and returns the residual of that proof term after the other. We define the projection operator by means of an inference system (postponing the proof that it is actually defined on orthogonal PRSs to the last part of the paper), prove that a PRS with projection operator is a residual system, and give an algorithm which calculates residuals.

An extended version of this paper was made available as technical report nr. 221 at `http://preprints.phil.uu.nl/lgps/`.

2 Preliminaries

2.1 Higher-Order Rewriting

We use Higher-order Rewriting Systems (HRSs) [7]. In fact, we consider HRSs as HORSs [12] with the simply typed λ-calculus as substitution calculus. We presuppose working knowledge of the λ-calculus, but in this section we will quickly recall the important notions of HRSs.

We fix in advance a signature Σ of simply typed constants (over a set of base types $\mathcal{B}$)[1]. *Preterms* are simply typed λ-terms over Σ. We identify α-equivalent preterms. We consider $\beta\eta$-equivalence classes of preterms. Since it is well-known that β-reduction combined with restricted η-expansion ($\beta\bar{\eta}$-reduction) is both confluent (modulo α-equivalence) and strongly normalizing, we can consider $\beta\bar{\eta}$-normal forms as unique representatives of the $\beta\eta$-equivalence classes. So, we define: *terms* are preterms in $\beta\bar{\eta}$-normal form. A *context* C is a term of the form $\lambda x.C_0$, such that x occurs free in C_0 exactly once.

We write stu for $(st)u$, and we use, for arbitrary (pre)terms $s, t_1, \ldots, t_n$, the following notation: $s(t_1, \ldots, t_n) = st_1 \ldots t_n$. Often, s will just be a function symbol, but the same notation is used if s is a term of the form $\lambda x_1 \ldots x_n.s_0$.

A term s is a *pattern* if all of its free variables x occur in some subterm of s of the form $x(y_1, \ldots, y_n)$, where the y_i are *distinct* bound variables.

Definition 2.1. *A rewrite rule is a tuple* $l = \lambda x_1 \ldots x_n.l_0 \rightarrow \lambda x_1 \ldots x_n.r_0 = r$, *where l (the left-hand side) and r (the right-hand side) are closed terms of the same type, and l is not η-equivalent to a variable. The rule is left-linear if* $x_1, \ldots, x_n$ *occur in l_0 exactly once.*

A Higher-order Rewrite System (HRS) $\mathcal{H}$ is a set of rewrite rules. $\mathcal{H}$ is left-linear, if all its rules are. An HRS is a Pattern Rewrite System (PRS) if, for all of its rules $\lambda x_1 \ldots x_n.l_0 \rightarrow \lambda x_1 \ldots x_n.r_0$, l_0 *is a pattern.*

---

[1] All definitions must be read as having the signature as an implicit parameter.

Let $\mathcal{H}$ be an HRS. We define the rewrite relation $\rightarrow_{\mathcal{H}}$ as follows [16]: s rewrites to t, written $s \rightarrow_{\mathcal{H}} t$ (the subscript is omitted if clear from the context), if there is a context C and a rule $l \rightarrow r \in R$, such that $s \twoheadleftarrow_\beta C(l)$ and $C(r) \twoheadrightarrow_\beta t$. By $\rightarrow_{\mathcal{H}}^*$ we denote the reflexive, transitive closure of $\rightarrow_{\mathcal{H}}$.

The most important reason one might have to use PRSs, is the following result of Miller [10]: unification of patterns is decidable, and if two patterns are unifiable, a most general unifier can be computed. This entails that the rewriting relation induced by a PRS is decidable.

We mention the following property of higher-order rewriting. It is non-trivial due to the implicit β-reductions in su and tv. Proofs can be found in [7,12].

Proposition 2.2. *Let s, t, u, v be terms. If $s \rightarrow^* t$ and $u \rightarrow^* v$ then $su \rightarrow^* tv$.*

2.2   Residual Theory

Residual theory was studied in, among others, [2,3,4,6,8]. In this section, we present residuals in an abstract setting, following [13,14], which was, in turn, based on [17]. If φ and ψ are reductions from the same object, in an arbitrary form of rewriting, then what can we tell in general of what the residual of φ after ψ must look like?

The most general form of rewriting system, which, for that reason, we will use in this section, is an *abstract rewriting system* (ARS). An ARS is a structure $\mathcal{R} = \langle A, R, \text{src}, \text{tgt} \rangle$ where A is a set of objects, R is a set of steps, and src and tgt are functions from R to A, specifying the source and target of the steps, respectively. Two steps are called *coinitial* if they start at the same object.

Definition 2.3. *A residual system is specified by a triple $\langle \mathcal{R}, 1, / \rangle$ where: $\mathcal{R}$ is an (abstract) rewriting system; 1 is a function from objects (of $\mathcal{R}$) to steps, such that $\text{src}(1(s)) = \text{tgt}(1(s)) = s$; and $/$, the projection function, is a function from pairs of coinitial steps to steps, with $\text{src}(\varphi/\psi) = \text{tgt}(\psi)$ and $\text{tgt}(\varphi/\psi) = \text{tgt}(\psi/\varphi)$, such that the following identities hold:*

$$1/\varphi = 1$$
$$\varphi/1 = \varphi$$
$$\varphi/\varphi = 1$$
$$(\varphi/\psi)/(\chi/\psi) = (\varphi/\chi)/(\psi/\chi)$$

The result of projecting φ over ψ (i.e. φ/ψ) is called the *residual* of φ after ψ. The intuitions behind the first three identities and the requirements to sources and targets are immediately clear. Noting that if we want to project φ over ψ and then over χ, we actually have to project φ over ψ and then over χ/ψ to make sure that the steps are coinitial, the last identity just states that projecting φ over ψ and then over χ yields the same result as projecting φ over ψ and χ in reverse order.

Theorem 2.4. *If $\langle \mathcal{R}, 1, / \rangle$ is a residual system, then $\mathcal{R}$ is confluent.*

Proof. Let $\langle \mathcal{R}, 1, / \rangle$ be a residual system, φ a step from a to b and ψ a step from a to c. Then ψ/φ is a step from b to some d and φ/ψ a step from c to the same object d.

Residual theory provides an elegant formalization of the notion of equivalence of reductions: two reductions are the same if the residual of the one after the other is an empty reduction, and vice versa. This formalization is called *permutation equivalence*. We define, for reductions φ, ψ:

$$\varphi \lesssim \psi \text{ if } \varphi/\psi = 1$$
$$\varphi \simeq \psi \text{ if } \varphi \lesssim \psi \text{ and } \psi \lesssim \varphi$$

It is not difficult to prove that $\lesssim$ is a quasi-order, and $\simeq$ is a congruence.

One of the side-effects of the main result of the paper, is that the above notion of permutation equivalence transfers directly to PRSs. Laneve & Montanari [5] give an axiomatic definition of permutation equivalence for the related format of orthogonal Combinatory Reduction Systems (CRSs), by translating CRS to first-order TRS and then using a first-order rewrite logic. We apply a higher-order rewrite logic to PRSs directly.

3   Higher-Order Rewrite Logic

In this section we give an alternative definition of the rewrite relation by means of a higher-order rewrite logic, i.e. a higher-order equational logic (see e.g. [11,19]) without the symmetry rule (cf. [9]). The rules of the higher-order rewrite logic are presented in Table 1, together with witnessing proof terms ($\rho : l \to r$ is a rule, and a is an arbitrary function symbol or variable). Note that $l(s_1, \ldots, s_n)$ is implicitly reduced to $\beta\overline{\eta}$-normal form. The rules don't include a symmetry rule; this rule can be easily simulated by the other rules, and is therefore left out. Note that the rule and apps rules function as axioms if $n = 0$. We write $s \geq t$ if there is a proof term φ such that $\varphi : s \geq t$.

Proposition 3.1. $s \to^* t$ *iff* $s \geq t$.

Table 1. Rewrite logic for HRSs with witnessing proof terms

$$\frac{\varphi_1 : s_1 \geq t_1 \ldots \varphi_n : s_n \geq t_n}{\rho(\varphi_1, \ldots, \varphi_n) : l(s_1, \ldots, s_n) \geq r(t_1, \ldots, t_n)} \text{ rule}$$

$$\frac{\varphi_1 : s_1 \geq t_1 \ldots \varphi_n : s_n \geq t_n}{a(\varphi_1, \ldots, \varphi_n) : a(s_1, \ldots, s_n) \geq a(t_1, \ldots, t_n)} \text{ apps}$$

$$\frac{\varphi : s \geq t}{\lambda x.\varphi : \lambda x.s \geq \lambda x.t} \text{ abs}$$

$$\frac{\varphi : s \geq u \quad \psi : u \geq t}{(\varphi \cdot \psi) : s \geq t} \text{ trans}$$

Proof. The left-to-right case of the proposition is trivial, and the right-to-left case is done by structural induction on the inference of $s \geq t$.

In the rest of the paper, the following conventions are used: f, g range over function symbols, x, y range over variables, a, b range over function symbols *and* variables, and ρ, θ are rule symbols, where l, r are the left- and right hand side of ρ. Suppose $\varphi : s \geq t$. The terms s and t will be called the source and target of φ, respectively, and we introduce the functions $\mathrm{src}(\varphi) = s$ and $\mathrm{tgt}(\varphi) = t$. It is easily seen that $s : s \geq s$. Thus, we define the unit function 1 as $1(t) = t$. We will write 1 for each reduction which is the unit of some term; usually the exact term can be found by looking at the source or the target.

Proof terms are convenient, because they are terms, and so we have technical machinery to deal with them [1,13,14]. We relate proof terms to the conventional rewriting terminology in the following way: a *multistep* (or just *step* for short) is a proof term which contains no $\cdot$'s; a *proper step* is a multistep with only one rule symbol in it, and a (multistep) *reduction* is a proof term of the form $\varphi_1 \cdot \ldots \cdot \varphi_n$ (modulo associativity of $\cdot$), where the φ_i are multisteps. Note that these notions intuitively correspond with the usual non proof term based notions.

We associate to each HRS $\mathcal{H}$ the following ARS $\hat{\mathcal{H}}$: terms are its objects, the *proof terms* of $\mathcal{H}$ are its *steps*, and the src and tgt functions simply are the ones introduced above. The translation of $\mathcal{H}$ into $\hat{\mathcal{H}}$ will be done implicitly.

4   Higher-Order Term Residual Systems

From now on, we restrict our attention to PRSs. Let a pre-slash-dot term be a proof term over an extended signature which includes a polymorphic *projection operator* $/ : \alpha \to \alpha \to \alpha$ (note that every proof term is a slash-dot term as well). Slash-dot terms are pre-slash-dot terms modulo the following equations:

$$f(\varphi_1 \cdot \psi_1, \ldots, \varphi_n \cdot \psi_n) = f(\varphi_1, \ldots, \varphi_n) \cdot f(\psi_1, \ldots, \psi_n)$$
$$\lambda x.(\varphi \cdot \psi) = \lambda x.\varphi \cdot \lambda x.\psi$$
$$1 \cdot \varphi = \varphi$$
$$\varphi \cdot 1 = \varphi$$

The first two of the equations are called the *functorial identities*, and the last two are called the *unit identities*.

We are interested in defining a projection function which associates to each slash-dot term the proof term which represents the desired residual reduction. We do this by first defining a simplification relation, and then proving that the 'normal forms' of this relation are proof terms, and unique for each slash-dot term. The projection function is then the function which associates to each slash-dot term this normal form.

4.1   A First Attempt

Simplification of terms is usually modelled as a rewriting system. In [13,14], a rewriting system is presented which reduces (first-order) slash-dot terms to their corresponding proof term. The naive method to transfer the system to the higher-order case, is to add the following rule:

$$(\lambda x.\varphi'(x)/\lambda x.\psi'(x))z \to \varphi'(z)/\psi'(z)$$

This rule pushes abstractions outwards. The variable z is used to correctly handle bound variables. However, the rule is not equipped to handle nesting correctly. Consider the following two-rule PRS:

$$\mu : \lambda z.\mathsf{mu}(\lambda x.z(x)) \to \lambda z.z(\mathsf{mu}(\lambda x.z(x)))$$
$$\rho : \qquad \lambda x.f(x) \to \lambda x.g(x)$$

and the following steps:

$$\mathsf{mu}(\lambda x.\rho(x)) : \mathsf{mu}(\lambda x.f(x)) \ge \mathsf{mu}(\lambda x.g(x))$$
$$\mu(\lambda x.f(x)) : \mathsf{mu}(\lambda x.f(x)) \ge f(\mathsf{mu}(\lambda x.f(x)))$$

Wee see that the proof term $\mathsf{mu}(\lambda x.\rho(x))/\mu(\lambda x.f(x))$ reduces in a number of steps to $\rho(\mathsf{mu}(\lambda x.\rho(x)/\lambda x.\rho(x)))$, and then in the final step the two copies of $\mathsf{mu}(\lambda x.\rho(x))$, which are not supposed to be further reduced, 'cancel each other out', resulting in the (incorrect) proof term $\rho(\mathsf{mu}(\lambda x.f(x)))$. Changing the fifth rule into

$$(\lambda x.\varphi'(x)/\lambda x.\psi'(x))z \to \varphi'(\bot z)/\psi'(\bot z)$$

where $\bot$ is a new symbol which makes sure that applications of the other rules are blocked, and adding rules to make sure that $\bot\varphi/\bot\varphi \to^* \varphi$, seems, at first sight, to solve the problem, but I have chosen another approach which I find more elegant.

4.2   Residuals of Compatible Reductions

We define the 'simplification' relation $\succcurlyeq$ between slash-dot terms and proof terms by means of the inference system Res given in Table 2 on page 129. We write $\vdash^{\mathcal{K}} \varphi \succcurlyeq \chi$ to denote that the inference $\mathcal{K}$ has $\varphi \succcurlyeq \chi$ as its final conclusion. The function $|\mathcal{K}|$ returns the 'depth' of an inference, i.e. if $|\mathcal{K}|$ is an inference with immediate subinferences $\mathcal{L}_1, \ldots, \mathcal{L}_n$, then $|\mathcal{K}| = \max_{0 < i \le n} |\mathcal{L}_i| + 1$. We write $\vdash^k \varphi \succcurlyeq \chi$ if an inference $\mathcal{K}$ exists such that $\vdash^{\mathcal{K}} \varphi \succcurlyeq \chi$ and $|\mathcal{K}| \le k$. If k is omitted, $\mathcal{K}$ may be of arbitrary size, and in this case the $\vdash$ will often be omitted as well. The *principal rule* of an inference $\mathcal{K}$ is the last rule which is applied, i.e. the rule which appears at the bottom of the inference. We will assume the function $\mathsf{pr}(\mathcal{K})$ which returns the principal rule of an inference $\mathcal{K}$.

Example 4.1. Consider the PRS from Sect. 4.1. The current framework yields the correct result:

$$\cfrac{\cfrac{\cfrac{x/x \succcurlyeq x}{\rho(x)/f(x) \succcurlyeq \rho(x)}\ R_1}{\lambda x.\rho(x)/\lambda x.f(x) \succcurlyeq \lambda x.\rho(x)}\ R_5}{\mathsf{mu}(\lambda x.\rho(x))/\mu(\lambda x.f(x)) \succcurlyeq \rho(\mathsf{mu}(\lambda x.\rho(x)))}\ R_4$$

Table 2. The inference rules for Res.

Residual rules:

$$\frac{\varphi_1/\psi_1 \succcurlyeq \chi_1 \cdots \varphi_n/\psi_n \succcurlyeq \chi_n}{a(\varphi_1,\ldots,\varphi_n)/a(\psi_1,\ldots,\psi_n) \succcurlyeq a(\chi_1,\ldots,\chi_n)} R_1$$

$$\frac{\varphi_1/\psi_1 \succcurlyeq \chi_1 \cdots \varphi_n/\psi_n \succcurlyeq \chi_n}{\rho(\varphi_1,\ldots,\varphi_n)/\rho(\psi_1,\ldots,\psi_n) \succcurlyeq r(\chi_1,\ldots,\chi_n)} R_2$$

$$\frac{\varphi_1/\psi_1 \succcurlyeq \chi_1 \cdots \varphi_n/\psi_n \succcurlyeq \chi_n}{\rho(\varphi_1,\ldots,\varphi_n)/l(\psi_1,\ldots,\psi_n) \succcurlyeq \rho(\chi_1,\ldots,\chi_n)} R_3$$

$$\frac{\varphi_1/\psi_1 \succcurlyeq \chi_1 \cdots \varphi_n/\psi_n \succcurlyeq \chi_n}{l(\varphi_1,\ldots,\varphi_n)/\rho(\psi_1,\ldots,\psi_n) \succcurlyeq r(\chi_1,\ldots,\chi_n)} R_4$$

$$\frac{\varphi/\psi \succcurlyeq \chi}{\lambda x.\varphi/\lambda x.\psi \succcurlyeq \lambda x.\chi} R_5$$

$$\frac{\varphi_1/\psi \succcurlyeq \varphi_1' \quad \psi/\varphi_1 \succcurlyeq \psi' \quad \varphi_2/\psi' \succcurlyeq \varphi_2'}{(\varphi_1 \cdot \varphi_2)/\psi \succcurlyeq \varphi_1' \cdot \varphi_2'} \cdot L \qquad \frac{\varphi/\psi_1 \succcurlyeq \varphi' \quad \varphi'/\psi_2 \succcurlyeq \chi}{\varphi/(\psi_1 \cdot \psi_2) \succcurlyeq \chi} \cdot R$$

$$\frac{\varphi \succcurlyeq \varphi' \quad \psi \succcurlyeq \psi' \quad \varphi'/\psi' \succcurlyeq \chi}{\varphi/\psi \succcurlyeq \chi} r{+}t/$$

Replacement rules:

$$\frac{\varphi_1 \succcurlyeq \psi_1 \cdots \varphi_n \succcurlyeq \psi_n}{a(\varphi_1,\ldots,\varphi_n) \succcurlyeq a(\psi_1,\ldots,\psi_n)} \text{repl}_a \qquad \frac{\varphi \succcurlyeq \psi}{\lambda x.\varphi \succcurlyeq \lambda x.\psi} \text{repl}_\lambda$$

$$\frac{\varphi_1 \succcurlyeq \psi_1 \cdots \varphi_n \succcurlyeq \psi_n}{\rho(\varphi_1,\ldots,\varphi_n) \succcurlyeq \rho(\psi_1,\ldots,\psi_n)} \text{repl}_\rho \qquad \frac{\varphi_1 \succcurlyeq \psi_1 \quad \varphi_2 \succcurlyeq \psi_2}{\varphi_1 \cdot \varphi_2 \succcurlyeq \psi_1 \cdot \psi_2} \text{repl}.$$

A slash-dot term φ is called *internally compatible* if there is a χ such that $\varphi \succcurlyeq \chi$. The source and target of an internally compatible slash-dot term φ with $\varphi \succcurlyeq \chi$ are defined as $\text{src}(\varphi) = \text{src}(\chi)$ and $\text{tgt}(\varphi) = \text{tgt}(\chi)$. Two slash-dot terms φ and ψ are *compatible* if φ/ψ is internally compatible. A PRS $\mathcal{H}$ is called compatible if all possible pairs of proof terms φ, ψ of $\mathcal{H}$ are compatible.

The following lemma expresses, in a sense, that proof terms are the 'final objects' of the relation $\succcurlyeq$ defined by the inference system.

Lemma 4.2. *Let φ be a proof term. Then:* $\vdash^{\mathcal{K}} \varphi \succcurlyeq \psi$ *if and only if $\varphi = \psi$.*

Proof. ($\Rightarrow$) by induction on $\mathcal{K}$, and ($\Leftarrow$) by induction on the length of φ.

Next, we prove a few standardization properties of the proposed inference system, which will come in handy in the later proofs. Given a desired outcome,

Lemma 4.3 and Lemma 4.4 are used to select the principal rule of a valid inference with the desired conclusion (if it exists).

Lemma 4.3. *Suppose* $\vdash^{\mathcal{K}} \varphi/\psi \succcurlyeq \chi$.

1. *If* $\varphi = a(\varphi_1, \ldots, \varphi_n)$ *and* $\psi = a(\varphi_1, \ldots, \varphi_n)$, *then there is an inference* $\mathcal{K}'$ *with* $|\mathcal{K}'| \le |\mathcal{K}|$ *such that* $\vdash^{\mathcal{K}'} \varphi/\psi \succcurlyeq \chi$ *and* $\mathsf{pr}(\mathcal{K}') = R_1$.
2. *If* $\varphi = \rho(\varphi_1, \ldots, \varphi_n)$ *and* $\psi = \rho(\varphi_1, \ldots, \varphi_n)$, *then there is an inference* $\mathcal{K}'$ *with* $|\mathcal{K}'| \le |\mathcal{K}|$ *such that* $\vdash^{\mathcal{K}'} \varphi/\psi \succcurlyeq \chi$ *and* $\mathsf{pr}(\mathcal{K}') = R_2$.
3. *If* $\varphi = \rho(\varphi_1, \ldots, \varphi_n)$ *and* $\psi = l(\varphi_1, \ldots, \varphi_n)$, *then there is an inference* $\mathcal{K}'$ *with* $|\mathcal{K}'| \le |\mathcal{K}|$ *such that* $\vdash^{\mathcal{K}'} \varphi/\psi \succcurlyeq \chi$ *and* $\mathsf{pr}(\mathcal{K}') = R_3$.
4. *If* $\varphi = l(\varphi_1, \ldots, \varphi_n)$ *and* $\psi = \rho(\varphi_1, \ldots, \varphi_n)$, *then there is an inference* $\mathcal{K}'$ *with* $|\mathcal{K}'| \le |\mathcal{K}|$ *such that* $\vdash^{\mathcal{K}'} \varphi/\psi \succcurlyeq \chi$ *and* $\mathsf{pr}(\mathcal{K}') = R_4$.
5. *If* $\varphi = \lambda x.\varphi_0$ *and* $\psi = \lambda x.\psi_0$, *then there is an inference* $\mathcal{K}'$ *with* $|\mathcal{K}'| \le |\mathcal{K}|$ *such that* $\vdash^{\mathcal{K}'} \varphi/\psi \succcurlyeq \chi$ *and* $\mathsf{pr}(\mathcal{K}') = R_5$.

Proof. By induction on $|\mathcal{K}|$.

Lemma 4.4. *Suppose* $\vdash^{\mathcal{K}} \varphi/\psi \succcurlyeq \chi$.

1. *If* $\varphi = \varphi_1 \cdot \varphi_2$, *then there is an inference* $\mathcal{K}'$ *with* $|\mathcal{K}'| \le |\mathcal{K}|$ *such that* $\vdash^{\mathcal{K}'} \varphi/\psi \succcurlyeq \chi$ *and* $\mathsf{pr}(\mathcal{K}) = \cdot L$.
2. *If* $\psi = \psi_1 \cdot \psi_2$, *then there is an inference* $\mathcal{K}'$ *with* $|\mathcal{K}'| \le |\mathcal{K}|$ *such that* $\vdash^{\mathcal{K}'} \varphi/\psi \succcurlyeq \chi$ *and* $\mathsf{pr}(\mathcal{K}) = \cdot R$.

Proof. By induction on $|\mathcal{K}|$.

Lemma 4.5. *If* $\varphi \succcurlyeq \chi$ *and* $\varphi \succcurlyeq \chi'$, *then* $\chi = \chi'$.

Proof. By induction on the sum of the sizes of the inferences.

We define the relation $\approx$ to be the reflexive, symmetric and transitive closure of $\succcurlyeq$. By Lemma 4.5 and the fact that if $\varphi \succcurlyeq \chi$ then χ is a proof term (easily proved by induction), we can take proof terms as the unique representatives of the classes of $\approx$-equivalent slash-dot terms. We can now define the projection operator $//$ as follows: $\varphi \mathbin{//} \psi = \chi$ if χ is the unique representative of the slash-dot term φ/ψ. Theorem 4.6 is proved in Sect. 4.3.

Theorem 4.6. $\langle \mathcal{H}, 1, // \rangle$ *is a residual system, if* $\mathcal{H}$ *is a compatible PRS.*

Corollary 4.7. *A compatible PRS is confluent.*

Proof. By Theorems 4.6 and 2.4.

4.3   Proof of Theorem 4.6

In this subsection we prove Theorem 4.6, i.e. we show that a compatible PRS together with unit and projection operator is a residual system. We mention the following two auxiliary lemmas, of which the proof is easy:

Lemma 4.8.

1. $(\varphi \cdot \psi)/\chi \approx \varphi/\chi \cdot \psi/(\chi/\varphi)$
2. $\chi/(\varphi \cdot \psi) \approx (\chi/\varphi)/\psi$

Lemma 4.9. $\approx$ *is a congruence.*

To prove that we are dealing with a residual system, we have to show that sources and targets match (Prop. 4.10), and that the residual axioms hold (Prop. 4.11).

Proposition 4.10. *Sources and targets match, i.e.:*

1. $\operatorname{src}(\varphi/\psi) = \operatorname{tgt}(\psi)$
2. $\operatorname{tgt}(\varphi/\psi) = \operatorname{tgt}(\psi/\varphi)$

Proof. By induction on the inferences of $\varphi/\psi \succcurlyeq \chi$ and $\psi/\varphi \succcurlyeq \xi$ we easily prove that $\operatorname{src}(\chi) = \operatorname{tgt}(\psi)$ and $\operatorname{tgt}(\chi) = \operatorname{tgt}(\xi)$.

Proposition 4.11. *The residual axioms hold, i.e.:*

1. $1/\varphi \approx 1$
2. $\varphi/1 \approx \varphi$
3. $\varphi/\varphi \approx 1$
4. $(\varphi/\psi)/(\chi/\psi) \approx (\varphi/\chi)/(\psi/\chi)$

Proof. (1)–(3) are proved by induction on the length of φ. In addition, (2) is based on (1), and (3) on (1) and (2).

In order to prove (4) we introduce the *layered size* $|\varphi|$ of a slash-dot term φ:

$$|f(\varphi_1, \ldots, \varphi_n)| = 1 + \max_{0 < i \leq n} |\varphi_i|$$
$$|x(\varphi_1, \ldots, \varphi_n)| = 1 + \max_{0 < i \leq n} |\varphi_i|$$
$$|\rho(\varphi_1, \ldots, \varphi_n)| = 1 + \max_{0 < i \leq n} |\varphi_i|$$
$$|\lambda x.\varphi| = |\varphi|$$
$$|\varphi \cdot \psi| = |\varphi| + 1 + |\psi|$$
$$|\varphi/\psi| = |\varphi|$$

Now (4) is verified by induction on the sum of the layered sizes of φ, ψ and χ.

The proof follows the same pattern as the one in [13]. Suppose that either φ, ψ or χ is a composite. If φ is a composite, we have the following, where the various (underlined) steps follow from Lemma 4.9 and either the induction hypothesis or Lemma 4.8:

$$((\varphi_1 \cdot \varphi_2)/\psi)/(\chi/\psi)$$
$$\approx \quad ((\varphi_1/\psi) \cdot (\varphi_2/(\psi/\varphi_1)))/(\chi/\psi)$$
$$\approx \quad (\varphi_1/\psi)/(\chi/\psi) \cdot ((\varphi_2/(\psi/\varphi_1))/((\chi/\psi)/(\varphi_1/\psi)))$$
$$\approx_{IH} (\varphi_1/\chi)/(\psi/\chi) \cdot ((\varphi_2/(\psi/\varphi_1))/((\chi/\varphi_1)/(\psi/\varphi_1)))$$
$$\approx_{IH} (\varphi_1/\chi)/(\psi/\chi) \cdot ((\varphi_2/(\chi/\varphi_1))/((\psi/\varphi_1)/(\chi/\varphi_1)))$$
$$\approx \quad ((\varphi_1/\chi) \cdot (\varphi_2/(\chi/\varphi_1)))/(\psi/\chi)$$
$$\approx \quad ((\varphi_1 \cdot \varphi_2)/\chi)/(\psi/\chi)$$

If ψ is a composite, we do:

$$(\varphi/(\psi_1 \cdot \psi_2))/(\chi/(\psi_1 \cdot \psi_2))$$
$$\approx \quad ((\varphi/\psi_1)/\psi_2)/((\chi/\psi_1)/\psi_2)$$
$$\approx_{IH} ((\varphi/\psi_1)/(\chi/\psi_1))/(\psi_2/(\chi/\psi_1))$$
$$\approx_{IH} ((\varphi/\chi)/(\psi_1/\chi))/(\psi_2/(\chi/\psi_1))$$
$$\approx \quad (\varphi/\chi)/(\psi_1/\chi \cdot \psi_2/(\chi/\psi_1))$$
$$\approx \quad (\varphi/\chi)/((\psi_1 \cdot \psi_2)/\chi)$$

The case that χ is a composite, is the inverse of this.

Now consider the case that none of φ, ψ, χ are composites. Suppose that $\varphi = f(\boldsymbol{\varphi})$, $\psi = f(\boldsymbol{\psi})$, and $\chi = f(\boldsymbol{\chi})$, where we use the notation $\boldsymbol{x}$ for the vector $x_1, \ldots, x_n$. By Lemma 4.3, the following inference must exist:

$$\frac{\dfrac{\cdots \ \varphi_i/\psi_i \succcurlyeq \zeta_{1,i} \ \cdots}{f(\boldsymbol{\varphi})/f(\boldsymbol{\psi}) \succcurlyeq f(\boldsymbol{\zeta_1})} \quad \dfrac{\cdots \ \chi_i/\psi_i \succcurlyeq \zeta_{2,i} \ \cdots}{f(\boldsymbol{\chi})/f(\boldsymbol{\psi}) \succcurlyeq f(\boldsymbol{\zeta_2})} \quad \dfrac{\cdots \ \zeta_{1,i}/\zeta_{2,i} \succcurlyeq \xi_{1,i} \ \cdots}{f(\boldsymbol{\zeta_1})/f(\boldsymbol{\zeta_2}) \succcurlyeq f(\boldsymbol{\xi_1})}}{(f(\boldsymbol{\varphi})/f(\boldsymbol{\psi}))/(f(\boldsymbol{\chi})/f(\boldsymbol{\psi})) \succcurlyeq f(\boldsymbol{\xi_1})}$$

and similarly we obtain an inference of $(f(\boldsymbol{\varphi})/f(\boldsymbol{\chi}))/(f(\boldsymbol{\psi})/f(\boldsymbol{\chi})) \succcurlyeq f(\boldsymbol{\xi_2})$. Using the same subinferences for $\varphi_i/\psi_i \succcurlyeq \zeta_{1,i}$, $\chi_i/\psi_i \succcurlyeq \zeta_{2,i}$ and $\zeta_{1,i}/\zeta_{2,i} \succcurlyeq \xi_{1,i}$, we easily obtain $(\varphi_i/\psi_i)/(\chi_i/\psi_i) \succcurlyeq \xi_{1,i}$, and similarly we show $(\varphi_i/\chi_i)/(\psi_i/\chi_i) \succcurlyeq \xi_{2,i}$. Since, by induction hypothesis, $(\varphi_i/\psi_i)/(\chi_i/\psi_i) \approx (\varphi_i/\chi_i)/(\psi_i/\chi_i)$, we know now that $\xi_{1,i} \approx \xi_{2,i}$, so there are $\xi_{3,i}$ such that $\xi_{1,i} \succcurlyeq \xi_{3,i} \preccurlyeq \xi_{2,i}$. Two easy inferences prove $f(\boldsymbol{\xi_1}) \succcurlyeq f(\boldsymbol{\xi_3})$ and $f(\boldsymbol{\xi_2}) \succcurlyeq f(\boldsymbol{\xi_3})$. We put everything together with transitivity and get:

$$(f(\boldsymbol{\varphi})/f(\boldsymbol{\psi}))/(f(\boldsymbol{\chi})/f(\boldsymbol{\psi})) \approx f(\boldsymbol{\xi_3}) \approx (f(\boldsymbol{\varphi})/f(\boldsymbol{\chi}))/(f(\boldsymbol{\psi})/f(\boldsymbol{\chi}))$$

The same strategy works in the other non-composite cases, e.g. if $\varphi = \rho(\boldsymbol{\varphi})$, $\psi = \rho(\boldsymbol{\psi})$, and $\chi = r(\boldsymbol{\chi})$, since the difficult nesting problems (duplicating behaviour within right-hand sides of rules) occur only on the right of the $\succcurlyeq$ symbols.

Now, Theorem 4.6 follows from Prop. 4.10 and Prop. 4.11. QED.

4.4 Computing Residuals

In Sect. 4.2 only a specification of the simplification relation was given, but Lemma 4.3 and Lemma 4.4 already hinted at the existence of an algorithm which effectively computes the representative of a slash-dot term. In this section, such an algorithm is indeed given. We also prove that it terminates for two special cases of slash-dot term, and show that if the algorithm terminates, it prints the correct answer.

Definition 4.12. *The (recursive) function* $\text{sim}(\pi)$ *on proof terms* π, *is defined by the following pseudo-program:*

$\text{sim}((\varphi_1/\varphi_2)/\psi)) = \text{sim}(\varphi'/\psi)$
   where $\varphi' = \text{sim}(\varphi_1/\varphi_2)$
$\text{sim}(\varphi/(\psi_1/\psi_2)) = \text{sim}(\varphi/\psi')$
   where $\psi' = \text{sim}(\psi_1/\psi_2)$
$\text{sim}(x(\varphi_1,\ldots,\varphi_n)/x(\psi_1,\ldots,\psi_n)) = x(\text{sim}(\varphi_1/\psi_1),\ldots,\text{sim}(\varphi_n/\psi_n))$
$\text{sim}(f(\varphi_1,\ldots,\varphi_n)/f(\psi_1,\ldots,\psi_n)) = f(\text{sim}(\varphi_1/\psi_1),\ldots,\text{sim}(\varphi_n/\psi_n))$
$\text{sim}(\rho(\varphi_1,\ldots,\varphi_n)/\rho(\psi_1,\ldots,\psi_n)) = r(\text{sim}(\varphi_1/\psi_1),\ldots,\text{sim}(\varphi_n/\psi_n))$
$\text{sim}(\rho(\varphi_1,\ldots,\varphi_n)/l(\psi_1,\ldots,\psi_n)) = \rho(\text{sim}(\varphi_1/\psi_1),\ldots,\text{sim}(\varphi_n/\psi_n))$
$\text{sim}(l(\varphi_1,\ldots,\varphi_n)/\rho(\psi_1,\ldots,\psi_n)) = r(\text{sim}(\varphi_1/\psi_1),\ldots,\text{sim}(\varphi_n/\psi_n))$
$\text{sim}(\lambda x.\varphi/\lambda x.\psi) = \lambda x.(\varphi/\psi)$
$\text{sim}((\varphi_1 \cdot \varphi_2)/\psi)) = \varphi'_1 \cdot \varphi'_2$
   where $\varphi'_1 = \text{sim}(\varphi_1/\psi)$
       $\varphi'_2 = \text{sim}(\varphi_2/\psi')$
       where $\psi' = \text{sim}(\psi/\varphi_1)$
$\text{sim}(\varphi/(\psi_1 \cdot \psi_2)) = \text{sim}(\varphi'/\psi_2)$
   where $\varphi' = \text{sim}(\varphi/\psi_1)$
$\text{sim}(f(\varphi_1,\ldots,\varphi_n)) = f(\text{sim}(\varphi_1),\ldots,\text{sim}(\varphi_n))$
$\text{sim}(\rho(\varphi_1,\ldots,\varphi_n)) = \rho(\text{sim}(\varphi_1),\ldots,\text{sim}(\varphi_n))$
$\text{sim}(\lambda x.\varphi) = \lambda x.\text{sim}(\varphi)$
if *none of the above cases apply* **then**
       print *"incompatible"*

Proposition 4.13.

1. *If* φ *and* ψ *are reductions, then* $\text{sim}(\varphi/\psi)$ *terminates.*
2. *If* φ *is internally compatible, then* $\text{sim}(\varphi)$ *terminates.*

Proof. We prove the first item first. If φ and ψ are reductions, then the computation of $\text{sim}(\varphi/\psi)$ proceeds in two stages: first the compositions on the outside of the terms are dealt with, and in this stage the number of composition symbols in the proof term strictly decreases in each step; and then, when φ and ψ are parallel steps, the length of the proof term strictly decreases in each step.

Secondly, if φ is internally compatible, then an inference $\mathcal{K}$ exists such that $\vdash^{\mathcal{K}} \varphi/ \succcurlyeq \chi$. The second item can be proved by induction on $\mathcal{K}$, using Lemma 4.3 and Lemma 4.4.

Termination *in general* is hard to show. If a proof term φ is not internally compatible, an inference of $\varphi \succcurlyeq \chi$ is not at our disposal, so we cannot use induction on the inference. The problem is then the cases which deal with composition. In these cases the size of the terms which are passed recursively to the function, may actually be larger than the size of the term under consideration.

Conjecture 4.14. $\text{sim}(\varphi)$ terminates for *all* slash-dot terms φ.

The main result of the paper does not depend on this conjecture, although, because of its not being proved, a small detour has to be followed in Sect. 5.1.

Proposition 4.15. $\text{sim}(\varphi) = \chi$ *if and only if* $\varphi \succcurlyeq \chi$.

Proof. The 'only if' side is proved by recursively building an inference of $\varphi \succcurlyeq \chi$. The 'if' side is easily proved by using Lemma 4.3 and Lemma 4.4.

5   Orthogonality

In this section we relate compatibility with the well-known notion of orthogonality. In order to define orthogonality, we need to define overlap, and this is done by associating with each proper step a set of redex positions, and then looking at the intersection of the redex positions of two coinitial proper steps.

Positions are sequences of natural numbers. If P is a set of positions, and p is a position, we write $p \star P$ for $\{pq \mid q \in P\}$. First, we need to define the set of all positions of a term. Let $\Box$ denote the empty context.

$$\mathcal{P}os(\Box) = \emptyset$$
$$\mathcal{P}os(x(s_1, \ldots, s_n)) = \{\epsilon\} \cup \bigcup_{0<i\leq n} i \star \mathcal{P}os(s_i)$$
$$\mathcal{P}os(f(s_1, \ldots, s_n)) = \{\epsilon\} \cup \bigcup_{0<i\leq n} i \star \mathcal{P}os(s_i)$$
$$\mathcal{P}os(\lambda x.s) = \{\epsilon\} \cup 1 \star \mathcal{P}os(s)$$

where x is a variable and f a function symbol.

Now, let φ be a proper step. We define the set of redex positions of φ, written $\mathcal{RP}os(\varphi)$, as:

$$\mathcal{RP}os(x(\varphi_1, \ldots, \varphi_n)) = \bigcup_{0<i\leq n} i \star \mathcal{RP}os(\varphi_i)$$
$$\mathcal{RP}os(f(\varphi_1, \ldots, \varphi_n)) = \bigcup_{0<i\leq n} i \star \mathcal{RP}os(\varphi_i)$$
$$\mathcal{RP}os(\lambda x.\varphi_0) = 1 \star \mathcal{RP}os(\varphi_0)$$
$$\mathcal{RP}os(\rho(\varphi_1, \ldots, \varphi_n)) = \mathcal{P}os(l(\Box, \ldots, \Box))$$

Note that, since φ is a proper step, in the last equation there are no more rule symbols in the φ_i.

Two coinitial proper steps φ and ψ are said to be *overlapping* if $\mathcal{RP}os(\varphi) \cap \mathcal{RP}os(\psi) \neq \emptyset$. A left-linear PRS is *orthogonal*, if all pairs of different, coinitial proper steps are non-overlapping.

This definition has an infinite flavour: there are infinitely many steps one has to check. Fortunately, it is well-known that an equivalent notion of orthogonality exists, based on critical pairs [7]. Since a finite PRS has only finitely many possible critical pairs, this makes the question whether a PRS is orthogonal or not decidable. We stick to the step-based definition for convenience.

5.1   Compatibility Is Orthogonality

In this subsection we will prove that compatibility and orthogonality coincide. The difficult part of the proof, but also the most important one, is to show that orthogonality implies compatibility. One way of doing so is by contraposition: we run the algorithm of Def. 4.12 and analyse in which situations it prints *incompatible*, and show that the PRS is not orthogonal in each of these cases. There is one problem: we have not succeeded in proving that the algorithm actually always terminates, so we have to follow a small detour: we transform the incompatible proof terms into incompatible reductions, and then feed those to the algorithm.

Lemma 5.1. *If $l(\varphi_1, \ldots, \varphi_n) \cdot \rho(\psi_1, \ldots, \psi_n)$ is compatible with χ, then $\rho(\varphi_1 \cdot \psi_1, \ldots, \varphi_n \cdot \psi_n)$ is compatible with χ.*

Proof. By constructing an inference. $\qquad \square$

Theorem 5.2. *Let $\mathcal{H}$ be an PRS. $\mathcal{H}$ is orthogonal, if and only if $\mathcal{H}$ is compatible.*

Proof. We first prove the right-to-left implication. Assume that all coinitial reductions are compatible. This implies that all coinitial multisteps φ, ψ are compatible, i.e. an inference $\mathcal{K}$ exists such that $\vdash^{\mathcal{K}} \varphi/\psi \succcurlyeq \chi$. We easily prove, by induction on $\mathcal{K}$, that φ, ψ are non-overlapping.

To show the left-to-right implication, assume, by contraposition, that φ, ψ are coinitial, but not compatible. Consider the (meta-level) rewrite system which consists of all rules of the form

$$\rho(\varphi_1 \cdot \psi_1, \ldots, \varphi_n \cdot \psi_n) \Rightarrow l(\varphi_1, \ldots, \varphi_n) \cdot \rho(\psi_1, \ldots, \psi_2)$$

where $\rho : l \to r$ is a rule. It is not difficult to see that this rewrite system is strongly normalizing, and that its normal forms are actually reductions. So, applying this rewriting system to φ and ψ yields reductions φ', ψ', respectively. By Prop. 4.13, $\mathrm{sim}(\varphi'/\psi')$ terminates, and by (the contraposition of) Lemma 5.1, φ' and ψ' are not compatible.

Let φ_0/ψ_0 be the slash-dot term which was passed to sim in the last step before it terminated; φ_0 and ψ_0 must be multisteps. By Prop. 4.15 the algorithm prints *incompatible*. By coinitiality of φ_0 and ψ_0, it cannot cannot be the case that $\varphi_0 = f(\varphi_1, \ldots, \varphi_n)$ and $\psi_0 = g(\psi_1, \ldots, \psi_n)$, where $f \neq g$. So, the following must apply: $\varphi_0 = \rho(\varphi_1, \ldots, \varphi_n)$ and $\psi_0 \neq_{\beta\eta} l(\psi_1, \ldots, \psi_n)$. There are two possible causes of this. The first is that ψ_0 has a rule symbol within the redex pattern of l. But then overlapping, coinitial proper steps φ_0' and ψ_0' can be constructed by replacing all rule symbols, except the overlapping ones, of φ_0 and ψ_0, respectively, by their left-hand sides. The second possible cause is that one of the ψ_i occurs twice in $l(\psi_1, \ldots, \psi_n)$. However, then l cannot be left-linear. Both cases imply non-orthogonality. (The third 'cause' is that ψ_0 has a $\cdot$ inside the redex pattern of φ_0, but this cannot happen because compositions are moved outwards over function symbols and abstractions by the functorial identities, and l consists only of function symbols and abstractions.) The same argument can be applied to the symmetrical case. $\qquad \square$

5.2   Residuals of Orthogonal PRSs

In this subsection we prove the main result of the paper, namely that an orthogonal PRS, together with the unit and projection operator, forms a residual system. The hard work has already been done; we just need to put together the results obtained so far.

Theorem 5.3. *If $\mathcal{H}$ is an orthogonal PRS, then $\langle \mathcal{H}, 1, // \rangle$ is a residual system.*

Proof. By Theorem 5.2, $\mathcal{H}$ is compatible, and thus, by Theorem 4.6, $\langle \mathcal{H}, 1, // \rangle$ is a residual system.

It is well-known that orthogonal PRSs are confluent, as was proved in, among others, [7,12,15]. Here, we obtain a new proof based on the residual theory developed in this paper. The proof emerges as a simple corollary of the main result.

Corollary 5.4. *Orthogonal PRSs are confluent.*

Proof. Let $\mathcal{H}$ be an orthogonal PRS. By Theorem 5.3, $\mathcal{H}$ is a residual system, and thus by Theorem 2.4, $\mathcal{H}$ is confluent.

6   Concluding Remarks

In this paper, we have shown that orthogonal PRSs form a residual system. As a consequence, all results for residual systems are inherited, such as the notion of permutation equivalence and confluence. We have also given an algorithm which simplifies slash-dot terms to proof terms, and we have proven, in two special cases, that the algorithm terminates.

For the future, the following research is interesting. Firstly, it is interesting to find a proof (or a refutation) of the claim that the algorithm mentioned in the previous paragraph does *always* terminate. Not only is this interesting in its own right, it is my view that such a proof may aid us in the understanding of termination of higher-order rewriting, and provide new proof methods.

Secondly, it is interesting to see if the framework can be generalized to non-orthogonal, left-linear PRSs, or even arbitrary PRSs. For this to work, an error symbol must be added, to indicate non-compatibility. For the first-order case, the same approach was succesfully applied to left-linear TRSs in [13].

Acknowledgements

I wish to thank Vincent van Oostrom and the anonymous referees for their valuable remarks on preliminary versions of this paper.

References

1. Barnaby P. Hilken. Towards a proof theory of rewriting: The simply typed 2λ-calculus. *Theoretical Computer Science*, 170:407–444, 1996.

2. Gérard Huet. Residual theory in λ-calculus: A formal development. *Journal of Functional Programming*, 4(3):371–394, 1994.
3. Gérard Huet and Jean-Jacques Lévy. Computations in orthogonal rewriting systems, part I + II. In J.L. Lassez and G.D. Plotkin, editors, *Computational Logic – Essays in Honor of Alan Robinson*. MIT Press, 1991.
4. Zurab Khasidashvili and John Glauert. Relating conflict-free stable transition systems and event models via redex families. *Theoretical Computer Science*, 286(1):65–95, 2002.
5. Cosimo Laneve and Ugo Montanari. Axiomatizing permutation equivalence. *Mathematical Structures in Computer Science*, 6(3):219–215, 1996.
6. Jean-Jacques Lévy. *Réductions correctes et optimales dans le λ-calcul*. Thèse de doctorat d'état, Université Paris VII, 1978.
7. Richard Mayr and Tobias Nipkow. Higher-order rewrite systems and their confluence. *Theoretical Computer Science*, 192:3–29, 1998.
8. Paul-André Melliès. Axiomatic rewriting theory VI: Residual theory revisited. In Sophie Tison, editor, *13th International Conference on Rewriting Techniques and Applications*, pages 24–50, 2002.
9. José Meseguer. Conditional rewriting logic as a unified model of concurrency. *Theoretical Computer Science*, 96:73–155, 1992.
10. Dale Miller. A logic programming language with lambda-abstraction, function variables, and simple unification. *Journal of Logic and Computation*, 1(4), 1991.
11. Tobias Nipkow and Christian Prehofer. Higher-order rewriting and equational reasoning. In W. Bibel and P. Schmitt, editors, *Automated Deduction — A Basis for Applications, Volume I: Foundations*, number 8 in Applied Logic Series, pages 399–430. Kluwer Academic Press, 1998.
12. Vincent van Oostrom. *Confluence for Abstract and Higher-Order Rewriting*. PhD thesis, Vrije Universiteit, Amsterdam, 1994.
13. Vincent van Oostrom and Roel de Vrijer. *Equivalence of Reductions*, chapter 8 of [18]. 2003.
14. Vincent van Oostrom and Roel de Vrijer. Four equivalent equivalences of reductions. In *Proceedings of WRS'02 (ENTCS 70.6)*, 2003. Downloadable at: http://www.elsevier.nl/locate/entcs/.
15. Femke van Raamsdonk. *Confluence and Normalisation for Higher-Order Rewriting*. PhD thesis, Vrije Universiteit, Amsterdam, 1996.
16. Femke van Raamsdonk. Higher-order rewriting. In *10th International Conference on Rewriting Techniques and Applications*, 1999.
17. Eugene W. Stark. Concurrent transition systems. *Theoretical Computer Science*, 64(3):221–269, 1989.
18. Terese. *Term Rewriting Systems*. Number 55 in Camb. Tracts in Theor. Comp. Sc. Cambridge University Press, 2003.
19. D. A. Wolfram. *The Clausal Theory of Types*. Number 21 in Camb. Tracts in Theor. Comp. Sc. Cambridge University Press, 1993.

Rewriting UNITY

Adam Granicz, Daniel M. Zimmerman, and Jason Hickey

California Institute of Technology
Computer Science Dept. MC 256-80
Pasadena CA 91125, USA
{granicz,dmz,jyh}@cs.caltech.edu

Abstract. In this paper we describe the implementation of the UNITY formalism as an extension of general-purpose languages and show its translation to C abstract syntax using PHOBOS, our generic front-end in the Mojave compiler. PHOBOS uses term rewriting to define the syntax and semantics of programming languages, and automates their translation to an internal compiler representation. Furthermore, it provides access to formal reasoning capabilities using the integrated MetaPRL theorem prover, through which advanced optimizations and transformations can be implemented or formal proofs derived.

1   Introduction

UNITY [3] is a powerful formalism for the specification of nondeterministic concurrent programs. The UNITY language and execution model are simple, yet there has been little effort directed toward the compilation of UNITY programs to executable code. In this paper we present a method that uses Phobos [7], the generic front-end of the Mojave [12] compiler, to translate UNITY programs into C abstract syntax suitable for code generation. Our method has concrete advantages over previously known techniques for generating executable code from UNITY programs: the implementation is quickly adaptable to different target languages, we can easily change the scheduling algorithm used in the generated code, and we can leverage the attached theorem prover to carry out transformations and proof derivations.

In our implementation we eliminate nondeterminism from UNITY programs by using a simple sequential scheduling of statements, which may consist of simple, conditional or quantified assignments as defined in the formalism. This particular scheduling is not an inherent property of the translation method, and can be easily modified as we describe later. The entire implementation is small, and can be tailored to different target languages with minimal effort. We do not address formal properties in this paper, but the implementation is designed to lay the groundwork for formal analysis in the MetaPRL system.

1.1   Related Work

Few compilers have been developed for the UNITY language. DeRoure's parallel implementation of UNITY [5] compiles UNITY to a common backend language,

R. Nieuwenhuis (Ed.): RTA 2003, LNCS 2706, pp. 138–147, 2003.

BSP-occam; Huber's MasPar UNITY [11] compiles UNITY to MPL for execution on MasPar SIMD computers; and Radha and Muthukrishnan have developed a portable implementation of UNITY for Von Neumann machines [17]. These UNITY compilers are not as easily adaptable to multiple target languages or multiple scheduling algorithms as the rewriting-based translator we describe, and none of them have the formal reasoning capabilities provided by an integrated theorem prover.

The construction of formal proofs for UNITY programs has been mechanized using various theorem proving environments. Anderson's HOL-UNITY [2] is an implementation of UNITY using the HOL system [6], Heyd and Cregut's Coq-UNITY [8] uses Coq, and Paulson has implemented UNITY within the Isabelle environment [15,16]. While these implementations provide assistance in proof generation for UNITY programs, they do not generate executable code.

2   The UNITY Formalism

The UNITY formalism consists of both a programming language (with accompanying execution model) and a proof logic. In this paper we are primarily concerned with the language and its execution model. For a discussion of the proof logic the reader is referred to Chandy [3].

2.1   Language

In the UNITY programming language, a program begins with a **program** declaration that specifies the program's name. This is followed by several program sections:

1. A **declare** section, which names the program variables and declares their types.
2. An optional **always** section, which defines program variables as functions of other variables. Variables defined in this section are essentially textual macros representing these functions, rather than actual state variables of the program.
3. An **initially** section, which specifies initial values for the variables from the **declare** section. Uninitialized variables have arbitrary initial values.
4. An **assign** section, the program's body, which consists of a set of assignment statements. These statements may be single or multiple assignments, and may be conditional through the use of an **if** construct. They may also be quantified over predetermined ranges using the $\|$ operator, which represents nondeterministic choice. In a multiple assignment statement, all the expressions on the right side and any subscripts on the left side are evaluated first, then the values of the expressions on the right side are assigned to the corresponding variables on the left side.

An example UNITY program that sorts an array of N elements is shown in Figure 1. The initialization sets the values for the elements of the array in

```
program array-sort

    declare
        a: array [N] of integer

    initially
        ⟨‖ i : 0 ≤ i < N :: a[i] = N − i⟩

    assign
        ⟨‖ i : 0 ≤ i < N − 1 :: a[i], a[i + 1] := a[i + 1], a[i]   if   a[i] > a[i + 1]⟩

end
```

Fig. 1. A UNITY program that sorts an array of N integers

parallel, and the quantified assignment is a nondeterministic choice among $N-1$ multiple assignment statements. In our implementation we do not deal with parallelism, but instead replace it with nondeterminism.

2.2 Execution Model

Execution of a UNITY program proceeds in the following way. First, the initialization statements are executed, simultaneously, to set the state variables to their initial values. Then, statements are repeatedly selected and executed atomically. Statement selection is subject to a weak fairness constraint, which requires that every statement is selected infinitely often in every infinite execution of the program. There are no other constraints on statement selection, so some statements may be executed far more often than others in any finite execution prefix.

It is possible for a UNITY program to reach a *fixed point*, where there is no statement whose execution would change the value of any state variable. When this occurs, we say that the program has terminated.

3   System Architecture

The Mojave compiler supports various front-end languages which are translated to a common functional intermediate representation. The typical code path through these source languages is shown in Figure 2 as (I). In addition, the integrated MetaPRL theorem prover can be used to perform transformation and formal reasoning of the programs under compilation. Phobos acts as a bridge between source languages and the formal system by providing generic parsing and transformation capabilities using the term rewriting mechanism of MetaPRL. Programming language syntax can be specified with context-free grammars where rewrite rules are used to describe parser actions, and the program is represented as a term in the formal system. Program transformations

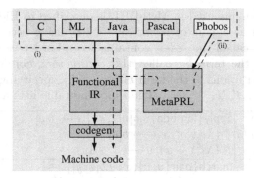

Fig. 2. The Mojave compiler architecture

and domain-specific knowledge can be specified using *formal* (which avoid capture and are guaranteed not to change binding) and *informal* (which are used
for parsing and can create binding) rewrite rules that are passed to MetaPRL for
execution. The final term is then converted to a specified compiler representation (in Figure 2 this is the functional IR) and compilation proceeds to generate
executable code.

3.1   Term Language

The term rewriting engine we use belongs to the MetaPRL logical framework [10,14].
All logical terms, including goals and subgoals, are expressed in the language of
terms. The general syntax of all terms has three parts. Each term has 1) an
operator-name, which is a unique name identifying the term; 2) a list of parameters representing constant values; and 3) a list of subterms with possible variable
binding occurrences. We use the following syntax to describe terms, based on
the NuPRL definition [1]:

$$\underbrace{opname}_{operator\ name}\ \underbrace{[p_1; \cdots ; p_n]}_{parameters}\underbrace{\{v_1.t_1; \cdots ; v_m.t_m\}}_{subterms}$$

Here are a few examples:

Shorthand	Term
1	`natural_number["1"]{}`
$\lambda x.b$	`lambda[]{x. b}`
$f(a)$	`apply[]{f; a}`
v	`variable["v"]{}`
$x + y$	`sum[]{x; y}`

Variables are terms with a string parameter giving their names; numbers
have an integer parameter with their value. The `lambda` term contains a binding
occurrence: the variable x is bound in the subterm b.

The rewriting engine used in MetaPRL is described in Hickey [9]. Rewriting rules are specified as a pair of terms $t_1 \longleftrightarrow t_2$ using second-order substitution. The term t_1, called the *redex*, contains second-order variables of the form $v[v_1; \cdots ; v_n]$; and the term t_2, called the *contractum*, contains corresponding second-order substitutions of the form $v[t_1'; \cdots ; t_n']$, specifying the simultaneous substitution $v[t_1', \ldots t_n'/v_1, \ldots, v_n]$. The following table lists a few examples:

Rewrite	$\mathsf{apply}\{\mathsf{lambda}\{v.b[v]\}; e\}\} \longleftrightarrow b[e]$
Shorthand	$(\lambda v.b[v])\ e \longleftrightarrow b[e]$
Example	$(\lambda x.x + x)\ 1 \longrightarrow 1 + 1$
Rewrite	$\mathsf{match}\{\mathsf{pair}\{u; v\}; x, y.b[x, y]\} \longleftrightarrow b[u, v]$
Shorthand	$(\mathbf{match}(u, v)\ \mathbf{with}\ x, y \to b[x, y]) \longleftrightarrow b[u, v]$
Example	$(\mathbf{match}(1, 2)\ \mathbf{with}\ x, y \to x + y) \longrightarrow (1 + 2)$

4   Implementation

We now describe the conversion of terms representing UNITY abstract syntax to C abstract syntax using source notation. The underlying actual term representation can be recovered in a straightforward manner. We also use the meta-syntax (::) to denote element insertion into a list, as used in OCaml. Occasionally, we show actual terms, in which case their names are underlined to distinguish them from abstract ones.

$$
\begin{array}{lll}
op ::= + \mid - \mid * \mid / \mid \mathbf{and} \mid \ldots \mid = \mid \neq \mid < \mid \leq \mid > \mid \geq & \text{binary operators} \\
r ::= e\ op\ v\ op\ e & \text{range} \\
\quad \mid\ e\ op\ v\ op\ e\ \&\ e & \text{range with condition} \\[6pt]
e ::= i \mid f \mid \mathbf{true} \mid \mathbf{false} & \text{numbers and Booleans} \\
\quad \mid\ v & \text{variables} \\
\quad \mid\ e\ op\ e & \text{binary operation} \\
\quad \mid\ e[e] & \text{subscripting} \\
\quad \mid\ e(e, \ldots, e) & \text{function application} \\[6pt]
assign ::= e, \ldots, e = e, \ldots, e & \text{Simple assignment} \\
\quad \mid\ e, \ldots, e = e, \ldots, e\ \mathbf{if}\ e & \text{Conditional assignment} \\
\quad \mid\ \langle \llbracket v, \ldots, v : r, \ldots, r :: assign \rangle & \text{Quantified assignment}
\end{array}
$$

Fig. 3. UNITY assignment grammar

4.1   The C Term Set

The C term set is a straightforward implementation of the Mojave C abstract syntax type. Each OCaml constructor name is defined as a term; for instance `C_declare of var * ty` is represented as $\underline{c\_declare}\{var; ty\}$, or `C_if of cond * true * false` is represented as $\underline{c\_if}\{cond; true; false\}$. When we can, we use C source syntax to denote these terms, for instance $\mathbf{if}\ (cond)\ true\ \mathbf{else}\ false$.

4.2   Design

The syntax we adopt for assignment statements in our implementation is defined in Figure 3. We achieve the independence of individual assignments in the same statement by keeping two sets of state variables. For each variable declared in the program we introduce an "alias," which stores the value of the aliased variable before entering a new statement. We use the alias for reading and the regular variable for writing, preserving the semantics of multiple assignment statements. The value of an alias may be different *only* when executing the statement that contains its aliased variable; upon exiting the statement, the two variables are synchronized. Throughout our discussion, we define the alias of variable v as **ALIAS**$[v]$, and that of UNITY expressions as shown below.

$$\textbf{ALIAS}[i \mid f \mid \textbf{true} \mid \textbf{false}] \rightarrow i \mid f \mid \textbf{true} \mid \textbf{false} \quad \textbf{ALIAS}[v] \rightarrow v\_alias$$
$$\textbf{ALIAS}[e_1 \, op \, e_2] \quad\quad \rightarrow \textbf{ALIAS}[e_1] \, op \, \textbf{ALIAS}[e_2]$$
$$\textbf{ALIAS}[e_1[e_2]] \quad\quad\quad \rightarrow \textbf{ALIAS}[e_1][\textbf{ALIAS}[e_2]]$$
$$\textbf{ALIAS}[e_f(e_1, \ldots, e_n)] \rightarrow \textbf{LV}[e_f](\textbf{ALIAS}[e_1], \ldots, \textbf{ALIAS}[e_n])$$

The lvalue expression **LV**$[\ldots]$ has all but the outmost variable replaced with aliases, since we want to use regular variables for writing but aliases for reading. For instance, **LV**$[\texttt{a[i]}] \rightarrow \texttt{a[i\_alias]}$.

$$\textbf{LV}[i \mid f \mid \textbf{true} \mid \textbf{false}] \rightarrow i \mid f \mid \textbf{true} \mid \textbf{false} \quad \textbf{LV}[v] \rightarrow v$$
$$\textbf{LV}[e_1 \, op \, e_2] \quad\quad \rightarrow \textbf{LV}[e_1] \, op \, \textbf{LV}[e_2]$$
$$\textbf{LV}[e_1[e_2]] \quad\quad\quad \rightarrow \textbf{LV}[e_1][\textbf{ALIAS}[e_2]]$$
$$\textbf{LV}[e_f(e_1, \ldots, e_n)] \rightarrow \textbf{LV}[e_f](\textbf{ALIAS}[e_1], \ldots, \textbf{ALIAS}[e_n])$$

We track any change in the global state by monitoring each assignment through **SYNCHRONIZE**. We update the alias for variable v with v itself if the two are different, in which case we set the global **CHANGED** variable to true. This allows us to identify changes to the state variables.

$$\textbf{SYNCHRONIZE}[v :: vars] \rightarrow \text{if } (\textbf{LV}[v] \neq \textbf{ALIAS}[v]) \, \{$$
$$\textbf{CHANGED} = \textbf{true};$$
$$\textbf{ALIAS}[v] = \textbf{LV}[v];$$
$$\} :: \textbf{SYNCHRONIZE}[vars]$$

The following illustrates how a simple statement with two conditional assignments is translated.

$$\texttt{x,y := y,x if x>y} \rightarrow \quad \begin{array}{l} \text{if } (\textbf{ALIAS}[x] > \textbf{ALIAS}[y]) \, \{ \\ \quad \textbf{LV}[x] = \textbf{ALIAS}[y]; \\ \quad \textbf{LV}[y] = \textbf{ALIAS}[x]; \\ \quad \textbf{SYNCHRONIZE}[x]; \\ \quad \textbf{SYNCHRONIZE}[y]; \\ \} \end{array}$$

4.3   Translation

After parsing, the original UNITY program is represented as a *program* term (which we have pretty-printed in the rule below) whose subterms correspond to the declarations, identities, initializations and assignments in the program. The main step required to translate this term into C abstract syntax terms can be expressed as:

$$
\begin{array}{ll}
& int\ main(\dots)\ \{ \\
\textbf{program}\ id & int\ \textbf{CHANGED}; \\
\quad \textbf{declare}\ v : ty, \dots & \mathbf{C}_1[v : ty, \dots] \\
\quad \textbf{always}\ v = e, \dots & \mathbf{C}_2[inits] \\
\quad \textbf{initially}\ inits \quad \rightarrow & \textbf{while}\ (!\,\textbf{CHANGED})\ \{ \\
\quad \textbf{assign}\ assigns & \quad \textbf{CHANGED} = false; \\
\textbf{end} & \quad \textbf{SUBST}[v = e, \dots; \mathbf{C}_3[assigns]]\ \} \\
& \}
\end{array}
$$

where $\mathbf{C}_1$, $\mathbf{C}_2$, $\mathbf{C}_3$ denote the translation process for declarations, initializations and assignments, respectively, as defined below:

$$\mathbf{C}_1[(v : ty) :: rest] \rightarrow \underline{c\_declare}\{var; ty\} :: \mathbf{C}_1[rest]$$
$$\mathbf{C}_1[\textbf{nil}] \rightarrow \textbf{nil}$$

$$\mathbf{C}_2[init :: rest] \rightarrow \textbf{ASSIGN}[init] :: \mathbf{C}_2[rest]$$
$$\mathbf{C}_2[\textbf{nil}] \rightarrow \textbf{nil}$$

$$\mathbf{C}_3[assign :: rest] \rightarrow \textbf{ASSIGN}[assign] :: \mathbf{C}_3[rest]$$
$$\mathbf{C}_3[\textbf{nil}] \rightarrow \textbf{nil}$$

Note that we use the same translation for initializations and assignments to simplify our discussion. In the actual implementation, we have omitted the code that tracks state changes from the initializations.

Identities. Given a list of variables and their identity expressions as defined in the **always** section of the source program, we simply substitute each expression in place of the variable.

$$\textbf{SUBST}[(v = exp) :: rest; prog[v]] \rightarrow \textbf{SUBST}[rest; prog[exp]]$$
$$\textbf{SUBST}[\textbf{nil}; prog] \rightarrow prog$$

Assignments. The heart of our implementation is the translation of assignment statements. Simple, conditional and quantified assignments are translated by $\mathbf{A}_1$, $\mathbf{A}_2$, $\mathbf{A}_3$, respectively.

$$\textbf{ASSIGN}[lvalues = values] \rightarrow \mathbf{A}_1[lvalues = values; lvalues]$$

$$\textbf{ASSIGN}[lvalues = values\ \textbf{if}\ cond] \rightarrow \mathbf{A}_2[lvalues = values\ \textbf{if}\ cond; lvalues]$$

$$\textbf{ASSIGN}[\langle\!\langle cvars : quants :: assign\rangle] \rightarrow \mathbf{A}_3[cvars; quants; assign]$$

Simple assignments are translated directly, followed by the synchronization of all left-hand side expressions:

$$\mathbf{A}_1[(v = exp) :: rest; lvalues] \rightarrow$$
$$(\mathbf{LV}[v] = \mathbf{ALIAS}[exp]) :: \mathbf{A}_1[rest; lvalues]$$

$$\mathbf{A}_1[\mathbf{nil}; lvalues] \rightarrow \mathbf{SYNCHRONIZE}[lvalues]$$

Conditional assignments are wrapped in an `if` statement:

$$\mathbf{A}_2[assigns \ \mathbf{if} \ cond; lvalues] \rightarrow \mathbf{if} \ (\mathbf{ALIAS}[cond]) \ \{$$
$$\mathbf{A}_1[assigns; lvalues]$$
$$\}$$

Quantified assignments involve the use of control variables over which we quantify expressions. We translate these by first declaring the control variables, then recursively turning each quantifier (which is of the form $e_1 \ op_1 \ v \ op_2 \ e_2$) into a for-loop. To compute the initial values and upper bound for the for-loop, we use $\mathbf{RANGE}_1$ and $\mathbf{RANGE}_2$, respectively, which are defined as:

$$\mathbf{RANGE}_1[lv; e; <] \rightarrow lv = e + 1$$
$$\mathbf{RANGE}_1[lv; e; \leq] \rightarrow lv = e$$

$$\mathbf{RANGE}_2[lv; e; <] \rightarrow lv < e$$
$$\mathbf{RANGE}_2[lv; e; \leq] \rightarrow lv \leq e$$

$$\mathbf{A}_3[cvars; quants; assigns] \rightarrow \mathbf{C}_1[cvars] @ \ \mathbf{A}_{3,1}[quants; assigns]$$

$$\mathbf{A}_{3,1}[(e_1 \ op_1 \ v \ op_2 \ e_2, \mathbf{none}) :: quants; assigns] \rightarrow$$
$$\mathbf{for} \ (\ \mathbf{RANGE}_1[\mathbf{ALIAS}[v]; \mathbf{ALIAS}[e_1]; op_1];$$
$$\mathbf{RANGE}_2[\mathbf{ALIAS}[v]; \mathbf{ALIAS}[e_2]; op_2];$$
$$\mathbf{ALIAS}[v] + +) \ \{$$
$$\mathbf{A}_{3,1}[quants; assigns]$$
$$\}$$

$$\mathbf{A}_{3,1}[\mathbf{nil}; assigns] \rightarrow \mathbf{ASSIGN}[assigns]$$

If the quantifier includes extra conditions (such as in `<| i: 0<=i<10 & odd(i) :: a[i] = i >`), we wrap the final assignment clause in a conditional statement:

$$\mathbf{A}_{3,1}[(e_1 \ op_1 \ v \ op_2 \ e_2, cond) :: quants; assigns] \rightarrow$$
$$\mathbf{for} \ (\ \mathbf{RANGE}_1[\mathbf{ALIAS}[v]; \mathbf{ALIAS}[e_1]; op_1];$$
$$\mathbf{RANGE}_2[\mathbf{ALIAS}[v]; \mathbf{ALIAS}[e_2]; op_2];$$
$$\mathbf{ALIAS}[v] + +) \ \{$$
$$\mathbf{if}(cond) \ \{$$
$$\mathbf{A}_{3,1}[quants; assigns]$$
$$\}$$
$$\}$$

When the translation terminates, Phobos attempts to convert the final term to C abstract syntax, and the resulting OCaml structure is passed to Mojave for optimization and code generation.

4.4   Further Considerations

Our use of the **CHANGED** variable to track changes in the program state is based on the assumption that executing all assignment statements must result in a state change unless the program has reached a fixed point. Although this only holds in the absence of randomness, we see the expected benefits in most programs. For instance, the sorting program shown in Figure 1 terminates after one iteration if the input array is initially sorted, while it takes N iterations for arrays sorted in reverse order.

Although we have described a concrete implementation for assignment translation, we can easily modify our approach to be more abstract. By overriding $\mathbf{A}_1$, $\mathbf{A}_2$, and $\mathbf{A}_3$ we may implement an alternative way of handling assignments. A simple modification would be to encode each assignment statement as a local function and store references to these functions in a global store. The main loop could then be modified to schedule assignment statements nondeterministically, by using a fair random number generator to determine the statement ordering and tracking state changes in a more sophisticated way.

We could also replace the main program loop with a call to a generic scheduler. This could be implemented as a C function to be linked against when compiling UNITY programs, providing full customization of the scheduler.

In addition, we can easily translate to any target abstract syntax supported by the Mojave compiler by modifying the various $\mathbf{A}$ and $\mathbf{C}$ operators in our implementation. Source-to-source translation from any target abstract syntax is available using Mojave's pretty-printing capabilities.

5   Conclusion

This paper has presented a method of translating UNITY programs into executable code, using term rewriting as an integral part of the compilation process. Our method has several advantages over other techniques for compiling UNITY programs, including easy translation to multiple languages and the ability to change the scheduler for UNITY statements. On the other hand, we have ignored rewriting termination or Church-Rosser properties of our implementation.

We intend to exploit Mojave's integrated MetaPRL theorem prover to carry out the derivation of formal proofs for properties of UNITY programs, and to apply our translation method to additional UNITY-based formalisms. Examples of such formalisms are the Communications and Control Language (CCL) [13], which we are using to specify and implement programs for multi-vehicle control systems [4], and Dynamic UNITY [18], a specification language and logic for message-passing systems that exhibit dynamic behavior (such as process creation and deletion).

We believe that translations from these formalisms can be carried out using methods similar to those we have applied to UNITY. The translation of Dynamic UNITY, in particular, will require significantly more runtime machinery than we have provided for UNITY programs; the presence of a weakly fair scheduler suffices to execute a UNITY program, but the execution of a Dynamic UNITY system requires additional constructs such as process tables and message queues.

References

1. Stuart F. Allen, Robert L. Constable, Douglas J. Howe, and William Aitken. The semantics of reflected proof. In *Proc. of Fifth Symp. on Logic in Comp. Sci.*, pages 95–197. IEEE, June 1990.
2. F. Andersen, K. Petersen, and J. Petterson. Program verification using HOL-UNITY. In *International Workshop on Higher Order Logic and its Applications*, volume 780 of *Lecture Notes in Computer Science*, pages 1–16. Springer–Verlag, Heidelberg, Germany, 1994.
3. K. Mani Chandy and Jayadev Misra. *Parallel Program Design: A Foundation.* Addison–Wesley Publishing Company, Reading, MA, USA, 1988.
4. Lars Cremean, William Dunbar, David van Gogh, Jason Hickey, Eric Klavins, Jason Meltzer, and Richard M. Murray. The Caltech multi-vehicle wireless testbed. In *Proceedings of the Conference on Decision and Control (CDC)*. IEEE Press, 2002. http://www.cs.caltech.edu/~mvwt/.
5. D. C. DeRoure. Parallel implementation of UNITY. In *The PUMA and GENESIS Projects*, pages 67–75, 1991.
6. M. J. C. Gordon and T. F. Melham. *Introduction to HOL—A theorem proving environment for higher order logic.* Cambridge University Press, Cambridge, England, 1993.
7. A. Granicz and J. Hickey. Phobos: A front-end approach to extensible compilers. In *36th Hawaii International Conference on System Sciences.* IEEE, 2002.
8. B. Heyd and P. Cregut. A modular coding of UNITY in Coq. In *Proceedings of the International Conference on Theorem Proving in Higher Order Logics (TPHOLs)*, 1996.
9. Jason Hickey and Alexey Nogin. Fast tactic-based theorem proving. In *Theorem Proving in Higher Order Logics (TPHOLs 2000)*, August 2000.
10. Jason J. Hickey. Nuprl-Light: An implementation framework for higher–order logics. In *14th International Conference on Automated Deduction.* Springer, 1997.
11. Martin Huber. MasPar UNITY version 1.0. ftp://sanfrancisco.ira.uka.de/pub/maspar/maspar_unity.tar.Z, 1992.
12. J. Hickey, J. D. Smith, A. Granicz, N. Gray, C. Tapus, and B. Aydemir. The Mojave Research Group Website. http://mojave.cs.caltech.edu/.
13. Eric Klavins. Communication complexity of multi-robot systems. In *Fifth International Workshop on the Algorithmic Foundations of Robotics*, Nice, France, December 2002. Proceedings to appear as a book in the Springer-Verlag series on advanced robotics.
14. Aleksey Nogin and Jason Hickey. Sequent schema for derived rules. In *Theorem Proving in Higher-Order Logics (TPHOLs '02)*, 2002.
15. Lawrence C. Paulson. *Isabelle: A Generic Theorem Prover.* Number 828 in Lecture Notes in Computer Science. Springer–Verlag, Heidelberg, Germany, 1994.
16. Lawrence C. Paulson. Mechanizing UNITY in Isabelle. *ACM Transactions on Computational Logic*, 1(1):3–32, 2000.
17. S. Radha and C. R. Muthukrishnan. A portable implementation of UNITY on Von Neumann machines. *Computer Languages*, 18(1):17–30, 1993.
18. Daniel M. Zimmerman. *Dynamic UNITY.* PhD thesis, Department of Computer Science, California Institute of Technology, 2001.

New Decidability Results
for Fragments of First-Order Logic
and Application to Cryptographic Protocols

Hubert Comon-Lundh and Véronique Cortier*

Laboratoire Spécification et Vérification, CNRS
Ecole Normale Supérieure de Cachan, France
{comon,cortier}@lsv.ens-cachan.fr

Abstract. We consider a new extension of the Skolem class for first-order logic and prove its decidability by resolution techniques. We then extend this class including the built-in equational theory of exclusive or. Again, we prove the decidability of the class by resolution techniques. Considering such fragments of first-order logic is motivated by the automatic verification of cryptographic protocols, for an arbitrary number of sessions; the first-order formalization is an approximation of the set of possible traces, for instance relaxing the nonce freshness assumption. As a consequence, we get some new decidability results for the verification of cryptographic protocols with exclusive or.

1 Introduction

The verification of cryptographic protocols deserved a lot of attention in the past few years, because of the huge application domain of secure communications via public channels. In this context, the full automation of verification tools is important because, in general, the same protocol appears in multiple contexts in a slightly altered form; each instance has to be verified since it is never clear whether a small modification has an impact on the security property or not.

Such verification problems are typically relevant to model checking: given a protocol P and a security property ϕ, does P satisfy ϕ ? And indeed, model-checking tools have been used successfully to find some attacks (the most famous one is due to G. Lowe [21]). However, *proving* the correctness of a protocol is much harder for several reasons. First of all, we must be very precise on the semantics of protocols and security properties; there is still today a debate on these aspects. Next, whatever model of the protocols is chosen, it is both infinite in depth (traces have an unbounded length, because arbitrarily many instances of the protocol, also called *sessions* can be involved) and infinitely branching (depending on an attacker's input). Finally most of the protocols use *nonces*, which are supposed to be randomly generated numbers. As demonstrated by several authors [10,16,1], this yields undecidability of model checking, even in very restricted cases.

---

* Partially supported by INRIA project SECSI and RNTL project EVA.

R. Nieuwenhuis (Ed.): RTA 2003, LNCS 2706, pp. 148–164, 2003.
© Springer-Verlag Berlin Heidelberg 2003

There are two possible research directions, which proved to be relevant: either consider a bounded number of sessions, which is sufficient to restore decidability as shown e.g. in [26], or to consider an abstraction of the model, which may be sufficient for proving the protocol correct, but may also output "dummy" attacks. This line of research is followed by e.g. [28,3,5] and that is also what we consider in this paper.

A first abstraction consists in replacing nonces with terms depending on the context. That is what is done in all abstraction techniques we know. Then, protocols can be modeled within first-order logic [4,28,3,8] and the satisfaction of most popular security properties such as secrecy and authentication reduces to satisfiability of a set of clauses (see e.g. [13]).

However, even for protocols without nonces (or considering the above abstraction), the verification of simple properties remains undecidable (e.g. [10]). On the other hand, experiments using general purpose automatic theorem provers such as SPASS, show that, most of the time, the proof search terminates. Trying to explain this phenomenon reduces to finding decidable fragments of first-order logic in which most of the protocols can be expressed (with the above sketched abstraction for nonces). For instance, we have shown in [9] that, for a significant class of protocols, the confidentiality problem can be reduced to the solvability of a class of set constraints with equality, itself shown to be decidable using tree automata with memory.

On the other hand, all automated verification results rely, so far, on the *perfect cryptography assumption*, which, roughly, says that the message algebra is a free term algebra. Such an hypothesis is too strong since many protocols use cryptographic primitives which do have algebraic properties. A typical example is the exclusive or. As an example, Bull's authentication protocol was proved to be secure with the perfect cryptography assumption, while there is an attack when the algebraic properties of xor are considered [24,27]. Up to our knowledge, there are very few results on verification of cryptographic protocols with xor: the only other result is a proof of decidability in case of a bounded number of sessions [14,6].

The work described in this paper has two motivations: on one hand to explain the reasons why first-order theorem provers often terminate on protocol verification, on the other hand study the extensions considering the algebraic properties of exclusive or and an unbounded number of sessions.

We already realized in [9] that one reason for undecidability, which does not occur in practice, is the agents ability to copy and locally modify two distinct pieces of a message, hence enabling the simulation of two counters machines. That is why we will consider here protocols in which an agent can copy "blindly" at most one piece of the message he receives. "Blindly" has the following (informal) meaning: protocols consist in message exchange between (say) two agents. Upon receiving some message m, agent A breaks m into pieces, decrypting what she can decrypt. Each piece she gets is either known to her (it can be a public value such as an agent name or a nonce she generated earlier,...) or something she does not know (a cyphertext that she cannot decrypt, a nonce generated by the other party). Such data are represented by variables: an intruder could for instance replace them by arbitrary values. If the message that A is supposed to send makes use of such variables, we say that she copies "blindly" their content.

Such an hypothesis on the uniqueness of blind copies seems relevant since most of the protocols of [7] falls into the class. On the model side, this corresponds to first-order clauses involving at most one variable. We will give more details in section 4. This is why we consider here the fragment of first-order logic consisting in clauses which contain at most one variable. Actually, we have to consider a larger fragment, because we need to express for instance intruder capabilities, which do not fall in this category. More precisely, we consider a clausal fragment in which every clause C either contains at most one variable or is such that every subterm t is either ground, a variable, or contains all variables of the clause. We prove that this fragment of first-order logic is decidable in section 2, using ordered resolution techniques. This fragment is actually similar to the extension $\mathcal{S}^+$ of the Skolem class as defined in [18]. Still, it is different since for instance, we will allow literals $P(x)$ in multiple variables clauses. We also allow arbitrary ground literals.

Our main result is however the extension of this decidable class, considering the algebraic properties of xor: we prove in section 3 the decidability of fragment of first-order logic, which contains both the above class and the equality axioms for xor. Therefore we design a set of deduction rules and an ordered strategy, which we prove complete and terminating.

One difficulty here is that there is almost no ordering on terms with variables, which is stable by substitution. Hence we use an ordering which is stable by "non-collapsing" substitutions, restoring completeness using a rule similar to narrowing. Another difficulty is to control the number of variables occurring in clauses, which we need for termination. To this end, we impose stronger restrictions on resolution and factorization, restoring completeness by *extensions*.

Termination relies on technical results on unification with associativity, commutativity, identity and nilpotence (ACUN) and free symbols (which is known to be in NP [23]), typically concerning the sizes of mgus. Finally, completeness is obtained via classical semantic trees methods.

In section 4, we show how the previous results apply to the verification of cryptographic protocols, hence providing the first decidability result for an unbounded number of sessions, and considering the algebraic properties of xor. We illustrate the result, proving the correctness of a simple protocol. Our result is disjoint from [14,6]. On one hand, we consider an unbounded number of sessions (while it is bounded in [14,6]). On the other hand, in [14,6], there is no hypothesis on the number of blind copies and the result relies on constraint solving techniques and locality properties in the spirit of [22]. Note that first-order logic is not relevant for a bounded number of sessions since it would require to give a bound on the number of times a clause is used (e.g. using rigid variables).

Due to space limitations, many proofs are only given in a technical report [12].

2   A Simple Decidable Fragment of First-Order Logic

2.1   Definitions

Let $\mathcal{F}$ be a finite set of function symbols, $\mathcal{V}$ a set of variables and $\mathcal{P}$ a finite set of unary predicates. For every clause C (resp. every term u), $V(C)$ (resp. $V(u)$) is the set of variables of C (resp. of u). $V(u, v)$ denotes $V(u) \cup V(v)$. If L is a positive literal, we write $L' = \pm L$ for $L' \in \{L, \neg L\}$. If u and t are terms of $\mathcal{T}(\mathcal{F} \cup \mathcal{V})$ and if x is in $V(u)$, $u[t/x]$ is the term u where every occurrence of x has been replaced by t.

Definition 1. *A clause set S belongs to the class $\mathcal{C}$ if for every clause C in S, either C contains at most one variable or, for every literal L in C :*

1. *either $L = \pm P(x_i)$ for some $P \in \mathcal{P}$;*
2. *or $L = \pm P(u[f(x_1, \ldots, x_n)/y])$ for some $P \in \mathcal{P}$ and some $f \in \mathcal{F}$ such that $\{x_1, \ldots, x_n\} = V(C)$ and u is some term of $\mathcal{T}(\mathcal{F} \cup \{y\})$.*

We may write that a clause C is in $\mathcal{C}$ instead of saying that the set $\{C\}$ is in $\mathcal{C}$ to express that C is a clause of the form described above.

This class is incomparable with the class $\mathcal{S}^+$ as described in [18]. We believe that, with some additional technical details, we can extend our result so that our class contains $\mathcal{S}^+$. This is however not relevant for our application nor for the extension of the next section. As examples of sets of clauses that can be expressed in this class, let us mention for instance two-way alternating tree automata (see e.g. [11], chapter 7); since the emptiness of the automaton can also be expressed as a clause in the class, the decidability of $\mathcal{C}$ implies the emptiness decidability for two-way alternating automata.

If $t \in \mathcal{T}(\mathcal{F} \cup \mathcal{V})$, $|t|$ is the *depth* of t (maximal size of its positions). For $x \in \mathcal{V}$, $|t|_x$ is the maximal depth of an occurrence of x in t. By convention, it is 0 if $x \notin V(t)$. $|.|$ and $|.|_x$ are extended to literals by $|P(t)| = |t|$ and $|P(t)|_x = |t|_x$.

We will prove the decision result by ordered resolution, using the ordering derived from the following definition.

Definition 2. *Let A, B be two literals.*

$$A < B \quad \text{if} \quad |A| < |B| \quad \text{and if} \quad \forall x \in V(A) \cup V(B) \quad |A|_x < |B|_x.$$

$A \leq B$ if $A < B$ or $A = B$.

Note that when $A \leq B$, we have in particular that $V(A) \subseteq V(B)$.

A sufficient condition for completeness of ordered resolution is to use a *liftable* ordering [20,18], also called *stable* ordering in [19].

Definition 3 (liftability). *An ordering $\leq_{\mathcal{R}}$ is liftable if, for all atoms A, B and all substitutions θ, $A \leq_{\mathcal{R}} B$ implies $A\theta \leq_{\mathcal{R}} B\theta$.*

Proposition 1. $\leq$ *is a liftable ordering.*

2.2   Decidability Result

Theorem 1 (decidability of $\mathcal{C}$). *Let S be a finite set of clauses such that S belongs to $\mathcal{C}$. The satisfiability of S is decidable.*

Proof sketch

We use splitting (see e.g. [29]), ordered factorization and ordered binary resolution (see e.g. [2]), w.r.t. the partial ordering defined above, using a classical redundancy criterion [2], also called *a posteriori criterion* in e.g. [18]; we apply resolution on two clauses C_1 and C_2 only if no atom of the resolvent is greater than the resolved atom. Such an ordered strategy is complete [2,18]. It only remains to show termination.

First, after splitting, we only generate clauses in $\mathcal{C}$. Then, define $\|C\|$ as the maximal depth of its literals and let N be the maximum of $\|C\|$ for clauses in S. We show that, for every generated clause C' (after splitting), either $\|C'\| \leq N$, or else C' is ground and $\|C'\| \leq 2 \times N$. This is a consequence of simple lemmas on the unifiers of terms containing at most one variable, for instance:

Lemma 1. *Let u, v be two terms such that $V(u) = \{x\}$ and $V(v) = \{y\}$. If they are unifiable with mgu σ, then either $u\sigma$ is ground and $|u\sigma| \leq 2 \times \max(|u|, |v|)$ or else $|u\sigma| \leq \max(|u|, |v|)$.*

Then, thanks to the ordered strategy, which only unifies maximal literals, we get the bound on $\|C\|$ for the generated clauses C.

The termination follows from the fact that there are only finitely many clauses in $\mathcal{C}$ whose size is bounded and to which splitting does not apply.

3   An Extension Including the Exclusive or

We are going to extend the result of the previous section, including algebraic properties of a binary symbol. We will proceed as in the previous section: we define an ordering and consider an ordered deduction strategy. There are however several additional problems:

- for termination purposes, we need to keep control of the number of variables in each clause. Therefore we restrict the applicability of e.g. resolution and restore completeness, adding extension rules.
- it is a hard task to find an ordering which is both liftable and compatible with the theory of xor. We use an ordering, which is stable only by substitutions which do not introduce any simplification. Considering substitutions which introduce redexes is handled separately as a pre-processing step
- for termination purposes, we need to control the size of unifiers, relying on the particular equational theory we consider. We will see the analogs of lemma 1 in section 3.2.

3.1   Definition of the Class of Clauses

In this part, we extend our class of clauses $\mathcal{C}$ to a class of clauses $\mathcal{C}^{\oplus}$ including the algebraic properties of $\oplus$ which are described in figure 1. The two last equations can be oriented from left to right and we get a convergent rewrite system modulo associativity and commutativity, provided we add the extended rule $y \oplus x \oplus x \rightarrow y$ (see e.g. [15] for definitions). For any term t in $T(\mathcal{F} \cup \{\oplus\} \cup \mathcal{V})$, we write $t \downarrow$ as its normal form w.r.t. these rules.

Formally, we consider a finite set $\mathcal{F}$ of function symbols containing the constant symbol 0, a set $\mathcal{V}$ of variables and a finite set $\mathcal{P}$ of predicate symbols. $\mathcal{C}^{\oplus}$ is a class of clauses extending $\mathcal{C}$, described below.

Definition 4. *A clause set S belongs to $\mathcal{C}^{\oplus}$ if for every clause C in S, either C contains at most one variable or for every literal L in C :*

1. *either $L = \pm P(x_i)$ for some $P \in \mathcal{P}$;*
2. *or $L = \pm P(u[f(x_1, \ldots, x_n)/y])$ for some $P \in \mathcal{P}$ and $f \in \mathcal{F}$ such that $\{x_1, \ldots, x_n\}$ $= V(C)$ and u is some term of $T(\mathcal{F} \cup \{\oplus\} \cup \{y\})$;*
3. *or $C = \neg P(x_1) \vee \neg P(x_2) \vee P(x_1 \oplus x_2)$ for some $P \in \mathcal{P}$.*

Remarks : Note that for the second type of clauses $(\pm P(u[f(x_1, \ldots, x_n)/y]))$, f is forbidden to be $\oplus$ but $\oplus$ may occur in u.

We will see in section 4 that the special clause $C_0 \stackrel{\text{def}}{=} \neg I(x) \vee \neg I(y) \vee I(x \oplus y)$ is used to encode the ability of the intruder to compute the xor of two terms.

In the following, S_0 denotes the set of clauses in S which are of the third type in the above definition.

From now on, $=$ denotes the equality between terms (or literals) modulo the (AC) properties of xor while $=_{\oplus}$ denotes the equality between terms (or literals) modulo the whole equational theory of xor.

Following the AC property of $\oplus$, we assume terms are written in flatten form: $\oplus$ may be considered as a variadic function symbol. Subterms are defined accordingly. For instance the subterms of $f(a \oplus b \oplus g(x))$ are $f(a \oplus b \oplus g(x)), a \oplus b \oplus g(x), a, b, g(x), x$. $a \oplus b$ and $a \oplus g(x)$ are not subterms.

We extend $|.|$ and $|.|_x$ on terms of $T(\mathcal{F} \cup \{\oplus\} \cup \mathcal{V})$. Informally, since $\oplus$ is now a variadic symbol, it may in particular have only one argument, in which case we don't write it, hence don't count it in the size of the terms; that is why the following measure computes the length of the longest path, not taking $\oplus$ into account.

Definition 5. $\|.\|$ *is defined inductively by:*

1. $\|a\| = 1$ *if $a \in \mathcal{V}$ or if a is a constant symbol of $\mathcal{F}$;*
2. $\|f(t_1, \ldots, t_k)\| = 1 + \max_{1 \leq i \leq k} \|t_i\|$ *for $f \in \mathcal{F}$;*

$$x \oplus (y \oplus z) = (x \oplus y) \oplus x \qquad x \oplus y = y \oplus x$$
$$x \oplus 0 = x \qquad x \oplus x = 0$$

Fig. 1. Equational theory of the xor function symbol

3. $\|t_1 \oplus \cdots \oplus t_n\| = \max_{1 \leq i \leq n} \|t_i\|$ if the head symbol of each t_i is not $\oplus$.

Then $|t|$ is defined as $\|t \downarrow \|$. $|.|_x$ is defined in the same way except for point 1: $\|x\|_x = 1$ and $\|a\|_x = 0$ if $a \in \mathcal{V}\text{-}\{x\}$ or if a is a constant symbol of $\mathcal{F}$. This is also extended to clauses by: $|C| = \max_{L \in C} |L|$ and $|\pm P(t)| = |t|$.

Then the definition of $\leq$ (definition 2) is unchanged. However, $\leq$ is no longer a liftable ordering.

Example 1. Let $L_1 = P(a \oplus b)$, $L_2 = P(f(x \oplus a) \oplus f(b \oplus a))$ and $x\theta = b$. Then $L_1 < L_2$ but $L_1\theta = P(a \oplus b) \not< L_2\theta = P(0)$.

Actually, there are few orderings which are liftable and compatible with the rules of figure 1. For instance there is no such ordering which contains the sub-term ordering: we would have $x \oplus f(a) > a$, but then $(a \oplus f(a)) \oplus f(a) > a$! That is why we introduce the notion of *narrow-liftable* ordering and *collapse-free* substitution.

Definition 6. *A substitution σ is* normalized *if, for every variable x, $x\sigma$ is in normal form. A substitution σ is* collapse-free *w.r.t. a set of terms S if, for every $t \in S$, $t\sigma \downarrow = t \downarrow \sigma$.*

We will write NS for the set of normalized substitutions and $CF(C_1, \ldots, C_n)$ for the set of collapse-free substitutions w.r.t. the set of subterms occurring in the clauses $C_1, \ldots, C_n$, which are supposed to be irreducible.

Definition 7. *An ordering $\leq_\mathcal{R}$ is* narrow-liftable *if, for every atom A, B and every substitution θ, which is collapse-free w.r.t. B, $A <_\mathcal{R} B$ implies $A\theta <_\mathcal{R} B\theta$.*

Proposition 2. $\leq$ *is a narrow-liftable ordering on literals of clauses of $\mathcal{C}^\oplus$.*

3.2   Some Useful Results on Unification

It is well known that unifiability modulo the theory of figure 1 is NP-complete in the presence of free function symbols and that unification is finitary [23]. We need however finer results (the analogs of lemma 1) to control the size of terms.

Lemma 2. *If $u \neq_\oplus v$ and $Var(u, v) \subseteq \{x\}$. Then either u and v are not unifiable (modulo the rules of figure 1) or else any (normalized) unifier $\sigma = \{x \mapsto w\}$ is such that w is a ground term and either w is a subterm of $u \oplus v$ or else $w = w_1 \oplus w_2$ is a normal form such that w_1 and $x \oplus w_2$ are subterms of u or v. Moreover, $|x\sigma| \leq \max\{|u|, |v|\}$.*

Note that $|u\sigma|$ may be strictly greater than $|u|$ and $|v|$.

Example 2. Let us consider $u = h^2(x) \oplus h^2(a) \oplus x$ and $v = h^2(x)$. The most general unifier of u and v is $\sigma(x) = h^2(a)$ and $u\sigma = h^4(a)$.

Lemma 3. *If $Var(u) \cap Var(v) = \emptyset$ and $Var(u) \subseteq \{x\}, Var(v) \subseteq \{y\}$, $u \neq_\oplus v$, then either u and v are not unifiable (modulo the rules of figure 1) or else every most general unifier θ of u, v is, up to variable renaming, such that:*

- *either there are ground subterms $w_1, \ldots, w_k$ of u, v such that $x\theta = w_1 \oplus \ldots \oplus w_k$ (resp. $y\theta = w_1 \oplus \ldots \oplus w_k$) and $y\theta$ is ground (resp. $x\theta$ is ground)*
- *or $x\theta = z \oplus t_1 \oplus \cdots \oplus t_k$, $y\theta = (u_1 \oplus \cdots \oplus u_n \oplus w_1 \oplus \cdots \oplus w_m)\theta$, where the t_i's and the w_i's are ground subterms of u, v, $n \geq 1$ and the u_i's are non-ground subterms of u or the converse, exchanging the roles of x and y (resp.of u and v).*

Example 3. $g(a \oplus f(y \oplus f(a)), f^n(y)) = g(x, f^n(x))$ has a solution $x = y = a \oplus f(a)$. Instantiating the original terms, their measure is growing.

A similar technique allows us to conclude when u or v is equal to $u'[x \rightarrow f(x_1, \ldots, x_n)]$. See the appendix for details.

We design the ordering $\leq$ in such a way that it is stable by collapse-free substitutions. Therefore, we have to show how it is possible to consider only such substitutions. A general result in [14] allows to focus on collapse-free substitutions, roughly guessing the shared parts and performing possible simplification beforehand. That is also what we (roughly) do here. However, we need also to control the size of the resulting clauses, taking advantage of our additional assumptions.

Lemma 4. *For every clause $C \in \mathcal{C}^\oplus$, there is a finite set of clauses $\{C_1, \ldots, C_n\}$, denoted by* narrow(C), *such that :*

$$\{C\sigma \downarrow \ | \ V(C\sigma) = \emptyset, \sigma \in NS\} = \bigcup_{i=1}^{n} \{C_i\sigma \ | \ V(C_i\sigma) = \emptyset, \sigma \in CF(C_1, \ldots, C_n)\}$$

Moreover, if $C \notin S_0$, every C_i falls in one of the three following cases: $C_i = C$, or C_i is ground and $|C_i| \leq 2 \times |C|$, or $V(C) = \{x\}$ and $C_i = C\{x \mapsto y \oplus t_i\} \downarrow$ for some sum t_i of ground subterms of C.

3.3   The Decidability Result

The goal of this section is to prove the following (main) result:

Theorem 2 (decidability of $\mathcal{C}^\oplus$). *Let S be a finite set of clauses such that S belongs to $\mathcal{C}^\oplus$. The satisfiability of S is decidable.*

Thanks to lemma 4 we can restrict our attention to collapse-free substitutions, provided that we apply the rule which replaces C with the set of clauses C_i constructed in lemma 4. This rule is called the *narrowing rule*.

But restricting ourself to "collapse-free" ordered resolution is still not sufficient to ensure termination. Indeed, only the repetitive resolution of renamings of C_0 with themselves yields an infinite set of clauses. That is why we will disallow resolution steps between clauses in S_0, restoring completeness using *extensions*.

The situation is similar to the transitivity rule for which a special inference rule is designed: ordered chaining [2]. Extensions aim at inferring $P(s \oplus u) \vee C \vee D$ from $P(s \oplus t) \vee C$ and $P(t \oplus u) \vee D$ when t is maximal among s, t, u. They consist in a short-cut of two resolution steps.

Example 4. Let us consider $C_1 = \neg P(s(h) \oplus x)$ and $C_2 = P(s(h(y)) \oplus s(y))$. Applying the rule Extension 1, we get the clause $C_3 = \neg P(h(y) \oplus s(y))$:

$$\frac{\neg P(s(x) \oplus x) \quad P(s(h(y)) \oplus s(y))}{\neg P(h(y) \oplus s(y))} \qquad \begin{array}{l} \text{with } t_1 = s(x), \ u_1 = s(h(y)) \\ \text{and } \theta = \{x \mapsto h(y)\}. \end{array}$$

C_3 could have been obtained by the two successive binary resolution rules if we had allowed for resolution with clauses in S_0.

$$\frac{\neg P(s(x) \oplus x) \quad \neg P(z) \vee \neg P(z') \vee P(z \oplus z')}{\neg P(s(h(y)) \oplus s(y)) \vee \neg P(h(y) \oplus s(y))} \qquad \begin{array}{l} \text{with } x = h(y), \ z = s(h(y)) \oplus \\ s(y) \text{ and } z' = h(y) \oplus s(y) \end{array}$$

$$\text{and} \quad \frac{\neg P(s(h(y)) \oplus s(y)) \vee \neg P(h(y) \oplus s(y)) \quad P(s(h(y)) \oplus s(y))}{\neg P(h(y) \oplus s(y))} .$$

Deduction rules are displayed in Figure 2. As usual (see e.g. [18]), repeatedly applying the deduction rules of figure 2 together with a splitting rule yields a set of sets of clauses: $\mathcal{E}_0 = \{S\}$ and $\mathcal{E}_{i+1}$ is obtained:

- either by replacing $S_j \in \mathcal{E}_i$ by $S_j \cup \{C\}$ if C can be inferred from S_i using a rule of figure 2,
- or by replacing some $S_j \cup \{C \vee C'\} \in \mathcal{E}_i$ with two sets $S_j \cup \{C\}$ and $S_j \cup \{C'\}$ if $Var(C) \cap Var(C') = \emptyset$.

We also remove redundant clauses at each step. For our purpose, it is sufficient to remove clauses $L \vee L \vee C$ when $L \vee C$ is in the set of clauses.

Lemma 5 (Correctness). *The narrowing rule and the deduction rules of figure 2 are correct (the set of models of one of the clause sets in $\mathcal{E}_i$ is the same as the set of models of one of the clause sets in $\mathcal{E}_{i+1}$) and, if every clause set in $\mathcal{E}_i$ is in $\mathcal{C}^{\oplus}$, then every clause set in $\mathcal{E}_{i+1}$ is in $\mathcal{C}^{\oplus}$.*

Lemma 6 (Termination). *The sequence $\mathcal{E}_i$ is finite when starting from $\mathcal{E}_0 = \{S\}$ and $S \in \mathcal{C}^{\oplus}$.*

Proof. (sketch) The sequence $\mathcal{E}_i$ is finite iff applying the rules of figure 2 together with the rule $C \vee C' \to C$ when $Var(C) \cap Var(C') = \emptyset$ terminates when starting from S.

We are going to give an upper bound on the size of a clause C in a set of $\mathcal{E}_i$. Let T the set of ground subterms of S and $N \stackrel{\text{def}}{=} \max_{L \in C, C \in S} |L|$. We show by induction on i that, for every clause C of a set of $\mathcal{E}_i$, either C is ground and $|C| \leq 2N$, or C is not ground and $|C| \leq N$, or C contains exactly one variable x and $|C\{x \mapsto x \oplus t\}| \leq N$ for some $t \in T$.

Binary Resolution

$$\frac{\neg P(t) \vee C \quad P(u) \vee C'}{C\sigma \vee C'\sigma}$$

If σ is collapse-free w.r.t. literals in C, C', $\sigma \in mgu(t, u)$, $P(t)\sigma \not< (C \vee C')\sigma$.

Factorization

$$\frac{L_1 \vee L_2 \vee C}{(L_1 \vee C)\sigma}$$

If $\sigma \in mgu(L_1, L_2)$, σ is collapse-free w.r.t. literals in the clause, and $L_1\sigma \not< C\sigma$.

Narrowing

$$\frac{C}{(C\sigma) \downarrow}$$

If $(C\sigma) \downarrow \in \mathsf{narrow}(C)$.

Explosion

$$\frac{P(t \oplus u) \vee C}{(P(t \oplus u) \vee C)\sigma}$$

If t is ground, $u\sigma$ is ground and $u\sigma < t$.

Extension 1

$$\frac{\neg P(t) \vee C \quad P(u_1 \oplus u_2) \vee C'}{(C \vee C' \vee \neg P(t_2 \oplus u_2))\theta}$$

If $\begin{cases} P(x \oplus y) \vee \neg P(x) \vee \neg P(y) \in S_0 \\ t = t_1 \oplus t_2 (\text{or } t = t_1 \text{ and } t_2 = 0) \\ Var(t) = Var(t_1), \theta \in mgu(t_1, u_1) \\ \theta \text{ collapse-free w.r.t. } t, u_1 \oplus u_2, t_2 \oplus u_2 \\ (C \vee C' \vee \neg P(t_2 \oplus u_2))\theta \not> t_1\theta. \end{cases}$

Extension 2

$$\frac{P(t) \vee C \quad P(u_1 \oplus u_2) \vee C'}{(C \vee C' \vee P(t_2 \oplus u_2))\theta}$$

If $\begin{cases} \neg P(x) \vee \neg P(y) \vee P(x \oplus y) \in S_0 \\ t = t_1 \oplus t_2 (\text{or } t = t_1 \text{ and } t_2 = 0) \\ Var(t) = Var(t_1), \theta \in mgu(t_1, u_1) \\ \theta \text{ collapse-free w.r.t. } t, u_1 \oplus u_2, t_2 \oplus u_2 \\ (C \vee C' \vee \neg P(t_2 \oplus u_2))\theta \not> t_1\theta. \end{cases}$

All rules only apply to non-splittable clauses, not belonging to S_0.

Fig. 2. Deduction rules.

To prove this, we investigate all possible cases (each deduction rule) and we rely on lemma 2 and 3 (detailed proof in [12]).

Then, we show that there are only finitely many ground clauses such that $|C| \leq 2N$ (this relies on the nilpotence of $\oplus$) and only finitely many non-ground clauses in $\mathcal{C}^\oplus$ such that $|C| \leq N$ or $|C\{x \mapsto x \oplus t\}| \leq N$ for some $t \in T$.

Thanks to lemma 6, the sequence $\mathcal{E}_i$ is finite. We let $\mathcal{E}^*(S)$ be its limit, when starting from $\mathcal{E}_0 = \{S\}$, $S \in \mathcal{C}^\oplus$.

Lemma 7 (Completeness). *Let $S \in \mathcal{C}^{\oplus}$. S is unsatisfiable if and only if for every set $S' \in \mathcal{E}^*(S)$, $\perp \in S'$.*

Proof (sketch): our deduction system is correct, thus if $\perp \in S^*$ for every set $S^* \in \mathcal{E}^*(S)$ then S is not satisfiable.

Assume S is not satisfiable and assume $\perp \notin S^* \in \mathcal{E}^*$.

We extend our partial ordering $\leq$ on literals to a total ordering $\overset{\sim}{\leq}$ on ground literals in the following way.

Let $\leq$ be any total ordering on the predicates $\mathcal{P}$ and on the function symbols $\mathcal{F}$. We extend $\leq$ on $\mathcal{F} \cup \{\oplus\}$ by $\oplus < f$ for all $f \in \mathcal{F}$. We then let $m(t)$ be the triple $(|t|, top(t), Sub(t))$ where $top(t)$ is the top symbol of t and $Sub(t)$ are its immediate (strict) subterms. For two ground terms in normal form, we let $t \overset{\sim}{<} t'$ if $m(t) < m(t')$ where the triples are lexicographically ordered, using the ordering on $\mathcal{F}$ for the second component, the lexicographic extension of $\leq$ on the subterms when the top symbol is not $\oplus$ and the multiset extension of $\overset{\sim}{\leq}$ otherwise.

Let L_1, L_2 be two ground positive literals : $L_1 = P_1(t_1)$ and $L_2 = P_2(t_2)$. Then $L_1 \overset{\sim}{<} L_2$ if either $t_1 \overset{\sim}{<} t_2$; or $t_1 = t_2$ and $P_1 < P_2$.

By definition, $\overset{\sim}{<}$ extends $<$ and $\overset{\sim}{\leq}$ is a total ordering. The Herbrand base is totally ordered accordingly as well as partial interpretations. As usual in semantic tree methods, since S is unsatisfiable, by correctness S^* is unsatisfiable, hence its semantic tree is finite (the set of partial interpretations which do not falsify a clause of S^*).

Then we consider a partial interpretation $\mathcal{I}$ whose two extensions to $P_1(v)$ falsify a clause of S^* and which is minimal w.r.t. the lexicographic ordering on partial interpretations. (This is a "leftmost" node whose two sons are failure nodes in the semantic tree). The lexicographic ordering on partial interpretations is defined by $I >_{lex} J$ if, when $P(u)$ is the maximal element of the Herbrand base such that I and J coincide on literals strictly smaller than $P(u)$, $I(P(u)) = 1$, $J(P(u)) = 0$.

By factorization we may assume that the two clauses C_1, C_2 falsified by the two extensions of $\mathcal{I}$ are such that $P_1(v) \vee C'_1 = C_1\sigma_1$ and $\neg P_1(v) \vee C'_2 = C_2\sigma_2$ for some $C_1, C_2 \in S^* \cup S_0$ such that $C'_1, C'_2 < P_1(v)$. By narrowing, we may assume that σ_1 is collapse-free w.r.t. C_1 and σ_2 is collapse-free w.r.t. C_2. We distinguish four cases: either $C_1, C_2 \in S_0$, or $C_1 \in S_0$ and $C_2 \notin S_0$, $C_1 \notin S_0$ and $C_2 \in S_0$ or else $C_1, C_2 \notin S_0$.

These cases are described in more details in the appendix, we sketch here the reasons why it works:

Case $C_1, C_2 \in S_0$: We prove directly that there is another smaller clause falsified by $\mathcal{I}$, simply recombining the terms in the right order. This corresponds to the uselessness of extensions of extensions.

Case $C_1 \in S_0, C_2 \notin S_0$: Let $C_1\sigma_1 = \neg P_0(x)\sigma_1 \vee \neg P_0(y)\sigma_1 \vee P_0(x \oplus y)\sigma_1$, $x\sigma_1 = v_1$, $y\sigma_1 = v_2$, and $(x\sigma_1 \oplus y\sigma_1) \downarrow = v$. There exist v'_1, v'_2, v' such that $v = v'_1 \oplus v'_2$, $v_1 = v'_1 \oplus v'$ and $v_2 = v'_2 \oplus v'$ without any collapse or $v = v_1 \oplus v_2$ without any collapse. We only consider the first case since the second one is similar. By hypothesis, $v_1 \overset{\sim}{<} v, v_2 \overset{\sim}{<} v$ and therefore $\mathcal{I}(P_0(v_1)) = \mathcal{I}(P_0(v_2)) = 1$.

Assume w.l.o.g that $P_0(v_1)\tilde{\leq}P_0(v_2)$. Now, by minimality of the interpretation $\mathcal{I}$ (w.r.t. lexicographic ordering), the partial interpretation $\mathcal{J}$ which coincides with $\mathcal{I}$ on literals strictly smaller than $P_0(v_1)$ and such that $\mathcal{J}(P_0(v_1)) = 0$ falsifies a clause $C_3 = P_0(u) \lor C'$ of S^*. We consider again two cases, depending on whether this clause is in S_0 or not.

Assume $C_3 \notin S_0$ and that no factorization can be applied. Also, by narrowing, $C_3\sigma_3$ does not contain any redex and $v_1 = u\sigma_3$. Moreover, $P_0(v_1)$ is maximal in $C_3\sigma_3$. We are going to show that we can apply **Extension 1** (possibly after **Explosion**) to C_2 and C_3 yielding a clause falsified by $\mathcal{I}$. We let $C_2 = \neg P_0(t) \lor C$. We have $v = t\sigma_2$ and σ_2 is collapse-free thus $t = t_1 \oplus t_2$ such that $t_1\sigma_2 = v_1'$ and $t_2\sigma_2 = v_2'$. In the same way, $u = u_1 \oplus u_2$ such that $u_1\sigma_3 = v_1'$ and $u_2\sigma_3 = v'$. This means in particular that t_1, u_1 are unifiable. By **Explosion**, we may assume that $V(t) = V(t_1)$ and, by lemma 3, that there is a $\theta \in mgu(t_1, u_1)$ such that $\sigma_2 \uplus \sigma_3 = \theta\theta'$. Moreover, let w be the maximal strict direct subterm of v. Since $v_2\tilde{<}v_1\tilde{<}v$, w is a strict direct subterm of v_1' thus $v_2 = v_2' \oplus v'\tilde{<}v_1'$. The inequality $v_2 = v_2' \oplus v'\tilde{<}v_1'$ gives $t_2\sigma_2 \oplus u_2\sigma_3\tilde{<}t_1\sigma_2$, hence $(t_2 \oplus u_2)\theta\theta'\tilde{<}t_1\sigma_2$. It follows that $(t_2 \oplus u_2)\theta \not> t_1$. In addition, θ is collapse-free w.r.t. t, $t_1 \oplus t_2$, $t_2 \oplus u_2$ and the clauses C and C'. Then, we can apply **Extension 1** and there is a clause $(C \lor C' \lor \neg P_0(t_2 \oplus u_2))\theta$, which is already falsified by $\mathcal{I}$.

The case $C_3 \in S_0$ yields to the previous case where $C_1, C_2 \in S_0$.

Case $C_1 \notin S_0, C_2 \in S_0$: this case is symmetric to the previous one, replacing **Explosion 1** with **Explosion 2**.

Case $C_1, C_2 \notin S_0$. We simply use **Resolution**; there is a smaller clause which is already falsified by $\mathcal{I}$.

4   Application to Cryptographic Protocols

We assume the reader familiar with the notion of agent, nonce, intruder, ... In this paragraph, we show how security properties for a class of protocols can be expressed as the satisfiability of a set of clauses $S \in \mathcal{C}^\oplus$. We also propose a simple (new) cryptographic protocol, which we prove correct using our technique.

We have presented in [13] a clausal model of cryptographic protocols. This model is a generalization of Paulson's model [25] and the strand spaces model [17]. Unfortunately, it is much too expressive for decidability results. That is why we use here an abstraction where the freshness of nonces is no longer guaranteed. It may induce false attacks but is correct: if an abstracted protocol is proven correct then it is correct in the general model.

Messages are terms constructed over the alphabet $\mathcal{F} = \{< \_,\_ >, \{\_\}\_, h\}$ and a finite set of constants C, depending on the protocol.

- $< m_1, m_2 >$ represents the concatenation of the two messages m_1 and m_2;
- $\{m_1\}_{m_2}$ represents the term m_1 encrypted by m_2;
- $h(m)$ represents the hash of m.

Note that we allow compound keys for example. We also could express asymmetric encryption but for the sake of simplicity, we do not present this in this paper. As explained in the introduction, this representation implicitly uses the perfect encryption assumption :

$$\{m\}_k = \{m'\}_{k'} \quad \Rightarrow \quad m = m' \;\&\; k = k'.$$

To relax this assumption, we add the $\oplus$ symbol together with its equational theory (described in Fig. 1) : $m_1 \oplus m_2$ represents the message m_1 xored with the message m_2. The xor function is widely used to encrypt messages by block [7]. It can also be used to implement a computationally cheap encryption: if K is a private key, then, instead of encrypting m with K, we may simply xor m and K. This is the case in the Bull protocol described in [24], which requires abstraction to fit in our class. We also propose the following protocol, which aims at sending a secret S_{ab}, shared by agents a, b, without using explicit encryption (hence using fewer time resources):

$$A \rightarrow B : N_a \oplus K_{ab}$$
$$B \rightarrow A : N_b \oplus N_a$$
$$A \rightarrow B : S_{ab} \oplus N_b$$

At the first step, the agent A sends a nonce N_a xored with the shared key between A and B.

We consider a predicate I which represents the set of messages possibly known to the intruder. Abstracting nonces by constants, the first rule of our protocol can be represented by the following clause:

$$\Rightarrow I(n_{ab}^1 \oplus K_{ab}), \tag{1}$$

where n_{ab}^1, K_{ab} are constant symbols. At the second step, the agent B can retrieve N_a by xoring the message he received by K_{ab}. Then he generates a new nonce N_b and sends the message $N_b \oplus N_a$. This can be represented by:

$$I(z) \Rightarrow I(z \oplus n_{ba}^2 \oplus K_{ab}), \tag{2}$$

where n_{ba}^2 is a constant symbol. Eventually, when the agent A receives B's message, she can retrieve N_b and send a secret S_{ab} by xoring it with N_b:

$$I(z) \Rightarrow I(z \oplus n_{ab}^1 \oplus S_{ab}). \tag{3}$$

These three clauses belong to our class $\mathcal{C}^\oplus$. Applying the reduction result of [13], we may assume that there are only two honest agents a, b and one dishonest agent c. We assume here that an honest agent is not allowed to speak with himself since we think this hypothesis is more realistic. Then, all clauses corresponding to the protocol rules are displayed in Figure 3. We use a finite set of constants $C = \bigcup_{i \in \{ab,ba,ac,ca,cb,bc\}} \{n_i^1, n_i^2, S_i\} \cup \{K_{ab}, K_{ac}, K_{bc}\}$.

Such a representation can be generalized to arbitrary protocols, and we stay within $\mathcal{C}^\oplus$ as soon as, at each step, at most one part of the message is blindly copied.

First rule:

$$\Rightarrow I(n_{ab}^1 \oplus K_{ab}) \qquad \Rightarrow I(n_{ba}^1 \oplus K_{ab}) \qquad \Rightarrow I(n_{ac}^1 \oplus K_{ac})$$
$$\Rightarrow I(n_{ca}^1 \oplus K_{ac}) \qquad \Rightarrow I(n_{cb}^1 \oplus K_{bc}) \qquad \Rightarrow I(n_{bc}^1 \oplus K_{bc})$$

Second rule:

$$I(z) \Rightarrow I(z \oplus n_{ab}^2 \oplus K_{ab}) \qquad I(z) \Rightarrow I(z \oplus n_{ba}^2 \oplus K_{ab})$$
$$I(z) \Rightarrow I(z \oplus n_{ac}^2 \oplus K_{ac}) \qquad I(z) \Rightarrow I(z \oplus n_{ca}^2 \oplus K_{ac})$$
$$I(z) \Rightarrow I(z \oplus n_{bc}^2 \oplus K_{bc}) \qquad I(z) \Rightarrow I(z \oplus n_{cb}^2 \oplus K_{bc})$$

Third rule:

$$I(z) \Rightarrow I(z \oplus n_{ab}^1 \oplus S_{ab}) \qquad I(z) \Rightarrow I(z \oplus n_{ba}^1 \oplus S_{ba})$$
$$I(z) \Rightarrow I(z \oplus n_{ac}^1 \oplus S_{ac}) \qquad I(z) \Rightarrow I(z \oplus n_{ca}^1 \oplus S_{ca})$$
$$I(z) \Rightarrow I(z \oplus n_{bc}^1 \oplus S_{bc}) \qquad I(z) \Rightarrow I(z \oplus n_{cb}^1 \oplus S_{cb})$$

Fig. 3. Rules representing our protocol for three participants a, b and c.

$$\Rightarrow I(K_{ac}) \quad \text{The intruder knows all keys of compro-}$$
$$\Rightarrow I(K_{bc}) \quad \text{mised agents.}$$

$$I(x), I(y) \Rightarrow I(x \oplus y) \quad \begin{array}{l}\text{The intruder may apply the \textbf{xor} function}\\ \text{to any messages.}\end{array}$$

$$I(x), I(y) \Rightarrow I(\{x\}_y) \quad \begin{array}{l}\text{The intruder can encrypt a known message}\\ \text{with a known key.}\end{array}$$

$$I(\{x\}_y), I(y) \Rightarrow I(x) \quad \begin{array}{l}\text{The intruder can retrieve the clear text of}\\ \text{a message encrypted with a known key.}\end{array}$$

Fig. 4. Some of the clauses defining I.

It remains to describe the intruder capabilities: he sees every message sent through the network and may send new messages. He knows private keys of dishonest agents. In addition, he is able to compose and decompose messages. Intruder capabilities can be encoded by clauses of $\mathcal{C}^\oplus$. In particular, the ability of the intruder to apply the **xor** function is described by the clause $\neg I(x) \vee \neg I(y) \vee I(x \oplus y)$. Some of the clauses are described Fig. 4. Actually, only the first three rules are relevant for our example since we only use the $\oplus$ symbol.

Now, we want to prove that S_{ab} remains unknown to the intruder when a and b are honest. Such a property may be expressed by the clause: $\phi_0 \stackrel{\text{def}}{=} \neg I(S_{ab})$. Let $\mathcal{C}_P$ be the clauses described in Fig. 3 and Fig. 4. The protocol satisfies our security property if and only if $\mathcal{C}_P \cup \{\phi_0\}$ is satisfiable: we are back to a satisfiability problem. Such a reduction actually works for any purely negative security property [13].

As a consequence, the security of our abstracted protocol can be decided by our decision procedure. And the answer is yes: our protocol preserves secrecy !

Proposition 3. *The set of clauses representing our protocol together with the security property $\mathcal{C}_P \cup \{\phi_0\}$ is satisfiable.*

Proof. We split the set of constants Γ into the set of (supposedly) secret data Γ_1 and known data Γ_2: $\Gamma_1 = \{n_{ab}^1, n_{ba}^1, n_{ab}^2, n_{ba}^2, S_{ab}, S_{ba}, K_{ab}\}$ and $\Gamma_2 = \Gamma \backslash \Gamma_1$. Jumping to the fixed point, we consider a set of terms T (resp. T') such that an even (resp. odd) number of "secrets" data is xored:

$$T = \{u_1 \oplus \cdots \oplus u_n \oplus t_1 \oplus \cdots \oplus t_k \mid n \text{ is even}, u_i \in \Gamma_1, t_j \in \Gamma_2, u_i, t_j \text{ distinct}\}.$$

Then we consider the following set of clauses:

$$S^* \overset{\text{def}}{=} \{I(m) \mid m \in T\} \cup \{\neg I(z \oplus m_1) \vee I(z \oplus m_2) \mid m_1 \oplus m_2 \in T\}$$
$$\cup \{\neg I(m_1) \vee I(m_2) \mid m_1 \oplus m_2 \in T\} \cup \{\neg I(m) \mid m \in T'\}.$$

S^* contains $\mathcal{C}_P \cup \{\phi_0\}$, thus it is sufficient to prove that S^* is satisfiable (actually S^* is obtained from $\mathcal{C}_P \cup \{\phi_0\}$ by applying our deduction rules thus S^* is satisfiable iff $\mathcal{C}_P \cup \{\phi_0\}$ is satisfiable). S^* is saturated by our inference rules (see [12] for more details). Applying theorem 2, since $\perp \notin S^*$, it follows that $\mathcal{C}_P \cup \{\phi_0\}$ is satisfiable. $\qquad \square$

Since the abstraction is an upper approximation, the above proposition shows that the protocol is secure.

Note: Instead of using the reduction result of [13], we could have introduced an arbitrary number of participants by adding new variables. For example, the second rule of our protocol could be represented by the clause:

$$A(x), A(y), I(z) \Rightarrow I(z \oplus n_2(x, y) \oplus K(x, y)),$$

where x nd y are variables representing agents. Such a clause does not belong to our class $\mathcal{C}^{\oplus}$ but we could extend $\mathcal{C}^{\oplus}$ to clauses with *basic variables* (like in [9]), representing restricted data like agents or nonces. We believe that the resulting class, which extends $\mathcal{C}^{\oplus}$, is still decidable.

5   Conclusion and Perspectives

We have proved the decidability of a new first-order logic fragment, including some algebraic properties. This result applies to the automatic verification of cryptographic protocols.

There are few extensions to be considered: first, adding basic variables, as explained in the above note would be useful for the application. On the theoretical side, there is no reason to restrict each clause of S_0 to use a single predicate symbol: it should be possible to allow clauses such as $\neg P_1(x) \vee \neg P_2(y) \vee P_3(x \oplus y)$ where P_1, P_2, P_3 are distinct. We didn't consider this extension here for sake of simplicity and because we do not need it in the application. Yet another natural extesion would be to consider the class $\mathcal{C}$, adding the algebraic properties of $\oplus$. This seems to be related to the above extension.

Finally, the complexity of the decision result looks prohibitive. Before implementing the decision procedure, we need some refinements. First, we actually use a refinement of the ordering used in section 3: we established a general termination result, however, completeness holds for any ordering which is narrow liftable and compatible with the ordering used in the completeness proof on the ground level.

A last question is of course to get similar results for other equational theories. In this paper, however, we heavily rely on the particular theory of xor.

References

1. R. Amadio and W. Charatonik. On name generation and set-based analysis in the dolev-yao model. In *Proc. CONCUR 02*, volume 1877 of *LNCS*, pages 380–394. Springer-Verlag, 2002.
2. L. Bachmair and H. Ganzinger. Resolution theorem proving. In A. Robinson and A. Voronkov, editors, *Handbook of Automated Reasoning*, volume 1, chapter 2, pages 19–100. North Holland, 2001.
3. B. Blanchet. Abstracting Cryptographic Protocols by Prolog Rules (invited +talk). In P. Cousot, editor, *8th International Static Analysis Symposium (SAS'2001)*, volume 2126 of *LNCS*, pages 433–436, Paris, France, July 2001. Springer Verlag.
4. D. Bolignano. Towards the mechanization of cryptographic protocol verificatio. In *9th. Conf. on Computer Aided Verification*, volume 1254 of *LNCS*, 1997.
5. L. Bozga, Y. Lakhnech, and M. Périn. Abstract interpretation for secrecy using patterns. In *Proc. TACAS*, LNCS, 2003. To appear.
6. Y. Chevalier, R. Kuester, M. Rusinowitch, and M. Turuani. An np decision procedure for protocol insecurity with xor. In *IEEE Logic in Comp. Science, to appear*, 2003.
7. J. Clark and J. Jacob. A survey of authentication protocol literature: Version, 1997.
8. E. Cohen. TAPS: A first-order verifier for cryptographic protocols. In *13th Computer Security Foundations Workshop (CSFW'00)*. IEEE Computer Society Press, 2000.
9. H. Comon and V. Cortier. Tree automata with one memory, set constraints and cryptographic protocols. Technical Report LSV-01-13, LSV, 2001. To appear in TCS.
10. H. Comon, V. Cortier, and J. Mitchell. Tree automata with memory, set constraints and ping pong protocols. In *Proc. ICALP 2001*, volume 2076 of *LNCS*. Springer Verlag, July 2001.
11. H. Comon, M. Dauchet, R. Gilleron, F. Jacquemard, D. Lugiez, S. Tison, and M. Tommasi. Tree automata techniques and applications. Available on: http://www.grappa.univ-lille3.fr/tata, 2002.
12. H. Comon-Lundh and V. Cortier. New decidability results for fragments of first-order logic and application to cryptographic protocols. Technical Report LSV-03-3, LSV, ENS de Cachan, Cachan, France, January 2003. 30 pages.
13. H. Comon-Lundh and V. Cortier. Security properties: two agents are sufficient. In *Proc. European Symposium on Programming*, volume 2618 of *LNCS*, pages 99–113. Springer Verlag, 2003.
14. H. Comon-Lundh and V. Shmatikov. Intruder deductions, constraint solving and insecurity decision in presence of exclusive or. In *Proc. IEEE Logic in Comp. Science, to appear*, 2003.

15. N. Dershowitz. Rewriting. In A. Robinson and A. Voronkov, editors, *Handbook of Automated Reasoning*, volume 1, chapter 9. North Holland, 2001.

16. N. Durgin, P. Lincoln, J. Mitchell, and A. Scedrov. Undecidability of bounded security protocols. In *Proc. Workshop on formal methods in security protocols*, 1999.

17. F. T. Fabrega, J. Herzog, and J. Guttman. Strand spaces: Proving security protocol correct. *Journal of Computer Security*, 7:191–230, 1999.

18. C. Fermuller, A. Leitsch, U. Hustadt, and T. Tamet. Resolution decision procedure. In A. Robinson and A. Voronkov, editors, *Handbook of Automated Reasoning*, volume 2, chapter 25, pages 1793–1849. North Holland, 2001.

19. J. Goubault-Larrecq and I. Mackie. *Proof Theory and Automated Deduction*, volume 6 of Applied Logic Series. Kluwer Academic, 1997.

20. R. Kowalski and P. Hayes. Semantic trees in automated theorem proving. In B. Meltzer and D. Michie, editors, *Machine Intelligence 4*, pages 87–101. Edinburgh University Press, 1969.

21. G. Lowe. Breaking and fixing the needham-schroeder public-key protocol using fdr. In Margaria and Steffen, editors, *Tools and Algorithms for the Construction and Analysis of Systems (TACAS)*, volume 1055 of *LNCS*, pages 147–166, 1996.

22. D. McAllester. Automatic recognition of tractability in inference relations. *J. ACM*, 40(2):284–303, 1993.

23. P. Narendran, Q. Guo, and D. Wolfram. Unification and matching modulo nilpotence. In *Proc. CADE-13*, volume 1104 of *LNCS*, pages 261–274, 1996.

24. L. Paulson. Mechanized proofs for a recursive authentication protocol. In *Proc. 10th IEEE Computer Security Foundations Workshop*, pages 84–95, 1997.

25. L. C. Paulson. The Inductive Approach to Verifying Cryptographic Protocols. *Journal of Computer Security*, 6(1):85–128, 1998.

26. M. Rusinowitch and M. Turuani. Protocol insecurity with finite number of sessions is NP-complete. In *14th IEEE Computer Security Foundations Workshop*, 2001.

27. P. Ryan and S. Schneider. An attack on a recursive authentication protocol: A cautionary tale. *Information Processing Letters*, 65(1):7–10, 1998.

28. C. Weidenbach. Towards an automatic analysis of security protocols in first-order logic. In H. Ganzinger, editor, *Proc. 16th Conference on Automated Deduction*, volume 1632 of *LNCS*, pages 314–328, 1999.

29. C. Weidenbach. Combining superposition, sorts and splitting. In A. Robinson and A. Voronkov, editors, *Handbook of Automated Reasoning*, volume 2, chapter 27. North Holland, 2001.

An E-unification Algorithm for Analyzing
Protocols That Use Modular Exponentiation

Deepak Kapur[1,*], Paliath Narendran[2,**], and Lida Wang[2,***]

[1] Department of Computer Science, University of New Mexico,
Albuquerque, NM 87131 USA,
kapur@cs.unm.edu
[2] Department of Computer Science, SUNY at Albany,
Albany, NY 12222 USA,
dran@cs.albany.edu, lidawang@cs.albany.edu

Abstract. Modular multiplication and exponentiation are common operations in modern cryptography. Unification problems with respect to some equational theories that these operations satisfy are investigated. Two different but related equational theories are analyzed. A unification algorithm is given for one of the theories which relies on solving syzygies over multivariate integral polynomials with noncommuting indeterminates. For the other theory, in which the distributivity property of exponentiation over multiplication is assumed, the unifiability problem is shown to be undecidable by adapting a construction developed by one of the authors to reduce Hilbert's 10th problem to the solvability problem for linear equations over semi-rings. A new algorithm for computing strong Gröbner bases of right ideals over the polynomial ring $Z<X_1, \ldots, X_n>$ is proposed; unlike earlier algorithms proposed by Baader as well as by Madlener and Reinert which work only for right admissible term orderings with the boundedness property, this algorithm works for *any* right admissible term ordering. The algorithms for some of these unification problems are expected to be integrated into Naval Research Lab.'s Protocol Analyzer (NPA), a tool developed by Catherine Meadows, which has been successfully used to analyze cryptographic protocols, particularly emerging standards such as the Internet Engineering Task Force's (IETF) Internet Key Exchange [11] and Group Domain of Interpretation [12] protocols. Techniques from several different fields – particularly symbolic computation (ideal theory and Gröebner basis algorithms) and unification theory — are thus used to address problems arising in state-based cryptographic protocol analysis.

* Research supported in part by the NSF grant nos. CCR-0098114 and CDA-9503064, the ONR grant no. N00014-01-1-0429, and a grant from the Computer Science Research Institute at Sandia National Labs.
** Research supported in part by NSF grant no. CCR-0098095 and ONR grant no. N00014-01-1-0430.
*** Research supported in part by NSF grant no. CCR-0098095.

R. Nieuwenhuis (Ed.): RTA 2003, LNCS 2706, pp. 165–179, 2003.
© Springer-Verlag Berlin Heidelberg 2003

1   Introduction

Modular arithmetic is the mainstay of many modern cryptographic algorithms. Arithmetical operations such as modular multiplication and exponentiation are part of several algorithms. For instance, the RSA and El Gamal algorithms use modular exponentiation for encryption/decryption, whereas the Diffie-Hellman and group Diffie-Hellman algorithms use it for key exchange. Abstracting equational properties of modular exponentiation and designing equational unification algorithms for the resulting theories for use in protocol analysis was initiated in [13]. Building on the work reported in [7], we have so far explored four related unification theories involving modular multiplication. These are described below.

The motivation for studying these equational theories comes from building a tool for analyzing authentication protocols against possible attack. The proposed unification algorithms are planned to be integrated into a software tool called the *NRL Protocol Analyzer* (*NPA*) developed by Catherine Meadows at the Naval Research Laboratory [10]. This tool employs a state-based approach for analyzing attacks on an authentication protocol, and has been used effectively to analyze, e.g., the Internet Engineering Task Force's (IETF) Internet Key Exchange [11], Group Domain of Interpretation [12] protocols, demonstrate known integrity flaws in the Encapsulating Security Protocol [19] (an Internet Standard), and discover a new attack on the Simmons Selective Broadcast Protocol [18]. Currently, the tool uses simple unification (over the empty theory) and a *narrowing* procedure for state exploration. Narrowing is used to find solutions with respect to (henceforth, abbreviated as *wrt*) a set of terminating rewrite rules capturing the semantics of primitive operations used in a protocol, thus simulating unification wrt the associated equational theory. However, if these primitive operations have the associativity and commutativity properties, which is often the case, then narrowing either does not work or is extremely inefficient.

To review the various equational theories discussed in this paper, consider the following set of axioms relating modular multiplication with modular exponentiation:

$$x \cdot (y \cdot z) = (x \cdot y) \cdot z \qquad A$$
$$x \cdot y = y \cdot x \qquad C$$
$$x \cdot 1 = x \qquad U$$
$$x \cdot x^{-1} = 1 \qquad Inv$$
$$x^1 = x \qquad Exp1$$
$$1^x = 1 \qquad Exp2$$
$$(x \cdot y)^z = (x^z) \cdot (y^z) \qquad Exp3$$
$$(x^y)^z = (x^z)^y \qquad Exp4$$
$$(x^y)^z = x^{y \circ z} \qquad Exp5$$
$$x \circ (y \circ z) = (x \circ y) \circ z \qquad A'$$
$$x \circ y = y \circ x \qquad C'$$
$$x \circ 1 = x \qquad U'$$

The first four equations (A, C, U, Inv) characterize an Abelian group with $\cdot$ representing multiplication modulo a prime number p; for brevity, this axiomatization is referred by AG. The last three equations characterize an Abelian monoid with ∘ standing for multiplication modulo $p-1$. Operators · and ∘ share the unit 1. Modular exponentiation is denoted by ^; $x\,\hat{}\,y$ is also written as x^y. Note also that $Exp5$ implies a 'kind of' associativity for ∘, since

$$x^{(u\circ(v\circ w))} =_{Exp5} ((x^u)^v)^w =_{Exp5} x^{((u\circ v)\circ w)}.$$

We have investigated various theories that are obtained by keeping AG fixed and varying the theories that ∘ satisfies. Our main results so far are:

(i) The unification problem for the equational theory consisting of AG and axioms $(Exp1, Exp2, Exp3)$ is decidable; this theory is denoted as $\mathcal{E}_3$. This theory is a subset of the equational theories in (ii) and (iii) below. A unification algorithm for this problem is given by reducing it to that of finding constrained solutions of linear equations over $Z<X_1, \ldots, X_n>$, an algebraic structure similar to a polynomial ring over the integers, except that the indeterminates do not commute (i.e., the multiplication operation on the terms is not commutative — this structure is often called a *monoid semiring*). This latter problem is solved by computing *strong* Gröbner bases[1] of right ideals over $Z<X_1, \ldots, X_n>$. A new algorithm for computing strong Gröbner bases for right ideals over $Z<X_1, \ldots, X_n>$ is given; in contrast to the earlier algorithms proposed by Baader [1] for weak Gröbner bases and by Madlener and Reinert [9] for strong Gröbner bases assuming right admissible orderings with the *boundedness property*[2], the proposed algorithm computes strong Gröbner bases using any right admissible ordering.

Techniques employed here for solving linear equations over $Z<X_1, \ldots, X_n>$ are novel since the variables of the equations being solved have additional constraints of the form that certain indeterminates cannot appear in their solutions (these constraints are related to the occur check condition in simple unification, i.e., over the empty theory[3]). Such constraints are ensured by defining somewhat *unusual* kinds of admissible term orderings reflecting such constraints. These term orderings are very different from usual term orderings typically used in the literature for computing Gröbner bases of ideals, such as total degree and lexicographic, pure lexicographic, reverse lexicographic as well as block orderings.

(ii) When axiom $Exp4$ is added to $\mathcal{E}_3$, the unification problem for the extended equational theory remains decidable, as shown in [7]; we will denote this

---

[1] A *weak* Gröbner basis of a (right) ideal simplifies polynomials in the (right) ideal to 0; however, polynomials equivalent with respect to the (right) ideal need not be simplified by the weak Gröbner basis to the *same* canonical form. In contrast, a *strong* Gröbner basis of a (right) ideal simplifies every polynomial to a unique canonical form such that equivalent polynomials with respect to the (right) ideal have the same canonical form; the canonical form of every polynomial in the (right) ideal is 0; see [6,1,9] for more details.

[2] An ordering has the boundedness property if and only if for every element, there are only finitely many elements smaller than the element in the ordering.

[3] and also the *linear constant restrictions* introduced by Baader and Schulz [3]

theory by $\mathcal{E}_{3,4}$. The unification algorithm uses an algorithm for computing strong Gröbner bases of polynomial ideals in $Z[x_1, \cdots, x_n]$ developed by one of the authors in 1984 [6]. Linear equations are solved under constraints in a way similar to (i) above. For details, the reader can refer to [7].

(iii) If the equational theory in (i) is extended by adding axioms $Exp5$, A', C' and U' instead of $Exp4$, then the unification problem for this equational theory, denoted by $\mathcal{E}_{3,5}$, is undecidable. (It is easy to see that $Exp4$ follows from C' and $Exp5$, thus implying that $Exp5$ is strictly stronger than $Exp4$ in this context.) The undecidability is mainly due to the distributivity property since if the distributivity axiom $Exp3$ is dropped from this equational theory—thus just keeping $Exp5$—then the unifiability problem is NP-complete [13].

The undecidability proof adapts an earlier proof showing the undecidability of the unification problem over the equational theory of isomorphisms over *Cartesian Closed Categories* developed by one of the authors [15]. Details can be found in [7].

(iv) If the equational theory in (i) is extended by adding axioms $Exp5$, A' and U' (in other words, $\cdot$ forms an Abelian group, whereas $\circ$ forms a *monoid*), denoted by $\mathcal{E}'_{3,5}$, the unification problem is still undecidable. This is shown by reducing Hilbert's tenth problem to the unification problem by adapting a construction developed by one of the authors [14] for showing undecidability of solving linear equations over polynomial semirings. In Section 2, we provide a sketch highlighting the main point; details can be found in [8].

The result mentioned in (ii) above was obtained earlier and is reported in [7] with detailed proofs. The undecidability result mentioned in (iii) is similar to the undecidability result reported in [7].

The paper thus brings together techniques from several different fields, particularly symbolic computation (ideal theory and Gröbner basis algorithms) and unification theory, to address problems arising in state-based cryptographic protocol analysis.

We state in the next section that unifiability for $\mathcal{E}'_{3,5}$ is undecidable. The rest of the paper focuses on the decidability of the unifiability check for $\mathcal{E}_3$. Section 3 relates unification over $\mathcal{E}_3$ to unification over $AGnH$ with an occur-check like condition. Section 4 discusses an algorithm for solving the unification problem over $AGnH$ with an occur-check-like condition. The algorithm uses a strong Gröbner basis algorithm to solve linear equations over a monoid semiring $Z<X_1, \ldots, X_n>$. To ensure that the solution to the unification problem satisfy the occur-check like condition, unusual term orderings capturing this constraint are defined. The Gröbner basis algorithm is discussed in Section 5. It is shown that the algorithm computes a Gröbner basis for a right ideal using arbitrary right admissible term orderings including those which do not have the boundedness property. This algorithm is new since earlier algorithms worked only for admissible term orderings satisfying the boundedness property.

2   Undecidability of Unification over $\mathcal{E}'_{3,5}$

We reduce Hilbert's tenth problem to it by simulating numbers as well as multiplication over numbers. In the following, for a natural number k, $\bigcirc_k(b)$ denotes $\underbrace{b \circ b \ldots \circ b}_{k}$.

Theorem 1. *Unification over $\mathcal{E}'_{3,5}$ is undecidable.*

Proof Sketch: The following equations

$$
\begin{array}{ll}
1.\ x_1{}^b \cdot a =^? x_1 \cdot a^{\bigcirc_{k_1}(b)} & 6.\ z_2{}^c \cdot v_2 =^? y_2 \cdot z_2 \\
2.\ x_2{}^c \cdot a =^? x_2 \cdot a^{\bigcirc_{k_2}(c)} & 7.\qquad s_1 =^? v_2 \cdot v_2 \\
3.\ y_1{}^b \cdot v_1 =^? x_1 \cdot y_1 & 8.\qquad s_2 =^? s_1 \cdot v_1 \\
4.\ y_2{}^c \cdot v_1 =^? x_2 \cdot y_2 & 9.\ x_3{}^b \cdot a =^? x_3 \cdot a^{w_2} \\
5.\ z_1{}^b \cdot v_2 =^? y_1 \cdot z_1 & 10.\ y_3{}^b \cdot s_2 =^? x_3 \cdot y_3,
\end{array}
$$

force w_2 to be $\bigcirc_{k_1^2}(b)$, thus simulating squaring. Using the construction proposed in [14] with the above way of encoding squaring of numbers, Hilbert's tenth problem can be formulated as a unification problem in $\mathcal{E}'_{3,5}$. For a detailed proof, please refer to [8].

3   Relating Unification over $\mathcal{E}_3$ to Unification over $AGnH$

We consider the theory $\mathcal{E}_3$ consisting of AG and axioms $Exp1$, $Exp2$ and $Exp3$. We show that the equational unification problem for $\mathcal{E}_3$ is equivalent to the unification problem wrt the theory of Abelian groups with *noncommuting* homomorphisms, denoted by $AGnH$, but with an additional constraint. (The n stands for the number of homomorphisms.)

It is shown in [2] that the theory $AGnH$ is *unitary* with respect to unification without constants and it is also unitary with respect to unification with constants[4]. In Section 5 of [1], Baader showed that the unification problem of $AGnH$ reduces to solving linear equations over the polynomial ring $Z<h_1, \ldots, h_n>$ where $h_1, \ldots, h_n$ are the noncommuting homomorphisms of $AGnH$, treated as indeterminates in the polynomial ring. He gave a unification algorithm for $AGnH$, which uses a weak Gröbner basis of a right ideal over $Z<h_1, \ldots, h_n>$ for solving linear equations; as a result, Baader also proposed an algorithm for computing a weak Gröbner basis. We generalize Baader's algorithm by adding an additional key step to ensure that a given *linear constraint* (capturing an occur-check like condition) is satisfied by the unifier, so as to apply it to the equational unification problem for $\mathcal{E}_3$. This generalization needs a strong Gröbner basis of a right ideal over $Z<h_1, \ldots, h_n>$. In a later section, we develop a new algorithm for computing a strong Gröbner basis of a right ideal over $Z<h_1, \ldots, h_n>$.

---

[4] A theory is unitary if a minimal complete set of unifiers always exists and its cardinality is at most one.

3.1   Unification over $\mathcal{E}_3$ as a Combination of Theories

Let $\Sigma = \{\cdot, ^{-1}, 1, \hat{\ }\}$, the signature of $\mathcal{E}_3$.

Definition 1. *An $\mathcal{E}_3$-unification problem S over Σ is called an AG-unification problem if each equation in S is of the form $x =^? t$, where x is a variable and t is a term over the signature of AG.*

Definition 2. *An $\mathcal{E}_3$-unification problem S on Σ is called an exponent $\mathcal{E}_3$-unification problem, abbreviated as EXP, if every equation in S is of the form $x =^? y^z$, where x and y are variables and z is a variable or a free constant. Also if z is a variable, z is called an* exponent variable; *otherwise, it is called an* exponent constant.

Definition 3. *An $\mathcal{E}_3$-unification problem S on Σ is called a* simple $\mathcal{E}_3$-unification problem *if $S = S_1 \bigcup S_2$, where S_1 is an AG-unification problem and S_2 is an exponent $\mathcal{E}_3$-unification problem.*

It is easy to see that using abstraction, any $\mathcal{E}_3$-unification problem can be transformed into a simple $\mathcal{E}_3$-unification problem. For example, consider $S = \{w =^? (x^{(y^{u \cdot v})^{-1} \cdot z^{u' \cdot v'}})^{-1}\}$. Using abstractions, S is transformed to S':

$$\{ \ 1.\ w =^? z_1^{-1}, \quad 2.\ z_1 =^? x^{z_2}, \quad 3.\ z_2 =^? z_3^{-1} \cdot z_4, \quad 4.\ z_3 =^? y^{z_5},$$
$$5.\ z_5 =^? u \cdot v, \quad 6.\ z_4 =^? z^{z_6}, \quad 7.\ z_6 =^? u' \cdot v' \ \},$$

where $z_1, z_2, z_3, z_4, z_5, z_6$ are new variables introduced for alien subterms in S.

3.2   Relating $AG + EXP$ to $AGnH$

Given a simple $\mathcal{E}_3$-unification problem S, for each equation of the form $x =^? y^w$ in S, we transform it into $x =^? h_w(y)$ where h_w is a homomorphism corresponding to the symbol w. Let $\mathcal{H}(S)$ denote the set of all homomorphisms introduced in this way, and, let $\Sigma_h = \{\cdot, ^{-1}, 1\} \cup \mathcal{H}(S)$. We call the transformed $AGnH$ problem a *h-image* of S.

For the above example, its *h-image* T is:

$$\{ \ 1.\ w =^? z_1^{-1}, \quad 2.\ z_1 =^? h_{z_2}(x), \quad 3.\ z_2 =^? z_3^{-1} \cdot z_4, \quad 4.\ z_3 =^? h_{z_5}(y),$$
$$5.\ z_5 =^? u \cdot v, \quad 6.\ z_4 =^? h_{z_6}(z), \quad 7.\ z_6 =^? u' \cdot v' \ \},$$

It is not hard to see that the unifiability of T wrt $AGnH$ does not necessarily imply that the original problem S has a unifier wrt $\mathcal{E}_3$. For instance, the problem $\{x =^? a^x\}$ has no unifier wrt $\mathcal{E}_3$, whereas its h-image $\{x =^? h_x(a)\}$, when simply taken as a unification problem wrt $AGnH$ (with $n = 1$) is solvable. Thus something like an extended occur check must be enforced; this is done by solving the unifiability problem of T wrt $AGnH$ subject to *linear* constraints (including) $x \succ h_x$ for every homomorphism $h_x \in \mathcal{H}(S)$, i.e., a unifier θ of T should satisfy the condition that for every $x \in Var(T)$, $\theta(x)$ *does not contain* any occurrence of h_x, where $Var(T)$ denotes the set of all variables in T.

Definition 4. *Given a simple $\mathcal{E}_3$-unification problem S and its h-image T wrt $AGnH$, a linear constraint C is a total ordering $\succ_C$ over $Var(T) \cup \mathcal{H}(S)$ such that $x \succ_C h_x$ for all exponent variables x in S.*

Definition 5. *A substitution β whose domain is $Var(T)$, is said to satisfy a linear constraint C if and only if the following holds: for every $x \in Var(T)$, $\beta(x)$ does not contain any of the function symbols below x in C. In other words, if $x \succ_C h_y$, then $\beta(x)$ does not contain any occurrence of h_y.*

Definition 6. *A unifier θ for a $\mathcal{E}_3$-unification problem S is said to be a discriminating unifier if and only if the following hold for all variables in $Var(S)$:*

1. *$\theta(u) \neq_{\mathcal{E}_3} 1$ for all u.*
2. *$\theta(v) =_{\mathcal{E}_3} \theta(w)$ iff $v = w$.*

   Theorems 2 and 3 below relate the unification problem S wrt $\mathcal{E}_3$ to its h-image T wrt $AGnH$.

Theorem 2. *Given a simple $\mathcal{E}_3$-unification problem S and its h-image T wrt $AGnH$, if S has a discriminating unifier, then T is unifiable. Furthermore, there is a linear constraint C that the unifier of T satisfies.*

A detailed proof of this theorem is discussed in [8].

Theorem 3. *Given a simple $\mathcal{E}_3$-unification problem S and its h-image T wrt $AGnH$, if T has a solution which satisfies a linear constraint, then S is solvable.*

Proof. Consider all exponent equations $\{x_{u_1} =^? x_{v_1}{}^{x_{w_1}}, \ldots, x_{u_k} =^? x_{v_k}{}^{x_{w_k}}\}$ in S; similarly, also consider their corresponding equations $\{x_{u_1} =^? h_{x_{w_1}}(x_{v_1}), \ldots, x_{u_k} =^? h_{x_{w_k}}(x_{v_k})\}$ in the h-image T for S.

Let β be a ground unifier of T that satisfies a linear constraint C. From C, we can get a subconstraint C' on variables in $Var(T)$. Let $Var(T) = \{x_1, \ldots, x_n\}$. Assume without loss of generality that $C' = x_n \succ_C \cdots \succ_C x_i \succ_C \cdots \succ_C x_1$. Now we will use induction on C' to form θ. As the basis step, consider the first variable x_n in C'. Since x_n is the first variable, $\beta(x_n)$ should not contain any item below x_n in C, implying that $\beta(x_n)$ is composed of constants. Define $\theta(x_n) = \beta(x_n)$.

Assume that $\theta(x_{j'})$ $(j \leq j' \leq n)$ is already defined. For variable x_{j-1}, the following cases arise:

1. $\beta(x_{j-1})$ is composed of constants. In this case, define $\theta(x_{j-1}) = \beta(x_{j-1})$.
2. $\beta(x_{j-1})$ is composed of constants and some $h_{x_{w_i}}$ $(1 \leq i \leq n)$ where each $h_{x_{w_i}} \succ_C x_{j-1}$. Since $x_{w_i} \succ_C h_{x_{w_i}}$, $x_{w_i} \succ_C h_{x_{w_i}} \succ_C x_{j-1}$. By the induction hypothesis, all these $\theta(x_{w_i})$ are already defined. Therefore, we can define $\theta(x_{j-1}) = repp\,(\beta(x_{j-1}))$ where the function $repp$ is defined as:

$repp(a) = a$, where a is a constant on Σ_h.

$repp(A \cdot B) = repp(A) \cdot repp(B)$, where A, B are terms on Σ_h.

$repp(h_{x_{w_i}}(A)) = repp(A)^{\theta(x_{w_i})}$, where A is a term on Σ_h.

It can be shown that $s =_{AGnH} t$ iff $repp(s) =_{\mathcal{E}_3} repp(t)$. Therefore, $repp(\beta(x_{u_i}))$ $=_{\mathcal{E}_3} repp(h_{x_{w_i}}(\beta(x_{v_i})))$ for all $1 \leq i \leq n$. So $\theta(x_{u_i}) =_{\mathcal{E}_3} (\theta(x_{v_i}))^{\theta(x_{w_i})}$ for all $1 \leq i \leq n$. Thus θ is a solution for S. $\square$

In the next section, we generalize Baader's algorithm for unifiability check for $AGnH$ to work with a linear constraint.

4   Unification over $AGnH$ with a Linear Constraint

The unifiers of a unification problem wrt $AGnH$, where $h_1, \ldots, h_n$ are the non-commuting homomorphisms, correspond to the solutions of (nonhomogeneous) linear equations over the polynomial ring $Z<h_1, \ldots, h_n>$ with $h_1, \ldots, h_n$ as indeterminates in the polynomial ring. The set of solutions of a homogeneous equation $p_1 X_1 + \ldots + p_k X_k = 0$, where $p_1, \ldots, p_k \in Z<h_1, \ldots, h_n>$ and $X_1, \ldots, X_k$ are variables, is a finitely generated right $Z<h_1, \ldots, h_n>$-semimodule. The nonhomogeneous equation $p_1 X_1 + \ldots + p_k X_k = p_0$ has a solution iff p_0 is a member of the right ideal generated by $p_1, \ldots, p_k$. And, the membership problem for finitely generated right ideals is decidable.

Let NHE be a set of linear equations $\{p_{11}X_1 + \cdots + p_{1k}X_k = p_1,$

$$\vdots \qquad \qquad \vdots$$

$$p_{m1}X_1 + \cdots + p_{mk}X_k = p_m\}$$

where $p_{11}, \cdots, p_{1k}, \cdots, p_{m1}, \cdots, p_{mk}, p_1, \cdots, p_m$ are in $Z<h_1, \ldots, h_n>$.

Baader [1] gave an algorithm for finding a solution for such nonhomogeneous linear equations. In his algorithm, he first computes a *weak Gröbner basis* G for a polynomial right ideal, then computes a right syzygy basis for homogeneous linear equations, and finally, a particular solution for the nonhomogeneous equations by using G. The algorithm is nontrivial; we will not discuss the details here but suggest the reader to refer to [1] for details. Let $\pi = (q_1, \ldots, q_k)$, where $\pi(X_i) = q_i$, be a particular solution for the above set NHE of nonhomogeneous equations obtained, for instance, using Baader's algorithm.

Let SB denote a right syzygy basis $\{(q_{11}, \cdots, q_{1k}), \ldots, (q_{w1}, \cdots, q_{wk})\}$ for the set HE of the homogeneous equations

$$\{p_{11}X_1 + \cdots + p_{1k}X_k = 0,$$

$$\vdots \qquad \qquad \vdots$$

$$p_{m1}X_1 + \cdots + p_{mk}X_k = 0\}.$$

Proposition 1. $\pi' = (q'_1, \ldots, q'_k)$ *is equivalent to π with respect to SB and hence is also a particular solution iff there exist multipliers $b_1, \cdots, b_w$ such that $q_i - q'_i = q_{1i}b_1 + \cdots + q_{wi}b_w$ for each $1 \le i \le k$.*

4.1 Solutions Satisfying a Linear Constraint

We discuss how a solution satisfying a linear constraint C, if any, is searched for among all solutions of NHE.

Let $z_1, \ldots, z_k$ be new indeterminates. Consider the following set MSB of polynomials in $Z{<}h_1, \ldots, h_n, z_1, \ldots, z_k{>}$ constructed from SB above:

$$\{z_1\, q_{11} + \ldots + z_k\, q_{1k}, \ \ldots, \ z_1\, q_{w1} + \ldots + z_k\, q_{wk}\}.$$

Note that we only have to consider terms of the form $z_j\, \omega$, where $\omega \in (\mathcal{H}(S))^*$, where $\mathcal{H}(S) = \{h_1, \cdots, h_n\}$. Below, we define a right compatible ordering $\succ_t$ on such linear terms to capture linear constraint C in the following sense: if in a term $z_j\, \omega_j$, $h_i \succ_C X_j$ for each h_i appearing in ω_j, whereas in another term $z_{j'}\, \omega_{j'}$ we have some $h_{i'}$ in $\omega_{j'}$ such that $X_{j'} \succ_C h_{i'}$ then $z_j\, \omega_j \prec_t z_{j'}\, \omega_{j'}$.

The ordering $\succ_t$ is used to construct a strong Gröbner basis $GMSB$ for the set MSB of polynomials. The polynomial $\pi_p = z_1 q_1 + \ldots z_k q_k$ corresponding to the particular solution π above is then normalized using the Gröbner basis $GMSB$. Since the equivalence relation induced by MSB preserves solutions of NHE, the canonical (normal) form of π_p wrt $GMSB$ also corresponds to a particular solution π'. If this particular solution π' satisfies C (i.e., all terms are *good* in the sense defined in the next subsection), then we get a unifier for the unification problem wrt $AGnH$ satisfying C. If π' does not satisfy C, then the unification problem wrt $AGnH$ does not have a solution satisfying C, since a polynomial corresponding to a solution satisfying C must be smaller than the canonical form of π_p wrt $\succ_t$.

In the next subsection, we introduce how to define a term ordering $\succ_t$ that capture linear constraint C.

4.2 A Term Ordering Capturing Occur-Check Condition

Among all possible solutions of nonhomogeneous linear equations, to search a solution that satisfies a given linear constraint C, we define below a right admissible term ordering in a radically different way. This is in contrast to term orderings including total degree ordering, pure lexicographic ordering, reverse lexicographic ordering and block ordering, typically used in the literature on Gröbner basis computations.

A linear constraint C on an extended alphabet

$$\Delta = \{Y_0, \ldots, Y_l, a_1, \ldots, a_l\},$$

where $\{X_1, \ldots, X_k\} \subseteq \{Y_0, \ldots, Y_l\}$ and $\{h_1, \ldots, h_n\} \subseteq \{a_1, \ldots, a_l\}$, is written as:

$$Y_l \succ_C a_l \succ_C \ldots \succ_C a_2 \succ_C Y_1 \succ_C a_1 \succ_C Y_0.$$

In the above, upper case symbols are used for variables, and lower case symbols are used for constants. Extra symbols are introduced to ensure that between every two variables, there is a constant in the ordering.

Consider any two terms s, t in $Z<h_1, \ldots, h_n, z_1, \ldots, z_k>$ which are linear in $\{z_1, \ldots, z_k\}$. Define $s \succ_t t$ iff $nf(s\#) >' nf(t\#)$, where nf stands for the normal form wrt the reduction rules defined below to capture the linear constraint C. After defining nf and $>'$, we show that $\succ_t$ is right admissible.

The term $nf(s\#)$ is over the extended alphabet

$$\Delta_1 = \{a_1, \ldots, a_l, v_1, \ldots, v_l, a'_1, \ldots, a'_l, z_1, \ldots, z_k, z'_1, \ldots, z'_k\},$$

where the a_i's in Δ_1 are copies of the corresponding a_i's in Δ; further, corresponding to every X_i in Δ, we have z_i, z'_i in Δ_1.

Below, *legal* term, *good* term, and *bad* term are defined on $\{a_1, \ldots, a_l, z_1, \ldots, z_k\}$ based on whether the term satisfies the linear constraint C.

Definition 7. *A term* $s = z_i \, s_a$, *where* $s_a \in \{a_1, \cdots, a_l\}^*$ *is called a* legal *term (only such terms appear in the polynomials in the basis MSB and in the computation of a Gröbner basis from MSB).*
A legal term $s = z_i \, s_a$ *is called a* good *term if for each a_j appearing in s_a, $a_j \succ_C X_i$ in C, i.e., s_a satisfies the linear constraint C with respect to X_i.*
A legal term $s = z_i \, s_a$ *is called a* bad *term if there exists a_j appearing in s_a such that it is not the case that $a_j \succ_C X_i$ in C, i.e., s_a does not satisfy the linear constraint C with respect to X_i. (A legal term that is not good, is bad.)*

To capture the restrictions imposed by the linear constraint C on terms, we define the reduction rules on legal terms as:

$$
\begin{aligned}
z_i \, a_j &\to a'_i \, z_j &&\text{if } a_j \succ_C X_i. \\
z_i \, a_j &\to v_j \, a'_j \, z_i &&\text{if } X_i \succeq_C a_j. \\
z_i \, \# &\to z'_i. \\
a'_i \, z'_j &\to z'_j \, a'_i. \\
a'_i \, v_j &\to v_j \, a'_i. \\
v_i \, v_j &\to v_j \, v_i &&\text{if } X_i \succ_C X_j.
\end{aligned}
$$

The normal form of a legal term $z_i \, s_a$ wrt the above rules is either

(i) $z_i' \, s_{a'}$, where $s_{a'}$ is obtained by systematically replacing every a_j in s_a by a'_j. or

(ii) $s_v \, z_i' \, s_{a'}$, where $s_{a'}$ is obtained from s_a as in (i) and s_v is a string of v_j's.

To compare $nf(s\#)$ with $nf(t\#)$ using the above reduction rules, we define the following ordering $>'$ on symbols in Δ_1:

$$v_1 >' \ldots >' v_l >' z_k' >' \ldots >' z_1' >' a'_1 >' \ldots >' a'_l$$

This ordering is *extended* to terms over Δ_1 using pure lexicographic comparison.

Definition 8. *Given two terms $s = x_1 \ldots x_m$, $t = y_1 \ldots y_r$ on Δ_1 and the alphabet ordering on Δ_1 as defined above, we define $s >' t$ iff t is a prefix of s or there exists a k such that $x_k > y_k$ and $x_{k'} = y_{k'}$ for all $1 \le k' < k$. Given two legal terms s, t on Δ_1, $s \succ_t t$ iff $nf(s\#) >' nf(t\#)$.*

By the above reduction rules, the normal form of a bad term $\succ_t$ the normal form of a good term because only the normal form of a bad term has some v_j's which are $>'$ all a_i'''s and z_i'''s. The ordering clearly does not have the boundedness property.

Below, we sketch a proof that the ordering $\succ_t$ on legal terms in $Z<h_1, \cdots, h_n, z_1, \ldots, z_k>$ is right admissible.

For any $s \neq 1$, it is easy to see that $s \succ_t 1$. The following lemma ensures that if $s \succ_t t$, then for any u, $s\, u \succ_t t\, u$, by proving that $nf(s\#) >' nf(t\#)$ iff $nf(su\#) >' nf(tu\#)$.

Lemma 1. *Let Δ_1, $>'$, and nf be as defined above. Then $nf(s\#) >' nf(t\#)$ iff $nf(su\#) >' nf(tu\#)$ for all legal terms s, t, su and tu.*

Proof-sketch: (i) If $nf(s\#) >' nf(t\#)$ then $nf(su\#) >' nf(tu\#)$: To prove this, it is enough to prove that for any symbol a_p in Δ_1, $nf(sa_p\#) >' nf(ta_p\#)$ if $nf(s\#) >' nf(t\#)$.

Since $nf(s\#) >' nf(t\#)$, right multiplying by a_p on both s and t could contribute either a_p' or $v_p a_p'$ to the normal form of $sa_p\#$ and $ta_p\#$. The only hard case is when $nf(s\#)$ contains z_i and $nf(t\#)$ contains z_j such that $X_j \succ_C X_i$ (i.e., X_j is 'more constrained' than X_i) and in addition, $a_p \succ_C X_i$ and $a_p \not\succ_C X_j$. Right multiplying both sides by a_p will contribute a_p' to $nf(sa_p\#)$ and $v_p a_p'$ to $nf(ta_p\#)$. But since $nf(s\#) >' nf(t\#)$ there must be some a_q in s such that $a_q \not\succ_C X_i$ and the number of a_q's in s is larger than the number of a_q's in t. Thus $nf(s\#)$ includes v_q whose power in $nf(s\#)$ is larger than its power in $nf(t\#)$. But since $a_p \succ_C X_i$, $v_q >' v_p$. Thus $nf(sa_p\#) >' nf(ta_p\#)$ since the terms are compared lexicographically.

(ii) If $nf(su\#) >' nf(tu\#)$, then $nf(s\#) >' nf(t\#)$: This is easier since $>'$ is a total ordering on terms. For a detailed proof, see [8]   □

5   A Gröbner Basis Algorithm for Right Ideals

Gröbner bases for polynomials over Z have been considered in for example [6], and more generally for polynomials over Euclidean rings. Here, we are interested in constructing Gröbner bases for finitely generated right ideals in $Z<X_1, \ldots, X_n>$, where $X_1, \ldots, X_n$ are the noncommuting indeterminates. In [1], Baader gave an algorithm for constructing weak Gröbner bases for right ideals in $Z<X_1, \ldots, X_n>$. But in his algorithm only right compatible orderings with the boundedness property can be used to construct weak Gröbner bases.[5] In [9], an algorithm for computing strong Gröbner bases for right ideals in $Z<X_1, \ldots, X_n>$ is given but that too is for right admissible term orderings with the boundedness property. In this section, we give an algorithm which can be used to construct Gröbner bases for polynomial right ideals in $Z<X_1, \ldots, X_n>$ based on any right admissible term ordering.

For $m, n \in Z$, we define the ordering $\succ_Z$ as follows: $m \succ_Z n$ if either $|m| > |n|$, or $|m| = |n|$ and $m < n$. Thus $-5 \succ_Z 5$.

---

[5] Recall that an ordering has the boundedness property if and only if for every element, there are only finitely many elements less than it in the ordering.

The set of terms we consider is the monoid $W_n = \{X_1, \ldots, X_n\}^*$.

Definition 9. *A total ordering $\succ$ on W_n is called right admissible iff it satisfies:*

1. *for any term $t \neq 1$, $t \succ 1$, and*
2. *for any terms s, t, u, if $s \succ t$, then $s\,u \succ t\,u$.*

A right admissible ordering $\succ$ on terms can be extended to monomials as follows: Let $a, b \in Z$ and $s, t \in W_n$. Then $as \succ bt$ iff

1. $s \succ t$, or
2. $s = t$ and $a \succ_Z b$.

Given an integer c, c induces an equivalence relation on Z as follows: $a =_c b$ iff there exists a k_1 such that $a = k_1 * c + b$ where $a, b, k_1 \in Z$. Using this equivalence relation $=_c$, we define the *remainders* with respect to c as follows: Consider all equivalence classes induced by $=_c$. From each equivalence class, the smallest element wrt $\succ_Z$ is a *remainder* of c. For example, the remainders of 5 are $0, 1, -1, 2, -2$; 3 is not a remainder of 5; similarly, the remainders of 4 are $0, 1, -1, 2$.

Let $\succ$ be a right admissible ordering and let $f = at + g$ be a polynomial in $Z{<}X_1, \ldots, X_n{>}$ such that $t \in W_n$ is the greatest term in f with respect to $\succ$ and $a \in Z\backslash\{0\}$ is the coefficient of t in f. Then t is called the *head term* of f, denoted as $HT(f)$; a is called the *head coefficient* of f, denoted as $HC(f)$; $a\,t$ is called the *head monomial* of f, denoted as $HM(f)$, and $g = f - a\,t$ is called the *rest* of f, denoted as $R(f)$.

A right-admissible ordering $\succ$ on monomials can be extended in the natural way to an ordering $\succ$ on polynomials by comparing head monomials first and if these are equal, recursively comparing the rest of the polynomials. Sets of polynomials can be compared using its multiset extension $\gg$. Since $\succ$ is well-founded, $\gg$ are well-founded too.

Definition 10. *Given a set F of polynomials, for any $f, g \in Z{<}X_1, \ldots, X_n{>}$, f can be reduced to g wrt F, denoted by $f \rightarrow_F g$, iff*

1. *f contains a term t with coefficient a, (i.e. f contains a monomial at).*
2. *F contains a polynomial h such that $t = HT(h) \cdot s$ for some s and a is not a remainder of $HC(h)$.*
3. *$g = f - b\,h\,s$ where $a = b\,HC(h) + c$ and c is a remainder of $HC(h)$.*

We use $nf_F(f)$ to denote a normal form of f with respect to $\rightarrow_F$.

Lemma 2. *Let $F = \{f_1, \ldots, f_k\}$ be a set of polynomials. For any $f_i\,(1 \leq i \leq k)$, if $f_i \rightarrow^*_{F\backslash\{f_i\}} f'_i$, then $F\backslash\{f_i\} \cup \{f'_i\}$ generates the same right ideal as F.*

Proof. Based on the definition of reduction rules $\rightarrow_{F\backslash\{f_i\}}$, $f_i = f'_i + \sum a_j\,f_{h_j}\,t_j)$ where $f_{h_j} \in F\backslash\{f_i\}$. So $F\backslash\{f_i\} \cup \{f'_i\}$ generates the same right ideal as F. $\square$

Algorithm 5.1: Gröbner Basis Algorithm for Right Polynomial Ideals.

In the beginning, $F_0 = \{p_1, \ldots, p_m\}$ and all pairs of indices are unmarked. Without loss of generality, we assume all $HC(p_i) > 0\ (1 \leq i \leq m)$. Assume that $F_k\ (k \leq 0)$ is already defined. If there is the zero polynomial 0 in F_k, we erase it. As long as there are $f = p_i$ and $g = p_j$ in F_k such that:

(a) (i,j) is not marked and

(b) $f = at + R(f)$ and $g = btr + R(g)$ for $a, b \in Z^+$, and $t, r \in W_n$, we do the following:

1. $a \leq b$. Let $b = c\, a + d$ for some c, d, where d is a remainder of a. Define $g_1 = g - c\, f\, r = d\, t\, r + R(g) - c\, R(f)\, r$. Reduce g_1 to its normal form wrt F_k. If $HC(nf_{F_k}(g_1)) \geq 0$, define $g_1' = nf_{F_k}(g_1)$. Otherwise define $g_1' = -nf_{F_k}(g_1)$. $F_{k+1} = (F_k \cup \{g_1'\} \setminus \{g, 0\})$. Since $g = g_1 + c\, f\, r$, F_{k+1} generates the same right ideal as F_k by **Lemma 1**. Note that $HM(g_1') \prec HM(g)$.

2. $r \neq 1, a > b$ and b does not divide a. Let $a = c\, b + d$ for some c, d, where d is a remainder of b. We define $g_1 = f\, r - c\, g = d\, t\, r + R(f)\, r - c\, R(g)$. Since $d < b$, g is reducible by g_1. Let $b = c_1\, d + d_1$ where d_1 is a remainder of d, and $g_2 = g - c_1\, g_1$. Reduce g_1, g_2 to their normal forms $g_1' = nf_{F_k}(g_1)$ and $g_2' = nf_{F_k}(g_2)$ wrt F_k. If $HC(g_1') \geq 0$, define $g_1'' = g_1'$, otherwise define $g_1'' = -g_1'$. Similarly if $HC(g_2') \geq 0$, define $g_2'' = g_2'$ and otherwise define $g_2'' = -g_2'$. Now $F_{k+1} = (F_k \cup \{g_1'', g_2''\} \setminus \{g, 0\})$. In other words, g is deleted and non-zero normal forms are added to F_k. Since $g = g_2 + c_1\, g_1$, F_{k+1} generates the same ideal as F_k by **Lemma 1**. Again, $HM(g_1'), HM(g_2') \prec HM(g)$

3. $r \neq 1, a > b$ and b divides a. That is, there exists c such that $a = c\, b$. Define $g_1 = f\, r - c\, g = R(f)\, r - c\, R(g)$. Reduce g_1 to its normal form wrt F_k. If $nf_{F_k}(g_1) \geq 0$, define $g_1' = g_1$, otherwise define $g_1' = -g_1$. Define $F_{k+1} = F_k \cup \{g_1'\}$. Since $g_1 = f\, r - c\, g$, F_{k+1} generates the same ideal as F_k by **Lemma 1**. Mark (i,j). Here $HT(g_1) \prec HT(g)$.

Note that there is no need to mark the pair in cases 1 and 2, since g is deleted in both cases. For cases $1, 2$, clearly $F_k \twoheadrightarrow F_{k+1}$. For case 3, however, it is possible that $F_{k+1} \twoheadrightarrow F_k$. It is easy to see that if $p, q \in F_k$ such that $HT(p) = HT(q)$, then due to case 1 above, eventually one of these polynomials will be deleted from the basis leaving at most one polynomial with any head term.

Lemma 3. *Algorithm 5.1 terminates on any finite input basis of polynomials.*

Proof-sketch: The proof follows from two crucial insights: (i) a new polynomial added to a basis during the algorithm (due to any of cases 1, 2 and 3) is smaller than the largest polynomial in the basis because its head term is lower than or equal to the head terms of the polynomials used in its generation, and (ii) the head term of any polynomial has only finitely many prefixes, and consequently, only finitely many new polynomials can be generated using any given polynomial.

The proof is by contradiction. Consider a run of the algorithm starting with a basis G_0: $G_0, G_1, \cdots, G_i, G_{i+1}, \cdots$, where G_{i+1} is obtained from G_i by one of the cases.

Claim: There exists an i such that every basis $G_{i'}, i' \geq i$, has the same largest polynomial, say f_i (since the ordering $\succ$ is well-founded)); furthermore, no overlaps involving f_i are considered subsequently, i.e., in all $G_{i'}, i' \geq i$.

It can then be shown that any Gröbner basis of $G_i \smallsetminus \{f_i\}$ when extended with f_i is a Gröbner basis of G_i.

Repeat the above argument on $G_i \smallsetminus \{f_i\}$. The largest polynomial in $G_i \smallsetminus \{f_i\}$ is lower in the ordering $\prec$ than f_i. This process must terminate because the term ordering is well-founded. This contradicts the assumption that the algorithm goes on forever.   □

The correctness of the above Gröbner basis algorithm is established by a series of lemmas, patterned after the proof in [1] using ideas from [6] to establish that the proposed algorithm indeed computes a strong Gröbner basis for a right ideal over $\mathsf{Z}<X_1, \ldots, X_n>$. Proofs had to be omitted because of space limitations; an interested reader can consult [8].

Lemma 4. *Starting with a finite input basis G, let Algorithm 5.1 terminate in G_n by generating a sequence of bases $G, G_1, \ldots, G_n$. For any term t, if $f = \sum_{g_i \in G} g_i a_i$ with $HT(g_i a_i) \prec t$, then $f = \sum_{g'_i \in G_n} g'_i a'_i$ with $HT(g'_i a'_i) \prec t$.*

Lemma 5. *Starting with a finite input basis G, let Algorithm 5.1 terminate in G_n. Assume $G_n = \{g_1, \cdots, g_m\}$. For any $f \in <G>$, there exist polynomials $a_1, \ldots, a_n$ such that $f = \sum_{g_i \in G_n} g_i a_i$ and $|\{i \mid HT(g_i a_i) = HT(f)\}| = 1$.*

Lemma 6. *Starting with a finite input basis G, let Algorithm 5.1 terminate in G_n. Assume $G_n = \{g_1, \cdots, g_m\}$. Any polynomial $f \in <G>$ can be reduced to 0 with respect to $\to_{G_n}$.*

Theorem 4. *Starting with a finite input basis G, let Algorithm 5.1 terminate in G_n by generating a sequence of bases $G, G_1, \ldots, G_n$. Then, G_n is a strong Gröbner basis.*

The key idea in the proof is that for any two polynomials p_1 and p_2, if $p_1 - p_2$ reduces to 0, then one of p_1 and p_2 are reducible by $\to_{G_n}$. Further, the ordering $\succ_\mathsf{Z}$ on Z satisfies the unique remainder property discussed in [6].

6   Conclusion

Unification problems for theories admitting modular multiplication and exponentiation are discussed. As shown above, for theories that admit the distributivity property of exponentiation over multiplication, unifiability checks are undecidable. However, if this property is excluded, then unification algorithms for various restricted theories, depending upon properties of exponentiation used, can be obtained. In most cases, these algorithms are of high complexity.

In order to integrate these unification algorithms into the NRL Protocol Analyzer (NPA) and effectively use them for cryptographic protocol analysis, it will be useful to further specialize these algorithms so as to keep their complexity manageable in practice. That is likely to be the main challenge in investigating the effectiveness of the approach proposed in [13]. This issue needs further investigation.

References

1. F. Baader. Unification in Commutative Theories, Hilbert's Basis Theorem, and Gröbner Bases. *J. ACM,* 40 (3), 1993, 477–503.
2. F. Baader and W. Nutt. Adding Homomorphisms to Commutative/Monoidal Theories, or: How Algebra Can Help in Equational Unification. Proc. *4th Intl. Conf. on Rewriting Techniques and Applications (RTA 91),* LNCS 488, 1991, 124–135.
3. F. Baader and K.U. Schultz. Unification in the Union of Disjoint Equational Theories: Combining Decision Procedures. Proc. *11th Conference on Automated Deduction (CADE-11),* Saratoga Springs, NY, Springer LNAI 607, 1992, 50–65.
4. J. Clark and J. Jacob. *A Survey of Authentication Protocol Literature: Version 1.0.* Unpublished Technical Report, Department of Computer Science, University of York, UK, Nov 1997. Available at the URL: `www-users.cs.york.ac.uk/~jac/papers/drareviewps.ps`.
5. M. Davis. *Computability and Unsolvability.* Dover Publications, 1982.
6. A. Kandri-Rody and D. Kapur. Computing the Gröbner Basis of a Polynomial Ideal over Integers. Proc. *Third MACSYMA Users' Conference,* Schenectady, NY, July 1984, 436–451. See also A. Kandri-Rody and D. Kapur. An Algorithm for Computing the Gröbner Basis of a Polynomial Ideal over an Euclidean Ring. Journal of *Symbolic Computation,* 6 (1), August 1988, 37-57.
7. D. Kapur, P. Narendran, and L. Wang. *A Unification Algorithm for Analysis of Protocols with Blinded Signatures.* TR 02-5, Department of Computer Science, SUNY, Albany, NY. To appear in the Festschrift for Jörg Siekmann (Dieter Hutter, Werner Stephan, eds.), Lecture Notes in Artificial Intelligence 2605, Springer.
8. D. Kapur, P. Narendran, and L. Wang. *Analyzing Protocols that use Modular Exponentiation: Semantic Unification Techniques* Technical Report, Department of Computer Science, SUNY, Albany, NY. An expanded version of this paper.
9. K. Madlener and B. Reinert. On Gröbner bases in Monoid and Group Rings. SEKI Report SR-93-08, Universität Kaiserslautern, Germany.
10. C. Meadows. The NRL Protocol Analyzer: An Overview. *J. Logic Programming,* 26(2), 1996, 113–131.
11. C. Meadows. Analysis of the Internet Key Exchange protocol using the NRL Protocol Analyzer. In: Proc. the 1999 Symp. on Security and Privacy, IEEE.
12. C. Meadows, P. Syverson and I. Cervesato. Formal Specification and Analysis of the Group Domain of Interpretation Protocol using NPATROL and the NRL Protocol Analyzer. To appear in the *Journal of Computer Security.*
13. C. Meadows and P. Narendran. A Unification Algorithm for the Group Diffie-Hellman Protocol. *Workshop on Issues in the Theory of Security (WITS 2002),* Portland, OR, Jan 2002.
14. P. Narendran. On solving linear equations over polynomial semirings. In: Proc. 11th Annual Symp. on Logic in Computer Science (LICS), NJ, July 96, 466–472.
15. P. Narendran, F. Pfenning, and R. Statman. On the Unification Problem for Cartesian Closed Categories. *Journal of Symbolic Logic,* 62 (2), June 97, 636–647.
16. O. Pereira and J.-J. Quisquater. A Security Analysis of the Cliques Protocols Suites. Proc. *14th IEEE Computer Security Foundations Workshop,* June 2001.
17. R.L. Rivest, A. Shamir, and L. Adleman. A Method for Obtaining Digital Signatures and Public Key Cryptosystems. CACM 21 (2), 1978, 120–126.
18. G. Simmons and C. Meadows. The Role of Trust in Information Integrity Protocols. *Journal of Computer Security* 3 (2), 1994.
19. S.G. Stubblebine and C. Meadows. On Searching for Known and Chosen Cipher Pairs using the NRL Protocol Analyzer. Presented at the DIMACS Workshop on Design and Formal Verification of Security Protocols, September 1997.

Two-Way Equational Tree Automata
for AC-Like Theories:
Decidability and Closure Properties*

Kumar Neeraj Verma

LSV/CNRS UMR 8643 & INRIA Futurs projet SECSI & ENS Cachan, France
verma@lsv.ens-cachan.fr

Abstract. We study two-way tree automata modulo equational theories. We deal with the theories of Abelian groups ($ACUM$), idempotent commutative monoids ($ACUI$), and the theory of exclusive-or ($ACUX$), as well as some variants including the theory of commutative monoids (ACU). We show that the one-way automata for all these theories are closed under union and intersection, and emptiness is decidable. For two-way automata the situation is more complex. In all these theories except $ACUI$, we show that two-way automata can be effectively reduced to one-way automata, provided some care is taken in the definition of the so-called push clauses. (The $ACUI$ case is open.) In particular, the two-way automata modulo these theories are closed under union and intersection, and emptiness is decidable. We also note that alternating variants have undecidable emptiness problem for most theories, contrarily to the non-equational case where alternation is essentially harmless.

1 Introduction

Tree automata [4,2] enjoy many good properties: emptiness is decidable, the class of recognizable languages is closed under Boolean operations notably. This extends to so-called *two-way* tree automata, where transitions may not only construct terms as in ordinary tree automata (call them *one-way* to distinguish them from two-way automata), but also destruct terms (see [2], Chapter 7, *Alternating Tree Automata*). The presence of these latter transitions sometimes make two-way automata more convenient to work with than one-way automata, although they are equally expressive.

A recent and important extension of the tree automata concept is that of *equational* tree automata [8,12] which recognize terms modulo an equational theory. Until now, all results on equational tree automata have been concerned with one-way automata only, see table below. The purpose of this paper is to fill this gap.

---

* Partially supported by the ACI "cryptologie" PSI-Robuste, ACI VERNAM, the RNTL project EVA and the ACI jeunes chercheurs "Sécurité informatique, protocoles cryptographiques et détection d'intrusions".

R. Nieuwenhuis (Ed.): RTA 2003, LNCS 2706, pp. 180–196, 2003.

	one-way	two-way	
non-equational	emptiness decidable, closed under ∪, ∩, **C** ⎤ [4,2]	emptiness decidable, closed under ∪, ∩, **C**, reduce to one-way automata ⎤	[2,3]
equational	[8,9,12,13]. (see related work section.)	This work.	

More specifically, we study the notion of two-way equational tree automata, modulo several theories extending the theory ACU of one associative, commutative operation $+$ with unit 0, which is defined by the axioms (A) $x + (y + z) = (x+y)+z$, (C) $x+y = y+x$ and (U) $x+0 = x$. These theories will be obtained by adding axioms to the base theory ACU, taken from the following: idempotence (I) $x + x = x$, the xor axiom (X) $x + x = 0$, more generally the cancellation axiom (X_n) $nx = 0$ (where nx denotes $x + x + \ldots + x$); the minus axiom (M) $x + (-x) = 0$, where $-$ is an additional unary symbol; and the minus distributivity axioms $(D)-(x + y) = (-x) + (-y)$, $-(-x) = x$, $-0 = 0$. We name a theory by the names of its axioms; e.g., $ACUM$ is the theory of Abelian groups. Note that D is implied by $ACUM$, so $ACUD$ is a (strictly) weaker theory than $ACUM$. Except for the axiom $-(-x) = x$, the theory $ACUD$ resembles the theory $ACUh$ (ACU with homomorphism) considered in some papers.

We first show that modulo ACU, $ACUI$, $ACUD$, $ACUM$ (Abelian groups), $ACUX$ (the theory of exclusive-or), and $ACUX_n$, the one-way automata are closed under intersection, union, and emptiness is decidable. In particular membership is decidable since trivially, the equational closure of a singleton set is accepted by our one-way automata. The hard part is in showing closure under intersection; this is in particular much more involved than in the non-equational case, although the technique we use can be thought of as a kind of souped-up product construction.

As far as *two-way* equational tree automata are concerned, we show that modulo all theories $\mathcal{E}$ above except $ACUI$, they are exactly as expressive as the corresponding one-way automata, and we describe effective reduction processes from two-way to one-way automata modulo $\mathcal{E}$. (The $ACUI$ case is currently still open.) For these reductions to work, and in fact for any reduction from two-way to one-way automata to work, special care has to be taken in the definition of the so-called *push clauses*, which are the kinds of transitions that are added in the two-way case compared to the one-way case. Indeed, we show that, had we been more sloppy, then emptiness of two-way automata modulo ACU, $ACUD$, $ACUM$ would have been undecidable. We also show that the emptiness question for the *alternating* variants of one-way automata modulo the latter theories are undecidable, too. This is in sharp contrast with the non-equational case, where emptiness is decidable for alternating, two-way tree automata.

Two-way tree automata have recently been used for verification of cryptographic protocols [6,11]. While they work in the case of perfect cryptographic primitives, more complex primitives with additional algebraic properties need to be modeled using equational theories. Two theories that occur often are the theories of exclusive-or and Abelian groups. This is not the topic of this paper and won't be pursued here.

Plan. After some material on related work, we define our one-way and two-way equational tree automata in Section 2, discussing basic properties and some undecidability results. To deal with decidable cases, we start with some easy results in Section 3, which shall form the basis for the rest of the paper; in particular, we show that the so-called *constant-only* one-way ACU automata recognize exactly the semilinear sets. These results are used in Section 4 to compute intersections of one-way automata modulo $ACUX$. From there, we deduce a procedure to convert two-way $ACUX$ automata to one-way $ACUX$ automata in Section 5; we also discuss generalizations to the theory $ACUX_n$ for any $n \geq 2$. The results and proofs in the Abelian groups case ($ACUM$) are exactly as in the $ACUX$ case, as we argue in Section 7. This however requires us to first deal with the constant-only $ACUD$ case in Section 6. The general ACU and $ACUD$ cases are simplified versions of the $ACUX$ and Abelian groups cases respectively and are dealt with in Section 8. Lastly we show that intersections of one-way $ACUI$ automata are also computable in Section 9, and discuss why translating two-way $ACUI$ to one-way $ACUI$ automata is troublesome. We conclude in Section 10.

Related work. The multitree automata of Lugiez [9], which extend his earlier work [8], correspond to our one-way ACU automata but with a much richer set of constraints including equality constraints, still keeping decidability, and are closed under boolean operations. This is incomparable to ours: our two-way automata cannot avoid undecidability in the presence of equality constraints. Ohsaki [12,13] considers a larger framework of (one-way) $\mathcal{E}$ tree automata, where $\mathcal{E}$ is an equational theory. Ohsaki's *regular* $\mathcal{E}$ automata coincide with our one-way $\mathcal{E}$ tree automata when $\mathcal{E}$ is linear (like AC, ACU), but this does *not* hold in all theories. For example, in Ohsaki's case, with transition rules $a \to q$, $b \to q$, $q + q \to q'$ and $0 \to q'$, and with the theory $ACUX$, we have $a + b \to^* q'$. In our case, with the corresponding clauses $q(a)$, $q(b)$, $q'(x+y) \Leftarrow q(x) \wedge q(y)$ and $q'(0)$, and with the theory $ACUX$, $a+b$ is not accepted at q'. For arbitrary $\mathcal{E}$ we do not know the relationship between our automata and Ohsaki's automata, and the two notions appear rather dissimilar. The multiset automata of Colcombet [1] correspond to the subclass of our one-way ACU automata in which all symbols other than $+, 0$ are unary. Note that the specific theories $ACUX$, $ACUM$, etc., that we consider here have traditionally not been considered in the framework of (one-way equational) tree automata; they give rise to specific technical problems and solutions. The notion of alternating two-way AC tree automata will be treated in detail in [7], which also considers some additional push clause formats which are not relevant in this paper.

2   Two-Way $\mathcal{E}$-Tree Automata

Fix a signature Σ of function symbols, each coming with a fixed arity, and let $\mathcal{E}$ be an equational theory, inducing a congruence $=_{\mathcal{E}}$ on the terms built from Σ. We will use clauses of first order logic as a general means of representing various classes of automata.

A *definite clause* is an implication of the form:

$$P(t) \Leftarrow P_1(t_1) \wedge ... \wedge P_n(t_n) \quad (1)$$

where $P, P_1, ..., P_n$ are predicates and $t, t_1, ..., t_n$ are terms built from Σ and variables. Given a finite set $\mathcal{C}$ of such definite clauses we define *derivations* of ground atoms using the following two rules:

$$\frac{P_1(t_1\sigma)...P_n(t_n\sigma)}{P(t\sigma)} \text{ if } P(t) \Leftarrow P_1(t_1) \wedge ... \wedge P_n(t_n) \in \mathcal{C} \qquad \frac{P(s)}{P(t)} \text{ if } s =_{\mathcal{E}} t$$

where σ is a ground substitution. Thus a derivation is a tree-like structure, which should not be confused with the trees which are the terms built from Σ. The connection of definite clauses with automata is as follows: predicates are states, finite sets of definite clauses are automata, and an atom $P(t)$ is derivable using $\mathcal{C}$, iff the term t is *accepted* at state P in the automaton $\mathcal{C}$. The derivations using $\mathcal{C}$ are sometimes called *runs* of the automaton $\mathcal{C}$. It is also easy to see that the set of derivable atoms is exactly the least Herbrand model of the set of clauses modulo $\mathcal{E}$.

The language $\mathcal{L}_P(\mathcal{C}/\mathcal{E})$ is the set of terms t such that $P(t)$ is derivable. When $\mathcal{E}$ is the empty theory, we shall call it $\mathcal{L}_P(\mathcal{C})$. If in addition some state P_f is specified as being *final* then the language *accepted* by $\mathcal{C}$ will be $\mathcal{L}(\mathcal{C}/\mathcal{E}) = \mathcal{L}_{P_f}(\mathcal{C}/\mathcal{E})$. Given a language $\mathcal{L}$ and an equational theory $\mathcal{E}$, $\mathcal{E}(\mathcal{L})$ denotes the set of terms t such that $t =_{\mathcal{E}} s$ for some $s \in \mathcal{L}$. A state or an automaton is called *empty* if it does not accept any term.

We will be especially interested in the following kind of clauses which we shall call *pop clauses*, *epsilon clauses* and *general push clauses* respectively.

$$P(f(x_1, ..., x_n)) \Leftarrow P_1(x_1) \wedge ... \wedge P_n(x_n) \quad (2)$$

$$P(x) \Leftarrow P_1(x) \quad (3)$$

$$P(x_i) \Leftarrow Q(f(x_1, ..., x_n)) \wedge P_1(x_{i_1}) \wedge ... \wedge P_k(x_{i_k}), \quad (4)$$

$$1 \leq i, i_1, ..., i_k \leq n$$

In both clauses (2) and (4), the variables $x_1, ..., x_n$ are distinct. We define *one-way automata* as consisting of clauses of kind (2) and (3), whereas *general two-way automata* in addition contain clauses of kind (4). We shall see that the general push clauses are problematic, hence we shall consider restricted forms called push clauses below. Our one-way automata (without equations) are exactly the classical tree automata usually described in the literature. Clauses 2 and 3 correspond to transition rules $f(P_1, ..., P_n) \rightarrow P$ and $P_1 \rightarrow P$ of classical tree automata. Note that the 'two-way automata' of [15] are a different notion from ours. The following result is an easy consequence of the above definitions, and is shown by induction on the derivations.

Lemma 1. *For any one-way automaton $\mathcal{C}$ and equational theory $\mathcal{E}$, $\mathcal{L}_P(\mathcal{C}/\mathcal{E}) = \mathcal{E}(\mathcal{L}_P(\mathcal{C}))$. In particular emptiness of one-way $\mathcal{E}$ tree-automata is decidable.*

The result does not hold for two-way automata in general.

We will sometimes need *extended epsilon clauses*:
$$P(x) \Leftarrow Q(x) \wedge P_1(x_1) \wedge ... \wedge P_n(x_n) \quad (5)$$

where the variables $x, x_1, ..., x_n$ are distinct. Intuitively, this is an epsilon clause $P(x) \Leftarrow Q(x)$ together with emptiness tests on the states $P_1, ..., P_n$. We have the easy:

Lemma 2. *For any one-way automaton $\mathcal{C}$ which in addition contains clauses (5), we can compute a one-way automaton $\mathcal{C}'$ such that for each P, $\mathcal{L}_P(\mathcal{C}/\mathcal{E}) = \mathcal{L}_P(\mathcal{C}'/\mathcal{E})$.*

Proof. Lemma 1 trivially extends to one-way automata with extra clauses (5), hence emptiness is decidable. Then remove all clauses (5) where some P_i is empty, $1 \leq i \leq n$, and remove all $P_i(x_i)$, $1 \leq i \leq n$, from the remaining clauses (5). $\square$

Since we are dealing with theories extending ACU, we assume that Σ contains symbols $+, 0$ and in case of equations D or M the symbol $-$. Note that we do not deal with the case of Σ containing several $+$ (resp. $-, 0$) symbols. Symbols in $\Sigma_f = \Sigma \setminus \{+, -, 0\}$, are called *free*. Free symbols of zero arity will be called *constants*. Terms of the form $f(t_1, ..., t_n)$ where f is free are called *functional terms*. Accordingly the pop and push clauses in our automata will be of the following form:

$$P(x + y) \Leftarrow P_1(x) \wedge P_2(y) \quad (6) \qquad P(a) \text{ where } a \text{ is a constant} \quad (8)$$

$$P(0) \quad (7) \qquad\qquad P(-x) \Leftarrow P_1(x) \quad (9)$$

$$P(f(x_1, ..., x_n)) \Leftarrow P_1(x_1) \wedge ... \wedge P_n(x_n), f \text{ being free} \quad (10)$$

$$Q(x_i) \Leftarrow P(f(x_1, ..., x_n)) \wedge Q_1(x_{i_1}) \wedge ... \wedge Q_k(x_{i_k}), \quad (11)$$
$$f \text{ being free}, i \in \{1, ..., n\} \setminus \{i_1, ..., i_k\}, 1 \leq i_1 < ... < i_k \leq n$$

While clauses (6)–(10) are pop clauses, we call (11) *push clauses*. The side conditions in (11) will be discussed at the end of this section.

Clauses (8) are special cases of clauses (10). Also the general push clause $P(x) \Leftarrow P_1(-x)$ is equivalent to (9) in the theories $ACUM$ and $ACUD$. One-way ACU (resp. $ACUI$, $ACUX$, $ACUX_n$) automata are sets of clauses (3), (6–8) and (10); one-way $ACUM$ and $ACUD$ automata in addition contain clauses (9). We define two-way automata by adding clauses (11) to one-way automata: hence *two-way* automata are sets of clauses (3) and (6–11)—with the proviso that (9) is only included when $- \in \Sigma$. *Constant-only* automata are one-way automata which contain clauses (8) instead of the general clauses (10) (the only free symbols in the signature are constants.) Given a two-way automaton $\mathcal{C}$ we define $\mathcal{C}_{one-way}$ to be the part of $\mathcal{C}$ without clauses (11). Also, given a one-way or two-way automaton $\mathcal{C}$, we define $\mathcal{C}_{eq}$ to be the part of $\mathcal{C}$ with clauses (3), (6), (7) and (9) (the equational part), and $\mathcal{C}_{free}$ is the remaining part.

The languages accepted by all our one-way or two-way automata are trivially closed under unions. As we have already dealt with emptiness of one-way automata (Lemma 1), we shall concentrate on intersection and reduction of two-way to one-way automata.

Negative Results. It is instructive to first consider constant-only ACU automata extended with *alternation clauses* of the form $P(x) \Leftarrow P_1(x) \wedge P_2(x)$. Then it is easy to encode reachable configurations of 2-counter automata $\mathcal{M}$ [10] using ACU automata (see [7].) It is not our purpose to replay the arguments of [7]. Instead here is the idea. We encode configurations $q(m, n)$ of $\mathcal{M}$ by atoms $q((x + m)a_1 + xa_2 + (y + n)b_1 + yb_2)$ for $x, y \geq 0$. To increment m we add a_1 and to decrement, we add a_2. Zero tests are done by alternation clauses, e.g., if $\mathcal{M}$ allows moving from state q to q' when $m = 0$, then we write a clause $q'(x) \Leftarrow q(x) \wedge zero_1(x)$ where $zero_1$ accepts all terms of the form $xa_1 + xa_2 + (y + n)b_1 + yb_2$. As reachability of states in two-counter automata is undecidable, emptiness of constant-only ACU automata with alternation clauses is undecidable. The same can be proved for $ACUM$ and $ACUD$ theories.

Now the above alternation clause can be coded as $Q(f(x)) \Leftarrow P_1(x), P(x) \Leftarrow Q(f(x)) \wedge P_2(x)$ for fresh Q. Accordingly, emptiness of constant-only ACU, $ACUM$, $ACUD$ automata with general push clauses is undecidable. This justifies the side-conditions $i \in \{1, ..., n\} \setminus \{i_1, ..., i_k\}, 1 \leq i_1 < ... < i_k \leq n$ in (11).

Note that we don't study automata with $+$-*push clauses*:
$$P(x) \Leftarrow P_1(x + y) \wedge P_2(y) \qquad (12)$$

In the $ACUX$ case, this has no impact as (12) is equivalent to (6). In the $ACUM$ case (12) can be coded as $P(x + y) \Leftarrow P_1(x) \wedge Q(y), Q(-y) \Leftarrow P_2(y)$. In the ACU and $ACUD$ cases, they strictly increase expressiveness as they at least encode Petri nets; this is postponed to a later paper.

Finally adding equality constraints between brothers, i.e. dropping the condition that the free variables in the pop clauses should be distinct, also leads to undecidability: the alternation clause above can be coded as $P(x) \Leftarrow Q(f(x, y))$, $Q(f(x, x)) \Leftarrow P_1(x) \wedge P_2(x)$ for fresh Q.

3   Starting Up: The Constant-Only ACU Case, and an Easy Lemma

In this section, we recall some important results on constant-only ACU automata which will be useful throughout the paper. If the set of constants in the signature is $\Sigma_f = \{a_1, ..., a_p\}$ then modulo ACU, the ground terms are of the form $\sum_{i=1}^{p} n_i a_i$ with $n_i \in \mathbb{N}$: equivalently p-tuples of natural numbers. Recall that a *linear set* is a set of the form $\{\nu + n_1\nu_1 + ... + n_k\nu_k \mid n_1, ..., n_k \in \mathbb{N}\}$ for some $\nu, \nu_1, ..., \nu_k \in \mathbb{N}^p$. A *semi-linear set* is a finite union of linear sets. The semi-linear sets are exactly the sets definable in Presburger arithmetic [5]. In particular they are closed under union, intersection, complementation and projection. We have the following result, also shown in [7] and corresponds to Corollary 6 of [13].

Lemma 3. *Constant-only ACU automata accept exactly semilinear sets.*

Proof. The proof uses Parikh's Theorem [14] which states that the commutative image of any context-free language is semi-linear, and in fact effectively so, together with the observation that the clauses (3), (6), (7) and (8) modulo *ACU* constitute exactly a context-free grammar modulo commutativity.   □

To prepare ourselves, we need another special property of *ACU*-automata which allows us to 'reuse' parts of derivations. This will be required very often in the paper.

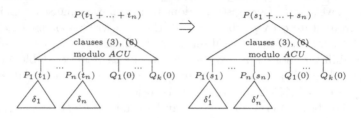

Fig. 1. Reuse of *ACU* derivations

Lemma 4. *Let $\mathcal{E}$ be any set of equations containing ACU. Consider a derivation δ of an atom $P(t)$ modulo $\mathcal{E}$. Let $\delta_1, ..., \delta_n$ be non-overlapping subderivations of δ such that outside the δ_i's, the only equations used are ACU and the set S of clauses used contains only clauses of kind (3), (6) and (7) (see Figure 1.) Suppose the conclusions of $\delta_1, ..., \delta_n$ are $P_1(t_1), ..., P_n(t_n)$. Then*

1. *$t =_{ACU} t_1 + ... + t_n$*
2. *If there are derivations $\delta_1', ..., \delta_n'$ of atoms $P_1(s_1), ..., P_n(s_n)$ modulo $\mathcal{E}$ then there is a derivation δ' of $P(s_1 + ... + s_n)$ modulo $\mathcal{E}$, containing δ_i''s as subderivations, such that outside the δ_i''s, the only equations used are ACU, and all clauses used belong to S.*

Proof. The first result follows from induction on δ. For the second, we replace the subderivations $\delta_1, ..., \delta_n$ by those of $P_1(s_1), ..., P_n(s_n)$ respectively. The atoms in the rest of the derivation need to be appropriately changed, keeping the clauses and equational rewritings applied at each step to be the same.   □

The following definition gives one way of computing such δ_i's and $P_i(t_i)$'s:

Definition 1. *Consider a derivation δ of an atom $P(t)$ in a one-way automaton modulo ACU. Let $\delta_1, ..., \delta_n$ be the set of maximal subderivations of δ in which the last step used is an application of clause (10) (or clause (8)). Suppose the conclusions of $\delta_1, ..., \delta_n$ are $P_1(t_1), ..., P_n(t_n)$ (in which case $t_1, ..., t_n$ must be functional.) Then we will say that the (unordered) list of atoms $P_1(t_1), ..., P_n(t_n)$ is the functional support of the derivation δ. (From Lemma 4 we have $t =_{ACU} t_1 + ... + t_n$.)*

4   One-Way $ACUX$ Case: Closure under Intersection

Consider a one-way $ACUX$ automaton $\mathcal{C}$ with predicates from some finite set $\mathbb{P}$. We introduce new predicate symbols (P,Q) and $\widehat{(P,Q)}$ for each $P,Q \in \mathbb{P}$, and sets of constants $S_1 = \{a_{P,Q} \mid P,Q \in \mathbb{P}\}$ and $S_2 = \{b_{P,Q} \mid P,Q \in \mathbb{P}\}$. The order of P,Q in all these is ignored. Instead of intersecting two distinct automata, we compute an automaton $\mathcal{C}_{inter}$ in which state (P,Q) represents intersection of P and Q for all P,Q. $\widehat{(P,Q)}$ accepts the functional terms among the terms accepted at (P,Q).

Consider the automaton $\mathcal{C}_{eq}^* = \mathcal{C}_{eq} \cup \{P(a_{P,Q}), P(b_{P,Q}) \mid P,Q \in \mathbb{P}\}$. The idea in defining $\mathcal{C}_{eq}^*$ and $\mathcal{C}_{P,Q,S,T}$ is to compute all possible derivations using clauses of the equational part. The $a_{P,Q}$'s and $b_{P,Q}$'s act as 'abstractions' for the functional terms accepted at both P and Q.

From Lemma 3 $\mathcal{L}_P(\mathcal{C}_{eq}^*/ACU)$ is a semilinear set for every P. For each $S \subseteq S_2$, we define $\mathcal{L}_{P,S}$ to be the set of those $t \in \mathcal{L}_P(\mathcal{C}_{eq}^*/ACU)$ such that each constant in S occurs in t a positive and even number of times and no constant from $S_2 \setminus S$ occurs in t. This operation is clearly Presburger-definable, and hence $\mathcal{L}_{P,S}$ is also a semilinear set. Define $\mathcal{L}'_{P,S}$ to be the language obtained from $\mathcal{L}_{P,S}$ by deleting all symbols of S_2, i.e., taking the image of $\mathcal{L}_{P,S}$ under the projection $\sum_{i,j} m_{ij}a_{P_i,Q_j} + \sum_{i,j} n_{ij}b_{P_i,Q_j} \mapsto \sum_{i,j} m_{ij}a_{P_i,Q_j}$. $\mathcal{L}'_{P,S}$ is again a semilinear set. Given $P,Q \in \mathbb{P}$ and $S,T \subseteq S_2$, clearly $\mathcal{L}'_{P,S} \cap \mathcal{L}'_{Q,T}$ is a semilinear set. By Lemma 3, we can construct a constant-only automaton $\mathcal{C}_{P,Q,S,T}$ with final state $F_{P,Q,S,T}$ such that $\mathcal{L}(\mathcal{C}_{P,Q,S,T}/ACU) = \mathcal{L}'_{P,S} \cap \mathcal{L}'_{Q,T}$. We assume that automata $\mathcal{C}_{P,Q,S,T}$'s are built from mutually disjoint sets of (fresh) states.

The required automaton $\mathcal{C}_{inter}$ has the following clauses:

- for each $P,Q \in \mathbb{P}$ and each $S,T \subseteq S_2$, the extended epsilon clause $(P,Q)(x) \Leftarrow F_{P,Q,S,T}(x) \wedge \bigwedge_{b_{R,R'} \in S \cup T}(R,R')(x_{R,R'})$.
- clauses (3), (6) and (7) (but not (8)) from each $\mathcal{C}_{P,Q,S,T}$.
- for each clause $R(a_{R',R''})$ in some $\mathcal{C}_{P,Q,S,T}$, the clause $R(x) \Leftarrow \widehat{(R',R'')}(x)$.
- for each pair of clauses $P(f(x_1,...,x_n)) \Leftarrow P_1(x_1) \wedge ... \wedge P_n(x_n)$ and $Q(f(x_1, ...,x_n)) \Leftarrow Q_1(x_1) \wedge ... \wedge Q_n(x_n)$ in $\mathcal{C}_{free}$, the clause $\widehat{(P,Q)}(f(x_1,...,x_n)) \Leftarrow (P_1,Q_1)(x_1) \wedge ... \wedge (P_n,Q_n)(x_n)$.

If $t =_{ACUX} t'$ then we must have $t =_{ACU} t_1 + ... + t_m + u_1 + v_1 + ... + u_n + v_n$, $t' = t'_1 + ... + t'_m + u'_1 + v'_1 + ... + u'_p + v'_p$, $t_i, t'_i, u_i, u'_i, v_i, v'_i$ being functional, such that $t_i =_{ACUX} t'_i, u_i =_{ACUX} v_i, u'_i =_{ACUX} v'_i$. The a's act as abstractions for the t_i, t'_i's and the b's for the u_i, v_i, u'_i, v'_i's. This is the reason we delete the b's from $\mathcal{L}_{P,S}$, representing the cancellations using X. Even though we can forget the actual values of u_i, v_i's, we need to be sure that there exist some terms to fill their place: this is the reason for the emptiness tests in the extended epsilon clauses of $\mathcal{C}_{inter}$. In this way we take care of the non-linearity and cancellation in the equation $x + x = 0$ using some kind of intersection-emptiness tests, and the remaining equations are dealt with using the results on ACU automata. This is made precise by Lemmas 5 and 6.

Lemma 5. *If $P(t')$ and $Q(t'')$ are derivable in $\mathcal{C}$ modulo ACU and $t' =_{ACUX} t''$, then for some $t =_{ACUX} t'$, $(P,Q)(t)$ is derivable in $\mathcal{C}_{inter}$ modulo ACU.*

Proof. By induction on the sum of the sizes of the derivations of $P(t')$ and $Q(t'')$. The derivations of $P(t')$ and $Q(t'')$ must have functional supports of the form $P_1(t'_1), ..., P_m(t'_m), I_1(u'_1), I'_1(u''_1), ..., I_n(u'_n), I'_n(u''_n)$ and $Q_1(t''_1), ..., Q_m(t''_m)$, $J_1(v'_1), J''_1(v''_1), ..., J_p(v'_p), J''_p(v''_p)$ respectively such that $t'_i =_{ACUX} t''_i$, $u'_i =_{ACUX} u''_i$ and $v'_i =_{ACUX} v''_i$ respectively. From Lemma 4, $P(a_{P_1,Q_1} + ... + a_{P_m,Q_m} + 2b_{I_1,I'_1} + ... + 2b_{I_n,I'_n})$ and $Q(a_{P_1,Q_1} + ... + a_{P_m,Q_m} + 2b_{J_1,J'_1} + ... + 2b_{J_p,J'_p})$ are derivable in $\mathcal{C}^*_{eq}$ modulo ACU. Let $S = \{b_{I_1,I'_1}, ..., b_{I_n,I'_n}\}$ and $T = \{b_{J_1,J'_1}, ..., b_{J_p,J'_p}\}$. $F_{P,Q,S,T}(a_{P_1,Q_1} + ... + a_{P_m,Q_m})$ is derivable in $\mathcal{C}_{P,Q,S,T}$ modulo ACU. We must have $t'_i = f_i(t'^1_i, ..., t'^{k_i}_i)$, $t''_i = f_i(t''^1_i, ..., t''^{k_i}_i)$, $t'^j_i =_{ACUX} t''^j_i$, the derivation of $P_i(t'_i)$ must use a clause $P_i(f_i(x_1, ..., x_{k_i})) \Leftarrow P^1_i(x_1) \wedge ... \wedge P^{k_i}_i(x_{k_i})$ and the derivation of $Q_i(t''_i)$ must use a clause $Q_i(f_i(x_1, ..., x_{k_i})) \Leftarrow Q^1_i(x_1) \wedge ... \wedge Q^{k_i}_i(x_{k_i})$. By induction hypothesis, we must have $t^j_i =_{ACUX} t'^j_i$ so that $(P^j_i, Q^j_i)(t^j_i)$ is derivable in $\mathcal{C}$ modulo ACU. Let $t_i = f_i(t^1_i, ..., t^{k_i}_i)$. $\widehat{(P_i, Q_i)}(t_i)$ is derivable in $\mathcal{C}$ modulo ACU using the clause $\widehat{(P_i, Q_i)}(f_i(x_1, ..., x_{x_i})) \Leftarrow (P^1_i, Q^1_i)(x^1_i) \wedge ... \wedge (P^{k_i}_i, Q^{k_i}_i)(x^{k_i}_i)$. Let the derivation of $F_{P,Q,S,T}(a_{P_1,Q_1} + ... + a_{P_m,Q_m})$ in $\mathcal{C}_{P,Q,S,T}$ have functional support $R_1(a_{P_1,Q_1}), ..., R_m(a_{P_m,Q_m})$. Then clauses $R_i(x) \Leftarrow \widehat{(P_i, Q_i)}(x)$ are in $\mathcal{C}_{inter}$. Hence $R_1(t_1), ..., R_m(t_m)$ are derivable in $\mathcal{C}_{inter}$ modulo ACU and from Lemma 4, $F_{P,Q,S,T}(t_1 + ... + t_m)$ is derivable in $\mathcal{C}_{inter}$ modulo ACU. Let the required t be $t_1 + ... + t_m$. Also by induction hypothesis we must have $u_j =_{ACUX} u'_j, v_k =_{ACUX} v'_k$ such that $(I_j, I'_j)(u_j)$ and $(J_k, J'_k)(v_k)$ are derivable in $\mathcal{C}_{inter}$ modulo ACU for $1 \leq j \leq n$ and $1 \leq k \leq p$. Using the clause $(P,Q)(x) \Leftarrow F_{P,Q,S,T}(x) \wedge \bigwedge_{b_{R,R'} \in S \cup T} (R, R')(x_{R,R'})$ we get a derivation of $(P,Q)(t)$ in $\mathcal{C}_{inter}$ modulo ACU. Also it is clear that $t =_{ACUX} t'$. $\square$

Lemma 6. *For $P, Q \in \mathbb{P}$, if $(P,Q)(t)$ is derivable in $\mathcal{C}_{inter}$ modulo ACU then for some $t' =_{ACUX} t'' =_{ACUX} t$, $P(t')$ and $Q(t'')$ are derivable in $\mathcal{C}$ modulo ACU.*

Proof. There must be some $S, T \subseteq S_2$ such that $F_{P,Q,S,T}(t)$ is derivable in $\mathcal{C}_{inter}$ modulo ACU (with a strictly smaller derivation), and terms $t_{R,R'}$ for each $b_{R,R'}$ in $S \cup T$, such that $(R, R')(t_{R,R'})$ is derivable in $\mathcal{C}_{inter}$ (with a strictly smaller derivation). From induction hypothesis we get terms $t'_{R,R'} =_{ACUX} t''_{R,R'} =_{ACUX} t_{R,R'}$ such that:
$R(t'_{R,R'})$ and $R'(t''_{R,R'})$ are derivable in $\mathcal{C}$ mod ACU, for each $b_{R,R'}$ in $S \cup T$. (*)
From the definition of $\mathcal{C}_{inter}$, the derivation of $F_{P,Q,S,T}(t)$ must have a functional support of the form $(\widehat{R'_1, R''_1})(t_1), ..., (\widehat{R'_m, R''_m})(t_m)$ for some $m \geq 0$, and the clause occurring immediately above the derivation of $(\widehat{R'_i, R''_i})(t_i)$ must be of the form $R_i(x) \Leftarrow (\widehat{R'_i, R''_i})(x)$. Then the clauses $R_i(a_{R'_i,R''_i})$ are in $\mathcal{C}_{P,Q,S,T}$ ($1 \leq i \leq m$). From Lemma 4 $F_{P,Q,S,T}(a_{R'_1,R''_1} + ... + a_{R'_m,R''_m})$ must be derivable in $\mathcal{C}_{P,Q,S,T}$. So $a_{R'_1,R''_1} + ... + a_{R'_m,R''_m} \in \mathcal{L}'_{P,S}$. Therefore we must have $b_{I_1,I'_1}, ..., b_{I_n,I'_n} \in S(n \geq 0)$ such that $a_{R'_1,R''_1} + ... + a_{R'_m,R''_m} + 2b_{I_1,I'_1} + ... + 2b_{I_n,I'_n} \in \mathcal{L}_P(\mathcal{C}^*_{eq}/ACU)$.

Since each t_i is functional, there are $f_i, t_i^1, ..., t_i^{k_i}$ such that $t_i = f_i(t_i^1, ..., t_i^{k_i})$ and the derivation of $(\widehat{R_i', R_i''})(t_i)$ in $\mathcal{C}_{inter}$ uses as last clause $(\widehat{R_i', R_i''})$ $(f_i(x_1, ..., x_{k_i})) \Leftarrow (R_i'^1, R_i''^1)(x_1) \wedge ... \wedge (R_i'^{k_i}, R_i''^{k_i})(x_{k_i})$ corresponding to clauses $R_i'(f_i(x_1, ..., x_{k_i})) \Leftarrow R_i'^1(x_1) \wedge ... \wedge R_i'^{k_i}(x_{k_i})$ and $R_i''(f_i(x_1, ..., x_{k_i})) \Leftarrow R_i''^1(x_1) \wedge ... \wedge R_i''^{k_i}(x_{k_i})$ of $\mathcal{C}_{free}$. Then $(R_i'^j, R_i''^j)(t_i^j)$ must be derivable in $\mathcal{C}_{inter}$ using derivations strictly smaller than that of $(P,Q)(t)$. Hence by induction hypothesis, we have $t_i'^j =_{ACUX} t_i''^j =_{ACUX} t_i^j$ such that $R_i'^j(t_i'^j), R_i''^j(t_i''^j)$ are derivable in $\mathcal{C}$ modulo ACU. Let $t_i' = f_i(t_i'^1, ..., t_i'^{k_i})$ and $t_i'' = f_i(t_i''^1, ..., t_i''^{k_i})$. $R_i'(t_i')$ is derivable in $\mathcal{C}$ using the clause $R_i'(f_i(x_1, ..., x_{k_i})) \Leftarrow R_i'^1(x_1) \wedge ... \wedge R_i'^{k_i}(x_{k_i})$. Similarly $R_i''(t_i'')$ is derivable in $\mathcal{C}$.

Now the derivation of $P(a_{R_1', R_1''} + ... + a_{R_m', R_m''} + 2b_{I_1, I_1'} + ... + 2b_{I_n, I_n'})$ in $\mathcal{C}_{eq}^*$ must have a functional support of the form $R_1^\dagger(a_{R_1', R_1''}), ..., R_m^\dagger(a_{R_m', R_m''})$, $I_1^\dagger(b_{I_1, I_1'}), I_1^\ddagger(b_{I_1, I_1'}), ..., I_n^\dagger(b_{I_n, I_n'}), I_n^\ddagger(b_{I_n, I_n'})$ where $R_i^\dagger \in \{R_i', R_i''\}$ and $I_i^\dagger, I_i^\ddagger \in \{I_i, I_i'\}$. Since each $b_{I, I'} \in S$, by ($\star$) $I_i(t_{I_i, I_i'}'), I_i'(t_{I_i, I_i'}')$ are derivable in $\mathcal{C}$ modulo ACU. Recall that $R_i'(t_i'), R_i''(t_i'')$ are derivable in $\mathcal{C}$ modulo ACU. So from Lemma 4 $P(t_1^\dagger + ... + t_m^\dagger + t_{I_1, I_1'}^\dagger + t_{I_1, I_1'}^\ddagger + ... + t_{I_n, I_n'}^\dagger + t_{I_n, I_n'}^\ddagger)$ is derivable in $\mathcal{C}$ modulo ACU, where $t_i^\dagger \in \{t_i', t_i''\}$ and $t_{I_i, I_i'}^\dagger, t_{I_i, I_i'}^\ddagger \in \{t_{I_i, I_i'}', t_{I_i, I_i'}''\}$. Let the required t' be $t_1^\dagger + ... + t_m^\dagger + t_{I_1, I_1'}^\dagger + t_{I_1, I_1'}^\ddagger + ... + t_{I_n, I_n'}^\dagger + t_{I_n, I_n'}^\ddagger)$. Then $t =_{ACUX} t'$ and $P(t')$ is derivable in $\mathcal{C}$. Similarly we can find t'' such that $t =_{ACUX} t''$ and $Q(t'')$ is derivable in $\mathcal{C}$. $\square$

From Lemma 1, $\mathcal{L}_P(\mathcal{C}/ACUX) \cap \mathcal{L}_Q(\mathcal{C}/ACUX) = \mathcal{L}_{(P,Q)}(\mathcal{C}_{inter}/ACUX)$ for $P, Q \in \mathbb{P}$. The extended epsilon clauses can be eliminated using Lemma 2. Hence:

Theorem 1. *One-way ACUX automata are closed under intersection.*

5   Two-Way ACUX Case: Translation to One-Way ACUX

Consider a two-way $ACUX$ automaton $\mathcal{C}$ with predicates from $\mathbb{P}$. To convert it to a automaton, we describe a saturation procedure which adds new epsilon clauses till the push clauses become redundant. The idea is that if any push clause is ever used then the corresponding free functional symbol must have been introduced by some pop clause. But the clauses from $\mathcal{C}_{eq}$ might have been used inbetween to add new terms, which eventually get canceled using X to leave only one functional term. Below, the b's act as abstractions for the terms that are canceled, and a's for the terms which remain.

We introduce new sets of constants $S_1 = \{a_P \mid P \in \mathbb{P}\}$ and $S_2 = \{b_{P,Q} \mid P, Q \in \mathbb{P}\}$. We do not distinguish between $b_{P,Q}$ and $b_{Q,P}$. We define $\mathcal{C}_{eq}^* = \mathcal{C}_{eq} \cup \{P(a_P) \mid P \in \mathbb{P}\} \cup \{P(b_{P,Q}) \mid P, Q \in \mathbb{P}\}$. $\mathcal{L}_P(\mathcal{C}_{eq}^*/ACU)$ is a semilinear set for every P. For $P, Q \in \mathbb{P}$ and $S \subseteq S_2$, define $\mathcal{L}_{P,Q,S,\mathcal{C}}$ to be the set of $t \in \mathcal{L}_P(\mathcal{C}_{eq}^*/ACU)$ such that

- a_Q occurs in t exactly once

- $\forall Q' \neq Q.a_{Q'}$ does not occur in t
- each constant in S occurs in t a positive and even number of times
- no constant from $S_2 \setminus S$ occurs in t.

Clearly $\mathcal{L}_{P,Q,S,\mathcal{C}}$ is also semilinear because it is Presburger-definable. In particular, we can effectively check its emptiness.

If $\mathcal{C}$ has a push clause $R(x_i) \Leftarrow P(f(x_1, ..., x_n)) \wedge R_1(x_{i_1}) \wedge ... \wedge R_k(x_{i_k})$, a pop clause $Q(f(x_1, ..., x_n)) \Leftarrow Q_1(x_1), ..., Q_n(x_n)$, and there is a set $S \subseteq S_2$ such that

- $\mathcal{L}_{P,Q,S,\mathcal{C}} \neq \emptyset$
- $\forall b_{Q',Q''} \in S.\exists t.$ both Q' and Q'' accept t in $\mathcal{C}_{one-way}$ modulo $ACUX$
- $\forall j \in \{1, ..., k\}.\exists t.$ both Q_{i_j} and R_j accept t in $\mathcal{C}_{one-way}$ modulo $ACUX$
- $\forall j \in \{1, ..., n\} \setminus \{i, i_1, ..., i_k\}.\exists t.Q_j$ accepts t in $\mathcal{C}_{one-way}$

then we will write $\mathcal{C} \triangleright \mathcal{C} \cup \{R(x_i) \Leftarrow Q_i(x_i)\}$, which we take to constitute one step of our saturation procedure. This can be effectively decided because of the fact that one-way $ACUX$-automata are closed under intersection and hence their intersection emptiness is decidable. The saturation step is harmless:

Lemma 7. *Let $\mathcal{C} \triangleright \mathcal{C} \cup \{R(x_i) \Leftarrow Q_i(x_i)\}$ as above. Then any atom derivable in $\mathcal{C} \cup \{R(x_i) \Leftarrow Q_i(x_i)\}$ modulo $ACUX$ is also derivable in $\mathcal{C}$ modulo $ACUX$.*

Proof. It is sufficient to show that for any t_i, if $Q_i(t_i)$ is derivable in $\mathcal{C}$, then $R(t_i)$ is derivable in $\mathcal{C}$. As in the definition above, let t_{i_j} be the term accepted at Q_{i_j} and R_j for $j \in \{1, ..., k\}$. Also let t_j be the term accepted at Q_j for $j \in \{1, ..., n\} \setminus \{i, i_1, ..., i_k\}$. $Q(f(t_1, ..., t_n))$ is derivable in $\mathcal{C}$ using the pop clause. As $L_{P,Q,S,\mathcal{C}} \neq \emptyset$, there must be an atom of the form $P(a_Q + 2b_{Q'_1,Q''_1} + ... + 2b_{Q'_p,Q''_p})$ derivable in $\mathcal{C}^*_{eq}$ modulo ACU, with $b_{Q'_i,Q''_i} \in S$. Let u_i be the term accepted at Q'_i and Q''_i in $\mathcal{C}_{one-way}$ modulo $ACUX$. The derivation of $P(a_Q + 2b_{Q'_1,Q''_1} + ... + 2b_{Q'_p,Q''_p})$ must have a functional support of the form $Q(a_Q), Q^{\dagger}_1(b_{Q'_1,Q''_1}), Q^{\ddagger}_1(b_{Q'_1,Q''_1}), ..., Q^{\dagger}_p(b_{Q'_p,Q''_p}), Q^{\ddagger}_p(b_{Q'_p,Q''_p})$ where $Q^{\dagger}_i, Q^{\ddagger}_i \in \{Q'_i, Q''_i\}$. From Lemma 4, we get a derivation of $P(f(t_1, ..., t_n) + 2u_1 + ... + 2u_p)$ in $\mathcal{C}$ modulo $ACUX$. Thus modulo $ACUX$, we have a derivation of $P(f(t_1, ..., t_n))$. Then we get a derivation of $R(t_i)$ using the push clause.   □

The converse is trivially true. Thus $\mathcal{C}$ and $\mathcal{C} \cup \{R(x_i) \Leftarrow Q_i(x_i)\}$ have the same set of derivable atoms modulo $ACUX$.

Given a two-way $ACUX$ automaton $\mathcal{C}$ our saturation procedure consists of (don't care non-deterministically) generating a sequence $\mathcal{C}_0(= \mathcal{C}) \triangleright \mathcal{C}_1 \triangleright \mathcal{C}_2...$ until no new clauses can be generated. This always terminates because there are only a finite number of epsilon clauses possible. Let the final (saturated) automaton be $\mathcal{D}$. Then we remove clauses (11) from $\mathcal{D}$ to get a one-way automaton $\mathcal{D}_{one-way}$. This step is also harmless:

Lemma 8. *If any atom is derivable in $\mathcal{D}$ modulo $ACUX$, then it is derivable in $\mathcal{D}_{one-way}$ modulo $ACUX$.*

Proof. It is sufficient to show that a derivation in $\mathcal{D}$, which has a push clause at the root and nowhere else, can be converted to a derivation in $\mathcal{D}_{one-way}$. Suppose we have a derivation of $R(t_i)$ from the derivations of $P(f(t_1, ..., t_n)), R_1(t_{i_1}), ...,$ $R_k(t_{i_k})$ using the push clause $R(x_i) \Leftarrow P(f(x_1, ..., x_n)) \wedge R_1(x_{i_1}) \wedge ... \wedge R_k(x_{i_k})$. Also, the latter derivations use only clauses from $\mathcal{D}_{one-way}$. Hence because of Lemma 1, we must have a derivation in $\mathcal{D}_{one-way}$ modulo ACU of an atom of the form $P(f(t'_1, ..., t'_n) + u_1 + v_1 + ... + u_p + v_p)$ with functional support of the form $Q(f(t'_1, ..., t'_n)), I_1(u_1), J_1(v_1), ..., I_k(u_p), J_k(v_p)$ such that $t_i =_{ACUX} t'_i$ and $u_i =_{ACUX} v_i$. By Lemma 4, $P(a_Q + 2b_{I_1,J_1} + ... + 2b_{I_p,J_p})$ is derivable in $\mathcal{D}^*_{eq}$ modulo ACU. Let $S = \{(I_1, J_1), ..., (I_p, J_p)\}$. Clearly $\mathcal{L}_{P,Q,S,\mathcal{D}} \neq \emptyset$. Now the derivation of $Q(f(t'_1, ..., t'_n))$ must be using some clause $Q(f(x_1, ..., x_n)) \Leftarrow$ $Q_1(x_1) \wedge ... \wedge Q_n(x_n)$ and the derivations of $Q_1(t'_1), ..., Q_n(t'_n)$ in $\mathcal{D}_{one-way}$. As $t'_i =_{ACUX} t_i$, we have that $\mathcal{D} \triangleright \mathcal{D} \cup \{R(x_i) \Leftarrow Q_i(x_i)\}$. But $\mathcal{D}$ is already saturated, hence $R(x_i) \Leftarrow Q_i(x_i) \in \mathcal{D}$. Also $Q_i(t_i)$ is derivable in $\mathcal{D}_{one-way}$. Hence $R(t_i)$ is derivable in $\mathcal{D}_{one-way}$. □

The converse is trivially true. Combining Lemmas 7 and 8, we get:

Theorem 2. *A two-way ACUX automaton can be effectively converted to a one-way ACUX automaton accepting the same language.*

The results of the $ACUX$ case are easily generalized to the $ACUX_n$ case for every $n \geq 2$ by computing intersections of n-tuples of states instead of pairs of states. Hence:

Theorem 3. *Two-way $ACUX_n$ automata have same expressiveness as one-way $ACUX_n$ automata, and are closed under intersection.*

6   Constant-Only $ACUD$ Automata

We shall see that as the ACU case helped us in dealing with the $ACUX$ case, the $ACUD$ case helps us in dealing with the Abelian groups case.

Let $\mathcal{C}$ be a constant-only $ACUD$ automaton with predicates in $\mathbb{P}$. Except for clauses (9) which introduce '$-$' symbols, $\mathcal{C}$ would have been just an ACU automaton. In the $ACUD$ case, the languages are in fact very similar to semilinear sets. We now make this more precise. Recall that Σ_f is the set of constants in our signature. Define a set of fresh constants $\overline{\Sigma}_f = \{\overline{a} \mid a \in \Sigma_f\}$. Terms built from $\Sigma_f \cup \{+, -, 0\}$ modulo $ACUD$ are of the form $a_1 + ... + a_m - b_1 - ... - b_n$ ($m, n \geq 0$ and $a_i, b_j \in \Sigma_f$) while those built from $\Sigma_f \cup \overline{\Sigma}_f \cup \{+, 0\}$ modulo ACU are of the form $a_1 + ... + a_m + \overline{b_1} + ... + \overline{b_n}$ ($m, n \geq 0$ and $a_i, b_j \in \Sigma_f$). Hence there is a natural 1-1 correspondence between terms (resp. languages) on $\Sigma_f \cup \{+, -, 0\}$ modulo $ACUD$ and terms (resp. languages) on $\Sigma \cup \overline{\Sigma}_f \cup \{+, 0\}$ modulo ACU.

Consider new predicate symbols $\overline{P}$ for every $P \in \mathbb{P}$. Define automaton $\mathcal{C}^\dagger$ to consist of the following clauses:

- for clause (3) in $\mathcal{C}$, the same clause, and $\overline{P}(x) \Leftarrow \overline{P_1}(x)$.

- for clause (6) in $\mathcal{C}$, the same clause, and $\overline{P}(x+y) \Leftarrow \overline{P_1}(x) \wedge \overline{P_2}(y)$
- for clause (7) in $\mathcal{C}$, the same clause, and $\overline{P}(0)$
- for clause (8) in $\mathcal{C}$, the same clause, and $\overline{P}(\overline{a})$.
- for clause (9) in $\mathcal{C}$, the clauses $P(x) \Leftarrow \overline{P_1}(x)$ and $\overline{P}(x) \Leftarrow P_1(x)$

By simple induction on the derivations, we can show:

Lemma 9. *(1) If $P(a_1 + ... + a_m - b_1... - b_n)$ is derivable in $\mathcal{C}$ modulo $ACUD$ then $P(a_1 + ... + a_m + \overline{b_1} + ... + \overline{b_n})$ and $\overline{P}(\overline{a_1} + ... + \overline{a_m} + b_1 + ... + b_n)$ are derivable in $\mathcal{C}^\dagger$ modulo ACU.*
(2) If $P(a_1 + ... + a_m + \overline{b_1} + ... + \overline{b_n})$ or $\overline{P}(\overline{a_1} + ... + \overline{a_m} + b_1 + ... + b_n)$ is derivable in $\mathcal{C}^\dagger$ modulo ACU then $P(a_1 + ... + a_m - b_1 - ... - b_n)$ is derivable in $\mathcal{C}$ modulo $ACUD$.

Hence modulo the correspondence of languages discussed above:

Corollary 1. *The language accepted by a constant-only $ACUD$ automata with constants from Σ_f is a semilinear set with constants from $\Sigma_f \cup \overline{\Sigma_f}$. Conversely, a semilinear set with constants from $\Sigma_f \cup \overline{\Sigma_f}$ can be represented as accepted by a constant-only $ACUD$ automaton with constants from Σ_f.*

7   Cancellative '−' Symbol: Abelian Groups Automata

The $ACUM$ equations are remarkably similar to $ACUX$: instead of canceling equal terms, we now cancel terms with opposite signs. In fact the constructions and proofs in this case are exactly the same as in the $ACUX$ case. As the ACU case helped in the $ACUX$ case, similarly the $ACUD$ case helps in the $ACUM$ case. Easy generalizations of Lemma 4 and Definition 1 to the $ACUD$ case are used.

The key new idea is that instead of canceling pairs of b's as in the $ACUX$ case, we cancel a b with a $\overline{b}$, where the $\overline{b}$'s act as abstractions for the negated terms. So we omit the full proofs of Theorems 4 and 5, but still make the constructions explicit.

Theorem 4. *One-way $ACUM$ automata are effectively closed under intersection.*

Proof. Let $\mathcal{C}$ be a one-way $ACUM$ automaton with predicates in $\mathbb{P}$. As in $ACUX$ case we use new predicate symbols (P,Q) and $\widehat{(P,Q)}$ for each $P, Q \in \mathbb{P}$. We will construct automaton $\mathcal{C}_{inter}$ which has states (P,Q) to accept intersection of P and Q. The new sets of constants used are $S_1 = \{a_{P,Q} \mid P, Q \in \mathbb{P}\}$, $S_2 = \{b_{P,Q} \mid P, Q \in \mathbb{P}\}$, $\overline{S_1} = \{\overline{a_{P,Q}} \mid P, Q \in \mathbb{P}\}$ and $\overline{S_2} = \{\overline{b_{P,Q}} \mid P, Q \in \mathbb{P}\}$.

Let $\mathcal{C}_{eq}^* = \mathcal{C}_{eq} \cup \{P(a_{P,Q}), P(b_{P,Q})\}$ for $P, Q \in \mathbb{P}$. From Corollary 1, for every P $\mathcal{L}_P(\mathcal{C}_{eq}^*/ACUD)$ is a semilinear set on the symbols from $S_1 \cup \overline{S_1} \cup S_2 \cup \overline{S_2}$. For each $S \subseteq S_2$, define $\mathcal{L}_{P,S}$ to be the set of those $t \in \mathcal{L}_P(\mathcal{C}_{eq}^*/ACUD)$ such that

- each $b_{P,Q} \in S$ occurs in t at least once

- no $b_{P,Q} \in S_2 \setminus S$ occurs in t
- for each $b_{P,Q} \in S_2$, $b_{P,Q}$ occurs exactly as many times as $\overline{b_{P,Q}}$ in t.

$\mathcal{L}_{P,S}$ is a semilinear set. Let $\mathcal{L}'_{P,S}$ be the language obtained from $\mathcal{L}_{P,S}$ by deleting all the symbols from $S_2 \cup \overline{S_2}$. This is again a semilinear set. For $P, Q \in \mathbb{P}$ and $S, T \subseteq S_2$ $\mathcal{L}'_{P,S} \cap \mathcal{L}'_{Q,T}$ is a semilinear set. By the second part of Corollary 1, we can construct a constant-only $ACUD$ automaton $\mathcal{C}_{P,Q,S,T}$ on signature $S_1 \cup \{+, -, 0\}$ with a final state $F_{P,Q,S,T}$ such that $\mathcal{L}(\mathcal{C}_{P,Q,S,T}/ACUD) = \mathcal{L}'_{P,S} \cap \mathcal{L}'_{Q,T}$. We assume that automata $\mathcal{C}_{P,Q,S,T}$'s are built from mutually disjoint sets of (fresh) states.

The required automaton $\mathcal{C}_{inter}$ has the following clauses:

- for each $P, Q \in \mathbb{P}$ and each $S, T \subseteq S_2$, the clause $(P, Q)(x) \Leftarrow F_{P,Q,S,T}(x) \wedge \bigwedge_{b_{R,R'} \in S \cup T}(R, R')(x_{R,R'})$.
- clauses (3, (6), (7) and (9) (but not (8)) from each $\mathcal{C}_{P,Q,S,T}$.
- for each clause $R(a_{R',R''})$ in some $\mathcal{C}_{P,Q,S,T}$, the clause $R(x) \Leftarrow \widehat{(R', R'')}(x)$.
- for each pair of clauses $P(f(x_1, ..., x_n)) \Leftarrow P_1(x_1) \wedge ... \wedge P_n(x_n)$ and $Q(f(x_1, ..., x_n)) \Leftarrow Q_1(x_1) \wedge ... \wedge Q_n(x_n)$ in $\mathcal{C}_{free}$ the clause $\widehat{(P, Q)}(f(x_1, ..., x_n)) \Leftarrow (P_1, Q_1)(x_1) \wedge ... \wedge (P_n, Q_n)(x_n)$. $\qquad \square$

Theorem 5. *Two-way $ACUM$ automata can be effectively converted to one-way $ACUM$ automata.*

Proof. Consider a two-way $ACUM$ automaton $\mathcal{C}$ with predicates in $\mathbb{P}$. As with $ACUX$ we describe the base step of the saturation procedure that adds epsilon clauses. (No new ideas are used.) The new sets of constants used are $S_1 = \{a_P \mid P \in \mathbb{P}\}$, $\overline{S_1} = \{\overline{a_P} \mid P \in \mathbb{P}\}$, $S_2 = \{b_{P,Q} \mid P, Q \in \mathbb{P}\}$, and $\overline{S_2} = \{\overline{b_{P,Q}} \mid P, Q \in \mathbb{P}\}$. We define $\mathcal{C}^*_{eq} = \mathcal{C}_{eq} \cup \{P(a_P) \mid P \in \mathbb{P}\} \cup \{P(b_{P,Q}) \mid P, Q \in \mathbb{P}\}$. From Corollary 1, for every P, $\mathcal{L}_P(\mathcal{C}^*_{eq}/ACUD)$ is a semilinear set on constants from $S_1 \cup S_2 \cup \overline{S_1} \cup \overline{S_2}$. For $P, Q \in \mathbb{P}$ and $S \subseteq S_2$, define $\mathcal{L}_{P,Q,S,\mathcal{C}}$ to be the set of $t \in \mathcal{L}_P(\mathcal{C}^*_{eq}/ACUD)$ such that

- a_Q occurs in t exactly once
- $\forall Q' \neq Q. a_{Q'}$ does not occur in t
- each constant in S occurs in t at least once
- no constant from $S_2 \setminus S$ occurs in t
- for each $b_{P,Q} \in S_2$, $b_{P,Q}$ occurs exactly as many times as $\overline{b_{P,Q}}$ in t.

$\mathcal{L}_{P,Q,S,\mathcal{C}}$ is also semilinear because the above conditions are definable using Presburger formulas. In particular, we can effectively check emptiness of $\mathcal{L}_{P,Q,S,\mathcal{C}}$.

If $\mathcal{C}$ contains a push clause $R(x_i) \Leftarrow P(f(x_1, ..., x_n)) \wedge R_1(x_{i_1}) \wedge ... \wedge R_k(x_{i_k})$, a pop clause $Q(f(x_1, ..., x_n)) \Leftarrow Q_1(x_1), ..., Q_n(x_n)$, and a set $S \subseteq S_2$ such that

- $\mathcal{L}_{P,Q,S,\mathcal{C}} \neq \emptyset$
- $\forall b_{Q',Q''} \in S. \exists t.$ both Q' and Q'' accept t in $\mathcal{C}_{one-way}$ modulo $ACUM$
- $\forall j \in \{1, ..., k\}. \exists t.$ both Q_{i_j} and R_j accept t in $\mathcal{C}_{one-way}$ modulo $ACUM$

- $\forall j \in \{1, ..., n\} \setminus \{i, i_1, ..., i_k\}.\exists t.Q_j$ accepts t in $\mathcal{C}_{one-way}$

then we write $\mathcal{C} \rhd \mathcal{C} \cup \{R(x_i) \Leftarrow Q_i(x_i)\}$, which is one step of our saturation procedure. The rest works as in the $ACUX$ case.   □

8   Simpler Cases: General ACU and $ACUD$ Automata

We observe that all the complications in the $ACUX$ and $ACUM$ cases were because of the equations $x + x = 0$ and $x - x = 0$ which cancel terms. Forgetting them (but keeping the distributivity of '$-$' symbol,) we get the ACU and $ACUD$ cases, which formed the basis of our results in the $ACUX$ and $ACUM$ cases. By looking at the proofs, it is easy to see that all the results proved for $ACUX$ and $ACUM$ automata continue to hold for ACU and $ACUD$ automata. In fact they become much simpler: all we need to do is to systematically ignore the parts about the $b, \bar{b}$'s which accounted for cancellations. For lack of space we content ourselves to summarize the results:

Theorem 6. *Two-way ACU (resp. $ACUD$) automata can be effectively converted to one-way ACU (resp. $ACUD$) automata and are effectively closed under intersection.*

9   Idempotence Axiom: $ACUI$ Automata

In the $ACUI$ case also we use techniques similar to the previous cases. We have:

Theorem 7. *One-way $ACUI$ automata are effectively closed under intersection.*

Proof. Let $\mathcal{C}$ be a one-way $ACUI$ automaton with predicates from $\mathbb{P}$. Instead of computing intersections of pairs of states, we will need to compute intersections of all tuples of states. Hence we introduce new predicates S and $\widehat{S}$ for every $\emptyset \neq S \subseteq \mathbb{P}$. A state $S = \{P_1, ..., P_n\}$ represents the intersection of states $P_1, ..., P_n$. $\widehat{S}$ accepts the functional terms among the terms accepted at S.

For each $\emptyset \neq S \subseteq \mathbb{P}$ we introduce a new constant a_S which will be used as an abstraction for the terms to be accepted at $\widehat{S}$. Let $\mathcal{C}_{eq}^* = \mathcal{C}_{eq} \cup \{P(a_S) \mid P \in S\}$. From Lemma 3 $\mathcal{L}_P(\mathcal{C}_{eq}^*/ACU)$ is a semilinear set for every P. Define $\mathcal{L}_P = \{n_1 a_{S_1} + ... + n_k a_{S_k} \mid$ some $m_1 a_{S_1} + ... + m_k a_{S_k} \in \mathcal{L}_P(\mathcal{C}_{eq}^*/ACU), 1 \leq n_i \leq m_i\}$. This step accounts for the contractions using the equation I. $\mathcal{L}_P$ is a semilinear set. For every $\emptyset \neq S \subseteq \mathbb{P}$, $\mathcal{L}_S = \bigcap_{P \in S} \mathcal{L}_P$ is a semilinear set. By Lemma 3, we can construct a constant-only ACU automaton $\mathcal{C}_S$ with final state F_S such that $\mathcal{L}(\mathcal{C}_S/ACU) = \mathcal{L}_S$. We assume that automata $\mathcal{C}_S$'s are built from mutually disjoint sets of (fresh) states.

The required automaton $\mathcal{C}_{inter}$ has the following clauses:

- for each $\emptyset \neq S \subseteq \mathbb{P}$, the clause $S(x) \Leftarrow F_S(x)$.
- clauses (3), (6) and (7) (but not (8)) from each $\mathcal{C}_S$.

- for each clause $R(a_S)$ in some $\mathcal{C}_S$, the clause $R(x) \Leftarrow \widehat{S}(x)$.
- for clauses $P^i(f(x_1, ..., x_n)) \Leftarrow P_1^i(x_1) \wedge ... \wedge P_n^i(x_n)$ in $\mathcal{C}$ for $1 \leq i \leq k, k \geq 1$, the clause $\widehat{S}(f(x_1, ..., x_n)) \Leftarrow S_1(x_1) \wedge ... \wedge S_n(x_n)$ where $S = \{P^1, ..., P^k\}$ and $S_j = \{P_j^1, ..., P_j^k\}$. □

While the one-way automata are closed under intersection, unlike in the other theories, we do not know whether the two-way automata have the same expressiveness as the one-way automata. Still we do know that the two-way $ACUI$ automata are powerful enough to encode alternation: the clause $P(x) \Leftarrow P_1(x) \wedge P_2(x)$ can be encoded as $Q_1(f(x)) \Leftarrow P_1(x), Q_2(f(x)) \Leftarrow P_2(x), Q(x + y) \Leftarrow Q_1(x) \wedge Q_2(y), P(x) \Leftarrow Q(f(x))$ for fresh predicates Q_1, Q_2, Q. We have already seen that alternation produces undecidability for ACU, $ACUD$ and $ACUM$ theories. This suggests that this problem is difficult and might require new techniques.

10   Conclusion

We have dealt with one-way and two-way tree automata modulo the equational theories ACU (associativity, commutativity, unit), $ACUD$ (ACU with a distributive '$-$' symbol), $ACUM$ (Abelian groups), $ACUX$ (exclusive-or), $ACUX_n$ (generalized exclusive-or, $n \geq 2$), and $ACUI$.

For each of these theories, we have shown that the languages accepted by one-way automata are effectively closed under union and intersection, and that emptiness is decidable. Also for all these theories except $ACUI$, the two-way automata can be translated to equivalent one-way automata. Care has been taken to suitably restrict the format of push clauses (look back at the side-conditions of (11)): without them emptiness would be undecidable in the ACU, $ACUD$ and $ACUM$ cases. In particular the corresponding two-way automata would not be reducible to one-way automata. We also saw that alternation leads to undecidable cases modulo these theories. In this sense, these automata have different behavior than classical (i.e. non-equational) automata.

Two questions remain to be answered. First, the equivalence between two-way and one-way $ACUI$ automata is conjectured. Second, the effect of adding clauses (12), which is trivial for the theories $ACUX$ and $ACUM$, is unknown for the others. Preliminary results show that this strictly increases expressiveness modulo ACU or $ACUD$.

Acknowledgements

I thank Jean Goubault-Larrecq for discussions and suggestions on previous drafts of the paper, as well as the anonymous referees for helpful comments.

References

1. T. Colcombet. Rewriting in the partial algebra of typed terms modulo AC. In A. Kucera and R. Mayr, editors, *Electronic Notes in Theoretical Computer Science*, volume 68. Elsevier Science Publishers, 2002.
2. H. Comon, M. Dauchet, R. Gilleron, F. Jacquemard, D. Lugiez, S. Tison, and M. Tommasi. Tree automata techniques and applications. www.grappa.univ-lille3.fr/tata, 1997.
3. T. Frühwirth, E. Shapiro, M. Y. Vardi, and E. Yardeni. Logic programs as types for logic programs. In *LICS'91*, 1991.
4. F. Gécseg and M. Steinby. Tree languages. In G. Rozenberg and A. Salomaa, editors, *Handbook of Formal Languages*, volume 3, pages 1–68. Springer Verlag, 1997.
5. S. Ginsburg and E. H. Spanier. Semigroups, Presburger formulas and languages. *Pacific Journal of Mathematics*, 16(2):285–296, 1966.
6. J. Goubault-Larrecq. A method for automatic cryptographic protocol verification. In *FMPPTA'2000, 15th IPDPS Workshops*, pages 977–984. Springer-Verlag LNCS 1800, 2000.
7. J. Goubault-Larrecq and K. N. Verma. Alternating two-way AC-tree automata. In preparation.
8. D. Lugiez. A good class of tree automata. Application to inductive theorem proving. In *ICALP'98*, pages 409–420. Springer-Verlag LNCS 1443, 1998.
9. D. Lugiez. Counting and equality constraints for multitree automata. In *FOS-SACS'03*. Springer-Verlag LNCS, 2003.
10. M. L. Minsky. Recursive unsolvability of Post's problem of "tag" and other topics in the theory of Turing machines. *Annals of Mathematics, Second Series*, 74(3):437–455, 1961.
11. D. Monniaux. Abstracting cryptographic protocols with tree automata. In *SAS'99*, pages 149–163. Springer-Verlag LNCS 1694, 1999.
12. H. Ohsaki. Beyond regularity: Equational tree automata for associative and commutative theories. In *CSL'01*, pages 539–553. Springer-Verlag LNCS 2142, 2001.
13. H. Ohsaki and T. Takai. Decidability and closure properties of equational tree languages. In *RTA'02*, pages 114–128. Springer-Verlag LNCS 2378, 2002.
14. R. J. Parikh. On context-free languages. *Journal of the ACM*, 13(4):570–581, 1966.
15. M. Y. Vardi. Reasoning about the past with two-way automata. In *ICALP'98*, pages 628–641. Springer Verlag LNCS 1443, 1998.

Rule-Based Analysis of Dimensional Safety*

Feng Chen, Grigore Roşu, and Ram Prasad Venkatesan

Department of Computer Science
University of Illinois at Urbana - Champaign, USA
{fengchen,grosu,rpvenkat}@uiuc.edu

Abstract. Dimensional safety policy checking is an old topic in software analysis concerned with ensuring that programs do not violate basic principles of units of measurement. Scientific and/or navigation software is routinely dimensional and violations of measurement unit safety policies can hide significant domain-specific errors which are hard or impossible to find otherwise. Dimensional analysis of programs written in conventional programming languages is addressed in this paper. We draw general design principles for dimensional analysis tools and then discuss our prototypes, implemented by rewriting, which include both dynamic and static checkers. Our approach is based on assume/assert annotations of code which are properly interpreted by our tools and ignored by standard compilers/interpreters. The output of our prototypes consists of warnings that list those expressions violating the unit safety policy. These prototypes are implemented in the rewriting system Maude.

1 Introduction

Checking software for measurement unit consistency, also known as dimensional analysis, is an old topic in software analysis. Software developed for scientific domains, such as physics, mechanics, mathematics or applications of those, often involves units of measurement despite the lack of support provided by underlying programming languages. Computations using entities having attached physical units can be quite complex; detecting dimensional inconsistencies in such computations, for example adding or comparing meters and seconds, can reveal deep domain-specific errors which can be hard, if not impossible, to find by just analyzing programs within their language's semantics, automatically or not.

To emphasize the importance and nontrivial nature of dimensional analysis, we recall two notorious real-life failures. NASA's Mars Climate Orbiter spacecraft crashed into Mars' atmosphere on 30 September 1999 due to a software navigation error; peer review findings indicate that one team used English units (e.g., inches, feet) while the other used metric units for a key spacecraft operation [24]. On 19 June 1985, the space shuttle Discovery flew upside down over Maui during an experiment, in an attempt to point the mirror to a spot 10,023 *nautical miles* above see level; that number was supplied in units of *feet* and then fed into the onboard guidance system, which unfortunately was expecting units

---

* This work is supported by joint NSF/NASA grant CCR-0234524.

R. Nieuwenhuis (Ed.): RTA 2003, LNCS 2706, pp. 197–207, 2003.
© Springer-Verlag Berlin Heidelberg 2003

in nautical miles, not feet [22]. These two failures, as well as many other lower magnitude ones, could have been avoided by using dimensional analysis tools.

There is much work on supporting measurement units in programming languages. The earliest mention of the idea of incorporating units in programming languages, to our knowledge was in 1960 [5]. Karr and Loveman [17] suggested a mechanism that allowed units to occur in programs. There have been proposals for dimensional checking within existing languages like Pascal [9,10] and Ada [11], and even in formal specification of software [14]. An intuitive approach to strengthen type checking in programming languages was also suggested in [16]. The Mission Data System (MDS) team at NASA JPL developed a C++ library incorporating hundres of classes representing typical units, like `MeterSecond`, together with appropriate methods to replace the arithmetic operators when measurement unit objects are involved. These techniques based on type checking, in addition to adding runtime overhead due to additional method calls (which can admittedly be minimized by optimized compilers), cause inconvenience to programmers and make the development of reusable software difficult. Furthermore, they limit the class of allowable (or type checkable) programs to an unacceptably low level. For example, a program calculating the geometric mean of the elements in a vector of meters needs a temporary variable which is multiplied incrementally by each element in the array; the unit of this temporary variable changes at each iteration, so it cannot be declared using any fixed type. The solution adopted by MDS is to remove and attach types to numerical values via appropriate extractors and constructors, which, of course, is a safety leak.

Packages for dimensional analysis and integrity in Ada have been proposed in [15,20], employing the use of Ada's abstraction facilities, such as operator overloading and type parameterization. Using a discipline of polymorphic programming, it was suggested in [21] that type checking can and should be supported by semantic proof and theory. This was extended in [23] using explicit type scheme annotations and type declarations and in [27] for type-indexed values in ML-like languages. The approach in [25] associated numeric types with polymorphic dimension parameters, avoiding dimension errors and unit errors. Kennedy proposed a formally verified method to incorporate, infer and check dimension types in ML-style languages [19], and provided a parametricity theorem saying that the behavior of programs is independent of the units used [18].

All the above study based on extensions, sometimes quite heavy, of programming languages, builds a foundation for languages equipped with dimensional information. However, due to practical, economical and/or taste reasons, these approaches have not been accepted by mainstream programmers and have not been widely used in applications. For instance, it is exceedingly inconvenient for programmers to rewrite a whole large application in another language – the one extended with unit types – just to avoid measurement unit conflicts. In this paper we propose a lighter-weight, rewriting-based approach to check measurement unit consistency, which has the main advantage that it does *not* modify the underlying programming language at all. The user interacts with our tools via code annotations, which are just comments, and via safety policy violation warning reports. We provide an integrated tool containing both dynamic and static checkers implemented by rewriting in Maude, and explain their trade-offs.

We mainly focus on examples and general concepts here, mentioning that our Maude rewriting implementation has more than 2,000 rewriting rules. One can find more information (including complete source code) and download our tools, at `http://fsl.cs.uiuc.edu`. The work presented in this paper has been started by the second author as a former researcher at NASA.

2 Preliminaries

In this section we recall the basics of the BC and Maude languages. BC is the language on which we applied our measurement unit safety checking approach presented in this paper, but an implementation targeting C is under current development and one targeting Java is under design. Maude is a rewriting based executable specification language that we used to implement our prototypes.

BC. Our domain-specific safety checking approach is general, both with respect to the domain of interest and with respect to the underlying programming language, but we firstly applied it to the GNU BC language, which comes with any Unix platform [1], because it is a simple but still practical language having most of the characteristics of current imperative languages. BC [1] is an arbitrary precision calculator language, typically used for mathematical and scientific computation. The most basic element in BC is the number. BC has only two types of variables, simple variables and arrays, which are used to store numbers. The syntax of expressions and statements in BC is very similar to that of C. It includes all the arithmetic, logical and relational operators found in C, in addition to the increment "++" and decrement "--" operators, and it also allows control structures for branching and looping through constructs like if, for and while. Comments start with the characters /* and end with */. BC programs are executed as the code is read, on a line by line basis; multiple instructions on a single line are allowed if separated by semicolon. It allows auto variables in functions, which are intended as variables for local usage; however, they are distinguished from the traditional local variables, their active range being extended over those functions called by the function in which they are defined, thus giving BC a dynamic scoping language flavor. By pushing auto variables and parameters of functions into stack dynamically, BC supports recursive functions. One can type man bc on any UNIX platform for more information on GNU BC. For some unexplained reason, only one-character identifiers are allowed by the BC implementation on Sun platforms; therefore we recommend the readers interested in experimenting with large examples to use the Linux version of BC.

Maude. Maude [6] is a high performance rewriting-based specification and verification system in the OBJ family [13]. We use Maude to specify BC along with its executable semantics and its domain-specific operational semantics w.r.t units of measurements. The following is a Maude module implemented in our unit safety analysis tool, defining a segment of the theory of units of measurement:

```
fmod UNITS is protecting INT .
  sorts BUnit SpecialUnit Unit UnitList .  subsorts BUnit SpecialUnit < Unit < UnitList .
  ops mile kg meter second Newton Celsius Fahrenheit : -> BUnit .
  ops noUnit any fail : -> SpecialUnit .   op _^_ : Unit Int -> Unit [prec 10] .
  op __ : Unit Unit -> Unit [assoc comm prec 15] .   op nil : -> UnitList .
  op _,_ : UnitList UnitList -> UnitList [assoc id: nil] .
  vars U U' : Unit .  vars N M : Int .        eq Newton = kg meter second ^ -2 .
  eq U noUnit = U .    eq U any = U .          eq U fail = fail .  eq fail ^ N = fail .
  eq any ^ N = any .   eq noUnit ^ N = noUnit .  eq U ^ 1 = U .     eq U U = U ^ 2 .
  ceq U ^ 0 = noUnit if ((U =/= fail) and (U =/= any)) .
  eq U (U ^ N) = U ^ (N + 1) .                 eq (U ^ N) (U ^ M) = U ^ (N + M) .
  eq (U U') ^ N = (U ^ N) (U' ^ N) .           eq (U ^ N) ^ M = U ^ (N * M) .
endfm
```

We assume the reader familiar with Maude. In the above module, we have different types (sorts) of data: BUnit for basic units, SpecialUnit, Unit and UnitList. Units like mile and noUnit have been declared as constants of sorts BUnit and SpecialUnit, respectively. The intuition for the special units is that they can be used in any unit context but can be distinguished from the basic units. The unit any is a unit which can be dynamically converted to any other unit, depending on the context; for example, in a BC statement like x++, the increment 1 is of unit any and is dynamically converted to the current unit associated to the variable x. The special unit noUnit is used to distinguish a cancelled unit (for example after calculating meter^(1-1)) from the unit any, in order to report appropriate warnings, and the special unit fail is attached to a variable in case its unit cannot be computed due to safety violations, such as, the unit of z after executing z = x + y in an environment in which x has the unit meter while y has the unit second. We claim, without proof, that the specification above is confluent and terminating, so it can be used as a computational model for unit equivalences.

3   Executable Semantics of Programming Languages

Equational logic is an important paradigm in computer science. It admits complete deduction and is efficiently mechanizable by rewriting: CafeOBJ [8], Maude [6] and Elan [3] are equational specification and verification systems in the OBJ [13] family that can perform millions and tens of millions of rewrites per second on standard PC platforms. It is expressive: Bergstra and Tucker [2] showed that any computable data type can be characterized by means of a finite equational specification, and Goguen and Malcolm [12], Wand [26], Broy, Wirsing and Pepper [4], and many others showed that equational logic is essentially strong enough to easily describe virtually all traditional programming language features.

Following the example in [12], we have defined the semantics of BC as an equational algebraic specification. Our BC specification has about 500 equations in Maude, all unconditional. Thanks to Maude's speed in executing unconditional equational specifications, we were able to run dozens of non-trivial, often recursive BC programs, directly within their semantics in Maude. The overall reduction in speed was a factor of about 25-30, which we found satisfactory for our prototypes, which essentially extend the executable semantics of BC with new, domain-specific definitions for safety policies.

Briefly, the executable semantics of BC declares an operation run which takes a program and a list of integers (its input) and returns another list of integers (its output). To execute programs properly, one needs to also define environments, which are sets of pairs (variable, integer). Because of recursive function calls, one needs to also stack these environments dynamically, as the program executes. Appropriate operations to update the environment are also defined, as well as operations to properly deal with return, break and continue statements.

4   Design Conventions and Annotation Schemas

The design of our prototypes has been influenced by three major factors: correctness, unchanged native programming language, and low amount of annotations.

Correctness. "Correctness" means that all violations of safety policy will be reported. We consider correctness a crucial aspect because, unlike other tools like ESC [7] intended to *help* users find many bugs with relatively little effort, our tools are intended to be used on safety critical software, such as air craft and navigation, where software developers want to be aware of any inconsistency.

Unmodified Programming Language. Another major influencing factor in our design was the decision to *not* modify the underlying programming language at all, for example by adding new types. Our reason for this decision is multiple. First, we do not want to worry about providing domain specific compilers; one can just use the state of the art optimized compilers for the specific programming language under consideration. Second, by enforcing an auxiliary typing policy on top of a programming language in order to detect unit inconsistencies via type checking, one should pay the price of some runtime overhead due to method calls that will replace all the normal arithmetic operators; our static prototype does not add any runtime overhead. Third and perhaps most importantly, since we do not add new types to the language, we do not put the user in the unfortunate situation to have a correct program rejected because it cannot be type checked, which is in our view the major drawback of typed approaches to unit safety; instead, our user has the option to either add auxiliary unit specific information to help the checker or to ignore some of the warning messages.

Annotation Schemas. The mechanism by which users can add auxiliary, in this case measurement unit specific, information to program is via annotations, which are special comments at appropriate places in the program. Annotations are introduced with the syntax /*U _ U*/, which is understood by our tools and ignored by compilers, and are of two kinds: assumptions and assertions.

Our annotation schemas are general and can be applied to any domain-specific safety policy checker, but in this paper we will focus on unit safety policy.

We now present an example showing some of the complex unit expressions that can be manipulated by our tool, and also emphasizing the importance of annotations. The program below provides functions to calculate distances, convert energy and calculate the angle under which a projectile of a given weight should be launched in order to travel a given distance:

```
define sqrtnaive(x) {
  auto temp; temp = 0;   /*U assume unit(temp) = sqrt(unit(x)) U*/
  while(1) {if (temp*temp>=x) return temp; if (temp*temp>x) return temp-1; temp += 1;}
}
define lb2kg(w) /*U assert unit(w)=lb U*/ /*U assume returns kg U*/ {return 10 * w / 22;}
define distance(x1, y1, x2, y2) {return sqrtnaive((x2-x1)^2 + (y2-y1)^2);}
define energy2speed(energy,weight) {return sqrtnaive(2 * energy / weight);}
define prjTangent(dist, speed, g) /*U assert unit(speed)^2 = unit(dist) unit(g) U*/
{ auto dx, dy; dx = speed*speed + sqrtnaive(speed^4 - (dist*g)^2); dy=dist*g;
return dx/dy}
projectilex = 0;        /*U assume unit(projectilex) = meter U*/
projectiley = 0;        /*U assume unit(projectiley) = unit(projectilex) U*/
targetx = 17;           /*U assume unit(targetx) = unit(projectilex) U*/
targety = 21;           /*U assume unit(targety) = unit(projectiley) U*/
dist = distance(projectilex, projectiley, targetx, targety);
projectileweight = 5;   /*U assume unit(projectileweight) = lb U*/
energy = 2560;          /*U assume unit(energy) = kg meter^2
second^-2 U*/ speed = energy2speed(energy, projectileweight);
g = 10;                 /*U assume unit(g) = meter second^-2 U*/
print(prjTangent(dist, speed, g));
```

The first function is the naive implementation of square root and the second one is a converting routine, from `lb` to `Kg`. The next function computes the distance between two points. No annotations are given, but a warning will be generated anyway if the arguments do not have the same unit. The fourth function computes the speed of an object, given the energy acting on it. The last function computes the tangent of the angle of a projectile, given a certain distance it wants to reach, an initial speed and a gravitational acceleration. This function is annotated with an assertion describing a unit invariant among its arguments. This allows one to use such functions in various contexts, such as under metric or English system conventions, as well as for other possible combinations of units. One can now assume a context in which these functions are called. The above code contains a unit safety violation, which is immediately reported by both checkers. The error will be reported when the function `projectileTangentAngle` is called, because the unit of speed is `Kg^(1/2) meter second^-1 lb^(-1/2)` so the assertion of function `projectileTangentAngle` will be violated. To correct this problem, the user should first properly convert the projectile weight to `Kg`, so the speed should be assigned the expression `energy2speed(energy, lb2kg(projectileWeight))`.

Reducing the Amount of Annotations. Influenced by the observed and sometimes openly declared reluctance of ordinary programmers and software engineers to modify or insert annotations in their programs, we paid special attention to reducing the amount of annotations to a minimum possible. As a consequence, every variable by default is considered to have its own unit, which is different from any other existing unit. This principle of course extends to auto variables, their units being considered different from the units of global variables having the same name. Our tool will therefore output a warning on the simple program `print(x+y)`, because x and y cannot be shown to have the same unit.

This brings us to a major design convention of our tool, called the *locality principle*, which assumes that the user understands what (s)he is doing locally, within a single instruction, with respect to constants. For example, if one writes x++, then one means to increase the value of x by 1, and this 1 has exactly the same unit as x. The same increment instruction can be reached several times during the execution of the program; each time the unit of the increment will be dynamically converted to the unit of x, which can be different each time. There is no difference between the statements x++ and x = x + 1, so we apply the same locality principle to numerical constants. That implies that in x = x + 5, the unit of 5 will be converted to the unit of x and no warning will be reported. Additionally, a constant assignment to a variable, such as x = 5, will not change the unit of x. Our motivation for these conventions is again to keep the amount of code annotation low, but the users thinking that our locality principle yields a safety leak have the option to always attach a unit to numerical values via appropriate assumptions, e.g., `temp = 5 ; /*U assume unit(temp) = second U*/`, and then execute x = x + temp; a warning will be reported in this case if the unit of x cannot be shown to be **second**. Based on these efforts, the following example of sorting needs only one assumption to satisfy the safety policy:

```
n = 25 ;   /*U assume unit(i) = any U*/
for (i = 1 ; i <= n ; i = i + 1) a[i] = n - i + 1 ;
for (i = 1 ; i < n ; i = i + 1)
  for (j = i + 1 ; j <= n ; j = j + 1)
    if (a[j] < a[i]) { temp = a[i] ; a[i] = a[j] ; a[j] = temp ; }
for (i = 1 ; i <= n ; i = i + 1) print(a[i]) ;
```

The only assumption needed, assigning the universal unit **any** to the counter i, guarantees the compatibility of i and n when they are compared later, within the loop conditions. The first loop, which assigns decreasing numbers to the elements of the array a, also assigns the unit of n, which is considered to be a fresh unit different from any other unit because no unit has been explicitly assigned to it, to each of the 25 elements of a. In the case of the static analyzer, the array a will be assigned the unit of n by executing the loop body symbolically only twice, regardless of the value of n (because the environment set stabilizes; see Subsection 5). Then the second loop is analyzed and no warning is reported because the nested loop assigns the unit of i, which is **any**, to j, so any subsequent comparisons of j are safe; the environment set also stabilizes in two iterations of the loop. Similarly the third loop can be certified without any auxiliary information. Without the assumption, 5 warnings would be reported.

5   Rule-Based Dynamic and Static Analysis Tool

The current version of our tool supports only the BC language, but it is being extended to support C and Java (see http://fsl.cs.uiuc.edu).

Tool Development. The tool is invoked with the command "`bc-unit [-so]` `filename`" where s and o are optional. By default, the tool starts its dynamic checker, which is described below, and its output consists of a list of warnings reported in the order of execution. A warning consists of the line number and the expression violating safety; the same warning can appear many times if the unsafe expression has been executed more than once. The option "`-o`" tells the tool to output the warning list ordered by line numbers without redundancy. The option "`-s`" triggers the static checking mode .

We used Maude as a rule-based programming language to implement both the dynamic and the static checkers. Since programs to be analyzed are expected to be provided as terms to Maude, we have implemented a simple wrapper (about 300 lines of PERL code), whose work-flow is the following:

1. Adjust the input program to be parsable by Maude, e.g., add spaces around BC symbols, add line numbers, delete unnecessary comments, detect the variable and function names and define them as appropriate constants, etc.;
2. Invoke either the dynamic or the static Maude checker (which are described below) to verify the generated program term;
3. Collect Maude's output, parse it and produce user friendly error messages.

This way users can use our tool in a push-button fashion, without seeing Maude.

Dynamic Checker. Our Maude dynamic unit safety checker interprets the BC program within its executable semantics enriched with the unit safety policy. This is realized by extending the executable semantics specification of BC discussed in Section 3. A major extension is with respect to execution environments. An execution environment is now a set of triples, each triple containing a variable, an integer value and a unit of measurement. The integer value is used to determine the execution flow of the analyzed program, while the unit is used to check the safety policy. For example, if the expression x + y is encountered at line number 15 and the execution environment contains the triples [x, 7, meter^2 second] and [y, 3, meter second] then the value 10 is correctly assigned to the sum of x and y but a warning message will be issued of the form 15 : x + y. If the expression x + y was assigned to a variable, say x, then the new environment will assign the value 10 and the unit `fail` to the variable x. Since BC supports recursive function calls and auto variables, all the environment stacking technique needs to be extended to the enriched environments.

Another major extension of the BC semantics is with respect to the newly introduced code annotations, which act like new, domain-specific instructions. An assumption /*U assume unit(Var) = UnitExp U*/ is interpreted by our dynamic checker as follows: 1) first evaluate the unit expression UnitExp in the current environment, hereby obtaining a result which is an expression using just basic units, then 2) modify the current environment by associating the newly calculated unit to the variable Var, without changing its current integer value; if UnitExp fails to evaluate to a correct unit, due to violations of the safety policy, then the unit `fail` will be assigned to Var. Due to its precision in analysis because of the exact execution path and environment, the dynamic checker can allow the user to assign different units to different elements in an array. In fact, any abstract memory location can have any unit associated with it. Assumptions /*U assume returns UnitExp U*/ are interpreted as follows: when a function call is invoked in an expression context, UnitExp is evaluated and returned as unit associated to the function call; the function call will also take place, and all additional warnings while executing the function are collected and reported. Assertions of boolean unit expressions are simply evaluated to boolean values and warnings are returned if they evaluate to false.

Static Checker. The main idea behind our static unit analyzer is that the concrete execution path of the program to be checked is entirely ignored; instead, all executions are considered in parallel. An immediate assumption is to also ignore all the numerical values and only consider the domain-specific, abstract values (units of measurement) of variables. Therefore, environments will now consist of pairs (variable, unit). Since the concrete indexes in arrays are not available anymore, it assumes that, unlike its dynamic version, all the elements in an array have the same unit. Due to the loss of precision, at each point in the program one has to consider a *set* of environments, namely all those in which a potential execution of the program can be. Each statement will be abstractly evaluated in all the environments. If the unit safety policy is violated in any of the environments then a warning will be output. A new set of environments will be computed after each statement. The treatment of loops is non-trivial. A general solution would involve loop invariants, which we would like to avoid as much as possible due to its lack of understanding by ordinary programmers and software engineers. Our alternative solution is based on *code patterns*. More precisely, we define loop patterns that we can efficiently analyze statically. One such pattern is a loop whose body, when symbolically executed under a set of possible environments, does not change that set of environments; if this is the case then the loop can be safely ignored. Another pattern is one which symbolically executes the loop until the set of environments stabilizes; this pattern for example is triggered in order to analyze the sorting algorithm in Subsection 4. If a certain loop does not fall under any of the provided patterns, then all the defined variables in the loop are invalidated (their unit is set to fail) and the static analysis process continues. The user can intervene and attach proper units to failed variables. The advanced user can add new patterns.

Some Experiments. In most of our experiments the Maude executable definition of BC was about 25-30 times slower than BC v1.06 on Linux platforms, which is a good factor considering that we build our tools directly on top of a mathematically clean setting. Adding measurement unit knowledge to the BC specification basically doubles its size and further increases the execution time of programs by a factor of 5. Since many physics programs essentially calculate a function and have just one execution path, one can argue that having a precise dynamic measurement unit safety checker is extremely useful, even if it slows down the execution of the program by 2-3 orders of magnitude. The static checker needs more axioms because it implements several patterns for loops. If a loop falls under a known pattern then it is discarded quickly; otherwise, the user intervention may be needed to add new assumptions as annotations. The killing complexity factor for the static checker is conditional branches when these modify the unit-specific environment differently, which in our experience happens very rarely. We tried examples where 10 worst-case 10 line conditionals were serialized, for a total of 1024 situations to analyze, and it took our static checker about 3 seconds to check it. On the other hand, if the two branches generate the same abstract environment, that is, if they both modify the units of variables in the same way, then we were able to analyze 1,000 repetitions of best-case 10 line conditionals, so a total of 10,000 lines of BC code, in about 1 second.

Discussion. The main advantage of the dynamic checker is the precision of its reported warnings: any reported warning represents a violation of the unit safety policy. The user should therefore consider these reports very seriously and should have strong reasons to ignore them. The main drawback of the dynamic checker is its coverage: it only covers the path that was traversed by the particular execution of the program. Therefore, other errors might exist in the analyzed program which were not revealed and which can appear when the program is executed with different input. Another drawback of the dynamic unit safety checker is that its execution time consists of the analyzed program execution time plus the runtime overhead. Therefore, if a program calculates a computationally complex function or does not terminate in a reasonable time, then so does the unit safety prototype, which can be a serious drawback in some applications.

An advantage of the static checker is that it covers all the potentially reachable code. So it will not miss any unsafe expression. A careful and patient analysis of the reported warnings can lead one to find all the unit safety leaks. Another advantage is its relative efficiency, because it does not execute the programs, so non-termination of the program does not imply non-termination of the tool. However, depending on the amount of theorem proving that one wants to put in such a static certifier, it can actually become rather inefficient. A major drawback of the static certifier is the potentially long list of false alarms that it reports.

6   Conclusion and Future Work

A promising annotation based approach to dimensional safety has been presented, together with a tool including both dynamic and static safety checkers implemented by rewriting in Maude. Future work includes extending the pattern database for the static checker and designing a general purpose invariant based loop analysis technique to be launched as a last pattern.

References

1. GNU BC. URL: http://www.gnu.org/software/bc/bc.html.
2. J. Bergstra and J.V. Tucker. Equational specifications, complete rewriting systems, and computable and semicomputable algebras. *JACM*, 42(6):1194–1230, 1995.
3. P. Borovanský, H. Cîrstea, H. Dubois, C. Kirchner, H. Kirchner, P.-E. Moreau, C. Ringeissen, and M. Vittek. ELAN. User manual – http://www.loria.fr.
4. M. Broy, M. Wirsing, and P. Pepper. On the algebraic definition of programming languages. *ACM Trans. on Prog. Lang. and Systems*, 9(1):54–99, January 1987.
5. T. Cheatham. Handling fractions and n-tuples in algebraic languages. Presented at the 15th ACM Annual Meeting, Aug. 1960.
6. M. Clavel, F. Durán, S. Eker, P. Lincoln, N. Martí-Oliet, J. Meseguer, and J. Quesada. Maude: spec. and progr. in rewriting logic. *J. of TCS*, 285(2):187–243, 2002.
7. Compaq. ESC for Java, 2000. URL: www.research.compaq.com/SRC/esc.
8. R. Diaconescu and K. Futatsugi. *CafeOBJ Report: The Language, Proof Techniques, and Methodologies for Object-Oriented Algebraic Specification.* World Scientific, 1998. AMAST Series in Computing, volume 6.
9. A. Dreiheller, M. Moerschbacher, and B. Mohr. Physcal - programming Pascal with physical units. *ACM SIGPLAN Notices*, 21(12):114–123, December 1986.
10. N. Gehani. Units of measure as a data attribute. *Comp. Lang.*, 2:93–111, 1977.
11. N. H. Gehani. Ada's derived types and units of measure. *Software: Practice and Experience*, 15(6):555–569, June 1985.
12. J. Goguen and G. Malcolm. *Alg. Semantics of Imperative Programs.* MIT, 1996.
13. J. Goguen, T. Winkler, J. Meseguer, K. Futatsugi, and J.-P. Jouannaud. Introducing OBJ. In *Software Eng. with OBJ: Alg. spec. in action.* Kluwer, 2000.
14. I. J. Hayes and B. P. Mahony. Units of measurement in formal specifications. Technical report, SVR Centre, University of Queensland, November 1994.
15. P. N. Hilfinger. An Ada package for dimensional analysis. *ACM Transactions on Programming Languages and Systems*, 10(2):189–203, April 1988.
16. R. T. House. A proposal for the extended form of type checking of expressions. *The Computer Journal*, 26(4):366–374, 1983.
17. M. Karr and D. B. Loveman III. Incorporation of units into programming languages. *Communications of the ACM*, 21(5):385–391, May 1978.
18. A. J. Kennedy. Relational parametricity and units of measure. In *POPL'97*. ACM.
19. A. J. Kennedy. *Programming Languages and Dimensions.* PhD thesis, St. Catherine's College, University of Cambridge, November 1995.
20. G. W. Macpherson. A reusable ada package for scientific dimensional integrity. *ACM Ada Letters*, XVI(3):56–69, 1996.
21. R. Milner. A theory of type polymorphism in programming languages. *Journal of Computer and System Sciences*, 17:348–375, 1978.
22. Peter G. Neumann. Letter from the editor - risks to the public. *ACM SIGSOFT Software Engineering Notes*, 10(3):10, July 1985.
23. M. Odersky and K. Läufer. Putting type annotations to work. TR, Newton Institute Workshop on Advances in Type Systems for Comp., Cambridge, 1995.
24. Mars Climate Orbiter. URL: http://mars.jpl.nasa.gov/msp98/orbiter.
25. M. Rittri. Dimensional inference under polymorphic recursion. In *Functional Programming Languages and Computer Architecture, 7th Conference.* ACM, 1995.
26. M. Wand. First-order identities as a defining language. *Acta Inf.* (14), 1980.
27. Z. Yang. Encoding types in ML-like languages. In *ICPF 98*. ACM, 1998.

Topological Collections, Transformations and Their Application to the Modeling and the Simulation of Dynamical Systems

Jean-Louis Giavitto

CNRS – LaMI, umr 8042, Université d'Évry – GENOPOLE
Tour Evry-2, 523 Place des Terrasses de l'Agora
91000 Évry, France
giavitto@lami.univ-evry.fr

1 Introduction

I take the opportunity given by this invited talk to promote two ideas: (1) a *topological point of view* can fertilize the notion of rewriting and (2) this topological approach of rewriting is at the core of the modeling and the simulation of an emerging class of dynamical systems (DS): the *DS that exhibit a dynamical structure* (or (DS)^2 in the rest of this paper).

This presentation is based upon the results of two research projects, 81/2 and MGS, that I have pursued hand in hand with Olivier Michel. The results and software tools presented here belong also to him and have been elaborated thanks to our long and fruitful collaboration.

I have voluntarily adopted in this presentation an informal style, including some non-technical considerations. Thus, the reader must take the opinions, subjective statements and positions expressed here with a grain of salt. For the technical details, he may refer to the papers published elsewhere. The MGS home page: http://mgs.lami.univ-evry.fr is a good starting point.

This presentation is organized as follows. Section 2 tries to develop an alternative understanding of the concept of a data structure: a data structure can be seen as a space where the computation moves following some path. This point of view is exemplified in section 3 on the design of a uniform data structure. The result, called a GBF, is funded on the group generated by the elementary moves (or displacements) in the data structure. The section 4 introduces the MGS experimental language used to investigate the idea of associating computations to paths through rules. The application of such rules can be seen as a kind of rewriting process on a collection of objects organized by a topological relationship (the neighborhood). Simple examples of MGS programs are given in section 4.4. However, a privileged application domain for MGS is the modeling and simulation of dynamical systems that exhibit a dynamic structure. Section 5 sketches this point and gives a short presentation of several models. We review to conclude some related and future work.

R. Nieuwenhuis (Ed.): RTA 2003, LNCS 2706, pp. 208–233, 2003.

2   Data Structures as Spaces

The fundamental concept of *data structure* is ubiquitous in computer science as well as in all branches of mathematics. Its characterization is then not easy. Some approaches emphasize on the construction of more sophisticated data structures from basic ones (e.g. domain theory); other approaches focus on the operations allowed on data structures (e.g. algebraic specification).

Species of structures. In [BLL97], a data structure s is presented as an *organization* or an *arrangement* o performed on a data set D. Quoting the introduction we can say that it is customary to consider the pair $s = (o, D)$ and to say that s is a structure o of D (for instance a *list* of *int*, an *array* of *float*, etc.). It is outlined that a customary approach consists in working with these pairs in the framework of axiomatic set theory. For example, the set $\mathcal{G}$ of simple directed graphs (directed graphs without multiple edges) can be defined by:

$$s = (o, D) \in \mathcal{G} \quad \Leftrightarrow \quad o \subseteq D \times D$$

This traditional approach consider equally the structure o and the set D and does not stress the structure o as a set of *places* or *positions*, independently of their occupation by elements of D. This last point of view is taken into account by the less traditional approach of *species of structures* [BLL97] motivated by the development of enumeration techniques and counting problems.

Space of a data structure. This point of view is also fruitful, even if one is not interested in counting the instances of a data structure. As a matter of fact, a lot of algorithms are structured following the structure of their data input or their data output and are largely insensitive to the precise values in their data set. This is obviously true for all polymorphic and polytypic functions, like `map`, `fold`, etc. [MFP91]. The notion of *shape* [Jay95] and *shape type* [FM97] also separates the set of places of a data structure from the values it contains.

Once we do not focus on the values manipulated in a program, we can analyze the previous notions as attempts to specify *classes of moves* or *paths* related to a given data structure. For example, there are two kinds of fold on lists: `fold_left` traverses the list from the head to the tail, and `fold_right` goes in the reverse direction. Another example: a shape type in [FM97] is defined as a grammar specifying the admissible paths resulting from following pointers in C data structures. So, in our context, the point of view is *topological* rather than combinatorial: *a data structure can be seen as a space*, the set of places or positions between which the programmers, the computation and the values, move.

At last, the notion of move or path relies on some notion of *neighborhood*: moving from one point to a neighbor point. Although speaking of *neighborhood* in a data structure is not usual, the relative accessibility from one element to another is a key point usually considered in a data structure. For example:

- In a simply linked list, the elements are accessed linearly (the second after the first, the third after the second, etc.).

- In a circular buffer, or in a double-linked list, computation goes from one element to the following *or* to the previous one.
- From a node in a tree, we can access the sons.
- The neighbors of a vertex V in a graph are visited after V when traveling through the graph.
- In a record, the various fields are locally related and this localization can be named by an identifier.
- Neighborhood relationships between array elements are left *implicit* in the array data structure. Implementing neighborhood on arrays relies on an index algebra: index computations are used to code the access to a neighbor. For example $(i-1, j)$ is the index used to access the "north neighbor" of point (i, j) (we assume that the "north" direction is mapped to the first element of the index tuple). The standard example of index algebra is integer tuples with linear mappings $\lambda x.x \pm 1$ along each dimension (called "Von Neumann" or "Moore" neighborhoods). More than 99% of array references are affine functions of array indexes in scientific programs [GG95].

This list of examples can be continued to convince ourselves that a notion of *logical neighborhood* is fundamental in the definition of a data structure. The concept of logical neighborhood in a data structure is not only an abstraction perceived by the programmer and vanishing at the execution, but it does have an actual meaning for the computation. The computation indeed complies with the logical neighborhood structure of the elements. For instance, recursive computations on a data structure respect so often the logical neighborhood, that standard high-order functions can be automatically defined from the data structure organization (think about catamorphisms and others polytypic functions on inductive types [FS96, NO94]).

Paths and Computations. In a sequential computation, elements of the data structure are visited one after the other. We assume that if element e' is visited just after element e in a data structure s, then e' must be a neighbor of e in some (concrete or abstract) way. We call the move from e to e' a *shift* and the succession of visited elements makes a path in s. The idea of sequential path can be extended to include parallel modes of computations: multi-dimensional paths must be used instead of one-dimensional paths [GJ92].

To summarize our presentation, we assume that a computation induces a path in a space defined by the neighborhood relationships between the elements of a data structure. At each shift, some elementary computation is done. Each topological operation used to build a path can then be turned into a new control structure that composes program fragments.

This schema is presented in an imperative setting but can be easily rephrased into the declarative programming paradigm by just specifying the linking of computational actions with path specifications. When a path specification matches an actual path in a data structure, then the corresponding action is triggered. It is very natural, especially in this topological framework, to require that the results of the computational action be *local*: the corresponding data structure transformation is restricted to the value of the the elements involved in the path and eventually to the organization of the path elements and their neighborhood relationships. Such transformation is qualified as local.

This declarative schema induces a rule-oriented style of programming: a rule defines a local transformation by specifying the path to be matched and the corresponding action. A program run consists in the transformation of a whole data structure by the simultaneous application of local transformations to non-intersecting paths. Obviously, such *global* transformation can then be iterated. Figures 1, 2 and 3 present three examples of algorithms where this topological emphasis is particularly relevant.

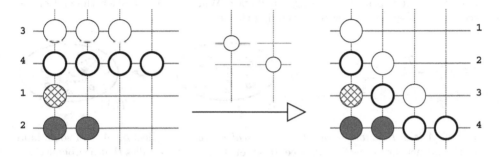

Fig. 1. Bead sort is a new sorting algorithm [ACD02]. The idea is to represent positive integers by a set of beads, like those used in an abacus. Beads are attached to vertical rods and appear to be suspended in the air just before sliding down (a number is read horizontally, as a row). After their falls, the rows of numbers have been rearranged such as the smaller numbers appears on top of greater numbers. The corresponding one-line MGS program is given in section 4.4.

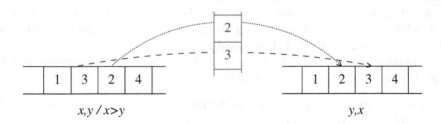

Fig. 2. A kind of bubble-sort is immediate in MGS; it is sufficient to specify the exchange of two non-ordered adjacent elements in a sequence. The corresponding one-line MGS program is given in section 4.4. This is not really bubble-sort because swapping of elements can take at arbitrary places; hence an out-of-order element does not necessarily bubble to the top in the characteristic way.)

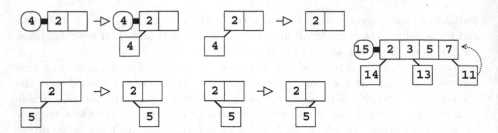

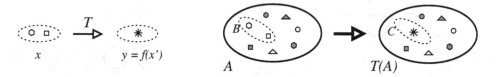

Fig. 3. Erastothene's sieve. The successive natural numbers are generated by the first cells (round box) and travel along a sequence of cells containing the previous prime number (square box). If a traveling number is divisible by the number in a cell, it is erased, else, it is passed to the right neighbor. When a number reach the end of the sequence, it becomes a new cell extending the sequence.

Fig. 4. *A local transformation of a topological collection.* Collection A is of some kind (set, sequence, array, cyclic grid, tree, term, etc). A rule T specifies that a subcollection B of A has to be substituted by a collection C computed from B. The right hand side of the rule is computed from the subcollection matched by the left hand side x and its possible neighbors x' in the collection A.

Rewriting and the Topological Approach. This topological approach shares many features with the idea of rewriting. Indeed, we can suppose that the computational action linked to a path is to replace this path by another one: this is the case for the four previous examples. Then, we retrieve the idea of rewriting, see figure 4 and 5, except that usually rewriting is described as the substitution of some sub-structure by another one (e.g. a sub-term by another term). What we gain with the topological emphasis is to focus on paths in the data structure instead of sub-structures [1]. Is this a real gain ?

The purpose of the MGS research project is to answer this question. To have a positive answer we have to show that:

1. it is possible to define a data structure through the specification of the neighborhood of its elements,
2. it is possible to define the substitution of a path by another one and to control the substitution strategy,
3. and this is useful in some application area.

The next section sketches the notion of *Group Based Datafield* (GBF) and is an example of a positive answer to question 1. This example is important also

---

[1] see however [Gia00].

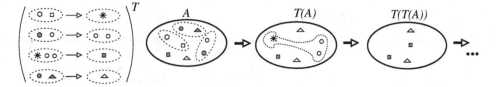

Fig. 5. *Transformation and iteration of a transformation.* A global transformation T is a set of local transformations applied in parallel and synchronously to make one evolution step. The local transformations do not interact together. A transformation can then be iterated.

because it integrates the array data structure, which opens the way to array rewriting and gives at least one answer to question 3. The section 4 introduces an experimental language, called also MGS, used to investigate the design space of question 2. The section 5 shows the use of the previous tools in the domain of dynamical systems modeling (especially in biology) and provide another answer to question 3.

3   The Example of Uniform Neighborhood Data Structures: GBF

From now on, we use the term *topological collection* to stress the topological organization of the data structure's elements. In this section, we will sketch a possible design for *uniform* topological collections. A topological collection is uniform if every element of the data structure has the same neighborhood structure. More precisely, we assume in this study that: (1) the set of places filled by the elements of the data structure is predefined (i.e. preexists to any occurrence of the data structure), and (2) the shifts followed to go from some place to a neighbor place can be named and (3) that the set **G** of shift's names, called *directions*, is the same for all places (like for example a "next neighbor" and a "previous neighbor" that exist for each element in a circular list).

The Group Structure of Uniform Neighborhood. Let "a", "b", "c"... be the direction's names and let $P\langle a\rangle$ be the "a" neighbor of the element P. Displacement operations can be composed: using a multiplicative notation, we write $P\langle a.b\rangle$ for $(P\langle a\rangle)\langle b\rangle$. Displacement composition is associative. We note 1 the null displacement, i.e. $P\langle 1\rangle = P$. Furthermore we will define a unique inverse displacement a^{-1} for each displacement a such that $P\langle a.a^{-1}\rangle = P\langle a^{-1}.a\rangle = P$. In other words, the displacements constitute a *group* $\mathcal{G}$ for the displacement composition, and the application $\cdot\langle\cdot\rangle$ of the displacements to the places is the *action of the group over the places of the data structure*. The simplest choice for the set of places $\mathcal{P}$ and the corresponding action is to let $\mathcal{P} = \mathcal{G}$ and $P\langle a\rangle = P.a$ (the group acts transitively on itself).

We assume that the group $\mathcal{G}$ is specified through a finite presentation with generators **G** (and $\mathcal{G}$ denotes indifferently the group and its presentation). Then,

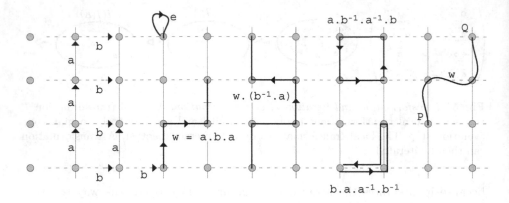

Fig. 6. Graphical representation of the relationships between Cayley graphs and group theory. A vertex is a group element. The label a of an edge corresponds to the generator a of the group. There is an edge between vertices P and Q labelled by a iff $P.a = Q$. A word (a product of generators) can be seen a path. Starting from vertex P, a path w ends in $P.w$. Path composition corresponds to word multiplication. A closed path (a cycle) is a word equal to e (the identity of the multiplication). An equation $v = w$ can be rewritten $v.w^{-1} = e$ and then corresponds to a cycle in the graph. There are two kinds of cycles in the graph: the cycles that are present in all Cayley graphs and corresponding to group laws (intuitively: a backtracking path like $b.a.a^{-1}.b^{-1}$) and closed paths specific to the own group equations (e.g.: $a.b^{-1}.a^{-1}.b$). The graph connexity (there is always a path going from P to Q) is equivalent to say that there is always a solution x to equation $P.x = Q$.

the discrete space spawned by $\mathcal{G}$ acting on itself is conveniently described by the *Cayley graph* associated to the presentation. See figure 6 for a dictionary between graph theory and group related concepts.

Group Indexed Data Structure. A GBF is an extension of the notion of array, where the elements are indexed by the elements of a group [GMS95, GM01a]. A GBF value g of type $\mathcal{G}$ is a partial function with a finite definition domain[2] that associates a value to some group elements. The group elements are the places of the collection. Thus the empty GBF is the everywhere undefined function. The acronym GBF stands for Group Based Datafield. The formalization of a data structure as a function is not new; it constitutes for instance, the foundation of the theory of *data fields* [Lis93] and is heavily used in [Gia00]. In computer science, it is common to think about a function as a rule to be performed in order to obtain a result starting from an argument: this is the *intensional* notion of functions. Here, we better rely on the *extensional* notion: a function is a set of pairs relating the argument and the result. This is closer to the concept of a data structure: for instance, an array tabulates the relationship between the set

---

[2] The definition domain of g is the subset of $\mathcal{G}$ of the elements having a well defined image by g.

of indices and the array elements and a GBF tabulates the relationship between the set of places $\mathcal{G}$ and their values (this is why GBFs are required to have a finite definition domain). We insist that the view of data structures as functions is only logical and appears only at the level of the data structure definition. It does not assume anything on the data structure implementation.

GBF in MGS. Here is an example. The finite presentation

```
gbf Grid2 = < north, east >
```

introduces in MGS (see section 4) a new collection type called *Grid2*, corresponding to the Von Neumann neighborhood in a classical array (a cell above, below, left or right – not diagonal) see figure 7. The two names **north** and **east** refer to the directions that can be followed to reach the neighbors of an element. These directions are the generators of the underlying group structure. The < and > brackets are used for the presentation of Abelian groups and to avoid the explicit writing of the commutation equations. In this presentation, there is no explicit equation (beside the implicit commutation of the generators): *Grid2* is a free Abelian group.

The following declaration defines a non-free Abelian group:

```
gbf Hexagon = < east, north, northwest; east + north = northwest >
```

The Cayley graph of *Hexagon* defines an hexagonal lattice that tiles the plane, see figure 7 and 8. Each cell has six neighbors (following the three generators and their inverses). The equation **east + north = northwest** specifies that a move following **northwest** is the same has a move following the **east** direction followed by a move following the **north** direction.

Uniform neighborhood and classical data structures. Free groups with n generators correspond to n-ary trees and Abelian GBF corresponds to twisted and circular grids (the free Abelian group with n generators generalizes n-dimensional

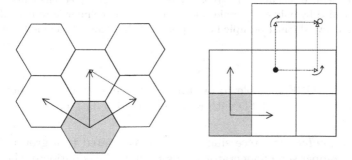

Fig. 7. These shapes correspond to a Cayley graph of *Hexagon* and *Grid2* with the following conventions: a vertex is represented as a face and two neighbors in the Cayley graphs share an edge in this representation. An empty cell has an undefined value. Only a part of the infinite domain is figured.

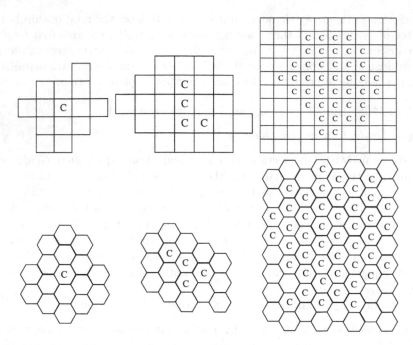

Fig. 8. Eden's model on a grid and on an hexagonal mesh (initial state, and states after the 3 and the 7 time steps). The Eden's aggregation process is a simple model of growth. The model has been used since the 1960's as a model for such things as tumor growth and growth of cities. In this model (specifically, a type B Eden model [Ede58]), a 2D space is partitioned in empty or occupied cells. We start with only one occupied cell. At each step, occupied cells with an empty neighbor are selected, and the corresponding empty cell is made occupied. This process simply described as *exactly the same* transformation for both cases:

$$\text{trans } Eden = \{ \quad \text{x,<undef> / x } \Rightarrow \text{ x,true} \quad \}$$

We assume that the boolean value **true** is used to represent an occupied cell, other cells are simply left undefined. Then the previous rule can be read: an occupied element x and an undefined neighbor are transformed into two occupied elements. This model cannot be coded by only one simple rule on a two-state cellular automata if one wants to avoid that two distinct occupied cells preempt the same unoccupied cell.

arrays). Thus, GBF are able to describe in the same formalism both tree and array, a feature not available with regular inductive data types.

GBF Implementations. Accessing the value associated to a group element requires the comparison of generator words modulo the equation of the GBF: this is the word problem for groups and it is undecidable in general. However, for large and interesting families of groups (e.g. free groups, Abelian groups, automatic groups) the problem is solvable. Actually the MGS implementation is restricted to Abelian groups.

4   Topological Collections and Their Transformations

In this section, we want to show how a declarative programming style, based on rules and a general notion of rewriting, can be developed on topological collections like the GBF presented in the previous section. The topological approach sketched in section 2 is investigated through an experimental declarative programming language called MGS [GM01c, GM02b]. MGS embeds the idea of topological collections and their transformations into the framework of a simple dynamically typed functional language. Collections are just new kinds of values and transformations are functions acting on collections and defined by a specific syntax using rules. Functions and transformations are first-class values and can be passed as arguments or returned as the result of an application. MGS is an applicative programming language: operators acting on values combine values to give new values, they do not act by side-effect. In our context, dynamically typed means that there is no static type checking and that type errors are detected at run-time during evaluation. Although dynamically typed, the set of values has a rich type structure used in the definition of pattern-matching, rule and transformations.

Transformation of a Topological Collection. The *global transformation* of a topological collection C consists in the parallel application of a set of *local transformations*. A local transformation is specified by a rewriting rule r that specifies the change of a subcollection. The application of a rewrite rule $r = \beta \Rightarrow f(\beta, ...)$ to a collection C:

1. selects a path B of C whose elements match the *path pattern* β,
2. computes a new collection B' as a function f of B and its neighbors,
3. and specifies the insertion of B' in place of B into C.

In the rest of this section, we first describe the topological collection types available in MGS beside the GBF. We introduce the notion of "Newtonian" and "Leibnizian" collection, because this distinction is crucial for the behavior of rule application. Subsection 4.2 sketches the most common pattern that can be used in the left hand side (l.h.s.) of a rule. Then we discuss some of the application strategy available in MGS. Finally, subsection 4.4 gives some simple examples of real MGS program.

4.1   Newtonian and Leibnizian Collection Types

There are several predefined collection types in MGS, and also several means to construct new collection types. The collection types can range in MGS from totally unstructured with sets and multisets to more structured with sequences and Abelian GBFs, Delaunay neighborhood and graphs (other topologies are currently under development). For any collection type T, the corresponding empty collection is written ():T. Elements in a collection T can be of any type, including collections, thus achieving *complex objects* in the sense of [BNTW95]. The name of a type is also a predicate used to test if a value has this type: T(v) returns true only if v has type T.

Monoidal Collections. Set, multiset (or bag) and sequences are members of the monoidal collection family. As a matter of fact, a sequence (resp. a multiset) (resp. a set) of values can be seen as an element of the free monoid (resp. the commutative monoid) (resp. the idempotent and commutative monoid). The join operation in V^* is written by a comma "," and induces the neighborhood of each element: let E be a monoidal collection, then elements x and y in E are neighbors iff $E = u,x,y,v$ for some u and v. This definition induces the following topology:

- for sets (type set), each element in the set is neighbor of any other element (because of the commutativity, the term describing a set can be reordered following any order);
- for multiset (type bag), each element is also neighbor of any other (however, the elements are not required to be distinct as in a set);
- for sequence (type seq), the topology is the expected one: an element not at the end has a neighbor at its right.

The comma operator is overloaded in MGS and can be used to build any monoidal collection (the type of the arguments disambiguate the collection built).

Newtonian and Leibnizian Collection Types. Coming back to the idea of seeing a data structure as a space, we can note a great difference between the "kind of space" involved by the GBFs and the monoidal collections. The two concepts of space involved by these data structure may be contrasted as follows:

1. in a GBF, the underlying space preexists (as the Cayley graph of the finite presentation) and is thought as a *container* for the collection elements;
2. in a monoidal collection, e.g. a set, the underlying space exists only by the virtue of the elements present in the collection.

The first notion as been advocated by Newton in opposition with Leibniz and Huygens [Jam93]. The last attributes a positional quality to the elements. In this approach, there is no such things like an empty place[3].

This distinction has several impacts on the management of the data structures. Consider the rule:

$$x, \; y \Rightarrow x$$

Intuitively it defines the erasure of an element y neighbor of an element x. This does not raise any difficulty in a Leibnizian collection: applied one time to a set with a cardinal greater than 2, this rule removes one randomly chosen element. However, in a Newtonian collection like an array, the erasure of y leave an empty cell, because the cell itself cannot disappear without breaking the neighborhood. The content of an empty cell is the special value <undef>.

Another distinction is that Newtonian collections correspond to an absolute space, where the place can be named, denoted and used in all the collections with the same type. There is no such thing for a Leibnizian collection: e.g. there is no notion of absolute place for the element of a multiset.

---

[3] An empty set/seq/bag is a space of a certain kind without any place, and not an empty space.

4.2   Path Patterns

A path is a sequence of elements and thus, a path pattern *Pat* is a sequence or a repetition *Rep* of *basic filters*. A basic filter *Bfilt* matches one element in a GBF. The grammar of path patterns reflects this decomposition:

$$Pat ::= Rep \mid Rep\ Dir\ Pat \mid Pat\ \text{as id} \mid (Pat)$$
$$Rep ::= Bfilt \mid Bfilt/exp \mid Bfilt\ Dir\text{+}$$
$$Bfilt ::= \text{cte} \mid \text{id} \mid \_ \mid \text{<undef>}$$
$$Dir ::= \text{,} \mid \text{|}u_1, \ \ldots, \ u_n\text{>}$$

where cte is a literal value, id ranges over the pattern variables, *exp* is a boolean expression, and u_i is a word of generators of a GBF. The following explanations give a systematic interpretation for these patterns.

literal: a literal value cte matches an element with the same value. For example, 123 matches an element in a GBF with value 123.

empty element the symbol <undef> matches an element with an undefined value, that is, an element whose position does not belong to the support of the GBF. The use of this basic filter is subject to some restriction: it can occur only as the neighbor of a defined element.

variable: a pattern variable a matches exactly one element with a well defined value. The variable a can then occur elsewhere in the rest of the rule and denotes the value of the matched element.

If the pattern variable a is not used in the rest of the rule, one can spare the effort of giving a fresh name using the anonymous filter _ that matches any element with a defined value. The position of a is accessible through the expression $pos(x)$.

neighbor: $b\ dir\ p$ is a pattern that matches a path with first element matched by b and continuing as a path matched by p with the first element p_0 such that p_0 is neighbor of b following the *dir* direction. The specification *dir* of a direction is interpreted as follows:

— the comma "," means that p_0 and b must be neighbors.

— the direction $|u_1, \ \ldots, \ u_n\text{>}$ means that p_0 must be a u_0-neighbor *or* a u_1-neighbor *or* ... *or* a u_n-neighbor of b;

For example, x, y matches two connected elements (i.e., x must be a neighbor of y). The pattern

```
1 |east> _ |north,east> 2
```

matches three elements. The first must have the value 1 and the third the value 2. The second is at the east of the first and the last is at the north *or* at the east of the second.

guard: p/exp matches a path matched by p if boolean expression *exp* evaluates to true. For instance, $x,\ y\ /\ y > x$ matches two neighbor elements x and y such that y is greater than x.

naming: a sub-pattern can be named using the as construct. For example, in the expression $(1,\ x\ \text{|north>+}\ ,\ 3)$ as P, the variable P is binded to the path matched by $1,\ x\ \text{|north>+},\ 3$.

repetition: pattern b $dir+$ matches a non-empty path b dir b $dir...dir$ b. If the basic filter b is a variable, then its value refers the sequence of matched elements and not to one of the individual values. The pattern $x+$ is an abbreviation for "`(_ ,+) as` x".

Elements matched by basic filters in a rule are distinct. So a matched path is without self-intersection. The identifier of a pattern variable can be used only once in the position of a filter. That is, the path pattern x,x is forbidden. However, this pattern can be rewritten for instance as: $x,y/y = x$.

4.3   Substitution and Application Strategies

Paths and Subcollections. A path pattern is used to find the occurrence of the specified path in a collection C. The matched path can be seen as a sequence of elements in C as well as a subcollection of C: the collection made of the elements in the path and inheriting its organization from C. Therefore, the right hand side (r.h.s.) can compute a sequence as well as a subcollection. If the r.h.s. is a sequence, then the nth element of the r.h.s. replaces the nth element of the matched path (this holds for Newtonian collections, Leibnizian collections are more flexible and allow the insertion or the deletion of elements). If the r.h.s is a collection, then this collection is pasted into C as a replacement for the matched path. The pasting operation depends of the collection kind and can be parameterized by giving explicit attributes to the arrow.

For example, suppose that we want to replace each 1 in a sequence by a series of three 1. The corresponding rule is:

```
1  ⇒  1, 1, 1
```

The behavior of the previous rule is the intended behavior. For example, applied to sequence 0, 1, 2, 1, 0 we obtain 0, 1, 1, 1, 2, 1, 1, 1, 0. However, there is a possible ambiguity with a rule that replaces each 1 by only one element which is, unfortunately, a sequence. That is, the desired result is a sequence of five elements: 0, (1, 1, 1), 2, (1, 1, 1), 0 (this sequence has for elements 3 integers and 2 sequences). This behavior is achieved by overriding the default pasting strategy of ⇒:

```
1  ={noflat}⇒  1, 1, 1
```

The attribute `noflat` enables the desired behavior.

Priorities and Application Order. Others attributes enable the control of the rule application strategy. For instance, rules can have a priority used to chose the next paths to match. However, the only property ensured by the MGS rewriting engine is the following: if no rule at all applies during the application of a transformation T on a collection C, then there is no occurrence in C of the paths specified by the l.h.s. of the rules of T. Nevertheless, if the l.h.s. of the T's rules specify only paths of length one, an additional property is satisfied: these rule are applied in a maximal parallel manner. For example

$$x \;\Rightarrow\; \mathtt{f}(x)$$

is a rule that implements a polytypic **map** f: this rule replaces each element x of a collection by $\mathtt{f}(x)$, for any collection type.

Iterations and Fixpoints. A transformation T is a function like any other function and a *first-class* value. For instance, a transformation can be passed as an argument to another function or returned as a result. It allows to sequence and compose transformations very easily.

The expression $T(c)$ denotes the application of one transformation step of the transformation T to the collection c. As said above, a transformation step consists in the parallel application of the rules (modulo the rule application's features). A transformation step can be easily iterated:

$$T[n]\,(c) \quad \text{denotes the application of } n \text{ transformation steps to } c$$
$$T[\mathtt{fixpoint}]\,(c) \quad \text{application of } T \text{ until a fixpoint is reached}$$
$$T[\mathtt{fixrule}]\,(c) \quad \text{idem but the fixpoint is detected when no rule applies}$$

4.4 Simple Examples

The path pattern language introduced above is largely enough to code the examples of figures 1, 2, and 3. We present the first three algorithms.

The transformation:

```
trans BeadSort = {   empty |north> 1  ⇒  1, empty   }
```

is applied on a *Grid2*. The constant **empty** is used to give a value to an empty place and the constant 1 is used to represent an occupied cell. The l.h.s. of the only rule of the transformation *BeadSort* selects the paths of length two, composed by an occupied cell at north of an empty cell. Such a path is replaced by a path computed in the r.h.s. of the rule. The r.h.s. in this example computes a path of length two with the occupied and the empty cell exchanged. Indeed, the comma in the MGS expression at the r.h.s. of a rule[4] is used to build a sequence by listing its elements.

The transformation *BubbleSort* acts on a sequence. Although the sequence collection type can be specified as a GBF with only one generator, the sequence type is predefined in MGS and has specific properties (see section 4.1). The transformation is defined as:

```
trans BubbleSort = {   x,y / x > y  ⇒  y,x   }
```

This is not really a bubble sort because swapping of elements can take at arbitrary places; hence an out-of-order element does not necessarily bubble to the top in the characteristic way.

---

[4] A comma is also used in a path expression to denote the neighborhood relationship between two elements in a collection in the l.h.s. The two usages agree, because in the sequence $a,\ b$ the elements a and b are neighbors.

The two previous examples do not create new elements in the collection. The *Erastothene* transformation computes the ordered sequence of the prime integers. Each element i in the sequence corresponds to the previously computed ith prime P_i and is represented by a record $\{p = P_i\}$. This element can receive a candidate number n and is then represented by a record $\{p = P_i, a = n\}$. If the candidate passes the test, then the element transforms itself to a record $r = \{x = P_i, b = n\}$. If the right neighbor of r is of form $\{x = P_{i+1}\}$, then the candidate n skip from r to the right neighbor. When there is no right neighbor to r, then n is prime and a new element is added at the end of the sequence. The first element of the sequence is distinguished and generates the candidates. Accordingly, the *Erastothene* transformation consists in 6 rules named *genere1*, *genere2*, *test1*, *test2*, *pass* and *create*:

```
trans Erastothene = {
    genere1:   n/int(n), <undef>  ⇒  n, {x=n}
    genere2:   n/int(n), {p=x, ~a, ~b}  ⇒  n, {x=n}
    test1:     {p=x, a=y, ~b} / y mod x == 0  ⇒  {p=x}
    test2:     {p=x, a=y, ~b} / y mod x <> 0  ⇒  {p=x, b=y}
    pass:      {p=x1, b=y}, {p=x2, ~a, ~b}  ⇒  {p=x1}, {p=x2, a=y}
    create:    {p=x, b=y}, <undef>  ⇒  {p=x}, {p=y}
}
```

The pattern $\{p=x, a=y, \~b\}$ matches a record with a field p (and the value of this field is binded to x), a field a and no field b. The pattern $n/\texttt{int}(n)$, <undef> matches a path reduced to a single integer (there is nothing at the right of this integer). Consequently, it matches the end of a sequence (if this end is an integer). The rule genere1 is used only once, at the beginning, when the transformation is applied to the sequence singleton 2,():seq.

5   Application to the Modeling of Dynamical Systems with a Dynamic Structure

Our topological approach is motivated by some considerations internal to computer science, and also by the needs expressed by some application domains. A target application domain for MGS is the modeling and simulation of dynamical systems (DS) and especially DS that exhibit a dynamic structure $((DS)^2)$. This kind of dynamical systems is very challenging to model and simulate. New programming concepts must be developed to ease their modeling and simulation.

Dynamical Systems with a Dynamical Structure. Intuitively, a dynamical system is a formal way to describe how a point (the state of the system) moves in the *phase space* (the space of all possible states of the system). It gives a rule, the *evolution function*, telling us where the point should go next from its current location. There exist several formalisms used to describe a DS: ordinary differential equations (ODE), partial differential equations (PDE), iterated equations (finite set of coupled difference equations), cellular automata, etc., following the discrete or continuous nature of the time, the space and the value used in the modeling.

Many DS systems are structured, which means that they can be decomposed into parts and *sometimes* the whole state s of the system is simply the product of the state of these parts. The evolution of the state of the whole system is then viewed as the result of the changes of the state of its parts. In this case, the evolution function h_i of a the state of a part o_i depends only on a subset $\{o_{i_j}\}$ of the state variables of the whole system. In this context, we say that the DS exhibits a *static structure* if:

1. the state of the system is statically described by the state of a fixed set of parts and this set does not change in time;
2. the relationships between the state of the parts, specified as the functions h_i between o_i and the arguments o_{i_j}, are also fixed and do not change in time.

Moreover, we say that the o_{i_j} are the *logical neighbors* of o_i (because very often, two parts of a system interact when they are physical neighbors). This situation is simple and arises often in elementary physics. For example, a falling stone is statically described by a position and a velocity and this set of variables does not change (even if the value of the position and the value of the velocity change in the course of time).

As pointed out by [GGMP02], many biological systems can be viewed as a dynamical system in which not only the values of state variables, but also the *set* of state variables *and/or* the evolution function, change over time. We call these systems *dynamical systems with a dynamic structure* following [GM01c], or $(DS)^2$ in short. An obvious example is given by the development of an embryo. Initially, the state of the system is described solely by the chemical state o_0 of the egg (no matter how complex this chemical state can be). After several divisions, the state of the embryo is given not only by the chemical state o_i of the cells, but also by their spatial arrangement[5]. The number of cells, their spatial organization and their interactions evolve constantly in the course of the development and is not handled by one fixed structure $\mathcal{O}$. On the contrary, the phase space $\mathcal{O}(t)$ used to characterize the structure of the state of the system at time t must be computed jointly with the running state of the system. In this kind of situation, the dynamic of the whole system is often specified as several local competing transformations occurring in an organized set of simpler entities. The organization of this set is subject to possible drastic changes in the course of time and is a plain part of the state of the DS.

The MGS approach. The main idea to model $(DS)^2$ is to follow an approach developed recently by several authors [FMP00, Man01, EKL$^+$02b, EKL$^+$02a]. The point is to use rewriting rules to model the parts of the system in interaction.

---

[5] The neighborhood of each cell is of paramount importance to evolution of the system because of the interplay between the shape of the system and the state of the cells. The shape of the system has an impact on the diffusion of the chemical signals and hence on the cells state. Reciprocally, the state of each cell determines the evolution of the shape of the whole system.

More specifically, we want to use an MGS topological collection S to represent the state of a dynamical system at a given time. The elements in the collection represent either entities (a subsystem or an atomic part of the dynamical system) or messages (signal, command, information, action, etc.) addressed to an entity.

A path or a subcollection in S represents a subset of interacting entities and messages in the system. The evolution of the system is achieved through transformations, where the l.h.s. of a rule typically matches an entity and a message addressed to it, and where the r.h.s. specifies the entity's updated state, and possibly other messages addressed to other entities.

If one uses a multiset organization for the collection, the entities interact in a rather unstructured way. More organized topological collections are used for more sophisticated spatial organizations and interactions (like GBFs or Delaunay).

More generally, many mathematical models of objects and processes are based on a notion of state that specifies the object or the process by assigning some data to each point of a physical or abstract space. The MGS programming language is designed to support this approach offering several mechanisms to build complex and evolving spaces and handling the maps between these spaces and the data.

In the rest of this section we present three examples involving various topology. The first one involves the use of sequences and multisets and is related to the cleavage of DNA strings floating in a chemical solution. The second example uses an hexagonal lattice to discretize the 2D formation of a snowflake. The last one sketch the trajectory of cells attracted by some neighbors. This example involves a dynamic topology computed as the result of the Delaunay triangulation of a set of points in Euclidean space.

5.1   Restriction Enzymes

This example shows the ability to nest different topologies to achieve the modeling of a biological structure. We want to represent the action of a set of restriction enzymes on the DNA. The DNA structure is simplified as a sequence of letters A, C, T and G. The DNA strings are collected in a multiset. Thus we have to manipulate a multiset of sequences. The following declarations:

```
collection DNA = seq;;
collection TUBE = bag;;
```

introduce a subtype called DNA of seq and a subtype of multisets called TUBE.

A restriction enzyme is represented as a rule that splits the DNA strings; for instance a rule like:

```
EcoRI = X+, ("G","A","A","T","T","C"), Y+
    ⇒ (X,"G") :: ("A","A","T","T","C",Y) :: ():TUBE ;
```

stands for the *EcoRI* restriction enzyme with recognition sequence G^AATTC (the point of cleavage is marked with ^). The X+ pattern filters the part of the DNA string before the recognition sequence. Identically, Y names the part of the string after the recognition sequence. The r.h.s. of the rule constructs a TUBE containing the two resulting DNA subsequences (the :: operator indicates the "consing" of an element at the head of a sequence).

We need an additional rule Void for specifying that a DNA string without a recognition sequence must be inserted wrapped in a TUBE. The two rules are collected into one transformation:

```
trans Restriction = {
    EcoRI = ...;
    Void = X+ ⇒ X :: ():TUBE ;
}
```

The rule specification order in a transformation is taken into account, and so, the rule Void is used only if rule EcoRI cannot be applied. In this way, the result of applying the transformation *Restriction* on a DNA string is systematically a sequence with only one element which is a TUBE.

The transformation *Restriction* can then be applied to the DNA strings floating in a TUBE using the simple transformation:

```
trans React = { dna ⇒ hd(Restriction(dna)) }
```

The operator hd gives the head of the result of the transformation *Restriction*, i.e. a TUBE containing one or two DNA strings. These elements are then merged with the content of the enclosing TUBE. The transformation can be iterated until a fixpoint is reached:

```
React[fixpoint]((
    ("C","C","C","G","A","A","T","T","C","A","A",():DNA),
    ("T","T","G","A","A","T","T","C","G","G","G",():DNA),
    ():TUBE ));;
```

returns a tube with four DNA strings:

```
("T","T","G",():DNA),
("C","C","C","G",():DNA),
("A","A","T","T","C","A","A",():DNA),
("A","A","T","T","C","G","G","G",():DNA),
():TUBE
```

5.2 The Formation of a Snowflake

A crystal forms when a liquid is cooled below its freezing point. Crystals start from a seed and then grows by progressively adding more molecules to their surface. As an idealization, the molecules of a snowflake lie on an hexagonal grid and when a piece of ice is added, to the snowflake, the heat released by this process inhibits the addition of ice nearby.

This phenomenon leads to the following cellular automata rule [Wol02]: a black cell (value 1) represents a place of the crystal filled with ice and a white cell

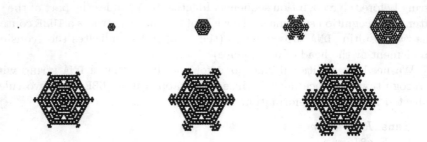

Fig. 9. Formation of a snowflake. See section 5.2 for the explanation. The transformation acts on a GBF *Hexagon* (cf. sec. 3). The pictured states are the step at time steps 1, 4, 8, 12, 16, 18, 20 and 23.

(value 0) is an empty place. A white cell becomes black if it has exactly one black neighbor, otherwise it remains white. The corresponding MGS transformation is:

```
trans SnowFlake = {
    0 as x / 1 == FoldNeighbor[\y.\acc.y+acc, 0](x)  ⇒  1
}
```

The construct `FoldNeighbor` is not a function but an operator available only within a rule: it enables to fold a function on the defined neighbors of an element matched in the l.h.s. Here, this operator is used to compute the number of neighbors (parameter y enumerates the neighbors and parameter `acc` acts as an accumulator). This transformation acts on a value of type *Hexagon* and a possible run is illustrated in figure 9.

5.3   System of Moving Cells Linked by Spring-Like Forces

We want to model the trajectory of a set of cells. A cell moves because it is attracted by its immediate neighbors (for example because the limited diffusion of a chemical that creates a gradient). The problem is that, due to the cell movements, the immediate neighbors of a cell can change. We use a Delaunay triangulation to compute the neighborhood of the cells. The Delaunay triangulation of a point set is a collection of edges satisfying an "empty circle" property: for each edge we can find a circle containing the edge's endpoints but not containing any other points.

In MGS, we start by defining the type of the value that represents a cell:

```
record Position = { x:float, y:float, z:float };;
record Cell = Position + {1};;
```

specify two record types, the first having the fields x, y and z, and the second having a field 1 in addition. The 1 field is used to associate an attractive force to each cell.

We then define a *Delaunay collection type*. The specification:

```
collection delaunay(3) D3 =
    \e.if Position(e)
        then (e.x, e.y, e.z)
        else ?("bad element type for D3 delaunay type") fi ;;
```

defines a new Delaunay collection type in 3 dimensions. The type, called *D3*, is parameterized by a user function that extracts from each element in the collection, an abstract coordinate. In this example, the coordinate are simply stored in the value that represents a cell and the function simply check that the cell's value has a correct type and returns its coordinate (as a sequence of 3 floats).

We assume that the interaction between two cells is computed by a function of two arguments called `interaction`. Then, the following MGS program fragment:

```
epsilon = 0.05;;
fun add(u, v, e) =
    u + { x = u.x + e*v.x, y = u.y + e*v.y, z = u.z + e*v.z };;
fun sum(x, u, acc) = add(acc, interaction(x,u), epsilon);;
trans evol = {
    c ⇒
    add(c, FoldNeighbor[sum(x), {x=0,y=0,z=0,l=c.l}](c), epsilon)
};;
```

defines *evol*, the system's evolution function. The function `add` takes two records u and v and a float e. The result is a record containing all the fields of u but where the fields x, y and z have been updated by a linear combination of the corresponding fields in u and v. The function sum adds to its first argument, the interaction between two cells. This function is called in the `FoldNeighbor` construct appearing in the transformation *evol*. This transformation compute the sum of the interaction between a cell *c* and a neighbor cell; this sum is then used to change the state of the cell *c*.

The result of 250 iteration steps of this program, assuming an `interaction` function computing a force corresponding to a spring parameterized by the l observable, is showed at figure 10.

Delaunay collections are Leibnizian, so it is easy to extend the model to take into account cellular division and death.

6   Related Works, Current Work and Future Work

The topological approach we have sketched here is part of a long term research effort [GMS95] developed for instance in [Gia00] where the focus is on the substructure, or in [GM01a] where a general tool for uniform neighborhood definition is developed. In this research program, a data structure is viewed as a space where some computation occurs and moves in this space. The notion of neighborhood is then used to control the computations.

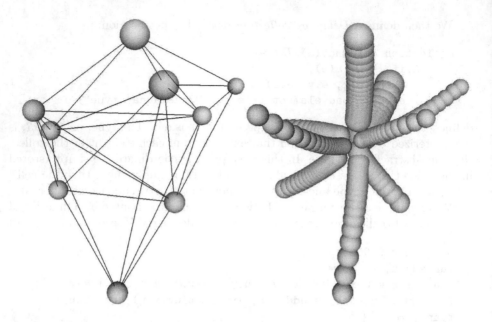

Fig. 10. Each sphere in the picture above corresponds to a cell attracted by its neighboring cells by a spring. The neighborhood of a cell is computed dynamically using a Delaunay triangulation built from the cells position. At each time step, this neighborhood can change. The first picture is the initial state and shows the neighborhood using links between the cells. The second picture shows the final state, when the system has reached an equilibrium (each "tube" in this picture represents the successive positions of a cell). In MGS, the Delaunay collection type is a type constructor corresponding to the building of collections with a neighborhood computed from the positions of the elements in a d-dimensional Euclidean space.

Related Works. Seeing a computation as a path in some abstract space is hardly new: the representation of the execution of a concurrent program as a trajectory in the Cartesian product of the sequential processes dates back to the 60's (in this representation, semaphore operations create topological obstructions and one can study the topology of theses obstructions to decide if a deadlock may occur). However, note that the considered space is based on the control structure, not on the involved data structure.

In the same line, the methods for building domains in denotational semantics have clearly topological roots, but they involve the *topology of the set of values*, not the *topology of a value*.

Transformation on multiset is reminiscent of multiset-rewriting (or rewriting of terms modulo AC). This is the main computational device of Gamma [BM86, BCM87], a language based on a chemical metaphor; the data are considered as a multiset M of molecules and the computation is a succession of chemical reactions according to a particular rule. The CHemical Abstract Machine (CHAM) extends these ideas with a focus on the expression of semantic of non deterministic processes [BB90]. The CHAM introduces a mechanism to isolate some parts of the chemical solution. This idea has been seriously taken into account in the notion of P systems. P systems [Pau98, Pau01] are a new distributed parallel computing model based on the notion of a membrane structure. A membrane structure is a nesting of cells represented, e.g, by a Venn diagram without intersection and with a unique superset: the skin. Objects are placed in the regions defined by the membranes and evolve following various transformations: an object can evolve into another object, can pass trough a membrane or dissolve its enclosing membrane. As for Gamma, the computation is finished when no object can further evolve. By using nested multisets, MGS is able to emulate more or less the notion of P systems. In addition, patterns like the iteration + go beyond what is possible to specify in the l.h.s. of a Gamma rule[6].

Lindenmayer systems [Lin68] have long been used in the modeling of $(DS)^2$ (especially in the modeling of plant growing). They loosely correspond to transformations on sequences or string rewriting (they also correspond to tree rewriting, because some standard features make particularly simple to code arbitrary trees, cf. the work of P. Prusinkiewicz [PLH$^+$90, PH92]). Obviously, L systems are dedicated to the handling of linear and tree-like structures.

There exists strong links between GBF and cellular automata (CA), especially considering the work of Z. Róka which has studied CA on Cayley graphs [Rók94]. However, our own works focus on the construction of Cayley graphs as the shape of a data structure and we develop an operator algebra and rewriting notions on this new data type. This is not in the line of Z. Róka which focuses on synchronization problems and establishes complexity results in the framework of CA.

Formalizations and Implementations. A unifying theoretical framework can be developed [GM01b, GM02b], based on the notion of *chain complex* developed in algebraic combinatorial topology [Hen94]. The topology needed to describe the neighborhood in a set or a sequence, or more generally the topology of the usual data structures, are fairly poor. However, the topological framework unifies various situations (see the paragraph above). Nevertheless, we do not claim that we have achieved a useful theoretical framework encompassing the previous paradigms. We advocate that few (topological) notions and a single syntax can be consistently used to allow the merging of several formalisms (CA, L systems, P systems, etc.) *for programming* purposes. All the examples presented here are running with one or the other of the two existing MGS interpreters. A new version of the interpreter is currently developed, written in OCAML (a dialect of ML): please visit the MGS home page: http://mgs.lami.univ-evry.fr.

Perspectives. The perspectives opened by this preliminary work are numerous. We want to develop several complementary approaches to defines new topological collection types. One approach to extend the GBF applicability is to consider

---

[6] For example the rule "x+ /n==length(x) $\Rightarrow$?(x)" can be used on a graph with n vertices to print an Hamiltonian path (function ? print its argument and function length gives the length of a sequence).

monoids instead of groups, especially automatic monoids which exhibit good algorithmic properties. Another direction is to handle general combinatorial spatial structures like simplicial complexes or G-maps [Lie91]. At the language level, the study of the topological collections concepts must continue with a finer study of transformation kinds. Several kinds of restriction can be put on the transformations, leading to various kind of pattern languages and rules. The complexity of matching such patterns has to be investigated. The efficient compilation of a MGS program is a long-term research. We have considered in this paper only one-dimensional paths, but a general n-dimensional notion of path exists and can be used to generalize the substitution mechanisms of MGS. From the applications point of view, we are targeted by the simulation of more complex developmental processes in biology [GGMP02].

To conclude, I want to promote the use of topological notions in computer science. The work sketched here is a modest step in this direction. I use the qualifier modest because the notions used here rely on very elementary notions taken in the domain of *combinatorial algebraic topology*. We do not use deep theorems but rather fundamental definitions that structure the field and clarify the objects and mechanisms to manage. This is why I want to advocate the development of alternative topological approaches of computation, confident on their heuristic, technical and pedagogical virtues.

Acknowledgments

I would like to reiterate my gratitude for Olivier Michel: our disputes are always fertile, frustrating and insightful. I am also grateful to P. Prusinkiewicz at University of Calgary, C. Godin at CIRAD Montpellier and F. Delaplace, J. Cohen, P. Legall, G. Bernot at LaMI, and the members of the "Simulation and Epigenesis" group at GENOPOLE-Evry for fruitful discussions, biological motivations, warm encouragements and challenging questions. The delightful questions and encouragements of D. Blasco have also raised many issues and motivated many developments of this work.

Many parts of this presentation have been developed in the following papers [GM01b, GM01c, GM01a, GM02b, GGMP02, GMC02, GM02a]. This research is supported in part by the CNRS, the GDR ALP, IMPG, GENOPOLE and the University of Evry.

References

ACD02.   J.J. Arulanandham, C.S. Calude, and M.J. Dinneen. Bead-sort: A natural sorting algorithm. *Bulletin of the European Association for Theoretical Computer Science*, 76:153–162, February 2002. Technical Contributions.

BB90.   G. Berry and G. Boudol. The chemical abstract machine. In *Conf. Record 17th ACM Symp. on Principles of Programmming Languages, POPL'90, San Francisco, CA, USA, 17–19 Jan. 1990*, pages 81–94. ACM Press, New York, 1990.

BCM87.   J. P. Banâtre, A. Coutant, and Daniel Le Métayer. Parallel machines for multiset transformation and their programming style. Technical Report RR-0759, Inria, 1987.

BLL97.   F. Bergeron, G. Labelle, and P. Leroux. *Combinatorial species and tree-like structures*, volume 67 of *Encyclopedia of mathematics and its applications*. Cambridge University Press, 1997. isbn 0-521-57323-8.

BM86.   J. P. Banâtre and Daniel Le Métayer. A new computational model and its discipline of programming. Technical Report RR-0566, Inria, 1986.

BNTW95.   Peter Buneman, Shamim Naqvi, Val Tannen, and Limsoon Wong. Principles of programming with complex objects and collection types. *Theoretical Computer Science*, 149(1):3–48, 18 September 1995.

Ede58.   M. Eden. In H. P. Yockey, editor, *Symposium on Information Theory in Biology*, page 359, New York, 1958. Pergamon Press.

EKL+02a.   S. Eker, M. Knapp, K. Laderoute, P. Lincoln, J. Meseguer, and J. Sonmez. Pathway logic: Symbolic analysis of biological signaling. In *Proceedings of the Pacific Symposium on Biocomputing*, pages 400 412, January 2002.

EKL+02b.   Steven Eker, Merrill Knapp, Keith Laderoute, Patrick Lincoln, , and Carolyn Talcott. Pathway logic: Executable models of biological networks. In *Fourth International Workshop on Rewriting Logic and Its Applications (WRLA'2002)*, volume 71 of *Electronic Notes in Theoretical Computer Science*. Elsevier, 2002.

FM97.   P. Fradet and D. Le Métayer. Shape types. In *Proc. of Principles of Programming Languages*, Paris, France, Jan. 1997. ACM Press.

FMP00.   Michael Fisher, Grant Malcolm, and Raymond Paton. Spatio-logical processes in intracellular signaling. *BioSystems*, 55:83–92, 2000.

FS96.   Leonidas Fegaras and Tim Sheard. Revisiting catamorphisms over datatypes with embedded functions (or, Programs from outer space). In *Conference Record of POPL '96: The 23rd ACM SIGPLAN-SIGACT Symposium on Principles of Programming Languages*, pages 284–294, St. Petersburg Beach, Florida, 21–24 January 1996.

GG95.   D. Gautier and C. Germain. A static approach for compiling communications in parallel scientific programs. *Scientific Programming*, 4:291–305, 1995.

GGMP02.   J.-L. Giavitto, C. Godin, O. Michel, and P. Prusinkiewicz. *Modelling and Simulation of biological processes in the context of genomics*, chapter "Computational Models for Integrative and Developmental Biology". Hermes, July 2002.

Gia00.   J.-L. Giavitto. A framework for the recursive definition of data structures. In *ACM-Sigplan 2nd International Conference on Principles and Practice of Declarative Programming (PPDP'00)*, pages 45–55, Montréal, September 2000. ACM-press.

GJ92.   E. Goubault and T. P. Jensen. Homology of higher-dimensional automata. In *Proc. of CONCUR'92*, Stonybrook, August 1992. Springer-Verlag.

GM01a.   J.-L. Giavitto and O. Michel. Declarative definition of group indexed data structures and approximation of their domains. In *Proceedings of the 3nd International ACM SIGPLAN Conference on Principles and Practice of Declarative Programming (PPDP-01)*. ACM Press, September 2001.

GM01b.   J.-L. Giavitto and O. Michel. MGS: a programming language for the transformations of topological collections. Technical Report 61-2001, LaMI – Université d'Évry Val d'Essonne, May 2001.

232   Jean-Louis Giavitto

GM01c.   Jean-Louis Giavitto and Olivier Michel. Mgs: a rule-based programming
           language for complex objects and collections. In Mark van den Brand and
           Rakesh Verma, editors, *Electronic Notes in Theoretical Computer Science*,
           volume 59. Elsevier Science Publishers, 2001.

GM02a.   J.-L. Giavitto and O. Michel. Data structure as topological spaces. In
           *Proceedings of the 3nd International Conference on Unconventional Mod-
           els of Computation UMC02*, volume 2509, pages 137–150, Himeji, Japan,
           October 2002. Lecture Notes in Computer Science.

GM02b.   J.-L. Giavitto and O. Michel. The topological structures of membrane
           computing. *Fundamenta Informaticae*, 49:107–129, 2002.

GMC02.   J.-L. Giavitto, O. Michel, and J. Cohen. Pattern-matching and rewriting
           rules for group indexed data structures. Technical Report 76-2002, LaMI
           – Université d'Évry Val d'Essonne, June 2002.

GMS95.   J.-L. Giavitto, O. Michel, and J.-P. Sansonnet. Group based fields. In
           I. Takayasu, R. H. Jr. Halstead, and C. Queinnec, editors, *Parallel Symbolic
           Languages and Systems (International Workshop PSLS'95)*, volume 1068
           of *LNCS*, pages 209–215, Beaune (France), 2–4 October 1995. Springer-
           Verlag.

Hen94.   M. Henle. *A combinatorial introduction to topology*. Dover publications,
           New-York, 1994.

Jam93.   Max Jammer. *Concepts of space – the history of theories of space in physics*.
           Dover, 1993. third enlarged edition (first edition 1954).

Jay95.   C. Barry Jay. A semantics of shape. *Science of Computer Programming*,
           25(2–3):251–283, 1995.

Lie91.   P. Lienhardt. Topological models for boundary representation: a com-
           parison with n-dimensional generalized maps. *Computer-Aided Design*,
           23(1):59–82, 1991.

Lin68.   A. Lindenmayer. Mathematical models for cellular interaction in develop-
           ment, Parts I and II. *Journal of Theoretical Biology*, 18:280–315, 1968.

Lis93.   B. Lisper. On the relation between functional and data-parallel program-
           ming languages. In *Proc. of the 6th. Int. Conf. on Functional Languages
           and Computer Architectures*. ACM, ACM Press, June 1993.

Man01.   Vincenzo Manca. Logical string rewriting. *Theoretical Computer Science*,
           264:25–51, 2001.

MFP91.   E. Meijer, M. Fokkinga, and R. Paterson. Functional Programming with
           Bananas, Lenses, Envelopes and Barbed Wire. In *5th ACM Conference
           on Functional Programming Languages and Computer Architecture*, volume
           523 of *Lecture Notes in Computer Science*, pages 124–144, Cambridge, MA,
           August 26–30, 1991. Springer, Berlin.

NO94.   Susumu Nishimura and Atsushi Ohori. A calculus for exploiting data par-
           allelism on recursively defined data (Preliminary Report). In *International
           Workshop TPPP '94 Proceedings (LNCS 907)*, pages 413–432. Springer-
           Verlag, November 94.

Pau98.   G. Paun. Computing with membranes. Technical Report TUCS-TR-208,
           TUCS - Turku Centre for Computer Science, November 11 1998.

Pau01.   G. Paun. From cells to computers: Computing with membranes (p sys-
           tems). *Biosystems*, 59(3):139–158, March 2001.

PH92. P. Prusinkiewicz and J. Hanan. L systems: from formalism to programming languages. In G. Ronzenberg and A. Salomaa, editors, *Lindenmayer Systems, Impacts on Theoretical Computer Science, Computer Graphics and Developmental Biology*, pages 193–211. Springer Verlag, February 1992.

PLH⁺90. P. Prusinkiewicz, A. Lindenmayer, J. S. Hanan, et al. *The Algorithmic Beauty of Plants*. Springer-Verlag, 1990.

Rók94. Zsuzsanna Róka. One-way cellular automata on Cayley graphs. *Theoretical Computer Science*, 132(1–2):259–290, 26 September 1994.

Wol02. Stephen Wolfram. *A new kind of science*. Wolfram Media, 2002.

On the Complexity of Higher-Order Matching in the Linear λ-Calculus

Sylvain Salvati and Philippe de Groote

LORIA UMR n° 7503 – INRIA
Campus Scientifique, B.P. 239
54506 Vandœuvre lès Nancy Cedex – France
salvati@loria.fr, degroote@loria.fr

Abstract. We prove that linear second-order matching in the linear λ-calculus with linear occurrences of the unknowns is NP-complete. This result shows that context matching and second-order matching in the linear λ-calculus are, in fact, two different problems.

1 Introduction

Higher-order unification, which consists in solving a syntactic equation between two simply-typed λ-terms (modulo β, or modulo $\beta\eta$), is undecidable [9], even in the second-order case [7]. Consequently, several restrictions of the problem have been introduced and studied in the literature(see [6] for a survey).

Higher-order matching is such a restriction. It consists in solving equations whose right-hand sides do not contain any unknown. This problem, which is indeed simpler, has been shown to be decidable in the second-order case [10], in the third-order case [5], and in the fourth order case [13]. Starting form the sixth-order case, higher-order matching modulo β is undecidable [12]. On the other-hand the decidability of higher-order matching modulo $\beta\eta$ is still open.

Another restriction consists in studying unification in the linear λ-calculus where every λ-abstraction $\lambda x.\, M$ is such that M contains exactly one free occurrence of x. The problem of unification in the linear λ-calculus, in the second order case, is related to context unification [1,2], which consists of unifying trees in which occur second-order variables (*i.e.*, variables ranging on "trees with holes"). It has been studied by Levy under the name of *linear second-order unification* [11]. Nevertheless, its decidability is still open. On the other hand, the more restricted problem of higher-order matching in the linear λ-calculus has been shown to be decidable and even NP-complete [8] which is also the case of context matching [15]. A related problem consists in deciding whether a matching problem between simply typed λ-terms admits a linear solution. This more general problem is also decidable [4].

Finally, several other restrictions concern the way the unknowns occur in the equation. In particular, another notion of linearity appears in the literature. Indeed, linear unification (or matching) also designates equations whose unknowns occur only once.

R. Nieuwenhuis (Ed.): RTA 2003, LNCS 2706, pp. 234–245, 2003.

In this paper, we will be concerned with these two different notions of linearity (equations between linear λ-terms, or linear occurrences of the unknowns). In order not to confuse them, we will speak of *matching in the linear λ-calculus*, in the first case, and we will use the expression *linear matching* for the second case. This question of vocabulary being settled, we may state our main result: *linear second-order matching in the linear λ-calculus is NP-complete.* Such a complexity, at first sight, might be surprising. Indeed, it seems to be folklore that context matching and second-order matching in the linear λ-calculus are equivalent problems. Our result, however, shows that this is not quite the case. Indeed, linear context matching is polynomial [15].

In fact, the key difference between a context $C[x_1, \ldots, x_n]$ and a second-order λ-term is the following : in a linear λ-term $\lambda x_1 \ldots x_n.C$, the order in which the λ-variables are abstracted does not especially correspond to the order in which these variables occur in the body of the term. This slight difference is sufficient to make our problem NP-complete while linear context matching is polynomial.

The paper is organized as follows. Section 2 contains prerequisite basic notions, and defines precisely what is linear second-order matching in the linear λ-calculus. In Section 3, we define a variant of the satifiability problem (which we call 1-neg-sat), and we prove its NP-completeness. Section 4 shows how to reduce 1-neg-sat to linear second-order matching in the linear λ-calculus, and Section 5 proves the correctness of the reduction. Finally, in Section 6, we state some related results.

2   Higher-Order Matching in the Linear λ-Calculus

This section reviews basic definitions and fixes the notations that we use in the sequel of the paper.

Definition 1. *Let $\mathcal{A}$ be a finite set, the elements of which are called* atomic types. *The set $\mathcal{F}$ of* linear functional types *built upon $\mathcal{A}$ is defined according to the following grammar:*

$$\mathcal{F} \quad ::= \quad \mathcal{A} \mid (\mathcal{F} \multimap \mathcal{F}).$$

∎

We let the lowercase Greek letters $(\alpha, \beta, \gamma, \ldots)$ range over $\mathcal{F}$, and we adopt the usual convention that $\alpha_1 \multimap \alpha_2 \multimap \cdots \alpha_n \multimap \alpha$ stands for $\alpha_1 \multimap (\alpha_2 \multimap (\cdots (\alpha_n \multimap \alpha) \cdots))$, and we write $\alpha^n \multimap \beta$ for:

$$\underbrace{\alpha \multimap \ldots \multimap \alpha}_{n\times} \multimap \beta$$

The order of such a linear functional type is defined as usual:

$$\text{order}(a) = 1 \text{ if } a \in \mathcal{A}$$
$$\text{order}(\alpha \multimap \beta) = \max(\text{order}(\alpha) + 1, \text{order}(\beta))$$

Then, the notion of raw λ-term is defined as follows.

Definition 2. *Let $(\Sigma_\alpha)_{\alpha\in\mathcal{F}}$ be a family of pairwise disjoint finite sets indexed by $\mathcal{F}$, whose almost every member is empty. Let $(\mathcal{X}_\alpha)_{\alpha\in\mathcal{F}}$ and $(\mathcal{Y}_\alpha)_{\alpha\in\mathcal{F}}$ be two families of pairwise disjoint countably infinite sets indexed by $\mathcal{F}$, such that $(\bigcup_{\alpha\in\mathcal{F}} \mathcal{X}_\alpha) \cap (\bigcup_{\alpha\in\mathcal{F}} \mathcal{Y}_\alpha) = \varnothing$. The set $\mathcal{T}$ of raw λ-terms is defined according to the following grammar:*

$$\mathcal{T} \;::=\; \Sigma \mid \mathcal{X} \mid \mathcal{Y} \mid \lambda\mathcal{X}.\mathcal{T} \mid (\mathcal{T}\,\mathcal{T}),$$

where $\Sigma = \bigcup_{\alpha\in\mathcal{F}} \Sigma_\alpha$, $\mathcal{X} = \bigcup_{\alpha\in\mathcal{F}} \mathcal{X}_\alpha$, and $\mathcal{Y} = \bigcup_{\alpha\in\mathcal{F}} \mathcal{Y}_\alpha$. ∎

In this definition, Σ is the set of constants, $\mathcal{X}$ is the set of λ-*variables*, and $\mathcal{Y}$ is the set of *meta-variables* or *unknowns*. We let the lowercase roman letters $(a, b, c, \ldots)$ range over the constants, the lowercase italic letters $(x, y, z, \ldots)$ range over the λ-variables, the uppercase bold letters $(\mathbf{X}, \mathbf{Y}, \mathbf{Z}, \ldots)$ range over the unknowns, and the uppercase italic letters $(M, N, O, \ldots)$ range over the λ-terms.

We write $h(M_1, \ldots, M_n)$ for a λ-term of the form $((\ldots(h\,M_1)\ldots)\,M_n)$, where h is either a constant, a λ-variable, or a meta-variable. Given such a term, h is called the head of the term.

The notions of free and bound occurrences of a λ-variable are defined as usual, and we write $\mathrm{FV}(M)$ for the set of λ-variables that occur free in a λ-term M. Finally, a λ-term that does not contain any meta-variable is called a *pure* λ-*term*.

We then define the notion of term of the linear λ-calculus..

Definition 3. *The family $(\mathcal{T}_\alpha)_{\alpha\in\mathcal{F}}$ of sets of terms of the linear λ-calculus is inductively defined as follows:*

1. *if $a \in \Sigma_\alpha$ then $a \in \mathcal{T}_\alpha$;*
2. *if $\mathbf{X} \in \mathcal{Y}_\alpha$ then $\mathbf{X} \in \mathcal{T}_\alpha$;*
3. *if $x \in \mathcal{X}_\alpha$ then $x \in \mathcal{T}_\alpha$;*
4. *if $x \in \mathcal{X}_\alpha$, $M \in \mathcal{T}_\beta$, and $x \in \mathrm{FV}(M)$, then $\lambda x.\,M \in \mathcal{T}_{(\alpha\multimap\beta)}$;*
5. *if $M \in \mathcal{T}_{(\alpha\multimap\beta)}$, $N \in \mathcal{T}_\alpha$, and $\mathrm{FV}(M) \cap \mathrm{FV}(N) = \varnothing$, then $(M\,N) \in \mathcal{T}_\beta$.* ∎

Clauses 4 and 5 imply that any term $\lambda x.\,M$ of the linear λ-calculus is such that there is exactly one free occurrence of x in M. Remark, on the other hand, that constants and unknowns may occur several times in the same linear λ-term.

We define the set of terms of the linear λ-calculus to be $\bigcup_{\alpha\in\mathcal{F}} \mathcal{T}_\alpha$. One easily proves that the sets $(\mathcal{T}_\alpha)_{\alpha\in\mathcal{F}}$ are pairwise disjoint. Consequently, we may define the type of a term M to be the unique linear type α such that $M \in \mathcal{T}_\alpha$. This allows the order of a term to be defined as the order of its type. In particular, we will speak about the order of a meta-variable.

The notions of α-conversion, η and β-reduction are defined as usual. In particular, we write $\twoheadrightarrow_\beta$ for the relation of β-reduction, and $=_\beta$ for the relation of β-conversion.

We let $M[x:=N]$ denote the usual capture-avoiding substitution of a λ-variable by a λ-term. Similarly, $M[\mathbf{X}:=N]$ denotes the capture-avoiding substitution of a meta-variable by a λ-term. We abbreviate $M[x_1:=N_1]\cdots[x_n:=N_n]$ as $M[x_i:=N_i]_{i=1}^n$.

We now give a precise definition of the matching problem with which we are concerned.

Definition 4. *A matching problem in the linear λ-calculus is a pair of terms of the linear λ-calculus* $\langle M, N \rangle$ *of the same type such that N is pure (i.e., does not contain any meta-variable).*

Such a problem admits a solution if and only if there exists a substitution $(\mathbf{X}_i := O_i)_{i=1}^n$ *such that* $M[\mathbf{X}_i := O_i]_{i=1}^n =_\beta N$, *where* $\{\mathbf{X}_1, \ldots, \mathbf{X}_n\}$ *is the set of meta-variables that occur in M.*   ∎

In the above definition, we have taken the relation of β-conversion to be the notion of equality between λ-terms. Nevertheless, all the results we will establish remain valid when taking the relation of $\beta\eta$-conversion as the notion of equality.

In the sequel of this paper, a pair of λ-terms $\langle M, N \rangle$ obeying the conditions of the above definition will also be called a *syntactic equation*. The order of such an equation is defined to be the maximum of the orders of the meta-variables occurring in left-hand side the equation. Finally, such an equation is said to be linear if the meta-variables occurring in its left-hand side occur only once.

In this paper, we will mainly be concerned with linear second-order matching in the linear λ-calculus, i.e, the problem of solving a linear second-order syntactic equation between terms of the linear λ-calculus.

3   1-Neg-sat

In this section, we define a variant of the satisfiability problem, due to Kilpeläinen [14].

We first remind the reader of some basic definitions. Given a finite set $\mathcal{A} = \{a_1, \ldots, a_n\}$ of boolean variables, a literal is defined to be either a boolean variable a_i or its negation $\neg a_i$. A clause is a finite set of literals, and a satisfiability problem consists in a finite set of clauses. A positive literal a_i is satisfied by a valuation $\eta : \mathcal{A} \to \{0, 1\}$ if and only if $\eta(a_i) = 1$, and a negative literal $\neg a_i$ is satisfied if and only if $\eta(a_i) = 0$, in which case we also write $\eta(\neg a_i) = 1$. Then, a satisfiability problem $\mathcal{C}$ admits a solution if and only if there exists a valuation $\eta : \mathcal{A} \to \{0, 1\}$ such that for all $C \in \mathcal{C}$ there exists $l \in C$ with $\eta(l) = 1$. As is well known, satisfiability is NP-complete [3].

We now introduce the variant of the satisfiability problem that we call *1-neg-sat*.

Definition 5. *Let* $\mathcal{A}$ *be a finite set of boolean variables, and* $\mathcal{C}$ *be a finite set of clauses over* $\mathcal{A}$. $\mathcal{C}$ *is called a 1-neg-sat problem if and only if for all* $a \in \mathcal{A}$, *there exists exactly one* $C \in \mathcal{C}$ *such that* $\neg a \in C$.   ∎

The next result is due to Kilpeläinen [14].

Lemma 1. *1-Neg-sat is NP-complete.*

Proof. We show that any satisfiability problem can be reduced to a 1-neg-sat-problem.

Let $\mathcal{C}$ be a finite set of clauses over the set of boolean variables $\mathcal{A} = \{a_1, \dots, a_n\}$. We introduce a set $\mathcal{B} = \{b_1, \dots, b_n\}$ of fresh boolean variables, and we define $\mathcal{D}$ to be the set of clauses $\bigcup_{i=1}^{n} \{\{a_i, b_i\}, \{\neg a_i, \neg b_i\}\}$. Clearly, any valuation η that satisfies $\mathcal{D}$ is such that $\eta(a_i) = 0$ if and only if $\eta(b_i) = 1$. Conversely, any valuation η such that $\eta(a_i) = 0$ if and only if $\eta(b_i) = 1$ satisfies $\mathcal{D}$.

Then we define $\mathcal{C}^*$ as the set of clauses obtained from $\mathcal{C}$ by replacing each occurrence of $\neg a_i$ by b_i. By construction, $\mathcal{C}^* \cup \mathcal{D}$ is a 1-neg-sat problem. Moreover, any valuation that satisfies this problem satisfies $\mathcal{C}$. Conversely, given a valuation η that satisfies $\mathcal{C}$, the valuation η' such that $\eta'(a_i) = \eta(a_i)$ and $\eta'(b_i) = \neg\eta(a_i)$ satisfies $\mathcal{C}^* \cup \mathcal{D}$. $\square$

4   Reduction of 1-neg-sat

In this section we show how to associate to any 1-neg-sat problem a linear second order syntactic equation in the linear λ-calculus.

Let $\mathcal{C} = \{C_1, \dots, C_m\}$ be a 1-neg-sat problem defined over the set of boolean variables $\mathcal{A} = \{a_1, \dots, a_n\}$. We define $\mathrm{neg} : \mathcal{A} \to \mathcal{C}$ to be the function such that:

$$\mathrm{neg}(a_i) = C_j \quad \text{if and only if} \quad \neg a_i \in C_j.$$

Similarly, we define $\mathrm{pos} : \mathcal{A} \to \mathcal{P}(\mathcal{C})$ such that:

$$\mathrm{pos}(a_i) = \{C_j \in \mathcal{C} \mid a_i \in C_j\}.$$

For each $i \in \{1, \dots, n\}$, let m_i be the cardinality of $\mathrm{pos}(a_i)$, and define $\psi_i : \{1, \dots, m_i\} \to \{1, \dots, m\}$ to be a function such that:

$$\mathrm{pos}(a_i) = \{C_{\psi_i(1)}, \dots, C_{\psi_i(m_i)}\}.$$

In case $m_i = 0$, by convention, ψ_i is defined to be the empty function.

Now, let o be an atomic type. In order to define the syntactic equation associated to $\mathcal{C}$, we introduce the following constants and meta-variables:

1. a constant a of type o;
2. a constant f of type $o^n \multimap o$;
3. for each clause $C \in \mathcal{C}$, a constant $\overline{C}$ of type $o^m \multimap o$;
4. a meta-variable $\mathbf{X}$ of type $o^m \multimap o$;
5. m^2 meta-variables $\mathbf{X}_{11}, \dots, \mathbf{X}_{1m}, \dots, \mathbf{X}_{m1}, \dots, \mathbf{X}_{mm}$ of type o.

For $(i, j) \in \{1, \dots, n\} \times \{1, \dots, m\}$, we define the following terms:

$$R_{ij} = \begin{cases} \overline{C_{\psi_i(j)}}(a, \dots, a) & \text{if } j \leq m_i \\ a & \text{otherwise.} \end{cases}$$

Then, for $i \in \{1, \dots, n\}$, we define:

$$R_i = \overline{\mathrm{neg}(a_i)}(R_{i1}, \dots, R_{im})$$

Finally, the syntactic equation $\langle L_\mathcal{C}, R_\mathcal{C} \rangle$, associated to $\mathcal{C}$, is defined as follows:

$$L_\mathcal{C} = \mathbf{X}(\overline{C_1}(\mathbf{X}_{11}, \ldots, \mathbf{X}_{1m}), \ldots, \overline{C_m}(\mathbf{X}_{m1}, \ldots, \mathbf{X}_{mm}))$$

$$R_\mathcal{C} = f(R_1, \ldots, R_n)$$

Let us illustrate the above reduction by an example. Consider the following clauses:

$$C_1 = \{a_1\}, C_2 = \{a_1, a_2\}, C_3 = \{\neg a_1, \neg a_2\}$$

to which we associate the constants $\overline{C_1}$, $\overline{C_2}$, and $\overline{C_3}$ of type $o \multimap o \multimap o \multimap o$, respectively. We have $\mathrm{neg}(a_1) = C_3$, $\mathrm{neg}(a_2) = C_3$, $\mathrm{pos}(a_1) = \{C_1, C_2\}$, and $\mathrm{pos}(a_2) = \{C_2\}$. If $\psi_1(1) = 1$, $\psi_1(2) = 2$ and $\psi_2(1) = 2$, the terms R_{ij} are the following:

$$R_{11} = \overline{C_1}(a, a, a) \quad R_{12} = \overline{C_2}(a, a, a) \quad R_{13} = a$$
$$R_{21} - \overline{C_2}(a, a, a) \quad R_{22} = a \quad R_{23} = a$$

Hence, the syntactic equation associated to this 1-neg-sat problem is as follows:

$$L_\mathcal{C} = \mathbf{X}(\overline{C_1}(\mathbf{X}_{11}, \mathbf{X}_{12}, \mathbf{X}_{13}), \overline{C_2}(\mathbf{X}_{21}, \mathbf{X}_{22}, \mathbf{X}_{23}), \overline{C_3}(\mathbf{X}_{31}, \mathbf{X}_{32}, \mathbf{X}_{33}))$$

$$R_\mathcal{C} = f(\overline{C_3}(\overline{C_1}(a, a, a), \overline{C_2}(a, a, a), a), \overline{C_3}(\overline{C_2}(a, a, a), a, a))$$

The intuition behind this reduction is the following. If the syntactic equation admits a solution, the term substituted for $\mathbf{X}$ must be of the form:

$$\lambda x_1 \ldots x_m . f(S_1, \ldots, S_n)$$

where each term S_i is either some λ-variable x_k, or some application of the form:

$$\overline{\mathrm{neg}(a_i)}(S_{i1}, \ldots, S_{im}).$$

The first case corresponds to a boolean variable a_i such that $\eta(a_i) = 0$, while the second case corresponds to a boolean variable a_i such that $\eta(a_i) = 1$.

Back to our example, one sees that the given equation admits the following solution:

$$\begin{cases} \mathbf{X} &:= \lambda x_1 \, x_2 \, x_3. \, f(c_3(x_1, x_2, a), \, x_3) \\ \mathbf{X}_{31} &:= c_2(a, a, a) \\ \mathbf{X}_{ij} &:= a \text{ for } i \neq 3 \text{ or } j \neq 1 \end{cases}$$

which corresponds, indeed, to the only valuation that satisfies $\mathcal{C}$, namely, the valuation η such that $\eta(a_1) = 1$ and $\eta(a_2) = 0$.

5   Correctness of the Reduction

Consider again a 1-neg-sat problem $\mathcal{C} = \{C_1, \ldots, C_m\}$ defined over the set of boolean variables $\mathcal{A} = \{a_1, \ldots, a_n\}$, and let the λ-terms R_{ij}, R_i, $L_\mathcal{C}$, and $R_\mathcal{C}$ be defined as in the previous section.

We first prove that the syntactic equation $\langle L_\mathcal{C}, R_\mathcal{C} \rangle$ admits a solution whenever $\mathcal{C}$ is satisfiable. To this end, suppose that $\mathcal{C}$ is satisfied by a valuation η.

Consequently, there exists a choice function ϕ that picks in each clause a literal that is satisfied by η. More precisely, we defined $\phi : \{1, \ldots, m\} \to \{1, \ldots, n\}$ to be a function such that

$$\text{either } \eta(a_{\phi(i)}) = 1 \text{ and } a_{\phi(i)} \in C_i, \text{ or } \eta(a_{\phi(i)}) = 0 \text{ and } \neg a_{\phi(i)} \in C_i.$$

Remark that this function is such that if $\phi(i) = \phi(j)$ and $\eta(a_{\phi(i)}) = 0$ then $i = j$. This is due to the constraint that a negative literal occurs in only one clause.

Given $\{x_1, \ldots, x_m\}$ a set of λ-variables, we define the family of terms S_i, for $i \in \{1, \ldots, n\}$, as follows:

$$S_i := \begin{cases} x_j \text{ if } \eta(a_i) = 0 \text{ and } j \text{ such that } \phi(j) = i \text{ exists} \\ \hline \overline{neg(a_i)}(S_{i1}, \ldots, S_{im}) \text{ otherwise} \end{cases}$$

where, in the second case, the family of terms S_{ij} is the following:

$$S_{ij} := \begin{cases} x_k \text{ if } \eta(a_i) = 1 \text{ and } k \text{ such that } \phi(k) = i \text{ and } R_{ij} = \overline{C_k}(a, \ldots, a) \text{ exists} \\ R_{ij} \text{ otherwise} \end{cases}$$

Finally, we define:
$$S = \lambda x_1 \ldots x_m . f(S_1, \ldots, S_n)$$

As we will show, the above term is the main ingredient of a solution to the syntactic equation $\langle L_C, R_C \rangle$. In order to establish this fact, we first prove that S is indeed a λ-term of the linear λ-calculus.

Lemma 2. *For all* $j \in \{1, \ldots, m\}$, $x_j \in \mathrm{FV}(S_{\phi(j)})$.

Proof. We proceed by case analysis, according to the value of $\eta(a_{\phi(j)})$.

Suppose that $\eta(a_{\phi(j)}) = 0$. Then, by definition, we have that $S_{\phi(j)} = x_j$. Hence, $x_j \in \mathrm{FV}(S_{\phi(j)})$.

On the other hand, when $\eta(a_{\phi(j)}) = 1$, we have, by definition of ϕ, that $C_j \in \mathrm{pos}(a_{\phi(j)})$. Consequently, there exists k such that $R_{\phi(j)k} = \overline{C_j}(a, \ldots, a)$. Therefore, by definition, $S_{\phi(j)k} = x_j$, which implies $x_j \in \mathrm{FV}(S_{\phi(j)})$.   □

Lemma 3. *If* $x_j \in \mathrm{FV}(S_i)$ *then* $\phi(j) = i$, *for any* $j \in \{1, \ldots, m\}$ *and any* $i \in \{1, \ldots, n\}$.

Proof. An immediate consequence of the definition of the family of terms S_j.   □

Lemma 4. *For all* $i \in \{1, \ldots, n\}$ *and all* $C_k \in \mathrm{pos}(a_i)$, *there exists exactly one* $j \in \{1, \ldots, m\}$ *such that* $R_{ij} = \overline{C_k}(a, \ldots, a)$.

Proof. An immediate consequence of the definition of the family of terms R_{ij}.

□

Lemma 5. $S = \lambda x_1 \ldots x_m . f(S_1, \ldots, S_n)$ *is a term of the linear* λ-*calculus.*

Proof. We have to prove that each of the λ-variables $x_1, \ldots, x_m$ has exactly one occurrence in $f(S_1, \ldots, S_n)$. By Lemma 2, we know that $x_1, \ldots, x_m \in \mathrm{FV}(f(S_1, \ldots, S_n))$. Hence, it remains to show that for any $j \in \{1, \ldots, m\}$, x_j occurs at most once in $f(S_1, \ldots, S_n)$. By Lemma 3, this amounts to prove that for any $i \in \{1, \ldots, n\}$, x_j occurs at most once in S_i. So, suppose that $x_j \in \mathrm{FV}(S_i)$. Then, either $x_j = S_i$, or $x_j = S_{ik}$ for some k. In the second case, k is such that $R_{ik} = \overline{C_j}(a, \ldots, a)$. Hence, it is unique by Lemma 4. Therefore, in both cases, there is only one occurence of x_j in S_i.   □

It appears in the proof of Lemma 2 that for all $i \in \{1, \ldots, m\}$ either there exists $k \in \{1, \ldots, n\}$ such that $x_i = S_k$, or there exists $k \in \{1, \ldots, n\}$ and $l \in \{1, \ldots, m\}$ such that $x_i = S_{kl}$. This fact allows the family of terms T_{ij} (for $i, j \in \{1, \ldots, m\}$) to be defined as follows:

$$T_{ij} = \begin{cases} R_{kj} & \text{if } k \text{ such that } x_i = S_k \text{ exists} \\ a & \text{if } k \text{ and } l \text{ such that } x_i = S_{kl} \text{ exist} \end{cases}$$

It is immediate that these terms are terms of the linear λ-calculus.

We are now in a position of establishing that the syntactic equation $\langle L_\mathcal{C}, R_\mathcal{C} \rangle$ admits a solution provided that $\mathcal{C}$ is satisfiable.

Proposition 1. *Let $\mathcal{C}$ be a 1-neg-sat problem, and $\langle L_\mathcal{C}, R_\mathcal{C} \rangle$ be the associated syntactic equation. If $\mathcal{C}$ is satisfiable, then $\langle L_\mathcal{C}, R_\mathcal{C} \rangle$ admits a solution.*

Proof. The fact that $\mathcal{C}$ is satisfiable allows the terms S, and T_{ij} to be defined, and we prove that

$$L_\mathcal{C}[\mathbf{X} := S][\mathbf{X}_{ij} := T_{ij}]_{i=1}^m {}_{j=1}^m \ \twoheadrightarrow_\beta \ R_\mathcal{C}$$

Indeed, we have:

$$\begin{aligned} L_\mathcal{C}[\mathbf{X} &:= S][\mathbf{X}_{ij} := T_{ij}]_{i=1}^m {}_{j=1}^m \\ &= S(\overline{C_1}(T_{11}, \ldots, T_{1m}), \ldots \overline{C_m}(T_{m1}, \ldots, T_{mm})) \\ &\twoheadrightarrow_\beta f(S_1, \ldots, S_n)[x_j := \overline{C_j}(T_{j1}, \ldots, T_{jm})]_{j=1}^m \end{aligned}$$

Then, it remains to show that for all $i \in \{1, \ldots, n\}$:

$$S_i[x_j := \overline{C_j}(T_{j1}, \ldots, T_{jm})]_{j=1}^m = R_i$$

There are two cases:

1. $S_i = x_k$, for some $k \in \{1, \ldots, m\}$.

   In this case, we have that $T_{kl} = R_{il}$, for all $l \in \{1, \ldots, m\}$. We also have $\eta(a_i) = 0$ and $\phi(k) = i$, which implies that $\mathrm{neg}(a_i) = C_k$. Consequently:

$$\begin{aligned} x_k[x_j := \overline{C_j}(T_{j1}, \ldots, T_{jm})]_{j=1}^m &= x_k[x_k := \overline{C_k}(R_{i1}, \ldots, R_{im})] \\ &= \overline{C_k}(R_{i1}, \ldots, R_{im}) \\ &= \overline{\mathrm{neg}(a_i)}(R_{i1}, \ldots, R_{im}) \\ &= R_i \end{aligned}$$

2. $S_i = \overline{\text{neg}(a_i)}(S_{i1}, \ldots, S_{im})$.

In this case, it is sufficient to show that for all $k \in \{1, \ldots, m\}$:

$$S_{ik}[x_j := \overline{C_j}(T_{j1}, \ldots, T_{jm})]_{j=1}^m = R_{ik}$$

There are two subcases. In the case $S_{ik} = x_l$, for some $l \in \{1, \ldots, m\}$, we have that $R_{ik} = \overline{C_l}(a, \ldots, a)$ and $T_{kj} = a$, for all $j \in \{1, \ldots, m\}$. Therefore:

$$
\begin{aligned}
x_l[x_j := \overline{C_j}(T_{j1}, \ldots, T_{jm})]_{j=1}^m &= x_l[x_l := \overline{C_l}(a, \ldots, a)] \\
&= \overline{C_l}(a, \ldots, a) \\
&= R_{ik}
\end{aligned}
$$

Otherwise, we have $S_{ik} = R_{ik}$, and the desired property follows immediately.
□

It remains to prove that $\mathcal{C}$ is satisfiable whenever $\langle L_{\mathcal{C}}, R_{\mathcal{C}} \rangle$ admits a solution. We first establish a technical lemma concerning the form of the possible solutions of $\langle L_{\mathcal{C}}, R_{\mathcal{C}} \rangle$.

Lemma 6. *If the equation $\langle L_{\mathcal{C}}, R_{\mathcal{C}} \rangle$ admits a solution then the variable $\mathbf{X}$ is substituted by a term of the form*

$$\lambda x_1 \ldots x_m.f(U_1, \ldots, U_n)$$

where the terms U_i are such that:

1. *either $U_i = x_k$ (for some $k \in \{1, \ldots, m\}$), in which case $\text{neg}(a_i) = C_k$,*
2. *or $U_i = \overline{\text{neg}(a_i)}(U_{i1}, \ldots, U_{im})$ where the terms U_{ij} are such that:*
   (a) either $U_{ij} = x_k$ (for some $k \in \{1, \ldots, m\}$), in which case $C_k \in \text{pos}(a_i)$,
   (b) or $U_{ij} = R_{ij}$.

Proof. Suppose that

$$\begin{cases} \mathbf{X} &= U \\ \mathbf{X}_{ij} &= V_{ij} \end{cases}$$

is a solution to the syntactic equation $\langle L_{\mathcal{C}}, R_{\mathcal{C}} \rangle$. Then, we must have:

$$U(\overline{C_1}(V_{11}, \ldots, V_{1m}), \ldots \overline{C_m}(V_{m1}, \ldots, V_{mm})) \twoheadrightarrow_\beta f(R_1, \ldots, R_n)$$

This implies that U is indeed of the form

$$\lambda x_1 \ldots x_m.f(U_1, \ldots, U_n)$$

where for all $i \in \{1, \ldots, n\}$:

$$U_i[x_j := \overline{C_j}(V_{j1}, \ldots, V_{jm})]_{j=1}^m \twoheadrightarrow_\beta R_i$$

Now, the head of each U_i is either some λ-variable x_k or some constant. In the first case, $U_i = x_k$, and we must have that

$$\overline{C_k}(V_{k1}, \ldots, V_{km}), = R_i$$

which implies that $\text{neg}(a_i) = C_k$. In the second case, the head of U_i must be the head of R_i, which implies that U_i is of the form

$$\overline{\text{neg}(a_i)}(U_{i1}, \ldots, U_{im})$$

Moreover, we must have that

$$U_{ik}[x_j := \overline{C_j}(V_{j1}, \ldots, V_{jm})]_{j=1}^m \twoheadrightarrow_\beta R_{ik}$$

Now, if the head of U_{ik} is some λ-variable x_l, we must have $U_{ik} = x_l$, and:

$$\overline{C_l}(V_{l1}, \ldots, V_{lm}) = R_{ik}$$

This implies that $C_l \in \text{pos}(a_i)$. Otherwise, we have

$$U_{ik} = R_{ik}.$$

$\square$

We are now in a position of proving the second half of our reduction result.

Proposition 2. *Let C be a 1-neg-sat problem, and $\langle L_C, R_C \rangle$ be the associated syntactic equation. If $\langle L_C, R_C \rangle$ admits a solution, then C is satisfiable.*

Proof. According to Lemma 6, if $\langle L_C, R_C \rangle$ admits a solution, then te term U substituted for **X** is of the form

$$\lambda x_1 \ldots x_m. f(U_1, \ldots, U_n)$$

where:

1. either $U_i = x_k$, for some $k \in \{1, \ldots, m\}$,
2. or $U_i = \overline{\text{neg}(a_i)}(U_{i1}, \ldots, U_{im})$.

We define a valuation η as follows:

$$\eta(a_i) = \begin{cases} 0 \text{ if } U_i = x_j \text{ for some } j \in \{1, \ldots, m\} \\ 1 \text{ otherwise} \end{cases}$$

Now, for every clause C_j such that $x_j = U_i$, for some $i \in \{1, \ldots, n\}$, we have, by Lemma 6, that $\text{neg}(a_i) = C_j$, i.e., $\neg a_i \in C_j$. Consequently, these clauses are satisfied by η.

As for the other clauses C_k, since U is a term of the linear λ-calculus, there must exists some term U_{ij} such that $U_{ij} = x_k$. In this case, according to Lemma 6, $C_k \in \text{pos}(a_i)$, i.e., $a_i \in C_k$. Consequently, these clauses are also satisfied by η. $\square$

As a consequence of Lemma 1, and Propositions 1, and 2, we get the main theorem of this paper.

Theorem 1. *Linear second-order matching in the linear λ-calculus is NP-complete.*

6   Related Results

The main difference between a context and a linear second-order λ-term is that the latter has the ability of rearranging its arguments in any order. This explains why linear second-order matching in the linear λ-calculus is NP-complete while linear context matching is not. Nevertheless, this difference is not significant when the arguments of the second-order meta-variable do not contain any meta-variable (first-order or second-order). Consider a second-order equation of the form:

$$\mathbf{X}(T_1, \ldots, T_n) = T$$

where $T_1, \ldots, T_n$, and T are first-order pure linear λ-terms (such an equation is called an interpolation equation). It is not difficult to see that it may be solved in polynomial time. Indeed, it amounts to check whether the union of the multisets of the subterms of $T_1, \ldots, T_n$ is included in the multiset of the subterms of T.

This polynomiality result, which is quite specific, cannot be generalized. Indeed, as we prove in the next proposition, interpolation in third-order case is NP-complete.

Proposition 3. *Third-order interpolation in the linear λ-calculus is NP-complete.*

Proof. The proof consists in a reduction of 1-Neg-sat that we obtain by reducing the equation $\langle L_\mathcal{C}, R_\mathcal{C} \rangle$ (as defined in section 4) to a third-order interpolation equation

Let $\mathcal{C} = \{C_1, \ldots, C_m\}$ be a 1-neg-sat problem defined over the set of boolean variables $\mathcal{A} = \{a_1, \ldots, a_n\}$. We build a third-order interpolation equation $\langle L, R \rangle$ which has a solution if and only if the equation $\langle L_\mathcal{C}, R_\mathcal{C} \rangle$ has a solution. From Propositions 1 and 2, this is equivalent to say that $\langle L, R \rangle$ has a solution if and only if $\mathcal{C}$ is satisfiable. Therefore, from Lemma 1, we obtain that third-order interpolation is NP-complete problem.

We first define

$$\begin{cases} L = Y(\lambda x_1 \ldots x_m.\overline{C_1}(x_1, \ldots, x_m), \ldots, \lambda x_1 \ldots x_m.\overline{C_m}(x_1, \ldots, x_m)) \\ R = R_\mathcal{C} \end{cases}$$

Then it remains to prove that $\langle L, R_\mathcal{C} \rangle$ has a solution if and only if $\langle L_\mathcal{C}, R_\mathcal{C} \rangle$ has a solution.

Suppose $\langle L_\mathcal{C}, R_\mathcal{C} \rangle$ has a solution :

$$\begin{cases} \mathbf{X} \ = U \\ \mathbf{X}_{ij} = V_{ij} \end{cases}$$

then the term

$$S = \lambda y_1 \ldots y_m.U(y_1(V_{11}, \ldots, V_{1m}), \ldots, y_m(V_{m1}, \ldots, V_{mm}))$$

is a solution of $\langle L, R_\mathcal{C} \rangle$. Indeed:

$$\begin{aligned} &S(\lambda x_1 \ldots x_m.C_1(x_1, \ldots, x_m), \ldots, \lambda x_1 \ldots x_m.C_m(x_1, \ldots, x_m)) \longrightarrow_\beta \\ &U(C_1(V_{11}, \ldots, V_{1m}), \ldots, C_m(V_{m1}, \ldots, V_{mm})) \qquad\qquad \longrightarrow_\beta R_\mathcal{C} \end{aligned}$$

Conversely if $\langle L, R_\mathcal{C} \rangle$ $[Y := S]$, then $S = \lambda y_1 \ldots y_m . S'$ and one can find terms of linear λ-calculus $U, V_{11}, \ldots, V_{1m}, \ldots, V_{m1}, \ldots, V_{mm}$ such that:

$$U(y_1(V_{11}, \ldots, V_{1m}), \ldots, y_m(V_{m1}, \ldots, V_{mm})) \twoheadrightarrow_\beta S'$$

and then
$$\begin{cases} \mathbf{X} &= U \\ \mathbf{X}_{ij} &= V_{ij} \end{cases}$$

is obviously a solution of $\langle L_\mathcal{C}, R_\mathcal{C} \rangle$. $\square$

References

1. H. Comon. Completion of rewrite systems with membership constraints. Part I: Deduction rules. *Journal of Symbolic Computation*, 25(4):397–419, 1998.
2. H. Comon. Completion of rewrite systems with membership constraints. Part II: Constraint solving. *Journal of Symbolic Computation*, 25(4):421–453, 1998.
3. S. A. Cook. The complexity of theorem proving procedures. *Proceedings of the 3rd annual ACM Symposium on Theory of Computing*, pages 151–158, 1971.
4. D. Dougherty and T. Wierzbicki. A decidable variant of higher order matching. In *Proc. 13th Conf. on Rewriting Techniques and Applications, RTA'02*, volume 2378, pages 340–351, 2002.
5. G. Dowek. Third order matching is decidable. *Annals of Pure and Applied Logic*, 69(2–3):135–155, 1994.
6. G. Dowek. Higher-order unification and matching. In A. Robinson and A. Voronkov (eds.), *Handbook of Automated Reasoning*, pp. 1009-1062, Elsevier, 2001.
7. W. D. Goldfarb. The undecidability of the second-order unification problem. *Theoretical Computer Science*, 13(2):225–230, 1981.
8. Ph. de Groote. Higher-order linear matching is np-complete. *Lecture Notes in Computer Science*, 1833:127–140, 2000.
9. G. Huet. The undecidability of unification in third order logic. *Information and Control*, 22(3):257–267, 1973.
10. G. Huet. *Résolution d'équations dans les langages d'ordre* $1, 2, \ldots, \omega$. Thèse de Doctorat d'Etat, Université Paris 7, 1976.
11. J. Levy. Linear second-order unification. In H. Ganzinger, editor, *Rewriting Techniques and Applications, RTA'96*, volume 1103 of *Lecture Notes in Computer Science*, pages 332–346. Springer-Verlag, 1996.
12. R. Loader. Higher order β matching is undecidable. *Logic Journal of the IGPL*, 11(1): 51–68, 2002.
13. V. Padovani. *Filtrage d'ordre supérieure*. Thèse de Doctorat, Université de Paris 7, 1996.
14. P. Kilpeläinen. Ordered and unordered tree inclusion. *SIAM. J. Comput.*, 24(2): 340–356, 1995.
15. M. Schmidt-Schauß and J. Stuber. On the complexity of linear and stratified context matching problems. Rapport de recherche A01-R-411, LORIA, December 2001.

XML Schema, Tree Logic and Sheaves Automata

Silvano Dal Zilio* and Denis Lugiez

Laboratoire d'Informatique Fondamentale de Marseille
CNRS (UMR 6166) and Université de Provence, France

Abstract. XML documents, and other forms of semi-structured data, may be roughly described as edge labeled trees; it is therefore natural to use tree automata to reason on them. This idea has already been successfully applied in the context of *Document Type Definition* (DTD), the simplest standard for defining XML documents validity, but additional work is needed to take into account XML Schema, a more advanced standard, for which regular tree automata are not satisfactory. In this paper, we define a tree logic that directly embeds XML Schema as a plain subset as well as a new class of automata for unranked trees, used to decide this logic, which is well-suited to the processing of XML documents and schemas.

1 Introduction

We describe a new class of tree automata, and a related logic on trees, with applications to the processing of XML documents and XML schemas. XML documents, and other forms of semi-structured data [1], may be roughly described as edge labeled trees. It is therefore natural to use tree automata to reason on them and try to apply the classical connection between automata, logic and query languages. This approach has already been followed by various researchers, both from a practical and a theoretical point of view, and has given some notable results, especially when dealing with *Document Type Definition* (DTD), the simplest standard for defining XML documents validity. A good example is the XDuce system of Pierce, Hosoya *et al.* [9], a typed functional language with extended pattern-matching operators for XML documents manipulation. In this tool, the types of XML documents are modeled by regular tree automata and the typing of pattern matching expressions is based on closure operations on automaton. Another example is given by the *hedge automaton* theory [11], an extension of regular tree automaton for unranked trees (that is, tree with nodes of unfixed and unbounded degrees). Hedge automata are at the basis of the implementation of RELAX-NG [6], an alternative proposal to XML Schema. Various extension of tree automata [2] and monadic tree logic have also been used to study the complexity of manipulating tree structured data but, contrary to our approach, these work are not directly concerned with schemas and are based

---

* work partially supported by ATIP CNRS "Fondements de l'Interrogation des Données Semi-Structurées" and by IST Global Computing PROFUNDIS.

R. Nieuwenhuis (Ed.): RTA 2003, LNCS 2706, pp. 246–263, 2003.

on ordered content models. More crucially, several mentions to automata theory appear in the XML specifications, principally to express restrictions on DTD and Schemas in order to obtain almost linear complexity for simple operations.

Document type definitions are expressed in a language akin to regular expressions and specify the set of elements that may be present in a valid document, as well as constraining their order of occurrence. Nonetheless, the "document types" expressible by means of DTD are sometimes too rigid and, for example, a document may become invalid after permutation of some of its elements. A new standard, XML Schema, has been proposed to overcome some of the limitations of the DTD model. In particular, we can interpret XML schemata as terms built using both associative and associative-commutative (AC) operators with unbounded arity, a situation for which regular tree automata are not satisfactory. Indeed, while regular tree automata constitute a useful framework, it has sometimes proved inadequate for practical purposes and many applications require the use of an extended model. To the best of our knowledge, no work so far has considered unranked trees with both associative and associative-commutative symbols, a situation found when dealing with XML Schemata.

We propose a new class of tree automata, named *sheaves automata*, for dealing with XML documents and schema. We believe it is the first work on automata theory applied to XML that consider the &-operator. By restricting our study to deterministic automata, we obtain a class of recognizable languages that enjoys good closure properties and we define a related modal logic for documents that is decidable and exactly matches the recognizable languages. A leading goal in the design of our logic is to include a simplified version of XML Schema as a plain subset.

The content of this paper is as follows. We start by defining the syntax of XML documents and XML schema. A distinctive aspect of our simplified schema language is to include the operator &. In Sect. 4, we present a tree logic intended for querying XML documents. This logic can be interpreted as a direct extension of the schema language with logical operators. The logic deliberately resembles (and extends on some points) TQL, a query language for semi-structured data based on the *ambient logic* [5,4]. We present a similar logic, with the difference that we deal both with ordered and unordered data structures, while TQL only deals with multisets of elements. Another difference with TQL lies in the addition of arithmetical constraints. In this extended logic, it becomes for instance possible to express constraints on the number of occurrences of an element, such as "there are more fields labeled a than labeled b" or "there is an even number of fields labeled a." While the addition of counting constraints is purely motivated by the presence of &, it incidentally provides a model for *cardinality constraint on repetitions*, $e\{m, n\}$, that matches k repetitions of the expression e, with $m \leqslant k \leqslant n$.

In Sect. 5, we introduce a new class of automata for unranked trees, called *Sheaves Automata* (SA), that is used to decide our extended tree logic. In the transition relation of SA, we combine the general rules for regular tree automata with regular word expression and counting constraints. In this framework, regular word expressions allow us to express constraints on sequences of elements and are used when dealing with sequential composition of documents, as in the *hedge automata* approach. Correspondingly, the counting constraints are used with the &-operator. The counting constraints are *Presburger arithmetic* formulas on the number of occurrences of each different type of elements. Intuitively, counting constraints appear as the counterpart of regular expressions in the presence of a commutative composition operator. Indeed, when the order of the elements becomes irrelevant, that is, when we deal with bags instead of sequences, the only pertinent constraints are numerical.

The choice of Presburger arithmetic is not exclusively motivated by the fact that it is a large class of constraints over natural numbers, which increases the expressiveness of our logic while still remaining decidable. Indeed, we prove that Presburger constraints arises naturally when we consider schemas that combine interleaving, &, and recursive definitions (see Sect. 3). Another reason is that this extension preserves many enjoyable properties of regular tree automata: the class of languages recognized by sheaves automata is closed under union and intersection, testing for emptiness is decidable, ..., while adding some new ones, like the fact that recognizable languages are closed by composition of sequential and commutative operators. Even so, the gain in expressiveness is significant as such. Indeed, Muscholl, Schwentick and Seidl have very recently proposed a new and independent class of automaton very close to our model for the sole purpose of making numerical queries on XML documents [12].

Before concluding, we give some results on the complexity of basic problems for schemas. By design, every formula of our extended tree logic directly relates to a deterministic sheaves automaton. As a consequence, we obtain the decidability of the *model-checking problem* for SL, that is finding the answers to a query, and of the *satisfiability problems*, that is finding if a query is trivially empty. Moreover, since schemas are directly embedded in the models of SL, we can relate a XML schema to an accepting sheaves automaton obtaining the decidability of all basic problems: typing a document by a schema, computing the set of documents typed by a schema, computing the set of documents typed by the difference of two schemas ... In proving these results, we also make clear how simple syntactical restrictions on schemas improve the complexity of simple operations.

Omitted proofs may be found in a long version of this paper [8].

2   Documents and Schemata

XML documents are a simple textual representation for unranked, edge labeled trees. In this report, we follow the notations found in the XDuce system [9] and choose a simplified version of XML documents by leaving aside attributes among other details. Most of the simplifications and notation conventions taken here are also found in the presentation of MSL [3], an attempt to formalize some of the core ideas found in XML Schema.

A document, d, is an ordered sequence of elements, $a_1[d_1] \cdot \ldots \cdot a_n[d_n]$, where a_i is a tag name and d_i is a sub-document. A document may also be empty, denoted

ϵ, or be a constant. We consider given sets of atomic data constant partitioned into primitive data types, like `String` or `Integer` for instance. Documents may be concatenated, denoted $d_1 \cdot d_2$, and this composition operation is associative with identity element ϵ.

Elements and Documents

$e ::=$	element or constant
$\quad a[d]$	element labeled a, containing d
$\quad$ cst	constant (any type)
$d ::=$	document
$\quad \epsilon$	empty document
$\quad e$	element
$\quad d_1 \cdot d_2$	document composition

Example 1. A typical entry of a bibliographical database could be the document·

$$book[\,auth[\text{"Knuth"}\,] \cdot title[\text{"Art of Computer Programming"}\,] \cdot year[1970]]$$

A schema may be interpreted as the type of a document. Our definition mostly follows the presentation made in MSL [3]. Nonetheless, we bring some simplifications and modifications to better fit our objective. In particular, we consider three separate syntactical categories: E for element schema definitions, S for (regular) schemata, and T for schemata that may only appear at top level of an element definition.

Schemas

$E ::=$	Element schema
$\quad a[T]$	element with tag a and interior matching T
$\quad a[T]?$	optional element
$\quad$ Datatype	datatype constant
$S ::=$	Regular schema
$\quad \epsilon$	empty schema
$\quad E$	element
$\quad S_1 \cdot S_2$	sequential composition
$\quad S + S$	choice
$\quad S*$	indefinite repetition
$T ::=$	Top-level schema
$\quad AnyT$	any type (match everything)
$\quad S$	regular schema
$\quad E_1 \& \ldots \& E_n$	interleaving composition

A schema is basically a regular expression that constrains the order and number of occurrences of elements in a document. An element, $a[T]$, describes documents that contain a single top element tagged with a and enclosing a sub-document satisfying the schema T. An optional element, $a[T]?$, matches one or zero occurrence of $a[T]$. The constructors for schemata include the standard operators found in regular expression languages, where $S \cdot S'$ stands for concatenation and $S + S'$ for choice. For simplicity reasons, we have chosen both iteration,

$S*$, and option, $a[T]?$, instead of the repetition operator $S\{m, n\}$ found in the Schema recommendation. The most original operator is the *interleaving operator*, $E_1 \& \ldots \& E_n$, which describes documents containing (exactly) elements matching E_1 to E_n regardless of their order. Our simplified Schema definition also contains a constant, $AnyT$, which stands for the most general type or *Any Type* in XML Schema terminology.

Example 2. Assuming that `String` and `Year` are the types associated to string and date constants, the following schema matches the book entry given in Example 1: $(book[title[\texttt{String}] \& auth[\texttt{String}] \& year[\texttt{Year}]?)$.

The distinction of a top-level schema allows us to express some of the constraints on the interleaving operator found in the XML specification. For example, $\&$ must appear as the sole child at the top of an element schema, that is, terms like $E_1 \cdot (E_2 \& E_3)$ or $(E_1 \& E_2)*$ are ill-formed.

To capture some situations arising in practice, we may enrich schemata by recursive definitions presented by a system of equations. This can be simply obtained by enriching the syntax with variables, $X, Y, \ldots$, and an operator for recursive schema definition, $(S \textbf{ where } X_1 = S_1, \ldots, X_n = S_n)$, where the X_i's are bound variable names.

Example 3. We may extend book entries with a *ref* element listing the entries cited in the book:

$$\mathcal{B}ook \textbf{ where } \mathcal{B}ook = book[auth[\texttt{String}] \& title[\texttt{String}] \& \mathcal{R}ef],$$
$$\mathcal{R}ef = ref[\mathcal{B}ook*]?$$

Next, we make explicit the role of schemas as a type system for documents and define the relation $d : S$, meaning that the document d satisfies the schema S. This relation is based on an auxiliary function, $inter(d)$, which computes the *interleaving* of the elements in d, that is the set of documents obtainable from d after permutation of its elements: $inter(e_1 \cdot \ldots \cdot e_n) = \{e_{\sigma(1)} \cdot \ldots \cdot e_{\sigma(n)} \mid \sigma \text{ permutation of } 1..n\}$.

In the long version of this paper [8], we define a more complex relation, $X_1 : S_1, \ldots, X_n : S_n \vdash d : S$, to type documents using recursive schemas.

Good Documents

$$\frac{d : T}{a[d] : a[T]} \qquad \frac{d : T}{a[d] : a[T]?} \qquad \frac{}{\epsilon : a[T]?} \qquad \frac{\texttt{cst} \in \texttt{Datatype}}{\texttt{cst} : \texttt{Datatype}} \qquad \frac{}{\epsilon : \epsilon} \qquad \frac{d_1 : S_1 \quad d_2 : S_2}{d_1 \cdot d_2 : S_1 \cdot S_2}$$

$$\frac{d : S}{d : S + S'} \qquad \frac{d : S'}{d : S + S'} \qquad \frac{d_1 : S, \ldots, d_n : S}{d_1 \cdot \ldots \cdot d_n : S*} \qquad \frac{}{d : AnyT} \qquad \frac{d \in inter(e_1 \cdot \ldots \cdot e_n)}{e_1 : E_1 \quad \ldots \quad e_n : E_n}{d : E_1 \& \ldots \& E_n}$$

In the next section, we introduce some basic mathematical tools that will be useful in the definition of both our tree logic and our new class of tree automata.

3   Basic Results on Presburger Arithmetic and Words

Some computational aspects of our tree automaton rely on arithmetical properties over the group $(\mathbb{N}, +)$ of natural numbers with addition. The first-order theory of equality on this structure, also known as Presburger arithmetic, is decidable. Formulas of Presburger arithmetic, also called *Presburger constraint*, are given by the following grammar. We use $N, M, \ldots$ to range over integer variables and $n, m, \ldots$ to range over integer values.

Presburger Constraint

$Exp ::=$	Integer expression
n	positive integer constant
N	positive integer variable
$Exp_1 + Exp_?$	addition
$\phi, \psi, \ldots ::=$	Presburger constraint
$(Exp_1 = Exp_2)$	test for equality
$\neg\phi$	negation
$\phi \vee \psi$	disjunction
$\exists N.\phi$	existential quantification

Presburger constraints allow us to define flexible, yet decidable, properties over positive integers like for example: the value of X is strictly greater than the value of Y, using the formula $\exists Z.(X = Y + Z + 1)$; or X is an odd number, $\exists Z.(X = Z + Z + 1)$. We denote $\phi(X_1, \ldots, X_p)$ a Presburger formula with free integer variables $X_1, \ldots, X_p$ and we shall simply write $\models \phi(n_1, \ldots, n_p)$ when $\phi(n_1, \ldots, n_p)$ is satisfied.

Decidability of Presburger arithmetic may be proved using a connection with *semilinear sets* of natural numbers. A *linear set* of $\mathbb{N}^n$, $L(\boldsymbol{b}, P)$, is a set of vectors generated by linear combination of the periods $P = \{\boldsymbol{p}_1, \ldots, \boldsymbol{p}_k\}$ (where $p_i \in \mathbb{N}^n$ for all $i \in 1..k$), with the base $\boldsymbol{b} \in \mathbb{N}^n$, that is, $L(\boldsymbol{b}, P) =_{\text{def}} \{\boldsymbol{b} + \sum_{i \in 1..k} \lambda_i \boldsymbol{p}_i \mid \lambda_1, \ldots, \lambda_k \in \mathbb{N}\}$. A *semilinear set* is a finite union of linear sets and the models of Presburger formulas (with p free variables) are semilinear sets of $\mathbb{N}^p$. An important result is that semilinear sets are closed under *union*, *sum* and *iteration*, where: $L + M = \{x + y \mid x \in L, y \in M\}$, and $L^n = L + \ldots + L$ (n times) and $L* = \bigcup_{n \geq 0} L^n$. In the case of iteration, the semilinear set $L*$ may be a union of exponentially many linear sets (in the number of linear sets in L).

3.1   Parikh Mapping

Another mathematical tool needed in the presentation of our new class of automaton is the notion of *Parikh mapping*. Given some finite alphabet $\Sigma = \{a_1, \ldots, a_n\}$, that we consider totally ordered, the Parikh mapping of a word w of $\Sigma*$ is a n-uple of natural numbers, $\#(w) = (m_1, \ldots, m_n)$, where m_i is the number of occurrences of the letter a_i in w. We shall use the notation $\#_a(w)$ for the number of occurrences of a in w, or simply $\# a$ when there is no ambiguity.

The *Parikh mapping* of a set of words is the set of Parikh mappings of its elements. When the set of words is a regular language, the Parikh mapping can be easily computed and it corresponds to the model of a Presburger formula. Furthermore, when the regular language is described by a regular expression, reg, we can compute the Parikh mapping in time $O(|reg|)$ (using regular expressions of semilinear sets). For example, if a_i is the ith letter in Σ, then $\#(a_i)$ is the linear set $L(\boldsymbol{u}_i, \emptyset)$, where $\boldsymbol{u}_i$ is the ith unit vector of $\mathbb{N}^n$, and the mapping of a sequential composition expression, $reg_1 \cdot reg_2$, is the linear set $\#(reg_1) + \#(reg_2)$.

Proposition 1. *The Parikh mapping of a regular language is a semilinear set.*

This property is useful when we consider the intersection of a regular word language with a set of words whose Parikh mapping satisfies a given Presburger constraint. This is the case in Sect. 4, for example, when we test the emptiness of the language accepted by a Sheaves automaton.

3.2   Relation with XML Schema

We clarify the relation between Presburger constraint, Parikh's mapping and the semantics of the interleaving operator and try to give an intuition on how the &-operator may add "counting capabilities" to schemas.

Let $a_1, \ldots, a_p$ be distinct element tags and d be a "flat document", i.e. of the form $a_{i_1}[\epsilon] \cdot \ldots \cdot a_{i_k}[\epsilon]$, then $\#(.)$ provides a straightforward mapping from d to $\mathbb{N}^p$. Suppose now that we slightly relax the syntactic constraints on schemas in order to accept expressions of the form $((E_1 \, \& \, \cdots \, \& \, E_n) + E)$ and $(E_1 \, \& \, \cdots \, \& \, E_n \, \& \, X)$. Then, for any Presburger constraint, ϕ, it is possible to define an (extended recursive) schema that matches the vectors of integers satisfying ϕ. For example, the schema X **where** $X = ((a_1 \, \& \, a_2 \, \& \, X) + \epsilon)$ is associated to the formula $\# a_1 = \# a_2$ (there are as many a_1's than a_2's) and X **where** $X = ((a_1 \, \& \, a_1 \, \& \, X) + \epsilon)$ is associated to $\exists N. \# a_1 = N + N$ (there is an even number of a_1's).

Proposition 2. *For every Presburger formula ϕ, there is a schema, S, such that $d : S$ iff $\models \phi \#(d)$.*

We conjecture that this ability to count is exactly circumscribed to Presburger arithmetic, that is, for every schema denoting a set of natural numbers, there is a Presburger formula denoting the same set.

In the next section, we introduce a modal logic for documents that directly embeds counting constraint. Indeed, Proposition 2 indicates that it is necessary to take into account Presburger constraints when dealing with the &-operator. Moreover, aside from the fact that counting constraints add expressiveness to our logic, another reason for adding Presburger formulas is that we extend the set of recognizable trees while still preserving good (and decidable) closure properties.

4   The Sheaves Logic

We extend our simplified version of XML Schema with a set of logical operators and relax some of its syntactical constraints in order to define a modal logic for documents, the *Sheaves Logic* (SL). The sheaves logic is a logic in the spirit of the Tree Query Logic (TQL) of Cardelli and Ghelli [4], a modal logic for unranked, edge-labeled trees that has recently been proposed as the basis of a query language for semi-structured data. A main difference between TQL and SL is that the latter may express properties on both ordered and unordered sets of trees. In contrast, our logic lacks some of the operators found in TQL like recursion or quantification over tag names, which could be added at the cost of some extra complexity.

The formulas of SL ranged over by $A, B, \ldots$ are given by the following grammar. The formulas are partitioned into three syntactical categories: (1) *elements formula*, E, to express properties of a single element in a document; (2) *regular formulas*, S, corresponding to regular expressions on sequences of elements; (3) *counting formulas*, T, to express counting constraints on bags of elements, that is in the situation where the order of the elements is irrelevant.

Logical Formulas

$E ::=$	Element
$\quad a[S]$	element with tag a and regular formula S
$\quad a[T]$	element with tag a and counting formula T
$\quad AnyE$	any element
$\quad$ **Datatype**	datatype constant
$S ::=$	Regular formula
$\quad \epsilon$	empty
$\quad E$	element
$\quad S \cdot S'$	sequential composition
$\quad S*$	indefinite repetition
$\quad S \vee S$	choice
$\quad \neg S$	negation
$T ::=$	Counting formula
$\quad \exists \boldsymbol{N} : \phi(\boldsymbol{N}) : N_1 E_1 \ \& \ \ldots \ \& \ N_p E_p$	generalized interleaving, $\boldsymbol{N} = (N_1, \ldots, N_p)$
$\quad T \vee T$	choice
$\quad \neg T$	negation
$A, B, \ldots ::= \quad S \mid T \mid A \vee A \mid \neg A$	Sheaves Logic Formula

Aside from the usual propositional logic operators, our main addition to the logic is the "Any Element" constant, $AnyE$, and a constrained form of existential quantification, $\exists \boldsymbol{N} : \phi(\boldsymbol{N}) : N_1 E_1 \ \& \ \ldots \ \& \ N_p E_p$, that matches documents made of $n_1 + \ldots + n_p$ elements, with n_1 elements matching E_1, ..., n_p elements matching E_p (regardless of their order), such that $(n_1, \ldots, n_p)$ satisfies the Presburger formula ϕ.

The generalized interleaving operator is inspired by the relation between schema and counting constraint given in Sect. 2. This operator is useful to express more liberal properties on documents than with Schemas. For example, it is now possible to define the type (an example of ill-formed schemas) $E_1* \ \& \ E_2$, of documents made only of elements matching E_1 but one matching E_2, using the formula $\exists N_1, N_2 : (N_1 \geqslant 0) \wedge (N_2 = 1) : N_1 E_1 \ \& \ N_2 E_2$. The $AnyE$ formula matches documents made of a single element. It has been chosen instead of the less general schema $AnyT$ since it could be used in a constrained existential quantification. It is possible to model $AnyT$ using the formulas $\exists N : (N \geqslant 0) : N AnyE$ and $AnyE*$.

Satisfaction Relation. We define the relation $d \models A$, meaning that the document d satisfies the formula A. This relation is defined inductively on the definition of A, and the rules shared for regular and counting formulas. In the following, we use the symbol Ψ to stand for formulas of sort S, T or A.

Satisfaction

$d \models a[\Psi]$	iff	$(d = a[d']) \wedge (d' \models \Psi)$
$d \models AnyE$	iff	$(d = a[d'])$
$d \models \mathtt{Datatype}$	iff	$(d = \mathrm{cst}) \wedge (\mathrm{cst} \in \mathtt{Datatype})$
$d \models \epsilon$	iff	$d = \epsilon$
$d \models S \cdot S'$	iff	$(d = d_1 \cdot d_2) \wedge (d_1 \models S) \wedge (d_2 \models S')$
$d \models S*$	iff	$(d = \epsilon) \vee$
		$((d = d_1 \cdot \ldots \cdot d_p) \wedge (\forall i \in 1..p, d_i \models S))$
$d \models \exists N : \phi(N) : N_1 E_1 \& \ldots \& N_p E_p$	iff	$\exists n_1, \ldots, n_p, \exists (e_1^j)_{j \in 1..n_1}, \ldots, (e_p^j)_{j \in 1..n_p}$
		$e_i^j \models E_i \wedge \models \phi(n_1, \ldots, n_p) \wedge$
		$d \in inter(e_1^1 \cdot \ldots \cdot e_p^{n_p})$
$d \models \Psi \vee \Psi'$	iff	$(d \models \Psi) \vee (d \models \Psi')$
$d \models \neg\Psi$	iff	not $(d \models \Psi)$

Example of Formulas. We start by defining some syntactic sugar. The formula *True* will be used for tautologies, that is formulas satisfied by all documents (like $T \vee \neg T$ for instance). We also define the notation $E_1 \& \ldots \& E_p$, for the formula satisfied by documents made of a sequence of p elements matching $E_1, \ldots, E_p$, regardless of their order.

$$(E_1 \& \ldots \& E_p) =_{\mathrm{def}} \exists N_1, ..., N_p : (N_1 = ... = N_p = 1) : N_1 E_1 \& \ldots \& N_p E_p$$

Likewise, we define the notation $(a[S] \& \cdots)$ for the formula satisfied by documents containing at least one element matching $a[S]$:

$$(a[S] \& \cdots) =_{\mathrm{def}} \exists M, N : (M = 1) \wedge (N \geqslant 0) : M a[S] \& N AnyE$$

For a more complex example, let us assume that a book reference is given by the schema in Example 2. The references may have been collected in several databases and we cannot be sure of the order of the fields. The following formula matches collections of books that contain at least 50 entries written by Knuth or Lamport.

$$\exists N, M, X : (N + M = 50 + X) : \left(\begin{array}{l} N book[(auth["\text{Knuth}"] \& \cdots)] \\ \& M book[(auth["\text{Lamport}"] \& \cdots)] \end{array} \right)$$

Next, we define a new class of tree automata that will be used to decide SL, in the sense that the set of documents matched by a formula will correspond to the set of terms accepted by an automaton.

5   A New Class of Tree Automata

We define a class of automata specifically designed to operate on XML schemata. A main distinction with other automata-theoretic approaches, like *hedge automata* [11] for example, is that we do not focus on regular expressions over paths but, instead, concentrate on the &-operator, which is one of the chief additions of XML Schema with respect to DTD. The definitions presented here have been trimmed down for the sake of brevity. For example, in the complete version of our class of automaton, we consider rich sets of constraints between subtrees [10]. Moreover, the definition of SA can be extended to any signature involving free function symbols and an arbitrary number of associative and AC symbols, giving an elegant way to model XML attributes.

A (bottom-up) sheaves automaton, $\mathcal{A}$, is a triple $\langle Q_{\mathcal{A}}, Q_{\text{fin}}, R \rangle$ where $Q_{\mathcal{A}}$ is a finite set of states, $\{q_1, \ldots, q_p\}$, Q_{fin} is a set of final states included in $Q_{\mathcal{A}}$, and R is a set of transition rules. Transition rules are of three kinds:

$$
\begin{array}{ll}
(1) & c \to q \\
(2) & a[q'] \to q \\
(3) & \phi(N_1, \ldots, N_p) \vdash Reg(Q_{\mathcal{A}}) \to q
\end{array}
$$

Type (1) and type (2) rules correspond to the transition rules found in regular tree automata for constants (leave nodes) and unary function symbols. Type (3) rules, also termed *constrained rules*, are the only addition to the regular tree automata model and are used to compute on nodes built using the concatenation operator (the only nodes with an unbounded arity). In type (3) rules, $Reg(Q_{\mathcal{A}})$ is a regular expression on the alphabet $\{q_1, \ldots, q_p\}$ and $\phi(N_1, \ldots, N_p)$ is a Presburger arithmetic formula with free variables $N_1, \ldots, N_p$. Intuitively, the variable N_i denotes the number of occurrences of the state q_i in a run of the automata. A type (3) rule may fire if we have a term of the form $d_1 \cdot \ldots \cdot d_n$ such that:

- each term d_i leads to a state $q_{j_i} \in Q_{\mathcal{A}}$;
- the word $q_{j_1} \cdot \ldots \cdot q_{j_n}$ is in the language defined by $Reg(Q_{\mathcal{A}})$;
- the formula $\phi \# (q_{j_1} \cdot \ldots \cdot q_{j_n})$ is satisfied, that is, $\models \phi(n_1, \ldots, n_p)$, where n_i is the number of occurrences of q_i in $q_{j_1} \cdot \ldots \cdot q_{j_n}$.

To stress the connection between variables in the counting constraint ϕ and the number of occurrences of q_i matched by $Reg(Q_{\mathcal{A}})$, we will use $\# q_i$ instead of N_i as the name of integer variables.

Example 4. An example of automaton on the signature $\{c, a[\_], b[\_]\}$ is given by the set of states $Q_{\mathcal{A}} = \{q_a, q_b, q_s\}$, the set of final states $Q_{\text{fin}} = \{q_s\}$ and the following set of five transition rules:

$$
\begin{array}{lll}
\epsilon \to q_s & a[q_s] \to q_a & (\# q_a = \# q_b) \wedge (\# q_s \geqslant 0) \vdash (q_a + q_b + q_s)* \to q_s \\
c \to q_s & b[q_s] \to q_b &
\end{array}
$$

We show in Example 5, after defining the transition relation, that this particular automaton accepts terms with as many a's than b's at each node, like for example $b[\epsilon] \cdot a[c \cdot b[\epsilon] \cdot c \cdot a[\epsilon]]$.

If we drop the Presburger arithmetic constraint and restrict to type (3) rules of the form $True \vdash Reg(Q_A) \rightarrow q$, we get *hedge automata* [11]. Conversely, if we drop the regular word expression and restrict to rules of the form $\phi(\# q_1, \ldots, \# q_p) \vdash (q_1 + \ldots + q_p)* \rightarrow q$, we get a class of automata which enjoys all the good properties of regular tree automata, that is closure under boolean operations, a determinisation algorithm, decidability of the test for emptiness, ... When both counting and regular word constraints are needed, some of these properties are no longer valid (at least in the case of non-deterministic SA).

Transition Relation. The *transition relation* of an automaton $\mathcal{A}$, denoted $d \rightarrow_{\mathcal{A}} q$, or simply $\rightarrow$ when there is no ambiguity, is the transitive closure of the relation defined by the following three rules.

Transition Relation: $\rightarrow$

<table>
<tr><td></td><td></td><td>(type 3)</td></tr>
<tr>
<td>(type 1)</td>
<td>(type 2)</td>
<td>$e_1 \rightarrow q_{j_1} \quad \cdots \quad e_n \rightarrow q_{j_n}$</td>
</tr>
<tr>
<td>$\dfrac{c \rightarrow q \in R}{c \rightarrow q}$</td>
<td>$\dfrac{d \rightarrow q' \quad n[q'] \rightarrow q \in R}{n[d] \rightarrow q}$</td>
<td>$\dfrac{q_{j_1} \cdot \ldots \cdot q_{j_n} \in Reg \quad \models \phi \#(q_{j_1} \cdot \ldots \cdot q_{j_n})}{\phi \vdash Reg \rightarrow q \in R \qquad (n \geqslant 2)}$
$\overline{\qquad e_1 \cdot \ldots \cdot e_n \rightarrow q \qquad}$</td>
</tr>
</table>

The rule for constrained transitions (type (3) rules), can only be applied to sequences of length at least 2. Therefore it could not be applied to the empty sequence, ϵ, or to sequence of only one element. It could be possible to extend the transition relation for type (3) rules to these two particular cases, but it would needlessly complicate our definitions and proofs without adding expressivity.

Example 5. Let $\mathcal{A}$ be the automaton defined in Example 4 and d be the document $a[c] \cdot b[a[c] \cdot b[c]]$. A possible accepting run of the automaton is given below:

$$d \rightarrow a[c] \cdot b[a[q_s] \cdot b[c]] \rightarrow a[q_s] \cdot b[a[q_s] \cdot b[c]] \rightarrow a[q_s] \cdot b[a[q_s] \cdot b[q_s]]$$
$$\rightarrow q_a \cdot b[a[q_s] \cdot b[q_s]] \rightarrow q_a \cdot b[a[q_s] \cdot q_b] \rightarrow q_a \cdot b[q_a \cdot q_b]$$
$$\xrightarrow{*} q_a \cdot b[q_s] \qquad \rightarrow q_a \cdot q_b \qquad \xrightarrow{*} q_s$$

Transitions marked with a $\star$-symbol (transitions 7 and 9) use the only constrained rule of $\mathcal{A}$. It is easy to check that, in each case, the word used in the constraints is $q_a \cdot q_b$, that this word belongs to $(q_a + q_b + q_s)*$ and that it contains as many q_a's than q_b's (its Parikh mapping is $(1, 1, 0)$).

Our example shows that SA can accept languages which are very different from regular tree languages, in fact closer to those accepted by context-free languages. In this example, we can recognize trees in which every sequences contains as many a's than b's as top elements. Indeed, the constrained rule in Example 4 can be interpreted as: "*the word $q_1 \cdot \ldots \cdot q_n$ belongs to the context-free language of words with as many q_a's than q_b's.*" It is even possible to write constraints defining languages which are not even context-free, like $q_a^n \cdot q_b^n \cdot q_c^n$ (just take the Presburger constraint $(\# q_a = \# q_b) \wedge (\# q_b = \# q_c)$ in Example 4).

As it is usual with automata, we say that a document d is *accepted* by a sheaves automaton $\mathcal{A}$ if there is a final state $q \in Q_{\text{fin}}$ such that $d \rightarrow_{\mathcal{A}} q$. The language $\mathcal{L}(\mathcal{A})$ is the set of terms accepted by $\mathcal{A}$. In the following, we will only consider *complete automaton*, such that every term reaches some state. This can be done without loss of generality since, for any SA, $\mathcal{A}$, it is always possible to build an equivalent complete automaton, $\mathcal{A}_c$ [8].

Proposition 3. *For any SA, $\mathcal{A}$, we can construct a complete automaton, $\mathcal{A}_c$, that accepts the language $\mathcal{L}(\mathcal{A})$ and it is deterministic if $\mathcal{A}$ is deterministic.*

Next, we enumerate of list of properties for our new class of automaton.

Deterministic SA Are Less Powerful Than Non-deterministic SA. A sheaves automaton is *deterministic* if and only if a term reaches at most one state. Contrary to regular tree automata, the class of deterministic sheaves automata is strictly weaker than the class of sheaves automata. In order to preserve determinism as much as possible, we will choose constructions for basic operations on automata that are a little bit more complex than the usual ones.

Proposition 4. *There is a language accepted by a sheaves automaton that can not be accepted by any deterministic sheaves automaton.*

Proof. Using an improved "pumping lemma" [8], we prove that the language L, consisting of the terms $a^n \cdot b^n \cdot a^m \cdot b^m$, with $n, m > 0$, is not recognizable by a deterministic SA, although there is a non-deterministic SA accepting L. □

Product, Union and Intersection. Given two automata $\mathcal{A} = \langle Q, Q_{\text{fin}}, R \rangle$ and $\mathcal{A}' = \langle Q', Q'_{\text{fin}}, R' \rangle$, we can construct the *product automaton*, $\mathcal{A} \times \mathcal{A}'$, that will prove useful in the definition of the automata for union and intersection. The product $\mathcal{A} \times \mathcal{A}'$ is the automaton $\mathcal{A}^{\times} = \langle Q^{\times}, \emptyset, R^{\times} \rangle$ such that:

- $Q^{\times} = Q \times Q' = \{(q_1, q'_1), \dots, (q_p, q'_l)\}$,
- for every type (1) rules $a \rightarrow q \in R$ and $a \rightarrow q' \in R'$, the rule $a \rightarrow (q, q')$ is in $R^{\times}$,
- for every type (2) rules $n[q] \rightarrow s \in R$ and $n[q'] \rightarrow s' \in R'$, the rule $n[(q, q')] \rightarrow (s, s')$ is in $R^{\times}$,
- for every type (3) rules $\phi \vdash Reg \rightarrow q \in R$ and $\phi' \vdash Reg' \rightarrow q' \in R$, the rule $\phi^{\times} \vdash Reg^{\times} \rightarrow (q, q')$ is in $R^{\times}$, where $Reg^{\times}$ is the regular expression corresponding to the product $Reg \times Reg'$ (this expression can be obtained from the product of an automaton accepting Reg by an automaton accepting Reg'). The formula $\phi^{\times}$ is the product of the formulas ϕ and ϕ' obtained as follows. Let $\#(q, q')$ be the name of the variable associated to the numbers of occurrences of the state (q, q'), then:

$$\phi^{\times} =_{\text{def}} \phi\Big(\sum_{q' \in Q'} \#(q_1, q'), \dots, \sum_{q' \in Q'} \#(q_p, q')\Big) \wedge \phi'\Big(\sum_{q \in Q} \#(q, q'_1), \dots, \sum_{q \in Q} \#(q, q'_l)\Big)$$

Proposition 5. *We have $d \to (q, q')$ in the automaton $A \times A'$, if and only if both $d \to_A q$ and $d \to_{A'} q'$.*

Given two automata, A and A', it is possible to obtain an automaton accepting the language $\mathcal{L}(A) \cup \mathcal{L}(A')$ and an automaton accepting $\mathcal{L}(A) \cap \mathcal{L}(A')$. The intersection $A \cap A'$ and the union $A \cup A'$ may be simply obtained from the product $A \times A'$ by setting the set of final states to:

$$Q_{\mathrm{fin}}^{\cap} =_{\mathrm{def}} \left\{ (q, q') \mid q \in Q_{\mathrm{fin}} \wedge q \in Q_{\mathrm{fin}}' \right\}$$
$$Q_{\mathrm{fin}}^{\cup} =_{\mathrm{def}} \left\{ (q, q') \mid q \in Q_{\mathrm{fin}} \vee q \in Q_{\mathrm{fin}}' \right\}$$

The union automaton may also be obtained using a simpler construction: take the union of the states of A and A' (supposed disjoint) and modify type (3) rules accordingly. It is enough to simply add the new states to each type (3) rules together with an extra counting constraint stating that the corresponding coefficients must be nil.

Proposition 6. *The automaton $A \cup A'$ accepts $\mathcal{L}(A) \cup \mathcal{L}(A')$ and $A \cap A'$ accepts $\mathcal{L}(A) \cap \mathcal{L}(A')$. Moreover, the union and intersection automaton are deterministic whenever both A and A' are deterministic.*

Complement. Given a deterministic automaton, A, we may obtain a deterministic automaton that recognizes the complement of the language $\mathcal{L}(A)$ simply by exchanging final and non-final states. This property does not hold for non-deterministic automata.

Proposition 7. *Non-deterministic Sheaves languages are not closed under complementation.*

Proof. We prove in [8] that given a two-counter machine, there is a non-deterministic automaton accepting exactly the bad computations of the machine. Thus, if the complement of this language was also accepted by some automaton, we could easily derive an automaton accepting the (good) computations reaching a final state, hence decide if the two-counter machine halts.   □

Membership. We consider the problem of checking whether a document, d, is accepted by a non-deterministic automaton A. We use the notation $|d|$ for the number of elements occurring in d and $|S|$ for the number of elements in a set S. The size of an automaton, $|A|$, is the number of symbols occurring in its definition.

Assume there is a function $Cost$ such that, for all constraints ϕ, the evaluation of $\phi(n_1, \ldots, n_p)$ can be done in time $O(Cost(p, n))$ whenever $n_i \leqslant n$ for all i in $1..p$. For quantifier-free Presburger formula (and if n is in binary notation) such a function is given by $K.p. \log(n)$, where K is the greatest coefficient occurring in ϕ. For arbitrary situations, that is for formulas involving any quantifiers alternation (which is very unlikely to occur in practice), the complexity is doubly exponential for a non-deterministic algorithm.

Proposition 8. *For an automaton* $\mathcal{A} = \langle Q, Q_{fin}, R \rangle$, *the problem* $d \stackrel{?}{\in} \mathcal{L}(\mathcal{A})$ *can be decided in time* $O(|d| \cdot |R| \cdot Cost(|Q|, |d|))$ *for a deterministic automaton and in time* $O(|d|^2 \cdot |Q| \cdot |R| \cdot Cost(|Q|, |d|))))$ *for a non-deterministic automaton.*

Proof. The proof is standard in the case of deterministic automata. Otherwise, there are $|d| \cdot |Q|$ possible labeling of the tree d by states of Q, and we check the applicability of each rules at each internal node.   □

Test for Emptiness. We give an algorithm for deciding emptiness that combines a marking algorithm with a test to decide if the combination of a regular expression and a Presburger constraint is satisfiable. We start by defining an algorithm for checking when a word on a sub-alphabet satisfies both a given regular word expression and a given counting constraint. We consider a set of states, $Q - \{q_1, \ldots, q_p\}$, that is also the alphabet for a regular expression Reg and a Presburger formula $\phi(\# q_1, \ldots, \# q_p)$. The problem is to decide whether there is a word on the sub-alphabet $Q' \subseteq Q$ satisfying both Reg and ϕ. We start by computing the regular expression $Reg_{|Q'}$ that corresponds to the words on the alphabet Q' satisfying Reg. This expression can be easily obtained from Reg by a set of simple syntactical rewritings. Then we compute the Parikh mapping $\#(Reg_{|Q'})$ as explained in Sect. 3 and test the satisfiability of the Presburger formula:

$$\phi(\# q_1, \ldots, \# q_p) \wedge \bigwedge_{q \notin Q'} (\# q = 0) \wedge \#(Reg_{|Q'})$$

When this formula is satisfiable, we say that the constraint $\phi \vdash Reg$ restricted to Q' is satisfiable. This notion is useful in the definition of an updated version of a standard marking algorithm for regular tree automaton. The marking algorithm computes a set $Q_M \subseteq Q$ of states and returns a positive answer if and only if there is a final state reachable in the automaton.

Algorithm 1. Test for Emptiness

$Q_M = \emptyset$

repeat   **if** $a \rightarrow q \in R$ **then** $Q_M = Q_M \cup \{q\}$
          if $n[q'] \rightarrow q \in R$ and $q' \in Q_M$ **then** $Q_M = Q_M \cup \{q\}$
          if $\begin{cases} \phi \vdash Reg \rightarrow q \in R \text{ and the constraint} \\ \phi \vdash Reg \text{ restricted to } Q_M \text{ is satisfiable} \end{cases}$ **then** $Q_M = Q_M \cup \{q\}$
until   no new state can be added to Q_M
         if Q_M contains a final state **then** return *not empty*   **else** return *empty*

Proposition 9. *A state q is marked by Algorithm 1, that is $q \in Q_M$, iff there exists a term t such that $t \rightarrow q$.*

We may prove this claim using a reasoning similar to the one for regular tree automata. We can also establish a result on the complexity of this algorithm. Let $Cost_{\mathcal{A}}$ denote the maximal time required to decide the satisfiability of the constraints occurring in the type (3) rules of $\mathcal{A} = (Q, Q_{fin}, R)$.

Proposition 10. *The problem $L(\mathcal{A}) \overset{?}{=} \emptyset$ is decidable in time $O(|Q| \cdot |R| \cdot Cost_{\mathcal{A}})$.*

The bound can be improved for regular tree automata, yielding a linear complexity. We could also get a linear bound if we have an oracle that, for each set of states $Q' \subseteq Q$ and each constraint, tells whether the constraint restricted to Q' is satisfiable.

6   Results on the Tree Logic and on XML Schema

We prove our main property linking sheaves automata and the sheaves logic and use this result to derive several important properties of the simplified schema language introduced in Sect. 2.

Theorem 1 (Definability). *For each formula Ψ of SL, we can construct a deterministic, complete, sheaves automaton $\mathcal{A}_\Psi$ accepting the models of Ψ.*

Proof. By structural induction on the definition of Ψ. Without loss of generality, we may strengthen the proposition with the following additional conditions: (1) a state q occurring in the right-hand side of a constrained rule may not occur in the left-hand side of a constrained rule; (2) a state occurring in the right-hand side of an unconstrained rule may not occur in the right-hand side of a constrained rule; (3) Presburger constraint may only occur when the right-hand side is not a final state, *i.e.* constrained rules are of the form $True \vdash Reg(Q) \rightarrow q$ whenever q is a final state. We only consider the difficult cases. For the case $\Psi = \Psi \vee \Psi$ or $\neg \Psi'$, we simply use the fact that deterministic SA are closed under union and complement.

$\Psi = a[T]$. Let $\mathcal{A}_T$ be the automaton constructed for T. Let q be a final state and q' be a state occurring in a rule $a[q] \rightarrow q'$ of $\mathcal{A}_T$. The idea is to choose the states of the form q' as the set of final states.

Let q be a final state occurring in a rule of the form $a[q] \rightarrow q'$. Whenever q' also occurs in a rule $c \rightarrow q'$ or $b[\ldots] \rightarrow q'$ of $\mathcal{A}_T$, we split q, q' in two states qa, qa' and $q\bar{a}, q\bar{a}'$ such that qa' occurs only in rules $a[qa] \rightarrow qa'$ and that $q\bar{a}'$ is used for the other rules, say $c \rightarrow q\bar{a}'$ or $b[\ldots] \rightarrow q\bar{a}'$. This is done for all such states q, q' of $\mathcal{A}$. The state-splitting is necessary to preserve determinism. The automaton $\mathcal{A}_\Psi$ is obtained by choosing the states qa' (where q is final in $\mathcal{A}_T$) as the set of final states.

$\Psi = S*, S \vee S, \bar{S}$ **or** S, S'. In this case, Ψ is a regular expression on some alphabet $E_1, \ldots, E_n$ where E_i are element formulas. By induction, there is a deterministic automaton $\mathcal{A}_i$ accepting the models of E_i for all $i \in 1..p$. Let $\mathcal{A}$ be the product automaton of the $\mathcal{A}_i$'s. A state $\mathcal{Q}$ of $\mathcal{A}$ is of the form $(q_1, ..., q_p)$, with q_i a state of $\mathcal{A}_i$. Therefore $\mathcal{Q}$ may represent terms accepted by several $\mathcal{A}_i$'s. We use the notation $\mathcal{Q} \in \text{fin}(\mathcal{A}_i)$ to say that the ith component of $\mathcal{Q}$ is a final state of $\mathcal{A}_i$.

We consider the regular expression Reg_S, with alphabet the set of states of $\mathcal{A}$, obtained by syntactically replacing E_i in Ψ with the expression $\bigcup \{\mathcal{Q} \mid \mathcal{Q} \in \text{fin}(\mathcal{A}_i)\}$. The complement of Reg_S is denoted $\overline{Reg}_S$.

For every state $\mathcal{Q}$ and rule $\phi \vdash Reg \rightarrow \mathcal{Q}$ of $\mathcal{A}$, we split $\mathcal{Q}$ into two states, $\mathcal{Q}_S$ and $\bar{\mathcal{Q}}_S$, and the constrained rule into two rules $\phi \vdash Reg \cap Reg_S \rightarrow \mathcal{Q}_S$ and $\phi \vdash Reg \cap \bar{Reg}_S \rightarrow \bar{\mathcal{Q}}_S$. To conclude, we choose the states of the form $\mathcal{Q}_S$ (where $\mathcal{Q}$ is final in $\mathcal{A}$) as the set of final states. This automaton is deterministic and complete and the property follows by showing that $d \models \Psi$ if and only if $d \in \mathcal{L}(\mathcal{A})$.

$\Psi = \exists \mathbf{N} : \phi : N_1 E_1 \& \ldots \& N_p E_p$. By induction, there is a deterministic automaton $\mathcal{A}_i$ accepting the models of E_i for all $i \in 1..p$. The construction is similar to a determinisation process. Let $\mathcal{A}$ be the product automaton of the $\mathcal{A}_i$'s and let $\{\mathcal{Q}_1, ..., \mathcal{Q}_m\}$ be the states of $\mathcal{A}$. A state $\mathcal{Q}$ of $\mathcal{A}$ is of the form $(q_1, ..., q_p)$, with q_i a state of $\mathcal{A}_i$, and it may therefore represent terms accepted by several $\mathcal{A}_i$'s. We use the notation $\mathcal{Q} \in \mathrm{fin}(\mathcal{A}_i)$ to say that the ith component of $\mathcal{Q}$ is a final state of $\mathcal{A}_i$.

The constrained rules of $\mathcal{A}$ are of the form $\psi(M_1, \ldots, M_m) \vdash Reg \rightarrow \mathcal{Q}$, where M_i stands for the number of occurrences of the state $\mathcal{Q}_i$ in a run. The idea is to define a Presburger formula, $\phi^{\exists}(M_1, \ldots, M_m)$, satisfied by configurations $\mathcal{Q}_{j_1} \cdot ... \cdot \mathcal{Q}_{j_n}$ containing a number of final states of the $\mathcal{A}_i$'s satisfying ϕ, and to augment all the type (3) rules with this counting constraint. To define $\phi^{\exists}$, we decompose M_i into a sum of integer variables, x_j^i for $j \in 1..p$, with x_j^i corresponding to a number of final states of $\mathcal{A}_j$ occurring in $\mathcal{Q}_i$.

$$\phi^{\exists} =_{\mathrm{def}} \exists (x_j^i)_{\substack{i \in 1..m \\ j \in 1..p}} \cdot \bigwedge_{i \in 1..m} \left(M_i = \sum_{\substack{j \in 1..p \\ \mathcal{Q}_i \in \mathrm{fin}(\mathcal{A}_j)}} x_j^i \right) \wedge \phi \left(\sum_{\substack{i \in 1..m \\ \mathcal{Q}_i \in \mathrm{fin}(\mathcal{A}_1)}} x_1^i, \; \ldots, \; \sum_{\substack{i \in 1..m \\ \mathcal{Q}_i \in \mathrm{fin}(\mathcal{A}_p)}} x_p^i \right)$$

Finally, we split each constrained rule $\psi \vdash Reg \rightarrow \mathcal{Q}$ of $\mathcal{A}$ into the two rules $\psi \wedge \phi^{\exists} \vdash Reg \rightarrow \mathcal{Q}_T$ and $\psi \wedge \neg \phi^{\exists} \vdash Reg \rightarrow \bar{\mathcal{Q}}_T$, splitting also the state $\mathcal{Q}$ into $\mathcal{Q}_T$ and $\bar{\mathcal{Q}}_T$. The automaton $\mathcal{A}_\Psi$ is obtained by choosing the states of the form $\mathcal{Q}_S$ (where $\mathcal{Q}$ is final in $\mathcal{A}$) as the set of final states. The automaton is deterministic and complete and the property follows by showing that $d \models \Psi$ if and only if $d \in \mathcal{L}(\mathcal{A})$.   □

As a direct corollary of Theorem 1 and Propositions 8 and 10, we obtain key results on the decidability and on the complexity of the sheaves logic. Let $|Q(\mathcal{A}_\Psi)|$ be the number of states of the SA associated to Ψ.

Theorem 2 (Decidability). *The logic SL is decidable.*

Theorem 3 (Model Checking). *For any document, d, and formula, Ψ, the problem $d \models \psi$ is decidable in time $O(|d| \cdot |\mathcal{A}_\psi| \cdot Cost(|Q(A_\Psi)|, |d|)|$.*

Since the schema language is a plain subset of our tree logic, we can directly transfer these results to schemas and decide the relation $d : S$ using sheaves automata.

Proposition 11. *For every schema, S, there is a deterministic SA, $\mathcal{A}$, such that $L(\mathcal{A}) = \{d \mid d : S\}$, and for every recursive schema, S, there is a SA such that $L(\mathcal{A}) = \{d \mid d : S\}$.*

Proof. Similar to the proof of Theorem 1. In the case of recursive schemas, we need to introduce a special state q_X for each definition $X = T$ in S. Then we construct the automata corresponding to T and replace q_X in $\mathcal{A}_S$ by any final state of $\mathcal{A}_T$. □

Combined with our previous results, we obtain several decidability properties on schemas, as well as automata-based decision procedures. We can, for example, easily define the intersection and difference of two schemas (that are not necessarily well-formed schemas).

Theorem 4 (XML Typing). *Given a document, d, and a schema, S, the problem $d : S$ is decidable.*

Theorem 5 (Satisfaction). *Given a schema S, the problem $\exists d \cdot d : S$ is decidable.*

7   Conclusion

Our contribution is a new class of automaton for unranked trees aiming at the manipulation of XML schemas. We believe it is the first work on applying tree automata theory to XML that considers the &-operator. This addition is significant in that interleaving is the source of many complications, essentially because it involves the combination of ordered and unordered data models. This led us to extend hedge automata [11] with counting constraints as a way to express properties on both sequences and multisets of elements. This extension appears quite natural since, when no counting constraints occurs, we obtain *hedge automata* and, when no constraints occur, we obtain regular tree automata.

The interleaving operator has been the subject of many controversial debates among the XML community, mainly because a similar operator was responsible for difficult implementation problems in SGML. Our work gives some justifications for these difficulties, like the undecidability of computing the complement of non-deterministic languages. To elude this problem, and in order to limit ourselves to deterministic automata, we have introduced two separate sorts for regular and counting formulas in our logic. It is interesting to observe that a stronger restriction appears in the schema specification, namely that & may only appears at top-level position in an element definition.

Another source of problems is related to the size and complexity of counting constraints. While the complexity of many operations on Presburger arithmetic is hyper-exponential (in the worst case), the constraints observed in practice are very simple and it seems possible to neglect the complexity of constraints solving in realistic circumstances. As a matter of fact, some simple syntactical restrictions on schemas yield simple Presburger formulas. For example, we may obtain polynomial complexity by imposing that each element tag in an expression $a_1[S_1]$ & ... & $a_p[S_p]$ be distinct, a restriction that also appears in the schema specification.

The goal of this work is not to devise a new schema or pattern language for XML, but rather to find an implementation framework compatible with schemas. An advantage of using tree automata theory for this task is that it also gives us complexity results on problems related to XML schema (and to possible extensions of schemas with logical operators). As indicated by our previous remarks, we may also hope to use our approach to define improved restrictions on schema and to give a better intuition on their impact. Another advantage of using tree automata is that it suggests multiple directions for improvements. Like for instance to add the capacity for the reverse traversal of a document or to extend our logic with some kind of path expression modality. These two extensions are quite orthogonal to what is already present in our logic and they could be added using some form of backtracking, like a parallel or alternating [7] variant of our tree automata, or by considering tree grammars (that is, equivalently, top-down tree automata). The same extension is needed if we want to process tree-structured data in a streamed way, a situation for which bottom-up tree automata are not well-suited.

References

1. S. Abiteboul, P. Buneman, and D. Suciu. *Data on the Web : From Relations to Semistructured Data and XML*. Morgan Kaufmann, 1999.
2. A. Berlea and H. Seidl. Binary queries. In *Extreme Markup Languages*, 2002.
3. A. Brown, M. Fuchs, J. Robie, and P. Wadler. MSL: A model for W3C XML schema. In WWW 10, 2001.
4. L. Cardelli and G. Ghelli. A query language based on the ambient logic. In *European Symposium on Programming (ESOP)*, volume 2028 of *LNCS*, pages 1–22, 2001.
5. L. Cardelli and A. Gordon. Anytime, anywhere: Modal logic for mobile ambients. In *Principles of Programming Languages (POPL)*. ACM Press, 2000.
6. J. Clark and M. Makoto, editors. *RELAX-NG Tutorial*. OASIS, 2001.
7. H. Comon, M. Dauchet, F. Jacquemard, D. Lugiez, S. Tison, and M. Tommasi. Tree Automata and their application. To appear as a book, 2003.
8. S. Dal Zilio and D. Lugiez. XML schema, tree logic and sheaves automata. Technical Report 4631, INRIA, 2002.
9. H. Hosoya and B. C. Pierce. Regular expression pattern matching for XML. In *Principles of Programming Languages (POPL)*, pages 67–80. ACM Press, 2001.
10. D. Lugiez and S. Dal Zilio. Multitrees automata, Presburger's constraints and tree logics. Technical Report 08-2002, LIF, 2002.
11. M. Makoto. Extended path expression for XML. In *Principles of Database Systems (PODS)*. ACM Press, 2001.
12. A. Muscholl, T. Schwentick, and H. Seidl. Numerical document queries. In *Principle of Databases Systems (PODS)*. ACM Press, 2003.

Size-Change Termination for Term Rewriting

René Thiemann and Jürgen Giesl

LuFG Informatik II, RWTH Aachen, Ahornstr. 55, 52074 Aachen, Germany
{thiemann|giesl}@informatik.rwth-aachen.de

Abstract. In [13], a new *size-change principle* was proposed to verify termination of functional programs automatically. We extend this principle in order to prove termination and innermost termination of arbitrary term rewrite systems (TRSs). Moreover, we compare this approach with existing techniques for termination analysis of TRSs (such as recursive path orderings or dependency pairs). It turns out that the size-change principle on its own fails for many examples that can be handled by standard techniques for rewriting, but there are also TRSs where it succeeds whereas existing rewriting techniques fail. In order to benefit from their respective advantages, we show how to combine the size-change principle with classical orderings and with dependency pairs. In this way, we obtain a new approach for automated termination proofs of TRSs which is more powerful than previous approaches.

1 Introduction

The size-change principle [13] is a new technique for automated termination analysis of functional programs, which raised great interest in the functional programming and automated reasoning community. However, up to now the connection between this principle and existing approaches for termination proofs of term rewriting was unclear. After introducing the size-change principle in Sect. 2, we show how to use it for (innermost) termination proofs of arbitrary TRSs in Sect. 3. This also illustrates how to combine the size-change principle with existing orderings from term rewriting. In Sect. 4 and 5 we compare the size-change principle with classical simplification orderings and with the dependency pair approach [1] for termination of TRSs. Finally, to combine their advantages, we developed a technique which integrates the size-change principle and dependency pairs. The combined technique was implemented in the system AProVE resulting in a very efficient and powerful automated method (details can be found in [14]).

2 The Size-Change Principle

We assume familiarity with term rewriting [3]. For a TRS $\mathcal{R}$ over a signature $\mathcal{F}$, the *defined symbols* $\mathcal{D}$ are the root symbols of the left-hand sides of rules and the *constructors* are $\mathcal{C} = \mathcal{F} \setminus \mathcal{D}$. We restrict ourselves to finite signatures and TRSs. $\mathcal{R}$ is a *constructor system* if the left-hand sides of its rules have the form $f(s_1, \ldots, s_n)$ where s_i are *constructor terms* (i.e., $s_i \in \mathcal{T}(\mathcal{C}, \mathcal{V})$). For a signature $\mathcal{F}$, the *embedding rules* $Emb_{\mathcal{F}}$ are $\{f(x_1, \ldots, x_n) \to x_i \mid f \in \mathcal{F}, n = \text{arity}(f), 1 \le i \le n\}$.

R. Nieuwenhuis (Ed.): RTA 2003, LNCS 2706, pp. 264–278, 2003.

In [13], the size-change principle was formulated for a functional programming language with eager evaluation strategy and without pattern matching. Such functional programs are easily transformed into TRSs which are orthogonal constructor systems whose ground normal forms only contain constructors (i.e., all functions are "completely" defined). In this section we present an extension of the original size-change principle which can be used for arbitrary TRSs.

We call $(\succsim, \succ)$ a *reduction pair* [11] on $\mathcal{T}(\mathcal{F}, \mathcal{V})$ if $\succsim$ is a quasi-ordering and $\succ$ is a well-founded ordering where $\succsim$ and $\succ$ are closed under substitutions and compatible (i.e., $\succsim \circ \succ \subseteq \succ$ or $\succ \circ \succsim \subseteq \succ$, but $\succ \subseteq \succsim$ is not required). In general, neither $\succsim$ nor $\succ$ must be closed under contexts. The reduction pair is *monotonic* if $\succsim$ is closed under contexts. In Sect. 3 we examine which additional conditions must be imposed on $(\succsim, \succ)$ in order to use the size-change principle for (innermost) termination proofs of TRSs. *Size-change graphs* denote how the size of function parameters changes when going from one function call to another.

Definition 1 (Size-Change Graph). *Let $(\succsim, \succ)$ be a reduction pair. For every rule $f(s_1, \ldots, s_n) \to r$ of a TRS $\mathcal{R}$ and every subterm $g(t_1, \ldots, t_m)$ of r where $g \in \mathcal{D}$, we define a size-change graph. The graph has n output nodes marked with $\{1_f, \ldots, n_f\}$ and m input nodes marked with $\{1_g, \ldots, m_g\}$. If $s_i \succ t_j$, then there is a directed edge marked with "$\succ$" from output node i_f to input node j_g. Otherwise, if $s_i \succsim t_j$, then there is an edge marked with "$\succsim$" from i_f to j_g. If f and g are clear from the context, then we often omit the subscripts from the nodes. So a size-change graph is a bipartite graph $G = (V, W, E)$ where $V = \{1_f, \ldots, n_f\}$ and $W = \{1_g, \ldots, m_g\}$ are the labels of the output and input nodes, respectively, and we have edges $E \subseteq V \times W \times \{\succsim, \succ\}$.*
Example 2. Let $\mathcal{R}$ consist of the following rules.

$$\mathsf{f}(\mathsf{s}(x), y) \to \mathsf{f}(x, \mathsf{s}(x)) \qquad (1) \qquad\qquad \mathsf{f}(x, \mathsf{s}(y)) \to \mathsf{f}(y, x) \qquad (2)$$

$\mathcal{R}$ has two size-change graphs $G_{(1)}$ and $G_{(2)}$ resulting from (1) and (2). Here, we use the embedding ordering on constructors $\mathcal{C}$, i.e., $(\succsim, \succ) = (\to^*_{Emb_\mathcal{C}}, \to^+_{Emb_\mathcal{C}})$.

To trace sizes of parameters along subsequent function calls, size-change graphs (V_1, W_1, E_1) and (V_2, W_2, E_2) can be concatenated to *multigraphs* if $W_1 = V_2$, i.e., if they correspond to arguments $\{1_g, \ldots, m_g\}$ of the same function g.
Definition 3 (Multigraph and Concatenation). *Every size-change graph of $\mathcal{R}$ is a multigraph of $\mathcal{R}$ and if $G = (\{1_f, \ldots, n_f\}, \{1_g, \ldots, m_g\}, E_1)$ and $H = (\{1_g, \ldots, m_g\}, \{1_h, \ldots, p_h\}, E_2)$ are multigraphs w.r.t. the same reduction pair $(\succsim, \succ)$, then the concatenation $G \cdot H = (\{1_f, \ldots, n_f\}, \{1_h, \ldots, p_h\}, E)$ is also a multigraph of $\mathcal{R}$. For $1 \le i \le n$ and $1 \le k \le p$, E contains an edge from i_f to k_h iff E_1 contains an edge from i_f to some j_g and E_2 contains an edge from j_g to k_h. If there is such a j_g where the edge of E_1 or E_2 is labelled with "$\succ$", then the edge in E is labelled with "$\succ$" as well. Otherwise, it is labelled with "$\succsim$". A multigraph G is called maximal if its input and output nodes are both labelled with $\{1_f, \ldots, n_f\}$ for some f and if it is idempotent, i.e., $G = G \cdot G$.*

Example 4. In Ex. 2 we obtain the following three maximal multigraphs:

$$G_{(1)} \cdot G_{(2)} : \quad 1_f \xrightarrow{\succsim} 1_f \qquad G_{(2)} \cdot G_{(1)} : \quad 1_f \qquad 1_f \qquad G_{(2)} \cdot G_{(2)} : \quad 1_f \xrightarrow{\succsim} 1_f$$
$$2_f \qquad 2_f \qquad\qquad 2_f \xrightarrow{\succ} 2_f \qquad\qquad 2_f \xrightarrow{\succsim} 2_f$$

For termination, in every maximal multigraph a parameter must be decreasing.[1]

Definition 5 (Size-Change Termination). *A TRS $\mathcal{R}$ over the signature $\mathcal{F}$ is* size-change terminating *w.r.t. a reduction pair $(\succsim, \succ)$ on $\mathcal{T}(\mathcal{F}, \mathcal{V})$ iff every maximal multigraph contains an edge of the form $i \xrightarrow{\succ} i$.*

In Ex. 4, each maximal multigraph contains the edge $1_f \xrightarrow{\succsim} 1_f$ or $2_f \xrightarrow{\succsim} 2_f$. So the TRS is size-change terminating w.r.t. the embedding ordering. Note that classical path orderings from term rewriting fail on this example (see Sect. 4).

Since there are only finitely many possible multigraphs, they can be constructed automatically. So for a given reduction pair, size-change termination is decidable. However, in general size-change termination does not imply termination.

Example 6. Consider the TRS with the rules $f(a) \to f(b)$ and $b \to a$. If we use the lexicographic path ordering $\succ_{LPO}$ [9] with the precedence $a > b$, then the only maximal multigraph is $1_f \xrightarrow{\succ_{LPO}} 1_f$. So size-change termination is proved, although the TRS is obviously not terminating.

3   Size-Change Termination and Termination of TRSs

In this section we develop conditions on the reduction pair used in Def. 5 which ensure that size-change termination indeed implies (innermost) termination. Then the size-change principle can be combined with classical orderings from term rewriting and it becomes a sound termination criterion.

In [13], the authors use reduction pairs $(\succsim, \succ)$ where $\succsim$ is the reflexive closure of $\succ$ and $\succ$ is defined in terms of a well-founded relation $>$ on (ground) normal forms of $\mathcal{R}$. We now show that such reduction pairs can be used for innermost termination proofs of arbitrary TRSs. Moreover, $\succsim$ can be any compatible quasi-ordering. We denote innermost reduction steps by $\xrightarrow{i}_{\mathcal{R}}$ and $s \xrightarrow{i}!_{\mathcal{R}} s'$ means that s' is a normal form reachable from s by innermost reduction. Thm. 7 will serve as the basis for the automation of the size-change principle in Thm. 8 afterwards.

Theorem 7 (Size-Change Termination and Innermost Termination).
Let $>$ be a well-founded ordering on normal forms of a TRS $\mathcal{R}$. For $s, t \in \mathcal{T}(\mathcal{F}, \mathcal{V})$ we define $\mathrm{NF}(s, t) = \{(s', t') \mid s\sigma \xrightarrow{i}!_{\mathcal{R}} s', t\sigma \xrightarrow{i}!_{\mathcal{R}} t', \sigma \text{ instantiates all variables of } s \text{ and } t \text{ with normal forms of } \mathcal{R}\}$. *Let $(\succsim, \succ)$ be a reduction pair where $s \succ t$ implies $s' > t'$ for all $(s', t') \in \mathrm{NF}(s, t)$. If $\mathcal{R}$ is size-change terminating w.r.t. $(\succsim, \succ)$, then $\mathcal{R}$ is innermost terminating.*

---

[1] Def. 5 corresponds to an equivalent characterization of size-change termination [13].

Proof. If $\mathcal{R}$ is not innermost terminating, then there is a minimal non-innermost terminating term v_0, i.e., all proper subterms of v_0 are innermost terminating. Let $\xrightarrow{\text{i}}_\epsilon$ denote root reductions and let $\xrightarrow{\text{i}}_{>\epsilon}$ denote reductions below the root. Then v_0's infinite innermost reduction starts with $v_0 \xrightarrow{\text{i}}{}^*_{>\epsilon} u_1 \xrightarrow{\text{i}}_\epsilon w_1$ where all proper subterms of u_1 are in normal form. Since w_1 is not innermost terminating, it has a minimal non-innermost terminating subterm v_1.

The infinite reduction continues in the same way. So for $i \geq 1$, we have $v_{i-1} \xrightarrow{\text{i}}{}^*_{>\epsilon} u_i = l_i\sigma_i$ and $v_i = r_i'\sigma_i$ for a rule $l_i \to r_i$, a subterm r_i' of r_i with defined root, and a substitution σ_i instantiating l_i's variables with normal forms.

For each step from u_i to v_i there is a corresponding size-change graph G_i. We regard the infinite graph resulting from $G_1, G_2, \ldots$ by identifying the input nodes of G_i with the output nodes of G_{i+1}. If $\mathcal{R}$ is size-change terminating, by [13, Thm. 4] resp. [14, Lemma 7], this infinite graph contains an infinite path where infinitely many edges are labelled with "$\succ$". Without loss of generality we assume that this path already starts in G_1. For every i, let a_i be the output node in G_i which is on this path. So we have $l_i|_{a_i} \succ r_i'|_{a_{i+1}}$ for all i from an infinite set $I \subseteq \mathbb{N}$ and $l_i|_{a_i} \succsim r_i'|_{a_{i+1}}$ for $i \in \mathbb{N} \setminus I$. Note that $l_i|_{a_i}\sigma_i = u_i|_{a_i}$ and $r_i'|_{a_{i+1}}\sigma_i = v_i|_{a_{i+1}}$ $\xrightarrow{\text{i}}{}^!_{\mathcal{R}} u_{i+1}|_{a_{i+1}}$. Thus, $(u_i|_{a_i}, u_{i+1}|_{a_{i+1}}) \in \mathrm{NF}(l_i|_{a_i}, r_i'|_{a_{i+1}})$. So for $I = \{i_1, i_2, \ldots\}$ we obtain $u_{i_1}|_{a_{i_1}} > u_{i_2}|_{a_{i_2}} > \ldots$ which contradicts well-foundedness of $>$. $\qquad\square$

Innermost termination is interesting, since then there are no infinite reductions w.r.t. eager evaluation strategies. Moreover, for non-overlapping TRSs, innermost termination already implies termination. However, Thm. 7 is not yet suitable for automation. To check whether $\succ$ satisfies the conditions of Thm. 7, one has to examine infinitely many instantiations of s and t and compute normal forms s' and t' although $\mathcal{R}$ is possibly not innermost terminating. Therefore, in the examples of [13], one is restricted to relations $\succsim$ and $\succ$ on constructor terms.

Thm. 8 shows how to use reduction pairs on $\mathcal{T}(\mathcal{C}, \mathcal{V})$ for possibly automated innermost termination proofs. A reduction pair $(\succsim, \succ)$ on $\mathcal{T}(\mathcal{G}, \mathcal{V})$ with $\mathcal{G} \subseteq \mathcal{F}$ can be *extended* to a (usually non-monotonic) reduction pair $(\succsim', \succ')$ on $\mathcal{T}(\mathcal{F}, \mathcal{V})$ by defining $s \succsim' t$ if $s = t$ or if there are $u, v \in \mathcal{T}(\mathcal{G}, \mathcal{V})$ with $u \succsim v$ and $s = u\sigma$, $t = v\sigma$ for some substitution σ. Moreover, $s \succ' t$ iff $u \succ v$ for u and v as above.

Theorem 8 (Innermost Termination Proofs). *Let $(\succsim, \succ)$ be a reduction pair on $\mathcal{T}(\mathcal{C}, \mathcal{V})$. If $\mathcal{R}$ is size-change terminating w.r.t. the extension of the reduction pair $(\succsim, \succ)$ to $\mathcal{T}(\mathcal{F}, \mathcal{V})$, then $\mathcal{R}$ is innermost terminating.*

Proof. Let $(\succsim', \succ')$ be the extension of $(\succsim, \succ)$ to $\mathcal{T}(\mathcal{F}, \mathcal{V})$. We show that $s \succ' t$ implies $s' \succ' t'$ for all $(s', t') \in \mathrm{NF}(s, t)$. Then the theorem follows from Thm. 7.

By the definition of extensions, $s \succ' t$ iff $s = u\sigma$, $t = v\sigma$, and $u \succ v$ for suitable u, v, and σ. In particular, u and v must be constructor terms and we also have $u \succ' v$ (as σ may also be the identity). Since $\mathrm{NF}(s, t) \subseteq \{(u\sigma, v\sigma) \mid \sigma$ instantiates u's and v's variables with normal forms$\}$, the claim follows from $u \succ' v$, because $\succ'$ is closed under substitutions. $\qquad\square$

For the TRS in Ex. 2, when using the extension of the reduction pair $(\to^*_{Emb_\mathcal{C}}, \to^+_{Emb_\mathcal{C}})$ on $\mathcal{T}(\mathcal{C}, \mathcal{V})$, we obtain the same size-change graphs as with

$(\rightarrow^*_{Emb_C}, \rightarrow^+_{Emb_C})$ on $T(\mathcal{F}, \mathcal{V})$. Ex. 4 shows that this TRS is size-change terminating w.r.t. this reduction pair and hence, by Thm. 8, this proves innermost termination. However, a variant of Toyama's example [15] shows that Thm. 7 and Thm. 8 are not sufficient to prove full (non-innermost) termination.

Example 9. Let $\mathcal{R} = \{f(c(a, b, x)) \rightarrow f(c(x, x, x)), g(x, y) \rightarrow x, g(x, y) \rightarrow y\}$. We define $\succsim = \rightarrow^*_S$ and $\succ = \rightarrow^+_S$ restricted to $T(\mathcal{C}, \mathcal{V})$, where S is the terminating TRS $c(a, b, x) \rightarrow c(x, x, x)$. The only maximal multigraph is $1_f \xrightarrow{\succ} 1_f$. So $\mathcal{R}$ is size-change terminating and innermost terminating by Thm. 8, but not terminating.

As in Ex. 9, reduction pairs $(\rightarrow^*_S, \rightarrow^+_S)$ satisfying the conditions of Thm. 8 can be defined using a terminating TRS S over the signature $\mathcal{C}$. The following theorem shows that if S is non-duplicating, then we may use the relation $\rightarrow_S$ also on terms with defined symbols and size-change termination even implies full termination. A TRS is *non-duplicating* if every variable occurs on the right-hand side of a rule at most as often as on the corresponding left-hand side. So size-change termination of the TRS in Ex. 2 and Ex. 4 using the reduction pair $(\rightarrow^*_{Emb_C}, \rightarrow^+_{Emb_C})$ implies that the TRS is indeed terminating.

To prove the theorem, we need a preliminary lemma which states that minimal non-terminating terms w.r.t. $\mathcal{R} \cup S$ cannot start with constructors of $\mathcal{R}$. Again, here S must be non-duplicating. Otherwise, in Ex. 9, $c(a, b, g(a, b))$ is a minimal non-terminating term w.r.t. $\mathcal{R} \cup S$ that starts with a constructor of $\mathcal{R}$.

Lemma 10. *Let $\mathcal{R}$ be a TRS over the signature $\mathcal{F}$ with constructors $\mathcal{C}$ and let S be a terminating non-duplicating TRS over $\mathcal{C}$. If $t_1, \ldots, t_n \in T(\mathcal{F}, \mathcal{V})$ are terminating w.r.t. $\mathcal{R} \cup S$ and $c \in \mathcal{C}$, then $c(t_1, \ldots, t_n)$ is also terminating w.r.t. $\mathcal{R} \cup S$.*

Proof. For any term $s \in T(\mathcal{F}, \mathcal{V})$, let M_s be the multiset of the maximal subterms of s whose root is defined, i.e., $M_s = \{s|_\pi \mid root(s|_\pi) \in \mathcal{D}$ and for all π' above π we have $root(s|_{\pi'}) \in \mathcal{C}\}$. Moreover, let s' be the term that results from s by replacing all maximal subterms with defined root by the same fresh special variable $x_\mathcal{C}$. Let $\twoheadrightarrow_{\mathcal{R} \cup S}$ be the extension of $\rightarrow_{\mathcal{R} \cup S}$ to multisets where $M \twoheadrightarrow_{\mathcal{R} \cup S} M'$ iff $M = N \cup \{s\}$ and $M' = N \cup \{t_1, \ldots, t_n\}$ with $n \geq 0$ and with $s \rightarrow_{\mathcal{R} \cup S} t_i$ for all i. We prove the following conjecture.

Let $s \in T(\mathcal{F}, \mathcal{V})$ such that all terms in M_s are terminating w.r.t. $\mathcal{R} \cup S$ and let $s \rightarrow_{\mathcal{R} \cup S} t$. Then all terms in M_t are also terminating w.r.t. $\mathcal{R} \cup S$.   (3)
Moreover, $M_s \twoheadrightarrow_{\mathcal{R} \cup S} M_t$ or both $M_s = M_t$ and $s' \rightarrow_S t'$.

Note that $\twoheadrightarrow_{\mathcal{R} \cup S}$ is well founded on multisets like M_s which only contain terminating terms. Termination of S implies that $\rightarrow_S$ is also well founded and the lexicographic combination of two well-founded orderings preserves well-foundedness. Hence, (3) implies that if all terms in M_s are terminating, then s is terminating as well. So the lemma immediately follows from Conjecture (3).

To prove (3), we distinguish according to the position π where the reduction $s \rightarrow_{\mathcal{R} \cup S} t$ takes place. If s has a defined symbol of $\mathcal{D}$ on or above position π, then this implies $M_s \twoheadrightarrow_{\mathcal{R} \cup S} M_t$ and all terms in M_t are also terminating. Otherwise, if π is above all symbols of $\mathcal{D}$ in s, then $s \rightarrow_{\mathcal{R} \cup S} t$ implies $s \rightarrow_S t$ and $M_s \supseteq M_t$ (since S is non-duplicating). Moreover, $s \rightarrow_S t$ also implies $s' \rightarrow_S t'$.   □

Theorem 11 (Termination Proofs). *Let $\mathcal{R}$ be a TRS over the signature $\mathcal{F}$ with constructors $\mathcal{C}$ and let $\mathcal{S}$ be a terminating non-duplicating TRS over $\mathcal{C}$. If $\mathcal{R}$ is size-change terminating w.r.t. the reduction pair $(\to_{\mathcal{S}}^{*}, \to_{\mathcal{S}}^{+})$ on $\mathcal{T}(\mathcal{F}, \mathcal{V})$, then $\mathcal{R}$ (and even $\mathcal{R} \cup \mathcal{S}$) is terminating.*

Proof. We define $\mathcal{R}' := \mathcal{R} \cup \mathcal{S}$. If $\mathcal{R}'$ is not terminating, then as in the proof of Thm. 7 we obtain an infinite sequence of minimal non-terminating terms u_i, v_i with $v_i \to_{>\epsilon, \mathcal{R}'}^{*} u_{i+1}$ where the step from u_i to v_i corresponds to a size-change graph of $\mathcal{R}'$. Thus, for all i there is a rule $l_i \to r_i$ in $\mathcal{R}'$ with $u_i = l_i \sigma_i$ and $v_i = r_i' \sigma_i$ for a subterm r_i' of r_i and a substitution σ_i.

By Lemma 10, the roots of u_i and v_i are defined symbols. So all these size-change graphs are from $\mathcal{R}$. As in Thm. 7's proof, there are a_i with $l_i|_{a_i} \to_{\mathcal{S}}^{+} r_i'|_{a_{i+1}}$ for all i from an infinite $I \subseteq \mathbb{N}$ and $l_i|_{a_i} \to_{\mathcal{S}}^{*} r_i'|_{a_{i+1}}$ for $i \in \mathbb{N} \setminus I$. Since $\to_{\mathcal{S}}$ is closed under substitution we have $u_i|_{a_i} \to_{\mathcal{S}}^{+} v_i|_{a_{i+1}}$ or $u_i|_{a_i} \to_{\mathcal{S}}^{*} v_i|_{a_{i+1}}$, respectively. Recall $v_i|_{a_{i+1}} \to_{\mathcal{R}'}^{*} u_{i+1}|_{a_{i+1}}$ and $\mathcal{S} \subseteq \mathcal{R}'$. So for $I = \{i_1, i_2, \dots\}$ we have $u_{i_1}|_{a_{i_1}} \to_{\mathcal{R}'}^{+} u_{i_2}|_{a_{i_2}} \to_{\mathcal{R}'}^{+} \dots$ contradicting the minimality of the terms u_i. $\square$

Thm. 8 and 11 offer two possibilities for automating the size-change principle. Even for innermost termination, they do not subsume each other. Ex. 9 cannot be handled by Thm. 11 and innermost termination of $\{g(f(a)) \to g(f(b)), f(x) \to x\}$ cannot be proved with Thm. 8, since $f(a) \not\succ f(b)$ for any extension $\succ$ of an ordering on constructor terms. But termination is shown with Thm. 11 using $\mathcal{S} = \{a \to b\}$. A variant of Thm. 11 for innermost termination holds if $\mathcal{S}$ is innermost terminating (and possibly duplicating). However, this variant only proves innermost termination of $\mathcal{R} \cup \mathcal{S}$ which does not imply innermost termination of $\mathcal{R}$.

So Thm. 8 and Thm. 11 are new contributions that show which reduction pairs are admissible in order to use size-change termination for termination or innermost termination proofs of TRSs. In this way, size-change termination becomes an automatic technique, since one can use classical techniques from termination of term rewriting to generate suitable reduction pairs automatically.

4   Comparison with Orderings from Term Rewriting

Traditional techniques for TRSs prove *simple termination* where $\mathcal{R}$ is simply terminating iff it is compatible with a *simplification ordering* (e.g., LPO or RPOS [5,9], KBO [10], most polynomial orderings [12]). Equivalently, $\mathcal{R}$ is simply terminating iff $\mathcal{R} \cup Emb_{\mathcal{F}}$ terminates for $\mathcal{R}$'s signature $\mathcal{F}$. Similar to traditional techniques, the size-change principle essentially only verifies simple termination.

Theorem 12 (Size-Change Principle and Simple Termination).

(a) *A TRS $\mathcal{R}$ over a signature $\mathcal{F}$ is size-change terminating w.r.t. a reduction pair $(\succsim, \succ)$ iff $\mathcal{R} \cup Emb_{\mathcal{F}}$ is size-change terminating w.r.t. $(\succsim, \succ)$.*

(b) *Let $\mathcal{S}$ be as in Thm. 11. If $\mathcal{S}$ is simply terminating and $\mathcal{R}$ is size-change terminating w.r.t. $(\to_{\mathcal{S}}^{*}, \to_{\mathcal{S}}^{+})$ on $\mathcal{T}(\mathcal{F}, \mathcal{V})$, then $\mathcal{R} \cup \mathcal{S}$ is simply terminating.*

Proof. (a) The "if" direction is obvious. For the "only if" direction, note that $Emb_{\mathcal{F}}$ yields no new size-change graphs. But due to $Emb_{\mathcal{C}}$, all constructors are transformed into defined symbols. So from the $\mathcal{R}$-rules we obtain additional size-change graphs whose input nodes are labelled with (former) constructors (i.e., $1_c, \ldots, n_c$ for $c \in \mathcal{C}$). However, since output nodes are never labelled with constructors, this does not yield new maximal multigraphs (since there, output and input nodes are labelled by the same function). Hence, size-change termination is not affected when adding $Emb_{\mathcal{F}}$.

(b) As in (a), adding $Emb_{\mathcal{D}}$ to $\mathcal{R}$ yields no new size-change graphs and thus, $\mathcal{R} \cup Emb_{\mathcal{D}}$ is also size-change terminating w.r.t. $(\rightarrow_{\mathcal{S}}^*, \rightarrow_{\mathcal{S}}^+)$ and hence, also w.r.t. $(\rightarrow_{\mathcal{S} \cup Emb_{\mathcal{C}}}^*, \rightarrow_{\mathcal{S} \cup Emb_{\mathcal{C}}}^+)$. Since $\mathcal{S} \cup Emb_{\mathcal{C}}$ is terminating, Thm. 11 implies termination of $\mathcal{R} \cup Emb_{\mathcal{D}} \cup \mathcal{S} \cup Emb_{\mathcal{C}}$, i.e., simple termination of $\mathcal{R} \cup \mathcal{S}$. $\square$

The restriction to simple termination excludes many relevant TRSs. Thm. 12 illustrates that the size-change principle cannot compete with new techniques (e.g., *dependency pairs* [1] or *monotonic semantic path ordering* [4]) where simplification orderings may be applied to non-simply terminating TRSs as well. However, these new techniques require methods to generate underlying base orderings. Hence, there is still an urgent need for powerful simplification orderings.

Now we clarify the connection between size-change termination and classical simplification orderings and show that they do not subsume each other in general.

A major advantage of the size-change principle is that it can simulate the basic ingredients of RPOS, i.e., the concepts of *lexicographic* and of *multiset*-comparison. Thus, by the size-change principle w.r.t. a very simple reduction pair like the embedding ordering we obtain an automated method for termination analysis which avoids the search problems of RPOS and which can still capture the idea of comparing tuples of arguments lexicographically or as multisets.

More precisely, for a reduction pair $(\succsim, \succ)$, let $\succ_{lex}$ and $\succ_{mul}$ result from comparing tuples s^* and t^* of terms lexicographically and as multisets, respectively. If $s_i^* \succ_{lex} t_i^*$ for all $1 \leq i \leq k$, then the TRS $\{f(s_1^*) \rightarrow f(t_1^*), \ldots, f(s_k^*) \rightarrow f(t_k^*)\}$ is size-change terminating w.r.t. $(\succsim, \succ)$. In particular, size-change termination w.r.t. the same reduction pair $(\succsim, \succ)$ can simulate $\succ_{lex}$ for *any permutation* used to compare the components of a tuple. Similarly, if $s_i^* \succ_{mul} t_i^*$ for all i, then this TRS is also size-change terminating w.r.t. $(\succsim, \succ)$.[2] For example, the TRS computing the Ackermann function as well as the TRS $\{\mathsf{plus}(0, y) \rightarrow y, \ \mathsf{plus}(\mathsf{s}(x), y) \rightarrow \mathsf{s}(\mathsf{plus}(y, x))\}$ are size-change terminating w.r.t. the embedding ordering on constructors whereas traditional rewriting techniques would need lexicographic and recursive (multiset) path ordering, respectively.

Since both lexicographic and multiset comparison are simulated by the size-change principle using the *same* reduction pair, one can also handle TRSs like Ex. 2 where traditional path orderings like RPOS (or KBO) fail. In the first rule $\mathsf{f}(\mathsf{s}(x), y) \rightarrow \mathsf{f}(x, \mathsf{s}(x))$ the arguments of f have to be compared lexicographically from left to right and in the second rule $\mathsf{f}(x, \mathsf{s}(y)) \rightarrow \mathsf{f}(y, x)$ they have to be compared as multisets. If one adds the rules for the Ackermann function then polynomial orderings fail as well, but size-change termination is proved as before.

However, compared to classical path orderings, the size-change principle also has several drawbacks. One problem is that it can only simulate lexicographic and

---

[2] Formal proofs for these observations can be found in [14, Thm. 14 and Thm. 15].

multiset comparison for the arguments of the *root* symbol. Hence, if one adds a new function on top of all terms in the rules, this simulation is no longer possible. For example, the TRS $\{f(plus(0, y)) \rightarrow f(y), f(plus(s(x), y)) \rightarrow f(s(plus(y, x)))\}$ is no longer size-change terminating w.r.t. the embedding ordering, whereas classical path orderings can apply lexicographic or multiset comparisons on all levels of the term. Thus, termination would still be easy to prove with RPO.

Perhaps the most serious drawback is that the size-change principle lacks concepts to compare defined function symbols syntactically. Consider a TRS with the rule $log(s(s(x))) \rightarrow s(log(s(half(x))))$ and rules for half such that $half(x)$ computes $\lfloor \frac{x}{2} \rfloor$. If a function (like log) calls another defined function (like half) in the arguments of its recursive calls, one has to check whether the argument $half(x)$ is smaller than the term $s(x)$ in the corresponding left-hand side. The size-change principle on its own offers no possibility for that and its mechanizable versions (Thm. 8 and Thm. 11) fail since they only use an underlying ordering on constructor terms. In contrast, classical orderings like RPO can easily show termination automatically using a *precedence* log > s > half on function symbols.

Finally, the size-change principle has the disadvantage that it cannot *measure* terms by combining measures of subterms as in polynomial orderings or KBO.

Example 13. Measures (*weights*) are especially useful if one parameter is increasing, but the decrease of another parameter is greater than this increase. So termination of $\{plus(s(s(x)), y) \rightarrow s(plus(x, s(y))), plus(x, s(s(y))) \rightarrow s(plus(s(x), y)), plus(s(0), y) \rightarrow s(y), plus(0, y) \rightarrow y\}$ is trivial to prove with polynomial orderings or KBO, but the TRS is not size-change terminating w.r.t. *any* reduction pair.

5   Comparison and Combination with Dependency Pairs

Now we compare the size-change principle with *dependency pairs*. In contrast to other recent techniques [4,6], dependency pairs and size-change graphs are both built from recursive calls which suggests to combine these approaches to benefit from their respective advantages. We recapitulate the concepts of dependency pairs; see [1,7,8] for refinements and motivations. Let $\mathcal{F}^\sharp = \{f^\sharp \mid f \in \mathcal{D}\}$ be a set of *tuple symbols*, where $f^\sharp$ has the same arity as f and we often write F for $f^\sharp$, etc. If $t = g(t_1, \ldots, t_m)$ with $g \in \mathcal{D}$, we write $t^\sharp$ for $g^\sharp(t_1, \ldots, t_m)$. If $l \rightarrow r \in \mathcal{R}$ and t is a subterm of r with defined root, then the rule $l^\sharp \rightarrow t^\sharp$ is a *dependency pair* of $\mathcal{R}$. So the dependency pairs of the TRS from Ex. 2 are

$$F(s(x), y) \rightarrow F(x, s(x)) \qquad (4) \qquad\qquad F(x, s(y)) \rightarrow F(y, x) \qquad (5)$$

We always assume that different occurrences of dependency pairs are variable disjoint. Then a TRS is (innermost) terminating iff there is no infinite (innermost) *chain* of dependency pairs. A sequence $s_1 \rightarrow t_1, s_2 \rightarrow t_2, \ldots$ of dependency pairs is a *chain* iff $t_i\sigma \rightarrow^*_{\mathcal{R}} s_{i+1}\sigma$ for all i and a suitable substitution σ. The sequence is an *innermost* chain iff $t_i\sigma \xrightarrow{i}^*_{\mathcal{R}} s_{i+1}\sigma$ and all $s_i\sigma$ are in normal form.

To estimate which dependency pairs may occur consecutively in chains, one builds a so-called dependency graph. Let CAP(t) result from replacing all subterms of t with defined root symbol by different fresh variables and let REN(t) result from replacing all occurrences of variables in t by different fresh variables.

For instance, $\text{CAP}(\mathsf{F}(x, \mathsf{s}(x))) = \mathsf{F}(x, \mathsf{s}(x))$ and $\text{REN}(\mathsf{F}(x, \mathsf{s}(x))) = \mathsf{F}(x_1, \mathsf{s}(x_2))$. The (estimated) *dependency graph* is the directed graph whose nodes are the dependency pairs and there is an arc from $s \to t$ to $v \to w$ iff $\text{REN}(\text{CAP}(t))$ and v are unifiable. In the (estimated) *innermost dependency graph* there is only an arc from $s \to t$ to $v \to w$ iff $\text{CAP}(t)$ and v are unifiable. For the TRS of Ex. 2, the dependency graph and the innermost dependency graph are identical and each dependency pair is connected with itself and with the other pair.

A non-empty set $\mathcal{P}$ of dependency pairs is a *cycle* if for any pairs $s \to t$ and $v \to w$ in $\mathcal{P}$ there is a non-empty path from $s \to t$ to $v \to w$ which only traverses pairs from $\mathcal{P}$. In our example we have the cycles $\{(4)\}$, $\{(5)\}$, and $\{(4), (5)\}$. If a cycle only contains dependency pairs resulting from the rules $\mathcal{R}' \subseteq \mathcal{R}$ we speak of an $\mathcal{R}'$-*cycle* of the dependency graph of $\mathcal{R}$. Finally, for $f \in \mathcal{D}$ we define its *usable rules* $\mathcal{U}(f)$ as the smallest set containing all f-rules and all rules that are usable for function symbols occurring in right-hand sides of f-rules. In our example, the usable rules for f are (1) and (2). For $\mathcal{D}' \subseteq \mathcal{D}$ let $\mathcal{U}(\mathcal{D}') = \bigcup_{f \in \mathcal{D}'} \mathcal{U}(f)$.

Theorem 14 (Dependency Pair Approach [1]). *A TRS $\mathcal{R}$ is terminating iff for each cycle $\mathcal{P}$ in the dependency graph there is a monotonic reduction pair $(\succsim, \succ)$ on $\mathcal{T}(\mathcal{F} \cup \mathcal{F}^{\sharp}, \mathcal{V})$ such that*

(a) $s \succsim t$ for all $s \to t \in \mathcal{P}$ and $s \succ t$ for at least one $s \to t \in \mathcal{P}$
(b) $l \succsim r$ for all $l \to r \in \mathcal{R}$.

$\mathcal{R}$ *is innermost terminating if for each cycle $\mathcal{P}$ in the innermost dependency graph there is a monotonic reduction pair $(\succsim, \succ)$ on $\mathcal{T}(\mathcal{F} \cup \mathcal{F}^{\sharp}, \mathcal{V})$ such that*

(c) $s \succsim t$ for all $s \to t \in \mathcal{P}$ and $s \succ t$ for at least one $s \to t \in \mathcal{P}$
(d) $l \succsim r$ for all $l \to r \in \mathcal{U}(\mathcal{D}')$,
   where $\mathcal{D}' = \{f \mid f \in \mathcal{D}$ occurs in t for some $s \to t \in \mathcal{P}\}$.

For the TRS of Ex. 2, in $\mathcal{P} = \{(4), (5)\}$ we must find a reduction pair where one dependency pair is weakly (w.r.t. $\succsim$) and one is strictly decreasing (w.r.t. $\succ$). Since $\succ$ does not have to be monotonic, one typically uses a standard simplification ordering combined with an *argument filtering* to eliminate argument positions of function symbols. For example, we may eliminate the second argument position of F. Then F becomes unary and every term $\mathsf{F}(s, t)$ is replaced by $\mathsf{F}(s)$. The constraint $\mathsf{F}(\mathsf{s}(x)) \succ \mathsf{F}(x)$ resulting from Dependency Pair (4) is easily satisfied but there is no reduction pair satisfying $\mathsf{F}(x) \succsim \mathsf{F}(y)$ from Dependency Pair (5). Indeed, there is no argument filtering such that the constraints of the dependency pair approach would be satisfied by a standard path ordering like RPOS or KBO. Moreover, if one adds the rules $\mathsf{f}(x, y) \to \mathsf{ack}(x, y)$, $\mathsf{ack}(\mathsf{s}(x), y) \to \mathsf{f}(x, x)$, and the rules for the Ackermann function ack, then the dependency pair constraints are not satisfied by any polynomial ordering either.

Thus, termination cannot be proved with dependency pairs in combination with classical orderings amenable to automation, whereas the proof is very easy with the size-change principle and a simple reduction pair like the embedding ordering on constructors. While the examples in [13] are easily handled by dependency pairs and RPOS, this shows that there exist TRSs where the size-change principle is preferable to dependency pairs and standard rewrite orderings.

In fact, size-change termination encompasses the concept of argument filtering for root symbols, since it concentrates on certain arguments of (root) function symbols while ignoring others. This is an advantage compared to dependency pairs where finding the argument filtering is a major search problem. Moreover, the size-change principle examines sequences of function calls in a more sophisticated way. Depending on the different "paths" from one function call to another, it can choose different arguments to be (strictly) decreasing. In contrast, in the dependency pair approach such choices remain fixed for the whole cycle.

But in addition to the drawbacks in Sect. 4, a disadvantage of the size-change principle is that it is not modular, i.e., one has to use the same reduction pair for the whole termination proof whereas dependency pairs permit different orderings for different cycles. The size-change principle also does not analyze arguments of terms to check whether two function calls can follow each other, whereas in dependency graphs, this is approximated using CAP and REN. Again, the most severe drawback is that the size-change principle offers no technique to compare terms with defined symbols, whereas dependency pairs use inequalities of the form $l \gtrsim r$ for this purpose. Therefore, only very restricted reduction pairs may be used for the size-change principle in Thm. 8 and 11, whereas one may use arbitrary monotonic reduction pairs for the dependency pair approach. In fact, dependency pairs are a *complete* technique which can prove termination of every TRS, which is not true for the size-change principle (see e.g., Ex. 13).

Therefore, we introduce a new technique to combine dependency pairs and size-change termination. A straightforward approach would be to use size-change termination as the "base ordering" when trying to satisfy the constraints resulting from the dependency pair approach. However, this would be very weak due to the restrictions on the reduction pairs in Thm. 8 and Thm. 11. Instead, we incorporate the size-change principle into the dependency pair approach and use it when generating the constraints. The resulting technique is stronger than both previous approaches: If (innermost) termination can be proved by the size-change principle or by dependency pairs using certain reduction pairs, then it can also be proved with our new technique using the *same* reduction pairs. On the other hand, there are many examples which cannot be proved by the size-change principle and where dependency pairs would require complicated reduction pairs (that can hardly be generated automatically), whereas with our combined technique the (automatic) proof works with very simple reduction pairs, cf. [14].

Obviously, size-change graphs and dependency pairs have a close correspondence, since they both represent a call of a defined symbol g in the right-hand side of a rewrite rule $f(s_1, \ldots, s_n) \rightarrow \ldots g(t_1, \ldots, t_m) \ldots$ Since we only need to concatenate size-change graphs which correspond to cycles in the (innermost) dependency graph, we now label size-change graphs by the corresponding dependency pair and multigraphs are labelled by the corresponding sequence of dependency pairs. Then two size-change graphs or multigraphs labelled with $(\ldots, D)$ and $(D', \ldots)$ may only be concatenated if there is an arc from D to D' in the (innermost)[3]

---

[3] Whether one regards the dependency graph or the innermost dependency graph depends on whether one wants to prove termination or innermost termination.

dependency graph. Another problem is that in size-change graphs one only has output nodes $1_f, \ldots, n_f$ and input nodes $1_g, \ldots, m_g$ to compare the *arguments* of f and g. Therefore, the size-change principle cannot deal with TRSs like Ex. 13 where one has to regard the *whole* term in order to show termination. For that reason we add another output node ϵ_f and input node ϵ_g which correspond to the whole terms (or more precisely, to the terms $F(s_1, \ldots, s_n)$ and $G(t_1, \ldots, t_m)$ of the corresponding dependency pair).

Definition 15 (Extended Size-Change Graphs). *Let* $(\succsim, \succ)$ *be a reduction pair on* $T(\mathcal{F} \cup \mathcal{F}^\sharp, \mathcal{V})$. *For every* $f(s_1, \ldots, s_n) \to r \in \mathcal{R}$ *and subterm* $g(t_1, \ldots, t_m)$ *of* r *with* $g \in \mathcal{D}$, *the extended size-change graph has* $n + 1$ *output nodes* i_f *and* $m + 1$ *input nodes* j_g *where* $i \in \{\epsilon, 1, \ldots, n\}$, $j \in \{\epsilon, 1, \ldots, m\}$. *Let* $s = F(s_1, \ldots, s_n)$ *and* $t = G(t_1, \ldots, t_m)$. *Then there is an edge* $i_f \xrightarrow{\succ} j_g$ *iff* $s|_i \succ t|_j$ *and otherwise, there is an edge* $i_f \xrightarrow{\succsim} j_g$ *iff* $s|_i \succsim t|_j$. *Every extended size-change graph is labelled by a one-element sequence* $(F(s_1, \ldots, s_n) \to G(t_1, \ldots, t_m))$.

Concatenation of extended size-change graphs to extended multigraphs works as in Def. 3. However, if G *is a multigraph labelled with* $(D_1, \ldots, D_n)$ *and* H *is labelled with* $(D'_1, \ldots, D'_m)$, *then they can only be concatenated if there is an arc from* D_n *to* D'_1 *in the (innermost) dependency graph. The concatenation* $G \bullet H$ *is labelled with* $(D_1, \ldots, D_n, D'_1, \ldots, D'_m)$.

In the remainder, when we speak of size-change graphs or multigraphs, we always mean *extended* graphs. To combine dependency pairs and the size-change principle now we only regard multigraphs labelled with a cycle $\mathcal{P}$ of the (innermost) dependency graph (i.e., they are labelled with $(D_1, \ldots, D_n)$ such that $\mathcal{P} = \{D_1, \ldots, D_n\}$). Moreover, one may use different reduction pairs for the multigraphs resulting from different cycles. To benefit from the advantages of the size-change principle (i.e., combining lexicographic and multiset comparison and using different argument filterings and strict inequalities within one cycle), we do not build inequalities but size-change graphs out of the dependency pairs.

The following theorem combines dependency pairs and the size-change principle for full termination (Thm. 11). In contrast to Thm. 11 we now allow arbitrary reduction pairs. However, to handle defined symbols properly, one then has to require that all rules are weakly decreasing (like in the dependency pair approach). Alternatively, as in Thm. 11 one may also use reduction pairs $(\to_{\mathcal{S}}^*, \to_{\mathcal{S}}^+)$ for a terminating non-duplicating TRS $\mathcal{S}$ over the constructors of $\mathcal{R}$ without requiring that $\mathcal{R}$'s rules are weakly decreasing. For example, in this way one can prove termination of the Ackermann TRS with the embedding ordering (i.e., $\mathcal{S} = Emb_\mathcal{C}$). However, in order to use $(\to_{\mathcal{S}}^*, \to_{\mathcal{S}}^+)$ for some cycles and other reduction pairs $(\succsim, \succ)$ for other cycles, one has to prove termination of $\mathcal{R} \cup \mathcal{S}$ instead of just $\mathcal{R}$.

Example 16. Let $\mathcal{R} = \{g(f(a)) \to g(f(b)), f(b) \to f(a)\}$ and $\mathcal{S} = \{a \to b\}$. For the only cycle $\{G(f(a)) \to G(f(b))\}$ of $\mathcal{R}$'s dependency graph, size-change termination can be shown by $(\to_{\mathcal{S}}^*, \to_{\mathcal{S}}^+)$. So if one only regards $\mathcal{R}$ instead of $\mathcal{R} \cup \mathcal{S}$, one could falsely "prove" termination of $\mathcal{R}$. Instead, $\{F(b) \to F(a)\}$ must also be regarded, since it is an $\mathcal{R}$-cycle of the dependency graph of $\mathcal{R} \cup \mathcal{S}$ (in $\mathcal{R} \cup \mathcal{S}$, a is a defined symbol). Moreover, for reduction pairs $(\succsim, \succ) \neq (\to_{\mathcal{S}}^*, \to_{\mathcal{S}}^+)$, one has to demand $l \gtrsim r$ not only for the rules $l \to r$ of $\mathcal{R}$, but for those of $\mathcal{S}$ as well. Otherwise, the constraints for the cycle $\{F(b) \to F(a)\}$ would falsely be satisfiable.

By Thm. 17, the resulting termination criterion is sound, complete, and more powerful than the size-change principle or dependency pairs on their own.

Theorem 17 (Termination Proofs). *Let $\mathcal{R}$ be a TRS over $\mathcal{F}$ with constructors $\mathcal{C}$ and let $\mathcal{S}$ be a terminating non-duplicating TRS over $\mathcal{C}$. $\mathcal{R}$ (and even $\mathcal{R} \cup \mathcal{S}$) is terminating iff for each $\mathcal{R}$-cycle $\mathcal{P}$ in the dependency graph of $\mathcal{R} \cup \mathcal{S}$ there is a monotonic reduction pair $(\gtrsim, \succ)$ on $\mathcal{T}(\mathcal{F} \cup \mathcal{F}^\sharp, \mathcal{V})$ such that*

(a) all maximal multigraphs w.r.t. $(\gtrsim, \succ)$ labelled with $\mathcal{P}$ contain an edge $i \xrightarrow{\succ} i$

(b) $\gtrsim = \to_{\mathcal{S}}^{*}$ and $\succ = \to_{\mathcal{S}}^{+}$ or $l \gtrsim r$ for all $l \to r \in \mathcal{R} \cup \mathcal{S}$

If $\mathcal{R}$ is size-change terminating w.r.t. $(\to_{\mathcal{S}}^{*}, \to_{\mathcal{S}}^{+})$ as in Thm. 11 or if a reduction pair satisfies Conditions (a) and (b) of Thm. 14 for termination with dependency pairs, then this reduction pair also satisfies the conditions of this criterion.

Proof. Thm. 17 simulates size-change termination (Thm. 11):If all maximal multigraphs contain $i \xrightarrow{\succ} i$, this also holds for maximal multigraphs labelled with $\mathcal{P}$. It simulates dependency pairs by choosing $\mathcal{S} = \varnothing$: By Thm. 14 (a), multigraphs labelled with $\mathcal{P}$ contain $\epsilon \xrightarrow{\succ} \epsilon$. As dependency pairs are *complete* for termination (even with estimated or no dependency graphs), this proves the "only if" part.

For the "if" direction, suppose that $\mathcal{R} \cup \mathcal{S}$ is not terminating. Since $\mathcal{S}$ terminates, by Lemma 10 and the soundness of dependency pairs, there is an infinite chain $s_1 \to t_1, s_2 \to t_2, \ldots$ of $\mathcal{R}$-dependency pairs such that $t_i \sigma \to_{\mathcal{R} \cup \mathcal{S}}^{*} s_{i+1} \sigma$ for all i and a substitution σ, and $s_1 = s^\sharp$ for a minimal non-terminating term s w.r.t. $\mathcal{R} \cup \mathcal{S}$. Moreover, there is an $\mathcal{R}$-cycle $\mathcal{P}$ consisting of those dependency pairs which occur infinitely often in this chain. Let $i_1 < i_2 < \ldots$ such that $\{s_{i_j} \to t_{i_j}, \ldots, s_{i_{j+1}-1} \to t_{i_{j+1}-1}\} = \mathcal{P}$ for all j, i.e., we partition the sequence into parts where all dependency pairs of $\mathcal{P}$ occur. For all j, let G_j be the multigraph resulting from the concatenation of the size-change graphs corresponding to $s_{i_j} \to t_{i_j}, \ldots, s_{i_{j+1}-1} \to t_{i_{j+1}-1}$. Note that all G_j are labelled with $\mathcal{P}$.

Due to (a), every multigraph H resulting from concatenation of size-change graphs contains an edge of the form $i \xrightarrow{\succ} i$, provided that $H = H \cdot H$ and that H is labelled with $\mathcal{P}$. Hence, every idempotent multigraph $H = H \cdot H$ resulting from concatenating graphs from $G_1, G_2, \ldots$ also contains an edge $i \xrightarrow{\succ} i$. The reason is that since all G_j are labelled with $\mathcal{P}$, then H is also labelled with $\mathcal{P}$.

From this, [13, Thm. 4] or [14, Lemma 7] implies that there is an infinite path with infinitely many "$\succ$"-edges in the infinite graph resulting from $G_1, G_2, \ldots$ by identifying the input nodes of G_j with the output nodes of G_{j+1}. Hence, there is also such a path in the infinite graph resulting from the size-change graphs corresponding to $s_1 \to t_1, s_2 \to t_2, \ldots$ Without loss of generality, we assume that the infinite path already starts in the size-change graph corresponding to $s_1 \to t_1$. For every i, let a_i be the output node in the size-change graph of $s_i \to t_i$ which is on this path. For infinitely many i we have $s_i|_{a_i}\sigma \succ t_i|_{a_{i+1}}\sigma$ and otherwise, we have $s_i|_{a_i}\sigma \gtrsim t_i|_{a_{i+1}}\sigma$, since $\gtrsim$ and $\succ$ are closed under substitutions.

If the reduction pair $(\gtrsim, \succ)$ is $(\to_{\mathcal{S}}^{*}, \to_{\mathcal{S}}^{+})$, then we obtain a contradiction to the minimality of s similar as in the proof of Thm. 11. Otherwise, $t_i|_{a_{i+1}}\sigma \gtrsim$

$s_{i+1}|_{a_{i+1}}\sigma$ due to (b) since $t_i|_{a_{i+1}}\sigma \to^*_{\mathcal{R}\cup\mathcal{S}} s_{i+1}|_{a_{i+1}}\sigma$. Hence, we have an infinite decreasing sequence w.r.t. $\succ$ which contradicts its well-foundedness.   □

For innermost termination, we integrate Thm. 8 with dependency pairs. (Integrating a variant of Thm. 11 for innermost termination would only prove innermost termination of $\mathcal{R}\cup\mathcal{S}$ which does not imply innermost termination of $\mathcal{R}$.) In the dependency pair approach for innermost termination, only the *usable* rules for defined symbols in right-hand sides t of dependency pairs $s \to t$ must be weakly decreasing. Here, one can benefit from the size-change principle, which restricts the comparison of terms to certain arguments. Symbols of t which do not occur in the arguments being compared do not have to be regarded as "usable". More precisely, if one uses the extension of a reduction pair which only compares terms with defined symbols from a subset $\mathcal{D}' \subseteq \mathcal{D}$, then one only has to require weak decreasingness of $\mathcal{U}(\mathcal{D}')$. So here the size-change principle has the advantage that one can reduce the set of usable rules.

For example, the Ackermann TRS has the rule $\mathsf{ack}(\mathsf{s}(x),\mathsf{s}(y)) \to \mathsf{ack}(x, \mathsf{ack}(\mathsf{s}(x),y))$ and therefore, we obtain the dependency pair $\mathsf{ACK}(\mathsf{s}(x),\mathsf{s}(y)) \to \mathsf{ACK}(x,\mathsf{ack}(\mathsf{s}(x),y))$. Since ack occurs in the right-hand side of this dependency pair, in the dependency pair approach we would have to require $l \succsim r$ for all ack-rules since they would be regarded as being usable. For this reason, we would need a lexicographic comparison. However, in our new technique, the ACK-dependency pairs are transformed into size-change graphs and size-change termination can easily be shown using the embedding ordering on constructor terms (i.e., $\mathcal{D}' = \varnothing$). In other words, the second argument of $\mathsf{ACK}(x,\mathsf{ack}(\mathsf{s}(x),y))$ is never regarded in this comparison and therefore, the ack-rules are no longer usable. So instead of LPO we only need the embedding ordering to satisfy the resulting constraints. Hence, in the combined technique one can often use much simpler reduction pairs than the reduction pairs needed with dependency pairs.

Here it is important that extensions are non-monotonic. Consider the TRS of Ex. 16 and a reduction pair on constructor terms (i.e., $\mathcal{D}' = \varnothing$) where a is greater than b. Hence, we do not have to regard any usable rules. In the extension $(\succsim,\succ)$ of this reduction pair we have $\mathsf{f}(\mathsf{a}) \not\succ \mathsf{f}(\mathsf{b})$. Thus, the dependency pair $\mathsf{G}(\mathsf{f}(\mathsf{a})) \to \mathsf{G}(\mathsf{f}(\mathsf{b}))$ is not decreasing, i.e., innermost termination is not proved. But if the extension were monotonic, we would falsely prove innermost termination of $\mathcal{R}$.

Theorem 18 (Innermost Termination Proofs). *A TRS $\mathcal{R}$ is innermost terminating if for each cycle $\mathcal{P}$ in the innermost dependency graph there is a reduction pair on $\mathcal{T}(\mathcal{C}\cup\mathcal{D}'\cup\mathcal{F}^\sharp,\mathcal{V})$ for some $\mathcal{D}' \subseteq \mathcal{D}$ which is monotonic if $\mathcal{D}' \neq \varnothing$, such that for its extension $(\succsim,\succ)$ to $\mathcal{T}(\mathcal{F}\cup\mathcal{F}^\sharp,\mathcal{V})$ we have*

(a) all maximal multigraphs w.r.t. $(\succsim,\succ)$ labelled with $\mathcal{P}$ contain an edge $i \xrightarrow{\succ} i$
(b) $l \succsim r$ for all $l \to r \in \mathcal{U}(\mathcal{D}')$

If $\mathcal{R}$ is size-change terminating w.r.t. a reduction pair as in Thm. 8 or if a reduction pair satisfies Conditions (c) and (d) of Thm. 14 for innermost termination with dependency pairs, then it also satisfies the conditions of this criterion.

Proof. Thm. 18 can simulate the size-change principle: As in Thm. 17, size-change termination implies (a). Moreover, if $(\succsim,\succ)$ is the extension of a reduction pair on $\mathcal{T}(\mathcal{C},\mathcal{V})$ as in Thm. 8, then $\mathcal{D}' = \varnothing$ and thus, (b) is also satisfied.

The simulation of dependency pairs and the soundness of the above criterion are shown as for Thm. 17. If $\mathcal{R}$ is not innermost terminating, then there is an infinite innermost chain $s_1 \to t_1, s_2 \to t_2, \ldots$ with $t_i\sigma \xrightarrow{i}_{\mathcal{R}}^* s_{i+1}\sigma$ and all $s_i\sigma$ are normal forms. As in Thm. 17's proof, this implies that in the infinite graph resulting from the corresponding size-change graphs there is an infinite path with infinitely many "$\succ$" labels. For every i, let a_i be the output node in the size-change graph corresponding to $s_i \to t_i$ which is on this infinite path. To conclude $t_i|_{a_{i+1}}\sigma \gtrsim s_{i+1}|_{a_{i+1}}\sigma$, note that $s_i|_{a_i} \gtrsim t_i|_{a_{i+1}}$ or $s_i|_{a_i} \succ t_i|_{a_{i+1}}$. According to the definition of extending reduction pairs, all subterms of $t_i|_{a_{i+1}}$ with root from $\mathcal{D} \setminus \mathcal{D}'$ also occur in $s_i|_{a_i}$. Hence, when instantiated by σ they are in normal form. Therefore, the only rules applicable to $t_i|_{a_{i+1}}\sigma$ are from $\mathcal{U}(\mathcal{D}')$. Moreover, above the redexes of $t_i|_{a_{i+1}}\sigma$ there are no symbols from $\mathcal{D} \setminus \mathcal{D}'$, since otherwise these redexes would also occur in the normal form $s_i|_{a_i}\sigma$. Now (b) ensures $t_i|_{a_{i+1}}\sigma \gtrsim s_{i+1}|_{a_{i+1}}\sigma$. The remainder is as in Thm. 17's proof.   □

The combined technique handles TRSs where both original techniques fail, since some rules require lexicographic or multiset comparison and others require polynomial orderings. In the combined technique, lexicographic or multiset comparison is implicit since the size-change principle is incorporated. Thus, the resulting constraints are often satisfied by simple polynomial orderings. For example, we unite the plus-TRS (Ex. 13) with the TRS for Ackermann's function, where $\mathsf{ack}(\mathsf{s}(x), \mathsf{s}(y)) \to \mathsf{ack}(x, \mathsf{ack}(\mathsf{s}(x), y))$ is replaced by $\mathsf{ack}(\mathsf{s}(x), \mathsf{s}(y)) \to \mathsf{ack}(x, \mathsf{plus}(y, \mathsf{ack}(\mathsf{s}(x), y)))$. In the original dependency pair approach, both the ack- and plus-rules are usable for the corresponding dependency pair and thus, no standard ordering amenable to automation fulfills the resulting constraints. But in the combined technique, there are no usable rules and hence, the innermost termination proof works with the simple polynomial ordering on constructors and tuple symbols where $\mathsf{s}(x)$ is mapped to $x + 1$ and $\mathsf{PLUS}(x, y)$ is mapped to $x + y$. In practice, there are many TRSs where the combined technique simplifies the termination proof significantly (e.g., TRSs for arithmetic operations, for sorting algorithms, for term manipulations in λ-calculus, etc., cf. [14]).

In [1,7], refinements to manipulate dependency pairs by narrowing, rewriting, and instantiation were proposed. These refinements directly carry over to our combined technique. To summarize, the combination of dependency pairs and the size-change principle has two main advantages: First, one can now prove (innermost) termination of TRSs automatically where up to now an automated proof was impossible. Second, for many TRSs where up to now the termination proof required complicated reduction pairs involving a large search space, one can now use much simpler orderings which increases efficiency.

6 Conclusion

We extended the size-change principle to prove (innermost) termination of arbitrary TRSs. Then we compared it with classical simplification orderings from rewriting: It is also restricted to simple termination, it incorporates lexicographic and multiset comparison for root symbols (although not below the root), but it cannot handle defined symbols or term measures and weights.

Nevertheless, there are even examples where the size-change principle is advantageous to dependency pairs, since it can simulate argument filtering for root symbols and it can investigate how the size of arguments changes in sequences of function calls. On the other hand, the size-change principle is not modular and it lacks a concept like the dependency graph to analyze which function calls can follow each other. Therefore, we developed a new approach to combine the size-change principle with dependency pairs. The combined approach is more powerful than both previous techniques and has the advantage that it often succeeds with much simpler argument filterings and base orderings than the dependency pair approach. We have implemented both the original dependency pair approach and the combined approach in the system AProVE and found that this combination often increases efficiency dramatically. With this combination and a reduction pair based on the lexicographic path ordering, 103 of the 110 examples in the collection of [2] could be proved innermost terminating fully automatically. Most of these proofs took less than a second; the longest took about 10 seconds. The remaining 7 examples only fail because of the underlying reduction pair (e.g., one would need polynomial orderings or KBO). For details on the experiments see [14].

References

1. T. Arts and J. Giesl. Termination of term rewriting using dependency pairs. *Theoretical Computer Science*, 236:133–178, 2000.
2. T. Arts and J. Giesl. A collection of examples for termination of term rewriting using dependency pairs. Technical Report AIB-2001-09, RWTH Aachen, 2001.
3. F. Baader and T. Nipkow. *Term Rewriting and All That*. Cambr. Univ. Pr., 1998.
4. C. Borralleras, M. Ferreira, and A. Rubio. Complete monotonic semantic path orderings. In *Proc. 17th CADE*, LNAI 1831, pages 346–364, 2000.
5. N. Dershowitz. Termination of rewriting. *J. Symbolic Comp.*, 3:69–116, 1987.
6. O. Fissore, I. Gnaedig, and H. Kirchner. Induction for termination with local strategies. In *Proc. 4th Int. Workshop Strategies in Aut. Ded.*, ENTCS 58, 2001.
7. J. Giesl and T. Arts. Verification of Erlang processes by dependency pairs. *Appl. Algebra in Engineering, Communication and Computing*, 12(1,2):39–72, 2001.
8. J. Giesl, T. Arts, and E. Ohlebusch. Modular termination proofs for rewriting using dependency pairs. *Journal of Symbolic Computation*, 34(1):21–58, 2002.
9. S. Kamin and J. J. Lévy. Two generalizations of the recursive path ordering. Unpublished Manuscript, University of Illinois, IL, USA, 1980.
10. D. Knuth and P. Bendix. Simple word problems in universal algebras. In J. Leech, editor, *Comp. Problems in Abstr. Algebra*, pages 263–297. Pergamon, 1970.
11. K. Kusakari, M. Nakamura, and Y. Toyama. Argument filtering transformation. In *Proc. 1st PPDP*, LNCS 1702, pages 48–62, 1999.
12. D. Lankford. On proving term rewriting systems are Noetherian. Technical Report MTP-3, Louisiana Technical University, Ruston, LA, USA, 1979.
13. C. S. Lee, N. D. Jones, and A. M. Ben-Amram. The size-change principle for program termination. In *Proc. POPL '01*, pages 81–92, 2001.
14. R. Thiemann and J. Giesl. Size-change termination for term rewriting. Report AIB-2003-02, RWTH Aachen, 2003. http://aib.informatik.rwth-aachen.de.
15. Y. Toyama. Counterexamples to the termination for the direct sum of term rewriting systems. *Information Processing Letters*, 25:141–143, 1987.

Monotonic AC-Compatible
Semantic Path Orderings

Cristina Borralleras[1] and Albert Rubio[2]*

[1] Universitat de Vic, Spain
cristina.borralleras@uvic.es
[2] Universitat Politècnica de Catalunya, Barcelona, SPAIN
rubio@lsi.upc.es

Abstract. Polynomial interpretations and RPO-like orderings allow one
to prove termination of Associative and Commutative (AC-)rewriting
by only checking the rules of the given rewrite system. However, these
methods have important limitations as termination proving tools.

To overcome these limitations, more powerful methods like the dependency pair method have been extended to the AC-case. Unfortunately,
in order to ensure AC-termination, the so-called extended rules, which,
in general, are hard to prove, must be added to the rewrite system.

In this paper we present a *fully monotonic AC-compatible semantic path
ordering*. This monotonic AC-ordering defines a new automatable termination proving method for AC-rewriting which does not need to consider
extended rules. As a hint of the power of this method, we can easily prove
several non-trivial examples appearing in the literature, including one
that, to our knowledge, can be handled by no other automatic method.

1 Introduction

In programming, as well as in theorem proving, it is very common to have binary
operators which satisfy the associative and commutative properties. However,
such axioms cannot be treated as additional rules in the rewrite system (e.g.,
commutativity cannot be oriented by any well-founded ordering), and hence
they require a special treatment. The most common approach to deal with AC
symbols is rewriting *modulo* AC, that is, rewriting using matching modulo associativity and commutativity to detect the applicability of the rules. The following
example (taken from [MU98]) describes addition $(+)$ and multiplication $(*)$ for
natural numbers in binary notation defined by a constant $\#$, denoting the empty
sequence of digits, and two unary postfixed functions $(\_)0$ and $(\_)1$, to add 0's
and 1's to the right. For instance, 5 is written as $(((\#)1)0)1$.

---

* Both authors partially supported by the spanish CICYT project MAVERISH ref.
TIC2001-2476-C03-01 and the spanish DURSI group 2001SGR 00254.

Example 1. In this example both $+$ and $*$ are AC-symbols.

$$(\#)0 \to \#$$
$$x + \# \to x$$
$$x * \# \to \#$$

$$(x)0 + (y)0 \to (x+y)0$$
$$(x)0 + (y)1 \to (x+y)1$$
$$(x)1 + (y)1 \to (x+y+(\#)1)0$$

$$x * (y)0 \to (x*y)0$$
$$x * (y)1 \to x + (x*y)0$$

Due to the fact that rewriting is performed modulo the AC-axioms, proving termination becomes a more difficult task. In particular, the applied method must be AC-compatible, which roughly means that all terms in the same AC-equivalent class are treated in the same way. When using an ordering-based termination proof method, AC-compatibility means that if some term s is greater than some term t, then any term that is AC-equivalent to s is greater than any term that is AC-equivalent to t.

Many efforts have been made[BCL87,BP85,KSZ95,DP93,RN95,KS00,Rub02] in order to obtain AC-compatible simplification orderings (i.e., monotonic orderings including the subterm relation) by extending the methods used for standard rewriting.

These methods are, in general, well suited for automation. However, as for standard rewriting, such AC-compatible simplification orderings have important limitations as termination proving tools. For instance, there are many term rewrite systems (TRSs) that are terminating but are not contained in any simplification ordering, i.e., they are not *simply terminating*.

In [MU98,KT01,Urb01] the dependency pair method [AG00], which can prove termination of TRSs that are not simply terminating, is adapted to deal with AC-rewriting, and in [GK01] it is adapted for rewriting modulo more general equational theories. All these AC-versions of the dependency pair method need to consider the so-called *extended rules*. For the AC-case this means to add to the set of rules one extended rule $f(l,x) \to f(r,x)$, where x is a new variable, for every rule $l \to r$ with l headed by an AC-symbol f. In the previous example we have to add

$$x + \# + z \to x + z$$
$$x * \# * z \to \# * z$$

$$(x)0 + (y)0 + z \to (x+y)0 + z$$
$$(x)0 + (y)1 + z \to (x+y)1 + z$$
$$(x)1 + (y)1 + z \to (x+y+(\#)1)0 + z$$

$$x * (y)0 * z \to (x*y)0 * z$$
$$x * (y)1 * z \to x + (x*y)0 * z$$

These extended rules are needed to ensure monotonicity with respect to the AC-symbols. But adding them to the system usually makes the termination proof harder.

An alternative to the dependency pair method is the use of the monotonic semantic path ordering (MSPO; [BFR00]), which is a monotonic version of the *semantic path ordering* (SPO; [KL80]). The SPO generalizes path orderings like Dershowitz's *recursive path ordering* (RPO; [Der82]) by replacing the use of a precedence by the use of any measure, defined by an *underlying quasi-ordering*, involving the whole term and not only the head symbol.

The aim of this paper is to adapt the MSPO to deal with AC symbols, obtaining a fully monotonic AC-ordering which allows us to avoid the use of extended rules. Following the ideas used to adapt RPO to the AC-case in [Rub02], SPO has been adapted to obtain an associative and commutative SPO (ACSPO). After that, a monotonic version of ACSPO, called ACMSPO, is obtained. Even though the ACSPO and the ACRPO share the same structure, finding the appropriate formulation of the ordering was not an easy task. In order to ensure the properties of the ACSPO and the ACMSPO, some new conditions on the underlying quasi-ordering used inside SPO are needed. These conditions have to be tight, otherwise the ordering becomes too weak. Additionally, to ensure stability under substitutions it is necessary to *linearize* some variables of the terms, but, fortunately, we have shown that this is only required in a single case.

With ACMSPO we have been able to obtain a simple termination proof for the *ternary integral arithmetic* example used in [CMR97] for computing addition and multiplication of integers in balanced ternary notation, where there are three unary postfixed functions $(x)0$, $(x)1$ and $(x)j$ representing respectively $3x$, $3x+1$ and $3x - 1$ (see also [Knu97], pages 207 and 208 for further details).

Example 2. Both $+$ and $*$ are AC-symbols.

$$
\begin{array}{ll}
(\#)0 \to \# & x - y \to x + opp(y) \\
x + \# \to x & opp(\#) \to \# \\
(x)0 + (y)0 \to (x + y)0 & opp((x)0) \to (opp(x))0 \\
(x)0 + (y)1 \to (x + y)1 & opp((x)1) \to (opp(x))j \\
(x)0 + (y)j \to (x + y)j & opp((x)j) \to (opp(x))1 \\
(x)1 + (y)j \to (x + y)0 & x * \# \to \# \\
(x)1 + (y)1 \to (x + y + (\#)1)j & x * (y)0 \to (x * y)0 \\
(x)j + (y)j \to (x + y + (\#)j)1 & x * (y)1 \to x + (x * y)0 \\
& x * (y)j \to (x * y)0 + opp(x)
\end{array}
$$

Proving termination of this example is not trivial at all. In [CMR97] there is a quite complex ad-hoc hand-tailored proof of termination based on a lexicographic combination of three interpretations on the non-negative integers. In [MU98] an AC-version of the *dependency pairs method* [AG00] was used for proving termination of this example (together with its extended rules), but the use of some AC-marked symbols, which was necessary to deal with the example, turned out to be unsound.

As shown for MSPO [BR02], the ACMSPO method can be fully automated in a constraint solving based system (see Section 6 for details).

The paper is organized as follows. The next section is devoted to preliminaries on orderings and AC-rewriting. In Section 3, the AC semantic path ordering (ACSPO), on which we will build our method, is introduced. A monotonic version of the ACSPO is given in Section 4. In Section 5, ACMSPO is used to check the termination of several examples and in Section 6 it is shown how ACMSPO can be implemented as a fully automated termination proving tool, using a constraint framework similar to the one of the dependency pair method. Finally, conclusions and further work are discussed in Section 7.

Due to the lack of space we have not included any proof of the properties of the orderings. They can all be found in [BR03].

2   AC-Rewriting and Termination

In the following we consider that $\mathcal{F}$ is a set of function symbols, $\mathcal{F}_{AC}$ the subset containing all the AC symbols, $\mathcal{X}$ a set of variables and $\mathcal{T}(\mathcal{F}, \mathcal{X})$ is the set of terms built from $\mathcal{F}$ and $\mathcal{X}$.

Rewriting modulo AC, or AC-rewriting, consists of rewriting over the equivalence classes defined by the associativity and commutativity axioms. Therefore, instead of syntactic equality, rewriting modulo AC considers $=_{AC}$, the congruence generated on $\mathcal{T}(\mathcal{F}, \mathcal{X})$ by the associativity and commutativity axioms for the symbols in $\mathcal{F}_{AC}$.

Given a TRS $\mathcal{R}$, a term $s \in \mathcal{T}(\mathcal{F}, \mathcal{X})$ rewrites to t with $\mathcal{R}$ modulo AC, denoted by $s \to_{\mathcal{R}/AC} t$ if $s =_{AC} s'$, $s'|_p = l\sigma$ for some rule $l \to r \in \mathcal{R}$, term s', position p and substitution σ, and $t =_{AC} s'[r\sigma]_p$.

Let s and t be arbitrary terms in $\mathcal{T}(\mathcal{F}, \mathcal{X})$, let f be a function symbol in $\mathcal{F}$ and let σ be a substitution. A quasi-ordering $\succeq$ is a transitive reflexive relation. Its *strict part* $\succ$ is the strict ordering $\succeq \setminus \preceq$ (i.e, $s \succ t$ iff $s \succeq t$ and $s \not\preceq t$). Its *equivalence* $\sim$ is $\succeq \cap \preceq$. Note that $\succeq$ is the disjoint union of $\succ$ and $\sim$, and that if $=$ denotes syntactic equality then $\succ \cup =$ is a quasi-ordering whose strict part is $\succ$. A quasi-ordering $\succeq$ is *monotonic* if $s \succeq t$ implies $f(\ldots s \ldots) \succeq f(\ldots t \ldots)$, and *stable under substitutions* if $s \succeq t$ implies $s\sigma \succeq t\sigma$.

A (strict partial) ordering $\succ$ is a transitive irreflexive relation. It is *monotonic* if $s \succ t$ implies $f(\ldots s \ldots) \succ f(\ldots t \ldots)$, and *stable under substitutions* if $s \succ t$ implies $s\sigma \succ t\sigma$. Monotonic orderings that are stable under substitutions are called *rewrite orderings*. A *reduction ordering* is a rewrite ordering that is *well-founded*: there are no infinite sequences $t_1 \succ t_2 \succ \ldots$

As the rewrite relation is defined over AC-equivalence classes, any ordering $\succ$ used to prove termination of AC-rewriting has to be *AC-compatible*.

Definition 1. *A relation is said to be AC-compatible if it is compatible with the $=_{AC}$ relation. In particular $\succ$ is AC-compatible if $s' =_{AC} s \succ t =_{AC} t'$ implies $s' \succ t'$; and $\succeq$ is AC-compatible if $s' =_{AC} s \succeq t =_{AC} t'$ implies $s' \succeq t'$.*

Theorem 1. *Let $\succ$ be an AC-compatible reduction ordering and let $\mathcal{R}$ be a TRS. If $l \succ r$ for all rules $l \to r \in \mathcal{R}$ then $\mathcal{R}$ is terminating for rewriting modulo AC.*

The AC-multiset extension of an AC-compatible ordering is defined in the standard way but using AC-equality instead of syntactic equality.

A very common way to easily obtain AC-compatibility is to consider the terms flattened wrt. the AC-symbols. The flat form of t, denoted by $\bar{t}$, is the normal form of t wrt. the (infinite set of) rules

$$f(x_1 \ldots x_{i-1}, f(y_1 \ldots y_k), x_{i+1} \ldots x_n) \to f(x_1 \ldots x_{i-1}, y_1 \ldots y_k, x_{i+1} \ldots x_n)$$

for each $f \in \mathcal{F}_{AC}$. E.g., let $t = +(g(+(a, +(b, c))), +(d, +(e, f)))$ then $\bar{t} = +(g(+(a, b, c)), d, e, f)$. Note that due to the flattening we need to consider variable arities (greater than or equal to 2) for symbols in $\mathcal{F}_{AC}$.

It follows from an easy induction that $s =_{AC} t$ iff $\bar{s}$ and $\bar{t}$ are equal up to permutation of arguments for the AC-symbols. We also denote by $=_{AC}$ this equality up to permutation of arguments for the AC symbols, and by $==_{AC}$ the standard extension of $=_{AC}$ to multisets. From now on, all terms are assumed to be in their flattened form.

However, when considering flattened terms the ordering frequently loses the monotonicity property. For instance, with the *recursive path ordering* (RPO) if a symbol f is greater than a symbol g and f is an AC-symbol, we have that $f(a, a) \succ_{rpo} g(a)$ but $f(f(a, a), b) \nsucc_{rpo} f(g(a), b)$ as the flattened form of $f(f(a, a), b)$ is $f(a, a, b)$ and $f(g(a), b) \succ_{rpo} f(a, a, b)$. The usual way to recover monotonicity consists of giving a special treatment to the small symbols like g when they occur below a big AC-symbol like f.

Remark that if we have a term s in flattened form, when adding a context $f(\ldots, s, \ldots)$, the flattening rules need to be applied at top position of the arguments only. Thus, we define the top-flattening of a term s wrt. an AC-symbol f, denoted by $tf_f(s)$, as $tf_f(f(s_1, \ldots, s_n)) = s_1, \ldots, s_n$ and $tf_f(s) = s$ if $top(s) \neq f$. Then $f(\ldots, tf_f(s), \ldots)$ is the flattened form of $f(\ldots, s, \ldots)$ for any given flattened term s and flattened context $f(\ldots[]\ldots)$.

Finally, let us give some definitions, which only concerns the AC-symbols. A strict ordering $\succ$ is AC-monotonic if $s \succ t$ implies $f(\ldots, tf_f(s), \ldots) \succ f(\ldots, tf_f(t), \ldots)$ for any $f \in \mathcal{F}_{AC}$. A quasi-ordering $\succeq$ is AC-monotonic if $s \succeq t$ implies $f(\ldots, tf_f(s), \ldots) \succeq f(\ldots, tf_f(t), \ldots)$ for any $f \in \mathcal{F}_{AC}$ and it fulfils the AC-deletion property if for all $f \in \mathcal{F}_{AC}$, if $n > m$ and $1 \leq i_1 < \ldots < i_m \leq n$ then $f(s_1, \ldots, s_n) \succeq f(s_{i_1}, \ldots, s_{i_m})$.

2.1   ACRPO

We give a restricted version of the ACRPO in [Rub02], where the *precedence*, i.e., the well-founded quasi-ordering on the set of function symbols, is total and the arguments are always compared as multisets.

In the definition of ACRPO the main difference with RPO appears when comparing two terms headed by some AC-symbol f.

In this case, in order to ensure monotonicity, we have to give a different treatment to the arguments headed by symbols bigger than f and the arguments headed by symbols smaller that f. For this reason we need to define the following (multi)sets of terms.

Definition 2. *Let s be a term of the form $f(s_1, \ldots, s_n)$ with $f \in \mathcal{F}_{AC}$.*

- *The multiset of arguments of s headed by a big symbol, which is denoted by $BigHead(s)$, is defined as $\{s_i \mid 1 \leq i \leq n \wedge top(s_i) \succ_{\mathcal{F}} f\}$*
- *The multiset of arguments of s headed by a symbol not smaller than f, denoted by $NoSmallHead(s)$, is defined as $\{s_i \mid 1 \leq i \leq n \wedge f \not\succ_{\mathcal{F}} top(s_i)\}$*
- *The set of terms embedded in s through an argument headed by a small symbol, denoted by $EmbSmall(s)$, is defined as $\{f(s_1, \ldots, tf_f(v_j), \ldots, s_n) \mid s_i = h(v_1, \ldots, v_r) \wedge f \succ_{\mathcal{F}} h \wedge j \in \{1, \ldots, r\}\}$*

Note that the difference between $NoSmallHead(s)$ and $BigHead(s)$ is that the former includes the variables which are arguments of s and the latter does not. For AC-equivalent terms all these three (multi)sets coincide (modulo AC). For instance, let $t = f(g(g(x, a), a), x, h(a), a)$ with $f \in \mathcal{F}_{AC}$, $h \succ_{\mathcal{F}} a \succ_{\mathcal{F}} f \succ_{\mathcal{F}} g$. Then $BigHead(t) = \{h(a), a\}$, $NoSmallHead(t) = \{x, h(a), a\}$ and $EmbSmall(t) = \{f(g(x, a), x, h(a), a), f(a, x, h(a), a)\}$.

Additionally, we need to count the number of arguments of a term t headed by an AC-symbol, but in order to preserve stability under substitutions we have to describe the counting by means of an expression with variables.

Definition 3. *Let s be a term of the form $f(s_1, \ldots, s_n)$ with $f \in \mathcal{F}_{AC}$. Then $\#(s)$ is an expression with variables on the positive integers, defined as $\#(f(s_1, \ldots, s_n)) = \#_v(s_1) + \ldots + \#_v(s_n)$, where $\#_v(x) = x$ and $\#_v(t) = 1$ if t is not a variable.*

For example, we have $\#(f(x, y, g(x))) = x + y + 1$, which means the arguments coming from x (when applying a substitution and flattening), the ones coming from y plus 1. Then we can compare the amount of arguments of two terms by checking $\#(f(x, y, g(x))) = x + y + 1 > x + y = \#(f(x, y))$, which is necessary to achieve stability under substitution. For AC-equivalent terms the counting coincides.

Definition 4. *Let $\succeq_{\mathcal{F}}$ be a well-founded total precedence and let s and t be terms in $\mathcal{T}(\mathcal{F}, \mathcal{X})$. Then $s = f(s_1 \ldots s_n) \succ_{ACRPO} t$ if and only if*

1. *$s_i \succeq_{ACRPO} t$ for some $i \in \{1 \ldots n\}$ or*
2. *$t = g(t_1 \ldots t_m)$, $f \succ_{\mathcal{F}} g$ and $s \succ_{ACRPO} t_i$ for all $i \in \{1 \ldots m\}$ or*
3. *$t = g(t_1 \ldots t_m)$, $f = g \notin \mathcal{F}_{AC}$ and $\{s_1, \ldots, s_n\} \gg_{ACRPO} \{t_1, \ldots, t_m\}$ or*
4. *$t = g(t_1 \ldots t_m)$, $f = g \in \mathcal{F}_{AC}$ and $s' \succeq_{ACRPO} t$ for some $s' \in EmbSmall(s)$ or*
5. *$t = g(t_1 \ldots t_m)$, $f = g \in \mathcal{F}_{AC}$, $s \succ_{ACRPO} t'$ for all $t' \in EmbSmall(t)$, $NoSmallHead(s) \succeq_{ACRPO} NoSmallHead(t)$ and either*
   (a) *$BigHead(s) \gg_{ACRPO} BigHead(t)$ or*
   (b) *$\#(s) > \#(t)$ or*
   (c) *$\#(s) \geq \#(t)$ and $\{s_1, \ldots, s_n\} \gg_{ACRPO} \{t_1, \ldots, t_m\}$*

where $\succeq_{ACRPO}$ *is* $\succ_{ACRPO} \cup =_{AC}$ *and* $\gg_{ACRPO}$ *is the AC-multiset extension of* $\succ_{ACRPO}$.

The condition $NoSmallHead(s) \succeq NoSmallHead(t)$ ensures that every variable in t is taken care of by a variable in s or by an argument of s headed by a big symbol. Then, if by instantiation, some variable becomes a term headed by a big symbol, we know that some argument of the (instantiation) of s headed by a big symbol takes care of it.

The following examples show the behavior of the ordering when comparing terms headed by the same AC-symbol.

Example 3. Let $f \in \mathcal{F}_{AC}$ and $h, g, a, b \in \mathcal{F} \setminus \mathcal{F}_{AC}$, and take the precedence $h \succ_{\mathcal{F}} f \succ_{\mathcal{F}} g \succ_{\mathcal{F}} a \succ_{\mathcal{F}} b$. Then we have

1. $s = f(g(f(h(a), a)), a) \succ_{ACRPO} f(h(a), a, a) = t$ by case 4 since $f \succ_{\mathcal{F}} g$ implies $f(tf_f(f(h(a), a)), a) = f(h(a), a, a) \in EmbSmall(s)$.

2. $s = f(h(a), g(a)) \succ_{ACRPO} f(g(h(a)), a) = t$ by case 5a, since we have that $s \succ_{ACRPO} f(h(a), a) \in EmbSmall(t)$ by case 4, $NoSmallHead(s) = \{h(a)\} \succeq_{ACRPO} \emptyset = NoSmallHead(t)$ and $BigHead(s) = \{h(a)\} \gg_{ACRPO} \emptyset = BigHead(t)$.

3. $s = f(g(h(a)), a, a, a) \succ_{ACRPO} f(g(f(h(a), a)), a) = t$ by case 5b, since we have $\#(s) = 4 > 2 = \#(t)$, $NoSmallHead(s) = \emptyset = NoSmallHead(t)$, $BigHead(s) = \emptyset = BigHead(t)$ and, finally, $s \succ_{ACRPO} f(h(a), a, a) = t' \subset EmbSmall(t)$ by applying first case 4 and then $s' = f(h(a), a, a, a) \succ_{ACRPO} f(h(a), a, a) = t'$ by case 5b, since $NoSmallHead(s') = BigHead(s') = \{h(a)\} = BigHead(t') = NoSmallHead(t')$, $EmbSmall(t') = \emptyset$ and $\#(s') = 4 > 3 = \#(t')$.

4. $s = f(h(a), a) \succ_{ACRPO} f(h(a), b) = t$, by case 5c, as $EmbSmall(t) = \emptyset$, $NoSmallHead(s) = BigHead(s) = \{h(a)\}$ and $NoSmallHead(t) = BigHead(t) = \{h(a)\}$, $\#(s) = 2 = \#(t)$ and $\{h(a), a\} \gg_{ACRPO} \{h(a), b\}$.

5. $s = f(h(x, y), a, y) \succ_{ACRPO} f(g(h(x, y)), y) = t$ by case 5a, since we have that $NoSmallHead(s) = \{h(x, y), y\} \succeq_{ACRPO} \{y\} = NoSmallHead(t)$, $BigHead(s) = \{h(x, y)\} \gg_{ACRPO} \emptyset = BigHead(t)$ and finally, $s \succ_{ACRPO} f(h(x, y), y) = t' \in EmbSmall(t)$ by case 5b, since $NoSmallHead(s) = \{h(x, y), y\} = NoSmallHead(t')$, $BigHead(s) = \{h(x, y)\} = BigHead(t')$, $EmbSmall(t') = \emptyset$ and $\#(s) = y + 2 > y + 1 = \#(t')$.

2.2   AC-Compatible Polynomial Interpretations

Polynomial interpretations can be used to prove AC-termination as well. To achieve AC-compatibility we need to define polynomial interpretations such that all AC-equivalent terms have the same interpretation. In this paper we will use polynomial interpretations as ingredient in our termination proofs.

Then, we can define a quasi-ordering and a strict ordering using this interpretations as follows:

- $s \succeq_\mu t$ iff $\mu(s) \geq \mu(t)$
- $s \succ_\mu t$ iff $\mu(s) > \mu(t)$

To ensure monotonicity of $\succeq_\mu$, we will only consider polynomial interpretations with non-negative integer coefficients.

Note that $\succ_\mu$ is included in $\succeq_\mu$ but does not coincide with the strict part of $\succeq_\mu$. The reason for making this distinction is that the given $\succ_\mu$ is stable under substitutions and the strict part of $\succeq_\mu$ is not, as shown in the example: if $\mu(f(x,y)) = x + y$, $\mu(g(x)) = x + 1$ and $\mu(h(x)) = 0$ then $\mu(g(f(z_1, z_2))) = z_1 + z_2 + 1$ and $\mu(g(z_1)) = z_1 + 1$, and hence, $\mu(g(f(z_1, z_2))) \geq \mu(g(z_1))$ and $\mu(g(z_1)) \not\geq \mu(g(f(z_1, z_2)))$, but replacing z_2 by $h(z_3)$ we have $\mu(g(f(z_1, h(z_3)))) = z_1 + 1 = \mu(g(z_1))$. Hence before the instantiation, $g(f(z_1, z_2))$ and $g(z_1)$ compare in the strict part of $\succeq_\mu$ and, after the instantiation, they do not. Finally, the defined strict ordering $\succ_\mu$ does not have this stability problem since $g(f(z_1, z_2)) \not\succ_\mu g(z_1)$.

The following lemma gives a sufficient condition to ensure AC-compatibility.

Lemma 1. *[BCL87] Let μ be a polynomial interpretation. If for all AC-symbol f we have that $\mu(f(x,y))$ is of the form $axy + b(x+y) + c$ with $b^2 = b + ac$ then $\succeq_\mu$ and $\succ_\mu$ are AC-compatible.*

For instance, if f and g are AC-symbols, the interpretation μ defined by $\mu(f(x,y)) = x + y + 1$ or by $\mu(f(x,y)) = 2 * x * y + x + y$ fulfills the aforemention conditions.

2.3   The SPO

To conclude the preliminaries we will recall briefly the definition of the semantic path ordering [KL80]. The SPO is a generalization of RPO where the comparison with the precedence is replaced by a comparison using an underlying quasi-ordering involving the whole term.

Here we will present a slightly modified version of SPO where instead of using only an underlying quasi-ordering we will use a compatible ordering pair which includes a quasi-ordering $\succeq_Q$ and a strict ordering $\succ_q$ which is compatible with $\succeq_Q$. This is done in order to use polynomial interpretations as underlying quasi-ordering, since as seen, the strict polynomial ordering we have defined (is included in, but) does not coincide with the strict part of the given polynomial quasi-ordering, since the latter is not stable under substitutions (see Section 2.2).

Definition 5. *Let $\succeq_Q$ be a quasi-ordering and let $\succ_q$ be an ordering. Then $\langle \succeq_Q, \succ_q \rangle$ is a compatible ordering pair if*

- *$\succ_q$ is compatible with $\succeq_Q$, i.e., $s' \succeq_Q s \succ_q t \succeq_Q t'$ implies $s' \succ_q t'$.*
- *$\succ_q$ is well-founded.*
- *$\succ_q$ and $\succeq_Q$ are stable under substitutions.*

Note that our notion of compatible ordering pair is similar to the notion of *weak reduction pair* given in [KNT99], but in our case we do not require monotonicity of $\succeq_Q$.

These compatible ordering pairs can be defined using polynomial interpretations or using standard term interpretations over some term ordering. Another possibility is to combine (lexicographically) a precedence with (quasi-)orderings obtained by using interpretations.

From a given compatible ordering pair we can build the SPO in a recursive way following a path ordering scheme.

Definition 6. (*The SPO*). *Let* $\langle \succeq_Q, \succ_q \rangle$ *be a compatible ordering pair. Let* s *and* t *be terms in* $\mathcal{T}(\mathcal{F}, \mathcal{X})$. *Then* $s = f(s_1...s_n) \succ_{spo} t$ *if and only if*

1. $s_i \succeq_{spo} t$ *for some* $i \in \{1...n\}$ *or*
2. $t = g(t_1, \ldots, t_m)$, $s \succ_q t$ *and* $s \succ_{spo} t_i$ *for all* $i \in \{1...m\}$ *and*
3. $t = g(t_1, \ldots, t_m)$, $s \succeq_Q t$ *and* $\{s_1, ..., s_n\} \succ\!\!\succ_{spo} \{t_1, ..., t_m\}$

where $\succeq_{spo}$ *is* $\succ_{spo} \cup =$ *and* $\succ\!\!\succ_{spo}$ *is the multiset extension of* $\succ_{spo}$.

The semantic path ordering is a well-founded ordering which is stable under substitutions. Unfortunately, it is, in general, not monotonic.

3   The AC-Semantic Path Ordering

In this section we will define an AC-compatible version of SPO, based on the definition of ACRPO. In this case, to be able to adapt the ACRPO scheme, we need to restrict the family of underlying orderings used inside SPO, to those using first a precedence and later (lexicographically) some quasi-ordering comparing the whole terms. Additionally, in order to ensure stability under substitutions we need to impose some extra conditions on this quasi-ordering.

Definition 7. *Let* $\succeq_Q$ *be a quasi-ordering and let* $\succ_q$ *be an ordering. Then* $\langle \succeq_Q, \succ_q \rangle$ *is an* AC-*compatible ordering pair if*

- $\langle \succeq_Q, \succ_q \rangle$ *is a compatible ordering pair.*
- $\succ_q$ *and* $\succeq_Q$ *are AC-compatible.*
- $\succeq_Q$ *fulfils the AC-deletion property.*

In addition, we say that $\langle \succeq_Q, \succ_q \rangle$ *is* AC-*monotonic if both* $\succeq_Q$ *and* $\succ_q$ *are* AC-*monotonic.*

Finally we have two more conditions relating the precedence and $\succeq_Q$.

(R1) $\forall g \in \mathcal{F}$ such that $f \succ_{\mathcal{F}} g$ for some $f \in \mathcal{F}_{AC}$,
   $g(x_1, \ldots, x_n) \succeq_Q x_i$ for all $i = 1 \ldots n$
(R2) $f(s_1, \ldots, x, \ldots, s_n) \succeq_Q g(t_1, \ldots, x, \ldots, t_m)$ implies
   $f(s_1, \ldots, y, \ldots, s_n) \succeq_Q g(t_1, \ldots, y, \ldots, t_m)$ for all $f =_{\mathcal{F}} g \in \mathcal{F}_{AC}$.

Due to the unavoidable condition of being AC-compatible, all other conditions except (R1) are easily satisfied. Condition (R1) has an impact on those symbols that are smaller, in the precedence, than an AC-symbol.

However, the allowed classes of quasi-orderings turn out to be powerful enough to obtain simple proofs of termination for the non-trivial examples given in the introduction.

Additionally, again due to the stability under substitutions, we need to *linearize* some variables when comparing two terms headed by equivalent AC-symbols. Condition (R2) above, relates to this linearization (note that the variable x may occur several times but we only replace one of them by y).

Definition 8. *Given two terms* $s = f(s_1, \ldots, s_n)$ *and* $t = g(t_1, \ldots, t_m)$ *such that* $f =_{\mathcal{F}} g \in \mathcal{F}_{AC}$ *and a set of variables* L, *the linearization of* s *and* t *wrt.* L *is defined as*

$$lin(s, t, L) = \begin{cases} lin(s', t', L) & \text{if } t_i = s_j \in L \text{ where} \\ & w \text{ is a fresh variable, } s' = s[w]_j, \ t' = t[w]_i \\ < s, t > & \text{otherwise} \end{cases}$$

Example 4. Let $f \in \mathcal{F}_{AC}$ and $h \succ_{\mathcal{F}} f \succ_{\mathcal{F}} g$. Given $s = f(h(x, y), g(z), z, y, z)$, $t = f(g(x), z, x, y, z)$ and $L = \{z\}$ we have that
$\langle \hat{s}, \hat{t} \rangle = lin(s, t, L) = \langle f(h(x, y), g(z), z_1, y, z_2), f(g(x), z_1, x, y, z_2) \rangle$.

We now give the definition of the ACSPO. For simplicity reasons, here we have only considered total precedences, but like for ACRPO this condition can be removed. On the other hand, since we consider $\succeq_{\mathcal{F}}$ as $\succ_{\mathcal{F}} \cup =_{\mathcal{F}}$ instead of $\succ_{\mathcal{F}}$ union syntactic equality then the flat form $\bar{t}$ of t has to be defined as the normal form of t wrt. the rules

$$f(x_1 \ldots x_{i-1}, g(y_1 \ldots y_k), x_{i+1} \ldots x_n) \rightarrow f(x_1 \ldots x_{i-1}, y_1 \ldots y_k, x_{i+1} \ldots x_n)$$

for each $f \in \mathcal{F}_{AC}$ and $g =_{\mathcal{F}} f$.

Definition 9. *(The ACSPO). Let* $\succeq_{\mathcal{F}}$ *be a total well-founded precedence such that for all* $f, g \in \mathcal{F}$, $f =_{\mathcal{F}} g$ *implies that either* $f, g \in \mathcal{F} \setminus \mathcal{F}_{AC}$ *or* $f, g \in \mathcal{F}_{AC}$, *and let* $\langle \succeq_Q, \succ_q \rangle$ *be an AC-monotonic and AC-compatible ordering pair, with* $\succeq_Q$ *fulfilling the above conditions (R1) and (R2).*
  Let s, t *be terms in* $\mathcal{T}(\mathcal{F}, \mathcal{X})$. *Then* $s = f(s_1 \ldots s_n) \succ_{acspo} t$ *if and only if*

1. $s_i \succeq_{acspo} t$ *for some* $i \in \{1 \ldots n\}$ *or*
2. $f \in \mathcal{F}_{AC}$ *and* $s' \succeq_{acspo} t$ *for some* $s' \in EmbSmall(s)$ *or*
3. $t = g(t_1 \ldots t_m)$ *and either* $f \succ_{\mathcal{F}} g$ *or* $(f =_{\mathcal{F}} g$ *and* $s \succ_q t)$, *and* $s \succ_{acspo} t_i$ *for all* $i \in \{1 \ldots m\}$, *or*
4. $t = g(t_1 \ldots t_m)$, $f =_{\mathcal{F}} g \notin \mathcal{F}_{AC}$, $s \succeq_Q t$ *and* $\{s_1, \ldots, s_n\} \gg_{acspo} \{t_1, \ldots, t_m\}$ *or*
5. $t = g(t_1 \ldots t_m)$, $f =_{\mathcal{F}} g \in \mathcal{F}_{AC}$, $s \succeq_Q t$, $\hat{s} \succ_{acspo} t'$ *for all* $t' \in EmbSmall(\hat{t})$, $NoSmallHead(s) \succeq_{acspo} NoSmallHead(t)$ *and either*
   (a) $BigHead(s) \gg_{acspo} BigHead(t)$ *or*
   (b) $\#(s) > \#(t)$ *or*
   (c) $\#(s) \geq \#(t)$ *and* $\{s_1, \ldots, s_n\} \gg_{acspo} \{t_1, \ldots, t_m\}$

where $\succeq_{acspo}$ *is* $\succ_{acspo} \cup =_{AC}$, $\gg_{acspo}$ *is the AC-multiset extension of* $\succ_{acspo}$ *and* $< \hat{s}, \hat{t} >= lin(s, t, L_{<s,t>})$ *where* $L_{<s,t>}$ *is the set of variables* $\{x \mid \exists t_i = x \in \mathcal{X}$ *and* $BigHead(s) \not\succ_{acspo} BigHead(t) \cup \{x\}\}$

The definition for *NoSmallHead*, *BigHead* and *EmbSmall* are given in Section 2. Note that linearization is only needed in case 5, when checking recursively the terms in *EmbSmall*. Remark that in this case, we have also required $NoSmallHead(s) \succeq_{acspo} NoSmallHead(t)$, which ensures that for any variable x occurring as argument of t such that $BigHead(s) \not\succ_{acspo} BigHead(t) \cup \{x\}$ there are, at least, as many occurrences of x as argument of s than as argument of t. Hence, after linearization all occurrences of variables in $L_{<s,t>}$ that are arguments in t have been renamed.

Theorem 2. $\succ_{acspo}$ *is a well-founded AC-compatible ordering which is stable under substitutions.*

4   The Monotonic AC-Semantic Path Ordering

Now we will obtain a monotonic version by using the same technique as for the MSPO in [BFR00] but considering AC-reduction triplets of the form $\langle \succeq_I, \succeq_Q , \succ_q \rangle$.

Definition 10. *A quasi-ordering $\succeq_Q$ is monotonic wrt. $\succeq_I$ if $s \succeq_I t$ implies $f(\ldots s \ldots) \succeq_Q f(\ldots t \ldots)$ for every $f \in \mathcal{F}$. Note that if $f \in \mathcal{F}_{AC}$ then we may need to apply some flattening.*

Then, $\langle \succeq_I, \succeq_Q, \succ_q \rangle$ is an AC-reduction triplet if $\langle \succeq_Q, \succ_q \rangle$ is an AC-monotonic AC-compatible ordering pair and $\succeq_I$ is an AC-compatible monotonic and stable under substitutions quasi-ordering and $\succeq_Q$ is monotonic wrt. $\succeq_I$.

Definition 11. *(The ACMSPO). Let $\succeq_{\mathcal{F}}$ be a precedence and $\langle \succeq_I, \succeq_Q, \succ_q \rangle$ be an AC-reduction triplet, where $\succeq_Q$ satisfies conditions (R1) and (R2).*

$$s \succ_{acmspo} t \quad iff \quad s \succeq_I t \text{ and } s \succ_{acspo} t$$

Note that $\succeq_{\mathcal{F}}$ must fulfil the same condition required in the definition of ACSPO.

Theorem 3. $\succ_{acmspo}$ *is an AC-compatible reduction ordering.*

This result implies that ACMSPO is a suitable method for proving AC-termination without the need of considering any extension rule, since by monotonicity they will be trivially included in ACMSPO. However, in order to use this method in practice we need to build actual adequate triplets $\langle \succeq_I, \succeq_Q, \succ_q \rangle$ fulfilling all requirements.

In most of the cases it is enough to define $\succeq_Q$ (respectively $\succ_q$) as the application of $\succeq_I$ (respectively $\succ_i$) on terms after applying a renaming of the non-AC head symbols (as in the dependency pair method). Hence we have $s \succeq_Q t$ iff $N(s) \succeq_I N(t)$ (respectively $s \succ_q t$ iff $N(s) \succ_i N(t)$) for some renaming mapping applied only at top positions for non-AC symbols. In this case, the monotonicity of $\succeq_Q$ wrt. $\succeq_I$ is implied by the monotonicity of $\succeq_I$.

In all examples considered in this paper, even the renaming is not needed, and hence $\langle \succeq_Q, \succ_q \rangle$ and $\langle \succeq_I, \succ_i \rangle$ coincide.

In this paper, the pair $\langle \succeq_I, \succ_i \rangle$ is defined by a polynomial interpretation μ as seen in Section 2.2. The pair $\langle \succeq_I, \succ_i \rangle$ can also be obtained by using standard term interpretations (with straightforward conditions to ensure AC-compatibility and the other properties) over an AC-compatible reduction ordering on terms like ACRPO (in a similar way as done for the dependency pair method and MSPO).

Furthermore, since $\langle \succeq_Q, \succ_q \rangle$ and $\langle \succeq_I, \succ_i \rangle$ coincide all conditions we have imposed on $\succeq_Q$ and $\succ_q$ should also be satisfied by $\succeq_I$ and $\succ_i$. Hence, we have to check that $\langle \succeq_I, \succ_i \rangle$ is an AC-monotonic AC-compatible ordering pair and $\succeq_I$, apart from monotonicity (which was already required), satisfies also R1 and R2.

The next lemma provides sufficient conditions for a polynomial interpretation to satisfy all required properties. A polynomial interpretations I is said to be *strictly positive* if no symbol is interpreted to 0 in I. The interpretation of a symbol f is said to be *fully argument dependent* if $I(f(x_1, \ldots, x_n))$ depends on all $x_1, \ldots, x_n$.

Lemma 2. *Let $\succeq_{\mathcal{F}}$ be a precedence and let I be a polynomial interpretation with non-negative integer coefficients. The pair $\langle \succeq_I, \succ_i \rangle$ is an AC-monotonic AC-compatible ordering pair and $\succeq_I$ is monotonic and satisfies R1 and R2 if*

- *for all AC-symbol f we have that $I(f(x,y)) = axy + b(x+y) + c$ with*
    1. *$b^2 = b + ac$ and*
    2. *either I is strictly positive and $a \neq 0$ or $b \neq 0$.*
- *for all symbol g s.t. $f \succ_{\mathcal{F}} g$ for some AC-symbol f we have that either*
    1. *I is strictly positive and the interpretation of g is fully argument dependent, or*
    2. *$I(g(x_1, \ldots, x_n)) = P + b_1 x_1 + \ldots + b_n x_n$ where P is a polynomial and all $b_i \neq 0$.*

Similarly, we can impose some simple condition on term interpretations in order to satisfy all required properties.

5   Examples

In this section we will present several examples together with the ingredients, i.e., a precedence and a polynomial interpretation, required to show its termination by ACMSPO. For these examples, we have checked that all rules are included in ACMSPO (this is detailed in the Example 6). In this section, we assume that the ingredients are provided by the user and, hence, we only need to check the rules following the definition of ACMSPO (as usually done for path orderings). In the following section a way to automatically generate these ingredients is studied. Let us start with a very simple example.

Example 5. Both $+$ and $*$ are AC-symbols.

$$x + 0 \to x$$
$$x + s(y) \to s(x + y)$$
$$x * 0 \to 0$$
$$x * s(y) \to x * y + x$$

$$minus(x, 0) \to x$$
$$minus(s(x), s(y)) \to minus(x, y)$$
$$quot(0, s(y)) \to 0$$
$$quot(s(x), s(y)) \to s(quot(minus(x, y), s(y)))$$

This rules are included in ACMSPO taking as precedence $quot \succ_{\mathcal{F}} minus \succ_{\mathcal{F}}$ $* \succ_{\mathcal{F}} + \succ_{\mathcal{F}} s$ and as $\langle \succeq_I, \succ_i \rangle = \langle \succeq_Q, \succ_q \rangle$ the polynomial interpretation $I(quot(x, y)) = x$, $I(minus(x, y)) = x$, $I(s(x)) - x \mid 1$, $I(0) = 1$, $I(x+y) = x+y$ and $I(x * y) = x * y + x + y$.

The following example comes with the complete proof showing that all rules are included in ACMSPO with the given ingredients (i.e., a precedence and a polynomial interpretation).

Example 6. Binary arithmetic (given in the introduction). Let us recall the rules ($+$ and $*$ are the only AC-symbols).

$$(\#)0 \to \#$$
$$x + \# \to x$$
$$x * \# \to \#$$

$$(x)0 + (y)0 \to (x + y)0$$
$$(x)0 + (y)1 \to (x + y)1$$
$$(x)1 + (y)1 \to (x + y + (\#)1)0$$

$$x * (y)0 \to (x * y)0$$
$$x * (y)1 \to x + (x * y)0$$

Take as precedence $* \succ_{\mathcal{F}} + \succ_{\mathcal{F}} 1 \succ_{\mathcal{F}} 0 \succ_{\mathcal{F}} \#$ and as $\langle \succeq_I, \succ_i \rangle = \langle \succeq_Q, \succ_q \rangle$ the polynomial interpretation $I(\#) = 1$, $I((x)0) = x$, $I((x)1) = x+2$, $I(x+y) = x+y$ and $I(x * y) = x * y + x + y$.

Now, we will show how the definition of ACMSPO is used for checking the rules. We have to check that all rules $l \to r$ are included in ACMSPO, which, by definition, means that $l \succeq_I r$ and $l \succ_{acspo} r$.

◇ First we prove $l \succeq_I r$ for all $l \to r \in \mathcal{R}$:

$$I((\#)0) = 1 \geq 1 = I(\#)$$
$$I(x + \#) = x + 1 \geq x = I(x)$$
$$I(x * \#) = x * 1 + x + 1 \geq 1 = I(\#)$$
$$I((x)0 + (y)0) = x + y \geq x + y = I((x + y)0)$$
$$I((x)0 + (y)1) = x + y + 2 \geq x + y + 2 = I((x + y)1)$$
$$I((x)1 + (y)1) = x + 2 + y + 2 \geq x + y + 1 + 2 = I((x + y + (\#)1)0)$$
$$I(x * (y)0) = x * y + x + y \geq x * y + x + y = I((x * y)0)$$
$$I(x * (y)1) = x * (y + 2) + x + y + 2 \geq x + x * y + x + y = I(x + (x * y)0)$$

$\diamond$ Now we show $l \succ_{acspo} r$ for all $l \to r \in \mathcal{R}$.
(1) $(\#)0 \succ_{acspo} \#$ by case 1,
(2) $x + \# \succ_{acspo} x$ by case 1,
(3) $x * \# \succ_{acspo} \#$ by case 1,

(4) $(x)0 + (y)0 \succ_{acspo} (x + y)0$ by case 3 :
$\quad + \succ_{\mathcal{F}} 0$ and $(x)0 + (y)0 \succ_{acspo} x + y$ by applying case 2 twice since
$\quad\quad (x)0 + y \in EmbSmall((x)0 + (y)0)$ and
$\quad\quad x + y \in EmbSmall((x)0 + y)$

(5) $(x)0 + (y)1 \succ_{acspo} (x + y)1$ by case 3 :
$\quad + \succ_{\mathcal{F}} 1$ and $(x)0 + (y)1 \succ_{acspo} x + y$ by applying case 2 twice since
$\quad\quad (x)0 + y \in EmbSmall((x)0 + (y)1)$ and
$\quad\quad x + y \in EmbSmall((x)0 + y)$

(6) $(x)1 + (y)1 \succ_{acspo} (x + y + (\#)1)0$ by case 3 :
$\quad + \succ_{\mathcal{F}} 0$ and $(x)1 + (y)1 \succ_{acspo} x + y + (\#)1$ by case 3:
$\quad + =_{\mathcal{F}} +$ and
$\quad I((x)1 + (y)1) = x + 2 + y + 2 > x + y + 1 + 2 = I(x + y + (\#)1)$ and
$\quad (x)1 + (y)1 \succ_{acspo} x$ by applying case 1 twice
$\quad (x)1 + (y)1 \succ_{acspo} y$ by applying case 1 twice
$\quad (x)1 + (y)1 \succ_{acspo} (\#)1$ by case 3 :
$\quad\quad + \succ_{\mathcal{F}} 1$ and
$\quad\quad (x)1 + (y)1 \succ_{acspo} \#$ by case 3 since $+ \succ_{\mathcal{F}} \#$

(7) $x * (y)0 \succ_{acspo} (x * y)0$ by case 3:
$\quad * \succ_{\mathcal{F}} 0$ and
$\quad x * (y)0 \succ_{acspo} x * y$ by case 2 since $x * y \in EmbSmall(x * (y)0)$

(8) $x * (y)1 \succ_{acspo} x + (x * y)0$ by case 3 :
$\quad * \succ_{\mathcal{F}} +$ and $x * (y)1 \succ_{acspo} x$ by case 1
$\quad x * (y)1 \succ_{acspo} (x * y)0$ by case 3 :
$\quad\quad * \succ_{\mathcal{F}} 0$ and
$\quad\quad x * (y)1 \succ_{acspo} x * y$ by case 2 since $x * y \in EmbSmall(x * (y)1)$

We come back to the second example of the introduction. Here we only provide the ingredients for the proof. Note that the polynomial interpretation we are using is very simple, which shows that the use of a precedence first is crucial.

Example 7. Ternary integral arithmetic (given in the introduction in Example 2).

It is proved included in $\succ_{acmspo}$ as follows : take as precedence $* \succ_{\mathcal{F}} - \succ_{\mathcal{F}} + \succ_{\mathcal{F}} opp \succ_{\mathcal{F}} 1 =_{\mathcal{F}} j \succ_{\mathcal{F}} 0 \succ_{\mathcal{F}} \#$ and as $\langle \succeq_I, \succ_i \rangle = \langle \succeq_Q, \succ_q \rangle$ the polynomial interpretation $I(\#) = 0$, $I(opp(x)) = x$, $I((x)0) = x$, $I((x)1) = I((x)j) = x + 1$, $I(x - y) = I(x + y) = x + y$ and $I(x * y) = x * y + x + y$.

6 Constraints

Proving termination with ACMSPO can be translated into a constraint solving problem in the same way as it is done for MSPO in [BFR00] and implemented in a fully automated system called *Termptation* [BR02]. The idea is to extract a set of constraints from the application of the definition of ACMSPO to the set of rules. Hence, if we can solve the constraints then there is a proof of termination of the given TRS using ACMSPO.

First, we obtain set of constraints on $\succeq_I$ from the first condition of the definition of ACMSPO applied to all rules. Then, we have to automatically generate a precedence to be used in the application of ACSPO. Note that, although theoretically there are exponentially many possibilities, in practice it can be done efficiently (like for the non-AC case). After that, we obtain constraints on $\succeq_I$ and $\succ_i$ by applying the definition of ACSPO. For instance, for the Example 6, after guessing the precedence $* \succ_{\mathcal{F}} + \succ_{\mathcal{F}} 1 \succ_{\mathcal{F}} 0 \succ_{\mathcal{F}} \#$ and assuming, for simplicity reasons, that $\succeq_I$ (resp. $\succ_i$) and $\succeq_Q$ (resp. $\succ_q$) coincide, we have the following constraints.

The first set is coming from the first condition of the definition of ACMSPO:

$$(\#)0 \succeq_I \#$$
$$x + \# \succeq_I x$$
$$x * \# \succeq_I \#$$

$$(x)0 + (y)0 \succeq_I (x + y)0$$
$$(x)0 + (y)1 \succeq_I (x + y)1$$
$$(x)1 + (y)1 \succeq_I (x + y + (\#)1)0$$

$$x * (y)0 \succeq_I (x * y)0$$
$$x * (y)1 \succeq_I x + (x * y)0$$

The second set is coming from the recursive application of the definition of ACSPO, by adding all conditions on $\succeq_I$ and $\succ_i$ (in fact, on $\succeq_Q$ and $\succ_q$) that we find in the chosen path of the definition of ACSPO (we have taken the same path as in the proof given in the example). In this example, since most of the comparisons are solved by subterm (case 1), AC-embedding (case 2) or precedence (case 3), we have only one constraint in this second set:

$$(x)1 + (y)1 \succ_i x + y + (\#)1$$

These constraints can be handled and solved by finding an appropriate polynomial interpretation (as done, for instance, in CiME system [CMMU00]). We are currently working on the implementation of this method inside the *Termptation* system.

7   Further Work and Conclusions

The ACMSPO is the first general method not being a simplification ordering that can prove AC-termination automatically without considering extended rules. This allows us to prove in a simple way several non-trivial examples of the literature. All alternative automatable methods we know of, based on dependency pair, require the addition of extended rules.

In order to ensure monotonicity and stability under substitutions we have needed to impose some additional conditions on the underlying orderings used in ACSPO. These conditions can be relaxed by adding more checking in the ACSPO and some more linearizations, which restrict the application of the method. This trade off between the conditions imposed on the underlying orderings and the conditions required in the checking of ACSPO have to be further analyzed.

Another nice property of our method is that we strongly believe that it can be easily combined with methods based on extended rules. In fact, we can obtain a much simpler AC-compatible version of SPO, called EACSPO, which needs to consider extended rules. In this case, we only need to flatten terms and require the underlying quasi-ordering to be AC-compatible. The resulting method is very similar to the existing AC-versions of the dependency pair method.

We are currently working on the combination of both AC-extensions of SPO, namely ACSPO and EACSPO, with the aim of obtaining a method such that for every AC-symbol we can choose whether we add the extended rules or not. Then an AC-symbol is treated like in the ACSPO if it has no extended rules included, otherwise is treated like in EACSPO, which is almost like the other symbols. In this way we can get the best of both methods.

References

AG00.   T. Arts and J. Giesl. Termination of term rewriting using dependency pairs. *Theoretical Computer Science*, 236:133–178, 2000.

BCL87.   A. Ben-Cherifa and P. Lescanne. Termination of rewriting systems by polynomial interpretations and its implementation. *Science of Computer Programming*, 9:137–160, 1987.

BFR00.   C. Borralleras, M. Ferreira, and A. Rubio. Complete monotonic semantic path orderings. Proc. of *17th Int. Conf. on Automated Deduction*, LNAI 1831:346–364, 2000.

BP85.   L. Bachmair and D.A. Plaisted. Termination orderings for associative-commutative rewriting systems. *Journal of Symbolic Computation*, 1:329–349, 1985.

BR01.   C. Borralleras and A. Rubio. A Monotonic Higher-Order Semantic Path Ordering. Proc. of *8th Int. Conf. on Logic for Programming, Artificial Intelligence and Reasoning (LPAR'01)* LNAI 2250:531–547, 2001.

BR02.   C. Borralleras and A. Rubio. TERMPTATION: TERMination Proof Techniques automATION. Available at //www.lsi.upc.es/~albert/.

BR03.   C. Borralleras and A. Rubio. Proving Termination of AC-rewriting without Extended Rules. Long version. Available at //www.lsi.upc.es/~albert/.

CMMU00.   E. Contejean, C. Marché, B. Monate and X. Urbain. CiME system. 2000. Available at //cime.lri.fr/.

CMR97.   E. Contejean, C. Marché and L. Rabehasaina. Rewrite systems for natural, integral, and rational arithmetic. Proc. of *8th Int. Conf. on Rewriting Techniques and Applications, RTA'97*, LNCS 1232:98–112, 1997.

Der82.   N. Dershowitz. Orderings for term-rewriting systems. *Theoretical Computer Science*, 17(3):279–301, 1982.

DP93.   C. Delor and L. Puel. Extension of the associative path ordering to a chain of associative commutative symbols. Proc. of *5th Int. Conf. on Rewriting Techniques and Applications RTA'93*, LNCS 690:389–404, 1993.

GK01.   J. Giesl and D. Kapur. Dependency pairs for Equational Rewriting. Proc. of *12th Int. Conf. on Rewriting Techniques and Applications, RTA'01*, LNCS 2051:93–108, 2001.

KL80.   S. Kamin and J. J. Levy. Two generalizations of the recursive path ordering. Unpublished note, Dept. of Computer Science, Univ. of Illinois, Urbana, IL, 1980.

KNT99.   K. Kusakari, M. Nakamura, and Y. Toyama. Argument filtering transformation. In *Proceedings of the International Conference on Principles and Practice of Declarative Programming, PPDP'99*, LNCS 1702:47–61. Springer-Verlag, 1999.

Knu97.   D. E. Knuth. The Art of Computer Programming. Vol. 2: Seminumerical Algorithms. Third Edition. Addison-Wesley, 1997.

KS00.   D. Kapur and G. Sivakumar. Proving Associative-Commutative Termination Using RPO-compatible Orderings. In *Proc. Automated Deduction in Classical and Non-Classical Logics*, LNAI 1761:40–62, 2000.

KSZ95.   D. Kapur, G. Sivakumar and H. Zhang. A Path Ordering for Proving Termination of AC Rewrite Systems. In *Journal of Automated Reasoning*, 14(2):293-316, 1995.

KT01.   K. Kusakari and Y. Toyama. On proving AC-termination by AC-dependency pairs. IEICE Transactions on Information and Systems, E84-D(5):604–612, 2001.

MU98.   C. Marché and X. Urbain. Termination of associative-commutative rewriting by dependency pairs. Proc. of *9th Int. Conf. on Rewriting Techniques and Applications, RTA'98*, LNCS 1379:241–255, 1998.

RN95.   A. Rubio and R. Nieuwenhuis. A total AC-compatible ordering based on RPO *Theoretical Computer Science*, 142(2):209–227, 1995.

Rub02.   A. Rubio. A fully syntactic AC-RPO. *Information and Computation*, 178(2):515-533, 2002.

Urb01.   X. Urbain. Approche incrémentale des preuves automatiques de terminaison. PhD thesis, Université Paris-Sud, UFR Scientifique d'Orsay, 2001.

Relating Derivation Lengths
with the Slow-Growing Hierarchy Directly

Georg Moser* and Andreas Weiermann**

WWU Münster
Institut für Mathematische Logik und Grundlagenforschung,
Einsteinstrasse 62, D-48149 Münster, Germany
{moserg,weierma}@math.uni-muenster.de

Abstract. In this article we introduce the notion of a generalized system of fundamental sequences and we define its associated slow-growing hierarchy. We claim that these concepts are genuinely related to the classification of the complexity—the derivation length— of rewrite systems for which termination is provable by a standard termination ordering. To substantiate this claim, we re-obtain multiple recursive bounds on the the derivation length for rewrite systems terminating under lexicographic path ordering, originally established by the second author.

1 Introduction

To show termination of a rewrite system R one usually shows that the induced reduction relation $\to_R$ is contained in some abstract ordering known to be well-founded. One way to assess the strength of such a termination ordering is to calculate its *order type*, cf. [7]. There appears to be a subtle relationship between these order types and the *complexity* of the rewrite system R considered. Cichon [5] discussed (and investigated) whether the complexity of a rewrite system for which termination is provable using a termination ordering of order type α is eventually dominated by a function from the *slow-growing hierarchy* along α. It turned out that this principle—henceforth referred to as (CP)—is valid for the (i) *multiset path ordering* ($\succ_{\mathrm{MPO}}$) and the (ii) *lexicographic path ordering* ($\succ_{\mathrm{LPO}}$).

More precisely, Hofbauer [9] proved that $\succ_{\mathrm{MPO}}$ as termination ordering implies primitive recursive derivation length, while the second author showed that $\succ_{\mathrm{LPO}}$ as termination ordering implies multiply-recursive derivation length [17]. If one regards the order types of $\succ_{\mathrm{MPO}}$ and $\succ_{\mathrm{LPO}}$, respectively, then these results imply the correctness of (CP) for (i) and (ii). Buchholz [3] has given an alternative proof of (CP) for (i) and (ii). His proof avoids the (sometimes lengthy) calculations with functions from subrecursive hierarchies in [9,17]. Instead a clever application of proof-theoretic results is used. Although this proof is of striking beauty, one might miss the link to term rewriting theory that is provided in [9,17].

---

* Supported by a Marie Curie fellowship, grant number HPMF-CT-2002-015777.
** Supported as a Heisenberg fellow of the DFG.

R. Nieuwenhuis (Ed.): RTA 2003, LNCS 2706, pp. 296–310, 2003.

The mentioned proofs [9,17,3] of (CP)—with respect to (i) and (ii)—are *indirect*. I.e. without direct reference to the slow-growing hierarchy. By now, we know from the work of Touzet [16] and Lepper [10,11] that (CP) fails to hold in general. However, our interest in (CP) is motivated by our strong belief that there exist reliable ties between *proof theory* and *term rewriting theory*. Ties which become particularly apparent if one studies those termination orderings for which (CP) holds.

To articulate this belief we give yet another *direct* proof of (CP) (with respect to (i) and (ii)). To this avail we introduce the notion of a *generalized system of fundamental sequences* and we define its associated *slow-growing hierarchy*. These concepts are genuinely related to classifying derivation lengths for rewrite systems for which termination is proved by a standard termination ordering. To emphasize this let us present the general outline of the proof method.

Let terms $s = t_0, t_1, \ldots, t_n$ be given, such that $s \to_R t_1 \to_R \cdots \to_R t_n$ holds, where t_n is in normal form and term-depth of s ($\tau(s)$) is $\leq m$. Assume $\to_R$ is contained in a termination ordering $\succ$. Hence $s \succ t_1 \succ \cdots \succ t_n$ holds. Assume further the sequence $(s, t_1, \ldots, t_n)$ is chosen so that n is maximal. Then in the realm of classifications of derivation lengths one usually defines an *interpretation* $\mathcal{I}: \mathcal{T}(\Sigma, \mathcal{V}) \to \mathbb{N}$ such that $\mathcal{I}(s) > \mathcal{I}(t_1) > \cdots > \mathcal{I}(t_n)$ holds. ($\mathcal{T}(\Sigma, \mathcal{V})$ denotes the term algebra over the signature Σ and the set of variables $\mathcal{V}$.) The existence of such an interpretation then directly yields a bound on the derivation length.

The problem with this approach is to guess the right interpretation from the beginning. More often than not this is not at all obvious. Therefore we want to generate the interpretation function directly from the termination ordering in an intrinsic way. To this avail we proceed as follows. We separate $\mathcal{I}$ into an *ordinal interpretation* $\pi: \mathcal{T}(\Sigma) \to T$ and an ordinal theoretic function $g: T \to \mathbb{N}$. (T denotes a suitable chosen set of terms representing an initial segment of the ordinals, cf. Definition 2.) This works smoothly. Firstly, we can employ the connection between the termination ordering $\succ$ and the ordering on the notation system T. This connection was already observed by Dershowitz and Okada, cf. [7]. Secondly, it turns out that g can be defined in terms of the slow-growing function $G_x: T \to \mathbb{N}; x \in \mathbb{N}$. (Note that we have swapped the usual denotation of arguments, see Definition 4 and Definition 9.)

To simplify the presentation we restrict our attention to a rewrite system R whose termination can be shown by a *lexicographic path ordering* $\succ_{\text{LPO}}$. It will become apparent later that the proof presented below is (relative) easily adaptable to the case where the rewrite relation $\to_R$ is contained in a *multiset path ordering* $\succ_{\text{MPO}}$. We assume the signature Σ contains at least one constant c.

Let R be a rewrite system over $\mathcal{T}(\Sigma, \mathcal{V})$ such that $\to_R$ is contained in a lexicographic path ordering. Let terms $s = t_0, t_1, \ldots, t_n$ be given, such that $s \to_R t_1 \to_R \cdots \to_R t_n$ holds, where t_n is in normal form and $\tau(s) \leq m$. By our choice of R this implies

$$s \succ_{\text{LPO}} t_1 \succ_{\text{LPO}} \cdots \succ_{\text{LPO}} t_n \quad . \tag{1}$$

We define a ground substitution $\rho: \rho(x) = c$, for all $x \in \mathcal{V}$. Let $>$ denote a suitable defined (well-founded) ordering relation on the ordinal notation system T. Let

$l, r \in \mathcal{T}(\Sigma, \mathcal{V})$. Depending on m and properties of R, we show the existence of a natural number h such that $l \succ_{\text{LPO}} r$ implies $\pi(l\rho) > \pi(r\rho)$ and $G_h(\pi(l\rho)) > G_h(\pi(r\rho))$, respectively. Employing this form of an *Interpretation Theorem* we conclude from (1) for some $\alpha \in T$

$$\alpha > \pi(s\rho) > \pi(t_1\rho) > \cdots > \pi(t_n\rho) \quad.$$

and consequently

$$G_h(\alpha) > G_h(\pi(s\rho)) > G_h(\pi(t_1\rho)) > \cdots > G_h(\pi(t_n\rho)) \quad.$$

Thus $G_h(\alpha)$ calculates an upper bound for n. Therefore the *complexity* of R can be measured in terms of the *slow-growing hierarchy* along the *order type* of T.

To see that this method calculates an optimal bound, it remains to relate the function $G_x \colon T \to \mathbb{N}$ to the multiply-recursive functions. We employ Girard's Hierarchy Comparison Theorem [8]. Due to (a variant) of this theorem any multiple-recursive function can be majorized by functions from the slow-growing hierarchy and vice versa.[1] (For further details see Section 4.)

Contrary to the original proof in[17], we can thus circumvent technical calculations with the F-hierarchy (the fast-growing hierarchy) and can shed light on the way the slow-growing hierarchy relates the order type of the termination ordering $\succ$ to the bound on the length of reduction sequences along $\to_R$.

2   The Lexicographic Path Ordering

We assume familiarity with the basic concepts of term rewriting. However, we fix some notations. Let $\Sigma = \{f_1, \ldots, f_K\}$ denote a finite signature such that any function symbol $f \in \Sigma$ has a unique *arity*, denoted as $\text{ar}(f)$. The cardinality K is assumed to be fixed in the sequel. To avoid trivialities we demand that Σ is non-empty and contains at least one constant, i.e. a function symbol of arity 0. We set $N := \max\{\text{ar}(f) \colon f \in \Sigma\}$.

The set of terms over Σ and the countably infinite set of variables $\mathcal{V}$ is denoted as $\mathcal{T}(\Sigma, \mathcal{V})$. We will use the meta-symbols $l, r, s, t, u, \ldots$ to denote terms. The set of variables occurring in a term t is denoted as $\text{var}(t)$. A term t is called *ground* or *closed* if $\text{var}(t) = \emptyset$. The set of ground terms over Σ is denoted as $\mathcal{T}(\Sigma)$. If no confusion can arise, the reference to the signature Σ and the set of variables $\mathcal{V}$ is dropped. With $\tau(s)$ we denote the *term depth* of s, defined as $\tau(s) := 0$, if $s \in \mathcal{V}$ or $s \in \Sigma$ and otherwise $\tau(f(s_1, \ldots, s_m)) := \max\{\tau(s_i) \colon 1 \leq i \leq m\} + 1$. A *substitution* $\sigma \colon \mathcal{V} \to \mathcal{T}$ is a mapping from the set of variables to the set of terms. The application of a substitution σ to a term t is (usually) written as $t\sigma$ instead of $\sigma(t)$.

A *term rewriting system* (or *rewrite system*) R over $\mathcal{T}$ is a finite set of rewrite rules (l, r). The *rewrite relation* $\to_R$ on $\mathcal{T}$ is the least binary relation on $\mathcal{T}$

---

[1] A k-ary function g is said to be *majorized* by a unary function f if there exists a number $n < \omega$ such that $g(x_1, \ldots, x_k) < f(\max\{x_1, \ldots, x_k\})$, whenever $\max\{x_1, \ldots, x_k\} \geq n$.

containing R such that (i) if $s \to_R t$ and σ a substitution, then $s\sigma \to_R t\sigma$ holds, and (ii) if $s \to_R t$, then $f(\ldots, s, \ldots) \to_R f(\ldots, t, \ldots)$. A rewrite system R is *terminating* if there is no infinite sequence $\langle t_i : i \in \mathbb{N} \rangle$ of terms such that $t_1 \to_R t_2 \to_R \cdots \to_R t_m \to_R \cdots$. Let $\succ$ denote a total order on Σ such that $f_j \succ f_i \leftrightarrow j > i$ for $i, j \in \{1, \ldots, K\}$. The *lexicographic path ordering* $\succ_{\mathrm{LPO}}$ on T (induced by $\succ$) is defined as follows, cf. [1].

Definition 1. $s \succ_{\mathrm{LPO}} t$ *iff*

1. $t \in \mathrm{var}(s)$ *and* $s \neq t$, *or*
2. $s = f_j(s_1, \ldots, s_m)$, $t = f_i(t_1, \ldots, t_n)$, *and*
   - *there exists* k $(1 \leq k \leq m)$ *with* $s_k \succeq_{\mathrm{LPO}} t$, *or*
   - $j > i$ *and* $s \succ_{\mathrm{LPO}} t_l$ *for all* $l = 1, \ldots, n$, *or*
   - $i = j$ *and* $s \succ_{\mathrm{LPO}} t_l$ *for all* $l = 1, \ldots, n$, *and there exists an* i_0 $(1 \leq i_0 \leq m)$ *such that* $s_1 = t_1, \ldots s_{i_0-1} = t_{i_0-1}$ *and* $s_{i_0} \succ_{\mathrm{LPO}} t_{i_0}$.

Proposition 1. *(Kamin-Levy).*

1. *If* $s \succ_{\mathrm{LPO}} t$, *then* $\mathrm{var}(t) \subseteq \mathrm{var}(s)$.
2. *For any total order* $\prec$ *on* Σ, *the induced lexicographic order* $\succ_{\mathrm{LPO}}$ *is a simplification order on* T.
3. *If* R *is a rewrite system such that* $\to_R$ *is contained in a lexicographic path ordering, then* R *is terminating.*

Proof. Folklore.

3   Ordinal Terms and the Lexicographic Path Ordering

Let N be defined as in the previous section. In this section we define a set of terms T (and a subset $P \subset T$) together with a well-ordering $<$ on T. The elements of T are built from 0, $+$ and the $(N+1)$-ary function symbol ψ. It is important to note that the elements of T are *terms* not ordinals. Although these terms can serve as representations of an initial segment of the set of ordinals ON, we will not make any use of this *interpretation*. In particular the reader not familiar with proof theory should have no difficulties to understand the definitions and propositions of this section. However some basic amount of understanding in proof theory may be useful to grasp the origin and meaning of the presented concepts, cf. [7,11,15]. For the reader familiar with proof theory: Note that P corresponds to the set of additive principal numbers in T, while ψ represents the (set-theoretical) fixed-point free Veblen function, cf. [15,11].

Definition 2. *Recursive definition of a set* T *of ordinal terms, a subset* $P \subset T$, *and a binary relation* $>$ *on* T.

1. $0 \in T$.
2. *If* $\alpha_1, \ldots, \alpha_m \in P$ *and* $\alpha_1 \geq \cdots \geq \alpha_m$, *then* $\alpha_1 + \cdots + \alpha_m \in T$.
3. *If* $\alpha_1, \ldots, \alpha_{N+1} \in T$, *then* $\psi(\alpha_1, \ldots, \alpha_{N+1}) \in P$ *and* $\psi(\alpha_1, \ldots, \alpha_{N+1}) \in T$.

4. $\alpha \neq 0$ implies $\alpha > 0$.
5. $\alpha > \beta_1, \ldots, \beta_m$ and $\alpha \in P$ implies $\alpha > \beta_1 + \cdots + \beta_m$.
6. Let $\alpha = \alpha_1 + \cdots + \alpha_m$, $\beta = \beta_1 + \cdots + \beta_n$. Then $\alpha > \beta$ iff
   - $m > n$, and for all i $(i \in \{1, \ldots, n\})$ $\alpha_i = \beta_i$, or
   - there exists i $(i \in \{1, \ldots, m\})$ such that $\alpha_1 = \beta_1, \ldots, \alpha_{i-1} = \beta_{i-1}$, and $\alpha_i > \beta_i$.
7. Let $\alpha = \psi(\alpha_1, \ldots, \alpha_{N+1})$, $\beta = \psi(\beta_1, \ldots, \beta_{N+1})$. Then $\alpha > \beta$ iff
   - there exists k $(1 \leq k \leq N+1)$ with $\alpha_k \geq \beta$, or
   - $\alpha > \beta_l$ for all $l = 1, \ldots, N+1$ and there exists an i_0 $(1 \leq i_0 \leq N+1)$ such that $\alpha_1 = \beta_1, \ldots \alpha_{i_0-1} = \beta_{i_0-1}$ and $\alpha_{i_0} > \beta_{i_0}$.

We use lower-case Greek letters to denote the elements of T. Furthermore we formally define $\alpha + 0 = 0 + \alpha = \alpha$ for all $\alpha \in T$.

We sometimes abbreviate sequences of (ordinal) terms like $\alpha_1, \ldots, \alpha_n$ by $\overline{\alpha}$. Hence, instead of $\psi(\alpha_1, \ldots, \alpha_{N+1})$ we may write $\psi(\overline{\alpha})$. To relate the elements of T to more expressive ordinal notations, we define $1 := \psi(\overline{0})$, $\omega := \psi(\overline{0}, 1)$, and $\epsilon_0 := \psi(\overline{0}, 1, 0)$. Let LIM be the set of elements in T which are neither 0 nor of the form $\alpha + 1$. Elements of LIM are called *limit* ordinal terms.

Proposition 2. *Let $(T, <)$ be defined as above. Then $(T, <)$ is a well-ordering.*

Proof. Let $|\alpha|$ denote the number of symbols in the ordinal term α. Exploiting induction on $|\alpha|$ one easily verifies that the ordering $(T, <)$ is well-defined. To show well-foundedness one uses induction on the lexicographic path ordering $\prec_{\text{LPO}}$, exploiting the close connection between Definition 1.2 in Section 2 and Definition 2.7 above. □

In the following proposition we want to relate the *order type* of the well-ordering $(T, <)$ and the well-partial ordering $\prec_{\text{LPO}}$. Concerning the latter it is best to momentarily restrict our attention to the well-ordering $(\mathcal{T}(\Sigma), \prec_{\text{LPO}})$. We indicate the arity of the function symbol ψ employed in Definition 2. We write $(T(N+1), <)$ instead of $(T, <)$. Similarly we write $(\mathcal{T}(\Sigma(N)), \prec_{\text{LPO}})$ to indicate the maximal arity of function symbols in the finite signature Σ. Let $\overline{\Theta}_{\Omega^\omega}(0)$ denote the small Veblen ordinal [15] and let **otyp**(M) denote the order type of a well-odering M.

Proposition 3. *1. For any number k, there exists an order isomorphic embedding from $(\mathcal{T}(\Sigma(k)), \prec_{\text{LPO}})$ into $(T(k+1), <)$.*
   2. For any number $k > 2$, there exists an order isomorphic embedding from $(T(k), <)$ into $(\mathcal{T}(\Sigma(k)), \prec_{\text{LPO}})$.
   3. $\sup_{k<\omega}(\mathbf{otyp}((T(k), <))) = \sup_{k<\omega}(\mathbf{otyp}((\mathcal{T}(\Sigma(k)), \prec_{\text{LPO}}))) = \overline{\Theta}_{\Omega^\omega}(0)$.

Proof. The first two assertions are a consequence of the well-ordering proof of $(T, <)$. We only comment on the stated lower bound in the second one. The statement fails for $(T(2), <)$ and $(\mathcal{T}(\Sigma(2)), \prec_{\text{LPO}})$. The presence of the binary function symbol $+$ in $T(2)$ can make the ordering $<$ more expressive than $\prec_{\text{LPO}}$. This difference vanishes for $k \geq 3$. The third assertion follows from [14]. □

4   Fundamental Sequences and Sub-recursive Hierarchies

To each ordinal term $\alpha \in T$ we assign a canonical sequence of ordinal terms $\langle \alpha[x] \colon x \in \mathbb{N} \rangle$, the *fundamental sequence*. The concept of fundamental sequences is a crucial one in (ordinal) proof theory. The main idea of utilizing fundamental sequences in term rewriting, is that the descent along the branches of such a sequence can, informally speaking, code rewriting steps. We have to wade through some technical definitions.

We define the set $\mathrm{IS}_{\overline{\alpha}}(\gamma)$, the set of *interesting subterms* of γ (relative to $\overline{\alpha}$) by induction on γ. We set $\mathrm{IS}_{\overline{\alpha}}(0) := \emptyset$, $\mathrm{IS}_{\overline{\alpha}}(\gamma_1 + \cdots + \gamma_m) := \bigcup_{i=1}^{m} \mathrm{IS}_{\overline{\alpha}}(\gamma_i)$, and finally

$$\mathrm{IS}_{\overline{\alpha}}(\psi(\gamma_1, \ldots, \gamma_{N+1})) := \begin{cases} \{\psi(\overline{\gamma})\} & \text{if } (\gamma_1, \ldots, \gamma_N) \geq_{\text{LEX}} (\alpha_1, \ldots, \alpha_N) \\ \bigcup_{i=1}^{N+1} \mathrm{IS}_{\overline{\alpha}}(\gamma_i) \text{ otherwise.} \end{cases}$$

The (relative to $\overline{\alpha}$) *maximal interesting subterm* $\mathrm{MS}_{\overline{\alpha}}(\gamma_1, \ldots, \gamma_n)$ of a nonempty sequence $(\gamma_1, \ldots, \gamma_n)$ is defined as the maximum of the terms occurring in $\mathrm{IS}_{\overline{\alpha}}(\gamma_i)$. Let $>_{\text{LEX}}$ denote the lexicographic ordering on sequences of ordinal terms induced by $>$. Let $\overline{\alpha} = \alpha_1, \ldots, \alpha_N \in T$ and $\beta \in T$. Then set

$$\mathrm{FIX}(\overline{\alpha}) := \{\psi(\overline{\gamma}, \delta) \colon \overline{\gamma} >_{\text{LEX}} \overline{\alpha} \text{ and } \psi(\overline{\gamma}, \delta) > \alpha_i \text{ for all } i = 1, \ldots, N\} \quad .$$

For a unary function symbol f we define the nth iteration f^n inductively as (i) $f^0(x) := x$, and (ii) $f^{n+1}(x) := f(f^n(x))$. We will make use of this notation for functions of higher arity by assuming that all but one argument remain fixed. We use $\cdot$ to indicate the free position. In the sequel λ (possibly extended by a subscript) will always denote a limit ordinal term.

Definition 3. *Recursive definition of $\alpha[x]$ for $x < \omega$.*

$$0[x] := 0$$
$$(\alpha_1 + \cdots + \alpha_m)[x] := \alpha_1 + \cdots + \alpha_m[x] \qquad m > 1, \alpha_1 \geq \cdots \geq \alpha_m$$
$$\psi(\overline{0})[x] := 0$$
$$\psi(\overline{0}, \beta + 1)[x] := \psi(\overline{0}, \beta) \cdot (x + 1)$$
$$\psi(\overline{0}, \lambda)[x] := \psi(\overline{0}, \lambda[x]) \qquad \lambda \notin \mathrm{FIX}(\overline{0})$$
$$\psi(\overline{0}, \lambda)[x] := \lambda \cdot (x + 1) \qquad \lambda \in \mathrm{FIX}(\overline{0})$$
$$\psi(\alpha_1, \ldots, \alpha_i + 1, \overline{0}, 0)[x] := \psi(\alpha_1, \ldots, \alpha_i, \cdot, \overline{0})^{x+1}(0)$$
$$\psi(\alpha_1, \ldots, \alpha_i + 1, \overline{0}, \beta + 1)[x] := \psi(\alpha_1, \ldots, \alpha_i, \cdot, \overline{0})^{x+1}(\psi(\alpha_1, \ldots, \alpha_i + 1, \overline{0}, \beta))$$
$$\psi(\alpha_1, \ldots, \alpha_i + 1, \overline{0}, \lambda)[x] := \psi(\alpha_1, \ldots, \alpha_i + 1, \overline{0}, \lambda[x]) \qquad \lambda \notin \mathrm{FIX}(\overline{\alpha}, \overline{0})$$
$$\psi(\alpha_1, \ldots, \alpha_i + 1, \overline{0}, \lambda)[x] := \psi(\alpha_1, \ldots, \alpha_i, \cdot, \overline{0})^{x+1}(\lambda) \qquad \lambda \in \mathrm{FIX}(\overline{\alpha}, \overline{0})$$
$$\psi(\alpha_1, \ldots, \lambda_i, \overline{0}, 0)[x] := \psi(\alpha_1, \ldots, \lambda_i[x], \overline{0}, \mathrm{MS}_{\overline{\alpha}, \lambda_i, \overline{0}}(\overline{\alpha}, \lambda_i))$$
$$\psi(\alpha_1, \ldots, \lambda_i, \overline{0}, \beta + 1)[x] := \psi(\alpha_1, \ldots, \lambda_i[x], \overline{0}, \psi(\alpha_1, \ldots, \lambda_i, \overline{0}, \beta))$$
$$\psi(\alpha_1, \ldots, \lambda_i, \overline{0}, \lambda)[x] := \psi(\alpha_1, \ldots, \lambda_i, \overline{0}, \lambda[x]) \qquad \lambda \notin \mathrm{FIX}(\overline{\alpha}, \overline{0})$$
$$\psi(\alpha_1, \ldots, \lambda_i, \overline{0}, \lambda)[x] := \psi(\alpha_1, \ldots, \lambda_i[x], \overline{0}, \lambda) \qquad \lambda \in \mathrm{FIX}(\overline{\alpha}, \overline{0})$$

The above definition is given in such a way as to simplify the comparison between the fundamental sequences for T and the fundamental sequences for the set of ordinal terms $T(2)$ (built from 0, +, and a 2-ary function symbol ψ) as presented in [18]. Note that our definition is equivalent to the more compact one presented in [11]. The following proposition is stated without proof. A proof (for a slightly different assignment of fundamental sequences) can be found in [4].

Proposition 4. *Let $\alpha \in T$ be given; assume $x < \omega$. If $\alpha > 0$, then $\alpha > \alpha[x]$. For $\alpha > 1$ we get $\alpha[x] > 0$, and if $\alpha \in \text{LIM}$, then $\alpha[x+1] > \alpha[x]$. Finally, if $\beta < \alpha \in \text{LIM}$, then there exists $x < \omega$, such that $\beta < \alpha[x]$ holds.*

In the definition of $\psi(\alpha_1, \ldots, \lambda_i, \overline{0}, 0)[x]$ we introduce at the last position of ψ the term $\text{MS}_{\overline{a}, \overline{0}}(\overline{\alpha})$. We cannot simply dispense of this term. To see this, we alter the definition of the crucial case. We momentarily consider only 3-ary ψ-functions; we set $\Gamma_0 := \psi(1, 0, 0)$ and calculate $\psi(0, \Gamma_0, 0)[x]$:

$$
\begin{aligned}
\psi(0, \Gamma_0, 0)[x] &= \psi(0, \psi(1,0,0)[x], 0) \\
&= \psi(0, \psi(0, \cdot, 0)^{x+1}(0), 0) \\
&= \psi(0, \cdot, 0)^{x+2}(0) \\
&< \psi(1, 0, 0) \quad .
\end{aligned}
$$

Hence for every $x < \omega$; $\psi(0, \Gamma_0, 0)[x] < \Gamma_0$ holds. This contradicts the last assertion of the proposition as $\Gamma_0 < \psi(0, \Gamma_0, 0)$. As a side-remark we want to mention that the given assignment of fundamental sequences even fulfills the *Bachmann* property, see [2]. Utilizing Definition 3 we are now in the position to define sub-recursive hierarchies of ordinal functions.

Definition 4. *(The slow-growing hierarchy). Recursive definition of the function $G_\alpha \colon \omega \to \omega$ for $\alpha \in T$.*

$$
\begin{aligned}
G_0(x) &:= 0 \\
G_{\alpha+1}(x) &:= G_\alpha(x) + 1 \\
G_\lambda(x) &:= G_{\lambda[x]}(x) \quad .
\end{aligned}
$$

Definition 5. *(The fast-growing hierarchy.) Recursive definition of the function $F_\alpha \colon \omega \to \omega$ for $\alpha \in T$.*

$$
\begin{aligned}
F_0(x) &:= x + 1 \\
F_{\alpha+1}(x) &:= F_\alpha^{x+1}(x) \\
F_\lambda(x) &:= F_{\lambda[x]}(x) \quad .
\end{aligned}
$$

It is easy to see that $G_\alpha(x) < F_\alpha(x)$ for all $\alpha > 0$. To see that the name of the hierarchy $\{G_\alpha \colon \alpha \in T\}$ is appropriate, it suffices to calculate some examples. Take e.g. $G_\omega \colon G_\omega(x) = G_{\psi(\overline{0}) \cdot (x+1)}(x) = G_{x+1}(x) = G_x(x) + 1 = x + 1$.

Recall that a function f is *elementary* (in a function g) if f is definable explicitly from 0, 1, +, $\dot{-}$ (and g), using bounded sum and product. $E(g)$

denotes the class of all such functions f. Then G_{ϵ_0} majorizes the elementary functions E. In contrast the function F_ω already majorizes the primitive recursive functions, i.e. its growth rate is comparable to the (binary) Ackermann function. Furthermore the class of multiple recursive functions can be characterized by the hierarchy $\{E(F_\gamma) : \gamma < \omega^\omega\}$, cf. [12,13].

However, the following theorem states a (surprising) connection between the slow- and fast-growing hierarchy. See e.g. [8,6,18] for further reading on the Hierarchy Comparison Theorem.

Theorem 1. *(The Hierarchy Comparison Theorem.)*

$$\bigcup_{\alpha \in T} E(G_\alpha) = \bigcup_{\gamma < \omega^{N+1}} E(F_\gamma) \quad .$$

Proof. We do not give a detailed proof, but only state the main idea. In [18] the hierarchy comparison theorem has been established for the set of ordinal terms $T(2)$ (built from 0, +, and the function symbol ψ, where $ar(\psi) = 2$). To extend the result to T it suffices to follow the pattern of the proof in [18].

The difficult direction is to show that every function in the hierarchy $\{F_\gamma : \gamma < \omega^{N+1}\}$ is majorized by some G_α. To show this one in particular needs to extend the proofs of Lemma 5 and Theorem 1 in [18] adequately. The reversed direction follows by standard techniques, cf. [6].   □

5   The Interpretation Theorem

For all $\alpha \in T$ there are uniquely determined ordinal terms $\alpha_1 \geq \cdots \geq \alpha_m \in P$ such that $\alpha = \alpha_1 + \cdots + \alpha_m$ holds. In addition, for every $\alpha \in P$ there exist unique $\alpha_1, \ldots, \alpha_{N+1}$ such that $\alpha = \psi(\alpha_1, \ldots, \alpha_{N+1})$. (This normal form property is trivial by definition.) Now assume $\alpha, \beta \in T$ with $\alpha = \gamma_1 + \cdots + \gamma_{m_0}$, $\beta = \gamma_{m_0+1} + \cdots + \gamma_m$. Then the *natural sum* $\alpha\#\beta$ is defined as $\gamma_{\rho(1)} + \cdots + \gamma_{\rho(m)}$, where ρ denotes a permutation on $\{1, \ldots, m\}$ such that $\gamma_{\rho(1)} \geq \cdots \geq \gamma_{\rho(m)}$ holds.

Let R denote a finite rewrite system whose induced rewrite relation is contained in $\succ_{\mathrm{LPO}}$.

Definition 6. *Recursive definition of the interpretation function $\pi \colon \mathcal{T}(\Sigma) \to T$. Let N denote the maximal arity of a function symbol in Σ. If $s = f_j \in \Sigma$, then set $\pi(s) := \psi(j, \overline{0})$. Otherwise, let $s = f_j(s_1, \ldots, s_m)$ and set*

$$\pi(s) := \psi(j, \pi(s_1), \ldots, \pi(s_m) + 1, \overline{0}) \quad .$$

In the sequel of this section we show that π defines an *interpretation* for R on $(T, <)$; i.e. we establish the following theorem.

Theorem 2. *For all $s, t \in \mathcal{T}(\Sigma)$ we have $s \to_R t$ implies $\pi(s) > \pi(t)$.*

Unfortunately this is not strong enough. The problem being that $\alpha > \beta$ implies that G_α majorizes G_β, only. Whereas to proceed with our general program—see Section 1—we need an interpretation theorem for a binary relation $\succ$ on T, such that $\alpha \succ \beta \Rightarrow G_\alpha(x) > G_\beta(x)$ holds for all x. We introduce a notion of a generalized system of fundamental sequences. Based on this generalized notion, it is then possible to define a suitable ordering $\succ$.

Definition 7. *(Generalized system of fundamental sequences for $(T, <)$.) Recursive definition of $(\alpha)^x$ for $x < \omega$.*

1. *$(0)^x := \emptyset$*
2. *Assume $\alpha = \alpha_1 + \cdots + \alpha_m$; $m > 1$. Then $\beta \in (\alpha)^x$ if either*
   - *$\beta = \alpha_1 \# \cdots \alpha_i^* \cdots \# \alpha_m$ and $\alpha_i^* \in (\alpha_i)^x$ holds, or*
   - *$\beta = \alpha_i$.*
3. *Assume $\alpha = \psi(\overline{\alpha})$. Then $\beta \in (\alpha)^x$ if*
   - *$\beta = \psi(\alpha_1, \ldots, \alpha_i^*, \ldots, \alpha_{N+1})$, and $\alpha_i^* \in (\alpha_i)^x$, or*
   - *$\beta = \alpha_i + x$, where $\alpha_i > 0$, or*
   - *$\beta = \psi(\overline{\alpha})[x]$.*

By recursion we define the *transitive closure* of the ownership $(\alpha)^x \ni \beta$: $(\alpha >_{(x)} \beta) \leftrightarrow (\exists \gamma \in (\alpha)^x (\gamma >_{(x)} \beta \vee \gamma = \beta))$. Let $\alpha, \beta \in T$. It is easy to verify that $\alpha >_{(x)} \beta$ (for some $x < \omega$) implies $\alpha > \beta$. If no confusion can arise we write α^x instead of $(\alpha)^x$.

Lemma 1. *(Subterm Property) Let $x < \omega$ be arbitrary.*

1. *$\alpha <_{(x)} \gamma_1 \# \cdots \alpha \cdots \# \gamma_m$.*
2. *$\alpha <_{(x)} \psi(\gamma_1, \ldots, \alpha, \ldots, \gamma_{N+1})$.*

Proof. The first assertion is trivial. The second assertion follows by the definition of $<_{(x)}$ and assertion 1.   □

Lemma 2. *(Monotonicity Property) Let $x < \omega$ be arbitrary.*

1. *If $\alpha >_{(x)} \beta$, then $\gamma_1 \# \cdots \alpha \cdots \# \gamma_m >_{(x)} \gamma_1 \# \cdots \beta \cdots \# \gamma_m$.*
2. *If $\alpha >_{(x)} \beta$, then $\psi(\gamma_1, \ldots, \alpha, \ldots, \gamma_{N+1}) >_{(x)} \psi(\gamma_1, \ldots, \beta, \ldots, \gamma_{N+1})$.*

Proof. We employ induction on α to prove 1). We write (ih) for induction hypothesis. We may assume that $\alpha > 0$. By definition of $\alpha >_{(x)} \beta$ we either have (i) that there exist $\delta \in \alpha^x$ and $\delta >_{(x)} \beta$ or (ii) $\beta \in \alpha^x$. Firstly, one considers the latter case. Then $(\gamma_1 \# \cdots \beta \cdots \# \gamma_m) \in (\gamma_1 \# \cdots \alpha \cdots \# \gamma_m)^x$ holds by Definition 7. Therefore $(\gamma_1 \# \cdots \beta \cdots \# \gamma_m) <_{(x)} (\gamma_1 \# \cdots \alpha \cdots \# \gamma_m)$ follows. Now, we consider the first case. By assumption $\delta >_{(x)} \beta$ holds, by (ih) this implies $(\gamma_1 \# \cdots \delta \cdots \# \gamma_m) >_{(x)} (\gamma_1 \# \cdots \beta \cdots \# \gamma_m)^x$. Now $(\gamma_1 \# \cdots \alpha \cdots \# \gamma_m) >_{(x)} (\gamma_1 \# \cdots \delta \cdots \# \gamma_m)$ follows by definition of $>_{(x)}$, if we replace β by δ in the proof of the second case. This completely proves 1).

To prove 2) we proceed by induction on α. By definition of $\alpha >_{(x)} \beta$ we have either (i) $\delta \in \alpha^x$ and $\delta >_{(x)} \beta$ or (ii) $\beta \in \alpha^x$. It is sufficient to consider the latter case, the first case follows from the second as above. By Definition 7, $\beta \in \alpha^x$ implies $\psi(\gamma_1, \ldots, \beta, \ldots, \gamma_{N+1}) \in \psi(\gamma_1, \ldots, \alpha, \ldots, \gamma_{N+1})^x$.   □

In the sequel we show the existence of a natural number e, such that for all $s, t \in \mathcal{T}$, and any ground substitution ρ, $s \to_R t$ implies $\pi(s\rho) >_{(e)} \pi(t\rho)$. Theorem 2 follows then as a corollary. The proof is involved, and makes use of a sequence of lemmas.

Lemma 3. *Assume* $\alpha, \beta \in \text{LIM}$; $x \geq 1$. *If* $\alpha >_{(x)} \beta$, *then* $\alpha >_{(x+1)} \beta + 1$ *holds.*

To prove the lemma we exploit the following auxiliary lemma.

Lemma 4. *We assume the assumptions and notation of Lemma 3; assume Lemma 3 holds for all* $\gamma, \delta \in \text{LIM}$ *with* $\gamma, \delta < \alpha$. *Then* $\alpha >_{(x+1)} \alpha[x+1] \geq_{(x+1)} \alpha[x] + 1$.

Proof. The lemma follows by induction on the form of α by analyzing all cases of Definition 3.   □

Proof. (of Lemma 3) The proof proceeds by induction on the form of α. We consider only the case where $\alpha = \psi(\alpha_1, \ldots, \alpha_{N+1})$. The case where $\alpha = \alpha_1 + \cdots + \alpha_m$ is similar but simpler.

By definition of $\alpha >_{(x)} \beta$ we have either (i) $\gamma \in \alpha^x$ and $\gamma >_{(x)} \beta$ or (ii) $\beta \in \alpha^x$. Assume for $\gamma \in \alpha^x$ we have already shown that $\gamma + 1 <_{(x+1)} \alpha$. Then for $\beta <_{(x)} \gamma$, we conclude by (ih) and the Subterm Property $\beta + 1 <_{(x+1)} \gamma <_{(x+1)} \gamma + 1 <_{(x+1)} \alpha$. Hence, it suffices to consider the second case. We proceed by case distinction on the form of β.

CASE $\beta = \psi(\alpha_1, \ldots, \alpha_i^*, \ldots, \alpha_{N+1})$ where $\alpha_i^* \in (\alpha_i)^x$ for some i ($1 \leq i \leq N+1$). Note that $\alpha_i < \alpha$, hence (ih) is applicable to establish $\alpha_i^* + 1 <_{(x+1)} \alpha_i$.

Furthermore by the Subterm Property follows $\alpha_i^* <_{(x+1)} \alpha_i^* + 1$ and therefore $\psi(\alpha_1, \ldots, \alpha_i^*, \ldots, \alpha_{N+1}) <_{(x+1)} \psi(\alpha_1, \ldots, \alpha_i^* + 1, \ldots, \alpha_{N+1})$ holds with Monotonicity. Applying (ih) with respect to $\psi(\alpha_1, \ldots, \alpha_i^* + 1, \ldots, \alpha_{N+1})$ we obtain

$$\psi(\alpha_1, \ldots, \alpha_i^*, \ldots, \alpha_{N+1}) + 1 <_{(x+1)} \psi(\alpha_1, \ldots, \alpha_i^* + 1, \ldots, \alpha_{N+1})$$
$$<_{(x+1)} \psi(\alpha_1, \ldots, \alpha_i, \ldots, \alpha_{N+1}) = \alpha \quad .$$

The last inequality follows again by an application of the Monotonicity Property.

CASE $\beta = \alpha_i + x$: Then $(\alpha_i + x) + 1 = \alpha_i + (x+1) <_{(x+1)} \alpha$.

CASE $\beta = \psi(\overline{\alpha})[x]$. Clearly $\beta \in \text{LIM}$. Then the auxiliary lemma becomes applicable. Thus $\psi(\overline{\alpha})[x] + 1 \leq_{(x+1)} \alpha[x+1] <_{(x+1)} \alpha$.   □

Lemma 5. *Let* $t \in \mathcal{T}(\Sigma)$ *be given. Assume* $\tau(t) \leq d$, *and* $f_j \in \Sigma$. *If* $f_j \succ_{\text{LPO}} t$, *then* $\pi(f_j) >_{(2d)} \pi(t)$.

Proof. We proceed by induction on $\tau(t)$. In the presentation of the argument, we will frequently employ the Subterm and the Monotonicity Property without further notice. Set $\alpha := \pi(f_j)$, and $\beta := \pi(t)$. Furthermore it is a crucial observation that $0 <_{(x)} \alpha$ holds for any $x < \omega$, $\alpha \in T$. (This follows by a simple induction on α.)

CASE $\tau(t) = 0$: Then by assumption $t = f_i \in \Sigma$, $i < j$. Hence $i <_{(2d)} j$ holds and we conclude $\pi(t) = \psi(i, \overline{0}) <_{(2d)} \psi(j, \overline{0}) = \pi(f_j)$.

CASE $\tau(t) > 0$: Let $t = f_i(t_1, \ldots, t_n)$. Set $\beta_l := \pi(t_l)$ for all $l = 1, \ldots, n$. By (ih) one obtains $\beta_l <_{(2(d-1))} \alpha$ for all l. For all l, we need only consider the case where $\beta_l \in \alpha^{2(d-1)}$. We consider $\psi(j, \overline{0})[2d]$ and apply the following sequence of descents via $>_{(2d)}$:

$$
\begin{aligned}
\psi(j, \overline{0})[2d] &= \psi(j-1, \cdot, \overline{0})^{2d+1}(0) \\
&= \psi(j-1, \psi(j-1, \cdot, \overline{0})^{2d}(0), \overline{0}) \\
&>_{(2d)} \psi(j-1, \psi(j-1, \cdot, \overline{0})^{2d-1}(0) + 1, \overline{0}) \\
&>_{(2d)} \psi(j-1, \underbrace{\psi(j-1, \cdot, \overline{0})^{2d-1}(0), \cdot, \overline{0})^{2d+1}(0)}_{\psi(j,\overline{0})[2(d-1)]} \quad .
\end{aligned}
$$

We define $\gamma_1 := \psi(j, \overline{0})[2(d-1)]$ and $\gamma_{k+1} := \psi(j-1, \gamma_1, \ldots, \gamma_k+1, \overline{0})[2(d-1)]$. By iteration of the above descent, we see

$$
\begin{aligned}
\alpha[2d] &= \psi(j, \overline{0})[2d] \\
&>_{(2d)} \psi(j-1, \gamma_1, \ldots, \gamma_n + 1, \overline{0}) \\
&>_{(2d)} \psi(j-1, \alpha[2(d-1)], \ldots, \alpha[2(d-1)] + 1, \overline{0}) \qquad (\delta) \quad .
\end{aligned}
$$

Let l $(1 \leq l \leq n)$ be fixed. By assumption we have $\beta_l \in (\alpha)^{2(d-1)}$. We proceed by case distinction on the definition of β_l.

Assume $\beta_l = \psi(j, \overline{0})[2(d-1)]$. Then $\delta = \psi(j-1, \alpha[2(d-1)], \ldots, \beta_l, \ldots, \alpha[2(d-1)] + 1, \overline{0})$. Assume $\beta_l = \psi(j^*, \overline{0})$, where $j^* \in (j)^{2(d-1)}$, i.e. $j^* \leq_{(2d)} j-1 <_{(2d)} j$. Therefore $\alpha[2(d-1)] >_{(2d)} \psi(j-1, \overline{0})$. Hence $\delta >_{(2d)} \psi(j-1, \alpha[2(d-1)], \ldots, \beta_l, \ldots, \alpha[2(d-1)] + 1, \overline{0})$. Finally assume $\beta_l = j + 2(d-1)$. Then $\beta_l <_{(2(d-1)+1)} \psi(j-1, \overline{0}) <_{(2(d-1)+1)} \psi(j-1, \cdot, \overline{0})^{2d-1}(0) = \alpha[2(d-1)]$. Hence $\beta_l <_{(2d)} \alpha[2(d-1)]$ by Lemma 3 and therefore $\delta >_{(2d)} \psi(j-1, \alpha[2(d-1)], \ldots, \beta_l, \ldots, \alpha[2(d-1)] + 1, \overline{0})$.

As l was fixed but arbitrary, the above construction is valid for all l. And the lemma follows. $\qquad \square$

Lemma 6. *Let $f_i(t_1, \ldots, t_n), f_j(s_1, \ldots, s_m) \in \mathcal{T}(\Sigma)$ be given; let $d > 0$. Then*

1. *If $i < j$, $\pi(f_j(\overline{s})) >_{(2(d-1))} \pi(t_l)$ for all $l = 1, \ldots, n$. Then $\pi(f_j(\overline{s})) >_{(2d)} \pi(f_i(\overline{t}))$ holds.*

2. *If $s_1 = t_1, \ldots, s_{i_0-1} = t_{i_0-1}$, $\pi(s_{i_0}) >_{(2(d-1))} \pi(t_{i_0})$, and $\pi(f_j(\overline{s})) >_{(2(d-1))} \pi(t_l)$, for all $l = i_0 + 1, \ldots, n$, then $\pi(f_j(\overline{s})) >_{(2d)} \pi(f_i(\overline{t}))$ holds.*

Proof. The proof of assertion 1) is similar to the proof of assertion 2) but simpler. Hence, we concentrate on 2). Set $\alpha := \pi(f_j(\overline{s}))$; $\beta := \pi(f_i(\overline{t}))$; finally set $\alpha_i := \pi(s_i)$ for all $i = 1, \ldots, m$, and $\beta_i := \pi(t : i)$ for all $i = 1, \ldots, n$. As above, we consider only the case where $\beta_l \in (\alpha)^{2(d-1)}$. The other case follows easily.

$$
\begin{aligned}
\alpha[2d] &= \psi(j, \alpha_1, \ldots, \alpha_m + 1, \overline{0})[2d] \\
&= \psi(j, \alpha_1, \ldots, \alpha_m, \psi(j, \alpha_1, \ldots, \alpha_m, \cdot, \overline{0})^{2d}(0), \overline{0}) \\
&>_{(2d)} \psi(j, \alpha_1, \ldots, \alpha_m, \psi(j, \alpha_1, \ldots, \alpha_m, \cdot, \overline{0})^{2d-1}(0) + 1, \overline{0}) \\
&= \psi(j, \alpha_1, \ldots, \alpha_m, \underbrace{\psi(j, \alpha_1, \ldots, \alpha_m + 1, \overline{0})[2(d-1)]}_{\alpha[2(d-1)]} + 1, \overline{0}) \quad .
\end{aligned}
$$

Similar to above, we define $\gamma_1 := \alpha[2(d-1)] = \psi(j, \alpha_1, \ldots, \alpha_m+1, \overline{0})[2(d-1)]$ and $\gamma_{k+1} := \psi(j, \alpha_1, \ldots, \alpha_m, \gamma_1, \ldots, \gamma_{k+1}+1, \overline{0})[2(d-1)]$ and obtain

$$\alpha[2d] >_{(2d)} \psi(j, \alpha_1, \ldots, \alpha_m, \gamma_1, \ldots, \gamma_{N-m}+1)$$
$$>_{(2d)} \psi(j, \alpha_1, \ldots, \alpha_m, \alpha[2(d-1)], \ldots, \alpha[2(d-1)]+1)$$
$$>_{(2d)} \psi(j, \alpha_1, \ldots, \alpha_{i_0}, \overline{0}, \alpha[2(d-1)]+1) \quad .$$

By assumption $\beta_{i_0} <_{(2(d-1))} \alpha_{i_0}$ and by Lemma 3 this implies $\beta_{i_0}+1 <_{(2d)} \alpha_{i_0}$. We set $\overline{\alpha} := \alpha_1, \ldots, \alpha_{i_0-1}$, then we obtain

$$\psi(j, \overline{\alpha}, \alpha_{i_0}, \overline{0}, \alpha[2(d-1)]+1) >_{(2d)} \psi(j, \overline{\alpha}, \beta_{i_0}+1, \overline{0}, \alpha[2(d-1)]+1)$$
$$>_{(2d)} \psi(j, \overline{\alpha}, \beta_{i_0}+1, \overline{0}, \alpha[2(d-1)]+1)[2d]$$
$$>_{(2d)} \psi(j, \overline{\alpha}, \beta_{i_0}, \psi(j, \overline{\alpha}, \beta_{i_0}+1, \overline{0}, \alpha[2(d-1)]), \overline{0})$$
$$>_{(2d)} \psi(j, \overline{\alpha}, \beta_{i_0}, \alpha[2(d-1)]+1), \overline{0})$$
$$= \psi(j, \beta_1, \ldots, \beta_{i_0}, \alpha[2(d-1)]+1), \overline{0}) \quad .$$

As in the first part of the proof, we obtain $\alpha[2d] >_{(2d)} \psi(j, \overline{\alpha}, \alpha_{i_0}, \overline{0}, \alpha[2(d-1)]+1) >_{(2d)}$

$$>_{(2d)} \psi(j, \beta_1, \ldots, \beta_{i_0}, \alpha[2(d-1)], \ldots, \alpha[2(d-1)]+1, \overline{0}) \quad .$$

By assumption we have $\beta_l <_{(2(d-1))} \alpha$ for all $l = 1, \ldots, n$. It remains to prove that this implies $\beta_l \leq_{(2d)} \gamma$. For this it is sufficient to consider the case where $\beta_l \in (\alpha)^{2(d-1)}$. The proof proceeds by case-distinction on the construction of β_l. The proof is similar to the respective part in the proof of Lemma 5, and hence omitted. □

Lemma 7. *Let $s, t \in \mathcal{T}$ be given. Assume $s = f_j(s_1, \ldots, s_m)$, ρ is a ground substitution, $\tau(t) \leq d$. Assume further $s_k \succ_{\mathrm{LPO}} u$ and $\tau(u) \leq d$ implies $\pi(s_k\rho) >_{(2d)} \pi(u\rho)$ for all $u \in \mathcal{T}$. Then $s \succ_{\mathrm{LPO}} t$ implies $\pi(s\rho) >_{(2d)} \pi(t\rho)$.*

Proof. The proof is by induction on d.

CASE $d = 0$: Hence $\tau(t) = 0$; therefore $t \in \mathcal{V}$ or $t = f_i \in \Sigma$. Consider $t \in \mathcal{V}$. Then t is a subterm of s. Hence there exists k ($1 \leq k \leq m$) s.t. t is subterm of s_k. Hence $s_k \succeq_{\mathrm{LPO}} t$, and by assumption this implies $\pi(s_k\rho) >_{(2d)} \pi(t\rho)$, and therefore $\pi(s\rho) >_{(2d)} \pi(t\rho)$ by the Subterm Property.

Now assume $t = f_i \in \Sigma$. As $s \succ_{\mathrm{LPO}} t$ by assumption either $i < j$ or $s_k \succeq_{\mathrm{LPO}} t$ holds. In the latter case, the assumptions render $\pi(s_k\rho) \geq_{(2d)} \pi(t\rho)$; hence $\pi(s\rho) >_{(2d)} \pi(t\rho)$. Otherwise, $\pi(s\rho) = \psi(j, \pi(s_1\rho), \ldots, \pi(s_m\rho)+1, \overline{0})$, while $\pi(t\rho) = \pi(t) = \psi(i, \overline{0})$. As $\pi(s_k\rho) >_{(x)} 0$ holds for arbitrary $x < \omega$, we conclude $\pi(s\rho) >_{(2d)} \pi(t\rho)$.

CASE $d > 0$: Assume $\tau(t) > 0$. (Otherwise, the proof follows the pattern of the case $d = 0$.) Let $t = f_i(t_1, \ldots, t_n)$, and clearly $\tau(t_l) \leq (d-1)$ for all $l = 1, \ldots, n$. We start with the following observation: Assume there exists i_0 s.t. $s \succ_{\mathrm{LPO}} t_l$ holds for all $l = i_0 + 1, \ldots, n$. Then by (ih) we have $\pi(s\rho) >_{(2(d-1))} \pi(t_l\rho)$.

We proceed by case-distinction on $s \succ_{\mathrm{LPO}} t$. Assume firstly there exists k ($1 \leq k \leq m$) s.t. $s_k \succeq_{\mathrm{LPO}} t$. Utilizing the assumptions of the lemma, we conclude $\pi(s\rho) >_{(2d)} \pi(t\rho)$. Now assume $i < j$ and $s \succ_{\mathrm{LPO}} t_l$ for all $l = 1, \ldots, n$. Clearly $s\rho, t\rho \in T(\Sigma)$. By the observation $\pi(s\rho) >_{(2(d-1))} \pi(t_l\rho)$ holds. Hence Lemma 6.1 becomes applicable and therefore $\pi(s\rho) >_{(2d)} \pi(t\rho)$ holds true. Finally assume $i = j$; $s_1 = t_1, \ldots, s_{i_0-1} = t_{i_0-1}$; $s_{i_0} \succ_{\mathrm{LPO}} t_{i_0}$; $s \succ_{\mathrm{LPO}} t_l$, for all $l = i_0 + 1, \ldots, m$. Utilizing the observation, we see that Lemma 6.2 becomes applicable and therefore $\pi(s\rho) >_{(2d)} \pi(t\rho)$.   □

Lemma 8. *Let $t \in T(\Sigma)$ be given, assume $\tau(t) \leq d$. Then $\psi(K+1, \overline{0}) >_{(2d)} \pi(t)$.*

Proof. The proof is by induction on $\tau(t)$ and follows the pattern of the proof of Lemma 5.   □

Theorem 3. *Let $l, r \in T$ be given. Assume ρ is a ground substitution, $\tau(t) \leq d$. Then $l \succ_{\mathrm{LPO}} r$ implies $\pi(l\rho) >_{(2d)} \pi(r\rho)$.*

Proof. We proceed by induction on $\tau(s)$.

CASE $\tau(s) = 0$: Then s can either be a constant or a variable. As $s \succ_{\mathrm{LPO}} t$ holds, we can exclude the latter case. Hence assume $s = f_j$. As $f_j \succ_{\mathrm{LPO}} t$, t is closed. Hence the assumptions of the theorem imply the assumptions of Lemma 5 and we conclude $\pi(s\rho) = \pi(s) >_{(2d)} \pi(t) = \pi(t\rho)$.

CASE $\tau(s) > 0$: Then s can be written as $f_j(s_1, \ldots, s_m)$. By (ih) $s_k \succ_{\mathrm{LPO}} u$ and $\tau(u) \leq d$ imply $\pi(s_k\rho) >_{(2d)} \pi(t\rho)$. Therefore the present assumptions contain the assumptions of Lemma 7 and hence $\pi(s\rho) >_{(2d)} \pi(t\rho)$ follows.   □

Theorem 4. *(The Interpretation Theorem.) Let R denote a finite rewrite system whose induced rewrite relation is contained in $\succ_{\mathrm{LPO}}$. Then there exists $k < \omega$, such that for all $l, r \in T$, and any ground substitution ρ $l \to_R r$ implies $\pi(l\rho) >_{(k)} \pi(r\rho)$.*

Proof. Set d equal to $\max\{\tau(r) \colon \exists l \ (l, r) \in R\}$. Then the theorem follows as a corollary to Theorem 3 if k is set to $2d$.   □

6   Collapsing Theorem

We define a variant of the slow-growing hierarchy, cf. Definition 4, suitable for our purposes.

Definition 8. *Recursive definition of the function $\widetilde{G}_\alpha \colon \omega \to \omega$ for $\alpha \in T$.*

$$\widetilde{G}_0(x) := 0$$
$$\widetilde{G}_\alpha(x) := \max\{\widetilde{G}_\beta(x) \colon \beta \in (\alpha)^x\} + 1 \quad .$$

Lemma 9. *Let $\alpha \in T$, $\alpha > 0$ be given. Assume $x < \omega$ is arbitrary.*

1. *$\widetilde{G}_\alpha$ is increasing. (Even strictly if $\alpha > \omega$.)*
2. *If $\alpha >_{(x)} \beta$, then $\widetilde{G}_\alpha(x) > \widetilde{G}_\beta(x)$.*

Proof. Both assertions follow by induction over $<$ on α.   □

We need to know that this variant of the slow-growing hierarchy is indeed slow-growing. We show this by verifying that the hierarchies $\{\widetilde{G}_\alpha \colon \alpha \in T\}$ and $\{G_\alpha \colon \alpha \in T\}$ coincide with respect to growth-rate. It is a triviality to verify that there exists $\beta \in T$ such that $\widetilde{G}_\beta$ majorizes G_α. (Simply set $\beta = \alpha$.) The other direction is less trivial. One first proves that for any $\alpha \in T$ there exists $\gamma < \omega^{N+1}$ such that $\widetilde{G}_\alpha(x) \leq F_\gamma(x)$ for almost all x. Secondly one employs the Hierarchy Comparison Theorem once more to establish the existence of $\beta \in T$ such that $\widetilde{G}_\alpha(x) \leq G_\beta(x)$ holds for almost all x.

Theorem 5.

$$\bigcup_{\alpha \in T} E(G_\alpha) = \bigcup_{\alpha \in T} E(\widetilde{G}_\alpha) = \bigcup_{\gamma < \omega^{N+1}} E(F_\gamma) \ .$$

7   Complexity Bounds

The *complexity* of a terminating finite rewrite system R is measured by the *derivation length* function.

Definition 9. *The derivation length function* $\mathrm{DL}_R \colon \omega \to \omega$. *Let* $m < \omega$ *be given.* $\mathrm{DL}_R(m) := \max\{n \colon \exists t_1, \ldots, t_n \in T \ ((t_1 \to_R \cdots \to_R t_n) \wedge (\tau(t_1) \leq m))\}$.

Let R be a rewrite system over T such that $\to_R$ is contained in a lexicographic path ordering. Now assume that there exist $s = t_0, t_1, \ldots, t_n \in T$ with $\tau(s) \leq m$ such that

$$s \to_R t_1 \to_R \cdots \to_R t_n$$

holds. By our choice of R this implies $s \succ_{\mathrm{LPO}} t_1 \succ_{\mathrm{LPO}} \cdots \succ_{\mathrm{LPO}} t_n$. By assumption on Σ there exists $c \in \Sigma$, with $\mathrm{ar}(c) = 0$. We define a ground substitution ρ: $\rho(x) = c$, for all $x \in V$. Let $k < \omega$ be defined as in Theorem 4. Recall that K denotes the cardinality of Σ. We conclude from the Interpretation Theorem and Lemma 8, $\pi(s\rho) >_{(k)} \pi(t_1\rho) >_{(k)} \cdots >_{(k)} \pi(t_n\rho)$ and $\psi(K+1,\bar{0}) >_{(2m)} \pi(s\rho)$. Setting $h := \max\{2m, k\}$ and utilizing Lemma 3, we obtain $\psi(K+1,\bar{0}) >_{(h)} \pi(s\rho) >_{(h)} \cdots >_{(h)} \pi(t_n\rho)$. An application of Lemma 9.2 yields

$$\widetilde{G}_{\psi(K+1,\bar{0})}(h) > \widetilde{G}_{\pi(s\rho)}(h) > \cdots > \widetilde{G}_{\pi(t_n\rho)}(h) \ .$$

Employing Theorem 5 we conclude the existence of $\gamma < \omega^\omega$, such that

$$F_\gamma(\max\{2m, k\}) \geq \widetilde{G}_{\psi(K+1,\bar{0})}(\max\{2m, k\}) \geq \mathrm{DL}_R(m) \ .$$

The class of multiply-recursive functions is captured by $\bigcup_{\gamma < \omega^\omega} E(F_\gamma)$, see [13]). Thus we have established a multiply-recursive upper bound for the derivation length of R if $\to_R$ is contained in a lexicographic path ordering. Furthermore, this bound is essentially optimal, cf. [17].

8   Conclusion

The presented proof method is generally applicable. Let R denote a rewrite system whose termination can be shown via $\succ_{\mathrm{MPO}}$. To yield a primitive recursive upper bound for the complexity of R the above proof can be employed. Firstly the definition of the interpretation function π has to be changed as follows. If $s = f_j(s_1, \ldots, s_m)$, then we set

$$\pi(s) := \psi(j, \pi(s_1)\# \cdots \#\pi(s_m)\#1) \quad .$$

Then the presented proof needs only partial changes. It suffices to reformulate (and reprove) Lemma 5, 6, 7, and 8, respectively.

Future work will be concerned with the *Knuth-Bendix ordering*. Due to the more complicated nature of this ordering the statement of the interpretation is not so simple. Still we believe that only mild alterations of the given proof are necessary.

References

1. F. Baader and T. Nipkow. *Term Rewriting and All That.* Cambridge Univeristy Press, 1998.
2. H. Bachmann. *Transfinite Zahlen.* Springer Verlag, 1955.
3. W. Buchholz. Proof-theoretical analysis of termination proofs. *APAL*, 75:57–65, 1995.
4. W. Buchholz. Ordinal notations and fundamental sequences. Unpublished manuscript; availabe at www.mathematik.uni-muenchen.de/~buchholz/, 2003.
5. E.A. Cichon. Termination orderings and complexity characterisations. In P. Aczel, H. Simmons, and S.S. Wainer, editors, *Proof Theory*, pages 171–193, 1992.
6. E.A. Cichon and S.S. Wainer. The slow-growing and the Grzegorczyk hierachies. *J. Symbolic Logic*, 48:399–408, 1983.
7. N. Dershowitz and M. Okada. Proof-Theoretic Techniques for Term Rewriting Theory. In *LICS 1998*, pages 104–111, 1988.
8. J.-Y. Girard. Π_2^1-logic I:Dilators. *Annals of Mathematical Logic*, 21:75–219, 1981.
9. D. Hofbauer. Termination proofs by multiset path orderings imply primitive recursive derivation lengths. *TCS*, 105:129–140, 1992.
10. I. Lepper. Derivation lengths and order types of Knuth-Bendix order. *Theoretical Computer Science*, 269:433–450, 2001.
11. I. Lepper. Simply terminating rewrite systems with long derivations. *Archive for Mathematical Logic*, 2003. To appear. www.math.uni-muenster.de/logik/publ/pre/3.html.
12. R. Péter. *Recursive Functions.* Academic Press, 1967.
13. J.W. Robbin. *Subrecursive Hierarchies.* PhD thesis, Princeton University, 1965.
14. D. Schmidt. Well-partial orderings and their maximal order types. Fakultät für Mathematik der Ruprecht-Karl-Universität Heidelberg, 1979. Habilitationsschrift.
15. Kurt Schütte. *Proof Theory.* Springer Verlag, Berlin and New York, 1977.
16. H. Touzet. Encoding the Hydra battle as a rewrite system. In *MFCS 1998*, LNCS 1450, pages 267–276. Springer Verlag, 1998.
17. A. Weiermann. Termination proofs for term rewriting systems with lexicographic path ordering imply multiply recursive derivation lengths. *TCS*, 139:355–362, 1995.
18. A. Weiermann. Some interesting connections between the slow growing hierarchy and the Ackermann function. *J. Symbolic Logic*, pages 609–628, 2001.

Tsukuba Termination Tool[*]

Nao Hirokawa[1] and Aart Middeldorp[2,**]

[1] Master's Program in Science and Engineering
University of Tsukuba, Tsukuba 305-8573, Japan
nao@score.is.tsukuba.ac.jp
[2] Institute of Information Sciences and Electronics
University of Tsukuba, Tsukuba 305-8573, Japan
ami@is.tsukuba.ac.jp

Abstract. We present a tool for automatically proving termination of first-order rewrite systems. The tool is based on the dependency pair method of Arts and Giesl. It incorporates several new ideas that make the method more efficient. The tool produces high-quality output and has a convenient web interface.

1 Introduction

Developing termination techniques for rewrite systems that can be automated has become an important research topic in the past few years. The dependency pair method of Arts and Giesl [3] is one of the most popular methods capable of automatically proving termination of first-order term rewrite systems (TRSs) that cannot be handled by traditional simplification orders. The dependency pair method has been implemented by Arts [1] and is part of the termination toolbox of CiME [5]. Tsukuba Termination Tool (T$_T$T in the sequel) is a new tool in which the dependency pair method takes center-stage. In the following sections we explain the features of T$_T$T, give some implementation details, report on some of the experiments that we performed, and provide a brief comparison with the tools described in [1,5]. We conclude with some ideas for future extensions of the tool. Familiarity with the dependency pair method will be helpful in the sequel.

2 Interface

We describe the features of T$_T$T by means of its web interface, displayed in Fig. 1.

TRS. The user inputs a TRS by typing the rules into the upper left text area or by uploading a file via the browse button. The input syntax is obtained by clicking the TRS link.

---

[*] http://www.score.is.tsukuba.ac.jp/ttt/

[**] Partially supported by the Grant-in-Aid for Scientific Research (C)(2) 13224006 of the Ministry of Education, Culture, Sports, Science and Technology of Japan.

R. Nieuwenhuis (Ed.): RTA 2003, LNCS 2706, pp. 311–320, 2003.
© Springer-Verlag Berlin Heidelberg 2003

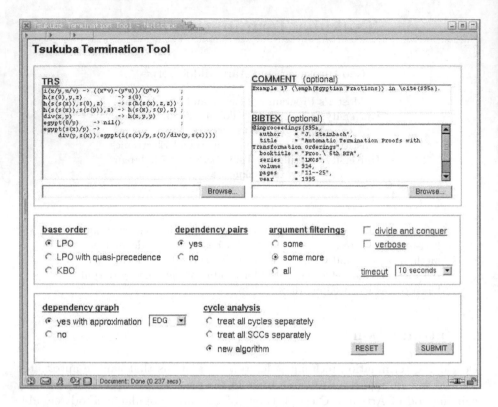

Fig. 1. A screen shot of the web interface of T$_T$T.

Comment and Bibtex. Anything typed into the upper right text area will appear as a footnote in the generated LaTeX code. This is useful to identify TRSs. LaTeX commands may be included. A typical example is a line like

```
Example 33 (\emph{Battle of Hydra and Hercules}) in \cite{D33}.
```

In order for this to work correctly, a bibtex entry for D33 should be supplied. This can be done by typing the entry into the appropriate text area or by uploading an appropriate bibtex file via the browse button.

Base Order. The current version of T$_T$T supports the following three base orders: LPO (lexicographic path order) with strict precedence, LPO with quasi-precedence, and KBO (Knuth-Bendix order) with strict precedence. The implementation of KBO is based on the polynomial-time algorithm of Korovin and Voronkov [11]. In Section 4 we comment on the implementation of LPO precedence constraint solving.

Dependency Pairs. Setting the dependency pair option activates the dependency pair technique of Arts and Giesl [2], which greatly enhances the termination proving power of the tool. The current version of T$_T$T supports the basic features of the dependency pair technique (argument filtering, dependency graph, cycle analysis) described below. Advanced features like narrowing, rewriting, and instantiation are not yet available. Also innermost termination analysis is not yet implemented.

Argument Filtering. A single function symbol f of arity n gives rise to $2^n + n$ different argument filterings:

- $f(x_1, \ldots, x_n) \to f(x_{i_1}, \ldots, x_{i_m})$ for all $1 \leqslant i_1 < \cdots < i_m \leqslant n$,
- $f(x_1, \ldots, x_n) \to x_i$ for all $1 \leqslant i \leqslant n$.

A moment's thought reveals that even for relatively small signatures, the number of possible argument filterings is huge. T$_T$T supports two simple heuristics to reduce this number.

- The *some* option considers for a function symbol f of arity n only the 'full' argument filtering $f(x_1, \ldots, x_n) \to f(x_1, \ldots, x_n)$ and the n 'collapsing' argument filterings $f(x_1, \ldots, x_n) \to x_i$ $(1 \leqslant i \leqslant n)$.
- The *some more* option considers the argument filtering $f(x_1, \ldots, x_n) \to f$ (when $n > 0$) in addition to the ones considered by the *some* option.

Dependency Graph. The dependency graph determines the ordering constraints that have to be solved in order to guarantee termination. Since the dependency graph is in general not computable, a decidable approximation has to be adopted. The current version of T$_T$T supplies two such approximations:

- EDG is the original estimation of Arts and Giesl [2, latter part of Section 2.4].
- EDG$*$ is an improved version of EDG described in [12, latter half of Section 6].

We refer to [9] for some statistics related to these two approximations.

Cycle Analysis. Once an approximation of the dependency graph has been computed, some kind of cycle analysis is required to generate the actual ordering constraints. T$_T$T offers three different methods:

1. The method described in [7] is to treat cycles in the approximated dependency graph separately. For every cycle $\mathcal{C}$, the dependency pairs in $\mathcal{C}$ and the rewrite rules of the given TRS must be weakly decreasing and at least one dependency pair in $\mathcal{C}$ must be strictly decreasing (with respect to some argument filtering and base order).
2. Another method, implemented in [1,5], is to treat all strongly connected components (SCCs) separately. For every SCC $\mathcal{S}$, the dependency pairs in $\mathcal{S}$ must be strictly decreasing and the rewrite rules of the given TRS must be weakly decreasing. Treating SCCs rather than cycles separately improves the efficiency at the expense of reduced termination proving power.
3. The third method available in T$_T$T combines the termination proving power of the cycle method with the efficiency of the SCC method. It is described in [9].

Divide and Conquer. The default option to find a suitable argument filtering that enables a group of ordering constraints to be solved by the selected base order is *enumeration*, which can be very inefficient, especially for larger TRSs where the number of suitable argument filterings is small. Setting the *divide and conquer* option computes all suitable argument filterings for each constraint separately and subsequently merges them to obtain the solutions of the full set of constraints. This can (greatly) reduce the execution time at the expense of an increased memory consumption. The divide and conquer option is described in detail in [9]. At the moment of writing it is only available in combination with LPO.

Verbose. Setting the verbose option generates more proof details. In combination with the divide and conquer option described above, the total number of argument filterings that enable the successive ordering constraints to be solved are displayed during the termination proving process.

Timeout. Every combination of options results in a finite search space for finding termination proofs. However, since it can take days to fully explore the search space, (the web version of) T$_T$T puts a strong upper bound on the permitted execution time.

3   Output

If T$_T$T succeeds in proving termination, it outputs a proof script which explains in considerable detail how termination was proved. This script is available in both HTML and LaTeX format. In the latter, the approximated dependency graph is visualized using the *dot* tool of the Graphviz toolkit [8]. Fig. 2 shows the generated output (with slightly readjusted vertical space to fit a single page) on Example 17 (*Egyptian Fractions*) in Steinbach [15] (in [15] the binary function symbol i is denoted by the infix operator ⋈). Here T$_T$T is used with the EDG approximation of the dependency graph, the SCC approach to cycle analysis, *some more* argument filterings, and without the verbose option. As can be seen from Fig. 2, we prefer to output LPO precedences compactly like div ≻ h ≻ s as opposed to div ≻ h; h ≻ s (or worse: div ≻ h; h ≻ s; div ≻ s). This is achieved by an obvious topological sorting algorithm.

4   Implementation

T$_T$T is written in Objective Caml [13], which is a strongly typed functional programming language extended with object-oriented features. We make use of the latter for the enumeration of argument filterings, but most of the code is written in a purely functional style. For instance, to compute SCCs and cycles in the approximated dependency graph the depth-first search algorithm described

Termination Proof Script[a]

We prove that the TRS $\mathcal{R}$ consisting of the 7 rewrite rules[b]

$$
\begin{aligned}
\mathsf{div}(x,y) &\rightarrow \mathsf{h}(x,y,y) \\
\mathsf{egypt}(0 \,/\, y) &\rightarrow \mathsf{nil} \\
\mathsf{egypt}(\mathsf{s}(x) \,/\, y) &\rightarrow \mathsf{div}(y,\mathsf{s}(x)) \cdot \mathsf{egypt}(\mathsf{i}(\mathsf{s}(x) \,/\, y, \mathsf{s}(0) \,/\, \mathsf{div}(y,\mathsf{s}(x)))) \\
\mathsf{h}(\mathsf{s}(0),y,z) &\rightarrow \mathsf{s}(0) \\
\mathsf{h}(\mathsf{s}(\mathsf{s}(x)),\mathsf{s}(0),z) &\rightarrow \mathsf{s}(\mathsf{h}(\mathsf{s}(x),z,z)) \\
\mathsf{h}(\mathsf{s}(\mathsf{s}(x)),\mathsf{s}(\mathsf{s}(y)),z) &\rightarrow \mathsf{h}(\mathsf{s}(x),\mathsf{s}(y),z) \\
\mathsf{i}(x \,/\, y, u \,/\, v) &\rightarrow ((x \times v) - (y \times u)) \,/\, (y \times v)
\end{aligned}
$$

is terminating. There are 6 dependency pairs:

$$
\begin{aligned}
1: &\qquad \mathsf{DIV}(x,y) \rightarrow \mathsf{H}(x,y,y) \\
2: &\qquad \mathsf{EGYPT}(\mathsf{s}(x) \,/\, y) \rightarrow \mathsf{DIV}(y,\mathsf{s}(x)) \\
3: &\qquad \mathsf{EGYPT}(\mathsf{s}(x) \,/\, y) \rightarrow \mathsf{EGYPT}(\mathsf{i}(\mathsf{s}(x) \,/\, y, \mathsf{s}(0) \,/\, \mathsf{div}(y,\mathsf{s}(x)))) \\
4: &\qquad \mathsf{EGYPT}(\mathsf{s}(x) \,/\, y) \rightarrow \mathsf{I}(\mathsf{s}(x) \,/\, y, \mathsf{s}(0) \,/\, \mathsf{div}(y,\mathsf{s}(x))) \\
5: &\qquad \mathsf{H}(\mathsf{s}(\mathsf{s}(x)),\mathsf{s}(0),z) \rightarrow \mathsf{H}(\mathsf{s}(x),z,z) \\
6: &\quad \mathsf{H}(\mathsf{s}(\mathsf{s}(x)),\mathsf{s}(\mathsf{s}(y)),z) \rightarrow \mathsf{H}(\mathsf{s}(x),\mathsf{s}(y),z)
\end{aligned}
$$

The EDG approximated dependency graph

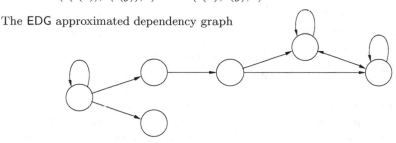

contains 2 SCCs: $\{5,6\}$, $\{3\}$.

- Consider the SCC $\{5,6\}$. By taking the AF $\cdot \mapsto []$ and LPO with precedence $\mathsf{div} \succ \mathsf{h} \succ \mathsf{s}$; $\mathsf{egypt} \succ \cdot$; $\mathsf{i} \succ \times$; $\mathsf{i} \succ -$; $\mathsf{i} \succ / \succ \mathsf{nil}$, the rules in $\mathcal{R}$ are weakly decreasing and the rules in $\{5,6\}$ are strictly decreasing.
- Consider the SCC $\{3\}$. By taking the AF $\times, \mathsf{i} \mapsto []$ and LPO with precedence $\mathsf{egypt} \succ \cdot$; $\mathsf{egypt} \succ \mathsf{div} \succ \mathsf{h} \succ \mathsf{s} \succ \mathsf{i} \succ \times$; $\mathsf{egypt} \succ \mathsf{nil}$; $\mathsf{i} \succ -$; $\mathsf{i} \succ /$, the rules in $\mathcal{R}$ are weakly decreasing and the rules in $\{3\}$ are strictly decreasing.

References

1. J. Steinbach. Automatic termination proofs with transformation orderings. In *Proc. 6th RTA*, volume 914 of *LNCS*, pages 11–25, 1995.

[a] http://www.score.is.tsukuba.ac.jp/ttt
[b] Example 17 (*Egyptian Fractions*) in [1].

Fig. 2. Output.

in [10] is used. Below we comment on the implementation of LPO precedence constraint solving.

The definition of LPO with strict precedence can be rendered as follows:

$$s >_{\text{lpo}} t \;=\; s >_{\text{lpo}}^{1} t \;\vee\; s >_{\text{lpo}}^{2} t$$

$$x >_{\text{lpo}}^{1} t \;=\; x >_{\text{lpo}}^{2} t \;=\; \bot$$

$$f(s_1,\ldots,s_n) >_{\text{lpo}}^{1} t \;=\; \exists i \, (s_i = t \vee s_i >_{\text{lpo}} t)$$

$$f(s_1,\ldots,s_n) >_{\text{lpo}}^{2} f(t_1,\ldots,t_n) \;=$$
$$(\forall i \; f(s_1,\ldots,s_n) >_{\text{lpo}} t_i) \wedge (s_1,\ldots,s_n) >_{\text{lpo}}^{\text{lex}} (t_1,\ldots,t_n)$$

$$f(s_1,\ldots,s_n) >_{\text{lpo}}^{2} g(t_1,\ldots,t_m) \;=\; (\forall i \; f(s_1,\ldots,s_n) >_{\text{lpo}} t_i) \wedge (f > g)$$

with $() \succ^{\text{lex}} () = \bot$ and $(s_1,\ldots,s_n) \succ^{\text{lex}} (t_1,\ldots,t_n) = s_1 \succ t_1 \vee (s_1 = t_1 \wedge (s_2,\ldots,s_n) \succ^{\text{lex}} (t_2,\ldots,t_n))$ for $n > 0$. Finding a precedence $>$ such that $s >_{\text{lpo}} t$ for concrete terms s and t is tantamount to solving the constraint that is obtained by unfolding the definition of $s >_{\text{lpo}} t$. The constraint involves the boolean connectives $\wedge$ and $\vee$, $\bot$, and atomic statements of the forms $f > g$ for function symbols f, g and $s = t$ for terms s, t. These symbols are interpreted as sets of precedences, as follows:

$$[\![C \vee D]\!] \;=\; \text{mins}\,([\![C]\!] \cup [\![D]\!]) \qquad\qquad [\![\bot]\!] \;=\; \varnothing$$
$$[\![C \wedge D]\!] \;=\; \text{mins}\,([\![C]\!] \otimes [\![D]\!]) \qquad\qquad [\![f > g]\!] \;=\; \{(f,g)\}$$

$$[\![s = t]\!] \;=\; \begin{cases} \{\varnothing\} & \text{if } s \text{ and } t \text{ are the same term} \\ \varnothing & \text{otherwise} \end{cases}$$

Here $O_1 \otimes O_2$ denotes the set of all strict orders $(>_1 \cup >_2)^{+}$ with $>_1 \in O_1$ and $>_2 \in O_2$. The purpose of the operator mins, which removes non-minimal precedences from its argument, is to avoid the computation of redundant precedences. For instance, one readily verifies that $[\![\mathsf{f(c)} >_{\text{lpo}} \mathsf{c}]\!] = \{\varnothing\}$ whereas without mins we would get $[\![\mathsf{f(c)} >_{\text{lpo}} \mathsf{c}]\!] = \{\varnothing, \{(\mathsf{f,c})\}\}$.

Now, by encoding the above definitions one almost immediately obtains an implementation of LPO precedence constraint solving. For instance, T_TT contains (a slightly optimized version of) the following OCaml code fragment:

```
let bottom   = empty
let disj c d = minimal (union c d)
let conj c d = minimal (combine c d)

let rec lex rel ss ts =
  match ss, ts with
  | s :: ss', t :: ts' when s = t -> lex rel ss' ts'
  | s :: ss', t :: ts'            -> rel s t

let rec lpo s t = disj (lpo1 s t) (lpo2 s t)
and lpo1 s t =
```

```
match s with
  | V _        -> bottom
  | F (f, ss) -> exists (fun s' -> disj (equal s' t) (lpo s' t)) ss
and lpo2 s t =
  match s, t with
  | F (f, ss), F (g, ts) when f = g
      -> conj ((for_all (fun t' -> lpo s t')) ts) (lex lpo ss ts)
  | F (f, ss), F (g, ts)
      -> conj ((for_all (fun t' -> lpo s t')) ts) (prec f g)
  | _ -> bottom
```

The point we want to emphasize is that other precedence-based syntactic orderings follow the same scenario and can thus be added very easily to T_T.

5   Experimental Results

We tested the various options of T_T on numerous examples. Here we consider 14 examples from the literature. Our findings are summarized in Tables 1 and 2. All experiments were performed on a notebook PC with an 800 MHz Pentium III CPU and 128 MB memory. The numbers in the two tables denote execution time in seconds. *Italics* indicate that T_T could not prove termination while fully exploring the search space implied by the options within the given time. Question marks denote a timeout of <u>one hour</u>. For the experiments in Table 1 we used LPO with strict precedence as base order, EDG as dependency graph approximation, and enumeration of argument filterings.

The three question marks for [6, Example 11] are explained by the fact that the dependency graph admits 4095 cycles (but only 1 strongly connected com-

Table 1. Argument filtering heuristics in combination with cycle analysis methods.

argument filterings cycle analysis	some			some more			all		
	cycle	scc	new	cycle	scc	new	cycle	scc	new
[3, Example 3.3]	0.02	*0.08*	0.02	0.14	*0.81*	0.13	5.72	5.68	5.78
[3, Example 3.4]	*0.01*	*0.01*	*0.01*	0.02	*0.02*	0.02	0.09	0.06	0.08
[3, Example 3.9]	0.28	*0.23*	0.13	1.94	*2.32*	0.86	9.79	4.38	4.48
[3, Example 3.11]	14.29	*9.35*	5.79	152.45	*209.10*	57.51	?	?	?
[3, Example 3.15]	*0.00*	*0.00*	*0.00*	*0.00*	*0.00*	*0.00*	*0.01*	*0.01*	*0.01*
[3, Example 3.38]	*0.01*	*0.02*	*0.01*	*0.05*	*0.05*	*0.05*	4.38	0.87	0.91
[3, Example 3.44]	*0.00*	*0.01*	*0.01*	0.01	0.00	0.01	0.00	0.00	0.01
[4, Example 6]	*0.06*	*0.05*	*0.05*	0.89	0.60	0.26	0.82	*2.97*	0.24
[6, Example 11]	?	0.08	0.08	?	0.08	0.08	?	16.46	15.21
[6, Example 33]	*0.05*	*0.05*	*0.05*	*0.13*	*0.13*	*0.12*	*0.48*	*0.44*	*0.48*
[15, Example 17]	*1.77*	*1.75*	*1.63*	4.41	4.39	4.19	1904.79	805.92	1045.75
[16, Example 4.27]	*0.00*	*0.01*	*0.01*	*0.01*	*0.01*	*0.01*	*0.03*	*0.04*	*0.03*
[16, Example 4.60]	*0.17*	*0.17*	*0.16*	0.23	0.13	0.14	41.19	21.50	21.42
[17, Example 58]	*0.00*	*0.00*	*0.00*	*0.00*	*0.00*	*0.00*	0.01	0.01	0.01

Table 2. Divide and conquer, KBO, and other tools.

	(1)	(2)	(3)	(4)	(5)	LPO	KBO	ARTS	CiME
[3, Example 3.3]	0.10	3.30	492.76	269.03	?	0.00	0.00	58.92	?
[3, Example 3.4]	0.01	0.02	0.08	3.13	25.51	0.00	0.00	2.76	0.19
[3, Example 3.9]	0.25	3.43	340.99	1183.73	?	0.00	0.00	391.18	?
[3, Example 3.11]	0.47	4.42	430.72	2.25	33.42	0.00	0.01	?	?
[3, Example 3.15]	0.01	0.00	0.01	0.24	0.24	0.00	0.03	?	0.08
[3, Example 3.38]	0.01	0.05	4.50	0.02	?	0.00	0.00	613.32	0.19
[3, Example 3.44]	0.00	0.04	0.04	6.55	10.16	0.00	0.87	0.60	0.02
[4, Example 6]	0.02	3.08	80.65	0.09	1783.14	0.00	0.00	?	440.39
[6, Example 11]	2.08	92.92	?	0.39	5.52	0.00	0.00	4.43	61.36
[6, Example 33]	0.02	0.12	0.89	0.18	593.26	0.00	0.00	?	0.78
[15, Example 17]	0.66	57.85	?	67.36	?	0.00	0.00	?	15.80
[16, Example 4.27]	0.01	0.05	0.29	202.65	396.36	0.00	5.17	?	1485.27
[16, Example 4.60]	0.04	0.36	23.14	0.28	387.01	0.00	0.00	6.44	1.74
[17, Example 58]	0.00	0.00	0.02	0.43	0.45	0.00	0.06	1.35	0.06

ponent, consisting of all 12 dependency pairs). The largest example in the collection, Example 3.11 (*Quicksort*) in [3], clearly reveals the benefits of the argument filtering heuristics as well as the new approach to cycle analysis.

From columns (1), (2), and (3) in Table 2 we infer that the divide and conquer option has an even bigger impact on this example, especially if one keeps in mind that all suitable argument filterings are computed. Here we used the new algorithm for cycle analysis, LPO with strict precedence as base order, EDG as dependency graph approximation, and *some* (1), *some more* (2), and *all* (3) argument filterings. The question marks in column (3) are largely explained by the large memory demands of the divide and conquer option. We will address this issue in the near future. Note that [6, Example 11] is the only example in the collection which can be directly handled by LPO.

In columns (4) and (5) we used KBO as base order and *some* respectively *some more* argument filterings (as well as the new algorithm for cycle analysis and EDG as dependency graph approximation). According to column (5) TᴛT requires 593.26 seconds to prove the termination of Example 33 (*Battle of Hydra and Hercules*) in [6]. This example nicely illustrates that the termination proving power of KBO, which is considered not to be very large, is increased significantly in combination with dependency pairs. The ARTS and CiME columns are described in the next section.

6   Comparison

TᴛT is not the first tool that implements the dependency pair method. The implementation of Arts [1] offers more refinements (like narrowing and termination via innermost termination) of the dependency pair method and, via its graphical user interface, allows the user to choose a particular argument filtering (separately for each group of ordering constraints). In contrast to the latter, T_TT offers improved algorithms for the automatic search for suitable argument filterings. For the ARTS column in Table 2 we used the only available automatic strategy in the distribution, which is (partly) described in [1, Section 3], and not guaranteed to terminate. Most of the successful termination proofs it generates use the refinements mentioned above.

The implementation of the dependency pair method in $CiME$ [5] uses weakly monotone polynomial interpretations as base order (which removes the need for argument filterings) and the SCC method for cycle analysis in the EDG approximated dependency graph. The search for a suitable polynomial interpretation can be restricted by specifying a certain class of simple polynomials as well as indicating a restricted range for the coefficients. Needless to say, the use of polynomial interpretations considerably restricts the class of terminating TRSs that can be proved terminating (automatically or otherwise). On the other hand, $CiME$ admits AC operators and supports powerful modularity criteria based on the dependency pair method (described in [18,19]), two extensions which are not (yet) available in T_TT. The data in the $CiME$ column was obtained by using the default options to restrict the search for polynomial interpretations: simple-mixed polynomials with coefficients in the range 0–6.

7   Future Extensions

In the near future we plan to add an option that makes T_TT search for a termination proof using everything in its arsenal. The challenge here is to develop a strategy that finds proofs quickly without compromising the ability to find proofs at all.

Other future extensions include adding more base orders, incorporating the refinements of the dependency pair method mentioned in the first paragraph of Section 6, and implementing the powerful modularity criteria based on the dependency pair method described in [14] and [19]. We also plan to add techniques for AC-termination. In Section 5 we already mentioned the reduction of the large memory requirements of the divide and conquer option as an important topic for future research.

Another interesting idea is to generate output that allows for an independent check of the termination proof. We plan to develop some kind of formal language in which all kinds of termination proofs can be conveniently expressed. This development may lead to cooperating rather than competing termination provers.

Acknowledgments

We thank the anonymous referees for several suggestions to improve the presentation.

References

1. T. Arts. System description: The dependency pair method. In *Proc. 11th RTA*, volume 1833 of *LNCS*, pages 261–264, 2001.
2. T. Arts and J. Giesl. Termination of term rewriting using dependency pairs. *Theoretical Computer Science*, 236:133–178, 2000.
3. T. Arts and J. Giesl. A collection of examples for termination of term rewriting using dependency pairs. Technical Report AIB-2001-09, RWTH Aachen, 2001. Available at http://aib.informatik.rwth-aachen.de/.
4. C. Borralleras, M. Ferreira, and A. Rubio. Complete monotonic semantic path orderings. In *Proc. 17th CADE*, volume 1831 of *LNAI*, pages 346–364, 2000.
5. E. Contejean, C. Marché, B. Monate, and X. Urbain. C*i*ME version 2, 2000. Available at http://cime.lri.fr/.
6. N. Dershowitz. 33 Examples of termination. In *French Spring School of Theoretical Computer Science*, volume 909 of *LNCS*, pages 16–26, 1995.
7. J. Giesl, T. Arts, and E. Ohlebusch. Modular termination proofs for rewriting using dependency pairs. *Journal of Symbolic Computation*, 34(1):21–58, 2002.
8. http://www.research.att.com/sw/tools/graphviz/.
9. N. Hirokawa and A. Middeldorp. Automating the dependency pair method. In *Proc. 19th CADE*, LNAI, 2003. To appear.
10. D.J. King and J. Launchbury. Structuring depth-first search algorithms in Haskell. In *Proc. 22nd POPL*, pages 344–354, 1995.
11. K. Korovin and A. Voronkov. Verifying orientability of rewrite rules using the Knuth-Bendix order. In *Proc. 12th RTA*, volume 2051 of *LNCS*, pages 137–153, 2001.
12. A. Middeldorp. Approximations for strategies and termination. In *Proc. 2nd WRS*, volume 70(6) of *Electronic Notes in Theoretical Computer Science*, 2002.
13. http://caml.inria.fr/ocaml/.
14. E. Ohlebusch. Hierarchical termination revisited. *Information Processing Letters*, 84(4):207–214, 2002.
15. J. Steinbach. Automatic termination proofs with transformation orderings. In *Proc. 6th RTA*, volume 914 of *LNCS*, pages 11–25, 1995.
16. J. Steinbach and U. Kühler. Check your ordering – termination proofs and open problems. Technical Report SR-90-25, Universität Kaiserslautern, 1990.
17. Joachim Steinbach. Simplification orderings: History of results. *Fundamenta Informaticae*, 24:47–87, 1995.
18. X. Urbain. Automated incremental termination proofs for hierarchically defined term rewriting systems. In *Proc. IJCAR*, volume 2083 of *LNAI*, pages 485–498, 2001.
19. X. Urbain. Modular & incremental automated termination proofs. *Journal of Automated Reasoning*, 2003. To appear.

Liveness in Rewriting

Jürgen Giesl[1] and Hans Zantema[2]

[1] LuFG Informatik II, RWTH Aachen, Ahornstr. 55, 52074 Aachen, Germany,
giesl@informatik.rwth-aachen.de
[2] Department of Computer Science, TU Eindhoven, P.O. Box 513,
5600 MB Eindhoven, The Netherlands, h.zantema@tue.nl

Abstract. In this paper, we show how the problem of verifying liveness properties is related to termination of term rewrite systems (TRSs). We formalize liveness in the framework of rewriting and present a sound and complete transformation to transform particular liveness problems into TRSs. Then the transformed TRS terminates if and only if the original liveness property holds. This shows that liveness and termination are essentially equivalent. To apply our approach in practice, we introduce a simpler sound transformation which only satisfies the 'only if'-part. By refining existing techniques for proving termination of TRSs we show how liveness properties can be verified automatically. As examples, we prove a liveness property of a waiting line protocol for a network of processes and a liveness property of a protocol on a ring of processes.

1 Introduction

Usually, *liveness* is roughly defined as: *"something will eventually happen"* [1] and it is often remarked that *"termination is a particular case of liveness"*. In this paper we present liveness in the general but precise setting of abstract reduction and TRSs and we study the relationship between liveness and termination. While classically, TRSs are applied to model evaluation in programming languages, we use TRSs to study liveness questions which are of high importance in practice (e.g., in protocol verification for distributed processes). In particular, we show how to verify liveness properties by existing termination techniques for TRSs.

In Sect. 2 we define a suitable notion of liveness to express eventuality properties using abstract reduction. Sect. 3 specializes this notion to the framework of term rewriting. In Sect. 4 we investigate the connection between a particular kind of liveness and termination, and present a sound and complete transformation which allows us to express liveness problems as termination problems of ordinary TRSs. Now techniques for proving termination of TRSs can also be used to infer liveness properties. To apply this approach in practice, based on our preceding results we present a sound (but incomplete) technique to perform termination proofs for liveness properties in Sect. 5, which is significantly easier to mechanize. In contrast to methods like model checking, our technique does not require finite state space. Our approach differs from other applications of term rewriting techniques to parameterized systems or infinite state spaces,

R. Nieuwenhuis (Ed.): RTA 2003, LNCS 2706, pp. 321–336, 2003.

where the emphasis is on verification of other properties like reachability [4]. We demonstrate our approach on two case studies of network protocols.

2   Liveness in Abstract Reduction

In this section we give a formal definition of liveness using the framework of abstract reduction. We assume a set S of states and a notion of computation that can be expressed by a binary relation $\to \subseteq S \times S$. So "$t \to u$" means that a computation step from t to u is possible. A *computation sequence* or *reduction* is defined to be a finite sequence $t_1, t_2, \ldots, t_n$ or an infinite sequence $t_1, t_2, t_3, \ldots$ with $t_i \to t_{i+1}$. We write $\to^*$ for the reflexive transitive closure of $\to$, i.e., $\to^*$ represents zero or more computation steps.

To define liveness we assume a set $G \subseteq S$ of 'good' states and a set $I \subseteq S$ of initial states. A reduction is *maximal* if it is either infinite or if its last element is in the set of *normal forms* $\mathsf{NF} = \{t \in S \mid \neg \exists u : t \to u\}$. The liveness property $\mathsf{Live}(I, \to, G)$ holds if every maximal reduction starting in I contains an element of G. Thus, our notion of liveness describes eventuality properties (i.e., it does not capture properties like starvation freedom which are related to fairness).

Definition 1 (Liveness). *Let S be a set of states, $\to \subseteq S \times S$, and $G, I \subseteq S$. Let "$t_1, t_2, t_3, \ldots$" denote an infinite sequence of states. Then $\mathsf{Live}(I, \to, G)$ holds iff*

1. $\forall t_1, t_2, t_3, \ldots : (t_1 \in I \land \forall i : t_i \to t_{i+1}) \Rightarrow \exists i : t_i \in G$, *and*
2. $\forall t_1, t_2, \ldots, t_n : (t_1 \in I \land t_n \in \mathsf{NF} \land \forall i : t_i \to t_{i+1}) \Rightarrow \exists i : t_i \in G$.

For example, *termination* (or *strong normalization* $\mathsf{SN}(I, \to)$) is a special liveness property describing the non-existence of infinite reductions, i.e.,

$$\mathsf{SN}(I, \to) = \neg(\exists t_1, t_2, t_3, \ldots : t_1 \in I \land \forall i : t_i \to t_{i+1}).$$

Theorem 2. *The property $\mathsf{SN}(I, \to)$ holds if and only if $\mathsf{Live}(I, \to, \mathsf{NF})$ holds.*

Proof. For the 'if'-part, if $\mathsf{SN}(I, \to)$ does not hold, then there is an infinite reduction $t_1 \to t_2 \to \cdots$ with $t_1 \in I$. Due to NF's definition, this infinite reduction does not contain elements of NF, contradicting Property 1 in Def. 1.

Conversely, if $\mathsf{SN}(I, \to)$ holds, then Property 1 in the definition of $\mathsf{Live}(I, \to, \mathsf{NF})$ holds trivially. Property 2 also holds, since $G = \mathsf{NF}$. $\square$

Thm. 2 states that termination is a special case of liveness. The next theorem proves a kind of converse. For that purpose, we restrict the computation relation $\to$ such that it may only proceed if the current state is not in G.

Definition 3 ($\to_G$). *Let S, $\to$, G be as in Def. 1. Then $\to_G \subseteq S \times S$ is the relation where $t \to_G u$ holds if and only if $t \to u$ and $t \notin G$.*

Now we show that $\mathsf{Live}(I, \to, G)$ is equivalent to $\mathsf{SN}(I, \to_G)$. The 'only if'-part holds without any further conditions. However, for the 'if'-part we have to demand that G contains all normal forms $\mathsf{NF}(I)$ reachable from I, where $\mathsf{NF}(I) = \{u \in \mathsf{NF} \mid \exists t \in I : t \to^* u\}$. Otherwise, if there is a terminating sequence $t_1 \to \ldots \to t_n$ with all $t_i \notin G$, we might have $\mathsf{SN}(I, \to_G)$ but not $\mathsf{Live}(I, \to, G)$.

Theorem 4. *Let* $\mathsf{NF}(I) \subseteq G$. *Then* $\mathsf{Live}(I, \to, G)$ *holds iff* $\mathsf{SN}(I, \to_G)$ *holds.*

Proof. For the 'if'-part assume $\mathsf{SN}(I, \to_G)$. Property 2 of Def. 1 holds since $\mathsf{NF}(I) \subseteq G$. If Property 1 does not hold then there is an infinite reduction without elements of G starting in I, contradicting $\mathsf{SN}(I, \to_G)$.

Conversely assume that $\mathsf{Live}(I, \to, G)$ holds and that $\mathsf{SN}(I, \to_G)$ does not hold. Then there is an infinite sequence $t_1, t_2, \ldots$ with $t_1 \in I \wedge \forall i : t_i \to_G t_{i+1}$. Hence, $t_i \notin G$ and $t_i \to t_{i+1}$ for all i, contradicting Property 1 in Def. 1. $\qquad\square$

Thm. 4 allows us to verify actual liveness properties: if $\mathsf{NF}(I) \subseteq G$, then one can instead verify termination of $\to_G$. If $\mathsf{NF}(I) \not\subseteq G$, then $\mathsf{SN}(I, \to_G)$ still implies the liveness property for all infinite computations. In Sect. 4 and 5 we show how techniques to prove termination of TRSs can be used for termination of $\to_G$.

3   Liveness in Term Rewriting

Now we focus on liveness in rewriting, i.e., we study the property $\mathsf{Live}(I, \to_R, G)$ where $\to_R$ is the rewrite relation corresponding to a TRS R. For an introduction to term rewriting, the reader is referred to [3], for example.

Let Σ be a signature containing a constant and let $\mathcal{V}$ be a set of variables. We write $\mathcal{T}(\Sigma, \mathcal{V})$ for the set of terms over Σ and $\mathcal{V}$ and $\mathcal{T}(\Sigma)$ is the set of ground terms. For a term t, $\mathcal{V}(t)$ and $\Sigma(t)$ denote the variables and function symbols occurring in t. Now $\mathcal{T}(\Sigma, \mathcal{V})$ represents computation states and $G \subseteq \mathcal{T}(\Sigma, \mathcal{V})$.

By Thm. 4, $\mathsf{Live}(I, \to, G)$ is equivalent to $\mathsf{SN}(I, \to_G)$, if $\mathsf{NF}(I) \subseteq G$. To verify liveness, we want to prove $\mathsf{SN}(I, \to_G)$ by approaches for termination proofs of ordinary TRSs. However, depending on the form of G, different techniques are required. In the remainder we restrict ourselves to sets G of the following form:

$$G = \{t \mid t \text{ does not contain an instance of } p\} \qquad \text{for some term } p.$$

In other words, G contains all terms which cannot be written as $C[p\sigma]$ for any context C and substitution σ. As before, $t \to_G u$ holds iff $t \to_R u$ and $t \notin G$. So a term t may be reduced whenever it contains an instance of the term p.

A typical example of a liveness property is that eventually all processes requesting a resource are granted access to the resource (see Sect. 5.3). If a process waiting for the resource is represented by the unary function symbol old and if terms are used to denote the state of the whole network, then we would define $G = \{t \mid t \text{ does not contain an instance of } \mathsf{old}(x)\}$. Now $\mathsf{Live}(I, \to_R, G)$ means that eventually one reaches a term without the symbol old.

However, for arbitrary terms and TRSs, the notion $\to_G$ is not very useful: if there is a symbol f of arity > 1 or if p contains a variable x (i.e., if p can be written as $C[x]$ for some context C), then termination of $\to_G$ implies termination of the full rewrite relation $\to_R$. The reason is that any infinite reduction $t_1 \to_R t_2 \to_R \cdots$ gives rise to an infinite reduction $f(t_1, p, \ldots) \to_R f(t_2, p, \ldots) \to_R \cdots$ or $C[t_1] \to_R C[t_2] \to_R \cdots$ where in both cases none of the terms is in G. Therefore we concentrate on the particular case of *top rewrite systems* in which there is a designated symbol top. (These TRSs can be regarded as special forms of *typed rewrite systems* [11].)

Definition 5 (Top Rewrite System). *Let Σ be a signature and let* top $\notin \Sigma$ *be a new unary function symbol. A term $t \in \mathcal{T}(\Sigma \cup \{\text{top}\}, \mathcal{V})$ is a top term if its root is* top *and* top *does not occur below the root. Let $\mathcal{T}_{\text{top}}$ denote the set of all ground top terms. A TRS R over the signature $\Sigma \cup \{\text{top}\}$ is a top rewrite system iff for all rules $l \to r \in R$ either*

- *l and r are top terms (in this case, we speak of a* top rule*) or*
- *l and r do not contain the symbol* top *(then we have a* non-top rule*)*

Top rewrite systems typically suffice to model networks of processes, since the whole network is represented by a top term [6]. Clearly, in top rewrite systems, top terms can only be reduced to top terms again. In such systems we consider liveness properties $\mathsf{Live}(\mathcal{T}_{\text{top}}, \to_R, G)$. So we want to prove that every maximal reduction of ground top terms contains a term without an instance of p.

Example 6 (Simple liveness example). Consider the following two-rule TRS R.

$$\text{top(c)} \to \text{top(c)} \qquad\qquad \text{f}(x) \to x$$

Clearly, R is not terminating and we even have infinite reductions within $\mathcal{T}_{\text{top}}$:

$$\text{top(f(f(c)))} \to_R \text{top(f(c))} \to_R \text{top(c)} \to_R \text{top(c)} \to_R \cdots$$

However, in every reduction one eventually reaches a term without f. Hence, if $p = \text{f}(x)$, then the liveness property is fulfilled for all ground top terms. Note that for $\Sigma = \{\text{c}, \text{f}\}$, we have $\mathsf{NF}(\mathcal{T}_{\text{top}}) = \varnothing$ and thus, $\mathsf{NF}(\mathcal{T}_{\text{top}}) \subseteq G$. Hence, by Thm. 4 it is sufficient to verify that $\to_G$ is terminating on $\mathcal{T}_{\text{top}}$. Indeed, the above reduction is not possible with $\to_G$, since top(c) is a normal form w.r.t. $\to_G$.

4   Liveness and Termination

In this section we investigate the correspondence between liveness and termination in the framework of term rewriting. As in the previous section, we consider liveness properties $\mathsf{Live}(\mathcal{T}_{\text{top}}, \to_R, G)$ for top rewrite systems R where G consists of those terms that do not contain instances of some subterm p. Provided that $\mathsf{NF}(\mathcal{T}_{\text{top}}) \subseteq G$, by Thm. 4 the liveness property is equivalent to $\mathsf{SN}(\mathcal{T}_{\text{top}}, \to_G)$.

Our aim is to prove termination of $\to_G$ on $\mathcal{T}_{\text{top}}$ by means of termination of TRSs. In this way one can use all existing techniques for termination proofs of term rewrite systems (including future developments) in order to prove liveness properties. A first step into this direction was taken in [6], where the termination proof technique of *dependency pairs* was used to verify certain liveness properties of telecommunication processes. However, now our aim is to develop an approach to connect liveness and termination in general.

Given a TRS R and a term p, we define a TRS $L(R, p)$ such that $L(R, p)$ terminates (on all terms) if and only if $\mathsf{SN}(\mathcal{T}_{\text{top}}, \to_G)$. A transformation where the 'only if'-direction holds is called *sound* and if the 'if'-direction holds, it is called *complete*. The existence of the sound and complete transformation $L(R, p)$ shows that for rewrite relations, liveness and termination are essentially equivalent.

The construction of $L(R, p)$ is motivated by an existing transformation [7,8] which was developed for a completely different purpose (termination of context-sensitive rewriting). We introduce a number of new function symbols resulting in an extended signature Σ_G. Here, $\mathsf{proper}(t)$ checks whether t is a ground term over the original signature Σ (Lemma 9) and $\mathsf{match}(p, t)$ checks in addition whether p matches t (Lemma 10). In this case, $\mathsf{proper}(t)$ and $\mathsf{match}(p, t)$ reduce to $\mathsf{ok}(t)$. To ease the formulation of the match-rules, we restrict ourselves to *linear* terms p, i.e., a variable occurs at most once in p. Moreover, for every variable x in p we introduce a fresh constant denoted by the corresponding upper-case letter X. We write $\bar{p}$ for the ground term obtained by replacing every variable in p by its corresponding fresh constant and in this way, it suffices to handle ground terms $\bar{p}$ in the match-rules. The new symbol check investigates whether its argument is a ground term over Σ which contains an instance of p (Lemma 11). In this case, $\mathsf{check}(t)$ reduces to $\mathsf{found}(t)$ and to find the instance of p, check may be propagated downwards through the term until one reaches the instance of p.

Finally, $\mathsf{active}(t)$ denotes that t may be reduced, since it contains an instance of p. Therefore, active may be propagated downwards to any desired redex of the term. After the reduction step, active is replaced by mark which is then propagated upwards to the top of the term. Now one checks whether the resulting term still contains an instance of p and none of the newly introduced function symbols. To this end, mark is replaced by check. If an instance of p is found, check is turned into found and found is propagated to the top of the term where it is replaced by active again. The TRS $L(R, p)$ has been designed in such a way that infinite reductions are only possible if this process is repeated infinitely often and Lemmata 12–14 investigate $L(R, p)$'s behavior formally.

Definition 7 ($L(R, p)$). *Let R be a top rewrite system over $\Sigma \cup \{\mathsf{top}\}$ with $\mathsf{top} \notin \Sigma$ and let $p \in T(\Sigma, V)$ be linear. The TRS $L(R, p)$ over the signature $\Sigma_G = \Sigma \cup \{\mathsf{top}, \mathsf{match}, \mathsf{active}, \mathsf{mark}, \mathsf{check}, \mathsf{proper}, \mathsf{start}, \mathsf{found}, \mathsf{ok}\} \cup \{X \mid x \in V(p)\}$ consists of the following rules for all non-top rules $l \to r \in R$, all top rules $\mathsf{top}(t) \to \mathsf{top}(u) \in R$, all $f \in \Sigma$ of arity $n > 0$ and $1 \le i \le n$, and all constants $c \in \Sigma_G$:*

$$\mathsf{active}(l) \to \mathsf{mark}(r)$$
$$\mathsf{top}(\mathsf{active}(t)) \to \mathsf{top}(\mathsf{mark}(u))$$
$$\mathsf{top}(\mathsf{mark}(x)) \to \mathsf{top}(\mathsf{check}(x)) \qquad (1)$$
$$\mathsf{check}(f(x_1, .., x_n)) \to f(\mathsf{proper}(x_1), .., \mathsf{check}(x_i), .., \mathsf{proper}(x_n))$$
$$\mathsf{check}(x) \to \mathsf{start}(\mathsf{match}(\bar{p}, x))$$
$$\mathsf{match}(f(x_1, .., x_n), f(y_1, .., y_n)) \to f(\mathsf{match}(x_1, y_1), .., \mathsf{match}(x_n, y_n)), \; \text{if } f \in \Sigma(p)$$
$$\mathsf{match}(c, c) \to \mathsf{ok}(c), \qquad \text{if } c \in \Sigma(p)$$
$$\mathsf{match}(c, x) \to \mathsf{proper}(x), \qquad \text{if } c \notin \Sigma \text{ and } c \in \Sigma(\bar{p})$$
$$\mathsf{proper}(c) \to \mathsf{ok}(c), \qquad \text{if } c \in \Sigma$$
$$\mathsf{proper}(f(x_1, \ldots, x_n)) \to f(\mathsf{proper}(x_1), \ldots, \mathsf{proper}(x_n))$$
$$f(\mathsf{ok}(x_1), \ldots, \mathsf{ok}(x_n)) \to \mathsf{ok}(f(x_1, \ldots, x_n))$$
$$\mathsf{start}(\mathsf{ok}(x)) \to \mathsf{found}(x)$$
$$f(\mathsf{ok}(x_1), .., \mathsf{found}(x_i), .., \mathsf{ok}(x_n)) \to \mathsf{found}(f(x_1, .., x_n))$$

$$\text{top}(\text{found}(x)) \rightarrow \text{top}(\text{active}(x)) \tag{2}$$
$$\text{active}(f(x_1,\dots,x_i,\dots,x_n)) \rightarrow f(x_1,\dots,\text{active}(x_i),\dots,x_n)$$
$$f(x_1,\dots,\text{mark}(x_i),\dots,x_n) \rightarrow \text{mark}(f(x_1,\dots,x_n))$$

Example 8 (Transformation of simple liveness example). Recall the TRS from Ex. 6 again. Here, the transformation yields the following TRS $L(R,p)$.

$$\text{active}(f(x)) \rightarrow \text{mark}(x) \qquad\qquad \text{proper}(c) \rightarrow \text{ok}(c)$$
$$\text{top}(\text{active}(c)) \rightarrow \text{top}(\text{mark}(c)) \qquad\qquad \text{proper}(f(x)) \rightarrow f(\text{proper}(x))$$
$$\text{top}(\text{mark}(x)) \rightarrow \text{top}(\text{check}(x)) \qquad\qquad f(\text{ok}(x)) \rightarrow \text{ok}(f(x))$$
$$\text{check}(f(x)) \rightarrow f(\text{check}(x)) \qquad\qquad \text{start}(\text{ok}(x)) \rightarrow \text{found}(x)$$
$$\text{check}(x) \rightarrow \text{start}(\text{match}(f(X),x)) \qquad f(\text{found}(x)) \rightarrow \text{found}(f(x))$$
$$\text{match}(f(x),f(y)) \rightarrow f(\text{match}(x,y)) \qquad \text{top}(\text{found}(x)) \rightarrow \text{top}(\text{active}(x))$$
$$\text{match}(X,x) \rightarrow \text{proper}(x) \qquad\qquad \text{active}(f(x)) \rightarrow f(\text{active}(x))$$
$$f(\text{mark}(x)) \rightarrow \text{mark}(f(x))$$

Note that it is really necessary to introduce the symbol proper and to check whether the whole term does not contain any new symbols from $\Sigma_G \setminus \Sigma$. If the proper-rules were removed, all remaining proper-terms were replaced by their arguments, and in $f(\text{ok}(x_1),\dots,\text{found}(x_i),\dots,\text{ok}(x_n)) \rightarrow \text{found}(f(x_1,\dots,x_n))$, the terms $\text{ok}(x_i)$ were replaced by x_i, then the transformation would not be complete any more. As a counterexample, regard $\Sigma = \{a, b, f\}$ and the TRS

$$\text{top}(f(b, x, y)) \rightarrow \text{top}(f(y, y, y))$$
$$\text{top}(f(x, y, z)) \rightarrow \text{top}(f(b, b, b))$$
$$\text{top}(a) \rightarrow \text{top}(b)$$

and let $p = a$. The TRS satisfies the liveness property since for any ground top term, after at most two steps one reaches a term without a (one obtains either $\text{top}(b)$ or $\text{top}(f(b, b, b))$). However, with the modified transformation we would get the following non-terminating cyclic reduction where u is the term $\text{found}(b)$:

$$\text{top}(\text{mark}(f(u, u, u))) \qquad \rightarrow \text{top}(\text{check}(f(u, u, u))) \qquad \rightarrow$$
$$\text{top}(f(u, \text{check}(u), u)) \qquad \rightarrow \text{top}(\text{found}(f(b, \text{check}(u), u))) \rightarrow$$
$$\text{top}(\text{active}(f(b, \text{check}(u), u))) \rightarrow \text{top}(\text{mark}(f(u, u, u))) \qquad\qquad \rightarrow \dots$$

To prove soundness and completeness of our transformation, we need several auxiliary lemmata about reductions with $L(R,p)$. The first lemma states that proper really checks whether its argument does not contain symbols from $\Sigma_G \setminus \Sigma$.

Lemma 9 (Reducing proper). *For $t \in \mathcal{T}(\Sigma_G)$ we have* $\text{proper}(t) \rightarrow^+_{L(R,p)} \text{ok}(u)$ *if and only if $t, u \in \mathcal{T}(\Sigma)$ and $t = u$.*

Proof. The proof is identical to the one in [7, Lemma 2] and [8]. $\qquad\qquad \square$

Now we show that $\text{match}(\overline{p}, t)$ checks whether p matches t and $t \in \mathcal{T}(\Sigma)$.

Lemma 10 (Reducing match). *Let $p \in T(\Sigma, \mathcal{V})$, let $q \in T(\Sigma(p), \mathcal{V})$ be linear, and let $t \in T(\Sigma_G)$. We have $\mathsf{match}(\overline{q}, t) \to^+_{L(R,p)} \mathsf{ok}(u)$ iff $t = u \in T(\Sigma)$ and $q\sigma = t$ for some σ.*

Proof. The 'if'-direction is an easy induction on the structure of the term t, see [9]. The 'only if'-direction is proved by induction on the length of the reduction. If the first reduction step is in t, then $\mathsf{match}(\overline{q}, t) \to_{L(R,p)} \mathsf{match}(\overline{q}, t') \to^+_{L(R,p)} \mathsf{ok}(u)$ for a term t' with $t \to_{L(R,p)} t'$. The induction hypothesis states $t' = u \in T(\Sigma)$ and $q\sigma = t'$. Note that $t' \in T(\Sigma)$ implies $t = t'$ which proves the lemma.

Otherwise, the first reduction step is on the root position (since $\overline{q}$ is in normal form). If q is a variable, then q obviously matches t and we obtain $\mathsf{match}(\overline{q}, t) \to_{L(R,p)} \mathsf{proper}(t) \to^+_{L(R,p)} \mathsf{ok}(u)$ and $t = u \in T(\Sigma)$ by Lemma 9. If q is a constant c, then a root reduction is only possible if $t = c$. We obtain $\mathsf{match}(\overline{q}, t) = \mathsf{match}(\overline{q}, c) \to_{L(R,p)} \mathsf{ok}(c)$. So in this case the lemma also holds.

Finally, if $q = f(q_1, \ldots, q_n)$, for a root reduction we have $t = f(t_1, \ldots, t_n)$. Then $\mathsf{match}(\overline{q}, t) = \mathsf{match}(f(\overline{q_1}, \ldots, \overline{q_n}), f(t_1, \ldots, t_n)) = f(\mathsf{match}(\overline{q_1}, t_1), \ldots,$ $\mathsf{match}(\overline{q_n}, t_n)) \to^+_{L(R,p)} \mathsf{ok}(u)$. To reduce $f(\ldots)$ to $\mathsf{ok}(\ldots)$, all arguments of f must reduce to ok-terms. Hence, $\mathsf{match}(\overline{q_i}, t_i) \to^+_{L(R,p)} \mathsf{ok}(u_i)$ for all i where these reductions are shorter than the reduction $\mathsf{match}(\overline{q}, t) \to^+_{L(R,p)} \mathsf{ok}(u)$. The induction hypothesis implies $t_i = u_i \in T(\Sigma)$ and that there are substitutions σ_i with $q_i \sigma_i = t_i$. Since q is linear, we can combine these σ_i to one σ such that $q\sigma = t$. Moreover, this implies $u = f(u_1, \ldots, u_n)$ which proves the lemma. $\square$

Based on the previous two lemmata, one can show that check works properly, i.e., it checks whether its argument is a term from $T(\Sigma)$ containing an instance of p. The proof is similar to the one of Lemma 10 and can be found in [9].

Lemma 11 (Reducing check). *Let $p \in T(\Sigma, \mathcal{V})$ be linear and $t \in T(\Sigma_G)$. We have $\mathsf{check}(t) \to^+_{L(R,p)} \mathsf{found}(u)$ iff $t = u \in T(\Sigma)$ and t contains a subterm $p\sigma$.*

Lemma 12 shows that the top-rules (1), (2) are applied in an alternating way.

Lemma 12 (Reducing active and check). *For all $t, u \in T(\Sigma_G)$ we have*

(a) $\mathsf{active}(t) \not\to^+_{L(R,p)} \mathsf{found}(u)$ *and* $\mathsf{active}(t) \not\to^+_{L(R,p)} \mathsf{ok}(u)$
(b) $\mathsf{check}(t) \not\to^+_{L(R,p)} \mathsf{mark}(u)$ *and* $\mathsf{proper}(t) \not\to^+_{L(R,p)} \mathsf{mark}(u)$

Proof. For (a), by induction on $n \in \mathbb{N}$, we show that there is no reduction from $\mathsf{active}(t)$ to $\mathsf{found}(u)$ or to $\mathsf{ok}(u)$ of length n. If the first reduction step is in t, then the claim follows from the induction hypothesis. Otherwise, the reduction starts with a root step. This first step cannot be $\mathsf{active}(t) \to_{L(R,p)} \mathsf{mark}(u)$, since the root symbol mark can never be reduced again. Hence, we must have $t = f(t_1, \ldots, t_i, \ldots, t_n)$ and $\mathsf{active}(t) = \mathsf{active}(f(t_1, \ldots, t_i, \ldots, t_n)) \to_{L(R,p)}$ $f(t_1, \ldots, \mathsf{active}(t_i), \ldots, t_n)$. In order to rewrite this term to a found- or ok-term, in particular $\mathsf{active}(t_i)$ must be rewritten to a found- or ok-term which contradicts the induction hypothesis. For the (similar) proof of (b), we refer to [9]. $\square$

We now prove that the top-rules are crucial for $L(R,p)$'s termination behavior.

Lemma 13. *Let $L'(R,p) = L(R,p) \setminus \{(1),(2)\}$. Then $L'(R,p)$ is terminating.*

Proof. Termination of $L'(R,p)$ can be proved by the recursive path order [5] using the precedence active > check > match > proper > start > f > ok > found > mark for all $f \in \Sigma \cup \{X \mid x \in \mathcal{V}(p)\}$. □

Before relating $L(R,p)$ and $\to_G$, we study the connection of $L(R,p)$ and $\to_R$.

Lemma 14. *Let $t, u \in \mathcal{T}(\Sigma)$. Then we have $\mathsf{active}(t) \to^+_{L(R,p)} \mathsf{mark}(u)$ iff $t \to_R u$ and $\mathsf{top}(\mathsf{active}(t)) \to^+_{L(R,p)} \mathsf{top}(\mathsf{mark}(u))$ iff $\mathsf{top}(t) \to_R \mathsf{top}(u)$.*

Proof. The 'if'-direction is easy by induction on t. For the 'only if'-direction, we prove that $\mathsf{active}(t) \to^+_{L(R,p)} \mathsf{mark}(u)$ implies $t \to_R u$ by induction on the length of the reduction. The proof that $\mathsf{top}(\mathsf{active}(t)) \to^+_{L(R,p)} \mathsf{top}(\mathsf{mark}(u))$ implies $\mathsf{top}(t) \to_R \mathsf{top}(u)$ is analogous [9]. Since $t \in \mathcal{T}(\Sigma)$, the first reduction step must be on the root position. If $\mathsf{active}(t) \to_{L(R,p)} \mathsf{mark}(u)$ on root position, then $t = l\sigma$ and $u = r\sigma$ for a rule $l \to r \in R$ and thus, $t \to_R u$. Otherwise, $t = f(t_1, \ldots, t_n)$ and $\mathsf{active}(t) = \mathsf{active}(f(t_1, \ldots, t_n)) \to_{L(R,p)} f(t_1, \ldots, \mathsf{active}(t_i), \ldots, t_n) \to^+_{L(R,p)} \mathsf{mark}(u)$. Thus, $\mathsf{active}(t_i) \to^+_{L(R,p)} \mathsf{mark}(u_i)$ and $u = f(t_1, \ldots, u_i, \ldots, t_n)$. The induction hypothesis implies $t_i \to_R u_i$ and hence, $t \to_R u$. □

Theorem 15 (Soundness and Completeness). *Let R be a top rewrite system over $\Sigma \cup \{\mathsf{top}\}$ with $\mathsf{top} \notin \Sigma$ and let $p \in \mathcal{T}(\Sigma, \mathcal{V})$ be linear. The TRS $L(R,p)$ is terminating (on all terms) iff the relation $\to_G$ is terminating on $\mathcal{T}_{\mathsf{top}}$.*

Proof. We first show the 'only if'-direction. If $\to_G$ does not terminate on $\mathcal{T}_{\mathsf{top}}$ then there is an infinite reduction $\mathsf{top}(t_1) \to_G \mathsf{top}(t_2) \to_G \ldots$ where $t_1, t_2, \ldots \in \mathcal{T}(\Sigma)$. By Lemma 14 we have $\mathsf{top}(\mathsf{active}(t_i)) \to^+_{L(R,p)} \mathsf{top}(\mathsf{mark}(t_{i+1}))$. Lemma 11 implies $\mathsf{check}(t_{i+1}) \to^+_{L(R,p)} \mathsf{found}(t_{i+1})$, since each t_{i+1} contains an instance of p. So we obtain the following contradiction to the termination of $L(R,p)$.

$$\mathsf{top}(\mathsf{active}(t_1)) \to^+_{L(R,p)} \mathsf{top}(\mathsf{mark}(t_2)) \to_{L(R,p)} \mathsf{top}(\mathsf{check}(t_2)) \to^+_{L(R,p)}$$
$$\mathsf{top}(\mathsf{found}(t_2)) \to_{L(R,p)} \mathsf{top}(\mathsf{active}(t_2)) \to^+_{L(R,p)} \cdots$$

For the 'if'-direction assume that $L(R,p)$ is not terminating. By type introduction [11] one can show that there exists an infinite $L(R,p)$-reduction of ground top terms. Due to Lemma 13 the reduction contains infinitely many applications of the rules (1) and (2). These rules must be applied in alternating order, since $\mathsf{active}(t)$ can never reduce to $\mathsf{found}(u)$ and $\mathsf{check}(t)$ can never reduce to $\mathsf{mark}(u)$ by Lemma 12. So the reduction has the following form where all reductions with the rules (1) and (2) are displayed.

$$\cdots \to^*_{L(R,p)} \mathsf{top}(\mathsf{mark}(t_1)) \to_{L(R,p)} \mathsf{top}(\mathsf{check}(t_1)) \to^+_{L(R,p)}$$
$$\mathsf{top}(\mathsf{found}(u_1)) \to_{L(R,p)} \mathsf{top}(\mathsf{active}(u_1)) \to^+_{L(R,p)}$$
$$\mathsf{top}(\mathsf{mark}(t_2)) \to_{L(R,p)} \mathsf{top}(\mathsf{check}(t_2)) \to^+_{L(R,p)}$$
$$\mathsf{top}(\mathsf{found}(u_2)) \to_{L(R,p)} \mathsf{top}(\mathsf{active}(u_2)) \to^+_{L(R,p)} \cdots$$

By Lemma 11 we have $t_i = u_i \in \mathcal{T}(\Sigma)$ and that t_i contains an instance of p. Lemma 14 implies $\mathsf{top}(u_i) \to_R \mathsf{top}(t_{i+1})$. Together, we obtain $\mathsf{top}(t_1) \to_G \mathsf{top}(t_2) \to_G \ldots$ in contradiction to the termination of $\to_G$ on $\mathcal{T}_{\mathsf{top}}$. □

By Thm. 15, one can now use existing techniques for termination proofs of TRSs to verify liveness of systems like Ex. 6. For instance, termination of the transformed TRS from Ex. 8 is easy to show with dependency pairs [2], cf. [9].

5 Proving Liveness

In Sect. 5.1 we present a sound transformation which is more suitable for mechanizing liveness proofs than the complete transformation from Sect. 4. The reason is that for this new transformation, termination of the transformed TRS is much easier to show. On the other hand, the approach in this section is incomplete, i.e., it cannot succeed for all examples. Subsequently, in Sect. 5.2 we introduce an automatic preprocessing technique based on *semantic labelling* [12] to simplify these termination proofs further. In this way, rewriting techniques can be used to mechanize the verification of liveness properties. To illustrate the use of our approach, in Sect. 5.3 we show how to verify liveness properties of a network of processes with a shared resource and of a token ring protocol.

5.1 A Sound Transformation for Liveness

To obtain a simple sound transformation, the idea is to introduce only one new symbol check. A new occurrence of check is created in every application of a top rule. If check finds an instantiation of p then check may be removed. Otherwise, check remains in the term where it may block further reductions.

Definition 16 ($LS(R, p)$). *For a top rewrite system R over $\Sigma \cup \{\mathsf{top}\}$ with $\mathsf{top} \notin \Sigma$ and $p \in \mathcal{T}(\Sigma, \mathcal{V})$, let $LS(R, p)$ consist of the following rules.*

$$
\begin{array}{ll}
l \to r & \text{for all non-top rules } l \to r \text{ in } R \\
\mathsf{top}(t) \to \mathsf{top}(\mathsf{check}(u)) & \text{for all top rules } \mathsf{top}(t) \to \mathsf{top}(u) \\
\mathsf{check}(f(x_1, .., x_n)) \to f(x_1, .., \mathsf{check}(x_i), .., x_n) & \text{for } f \in \Sigma \text{ of arity } n \geq 1,\ i = 1, .., n \\
\mathsf{check}(p) \to p &
\end{array}
$$

Example 17 (Simple example revisited). To illustrate the transformation, reconsider the system from Ex. 6. Here, $LS(R, \mathsf{f}(x))$ is the following TRS whose termination can be proved by dependency pairs and the recursive path order.

$$
\begin{array}{llll}
\mathsf{top}(\mathsf{c}) \to \mathsf{top}(\mathsf{check}(\mathsf{c})) & (3) & \mathsf{check}(\mathsf{f}(x)) \to \mathsf{f}(\mathsf{check}(x)) & (5) \\
\mathsf{f}(x) \to x & (4) & \mathsf{check}(\mathsf{f}(x)) \to \mathsf{f}(x) & (6)
\end{array}
$$

Now we show that this transformation is indeed sound. In other words, the above termination proof verifies the liveness property of our example.

Theorem 18 (Soundness). *Let R be a top rewrite system over $\Sigma \cup \{\text{top}\}$ with* top $\notin \Sigma$, *let $p \in \mathcal{T}(\Sigma, \mathcal{V})$, and let $G = \{t \mid t \text{ does not contain an instance of } p\}$.* *If $LS(R, p)$ is terminating then there is no infinite $\to_G$-reduction of top terms.*

Proof. Assume there is an infinite $\to_G$-reduction of top terms $\text{top}(t_1) \to_G \text{top}(t_2)$ $\to_G \cdots$ Since top does not occur in p, every t_i has the form $C_i[p\sigma_i]$ for some context C_i and substitution σ_i. To prove the theorem, we show that $\text{top}(t_i) \to_{LS(R,p)}^+$ $\text{top}(t_{i+1})$ for every i, by which we obtain an infinite $LS(R, p)$-reduction.

If $\text{top}(t_i) \to_R \text{top}(t_{i+1})$ by the application of a non-top rule $l \to r$ then we also have $\text{top}(t_i) \to_{LS(R,p)} \text{top}(t_{i+1})$ since $l \to r$ is also contained in $LS(R, p)$. Otherwise, $\text{top}(t_i) \to_R \text{top}(t_{i+1})$ by a top rule $\text{top}(t) \to \text{top}(u)$. Hence, $t_i = t\sigma$ and $t_{i+1} = u\sigma$ for some σ. Since $LS(R, p)$ contains the rules $\text{check}(f(x_1, \ldots, x_n))$ $\to f(x_1, \ldots, \text{check}(x_i), \ldots, x_n)$ for all f with arity ≥ 1, we obtain

$$
\begin{aligned}
\text{top}(t_i) = \text{top}(t\sigma) &\to_{LS(R,p)} \text{top}(\text{check}(u\sigma)) &&= \text{top}(\text{check}(C_{i+1}[p\sigma_{i+1}])) \\
&\to_{LS(R,p)}^* \text{top}(C_{i+1}[\text{check}(p)\sigma_{i+1}]) \\
&\to_{LS(R,p)} \text{top}(C_{i+1}[p\sigma_{i+1}]) &&= \text{top}(t_{i+1}) \qquad \square
\end{aligned}
$$

Example 19 (Sound transformation is not complete). However, this transformation is incomplete as can be shown by the following top rewrite system R

$$\text{top}(\mathsf{f}(x, \mathsf{b})) \to \text{top}(\mathsf{f}(\mathsf{b}, \mathsf{b})) \qquad\qquad \mathsf{a} \to \mathsf{b}$$

where $\Sigma = \{\mathsf{a}, \mathsf{b}, \mathsf{f}\}$ and $p = \mathsf{a}$. In this example, normal forms do not contain a any more and every infinite reduction of top terms reaches the term $\text{top}(\mathsf{f}(\mathsf{b}, \mathsf{b}))$ which does not contain the symbol a either. Hence, the liveness property holds. However, $LS(R, p)$ admits the following infinite reduction:

$$\text{top}(\mathsf{f}(\mathsf{b}, \mathsf{b})) \to \text{top}(\text{check}(\mathsf{f}(\mathsf{b}, \mathsf{b}))) \to \text{top}(\mathsf{f}(\text{check}(\mathsf{b}), \mathsf{b})) \to \text{top}(\text{check}(\mathsf{f}(\mathsf{b}, \mathsf{b}))) \to \ldots$$

Thus, the transformation of Def. 16 is incomplete, because even if check remains in a term, this does not necessarily block further (infinite) reductions.

5.2 A Preprocessing Procedure for Verifying Liveness

The aim of our sound transformation from Def. 16 is to simplify (and possibly automate) the termination proofs which are required in order to show liveness properties. Since the TRSs resulting from our transformation have a particular form, we now present a method to preprocess such TRSs. This preprocessing is especially designed for this form of TRSs and in this way, their termination proofs can often be simplified significantly. The method consists of four steps which can be performed automatically:

(a) First one deletes rules which cannot cause non-termination.
(b) Then one applies the well-known transformation technique of *semantic labelling* [12] with a particularly chosen model and labelling. (This restricted form of semantic labelling can be done automatically.)

(c) Then one again deletes rules which cannot cause non-termination.
(d) Finally one uses an existing automatic technique (e.g., the recursive path order or dependency pairs) to prove termination of the resulting TRS.

To delete rules in Step (a) and (c) we use the following lemma. For a function symbol $f \in \Sigma$ and a term $t \in \mathcal{T}(\Sigma, \mathcal{V})$, let $\#_f(t)$ be the number of f-symbols occurring in t. For $\varnothing \neq \Sigma' \subseteq \Sigma$ let $\#_{\Sigma'}(t) = \sum_{f \in \Sigma'} \#_f(t)$.

Lemma 20. *Let R be a TRS such that*

- *R is* non-duplicating, *i.e., for every rule $l \to r$, no variable occurs more often in r than in l, and*
- *$\#_{\Sigma'}(l) \geq \#_{\Sigma'}(r)$ for all rules $l \to r$ in R*

for some $\Sigma' \subseteq \Sigma$. Let R' consist of those rules $l \to r$ from R which satisfy $\#_{\Sigma'}(l) > \#_{\Sigma'}(r)$. Then R is terminating if and only if $R \setminus R'$ is terminating.

Proof. The 'only if'-part holds since $R \setminus R' \subseteq R$. For the 'if'-part assume that $R \setminus R'$ is terminating and that we have an infinite R-reduction. Due to the conditions of the lemma we have $\#_{\Sigma'}(t) \geq \#_{\Sigma'}(u)$ for every step $t \to_R u$ and $\#_{\Sigma'}(t) > \#_{\Sigma'}(u)$ for every step $t \to_{R'} u$. Hence, due to well-foundedness of the natural numbers, the infinite R-reduction contains only finitely many R'-steps. After removing the finite initial part containing all these R'-steps, the remaining part is an infinite $R \setminus R'$-reduction, which gives a contradiction. □

The application of Lemma 20 is easily automated as follows: for all sets $\Sigma' \subseteq \Sigma$ with $|\Sigma'| \leq n$ for some (small) $n \in \mathbb{N}$, it is checked whether $\#_{\Sigma'}(l) \geq \#_{\Sigma'}(r)$ for all rules $l \to r$. If so, then all rules $l \to r$ satisfying $\#_{\Sigma'}(l) > \#_{\Sigma'}(r)$ are removed. This process is repeated until no rule can be removed any more.

As a first example, we apply Lemma 20 to the TRS from Ex. 17. By counting the occurrences of f, we note that the number of f-symbols strictly decreases in Rule (4) and it remains the same in all other rules. Hence, due to Lemma 20 we can drop this rule when proving termination of the TRS. It turns out that in this case repetition of this process does not succeed in removing more rules.

In our termination procedure, in Step (b) we apply a particular instance of *semantic labelling* [12]. Before describing this instance we briefly explain how semantic labelling works as a tool to prove termination of a TRS R over the signature Σ: One starts by choosing a *model* for the TRS R. Thus, one defines a non-empty carrier set M and for every function symbol $f \in \Sigma$ of arity n, an interpretation $f_M : M^n \to M$ is chosen. As usual, every variable assignment $\alpha : \mathcal{V} \to M$ can be extended to terms from $\mathcal{T}(\Sigma, \mathcal{V})$ by inductively defining $\alpha(f(t_1, \ldots, t_n)) = f_M(\alpha(t_1), \ldots, \alpha(t_n))$. The interpretation is a *model* for R if $\alpha(l) = \alpha(r)$ for every rule $l \to r$ in R and every variable assignment $\alpha : \mathcal{V} \to M$.

Using this model, the TRS R over the signature Σ is transformed into a *labelled* TRS $\overline{R}$ over the *labelled* signature $\overline{\Sigma}$. Here, every function symbol $f \in \Sigma$ of arity n may be labelled by n elements from M, i.e., $\overline{\Sigma} = \{f_{a_1, \ldots, a_n} \mid f \in \Sigma, n = \text{arity}(f), a_i \in M\}$ where the arity of $f_{a_1, \ldots, a_n}$ is the same as the arity of f. For any variable assignment $\alpha : V \to M$, we define a function $\mathsf{lab}_\alpha : T(\Sigma, V) \to T(\overline{\Sigma}, V)$ which labels every function symbol by the interpretations of its arguments:

$$\mathsf{lab}_\alpha(x) \qquad\qquad = x, \text{ for } x \in V$$
$$\mathsf{lab}_\alpha(f(t_1, \ldots, t_n)) = f_{\alpha(t_1), \ldots, \alpha(t_n)}(\mathsf{lab}_\alpha(t_1), \ldots, \mathsf{lab}_\alpha(t_n))$$

Now the TRS $\overline{R}$ is defined to consist of all rules $\mathsf{lab}_\alpha(l) \to \mathsf{lab}_\alpha(r)$ for all variable assignments $\alpha : V \to M$ and all rules $l \to r$ in R. The main theorem of semantic labelling states that R is terminating if and only if $\overline{R}$ is terminating.

In general, semantic labelling permits a lot of freedom and is hard to automate, since one may choose arbitrary models. Moreover, in full semantic labelling one may also use arbitrary labellings. However, we will restrict ourselves to the case where $M = \{0, 1\}$. Now there are only finitely many possibilities for the interpretations f_M in the model. This means that with this restriction the termination method consisting of the steps (a) - (d) is fully decidable.

To improve efficiency and to avoid checking all possibilities of a two-element model for semantic labelling, we now propose heuristics for choosing the interpretations f_M in such a model. These heuristics are adapted to the special form of TRSs resulting from our transformation in Def. 16 when verifying liveness properties. The main objective is that we want to distinguish between terms that contain instances of p and terms that do not. Therefore, our aim is to interpret the former terms by 0 and the latter terms by 1. Since the intention of check is that an occurrence of p should be found, $\mathsf{check}(x)$ will be interpreted as the constant function 0. Since top only occurs at the top, for $\mathsf{top}(x)$ we may also choose a constant function. Having these objectives in mind, we arrive at the following heuristic for choosing the operations f_M in the model $M = \{0, 1\}$:

- $\mathsf{top}_M(x) = \mathsf{check}_M(x) = f_M(x_1, \ldots, x_n) = 0$ for $x = 0, 1$, where f is the root symbol of p;
- $c_M = 1$ for every constant c, except if $p = c$;
- $f_M(x_1, \ldots, x_n) = \min(x_1, \ldots, x_n)$ for all other symbols f as long as this does not conflict with the model requirement $\alpha(l) = \alpha(r)$. In particular, for the remaining unary symbols f one tries to choose $f_M(x) = x$.

Applying these heuristics to our example results in the following interpretation:

$$\mathsf{top}_M(x) = \mathsf{check}_M(x) = f_M(x) = 0 \quad \text{for } x \in M = \{0, 1\} \quad \text{and} \quad c_M = 1$$

One checks that this is a model for the TRS. Here it is essential that we first removed Rule (4), since $f_M(x) = 0 \neq x$ if $x = 1$. The labelling results in the TRS

$$\mathsf{top}_1(c) \to \mathsf{top}_0(\mathsf{check}_1(c))$$
$$\mathsf{check}_0(f_i(x)) \to f_0(\mathsf{check}_i(x)) \qquad \text{for } i \in \{0, 1\}$$
$$\mathsf{check}_0(f_i(x)) \to f_i(x) \qquad\qquad \text{for } i \in \{0, 1\}$$

In Step (c) of our termination procedure, we apply Lemma 20 again. By counting the occurrences of top_1, we can drop the first rule. By counting f_1, the second rule can be removed if i is 1, and by counting check_0 we can delete the third rule. So the remaining TRS just contains the rule $\mathsf{check}_0(\mathsf{f}_0(x)) \to \mathsf{f}_0(\mathsf{check}_0(x))$ whose termination is trivial to prove by the recursive path order.

This example indicates that preprocessing a TRS according to Steps (a) - (c) often simplifies the termination proof considerably. For the original TRS of Ex. 17, one needs dependency pairs for the termination proof, whereas after the transformation a very simple recursive path order is sufficient.

5.3   Two Case Studies of Liveness

To demonstrate the applicability of our approach, we regard two case studies. The first one is motivated by verification problems of protocols similar to the *bakery protocol* [10]. We describe a network of processes which want to gain access to a shared resource. The processes waiting for the resource are served one after another. Since the maximal size of the waiting line is fixed, a new process can only enter the waiting line if a process in the current line has been "served" (i.e., if it has been granted access to the resource). The maximal length n of the waiting line is arbitrary, and we will show that the liveness property holds for all $n \in \mathbb{N}$. Hence, techniques like classical model checking are not applicable here.

The processes in the line are served on a "first in - first out" basis (this corresponds to the serving of clients in a shop). So at the front end of the waiting line, a process may be served, where serving is denoted by a constant **serve**. If a process is served, its place in the line is replaced by a free place, denoted by **free**. If the place in front of some process is free, this process may take the free place, creating a free place on its original position. If the line has a free place at its back end, a new process **new** may enter the waiting line, taking over the position of the free place. Apart from new processes represented by **new** we also consider old processes represented by **old**, which were already in the line initially. We want to verify the liveness property that eventually all old processes will be served. To model protocols with TRSs, we represent the state of the whole network by a top term. Introducing the symbol **top** at the back end of the waiting line, this network is described by the following top rewrite system R:

$$\mathsf{top}(\mathsf{free}(x)) \to \mathsf{top}(\mathsf{new}(x)) \qquad \mathsf{new}(\mathsf{serve}) \to \mathsf{free}(\mathsf{serve})$$
$$\mathsf{new}(\mathsf{free}(x)) \to \mathsf{free}(\mathsf{new}(x)) \qquad \mathsf{old}(\mathsf{serve}) \to \mathsf{free}(\mathsf{serve})$$
$$\mathsf{old}(\mathsf{free}(x)) \to \mathsf{free}(\mathsf{old}(x))$$

Note that the above TRS admits infinite reductions of top terms. For instance,

$$\mathsf{top}(\mathsf{new}(\mathsf{serve})) \to_R \mathsf{top}(\mathsf{free}(\mathsf{serve})) \to_R \mathsf{top}(\mathsf{new}(\mathsf{serve})) \to_R \cdots$$

describes that the protocol for serving processes and for letting new processes enter may go on forever. But we will prove that after finitely many steps one reaches a term without the symbol old, i.e., eventually all old processes are served. In our terminology this liveness property is represented by $\mathsf{Live}(\mathcal{T}_{\mathsf{top}}, \to_R, G)$ where $G = \{t \mid t \text{ does not contain an instance of } \mathsf{old}(x)\}$. Note that this liveness property does not hold for various variations of this system. For instance, if processes are allowed to swap by $\mathsf{new}(\mathsf{old}(x)) \to \mathsf{old}(\mathsf{new}(x))$, or if new processes are always allowed to line up by $\mathsf{top}(x) \to \mathsf{top}(\mathsf{new}(x))$, then liveness is destroyed.

Since $\mathsf{top}(\mathsf{serve})$ is the only ground top term that is in normal form, we conclude that $\mathsf{NF}(\mathcal{T}_{\mathsf{top}}) \subseteq G$. Hence by Thm. 4 the required liveness property is equivalent to $\mathsf{SN}(\mathcal{T}_{\mathsf{top}}, \to_G)$. To prove this termination property of $\to_G$, according to Thm. 18 we may prove termination of the TRS $LS(R, p)$:

$$\mathsf{top}(\mathsf{free}(x)) \to \mathsf{top}(\mathsf{check}(\mathsf{new}(x)))\ (7) \qquad \mathsf{old}(\mathsf{free}(x)) \to \mathsf{free}(\mathsf{old}(x))\quad (9)$$
$$\mathsf{new}(\mathsf{free}(x)) \to \mathsf{free}(\mathsf{new}(x)) \qquad\ (8) \qquad \mathsf{new}(\mathsf{serve}) \to \mathsf{free}(\mathsf{serve})\quad (10)$$

$$\mathsf{old}(\mathsf{serve}) \to \mathsf{free}(\mathsf{serve}) \qquad (11)$$
$$\mathsf{check}(\mathsf{free}(x)) \to \mathsf{free}(\mathsf{check}(x))\,(12) \qquad \mathsf{check}(\mathsf{old}(x)) \to \mathsf{old}(\mathsf{check}(x))\ (14)$$
$$\mathsf{check}(\mathsf{new}(x)) \to \mathsf{new}(\mathsf{check}(x))\,(13) \qquad \mathsf{check}(\mathsf{old}(x)) \to \mathsf{old}(x) \qquad\qquad (15)$$

While standard techniques for automated termination proofs of TRSs do not succeed for this TRS, with the preprocessing steps (a) - (c) termination can easily be shown automatically.

According to (a), we first delete rules which do not influence termination. By counting the occurrences of old, with Lemma 20 we can remove Rule (11). Then in Step (b), we apply the heuristics for semantic labelling and arrive at

$$\mathsf{top}_M(x) = \mathsf{check}_M(x) = \mathsf{old}_M(x) = 0, \quad \mathsf{new}_M(x) = \mathsf{free}_M(x) = x, \quad \mathsf{serve}_M = 1$$

for $x \in M = \{0, 1\}$. Indeed this is a model for the TRS. For that purpose, we had to remove Rule (11) since $\mathsf{old}_M(\mathsf{serve}_M) = 0 \neq 1 = \mathsf{free}_M(\mathsf{serve}_M)$. The corresponding labelled TRS $\overline{R}$ is

$$\mathsf{top}_i(\mathsf{free}_i(x)) \to \mathsf{top}_0(\mathsf{check}_i(\mathsf{new}_i(x)))\ (7_i) \quad \mathsf{check}_i(\mathsf{free}_i(x)) \to \mathsf{free}_0(\mathsf{check}_i(x))\ (12_i)$$
$$\mathsf{new}_i(\mathsf{free}_i(x)) \to \mathsf{free}_i(\mathsf{new}_i(x)) \qquad\quad (8_i) \quad \mathsf{check}_i(\mathsf{new}_i(x)) \to \mathsf{new}_0(\mathsf{check}_i(x))\ (13_i)$$
$$\mathsf{old}_i(\mathsf{free}_i(x)) \to \mathsf{free}_0(\mathsf{old}_i(x)) \qquad\qquad (9_i) \quad \mathsf{check}_0(\mathsf{old}_i(x)) \to \mathsf{old}_0(\mathsf{check}_i(x))\ (14_i)$$
$$\mathsf{new}_1(\mathsf{serve}) \to \mathsf{free}_1(\mathsf{serve}) \qquad\qquad\quad (10) \quad \mathsf{check}_0(\mathsf{old}_i(x)) \to \mathsf{old}_i(x), \qquad\qquad (15_i)$$

for $i \in \{0, 1\}$. It remains to prove termination of this TRS of 15 rules. According to Step (c) we repeatedly apply Lemma 20. By consecutively choosing $\Sigma' = \{f\}$ for f being top_1, old_1, new_1, free_1, free_0, and check_0, the rules (7_1), (14_1), (10) and (13_1), (9_1) and (12_1), (7_0), and finally (15_0) and (15_1) are removed. Termination of the remaining system consisting of the rules (8_0), (8_1), (9_0), (12_0), (13_0), and (14_0) is easily proved by the recursive path order, using a precedence satisfying $\mathsf{check}_0 > \mathsf{old}_0 > \mathsf{free}_0$, $\mathsf{check}_0 > \mathsf{new}_0 > \mathsf{free}_0$, and $\mathsf{new}_1 > \mathsf{free}_1$. Hence, the liveness property of this example can be proved automatically.

As a second case study we consider the following protocol on a ring of processes (similar to a token ring protocol). Every process is in one of the three states sent, rec (received), or no (nothing). Initially at least one of the processes is in state rec which means that it has received a message (token). Now the protocol is defined as follows:

> If a process is in state rec then it may send its message to its right neighbor which then will be in state rec, while the process itself then will be in state sent.

Clearly, at least one process will always be in state rec, and this procedure can go on forever; we will prove that eventually no process will be in state no. This means that eventually all processes have received the message; a typical liveness property to be proved. The requirement $\mathsf{NF}(I) \subseteq G$ and in fact $\mathsf{NF}(I) = \varnothing$ (for I consisting of all configurations containing rec) is easily seen to hold on the protocol level. According to Thm. 4, for proving the desired liveness property it suffices to show $\mathsf{SN}(I, \to_G)$. The protocol is encoded by unary symbols sent, rec, and no, where the right neighbor of each of these symbols corresponds to the root of its argument. To obtain a ring topology we add a unary symbol top and a constant bot. For a symbol with the argument bot, its right neighbor is defined to be the symbol just below top. So again the state of the whole ring network is represented by a top-term $\mathsf{top}(f_1(\ldots(f_n(\mathsf{bot}))\ldots))$. Here the size n of the ring is arbitrary. In order to pass messages from the bot-process n to the top-process 1, an auxiliary unary symbol up is introduced.

$$
\begin{aligned}
\mathsf{rec}(\mathsf{rec}(x)) &\to \mathsf{sent}(\mathsf{rec}(x)) \quad (16) & \mathsf{sent}(\mathsf{up}(x)) &\to \mathsf{up}(\mathsf{sent}(x)) \ (21) \\
\mathsf{rec}(\mathsf{sent}(x)) &\to \mathsf{sent}(\mathsf{rec}(x)) \quad (17) & \mathsf{no}(\mathsf{up}(x)) &\to \mathsf{up}(\mathsf{no}(x)) \quad (22) \\
\mathsf{rec}(\mathsf{no}(x)) &\to \mathsf{sent}(\mathsf{rec}(x)) \quad (18) & \mathsf{top}(\mathsf{rec}(\mathsf{up}(x))) &\to \mathsf{top}(\mathsf{rec}(x)) \ (23) \\
\mathsf{rec}(\mathsf{bot}) &\to \mathsf{up}(\mathsf{sent}(\mathsf{bot})) \ (19) & \mathsf{top}(\mathsf{sent}(\mathsf{up}(x))) &\to \mathsf{top}(\mathsf{rec}(x)) \ (24) \\
\mathsf{rec}(\mathsf{up}(x)) &\to \mathsf{up}(\mathsf{rec}(x)) \quad (20) & \mathsf{top}(\mathsf{no}(\mathsf{up}(x))) &\to \mathsf{top}(\mathsf{rec}(x)) \ (25)
\end{aligned}
$$

Now we prove that every infinite top reduction reaches a term without no, proving the desired liveness property. Applying Thm. 18 for $p = \mathsf{no}(x)$, this can be done by proving termination of $LS(R, p)$, which consists of Rules (16) - (22) and

$$
\begin{aligned}
\mathsf{top}(\mathsf{rec}(\mathsf{up}(x))) &\to \mathsf{top}(\mathsf{check}(\mathsf{rec}(x))) \ (23\mathrm{a}) & \mathsf{check}(\mathsf{sent}(x)) &\to \mathsf{sent}(\mathsf{check}(x)) \ (27) \\
\mathsf{top}(\mathsf{sent}(\mathsf{up}(x))) &\to \mathsf{top}(\mathsf{check}(\mathsf{rec}(x))) \ (24\mathrm{a}) & \mathsf{check}(\mathsf{rec}(x)) &\to \mathsf{rec}(\mathsf{check}(x)) \ (28) \\
\mathsf{top}(\mathsf{no}(\mathsf{up}(x))) &\to \mathsf{top}(\mathsf{check}(\mathsf{rec}(x))) \ (25\mathrm{a}) & \mathsf{check}(\mathsf{no}(x)) &\to \mathsf{no}(\mathsf{check}(x)) \ (29) \\
\mathsf{check}(\mathsf{up}(x)) &\to \mathsf{up}(\mathsf{check}(x)) \quad\quad\quad (26) & \mathsf{check}(\mathsf{no}(x)) &\to \mathsf{no}(x) \quad\quad\quad (30)
\end{aligned}
$$

Termination is easily proved completely automatically according to our heuristics: by respectively choosing Σ' to be $\{\mathsf{no}\}$ and $\{\mathsf{rec}, \mathsf{up}\}$ in Lemma 20, the rules (16), (18), (23a), and (25a) can be removed. After applying labelling according to our heuristics a TRS is obtained for which termination is proved automatically by applying Lemma 20 and the recursive path order, cf. [9].

6   Conclusion and Further Research

We showed how to relate liveness and termination of TRSs and presented a sound and complete transformation such that liveness holds iff the transformed TRS is terminating. By a simpler sound transformation and by refining termination techniques for TRSs we developed an approach to verify liveness mechanically.

Our results can be refined in several ways. For instance, instead of one unary top symbol one can regard several top symbols of arbitrary arity and one can extend the framework to liveness w.r.t. several terms $p_1, \ldots, p_n$ instead of just one p. Such refinements and further examples of liveness properties verified by our method can be found in [9]. For example, we show liveness in a network with several waiting lines of processes which want to gain access to a shared resource.

This problem is considerably more difficult than the waiting line protocol in Sect. 5.3, since liveness only holds if the lines are synchronized in a suitable way.

References

1. B. Alpern and F. B. Schneider. Defining liveness. *Inf. Pr. Lett.*, 21:181–185, 1985.
2. T. Arts and J. Giesl. Termination of term rewriting using dependency pairs. *Theoretical Computer Science*, 236:133–178, 2000.
3. F. Baader and T. Nipkow. *Term Rewriting and All That*. Cambr. Univ. Pr., 1998.
4. A. Bouajjani. Languages, rewriting systems, and verification of infinite-state systems. In *Proc. ICALP '01*, volume 2076 of *LNCS*, pages 24–39, 2001.
5. N. Dershowitz. Termination of rewriting. *J. Symb. Comp.*, 3:69–116, 1987.
6. J. Giesl and T. Arts. Verification of Erlang processes by dependency pairs. *Applicable Algebra in Engineering, Communication and Comp.*, 12(1,2):39–72, 2001.
7. J. Giesl and A. Middeldorp. Transforming context-sensitive rewrite systems. In *Proc. 10th RTA*, volume 1631 of *Lecture Notes in Comp. Sc.*, pages 271–285, 1999.
8. J. Giesl and A. Middeldorp. Transformation techniques for context-sensitive rewrite systems. *Journal of Functional Programming*, 2003. To appear. Preliminary extended version in Technical Report AIB-2002-02, RWTH Aachen, Germany.
9. J. Giesl and H. Zantema. Liveness in rewriting. Technical Report AIB-2002-11, RWTH Aachen, Germany, 2002. http://aib.informatik.rwth-aachen.de.
10. L. Lamport. A new solution to Dijkstra's concurrent programming problem. *Communications of the ACM*, 17(8):453–455, 1974.
11. H. Zantema. Termination of term rewriting: Interpretation and type elimination. *Journal of Symbolic Computation*, 17:23–50, 1994.
12. H. Zantema. Termination of term rewriting by semantic labelling. *Fundamenta Informaticae*, 24:89–105, 1995.

Validation of the JavaCard Platform
with Implicit Induction Techniques

Gilles Barthe[1] and Sorin Stratulat[2]

[1] INRIA Sophia-Antipolis, France
`Gilles.Barthe@inria.fr`
[2] LITA, Université de Metz, France
`stratula@sciences.univ-metz.fr`

Abstract. The bytecode verifier (BCV), which performs a static analysis to reject potentially insecure programs, is a key security function of the Java(Card) platform. Over the last few years there have been numerous projects to prove formally the correctness of bytecode verification, but relatively little effort has been made to provide methodologies, techniques and tools that help such formalisations. In earlier work, we develop a methodology and a specification environment featuring a neutral mathematical language based on conditional rewriting, that considerably reduce the cost of specifying virtual machines.
In this work, we show that such a neutral mathematical language based on conditional rewriting is also beneficial for performing automatic verifications on the specifications, and illustrate in particular how implicit induction techniques can be used for the validation of the Java(Card) Platform. More precisely, we report on the use of SPIKE, a first-order theorem prover based on implicit induction, to establish the correctness of the BCV. The results are encouraging, as many of the intermediate lemmas required to prove the BCV correct can be proved with SPIKE.

1 Introduction

Virtual machines, such as the Java(Card) Virtual Machine, provide a means to ensure security of mobile code, because the virtual machine controls the interaction between the applet and its environment and hence reduces the risk of malicious applets performing a security attack. Furthermore, such architectures rely on several mechanisms, known as security functions. A crucial such security function of the Java(Card) architecture is the bytecode verifier which performs a static analysis on programs and rejects potentially insecure programs.

Over the last few years there have been numerous projects to specify such virtual machines and their bytecode verifiers, and to prove the correctness of bytecode verification. While several projects have been very successful in their work, such endeavours are labour-intensive and suffer from the lack of adequate tool support, see Section 5.1. Our line of work is precisely to develop methodologies, techniques and tools that reduce the cost of developing and maintaining such formalisations.

R. Nieuwenhuis (Ed.): RTA 2003, LNCS 2706, pp. 337–351, 2003.

CertiCartes In early work [5,4], we have developed a robust methodology to validate bytecode verifiers. The methodology consists in defining three virtual machines:
- a reference, so-called defensive, virtual machine where values are tagged by their type and where typing information is verified at run-time;
- an abstract virtual machine that manipulates types and that is used for bytecode verification;
- a "standard", so-called offensive, virtual machine, where values are untyped, and which relies on successful bytecode verification to eliminate type verification at run-time.

The advantages of our methodology is three-fold:
1. the offensive and abstract virtual machines can be derived from the defensive virtual machine using abstraction techniques;
2. the correctness of bytecode verification is now crisply stated as: "the offensive and defensive virtual machines coincide on those programs that pass bytecode verification";
3. the correctness of bytecode verification follows from the correctness of the abstractions of the defensive virtual machine into an offensive and an abstract virtual machine respectively, and from a generic development that establishes the correctness of the derivation of the bytecode verifier from the abstract virtual machine—the development is presented in [18] and further refined in [2,15].

Jakarta In previous work [1,3], we argue that a neutral mathematical language is beneficial for performing automatic transformations on the specifications. Further, we introduce the Jakarta Specification Language (JSL), a simple typed specification language based on conditional rewriting, and the Jakarta Transformation Kit (JTK), an abstraction engine which constructs an offensive and an abstract virtual machine from the defensive virtual machine. The results with the JTK are encouraging, as it automates to a large extent the derivation of the offensive and abstract virtual machine; indeed, user interaction is limited to abstraction scripts that contain information on how the abstractions are to be constructed, and that are typically 10 times shorter than the latter.

SPIKE In this work, we show that the choice of a neutral mathematical language based on conditional rewriting is also beneficial for performing automatic verifications on the specifications, and illustrate in particular how SPIKE, a first-order theorem prover based on implicit induction techniques [7,20], can be used for the validation of the JavaCard Platform. Results are encouraging, as many of the intermediate lemmas required to prove the correctness of the BCV, are proved by SPIKE with very limited user interaction; we return to this point in Section 5.

The remaining of the paper is organised as follows: Section 2 provides the necessary background on CertiCartes and introduces the problem to be addressed. Section 3 gives a brief introduction to SPIKE, and describes the main improvements that were implemented to handle the specification and validation of virtual machines. In Section 4, we turn to the application of SPIKE for proving the cross-validation of virtual machines. Finally, we conclude in Section 5 with related work and directions for future work.

Acknowledgments We would like to thank Guillaume Dufay for providing the specifications of the JCVMs in Coq, and for many useful discussions on JavaCard. We would also like to thank Pierre Courtieu for useful discussions, and the referees for their comments. This work is partially supported by the VerifiCard Project IST-2000-26328.

2   A Primer on CertiCartes

CertiCartes is an in-depth feasibility study in the formal verification, using the Coq proof assistant [12], of the JavaCard Platform—recall that JavaCard is a dialect of Java tailored towards programming multi-application smartcards. In a nutshell, CertiCartes contains formal specifications of (one-step execution of) a defensive, an abstract and an offensive JavaCard Virtual Machine (JCVM) and of the BCV, and a proof that the defensive and offensive VMs coincide on those programs that pass bytecode verification.

Virtual Machines In order to formalize the semantics of the virtual machines:

- we model programs as a triple consisting of a list of classes, a list of interfaces, and a list of methods. Classes, interfaces and methods are represented likewise as appropriate tuples;
- we define for each machine a notion of state: $dstate$ which builds upon typed values for the defensive machine, $astate$ which takes types as values for the abstract machine, and $ostate$ which builds upon untyped values for the offensive machine. Further, we define an associated notion of return states: $drstate$ for the defensive machine, $arstate$ for the abstract machine, and $orstate$ for the offensive machine, that extends states with a tag to account for normal/abnormal termination, and in the case of the abstract machine returns lists of states to account for non-determinism;
- we model the semantics of each JavaCard bytecode b as a function $?exec\_b$: $?state \rightarrow r?state$, where ? ranges over d, a and o—note that in our formalisation, the JCVM instruction set is factorized into 45 generic instructions, as many instructions only differ by the type of their arguments, and can be factorized using a polymorphic instruction. Typically, the function $?exec\_b$ extracts values from the state, performs type verification on these values, and extends/updates the state with the results of executing the bytecode;
- we model one-step execution as a function $?exec$: $?state \rightarrow r?state$ which inspects the state to extract the JavaCard bytecode b to be executed and then calls the corresponding function $?exec\_b$.

In order to prove the correctness of the BCV, we must prove three crucial properties about virtual machines:

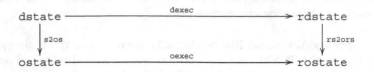

Fig. 1. Commutative diagram of defensive and offensive execution.

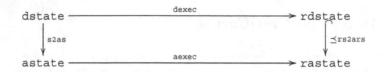

Fig. 2. Commutative diagram of defensive and abstract execution.

- **CDO:** the offensive abstract virtual machine is a sound abstraction of the defensive virtual machine, as illustrated by the commuting (up to the absence of typing error in the defensive execution) diagram in Fig. 1, where s2os is the function mapping states to offensive states (by omitting types from values), and rs2ors denotes its lifting to return states;
- **CDA:** the abstract virtual machine is a sound abstraction of the defensive virtual machine, as illustrated by the commuting (up to subtyping, as indicated by the $\preceq$ relation in the right arrow, and under suitable conditions, e.g. that execution does not raise an exception and keeps in the same frame) diagram in Fig. 2, where s2as is the function mapping states to abstract states (by projecting values to types), and rs2ars denotes its lifting to return states;
- **MON:** the abstract virtual machine is monotonic w.r.t. the order induced by the inheritance relations on classes and interfaces.

For each of the properties considered, the proof proceeds by a case analysis on the bytecode to be executed, and then by an analysis of the possible outcomes of execution.

Bytecode verifier The BCV is derived by instantiating a dataflow analyser with the abstract JCVM, and its correctness is derived from CDO, CDA and MON, using a generic (i.e. independent from the specifics of the JCVM) proof that justifies the dataflow analysis and the compositional, method-by-method, algorithm underlying bytecode verification, see [2,16,18].

3   SPIKE

SPIKE provides an environment to verify clausal formulas in the initial model of many-sorted constructor-based theories presented by first-order conditional rules, and hence seems to be a good candidate for proving CDA, CDO and MON. Nevertheless, the standard distribution of SPIKE could not be used, since its specification language is too restricted, and its proof engine is not sufficiently optimized. Below we report on a number of improvements that were undertaken in order to apply SPIKE to our problem.

3.1   Specification Language

Parameterized Specifications The JavaCard VMs specifications are based on an important number of parameterized datatypes and functions. In particular, polymorphic lists are used intensively in the memory model: for example the heap is described as a list of objects, and the stack as a list of frames; further, each frame comes up with an operand stack and a set of local variables, each of which is described as a list of values. However, such parameterized specifications are not handled by the standard version of SPIKE. In order to perform our case study, we had to extend the syntax, type checking and inference system of SPIKE to deal with parameterized specifications—a similar work is described in detail in [6], but had not been integrated in the standard version of SPIKE.

Introduction of Existential Variables The axioms of standard SPIKE specifications consist in conditional rewrite rules of the form

$$l_1 = r_1, \ \ldots \ , l_n = r_n \Rightarrow g \rightarrow d$$

where all variables in conditions and d are required to occur in g. Formally, SPIKE requires that $\mathsf{var}(d) \subseteq \mathsf{var}(g)$ and that for $1 \leq i \leq n$, $\mathsf{var}(l_i) \subseteq \mathsf{var}(g)$ and $\mathsf{var}(r_i) \subseteq \mathsf{var}(g)$. However, most functions defining the semantics of the JCVM fail to meet this requirement, as variables in the r_is are fresh. In order to handle the JCVM specifications, we have enhanced SPIKE with the ability to handle such variables, which we call *existential*.

Obtaining SPIKE *specifications of the JCVMs* We have implemented mechanisms that may be used to compile a large class of Coq specifications to JSL and SPIKE, and that have been used to produce SPIKE specifications of the JCVMs from CertiCartes.

3.2   Description of SPIKE's Proof Engine

In order to motivate and explain our extensions to SPIKE, we begin with a short description of its proof engine.

Principles SPIKE's proof method is based on Cover Set Induction which encompasses different reasoning techniques, most of them based on conditional rewriting, case analysis and subsumption, and combines the advantages of explicit induction and of proofs by consistency [7,20].

In a nutshell, the method is parameterized by a set of axioms Ax, and proceeds by modifying incrementally two sets of clauses, (E, H), where E contains the conjectures to be checked and H contains clauses, previously in E, that have been reduced. The method is modelled by means of the relation $(E, H) \xrightarrow[Ax]{spike} (E', H')$ which is described below. We say that a formula ϕ is an inductive theorem w.r.t. Ax if there exists a finite derivation of the form $(\{\phi\}, \emptyset) \xrightarrow[Ax]{spike} \cdots \xrightarrow[Ax]{spike} (\emptyset, H)$; we call this derivation a proof of ϕ.

Proof system Given a set of conditional rules R derived from the orientation of Ax, SPIKE computes covering substitutions which is a family of substitutions covering all possible cases for induction variables. These substitutions are applied to conjectures *generating* special instances which are then *simplified* by rules, lemmas and induction hypotheses. This instantiation/simplification operation creates new subgoals that are processed in the same way in the following steps. Concretely, the relation $(E \cup \{C\}, H) \xrightarrow[Ax]{spike} (E', H')$, that transforms the current conjecture C, is defined by the rules of Fig. 3. The GENERATE inference rule computes appropriate covering substitutions which are then applied to C. These so-built instances are then simplified by rules and lemmas and appropriate instances of E and H. The set of induction hypotheses available for the simplification of the cover-set instance $C\sigma$ are ad-hoc instances of the current set of E, $\{C\}$ and H, strictly smaller (w.r.t. a decreasing order over clauses $\prec_c$) than $C\sigma$. The SIMPLIFY inference rule transforms a conjecture into a (potentially empty) set of new and simpler conjectures.

Strategies SPIKE offers the user limited, but crucial, mechanisms to interact with the proof engine. For each conjecture, the user can i) introduce intermediate lemmas that are first proven automatically and then used to establish the conjecture; ii) define a particular proof strategy that gives the order of execution for inference rules; iii) influence the inner mechanisms of some inference rules; for example the user can specify the order in which reducible terms are rewritten or the way the induction variables are chosen. These interaction mechanisms are crucial to guarantee that proof runs finish with success—when an empty set of conjectures is obtained. Of course, not all proof runs are successful; they may also diverge, or finish with failure; in the latter case the prover provides (under certain conditions) a counterexample to the initial conjectures.

Soundness SPIKE's inference engine is:

- sound, i.e. every conjecture that is successfully processed is valid;
- refutationally sound, i.e. the detection of a counterexample implies the existence of a counterexample in the initial conjectures [6].

3.3   Extensions of SPIKE's Proof Engine

We only provide a concise and informal description of the extensions that we have implemented, and briefly indicate their impact on soundness; a more detailed and formal description of these extensions can be found in [21].

$\text{Generate:} \ (E \cup \{C\}, H) \xrightarrow[Ax]{spike} (E \cup \bigcup_{\sigma \in CS\Sigma(C)} E_\sigma, H \cup \{C\})$

$$\text{if } \{C\sigma\} \xrightarrow[R;(E \cup H \cup \{C\})_{\prec_c C\sigma}]{simplify} E_\sigma \text{ for } \sigma \in CS\Sigma(C)$$

$\text{Simplify:} \ (E \cup \{C\}, H) \xrightarrow[Ax]{spike} (E \cup E', H)$

$$\text{if } \{C\} \xrightarrow[R;H_{\prec_c C} \cup E_{\prec_c C}]{simplify} E'$$

Recall that:

- a term t is said to be *inductively R-reducible (resp. R-irreducible)* if, for each substitution γ mapping variables to R-irreducible terms, $t\gamma$ is R-reducible (resp. R-irreducible);
- a *cover set for a conditional rewrite system* R, $CS(R)$, is a finite set of R-irreducible terms such that for all ground R-irreducible term s, there is a term t in $CS(R)$ and a ground substitution σ such that $Ax \models t\sigma = s$. From a cover set for a conditional rewrite system, we can build cover sets for clauses;
- a *cover substitution for a clause* C instantiates a particular subset of $Var(C)$ (called induction variables) by terms obtained from $CS(R)$ whose variables are replaced by fresh ones. We will denote by $CS\Sigma(C)$ the set of all possible cover substitutions for C.
- the set $\{C\sigma \mid \sigma \in CS\Sigma(C)\}$ is a *cover set for the clause* C.

Fig. 3. SPIKE's inference system.

Adaptation of the Inference System. In order to handle the extensions of the specification language, we have modified the inference system, and in particular the GENERATE rule. First, the parameterized variables cannot be instantiated by GENERATE rules during the proofs. Second, the GENERATE rule is modified so that SPIKE i) forbids the instantiation of existential variables, unless all induction variables are tagged as existential; ii) does not put the current conjecture in the set of premises if its cover-set instances are simplified with conditional rewrite rules introducing existential variables. W.r.t. i), observe that if no special provision were made, no inference rule could be applied if all induction variables are tagged as existential. In some circumstances however, we may want the proof to proceed, and so we force such a behavior by generalizing existential variables to universal ones in order to perform GENERATE. One drawback of this solution is the loss of refutational soundness, as the new rule potentially introduces new artificial counterexamples in the derivation by a generalization operation. Nevertheless, the new rule preserves the soundness of the system. W.r.t. ii), existential variables break the order condition requiring that the left hand side be greater than the conditions and the right hand side. This implies that if the current conjecture would contain a counterexample, the new set of conjectures cannot guarantee a smaller one. However, this condition is crucial for allowing the current conjecture to participate to further inferences [20]. In such cases, the transformation of a cover-set instance $C\sigma$ can be considered as an instance of SIMPLIFY rule, which in addition (w.r.t. the GENERATE rule) allows the use of H instances equivalent to $C\sigma$. Summing up, the resulting system is sound, but not refutationally sound.

Improvements over the Inference System

New Induction Schemas In the standard implementation, each cover substitution for a clause C should instantiate all the induction variables from C. Therefore, the number of cover substitutions is exponential w.r.t. number of induction variables. For real applications such as the cross-validation of the JCVMs, this induction scheme generates thousands of cover substitutions and the prover performances become unacceptably poor.

In order to overcome this problem, we have implemented the following induction scheme, which leads to a major improvement in terms of performance: assume that there exists a (sub)term t of C whose head symbol is defined and that unifies with left-hand sides of the axioms defining the head symbol. From the most general unifier, we can immediately deduce that the cover substitution σ and the axiom that can simplify $C\sigma$. Therefore, the number of cover substitutions is limited to the number of axioms defining the head symbol, usually ranged to tens. As explained above, the improved schema is sound because the specification is constructor-based, complete and strongly complete. The last property guarantees that the disjunction of the conditions related to instances of axioms having the same left-hand side is valid.

Although of no incidence for our purpose, this scheme is not fit to prove conjectures having different (sub)terms that share induction variables, as for the associativity of the addition over naturals; it leads to a proof divergence. Therefore, we have adapted the following heuristics: recursively, if the (sub)term t shares induction variables with other (sub)term t' of C, compute also the cover substitutions and apply the heuristics for t' as for t. Since the number of (sub)terms of C is finite, this heuristics terminates. At the end, by the combination of the partial cover substitutions, it returns a set of cover substitutions such that the resulted instances of C can be simplified at any position corresponding to the terms treated by the heuristics (like t and t'). In our proofs, the number of cover substitutions still remains ranged to tens.

New Inference Rules The following inference rules, illustrated in Fig. 4, have been added in order to exploit the conditions of conjectures:

1. **auto simplification**. It allows the rewriting of a conjecture with its negative literals, and allows to eliminate an existential variable from the rest of a conjecture as soon as it appears in a top position in equalities. Note that the order $>_e$ is an extension of the usual recursive path ordering to existential variables: for example, an existential variable x is always greater than any term that does not contain x and is not itself an existential variable;

2. **congruence closure**. If a conjecture contains as conditions the literals of the form $s = t$ and $t = u$ then the new literal $s = u$ is added to the conditions. The new literals are built using a completion algorithm having as input all

AUTO SIMPLIFICATION: $(E \cup \{C[\overline{s = t}]\}, H) \xrightarrow[Ax]{spike} (E \cup \{C'\}, H)$

$$\text{if } s >_e t \text{ and } C' \text{ is the clause } C \text{ rewritten}$$
$$\text{with } s \to t, \text{ excepting the term } s \text{ of } s = t$$

CONGRUENCE CLOSURE: $(E \cup \{\dots s = t \dots \wedge t = u \wedge \dots \Rightarrow l\}, H) \xrightarrow[Ax]{spike} (E \cup \{C'\}, H)$

$$\text{where } C' \equiv \dots s = t \dots \wedge t = u \wedge \dots s = \mathbf{u} \Rightarrow l$$

AUGMENTATION: $(E \cup \{\underbrace{cond \Rightarrow l}_{C}\}, H) \xrightarrow[Ax]{spike} (E \cup \{cond \wedge t \Rightarrow l\}, H)$

$$\text{if there exists a clause } cond' \Rightarrow p \text{ of } R \cup H_{\preceq_c C} \cup E_{\prec_c C}$$
$$\text{s.t. every literal of } cond' \text{ is subsumed by } cond$$

Fig. 4. New inference rules.

the negative literals of the current conjecture. The procedure is refined by looking in priority for new equalities between constructor terms. If the head symbols of the both sides of a new equality are the same, we can derive new equalities by a decomposition operation, otherwise the clause is eliminated from the set of conjectures;

3. **augmentation**. Given a conditional clause, its conclusion can be added to the conditions *cond* of a conjecture if the conditions of the clause are discharged by *cond* [8]. The typical use of this rule in our applications is when the clause is a non-orientable user-defined lemma.

Additional applicability conditions are put such that each of these inference rules is an instance of the SIMPLIFY rule. Hence the soundness of these rules follows from the soundness of the abstract inference system of Figure 3.

The application strategy of the inference rules is standard, by trying firstly the SIMPLIFY rules that do not add new conjectures, then the other SIMPLIFY rules and, finally, the GENERATE rules.

Implementation Optimisations Another major improvement in terms of execution time is the recording of the failures of the inference rules application in order to avoid useless computation. Some of the recordings are performed at the level of clauses (for example, for subsumption), others at the level of terms (for example, for rewriting). If a rewrite operation with an unconditional rule fails at a given position of a conjecture, the rule's identification number is associated to that position such that the rule is avoided in the further rewriting operations as long as the term containing the position does not change.

4   Applications to JavaCard

In this section, we describe the results of our experiments of using the extended version of SPIKE to prove CDO, CDA and MON. For each instruction, we have three modules, one for each property CDA, CDO, and MON; this separation has no other purpose than convenience for carrying our experiments and collecting statistics. Each module consists of three parts: an algebraic specification, in our case parts of the description of the JCVMs, a logical theory to be proven, in our case some assumptions about the program and statements of CDA, CDO and MON, and a strategy that determines the prover's behavior during the proofs. The modules are available at www.loria.fr/~stratula/verificard.

4.1   CDO

The new version of SPIKE has been used to verify CDO for most instructions (41 out of 45). Figure 5 provides an excerpt of the SPIKE module used to prove CDO for the function CONV, that factors several of the conversion bytecodes of the JCVM: s2b (short to bytes), s2i (short to integers), i2b (integers to bytes), i2s (integers to short). Figure 1 provides some statistics about this experiment. In the second column, we indicate if the proof has been already done (yes) or not yet (n.y.). The third column presents the number of lemmas introduced by the user (and proved previously by SPIKE), while the other columns show respectively the number of GENERATE rules, normalization operations with unconditional rules, case rewriting with conditional rules, syntactic subsumption rules, tautology elimination rules and the execution time. Note that most proofs are automatic, i.e. do not require users to provide SPIKE with additional lemmas, and done in a reasonable time.

4.2   CDA and MON

We are now working on the proofs of CDA and MON, and have proven both properties for around half of the instructions. These properties are more challenging to prove than CDO, in particular because they rely on a number of invariants about JavaCard programs and the JCVM memory model. Thus users must provide appropriate invariants for the proofs to go through; as the formulation of such invariants can only be made during proofs, the benefits of automation are less clear for CDA and MON.

4.3   Assessment

We briefly comment on the effectiveness of the tool, and establish a comparison with our work on CertiCartes.

Automation SPIKE provides a reasonable level of automation, and there is no need to tune the strategy for each lemma to be proved. The best results are achieved with CDO, which for many bytecodes can be proved automatically, i.e. without requiring the users to provide intermediate lemmas. As explained above, the level of automation is lower for CDA and CDO. We detail below two directions for improvement.

The module begins with the name of the specification, and follows by declaring the types (or sorts), constructor symbols, and defined functions of the specification. Then the behavior of defined functions is specified by means of clauses. The module is completed by fixing a proof strategy, and by declaring of the conjectures to be proven; note that conjectures are formulated as equational clauses.

```
specification : CONV

sorts : list type_prim jcvm_state   ...

constructors :
Nil: -> (list 'A ); Cons__:  'A (list 'A) -> (list 'A );...

defined functions :
CONV___ : type_prim type_prim jcvm_state -> returned_state;...

axioms :

% cONV :1

stack_f (u1) = Nil =>
cONV (u2, u3, u1) -> abortCode (State_error, u1) ;

% cONV :2

stack_f (u1) = Cons (e2, e3),
extr_from_opstack (u4, opstack(e2)) = Inl (Pair (e5, e6))
=> cONV (u4, u7, u1) -> update_frame
(push_opstack (VPrim (tpz2vp (u7, t_convert (u4, u7, e5))), e6,
e2), u1) ;

% cONV :3

stack_f (u1) = Cons (e2, e3),
extr_from_opstack (u4, opstack (e2)) = Inr (e5)
=> cONV (u4, u6, u1) -> abortCode (e5, u1) ;


strategy : ...

conjectures :

state = Build_jcvm_state( sh, hp, Cons (h, lf)),
res = cONV(n, z0, state) =>
res = abortCode( Type_error, state),
res = abortCode( Signature_error, state),
rs2ors( res) = ocONV (n, z0, s2os(state));
```

Fig. 5. An excerpt of a SPIKE specification formalizing the instruction CONV.

Table 1. Statistics for CDO proofs carried on a PC equipped with a 3.06 GHz Pentium processor and 512 Mbytes RAM.

instruction	proved	lemmas	Generate	U. R.	C. R.	Subsumption	Taut.	time
ACONST_NULL	yes	0	0	4	1	0	1	0.5s
ALOAD	n.y.	0	0	0	0	0	0	0.0
ARITH	yes	33	100	8771	2893	979	2178	8m
ARRAYLENGTH	yes	22	23	880	199	105	567	16s
ASTORE	n.y.	0	0	0	0	0	0	0.0
ATHROW	yes	24	24	2021	29	168	3496	1m42s
CHECKCAST	yes	79	88	1531	382	153	4741	1m44s
CONST	yes	0	1	24	7	0	7	0.5s
CONV	yes	0	94	999	405	12	495	0.54s
DUP	yes	0	4	21	3	2	26	0.13s
DUP2	yes	0	4	45	4	4	62	0.25s
GETFIELD	yes	24	49	4080	1074	347	4581	1m57s
GETFIELD_THIS	yes	24	49	4080	1074	347	4581	1m56s
GETSTATIC	yes	0	22	313	25	23	543	2.58s
GOTO	yes	0	0	4	1	0	1	0.07s
ICMP	yes	0	93	283	6	135	156	1.9s
IFNONNULL	yes	0	20	85	23	13	54	0.47s
IFNULL	yes	0	22	89	15	13	56	0.85s
IF_ACMP_COND	yes	13	38	147	31	48	99	1.3s
IF_COND	yes	0	46	175	117	97	81	0.4s
IF_SCMP_COND	yes	0	75	288	130	116	163	1.3s
INC	yes	0	10	217	29	22	566	1.5s
INSTANCEOF	yes	66	72	4173	1838	1203	5388	297m
INVOKEINTERFACE	yes	47	53	951	171	261	2026	0.38s
INVOKESPECIAL	yes	41	54	633	103	166	1097	13s
INVOKESTATIC	yes	8	12	42	7	13	72	0.4s
INVOKEVIRTUAL	yes	49	57	891	172	251	1576	31s
JSR	yes	0	0	4	1	0	1	0.15s
LOAD	yes	0	17	196	25	20	417	1.7s
LOOKUPSWITCH	yes	19	33	3434	1208	372	7414	52.4s
NEG	yes	2	16	87	38	24	76	1.2s
NEW	yes	1	7	26	3	4	33	0.17s
NEWARRAY	yes	22	31	4239	435	574	7540	1m07s
NOP	yes	0	0	4	1	0	1	0.05s
POP	yes	0	6	25	3	3	26	0.1s
POP2	yes	0	9	31	3	3	27	0.1s
PUSH	yes	0	1	9	1	0	10	0.4s
PUTFIELD	n.y.	0	0	0	0	0	0	0.0
PUTFIELD_THIS	n.y.	0	0	0	0	0	0	0.0
PUTSTATIC	yes	21	57	643	155	124	1096	9s
RET	yes	0	6	36	3	4	37	0.14s
RETURN	yes	8	11	200	33	2	199	0.92s
STORE	yes	0	55	554	139	95	2028	9.8s
SWAP	yes	0	13	51	4	5	64	0.3s
TABLESWITCH	yes	17	86	13651	10830	1190	4302	15m43

Counterexamples SPIKE provides useful feedback to the specifier. By permitting the automatic refutation of false conjectures, SPIKE highlights, at a relatively low cost, possible problems in the specifications. This is essential for complex, large-scale formalisations which are bound to contain bugs, at least in their initial stages.

Expressivity SPIKE is expressive enough for specifying the virtual machines, and the properties CDO, CDA and MON. However it is not expressive enough to prove the correctness of the BCV, see below.

Comparison with CertiCartes CDA, CDO and MON have been proved independently in the Coq proof assistant. The comparison is without surprise, e.g. SPIKE provides a better level of automation than Coq, but on the other hand proofs that are not automatic may be harder to go through in SPIKE. Further, Coq is more expressive than SPIKE, and provides an adequate environment to specify (and prove) some properties of the JavaCard platform that cannot even stated in SPIKE—most of the work reported in [2] cannot be cast in SPIKE.

Directions for improvement We see two directions of work for optimizing the usefulness of SPIKE in the context of the certification of the JavaCard Platform:

- **Automatic generation of intermediate lemmas:** for a number of byte-codes, SPIKE requires users to provide intermediate results for establishing CDO, CDA and MON. Many of such lemmas are of a similar shape, and could be generated automatically so as to minimize user interactions. One possibility that we are exploring is to exploit the abstraction script used to generate the offensive/abstract machine from the defensive one for generating such lemmas;
- **Connection with Coq:** while SPIKE provides a reasonable level of automation, not all proofs can be performed automatically. Further, Coq is more expressive than SPIKE, as explained above. In this respect, it may be beneficial to connect Coq and SPIKE so that Coq users may appeal to SPIKE to discharge some proof obligations automatically, as is done for example for Coq and Elan [17]. In particular, such a connection would allow users to discharge automatically many trivial (sub)cases of CDA and MON, namely those which do not rely on any invariant.

5   Conclusion and Future Work

5.1   Related Work

Our work is an attempt to apply rewriting techniques to validate security architectures for low-level languages used in smartcards. There have been a number of other applications of rewriting techniques to security, but these works focus on different aspects of security, such as network security and cryptographic protocols, see e.g. [10,13].

Our work is related to existing efforts to provide formal specification and correctness proofs for open platforms, including those carried by E. Giménez and co-authors at Trusted Logic, by J.-L. Lanet and co-workers at Gemplus [9] (abstract B machines for the JCVM and BCV), by T. Nipkow and co-workers at Munich [16] (Java, JVM, BCV, and compiler in Isabelle), by J. Strother Moore and co-workers at U. of Texas (JVM and BCV in ACL2)—note that some other works, e.g. [19,11] provide machine executable semantics, but pencil-and-paper formal proofs. For lack of space, we refer to [14] for further information, and limit ourselves to notice that most of these specifications implicitly use a restricted framework, but our work is distinctive by expliciting and taking advantage of this restricted framework.

Closest to our work is the work by A. Gordon and D. Syme [22], which aims at automatic type-safety proofs for low-level languages. They identify a restricted framework in which specifications and properties can be expressed, and enhance the proof assistant HOL with suitable decision procedures, inspired from SVC (Stanford Validity Checker), to achieve a high degree of automation. Our methodology, which aims at validating automatically derived abstractions, seems crisper but we lack grounds for comparison —it would be interesting to validate, as they do, the .NET virtual machine, for carrying such a comparison.

5.2   Future Work

Further case studies. Our current focus with Jakarta is to provide automatic support for the construction and cross-validation of the virtual machines for properties other than typing, e.g. initialization or non-interference. As such efforts rely on a similar methodologies, it seems interesting to use SPIKE to prove appropriate versions of the CDO, CDA and MON properties.

Domain-specific proof environment for certifying low-level languages. A longer term objective is to enhance the Jakarta toolset towards an environment that provides automatic support for certifying low-level languages. We expect the restricted format of JSL will prove useful for this task.

References

1. G. Barthe, P. Courtieu, G. Dufay, and S. Melo de Sousa. Tool-Assisted Specification and Verification of the JavaCard Platform. In H. Kirchner and C. Ringessein, editors, *Proceedings of AMAST'02*, volume 2422 of *Lecture Notes in Computer Science*, pages 41–59. Springer-Verlag, 2002.
2. G. Barthe and G. Dufay. Verified ByteCode Verifiers Revisited. Manuscript, 2003.
3. G. Barthe, G. Dufay, M. Huisman, and S. Melo de Sousa. Jakarta: a toolset to reason about the JavaCard platform. In I. Attali and T. Jensen, editors, *Proceedings of e-SMART'01*, volume 2140 of *Lecture Notes in Computer Science*, pages 2–18. Springer-Verlag, 2001.
4. G. Barthe, G. Dufay, L. Jakubiec, and S. Melo de Sousa. A formal correspondence between offensive and defensive JavaCard virtual machines. In A. Cortesi, editor, *Proceedings of VMCAI'02*, volume 2294 of *Lecture Notes in Computer Science*, pages 32–45. Springer-Verlag, 2002.

5. G. Barthe, G. Dufay, L. Jakubiec, B. Serpette, and S. Melo de Sousa. A Formal Executable Semantics of the JavaCard Platform. In D. Sands, editor, *Proceedings of ESOP'01*, volume 2028 of *Lecture Notes in Computer Science*, pages 302–319. Springer-Verlag, 2001.
6. A. Bouhoula. Using induction and rewriting to verify and complete parameterized specifications. *Theoretical Computer Science*, 1-2(170):245–276, 1996.
7. A. Bouhoula. Automated theorem proving by test set induction. *Journal of Symbolic Computation*, 23(1):47–77, January 1997.
8. R. S. Boyer and J S. Moore. Integrating decision procedures into heuristic theorem provers: A case study with linear arithmetic. ICSCA-CMP-44, University of Texas at Austin, 1985. Also published in *Machine Intelligence 11*, Oxford University Press, 1988.
9. L. Casset, L. Burdy, and A. Requet. Formal Development of an Embedded Verifier for JavaCard ByteCode. In *Proceedings of DSN'02*. IEEE Computer Society, 2002.
10. I. Cervesato, N. A. Durgin, P. D. Lincoln, J. C. Mitchell, and A. Scedrov. A meta-notation for protocol analysis. In *12th IEEE Computer Security Foundations Workshop*. IEEE Computer Society Press, June 1999.
11. A. Coglio, A. Goldberg, and Z. Qian. Towards a Provably-Correct Implementation of the JVM Bytecode Verifier. In *Formal Underpinnings of Java Workshop at OOPSLA*, 1998.
12. Coq Development Team. *The Coq Proof Assistant User's Guide. Version 7.4*, February 2003.
13. G. Denker, J. Meseguer, and C. Talcott. Formal specification and analysis of active networks and communication protocols: The maude experience. In *DARPA Information Survivability Conference and Exposition (DISCEX 2000)*. IEEE, 2000.
14. P. Hartel and L. Moreau. Formalizing the Safety of Java, the Java Virtual Machine and Java Card. *ACM Computing Surveys*, 33(4):517–558, December 2001.
15. G. Klein. *Verified Java Bytecode Verification*. PhD thesis, Technical University Munich, 2003.
16. G. Klein and T. Nipkow. Verified bytecode verifiers. *Theoretical Computer Science*, 2003. To appear.
17. Q.-H. Nguyen, C. Kirchner, and H. Kirchner. External rewriting for skeptical proof assistants. *Journal of Automated Reasoning*, 29(3-4):309–336, 2002.
18. T. Nipkow. Verified Bytecode Verifiers. In F. Honsell and M. Miculan, editors, *Proceedings of FOSSACS'01*, volume 2030 of *Lecture Notes in Computer Science*, pages 347–363. Springer-Verlag, 2001.
19. R. Stärk, J. Schmid, and E. Börger. *Java and the Java Virtual Machine - Definition, Verification, Validation*. Springer-Verlag, 2001.
20. S. Stratulat. A general framework to build contextual cover set induction provers. *Journal of Symbolic Computation*, 32(4):403–445, September 2001.
21. S. Stratulat. New uses of existential variables in implicit induction. In preparation.
22. D. Syme and A. D. Gordon. Automating type soundness proofs via decision procedures and guided reductions. In M. Baaz and A. Voronkov, editors, *Proceedings of LPAR'02*, volume 2514 of *Lecture Notes in Computer Science*, pages 418–434, 2002.

"Term Partition" for Mathematical Induction

Urso Pascal and Kounalis Emmanuel

Université de Nice - Sophia Antipolis, Laboratoire I3S
Dpt. Informatique, Parc Valrose
06108 Nice CEDEX 2, France
urso@unice.fr, kounalis@unice.fr

Abstract. A key new concept, *term partition*, allows to design a new method for proving theorems whose proof usually requires mathematical induction. A term partition of a term t is a well-defined splitting of t into a pair (a, b) of terms that describes the *language of normal forms of the ground instances of t*.
If $\mathcal{A}$ is a *monomorphic* set of axioms (rules) and (a, b) is a term partition of t, then the normal form (obtained by using $\mathcal{A}$) of any ground instance of t can be "divided" into the normal forms (obtained by using $\mathcal{A}$) of the corresponding ground instances of a and b. Given a conjecture $t = s$ to be checked for inductive validity in the theory of $\mathcal{A}$, a partition (a, b) of t and a partition (c, d) of s is computed. If $a = c$ and $b = d$, then $t = s$ is an inductive theorem for $\mathcal{A}$.
The method is conceptually different to the classical theorem proving approaches. It allows to obtain proofs of a large number of conjectures (including non-linear ones) without additional lemmas or generalizations.

1 Introduction

The need to be able to prove theorems by induction appears in many applications including number theory, program verification, and program synthesis. We assume familiarity with the basic notion of equational logic and rewrite systems (see for instance [9]).

A many-sorted signature Σ is a pair $(\mathcal{S}, \mathcal{F})$ where $\mathcal{S}$ is a set of *sorts* and $\mathcal{F}$ is a finite vocabulary of *functions symbols*. Each symbol $f \in \mathcal{F}$ is associated with a type denoted $s_1 \times \ldots \times s_n \to s$ such that s and every s_i belong to $\mathcal{S}$. n is the *arity* of f and s is the value (i.e. the *coarity*) of f. Let $T(\mathcal{F}, \mathcal{X})$ denote the set of well-sorted *terms* built out of function symbols taken from $\mathcal{F}$ and a denumerable set $\mathcal{X}$ of free-sorted *variables*. We assume that $\mathcal{F}$ contains at least one constant symbol by sort. Thus, the set $T(\mathcal{F})$ of *ground* terms (variable-free), is non-empty. If t is a term and θ is a (ground) substitution of (ground) term for variables in t, then $t\theta$ is a *(ground) instance* of t. Finally, an *equation* e is an element of $T(\mathcal{F}, \mathcal{X}) \times T(\mathcal{F}, \mathcal{X})$ and is written as $t = s$.

An equation $t = s$ is a *deductive consequence* of a set $\mathcal{A}$ of equations if it is valid in any model of $\mathcal{A}$. It is well known that $t = s$ is a deductive consequence of $\mathcal{A}$ if and only if $t =_{\mathcal{A}} s$. Here, $=_{\mathcal{A}}$ denotes the smallest monotonic congruence that contains $\mathcal{A}$. An equation is an *inductive consequence* of a set $\mathcal{A}$ of equations if

R. Nieuwenhuis (Ed.): RTA 2003, LNCS 2706, pp. 352–366, 2003.

it is valid in the initial (standard) model. In proof theoretical terms, an equation $t = s$ is said to be an ***inductive theorem***, denoted $t =_{ind(\mathcal{A})} s$, if and only if $t\sigma =_{\mathcal{A}} s\sigma$ for all ground instance of $t\sigma = s\sigma$ of $t = s$. Thus, the proof of $t = s$ depends on the proof of infinite number of ground instances of $t = s$.

To establish inductive consequences, classical theorem proving provides either explicit induction [1,5,16] or implicit induction [2,3,4,6,7,8,11]. However, inductive proofs often diverge. The hardest problem in using either approach is to find the appropriate *induction schemes* as well as the suitable *lemmas* needed for the proof. As a "simple" example, consider the theorem:

$$x * (x + (x * x)) = (x * x) + (x * (x * x)) \tag{1}$$

Addition $(+)$, and multiplication $(*)$ are defined by means of the equations, $\mathcal{A} = \{x + 0 = x;\ x + s(y) = s(x + y);\ x * 0 = 0;\ x * s(y) = x * y + x\}$, where $s(x)$ represents the successor of x (i.e $x + 1$).

The proof attempt begins with a simple induction step on x. The proof of basis case $0 * (0 + (0 * 0)) = (0 * 0) + (0 * (0 * 0))$ is trivial. In the step case, the induction hypothesis is (1) and the induction conclusion is $s(x) * (s(x) + (s(x) * s(x))) = (s(x) * s(x)) + (s(x) * (s(x) * s(x)))$. Simplifying the induction conclusion with the definitions above gives:

$$s(s(x)*(s(x)+((s(x)*x)+x))+x) = s(s((s(x)*x)+x)+(s(x)*((s(x)*x)+x)+x))$$

This equation cannot be simplified furthermore because the both sides of this equation doesn't contain any subterm which is an instance of an equation of $\mathcal{A}$ or of the induction hypothesis (1). So, another induction step on x is performed. Unfortunately this generates a diverging sequences of subgoals. The proof of (1) simply fails. The problem is that the prover repeatedly tries an induction on x but is unable to simplify the successor functions that it introduces on the first positions of $+$ and $*$. *This failure is especially tied to the classical induction setting which is based on the explicit or implicit use of induction hypothesis.* Equation (1) cannot be proven when given just the above definitions without a suitable *generalization* of the induction hypothesis[1]. For instance, to prove this equation the user has to provide the lemmas $x * (y + z) = x * y + x * z$ and $(w + (x * y')) + v = w + ((x * y') + v)$.

A *rewrite system* $\mathcal{R}$ is a set of oriented equations $\{l \to r\}$ called *rewrite rules*. A rule is applied to a term t by finding a subterm s of t that is an instance of the left side l (i.e., $s = l\sigma$) and replacing s with the corresponding instance $(r\sigma)$ of the rule's right side. If $\mathcal{R}$ terminates, one computes with $\mathcal{R}$ by repeatedly applying rules to rewrite an input term until a *normal form* (unrewritable term) is obtained. In case where $\mathcal{A}$ can be compiled into a ground convergent $\mathcal{R}$ rewrite system, for a ground substitution σ, we can decide $t\sigma =_{\mathcal{A}} s\sigma$ by testing for syntactic identity of the $\mathcal{R}$-normal forms of $t\sigma$ and $s\sigma$ (i.e. Is $t\sigma{\downarrow}_{\mathcal{R}} \equiv s\sigma{\downarrow}_{\mathcal{R}}$? where $t\sigma{\downarrow}_{\mathcal{R}}$ denotes the $\mathcal{R}$-normal form of $t\sigma$).

---

[1] Please note that the most advanced heuristic-based methods ([10,12,14,15]) fail also to produce the necessary lemmas and/or generalizations for the proof to go through for all the examples of the present paper (especially non-linear ones).

In terms of these definitions, a deep analysis of the normal forms of the ground instances of the both sides of (1) shows the existence of two terms $a = x * x$ and $b = x * (x * x)$ that satisfy the following property: for all ground substitutions θ,

$$(x * (x + (x * x)))\theta\downarrow_{\mathcal{R}} = (x * x)\theta\downarrow_{\mathcal{R}} \otimes (x * (x * x))\theta\downarrow_{\mathcal{R}}$$
$$\text{and } ((x * x) + (x * (x * x)))\theta\downarrow_{\mathcal{R}} = (x * x)\theta\downarrow_{\mathcal{R}} \otimes (x * (x * x))\theta\downarrow_{\mathcal{R}}$$

Roughly speaking, the normal form of a ground instance of $x * (x + (x * x))$ is obtained by replacing the innermost symbol (i.e. 0) of the normal form of the corresponding ground instance of a by the normal form of the corresponding ground instance of b (the semantics of $\otimes$). Similarly, the normal form of a ground instance of $(x * x) + (x * (x * x))$ is obtained by replacing the innermost symbol of $a\theta\downarrow$ by $b\theta\downarrow$. Since both sides of (1) can be divided into terms $a = x * x$ and $b = x * (x * x)$ we may conclude that (1) is an inductive theorem (see theorem 1).

Our *approach tries to capture this intuition as to why the above equation is an inductive theorem*. The central part of this paper is to show how our method enables to obtain inductive validity of theorems, completely automatically from the functions definitions alone.

The organization of this paper is as follows. In Sect. 2, the class of monomorphic rewrite system is provided. In Sect. 3, an outline of our approach with a "simple" example is presented. Section 4 introduces the key concept of term partition and shows how to use it to prove inductive theorems. Section 5 describes how to compute a term partition. In Sect. 6 we present our general inductive procedure and applies it to some *hard* examples[2]. The formal proofs that are too long to appear in the body of our paper are given in the appendix that can be found at http://www-sop.inria.fr/coprin/urso/papers.html.

2   Monomorphic Rewrite Systems

A *ground convergent* rewrite system $\mathcal{R}$ over a set of function symbols $\mathcal{F}_{\mathcal{R}}$ is *terminating* – w.r.t. a reduction ordering $\succ$ – and *ground confluent* – i.e. $\mathcal{R}$ has the Church-Rosser property on ground terms. Termination implies that there is at least one $\mathcal{R}$-normal form for any term. From now, we assume that $\mathcal{F}_{\mathcal{R}}$ can be partitioned into *free constructors* $\mathcal{C}_{\mathcal{R}}$ and *defined symbols* $\mathcal{D}_{\mathcal{R}}$, such that every ground term with a defined symbol can be made equal (using $\mathcal{R}$) to a ground term built upon constructors only (*sufficient completeness*). We shall from now on regard our set $\mathcal{A}$ of equations as a rewrite system $\mathcal{R}$.

The set $TS(\mathcal{R}) = \{t \mid t$ is constant or t is of the form $c(x_1, x_2, \ldots, x_n$ with $c \in \mathcal{C}_{\mathcal{R}}$ and $x_1, \ldots, x_n) \in \mathcal{X}\}$ is a *test set* for $\mathcal{R}$ [13]. A *test set substitution* σ is a substitution with values in $TS(\mathcal{R})$. $t\downarrow_{\mathcal{R}}$ denotes the normal form of term t using $\mathcal{R}$ (when R is unambiguous it is just denoted $t\downarrow$). Let $(t = s)^{\prec}$ denote the instances of equation $t = s$ that are smaller (w.r.t. the extension of $\succ$ to

---

[2] A hard theorem requires either a change of induction rule, or additional lemmas and generalizations for the proof to go through.

equations) than $t = s$. The following function GEN encompasses the classical definition of induction.

Definition 1. GEN$(\mathbf{t} = \mathbf{s}, \mathcal{R}) = \{t\sigma\!\downarrow_{\mathcal{R}} = s\sigma\!\downarrow_{\mathcal{R}} \mid \sigma$ *is test set substitution,* $t\sigma\!\downarrow_{\mathcal{R}} \neq s\sigma\!\downarrow_{\mathcal{R}}$, *and* $t\sigma\!\downarrow_{\mathcal{R}}$ *(resp.* $s\sigma\!\downarrow_{\mathcal{R}}$*) is computed using* $T = \mathcal{R} \cup \{(t = s)^{\prec}\}$.

If t is a term, $type(t)$ denotes the sort of t (i.e. the coarity of the root of t) and $dom(t)$ is the set of positions of t. ε denotes the *empty position*, p, q, $\ldots$ denote *positions* in a term. $|p|$ is the length of position p and $<$ is the *prefix ordering*. For notational convention, we shall represent positions as lists of digits from $\{1 \ldots 9\}$. t/p denotes the *subterm of t at position p*. We write $t[s]_p$ the result of replacing the subterm of t at position p by s. Finally $t(p)$ denotes the *symbol of t at position p*.

The **monomorphic rewrite systems** are a subset of ground convergent and sufficiently complete rewrite systems. Their main interest is that their ground normalized terms can be viewed as "lists". Now, *in a list we are able to identify a "head" and a "tail" part and then to split a ground normalized term.*

Definition 2. *A ground convergent and sufficiently complete (over free constructor) rewrite system $\mathcal{R}$ is* monomorphic *if there is only one constant by sort $\mathcal{T}$ – denoted $\bot_{\mathcal{T}}$ – and every ground term t in $\mathcal{R}$-normal form has only one leaf labelled by $\bot_{type(t)}$.*

Example 1. Let $\mathcal{R}$ be the following monomorphic system (with $\mathcal{S} = \{nat, list\}$):

$$\begin{cases} x{+}s(y) \rightarrow s(x{+}y); & x{+}0 \rightarrow x; & e(x, s(y)) \rightarrow e(x, y) * x; & e(x, 0) \rightarrow s(0); \\ x * s(y) \rightarrow (x * y){+}x; & x * 0 \rightarrow 0; & m(x, s(y)) \rightarrow x{+}m(x, y); & m(x, 0) \rightarrow 0; \\ \Sigma(s(x)) \rightarrow s(x){+}\Sigma(x); & \Sigma(0) \rightarrow 0; & \Sigma I(s(x), y) \rightarrow \Sigma I(x, s(y{+}x)); & \Sigma I(0, y) \rightarrow y; \\ r(c.l) \rightarrow ap(r(l), c.\varnothing); & r(\varnothing) \rightarrow \varnothing; & ap(c.l, L) \rightarrow c.ap(l, L); & ap(\varnothing, L) \rightarrow L; \\ R(c.l, L) \rightarrow R(l, c.L); & R(\varnothing, L) \rightarrow L \end{cases}$$

$$\mathcal{C}_{\mathcal{R}} = \begin{cases} 0: \rightarrow nat; & s: \quad nat \rightarrow nat; \\ \varnothing: \rightarrow list; & .: nat \times list \rightarrow list \end{cases}$$

$$\text{and } \mathcal{D}_{\mathcal{R}} = \begin{cases} \Sigma: nat \rightarrow nat; & +, *, m, e, \Sigma I: nat \times nat \rightarrow nat; \\ r: list \rightarrow list; & R, ap: \quad list \times list \rightarrow list \end{cases}$$

Further, $TS(\mathcal{R}) = \{0, s(x), \varnothing, c.l\}$. Throughout of this paper we shall make free use of rules in $\mathcal{R}$.

According to the above definition, *a rewrite system is monomorphic only if its non-constant constructors have exactly one argument of their own sort*; this argument is called "reflexive".

Definition 3. *Let $\mathcal{R}$ be a monomorphic rewrite system and let $f: s_1 \times \ldots \times s_n \rightarrow s$ be a non-constant function symbol in $\mathcal{C}_{\mathcal{R}}$. The unique position $i \leq n$ that verifies $s_i = s$ is called the* reflexive argument position *of f, and is denoted $RA(\mathcal{R}, f)$.*
Let $C \in T(\mathcal{C}_{\mathcal{R}}, \mathcal{X})$, the term $C[t]_{RA(\mathcal{R}, C(\varepsilon))}$ is simply denoted $C[t]$.

For the above rewrite system, we get that $RA(\mathcal{R}, .) = 2$ and $RA(\mathcal{R}, s) = 1$.

Finally, the "join" of two ground normalized terms in a monomorphic theory is defined as follows.

Definition 4. *Let $\mathcal{R}$ be a monomorphic rewrite system and let A and B be two ground terms in $\mathcal{R}$-normal form, both of sort T; the join of A and B denoted $A \otimes B$ is the term $A[B]_p$ such that $A/p = \perp_T$.*

For instance, $s(0).(0.\underline{\varnothing}) \otimes s(s(0)).\varnothing = s(0).(0.(\underline{s(s(0)).\varnothing}))$.

3   Outline of Our Approach: An Example

The key concept underlying our approach is to split both sides of a given equation $t = s$ into pairs (a, b) and (c, d) and to recursively check whether $a = c$ and $b = d$ (see Theorem 1). Here, a and c are the *head parts* of t and s. b and d are theirs *tail parts*. To obtain a pair that describes the head and the tail part of the normal form of the ground instances of a term t we have to identify which particular combination of subterms of t "creates" these parts. Further, to find these subterms we have to understand how each function in the rewrite system manages its arguments.

To illustrate the essential ideas behind our method let us outline it on a "tricky" example. Assume we wish to prove the non-linear equation $t = s$:

$$r(ap(l, r(l)) = ap(l, r(l)) \tag{2}$$

Our approach to induction consists in computing a suitable term partition for each side of (2). Actually, we compute a set of partitions (DEC) for each side and try to find in these sets two head or tail parts syntactically equal (see induction procedure in Sect. 6). A set of partitions is computed in two phases.

• In the *first* phase, the type of the argument positions of the defined function symbols appearing in $\mathcal{R}$ is characterized. Intuitively, this characterization indicates how each function argument is moved onto another argument position at each step of a rewriting sequence. This type can be precompiled using the definitions 6, 7, and 8 (see Sect. 5).

In our example, position 1 is the upward argument of ap; position 2 is the downward argument of ap; and position 1 is the down-contextual argument of r. Roughly speaking, the *upward* argument position of a function symbol f indicates which subterm in a ground term (with f as root symbol) moves towards the head of the normal form in a rewriting sequence. The *downward* argument position indicates which subterm in a ground term moves down towards the tail of the normal form in a rewriting sequence. The *down-contextual* argument position indicates which subterm in a ground term is used to create a regular series of elements whose normalization leads to the tail of the normal form[3].

---

[3] A fourth type of argument position – *up-contextual* – is not present in these terms, it indicates which subterm is used to create a regular series of elements whose normalization leads to the head of the normal form.

- In the *second* phase, "combinations" of subterms of each side of the equation to split are identified. These combinations are represented by the *top* and *bot* function (see Definition 10) and computed upon a *"top"* (TP) and *"bottom"* (BP) paths (see definition 9). For instance, we get the following paths: $TP(r(ap(l, r(l)))) = 12$, $TP(ap(l, r(l))) = 1$, $BP(r(ap(l, r(l)))) = 11$, and $BP(ap(l, r(l))) = 21$. Roughly speaking, a TP (resp. BP) path shows where to look for the subterms that creates the head (resp. the tail) of a normal form of a ground instance of a term. For instance, the head of the normal form of a ground instance of $r(ap(l, r(l)))$ will be the result of computing the normal forms of the ground instance of $r(l)$ (at position 2 for ap) and then applying the definition of r to position 1 (path 12). Similarly, the tail of the normal form of a ground instance of $r(ap(l, r(l)))$ can be found by applying the rules of the function symbols that label each position along the path 12. Each path allows us to compute (see definition 11) the following sets:

$$DEC(t) = \{(r(ap(l,r(l))),\varnothing); (r(r(l)),r(ap(l,\varnothing))); (\varnothing,r(ap(l,r(l)))); (r(r(l)),r(l))\}$$
$$DEC(s) = \{(ap(l,r(l)),\varnothing); (l,r(l)); (\varnothing,ap(l,r(l))); (ap(l,\varnothing),r(l))\}$$

Each element of these sets constitutes a partition of t and s (see proposition 1). Since $(r(r(l)), \mathbf{r(l)})$ is a partition of $r(ap(l, r(l)))$ and $(l, \mathbf{r(l)})$ is a partition of $ap(l, r(l))$, we may reduce – by "taking off" the tail parts $r(l)$ – the proof of (2) to the proof of $t' = s'$ (see theorem 1):

$$r(r(l)) = l \tag{3}$$

So, we need to check (3) for inductive validity. We iterate the process of computation of a term partition of both sides of (3) using definition 11. Since a suitable partition for both terms cannot be found using the definition of DEC, the next step of our induction procedure consists of computing the *"patterns"* (see definition 12) of both sides of (3). Roughly speaking, since ground normal forms of terms in monomorphic systems can be viewed as "lists", they can thus be made up of a regular series of similar elements. Intuitively, a pattern is a representation of these elements when they exist.

To compute patterns, two positions $p \in dom(t')$ and $q \in dom(s')$ such that $t'/p \equiv s'/q$ are first chosen. Then, the normal forms of terms $t'[c.x]_p$ and $s'[c.x]_q$ are computed, where $c.x$ is a non-constant element of $TS(\mathcal{R})$ (see Sect. 2). Finally, we have to find a suitable partition for $t'[c.x]_p$ that contains $\mathbf{t[x]_p}$. Since $t'[c.x]_{11}\downarrow = r(ap(r(l), c.\varnothing))$, we get that $(\mathbf{r(r(x))}, c.\varnothing) \in DEC(t'[c.x]_{11}\downarrow)$, and a pattern of t is $c.\varnothing$. Similarly, since $s'[c.x]_\varepsilon\downarrow = c.x$, we get that $(\mathbf{x}, c.\varnothing) \in DEC(s'[c.x]_\varepsilon\downarrow)$, and thus $c.\varnothing$ is also a pattern of s. Intuitively, the reason for such a computation is to find a term *pat* that have the following property (where θ is a ground substitution, and each θ_i depends on each element of the list of length n that represents the term $(t/p)\theta\downarrow$):

$$t\theta\downarrow \equiv t[\bot]_p\theta\downarrow \otimes pat\theta_1 \otimes \ldots \otimes pat\theta_n$$
$$s\theta\downarrow \equiv s[\bot]_q\theta\downarrow \otimes pat\theta_1 \otimes \ldots \otimes pat\theta_n$$

$$\text{e.g. } (t'/p)\theta\downarrow \equiv c_1.\ldots.c_n.\varnothing \implies \begin{cases} t'\theta\downarrow \equiv r(r(\varnothing))\downarrow \otimes c_1.\varnothing \otimes \ldots \otimes c_n.\varnothing \\ s'\theta\downarrow \equiv \varnothing\downarrow \otimes c_1.\varnothing \otimes \ldots \otimes c_n.\varnothing \end{cases}$$

Since both sides of (3) have a common pattern, we have to check whether $r(r(\varnothing)) = \varnothing$ is an inductive theorem (see theorem 2). Now, $r(r(\varnothing)) = \varnothing$ trivially holds. Therefore (3) is an inductive theorem. Hence (2) is so.

4   Induction Using "Term Partition"

In this section, we define our approach to mathematical induction that is directly based on the finite specification of the language of the normal forms of the infinitely many ground instances of a term.

Definition 5. *If $\mathcal{R}$ is a rewrite system and t is a term, then a* partition *of t with respect to $\mathcal{R}$ is an ordered pair (a, b) where a and b are terms such that $var(a) \cup var(b) \subseteq var(t)$ and for every ground substitution θ the following holds: $t\theta{\downarrow} = a\theta{\downarrow} \otimes b\theta{\downarrow}$.*

For instance, $(r(m), r(l))$ is a partition of $r(ap(l, m))$: the normal forms of the ground instances of t are equal to the normal forms of the corresponding ground instances of $r(m)$ followed by those of $r(l)$. Similarly, $(r(m), r(l))$ is also a partition of $ap(r(m), r(l))$. The key property of term partition is the theorem 1.

Theorem 1. *Let $\mathcal{R}$ be a monomorphic ground convergent rewrite system and $t = s$ be an equation. Assume that (a, b) is a partition of t and (c, d) is a partition of s. If $a =_{ind(\mathcal{R})} c$ then, $t =_{ind(\mathcal{R})} s$ if and only if $b =_{ind(\mathcal{R})} d$. Respectively, if $b =_{ind(\mathcal{R})} d$ then, $t =_{ind(\mathcal{R})} s$ if and only if $a =_{ind(\mathcal{R})} c$.*

Proof. Let θ be a ground substitution. Since (c, d) is a partition of s, $s\theta{\downarrow} = c\theta{\downarrow} \otimes d\theta{\downarrow}$. Since (a, b) is a partition of t, $t\theta{\downarrow} = a\theta{\downarrow} \otimes b\theta{\downarrow}$.

Assume first that $t =_{ind(\mathcal{R})} s$. Since $\mathcal{R}$ is ground convergent, we get that $t\theta{\downarrow} = s\theta{\downarrow}$. Therefore, we have $a\theta{\downarrow} \otimes b\theta{\downarrow} = c\theta{\downarrow} \otimes d\theta{\downarrow}$.

- If $a =_{ind(\mathcal{R})} c$ we then have $a\theta{\downarrow} = c\theta{\downarrow}$. So $a\theta{\downarrow} \otimes b\theta{\downarrow} = a\theta{\downarrow} \otimes d\theta{\downarrow}$. By definition 4 we get $b\theta{\downarrow} = d\theta{\downarrow}$, and therefore $b =_{ind(\mathcal{R})} d$.
- Similarly, $b =_{ind(\mathcal{R})} d$ implies $b\theta{\downarrow} = d\theta{\downarrow}$. So $a\theta{\downarrow} \otimes b\theta{\downarrow} = c\theta{\downarrow} \otimes b\theta{\downarrow}$. By definition 4 we get $a\theta{\downarrow} = c\theta{\downarrow}$, and therefore $a =_{ind(\mathcal{R})} c$.

Assume now $a =_{ind(\mathcal{R})} c$ and $b =_{ind(\mathcal{R})} d$. Since $\mathcal{R}$ is monomorphic, we get an unique position p such that $a\theta{\downarrow}/p = c\theta{\downarrow}/p = \bot$. We then have, $t\theta{\downarrow} = a\theta{\downarrow} \otimes b\theta{\downarrow} = c\theta{\downarrow} \otimes d\theta{\downarrow} = s\theta{\downarrow}$.   □

For instance, since $(r(m), r(l))$ is a common partition of $r(ap(l, m))$ and $ap(r(m), r(l))$, theorem 1 says that $r(ap(l, m)) =_{ind(\mathcal{R})} ap(r(m), r(l))$.

5   Computing "Term Partitions"

As seen in Sect. 2, a term partition is computed in two phases. The first phase is to understand how the normal forms of the ground instances of a term are built up. The second phase uses the first one to extract from a term the combination of subterms that form the partition.

Parsing the Rewrite System. Let $\mathcal{R}$ be a ground convergent rewrite system, and let $\mathcal{R}_f = \{l \rightarrow r \in \mathcal{R} \mid l = f(t1,\ldots,tn) \text{ with } f \in \mathcal{D}_\mathcal{R} \text{ and } t1,\ldots,tn \in T(\mathcal{C}_\mathcal{R}, \mathcal{X})\}$ be the *definition* of f. Assume that t is a term and θ is a ground constructor substitution. If we were able to identify the subterms in $t\theta$ which could be moved (possibly changed) towards the "top" of the $t\theta\!\downarrow$ or down towards the "bottom" of the $t\theta\!\downarrow$ in any rewriting sequence, then we would be able to obtain a term partition.

The type of an argument position allows us to know how each function argument is moved onto another argument position in a rewriting step. Let $\mathcal{R}$ be a monomorphic rewrite system. Let P_f be the *argument position set* of f, define $P_f = \{1,\ldots,n\}$ where n is the arity of symbol f. Remember that $RA(R,f)$ is the reflexive argument position of $f \in \mathcal{C}_\mathcal{R}$ (see Sect. 2).

Definition 6. *Let $\mathcal{R}$ be a monomorphic rewrite system, let f be a function symbol in $\mathcal{D}_\mathcal{R}$. $p \in P_f$ is a downward position, denoted by $DP(\mathcal{R}, f)$, if for all $l \rightarrow r \in \mathcal{R}_f$, l/p is a variable and there exists just one position q such that $l/p = r/q$ and*
- *Either $q = \varepsilon$,*
- *Or $q = q_1 \ldots q_n$ with for all $i \leq n$, $|q_i| = 1$ and $q_i = RA(\mathcal{R}, r(q_1 \ldots q_{i-1}))$, $q_i = DP(\mathcal{R}, r(q_1 \ldots q_{i-1}))$, or $q_i = p$ with $r(q_1 \ldots q_{i-1}) = f$.*

Example 2. If $\mathcal{R}_R = \{R(c.l, L) \rightarrow R(l, c.L); \; R(\varnothing, L) \rightarrow L\}$, then by taking $p = 2$ we get $q = 22$ or $q = \varepsilon$. Thus $DP(\mathcal{R}, R) = 2$.

Definition 7. *Let $\mathcal{R}$ be a monomorphic rewrite system, let f be a function symbol in $\mathcal{D}_\mathcal{R}$. $p \in P_f$ is an upward position, denoted by $UP(\mathcal{R}, f)$, if for all $l \rightarrow r \in \mathcal{R}_f$,*
- *Either $l/p = \perp_{type(l)}$,*
- *Or $l/p = C[x]$ and $r = C[l[x]_p]$.*

Example 3. If $\mathcal{R}_{ap} = \{ap(\varnothing, L) \rightarrow L; \; ap(c.l, L) \rightarrow c.ap(l, L)\}$, then by taking $p = 1$ we get $l/p = \varnothing$ or $l/p = c.l$ and $r = c.\mathbf{ap}(\mathbf{l}, \mathbf{L})$. Thus $UP(\mathcal{R}, ap) = 1$.

Definition 8. *Let $\mathcal{R}$ be a monomorphic rewrite system, let f be a function symbol in $\mathcal{D}_\mathcal{R}$. For a position $p \in P_f$, if for all $l \rightarrow r \in \mathcal{R}_f$*
- *Either $l/p = \perp_{type(l)}$ and $r = \perp_{type(l)}$*
- *Or $l/p = C[x]$ and there exists just one position q s.t. $r/q = l[x]_p$. Then p is*
  - *an up-contextual position and denoted by $UCP(\mathcal{R}, f)$ if $q = DP(\mathcal{R}, r(\varepsilon))$,*
  - *a down-contextual position and denoted by $DCP(\mathcal{R}, f)$ if $q = UP(\mathcal{R}, r(\varepsilon))$.*

Example 4. If $\mathcal{R}_* = \{x * 0 \rightarrow 0; \; x * s(y) \rightarrow (x * y) + x\}$, then by taking $p = 2$ we get $l/p = r = 0$ or $l/p = s(y)$ and $r/q = (x * y)$ with $q = DP(\mathcal{R}, +) = 1$. Thus $UCP(\mathcal{R}, *) = 2$.

Example 5. If $\mathcal{R}_m = \{m(x, 0) \rightarrow 0; \; m(x, s(y)) \rightarrow x + m(x, y)\}$, then by taking $p = 2$ we get $l/p = r = 0$ or $l/p = s(y)$ and $r/q = m(x, y)$ with $q = UP(\mathcal{R}, +) = 2$. Thus $DCP(\mathcal{R}, m) = 2$.

Table 1. Argument positions for $\mathcal{R}$ (see Example 1).

f	$RA(\mathcal{R},f)$	$DP(\mathcal{R},f)$	$UP(\mathcal{R},f)$	$UCP(\mathcal{R},f)$	$DCP(\mathcal{R},f)$
s	1				
$+$		1	2		
$*$				2	
e					
m					2
Σ					
ΣI		2			
$.$	2				
ap		2	1		
r					1
R		2			

Terms with downwards, upward, up-contextual, and down-contextual argument positions may be divided into two parts as the following lemma shows:

Lemma 1. *Let $\mathcal{R}$ be a monomorphic rewrite system, let t be a term, and let p a position in $P_{t(\varepsilon)}$. For any ground substitution θ, and for any ground terms in $\mathcal{R}$-normal form A and B,*

1. *if $p = DP(\mathcal{R}, t(\varepsilon))$, then $t[A]_p\theta\downarrow = t[\bot_{type(t)}]_p\theta\downarrow \otimes A$*
2. *if $p = UP(\mathcal{R}, t(\varepsilon))$, then $t[A]_p\theta\downarrow = A \otimes t[\bot_{type(t)}]_p\theta\downarrow$*
3. *if $p = UCP(\mathcal{R}, t(\varepsilon))$, then $t[A \otimes B]_p\theta\downarrow = t[A]_p\theta\downarrow \otimes t[B]_p\theta\downarrow$*
4. *if $p = DCP(\mathcal{R}, t(\varepsilon))$, then $t[A \otimes B]_p\theta\downarrow = t[B]_p\theta\downarrow \otimes t[A]_p\theta\downarrow$*

Partition Sets. At the second step, we have to know how each function symbol argument is moved at each step of rewriting sequence of a ground instance $t\theta$ of a term t. The mechanism is directly based on the argument positions as defined above, since they point out the subterms of t that will constitute identified parts – by lemma 1 – of $t\theta\downarrow$. To construct the path leading to the innermost subterms that participate to the "head" or to the "tail" of $t\theta\downarrow$ we follow recursively the tree representing t .

Definition 9. *Let $\mathcal{R}$ be a monomorphic rewrite system, let t be a term. The* maximum top path *of t, denoted by $TP(t)$, and the* maximum bottom path *of t denoted by $BP(t)$, are computed recursively by the following functions.*

Function TP(t) : path

Let $f := t(\varepsilon)$;
For all $q \in P_f$
    If $(q = RA(\mathcal{R}, f))$ **or** $(q = UP(\mathcal{R}, f))$ **or** $(q = UCP(\mathcal{R}, f))$ **Then**
        Return $q.TP(t/q)$;
    Else If $q = DCP(\mathcal{R}, f)$ **Then Return** $q.BP(t/p)$;
Return ε;

Function BP(t) : path

Let $f := t(\varepsilon)$;
 For all $q \in P_f$
      If $(q = RA(\mathcal{R}, f))$ **or** $(q = DP(\mathcal{R}, f))$ **or** $(q = UCP(\mathcal{R}, f))$ **Then**
          Return $q.BP(t/q)$;
      Else If $q = DCP(\mathcal{R}, f)$ **Then Return** $q.TP(t/p)$;
 Return ε;

Example 6. $ap(r(ap(l, n)), R(n, l))$

- $TP(ap(r(ap(l, n)), R(n, l))) = 1TP(r(ap(l, n))) = 11BP(ap(l, n)) = 112BP(n)$
$= 112$
- $BP(ap(r(ap(l, n)), R(n, l))) = 2BP(R(n, l)) = 22BP(l) = 22$

Example 7. $x * m(y, z + x)$

- $TP(x * m(y, z + x)) = 2TP(m(y, z + x)) - 22BP(z \mid x) = 221BP(z) = 221$
- $BP(x * m(y, z + x)) = 2BP(m(y, z + x)) = 22TP(z + x) = 222TP(x) = 222$

We are now ready to specify the "heads" and the "tails" of the normal forms of the ground instances of a term t having a top or a bottom path. To represent these parts of every $t\theta\!\downarrow$, we compute terms of which ground instances in normal form will be at the head or at the tail of $t\theta\!\downarrow$. These terms are built up recursively following a top or a bottom path.

Definition 10. *Let* $\mathcal{R}$ *be a monomorphic rewrite system, let* t *be a term, and let* p *be a top path (resp. a bottom path). The* head part *denoted by* $top(t, p)$ *(resp. the* tail part *denoted by* $bot(t, p)$*) is the term computed as*[4]

$$
\begin{array}{l|l}
q = RA(\mathcal{R}, t(\varepsilon)) \Rightarrow top(t, q.p) = t[top(t/q, p)]_q & bot(t, q.p) = bot(t/q, p) \\
q = DP(\mathcal{R}, t(\varepsilon)) \Rightarrow & bot(t, q.p) = bot(t/q, p) \\
q = UP(\mathcal{R}, t(\varepsilon)) \Rightarrow top(t, q.p) = top(t/q, p) & \\
q = UCP(\mathcal{R}, t(\varepsilon)) \Rightarrow top(t, q.p) = t[top(t/q, p)]_q & bot(t, q.p) = t[bot(t/q, p)]_q \\
q = DCP(\mathcal{R}, t(\varepsilon)) \Rightarrow top(t, q.p) = t[bot(t/q, p)]_q & bot(t, q.p) = t[top(t/q, p)]_q \\
\qquad\qquad top(t, \varepsilon) = t & bot(t, \varepsilon) = t
\end{array}
$$

The complement of the head part *denoted by* $ntp(t, p)$ *(resp. the* complement of the tail part *denoted by* $nbt(t, p)$*) is the term computed as*

$$
\begin{array}{l|l}
q = RA(\mathcal{R}, t(\varepsilon)) \Rightarrow ntp(t, q.p) = ntp(t/q, p) & nbt(t, q.p) = t[nbt(t/q, p)]_q \\
q = DP(\mathcal{R}, t(\varepsilon)) \Rightarrow & nbt(t, q.p) = t[nbt(t/q, p)]_q \\
q = UP(\mathcal{R}, t(\varepsilon)) \Rightarrow ntp(t, q.p) = t[ntp(t/q, p)]_q & \\
q = UCP(\mathcal{R}, t(\varepsilon)) \Rightarrow ntp(t, q.p) = t[ntp(t/q, p)]_q & nbt(t, q.p) = t[nbt(t/q, p)]_q \\
q = DCP(\mathcal{R}, t(\varepsilon)) \Rightarrow ntp(t, q.p) = t[nbt(t/q, p)]_q & nbt(t, q.p) = t[ntp(t/q, p)]_q \\
\qquad\qquad ntp(t, \varepsilon) = \bot_{type(t)} & nbt(t, \varepsilon) = \bot_{type(t)}
\end{array}
$$

The following definition and proposition *implement* the concept of term partition.

---

[4] The way to compute *top* and *bot* is similar to function TP and BP. The presentation is different to reduce the size of the definition.

Definition 11. *Let t be a term, then the* partition set *of t, denoted $DEC(t)$, is*

$$\{(top(t,p),\ ntp(t,p)\!\downarrow) \mid p \leq TP(t)\} \cup \{(nbt(t,q)\!\downarrow,\ bot(t,q)) \mid q \leq BP(t)\}$$

Proposition 1. *Every element of $DEC(t)$ is a partition of t.*

Example 8. Consider the term $t = ap(r(ap(l,n)), R(n,l))$ and the path $11 \leq TP(t)$.
- $top(t,11) = top(r(ap(l,n)),1) = r(\underline{bot}(ap(l,n),\varepsilon)) = r(\underline{ap(l,n)})$
- $ntp(t,11)\!\downarrow = ap(ntp(r(ap(l,n)),1), R(n,l))\!\downarrow = ap(r(\underline{nbt}(ap(l,n),\varepsilon)), R(n,l))\!\downarrow$
  $= ap(r(\varnothing), R(n,l))\!\downarrow = R(n,l)$

Thus, $(r(ap(l,n)),\ R(n,l))$ is a partition of t.

Example 9. Consider the term $t = x * m(y, z + x)$ and the path $222 \leq BP(t)$.
- $nbt(t,222)\!\downarrow = (x * \underline{nbt}(m(y, z+x), 22))\!\downarrow = (x * m(y, \underline{ntp}(z+x,2)))\!\downarrow$
  $= (x * m(y, z + \underline{ntp}(x,\varepsilon)))\!\downarrow = (x * m(y, z + \underline{0}))\!\downarrow = x * \underline{m(y,z)}$
- $bot(t,222) = x * \underline{bot}(m(y, z+x), 22) = x * m(y, \underline{top}(z+x, 2))$
  $= x * m(y, \underline{top}(x,\varepsilon)) = x * m(y, \underline{x})$

Thus, $(x * m(y,z),\ x * m(y,x))$ is a partition of s.

Patterns. In some cases, Definition 10 does not provide us with a suitable term partition. A reason for this is that $\{(t, \bot), (\bot, t)\}$ may be the only elements of $DEC(t)$. Another reason is that the type of the arguments of some function symbols (e.g. e, ΣI, ...) cannot be specified[5] . A pattern of t is computed using a partition of the instances of t obtained by replacing a variable in t by a non-constant element of the test set.

Definition 12. *Let $\mathcal{R}$ is a monomorphic rewrite system, t be a term, $C[y] \in TS(\mathcal{R})$, and $p \in dom(t)$. The* left-pattern *(resp. the* right-pattern*) of t, denoted $lpat(t,p,C[y])$ (resp. $rpat(t,p,C[y])$), with respect to $C[y]$ and p is the term α such that $(\alpha, t[y]_p)$ (resp. $(t[y]_p, \alpha)$) is a partition of $t[C[y]]_p\!\downarrow$.*

Example 10. Consider the term $t = x * (x * x)$. Assume that $s(y) \in TS(\mathcal{R})$. We then have $t[s(y)]_{22}\!\downarrow = x * ((x * y) + x)$. Since $ntp(x * ((x * y) + x), 22)\!\downarrow = (x * ((x * y) + 0))\!\downarrow = x * (x * y) = t[y]_{22}$, the left-pattern of t at position 22 is $top(x * ((x * y) + x), 22) = x * x$. Thus, for any ground substitution θ we get:

$$t\theta\!\downarrow \equiv (x*x)\theta\!\downarrow \otimes \ldots \otimes (x*x)\theta\!\downarrow \otimes (x*(x*0))\theta\!\downarrow \text{ with } (x * x)\theta\!\downarrow \text{ repeated } |x\theta\!\downarrow| \text{ times.}$$

Example 11. Consider the term $t = r(ap(l, r(l)))$. Assume that $c.x \in TS(\mathcal{R})$. We then have $t[c.y]_{11}\!\downarrow = ap(r(ap(y, r(l))), c.\varnothing)$. Since $top(ap(r(ap(y, r(l))), c.\varnothing), 1) = t[y]_{11}$, the right-pattern of t at position 11 is $ntp(ap(r(ap(y, r(l))), c.\varnothing), 11)\!\downarrow = ap(\varnothing, c.\varnothing)\!\downarrow = c.\varnothing$. Thus, for any ground substitution θ we get:

$$t\theta\!\downarrow \equiv r(ap(\varnothing, r(l)))\!\downarrow \otimes c_1.\varnothing \otimes \ldots \otimes c_n.\varnothing \text{ with } l\theta\!\downarrow = c_1.\ldots.c_n.\varnothing.$$

---

[5] Of course, definition 10 can handle these functions if they do not occur at the root.

Theorem 2. *Let $\mathcal{R}$ be a monomorphic system and $t = s$ be an equation. Assume that there is a pair $(p, q) \in (dom(t), dom(s))$ such that $t/p =_{ind(\mathcal{R})} s/q$.*

- *If for all $C[y] \in TS(\mathcal{R})$ one has $lpat(t, p, C[y]) =_{ind(\mathcal{R})} lpat(s, q, C[y])$ or $rpat(t, p, C[y]) =_{ind(\mathcal{R})} rpat(s, q, C[y])$ then,*

$$t =_{ind(\mathcal{R})} s \text{ if and only if } t[\perp_{type(t)}]_p =_{ind(\mathcal{R})} s[\perp_{type(t)}]_q.$$

- *Similarly, if $t[\perp_{type(t)}]_p =_{ind(\mathcal{R})} s[\perp_{type(s)}]_q$ then, $t =_{ind(\mathcal{R})} s$ if and only if for all $C[y] \in TS(\mathcal{R})$ one has $lpat(t, p, C[y]) =_{ind(\mathcal{R})} lpat(s, q, C[y])$ or $rpat(t, p, C[y]) =_{ind(\mathcal{R})} rpat(s, q, C[y])$.*

Proof. Let θ be a ground substitution. $t/p =_{ind(\mathcal{R})} s/p$ implies $(t/p)\theta\downarrow = (s/q)\theta\downarrow$. Let A be a ground term in $\mathcal{R}$-normal form such that $A = (t/p)\theta\downarrow$. Since $\mathcal{R}$ is ground convergent, we get, by substitution property, that $t\theta\downarrow = t\theta[(t/p)\theta\downarrow]_p\downarrow = t\theta[A]_p\downarrow$. Similarly $s\theta\downarrow = s\theta[A]_q\downarrow$. We proceed by induction on the structure of A (remember $\mathcal{R}$ is monomorphic and then sufficiently complete, so $A \in T(\mathcal{C}_\mathcal{R})$) [6].

- Basis case: $t[\perp]_p =_{ind(\mathcal{R})} s[\perp]_q$ implies $t\theta[\perp]_p\downarrow = s\theta[\perp]_q\downarrow$.
- Induction case: for all A' such that $A = C[A']$ we have that
  - either $lpat(t, p, C[y])\theta\downarrow = lpat(s, q, C[y])\theta\downarrow = B$ and $t\theta\downarrow = t\theta[C[A']]_p\downarrow = B \otimes t\theta[A']_p\downarrow$. Similarly, $s\theta\downarrow = B \otimes s\theta[A']_q\downarrow$,
  - or $rpat(t, p, C[y])\theta\downarrow = rpat(s, q, C[y])\theta\downarrow = B$ and $t\theta\downarrow = t\theta[C[A']]_p\downarrow = t\theta[A']_p\downarrow \otimes B$. Similarly, $s\theta\downarrow = s\theta[A']_q\downarrow \otimes B$.

  Therefore, by induction hypothesis $t\theta[A']_p\downarrow = s\theta[A']_q\downarrow$.
  And $\forall C[x]$, $lpat(t, p, C[x]) =_{ind(\mathcal{R})} lpat(s, q, C[x])$ or $rpat(t, p, C[x]) =_{ind(\mathcal{R})} rpat(s, q, C[x])$ implies $t =_{ind(\mathcal{R})} s$ if and only if $t[\perp]_p =_{ind(\mathcal{R})} s[\perp]_q$. $\square$

6   Organizing the Inductive Proofs

In this section we show how to organize inductive proofs. Assume we are working with a monomorphic $\mathcal{R}$ (see Sect. 2). To verify whether $t =_{ind(\mathcal{R})} s$ we run the following procedure:

Function inductive($t = s$) : boolean

If $t\downarrow \equiv s\downarrow$ **Then Return** TRUE;
 If $vars(t) = \varnothing$ and $vars(s) = \varnothing$ **Then Return** FALSE;
 For all $(a, b) \in DEC(t)$ and all $(c, d) \in DEC(s)$
     If $a \equiv c$ **Then Return** inductive($b = d$);
     If $b \equiv d$ **Then Return** inductive($a = c$);
 For all $p \in dom(t)$ and all $q \in dom(s)$ **with** $t/p \equiv s/q$
     If $\forall C[x] \in TS(\mathcal{R})$. $pat(t, p, C[x]) \not\equiv$ null **Then**
         If $\forall C[x] \in TS(\mathcal{R})$. $pat(t, p, C[x]) \equiv pat(s, q, C[x])$ **Then**
             Return inductive($t[\perp_{type(t)}]_p = s[\perp_{type(t)}]_q$);
         Else If $t[\perp_{type(t)}]_p\downarrow \equiv s[\perp_{type(t)}]_q\downarrow$ **Then**
             Return $\forall C[x] \in TS(\mathcal{R})$. inductive($pat(t, p, C[x]) = pat(s, q, C[x])$);
 Return inductive(GEN($t = s$));

---

[6] In the proofs, since we deal with only one sort, we note $\perp$ the constant of that sort.

To compute patterns, we define one function that returns the term and the side (left or right) defining the pattern. In the inductive function defined above, the equality test ($\equiv$) compares both terms and sides but the inductive call on patterns is only applied on terms[7].

Function pat(t, p, C[x]) : (side, term)

For all $(a, b) \in DEC(t[C[x]]_p \downarrow)$
    If $a \equiv t[x]_p$ **Then Return** $(right, b)$;
    Else If $b \equiv t[x]_p$ **Then Return** $(left, a)$;
Return $null$;

Let us illustrate how our framework succeeds in some hard examples:

Example 12. Consider the equation $t = s$: $\boxed{ap(r(l), ap(l, l)) = ap(ap(r(l), l), l)}$.
- $(nbt(t, 1)\downarrow,\ bot(t, 1)) = (r(l),\ ap(l, l)) \in DEC(t)$
- $(nbt(s, 11)\downarrow,\ bot(s, 11)) = (r(l),\ ap(l, l)) \in DEC(s)$

Example 13. Let $t = s$ be $\boxed{r(ap(l, l)) = ap(r(l), r(l))}$.
- $(nbt(t, 11)\downarrow,\ bot(t, 11)) = (r(l),\ r(l)) \in DEC(t)$
- $(top(s, 1),\ ntp(s, 1)\downarrow) = (r(l),\ r(l)) \in DEC(s)$

In the two examples above, we get two partitions (a, b) of t and (c, d) of s such that $a \equiv c$, so the inductive procedure is called again on b and d which are also syntactically equal.

Example 14. Let $t = s$ be $\boxed{R(l, \varnothing) = r(l)}$. With patterns, $t[c.l']_1\downarrow = R(l', c.\varnothing)$ and $s[c.l']_1\downarrow = ap(r(l'), c.\varnothing)$, then
- $(nbt(t[c.l']_1\downarrow, 2)\downarrow,\ bot(t[c.l']_1\downarrow, 2)) = (R(l', \varnothing),\ c.\varnothing)$ and
- $(top(s[c.l']_1\downarrow, 1),\ ntp(s[c.l']_1\downarrow, 1)\downarrow) = (r(l'),\ c.\varnothing)$.
Since $R(\varnothing, \varnothing)\downarrow \equiv r(\varnothing)\downarrow \equiv \varnothing$, we get that $t =_{ind(\mathcal{R})} s$.

We get two right-patterns syntactically equals $(c.\varnothing)$, so the inductive procedure is called again on the base cases $(R(\varnothing, \varnothing)$ and $r(\varnothing))$ of which normal forms are equal to $\varnothing$.

Example 15. Let $r = l$ be $\boxed{s(x + m(x, e(x, y) + y)) = s(m(x, s(e(x, y)) + y))}$
- $(top(r, 1221),\ ntp(r, 1221)\downarrow) = (s(m(x, e(x, y))),\ x + m(x, 0 + y)) \in DEC(r)$
- $(top(l, 1211),\ ntp(l, 1211)\downarrow) = (s(m(x, e(x, y))),\ m(x, s(0) + y)) \in DEC(l)$
We have now to prove $r' = l'$: $x + m(x, 0 + y)) = m(x, s(0) + y)$
- $(top(r', 22),\ ntp(r', 22)\downarrow) = (m(x, y),\ x) \in DEC(r')$
- $(top(l', 22),\ ntp(l', 22)\downarrow) = (m(x, y),\ x) \in DEC(l')$

In this example, induction procedure simply uses two couples of partitions.

Example 16. Let $r = l$ be $\boxed{\Sigma(x) = \Sigma I(x, 0)}$. With patterns, $r[s(y)]_1\downarrow = s(y) + \Sigma(y)$ and $l[s(y)]_1\downarrow = \Sigma I(y, s(0 + y))$ then
- $(top(r[s(y)]_1\downarrow, 2),\ ntp(r[s(y)]_1\downarrow, 2)\downarrow) = (\Sigma(y),\ s(y))$ and

---

[7] In an actual implemented algorithm, we can, for more efficiency, compute DEC sets just once for every term or patterns. We can also, not compute patterns for every position in *dom* but just for *inductive positions* as defined in [14].

- $(nbt(l[s(y)]_1 \downarrow, 211) \downarrow, bot(l[s(y)]_1 \downarrow, 211)) = (\Sigma I(y, 0), s(0 + y))$.

Since $\Sigma(0) \downarrow \equiv \Sigma I(0, 0) \downarrow \equiv 0$, we have to verify $r' = l'$: $s(y) =_{ind(\mathcal{R})} s(0 + y)$.
Since $(s(y), 0)$ is a common partition of r' and l', we get that $r =_{ind(\mathcal{R})} l$.

We get two right-patterns ($s(y)$ and $s(0+y)$) syntactically different but two base cases ($\Sigma(0)$ and $\Sigma I(0, 0)$) of which normal form are equals, so the procedure is called on the two patterns. These patterns are proved inductively equal with a simple partition.

Example 17. Let $r = l$ be $\boxed{(x * x) * (x * x) = x * (x * (x * x))}$. With patterns, $r[s(y)]_{22} \downarrow = (x * x) * (x * y + x)$ and $l[s(y)]_{222} \downarrow = x * (x * (x * (y + x)))$, then

- $(nbt(r[s(y)]_{22} \downarrow, 222) \downarrow, bot(r[s(y)]_{22} \downarrow, 222)) = ((x * x) * x, (x * x) * (x * y))$
- $(nbt(l[s(y)]_{222} \downarrow, 2222) \downarrow, bot(l[s(y)]_{222} \downarrow, 2222)) = (x * (x * x), x * (x * (x * y)))$.

Since $((x * x) * (x * 0)) \downarrow \equiv (x * (x * (x * 0))) \downarrow \equiv 0$, we have now to verify $r' = l'$: $(x * x) * x = x * (x * x)$.

With patterns, $r'[s(y)]_2 \downarrow = x * (x * y + x)$ and $l'[s(y)]_{22} \downarrow = x * (x * (y + x))$,

- $(nbt(r'[s(y)]_2 \downarrow, 22) \downarrow, bot(r'[s(y)]_2 \downarrow, 22)) = (x * x, (x * x) * y)$ and
- $(nbt(l'[s(y)]_{22} \downarrow, 222) \downarrow, bot(l'[s(y)]_{22} \downarrow, 222)) = (x * x, x * (x * y))$.

Since $((x * x) * 0) \downarrow \equiv (x * (x * 0)) \downarrow \equiv 0$, we get that $r =_{ind(\mathcal{R})} l$.

Again, we have two patterns different but two base cases equal (w.r.t. $\mathcal{R}$), so the procedure is called on the two left-patterns ($(x * x) * x$ and $x * (x * x)$). These new terms share a common left-pattern $(x * x)$, so the procedure is called again on the base cases ($(x * x) * 0$ and $x * (x * 0)$) of which normal forms are equal.

Example 18. Let $r = l$ be $\boxed{e(x, y + z) = e(x, y) * e(x, z)}$. Since no partition or pattern can be defined, we apply GEN function. We get the equation $r' = l'$: $(e(x, y) * e(x, z)) * x = e(x, y) * (e(x, z) * x)$. With patterns,

- $r'[s(x')]_2 \downarrow = ((e(x, y) * e(x, z)) * x') + (e(x, y) * e(x, z))$ and
- $l'[s(x')]_{22} \downarrow = e(x, y) * ((e(x, z) * x') + e(x, z))$

We then have $lpat(r', 2, s(x')) = e(x, y) * e(x, z) = lpat(l', 22, s(x'))$. Thus, since $((e(x, y) * e(x, z)) * 0) \downarrow \equiv (e(x, y) * (e(x, z) * 0)) \downarrow \equiv 0$, we get that $r =_{ind(\mathcal{R})} l$.

The last example represents $x^{y+z} = x^y * x^z$. The function GEN applied on variable z returns only one equation (since $e(x, y + 0) \downarrow = (e(x, y) * e(x, 0)) \downarrow = e(x, y)$). The both sides of this equation $r' = l'$ share a common left-pattern $(e(x, y) * e(x, z))$, so the procedure is called again on the two base cases $(e(x, y) * e(x, z)) * 0$ and $e(x, y) * (e(x, z) * 0)$. Since their normal forms are equal to 0, the conjecture $r = l$ is an inductive theorem.

7 Conclusion

We have presented in this paper a new method to construct proofs that usually require mathematical induction with strong generalized hypotheses and additional lemmas. The method is simple and allows us to obtain very elegant and natural proofs. We know how to handle simple fragments of arithmetic and how to apply the method to proofs of properties of programs computing over lists.

The method has some limitations, however. The requirement on the monomorphic rewrite systems must be generalized to handle general recursive definitions.

Further, we do not treat multiple conjectures whose proofs use each other in a mutually recursive fashion. Finally, most nontrivial program proofs involve conditional reasoning: it may be possible to generalize this method in some simple cases. An implementation of the method in the NICE-system has been realized[8].

References

1. R. Aubin, *Mechanizing structural induction*, Theorical Computer Science **9** (1979), 329–362.
2. L. Bachmair, *Proof by consistency in equational theories*, Proceedings of Third IEEE LICS, 1988, pp. 228–233.
3. A. Bouhoula and J.P. Jouannaud, *Automata-driven automated induction*, Information and Computation **169(1)** (2001), 1–22.
4. A. Bouhoula, E. Kounalis, and M. Rusinowitch, *Automated mathematical induction*, Journal of Logic and Computation **5(5)** (1995), 631–668.
5. R.S. Boyer and J.S. Moore, *A computational logic*, Academic Press, NY, 1979.
6. F. Bronsard, U. Reddy, and R. Hasker, *Induction using term orders*, Journal of Automated Reasoning **16** (1996), 3–37.
7. H. Comon, *Inductionless induction*, Handbook of Automated Reasoning (J. A. Robinson and A. Voronkov, eds.), vol. 1, Elsevier and MIT Press, 2001, pp. 913–962.
8. N. Dershowitz, *Completion and its applications*, Actes du Séminaire d'Informatique Théorique (Paris), 1997.
9. N. Dershowitz and J.P. Jouannaud, *Rewriting systems*, Handbook of Theoretical Computer Science (J. van Leeuwen, ed.), vol. B, North-Holland, 1990, pp. 243–320.
10. A. Ireland and A. Bundy, *Using failure to guide inductive proof*, Journal of Automated Reasoning **16** (1996), 38–85.
11. J.P. Jouannaud and E. Kounalis, *Automatic proofs by induction in theories without constructor*, Information and Computation **82(1)** (1989), 1–33.
12. D. Kapur and M. Subramaniam, *Lemma discovery in automating induction*, Proceedings of Thirteenth Int. CADE, 1996, pp. 538–552.
13. E. Kounalis, *How to check for the ground-reducibility property in term rewriting systems*, TCS **106 (1)** (1992), 87–117.
14. E. Kounalis and P. Urso, *Generalization discovery for proofs by induction in conditional theories*, Proceedings of FLAIRS-99, AAAI Press, 1999, pp. 250–256.
15. T. Walsh, *A divergence critic for inductive proof*, Journal of Artificial Intelligence Research **4** (1996), 209–235.
16. H. Zhang, D. Kapur, and M.S. Krishnamoorthy, *A mechanizable induction principle for equational specification*, Proceedings of Ninth Int. CADE, 1988, pp. 162–181.

---

[8] NICE can downloaded at http://www-sop.inria.fr/coprin/urso/logiciels.

Equational Prover of THEOREMA[*]

Temur Kutsia

Research Institute for Symbolic Computation
Johannes Kepler University
A-4040, Linz, Austria
kutsia@risc.uni-linz.ac.at

Abstract. The equational prover of the THEOREMA system is described. It is implemented on Mathematica and is designed for unit equalities in the first order or in the applicative higher order form. A (restricted) usage of sequence variables and Mathematica built-in functions is allowed.

1 Introduction

The THEOREMA[1] system [7] is an integrated environment for proving, solving and computing built on the top of Mathematica [32]. It is based on early papers by Buchberger (e.g. [5,6]) and provides a front end for composing formal mathematical text consisting of a hierarchy of axioms, propositions, algorithms etc. in a common logic frame with user-extensible syntax, and a library of provers, solvers and simplifiers for proving, solving and simplifying mathematical formulae.

The equational prover of THEOREMA is one of such provers, designed for unit equality problems in the first order or in the applicative higher order form. The input may contain sequence variables. A (restricted) usage of Mathematica built-in functions is allowed. The prover has two proving modes: unfailing completion [3] and simplification (rewriting/narrowing). It consists of the preprocessor, the kernel and the proof presenter parts. The preprocessor checks the input syntax, sets option values, Skolemizes, chooses a proving mode, an ordering and passes the preprocessed input to the kernel. The kernel runs a proof procedure with the chosen settings and passes the output to the proof presenter, which structures it, deletes redundant steps, introduces lemmata and constructs the proof object.

2 Proof Procedure: Algorithm and Implementation

The unfailing completion procedure is implemented as a given-clause algorithm [23], where proof search is organized as a DISCOUNT [1] loop. The input of the procedure is a set of (implicitly) universally closed equalities $\mathcal{E}$, a ground goal $\mathcal{G}$ and a (ground total) reduction ordering $>$, which can be either the lexicographic path ordering (LPO), Knuth-Bendix ordering (KBO) or the lexicographic extension of the multiset path ordering with sequence variables (MPOSV [18]). Before

---

[*] Supported by the Austrian Science Foundation (FWF) under Project SFB F1302.
[1] http://www.theorema.org/.

calling the completion procedure, we Skolemize all equations in the given proving problem. If the equation in the hypothesis contains existentially quantified variables, we proceed in a standard way introducing a new function symbol eq and two new constants, $true$ and $false$. Then we add two new equations $eq(x, x) = true$ and $eq(s, t) = false$ to $\mathcal{E}$, where x is a variable and s and t are sides of the hypothesis, and $true = false$ becomes a goal.

The proving procedure saturates $\mathcal{E}$ and works on a set of active facts $\mathcal{A}$, participating in the inference, and on a set of passive facts $\mathcal{P}$, waiting to become members of $\mathcal{A}$. The completion loop is shown on Fig. 1. It is essentially the same as the loop WALDMEISTER implements (see [20]).

Algorithm 1. Completion Loop

Function ProveByCompletion($\mathcal{E}, \mathcal{G}, >$)

1: $(\mathcal{A}, \mathcal{P}) := (\emptyset, \mathcal{E})$
2: **while** $\neg\text{trivial}(\mathcal{G}) \wedge \mathcal{P} \neq \emptyset$ **do**
3:      $e := \text{Select}(\mathcal{P}); \mathcal{P} := \mathcal{P} \backslash \{e\}$
4:      **if** $\neg\text{orphan}(e)$ **then**
5:          $e := \text{Normalize}^>_{\mathcal{A}}(e)$
6:          **if** $\neg\text{redundant}(e)$ **then**
7:              $(\mathcal{A}, \mathcal{P}_1) := \text{Interred}^>(\mathcal{A}, e)$
8:              $\mathcal{A} := \mathcal{A} \cup \{\text{Orient}^>(e)\}$
9:              $\mathcal{P}_2 := CP^>(e, \mathcal{A})$
10:              $\mathcal{P} := \mathcal{P} \cup \text{Normalize}^>_{\mathcal{A}}(\mathcal{P}_1 \cup \mathcal{P}_2)$
11:              $\mathcal{G} := \text{Normalize}^>_{\mathcal{A}}(\mathcal{G})$
12:          **end**
13:      **end**
14: **end**
15: **return** trivial($\mathcal{G}$)

Fig. 1. Main loop for proving by unfailing completion mode.

The predicate *trivial* on line 2 is true on an equality $s = t$ iff s and t are identical. The function *Select* on line 3 decides which equality should be selected from passive facts for activation. It has to guarantee that every passive fact eventually becomes active, thus ensuring the fairness of the procedure. This function selects a fact with the minimal weight. If there are several such facts, then it chooses the oldest one. Moreover, once in each five iterations *Select* takes the smallest fact where *false* occurs, if there is such a fact in $\mathcal{P}^2$. The predicate *orphan* on line 4 is true on e iff a parent equation of e has been reduced. The predicate *redundant* on line 6 is true on e iff either e is trivial, is subsumed by an equation in $\mathcal{A}$ or is ground joinable. The interreduction function *Interred* on line 7 takes active facts that are reducible by e out of $\mathcal{A}$ and puts them into $\mathcal{P}_1$. The *Orient* function on line 8 orients e with respect to $>$, if possible. The function CP on line 9 generates all possible critical pairs between e and $\mathcal{A}$. The

---

² BARCELONA and FIESTA implement such a selection criterion [26].

function *Normalize* does normalization with the active facts only. Passive facts are normalized only on their generation and after selection.

We store $\mathcal{P}$ as a heap of heaps, following the WALDMEISTER approach. It allows efficient "orphan murder" and fast selection of the minimal equation. We use Mathematica arrays to implement the heap. Terms are kept as stringterms.

Normalization of the selected equation, new critical pairs or the goal, using active facts, is an example of forward simplification. Since the set of active facts grows larger and larger, fast identification of the appropriate fact for rewriting (generalization retrieval) becomes crucial. There are various indexing techniques suitable for this operation, like code trees [30], substitution trees [14], context trees [12] or various versions of discrimination trees [9,22,15]. However, in our case, instead of implementing an indexing technique, we decided to rely on Mathematica rewriting tools, as its programming language is a rewrite language [4][3]. This approach is similar to what Stickel proposed in [27], using the Prolog implementation technology for model elimination. We call it Mathematica Technology Term Rewriting (MTTR) and show on the example below how it works.

Let R and E be respectively the set of rules and the set of equations in $\mathcal{A}$. Assume we have a rule for the associativity law in R: $f(f(x,y),z) \rightarrow f(x,f(y,z))$. Every active and passive fact has its unique label, an integer associated with it. Let the label for the rule above be 5. Then we transform the rule into a Mathematica assignment as follows: First, we normalize the variable names and transform each variable in the left hand side of the rule into Mathematica patterns getting $\mathtt{f[f[x1\_,x2\_],x3\_]}$. Next, we make the Mathematica assignment:

$\mathtt{f[f[x1\_,x2\_],x3\_,\_:\{5\}]}$ $:=(\mathtt{AppendTo[\$LABELS,\{5\}];f[x1,f[x2,x3]]})/;$
$\qquad(\mathtt{\$PHASE === \text{"Rewriting"}})$

where $\mathtt{\$LABELS}$ is a global variable, initialized with the empty list every time before normalizing a term. After a term is normalized, $\mathtt{\$LABELS}$ stores the list of labels of those active facts which participated in the normalization. In the condition, $\mathtt{\$PHASE}$ is a global variable specifying the deduction phase. It prevents unexpected evaluations. In the example above, the assignment becomes applicable only at the "Rewriting" phase and not, for instance, at the "Subconnectedness checking" phase, where we only need reducibility. The entire main loop runs in the "Neutral" phase, switching to the specific phases when needed.

Transformation of equalities from E into delayed assignments is done in the similar manner, but we add the ordering check additionally. For instance, an equality $f(x,f(y,z) = f(y,f(z,x))$ is transformed into two assignments:

$\mathtt{f[x1\_,f[x2\_,x3\_],\_:\{\text{"L"},6\}]}:=$
$\qquad(\mathtt{AppendTo[\$LABELS,\{\text{"LR"},6\}];f[x2,f[x3,x1]]})/;$
$\qquad(\mathtt{\$PHASE ==\text{"Rewriting"}} \wedge \mathtt{\$GREATER[f[x1,f[x2,x3]],f[x2,f[x3,x1]]]})$

$\mathtt{f[x1\_,f[x2\_,x3\_],\_:\{\text{"RL"},6\}]}:=$
$\qquad(\mathtt{AppendTo[\$LABELS,\{\text{"RL"},6\}];f[x3,f[x1,x2]]})/;$
$\qquad(\mathtt{\$PHASE === \text{"Rewriting"}} \wedge \mathtt{\$GREATER[f[x1,f[x2,x3]],f[x3,f[x1,x2]]]})$

---

[3] We tried to implement discrimination trees, but since the low-level programming capabilities are very restricted in the high-level Mathematica programming language, which itself is not very fast, we did not get a reasonable performance.

where $GREATER is a global variable whose value is the function specifying the given reduction ordering. We make sure that for equalities like the commutativity law, only one delayed assignment is made, instead of two. Note that MTTR approach treats constants as nullary function symbols.

When we need to rewrite a term t in a phase p, we simply call the function rewrite on t and p. rewrite is implemented as follows:

```
Clear[rewrite];
rewrite[term_, phase_] := Module[{ans},
    With[{y = $SIGNATURE}, $PHASE = phase; Map[Update, y]];
    ans = term; $PHASE = "Neutral"; ans];
```

where $SIGNATURE is a global variable whose value is a list of all constants and function symbols occurring in the problem.

MTTR is probably one of the fastest ways of doing rewriting in Mathematica, but it has disadvantages as well, namely, we have minimal control on rewriting strategies, can not keep track of results of single rewrite steps, and should put additional control to prevent unexpected evaluation.

We found useful to use Mathematica matching mechanism in forward subsumption as well, which is one of the redundancy criteria for the selected equation. Another redundancy criterion is the ground joinability test [2], implemented for associative-commutative symbols only: we add to the active facts a ground complete subset for an AC symbol f consisting of AC axioms and the additional equation $f(x, f(y, z)) = f(y, f(x, z))$. Any other equation joinable modulo AC can be deleted. Such an equation is called ground joinable. To test ground joinability we use the following trick: for each AC symbol f we create a new function symbol nf, make a list of transformation rules $AC-SYMBOLS={f → nf, ...} and set attributes of nf to {Flat, Orderless, OneIdentity}. Then testing whether s=t is ground joinable reduces to testing whether s/.$AC-SYMBOLS and t/.$AC-SYMBOLS are identical[4].

Mathematica delayed assignment rules are employed also in caching for term orderings. The orderings like LPO or MPOSV compare the same term pairs many times. To avoid a repeated work we store the result of comparison between two terms s and t as cachedComparison[s,t]:=result, where result is either True or False and look it up whenever s and t have to be compared again[5].

With interreduction and critical pair generation the situation becomes more complicated. Here we need to perform instance and unifiable retrieval on the set of active facts. Mathematica does not provide mechanisms which would make possible to implement these operations in the same spirit as we did for generalization retrieval. In order to perform instance retrieval in more or less reasonable way, we had to implement some kind of indexing for the terms in active facts. We chose path indexing [28], because it does not involve backtracking, insertion and deletion can be done more efficiently than for other indexing techniques, is economical in terms of memory usage, and is useful for retrieving instances (see [25]). One of the main disadvantages of path indexing is that it requires costly

---

[4] in Mathematica /. is a short notation for the function ReplaceAll.

[5] The idea of caching was implemented earlier in Dedam by RPO caching [26].

union and intersection operations to combine intermediate results. We use Mathematica built-in functions `Union` and `Intersection` for these operations.

The main loop for proving by simplification, unlike Algorithm 1, does not perform interreduction and orphan testing, and does not generate critical pairs unless at least one of the parent equations contains a term with the head *eq*. The simplification mode has one more specific feature: optionally, all equations can be oriented from left to right. In this case, of course, termination of rewriting is not guaranteed and the prover issues the corresponding warning.

3   Extensions

3.1   Sequence Variables

A sequence variable is a variable that can be instantiated with an arbitrary finite, possibly empty, sequence of terms. To distinguish, we call ordinary variables individual variables. Sequence variables are allowed to appear only as arguments of flexible arity symbols. The main difficulty in deduction with sequence variables is infinitary unification, even in the syntactic case ([19]). However, it was shown to be decidable in [17] and a theorem proving procedure with constraints à la Nieuwenhuis/Rubio [24] was proposed in [18].

The equational prover of THEOREMA implements unfailing completion with sequence variables, occurring only in the last argument positions in terms (as, e.g. in $f(a, f(x, \overline{x}), g(\overline{x}), \overline{y})$, where $\overline{x}$ and $\overline{y}$ are sequence variables). It makes unification unitary. A rule-based unification algorithm is shown on Fig. 2.

Algorithm 2. Unification with sequence variables in the last argument positions

Function unify(s, t), s and t are not sequence variables

1: unify(t, t) := $\{\}$
2: unify(x, t) := $\{x \leftarrow t\}$ if $x \neq t$ and $x \notin vars(t)$
3: unify(t, x) := $\{x \leftarrow t\}$ if $x \neq t$ and $x \notin vars(t)$
4: unify($f(s, \tilde{s}), f(t, \tilde{t})$) :=   if $\sigma = $ unify(s, t) and $\sigma \neq$ **fail**
       compose(σ, unify($f'(\tilde{s})\sigma, f'(\tilde{t})\sigma)$))
5: unify($f(\overline{x}), f(\tilde{t})$) := $\{\overline{x} \leftarrow \tilde{t}\}$ if $\overline{x} \neq \tilde{t}$ and $\overline{x} \notin vars(\tilde{t})$
6: unify($f(\tilde{t}), f(\overline{x})$) := $\{\overline{x} \leftarrow \tilde{t}\}$ if $\overline{x} \neq \tilde{t}$ and $\overline{x} \notin vars(\tilde{t})$
7: unify(s, t) := **fail**   otherwise

Fig. 2. Unification for terms with sequence variables in the last argument position

The input of the algorithm are two terms, which are not sequence variables themselves and all occurrences of sequence variables happen only in the last argument positions of subterms. The *compose* function on Line 3 returns **fail**, if at least one of its arguments is **fail**, otherwise it composes substitutions in its first and second arguments. $\tilde{s}$ and $\tilde{t}$ denote arbitrary finite, possibly empty, sequences of terms. $vars(t)$ (resp. $vars(\tilde{t})$) is a set of all individual and sequence variables of a term t (resp. sequence of terms $\tilde{t}$). x is an individual variable, $\overline{x}$

is a sequence variable. The function symbol f' on line 4 is a new flexible arity symbol, if the symbol f on the same line has a fixed arity, otherwise f' and f are the same. The function symbol f on 5 and 6 has a flexible arity.

In the simplification mode we use sequence variables without any restrictions on their occurrence. It means that in this case unification is infinitary and matching is finitary. For the moment we do not allow existential goals in this setting, and therefore unification problems do not appear. As for matching/rewriting, MTTR follows the Mathematica strategy, choosing from the finite alternatives the matcher that assigns the shortest sequences of terms to the first sequence variables that appear in the pattern[6].

Unrestricted quantification over sequence variables takes the language beyond first-order expressiveness. In [17] we considered an extension of the language with constructs called pattern-terms, which abbreviate term sequences of unknown length matching certain "pattern", like, for instance, all the terms in the sequence having the same arguments, but different top function symbols. Such pattern-terms are naturally introduced via Skolemization. In the unfailing completion mode of the prover we allow pattern-terms to occur only in the last argument positions in terms whose top function symbol has a flexible arity. A pattern-term can be unified only with a sequence variable which does not occur in it, or with an identical pattern-term.

The MTTR technique has to be extended to terms with sequence variables and pattern-terms. First, each sequence variable should be transformed into the corresponding pattern (an identifier with three underscores). Second, since individual variables match neither sequence variables nor pattern-terms, we have to restrict Mathematica patterns that correspond to individual variables. Thus, a term $f(x, f(\overline{g(\overline{x})}), \overline{x})$, where $\overline{x}$ is a sequence variable, $\overline{g(\overline{x})}$ is a pattern-term and x is an individual variable, will be transformed into the pattern $\texttt{f[x1\_?}\neg\texttt{MatchQ[\#,.var[.seq[\_]]]} \land \neg\texttt{MatchQ[\#,.seq[\_]]\&,.seq[g[x2\_\_\_]],x2\_\_\_]}$[7].

We also extended the path indexing technique to index terms with sequence variables and pattern-terms in the last argument positions. However, more effort has to be made here to improve efficiency of retrieval operations.

3.2   Problems in Applicative Higher Order Form

Warren introduced in [31] a method to translate expressions from higher order applicative form into first order syntax, preserving both declarative and narrowing semantics [13]. With this translation, for example, the higher order equation $twice(F)(X) = F(F(X))$ is translated into the equations $twice(F, X) = apply(F, apply(F, X))$, $apply(twice_0, F) = twice_1(F)$, $apply(twice_1(F), X) = twice(F, X)$, where $apply$ is a new binary function and $twice_0$ and $twice_1$ are new

---

[6] Recently, [21] proposed an approach to gain more control on rewriting with sequence variables in Mathematica.

[7] .var and .seq are THEOREMA tags respectively for variables and for sequences. .var[.seq[_]] is a Mathematica pattern which can match any THEOREMA sequence variable and .seq[_] can match any THEOREMA pattern-term.

constructors representing partial applications. Since THEOREMA syntax allows higher order expressions, the equational prover can accept such an input. Then the input is translated by Warren's method into the first order form, on which the proving procedure is applied. The output is translated back into higher order form. Thus, the user sees only higher order input and output.

Optionally, if the proving mode is simplification and the goal is universal, MTTR can be applied immediately, without Warren's translation, because the Mathematica programming language supports rewriting with higher order constructs. In this case currently the equalities are oriented from left to right, but we intend to implement HORPO [16] as well.

At the current stage sequence variables and pattern-terms can be used in higher order problems only in the simplification mode with universal goals.

3.3 Using Mathematica Built in Functions

We incorporate Mathematica built in functions in the proving task in the following way: On the one hand, to be interpreted as a Mathematica built-in function it is not enough for a function in the proving problem to have a syntax of a Mathematica function. It has to be stated explicitly that it is a built-in function (THEOREMA has a special construct built-in for that). Moreover, a function can get its built-in meaning only when it appears in the goal. After normalization, the goal is checked on joinability modulo built-in meaning of the Mathematica functions in it, but the built-ins are not used to derive new goals. On the other hand, the approach is not completely sceptical: after a built-in function is identified, it is trusted and the result of computation is not checked. Therefore, when Mathematica functions are involved in the task, in the prover output it is stated: "If the built-in computation is correct, the following theorem holds...". The integration tool is still at the experimental level and needs further development, e.g. integrating existing frameworks of combining computer algebra and theorem proving/rule based reasoning (with [8] as a particular example).

4   Proof Presentation

We use the Proof Communication Language (PCL) [11] to describe proofs. A slight modification is needed to represent reduction steps, because MTTR does not show intermediate rewriting results. Proofs are structured into lemmata. Proofs of universally closed theorems are displayed as equational chains, while those of existential theorems represent sequences of equations. The symbols eq, $true$ and $false$ are not shown. In failing proofs, on the one hand, the theorems which have been proved during completion are given, and on the other hand, failed propositions whose proving would lead to proving the original goal are displayed, if there are any. They are obtained from descendants of the goal and certain combinations of their sides.

5 Examples

Example 1 (Insertion sort). This is an example of using sequence variables and Mathematica functions. The assumptions specify the insertion sort:

Assumption["1", $\underset{n}{\forall}(\texttt{insert}[n, \langle\rangle] = \langle n\rangle)$]

Assumption["2", $\underset{n,m,\overline{x}}{\forall}(\texttt{insert}[n, \langle m, \overline{x}\rangle] =$

$\qquad\qquad\qquad\texttt{prepend}[\texttt{max}[m, n], \texttt{insert}[\texttt{min}[n, m], \langle \overline{x}\rangle]])$]

Assumption["3", $\texttt{sort}[\langle\rangle] = \langle\rangle$]

Assumption["4", $\underset{x,\overline{y}}{\forall}(\texttt{sort}[\langle x, \overline{y}\rangle] = \texttt{insert}[x, \texttt{sort}[\langle \overline{y}\rangle]])$]

Assumption["5", $\underset{x,\overline{y}}{\forall}(\texttt{prepend}[x, \langle \overline{y}\rangle] = \langle x, \overline{y}\rangle)$]

where min and max are interpreted as the Mathematica Min and Max functions:

Built-in["MinMax",
  min $\rightarrow$ Min "Minimum"
  max $\rightarrow$ Max "Maximum"]

We would like to prove the following proposition:

Proposition["sort", $\underset{\overline{x}}{\exists}(\texttt{sort}[\langle 1, 3, 2.4, -4\rangle] = \langle \overline{x}\rangle)$]

The equational prover is called to prove the proposition under the given assumptions and built-ins. In addition, numbers are treated in the Mathematica built-in way and all the equations are oriented from left to right:

Prove[Proposition["sort"], using $\rightarrow$ {Assumption["1"], Assumption["2"],
  Assumption["3"], Assumption["4"], Assumption["5"]},
  by $\rightarrow$ EquationalProver,
  built-in$\rightarrow${Built-in["MinMax"], Built-in["Numbers"]},
  ProverOptions $\rightarrow$ {EqPrOrdering $\rightarrow$ "LeftToRight"}]

The output of the prove call is placed in a new notebook. THEOREMA displays it in an elegant way, with natural language text, hierarchically nested cells, hyperlinks, colors, etc. We show the (final part of the) generated proof below [8]:

. . .

To prove (Proposition (sort)), we have to find $\overline{x}^*$ such that

(1) $sort[\langle 1, 3, 2.4, -4\rangle] = \langle \overline{x}^*\rangle.$

We will use the following assumptions, referring to them as axioms:

(Axiom 1) $sort[\langle\rangle] = \langle\rangle.$

(Axiom 2) $\underset{x1}{\forall}(insert[x1, \langle\rangle] = \langle x1\rangle).$

(Axiom 3) $\underset{x1,\overline{x2}}{\forall}(prepend[x1, \langle \overline{x2}\rangle] = \langle x1, \overline{x2}\rangle).$

---

[8] Koji Nakagawa provided a tool to translate the proofs from the THEOREMA proof format into LATEX form.

(Axiom 4) $\forall_{x1,\overline{x2}}(sort[\langle x1, \overline{x2}\rangle] = insert[x1, sort[\langle \overline{x2}\rangle]])$.

(Axiom 5) $\forall_{x1,x2,\overline{x3}}(insert[x1, \langle x2, \overline{x3}\rangle] =$

$$prepend[max[x2, x1], insert[min[x1, x2], \langle \overline{x3}\rangle]])$$.

We choose

$$\overline{x}^* = Sequence[3, 2.4, 1, -4]$$

and show that the equality (1) holds for this value (assuming that the built-in simplification/decomposition is sound):

(Theorem) $sort[\langle 1, 3, 2.4, -4\rangle] = \langle 3, 2.4, 1, -4\rangle$.

Proof.

$$sort[\langle 1, 3, 2.4, -4\rangle] = \langle 3, 2.4, 1, -4\rangle$$

if and only if (by (Axiom 4) LR, (Axiom 4) LR, (Axiom 4) LR, (Axiom 4) LR, (Axiom 1) LR, (Axiom 2) LR)

$$insert[1, insert[3, insert[2.4, \langle -4\rangle]]] = \langle 3, 2.4, 1, -4\rangle$$

if and only if (by (Axiom 5) LR, (Axiom 2) LR, (Axiom 3) LR)

$$insert[1, insert[3, \langle max[-4, 2.4], min[2.4, -4]\rangle] = \langle 3, 2.4, 1, -4\rangle$$

if and only if (by (Axiom 5) LR, (Axiom 5) LR, (Axiom 2) LR, (Axiom 3) LR, (Axiom 3) LR, (Axiom 5) LR, (Axiom 5) LR, (Axiom 5) LR, (Axiom 2) LR, (Axiom 3) LR, (Axiom 3) LR, (Axiom 3) LR)

$$\langle max[max[max[-4, 2.4], 3], 1], max[max[min[2.4, -4],$$
$$min[3, max[-4, 2.4]]], min[1, max[max[-4, 2.4], 3]]],$$
$$max[min[min[3, max[-4, 2.4]], min[2.4, -4]],$$
$$min[min[1, max[max[-4, 2.4], 3]], max[min[2.4, -4],$$
$$min[3, max[-4, 2.4]]]]], min[min[min[1, max[max[-4, 2.4], 3]],$$
$$max[min[2.4, -4], min[3, max[-4, 2.4]]]], min[min[3, max[-4, 2.4]],$$
$$min[2.4, -4]]]\rangle = \langle 3, 2.4, 1, -4\rangle$$

if and only if (by the built-in simplification/decomposition)

$$\langle 3, 2.4, 1, -4\rangle = \langle 3, 2.4, 1, -4\rangle$$

which, by reflexivity of equality, concludes the proof.   □

Example 2 (Combinatory logic). This is an example of a problem in applicative higher order form. The strong fixpoint property holds for the set consisting of the combinators B and W only[9]. The prover uses Warren's method to translate the problem into first order form, proves it with unfailing completion procedure and shows the output again in the higher order form. The proof is given below:

Prove:

(Proposition (goal)) $strong\text{-}fixed\text{-}point[fixed\text{-}pt] =$

$$fixed\text{-}pt[strong\text{-}fixed\text{-}point[fixed\text{-}pt]]$$

...

We will use the following assumptions, referring to them as axioms:

(Axiom 1) $\underset{x,y}{\forall}\,(x[y][y] = W[x][y]).$

(Axiom 2) $\underset{x,y,z}{\forall}\,(B[x][y][z] = x[y[z]]).$

(Axiom 3) $B[W[W]][B[W][B[B][B]]] = strong\text{-}fixed\text{-}point.$

We need the following propositions:

(Lemma 1) $\underset{x1}{\forall}\,(W[W][W[B[B[x1]]]] = strong\text{-}fixed\text{-}point[x1])$

Proof.   We take all variables arbitrary but fixed.

$W[W][W[B[B[x_1]]]] =$ (by (Axiom 2) RL,(Axiom 2) RL)

$W[W][B[W][B[B][B]][x_1]] =$ (by (Axiom 2) RL)

$B[W[W]][B[W][B[B][B]]][x_1] =$ (by (Axiom 3) LR)

$strong\text{-}fixed\text{-}point[x_1].$ □

(Lemma 2) $\underset{x1,x2}{\forall}\,(x1[W[x2][x2]] = W[W[B[B[x1]]]][x2])$

Proof.   We take all variables arbitrary but fixed.

$x_1[W[x_2][x_2]] =$ (by (Axiom 1) RL)

$x_1[x_2[x_2][x_2]] =$ (by (Axiom 2) RL)

$B[B[x_1]][x_2][x_2][x_2] =$ (by (Axiom 1) LR)

$W[W[B[B[x_1]]]][x_2].$ □

---

[9] In TPTP this problem is stated in the first order form in COL003-12.pr.

(Lemma 3) $W[W][W[B[B[fixed\text{-}pt]]]] = fixed\text{-}pt\ [W[W][W[B[B[fixed\text{-}pt]]]]]$

Proof.

$W[W][W[B[B[fixed\text{-}pt]]]] =$ $\qquad\qquad\qquad$ (by (<u>Axiom 1</u>) RL)

$W[W[B[B[fixed\text{-}pt]]]][W[B[B[fixed\text{-}pt]]]] =$ $\qquad\quad$ (by (<u>Lemma 2</u>) RL)

$fixed\text{-}pt[W[W[B[B[fixed\text{-}pt]]]][W[B[B[fixed\text{-}pt]]]]] =$ (by (<u>Axiom 1</u>) LR)

$fixed\text{-}pt[W[W][W[B[B[fixed\text{-}pt]]]]]$. $\qquad\qquad\qquad$ □

(Proposition 1) $fixed\text{-}pt[strong\text{-}fixed\text{-}point[fixed\text{-}pt]] = strong\text{-}fixed\text{-}point[fixed\text{-}pt]$.

Proof.

$fixed\text{-}pt[strong\text{-}fixed\text{-}point[fixed\text{-}pt]] =$ $\qquad$ (by (<u>Lemma 1</u>) RL)

$fixed\text{-}pt[W[W][W[B[B[fixed\text{-}pt]]]]] =$ $\qquad$ (by (<u>Lemma 3</u>) RL)

$W[W][W[B[B[fixed\text{-}pt]]]] =$ $\qquad\qquad\qquad$ (by <u>Lemma 1</u> LR)

$strong\text{-}fixed\text{-}point[fixed\text{-}pt]$. $\qquad\qquad\qquad$ □

Now, we prove (<u>Proposition (goal)</u>).

(Theorem) $strong\text{-}fixed\text{-}point[fixed\text{-}pt] = fixed\text{-}pt[strong\text{-}fixed\text{-}point[fixed\text{-}pt]]$

Proof.

$strong\text{-}fixed\text{-}point[fixed\text{-}pt] =$ $\qquad\qquad$ (by (<u>Proposition 1</u>) RL)

$fixed\text{-}pt[strong\text{-}fixed\text{-}point[fixed\text{-}pt]]$. $\qquad$ □

6   Performance and Future Development

From 431 unit equality problems in TPTPv2.4.0 [29] the prover solved 180 (42%) within 300 seconds on a Linux PC, Intel Pentium 4, 1.5GHz, 128Mb RAM[10]. The performance is lower than the one of, for instance, Waldmeister (85%), Discount (70%), Fiesta (68%) or CiME [10] (53%), but it should be taken into account that Mathematica is fundamentally an interpreter, the prover does not have many heuristics and is not tuned for any specific class of problems. It

---

[10] This does not include problems proved with some user interaction (e.g., choosing appropriate precedence, ordering, age-weight ratio, etc.), but only those ones proved in the autonomous mode.

is still at the experimental level, and there is a room to improve in many parts of it. Especially, the autonomous mode can be strengthened with a structure detection facility, and instance and unification retrievals can be done more efficiently. Proving with constraints involving sequence variables might be another interesting future development.

Strong sides of the prover are its abilities to handle sequence variables and problems in applicative higher form, and to interface Mathematica functions. THEOREMA provides yet another advantage – a convenient, user-friendly interface, and human-oriented proof presentation tools.

Acknowledgments

My thanks go to Prof. Bruno Buchberger and all the THEOREMA group members.

References

1. J. Avenhaus, J. Denzinger, and M. Fuchs. DISCOUNT: a system for distributed equational deduction. In J. Hsiang, editor, *Proceedings of the 6th RTA*, volume 914 of *LNCS*, pages 397–402, Kaiserslautern, Germany, 1995. Springer.
2. J. Avenhaus, Th. Hillenbrand, and B. L"ochner. On using ground joinable equations in equational theorem proving. *J. Symbolic Computation*, 2002. To appear.
3. L. Bachmair, N. Dershowitz, and D. Plaisted. Completion without failure. In H. A"ıt-Kaci and M. Nivat, editors, *Resolution of Equations in Algebraic Structures*, volume 2, pages 1–30. Elsevier Science, 1989.
4. B. Buchberger. Mathematica as a rewrite language. In T. Ida, A. Ohori, and M. Takeichi, editors, *Proceedings of the 2nd Fuji Int. Workshop on Functional and Logic Programming*, pages 1–13, Shonan Village Center, Japan, 1–4 November 1996. World Scientific.
5. B. Buchberger. Symbolic computation: Computer algebra and logic. In F. Baader and K.U. Schulz, editors, *Frontiers of Combining Systems*, Applied Logic Series, pages 193–220. Kluwer Academic Publishers, 1996.
6. B. Buchberger. Using Mathematica for doing simple mathematical proofs (invited paper). In *Proceedings of the 4th Mathematica Users' Conference*, pages 80–96, Tokyo, Japan, 2 November 1996. Wolfram Media Publishing.
7. B. Buchberger, C. Dupré, T. Jebelean, F. Kriftner, K. Nakagawa, D. Vasaru, and W. Windsteiger. The Theorema project: A progress report. In M. Kerber and M. Kohlhase, editors, *Proceedings of Calculemus'2000 Conference*, pages 98–113, St. Andrews, UK, 6–7 August 2000.
8. R. Bündgen. Combining computer algebra and rule based reasoning. In J. Calmet and J. A. Campbell, editors, *Integrating Symbolic Mathematical Computation and Artificial Intelligence. Proceedings of AISMC-2*, volume 958 of *LNCS*, pages 209–223, Cambridge, UK, 3–5 August 1994. Springer.
9. J. Christian. Flatterms, discrimination trees, and fast term rewriting. *J. Automated Reasoning*, 10(1):95–113, 1993.
10. E. Contejean, C. Marche, B. Monate, and X. Urbain. CiME version 2, 2000. http://cime.lri.fr/.
11. J. Denzinger and S. Schulz. Analysis and representation of equational proofs generated by a distributed completion based proof system. SEKI-report SR-94-05, University of Kaiserslautern, Germany, 1994.

12. H. Ganzinger, R. Nieuwenhuis, and P. Nivela. Context trees. In R. Gore, A. Leitsch, and T. Nipkow, editors, *Automated Reasoning. Proceedings of the IJCAR'01*, volume 2083 of *LNAI*, pages 242–256, Siena, Italy, June 2001. Springer.

13. J. C. González-Moreno. A correctness proof for Warren's HO into FO translation. In D. Saccà, editor, *Proc. of the 8th Italian Conference on Logic Programming (GULP'93)*, pages 569–585, Gizzeria Lido, Italy, June 1993. Mediterranean Press.

14. P. Graf. Substitutin tree indexing. In J. Hsiang, editor, *Proceedings of the 6th RTA*, volume 914 of *LNCS*, pages 117–131, Kaiserslautern, Germany, 1995. Springer.

15. T. Hillenbrand, A. Buch, R. Vogt, and B. Löchner. WALDMEISTER – high-performance equational deduction. *J. Automated Reasoning*, 18(2):265–270, 1997.

16. J.-P. Jouannaud and A. Rubio. The higher order recursive path ordering. In *Proceedings of the 14th annual IEEE symposium LICS*, Trento, Italy, 1999.

17. T. Kutsia. Solving and proving in equational theories with sequence variables and flexible arity symbols. Technical Report 02-09, PhD Thesis. Research Institute for Symbolic Computation, Johannes Kepler University, Linz, Austria, 2002.

18. T. Kutsia. Theorem proving with sequence variables and flexible arity symbols. In M. Baaz and A. Voronkov, editors, *Logic in Programming, Artificial Intelligence and Reasoning. International Conference LPAR'02*, volume 2514 of *LNAI*, pages 278–291, Tbilisi, Georgia, 2002. Springer.

19. T. Kutsia. Unification with sequence variables and flexible arity symbols and its extension with pattern-terms. In J. Calmet, B. Benhamou, O. Caprotti, L. Henocque, and V. Sorge, editors, *Proceedings of Joint AISC'2002 – Calculemus'2002 conference*, volume 2385 of *LNAI*, Marseille, France, 1–5 July 2002. Springer.

20. B. L¨ochner and Th. Hillenbrand. A phytography of WALDMEISTER. *AI Communications*, 15(2,3):127–133, 2002.

21. M. Marin. Introducing Sequentica, 2002. http://www.score.is.tsukuba.ac.jp/~mmarin/Sequentica/.

22. W. W. McCune. Experiments with discrimination-tree indexing and path-indexing for term retrieval. *J. Automated Reasoning*, 9(2):147–167, 1992.

23. W. W. McCune. OTTER 3.0 reference manual and guide. Technical Report ANL-94/6, Argonne National Laboratory, Argonne, US, January 1994.

24. R. Nieuwenhuis and A. Rubio. Theorem proving with ordering and equality constrained clauses. *J. Symbolic Computation*, 19:321–351, 1995.

25. I. V. Ramakrishnan, R. Sekar, and A. Voronkov. Term indexing. In A. Robinson and A. Voronkov, editors, *Handbook of Automated Reasoning*, volume II, pages 1853–1964. Elsevier Science, 2001.

26. J. M. Rivero. Data structures and algorithms for automated deduction with equality. PhD Thesis. Universitat Politècnica de Catalunya, Barcelona, Spain, 2000.

27. M. Stickel. A Prolog Technology Theorem Prover: implementation by an extended Prolog compiler. *J. Automated Reasoning*, 4:353–380, 1988.

28. M. Stickel. The path indexing method for indexing terms. Technical Report 473, Artificial Intelligence Center, SRI International, Menlo Park, CA, October 1989.

29. G. Sutcliffe and C. Suttner. The TPTP Problem Library for Automated Theorem Proving. http://www.cs.miami.edu/~tptp/.

30. A. Voronkov. The anatomy of Vampire: Implementing bottom-up procedures with code trees. *J. Automated Reasoning*, 15(2):237–265, 1995.

31. D. H. D. Warren. Higher-order extensions to PROLOG: are they needed? In *Machine Intelligence*, volume 10, pages 441–454. Edinburgh University Press, Edinburgh, UK, 1982.

32. S. Wolfram. *The Mathematica Book*. Cambridge University Press and Wolfram Research, Inc., fourth edition, 1999.

Termination of Simply Typed Term Rewriting by Translation and Labelling[*]

Takahito Aoto[1] and Toshiyuki Yamada[2]

[1] Research Institute of Electrical Communication, Tohoku University, Japan
aoto@nue.riec.tohoku.ac.jp
[2] Faculty of Engineering, Mie University, Japan
toshi@cs.info.mie-u.ac.jp

Abstract. Simply typed term rewriting proposed by Yamada (RTA 2001) is a framework of term rewriting allowing higher-order functions. In contrast to the usual higher-order term rewriting frameworks, simply typed term rewriting dispenses with bound variables. This paper presents a method for proving termination of simply typed term rewriting systems (STTRSs, for short). We first give a translation of STTRSs into many-sorted first-order TRSs and show that termination problem of STTRSs is reduced to that of many-sorted first-order TRSs. Next, we introduce a labelling method which is applied to first-order TRSs obtained by the translation to facilitate termination proof of them; our labelling employs an extension of semantic labelling where terms are interpreted on a many-sorted algebra.

1 Introduction

Simply typed term rewriting proposed by Yamada [10] is a simple extension of first-order term rewriting. It can deal with higher-order functions. Equational specification using higher-order functions, like functional programs, are naturally expressed in this framework. In contrast to the usual higher-order term rewriting frameworks [5,7,9], simply typed term rewriting dispenses with bound variables. In this respect, simply typed term rewriting reflects limited higher-order features. On the other hand, simply typed term rewriting framework is succinct and theoretically much more easier to deal with.

This paper presents a method for proving termination of simply typed term rewriting systems (STTRSs, for short). Termination of STTRSs based on monotone interpretation has been investigated in [10]. We are concerned here with syntactic methods and propose techniques which are more suitable for automated termination proof.

We first give a translation of STTRSs into many-sorted first-order TRSs such that the termination of an STTRS is induced from that of the many-sorted first-order TRS obtained by this translation. Since a many-sorted first-order TRS is

---

[*] This work was partially supported by a grant from Japan Society for the Promotion of Science, No. 14780187.

R. Nieuwenhuis (Ed.): RTA 2003, LNCS 2706, pp. 380–394, 2003.

terminating whenever the underlying first-order TRS obtained by omitting the sort information is terminating, one can apply any known methods for proving termination of ordinary TRSs to infer the termination of STTRSs based on our translation. Next, we introduce a labelling method which is applied to first-order TRSs obtained by the translation to facilitate termination proof of them. Our labelling method is based on semantic labelling proposed by Zantema [11]— in fact, it is a particular kind of the semantic labelling over fixed models and labels (determined by the signature of STTRSs). However, the original semantic labelling method for unsorted TRSs is insufficient for our purpose and thus our labelling employs an extension of semantic labelling where terms are interpreted on a many-sorted algebra.

The remainder of the paper is organized as follows: In Section 2, we review the basic notions and terminology of simply typed term rewriting. In Section 3, we give a translation of STTRSs into many-sorted first-order TRSs such that the termination problem of an STTRS is reduced to that of the corresponding many-sorted TRS. In Sections 4 and 5, we present a labelling method that facilitates termination proof of many-sorted TRSs obtained by our translation. We first introduce our labelling method in unsorted setting using the original semantic labelling, and examine why the labelling in this setting is not often useful (in Section 4). Then the labelling method is improved based on the many-sorted version of semantic labelling (in Section 5).

2   Preliminaries

In this section, we recall the basic notions and terminology of simply typed term rewriting, which were introduced in [10]. We assume the reader to be familiar with (first-order) term rewriting [3,4,8].

For a set B of *basic types*, the set of *simple types* is the smallest set $\mathrm{ST}(B)$ such that (1) $B \subseteq \mathrm{ST}(B)$, and (2) $\tau_1 \times \cdots \times \tau_n \to \tau_0 \in \mathrm{ST}(B)$ whenever $\tau_0, \tau_1, \ldots, \tau_n \in \mathrm{ST}(B)$. Note that our definition allows multiple basic types whereas the original one in [10] is based on a single basic type. When clear, simple type is abbreviated as *type*, and $\mathrm{ST}(B)$ is written as ST.

Each *constant* or *variable* is associated with its type; the sets of constants and variables of type τ are denoted by C^τ and V^τ, respectively. C and V stand for the sets of all constants and variables, respectively: $C = \bigcup_{\tau \in \mathrm{ST}} C^\tau$ and $V = \bigcup_{\tau \in \mathrm{ST}} V^\tau$. We assume that V^τ is countably infinite for any $\tau \in \mathrm{ST}$. The set $\mathrm{T}_{\mathrm{ST}}(C, V)^\tau$ of *simply typed terms* of type τ over C, V is defined as follows: (1) $C^\tau \cup V^\tau \subseteq \mathrm{T}_{\mathrm{ST}}(C, V)^\tau$, and (2) if $s \in \mathrm{T}_{\mathrm{ST}}(C, V)^{\tau_1 \times \cdots \times \tau_n \to \tau}$ and $t_i \in \mathrm{T}_{\mathrm{ST}}(C, V)^{\tau_i}$ for all $i \in \{1, \ldots, n\}$ then $(s\, t_1 \cdots t_n) \in \mathrm{T}_{\mathrm{ST}}(C, V)^\tau$. The outermost parenthesis of simply typed terms may be omitted when no confusion arises. A simply typed term s has type τ (denoted by s^τ) when $s \in \mathrm{T}_{\mathrm{ST}}(C, V)^\tau$. It is clear that each simply typed term has a unique type; thus τ is also referred to as the type of s. The set $\mathrm{T}_{\mathrm{ST}}(C, V)$ of all simply typed terms is $\bigcup_{\tau \in \mathrm{ST}} \mathrm{T}_{\mathrm{ST}}(C, V)^\tau$; when clear, $\mathrm{T}_{\mathrm{ST}}(C, V)$ is abbreviated as T_{ST}. The *head symbol* of a simply typed term is defined as follows: (1) $\mathrm{head}(t) = t$ if $t \in C \cup V$, and (2) $\text{head}((s\, t_1 \cdots t_n)) = \text{head}(s)$. The set of variables occurring in a term t is written as $V(t)$.

A pair $\langle l, r \rangle$ of simply typed terms is a *simply typed rewrite rule* when (1) l and r have the same type, (2) $\text{head}(l) \in C$, and (3) $V(r) \subseteq V(l)$. A simply typed rewrite rule $\langle l, r \rangle$ will be often written as $l \to r$. A triple $\langle B, C, R \rangle$ consisting of a set B of basic types, a set C of constants, and a set R of simply typed rewrite rules is called a *simply typed term rewriting system* (STTRS, for short).

A *substitution* is a mapping $\sigma : V \to \text{T}_{\text{ST}}(C, V)$ that satisfies the following conditions: (1) $\text{Dom}(\sigma) = \{x \mid \sigma(x) \neq x\}$ is finite; and (2) for each $x \in \text{Dom}(\sigma)$, x and $\sigma(x)$ have the same type. The homomorphic extension of σ to $\text{T}_{\text{ST}}(C, V)$ is also denoted by σ. As usual, $\sigma(t)$ is written as $t\sigma$. The *rewrite relation* $\to_{\mathcal{R}}$ induced by a simply typed term rewriting system $\mathcal{R} = \langle B, C, R \rangle$ is the smallest relation over $\text{T}_{\text{ST}}(C, V)$ satisfying the following conditions: (1) $l\sigma \to_{\mathcal{R}} r\sigma$ for all $l \to r \in R$ and for all substitutions σ, and (2) if $s \to_{\mathcal{R}} t$ then $(s_0 \cdots s \cdots s_n) \to_{\mathcal{R}} (s_0 \cdots t \cdots s_n)$ for all $s_0, \ldots, s_n$. An STTRS $\mathcal{R}$ is *terminating* if there is no infinite reduction sequences $s_0 \to_{\mathcal{R}} s_1 \to_{\mathcal{R}} \cdots$.

Example 1 (simply typed term rewriting). Let $\mathcal{R} = \langle B, C, R \rangle$ be an STTRS where $B = \{\, Nat, List \,\}$, $C = \{\, 0^{Nat},\ \text{s}^{Nat \to Nat},\ []^{List},\ :^{Nat \times List \to List},\ \text{map}^{(Nat \to Nat) \times List \to List},\ \circ^{(Nat \to Nat) \times (Nat \to Nat) \to (Nat \to Nat)},\ \text{twice}^{(Nat \to Nat) \to (Nat \to Nat)} \,\}$, and

$$
R = \begin{cases}
\text{map } F\ [] & \to & [] \\
\text{map } F\ (x : xs) & \to & (F\ x) : (\text{map } F\ xs) \\
(F \circ G)\ x & \to & F\ (G\ x) \\
\text{twice } F & \to & F \circ F
\end{cases}
$$

Here is a rewrite sequence of $\mathcal{R}$:

$$
\begin{aligned}
\text{map (twice s) } (0 : []) \ &\to_{\mathcal{R}} \ \text{map (s} \circ \text{s)} \ (0 : []) \\
&\to_{\mathcal{R}} \ ((\text{s} \circ \text{s})\ 0) : (\text{map (s} \circ \text{s)} \ []) \\
&\to_{\mathcal{R}} \ (\text{s (s 0)}) : (\text{map (s} \circ \text{s)} \ []) \\
&\to_{\mathcal{R}} \ (\text{s (s 0)}) : [].
\end{aligned}
$$

3   Translating STTRSs to Many-Sorted TRSs

The framework of STTRSs can deal with higher-order variables and thus it is not within the framework of (usual) first-order term rewriting. However, this does not necessarily imply that STTRSs can not be seen as TRSs via suitable encoding. In this section, we will see that STTRSs can be encoded into many-sorted TRSs.

First, we define the notion of arity, which will be used to reflect the type information of the simply typed terms in our encoding.

Definition 1 (arity). *The set of* arities *is the smallest set* $\text{Ar}(B)$ *such that* (1) $B \subseteq \text{Ar}(B)$, *and* (2) *if* $n \geq 1$ *and* $a_0, a_1, \ldots, a_n \in \text{Ar}(B)$ *then* $\langle a_1 \cdots a_n\, a_0 \rangle \in \text{Ar}(B)$. *The mapping* $\text{ar} : \text{ST}(B) \to \text{Ar}(B)$ *is defined as follows:*

$$
\text{ar}(\tau) = \begin{cases}
\tau & \text{if } \tau \in B, \\
\langle \text{ar}(\tau_1) \cdots \text{ar}(\tau_n)\, \text{ar}(\tau_0) \rangle & \text{if } \tau = \tau_1 \times \cdots \times \tau_n \to \tau_0.
\end{cases}
$$

Arities can denote simple types concisely. For example, $\mathrm{ar}((Nat \to Nat) \times List \to List) = \langle\langle Nat\ Nat\rangle List\ List\rangle$. We also employ the following conventions for simplicity:

1. $Nat, List$, etc. are abbreviated as N, L, etc. when no confusion arises.
2. $\langle a_1 \cdots a_n\rangle$ is abbreviated as a_1^n when $a_1 = \cdots = a_n$. (Note that this implies that $(N^2)^2$ differs from N^4; the former denotes $\langle\langle NN\rangle\langle NN\rangle\rangle$ while the latter is $\langle NNNN\rangle$.)
3. Outer most brackets of arities are omitted. (Thus, for example, $\langle\langle NL\rangle LL\rangle$ is written as $\langle NL\rangle LL$.)

These conventions are illustrated in the following table, which contains some examples of arities.

symbol $c \in C$	simple type τ	arity $\mathrm{ar}(\tau)$
0	Nat	N
s	$Nat \to Nat$	N^2
:	$Nat \times List \to List$	NLL
map	$(Nat \to Nat) \times List \to List$	N^2LL
twice	$(Nat \to Nat) \to (Nat \to Nat)$	$(N^2)^2$

We next give a translation from STTRSs to many-sorted TRSs. A many-sorted TRS is specified by a triple $\langle S, F, R\rangle$ where S is a set of sorts, F a set of S-sorted function symbols, and R a set of rewrite rules.

Definition 2 (translation). *We define a translation Θ from simply typed signature (terms, STTRSs) to many-sorted signature (terms, many-sorted TRSs, respectively).*

1. $\Theta(C) = C \cup \{\ @_a \mid a \in \mathrm{Ar}(B) \setminus B\ \}$
   where each function symbol in $\Theta(C)$ is associated with its sort as follows:
   $$\mathrm{sort}(f) = \begin{cases} \mathrm{ar}(\tau) & \text{if } f \in C^\tau \\ \langle a_1 \cdots a_n a_0\rangle \times a_1 \times \cdots \times a_n \to a_0 & \text{if } f = @_{\langle a_1 \cdots a_n a_0\rangle} \end{cases}$$
2. $\Theta(t) = \begin{cases} t & \text{if } t \in C \cup V \\ @_{\mathrm{ar}(\tau)}(\Theta(s), \Theta(t_1), \ldots, \Theta(t_n)) & \text{if } t = (s^\tau\ t_1 \cdots t_n) \end{cases}$
3. $\Theta(R) = \{\ \Theta(l) \to \Theta(r) \mid l \to r \in R\ \}$
4. $\Theta(\langle B, C, R\rangle) = \langle \mathrm{Ar}(B), \Theta(C), \Theta(R)\rangle$

The following table shows examples of symbols and their sorts in a translated signature.

symbol $f \in \Theta(C)$	sort $\mathrm{sort}(f)$
0	N
s	N^2
map	N^2LL
$@_{N^2}$	$N^2 \times N \to N$
$@_{NLL}$	$NLL \times N \times L \to L$

Example 2 (translation). Let $\mathcal{R}$ be an STTRS given in Example 1. Given below is the rewrite rules of $\Theta(\mathcal{R})$.

$$
\begin{cases}
@_{N^2LL}(\mathsf{map}, F, []) & \rightarrow \quad [] \\
@_{N^2LL}(\mathsf{map}, F, @_{NLL}(:, x, xs)) & \rightarrow \quad @_{NLL}(:, @_{N^2}(F, x), @_{N^2LL}(\mathsf{map}, F, xs)) \\
@_{N^2}(@_{(N^2)^3}(\circ, F, G), x) & \rightarrow \quad @_{N^2}(F, @_{N^2}(G, x)) \\
@_{(N^2)^2}(\mathsf{twice}, F) & \rightarrow \quad @_{(N^2)^3}(\circ, F, F)
\end{cases}
$$

Theorem 1 (completeness of translation). *Let $\mathcal{R}$ be an STTRS. Then $\Theta(\mathcal{R})$ is terminating if and only if $\mathcal{R}$ is terminating.*

Proof. Easy. □

Thus, the termination problem of STTRSs is reduced to the termination problem of many-sorted TRSs. Clearly, many-sorted TRS is terminating when its underlying unsorted TRS obtained by eliminating its sort information is terminating. Therefore, for proving termination of an STTRS, any existing proof techniques can be applied to the TRS obtained by the translation Θ.

Example 3 (termination of STTRS by translation). Let $\mathcal{R}$ be the STTRS in Example 1. Termination of $\Theta(\mathcal{R})$ is shown, for example, by the lexicographic path order (LPO) [6] and thus, $\mathcal{R}$ is terminating.

4   Primary Symbol Labelling on Single Sort

In simply typed term rewriting, the usual expression $f(s_1, \ldots, s_n)$ of terms is changed to $(f\ s_1\ \cdots\ s_n)$ so that function variables does not appear as a node of tree structure of terms like $F(s_1, \ldots, s_n)$ but as a leaf like $(F\ s_1\ \cdots\ s_n)$. Similarly, for TRSs of the form $\Theta(\mathcal{R})$, the terms are of the form $@_a(f, s_1, \ldots, s_n)$. Then, contrasted to the usual first-order term formulation, when one tries to compare terms using path-orders like RPO, LPO, etc., each leading symbol f is no longer compared before its arguments $s_1, \ldots, s_n$, and only application symbols with type information are compared before their arguments. Since the type information of a term is more common information compared to the function symbol, path-orders are not effectively applied to TRSs obtained by the translation.

Example 4 (motivation for labelling). Let $B = \{\ Nat\ \}$, $C = \{\ 0^{Nat},\ \mathsf{s}^{Nat \rightarrow Nat},\ +^{Nat \rightarrow (Nat \rightarrow Nat)},\ *^{Nat \rightarrow (Nat \rightarrow Nat)}\ \}$, and

$$
R = \begin{cases}
(+\ 0)\ y & \rightarrow \quad y \\
(+\ (\mathsf{s}\ x))\ y & \rightarrow \quad \mathsf{s}\ ((+\ x)\ y) \\
(*\ 0)\ y & \rightarrow \quad 0 \\
(*\ (\mathsf{s}\ x))\ y & \rightarrow \quad +\ ((*\ x)\ y)\ y
\end{cases}
$$

Then $\Theta(\mathcal{R})$ has the following rewrite rules:

$$
\begin{cases}
@_{N^2}(@_{NN^2}(+, 0), y) & \rightarrow \quad y \\
@_{N^2}(@_{NN^2}(+, @_{N^2}(\mathsf{s}, x)), y) & \rightarrow \quad @_{N^2}(\mathsf{s}, @_{N^2}(@_{NN^2}(+, x), y)) \\
@_{N^2}(@_{NN^2}(*, 0), y) & \rightarrow \quad 0 \\
@_{N^2}(@_{NN^2}(*, @_{N^2}(\mathsf{s}, x)), y) & \rightarrow \quad @_{N^2}(@_{NN^2}(+, @_{N^2}(@_{NN^2}(*, x), y)), y)
\end{cases}
$$

The fourth rule can not be made decreasing by LPO at any precedence—this is because $+$ and $*$ have the same type (i.e. both lhs and rhs of the rule have the same root symbol $@_{N^2}$).

This observation leads us to the idea of labelling application symbols not only by types but also head symbols. That is, we label each application symbol by the leftmost non-application symbol in its first argument. For example, the fourth rule of the TRS above becomes

$$@_{N^2*}(@_{NN^2*}(*, @_{N^2\mathsf{s}}(\mathsf{s}, x)), y)$$
$$\rightarrow @_{N^2+}(@_{NN^2+}(+, @_{N^2*}(@_{NN^2*}(*, x), y)), y)$$

and the root symbols of lhs and rhs of the rule get distinguished. For this purpose, semantic labelling [11] seems to be helpful.

In this section, we define this particular labelling, called primary symbol labelling, for first-order TRSs. Our labelling method is obtained from semantic labelling by fixing ordered algebra and a labelling specification. It turns out that the labelling method obtained from the original semantic labelling is not useful in many cases. In the end of the section, we will exhibit by examples why this naive approach is unsatisfactory. The labelling method in this section will be modified in the next section.

In semantic labelling, algebra operations are used to determine a label of a function symbol. Since our labelling is based on the quasi-model version of semantic labelling, the carrier of an algebra for labelling need to be partially ordered. Let Σ be a first-order signature. A *weakly monotone Σ-algebra* $\mathcal{A} = \langle A, \geq_{\mathcal{A}}, \{f_{\mathcal{A}}\}_{f \in \Sigma} \rangle$ consists of a non-empty carrier set A, a partial order $\geq_{\mathcal{A}}$ on A, and a family $\{f_{\mathcal{A}}\}_{f \in \Sigma}$ of interpretations. Each $f \in \Sigma$ takes a fixed number of arguments and the set of all function symbols in Σ taking n arguments is denoted by Σ_n. Each constant $c \in \Sigma_0$ is interpreted as an element $c_{\mathcal{A}} \in A$ and each $f \in \Sigma_n$ $(n \geq 1)$ is interpreted as an algebra operation $f_{\mathcal{A}} : A^n \to A$. All operations need to be weakly monotone, i.e., if $a_i \geq_{\mathcal{A}} b_i$ for $i = 1, \dots, n$ then $f_{\mathcal{A}}(a_1, \dots, a_n) \geq_{\mathcal{A}} f_{\mathcal{A}}(b_1, \dots, b_n)$. The result of evaluating a term t in $\mathcal{A}$ is denoted by $[\![t]\!]_{\mathcal{A}}$. The subscript $\mathcal{A}$ will be omitted when no confusion occurs.

We define a particular ordered algebra suitable for our labelling.

Definition 3 (algebra for primary symbol labelling). *Let Σ be a first-order signature and $\geq$ a partial order on the set Σ_0 of all constant symbols. The Σ-algebra* **Pri** *is defined as $\langle \Sigma_0, \geq, \{f_{\mathbf{Pri}}\}_{f \in \Sigma} \rangle$ where the interpretation of a function symbol $f \in \Sigma_n$ is defined as follows:*

$$f_{\mathbf{Pri}}(a_1, \dots, a_n) = \begin{cases} f & \text{if } n = 0, \\ a_1 & \text{if } n \geq 1. \end{cases}$$

Observe that $f_{\mathbf{Pri}}$ is weakly monotone for any partial order $\geq$.

Example 5 (Σ-algebra **Pri**). *Let Σ be the signature of $\Theta(\mathcal{R})$ in Example 4, namely, $\Sigma = \{ 0, \mathsf{s}, +, *, @_{N^2}, @_{NN^2}, \dots \}$ and $\Sigma_0 = \{ 0, \mathsf{s}, +, * \}$. Let $\geq$ be any* partial order on Σ_0. Terms are evaluated in **Pri** as follows: $[\![0]\!] = 0$, $[\![s]\!] = s$, $[\![@_{N^2}(s, 0)]\!] = s$, $[\![@_{NN^2}(*, @_{N^2}(s, 0))]\!] = *$, and $[\![@_{N^2}(@_{NN^2}(*, @_{N^2}(s, 0)), 0)]\!] = *$. Note that $\mathrm{head}(t) = [\![\Theta(t)]\!]$ holds for all simply typed term t without variables.

Now let us consider labelling for terms and rewrite rules. The set of first-order variables is denoted by X. An *assignment* on A is a function from X to A. The result of evaluating a term t in a Σ-algebra $\mathcal{A}$ under an assignment α is denoted by $[\![t]\!]_{\mathcal{A},\alpha}$, or simply $[\![t]\!]_\alpha$. Let $\mathcal{R} = \langle \Sigma, R \rangle$ be a first-order TRS. A weakly monotone Σ-algebra $\mathcal{A}$ is a *quasi-model* of $\mathcal{R}$ if $[\![l]\!]_\alpha \geq [\![r]\!]_\alpha$ for all rewrite rule $l \to r \in R$ and assignments α on the carrier of $\mathcal{A}$.

Definition 4 (primary symbol). *Let Σ be a first-order signature, $\geq$ a partial order on the set Σ_0 of constant symbols. For any assignment α on Σ_0, the primary symbol of a first-order term t is defined as $[\![t]\!]_{\mathbf{Pri},\alpha} \in \Sigma_0$.*

Example 6 (primary symbol). Let Σ be the signature of $\Theta(\mathcal{R})$ in Example 4 and $\geq$ be any partial order on Σ_0. Suppose an assignment α satisfies $\alpha(F) = *$. The primary symbol of a term is computed as follows: $[\![@_{N^2}(s, 0)]\!]_\alpha = s$, $[\![@_{N^2}(@_{NN^2}(F, @_{N^2}(s, x)), 0)]\!]_\alpha = *$. Note that, if the head symbol of a simply typed term t is a constant, then it is identical to the primary symbol of $\Theta(t)$; otherwise, the assignment determines the primary symbol of $\Theta(t)$.

In our labelling method, every function symbol in a term is labelled by the primary symbol of its first argument.

Definition 5 (primary symbol labelling for terms). *Let Σ be a first-order signature and $\geq$ a partial order on Σ_0. The set $\mathrm{Lab}(\Sigma)$ of labelled function symbols is defined as*

$$\mathrm{Lab}(\Sigma) = \Sigma_0 \cup \{ f_\ell \mid f \in \Sigma_n, \ n \geq 1, \ \ell \in \Sigma_0 \}$$

where f_ℓ has the same arity as f. For each assignment α on Σ_0, we define the labelling function $\mathrm{lab}_\alpha : \mathrm{T}(\Sigma, X) \to \mathrm{T}(\mathrm{Lab}(\Sigma), X)$ as follows:

$$\mathrm{lab}_\alpha(t) = \begin{cases} t & \text{if } t \in \Sigma_0 \cup X, \\ f_{[\![t_1]\!]_\alpha}(\mathrm{lab}_\alpha(t_1), \dots, \mathrm{lab}_\alpha(t_n)) & \text{if } t = f(t_1, \dots, t_n), n \geq 1. \end{cases}$$

Example 7 (primary symbol labelling for terms). Let Σ be the signature of $\Theta(\mathcal{R})$ in Example 4. Then, for any assignment α on Σ_0, we have $\mathrm{lab}_\alpha(@_{N^2}(s, 0)) = @_{N^2 s}(s, 0)$, and $\mathrm{lab}_\alpha(@_{N^2}(@_{NN^2}(*, 0), x)) = @_{N^2 *}(@_{NN^2 *}(*, 0), x)$.

Definition 6 (primary symbol labelling for rewrite systems). *For any TRS $\langle \Sigma, R \rangle$ and any partial order $\geq$ on Σ_0, we define*

$$\mathrm{LabDec}(\langle \Sigma, R \rangle) = \langle \mathrm{Lab}(\Sigma), \mathrm{Lab}(R) \cup \mathrm{Dec}(R) \rangle$$

where

$$\mathrm{Lab}(R) = \{ \mathrm{lab}_\alpha(l) \to \mathrm{lab}_\alpha(r) \mid l \to r \in R, \ \alpha : X \to \Sigma_0 \},$$
$$\mathrm{Dec}(R) = \{ f_\ell(x_1, \dots, x_n) \to f_{\ell'}(x_1, \dots, x_n) \mid$$
$$f \in \Sigma_n, \ n \geq 1, \ \ell, \ell' \in \Sigma_0, \ \ell > \ell' \}.$$

Theorem 2 (soundness of primary symbol labelling). *Let $\mathcal{R} = \langle \Sigma, R \rangle$ be a first-order TRS and $\geq$ a partial order on Σ_0. If the Σ-algebra $\mathbf{Pri}$ is a quasi-model of $\mathcal{R}$ and $\mathrm{LabDec}(\mathcal{R})$ is terminating, then $\mathcal{R}$ is terminating.*

Proof. We use the quasi-order version of semantic labelling [11]. For all function symbols $f \in \Sigma \setminus \Sigma_0$, take $\langle \Sigma_0, \geq \rangle$ as the partially ordered set of labels. For the mapping $\pi_f : \Sigma_0{}^n \to \Sigma_0$ $(n \geq 1)$, which determines a label for f, we choose the projection to the first argument: $\pi_f(\ell_1, \ldots, \ell_n) = \ell_1$. $\qquad\square$

Corollary 1 (termination of STTRS by labelling). *Let $\mathcal{R}$ be an STTRS, $\mathcal{R}' = \langle \Sigma, R' \rangle$ the unsorted version of $\Theta(\mathcal{R})$, and $\geq$ a partial order on Σ_0. If $\mathbf{Pri}$ is a quasi-model of $\mathcal{R}'$ and $\mathrm{LabDec}(\mathcal{R}')$ is terminating, then $\mathcal{R}$ is terminating.*

As mentioned in the beginning of this section, the naive labelling presented in this section is not successfully applied. Let us illustrate why the primary symbol labelling defined in this section is ineffective.

Example 8 (drawback of naive labelling). Consider the STTRS $\mathcal{R}$ in Example 4. The set of constant symbols of $\Theta(\mathcal{R})$ is $\Sigma_0 = \{\, 0, \mathsf{s}, +, * \,\}$. To guarantee that $\mathbf{Pri}$ is a quasi-model of the unsorted version of $\Theta(\mathcal{R})$, the partial order $\geq$ on Σ_0 should satisfy the following constraints.

1. $+ \geq 0, \mathsf{s}, +, *$ from the first rule, and
2. $* \geq +$ from the fourth rule.

This is impossible because $+ \geq *$ and $* \geq +$ can not be satisfied at the same time. Since every rule should be decreasing w.r.t. the interpretation, only very restricted partial orders are possible (especially, when collapsing rules are contained as above), and often the labelling is useless.

Example 9 (termination of STTRS by labelling). Consider the STTRS $\mathcal{R}$ in Example 1. Then $\mathrm{LabDec}(\Theta(\mathcal{R}))$ has the following rewrite rules:

$$
\left\{
\begin{array}{rcl}
@_{N^2 LL\mathsf{map}}(\mathsf{map}, F, [\,]) & \to & [\,] \\[2pt]
@_{N^2 LL\mathsf{map}}(\mathsf{map}, F, @_{NLL:}(:, x, xs)) & & \\
& \to & @_{NLL:}(:, @_{N^2\mathsf{s}}(F, x), @_{N^2 LL\mathsf{map}}(\mathsf{map}, F, xs)) \\[2pt]
@_{N^2 LL\mathsf{map}}(\mathsf{map}, F, @_{NLL:}(:, x, xs)) & & \\
& \to & @_{NLL:}(:, @_{N^2\mathsf{map}}(F, x), @_{N^2 LL\mathsf{map}}(\mathsf{map}, F, xs)) \\[4pt]
& \vdots & \\[4pt]
@_{N^2\circ}(@_{(N^2)^3\circ}(\circ, F, G), x) & \to & @_{N^2\mathsf{s}}(F, @_{N^2\mathsf{s}}(G, x)) \\[2pt]
@_{N^2\circ}(@_{(N^2)^3\circ}(\circ, F, G), x) & \to & @_{N^2\mathsf{s}}(F, @_{N^2\mathsf{map}}(G, x)) \\[2pt]
@_{N^2\circ}(@_{(N^2)^3\circ}(\circ, F, G), x) & \to & @_{N^2\mathsf{s}}(F, @_{N^2:}(G, x)) \\[4pt]
& \vdots & \\[4pt]
@_{(N^2)^2\mathsf{twice}}(\mathsf{twice}, F) & \to & @_{(N^2)^3\circ}(\circ, F, F)
\end{array}
\right.
$$

When labelling rewrite rules, we have to consider all assignments for variables. This gives rise to making a large number of labelled rules from a rewrite rule containing function variables.

However, these drawbacks can be avoided by restricting possibility of labelling by using sort information. To do so, we use the many-sorted version of semantic labelling.

5   Primary Symbol Labelling on Multiple Sorts

In [11], semantic labelling is developed for unsorted TRSs. The many-sorted version of semantic labelling is verified exactly in the same way as in the unsorted case. In this section, we apply the many-sorted version of semantic labelling to improve the labelling method introduced in the previous section.

Let S be a set of sorts, Σ be an S-sorted first-order signature. A *weakly monotone S-sorted Σ-algebra* $\mathcal{A} = \langle \{A^a\}_{a \in S}, \geq_{\mathcal{A}}, \{f_{\mathcal{A}}\}_{f \in \Sigma} \rangle$ consists of a family $\{A^a\}_{a \in S}$ of non-empty carrier sets, a partial order $\geq_{\mathcal{A}}$ on $A = \bigcup \{A^a \mid a \in S\}$, and a family $\{f_{\mathcal{A}}\}_{f \in \Sigma}$ of interpretations. Each constant $c \in \Sigma$ of sort a is interpreted as an element $c_{\mathcal{A}} \in A^a$, and each function symbol $f \in \Sigma$ of sort $a_1 \times \cdots \times a_n \to a_0$ is interpreted as an algebra operation $f_{\mathcal{A}} : A^{a_1} \times \cdots \times A^{a_n} \to A^{a_0}$. Similarly to the unsorted case, the operations need to be weakly monotone. Although many-sorted algebras allow pairwise disjoint domains, below we will choose carrier sets that overlap each other. In order to deal with such a case easily, we use a single partial order $\geq_{\mathcal{A}}$ over A.

Since a simply typed term, with B a set of basic types, is transformed into an $\mathrm{Ar}(B)$-sorted term by the translation Θ, we take $\mathrm{Ar}(B)$ as the set of sorts. We now verify how to fix carrier sets of many-sorted algebra, motivated by the following two observations.

Observation 1. *Constants that may occur as the primary symbol of t is restricted by the sort of t.*

Example 10 (restricting terms by sort information). Let $B = \{Nat\}$ and $C = \{\, 0^{Nat}, +^{Nat \times Nat \to Nat}, \mathsf{curry}^{(Nat \times Nat \to Nat) \to (Nat \to (Nat \to Nat))} \,\}$. Terms with the constant curry appearing as the primary symbol are limited to those having sorts $N^3 \langle NN^2 \rangle$, NN^2, N^2, or N. For example,

term	sort
curry	$N^3 \langle NN^2 \rangle$
$@_{N^3 \langle NN^2 \rangle}(\mathsf{curry}, +)$	$\langle NN^2 \rangle$
$@_{\langle NN^2 \rangle}(@_{N^3 \langle NN^2 \rangle}(\mathsf{curry}, +), 0)$	N^2
$@_{N^2}(@_{\langle NN^2 \rangle}(@_{N^3 \langle NN^2 \rangle}(\mathsf{curry}, +), 0), 0)$	N

This observation leads to the following definition.

Definition 7 (range-order). *The* range-order $\trianglerighteq$ *on the set* $\mathrm{Ar}(B)$ *is the smallest partial order such that* $\langle a_1 \cdots a_n a_0 \rangle \trianglerighteq a_0$.

Example 11 (range-order). Let $B = \{Nat, List\}$. Then $N^3 \langle NN^2 \rangle \trianglerighteq NN^2 \trianglerighteq N^2 \trianglerighteq N$. Also we have $\langle NN \rangle LL \trianglerighteq L$.

Thus, in contrast with the unsorted case, we can restrict carrier sets based on the sort information. We tentatively fix the carrier sets as $A^a = \{\, c \in C^\tau \mid \mathrm{ar}(\tau) \unrhd a \,\}$ for all sorts $a \in \mathrm{Ar}(B)$.

The first observation gives rise to unnecessarily large carrier sets $A^{\mathrm{ar}(\tau)} (= A^\tau)$ for basic types τ. Because usually most of rewrite rules are of basic types, this will impose many restrictions to our choice of the partial order. However, the following observation reveals that elements in a carrier set of a basic type need not to be distinguished.

Observation 2. *No constant of basic type is used as a label.*

Any constant of basic type, like 0 and [], does not occur as a primary symbol in a translated term except for a constant itself, because it does not appear at the first argument of an application symbol $@_a$. This means that elements of A^τ are not used as labels whenever τ is a basic type, and thus there is no need to distinguish them. Therefore, we can take the singleton set $A^\tau = \{\bullet\}$ for every basic type τ. This in particular implies that the rewrite rules of basic types do not impose any restriction on the selection of the partial order of the many-sorted algebra.

Now, based on the observations so far, we define a many-sorted algebra.

Definition 8 (many-sorted algebra for primary symbol labelling). *Let B be a set of basic types and C a set of constants for simply typed terms. Then a many-sorted algebra $\mathbf{Pri}(B, C)$ is a weakly monotone S-sorted Σ-algebra $\langle \{A^a\}_{a \in S}, \geq, \{f_{\mathbf{Pri}(B,C)}\}_{f \in \Sigma} \rangle$ where*

- *$S = \mathrm{Ar}(B)$ and $\Sigma = \Theta(C)$,*
- *$\bullet$ is an element not contained in C and $\geq$ is a partial order on $A = \{\bullet\} \cup C$,*
- *The carrier set A^a of sort a is defined as:*

$$A^a = \begin{cases} \{\bullet\} & \text{if } a \in B \text{ or } C^{\unrhd a} = \emptyset, \\ C^{\unrhd a} & \text{otherwise,} \end{cases}$$

where $C^{\unrhd a} = \{\, c \in C^\tau \mid \mathrm{ar}(\tau) \unrhd a \,\}$,
- *The interpretation of a function symbol $f \in \Sigma$ of sort $a_1 \times \cdots \times a_n \to a_0$ is defined as follows:*

$$f_{\mathbf{Pri}(B,C)}(a_1, \ldots, a_n) = \begin{cases} f & \text{if } n = 0, \\ \bullet & \text{if } n \geq 1 \text{ and } A^{a_0} = \{\bullet\}, \\ d & \text{if } n \geq 1 \text{ and } A^{a_0} \neq \{\bullet\} \text{ and } A^{a_1} = \{\bullet\}, \\ a_1 & \text{otherwise,} \end{cases}$$

where d is an arbitrarily fixed element in A^{a_0}. It is easy to see that every $f_{\mathbf{Pri}(B,C)}$ is weakly monotone.

Example 12 (many-sorted Σ-algebra $\mathbf{Pri}(B,C)$). Let $B = \{\, Nat \,\}$, and $C = \{\, 0^{Nat},\ s^{Nat \to Nat},\ +^{Nat \times Nat \to Nat},\ *^{Nat \times Nat \to Nat} \,\}$. Then $A = \{\, \bullet, 0, s, +, * \,\}$. $A^{N^2} = \{\, s \,\}$, $A^{N^3} = \{\, +, * \,\}$, and $A^a = \{\, \bullet \,\}$ for $a \notin \{\, N^2, N^3 \,\}$. The order $\geq$ can be any partial order on A.

The set of many-sorted variables is denoted by X. An *assignment* on A is a function $\alpha : X \to A$ such that $x \in X^a$ implies $\alpha(x) \in A^a$. The notions of interpretation, quasi-model, and the primary symbol of a many-sorted term are defined similarly to the unsorted case.

Example 13 (interpretation). Let B and C be the ones in Example 10, and α be any assignment. Then $[\![@_{N^2}(\mathsf{s}, 0)]\!]_\alpha = [\![@_{N^3}(+, 0, 0)]\!]_\alpha = \bullet$. Also, $[\![+]\!]_\alpha = +$, and $[\![@_{N^3\langle NN^2\rangle}(\mathsf{curry}, +)]\!]_\alpha = [\![@_{\langle NN^2\rangle}(@_{N^3\langle NN^2\rangle}(\mathsf{curry}, +), 0))]\!]_\alpha = \mathsf{curry}$. Note that by definition $[\![\Theta(t)]\!]_\alpha = \bullet$ for all simply typed term t of basic type.

The set of labels and labelling functions are chosen similarly to the unsorted case.

Definition 9 (primary symbol labelling for terms). *Let B be a set of basic types and C a set of constants for simply typed terms, and suppose that $S = \mathrm{Ar}(B)$ and $\Sigma = \Theta(C)$. The set $\mathrm{Lab}(\Sigma)$ of S-sorted labelled function symbols is defined as*

$$\mathrm{Lab}(\Sigma) = \Sigma_0 \cup \{f_\ell \mid f \in \Sigma, \mathrm{sort}(f) = a_1 \times \cdots \times a_n \to a_0, n \geq 1, \ell \in A^{a_1}\}$$

where each f_ℓ has the same sort as f. The labelling function is defined in the same way as the unsorted case.

Definition 10 (primary symbol labelling for rewrite systems). *Let B be a set of basic types and C a set of constants for simply typed terms, and suppose that $S = \mathrm{Ar}(B)$ and $\Sigma = \Theta(C)$. For any many-sorted TRS $\langle S, \Sigma, R\rangle$, define*

$$\mathrm{LabDec}(\langle S, \Sigma, R\rangle) = \langle S, \mathrm{Lab}(\Sigma), \mathrm{Lab}(R) \cup \mathrm{Dec}(R)\rangle$$

where $\mathrm{Lab}(R)$ and $\mathrm{Dec}(R)$ are defined in the same way as unsorted case.

Theorem 3 (soundness of primary symbol labelling). *Let $\mathcal{R} = \langle B, C, R\rangle$ be an STTRS, and $\geq$ be a partial order on $C \cup \{\bullet\}$. If the many-sorted algebra $\mathbf{Pri}(B, C)$ is a quasi-model of $\Theta(\mathcal{R})$ and $\mathrm{LabDec}(\Theta(\mathcal{R}))$ is terminating then $\Theta(\mathcal{R})$ is terminating.*

Proof. We use the many-sorted version of semantic labelling. The partially ordered set of labels $\mathcal{L}_f = \langle L_f, \geq\rangle$ of labels for each $f \in \Sigma$ of sort $a_1 \times \cdots \times a_n \to a_0$ $(n \geq 1)$ consists of $L_f = A^{a_1}$ and the partial order $\geq$ given by the restriction of $\geq_A$ on A^{a_1}. Take the labelling function $\pi_f : A^{a_1} \times \cdots \times A^{a_n} \to L_f$ for each $f \in \Sigma$ of sort $a_1 \times \cdots \times a_n \to a_0$ $(n \geq 1)$ is defined as: $\pi_f(\ell_1, \ldots, \ell_n) = \ell_1$. $\square$

Example 14 (termination of STTRS by labelling). Let $\mathcal{R} = \langle B, C, R\rangle$ be an STTRS where $B = \{Nat\}$ and $C = \{0^{Nat}, \mathsf{s}^{Nat\to Nat}, +^{Nat\times Nat\to Nat}, *^{Nat\times Nat\to Nat}, \mathsf{curry}^{(Nat\times Nat\to Nat)\to(Nat\to(Nat\to Nat))}, \mathsf{add}^{Nat\to(Nat\to Nat)}, \mathsf{mult}^{Nat\to(Nat\to Nat)}\}$, and

$$R = \begin{cases} + \; 0 \; y & \to & y \\ + \; (\mathsf{s} \; x) \; y & \to & \mathsf{s} \; (+ \; x \; y) \\ * \; 0 \; y & \to & 0 \\ * \; (\mathsf{s} \; x) \; y & \to & + \; y \; (* \; x \; y) \\ ((\mathsf{curry} \; F) \; x) \; y & \to & F \; x \; y \\ \mathsf{add} & \to & \mathsf{curry} \; + \\ \mathsf{mult} & \to & \mathsf{curry} \; * \end{cases}$$

Note that one can not prove termination of $\Theta(\mathcal{R})$ by LPO.

Since the first five rules are of basic type, both sides evaluate to • in the algebra. Hence, in order to fix the partial order, we only need to focus on the last two rules, which are of non-basic types. Based on the interpretations of the both hand sides, we take the smallest partial order satisfying add > curry and mult > curry, by which the many-sorted algebra $\mathbf{Pri}(B, C)$ is a quasi-model of $\Theta(\mathcal{R})$. Then $\mathrm{LabDec}(\Theta(\mathcal{R}))$ has the following rewrite rules:

$$
\begin{cases}
@_{N^3+}(+, 0, y) & \rightarrow \quad y \\
@_{N^3+}(+, @_{N^2s}(\mathsf{s}, x), y) & \rightarrow \quad @_{N^2s}(\mathsf{s}, @_{N^3+}(+, x, y)) \\
@_{N^3*}(*, 0, y) & \rightarrow \quad 0 \\
@_{N^3*}(*, @_{N^2s}(\mathsf{s}, x), y) & \rightarrow \quad @_{N^3+}(+, y, @_{N^3*}(*, x, y)) \\
@_{N^2\mathsf{curry}}(@_{NN^2\mathsf{curry}}(@_{N^3\langle NN^2\rangle\mathsf{curry}}(\mathsf{curry}, F), x), y) & \rightarrow \quad @_{N^3+}(F, x, y) \\
@_{N^2\mathsf{curry}}(@_{NN^2\mathsf{curry}}(@_{N^3\langle NN^2\rangle\mathsf{curry}}(\mathsf{curry}, F), x), y) & \rightarrow \quad @_{N^3*}(F, x, y) \\
\mathsf{add} & \rightarrow \quad @_{N^3\langle NN^2\rangle\mathsf{curry}}(\mathsf{curry}, \mathsf{I}) \\
\mathsf{mult} & \rightarrow \quad @_{N^3\langle NN^2\rangle\mathsf{curry}}(\mathsf{curry}, *) \\
@_{N^2\mathsf{add}}(F, x) & \rightarrow \quad @_{N^2\mathsf{curry}}(F, x) \\
@_{N^2\mathsf{mult}}(F, x) & \rightarrow \quad @_{N^2\mathsf{curry}}(F, x) \\
@_{NN^2\mathsf{add}}(F, x) & \rightarrow \quad @_{NN^2\mathsf{curry}}(F, x) \\
@_{NN^2\mathsf{mult}}(F, x) & \rightarrow \quad @_{NN^2\mathsf{curry}}(F, x)
\end{cases}
$$

The last four rules of $\mathrm{LabDec}(\Theta(\mathcal{R}))$ are required, since the last two rules of $\mathcal{R}$ have non-basic type. In contrast to $\Theta(\mathcal{R})$, termination of $\mathrm{LabDec}(\Theta(\mathcal{R}))$ can be shown by LPO. Thus, by Theorem 3, $\mathcal{R}$ is terminating. Note that $A^{N^3\langle NN^2\rangle} = \{\mathsf{curry}\}$, $A^{NN^2} = \{\mathsf{curry}, \mathsf{add}, \mathsf{mult}\}$, $A^{N^2} = \{\mathsf{curry}, \mathsf{add}, \mathsf{mult}, \mathsf{s}\}$, $A^{N^3} = \{+, *\}$, and $A^a = \{\bullet\}$ for any $a \notin \{\, N^3\langle NN^2\rangle, NN^2, N^2, N^3 \,\}$.

Corollary 2 (soundness of primary symbol labelling). *Let $\mathcal{R}$ be an STTRS such that all rules are of basic types. Then, if $\mathrm{Lab}(\Theta(\mathcal{R}))$ is terminating then $\mathcal{R}$ is terminating.*

Proof. Take the discrete order as the partial order $\geq$ on the many-sorted algebra $\mathbf{Pri}(B, C)$. □

Example 15 (termination of STTRS by labelling). Let STTRS $\mathcal{R}$ be the one in Example 4. Then $\mathrm{Lab}(\Theta(\mathcal{R}))$ has the following rewrite rules:

$$
\begin{cases}
@_{N^2+}(@_{NN^2+}(+, 0), y) & \rightarrow \quad y \\
@_{N^2+}(@_{NN^2+}(+, @_{N^2s}(\mathsf{s}, x)), y) & \rightarrow \quad @_{N^2s}(\mathsf{s}, @_{N^2+}(@_{NN^2+}(+, x), y)) \\
@_{N^2*}(@_{NN^2*}(*, 0), y) & \rightarrow \quad 0 \\
@_{N^2*}(@_{NN^2*}(*, @_{N^2s}(\mathsf{s}, x)), y) & \\
\quad \rightarrow \quad @_{N^2+}(@_{NN^2+}(+, @_{N^2*}(@_{NN^2*}(*, x), y)), y)
\end{cases}
$$

Termination of $\mathrm{Lab}(\Theta(\mathcal{R}))$ can be shown by LPO and therefore $\mathcal{R}$ is terminating by Theorem 2.

Example 16 (termination of STTRS by labelling). Let $\mathcal{R} = \langle B, C, R \rangle$ be an STTRS where $B = \{Nat, Bool, List\}$, $C = \{\ 0^{Nat},\ \mathsf{s}^{Nat \rightarrow Nat},\ \mathsf{true}^{Bool},\ \mathsf{false}^{Bool},\ \mathsf{gt}^{Nat \times Nat \rightarrow Bool},\ \mathsf{le}^{Nat \times Nat \rightarrow Bool},\ []^{List},\ :^{Nat \times List \rightarrow List},\ \mathsf{filter}^{(Nat \times Nat \rightarrow Bool) \times Nat}$

$\times List \rightarrow List$, $\mathsf{filtersub}^{Bool \times (Nat \times Nat \rightarrow Bool) \times Nat \times List \rightarrow List}$, $\mathsf{high}^{Nat \times List \rightarrow List}$, low^{Nat}
$\times List \rightarrow List$, $\mathsf{append}^{List \times List \rightarrow List}$, $\mathsf{qsort}^{List \rightarrow List}$ }, and

$$
R = \begin{cases}
\mathsf{gt}\ 0\ x & \rightarrow & \mathsf{false} \\
\mathsf{gt}\ (\mathsf{s}\ x)\ 0 & \rightarrow & \mathsf{true} \\
\mathsf{gt}\ (\mathsf{s}\ x)\ (\mathsf{s}\ y) & \rightarrow & \mathsf{gt}\ x\ y \\
\mathsf{le}\ 0\ x & \rightarrow & \mathsf{true} \\
\mathsf{le}\ (\mathsf{s}\ x)\ 0 & \rightarrow & \mathsf{false} \\
\mathsf{le}\ (\mathsf{s}\ x)\ (\mathsf{s}\ y) & \rightarrow & \mathsf{le}\ x\ y \\
\mathsf{filter}\ F\ x\ \mathsf{nil} & \rightarrow & \mathsf{nil} \\
\mathsf{filter}\ F\ x\ (y:ys) & \rightarrow & \mathsf{filtersub}\ (F\ x\ y)\ F\ x\ (y:ys) \\
\mathsf{filtersub}\ \mathsf{true}\ F\ x\ (y:ys) & \rightarrow & y:(\mathsf{filter}\ F\ x\ ys) \\
\mathsf{filtersub}\ \mathsf{false}\ F\ x\ (y:ys) & \rightarrow & \mathsf{filter}\ F\ x\ ys \\
\mathsf{high}\ x\ xs & \rightarrow & \mathsf{filter}\ \mathsf{gt}\ x\ xs \\
\mathsf{low}\ x\ xs & \rightarrow & \mathsf{filter}\ \mathsf{le}\ x\ xs \\
\mathsf{append}\ [\,]\ xs & \rightarrow & xs \\
\mathsf{append}\ (x:xs)\ ys & \rightarrow & x:(\mathsf{append}\ xs\ ys) \\
\mathsf{qsort}\ [\,] & \rightarrow & [\,] \\
\mathsf{qsort}\ (x:xs) & & \\
\quad \rightarrow\ \mathsf{append}\ (\mathsf{qsort}\ (\mathsf{low}\ x\ xs))\ (x:(\mathsf{qsort}\ (\mathsf{high}\ x\ xs))) &&
\end{cases}
$$

Using the dependency pair method [2], the inequality required to show termination of $\mathrm{Lab}(\Theta(\mathcal{R}))$ is reduced to the following:

$$
\begin{aligned}
@_{NNB\,\mathsf{gt}}(\mathsf{gt}, 0, x) &\geq \mathsf{false} \\
@_{NNB\,\mathsf{gt}}(\mathsf{gt}, @_{N^2\mathsf{s}}(\mathsf{s}, x), 0) &\geq \mathsf{true} \\
@_{NNB\,\mathsf{gt}}(\mathsf{gt}, @_{N^2\mathsf{s}}(\mathsf{s}, x), @_{N^2\mathsf{s}}(\mathsf{s}, y)) &\geq @_{NNB\mathsf{gt}}(\mathsf{gt}, x, y) \\
@_{NNB\,\mathsf{le}}(\mathsf{le}, 0, x) &\geq \mathsf{true} \\
@_{NNB\,\mathsf{le}}(\mathsf{le}, @_{N^2\mathsf{s}}(\mathsf{s}, x), 0) &\geq \mathsf{false} \\
@_{NNB\,\mathsf{le}}(\mathsf{le}, @_{N^2\mathsf{s}}(\mathsf{s}, x), @_{N^2\mathsf{s}}(\mathsf{s}, y)) &\geq @_{NNB\,\mathsf{le}}(\mathsf{le}, x, y) \\
[\,] &\geq [\,] \\
@_{NLL:}(:, y, ys) &\geq @_{NLL:}(:, y, ys) \\
@_{NLL:}(:, y, ys) &\geq ys \\
@_{NLL\,\mathsf{high}}(\mathsf{high}, x, xs) &\geq xs \\
@_{NLL\,\mathsf{low}}(\mathsf{low}, x, xs) &\geq xs \\
@_{L^3\mathsf{append}}(\mathsf{append}, [\,], xs) &\geq xs \\
@_{L^3\mathsf{append}}(\mathsf{append}, @_{NLL:}(:, x, xs), ys) &\geq @_{NLL:}(:, x, @_{L^3\mathsf{append}}(\mathsf{append}, xs, ys)) \\
@_{L^2\mathsf{qsort}}(\mathsf{qsort}, [\,]) &\geq [\,] \\
@_{L^2\mathsf{qsort}}(\mathsf{qsort}, @_{NLL:}(:, x, xs)) &
\end{aligned}
$$

$$
\begin{aligned}
\geq\ & @_{L^3\mathsf{append}}(\mathsf{append}, @_{L^2\mathsf{qsort}}(\mathsf{qsort}, @_{NLL\,\mathsf{low}}(\mathsf{low}, x, xs)), \\
& \qquad @_{NLL\,\mathsf{cons}}(\mathsf{cons}, x, @_{L^2\mathsf{qsort}}(\mathsf{qsort}, @_{NLL\,\mathsf{high}}(\mathsf{high}, x, xs))))
\end{aligned}
$$

$$
\begin{aligned}
A_{NNB\,\mathsf{gt}}(\mathsf{gt}, @_{N^2\mathsf{s}}(\mathsf{s}, x), @_{N^2\mathsf{s}}(\mathsf{s}, y)) &> A_{NNB\,\mathsf{gt}}(\mathsf{gt}, x, y) \\
A_{NNB\,\mathsf{le}}(\mathsf{le}, @_{N^2\mathsf{s}}(\mathsf{s}, x), @_{N^2\mathsf{s}}(\mathsf{s}, y)) &> A_{NNB\,\mathsf{le}}(\mathsf{le}, x, y) \\
@_{NLL:}(:, y, ys) &> ys
\end{aligned}
$$

$$
\begin{aligned}
A_{L^3\mathsf{append}}(\mathsf{append}, @_{NLL:}(:, x, xs), ys) &> A_{L^3\mathsf{append}}(\mathsf{append}, xs, ys) \\
@_{NLL:}(:, x, xs) &> @_{NLL\,\mathsf{low}}(\mathsf{low}, x, xs) \\
@_{NLL:}(:, x, xs) &> @_{NLL\,\mathsf{high}}(\mathsf{high}, x, xs)
\end{aligned}
$$

where $A_{a\ell}$ denotes the tuple symbol for $@_{a\ell}$. The following argument filtering is used: $\pi(@_{\langle NNB\rangle NLL}) = \pi(A_{\langle NNB\rangle NLL}) = 4$, $\pi(@_{B\langle NNB\rangle NLL}) = \pi(A_{B\langle NNB\rangle NLL}) = 5$, $\pi(A_{L^2\mathsf{qsort}}) = 2$. These inequalities are satisfied by LPO based on the following precedence: gt > false, gt > true, le > false, le > true, $@_{L^2\mathsf{qsort}} > @_{L^3\mathsf{append}} > @_{NLL:} > @_{NLL\mathsf{low}}$, $@_{L^2\mathsf{qsort}} > @_{L^3\mathsf{append}} > @_{NLL:}$, qsort > append > : > low, qsort > append > :, $@_{NLL:} > @_{NLL\mathsf{high}}$, : > high. Thus $\Theta(\mathcal{R})$ is terminating and therefore $\mathcal{R}$ is terminating by Theorem 2.

6   Concluding Remarks

In this paper, we have presented a method to prove termination of simply typed term rewriting systems.

We have defined a translation Θ from STTRSs $\mathcal{R}$ to many-sorted first-order TRSs $\Theta(\mathcal{R})$, and showed that $\Theta(\mathcal{R})$ is terminating if and only if $\mathcal{R}$ is terminating. The translation Θ is easily automated and thus termination of STTRSs can be proved automatically using any known automated methods for proving termination of first-order term rewriting systems.

We further presented a labelling method that facilitates termination proof of many-sorted TRSs obtained by our translation. For this, we use the many-sorted extension of semantic labelling method which is originally proved for unsorted term rewriting. We defined the labelling LabDec and Lab of many-sorted TRSs such that $\mathrm{Lab}(\Theta(\mathcal{R})) \subseteq \mathrm{LabDec}(\Theta(\mathcal{R}))$, and showed that any STTRS $\mathcal{R}$ is terminating whenever $\mathrm{LabDec}(\Theta(\mathcal{R}))$ is terminating and that any STTRS $\mathcal{R}$ whose all rules are of basic type is terminating whenever $\mathrm{Lab}(\Theta(\mathcal{R}))$ is terminating.

We have demonstrated that useful labelling by primary symbol is not implemented using unsorted semantic labelling and proposed the one using many-sorted semantic labelling. However, there is another direction to overcome this defect—that is to restrict labels so that there are just two kinds of labels p and n that distinguish defined primary symbols and constructor primary symbols. Then the soundness theorem like Theorem 3 is proved using the original semantic labelling method and that like Theorem 2 is proved by slightly modifying the original semantic labelling proof [1].

Finally we also note that another termination proof technique for STTRSs, called monotone interpretation, has been proposed in [10]. Unlike our method, the one in [10] is a semantical method and we think our techniques are more suitable for automated termination proof.

References

1. T. Aoto and T. Yamada. Proving termination of simply typed term rewriting systems automatically. *IPSJ Transactions on Programming*, 44(SIG 4 PRO 17):67–77, 2003. In Japanese.
2. T. Arts and J. Giesl. Termination of term rewriting using dependency pairs. *Theoretical Computer Science*, 236:133–178, 2000.
3. F. Baader and T. Nipkow. *Term Rewriting and All That*. Cambridge University Press, Cambridge, 1998.

4. N. Dershowitz and J.-P. Jouannaud. Rewrite systems. In J. van Leeuwen, editor, *Handbook of Theoretical Computer Science*, volume B, pages 243–320. Elsevier Science Publishers, 1990.
5. J.-P. Jouannaud and M. Okada. Executable higher-order algebraic specification languages. In *Proceedings of the 6th IEEE Symposium on Logic in Computer Science (LICS'91)*, pages 350–361, 1991.
6. S. Kamin and J.-J. Lévy. Two generalizations of the recursive path ordering. Unpublished manuscript, University of Illinois, 1980.
7. J. W. Klop. *Combinatory Reduction Systems*. PhD thesis, Rijksuniversiteit, Utrecht, 1980.
8. J. W. Klop. Term rewriting systems. In S. Abramsky, D. Gabbay, and T. Maibaum, editors, *Handbook of Logic in Computer Science*, volume 2, pages 1–116. Oxford University Press, 1992.
9. R. Mayr and T. Nipkow. Higher-order rewrite systems and their confluence. *Theoretical Computer Science*, 192:3–29, 1998.
10. T. Yamada. Confluence and termination of simply typed term rewriting systems. In *Proceedings of the 12th International Conference on Rewriting Techniques and Applications (RTA'01)*, volume 2051 of *Lecture Notes in Computer Science*, pages 338–352. Springer-Verlag, 2001.
11. H. Zantema. Termination of term rewriting by semantic labelling. *Fundamenta Informaticae*, 24:89–105, 1995.

Rewriting Modulo in Deduction Modulo

Frédéric Blanqui

Laboratoire d'Informatique de l'École Polytechnique
91128 Palaiseau Cedex, France

Abstract. We study the termination of rewriting modulo a set of equations in the Calculus of Algebraic Constructions, an extension of the Calculus of Constructions with functions and predicates defined by higher-order rewrite rules. In a previous work, we defined general syntactic conditions based on the notion of computability closure for ensuring the termination of the combination of rewriting and β-reduction.
Here, we show that this result is preserved when considering rewriting modulo a set of equations if the equivalence classes generated by these equations are finite, the equations are linear and satisfy general syntactic conditions also based on the notion of computability closure. This includes equations like associativity and commutativity and provides an original treatment of termination modulo equations.

1 Introduction

The Calculus of Algebraic Constructions (CAC) [2,3] is an extension of the Calculus of Constructions (CC) [9] with functions and predicates defined by (higher-order) rewrite rules. CC embodies in the same formalism Girard's polymorphic λ-calculus and De Bruijn's dependent types, which allows one to formalize propositions and proofs of (impredicative) higher-order logic. In addition, CAC allows functions and predicates to be defined by any set of (higher-order) rewrite rules. And, in contrast with (first-order) Natural Deduction Modulo [13], proofs are part of the terms.

Very general conditions are studied in [2,4] for preserving the decidability of type-checking and the logical consistency of such a system. But these conditions do not take into account rewriting modulo equations like associativity and commutativity (AC), which would be very useful in proof assistants like Coq [22] since it increases automation and decreases the size of proofs. We already used the rewriting engine of CiME [8], which allows rewriting modulo AC, for a prototype implementation of CAC, and now work on a new version of Coq including rewriting modulo AC. In this paper, we extend the conditions given in [2] to deal with rewriting modulo equations.

2 The Calculus of Algebraic Constructions

We assume the reader familiar with typed λ-calculi [1] and rewriting [11]. The Calculus of Algebraic Constructions (CAC) [2] simply extends CC by considering

R. Nieuwenhuis (Ed.): RTA 2003, LNCS 2706, pp. 395–409, 2003.
© Springer-Verlag Berlin Heidelberg 2003

a set $\mathcal{F}$ of *symbols* and a set $\mathcal{R}$ of *rewrite rules*. The terms of CAC are:

$$t, u \in \mathcal{T} ::= s \mid x \mid f \mid [x : t]u \mid tu \mid (x : t)u$$

where $s \in \mathcal{S} = \{\star, \square\}$ is a *sort*, $x \in \mathcal{X}$ a *variable*, $f \in \mathcal{F}$, $[x : t]u$ an *abstraction*, tu an *application*, and $(x : t)u$ a *dependent product*, written $t \Rightarrow u$ if x does not freely occur in u.

The sort $\star$ denotes the universe of types and propositions, and the sort $\square$ denotes the universe of predicate types (also called *kinds*). For instance, the type *nat* of natural numbers is of type $\star$, $\star$ itself is of type $\square$ and $nat \Rightarrow \star$, the type of predicates over *nat*, is of type $\square$.

We use bold face letters for denoting sequences of terms. For instance, t is the sequence $t_1 \ldots t_n$ where $n = |t|$ is the length of t, and $(x : T)U$ is the term $(x_1 : T_1) \ldots (x_n : T_n)U$ (we implicitly assume that $|x| = |T| = n$).

We denote by $\mathrm{FV}(t)$ the set of free variables of t, by $\mathrm{dom}(\theta)$ the *domain* of a substitution θ, by $\mathrm{Pos}(t)$ the set of Dewey's positions of t, by $t|_p$ the subterm of t at position p, and by $t[u]_p$ the replacement of $t|_p$ by u.

Every symbol f is equipped with a sort s_f, an *arity* α_f and a type τ_f which may be any closed term of the form $(x : T)U$ with $|x| = \alpha_f$. The terms only built from variables and applications of the form ft with $|t| = \alpha_f$ are *algebraic*.

A *typing environment* Γ is an ordered list of type declarations $x : T$. If f is a symbol of type $\tau_f = (x : T)U$, we denote by Γ_f the environment $x : T$.

A rule for typing symbols is added to the typing rules of CC:

$$\text{(symb)} \quad \frac{\vdash \tau_f : s_f}{\vdash f : \tau_f}$$

A *rewrite rule* is a pair $l \to r$ such that (1) l is algebraic, (2) l is not a variable, and (3) $\mathrm{FV}(r) \subseteq \mathrm{FV}(l)$. Only l has to be algebraic: r may contain applications, abstractions and products. This is a particular case of Combinatory Reduction System (CRS) [18] which does not need *higher-order pattern-matching*.

If $\mathcal{G} \subseteq \mathcal{F}$, $\mathcal{R}_\mathcal{G}$ is the set of rules whose left-hand side is headed by a symbol in $\mathcal{G}$. A symbol f with $\mathcal{R}_{\{f\}} = \emptyset$ is *constant*, otherwise it is (partially) *defined*.

A rule is *left-linear* (resp. *right-linear*) if no variable occurs more than once in the left-hand side (resp. right-hand side). A rule is *linear* if it is both left-linear and right-linear. A rule is *non-duplicating* if no variable occurs more in the right-hand side than in the left-hand side.

A term t $\mathcal{R}$-*rewrites* to a term t', written $t \to_\mathcal{R} t'$, if there exists a position p in t, a rule $l \to r \in \mathcal{R}$ and a substitution σ such that $t|_p = l\sigma$ and $t' = t[r\sigma]_p$. A term t β-*rewrites* to a term t', written $t \to_\beta t'$, if there exists a position p in t such that $t|_p = ([x : U]v \, u)$ and $t' = t[v\{x \mapsto u\}]_p$. Given a relation $\to$ and a term t, let $\to(t) = \{t' \in \mathcal{T} \mid t \to t'\}$.

Finally, in CAC, $\beta\mathcal{R}$-equivalent types are identified. More precisely, in the type conversion rule of CC, $\downarrow_\beta$ is replaced by $\downarrow_{\beta\mathcal{R}}$:

$$\text{(conv)} \quad \frac{\Gamma \vdash t : T \quad T \downarrow_{\beta\mathcal{R}} T' \quad \Gamma \vdash T' : s}{\Gamma \vdash t : T'}$$

where $u \downarrow_{\beta\mathcal{R}} v$ iff there exists a term w such that $u \to^*_{\beta\mathcal{R}} w$ and $v \to^*_{\beta\mathcal{R}} w$, $\to^*_{\beta\mathcal{R}}$ being the reflexive and transitive closure of $\to_\beta \cup \to_\mathcal{R}$. This rule means that any term t of type T in the environment Γ is also of type T' if T and T' have a common reduct (and T' is of type some sort s). For instance, if t is a proof of $P(2+2)$ then t is also a proof of $P(4)$ if $\mathcal{R}$ contains the following rules:

$$x + 0 \quad \to \quad x$$
$$x + (s\ y) \quad \to \quad s\ (x+y)$$

This decreases the size of proofs and increases automation as well.

A substitution θ *preserves typing from* Γ *to* Δ, written $\theta : \Gamma \rightsquigarrow \Delta$, if, for all $x \in \mathrm{dom}(\Gamma)$, $\Delta \vdash x\theta : x\Gamma\theta$, where $x\Gamma$ is the type associated to x in Γ. Type-preserving substitutions enjoy the following important property: if $\Gamma \vdash t : T$ and $\theta : \Gamma \rightsquigarrow \Delta$ then $\Delta \vdash t\theta : T\theta$.

For ensuring the *subject reduction* property (preservation of typing under reduction), every rule $fl \to r$ is equipped with an environment Γ and a substitution ρ such that,[1] if $f : (\boldsymbol{x} : \boldsymbol{T})U$ and $\gamma = \{\boldsymbol{x} \mapsto \boldsymbol{l}\}$ then $\Gamma \vdash fl\rho : U\gamma\rho$ and $\Gamma \vdash r : U\gamma\rho$. The substitution ρ allows to eliminate non-linearities only due to typing and thus makes rewriting more efficient and confluence easier to prove. For instance, the concatenation on polymorphic lists (type $list : \star \Rightarrow \star$ with constructors $nil : (A : \star)listA$ and $cons : (A : \star)A \Rightarrow listA \Rightarrow listA$) of type $(A : \star)listA \Rightarrow listA \Rightarrow listA$ can be defined by:

$$app\ A\ (nil\ A')\ l' \quad \to \quad l'$$
$$app\ A\ (cons\ A'\ x\ l)\ l' \quad \to \quad cons\ A\ x\ (app\ A\ x\ l\ l')$$
$$app\ A\ (app\ A'\ l\ l')\ l'' \quad \to \quad app\ A\ l\ (app\ A\ l'\ l'')$$

with $\Gamma = A : \star, x : A, l : listA, l' : listA$ and $\rho = \{A' \mapsto A\}$. For instance, $app\ A\ (nil\ A')$ is not typable in Γ (since $A' \notin \mathrm{dom}(\Gamma)$) but becomes typable if we apply ρ. This does not matter since, if an instance $app\ A\sigma\ (nil\ A'\sigma)$ is typable then $A\sigma$ is convertible to $A'\sigma$.

3   Rewriting Modulo

Now, we assume given a set $\mathcal{E}$ of *equations* $l = r$ which will be seen as a set of *symmetric* rules, that is, a set such that $l \to r \in \mathcal{E}$ iff $r \to l \in \mathcal{E}$. The conditions on rules imply that, if $l = r \in \mathcal{E}$, then (1) both l and r are algebraic, (2) both l and r are headed by a function symbol, (3) l and r have the same (free) variables.

Examples of equations are:

$$x + y = y + x \qquad \text{(commutativity of } +)$$
$$x + (y + z) = (x + y) + z \qquad \text{(associativity of } +)$$
$$x \times (y + z) = (x \times y) + (x \times z) \qquad \text{(distributivity of } \times)$$
$$x + 0 = x \qquad \text{(neutrality of } 0)$$

---

[1] Other conditions are necessary that we do not detail here.

$$add\ A\ x\ (add\ A'\ y\ S) = add\ A\ y\ (add\ A'\ x\ S)$$
$$union\ A\ S\ S' = union\ A\ S'\ S$$
$$union\ A\ S\ (union\ A'\ S'\ S'') = union\ A\ (union\ A'\ S\ S')\ S''$$

where $set : \star \Rightarrow \star$, $empty : (A : \star)setA$, $add : (A : \star)A \Rightarrow setA \Rightarrow setA$ and $union : (A : \star)setA \Rightarrow setA \Rightarrow setA$ formalize finite sets of elements of type A. Except for distributivity which is not linear, and the equation $x + 0 = x$ whose equivalence classes are infinite, all the other equations will satisfy our strong normalization conditions. Note however that distributivity and neutrality can always be used as rules when oriented from left to right. Hence, the word problem for abelian groups or abelian rings for instance can be decided by using *normalized rewriting* [19].

On the other hand, the following expressions are not equations since left and right-hand sides have distinct sets of variables:

$$x \times 0 = 0 \quad (0 \text{ is absorbing for } \times)$$
$$x + (-x) = 0 \quad (\text{inverse})$$

Let $\sim$ be the reflexive and transitive closure of $\rightarrow_\mathcal{E}$ ($\sim$ is an equivalence relation since $\mathcal{E}$ is symmetric). We are now interested in the termination of $\blacktriangleright = \rightarrow_\beta \cup \sim \rightarrow_\mathcal{R}$ (instead of $\rightarrow_\beta \cup \rightarrow_\mathcal{R}$ before). In the following, we may denote $\rightarrow_\mathcal{E}$ by $\mathcal{E}$, $\rightarrow_\mathcal{R}$ by $\mathcal{R}$ and $\rightarrow_\beta$ by β.

In order to preserve all the basic properties of the calculus, we do not change the shape of the relation used in the type conversion rule (conv): two types T and T' are convertible if $T \downarrow T'$ with $\rightarrow = \rightarrow_\beta \cup \rightarrow_\mathcal{R} \cup \rightarrow_\mathcal{E}$. But this raises the question of how to check this condition, knowing that $\rightarrow$ may be not terminating. We study this problem in Section 6.

4   Conditions of Strong Normalization

In the strong normalization conditions, we distinguish between *first-order* symbols (set $\mathcal{F}_1$) and *higher-order* symbols (set $\mathcal{F}_\omega$). To precisely define what is a first-order symbol, we need a little definition before. We say that a constant predicate symbol is *primitive* if it is not polymorphic and if its constructors have no functional arguments. This includes in particular any first-order data type (natural numbers, lists of natural numbers, etc.). Now, a symbol f is *first-order* if it is a predicate symbol of *maximal arity*,[2] or if it is a function symbol whose output type is a primitive predicate symbol. Any other symbol is *higher-order*. Let $\mathcal{R}_\iota = \mathcal{R}_{\mathcal{F}_\iota}$ and $\mathcal{E}_\iota = \mathcal{E}_{\mathcal{F}_\iota}$ for $\iota \in \{1, \omega\}$.

Since the pioneer works on the combination of λ-calculus and first-order rewriting [7,20], it is well known that the addition at the object level of a strongly normalizing first-order rewrite system preserves strong normalization. This comes from the fact that first-order rewriting cannot create β-redexes. On

---

[2] A predicate symbol f of type $(\boldsymbol{x} : \boldsymbol{T})U$ is of *maximal arity* if $U = \star$, that is, if the elements of type ft are not functions.

the other hand, higher-order rewriting can create β-redexes. This is why we have other conditions on higher-order symbols than merely strong normalization. Furthermore, in order for the two systems to be combined without losing strong normalization [23], we also require first-order rules to be non-duplicating [21]. Note however that a first-order symbol can always be considered as higher-order (but the strong normalization conditions on higher-order symbols may not be powerful enough for proving the termination of its defining rules).

The strong normalization conditions on higher-order rewrite rules are based on the notion of *computability closure* [5]. We are going to use this notion for the equations too.

Typed λ-calculi are generally proved strongly normalizing by using Tait and Girard's technique of *computability predicates/reducibility candidates* [14]. Indeed, a direct proof of strong normalization by induction on the structure of terms does not work. The idea of Tait, later extended by Girard to the polymorphic λ-calculus, is to strengthen the induction hypothesis as follows. To every type T, one associates a set $[\![T]\!] \subseteq \mathcal{SN}$ (set of strongly normalizing terms), and proves that every term of type T is *computable*, that is, belongs to $[\![T]\!]$.

Now, if we extend such a calculus with rewriting, for preserving strong normalization, a rewrite rule has to preserve computability. The *computability closure* of a term t is a set of terms that are computable whenever t itself is computable. So, if the right-hand side r of a rule $fl \to r$ belongs to the computability closure of l, a condition called the *General Schema*, then r is computable whenever the terms in l are computable.

Formally, the computability closure for a rule $(fl \to r, \Gamma, \rho)$ with $\tau_f = (\boldsymbol{x} : \boldsymbol{T})U$ and $\gamma = \{\boldsymbol{x} \mapsto l\}$ is the set of terms t such that the judgment $\vdash_c t : U\gamma\rho$ can be deduced from the rules of Figure 1, where the variables of dom(Γ) are considered as symbols $(\tau_x = x\Gamma)$, $>_{\mathcal{F}}$ is a well-founded quasi-ordering (precedence) on symbols, with $x <_{\mathcal{F}} f$ for all $x \in$ dom(Γ), $>_f$ is the multiset or lexicographic extension[3] of the subterm ordering[4] $\rhd$, and $T \downarrow_f T'$ iff T and T' have a common reduct by $\to_f = \to_\beta \cup \to_{\mathcal{R}_f^<}$ where $\mathcal{R}_f^< = \{gu \to v \in \mathcal{R} \mid g <_{\mathcal{F}} f\}$.

In addition, every variable $x \in$ dom(Γ) is required to be *accessible* in some l_i, that is, $x\sigma$ is computable whenever $l_i\sigma$ is computable. The arguments of a constructor-headed term are always accessible. For a function-headed term ft with $f : (\boldsymbol{x} : \boldsymbol{T})C\boldsymbol{v}$ and C constant, only the t_i's such that C occurs positively in T_i are accessible (X occurs positively in $Y \Rightarrow X$ and negatively in $X \Rightarrow Y$).

The relation $\vdash_c$ is similar to the typing relation $\vdash$ of CAC except that symbol applications are restricted to symbols smaller than f, or to arguments smaller than l in the case of an application of a symbol equivalent to f. So, verifying that a rule satisfies the General Schema amounts to check whether r has type $U\gamma\rho$ with the previous restrictions on symbol applications. It therefore has the same complexity.

---

[3] Or a simple combination thereof, depending on the *status* of f.

[4] We use a more powerful ordering for dealing with recursive definitions on types whose constructors have functional arguments.

$$(\text{ax}) \qquad \frac{}{\vdash_c \star : \square}$$

$$(\text{symb}^<) \qquad \frac{\vdash_c \tau_g : s_g}{\vdash_c g : \tau_g} \qquad (g <_{\mathcal{F}} f)$$

$$(\text{symb}^=) \qquad \frac{\vdash_c \tau_g : s_g \quad \delta : \Gamma_g \leadsto_c \Delta}{\Delta \vdash_c gy\delta : V\delta} \qquad \begin{array}{l}(\tau_g = (\boldsymbol{y} : \boldsymbol{U})V, \\ g =_{\mathcal{F}} f \text{ and } \boldsymbol{y}\delta <_f \boldsymbol{l})\end{array}$$

$$(\text{var}) \qquad \frac{\Delta \vdash_c T : s}{\Delta, x : T \vdash_c x : T} \qquad (x \notin \text{dom}(\Delta))$$

$$(\text{weak}) \qquad \frac{\Delta \vdash_c T : s \quad \Delta \vdash_c u : U}{\Delta, x : T \vdash_c u : U} \qquad (x \notin \text{dom}(\Delta))$$

$$(\text{abs}) \qquad \frac{\Delta, x : U \vdash_c v : V \quad \Delta \vdash_c (x : U)V : s}{\Delta \vdash_c [x : U]v : (x : U)V}$$

$$(\text{app}) \qquad \frac{\Delta \vdash_c t : (x : U)V \quad \Delta \vdash_c u : U}{\Delta \vdash_c tu : V\{x \mapsto u\}}$$

$$(\text{prod}) \qquad \frac{\Delta, x : U \vdash_c V : s}{\Delta \vdash_c (x : U)V : s}$$

$$(\text{conv}) \qquad \frac{\Delta \vdash_c t : T \quad \Delta \vdash_c T : s \quad \Delta \vdash_c T' : s}{\Delta \vdash_c t : T'} \qquad (T \downarrow_f T')$$

Fig. 1. Computability closure for $(fl \to r, \Gamma, \rho)$

Now, how the computability closure can help us in dealing with rewriting modulo equations? When one tries to prove that every term is computable, in the case of a term ft, it is sufficient to prove that every reduct of ft is computable. In the case of a head-reduct $fl\sigma \to r\sigma$, this follows from the fact that r belongs to the computability closure of l since, by induction hypothesis, the terms in $l\sigma$ are computable.

Now, with rewriting modulo, a $\mathcal{R}$-step can be preceded by $\mathcal{E}$-steps: $ft \to^*_{\mathcal{E}} gu \to_{\mathcal{R}} t'$. To apply the previous method with gu, we must prove that the terms in $\boldsymbol{u}$ are computable. This can be achieved by assuming that the equations also satisfy the General Schema in the following sense: an equation $(fl \to gm, \Gamma, \rho)$ with $\tau_g = (\boldsymbol{x} : \boldsymbol{T})U$ and $\gamma = \{\boldsymbol{x} \mapsto \boldsymbol{m}\}$ satisfies the General Schema if, for all i, $\vdash_c m_i : T_i\gamma\rho$, that is, the terms in $\boldsymbol{m}$ belong to the computability closure of l. By symmetry, the terms in l belong to the computability closure of $\boldsymbol{m}$.

One can easily check that this condition is satisfied by commutativity (whatever the type of $+$ is) and associativity (if both y and z are accessible in $y + z$):

$$\begin{aligned} x + y &= y + x \\ x + (y + z) &= (x + y) + z \end{aligned}$$

For commutativity, this is immediate and does not depend on the type of $+$: both y and x belong to the computability closure of x and y.

For associativity, we must prove that both $x + y$ and z belong to the computability closure $\mathcal{CC}$ of x and $y+z$. If we assume that both y and z are accessible in $y + z$ (which is the case for instance if $+ : nat \Rightarrow nat \Rightarrow nat$), then z belongs to $\mathcal{CC}$ and, by using a multiset status for comparing the arguments of $+$, $x + y$ belongs to $\mathcal{CC}$ too since $\{x, y\} \lhd_{\mathrm{mul}} \{x, y + z\}$.

We now give all the strong normalization conditions.

Theorem 1 (Strong normalization of $\beta \cup \sim \mathcal{R}$). *Let $\sim_1$ be the reflexive and transitive closure of $\mathcal{E}_1$. The relation $\blacktriangleright\ =\to_\beta \cup \sim \to_\mathcal{R}$ is strongly normalizing if the following conditions adapted from [2] are satisfied:*

- $\to\ =\to_\beta \cup \to_\mathcal{R} \cup \to_\mathcal{E}$ *is confluent,*[5]
- *the rules of $\mathcal{R}_1$ are non-duplicating,*[6] $\mathcal{R}_1 \cap \mathcal{F}_\omega = \mathcal{E}_1 \cap \mathcal{F}_\omega = \emptyset$[7] *and $\sim_1 \to_{\mathcal{R}_1}$ is strongly normalizing on first-order algebraic terms,*
- *the rules of $\mathcal{R}_\omega$ satisfy the General Schema and are safe,*[8]
- *rules on predicate symbols have no critical pair, satisfy the General Schema*[9] *and are small,*[10]

and if the following new conditions are satisfied too:

- *there is no equation on predicate symbols,*
- *$\mathcal{E}$ is linear,*
- *the equivalence classes modulo $\sim$ are finite,*
- *every rule $(fl \to gm, \Gamma, \rho) \in \mathcal{E}$ satisfies the General Schema in the following sense: if $\tau_g = (\boldsymbol{x} : \boldsymbol{T})U$ and $\gamma = \{\boldsymbol{x} \mapsto \boldsymbol{m}\}$ then, for all i, $\vdash_c m_i : T_i \gamma \rho$.*

Not allowing equations on predicate symbols is an important limitation. However, one cannot have equations on connectors if one wants to preserve the Curry-Howard isomorphism. For instance, with commutativity on $\wedge$, one looses subject reduction. Take $\wedge : \star \Rightarrow \star \Rightarrow \star$, $pair : (A : \star)(B : \star)A \Rightarrow B \Rightarrow A \wedge B$ and $\pi_1 : (A : \star)(B : \star)A \wedge B \Rightarrow A$ defined by $\pi_1\ A\ B\ (pair\ A'\ B'\ a\ b) \to a$. Then, $\pi_1\ B\ A\ (pair\ A\ B\ a\ b)$ is of type B but a is not.

5   Strong Normalization Proof

The strong normalization proof follows the one given in [6] very closely.[11] We only give the definitions and lemmas that must be modified. As previously explained, the strong normalization is obtained by defining an interpretation $[\![T]\!] \subseteq \mathcal{SN}$ for every type T, and by proving that every term of type T belongs to $[\![T]\!]$.

---

[5] If there are type-level rewrite rules.

[6] If there are higher-order rules.

[7] First-order rules/equations only contain first-order symbols.

[8] No pattern-matching on predicates.

[9] There are other possibilities. See [2] for more details.

[10] A rule $fl \to r$ is *small* if every predicate variable in r is equal to one of the l_i's.

[11] The proof given in [6] is an important simplification of the one given in [2].

More precisely, for every type T, we define the set $\mathcal{R}_T$ of the possible interpretations, or *candidates*, for the terms of type T. $\mathcal{R}_{(x:U)V}$ is the set of functions R from $\mathcal{T} \times \mathcal{R}_U$ to $\mathcal{R}_V$ that are stable by reduction: if $u \to u'$ then $R(u, S) = R(u', S)$. A term t is *neutral* if it is distinct from an abstraction or a constructor. $\mathcal{R}_\star$ is the set of sets $R \subseteq \mathcal{T}$ such that:

(R1) Strong normalization: $R \subseteq \mathcal{SN}$.
(R2) Stability by reduction: if $t \in R$ then $\to(t) \subseteq R$.
(R3) Neutral terms: if t is neutral and $\blacktriangleright(t) \subseteq R$ then $t \in R$.

Candidates form a complete lattice. A *candidate assignment* ξ is a function which associates a candidate to every variable. Given an interpretation I for predicate symbols, a candidate assignment ξ and a substitution θ, the *interpretation* of a type T, written $\llbracket T \rrbracket_{\xi,\theta}^I$, is defined in [4]. The elements of $\llbracket T \rrbracket_{\xi,\theta}^I$ are said *computable*. A pair (ξ, θ) is Γ-*valid*, written $\xi, \theta \models \Gamma$, if, for all $x \in \mathrm{dom}(\Gamma)$, $x\xi \in \mathcal{R}_{x\Gamma}$ and $x\theta \in \llbracket x\Gamma \rrbracket_{\xi,\theta}^I$.

Then, strong normalization is obtained by defining an interpretation $I_f \in \mathcal{R}_{\tau_f}$ for every predicate symbol f, and by proving that every symbol f is computable, that is, $f \in \llbracket \tau_f \rrbracket$. If $\tau_f = (\boldsymbol{x} : \boldsymbol{T})U$, it amounts to check that, for all Γ_f-valid pair (ξ, θ), $f\boldsymbol{x}\theta \in \llbracket U \rrbracket_{\xi,\theta}$. For the interpretation, we keep the one for constant predicate symbols given in [6] but slightly modify the interpretation of defined predicate symbols for taking into account the new reduction relation.

Although we do not change the interpretation of constant predicate symbols, we must check that the interpretation of *primitive* predicate symbols is still $\mathcal{SN}$ (hence that, for primitive predicate symbols, computability is equivalent to strong normalization), since this property is used for proving that a terminating and non-duplicating (if there are higher-order rewrite rules) first-order rewrite system preserves strong normalization. The verification of the former property is easy. We now prove the latter.

Lemma 2. [16] *If the $\sim$-classes are finite then $\sim\rhd$ is strongly normalizing.*

Proof. We prove that $(\sim\rhd)^n \subseteq \sim\rhd^n$ by induction on n. For $n = 0$, this is immediate. For $n + 1$, $(\sim\rhd)^{n+1} \subseteq \sim\rhd\sim\rhd^n \subseteq \sim\sim\rhd\rhd^n \subseteq \sim\rhd^{n+1}$.   □

Lemma 3. [12] *If $t \in \mathcal{SN}(\beta)$ and $t \to_{\mathcal{R}_1} u$ then $\beta(t) \to_{\mathcal{R}_1}^* \beta(u)$.*

Proof. Dougherty proves this result in [12] (Proposition 4.6 and Theorem 4.7) for the untyped λ-calculus. The proof can clearly be extended to the Calculus of Algebraic Constructions. We inductively define $\twoheadrightarrow$ as follows:

- $a \twoheadrightarrow a$;
- if $l \to r \in \mathcal{R}_1$ and $\sigma \twoheadrightarrow \theta$ then $l\sigma \twoheadrightarrow r\theta$;
- if $a \twoheadrightarrow b$ and $c \twoheadrightarrow d$ then $ac \twoheadrightarrow bd$, $[x : a]c \twoheadrightarrow [x : b]d$ and $(x : a)c \twoheadrightarrow (x : b)d$;
- if $a \twoheadrightarrow b$ then $fa \twoheadrightarrow fb$.

We now prove that, if $t \to_\beta t'$ and $t \twoheadrightarrow u$ then there exist t'' and u' such that $t' \to_\beta^* t'' \twoheadrightarrow u'$ and $u \to_\beta^* u'$ by induction on $t \twoheadrightarrow u$.

- $u = t$. Immediate.
- $t = l\sigma$, $u = r\theta$ and $\sigma \twoheadrightarrow \theta$. Since left-hand sides of rules are algebraic, the β-reduction must take place in an occurrence of a variable $x \in \mathrm{FV}(l)$. Let v' be the β-reduct of $x\sigma$. By induction hypothesis, there exists v'' and w such that $v' \rightarrow^*_\beta v'' \twoheadrightarrow w$ and $x\theta \rightarrow^*_\beta w$. Let σ'' such that $x\sigma'' = v''$ and $y\sigma'' = y\sigma$ if $y \neq x$, and θ' such that $x\theta' = w$ and $y\theta' = y\theta$ if $y \neq x$. We have $\sigma'' \twoheadrightarrow \theta'$. By β-reducing all the instances of the occurrences of x in l to v'', we get $t' \rightarrow^*_\beta l\sigma'' \twoheadrightarrow r\theta'$ and, by reducing all the instances of the occurrences of x in r to w, we get $u = r\theta \rightarrow^*_\beta r\theta'$.
- Assume that $t = [x : a]c\ k$, $u = v\ l$, $[x : a]c \twoheadrightarrow v$, $k \twoheadrightarrow l$ and $t' = c\{x \mapsto k\}$. Then, $v = [x : b]d$ with $a \twoheadrightarrow b$ and $c \twoheadrightarrow d$. Therefore, $c\{x \mapsto k\} \twoheadrightarrow d\{x \mapsto l\}$ and $u \rightarrow_\beta d\{x \mapsto l\}$.
  Assume now that $t = ac$, $u = bd$, $a \twoheadrightarrow b$, $c \twoheadrightarrow d$ and $a \rightarrow_\beta a'$. The other cases are similar. By induction hypothesis, there exist a'' and b' such that $a' \rightarrow^*_\beta a'' \twoheadrightarrow b'$ and $b \rightarrow^*_\beta b'$. Therefore, $a'c \rightarrow^*_\beta a''c \twoheadrightarrow b'd$ and $bd \rightarrow^*_\beta b'd$.
- $t = \boldsymbol{f}\boldsymbol{a}$, $u = \boldsymbol{f}\boldsymbol{b}$ and $\boldsymbol{a} \twoheadrightarrow \boldsymbol{b}$. Then, there is i such that $t' = \boldsymbol{f}\boldsymbol{a}'$, $a_i \rightarrow_\beta a'_i$ and $a_j = a'_j$ if $j \neq i$. By induction hypothesis, there exists a''_i and b'_i such that $a'_i \rightarrow^*_\beta a''_i \twoheadrightarrow b'_i$ and $b_i \rightarrow^*_\beta b'_i$. Let $a''_j = a_j$ and $b'_j = b_j$ if $j \neq i$. Then, $\boldsymbol{a}'' \twoheadrightarrow \boldsymbol{b}'$, $t' = \boldsymbol{f}\boldsymbol{a}' \rightarrow^*_\beta \boldsymbol{f}\boldsymbol{a}'' \twoheadrightarrow \boldsymbol{f}\boldsymbol{b}'$ and $u = \boldsymbol{f}\boldsymbol{b} \rightarrow^*_\beta \boldsymbol{f}\boldsymbol{b}'$.

Now, since t is β-strongly normalizable, we can prove the lemma by induction on $\rightarrow_\beta$. If t is in β-normal form then u also is in β-normal form since $\mathcal{R}_1$-reductions preserve β-normal forms. Hence, $\beta(t) = t \twoheadrightarrow u = \beta(u)$. Now, if $t \rightarrow_\beta t'$ then there exist t'' and u' such that $t' \rightarrow^*_\beta t'' \twoheadrightarrow u'$ and $u \rightarrow^*_\beta u'$. By induction hypothesis, $\beta(t'') \twoheadrightarrow \beta(u')$. Therefore, $\beta(t) \twoheadrightarrow \beta(u)$. □

Definition 4 (Cap and aliens). *Let ζ be an injection from the classes of terms modulo $\downarrow^*$ to $\mathcal{X}$. The* cap *of a term t is the biggest first-order algebraic term $cap(t) = t[x_1]_{p_1} \ldots [x_n]_{p_n}$ such that $x_i = \zeta(t|_{p_i})$. The $t|_{p_i}$'s are called the* aliens *of t. We denote by $\beta(t)$ the β-normal form of t, by $cap\beta(t)$ the cap of $\beta(t)$, by $Cap(t)$ (resp. $Cap\beta(t)$) the $\sim_1$-equivalence class of $cap(t)$ (resp. $cap\beta(t)$), by $aliens(t)$ the multiset of the aliens of t, and by $Aliens(t)$ the multiset union of the (finite) $\sim$-equivalence classes of the aliens of t.*

Theorem 5 (Computability of first-order symbols). *If $f \in \mathcal{F}_1$ and $\boldsymbol{t} \in \mathcal{SN}$ then $f\boldsymbol{t} \in \mathcal{SN}$.*

Proof. We prove that every $\blacktriangleright$-reduct t' of $t = f\boldsymbol{t}$ is strongly normalizable. In the following, $(>_a, >_b)_{\mathrm{lex}}$ denotes the lexicographic ordering built with $>_a$ and $>_b$, and $>_{\mathrm{mul}}$ denotes the multiset extension of $>$.

    Case $\mathcal{R}_\omega \neq \emptyset$. By induction on $(Aliens(t), Cap(t))$ with $((\rightarrow_\beta\sim \cup \rightarrow_{\mathcal{R}}\sim \cup \triangleright\sim)_{\mathrm{mul}}, (\rightarrow_{\mathcal{R}_1}\sim_1)_{\mathrm{mul}})_{\mathrm{lex}}$ as well-founded ordering. It is easy to see that the aliens are strongly normalizable for $\rightarrow_\beta\sim$, $\rightarrow_{\mathcal{R}}\sim$ and $\triangleright\sim$ since they are so for $\sim\rightarrow_\beta$ (Lemma 7), $\sim\rightarrow_{\mathcal{R}}$ and $\sim\triangleright$ (Lemma 2) respectively.

    If $t \rightarrow_\beta t'$ then the reduction takes place in an alien v. Let v' be its β-reduct. If v' is not headed by a symbol of $\mathcal{F}_1$ then $Aliens(t)$ $(\rightarrow_\beta\sim)_{\mathrm{mul}}$ $Aliens(u)$.

Otherwise, its cap increases the cap of t' but, since the aliens of t' are then strict subterms of v', we have $Aliens(t)$ $(\rightarrow_\beta\sim \cup \rhd\sim)_{\mathrm{mul}}$ $Aliens(u)$.

Assume now that $t \rightarrow^*_{\mathcal{E}} u \rightarrow_{\mathcal{R}} t'$. We first look at what happens when $t \rightarrow_{\mathcal{E}} u$. There are two cases:

- If the reduction takes place in the cap then this is a $\mathcal{E}_1$-reduction. Since both the left-hand side and the right-hand side of a first-order rule are first-order algebraic terms, we have $cap(t) \rightarrow_{\mathcal{E}_1} cap(u)$ and, since the rules of $\mathcal{E}$ are linear, we have $aliens(t) = aliens(u)$.

- If the reduction takes place in an alien then $cap(t) = cap(u)$ and $aliens(t)$ $(\rightarrow_{\mathcal{E}})_{\mathrm{mul}}$ $aliens(u)$.

So, in both cases, $Cap(t) = Cap(u)$ and $Aliens(t) = Aliens(u)$. Therefore, by induction on the number of $\mathcal{E}$-steps, if $t \rightarrow^*_{\mathcal{E}} u$ then $Cap(t) = Cap(u)$ and $Aliens(t) = Aliens(u)$. We now look at the $\mathcal{R}$-reduction. There are two cases:

- If the reduction takes place in the cap then it is a $\mathcal{R}_1$-reduction. Since both the left-hand side and the right-hand side of a first-order rule are first-order algebraic terms, we have $cap(u) \rightarrow_{\mathcal{R}_1} cap(t')$ and, since the rules of $\mathcal{R}_1$ are non-duplicating, we have $aliens(u) \subseteq aliens(t')$. If $aliens(u) \subsetneq aliens(t')$ then $Aliens(u) \subsetneq Aliens(t')$. Otherwise, $Cap(u)$ $(\rightarrow_{\mathcal{R}_1}\sim_1)_{\mathrm{mul}}$ $Cap(t')$.

- If the reduction takes place in an alien then, as in the case of a β-reduction, we have $Aliens(t)$ $(\rightarrow_{\mathcal{R}}\sim \cup \rhd\sim)_{\mathrm{mul}}$ $Aliens(u)$.

Case $\mathcal{R}_\omega = \emptyset$. Since the t_i's are strongly normalizable and no β-reduction can take place at the top of t, t has a β-normal form. We prove that every $\blacktriangleright$-reduct t' of t is strongly normalizable, by induction on $(Cap\beta(t), Aliens(t))$ with $((\rightarrow_{\mathcal{R}_1}\sim_1)_{\mathrm{mul}}, (\rightarrow_\beta\sim \cup \rightarrow_{\mathcal{R}}\sim \cup \rhd\sim)_{\mathrm{mul}})_{\mathrm{lex}}$ as well-founded ordering.

If $t \rightarrow_\beta t'$ then $cap\beta(t) = cap\beta(t')$ and, as seen in the previous case, $Aliens(t)$ $(\rightarrow_\beta\sim \cup \rhd\sim)$ $Aliens(u)$.

Otherwise, $t \rightarrow^*_{\mathcal{E}} u \rightarrow_{\mathcal{R}_1} t'$. As seen in the previous case, $cap(t) \rightarrow^*_{\mathcal{E}_1} cap(u)$ and $Aliens(t) = Aliens(u)$. Since β and $\mathcal{E}$ commute and $\mathcal{E}$ preserves β-normal forms, we have $cap\beta(t) \rightarrow^*_{\mathcal{E}_1} cap\beta(u)$ and thus $Cap\beta(t) = Cap\beta(u)$. We now look at the $\mathcal{R}_1$-reduction. There are two cases:

- The reduction takes place in the cap. Since both the left-hand side and the right-hand side of a first-order rule are first-order algebraic terms, we have $cap(u) \rightarrow_{\mathcal{R}_1} cap(t')$ and, since β-reductions cannot reduce the cap, we have $cap\beta(u) \rightarrow_{\mathcal{R}_1} cap\beta(t')$ and thus $Cap\beta(t)$ $(\rightarrow_{\mathcal{R}_1}\sim_1)_{\mathrm{mul}}$ $Cap\beta(t')$.

- If the reduction takes place in an alien then $Aliens(t)$ $(\rightarrow_{\mathcal{R}}\sim)_{\mathrm{mul}}$ $Aliens(u)$ and, after Lemma 3, $\beta(u) \rightarrow^*_{\mathcal{R}_1} \beta(t')$. Therefore, $cap\beta(u) \rightarrow^*_{\mathcal{R}_1} cap\beta(t')$ and $Cap\beta(u)$ $(\rightarrow_{\mathcal{R}}\sim)_{\mathrm{mul}}$ $Cap\beta(t')$. $\square$

We now come to the interpretation of defined predicate symbols. Let f be a defined predicate of type $(\boldsymbol{x} : \boldsymbol{T})U$. We define $I_f(\boldsymbol{t}, \boldsymbol{S})$ by induction on $\boldsymbol{t}, \boldsymbol{S}$ as follows. If there exists a rule $(f\boldsymbol{l} \rightarrow r, \Gamma, \rho)$ and a substitution σ such that $\boldsymbol{t} \blacktriangleright^* \sim \boldsymbol{l}\sigma$ and $\boldsymbol{l}\sigma$ is in $\blacktriangleright$-normal form, then $I_f(\boldsymbol{t}, \boldsymbol{S}) = [\![r]\!]^I_{\xi,\sigma}$ with $\sigma = \{\boldsymbol{x} \mapsto \boldsymbol{t}\}$ and $x\xi = S_{\kappa_x}$ where κ_x is given by smallness. Otherwise, we take the greatest element of $\mathcal{R}_U$.

We must make sure that the definition does not depend on the choice of the rule. Assume that there is another rule $(fl' \rightarrow r', \Gamma', \rho')$ and a substitution σ' such that $t \blacktriangleright^* \sim l'\sigma'$ in normal form. By confluence and Lemma 10, we have $l\sigma \sim l'\sigma'$. Since $\rightarrow$ is confluent and rules on predicate symbols have no critical pair, there exists σ'' such that $\sigma \rightarrow^*_\mathcal{E} \sigma''$, $\sigma' \rightarrow^*_\mathcal{E} \sigma''$ and $l\sigma'' = l'\sigma''$. Therefore, for the same reason, we must have $l = l'$ and $r = r'$.

Finally, we check that the interpretation is stable by reduction: if $t \rightarrow t'$ then, since $\rightarrow$ is confluent, t has a $\blacktriangleright$-normal form iff t' has a $\blacktriangleright$-normal form too.

We now prove the computability of higher-order symbols.

Theorem 6 (Computability of higher-order symbols). *If $f \in \mathcal{F}_\omega$, $\tau_f = (x : T)U$ and $\xi, \theta \models \Gamma_f$ then $fx\theta \in [\![U]\!]_{\xi,\theta}$.*

Proof. The proof follows the one given in [6] except that $\rightarrow$ is replaced by $\blacktriangleright$. We examine the different $\blacktriangleright$-reducts of $fx\theta$. If this is a β-reduction, it must take place in one $x_i\theta$ and we can conclude by induction hypothesis. Otherwise, we have $fx\theta \rightarrow^*_\mathcal{E} gu \rightarrow_\mathcal{R} t'$. Since the equations satisfy the General Schema, the u_i's are computable. Now, if the $\mathcal{R}$-reduction takes place in one u_i, we can conclude by induction hypothesis. Otherwise, this is a head-$\mathcal{R}$-reduction and we can conclude by correctness of the computability closure.   □

6   Confluence

We now study the confluence of $\rightarrow$ and the decidability of $\downarrow^*$. Let R be a relation. $\overline{R}$, R^+, R^* respectively denote the inverse, the transitive closure, and the reflexive and transitive closure of R. Composition is denoted by juxtaposition.

- R is *confluent* if $\overline{R}^* R^* \subseteq R^* \overline{R}^*$.
- R is *confluent modulo* $\sim$ or $\sim$-*confluent*[12] if $\overline{R}^* R^* \subseteq R^* \sim \overline{R}^*$.
- R is $\sim$-*confluent on* $\sim$-*classes* if $\overline{R}^* \sim R^* \subseteq R^* \sim \overline{R}^*$.
- R is *locally confluent* if $\overline{R}R \subseteq R^* \overline{R}^*$.
- R is *locally* $\sim$-*confluent* if $\overline{R}R \subseteq R^* \sim \overline{R}^*$.
- R is *locally* $\sim$-*confluent on* $\sim$-*classes* if $\overline{R} \sim R \subseteq R^* \sim \overline{R}^*$.
- R is *locally* $\sim$-*coherent* if $\mathcal{E}R \subseteq R^* \sim \overline{R}^*$.
- R and S *commute* if $\overline{R}S \subseteq S\overline{R}$.
- R $\sim$-*commutes on* $\sim$-*classes* if $\overline{R} \sim R \subseteq R \sim \overline{R}$.

Lemma 7. *If $\mathcal{E}$ is linear then $\sim$ commutes with β and $\blacktriangleright$.*

Proof. Assume that $t \rightarrow_{\beta,p} u$ (β-reduction at position p) and $t \rightarrow_{\mathcal{E},q} v$ ($\mathcal{E}$-reduction at position q). There are several cases depending on the relative positions of the different reductions.

---

[12] The definitions of confluence modulo and local confluence modulo are those of [16]. They differ from Huet's definition [15]. Huet's confluence modulo corresponds to our confluence modulo on equivalence classes, but Huet's local confluence modulo does not correspond to our local confluence modulo on equivalence classes.

- p and q have no common prefix. Then the reductions clearly commute and $\mathcal{E}\beta \subseteq \beta\mathcal{E}$ in this case (remember that $\overline{\mathcal{E}} = \mathcal{E}$).
- $p = q$: not possible since left-hand sides of rules are algebraic and distinct from a variable.
- $p < q$: $t|_p = [x : A]b\ a$ and $u = t[b\theta]_p$ with $\theta = \{x \mapsto a\}$.
  - Reduction in A: $v = t[[x : A']b\ a]_p$ with $A \to_{\mathcal{E}} A'$. Then, $v \to_\beta u$ and $\mathcal{E}\beta \subseteq \beta$.
  - Reduction in b: $v = t[[x : A]b'\ a]_p$ with $b \to_{\mathcal{E}} b'$. Then, $v \to_\beta t[b'\theta]_p\ {}_{\mathcal{E}}\!\leftarrow u$ and $\mathcal{E}\beta \subseteq \beta\mathcal{E}$.
  - Reduction in a: $v = t[[x : A]b\ a']_p$ with $a \to_{\mathcal{E}} a'$. Let $\theta' = \{x \mapsto a'\}$. Then, $v \to_\beta t[b\theta']_p\ {}_{\mathcal{E}}^*\!\leftarrow u$ and $\mathcal{E}\beta \subseteq \beta\mathcal{E}^*$.
- $p > q$: $t = t[l\sigma]_q$ and $v = t[r\sigma]_q$. Since left-hand sides of rules are algebraic, there is one occurrence of a variable $x \in \mathrm{FV}(l)$ such that $x\sigma \to_\beta w$. Let σ' be the substitution such that $x\sigma' = w$ and $y\sigma' = y\sigma$ if $y \neq x$. Let a (resp. b) be the number of occurrences of x in l (resp. r). Then, $u \to_\beta^{a-1} t[l\sigma']_q \to_{\mathcal{E}} t[r\sigma']_q\ {}_\beta^b\!\leftarrow v$. Since $\mathcal{E}$ is linear, we have $a = b = 1$ and thus $\mathcal{E}\beta \subseteq \beta\mathcal{E}$.

In conclusion, in every case, we have $\mathcal{E}\beta \subseteq \beta\mathcal{E}^*$. By induction on the number of $\mathcal{E}$-steps, we get $\mathcal{E}^*\beta \subseteq \beta\mathcal{E}^*$, that is, $\sim \beta \subseteq \beta \sim$. Therefore, $\sim \blacktriangleright\ \subseteq\ \blacktriangleright \sim$ since $\blacktriangleright = \beta \cup \sim\mathcal{R}$, $\sim \beta \subseteq \beta \sim\ \subseteq\ \blacktriangleright \sim$ and $\sim\sim\mathcal{R} \subseteq\ \blacktriangleright \sim$. □

Corollary 8. *If $\mathcal{E}$ is linear and $t \in \mathcal{SN}(\beta)$ then $t \in \mathcal{SN}(\sim\beta)$.*

Proof. Assume that $t \in \mathcal{SN}(\beta)$. We prove that $(\sim\beta)^n \subseteq \beta^n\sim$ by induction on n. For $n = 0$, this is immediate. For $n + 1$, $(\sim \beta)^{n+1} = (\sim \beta)^n \sim \beta \subseteq \beta^n \sim\sim \beta \subseteq \beta^{n+1} \sim$. Therefore, $t \in \mathcal{SN}(\sim \beta)$. □

Lemma 9. *If $\mathcal{E}$ is linear then $\to^*\subseteq\ \blacktriangleright^* \sim$ and $\downarrow = \blacktriangleright^* \sim {}^*\!\blacktriangleleft$.*

Proof. $\to^*\ \subseteq\ (\beta \cup \mathcal{E} \cup \sim\mathcal{R})^*$. Since $\sim \beta^* \subseteq \beta^* \sim$ and $\sim \sim\mathcal{R} \subseteq \sim\mathcal{R}$, we get $\to^*\subseteq\ \sim \cup (\sim\mathcal{R})^*\to^* \cup \beta^*\to^*$. Therefore, $\to^*\subseteq\ \blacktriangleright^* \sim$. □

Lemma 10. *If $\mathcal{E}$ is linear then the following propositions are equivalent: $\to$ is confluent, $\blacktriangleright$ is $\sim$-confluent, $\blacktriangleright$ is $\sim$-confluent on $\sim$-classes.*

Proof. Since $\mathcal{E}$ is linear, we have $\to^*\subseteq\ \blacktriangleright^* \sim$ and $\sim \blacktriangleright^*\ \subseteq\ \blacktriangleright^* \sim$. We prove that $\blacktriangleright$ is $\sim$-confluent if $\to$ is confluent: ${}^*\!\blacktriangleleft \blacktriangleright^*\ \subseteq\ {}^*\!\leftarrow\to^*\ \subseteq\to^*\ {}^*\!\leftarrow\ \subseteq\ \blacktriangleright^* \sim\sim\ {}^*\!\blacktriangleleft$. We prove that $\to$ is confluent if $\blacktriangleright$ is $\sim$-confluent: ${}^*\!\leftarrow\to^*\ \subseteq\ \sim\ {}^*\!\blacktriangleleft \blacktriangleright^*\!\sim\ \subseteq\ \sim\ \blacktriangleright^* \sim\ {}^*\!\blacktriangleleft \sim\ \subseteq\ \blacktriangleright^* \sim\sim\sim\ {}^*\!\blacktriangleleft$. We now prove that $\blacktriangleright$ is $\sim$-confluent on $\sim$-classes if $\blacktriangleright$ is $\sim$-confluent (the inverse is trivial): ${}^*\!\blacktriangleleft \sim \blacktriangleright^*\ \subseteq\ {}^*\!\blacktriangleleft\blacktriangleright^*\ \sim\ \subseteq\ \blacktriangleright^* \sim\ {}^*\!\blacktriangleleft \sim\ \subseteq\ \blacktriangleright^* \sim\sim\ {}^*\!\blacktriangleleft$. □

Theorem 11. *Type-checking is decidable if $\blacktriangleright$ is weakly normalizing, $\mathcal{R}$ is finitely branching, $\blacktriangleright$ is $\sim$-confluent on $\sim$-classes, $\mathcal{E}$ is linear and $\sim$ is decidable.*

Proof. Type-checking is deciding whether a term t has type T in an environment Γ. A type for t can be easily inferred. Then, one checks that it is equivalent to T

(see [10] for more details). Thus, we are left to prove that $\downarrow^*$ is decidable. Since $\mathcal{E}$ is linear and $\blacktriangleright$ is $\sim$-confluent on $\sim$-classes, by Lemma 10, $\rightarrow$ is confluent and $\downarrow^* = \downarrow$. Since $\mathcal{E}$ is linear, by Lemma 9, $\downarrow \; = \; \blacktriangleright^* \sim \; ^*\blacktriangleleft$. Since $\blacktriangleright$ is weakly normalizing and finitely branching ($\sim$-classes are finite and β and $\mathcal{R}$ are finitely branching), one can define a function nf computing a $\blacktriangleright$-normal form of a term. We prove that $t \downarrow^* u$ only if $nf(t) \sim nf(u)$ (the inverse is trivial). Assume that $t \blacktriangleright^* t' \sim u' \; ^*\blacktriangleleft u$. Since $\blacktriangleright$ is $\sim$-confluent on $\sim$-classes, $nf(t) \sim nf(t') \; ^*\blacktriangleleft t' \sim u' \blacktriangleright^* nf(u') \sim nf(u)$. Again, since $\blacktriangleright$ is $\sim$-confluent on $\sim$-classes, there exist t'' and u'' such that $nf(t) \sim nf(t') \blacktriangleright^* t'' \sim u'' \; ^*\blacktriangleleft nf(u') \sim nf(u)$. Since $nf(t')$ and $nf(u')$ are $\blacktriangleright$-normal forms, we have $nf(t) \sim nf(u)$.   □

Lemma 12. *For all relation R, if R $\sim$-commutes on $\sim$-classes then $\sim R$ is $\sim$-confluent on $\sim$-classes.*

Proof. Let $S = \; \sim R$. We prove that $\overline{S}^p \sim S^n \subseteq S^n \sim \overline{S}^p$ by induction on n.

- Case $n = 0$. By induction on p. The case $p = 0$ is immediate. Case $p + 1$: $\overline{S}^{p+1} \sim \; = \overline{SS}^p \sim \; \subseteq \; \sim \overline{S} \sim \overline{S}^p \; \subseteq \; \sim \overline{SS}^p$ since $\overline{S} \sim \; = \overline{R} \sim\sim \; = \overline{R} \sim \; = \overline{S} \subseteq \; \sim \overline{S}$.

- Case $n = 1$. By induction on p.
  - Case $p = 0$. $\sim S = \; \sim\sim R = \; \sim R = S \subseteq S \sim$.
  - Case $p + 1$. $\overline{S}^{p+1} \sim S = \overline{SS}^p \sim S \subseteq \overline{SS} \sim \overline{S}^p \subseteq S \sim \overline{SS}^p$ since $\overline{SS} \sim \; = \overline{R} \sim\sim R \sim \; = \overline{R} \sim R \sim \; \subseteq R \sim \overline{R} \sim \; \subseteq S \sim \overline{S}$.

- Case $n+1$. $\overline{S}^p \sim S^{n+1} = \overline{S}^p \sim SS^n \subseteq S \sim \overline{S}^p S^n \subseteq S \sim \overline{S}^p \sim S^n \subseteq S \sim S^n \sim \overline{S}^p$ and we prove that $S \sim S^n \sim \; \subseteq S^{n+1} \sim$ by induction on n. The case $n = 0$ is immediate. Case $n + 1$: $S \sim S^{n+1} \sim \; \subseteq S \sim S^n \sim S \sim \; \subseteq S^{n+1} \sim S \sim \; \subseteq S^{n+1} S \sim$ since $\sim S = \; \sim\sim R = \; \sim R = S$.   □

Lemma 13. *For all relation R, if R is $\sim$-confluent on $\sim$-classes then $\sim R$ is $\sim$-confluent on $\sim$-classes.*

Proof. If R is $\sim$-confluent on $\sim$-classes then R^* $\sim$-commutes on $\sim$-classes. Hence, by Lemma 12, $\sim R^*$ is $\sim$-confluent on $\sim$-classes. Therefore, $\sim R$ is $\sim$-confluent on $\sim$-classes since $(\sim R)^* \subseteq (\sim R^*)^*$ and $(\sim R^*)^* \subseteq (\sim R)^* \sim$.   □

Theorem 14. $\blacktriangleright$ *is $\sim$-confluent on $\sim$-classes if $\blacktriangleright$ is strongly normalizing, $\mathcal{E}$ is linear, $\mathcal{R}$ is locally $\sim$-confluent and $\mathcal{R}$ is locally $\sim$-coherent.*

Proof. We first prove that $\beta \cup \mathcal{R}$ is $\sim$-confluent on $\sim$-classes. In [15], Huet proves that a relation R is $\sim$-confluent on $\sim$-classes if $R \sim$ is strongly normalizing, R is locally $\sim$-confluent and R is locally $\sim$-coherent. We take $R = \beta \cup \mathcal{R}$ and check the conditions. $R\sim$ is strongly normalizing since $\blacktriangleright$ is strongly normalizing and β and $\sim$ commute ($\mathcal{E}$ is linear). Local confluence: $\overline{\beta}\beta \subseteq \beta^*\overline{\beta}^*$ since β is locally confluent, $\overline{\mathcal{R}}\beta \subseteq \beta^*\overline{\mathcal{R}}^*\overline{\beta}^*$ after the proof of Lemma 7, and $\overline{\mathcal{R}}\mathcal{R} \subseteq \mathcal{R}^* \sim \overline{\mathcal{R}}^*$ by assumption. Local coherence: $\mathcal{E}\beta \subseteq \beta\mathcal{E} \subseteq \beta \sim$ since $\mathcal{E}$ is linear, and $\mathcal{E}\mathcal{R} \subseteq \mathcal{R}^* \sim \overline{\mathcal{R}}^*$ by assumption.

So, $R = \beta \cup \mathcal{R}$ is $\sim$-confluent on $\sim$-classes. Therefore, by Lemma 13, $\sim R$ is $\sim$-confluent on $\sim$-classes. We now prove the theorem. We have $\blacktriangleright^* \subseteq (\sim R)^*$ and $(\sim R)^* \subseteq \blacktriangleright^* \sim$ (β and $\sim$ commute since $\mathcal{E}$ is linear). Thus, $^*\blacktriangleleft \sim \blacktriangleright^* \subseteq \overline{(\sim R)}^* \sim (\sim R)^* \subseteq (\sim R)^* \sim \overline{(\sim R)}^* \subseteq \blacktriangleright^* \sim\sim \; ^*\blacktriangleleft$.   □

Huet also proves in [15] that $\mathcal{R}$ is locally $\sim$-confluent iff its critical pairs are $\sim$-confluent, and that $\mathcal{R}$ is locally $\sim$-coherent if $\mathcal{R}$ is left-linear and the critical pairs between $\mathcal{R}$ and $\mathcal{E}$ are $\sim$-confluent. So, $\sim$-confluence is decidable whenever $\blacktriangleright$ is strongly normalizing, $\sim$ is decidable and $\mathcal{R} \cup \mathcal{E}$ is finite: it amounts to checking whether the critical pairs between the rules, and between the rules and the equations (in both directions), are $\sim$-confluent.

Unfortunately, when considering type-level rewriting, confluence is required for proving strong normalization. Whether strong normalization can be proved by using local confluence only is an open problem. Fortunately, confluence can be proved for a large class of rewrite systems without using strong normalization, namely the left-linear systems.

Theorem 15. $\blacktriangleright$ *is* $\sim$-*confluent on* $\sim$-*classes if* $\mathcal{E}$ *is linear,* $\mathcal{R}$ *is left-linear and* $\mathcal{R}$ *is* $\sim$-*confluent on* $\sim$-*classes.*

Proof. In [24], Van Oostrom and Van Raamsdonk prove that the combination of two left-linear and confluent Combinatory Reduction Systems (CRS) $\mathcal{H}$ and $\mathcal{J}$ is confluent if all the critical pairs between the rules of $\mathcal{H}$ and the rules of $\mathcal{J}$ are trivial. We prove the theorem by taking $\mathcal{H} = \mathcal{R} \cup \mathcal{E}$ and $\mathcal{J} = \beta$, and by proving that $\mathcal{H}$ is confluent. Since $\mathcal{H}^* \subseteq (\sim\mathcal{R})^* \sim$, we have $\overline{\mathcal{H}}^* \mathcal{H}^* \subseteq \sim (\overline{\sim\mathcal{R}})^* (\sim\mathcal{R})^* \sim$. Since $\mathcal{R}$ is $\sim$-confluent on $\sim$-classes, by Lemma 13, $\sim\mathcal{R}$ is $\sim$-confluent on $\sim$-classes. Therefore, $\sim (\overline{\sim\mathcal{R}})^*(\sim\mathcal{R})^* \sim \subseteq \sim (\sim\mathcal{R})^* \sim (\overline{\sim\mathcal{R}})^* \sim \subseteq \mathcal{H}^* \overline{\mathcal{H}}^*$.   □

Again, $\mathcal{R}$ is $\sim$-confluent on $\sim$-classes if $\sim\mathcal{R}$ is strongly normalizing and $\mathcal{R}$ is locally confluent and $\sim$-coherent, which can be proved by analyzing the critical pairs between the rules and between the rules and the equations (when $\mathcal{R}$ is left-linear) [15].

7   Conclusion

In [3,2], we give general syntactic conditions based on the notion of computability closure for proving the strong normalization of β-reduction and (higher-order) rewriting. In this paper, we show that the notion of computability closure can also be used for proving the strong normalization of β-reduction and (higher-order) rewriting modulo (higher-order) equations. It is interesting to note that, in our approach, the introduction of equations does not affect the conditions on rules: although based on the same notion, equations and rules are dealt with separately. Finally, one may wonder whether our method could be extended to Jouannaud and Rubio's Higher-Order Recursive Path Ordering (HORPO) [17,25], which also uses the notion of computability closure for increasing its expressive power.

Acknowledgments

I thank J.-P. Jouannaud, F. van Raamsdonk and the referees for their useful comments on previous versions of this paper. Part of this work was performed during my stay at Cambridge (UK) thanks to a grant from the INRIA.

References

1. H. Barendregt. Lambda calculi with types. In S. Abramski, D. Gabbay, and T. Maibaum, editors, *Handbook of logic in computer science*, volume 2. Oxford University Press, 1992.
2. F. Blanqui. *Théorie des Types et Récriture*. PhD thesis, Université Paris XI, Orsay, France, 2001. Available in english as "Type Theory and Rewriting".
3. F. Blanqui. Definitions by rewriting in the Calculus of Constructions (extended abstract). In *Proc. of LICS'01*.
4. F. Blanqui. Definitions by rewriting in the Calculus of Constructions, 2002. Journal submission, 68 pages.
5. F. Blanqui, J.-P. Jouannaud, and M. Okada. Inductive-data-type Systems. *Theoretical Computer Science*, 272:41–68, 2002.
6. F. Blanqui. A short and flexible strong normalization proof for the Calculus of Algebraic Constructions with curried rewriting, 2003. Draft.
7. V. Breazu-Tannen and J. Gallier. Polymorphic rewriting conserves algebraic strong normalization. In *Proc. of ICALP'89*, LNCS 372.
8. E. Contejean, C. Marché, B. Monate, and X. Urbain. CiME, 2000.
9. T. Coquand and G. Huet. The Calculus of Constructions. *Information and Computation*, 76(2–3):95–120, 1988.
10. T. Coquand. An algorithm for testing conversion in type theory. In G. Huet, G. Plotkin, editors, *Logical Frameworks*, p. 255–279. Cambridge Univ. Press, 1991.
11. N. Dershowitz and J.-P. Jouannaud. Rewrite systems. In J. van Leeuwen, editor, *Handbook of Theoretical Computer Science*, vol. B, chap. 6. North-Holland, 1990.
12. D. Dougherty. Adding algebraic rewriting to the untyped lambda calculus. *Information and Computation*, 101(2):251–267, 1992.
13. G. Dowek, T. Hardin, and C. Kirchner. Theorem proving modulo. Technical Report 3400, INRIA Rocquencourt, France, 1998.
14. J.-Y. Girard, Y. Lafont and P. Taylor. *Proofs and Types*. Cambridge University Press, 1988.
15. G. Huet. Confluent reductions: Abstract properties and applications to term-rewriting systems. *Journal of the ACM*, 27(4):797–821, 1980.
16. J.-P. Jouannaud and H. Kirchner. Completion of a set of rules modulo a set of equations. *SIAM Journal on Computing*, 15(4):1155–1194, 1986.
17. J.-P. Jouannaud and A. Rubio. The Higher-Order Recursive Path Ordering. In *Proc. of LICS'99*.
18. J. W. Klop, V. van Oostrom, F. van Raamsdonk. Combinatory reduction systems: introduction and survey. *Theoretical Computer Science*, 121:279–308, 1993.
19. C. Marché. Normalised rewriting and normalised completion. In *Proc. of LICS'94*.
20. M. Okada. Strong normalizability for the combined system of the typed lambda calculus and an arbitrary convergent term rewrite system. In *Proc. of ISSAC'89*.
21. M. Rusinowitch. On termination of the direct sum of term-rewriting systems. *Information Processing Letters*, 26(2):65–70, 1987.
22. Coq Development Team. *The Coq Proof Assistant Reference Manual – Version 7.4*. INRIA Rocquencourt, France, 2003. http://coq.inria.fr/.
23. Y. Toyama. Counterexamples to termination for the direct sum of term rewriting systems. *Information Processing Letters*, 25(3):141–143, 1987.
24. V. van Oostrom and F. van Raamsdonk. Weak orthogonality implies confluence: the higher-order case. In *Proc. of LFCS'94*, LNCS 813.
25. D. Walukiewicz-Chrząszcz. Termination of rewriting in the Calculus of Constructions. *Journal of Functional Programming*, ?(?):?–?, 2002.

Termination of String Rewriting Rules That Have One Pair of Overlaps*

Alfons Geser**

National Institute for Aerospace, Hampton VA, USA***

Abstract. This paper presents a partial solution to the long standing open problem whether termination of one-rule string rewriting is decidable. Overlaps between the two sides of the rule play a central role in existing termination criteria. We characterize termination of all one-rule string rewriting systems that have one such overlap at either end. This both completes a result of Kurth and generalizes a result of Shikishima-Tsuji et al.

Key Words and Phrases: semi-Thue system, string rewriting, one-rule, single-rule, termination, uniform termination, overlap

1 Introduction and Related Work

Whether termination of one-rule string rewriting systems (SRSs) is decidable or not, is a long standing open problem [2,3,4,6,10,11,12,13,14,15,17]. A systematic approach was started by Kurth [7]. Kurth introduced a number of termination criteria to decide termination for all $\ell \to r$ where $|r| \leq 6$.[1]

Most of Kurth's criteria (5 out of 8), and indeed most of the criteria introduced since, are based on two sets: the set of overlaps of the left hand side (from the left end) with the right hand side (from the right end); and the set of overlaps of the right hand side (from the left end) with the left hand side (from the right end). Kurth's Criterion D states that we have termination if one or both of the two sets are empty.

In the case where both sets are singletons, we say that the one-rule SRS has *one pair of overlaps*. Kurth [7] provides Criterion F specifically for this case. As Criterion F can only prove termination of rules that are left barren or right barren, it is incomplete as we will show (Example 2). Shikishima-Tsuji et al. [15, Theorem 2] show that a *confluent* one-rule SRS with one pair of overlaps

---

* This work was supported by the National Aeronautics and Space Administration under NASA Contract No. NAS1-97046 while the author was in residence at ICASE, NASA Langley Research Center, Hampton, VA 23681-2199, USA.

** Address: National Institute for Aerospace, 144 Research Drive, Hampton, VA 23666. geser@nianet.org

*** Address: 144 Research Drive, Hampton, VA 23666. E-mail: geser@nianet.org

[1] An English presentation of Kurth's chapter on termination can be found in the author's habilitation thesis [3].

R. Nieuwenhuis (Ed.): RTA 2003, LNCS 2706, pp. 410–423, 2003.

terminates if and only if there are no loops of lengths 1 or 2. As a consequence termination of such SRSs is decidable.

This paper completely solves the termination problem for one-rule SRSs with one overlap pair. We prove that such an SRS terminates if and only if it has no loop of lengths 1, 2 or 3 (Theorem 6). This implies decidability of the termination problem.

It turns out that the extension is non-trivial. There are two behaviours that were observed neither by Kurth nor by Shikishima-Tsuji et al. Loops of length 3 is one of them; the other is terminating non-tame rules.

This paper makes the following original contributions:

1. Termination of one-rule SRSs with one overlap pair is shown decidable.
2. Termination of one-rule SRSs with one overlap pair is shown equivalent to the non-existence of loops of length 3 or less.
3. Terminating one-rule SRSs with one overlap pair are shown to have linear derivation lengths, unless they are left barren or right barren.
4. For the first time, a termination criterion for a class of non-tame one-rule SRSs is presented.

The paper is organized as follows. After the preliminaries (Section 2) and an introduction to left barren and tame rules (Section 3), we focus on the interesting non-tame case. In Section 4, we derive a pattern that describes the non-tame rules. In Sections 5 and 6, we solve the non-terminating and terminating non-tame rules, respectively. Section 7 finally shows the main theorem of the paper and its ramifications.

2   Preliminaries

A *string rewriting rule* is a pair $\ell \rightarrow r$ of strings, $\ell, r \in \Sigma^*$ where Σ is a given alphabet. A set of string rewriting rules is called a *string rewriting system* (SRS). An SRS R induces a *rewrite step* relation $\rightarrow$ defined by $s \rightarrow t$ if there are $u, v \in \Sigma^*$ and a rule $\ell \rightarrow r$ in R such that $s = u\ell v$ and $t = urv$. The SRS R is said to *terminate* if there is no infinite sequence of rewrite steps $s_1 \rightarrow s_2 \rightarrow \ldots$.

The length of a string u is denoted by $|u|$. A string u is called a *factor* of v if $v = sut$ for some $s, t \in \Sigma^*$; a *prefix* if $v = ut$ for some $t \in \Sigma^*$; a *suffix* if $v = su$ for some $s \in \Sigma^*$. The prefix or suffix u of v is called *proper* if $u \neq v$. The set of *overlaps* of a string u with a string v is defined by

$$\mathrm{OVL}(u, v) = \{w \in \Sigma^+ \mid u = u'w, v = wv', u'v' \neq \varepsilon, u', v' \in \Sigma^*\}.$$

3   Left Barren Rules

For a fixed one-rule SRS $\{\ell \rightarrow r\}$ let $A = \mathrm{OVL}(r, \ell) \times \{0\}$ and $B = \mathrm{OVL}(\ell, r) \times \{1\}$. The labels 0 and 1 are there to make A and B disjoint. By abuse of notation, we will confuse elements of A and B with elements of $\mathrm{OVL}(r, \ell)$ and $\mathrm{OVL}(\ell, r)$, respectively.

For all $\alpha \in A$, the strings ℓ_α and r_α are defined by $\ell = \alpha\ell_\alpha$ and $r = r_\alpha\alpha$, respectively. Likewise, for all $\beta \in B$, the strings ℓ_β and r_β are defined by $\ell = \ell_\beta\beta$ and $r = \beta r_\beta$, respectively.

The following definition of "left barren" is after McNaughton's corrected version. The original definition is renamed to "left s-barren" (see Definition 2), following a suggestion of Kobayashi et al. [6].

Definition 1 (Left barren, right barren [10]). *A one-rule SRS $\{\ell \to r\}$ is called* left barren *if ℓ is not a factor of r and no $\ell_\alpha, \alpha \in A$ is a prefix of any concatenation $r_{\beta_1} \ldots r_{\beta_k}$ where $\beta_1, \ldots, \beta_k \in B, k \geq 1$. Dually, $\{\ell \to r\}$ is called* right barren *if ℓ is not a factor of r and no $\ell_\beta, \beta \in B$ is a suffix of any concatenation $r_{\alpha_1} \ldots r_{\alpha_k}$ where $\alpha_1, \ldots, \alpha_k \in A, k \geq 1$.*

A one-rule SRS $\{\ell \to r\}$ is called *non-overlapping* if $\mathrm{OVL}(\ell, \ell) = \emptyset$.

Theorem 1 ([10]). *Every non-overlapping, left barren, one-rule SRS terminates.*

Theorem 2 ([3]). *Every left barren one-rule SRS terminates.*

By symmetry w.r.t. reversal of strings also every right barren one-rule SRS terminates.

Definition 2 (Left s-barren, right s-barren [10,6]). *A rule $\ell \to r$ is called* left s-barren *if ℓ is not a factor of r and no $\ell_\alpha, \alpha \in A$ is a prefix of any $r_\beta, \beta \in B$. Dually $\ell \to r$ is called* right s-barren *if ℓ is not a factor of r and no $\ell_\beta, \beta \in B$ is a suffix of any $r_\alpha, \alpha \in A$.*

A left barren rule is left s-barren, but the converse usually does not hold. Indeed we will encounter left s-barren, not left barren rules later in this paper. They belong to a class of rules whose termination is particularly difficult to show. Next we will define this class.

In the following definition we consider A, B as alphabets. For $\overline{\alpha} = \alpha_1\alpha_2 \ldots \alpha_k \in A^*$ we define $\ell_{\overline{\alpha}}$ by $\ell_{\overline{\alpha}} = \ell_{\alpha_1}\ell_{\alpha_2} \ldots \ell_{\alpha_k}$. And dually, for $\overline{\beta} = \beta_1\beta_2 \ldots \beta_k \in B^*$ we define $\ell_{\overline{\beta}}$ by $\ell_{\overline{\beta}} = \ell_{\beta_1}\ell_{\beta_2} \ldots \ell_{\beta_k}$.

Kobayashi et al. [6] introduced the notion of tame, non-overlapping one-rule SRSs.

Definition 3 (Tame [3]). *Let $\{\ell \to r\}$ be a one-rule SRS. The sets C and D are defined by*

$$C = \{r' \in \Sigma^* \mid r = \beta\ell_{\overline{\alpha}}r', \beta \in B, \overline{\alpha} \in A^*\},$$
$$D = \{r' \in \Sigma^* \mid r = r'\ell_{\overline{\beta}}\alpha, \alpha \in A, \overline{\beta} \in B^*\}.$$

Then $\ell \to r$ is called tame *if ℓ is neither of the form*

$$\alpha r_1 r_2 \ldots r_k w, \tag{1}$$

for any $\alpha \in A$, $k \geq 1$, $r_1, \ldots, r_k \in C$, *and non-empty prefix* w *of an element of* C; *nor of the form*

$$wr_1 r_2 \ldots r_j \beta, \tag{2}$$

for any $\beta \in B$, $j \geq 1$, $r_1, \ldots, r_j \in D$, *and non-empty suffix* w *of an element of* D.

The following result is implicit in Kobayashi et al. [6, Cor. 5.9].

Theorem 3. *Every non-overlapping, tame, left s-barren one-rule SRS is left barren.*

Theorem 4 ([3]). *Every tame, left s-barren one-rule SRS is left barren.*

By symmetry, every tame, right s-barren one-rule SRS is right barren.

Proof. For a proof by contradiction, assume that $\ell \to r$ is not left barren, i.e., some ℓ_α is a prefix of some concatenation $r_{\beta_1} r_{\beta_2} \cdots r_{\beta_n}$. Let n be minimal. If $n = 1$ then $\ell \to r$ is not left s-barren. So $n \geq 2$ whence ℓ_α is of the form $r_{\beta_1} r_{\beta_2} \cdots r_{\beta_{n-1}} w$ where w is a nonempty prefix of r_{β_n}. Hence ℓ is of the form (1) and so $\ell \to r$ is not tame. □

4 A Reduction of the Problem

Throughout the remainder of this paper we assume a one-rule SRS $\{\ell \to r\}$ that has one pair of overlaps, i.e., $|\operatorname{OVL}(r, \ell)| = |\operatorname{OVL}(\ell, r)| = 1$. Let then $\alpha, \beta \in \Sigma^+$ be defined by $\operatorname{OVL}(r, \ell) = \{\alpha\}$ and $\operatorname{OVL}(\ell, r) = \{\beta\}$.

We will devote the greater part of the paper to solving the interesting case: rules that are left s-barren but neither left barren nor right s-barren. According to Theorem 4, these are non-tame, specifically they are of the form (1). In this section we will derive the general pattern of such rules. Let us henceforth assume that ℓ is not a factor of r and that $|\ell| < |r|$.

The first pattern is derived without the non-right-s-barren hypothesis.

Lemma 1. *Let* $\ell \to r$ *be left s-barren but not left barren. Then* $|\beta| > |\alpha|$ *and* $\ell \to r$ *is of the form*

$$\alpha(ww')^{n-1} w \to \beta ww' \tag{3}$$

for some $n \geq 2$, $w' \in \Sigma^*$, *and* $w \in \Sigma^+$.

Proof. Let $\ell \to r$ be left s-barren but not left barren. Then we get by the respective definitions that ℓ_α is not a prefix of r_β and that ℓ_α is a prefix of r_β^n form some $n \geq 1$. Hence r_β is a proper prefix of ℓ_α. So let $\ell_\alpha = r_\beta^{n-1} w$ where $n \geq 2$, and w is a non-empty prefix of r_β. Let $w' \in \Sigma^*$ be defined by $r_\beta = ww'$. By back-substitution we get the form (3). From $|\beta r_\beta| = |r| > |\ell| = |\alpha r_\beta^{n-1} w|$ we conclude $|\beta| > |\alpha|$. □

We can rule out the case where α and β overlap in ℓ.

Lemma 2. *If $\ell \to r$ is left s-barren but not left barren then $|\alpha| + |\beta| \le |\ell|$.*

Proof. Let $\ell \to r$ be left s-barren but not left barren. By Lemma 1 we get that $\ell \to r$ has the form (3). For a proof by contradiction assume $|\alpha| + |\beta| > |\ell|$. Then there is a non-empty suffix u of α such that $\beta = u(ww')^{n-1}w$. Define $\alpha' \in \Sigma^*$ by $\alpha = \alpha'u$. The string α' is non-empty by $\beta \ne \ell$. Thus ℓ and r are of the form

$$\ell = \alpha'u(ww')^{n-1}w,$$
$$r = u(ww')^{n-1}www',$$

for some $n \ge 2$, $w' \in \Sigma^*$, and $\alpha', u, w \in \Sigma^+$.

Now we use the fact that $\alpha = \alpha'u$, and so u, is a suffix of $r = u(ww')^{n-1}www'$. Let $m \ge 0$ be maximal such that $((ww')^{n-1}www')^m$ is a suffix of u. Define $u_1 \in \Sigma^*$ by $u = u_1((ww')^{n-1}www')^m$. Then u_1 is a proper suffix of $(ww')^{n-1}www'$. If u_1 is a suffix of ww' then $u_1w \in \mathrm{OVL}(\ell, r)$, a contradiction. So ww' is a proper suffix of u_1. Let $u_2 \in \Sigma^+$ be defined by $u_1 = u_2ww'$. Then u_2 is a proper suffix of $(ww')^{n-1}w$. Hence $u_2 \in \mathrm{OVL}(\ell, r)$, a contradiction. □

Knowing that α and β do not overlap in ℓ, we can narrow the pattern for the rule:

Lemma 3. *Let $\ell \to r$ be left s-barren but not left barren. Then $\ell \to r$ is of the form*

$$\alpha wxy\alpha w \to y\alpha wwxy\alpha \qquad (4)$$

for some $x \in \Sigma^*$ and $y, \alpha, w \in \Sigma^+$.

Proof. Let $\ell \to r$ be left s-barren but not left barren. By Lemma 1 we get that $\ell \to r$ has the form (3). Lemma 2 yields $|\alpha| + |\beta| \le |\ell|$, so β is a suffix of $(ww')^{n-1}w$. We distinguish cases whether β starts in some w or in some w'.

Case 1: $\beta = w''(w'w)^i$ for some $0 \le i \le n-1$, and some non-empty suffix w'' of w. If $i \ge 1$ then $w'' \in \mathrm{OVL}(\ell, r)$, a contradiction. So $i = 0$ and $\beta = w''$. Then

$$|r| - |\ell| = |w''| + |w| + |w'| - (|\alpha| + n|w| + (n-1)|w'|) < 0,$$

again a contradiction.

Case 2: $\beta = w''w(w'w)^i$ for some $0 \le i \le n-2$, and some nonempty suffix w'' of w'. If $i \ge 1$ then $w''w \in \mathrm{OVL}(\ell, r)$, a contradiction. So $i = 0$ and $\beta = w''w$. Let $w' = xw''$ for some string x. Then we have

$$\ell = \alpha(wxw'')^{n-1}w,$$
$$r = w''wwxw'',$$

and so

$$|r| - |\ell| = 2|w''| + 2|w| + |x| - (|\alpha| + (n-1)|w''| + (n-1)|x| + n|w|)$$
$$= (3-n)|w''| + (2-n)|w| + (2-n)|x| - |\alpha|.$$

If $n \geq 3$ then $|r| - |\ell| < 0$. So $n = 2$ and $|r| - |\ell| = |w''| - |\alpha| > 0$ whence $|w''| > |\alpha|$. By definition of α now α is a proper suffix of w''. Let $w'' = y\alpha$ for some $y \in \Sigma^+$. We conclude that $\ell \to r$ is of the form (4). $\square$

Adding the non-right-s-barren premise allows us to narrow the rule pattern further:

Lemma 4. *If $\ell \to r$ is left s-barren but neither left barren nor right s-barren then $\ell \to r$ is of the form*

$$\alpha wx(y\alpha wx)^{m+1}\alpha w \to y\alpha wx\alpha wwx(y\alpha wx)^{m+1}\alpha \qquad (5)$$

for some $m \geq 0$, $x \in \Sigma^*$, and $\alpha, w, y \in \Sigma^+$.

Proof. Let $\ell \to r$ be left s-barren but neither left barren nor right s-barren. By Lemma 3 we get that $\ell \to r$ has the form (4)

The property that $\ell \to r$ is not right s-barren means that $\ell_\beta = \alpha wx$ is a suffix of $r_\alpha = y\alpha wwxy$. Recall that $x \in \Sigma^*$ and $\alpha, w, y \in \Sigma^+$. Let $m \geq 0$ be maximal such that y^m is a suffix of x. Define $x_1 \in \Sigma^*$ by $x = x_1 y^m$. Then αwx_1 is a suffix of $y\alpha wwx_1 y$ and x_1 is a proper suffix of y. Define $y_1 \in \Sigma^+$ by $y = y_1 x_1$. Then αw is a suffix of $y_1 x_1 \alpha wwx_1 y_1$. If y_1 is a suffix of w then $y_1 \in \mathrm{OVL}(\ell, r)$, a contradiction. So w is a proper suffix of y_1. Define $y_2 \in \Sigma^+$ by $y_1 = y_2 w$. Then α is a suffix of $y_2 wx_1 \alpha wwx_1 y_2$. If y_2 is a suffix of α then $y_2 w \in \mathrm{OVL}(\ell, r)$, a contradiction. So α is a proper suffix of y_2. Define $y_3 \in \Sigma^+$ by $y_2 = y_3 \alpha$.

By back-substitution we get

$$y = y_1 x_1 = y_2 wx_1 = y_3 \alpha wx_1,$$
$$x = x_1 y^m = x_1 (y_3 \alpha wx_1)^m,$$
$$\ell = \alpha wxy\alpha w = \alpha wx_1(y_3 \alpha wx_1)^{m+1}\alpha w,$$
$$r = y\alpha wwxy\alpha = y_3 \alpha wx_1 \alpha wwx_1(y_3 \alpha wx_1)^{m+1}\alpha.$$

and thus the form (5) by the renaming $\{x_1 \mapsto x, y_3 \mapsto y\}$. $\square$

The following is interesting to note. It explains why rules of the form (5) were not observed by Shikishima-Tsuji et al.

Theorem 5. *All rules of the form* (5) *are non-confluent.*

Proof. A one-rule SRS $\{\ell \to r\}$ where $|\ell| < |r|$ is confluent if and only if $\mathrm{OVL}(\ell, \ell) \subseteq \mathrm{OVL}(r, r)$ by a result of Wrathall [16]. A rule of the form (5) satisfies $\alpha w \in \mathrm{OVL}(\ell, \ell)$. If $\alpha w \in \mathrm{OVL}(r, r)$ then $\alpha w \in \mathrm{OVL}(r, \ell)$, a contradiction to $\mathrm{OVL}(r, \ell) = \{\alpha\}$. So $\alpha w \in \mathrm{OVL}(\ell, \ell) \setminus \mathrm{OVL}(r, r)$ whence $\ell \to r$ is not confluent. $\square$

In the next two sections we are going to identify the non-terminating and the terminating instances of the form (5).

5   The Non-terminating Case

A rule of the form (5) loops in the following case:

Lemma 5. *Let $\ell \to r$ be left s-barren but neither left barren nor right s-barren. If $\ell_\beta \ell_\beta$ is a suffix of r_α, then the one-rule SRS $\{\ell \to r\}$ has a loop of length 3.*

Proof. Like in the proof of Lemma 1, we get $\ell_\alpha = r_\beta^{n-1} w$ and $r_\beta = ww'$ for some $w \in \Sigma^+, w' \in \Sigma^*, n \geq 2$. In the proof of Lemma 3 we showed $n = 2$. With $r_\alpha = v\ell_\beta\ell_\beta$ for some $v \in \Sigma^*$, we then get a loop:

$$\ell\ell_\alpha \to r_\alpha\alpha\ell_\alpha \to r_\alpha r = v\ell_\beta\ell_\beta\beta r_\beta \to v\ell_\beta rr_\beta = v\ell_\beta\beta r_\beta r_\beta = v\ell r_\beta r_\beta$$
$$= v\ell\ell_\alpha w'. \quad \square$$

These loops are also instances of Kurth's criterion for loops of length 3 [8, Theorem 2, Case A]. The following little result provides an alternative criterion to Lemma 5.

Lemma 6. *If $\ell \to r$ has the form (5) then the following are equivalent:*

1. *$\ell_\beta \ell_\beta$ is a suffix of r_α,*
2. *$m = 0$ and $y = y'\alpha wx$ for some $y' \in \Sigma^+$.*

Proof. Obviously (2) implies (1). Next we show the converse by contradiction. Let $\ell \to r$ have the form (5) and let $\ell_\beta\ell_\beta$ be a suffix of r_α. Define $v \in \Sigma^*$ by $r_\alpha = v\ell_\beta\ell_\beta$. If $m > 0$ then y is a suffix of $y\alpha w$ and then $y\alpha w \in \mathrm{OVL}(\ell, r)$, a contradiction. With $m > 0$, the string αwx is a suffix of $\alpha wwxy$. If y is a suffix of αwx then $y\alpha w \in \mathrm{OVL}(\ell, r)$, a contradiction. So αwx is a proper suffix of y, i.e., there is $y' \in \Sigma^+$ such that $y = y'\alpha wx$. $\quad \square$

Example 1. The one-rule SRS

$$bcabcbcbc \to abcbcbccabcbcb$$

has a loop of length 3:

$$\underline{bcabcbcbc}cabcbcbc \to$$
$$abcbcbccabcbc\underline{bcabcbcbc} \to$$
$$abcbcbccabcbc\underline{bcabcbcbc}ccabcbcb \to$$
$$abcbcbcca\,\boxed{bcabcbcbccabcbcbc}\,abcbcb.$$

Redexes are underlined. The re-occurrence of the start string is indicated by a box. This example provides the smallest non-terminating witness ($|r| = 14$) of Lemma 4.

6   The Terminating Case

For this section let us assume a rule of the form (5) where $\ell_\beta \ell_\beta$ is not a suffix of r_α. We are going to reduce termination of such a rule to termination of an SRS R over a different alphabet. Termination of R will be easy to prove.

Define r_δ, $r_{\beta,\alpha}$, and $r_{\beta,\delta}$ by

$$r = r_\delta \ell_\beta \alpha, \qquad r = \beta r_{\beta,\alpha} \alpha, \qquad r = \beta r_{\beta,\delta} \ell_\beta \alpha.$$

These definitions are sound as witnessed by

$$\beta = y\alpha wx\alpha w,$$
$$\ell_\beta = \alpha wx(y\alpha wx)^m,$$
$$r_\delta = y\alpha wx\alpha wwxy,$$
$$r_{\beta,\alpha} = wx(y\alpha wx)^{m+1},$$
$$r_{\beta,\delta} = wxy.$$

Lemma 7. *Let $\ell \to r$ have the form (5). Then the following rewrite steps exist:*

$$r_\alpha r \to_{\ell \to r} r_\delta rr_\beta, \qquad r_\alpha r_\alpha \to_{\ell \to r} r_\delta rr_{\beta,\alpha}, \qquad r_\alpha r_\delta \to_{\ell \to r} r_\delta rr_{\beta,\delta},$$
$$r_{\beta,\alpha} r \to_{\ell \to r} r_{\beta,\delta} rr_\beta, \qquad r_{\beta,\alpha} r_\alpha \to_{\ell \to r} r_{\beta,\delta} rr_{\beta,\alpha}, \qquad r_{\beta,\alpha} r_\delta \to_{\ell \to r} r_{\beta,\delta} rr_{\beta,\delta}.$$

Proof. Routine. □

Lemma 8. *Let $\ell \to r$ have the form (5) and let $\ell_\beta \ell_\beta$ not be a suffix of r_α. Then ℓ is not a factor of any of the following: (1) $r_\delta^i r$, (2) rr_β, (3) $rr_{\beta,\delta} r_\delta^i r$ for any $i \geq 0$.*

Proof. For Claim 1, let $i \geq 1$ be least such that ℓ is a factor of $r_\delta^i r$. Then ℓ_β is a suffix of r_δ^i because β is the only overlap of ℓ with r. Since $\ell_\beta \ell_\beta$ is not a suffix of $r_\alpha = r_\delta \ell_\beta$, ℓ_β is not a suffix of y. Hence y is a proper suffix of ℓ_β and so of $y\alpha wx$. So $y\alpha w \in \mathrm{OVL}(\ell, r)$, a contradiction.

For Claim 2, let ℓ be a factor of rr_β. Because α is the only overlap between r and ℓ, we have $|\ell_\alpha| \leq |r_\beta|$, a contradiction.

For Claim 3 assume that ℓ is a factor of $rr_{\beta,\delta} r_\delta^i r$ for some $i \geq 0$. By Claims 1 and 2, ℓ is neither a factor of $r_{\beta,\delta} r_\delta^i r$ nor of $rr_{\beta,\delta}$; so ℓ is of the form $\ell' r_{\beta,\delta} r_\delta^j \ell''$ for some $0 \leq j \leq i$ and some non-empty suffix ℓ' of r and some non-empty prefix ℓ'' of r. Thus ℓ is of the form $\alpha r_{\beta,\delta} r_\delta^j \beta$. If $j = 0$ then $wx(y\alpha wx)^m = wxy$ which contradicts $y, \alpha \in \Sigma^+$. So $j > 0$ and y is a proper suffix of ℓ_β. We get a contradiction by $y\alpha w \in \mathrm{OVL}(\ell, r)$. □

The six-rule SRS R over $\Omega = \{a, b, c, d, e, f\}$ is defined as follows:

$$R = \{g'g'' \to h'fh'' \mid (g', h') \in \{(a, d), (c, e)\},$$
$$(g'', h'') \in \{(a, c), (d, e), (f, b)\}\}$$

Define the weight $wt^*(x)$ of a string x by $wt(a) = wt(c) = 3$, $wt(b) = wt(d) = wt(e) = wt(f) = 1$, and $wt^*(x_1 \ldots x_k) = \sum_{i=1}^k wt(x_i)$. Then R terminates by

$$wt^*(u) - wt^*(v) = (wt(g') - wt(h')) - wt(f) + (wt(g'') - wt(h''))$$
$$= 2 - 1 + 0 > 0$$

for all rewrite steps $u \to_R v$.

Let the string homomorphism $\phi : \Omega^* \to \Sigma^*$ be defined by $\phi(a) = r_\alpha, \phi(b) = r_\beta, \phi(c) = r_{\beta,\alpha}, \phi(d) = r_\delta, \phi(e) = r_{\beta,\delta}, \phi(f) = r$. By Lemma 7, $u \to_R v$ implies $\phi(u) \to_{\ell \to r} \phi(v)$ for all $u, v \in \Omega^*$. However we will need the converse direction. To this end let us define the regular language $\mathcal{M}$ by

$$\mathcal{M} = (a + d(fe)^* + d(fe)^* fc)^* (af + d(fe)^* f(cf + b)) + f.$$

Let $\phi[\mathcal{M}]$ denote the set $\{\phi(u) \mid u \in \mathcal{M}\}$. We are going to show that $\{\ell \to r\}$-reduction steps on $\phi[\mathcal{M}]$ can be simulated by R-reduction steps. First we show that R-reduction preserves $\phi[\mathcal{M}]$.

Lemma 9. *If $u \in \mathcal{M}$ and $u \to_R v$ then $v \in \mathcal{M}$.*

Proof. Let $(g', h') \in \{(a, d), (c, e)\}$ and $(g'', h'') \in \{(a, c), (d, e), (f, b)\}$. Let $u = u'g'g''u'' \in \mathcal{M}$ and $v = u'h'fh''u''$. Then we derive

$$u' \in (a + d(fe)^* + d(fe)^* fc)^* \qquad \text{if } g' = a,$$
$$u' \in (a + d(fe)^* + d(fe)^* fc)^* d(fe)^* f \qquad \text{if } g' = c.$$

Case 1: $g'' = a$. If $g' = a$ then $u'' \in \mathcal{M}$ whence $v = u'dfcu'' \in \mathcal{M}$. If $g' = c$ then $u'' = f$ whence $v = u'efcu'' \in \mathcal{M}$.

Case 2: $g'' = d$. Then

$$u'' \in ((fe)^* + (fe)^* fc)(a + d(fe)^* + d(fe)^* fc)^* (af + d(fe)^* f(cf + b))$$
$$+ (fe)^* f(cf + b).$$

If $g' = a$ then $v = u'dfeu'' \in \mathcal{M}$. If $g' = c$ then $v = u'efeu'' \in \mathcal{M}$.

Case 3: $g'' = f$. If $g' = a$ then u'' is the empty string and $v = u'dfbu'' \in \mathcal{M}$. If $g' = c$ then u'' is again the empty string and $v = u'efbu'' \in \mathcal{M}$. $\square$

Next we derive a few properties of $u \in \mathcal{M}$ if $\phi(u)$ contains a factor ℓ.

Lemma 10. *Let $u \in \mathcal{M}$ and $s', s'' \in \Sigma^*$. If $\phi(u) = s'\ell s''$ then $u = u'g'g''u''$, $|\phi(u')| \le |s'| < |\phi(u'g')|$, $|\phi(u'')| \le |s''| < |\phi(g''u'')|$ for some $u', u'' \in \Omega^*$, $g' \in \{a, c\}$, $g'' \in \{a, d, f\}$.*

Proof. Suppose that $u \in \mathcal{M}$, $s', s'' \in \Sigma^*$, and $\phi(u) = s'\ell s''$. Let $u' \in \Omega^*$ be the longest prefix of u such that $|\phi(u')| \le |s'|$. Let $u'' \in \Omega^*$ be the longest suffix of u such that $|\phi(u'')| \le |s''|$. By $|\phi(u)| > |\phi(u'u'')|$ there is $v \in \Sigma^+$ such that $u = u'vu''$. Define $t', t'' \in \Sigma^*$ by $s' = \phi(u')t'$ and $s'' = t''\phi(u'')$. Then

$$\phi(u) = \phi(u')\phi(v)\phi(u'') = \phi(u')t'\ell t''\phi(u''),$$

whence $\phi(v) = t'\ell t''$. The case $|v| = 1$ implies that ℓ is a factor of r, so $|v| \geq 2$. We distinguish cases on the form of v.

Case 1: $v \in \Omega^*(a+c)(a+d+f)\Omega^*$. Let $g' \in \{a, c\}$, $g'' \in \{a, d, f\}$, $v', v'' \in \Omega^*$, and let $v = v'g'g''v''$. We further distinguish cases whether v', v'' are empty strings or not.

Case 1.1: $|v'| = |v''| = 0$. Then $v = g'g''$. By definition of u' we get $|t'| < |\phi(g')|$. By definition of u'' we get $|t''| < |\phi(g'')|$. The claim follows.

Case 1.2: $|v'| = 0$, $|v''| > 0$. By $|r| > |\ell|$ and $|r_\alpha| > |\ell|$ and $u \in \mathcal{M}$ we get $v \in (a+c)d^+(a+d+f)$. Let $v = v_0g_0$ for some $v_0 \in (a+c)d^+$, and $g_0 \in \{a, d, f\}$. Then there are $\ell', \ell'' \in \Sigma^+$ such that $\ell = \ell'\ell''$, $\phi(v_0) = t'\ell'$, and $\phi(g_0) = \ell''t''$. Since $\phi(g_0)$ is a prefix of r, we obtain $\ell'' \in \mathrm{OVL}(\ell, r)$, so $\ell'' = \beta$ and $\ell' = \ell_\beta$. By definition of v_0, now $\phi(d) = r_\delta = yawxawwxy$ is a suffix of $\ell_\beta = \alpha wx(yawx)^m$. So $m > 0$ and y is a suffix of $yawx$. Then $yaw \in \mathrm{OVL}(\ell, r)$, a contradiction.

Case 1.3: $|v'| > 0$, $|v''| = 0$. Let $v = v_0g_0$ for some $v_0 \in \Omega^+(a+c)$, and $g_0 \in \{a, d, f\}$. Then there are $\ell', \ell'' \in \Sigma^+$ such that $\ell = \ell'\ell''$, $\phi(v_0) = t'\ell'$, and $\phi(g_0) = \ell''t''$. Since $\phi(g_0)$ is a prefix of r, we obtain $\ell'' \in \mathrm{OVL}(\ell, r)$, so $\ell'' = \beta$ and $\ell' = \ell_\beta$. Then

$$|\ell_\beta| = |\phi(v_0)| > |\phi(c)| = |r_{\beta,\alpha}| > |\ell_\beta|,$$

a contradiction.

Case 1.4: $|v'|, |v''| > 0$. By $|r| > |\ell|$ and $|r_\alpha| > |\ell|$ and $u \in \mathcal{M}$ we get $g' = c$ and $g'' = d$. So $\phi(cd) = r_{\beta,\alpha}r_\delta$ is a factor of ℓ, whence $|r_{\beta,\alpha}r_\delta| \leq |\ell|$, a contradiction.

Case 2: $v \in \Omega^+ \setminus \Omega^*(a+c)(a+d+f)\Omega^*$. Define the set of fragments $\mathcal{F}(z)$ of a string $z \in \Omega^*$ as follows. If $z \in (\Omega \setminus \{f\})^*$ then $\mathcal{F}(z) = \{z\}$. Else $z = z_0fz_1 \ldots fz_n$ for some $n \geq 1$ and unique $z_0, \ldots, z_n \in (\Omega \setminus \{f\})^*$; then

$$\mathcal{F}(z) = \{z_0f, fz_1f, \ldots, fz_{n-1}f, fz_n\}.$$

From $u \in \mathcal{M}$ then

$$\mathcal{F}(u) \in (a+d)^*f + f(e+c)(a+d)^*f + fb.$$

Because $|r| > |\ell|$, and ℓ is not a factor of r, we obtain $v \in \mathcal{F}(u)$. So

$$v \in \mathcal{F}(u) \setminus \Omega^*(a+c)(a+d+f)\Omega^* = d^*f + fed^*f + fb.$$

By Lemma 8, $\phi(v)$ has no factor ℓ, so this case is void. $\qquad\square$

Now we are ready to state the simulation lemma.

Lemma 11. *Let $u \in \mathcal{M}$ and $t \in \Sigma^*$. If $\phi(u) \to_{\ell \to r} t$ then $\phi(v) = t$ and $u \to_R v$ for some $v \in \mathcal{M}$.*

Proof. Let $u \in \mathcal{M}$ and $s', s'', t \in \Sigma^*$, and let $\phi(u) = s'\ell s''$ and $t = s'rs''$. By Lemma 10 there are $u', u'' \in \Omega^*$, $g' \in \{a, c\}$, $g'' \in \{a, d, f\}$ such that $u = u'g'g''u''$ and $|\phi(u')| \leq |s'| < |\phi(u'g')|$ and $|\phi(u'')| \leq |s''| < |\phi(g''u'')|$. Define $t', t'' \in \Sigma^*$ by $s' = \phi(u')t'$ and $s'' = t''\phi(u'')$. Then

$$\phi(u) = \phi(u')\phi(g')\phi(g'')\phi(u'') = \phi(u')t'\ell t''\phi(u''),$$

so $\phi(g')\phi(g'') = t'\ell t''$. By $|s''| < |\phi(g''u'')|$ we get $|t''| < |\phi(g'')|$. Define $\ell'' \in \Sigma^+$ by $\phi(g'') = \ell''t''$. Define $\ell' \in \Sigma^*$ by $\ell = \ell'\ell''$. So $\phi(g') = t'\ell'$. By $|s'| < |\phi(u'g')|$ we get $|t'| < |\phi(g')|$ and so $\ell' \in \Sigma^+$.

Since $\phi(g'')$ is a prefix of r, we obtain $\ell'' \in \mathrm{OVL}(\ell, r)$, so $\ell'' = \beta$ and $\ell' = \ell_\beta$. Define $h', h'' \in \Omega$ by

$$h' = \begin{cases} d & \text{if } g' = a, \\ e & \text{if } g' = c, \end{cases} \qquad h'' = \begin{cases} c & \text{if } g'' = a, \\ e & \text{if } g'' = d, \\ b & \text{if } g'' = f. \end{cases}$$

Then $g'g'' \to h'fh''$ is in R, and moreover $\phi(g') = \phi(h')\ell_\beta = t'\ell_\beta$ and $\phi(g'') = \beta\phi(h'') = \beta t''$. So $t' = \phi(h')$ and $t'' = \phi(h'')$ and so

$$t = s'rs'' = \phi(u')\phi(h')\phi(f)\phi(h'')\phi(u'') = \phi(v)$$

for $v = u'h'fh''u''$. So $u \to_R v$. By Lemma 9 we get $v \in \mathcal{M}$. $\qquad\square$

We are about to prove termination of $\ell \to r$ by a reduction to termination of R. For this purpose we still need $\{\ell \to r\}$-reductions that start in $\phi[\mathcal{M}]$. Such reductions are provided by forward closures [9,1] as we will show next. We use the following characterization of forward closures by Hermann.

Definition 4 ([5, Corollaire 2.16]). *The set of forward closures of a string rewriting rule $\ell \to r$ over alphabet Σ is the least set $\mathrm{FC}(\ell \to r)$ of $\ell \to r$-reductions such that*

fc1. $(\ell \to r) \in \mathrm{FC}(\ell \to r)$,
fc2. *if* $(s_1 \to^+ t_1'\ell') \in \mathrm{FC}(\ell \to r)$ *and* $\ell = \ell'\ell''$ *for some* $\ell', \ell'' \in \Sigma^+$ *then* $(s_1\ell'' \to^+ t_1'\ell'\ell'' \to^+ t_1'r) \in \mathrm{FC}(\ell \to r)$,
fc3. *if* $(s_1 \to^+ t_1'\ell t_1'') \in \mathrm{FC}(\ell \to r)$ *then* $(s_1 \to^+ t_1'\ell t_1'' \to^+ t_1'r t_1'') \in \mathrm{FC}(\ell \to r)$.

Lemma 12. *Every forward closure of a rule $\ell \to r$ of the form (5) where $\ell_\beta\ell_\beta$ is not a suffix of r_α, has a right hand side in $\phi[\mathcal{M}]$.*

Proof. By induction along the definition of forward closure. Let $(s \to^+ t) \in \mathrm{FC}(\ell \to r)$. In Case (fc1) we have $t = r = \phi(f)$. In Case (fc3) the claim follows from Lemma 11. This leaves to prove Case (fc2).

Suppose that $s = s_1\ell''$, $t = t_1'r$, $(s_1 \to^+ t_1'\ell') \in \mathrm{FC}(\ell \to r)$, and $\ell = \ell'\ell''$ for some $\ell', \ell'' \in \Sigma^+$. By inductive hypothesis, there is $u \in \mathcal{M}$ such that $t_1'\ell' = \phi(u)$. By definition of $\mathcal{M}$, u has suffix f or fb.

Case 1: u has suffix fb. Define $g' \in \Omega^*$ by $u = g'fb$. Then

$$g' \in (a + d(fe)^* + d(fe)^*fc)d(fe)^*$$

by definition of $\mathcal{M}$. We distinguish cases whether $|\ell'| > |r_\beta|$ or not.

Case 1.1: $|\ell'| > |r_\beta|$. The string $t_1'\ell'$ has suffix $\phi(fb) = rr_\beta$. By $|\ell| < |r|$ and $|\ell'| > |r_\beta|$ we get $\ell' = zr_\beta$ for some non-empty suffix z of r. Now $z \in \mathrm{OVL}(r, \ell)$, so $z = \alpha$. So $t_1'\ell' = \phi(g')rr_\beta = \phi(g')r_\alpha\ell'$, whence $t_1' = \phi(g')r_\alpha = \phi(g'a)$. So $t_1'r = \phi(g'a)r = \phi(g'af)$ for $g'af \in \mathcal{M}$.

Case 1.2: $|\ell'| \leq |r_\beta|$. Then ℓ' is a suffix of r_β and so of r. So $\ell' \in \mathrm{OVL}(r, \ell)$ whence $\ell' = \alpha$. So $t_1'\ell' = \phi(g'f)r_\beta = \phi(g'f)r_{\beta,\alpha}\ell'$, whence $t_1' = \phi(g'f)r_{\beta,\alpha} = \phi(g'fc)$. So $t_1'r = \phi(g'fc)r = \phi(g'fcf)$ for $g'fcf \in \mathcal{M}$.

Case 2: u has suffix f. Define $g' \in \Omega^*$ by $u = g'f$. Then

$$g' \in (a + d(fe)^* + d(fe)^*fc)^*$$

by definition of $\mathcal{M}$. By $|\ell| < |r|$ we get that $\ell' \in \mathrm{OVL}(r, \ell)$, whence $\ell' = \alpha$. So $t_1'\ell' = \phi(g'f) = \phi(g')r = \phi(g')r_\alpha\ell'$, whence $t_1' = \phi(g')r_\alpha = \phi(g'a)$. So $t_1'r = \phi(g'a)r = \phi(g'af)$ for $g'af \in \mathcal{M}$.   □

Lemma 13. *A rule $\ell \to r$ of the form (5) terminates if $\ell_\beta\ell_\beta$ is not a suffix of r_α.*

Proof. If $\ell \to r$ is non-terminating then there is an infinite rewriting sequence $s_1 \to_{\ell \to r} s_2 \to_{\ell \to r} \dots$ starting from a right hand side of a forward closure [1]. By Lemma 12 $s_1 \in \phi[\mathcal{M}]$, i.e., there is $u_1 \in \mathcal{M}$ such that $\phi(u_1) = s_1$. By induction on i, using Lemma 11, one easily proves that for every i there is an $u_{i+1} \in \mathcal{M}$ such that both $u_i \to_R u_{i+1}$ and $\phi(u_{i+1}) = s_{i+1}$. Hence we get an infinite reduction sequence $u_1 \to_R u_2 \to_R \dots$. Contradiction to termination of R.   □

Example 2. For every $m \geq 0$, the one-rule SRS

$$bc(abc)^{m+1}bc \to abcbcc(abc)^{m+1}b$$

is terminating by Lemma 13. With $m = 0$ we get the smallest terminating witness ($|r| = 10$) of Lemma 4.

This example also proves that Kurth's [7] Criterion F is incomplete, for Criterion F applies only to the left barren or right barren cases [3, Theorem 6.31].

We note moreover that the maximal length of a derivation starting with $s \in \Sigma^*$ is linear in $|s|$. This is a direct consequence of the decreasing weight associated with a step $u \to_R v$.

7   The Main Theorem

Now we have all material together to prove our claim.

Theorem 6. *Let $|\mathrm{OVL}(r, \ell)| = |\mathrm{OVL}(\ell, r)| = 1$. Then $\{\ell \to r\}$ terminates if and only if it has no loop of lengths 1, 2, or 3.*

Proof. Let $\mathrm{OVL}(r, \ell) = \{\alpha\}$ and $\mathrm{OVL}(\ell, r) = \{\beta\}$. If ℓ is a factor of r then $\{\ell \to r\}$ has a loop of length 1 [7]. Else if $|\ell| \geq |r|$ then $\{\ell \to r\}$ terminates. If $\ell \to r$ is left barren or right barren then $\{\ell \to r\}$ terminates. So suppose that ℓ

is not a factor of r; that $|\ell| < |r|$; and that $\ell \to r$ is neither left barren nor right barren. We distinguish cases:

Case 1: $\ell \to r$ is neither left s-barren nor right s-barren. Then $r = r'\ell_\beta \alpha$ and $r = \beta\ell_\alpha r''$ for some strings r', r''. There is a loop of length 2:

$$\ell\ell_\alpha \to r\ell_\alpha = r'\ell_\beta\alpha\ell_\alpha = r'\ell_\beta\ell \to r'\ell_\beta r = r'\ell_\beta\beta\ell_\alpha r'' = r'\ell\ell_\alpha r''.$$

Case 2: $\ell \to r$ is left s-barren but not right s-barren. Then $\ell \to r$ has the form (5). If $\ell_\beta\ell_\beta$ is a suffix of r_α then $\{\ell \to r\}$ has a loop of length 3 by Lemma 5. Else $\{\ell \to r\}$ terminates by Lemma 13.

Case 3: $\ell \to r$ is not left s-barren but right s-barren. This case is symmetric to Case 2: We have a loop of length 3 if $\ell_\alpha\ell_\alpha$ is a prefix of r_β, otherwise termination.

Case 4: $\ell \to r$ is both left s-barren and right s-barren. Then Lemma 1 and its dual apply, showing $|\beta| > |\alpha|$ and $|\alpha| > |\beta|$, a contradiction. So this case does not exist. This finishes the proof.   □

Since the left barren, right barren, left s-barren, right s-barren properties are decidable, one may conclude:

Corollary 1. *Termination is decidable for one-rule SRSs $\{\ell \to r\}$ that satisfy $|\operatorname{OVL}(r, \ell)| = |\operatorname{OVL}(\ell, r)| = 1$.*

Corollary 1 also follows directly from Theorem 6 by the decidability of the existence of loops of lengths 1, 2, or 3 for one-rule SRSs [8].

At the end of the previous section we noted that terminating one-rule SRSs that are left s-barren but neither left barren nor right s-barren have linear derivation lengths. So terminating one-rule SRSs $\{\ell \to r\}$ that satisfy $|\operatorname{OVL}(r, \ell)| = |\operatorname{OVL}(\ell, r)| = 1$ have linear derivation lengths, unless they are left barren or right barren. A right barren rule with one pair of overlaps may have exponential derivation lenghts: $ba \to aab$ admits derivations $b^n a \to^{2^n - 1} a^{2^n} b^n$.

8   Conclusion

We proved that termination of one-rule SRSs with one pair of overlaps is equivalent to the non-existence of loops of length less than or equal to 3. Thus we showed that termination is decidable for one-rule SRSs with one pair of overlaps. A surprising observation in this investigation was the emergence of non-tame rules, some admitting loops of length 3, and some terminating. Such rules were not covered by the two precursor results by Kurth and by Shikishima-Tsuji et al.

Acknowledgements

Robert McNaughton gave me an appreciation of the intricacy of the problem.

References

1. N. DERSHOWITZ, *Termination of linear rewriting systems*, in Proc. 8th Int. Coll. Automata, Languages and Programming, LNCS 115, Springer, 1981, pp. 448–458.

2. A. GESER, *Decidability of termination of grid string rewriting rules*, SIAM J. Comput., 31 (2002), pp. 1156–1168.

3. ——, *Is termination decidable for string rewriting with only one rule?*, habilitation thesis, Wilhelm-Schickard-Institut, Universität Tübingen, Germany, Jan. 2002. 201 pages.

4. ——, *Loops of superexponential lengths in one-rule string rewriting*, in Proc. 13th Int. Conf. Rewriting Techniques and Applications, S. Tison, ed., LNCS 2378, Springer, 2002, pp. 267–280.

5. M. HERMANN, *Divergence des systèmes de réécriture et schématisation des ensembles infinis de termes*, habilitation, Université de Nancy, France, Mar. 1994.

6. Y. KOBAYASHI, M. KATSURA, AND K. SHIKISHIMA-TSUJI, *Termination and derivational complexity of confluent one-rule string rewriting systems*, Theoret. Comput. Sci., 262 (2001), pp. 583–632.

7. W. KURTH, *Termination und Konfluenz von Semi-Thue-Systemen mit nur einer Regel*, dissertation, Technische Universität Clausthal, Germany, 1990.

8. ——, *One-rule semi-Thue systems with loops of length one, two, or three*, RAIRO Inform. Théor., 30 (1995), pp. 415–429.

9. D. S. LANKFORD AND D. R. MUSSER, *A finite termination criterion*, tech. rep., Information Sciences Institute, Univ. of Southern California, Marina-del-Rey, CA, 1978.

10. R. MCNAUGHTON, *The uniform halting problem for one-rule Semi-Thue Systems*, Tech. Rep. 94-18, Dept. of Computer Science, Rensselaer Polytechnic Institute, Troy, NY, Aug. 1994. See also "Correction to 'The Uniform Halting Problem for One-rule Semi-Thue Systems'", unpublished paper, Aug., 1996.

11. ——, *Well-behaved derivations in one-rule Semi-Thue Systems*, Tech. Rep. 95-15, Dept. of Computer Science, Rensselaer Polytechnic Institute, Troy, NY, Nov. 1995. See also "Correction by the author to 'Well-behaved derivations in one-rule Semi-Thue Systems'", unpublished paper, July, 1996.

12. ——, *Semi-Thue Systems with an Inhibitor*, J. Automated Reasoning, 26 (1997), pp. 409–431.

13. W. MOCZYDŁOWSKI, JR AND A. GESER, *Termination of single-threaded one-rule Semi-Thue systems*, Tech. Rep. TR 02-08 (273), Warsaw University, Dec. 2002. Available electronically at `research.nianet.org/~geser/papers/single.html`.

14. G. SÉNIZERGUES, *On the termination problem for one-rule Semi-Thue Systems*, in Proc. 7th Int. Conf. Rewriting Techniques and Applications, H. Ganzinger, ed., LNCS 1103, Springer, 1996, pp. 302–316.

15. K. SHIKISHIMA-TSUJI, M. KATSURA, AND Y. KOBAYASHI, *On termination of confluent one-rule string rewriting systems*, Inform. Process. Lett., 61 (1997), pp. 91–96.

16. C. WRATHALL, *Confluence of one-rule Thue systems*, in Word Equations and Related Topics, K. U. Schulz, ed., LNCS 572, Springer, 1992.

17. H. ZANTEMA AND A. GESER, *A complete characterization of termination of $0^p 1^q \to 1^r 0^s$*, Applicable Algebra in Engineering, Communication, and Computing, 11 (2000), pp. 1–25.

Environments for Term Rewriting Engines for Free!

Mark van den Brand[1,3], Pierre-Etienne Moreau[2], and Jurgen Vinju[1]

[1] CWI, Kruislaan 413,
NL-1098 SJ Amterdam, The Netherlands
{Mark.van.den.Brand,Jurgen.Vinju}@cwi.nl
[2] LORIA-INRIA, 615, rue du Jardin Botanique,
BP 101, 54602 Villers-lès-Nancy Cedex France
Pierre-Etienne.Moreau@loria.fr
[3] Vrije Universiteit, De Boelelaan 1081A,
NL-1081 HV Amsterdam, The Netherlands

Abstract. Term rewriting can only be applied if practical implementations of term rewriting engines exist. New rewriting engines are designed and implemented either to experiment with new (theoretical) results or to be able to tackle new application areas. In this paper we present the Meta-Environment: an environment for rapidly implementing the syntax and semantics of term rewriting based formalisms. We provide not only the basic building blocks, but complete interactive programming environments that only need to be instantiated by the details of a new formalism.

1 Introduction

Term rewriting can only be applied if practical implementations of term rewriting engines exist. New rewriting engines are designed and implemented either to experiment with new (theoretical) results or to be able to tackle new application areas, e.g., protocol verification, software renovation, etc. However, rewrite engines alone are not enough to implement real applications.

An analysis of existing applications of term rewriting, e.g. facilitated by formalisms like ASF+SDF [11], ELAN [3], MAUDE [9], RRL [14], STRATEGO [18], TXL [10], reveals the following four required aspects:

- a *formalism* that can be executed by a rewriting engine.
- *parsers* to implement the syntax of the formalism and the terms.
- a *rewriting engine* to implement the semantics of the formalism.
- a *programming environment* for supporting user-interaction.

A formalism introduces the syntactic notions that correspond to the operational semantics of the rewriting engine. This allows the user to write readable specifications. The parsers provide the connection from the formalism to the rewriting engine via abstract syntax trees. The programming environment can be either a set of practical command line tools, an integrated system with a graphical

R. Nieuwenhuis (Ed.): RTA 2003, LNCS 2706, pp. 424–435, 2003.

user-interface, or some combination. It offers a user-interface tailored towards the formalism for interacting with the rewriting engine. For a detailed overview of rewriting-based systems we refer to [12].

Implementing the above four entities is usually a major research and software engineering effort, even if we target only small but meaningful examples. It is a long path from a description of a term rewriting engine, via language design for the corresponding formalism, to a usable programming environment.

In this paper we present the Meta-Environment: *An open architecture of tools, libraries, user-interfaces and code generators targeted to the design and implementation of term rewriting environments.*

We show that by using the Meta-Environment a mature programming environment for a new term rewriting formalism can be obtained in a few steps. Our approach is based on well-known software engineering concepts: standardization (of architecture and exchange format), software reuse (component based development), source code generation and parameterization.

1.1   Requirements

Real-world examples of term rewriting systems are to be found in many areas, including the following ([12]): rewriting workbenches, computer algebra, symbolic computation, functional programming, definition of programming languages, theorem proving, and generation, analysis, and transformation of programs.

These application areas are quite different, which explains the existence of several formalisms each tailored for a certain application domain. Each area influences the design and implementation of a term rewriting environment in several ways. We identify the following common requirements:

- *Openness.* Collaboration with unforseen components is often needed. It asks for an open architecture to facilitate communication between the environment, the rewriting engine, and foreign tools.
- *Readable syntax.* Syntax is an important design issue for term rewriting formalisms. Although conceptually syntax might be a minor detail, a formalism that has no practical and readable syntax is not usable.
- *Scalability.* Most real-world examples lead to big specifications or big terms. Scalability means that the implementation is capable of handling such problems using a moderate amount of resources.
- *Graphical User Interface.* A GUI with editors is needed. It automates as much of the browsing, editing and testing, of specifications as possible.

The above four issues offer no deep conceptual challenges, but still they stand for a considerable design and engineering effort. We offer immediately usable solutions concerning each of those issues in this paper. This paves the way for the application of new experiments concerning term rewriting that would otherwise have cost months to implement. In that sense, this paper contributes to the promotion and the development of rewriting techniques and their applications.

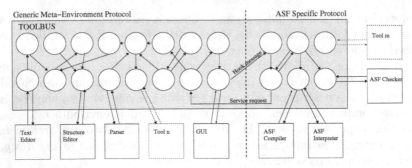

Fig. 1. A complete environment consisting of a generic part and an ASF specific part

2   Architecture for an Open Environment

In Section 3 we discuss the specific components of the Meta-Environment that can be used to implement a new term rewriting environment. An example environment is implemented in Section 4. Here we discuss the general architecture of the Meta-Environment.

The main issue is to separate computation from communication. This separation is achieved by means of a software coordination architecture and a generic data exchange format. An environment is obtained by plugging in the appropriate components into this architecture.

ToolBus. To prevent entangling of coordination with computation in components we introduce a software coordination architecture, the ToolBus [1]. It is a programmable software bus based on Process Algebra. Coordination is expressed by a formal description of the cooperation protocol between components while computation is expressed inside the components that may be written in any language. Figure 1 visualizes a ToolBus application (to be discussed below).

Separating computation from communication means that each of these components is made as *independent* as possible from the others. Each component provides a certain service to the other components via the software bus. They interact with each other using messages. The organization of this interaction is fully described using a script that corresponds to a collection of process algebra expressions.

ATERMS. Coordination protocol and components have to share data. We use ATERMS [5] for this purpose. These are normal prefix terms with optional annotations added to each node. The annotations are used to store tool-specific information such as text coordinates or proof obligations. All data that is communicated via the ToolBus is encoded as ATERMS. ATERMS are comparable to XML, both are generic data representations. Although there are tools for conversions between these formats, we prefer ATERMS for efficiency reasons. They can be linearized using either a readable representation or a very dense binary encoding.

ATERMS can not only be used as a generic data exchange format but also to implement an efficient term data structure in rewriting engines. The ATERM library offers a complete programming interface to the term data structure. It is used to implement term rewriting interpreters or run-time support for compiled rewriting systems. The following three properties of the ATERM library are essential for term rewriting:

- Little memory usage per node.
- Maximal sub-term sharing.
- Automatic garbage collection.

Maximal sharing has proven to be a very good method for dealing with large amounts of terms during term rewriting [4,18]. It implies that term equality reduces to *pointer equality*. Automatic garbage collection is a very practical feature that significantly reduces the effort of designing a new rewriting engine or compiler.

Meta-Environment Protocol. The ToolBus and ATERMS are more widely applicable than just for term rewriting environments. To instantiate this generic architecture, the Meta-Environment ToolBus scripts implement a coordination protocol between its components. Together with the tools, libraries and program generators this protocol implements the basic functionality of an interactive environment.

The Meta-Environment protocol makes no assumptions about the rewriting engine and its coordination with other tools. In order to make a complete term rewriting environment we must complement the generic protocol with specific coordination for every new term rewriting formalism.

For example, the architecture of the ASF+SDF Meta-Environment is shown in Figure 1. The ToolBus executes the generic Meta-Environment protocol, depicted by the circles in the left-hand side of the picture. It communicates with external tools, depicted by squares. The right-hand side of the picture shows a specific extension of the Meta-Environment protocol, in this example it is designed for the ASF+SDF rewriting engines. It can be replaced by another protocol in order to construct an environment for a different rewriting formalism.

Hooks. The messages that can be received by the generic part are known in advance, simply because this part of the system is fixed. The reverse is not true, the generic part can make no assumptions about the other part of the system.

We identify messages that are sent from the generic part of the Meta-Environment to the rewriting formalism part as so-called *hooks*. Each instance of an environment should *at least* implement a receiver for each of these hooks. Table 1 shows the basic Meta-Environment hooks. The first four hooks instantiate parameters of the GUI and the editors. The last four hooks are events that need to be handled in a manner that is specific for the rewriting formalisms.

Table 1. The Meta-Environment hooks: the hooks that parameterize the GUI (top half), and events concerning the syntax and semantics of a term rewriting formalism (bottom half).

Hook	Description
`environment-name(Name)`	The main GUI window will display this name
`extensions(Sig, Sem, Term)`	Declares the extensions of different file types
`stdlib-path(Path)`	Sets the path to a standard library
`semantics-top-sort(Sort)`	Declares the top non-terminal of a specification
`rewrite(Sig, Sem, Term)`	Rewrite a term using a specification
`pre-parser-generation(Sig)`	Manipulate the syntax before parser generation
`rename-semantics(Sig,Binds,Sem)`	Implement module parameterization
`pre-rewrite(Sig,Spec)`	Actions to do before rewriting

3   Reusable Components

In this section we present reusable components to implement each aspect of the design of a term rewriting environment. The components are either tools, libraries or code generators. In Section 4 we explain how to use these components to create a programming environment using an example term rewriting formalism.

3.1   Generalized Parsing for a Readable Formalism

We offer generic and reusable parsing technology. An implementation of parsing usually consists of a syntax definition formalism, a parser generator, and run-time support for parsing. Additionally, automated parse tree construction and abstract syntax tree construction are offered. Table 2 shows a list of components related to parsing.

Syntax. SDF is a declarative syntax definition formalism used to define modular context-free grammars. Both lexical syntax and context-free syntax can be expressed in a uniform manner. Among other disambiguation constructs, notions for defining associativity and relative priority of operators are present.

Furthermore, SDF offers a simple but effective parameterization mechanism. A module may be parameterized by formal parameters attached to the module name. Using the import mechanism of SDF this parameter can be bound to an actual non-terminal.

Programs that deal with syntax definitions can use the SDF library. It provides a complete high-level programming interface for dealing with syntax definitions.

Concrete syntax. Recall that a syntax definition can serve as a many-sorted signature for a term rewriting system. The grammar productions in the definition are the operators of the signature and the non-terminals are the sorts.

Table 2. A list of the most frequently used components for SDF and ASFIX

Tool	Type		Description
pgen	SDF	→ Table	Generates a parse table from a syntax definition
sglr	Table×Str	→ AsFix	parses an input string and yields a derivation
implode	AsFix	→ ATerm	Maps a parse tree to an abstract term
posinfo	AsFix	→ AsFix	Adds line and column annotations
unparse	AsFix	→ Str	Yields the string that is derived by a parse tree

The number of non-terminals used in a grammar production is the arity of an operator.

Concrete syntax for any term rewriting formalism can be obtained by simply expressing both the fixed syntax of the formalism and the user defined syntax of the terms in SDF. A parameterized SDF module is used to describe the fixed syntax. This module can be imported for every sort in the user-defined syntax. An example is given in Section 4.

SGLR. To implement the SDF formalism, we use scannerless generalized LR parsing [7]. The result is a simple parsing architecture, but capable of handling any modular context-free grammar.

ASFIX. SGLR produces parse trees represented as ATERMS. This specific class of ATERMS is called ASFIX. Every ASFIX parse tree explains exactly, for each character of the input, which SDF productions were applied to obtain a derivation. A library is offered to be able to create components that deal with ASFIX.

3.2 Establishing the Connection between Parsing and Rewriting

The SDF library and the ASFIX library can be used to implement the connection between the parser and a rewriting engine. Furthermore, we can also automatically generate new libraries specifically tailored towards the rewriting formalism that we want to implement [13].

We use an SDF definition of the new formalism to generate C or Java libraries that hide the actual ATERM representation of a parse tree of a specification behind a typed interface. The generated interfaces offer: reading in parse trees, constructors, getters and setters for each operator of the new formalism. Apart from saving a lot of time, using these code generators has two major advantages:

– The term rewriter can be developed at a higher level of abstraction.
– Programming errors are prevented by the strictness of the generated types.

3.3 Graphical User Interface

MetaStudio. The Meta-Environment contains a user-interface written in Java (Figure 2). It can be used to browse modules. Every module has a number of actions that can be activated using the mouse. The actions are sent to the ToolBus. MetaStudio has parameters to configure the name of the environment, the typical file extensions, etc.

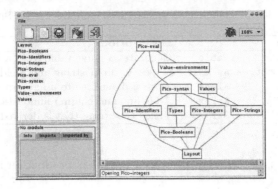

Fig. 2. GUI of the Meta-Environment displaying an import relation.

Editors. Editing of specifications and terms is done via XEmacs[1]. To implement structure-editing capabilities, XEmacs communicates with another component that holds a tree representation of the edited text.

Utilities. Among other utilities, we offer file I/O and in-memory storage that aid in the implementation of an interactive environment.

4   A New Environment in a Few Steps

In this section we show the steps involved in designing a new environment. We take a small imaginary formalism called "RHO" as a running example. It is a subset of the ρ-calculus [8], having first-class rewrite rules and an explicit application operator. The recipe to create a RHO environment is:

1. Instantiate the parameters of the GUI.
2. Define the syntax of RHO.
3. Write some small RHO specifications.
4. Implement and connect a RHO interpreter.
5. Connect other components.

1. Instantiate the parameters of the GUI: We start from a standard Tool-Bus script that implements default behavior for all the hooks of Table 1. We can immediately bind some of the configuration parameters of the GUI. In the case of RHO, we can instantiate two hooks: environment-name("The RHO Environment") and extensions(".sdf",".rho",".trm").

Using the RHO Meta-Environment is immediately possible. It offers the user three kinds of syntax-directed editors that can be used to complete the rest of the recipe: SDF editors, editors for the (yet unspecified) RHO formalism, and term editors.

---

[1] http://www.xemacs.org

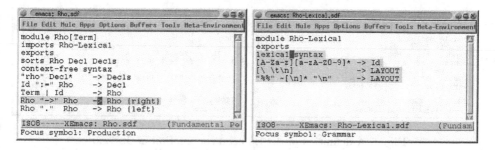

Fig. 3. A parameterized syntax definition of the formalism RHO.

2. Define the syntax of RHO: Figure 3 shows how the SDF editors can be used to define the syntax of RHO[2]. It has some predefined operators like assignment ("`:=`"), abstraction ("`->`") and application ("`.`"), but also concrete syntax for basic terms. So, a part of the syntax of a RHO term is user-defined. The parameterization mechanism of SDF is used to leave a placeholder (`Term`) at the location where user-defined terms are expected[3]. The `Term` parameter will later be instantiated when writing RHO specifications.

To make the syntax-directed editors for RHO files work properly we now have to instantiate the following hook: `semantic-top-sort("Decls")`. The parameter `"Decls"` refers to the top sort of the definition in Figure 3.

3. Write some small RHO *specifications:* We want to test the syntax of the new formalism. Figure 4 shows how two editors are used to specify the signature and some rules for the Boolean conjunction. Notice that the `Rho` module is imported explicitly by the `Booleans` module, here we instantiate the `Term` placeholder for the user-defined syntax. In Section 3 we explain how to add the imports implicitly.

We can now experiment with the syntax of RHO, define some more operators, basic data-types or start a standard library of RHO specifications. For the GUI, the location of the library should be instantiated using the `stdlib-path` hook.

4. Implement and connect a RHO *interpreter:* As mentioned in Section 2, the ATERM library is an efficient choice for a term implementation. Apart from that we present the details of the connection between a parsed specification and an implementation of the operational semantics of RHO. The algorithmic details of evaluating RHO are left to the reader, because that changes with each instance of a new formalism.

The **rewrite** hook connects a rewriting engine to the RHO environment: `rewrite(Syntax,Semantics,Term)` From this message we receive the information that is to be used by the rewriting engine. Note that this does not prohibit to request any other information from other components using extra messages.

---

[2] For the sake of brevity, Figure 3 does not show any priorities between operators.

[3] Having concrete syntax of terms is not obligatory.

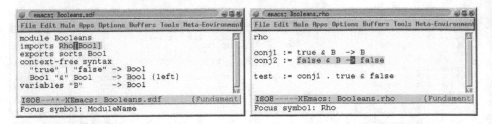

Fig. 4. A definition of the Boolean conjunction in SDF+RHO.

The input data that is received can be characterized as follows: `Syntax` is a list of all SDF modules (the parse-trees of `Rho.sdf` and `Booleans.sdf`). `Semantics` is a list of all RHO modules (the parse-tree of `Booleans.rho`). `Term` is the expression that is to be normalized (for example a parse-tree of a file called `test.trm`).

Two scenarios are to be considered: either a RHO engine already exists, or a new engine has to be designed from scratch. In the first case, the data-types of the Meta-Environment will be converted to the internal representation of the existing engine. In the second case, we can implement a new engine based on the data-types of the Meta-Environment directly. In both cases the three data-types of the Meta-Environment are important: SDF, ASFIX and ATERMS. The libraries and generators ensure that these cases can be specified on a high level of abstraction. We split the work into the signature and semantics parts of RHO.

Signature. To extract the needed information from the user-defined signature the SDF modules should be analyzed. The SDF library is the appropriate mechanism to inspect them in a straightforward manner.

Semantics. Due to having concrete syntax, the list of parse trees that represent RHO modules is not defined by a fixed signature. We can divide the set of operators in two categories:

- *A fixed* set of operators that correspond to the basic operators of the formalism. Each fixed operator represents a syntactical notion that should be given a meaning by the operational semantics. For RHO, assignment, abstraction, and application are examples of fixed operators.
- *Free* terms occur at the location where the syntax is user-defined. In RHO this is either as the right-hand side of an assignment or as a child of the abstraction or application operators.

There is a practical solution for dealing with each of these two classes of operators. Firstly, from an SDF definition for RHO we generate a library specifically tailored for RHO. This library is used to recognize the operators of RHO and extract information via an abstract typed interface. For example, one of the C function headers in this generated library is: `Rho getRuleLhs(Rho rule)`. A RHO interpreter can use it to retrieve the left-hand side of a rule.

Secondly, the free terms can be mapped to simple prefix ATERMS using the component `implode`, or they can be analyzed directly using the ASFIX library.

The choice depends on the application area. E.g., for source code renovation details such as white space and source code comments are important, but for symbolic computation this information might as well be thrown away in favor of efficiency.

In the case of an existing engine, the above interfaces are used to extract information before providing it to the engine. In the case of a new engine, the interfaces are used to directly specify the operational semantics of RHO.

5. *Connect other components:* There are some more hooks that can be instantiated in order to influence the behavior of the Meta-Environment. Also, the RHO part of the newly created environment might introduce other components besides the rewriting engine.

We give two examples here. The **pre-parser-generation** hook can be used to extend the user-defined syntax with imports of the RHO syntax automatically for each non-terminal. Secondly, the **pre-rewrite** hook hook can be used to connect an automatic verifier or prover like a Knuth-Bendix completion procedure.

Adding unanticipated tools is facilitated at three levels by the Meta-Environment. Firstly, an SDF production can have any attribute to make it possible to express special properties of operators for the benefit of new tools. An example: B ''&" B -> B { left, lpo-precedence(42) }. Secondly, any ATERM can be annotated with extra information without affecting the other components. For example: and(true,false){not-reduced}. Finally, all existing services of the Meta-Environment are available to the new tool. It can for example open a new editor to show its results using this message: new-editor(Contents)

5   Instantiations of the Meta-environment

We now introduce the four formalisms we have implemented so far using the above recipe. We focus on the discriminating aspects of each language.

ASF [11] is a term rewriting formalism based on leftmost-innermost normalization. The rules are called equations and are written in concrete syntax. Equations can have a list of conditions which must all evaluate to true before a reduction succeeds. The operational semantics of ASF also introduces *rewriting with layout* and *traversal functions* [6], operators that traverse the subterm they are applied to.

The above features correspond to the application areas of ASF. It is mainly used for design of the syntax and semantics of domain specific languages and analysis and transformation of programs in existing programming languages. From the application perspective ASF is an expressive form of first-order functional programming. The Meta-Environment serves as a programming environment for ASF.

ELAN [3] is based on rewrite rules too. It provides a strategy language, allowing to control the application of rules instead of leaving this to a fixed normalization strategy. Primitive strategies are labelled rewrite rules, which can be combined using strategy basic operators. New strategy operators can be expressed by defining them in terms of less complex ones. ELAN supports the design of theorem provers, logic programming languages, constraint solvers and decision procedures and offers a modular framework for studying their combination.

In order to improve the architecture, and to make the ELAN system more interactive, it was decided to redesign the ELAN system based on the Meta-Environment. The instantiation of the ELAN environment involved the implementation of several new components, among others an interpreter. Constructing the ELAN environment was a matter of a few months.

The ρ-calculus [8] integrates in a uniform and simple setting first-order rewriting, lambda-calculus and non-deterministic computations. Its abstraction mechanism is based on the rewrite rule formation. The application operator is explicit, allowing to handle sets of results explicitly.

The ρ-calculus is typically a new rewriting formalism which can benefit from the the Meta-Environment. We have prototyped a workbench for the complete ρ-calculus. After that, we connected an existing ρ-calculus interpreter. This experiment was realized in one day.

The JITty interpreter [17] is a part of the μCRL [2] toolset. In this toolset it is used as an execution mechanism for rewrite rules. JITty is not supported by its own formalism or a specialized environment. However, the ideas of the JITty interpreter are more generally applicable. It implements an interesting normalization strategy, the so-called `just-in-time` strategy. A workbench for the JITty interpreter was developed in a few hours that allowed to perform experiments with the JITty interpreter.

6   Conclusions

Experiments with and applications of term rewriting engines are within much closer reach using the Meta-Environment, as compared to designing and engineering a new formalism from scratch.

We have presented a generic approach for rapidly developing the three major ingredients of a term rewriting based formalism: syntax, rewriting, and an environment. Using the scalable technology of the Meta-Environment significantly reduces the effort to develop them. We used our approach to build four environments. Two of them are actively used by their respective communities. The others serve as workbenches for new developments in term rewriting.

The Meta-Environment and its components can now support several term rewriting formalisms. A future step is to build environments for languages like Action Semantics [15] and TOM [16]. Apart from more environments, other future work consists of even further parameterization and modularization of the Meta-Environment. Making the Meta-Environment open to different syntax definition formalisms is an example. The Meta-Environment can be downloaded via: `http://www.cwi.nl/projects/MetaEnv`

References

1. J. Bergstra and P. Klint. The discrete time ToolBus – a software coordination architecture. *Science of Computer Programming*, 31(2-3):205–229, July 1998.
2. S. Blom, W. Fokkink, J. Groote, I. van Langevelde, B. Lisser, and J. van de Pol. μCRL: A toolset for analysing algebraic specifications. In G. Berry, H. Comon, and A. Finkel, editors, *CAV 2001*, volume 2102 of *LNCS*, pages 250–254. Springer-Verlag, 2001.
3. P. Borovanský, C. Kirchner, H. Kirchner, P.-E. Moreau, and C. Ringeissen. An overview of ELAN. In C. Kirchner and H. Kirchner, editors, *WRLA*, volume 15 of *ENTCS*. Elsevier Sciences, 1998.
4. M. v. d. Brand, J. Heering, P. Klint, and P. Olivier. Compiling language definitions: The ASF+SDF compiler. *ACM Transactions on Programming Languages and Systems*, 24(4):334–368, 2002.
5. M. v. d. Brand, H. d. Jong, P. Klint, and P. Olivier. Efficient Annotated Terms. *Software, Practice & Experience*, 30:259–291, 2000.
6. M. v. d. Brand, P. Klint, and J. Vinju. Term rewriting with traversal functions. Technical Report SEN-R0121, Centrum voor Wiskunde en Informatica, 2001.
7. M. v. d. Brand, J. Scheerder, J. Vinju, and E. Visser. Disambiguation Filters for Scannerless Generalized LR Parsers. In R. N. Horspool, editor, *Compiler Construction (CC'02)*, volume 2304 of *LNCS*, pages 143–158. Springer-Verlag, 2002.
8. H. Cirstea, C. Kirchner, and L. Liquori. Matching Power. In A. Middeldorp, editor, *RTA'01*, volume 2051 of *LNCS*, pages 77–92. Springer-Verlag, 2001.
9. M. Clavel, S. Eker, P. Lincoln, and J. Meseguer. Principles of Maude. In J. Meseguer, editor, *First international workshop on rewriting logic*, volume 4, Asilomar (California), 1996. ENTCS.
10. J. Cordy, C. Halpern-Hamu, and E. Promislow. TXL: A rapid prototyping system for programming language dialects. *Computer Languages*, 16(1):97–107, 1991.
11. A. v. Deursen, J. Heering, and P. Klint, editors. *Language Prototyping: An Algebraic Specification Approach*, volume 5 of *AMAST Series in Computing*. World Scientific, 1996.
12. J. Heering and P. Klint. *Term Rewriting Systems*, chapter 15, pages 787–808. Cambridge University Press, 2003.
13. H. d. Jong and P. Olivier. Generation of abstract programming interfaces from syntax definitions. Technical Report SEN-R0212, Centrum voor Wiskunde en Informatica (CWI), Aug. 2002.
14. D. Kapur and H. Zhang. An overview of Rewrite Rule Laboratory (RRL). *J. Computer and Mathematics with Applications*, 29(2):91–114, 1995.
15. S. Lassen, P. Mosses, and D. Watt. An introduction to AN-2, the proposed new version of Action Notation. In *Proc. 3rd International Workshop on Action Semantics*, volume NS-00-6 of *Notes Series*, pages 19–36. BRICS, 2000.
16. P.-E. Moreau, C. Ringeissen, and M. Vittek. A Pattern Matching Compiler for Multiple Target Languages. In G. Hedin, editor, *12th Conference on Compiler Construction, Warsaw (Poland)*, volume 2622 of *LNCS*, pages 61–76. Springer-Verlag, May 2003.
17. J. v. d. Pol. JITty: a Rewriter with Strategy Annotations. In S. Tison, editor, *Rewriting Techniques and Applications*, volume 2378 of *LNCS*, pages 367–370. Springer-Verlag, 2002.
18. E. Visser. Stratego: A language for program transformation based on rewriting strategies. System description of Stratego 0.5. In A. Middeldorp, editor, *RTA'01*, volume 2051 of *LNCS*, pages 357–361. Springer-Verlag, 2001.

A Logical Algorithm for ML Type Inference

David McAllester

Toyota Technological Institute at Chicago
mcallester@tti-c.org

Abstract. This paper gives a bottom-up logic programming formulation of the Hindley-Milner polymorphic type inference algorithm. We show that for programs of bounded order and arity the given algorithm runs in $O(n\alpha(n) + dn)$ time where n is the length of the program, d is the "scheme depth" of the program, and α is the inverse of Ackermann's function. It is argued that for practical programs d will not exceed 5 even for programs with hundreds of module layers. This formulation of the Hindley-Milner algorithm is intended as a case study in "logical algorithms", i.e., algorithms presented and analyzed as bottom-up inference rules.

1 Introduction

This paper is a case study in the use of bottom-up logic programming for the presentation and analysis of complex algorithms. The use of bottom-up logic programming for algorithm presentation has been developed in a recent series of papers whose main contributions are theorems governing the running time of these programs [6,1,2]. This paper explores the use of these run time theorems for the presentation and analysis of the Hindley-Milner type inference algorithm used in the ML and Caml programming languages [7]. It is known that for programs where procedures can take an unbounded number of arguments and be of unboundedly high order (procedures which take procedures which take procedures ...) the type inference problem is complete for exponential time [4,5]. In practice human written procedures never take more than twenty arguments and are never more than fifth order. It is known that for bounded order and arity the type inference problem can be done in polynomial time [3]. However, I am not aware of a published analysis giving a particular polynomial running time for this problem. This paper gives an inference rule presentation of a version of the Hindley-Milner type inference algorithm and shows that this version runs in time $O(n\alpha(n) + dn)$ where d is the "scheme depth" of the program. The algorithm presented here is very similar to the one described in [8] although no formal analysis of running time is given there. Section 5 defines scheme depth and argues that it can be expected to be less than 5 even for programs with hundreds of module layers.

R. Nieuwenhuis (Ed.): RTA 2003, LNCS 2706, pp. 436–451, 2003.

2   The LDP Programming Language

Here we use (essentially) the logic programming language and run time model specified in [2]. For convenience we will here refer to this programming language as LDP for Logic programs with Deletions and Priorities. It is important to note that deletions and priorities have been widely discussed in the logic programming literature. The main contribution of [2] is the definition of an abstract notion of running time and a proof that this abstract definition of running time can be implemented on a conventional random access computer. This run time result is stated in section 3. We now define an LDP program to be a set of inference rules where an inference rule is specified by the category r in the following grammar.

$$N \equiv i \mid n \mid N_1 + N_2 \mid N_1 * N_2$$
$$H \equiv x \mid f(\tau_1, \ldots, \tau_k)$$
$$\tau \equiv H \mid N$$
$$A \equiv P(\tau_1, \ldots, \tau_k) \mid N_1 \leq N_2$$
$$C \equiv P(\tau_1, \ldots, \tau_k) \mid \mathrm{del}(P(\tau_1, \ldots, \tau_k))$$

$r \equiv A_1, \ldots, A_n \rightarrow C_1, \ldots, C_k$ with priority N

Every variable in the priority N occurs in A_1.

If $A_i = P(t_1, \ldots t_k)$ then A_i does not contain $+$ or $*$.

If $A_i = N_1 \leq N_2$ then every variable in A_i occurs in some A_j for $j < i$.

Every variable in C_i occurs in some A_j.

This is two-sorted grammar with a sort for Herbrand terms (H) and a separate sort for integers (N). There are two sorts of variables — Herbrand variables such as x in the grammar for H and integer variables such as i in the grammar for N. In the grammar for integers, n ranges over any integer constant. We allow predicates and functions to take either sort as arguments although we assume that each predicate and function symbol has a specified arity and a specified sort for each argument and all applications of predicate and function symbols must respect this specification to be well formed. The function symbol f in the grammar for Herbrand terms should be viewed as a data constructor.

The inference rules are to be run bottom-up. For rules not involving deletion, a state of the system is a database of assertions which grows monotonically by adding new assertions derivable from some rule and assertions already in the database. When deletion is involved each rule states that its conclusion actions are to be taken taken whenever its antecedents are satisfied. The actions are either additions to, or removals from, a database of assertions of the form $P(\tau_1, \ldots, \tau_n)$. A particular use (instance) of a rule involves particular values for all the variables of that rule. Given values for the variables in the first antecedent, a rule is associated with an integer priority where the integer 1 is the highest priority (priority 1 rules run first). Priorities smaller than 1 are treated

$$(D1,1) \quad \frac{\text{source}(v)}{\text{dist}(v,0)} \qquad (D2,1) \quad \frac{\begin{array}{c}\text{dist}(v,d)\\ \text{dist}(v,d')\\ d' < d\end{array}}{\text{del}(\text{dist}(v,d))} \qquad (D3,d+2) \quad \frac{\begin{array}{c}\text{dist}(v,d)\\ E(v,c,u)\end{array}}{\text{dist}(u,d+c)}$$

Fig. 1. Dijkstra Shortest Path.

as equivalent to 1 but (instances of) rules with larger priority values run only if no higher priority rule instance can run.

Figure 1, taken from [2], gives an LDP implementation of the Dijkstra shortest path algorithm. The input is an initial database containing assertions of the form $E(v,c,u)$ stating that there is an edge from v to u of cost c plus an assertion of the form source(v) stating that v is the source node. In the figure each rule is given a name and a priority. For example, rule D2 has priority 1 while rule D3 has priority $d+2$ where the integer variable d occurs in the first antecedent of the rule. Different uses of the rule D3 run at different priorities. This has the effect that distances are established in a shortest-first order as in the normal Dijkstra shortest path algorithm. The general run time model for inference rules given in section 3 implies that these rules run in $O(e \log e)$ where e is the number of initial assertions. Note that $d' < d$ can be written as $d' + 1 \le d$.

We now consider the operational semantics an arbitrary set of LDP rules in more detail. A ground assertion is one not containing variables or arithmetic operations. A program state is a set S of ground assertions of the form $P(t_1, \ldots, t_k)$ and deletion assertions of the form $\text{del}(P(t_1, \ldots, t_k))$. Deletion actually adds an assertion of the form $\text{del}(P(t_1, \ldots, t_k))$ so that the set D grows monotonically over the execution of the algorithm. However, only the positive elements of D that have not been deleted are "visible" to the antecedents of the inference rules. Once a ground assertion has been both asserted and deleted new assertions or deletions of that ground assertion do not change the state of the database. Let r be the rule $A_1, \ldots, A_n \to C_1, \ldots, C_m$ at priority N. Let σ be a substitution assigning (ground) values to all the variables in the rule r. The pair $\langle r, \sigma \rangle$ will be called an instance of r. The instance $\langle r, \sigma \rangle$ is called *pending* at state S if each antecedent $\sigma(A_i)$ holds in the state S and firing the rule would change the state, i.e., $S \ne S \cup \{\sigma(C_1), \ldots, \sigma(C_m)\}$. We say that state S can make an R-transition to state S', written $S \xrightarrow{R} S'$, if there exists a pending rule instance $\langle r, \sigma \rangle$ with $r \in R$ such that no pending stance of a rule in R has higher priority and S' is $S \cup \{\sigma(C_1), \ldots, \sigma(C_m)\}$ where $C_1, \ldots, C_m$ is the conclusion of r. We say that W is a final state for R on input S if no rule instances are pending in W and W is reachable from S by a sequence of R-transitions. One should think of R as a (don't care) nondeterministic procedure for mapping input S to output W.

3   The Running Time of LDP Programs

We say that R terminates on input S if there is no infinite sequence S_1, S_2, S_3, ... such that $S = S_1$ and $S_i \xrightarrow{R} S_{i+1}$. The Dijkstra shortest path algorithm in figure 1 terminates even if we assign all rules priority 1 so that they can fire in any order. However, we are interested here in much more refined analysis of running time when the rule set is implemented on a conventional random access computer. To make statements about conventional running time we introduce the notion of a prefix firing. A *prefix instance* of r with n antecedents is a triple $\langle r, i, \sigma \rangle$ where $1 \leq i \leq n$ and σ is a ground substitution defined on (only) the variables occurring in the antecedent prefix A_1, ..., A_i of r. Intuitively, a prefix instance is a way of instantiating the first i antecedents of the rule. Let W be a final state of input S for rule set R. An atomic formula $P(t_1, \ldots, t_k)$ in W will be said to have been asserted and will be said to have been deleted if W contains $del(P(t_1, \ldots, t_k))$. An assertion is visible to the antecedents of rules if it has been asserted but has not been deleted.

> **Definition:** A *prefix firing* of a rule r over a final state W is a prefix instance $\langle r, i, \sigma \rangle$ of r such that $\sigma(A_1)$, ..., $\sigma(A_i)$ have all been asserted (and possibly also deleted) where A_1, ..., A_i are the first i antecedents of r.

The basic result in [6] is that for a rule set R in which all rules have priority 1 (and can therefore fire in any order), and where no rule involves deletion, the (unique) final state can be computed time proportional to the number of prefix firings over the final state. This bound also holds for rules with fixed priorities (no variables in the priority expressions) and deletions. However the run time bound from this "naive" count of prefix firings is typically quite loose for rule sets involving deletions and priorities. Rather than count all prefix firings we want to only count the "visible" prefix firings. To define the visible prefix firings we consider computation histories. A complete R-computation from S is a sequence S_1, S_2, ..., S_T such that $S_1 = S$, $S_i \xrightarrow{R} S_{i+1}$ and S_T is a final value of S, i.e., there are no instances of rules in R that are pending in S_T.

> **Definition:** A state S is said to be visible to a prefix instance $\langle r, i, \sigma \rangle$ if no pending instance of a rule in R has priority higher than the priority of $\langle r, i, \sigma \rangle$. A prefix firing $\langle r, i, \sigma \rangle$ over the final state of a computation is said to be visible in a computation if either $i = 1$ and r is variable priority or the computation contains a state S visible to $\langle r, i, \sigma \rangle$ such that $\sigma(A_1)$, ... $\sigma(A_i)$ all hold in S (have been asserted but not deleted) where A_1, ..., A_i are the first i antecedents of r.

Every visible prefix firing is a prefix firing over the final state, but the visible prefix firings are usually only a small fraction of the prefix firings. A first-antecedent prefix firing is just a prefix firing $\langle r, i, \sigma \rangle$ with $i = 1$. The following is the main theorem of [2].

Theorem 1. *If the rule set R terminates on initial state S then a complete R-computation from S can be computed on a RAM machine extended with constant time hash table operations in time proportional to $|S| + P_1 + P_2 \log N$ where $|S|$ is the number of assertions in S, P_1 is the number of visible prefix firings of fixed priority rules; P_2 is the number of visible prefix firings of variable priority rules; and N is the number of distinct priorities of first-antecedent prefix firings of variable priority rules.*

To see how this theorem can be applied we now give a running time analysis of the Dijkstra shortest path algorithm shown in Figure 1. Note that for a state to be visible to (an instance of) a rule there must not be any pending higher priority rule. States where no high-priority rule is pending often satisfy certain invariants. The priority of a state is the priority of a highest-priority (lowest integer) pending rule instance (or $+\infty$ if there are no pending rule instances). The rule D2 ensures that in any state with priority 2 or larger we have at most one distance associated with each node. So this invariant holds in any state visible to the rule D3. The priority of an instance of rule D3 is determined by the value of the integer variable d appearing in the first antecedent — shorter distances get higher priority. Note that when an instance of D3 runs all pending rule firings involve priorities at least as large as d. Since an invocation of rule D3 must generate a bound at least as large as d, all future bounds will be at least as large as d. Hence, in any state with priority $d+2$ or greater, any visible assertion of the form $\mathsf{dist}(u, d)$ must have the property that d is the actual shortest distance to the node u. Hence, for a given node u there is only one value of d used in a full firing of rule D3. This implies that the total number of firings of the first two antecedents of D3 is at most the number of edges in the graph. Each firing of D2 occurs in a state immediately following a firing of D3 and for each firing of D3 there is at most one firing of D2. Hence the total number of firings of D2 is also at most the total number of edges. Furthermore, this implies that the total number of assertions of the form $\mathsf{dist}(u, d)$ ever asserted is at most e. All of these "ever-asserted" assertions must be included as prefix firings of the first antecedent of the variable priority rule D3. However, for the two antecedent prefix firings of D3 we need only consider a single value of d for each value of u. Hence the total number of prefix firings is $O(e)$. The number of distinct priorities associated with rule D3 is at most e. So the abstract run time of rule D3 is $O(e \log e)$. The run time of D3 dominates and the algorithm runs in $O(e \log e)$ time.

4   Union-Find

Figure 2, taken from [2], gives an LDP implementation of the union-find algorithm. The algorithm is not particularly elegant, but it does show that LDP with its associated abstraction notion of run time is sufficiently powerful to express a useful implementation of union-find. Note that these rules all have priority either 1 or 2. The rules take as input assertions of the form $\mathsf{union}(x, y)$ and produce as output assertions of the form $\mathsf{find}(x, f)$. Any state in which no union-find rules are pending, e.g., any state with priority 3 or lower (numerically larger), satisfies

$$(\text{UF1,1}) \quad \frac{\text{union}(x,y)}{\begin{array}{l}\text{nofind}(x)\\\text{nofind}(y)\end{array}}$$

$$(\text{UF2,1}) \quad \frac{\text{find}(x,y)}{\text{del}(\text{nofind}(x))}$$

$$(\text{UF3,1}) \quad \frac{\begin{array}{l}\text{find}(x,y)\\\text{find.arc}(y,z)\end{array}}{\begin{array}{l}\text{find}(x,z)\\\text{del}(\text{find}(x,y))\end{array}}$$

$$(\text{UF4,1}) \quad \frac{\begin{array}{l}\text{union}(x,y)\\\text{find}(x,z)\\\text{find}(y,z)\end{array}}{\text{del}(\text{union}(x,y))}$$

$$(\text{UF5,2}) \quad \frac{\text{nofind}(x)}{\begin{array}{l}\text{find}(x,x)\\\text{size}(x,1)\end{array}}$$

$$(\text{UF6,2}) \quad \frac{\begin{array}{l}\text{union}(x,y)\\\text{find}(x,x')\\\text{find}(y,y')\end{array}}{\text{merge}(x',y')}$$

$$(\text{UF7,1}) \quad \frac{\begin{array}{l}\text{merge}(x,y)\\\text{size}(x,s1)\\\text{size}(y,s2)\\s1 \le s2\end{array}}{\begin{array}{l}\text{del}(\text{merge}(x,y))\\\text{find.arc}(x,y)\\\text{del}(\text{size}(y,s2))\\\text{size}(y,s1+s2)\end{array}}$$

$$(\text{UF8,1}) \quad \frac{\begin{array}{l}\text{merge}(x,y)\\\text{size}(x,s1)\\\text{size}(y,s2)\\s2 < s1\end{array}}{\begin{array}{l}\text{del}(\text{merge}(x,y))\\\text{find.arc}(y,x)\\\text{del}(\text{size}(x,s1))\\\text{size}(x,s1+s2)\end{array}}$$

Fig. 2. Union-Find

$$(\text{ST1,3}) \quad \frac{\begin{array}{l}E(x,c,y)\\\text{find}(x,z)\\\text{find}(y,z)\end{array}}{\text{del}(E(x,c,y))}$$

$$(\text{ST2,c+4}) \quad \frac{E(x,c,y)}{\begin{array}{l}\text{union}(x,y)\\\text{out}(x,c,y)\end{array}}$$

Fig. 3. Minimum Spanning Tree

the invariant that for any x there is at most one y satisfying $\text{find}(x,y)$ and that the find map defined by the find relation implements the equivalence relation defined by the input union assertions. This implementation uses greedy path compression. The number of visible prefix firings (the abstract running time for fixed priority rules) is $O(n \log n)$ where n is the number of union operations. Figure 3, also taken from [2], shows an $O(n \log n)$ LDP implementation of a minimum spanning tree algorithm based on this implementation of union-find. The input is a set of assertion of the form $E(x,c,y)$ and the output spanning tree is a set of assertions of the form $\text{out}(x,c,y)$. An $O(n\alpha(n))$ implementation of union-find can also be given in LDP but requires that union assertions carry time stamps and that a time-stamped find request is made each time one accesses the find relation. This makes it difficult to write rules, such as rule ST1 in figure 3, whose antecedents notice changes in the find map. In many applications of union-find, such as the spanning tree algorithm in figure 3, the union-find processing time is dominated by other computations (such as the priority queue implicit in rule ST2) and the $O(n \log n)$ implementation of union-find suffices.

5   Polymorphic Type Inference

Polymorphic type inference can be formulated for the lambda calculus extended with an explicit let constructor and a constant for the numeral zero. The lambda calculus with let and zero is the set of expressions defined by the following grammar.

$$x \equiv \mathsf{termvar(id)}$$
$$e \equiv x \mid 0 \mid \mathsf{lambda}(x,\, e) \mid \mathsf{let}(x,\, e_1,\, e_2) \mid \mathsf{apply}(e_1,\, e_2)$$

Note that this grammar represents each expression of the lambda calculus explicitly as an LDP data structure. Variables are represented by LDP data structures of the form $\mathsf{termvar(id)}$ where id is the "identifier" of the variable and can be any LDP data structure (ground term). It is interesting to note that one can easily write LDP programs that "gensym" new variables to avoid variable capture in operations such as substitution. More specifically, in implementing substitution on the lambda calculus one must be able to construct a variable x that is guaranteed not to occur in a given expression e. But note that the variable $\mathsf{termvar}(e)$ cannot occur in e. I will write $(e_1\ e_2)$ as an abbreviation for $\mathsf{apply}(e_1,\, e_2)$ and write $(fe_1,\, e_2,\, \ldots,\, e_n)$ as an abbreviation for the "Curried application" $(\ldots((fe_1)e_2)\ldots e_n)$. I will also sometimes write $\lambda x.\ e$ as an abbreviation for $\mathsf{lambda}(x,\, e)$. I will also write $\lambda x_1 x_2.\ e$ for $\lambda x_1.\ \lambda x_2.\ e$

The type inference algorithm described here runs in $O(n\alpha(n) + dn)$ time where d is the scheme depth of the input program. To define scheme depth we first say that the position of e_1 in the let expression $\mathsf{let}(x,\, e_1,\, e_2)$ is a scheme formation position. As described below, these scheme formation positions are the position in the program where polymorphic type inference creates a type scheme. The scheme depth of a position ρ in the program is the number of scheme formation positions above ρ. For example, one might have a sequence of module definitions where each module can use definitions from the previous module. Conceptually, the sequence of module definitions is analogous to the following pattern of let bindings.

$$\mathsf{let}(m_1,\, M_2,\, \mathsf{let}(m_2,\, M_2,\, \mathsf{let}(m_3,\, M_3 \ldots)))$$

Each module M_i might consist of a sequence of procedure definitions analogous to the following let bindings.

$$M_i = \mathsf{let}(f_1,\, F_1,\, \mathsf{let}(f_2,\, F_2,\, \mathsf{let}(f_3,\, F_3,\, \ldots)))$$

Each procedure might be defined with a sequence of let expressions as follows

$$f_i = \lambda x_1, \ldots x_n \; \mathsf{let}(y_1, \; e_1, \; \mathsf{let}(y_2, \; e_2, \; \mathsf{let}(y_3, \; e_3, \; \ldots)))$$

Typically the expressions e_i that give the values of let-bound variables inside individual procedure definitions do not themselves contain let expressions. So an arbitrarily long sequence of dependent models, each consisting of an arbitrarily long sequence of dependent procedure definitions, each consisting of an arbitrarily sequence of dependent let expressions, only has scheme depth 3. It seems unlikely that the scheme depth ever exceeds 5 in human written programs.

Hindley-Milner type inference is a process by which the various variables and subexpressions of a given input expression are assigned types. Here we consider only one primitive data type — the type of integers. Finite (nonrecursive) types are generated by the following grammar.

$$\tau \equiv \alpha \;\mid\; \mathsf{int} \;\mid\; \mathsf{arrow}(\tau_1, \; \tau_2)$$

In this grammar α ranges over type variables. The type $\mathsf{arrow}(\tau_1, \; \tau_2)$ is the type assigned to procedures which take as an argument a value in the type τ_1 and produce as an output a value in the type τ_2. I will often write $\tau_1 \rightarrow \tau_2$ as an alternate notation for $\mathsf{arrow}(\tau_1, \; \tau_2)$ and write $\tau_1 \times \cdots \times \tau_n \rightarrow \sigma$ as an alternate notation for $\tau_1 \rightarrow (\tau_2 \rightarrow \cdots \sigma)$. If τ is the type $\sigma \rightarrow \gamma$ then I will sometimes write $\mathsf{domain}(\tau)$ for the type σ and $\mathsf{range}(\tau)$ for the type γ.

The basic constraint in type inference is that in each application $(e_1, \; e_2)$ the expression e_1 must be assigned a type of the form $\tau \rightarrow \sigma$ where e_2 is assigned the type τ and the application $(e_1, \; e_2)$ is assigned the type σ. Type inference is done by unification of type expressions. For each application $(e_1 \; e_2)$ we introduce the following constraints.

$$\mathsf{type.of}(e_1, \; \rho_1) = \mathsf{domain}(\mathsf{type.of}(e_1, \; \rho_1)) \rightarrow \mathsf{range}(\mathsf{type.of}(e_1, \; \rho_1))$$
$$\mathsf{type.of}(e_2, \; \rho_2) = \mathsf{domain}(\mathsf{type.of}(e_1, \; \rho_1))$$
$$\mathsf{type.of}((e_1 \; e_2), \; \rho_3) = \mathsf{range}(\mathsf{type.of}(e_1, \; \rho_1))$$

Expressions of the form $\mathsf{type.of}(e, \; \rho)$ are treated as type variables. In polymorphic type inference different occurrences of the same expression can be assigned different types as will be explained below. In a type variable of the form $\mathsf{type.of}(e, \; \rho)$ we have that ρ names a position in the input expression at which the expression e occurs. Unification is used to construct the most general solution to the type constraints.

Figure 4 gives the top level structure of the polymorphic type inference procedure. The procedure definitions are abbreviations for inference rules given in figure 5. The input to the top level procedures in figure 4 is a single expression of the form $\mathsf{do}(\mathsf{analyze}(e, \; \mathsf{root}))$ where e is a closed lambda expression whose variables have been renamed so that each variable is bound at only one position in e. The basic constraints for application are installed by the first procedure in figure 4. The input expression e is typable by polymorphic recursive types if and only if the rules in figures 4, 6, 7, 8, and 9 do not generate clash. These

```
procedure analyze(apply(e₁, e₂), ρ)
   [analyze(e₁, down(ρ, 1));
    analyze(e₂, down(ρ, 2));
    assert.declare.arrow(type.of(e₁, down(ρ, 1)));
    assert.eq.types(type.of(e₂, down(ρ, 2)),
                      domain(type.of(e₁, down(ρ, 1))));
    assert.eq.types(type.of(apply(e₁, e₂), ρ),
                      range(type.of(e₁, down(ρ, 1))))]

procedure analyze(0, ρ)
   [assert.int.type(type.of(0, ρ))]
```

$$\text{(A1, 4)} \quad \frac{\begin{array}{l} \text{do(analyze(termvar(id), } \rho)) \\ \text{monomorphic(termvar(id))} \end{array}}{\begin{array}{l} \text{eq.types(type.of(termvar(id), } \rho), \text{ type.of(termvar(id)))} \\ \text{done(analyze(termvar(id), } \rho)) \end{array}}$$

$$\text{(A2, 4)} \quad \frac{\begin{array}{l} \text{do(analyze(termvar(id), } \rho)) \\ \text{polymorphic(termvar(id), } s) \end{array}}{\begin{array}{l} \text{make.copy(}s, \rho) \\ \text{eq.types(type.of(termvar(id), } \rho), \text{ , copy(}s, \rho)) \\ \text{done(analyze(termvar(id), } \rho)) \end{array}}$$

```
procedure analyze(lambda(x, e), ρ)
   [assert.monomorphic(x);
    analyze(e, down(ρ, 2));
    assert.declare.arrow(type.of(lambda(x, e), ρ));
    assert.eq.types(type.of(x), domain(type.of(lambda(x, e), ρ)));
    assert.eq.types(type.of(e, down(ρ, 2)), range(type.of(lambda(x, e), ρ))) ]

procedure analyze(let(x, e₁, e₂), ρ)
   [analyze(e₁, down(ρ, 2));
    assert.make.scheme(type.of(e₁, down(ρ, 2)), ρ);
    assert.polymorphic(x, sch(type.of(e₁, down(ρ, 2)), ρ));
    analyze(e₂, down(ρ, 3));
    eq.types(type.of(let(x, e₁, e₂), ρ), type.of(e₂, down(ρ, 3))) ]
```

Fig. 4. Hindley-Milner Type Inference: Fundamental Structure

figures give a complete machine-executable implementation of the polymorphic type inference procedure. This procedure allows recursive types by not performing any occurs-check in the unification procedure. Recursive types can be viewed as infinite type expressions with a finite number of distinct subexpressions. For

$$(P1,4) \quad \frac{\mathsf{do}(f(t_1, \ldots, t_n))}{\mathsf{do}([a_1; \ldots; a_n])}$$

$$(P2,4) \quad \frac{\begin{array}{c} \mathsf{do}(f(t_1, \ldots, t_n)) \\ \mathsf{done}([a_1; \ldots; a_n]) \end{array}}{\mathsf{done}(f(t_1, \ldots, t_n))}$$

$$(P3,4) \quad \frac{\mathsf{do}(\mathsf{sequence}(a1, a_2))}{\mathsf{do}(a_1)}$$

$$(P4,4) \quad \frac{\begin{array}{c} \mathsf{do}(\mathsf{sequence}(a_1, a_2)) \\ \mathsf{done}(a_1) \end{array}}{\mathsf{do}(a_2)}$$

$$(P5,4) \quad \frac{\begin{array}{c} \mathsf{do}(\mathsf{sequence}(a_1, a_2)) \\ \mathsf{done}(a_1) \\ \mathsf{donc}(a_2) \end{array}}{\mathsf{done}(\mathsf{sequence}(a_1, a_2))}$$

$$(P6 \ 1) \quad \frac{\mathsf{do}(\mathsf{assert.P}(x_1, \ldots, x_n))}{\begin{array}{c} P(x_1, \ldots, x_n) \\ \mathsf{done}(\mathsf{assert.P}(x_1, \ldots, x_n)) \end{array}}$$

Fig. 5. Implementing Procedures. Defining $f(t_1, \ldots, t_n)$ to be $[a_1; \ldots; a_n]$ abbreviates the rules P1 and P2 above. The notation $[a_1; a_2]$ abbreviates $\mathsf{sequence}(a_1, a_2)$ and $[a_1; a_2; \ldots; a_n]$ abbreviates $[a_1; [a_2; \ldots; a_n]]$. Rule P6 is assumed to be present for every action constructor of the form assert.P.

$$(U1,1) \quad \frac{\mathsf{eq.types}(\tau, \sigma)}{\begin{array}{c} \mathsf{type.var}(\tau) \\ \mathsf{type.var}(\sigma) \\ \mathsf{union}(\tau, \sigma) \end{array}}$$

$$(U2, 1) \quad \frac{\mathsf{declare.arrow}(\tau)}{\begin{array}{c} \mathsf{type.var}(\tau) \\ \mathsf{type.var}(\mathsf{domain}(\tau)) \\ \mathsf{type.var}(\mathsf{range}(\tau)) \\ \mathsf{decl.struct}(\tau, \mathsf{domain}(\tau), \mathsf{range}(\tau)) \end{array}}$$

$$(U3, 1) \quad \frac{\mathsf{int.type}(\tau)}{\mathsf{type.var}(\tau)}$$

$$(U4,1) \quad \frac{\mathsf{type.var}(\alpha)}{\mathsf{no.struct}(\alpha)}$$

$$(U5,1) \quad \frac{\mathsf{struct}(\alpha, \beta, \gamma)}{\mathsf{del}(\mathsf{no.struct}(\alpha))}$$

$$(U6,2) \quad \frac{\begin{array}{c} \mathsf{decl.struct}(\alpha, \beta, \gamma) \\ \mathsf{no.struct}(\alpha) \end{array}}{\mathsf{struct}(\alpha, \beta, \gamma)}$$

$$(U7,1) \quad \frac{\begin{array}{c} \mathsf{decl.struct}(\alpha, \beta, \gamma) \\ \mathsf{struct}(\alpha, \beta', \gamma') \end{array}}{\begin{array}{c} \mathsf{union}(\beta, \beta') \\ \mathsf{union}(\gamma, \gamma') \end{array}}$$

$$(U8,1) \quad \frac{\begin{array}{c} \mathsf{struct}(\alpha, \beta, \gamma) \\ \mathsf{find.arc}(\alpha, \alpha') \end{array}}{\mathsf{decl.struct}(\alpha', \beta, \gamma)}$$

$$(U9,1) \quad \frac{\begin{array}{c} \mathsf{int.type}(\tau) \\ \mathsf{find.arc}(\tau, \sigma) \end{array}}{\mathsf{int.type}(\sigma)}$$

$$(U10,1) \quad \frac{\begin{array}{c} \mathsf{struct}(\alpha, \beta, \gamma) \\ \mathsf{int.type}(\alpha) \end{array}}{\mathsf{clash}}$$

Fig. 6. Type Unification

example there is a recursive type τ satisfying the following fixed point equation.

$$\tau = \text{int} \rightarrow \tau$$

It is possible to add occurs-check rules if one wishes to avoid recursive types.

In Hindley-Milner type inference, expressions can have polymorphic types — different occurrences of a procedure can have different types. For example, consider a composition operator comp satisfying the following equation.

$$((\text{comp } f \ g) \ x) = (f \ (g \ x))$$

For any types τ_1 and τ_2 the composition operator can be assigned the type $(\tau_1 \rightarrow \tau_2) \times (\tau_1 \rightarrow \tau_2) \rightarrow (\tau_1 \rightarrow \tau_2)$. For the polymorphic composition operator the types τ_1 and τ_2 can be different for different uses of the operator. For example, the same composition operator can be used to compose functions from integers to integers in one place and to compose functions on floating points in another place (in a language with floating point numbers). The type of the polymorphic composition operator is often written as follows.

$$\text{comp} \ : \ \forall \alpha, \ \beta, \ (\alpha \rightarrow \beta) \times (\alpha \rightarrow \beta) \rightarrow (\alpha \rightarrow \beta)$$

In Hindley-Milner type inference polymorphism is restricted to let-bound variables. If the top level expression does not involve let then the rules in figures 4 and 6 suffice for type inference. Figures 7, 8, and 9 handle polymorphism. The basic idea is that when the procedure analyzes a let expression it makes the type of the let-bound variable polymorphic. This is done by converting the type to a type scheme which is then instantiated with fresh type variables for each use of the let bound variable.

It is instructive to first consider the case of expressions without let. In this case we can ignore rule A2 and the last procedure definition in figure 4. Since the rules for polymorphic type inference do not involve variable-priority rules, to analyze the run time of the procedure it suffices to count the number of visible prefix firings. The number of prefix firings of the rules implicit in figure 4 is proportional to the number of expressions analyzed, i.e., the number of positions occupied in the input expression. The number of occupied positions corresponds to the written length of the expression and I will simple call this number "the size of the input" and denote it by n. To finish the analysis it suffices to count the number of visible prefix firings in the union-find rules in figure 2 and of the unification rules in figure 6. The input to the unification module consists of assertions of the form declare.arrow(σ), int.type(σ) and eq.types(σ, τ). The output is the assertion clash if the constraints are unsatisfiable and otherwise the output consists of the union-find equivalence relation on the set of type expressions plus assertions of the form struct(α, β, γ) which implies that $\alpha = \beta \rightarrow \gamma$. The rules maintain the invariant that for any α there is at most one assertion of the form struct(α, β, γ). Note that, with the exception of rule U2, the unification rules do not introduce new expressions. In fact the number of expressions generated by the rules is no more than linear in the number

$$(\text{MS1},1) \; \frac{\text{type.var}(\alpha)}{\text{unbound}(\alpha)}$$

$$(\text{MS2},1) \; \frac{\text{arrow.type}(\alpha)}{\text{del}(\text{unbound}(\alpha))}$$

$$(\text{MS3},1) \; \frac{\text{int.type}(\alpha)}{\text{del}(\text{unbound}(\alpha))}$$

$$(\text{MS4},1) \; \frac{\begin{array}{l}\text{make.scheme}(\tau,\ \rho)\\ \text{find}(\tau,\ \tau')\\ \text{struct}(\tau',\ \sigma,\ \gamma)\end{array}}{\begin{array}{l}\text{sch.struct}(\text{sch}(\tau,\ \rho),\ \text{sch}(\sigma,\ \rho),\ \text{sch}(\gamma,\rho))\\ \text{make.scheme}(\sigma,\ \rho)\\ \text{make.scheme}(\gamma,\ \rho)\end{array}}$$

$$(\text{MS5},1) \; \frac{\begin{array}{l}\text{make.scheme}(\tau,\ \rho)\\ \text{find}(\tau,\ \tau')\\ \text{int.type}(\tau')\end{array}}{\text{int.scheme}(\text{sch}(\tau,\ \rho))}$$

$$(\text{MS6},2) \; \frac{\begin{array}{l}\text{make.scheme}(\tau,\ \rho)\\ \text{find}(\tau,\ \tau')\\ \text{unbound}(\tau')\\ \text{scheme.depth}(\tau',\ i)\\ \text{scheme.depth}(\rho,\ j)\\ i < j\end{array}}{\text{free.var}(\text{sch}(\tau,\ \rho),\ \tau')}$$

$$(\text{MS7},2) \; \frac{\begin{array}{l}\text{make.scheme}(\tau,\ \rho)\\ \text{find}(\tau,\ \tau')\\ \text{unbound}(\tau')\\ \text{scheme.depth}(\tau',\ i)\\ \text{scheme.depth}(\rho,\ j)\\ j \le i\end{array}}{\text{bound.var}(\text{sch}(\tau,\ \rho),\ \text{sch}(\tau',\ \rho))}$$

Fig. 7. Making a Type Scheme

$$(\text{C1},3) \; \frac{\begin{array}{l}\text{make.copy}(s,\ \rho)\\ \text{sch.struct}(s,\ t,\ v)\end{array}}{\begin{array}{l}\text{declare.arrow}(\text{copy}(s,\ \rho))\\ \text{eq.types}(\text{domain}(\text{copy}(s,\ \rho)),\ \text{copy}(t,\ \rho))\\ \text{eq.types}(\text{range}(\text{copy}(s,\ \rho)),\ \text{copy}(v,\ \rho))\\ \text{make.copy}(t,\ \rho)\\ \text{make.copy}(v,\ \rho)\end{array}}$$

$$(\text{C2},3) \; \frac{\begin{array}{l}\text{make.copy}(s,\ \rho)\\ \text{int.scheme}(s)\end{array}}{\text{int.type}(\text{copy}(s,\rho))}$$

$$(\text{C3},3) \; \frac{\begin{array}{l}\text{make.copy}(s,\ \rho)\\ \text{free.var}(s,\ \tau')\end{array}}{\text{eq.types}(\text{copy}(s,\rho),\ \tau')}$$

$$(\text{C4},3) \; \frac{\begin{array}{l}\text{make.copy}(s,\ \rho)\\ \text{bound.var}(s_1,\ s_2)\end{array}}{\text{eq.types}(\text{copy}(s_1,\rho),\ \text{copy}(s_2,\ \rho))}$$

Fig. 8. Copying a Type Scheme at Program Position ρ

$(D1,1)$ ——————
$$\text{scheme.depth}(\text{root},\ 0)$$

$$\text{do}(\text{analyze}(\text{let}(x,\ e_1,\ e_2),\ \rho))$$
$$\text{scheme.depth}(\rho,\ d)$$
$(D2,1)$ ——————
$$\text{scheme.depth}(\text{down}(\rho,\ 2),\ d+1)$$
$$\text{scheme.depth}(\text{down}(\rho,\ 3),\ d)$$

$$\text{do}(\text{analyze}(\text{lambda}(x,\ e),\ \rho))$$
$$\text{scheme.depth}(\rho,\ d)$$
$(D3,1)$ ——————
$$\text{scheme.depth}(\text{down}(\rho,\ 2),\ d)$$

$$\text{do}(\text{analyze}(\text{apply}(e_1,\ e_2),\ \rho))$$
$$\text{scheme.depth}(\rho,\ d)$$
$(D4,1)$ ——————
$$\text{scheme.depth}(\text{down}(\rho,\ 1),\ d)$$
$$\text{scheme.depth}(\text{down}(\rho,\ 2),\ d)$$

$$\text{type.var}(\text{type.of}(e,\ \rho))$$
$$\text{scheme.depth}(\rho,\ d)$$
$(D5,1)$ ——————
$$\text{scheme.depth}(\text{type.of}(e,\ \rho),\ d)$$

$$\text{type.var}(\text{copy}(s,\ \rho))$$
$$\text{scheme.depth}(\rho,\ d)$$
$(D6,1)$ ——————
$$\text{scheme.depth}(\text{copy}(s,\ \rho),\ d)$$

$$\text{scheme.depth}(x,\ d_1)$$
$$\text{scheme.depth}(x,\ d_2)$$
$$d_1 < d_2$$
$(D7,1)$ ——————
$$\text{del}(\text{scheme.depth}(x,\ d_2))$$

$$\text{scheme.depth}(x,\ d)$$
$$\text{find.arc}(x,\ y)$$
$(D8,2)$ ——————
$$\text{scheme.depth}(y,\ d)$$

$$\text{scheme.depth}(\alpha,\ d)$$
$$\text{struct}(\alpha,\ \beta,\ \gamma)$$
$(D9,3)$ ——————
$$\text{scheme.depth}(\beta,\ d)$$
$$\text{scheme.depth}(\gamma,\ d)$$

Fig. 9. The Computation of Scheme Depth

of assertions input to the unification process. This implies that the number of (uncompressed) underlying find arcs in the union-find assertions is also no more than linear in the number of inputs to unification. The number of prefix firings of the unification rules can be seen to be proportional to the number of find arcs and hence the number of prefix firings of the unification rules is proportional to the number of input assertions. In let-free programs the number of inputs to unification is proportional to the number of positions occupied in the input expression. Because the unification rules use only the uncompressed find arcs a lazy path compression unification algorithm can be used. This gives $n\alpha(n)$ type inference procedure for let-free programs. The lazy path compression algorithm can also be used with the full polymorphic type inference procedure. While linear time unification is appropriate for let-free programs, in the presence of polymorphism one must alternate unification processing with type scheme construction and this alternation prevents the use of linear time unification.

To understand the subtleties of the polymorphic case consider the following expression.

$$\lambda y.\mathsf{let}(f,\ \lambda x.y,\ e)$$

In this case multiple occurrences of f in e can have different domain types but must all have the same range type. The range type of f is the type of the lambda-bound variable y which can be determined from the contexts into which the overall lambda expression is embedded. In the Hindley-Milner type inference algorithm we assign f and y the following type.

$$y : \beta$$
$$f : \forall \alpha,\ \alpha \to \beta$$

Note that in this type α is a bound type variable while β is a free type variable. In general, when the procedure constructs a type scheme it must distinguish type variables which can be universally quantified (the bound type variables) from the type variables which must be left free. Each type variable has a position in the program where it is created. In a let expression $\mathsf{let}(x, e_1, e_2)$ type variables created in e_1 are candidates for quantification in the type scheme. However, the expression e_1 usually contains free variables such as y in the above example. The types associated with the free variables in e_1 cannot be generalized. A type that is provably equal to a range type or a domain type of an ungeneralizable type is also ungeneralizable. To determine which types are generalizable we us the notion of scheme depth defined earlier. The formal definition of the scheme depth of a position is given by rules D1 through D4 in figure 9. We first say that a type α is provably a subexpression of a type β if α is provably equal to β (the union-find structure equates them) or α is of the form $\mathsf{domain}(\gamma)$ or $\mathsf{range}(\gamma)$ where γ is provably a subexpression of β. Each type variable has a creation depth and an inferred depth. The inferred depth of α is the creation depth of the shallowest type variable β such that α is provably a subexpression of β. Rules D5 and D6 in figure 9 install the creation depth of type variables and rules D7, D8, and D9 compute inferred depth. A variable can be bound by the universal quantifier at scheme creation time as long as its inferred depth is no less than the depth of position at which the scheme is being created.

Figure 7 gives rules for creating type schemes. We leave it to reader to decipher the meaning of these rules. One point concerning their complexity should be noted however. The find assertions in the antecedents of these rules obviously should only be instantiation with the find values that are in place when the scheme is constructed. This can be achieved by adding an antecedent of the form $\mathsf{active}(\rho)$ to each rule where this assertion is only true during the computation of the scheme for position ρ. With this modification it is easy to check that the number of visible prefix firings of the rules in figure 7 is proportional to the number of nodes in the scheme created. For programs of bounded order and arity there is a constant upper bound on the number of nodes in each scheme. The rules for making a scheme are consistent with the use a lazy path compression version of union-find.

The rules in figure 8 copy a type scheme at a particular program location. The number of visible prefix firings of these rules is proportional to the size of the scheme being copied. If schemes have a bounded size then the total time taken to create and copy schemes is proportional to the size of the input program (the number of occupied positions). In this case the total number of type variables is also proportional the size of the input program so the time spent inside a lazy path compression version of union-find is $O(n\alpha(n))$. The number of visible prefix firings of rule D7, D8, and D9 in bounded by the size of the program (the number of type variables) times the number of depths, i.e., the scheme depth of the deepest scheme position. This gives a total running time of $O(n\alpha(n) + dn)$ where n is the length of the program and d is the scheme depth of the program.

6   Conclusions

This paper is a case study in the use of bottom-up logic programming extended with priorities and deletions in presenting and analyzing algorithms. Efficient Hindley-Miler type inference seems to be a challenging algorithm to both formulate and analyze. The algorithm presented here is essentially the one used in ML and Caml implementations. Although beauty is in the eye of the beholder, it can at least be argued that the inference rule presentation of the algorithm is clearer both respect to its correctness *and with respect to its running time* than is any presentation of the algorithm using traditional control structures. Of course the top level procedure in figure 4 uses classical procedural control structures. However, the implementation of unification and the depth propagation seems easier in inference rules that classical control structures. Also, inference rules provide a different form of modularity than is possible in classical programs. The unification algorithm can be given as a separate module that uses a union-find module without modification. Depth propagation can be done with yet another module. The complexity analysis of these modules can be done separately (modularly). This modularization seems difficult with classical control structures. The use of inference rules also seems to facilitates the treatment of recursive types.

In comparing the algorithm in figures 4, 6, 7, 8, and 9 to other presentations it is important to keep in mind that the these figures contain machine readable code. Machine readable code is usually less clear than informal descriptions of algorithms written in English. A fair comparison would require comparing these figures to a machine-readable implementation in an some more traditional programming language.

Bottom-up logic programming is clearly not the best tool for all applications. However, it is hoped that this case study demonstrates that presenting and analyzing complex algorithms as bottom-up logic programs is indeed feasible and perhaps provides greater clarity than traditional approaches.

References

1. H. Ganzinger and D. McAllester. A new meta-complexity theorem for bottom-up logic programs. In *Proc. International Joint Conference on Automated Reasoning*, volume 2083 of *Lecture Notes in Computer Science*, pages 514–528. Springer-Verlag, 2001.
2. H. Ganzinger and D. McAllester. Logical algorithms. In *Proc. International Conference on Logic Programming (ICLP)*, 2002.
3. F. Henglein. Type inference with polymorphic recursion. *Transactions on Programming Languages and Systems (TOPLAS)*, 15(2):253–289, 1993.
4. A. Kfoury, J. Tiuryn, and P. Urzyczyn. Ml typability is dexptime complete. In *Proceedings of the 15th Colloquium on Trees in Algebra and Programming (CAAP)*, pages 468–476. ACM, 1990.
5. H. Mairson. Deciding ml typability is complete for deterministic exponential time. In *ACM Symposium on Principles of Programming Languages*. Association for Computing Machinery, 1990.
6. David McAllester. On the complexity analysis of static analyses. *Journal of the ACM (JACM)*, 49(4):512–537, 2002. A short version appeared in SAS99.
7. Robin Milner. A theory of type polymorphism in programming. *JCSS*, 17:348–375, 1978.
8. Didier Rémy. Extending ML type system with a sorted equational theory. Research Report 1766, Institut National de Recherche en Informatique et Automatisme, Rocquencourt, BP 105, 78 153 Le Chesnay Cedex, France, 1992.

A Rewriting Alternative
to Reidemeister-Schreier

Neil Ghani and Anne Heyworth

Department of Mathematics and Computer Science,
University of Leicester

Abstract. One problem in computational group theory is to find a presentation of the subgroup generated by a set of elements of a group. The
Reidemeister-Schreier algorithm was developed in the 1930's and gives
a solution based upon enumerative techniques. This however means the
algorithm can only be applied to finite groups. This paper proposes a
rewriting based alternative to the Reidemeister-Schreier algorithm which
has the advantage of being applicable to infinite groups.

1   Introduction

In computational group theory [3], one tries to reason about various properties
of groups which are finitely presentable, ie groups defined as the quotient of the
free group on a set of generators by a set of relations. One of the most common
approaches to these sorts of problems is based upon enumerative techniques [7]
with another being based upon string rewriting [2,11]. Although the former are
more widely used, their enumerative nature means they are limited to groups
with finitely many elements.

One problem in computational group theory is to find a presentation of the
subgroup generated by a set of elements of a group. The Reidemeister-Schreier
algorithm [7] was developed in the 1930's and gives a solution based upon enumerative techniques. This paper proposes a rewriting based alternative to the
Reidemeister-Schreier algorithm which has the advantage of being applicable to
infinite groups. A prototype has been implemented and we are currently discussing with the GAP-group how to bring it up to the standard required for
integration into the GAP [4] distribution.

Typically a group is given by a monoid presentation consisting of a set of
generators X and equations R and we are interested in finding a presentation
of the subgroup H generated by a set of words $Y \subseteq X^*$. It is clear that in general one can take as a generating set for H the disjoint union of Y with itself.
One half of this union will represent the elements of Y in H while the other
half will represent their inverses. However, the difficult question is to take the
relations of R, which may refer to words not in Y, and recast them so that they
only mention words built from Y and its inverses. To do this, words w_1 and w_2
built from Y but equal under R are considered as rewrite sequences and thus
the question becomes when should two rewrite sequences be equal. This takes

R. Nieuwenhuis (Ed.): RTA 2003, LNCS 2706, pp. 452–466, 2003.

us into the world of logged [6] or labelled rewriting as is found in Levy equivalence [9], rewriting logic [10] and 2-categorical models of rewriting [12]. Our central idea is that two rewrite sequences are equal if they arise through the analysis of critical pairs as found in Knuth-Bendix completion [8]. Thus, Knuth-Bendix completion is not only a mechanism for completing rewrite systems, but in addition the process of how this completion occurs contains valuable computational information. Since our equations are a by-product of Knuth-Bendix completion, our algorithm can be applied to infinite groups unlike the standard Reidemeister-Schreier algorithm. In more detail, our algorithm is broken down onto three parts.

- Subgroups are intimately connected with the behaviour of the associated cosets. The first step of our procedure is to define a *coset rewriting system* to solve the coset membership problem which asks when two elements of the group belong to the same coset.
- By attaching labels to the rewrites of the coset rewriting system we obtain witnesses to the solution of the coset membership problem.
- Finally, the critical pairs of the coset rewriting system, when labelled, yield the presentation of the subgroup.

As well as providing an application of rewriting, we were pleasantly surprised that our algorithm used some of the theory of rewriting, in particular sesqui-categories [12], Levy equivalence [9] and the interaction of these structures with Knuth-Bendix completion. We are aware that certain readers will not be familiar with these sesqui-categories but we only use the language of sesqui-categories to organise definitions and there is no deep categorical content which could put the reader off. Possibly more of a problem is the group theory used here which, although only of an undergraduate level, some readers may not have met. We have addressed this issue by including all relevant definitions and giving references. However, in the end, it is the nature of applications of rewriting to use concepts from outside the core of rewriting.

The paper is structured as follows. Section 2 contains all the group theoretic definitions required, while Section 3 addresses the coset membership problem. Section 4 gives our algorithm for obtaining a presentation of a subgroup while Section 5 contains two examples which we hope the reader will use to help understand the paper. We finish in Section 6 with some concluding remarks.

2   A Brief Introduction to Group Theory

This section contains all the basic definitions from group theory needed within this paper. A more detailed exposition of this material can be found in any text on computational group theory [3]. Since this paper is addressed to a rewriting audience, standard rewriting knowledge as in [1,2] will be assumed.

A monoid M consists of a triple $M = \langle X, \circ, e \rangle$ where $\circ$ is an associative binary operation on X with unit e. A group G consists of a quadruple $G = \langle X, \circ, \_^{-1}, e \rangle$ where $\langle X, \circ, e \rangle$ is a monoid and $\_^{-1}$ is a unary operation on X such that for all

$x \in X$, x^{-1} is an inverse for x under $\circ$. As is common practice, we use the same notation for a group and its underlying carrier set. A monoid homomorphism $f :$ $M_1 \to M_2$ between monoids is a function on the underlying sets which preserves the unit and composition. A group homomorphism is a monoid homomorphism between the underlying monoids as such monoid homomorphisms automatically preserve the inverse operation. We use the group S_3 of rotations and reflections of an equilateral triangle as a running example throughout this paper.

Example 1. *The group S_3 of rotations and reflections of an equilateral triangle has as elements $\{1, a, aa, ab, ba, b\}$ where a is a rotation by 120 degrees and b is a reflection around one axis. Composition, inverses etc are left to the reader.*

Given a set X, the free monoid X^* on X consists of finite sequences of elements of X. This set is also called the set of words over X. The monoid structure on X^* has as unit the empty word 1 and composition given by concatenation of words. Given a set X, we write $X + X$ for the disjoint union of X with itself. Typical elements of $(X + X)^*$ are written $x_1^{\epsilon_1} \cdots x_n^{\epsilon_n}$ where each $x_i \in X$ and $\epsilon_i \in \{+, -\}$ to denote which half of the disjoint union each element comes from. In practice we write x^+ simply as x. The free group $F_{\mathcal{G}}(X)$ on a set X is the quotient of $(X + X)^*$ by the relations $xx^- = 1 = x^-x$. Freeness of these structures allow us to define monoid homomorphisms $X^* \to M$ by giving functions $X \to M$ and group homomorphisms $F_{\mathcal{G}}(X) \to G$ by giving functions $X \to G$.

2.1   Monoid Presentations and Group Presentations

Most groups are not free. A larger class of groups which include many of practical importance and for which effective computational methods exist are the finitely presentable groups. These are defined via monoid presentations [3].

Definition 2 (Monoid Presentation). *A monoid presentation for a group G is of the form $mon\langle X|R \rangle$, where X is a finite set and R is a finite subset of $X^* \times X^*$ such that G is isomorphic (as a monoid, and hence a group) to the quotient of X^* by the least congruence containing R.*

Given a monoid presentation of a group G by $mon\langle X|R \rangle$ we denote by $\theta :$ $X^* \to G$ the quotient morphism assigning to each word its equivalence class in the group. Note that θ is surjective and a monoid homomorphism. Also given $w \in X^*$, we know that $\theta(w)^{-1} \in G$ and by surjectivity there is a word $z \in X^*$ such that $\theta(z) = \theta(w)^{-1}$. Abusing notation, we denote this word by w^- since it is a word representing the inverse of the word w under θ in G. Of course, w^- is not uniquely defined and we ensure we deal with this whenever required.

As an example of a monoid presentation, consider S_3. Three rotations produce the identity transformation of the triangle, so do two reflections and also a rotation, reflection, rotation and reflection. In fact all other equivalences of rotations and reflections can be deduced from these facts. Thus,

Example 3. *S_3 is presented by $mon\langle\, a, b \mid a^3 = 1,\ b^2 = 1,\ abab = 1 \,\rangle$.*

The most famous problem in computational group theory is the word problem: *Given a group presentation* $mon\langle X|R\rangle$ *and any two words w and w' in X^*, is it the case that $w \sim_R w'$* where $\sim_R$ is the least congruence on X^* containing R. This problem is in general undecidable but there are a number of approaches which solve the problem under certain circumstances. The most common is based upon *string rewriting* and *Knuth-Bendix completion* [1,2]. Given a monoid presentation, one orients each pair $(u, v) \in R$ as a rewriting rule $u \to_R v$, and proves the resulting rewriting relation is strongly normalising and confluent. Then every word has a computable unique normal form and $w \sim_R w'$ iff the normal form of w is equal to that of w'. If, as is most likely, the rewriting relation is not strongly normalising and confluent, Knuth-Bendix completion can attempt to obtain a rewriting relation $\to_{R'}$ which is strongly normalising, confluent and which generates the same congruence as $\to_R$.

Example 4. *Knuth-Bendix completion (with word length as termination order) of the presentation of S_3 gives the following complete rewriting system.*

$$
\begin{array}{lll}
aaa \to 1 & bb \to 1 & aab \to ba \\
aba \to b & baa \to ab & bab \to aa
\end{array}
$$

This paper tackles the problem of finding a presentation for a subgroup of a finitely presentable group. Subgroups are intimately connected with cosets and so we turn to the definition of these concepts.

Definition 5 (Subgroup). *A subgroup of a group G is a non-empty subset $H \subseteq G$ such that $e \in H$ and H is closed under composition and inverses.*

Examples of subgroups of S_3 are $\{1\}, \{1, a, aa\}$ and $\{1, b\}$. If H is a subgroup of G, we can divide or partition G by H into what are called *cosets*.

Definition 6 (Cosets). *Let H be a subgroup of G. Define an equivalence relation on G by $x \sim_H x'$ iff there is an $h \in H$ such that $x = hx'$. The cosets of H in G are written as G/H and defined to be the equivalence classes of G under $\sim_H$. The coset of an element $x \in G$ is written Hx.*

The data used in our rewriting alternative to Reidemeister-Schreier consists of a presentation of the group and a set of words which generate the subgroup.

Definition 7 (Coset Presentation). *A coset presentation is a triple $\langle X, S, Y \rangle$ where X is a set, $S \subseteq X^* \times X^*$ and $Y \subseteq X^*$.*

Implicitly a coset presentation P is assumed to determine the following:

- A group G_P defined via the monoid presentation $\langle X, S \rangle$.
- A monoid homomorphism $\theta : X^* \to G_P$.
- A subgroup H_P of G_P defined to be the least subgroup of G_P containing the set $\theta(Y)$. Alternatively, H_P consists of all elements of G_P of the form $\theta(y_1)^{\pm 1} \cdots \theta(y_n)^{\pm 1}$ where each $y_i \in Y$.

We now fix a coset presentation $\langle X, S, Y \rangle$, omit the subscript P and speak simply of the group G and the subgroup H. Any set of generators for H must have enough words to represent each element of H. Clearly $Y + Y$ provides such a set since $\theta(y)$ can be represented by y, $\theta(y)^{-1}$ by y^- and composites of the form $\theta(y_1)^{\pm 1} \cdots \theta(y_n)^{\pm 1}$ can be represented by words over $Y + Y$. Of course θ restricts to a map $Y \to H$ which extends uniquely to a monoid homomorphism $\hat{\theta} : (Y + Y)^* \to H$ by setting $\hat{\theta}(y^-) = \theta(y)^{-1}$. Further evidence that H can be expressed as a quotient of $(Y + Y)^*$ is the following lemma:

Lemma 8. *Let $\sim_{\hat{\theta}}$ be the kernel of $\hat{\theta}$. Then H is isomorphic to $(Y+Y)^*/\sim_{\hat{\theta}}$.*

Proof. We construct a bijection between $(Y+Y)^*/\sim_{\hat{\theta}}$ and H. Given $h \in H$, we have seen that h is of the form $\theta(w)$ for some $w \in (Y+Y)^*$. Thus h is mapped to the equivalence class of w under $\sim_{\hat{\theta}}$. In the reverse direction, given any equivalence class $[w] \in (Y+Y)^*/\sim_{\hat{\theta}}$, we map $[w]$ to $\hat{\theta}(w)$. That these definitions are independent upon the various choices and are mutually inverse are straightforward and left to the reader.

Unfortunately the congruence $\sim_{\hat{\theta}}$ does not give us a presentation and thus we must try to re-axiomatise it as equations using only symbols from $Y + Y$.

3   The Coset Membership Problem

The first step of our algorithm for obtaining a presentation of the subgroup H is to solve the coset membership problem which asks when two elements of the group belong to the same coset. We do this by rewriting over the set HX^* defined by introducing the formal symbol H and defining

$$HX^* = \{Hw \mid w \in X^*\}$$

We stress that in this context, H is just a formal symbol in the same way that elements of X^* are just formal words. The distinction between H used here as such a formal word and H used elsewhere as a subgroup mirrors the distinction between the words in X^* and their equivalence classes as elements of a group. Coset rewriting systems are defined as follows:

Definition 9 (Coset Rewriting System). *If $P = \langle X, S, Y \rangle$ is a coset presentation, a coset rewriting system (CRS) for P consists of a pair $R = \langle R_G, R_H \rangle$ where $R_G \subseteq X^* \times X^*$ and $R_H \subseteq HX^* \times HX^*$ such that:*

- *The relations R_G and S generate the same congruence. That is $\sim_S$ and $\sim_{R_G}$ are the same or, equivalently, $\langle X, R_G \rangle$ is a monoid presentation of G.*
- *If $(Hw, Hw') \in R_H$, then (as cosets) $H\theta(w) = H\theta(w')$.*
- *If $h \in H$, then there is a $w \in X^*$ such that $h = \theta(w)$ and $Hw \sim_R H$.*

The congruence $\sim_R$ used in the third clause of Definition 9 is generated from the rewriting relation $\to_R$ defined as the union of the rewriting relations $\to_{R_G}$ and $\to_{R_H}$ on HX^*. In turn these are defined as follows:

- $\rightarrow_{R_G}= \{ \ (Hulv, Hurv) \ | \ (l,r) \in R_G, \ u,v \in X^* \ \}$,
- $\rightarrow_{R_H}= \{ \ (Hwv, Hw'v) \ | \ (Hw, Hw') \in R_H, \ v \in X^* \ \}$.

The intuition underlying Definition 9 is that R_G gives another presentation of G — since we will be using Knuth-Bendix completion R_G cannot simply be taken to be S. We may then think of R_H as performing computation on G, ie rewriting on R_G-equivalence classes. By regarding a CRS as a proof system, the first of the conditions of Definition 9 is the soundness and completeness of R_G with respect to S, the second condition is the soundness of R_H with respect to the subgroup H while the final condition is the completeness of R wrt H.

As with usual rewriting systems, CRSs are closed under inverses and disjoint unions. Formally, if R is a CRS its inverse R^{-1} is the CRS with rules in the reverse direction. Similarly, given two CRSs R_1 and R_2 for the same coset presentation, the union $R_1 + R_2$ is the CRS whose rules are the union of the rules of R_1 and R_2. The following is an easy lemma.

Lemma 10. *If R is a CRS, so is its inverse R^{-1}. Similarly, if R_1 and R_2 are CRSs for the same coset presentation, so is $R_1 + R_2$.*

There are two key lemmas we wish to establish about CRSs; firstly that CRSs can be used to decide the coset membership problem and secondly that a coset presentation defines an initial CRS.

Lemma 11. *If $R = \langle R_G, R_H \rangle$ is a CRS for a coset presentation $\langle X, S, Y \rangle$, then the cosets G/H are in 1-1 correspondence with the equivalence classes $HX^*/ \sim_R$.*

Proof. We define functions $\phi : G/H \rightarrow HX^*/ \sim_R$ and $\psi : HX^*/ \sim_R \rightarrow G/H$; check they are well defined given that their definitions depend upon representatives of cosets and equivalence classes; and prove they are mutually inverse.

To define ϕ consider a coset Hg. Surjectivity of θ means there is an $x_g \in X^*$ such that $\theta(x_g) = g$. Set $\phi(Hg) = [Hx_g]$. We show this definition is independent of the choice of g and the word x_g. Given a y_g such that $\theta(y_g) = g$, then $y_g \sim_S x_g$ and hence $y_g \sim_{R_G} x_g$. Thus $[Hx_g] = [Hy_g]$. Given a g' such that $Hg' = Hg$, there is an $h \in H$ such that $g' = hg$. Thus there is a $w \in X^*$ such that $\theta(w) = h$ and $Hw \sim_R H$. Thus $\theta(wx_g) = g'$ and hence $\phi(Hg') = [Hwx_g] = [Hx_g] = \phi(Hg)$.

Define ψ by mapping an equivalence class $[Hw]$ to the coset $H\theta(w)$. If $[Hw] = [Hw']$ we must show that $H\theta(w) = H\theta(w')$. Without loss of generality, assume Hw' is a one-step rewrite of Hw using either $\rightarrow_{R_H}$ or $\rightarrow_{R_G}$. Either i) $Hw = Hlv \rightarrow_{R_H} Hrv = Hw'$ where $(Hl, Hr) \in R_H$ in which case $H\theta(w) = H\theta(lv) = H\theta(l)\theta(v) = H\theta(r)\theta(v) = H\theta(rv) = H\theta(w')$ where $H\theta(l) = H\theta(r)$ is the second condition in a CRS; ii) $Hw = Hulv \rightarrow_{R_G} Hurv = Hw'$ where $(l,r) \in R_G$ in which case $\theta(w) = \theta(w')$ since $\sim_{R_G}=\sim_S$ and θ identifies S-equivalent words.

Finally, $\phi(\psi[Hw]) = \phi(H\theta(w)) = [Hw]$ since we may choose w from the preimage of $\theta(w)$. In the other direction $\psi(\phi(Hg)) = \psi([Hx_g]) = H\theta(x_g) = Hg$ where x_g is an arbitrary element such that $\theta(x_g) = g$.

The other lemma we want is that CRSs actually exist. In fact, a coset presentation actually defines an associated CRS.

Lemma 12. *If $P = \langle X, S, Y \rangle$ is a coset presentation, define*

$$P_G = S \quad and \quad P_H = \{(Hy, H) \mid y \in Y\} \cup \{(Hy^-, H) \mid y \in Y\}$$

Then $P_0 = \langle P_G, P_H \rangle$ is a CRS henceforth called the initial CRS generated by P.

Proof. We have three conditions to verify. The first is trivial and so is the second since if $y \in Y$, then $\theta(y), \theta(y)^{-1} \in H$. Next, let K consist of those elements $h \in H$ such that there is a word z such that $\theta(z) = h$ and $Hz \sim_R H$. We want to prove $H \subseteq K$. Clearly K contains all elements of the form $\theta(y)$ for $y \in Y$. K is also trivially closed under multiplication. We finish by showing K is closed under inverses. So let $h \in K$ with, say, $\theta(z) = h$ and $Hz \sim_R H$. Recall there is a $z^- \in X^*$ such that $\theta(z^-) = h^{-1}$ and hence $\theta(zz^-) = 1$. Thus $zz^- \sim_S 1$ and

$$Hz^- \sim_{P_H} Hzz^- \sim_S H$$

and so $Hz^- \sim_{P_0} H$ with $\theta(z^-) = h^{-1}$ as required.

We define $P^= = P_0 + P_0^{-1}$ which, by lemma 10, is also a CRS. The final part of the lemma follows from lemma 10. Given that a coset presentation defines an initial CRS, we now prove that Knuth-Bendix completion of a CRS produces a CRS. We do this in two stages to ensure that we get a complete rewriting system to decide the equality $\sim_S$ defining the group G.

Lemma 13. *Let $R = \langle R_G, R_H \rangle$ be a CRS for a coset presentation $P = \langle X, S, Y \rangle$. If R_G^c is the Knuth-Bendix completion of R_G then $\langle R_G^c, R_H \rangle$ is a CRS for P.*

Proof. Knuth-Bendix completion doesn't alter the strength of the associated congruence. Thus $\sim_{R_G^c}$ is the same as $\sim_{R_G}$. The second property trivially holds, while the third property follows for the same reason as the first.

Knuth-Bendix completion of a CRS also involves an analysis for $R_G - R_H$ critical pairs and $R_H - R_H$ critical pairs and consequently adding new R_H-rewrites to the CRS. The iterative step of this part of the completion considers spans $Hw \to_R^* Hu$ and $Hw \to_R^* Hv$ where Hu and Hv are $\to_R$ normal forms and adds a rewrite $Hu \to_{R_H} Hv$ or $Hv \to_{R_H} Hu$ depending on which term is larger in the termination order.

Lemma 14. *Knuth-Bendix completion of a CRS results in a CRS.*

Proof. We have already dealt with the analysis of $R_G - R_G$ critical pairs. Assume we have a CRS R_n and a critical pair $Hw \to_{R_n}^* Hu$ and $Hw \to_{R_n}^* Hv$ which cannot be completed. We then introduce a new R_H-rewrite $Hu \to Hv$ or vice versa depending upon the termination order. Clearly the first and third condition of a CRS holds after the addition of this rewrite. For the second condition, note that Hu and Hv belong to the same $\sim_{R_n}$ equivalence class. From lemma 11, we conclude that $\psi(Hu) = \psi(Hv)$. Since $H\theta(u) = \psi(Hu)$ and $H\theta(v) = \psi(Hv)$, the second condition is also preserved by the addition of this new rewriting rule.

We now have our first key theorem, namely that if the Knuth-Bendix procedure terminates, coset equivalence is decidable.

Theorem 15. *Assume the Knuth-Bendix procedure terminates. Then given two elements $g, g' \in G$, it is decidable if $Hg = Hg'$.*

Proof. Let R be the CRS resulting from Knuth-Bendix completion in lemma 14 of the initial CRS arising from the coset presentation as described in lemma 12. Further, let $\theta(x_g) = g$ and $\theta(x_{g'}) = g'$. Then $Hg = Hg'$ iff $Hx_g \sim_R Hx_{g'}$ and this later condition can be decided by reducing to normal form.

4   Logged Coset Rewriting System

The second step in our algorithm is to label the rewrites of a CRS which provides proof terms or witnesses for the coset membership problem. By equating those labels which arise from critical pair completion we get our presentation for the subgroup of a coset presentation.

A logged coset rewriting system is simply a rewriting system with proof terms attached to indicate why a term rewrites to another. This is similar in nature to what happens in *rewriting logic* [10] and can be traced back to Levy's *permutation equivalence* [9]. In a different context, the same idea also arises in 2-categorical and sesqui-categorical models of rewriting [12,13]. Although we use the formal language of sesqui-categories because they provide the most concise language to express our constructions, they do not hide any difficult mathematics and are simply an efficient organisational device. Readers not familiar with sesqui-categories should therefore still be able to follow the argument.

Firstly we give the labels for rewrites. A one-step rewrite will be labelled by the rewrite used and the context within which it is used. For a CRS $\langle R_G, R_H \rangle$, this context is a pair of words if the rule comes from R_G and simply a word if the rule is in R_H. A rewrite sequence will be labelled by a sequence of such one-step labels making sure that the sources and targets match for the sake of well-formedness.

Definition 16 (Theory of a CRS). *Given a CRS $R = \langle R_G, R_H \rangle$ for a coset presentation $P = \langle X, S, Y \rangle$, the theory of R, written S_R, consists of all elements of the following form: $u_1 \rho_1 v_1 \dots u_n \rho_n v_n$ where*

- *Each $\rho_i \in R_G$ or $\rho_i \in R_H$.*
- *If $\rho_i \in R_G$, then $u_i \in HX^*$ and $v_i \in X^*$.*
- *If $\rho_i \in R_H$, then $u_i = 1$ and $v_i \in X^*$.*
- *Sources/targets of adjacent rewrites match: $u_i tgt(\rho_i) v_i = u_{i+1} src(\rho_{i+1}) v_{i+1}$*

An abstract definition of S_R is as the free sesqui-category on the following graph:

$$\bullet \xrightarrow{\quad H \quad} \bullet \; \circlearrowright \, X^*$$

with 2-cells consisting of the rewriting rules of $\to_R$. That S_R is a sesqui-category is just a quick way of saying that rewrite sequences with adjacent sources and targets can be composed in an associative manner with a unit, and that rewrites can be composed on the left and right by words, ie rewrites can be placed in context. The arrow H reflects the fact that R_H rewritings can only be composed on the right. S_R is not a 2-category as the permutation law of Levy equivalence or, equivalently, the interchange laws of a 2-category [13] do not hold.

These labels contain too much information for obtaining a presentation of the subgroup of a coset presentation. For example when we perform Knuth-Bendix completion we don't want to add new labels for the rewriting rules added by the completion process. Rather we want to use the span which led to the addition of a new rewriting rule as its label. We describe the quotienting of this extra information by a sesqui-functor and call this a logged coset rewriting system.

Definition 17 (Logged Coset Rewriting System). *Given a coset presentation $P = \langle X, S, Y \rangle$, a logged coset rewriting system (LCRS) consists of a CRS R and a sesqui-functor $F : S_R \longrightarrow S_{P=}$ which is the identity on 0- and 1-cells.*

The fact that F is an identity on 0-cells and 1-cells means all F does is to associate each label from a CRS R with a label from the CRS $P^=$ which recall is the symmetric closure of the initial CRS P_0. We call the functor F, the log functor of the LCRS. Of course, the initial CRS P_0 is a logged CRS with the obvious inclusion functor $F : S_{P_0} \longrightarrow S_{P=}$. As implied above, Knuth-Bendix completion not only maps CRSs to CRSs, but also LCRSs to LCRSs by replacing the label of each new rewriting rule by the span which it completed.

Lemma 18. *Let $L = \langle R, F \rangle$ be a LCRS. If R^c is the Knuth-Bendix completion of R, then there is a canonical LCRS $L^c = \langle R^c, F^c \rangle$.*

Proof. Assume at stage n, we have a CRS R_n and log functor $F_n : S_{R_n} \longrightarrow S_{P=}$. Given a span $\alpha_1, \alpha_2 : Hw \rightarrow^*_{R_n} Hw_1, Hw_2$ with Hw_1 and Hw_2 in R_n-normal form, not only do we form the new CRS by adding a rule, say, $Hw_1 \rightarrow Hw_2$ to obtain the CRS R_{n+1}, but we also freely generate a log functor $F_{n+1} : S_{R_{n+1}} \longrightarrow S_{P=}$ by setting the log of the rewrite $Hw_1 \rightarrow Hw_2$ to be $(F_n\alpha_1)^{-1}F_n\alpha_2$.

So the log functor translates the rewrites of a Knuth-Bendix completed CRS into rewrites and their inverses from the initial CRS. The examples of Section 5 show how the logs for specific completed LCRSs are calculated. However, there is more information we wish to delete. For example all the rewrites in R_G describe the construction of the group G from words but tell us nothing about the subgroup H. Thus for the purposes of obtaining a presentation of H they have no computational content and hence we want to ignore them. To do this we wish to set their logs to 1. We also wish to throw away the context from a P_H rewrite and simply record the particular rules from P_H which were used. Thus we define a map $[\![.]\!] : S_{P=} \longrightarrow (Y + Y)^*$ as follows:

$$\begin{aligned}
[\![\alpha w]\!] &= y & \text{if there is a } y \in Y + Y \text{ such that } \alpha = (Hy, H) \in P_H \\
[\![\alpha^{-1} w]\!] &= y^- & \text{if there is a } y \in Y + Y \text{ such that } \alpha^{-1} = (H, Hy) \in P_H^{-1} \\
[\![\alpha^{-1} w]\!] &= 1 & \text{if } \alpha \in P_G + (P_G)^{-1}
\end{aligned}$$

We get a map $[\![.]\!] : S_{P=} \to (Y + Y)^*$ by applying $[\![.]\!]$ as defined above to each logged rewrite in a rewrite sequence. Putting these maps together, for every LCRS $\langle R, F \rangle$, we have the following chain:

$$S_R \xrightarrow{\ F\ } S_{P=} \xrightarrow{\ [\![.]\!]\ } (Y + Y)^* \xrightarrow{\ \hat{\theta}\ } H \qquad (1)$$

A category theorist will notice that we are abusing notation here in that F is a sesqui-functor, while $[\![.]\!]$ is mapping the 2-cells/logged rewrites of $S_{P=}$ to a monoid and $\hat{\theta}$ is a monoid homomorphism. Nevertheless, equation 1 shows how rewrites in a LCRS are converted into words in $(Y + Y)^*$.

A crucial part of our algorithm is that elements of the generating set $(Y+Y)^*$, while usually regarded as either atomic symbols or words in X^*, can also be regarded as rewrites in Γ_0 and thus equality on such words can be axiomatised via equality of rewrites generated from Knuth-Bendix completion. This is shown by the following simple lemma:

Lemma 19. *Let $w \in (Y + Y)^*$ be a word. Then there is a rewrite sequence $r_w : Hw \to^*_{P_H} H$. Furthermore, $[\![r_w]\!] = w$.*

Proof. Define r_w by induction. If $w = 1$, set r_w to be the identity rewrite $H \to^*_{P_H} H$. If w is of the form yw' where $y \in Y + Y$, then we have a P_H-rewrite $\alpha_y : Hy \longrightarrow H$ and r_w can be defined as follows:

$$Hyw' \xrightarrow{\ \alpha_y w'\ } Hw' \xrightarrow{\ r_{w'}\ } H$$

The second half of the lemma is a trivial calculation.

By lemma 8, we know that H is the quotient of $(Y+Y)^*$ by $\sim_{\hat{\theta}}$. Since critical pair completion results in parallel pairs, proving that the equality derived from critical pair completion is contained in $\sim_{\hat{\theta}}$ is essentially the following lemma.

Lemma 20. *If $\beta : Hw \to^* Hz$ in the LCRS $P^=$, then $w \sim_{\hat{\theta}} [\![\beta]\!]z$. Thus if $\beta, \beta' : Hw \to^* Hz$, then $[\![\beta]\!] \sim_{\hat{\theta}} [\![\beta']\!]$.*

Proof. The first part of the lemma is clearly true if β is a one-step rewrite since i) if β is of the form urv for $r \in P_G$, then $[\![\beta]\!] = 1$ and $w \sim_S z$; ii) if β is of the form rv for $r = (Hy, H)$ for $y \in Y$, then $w = yv$, $[\![\beta]\!] = y$ and $z = v$; and iii) a similar argument holds when β is of the form rv for $r = (H, Hy) \in P_H^{-1}$. The result holds for many-step rewrites since the action of $[\![.]\!]$ on a sequence of rewrites is just the composition of the action of $[\![.]\!]$ on each one-step rewrite. For the second part of the lemma, we have $[\![\beta]\!]z \sim_{\hat{\theta}} w \sim_{\hat{\theta}} [\![\beta']\!]z$. The result follows from cancellation of z using a word $z^- \in X^*$ such that $\theta(z^-) = \theta(z)^{-1}$

$$[\![\beta]\!] \sim_{\hat{\theta}} [\![\beta]\!]zz^- \sim_{\hat{\theta}} [\![\beta']\!]zz^- \sim_{\hat{\theta}} [\![\beta']\!]$$

We now give a presentation of the subgroup generated from a coset presentation.

Definition 21. *Let* $L^c = \langle R^c, F^c \rangle$ *be the LCRS arising from Knuth-Bendix completion of the initial LCRS. For each critical pair in* R^c, $\alpha_1, \alpha_2 : Hw \to Hw_1, Hw_2$, *there are completions* $\beta_1, \beta_2 : Hw_1, Hw_2 \to Hw'$. *Define* $\mathcal{C}$ *as follows:*

$$\mathcal{C} = \{(\alpha_1.\beta_1, \alpha_2.\beta_2) \mid \alpha_1, \alpha_2 \text{ is such a critical pair }\}$$

and the equations R_L *by:*

$$R_L = \{([\![F^c\gamma]\!], [\![F^c\gamma']\!]) \mid (\gamma, \gamma') \in \mathcal{C}\}$$

All that is left to do is prove that this really is a presentation for the subgroup H. Lemma 20 is the key to proving that critical pair equality is contained in $\sim_{\hat{\theta}}$ so not surprisingly the reverse inclusion depends upon what looks like a partial converse to lemma 20.

Lemma 22. *Let* $\langle R^c, F^c \rangle$ *be a complete logged rewriting system and assume there are rewrites* $r_1 : Hw_1 \to^*_{R^c} H$ *and* $r_2 : Hw_2 \to^*_{R^c} H$ *where* $w_1 \sim_{R^c_G} w_2$. *Then* $[\![F^c r_1]\!] \sim_{R_L} [\![F^c r_2]\!]$.

Proof. We first prove the lemma when $w_1 = w_2$ using a simple tiling argument by induction on the rank of w. If either rewrite has length 0, then so does the other (because of termination) and so the result is trivial. Otherwise we have the following situation:

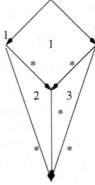

where the first rewrite of r_1 and the first rewrite of r_2 have been completed via a critical pair in cell (1), while cells (2) and (3) are formed because the completion of this critical pair must rewrite to H. After applying $[\![F^c\_]\!]$ to the rewrites in this diagram, cell (1) commutes up to $\sim_{R_L}$ since it is formed by a critical pair, while cells (2) and (3) commute up to $\sim_{R_L}$ by induction. Thus $[\![F^c r_1]\!] \sim_{R_L} [\![F^c r_2]\!]$. For the general case, w_1 and w_2 have a common R^c_G reduct and the lemma then follows from the argument above and the observation that for any R^c_G-rewrite sequence r, $[\![F^c r]\!] = 1$.

Finally, we prove our main theorem:

Theorem 23. *Assume* $P = \langle X, S, Y \rangle$ *is a coset presentation for a subgroup H of G which generates a complete logged rewriting system* $L^c = \langle R^c, F^c \rangle$ *as described above. Then* $\langle Y + Y, R_L \rangle$ *is a monoid presentation for H.*

Proof. By lemma 8, we know that $H = (Y + Y)^*/ \sim_{\hat{\theta}}$ so the result follows by proving that the congruences $\sim_{\hat{\theta}}$ and $\sim_{R_L}$ are equal.

In one direction, consider a critical pair α_1, α_2 with completions β_1, β_2. Now $(\alpha_1.\beta_1, \alpha_2.\beta_2)$ is a parallel pair and hence by lemma 20 $[\![F^c(\alpha_1.\beta_1)]\!] \sim_{\hat{\theta}} [\![F^c(\alpha_2.\beta_2)]\!]$.

In the reverse direction, let $h \sim_{\hat{\theta}} k$. By lemma 19, there are logged rewrites in P_0 of the form $r_h : Hh \to H$ and $r_k : Hk \to H$. Since P_0 is a CRS, we also have that $Hh \sim_{P_G} Hk$. By lemma 22, $[\![r_h]\!] \sim_{R_L} [\![r_k]\!]$. Since $[\![r_h]\!] = h$ and $[\![r_k]\!] = k$ $h \sim_{R_L} k$ and hence $\sim_{\hat{\theta}}$ is contained in $\sim_{R_L}$.

5 S_3 and an Example with Infinite Cosets

We illustrate our algorithm with our running example of S_3 and another example showing the applicability of our algorithm to a situation where one has an infinite number of cosets. We have kept the examples simple so the reader can follow the examples without too many exhaustive Knuth-Bendix calculations.

Example 1: For S_3, we use the following coset presentation $P = \langle X, S, Y \rangle$:

$$X = \{a, b\} \quad S = \{(aaa, 1), (bb, 1), (abab, 1)\} \quad Y = \{a\}$$

The subgroup generated by a is $\{1, a, aa\}$ which has as presentation $mon\langle \ a \ | \ (aaa, 1) \ \rangle$. Our algorithm attempts to build a presentation based upon 2 generators a and a^-. Since $\theta(aa) = \theta(a)^{-1}$, the initial CRS $P_0 = \langle P_G, P_H \rangle$ is:

$$P_G = \{(aaa, 1), (bb, 1), (abab, 1)\} \qquad P_H = \{(Ha, H), (Haa, H)\}$$

To complete P_G, add rules $\{(bab, a^2), (ba^2, ab), (a^2b, ba), (aba, b)\}$,. To complete the CRS P_0 add the rule (Hba, Hb) since we have the span $r_a ba : Haba \to Hba$ and $Haba \to_{P_G^c} Hb$. As described in the proof of lemma 18, the application of $[\![F^c_-]\!]$ to any rewrite built from this new rewriting rule will be a^-. The equations of the presentation then come from analysis of the critical pairs. Two of these are given below where we have already applied $[\![F^c_-]\!]$ to the rewrites.

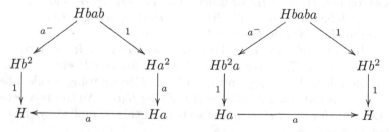

The first diagram above comes from resolving the critical pair that occurs on $Hbab$ when the rules $Hba \to Hb$ and $bab \to a^2$ are applied. This gives us the relation $aa = a^-$. The second diagram shows the resolution of the pair $Hba \to Hb$ and $aba \to b$ on $Hbaba$, which gives us the relation $a^-a = 1$. Combining these we get $aaa = 1$. Analysis of other critical pairs gives no new equations and since a^- is definable from a we can delete this generator. Thus the subgroup generated by this coset presentation is the cyclic group of order 3.

Example 2: This example shows how the rewriting methods we describe can be applied to the problem of finding a presentation of a subgroup when the group, subgroup and the number of cosets are infinite.

Let G be the group generated by four elements $\{a, b, c, d\}$ of which the first pair a and b, commute with each other and the second pair c and d, also commute with each other. Let H be the subgroup generated by the four elements $\{ac, ca, bd, db\}$. The initial coset rewrite system then includes the rewrite rules for the group:

$$\{ (aa^-, 1), (a^-a, 1), (bb^-, 1), (b^-b, 1), (cc^-, 1), (c^-c, 1), (dd^-, 1), (d^-d, 1),$$
$$(ba, ab), (ba^-, a^-b), (b^-a, ab^-), (b^-a^-, a^-b^-),$$
$$(dc, cd), (dc^-, c^-d), (d^-c, cd^-), (d^-c^-, c^-d^-)\}$$

This system is in fact complete. The rules of this type do not give us information about the subgroup, so we assign to each of them the identity label. The four generators of the subgroup give us four initial H-rules:

$$\{(Hac, H), (Hca, H), (Hbd, H), (Hdd, H)\},$$

which we label $\alpha_1, \ldots, \alpha_4$ respectively. These are the generators for our presentation of the group H. Their inverses, $\alpha_1^{-1}, \ldots, \alpha_4^{-1}$ are the following rules:

$$\{(Hc^-a^-, H), (Ha^-c^-, H), (Hd^-b^-, H), (Hb^-d^-, H)\}.$$

Logged completion uses the shortlex order with $a < a^- < b < b^- < \cdots < d^- < H$, identifies critical pairs and resolves them, adding new logged rules to the system. For example, $Ha^-c^- \to H$ by α_2^{-1} overlaps with $c^-c \to 1$ by 1. The resolution of this is as follows: $Ha^-c^-c \to Hc^-$ by using a rule labelled by α_2^{-1} and $Ha^-c^-c \to Ha^-$ by using a rule labelled by 1. This gives us the new rule $Hc \to Ha^-$ by α_2.

Similarly, $Hbd \to H$ by α_3 overlaps with $dc \to cd$ by 1. The resolution of this is as follows: $Hbdc \to Hc$ by using a rule labelled by α_3 and $Hc \to Ha^-$ by using a rule labelled by α_2 while $Hbdc \to Hbcd$ by using a rule labelled by 1. This gives us the new rule $Hbcd \to Ha^-$ by $\alpha_3\alpha_2$.

As a final example, the rule obtained above $Hbcd \to H$ by $\alpha_3\alpha_2^{-1}$ overlaps with $dd^- \to 1$ by 1. The resolution of this is as follows: $Hbcdd^- \to Ha^-d^-$ by using a rule labelled by $\alpha_3\alpha_2$ and $Hbcdd^- \to Hbc$ by using a rule labelled by 1. This gives us the new rule $Hbc \to Ha^-d^-$ by $\alpha_3\alpha_2$. We can now remove the previous rule $Hbcd \to Ha^-$ from the system, as this is implied by the new rule, together with $dd^- \to 1$.

After a few passes of the logged Knuth-Bendix algorithm we have the same group rules and the following H-rules:

$$\{ (Hac, H), (Ha^-c^-, H), (Hbd, H), (Hb^-d^-, H), (Hc^-, Ha), (Hc, Ha^-), (Hd^-, Hb),$$
$$(Hd, Hb^-), (Hbc, Ha^-d^-), (Hbc^-, Had^-), (Hb^-c, Ha^-d), (Hb^-c^-, Had) \}$$

with various labels. Now we seek the relations for the subgroup, by looking at the critical pairs of the completed system and noting the labelled rules which are used in resolving them. For example, $Hac \to H$ overlaps with $cc^- \to 1$. The resolution of this is as follows: $Hacc^- \to Hc^-$ by using the rule labelled by α_1 and $Hc^- \to Ha$ by using the rule labelled by α_1^{-1} and $Hacc^- \to Ha$ by using a rule labelled by 1. This gives us the relation $\alpha_1 \alpha_1^{-1} = 1$. If we continue, checking all critical pairs, we find that every critical pair yields a trivial relation. Thus, H can be proven to be the free group on four generators.

6   Conclusion

We have presented an algorithm based upon rewriting for calculating a presentation for a subgroup of a finitely presentable group. Within this framework, the number of relations is computed via the critical pairs of a certain rewriting system. This makes it applicable to situations where the group, subgroup and the number of cosets are infinite. These examples cannot be tackled by the traditional Reidemeister-Schreier algorithm which has at its core an enumeration of the elements of the group. The key theoretical idea underpinning our algorithm is that the Knuth-Bendix completion procedure can give us not only a complete rewriting system, but also the nature of these completions contain valuable information.

We are currently thinking of taking this research in two directions. Firstly we wish to see our algorithm implemented and distributed so that it can be used by group theorists. A prototype has already been written for the GAP system and we are currently discussing with the GAP group ways to optimise it so as to improve its efficiency, etc. A couple of referees did comment on the practical viability of our algorithm. The general consensus [5] seems to be a practical one, namely that in any given situation we want to have as many methods available to try and the best solution may well be a mixture of several approaches.

In a more theoretical direction, there are a number of other algebraic structures, eg rings, modules, algebras, where the same problem of obtaining presentations for substructures arise and we are developing analogues of the algorithm presented in this paper to tackle these questions.

References

1. F.Baader and T. Nipkow : Term Rewriting and all That, *Cambridge University Press* 1998.
2. R. Book and F. Otto : String-Rewriting Systems, *Springer-Verlag, New York* 1993.
3. D.B.A. Epstein with J.W.Cannon et al : Word processing in groups, *Jones and Bartlett, Boston* 1992.
4. THE GAP GROUP, 'GAP – Groups, Algorithms, and Programming, Version 4', Aachen, St Andrews, 1998, (http://www-gap.dcs.st-and.ac.uk/~gap).
5. Havas, Holt, Keene and Rees: Australian Mathematical Society 0263-6115/0 (1999) http://www.mas.ncl.ac.uk/ nser/abstracts/jams.ps.gz

6. A. Heyworth and C. D. Wensley : Logged rewriting with applications to identities among relations, *Groups St Andrews 2001 in Oxford, eds C. Campbell, E. Robertson and G. Smith, Cambridge University Press* (to appear).
7. D. Johnson : Presentations of Groups, *Cambridge University Press* 1990.
8. M. Johnson : Pasting diagrams in n-categories with applications to coherence theorems and categories of paths, *PhD thesis, University of Sydney*, 1988.
9. J.J. Levy: *Réductions correctes et optimales dans le λ-calcul*, Thèse d'Etat, Paris (1978).
10. J. Meseguer: Research Directions in Rewriting Logic, *Computational Logic, NATO Advanced Study Institute Series F, Vol. 165, pp. 345-398, Springer-Verlag*, 1999.
11. C. C. Sims : Computation with Finitely Presented Groups, *Cambridge University Press*, 1994.
12. J. G. Stell : *Modelling Term Rewriting Systems by Sesquicategories*, Technical Report TR94-02, University of Keele, 1994.
13. R. Street : *Categorical structures*, Handbook of Algebra, Vol. 1 pp.529–577, 1996.

Stable Computational Semantics
of Conflict-Free Rewrite Systems
(Partial Orders with Duplication)

Zurab Khasidashvili[1] and John Glauert[2]

[1] Logic and Validation Technology
Intel, IDC, Haifa, Israel
Zurab.Khasidashvili@intel.com
[2] School of Computing Sciences, UEA
Norwich NR4 7TJ, UK
J.Glauert@uea.ac.uk

Abstract. We study orderings $\trianglelefteq_S$ on reductions in the style of Lévy reflecting the growth of information w.r.t. *(super)stable* sets S of 'values' (such as head-normal forms or Böhm-trees). We show that sets of co-initial reductions ordered by $\trianglelefteq_S$ form finitary ω-algebraic complete lattices, and hence form computation and Scott domains. As a consequence, we obtain a relativized version of the *computational semantics* proposed by Boudol for term rewriting systems. Furthermore, we give a pure domain-theoretic characterization of the orderings $\trianglelefteq_S$ in the spirit of Kahn and Plotkin's *concrete domains*. These constructions are carried out in the framework of *Stable Deterministic Residual Structures*, which are abstract reduction systems with an axiomatized residual relations on redexes, that model all orthogonal (or conflict-free) reduction systems as well as many other interesting computation structures.

1 Introduction

The idea of representing or identifying a process (or a program, or a term) with the domain of all its computations is not new in semantics: it is central to the study of event structure semantics of programming languages developed by Winskel, Nielsen and Plotkin [Win80,NPW81,Win89]. Berry and Lévy [BL79] were the first to base algebraic semantics [NR85] of recursive programs on an ordering on the set of *computations* rather than on the set of *terms*; they used Lévy's [Lév78,Lév80] *embedding* relation $\trianglelefteq_L$ on reductions, and *Lévy-* or *permutation-equivalence* $\approx_L$ on reductions which is the largest symmetric relation contained in $\trianglelefteq_L$. Permutation-equivalent reductions result from one another by permuting concurrent consecutive steps, hence the name. Developing these ideas further, Boudol [Bou85] proposed a *computational* approach to semantics of term rewriting systems [Ter03] in general. Boudol's idea was to define the semantics of a term t in a term rewriting system (Σ, R) (where Σ is an alphabet and R is a set of rewrite rules) via the set of $\approx_L$-classes of all $\trianglelefteq_L$-maximal computations starting from t. In the case of deterministic (or conflict-free or

R. Nieuwenhuis (Ed.): RTA 2003, LNCS 2706, pp. 467–482, 2003.
© Springer-Verlag Berlin Heidelberg 2003

orthogonal) TRSs, a term has exactly one $\trianglelefteq_L$-maximal computation (up to $\approx_L$), which corresponds to a *fair* computation [Ter03]. To support his computational approach to semantics, Boudol defined *interpretations* of TRSs in the usual algebraic style (i.e., the class of interpretations coincides with the class of Σ-algebras) and showed that the computational semantics coincides with the algebraic one.

However, Boudol [Bou85] remarked that, besides being a cpo, "$\trianglelefteq_L$ *seems to have generally no 'good' properties (even for deterministic TRSs)*". To clarify the problem, we observe that, according to Kahn and Plotkin [KP93], a 'good' domain into which to interpret programs must be at least *coherent* and ω-*algebraic*; they call such domains *computation domains*. According to Scott [Sco82], 'good' domains are *consistently complete* ω-algebraic cpos, now termed *Scott domains*. To quote Plotkin, 'Algebraicity is an important idea which formalizes some intuitive ideas of *finiteness* and objects as *limits* of their finite approximations. Algebraicity allows definitions of *computability* to provide links with recursion function theory and allow results on *definability*. It allows easy consideration of constructions as *powerdomains* and enables us to visualize domains as *completions* of structures of finite information' [Plo83]. Further, Kahn and Plotkin [KP93], Girard [Gir87], Winskel [Win89], and many others argue that it is reasonable to require 'good' domains to be *finitary*, because in this way finite elements are 'really' finite, i.e., represent only a finite amount of information (built up from a finite number of components), and thus cannot be decomposed infinitely. But $\trianglelefteq_L$ is not finitary, and the $\trianglelefteq_L$-glb of two finite elements needs not be finite. To recover 'good' properties of the reduction space, Boudol [Bou85] studied the sub-space of all *strongly needed* reductions [HL91] and proved that a reduction space thus restricted is finitary and ω-algebraic, and conjectured that it corresponds to the domain of configurations of an event structure and moreover forms a *concrete domain* [KP93].

There have been other similar proposals to construct domains with rich algebraic properties out of the reduction space of a reduction system. For example, in order to construct an event structure semantics for orthogonal (term graph) rewriting systems with non-duplicating residual relation, Kennaway et al. [KKSV93] restrict themselves to needed reductions of normalizable terms; the resulting domain is finitary and *distributive* (or equivalently, *prime algebraic*). Finitary distributive domains (also called *dI-domains* or *stable domains*) are exactly domains of configurations/states (ordered by the subset relation) generated by *stable* event structures [Win80,NPW81,Win89], and are commonly accepted domains to model concurrency.

Thus in all these cases, a *linear* subspace of reductions is identified on which $\trianglelefteq_L$ forms *dI*-domains. This works because event structures are equivalent to linear reduction systems (where there is no erasure or duplication of redexes): in linear systems, $\trianglelefteq_L$ corresponds to the subset ordering on states of an event structure, all permutation-equivalent reductions correspond to the same state, *prime intervals* of the event structure represent reduction steps [Win89], and events can be seen as equivalence-classes of prime-intervals [Win89], which are nothing but *zig-zag*-classes [Lév78,Lév80] of the corresponding reduction steps [Cur86]. This correspondence is further extended in [KG02] (for the case of stable conflict-free systems), where prime event structures (which are equivalent to stable ones [Win89]), with an axiomatized *erasure* relation, are defined. These are to non-duplicating reduction systems what event structures are to linear ones.

In order to achieve a stable event structure semantics, or equivalently, to construct a *dI*-domain out of a reduction space, rather than restricting the reduction space, one could weaken permutation-equivalence into an equivalence relation whose equivalence classes would correspond to the same state of a stable event structure. This observation led Laneve [Lan94] to introduce *distributive permutation equivalence* in the λ-calculus which only equates reductions resulting one from another by permutation of steps that cannot erase or duplicate one another. The distributive equivalence coincides with permutation-equivalence on needed reductions in non-duplicating orthogonal rewriting systems, but is strictly weaker in the case of even λ_I-calculus, where there is no erasure of redexes. Similarly, Corradini et al [CGM95] based their construction on an equivalence relation generated by permutations of disjoint redexes only, in a general categorical model of rewriting.

In this paper we propose a general method to construct finitary computation domains from computation spaces based on new orderings which, unlike Lévy's permutation embedding and Laneve's distributive embedding, we believe *truly* express the growth of information along computations, in the spirit of Scott's idea of Information Systems [Sco82] which underlies the whole theory of semantics of programming languages. We thereby further extend Boudol's computational approach to semantics, and develop a 'relativized' version for calculi where redexes can be duplicated and erased. We restrict ourselves to the conflict-free case, but hope our constructions can be generalized based on [Bou85,Mel96].

To fully understand the problem, let us examine once again Lévy's hugely successful idea of '*less work* $\unlhd_L$' and of '*the same work* $\approx_L$'. For co-initial finite reductions P, Q in an orthogonal rewrite system (e.g. the λ-calculus), P is less than Q, written $P \unlhd_L Q$, if what remains of P after Q, the *residual* P/Q of P after Q, is empty. And P and Q do the same work, $P \approx_L Q$, if $P \unlhd_L Q$ and $Q \unlhd_L P$. The 'real life' counterparts of an ordering relation, such as 'greater', 'older', 'stronger', refers to, or is *relative* with respect to, a *particular* aspects of the object/subject one is interested in. But Lévy's ordering lacks that relativity property: Suppose we are interested in computing the normal forms of a λ-term $t = Kx(IIx)$, where $K = \lambda x.\lambda y.x$ and $I = \lambda x.x$. Let $P : t \xrightarrow{I} Kx(Ix)$ and $Q : t \xrightarrow{I} Kx(Ix) \xrightarrow{I} Kxx$. Clearly $P \lhd_L Q$. But both P and Q are unneeded, and neither makes progress towards computation of the normal form obtainable from t in one K-step $t \xrightarrow{K} x$. In this circumstances, does it really make sense to say that 'Q is *greater* (i.e., does *more* work) than P'?

To correct this situation, we introduced in [GK02] orderings $\unlhd_S$ on reductions relative to particular sets S of finite or infinite *values* one may be interested in, such as normal forms, head-normal forms, weak head-normal forms, *Böhm-trees* [Bar84], *Lévy-Longo-trees* [Lév76,Lon83], or *Berarducci-trees* [Ber96], in the λ-calculus, or root-stable forms [Mid97] in orthogonal TRSs. Such values are expressed via *(super)stable* sets of reductions in *Stable Deterministic Residual Structures* (SDRSs) [GK96]. SDRSs are Abstract Reduction Systems [Ter03] with an axiomatized *residual* relation on redexes, enabling one to define permutation equivalence on reductions. SDRSs cover all conflict-free term and (sharing-) graph/net rewrite systems, and many other interesting computational structures, and we abstract from inessential syntactic structure of the objects. In SDRSs one can give abstract proofs of the normalization and minimality theorems [GK96,GK02], relative to (super)stable sets of reductions. Recall from [Win89] that families of configurations in stable event structures whose enabling relation have a similar 'minimality' property generate dI-domains. The concept of *stability* of an event structure can be expressed in terms of our concept of stable reduction (configuration) sets: it is trivial to check that an event structure is stable [Win89] iff for any event e, the set of all configurations containing e is stable (in our sense).

Here we show that the orderings $\trianglelefteq_S$, which we name (temporarily) *reduction orderings*, form finitary ω-algebraic complete lattices on $\approx_S$-equivalence classes of co-initial reductions (where $\approx_S = \trianglelefteq_S \cap \trianglerighteq_S$). An ordering $\trianglelefteq_S$ need not be distributive in general, since for example if we take for S the set of all normalizing reductions in the λ_I-calculus, then $\trianglelefteq_S$ coincides with $\trianglelefteq_L$, and Laneve [Lan94] has demonstrated that $\trianglelefteq_L$ is not distributive (even) for the case of λ_I-calculus. However, any $\trianglelefteq_S$ contains a substructure which is a dI-domain. This substructure corresponds to S-needed complete-family reductions [Lév78,Lév80]. (The subspace of complete-family reductions generates a non-duplicating computation space as families do not duplicate one another; as we have already mentioned, non-duplicating reduction systems are equivalent to event structures with erasure, and the glb operation can simply be expressed via ordinary set-theoretic intersection on S-needed events/families [KG02].) Thus the reduction orderings can be seen as a *refinement* of dI-domains which reflect computations more closely: they *directly* reflect duplication of redexes which dI-domains cannot, and this is the reason for the loss of the distributivity property.

Furthermore, we show that reduction orderings can be generated by the permutation ordering $\trianglelefteq_L$ on *non-erasing* conflict-free reduction systems that are free from *(syntactic) accidents* (i.e., co-initial reductions that end at the same term are permutation-equivalent). The name reduction ordering was chosen because in such systems, $\trianglelefteq_L$ coincides with the reduction relation $\twoheadrightarrow$, which enables us to give an equivalent domain-theoretic definition of reduction orderings. This result is an analog of the well known *representation theorems* for concrete domains [KP93], dI-domains [Win89] and Scott-domains [Sco82,LW93], and the key idea is to equip partial orders with a well-behaved *residual information*.

The following example demonstrates the differences between the domain constructions for duplicating systems discussed above.

Example 1.1 Consider the λ_I-term $t = (\lambda x.xx)(Iz)$, where $I = \lambda x.x$, used by Laneve [Lan94] to demonstrate that Lévy-equivalence need not generate a dI-domain from the reduction space of a λ-term. Figure 1 displays the Hasse diagrams corresponding to the reduction ordering (w.r.t. normal forms), to Laneve's *distributive permutation ordering*, to Khasidashvili and Glauert's *event ordering* [KG02], and Boudol and Melliès' *external ordering* [Bou85,Mel97]. Clearly, the reduction ordering describes the computation space of t most closely (the corresponding Hasse diagram coincides with the reduction graph of t). The distributive permutation ordering is not even a lattice (despite the fact that the λ-calculus is conflict-free), but the downward closure of any element is a distributive lattice. The external ordering (roughly) corresponds to call-by-name computation and cannot adequately account for either call-by-value computation from t or for all needed ones (note that call-by-value computation from t to normal form is shorter than the two external computations to normal form, hence is computationally interesting). The event ordering cannot adequately account for call-by-need computation; it accounts well for call-by-value and needed complete family computations from t, but this need not be true for all terms since complete family-reductions fail in general to compute minimal normal forms (see [GKK00,GK02]). None of these orderings can account for unneeded steps, but such steps do not make any progress towards the normal form.

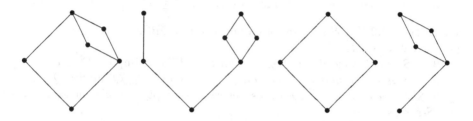

Fig. 1. The orderings

In the next section, we recall some relevant concepts briefly. Section 3 contains the construction of finitary ω-algebraic complete lattices based on reduction orderings. In Section 4 we give a domain-theoretic definition of reduction orderings. Conclusions appear in Section 5. Missing definitions and proofs can be found in [KG03], as well as in our earlier work [GK96,GK02].

2   Preliminaries

Notation 2.1 *We write $u \in t$ if u is a member of the redexes of term t, and write $U \subseteq t$ if U is a subset of the redexes. One can identify u with the triple $t \xrightarrow{u} s$ (the reduction that contracts u). Similarly, U may also denote a complete development of the set U. A reduction is a sequence $t \xrightarrow{u_1} t_2 \xrightarrow{u_2} \dots$. Reductions are denoted by P, Q, N. We write $P : t \twoheadrightarrow s$ or $t \xrightarrow{P} s$ if P denotes a reduction from t to s. $Q : t \twoheadrightarrow$ may be finite as well as infinite. $P + Q$ denotes the concatenation of P and Q. Further, for any reduction Q, $\lceil Q \rceil^k$ will denote the* *initial part of Q of length k, provided $k \leq |Q|$ (the length of Q), and $\lceil Q \rceil_k$ will denote the tail of Q starting from the $(k+1)$th step; thus $Q = \lceil Q \rceil^k + \lceil Q \rceil_k$. Finally, we write $P \leq Q$ if P is an initial part of Q.*

Definition 2.2 Let S be a set of reductions in a DRS.

(1) Let $u \in U \subseteq t$ and $P : t \twoheadrightarrow$. We call P *external* to U (resp. u) if P does not contract residuals of redexes in U (resp. residuals of u).

(2) We call $u \in t$ S-*unneeded* if there is a reduction $Q \in S$ starting from t that is external to u, and call it S-*needed* otherwise. We say a reduction P is S-*needed* if all its steps contract S-needed redexes. The S-*needed part of* P, $[P]_S$, is a finite or infinite reduction defined by: $[P]_S = u + [P/u]_S$, where $u \in t$ is the redex whose residual is contracted first among S-needed steps in P.

(3) Let P, Q be co-initial reductions. If P and Q are both finite, then we define $P \trianglelefteq_S Q$ if P/Q is S-unneeded. Otherwise, $P \trianglelefteq_S Q$ if for any finite $P' \leq P$ there is a finite $Q' \leq Q$ such that $P' \trianglelefteq_S Q'$. Further, $P \approx_S Q$ iff $P \trianglelefteq_S Q$ and $Q \trianglelefteq_S P$. We call $\trianglelefteq_S$ and $\approx_S$ respectively S-*embedding* and S-*equivalence*. $\langle P \rangle_S$ denotes the $\approx_S$-equivalence class of P (we will show below that $\approx_S$ is an equivalence relation). We write $\langle P \rangle_S \trianglelefteq_S \langle Q \rangle_S$ if $P \trianglelefteq_S Q$.

It is immediate from the definition that $\trianglelefteq_L \subseteq \trianglelefteq_S$.

Definition 2.3 Let S be a set of reductions in a DRS.
(1) We call S *stable* iff:
  [CS] S *is suffix-closed*: if $P' \notin S$, then $P' + P'' \in S$ implies $P'' \in S$.
  [CE] S *is closed under S-embedding*: $P \in S$ and $P \trianglelefteq_S Q$ implies $Q \in S$.
  [CN] S *is closed under neededness*: every non-empty $P \in S$ contracts at least one S-needed redex.
(2) We call S *regular* iff:
  [Reg] In no term can an S-unneeded redex duplicate an S-needed one.
(3) We call S *superstable* iff:
  [Min] For any S-normalizable term t, S contains a unique, up to $\approx_L$, $\trianglelefteq_L$-minimal element starting from t. Such reductions are called S-*minimal*.

We call a (regular, super) stable set of reductions in a DRS $\mathcal{R}$ a *(regular, super) stable semantics* of $\mathcal{R}$. Below S will denote a stable (regular or superstable) semantics of a DRS.

The following lemma is required from earlier work:

Lemma 2.4 ([GK02]) Let S be a stable semantics of an SDRS, and let $P :$ $t \xrightarrow{u} s \twoheadrightarrow \in S$. Further:

(1) Let v' be a u-residual of $v \in t$, and let v be S-unneeded. Then so is v'.

(2) Let u create $v \in s$, and let u be S-unneeded. Then so is v.

(3) Let S be regular, let $u \neq v \in t$, and let v be S-needed. Then v has at least one S-needed residual in s.

(4) Let S be regular. Then $[P]_S$ is an S-needed reduction whose length coincides with the number of S-needed steps in P, and $P \approx_S [P]_S$.

3   Properties of Reduction Orderings

This section contains the construction of ω-algebraic finitary complete lattices from the reduction spaces of SDRSs.

First of all, we show that $\trianglelefteq_S$ is a partial order, which requires the following characterization of $\trianglelefteq_S$ via $\trianglelefteq_L$.

Lemma 3.1 Let P and Q be finite co-initial reductions in an SDRS $\mathcal{R}$ with regular stable semantics $\mathcal{S}$. Then $P \trianglelefteq_S Q$ iff $P \trianglelefteq_L Q + Q'$ for some $\mathcal{S}$-unneeded Q'.

Lemma 3.2 Let P, Q and N be co-initial reductions in an SDRS $\mathcal{R}$ with regular stable semantics $\mathcal{S}$, and let $P \trianglelefteq_S Q \trianglelefteq_S N$. Then $P \trianglelefteq_S N$.

Corollary 3.3 Let $\mathcal{S}$ be a regular stable semantics of an SDRS $\mathcal{R}$. Then $\approx_S$ is an equivalence relation, and consequently $\mathcal{L}^{\trianglelefteq_S}(\mathcal{R}) = (\mathcal{L}^{\approx_S}(\mathcal{R}), \trianglelefteq_\mathcal{E})$ is a partial order, where $\mathcal{L}^{\approx_S}(\mathcal{R}) = \mathcal{L}(\mathcal{R})/_{\approx_S}$ and $\mathcal{L}(\mathcal{R})$ is a set of co-initial reductions in $\mathcal{R}$.

Recall the definition of the $\trianglelefteq_L$-meet operation from [GK02]. Let Φ be a set of reductions starting from t, in a DRS. Then the $\trianglelefteq_L$-*meet* of reductions in Φ, written $\sqcap_L \Phi$, is defined as follows: Let $U \subseteq t$ be the maximal subset such that $U \trianglelefteq_L \Phi$, and let $t \overset{U}{\twoheadrightarrow} s$ be a complete development of U (or the multi-step contracting U). Then $\sqcap_L \Phi = U + \sqcap_L(\Phi/U)$.

Note that $P \sqcap_L Q$ need not be a $\trianglelefteq_S$-glb of P and Q even in a DRS corresponding to a Recursive Program Scheme: Let $R = \{g(x) \to h(x, E(x)), E(x) \to a\}$, let $t = g(g(g(x)))$, let $P : t \to h(g(g(x)), E(g(g(x)))) \to h(g(h(x, E(x))), E(g(g(x))))$, and let $Q : t \to g(h(g(x), E(g(x)))) \to g(h(h(x, E(x)), E(g(x))))$. Then t contains three redexes: u, v and w, listed in the top-down order, and none of them are erased in both P and Q, thus $P \sqcap_L Q = \emptyset$, while $w \trianglelefteq_S P, Q$ for the set $\mathcal{S}$ of all normalizing reductions. This suggests the following definition:

Definition 3.4 Let $\mathcal{S}$ be a stable semantics of an SDRS $\mathcal{R}$, and let Φ be a set of reductions in $\mathcal{R}$ starting from t. Then:

(1) (**$\mathcal{S}$-meet**) $\mathcal{S}$-*meet* of Φ, written $\sqcap_S \Phi$, is defined as follows: Let $U \subseteq t$ be the maximal subset such that $U \trianglelefteq_S \Phi$, and let $t \overset{U}{\twoheadrightarrow} s$. Then $\sqcap_S \Phi = U + \sqcap_S(\Phi/U)$.

(2) (**$\mathcal{S}$-join**) $\mathcal{S}$-*join* of reductions in Φ, written $\sqcup_S \Phi$, is defined as follows: Let $V \subseteq t$ be the set of all redexes that are contracted in the first step of one of the reductions in Φ, and let $t \overset{V}{\twoheadrightarrow} s$. Then $\sqcup_S \Phi = V + \sqcup_S(\Phi/V)$.

(3) (**L-join**) We define $\sqcup_L \Phi = \sqcup_S \Phi$.

We need the following two simple lemmas to prove that $\sqcap_S$ and $\sqcup_S$ are indeed meet and join operations for $\trianglelefteq_S$.

Lemma 3.5 Let P, Q be finite reductions in an SDRS with regular stable semantics $\mathcal{S}$, let $P \trianglelefteq_L Q$, and let Q be $\mathcal{S}$-unneeded. Then so is P.

Lemma 3.6 Let $P \trianglelefteq_S Q$ in an SDRS with a regular stable semantics $\mathcal{S}$, and let N be finite and co-initial with P. Then $P/N \trianglelefteq_S Q/N$.

Below we use Φ to denote sets of co-initial reductions. Further, for example we write $P \trianglelefteq_L \Phi$ iff $\forall Q \in \Phi.\, Q \trianglelefteq_L P$; $\lceil \Phi \rceil^k$ will denote the set of initial parts, of the length k, of reductions in Φ; etc.

First note that if Φ consists of two finite reductions P and Q, then $P \sqcup Q \approx_L P \sqcup_L Q$, although $P \sqcup Q$ and $P \sqcup_L Q$ are different as multi-step reductions. Further, since every term contains a finite number of redexes, a finite subset of Φ is enough to generate any particular step in $\sqcup_L \Phi$ (even if Φ contains an infinite number of reductions). More precisely:

Lemma 3.7 Let Φ be a set of reductions in a DRS. Then for any $k \leq |\sqcup_L \Phi|$, there is a finite subset $\Phi[k] \subseteq \Phi$ such that $\lceil \sqcup_L \Phi \rceil^k = \sqcup_L \lceil \Phi[k] \rceil^k \approx_L \sqcup \lceil \Phi[k] \rceil^k$.

Lemma 3.8 Let Φ be a set of co-initial reductions in a DRS. Then $\sqcup_L \Phi$ is a (unique up to $\approx_L$) $\trianglelefteq_L$-lub of Φ.

Proof It is immediate from the definition of $\sqcup_L$ that $\Phi \trianglelefteq_L \sqcup_L \Phi$. Now let $\Phi \trianglelefteq_L P$ and let us show $\sqcup_L \Phi \trianglelefteq_L P$, i.e., that $\lceil \sqcup_L \Phi \rceil^k \trianglelefteq_L \lceil P \rceil^{l_k}$ for any k and some l_k. By Lemma 3.7, $\lceil \sqcup_L \Phi \rceil^k = \sqcup_L \lceil \Phi[k] \rceil^k \approx_L \sqcup \lceil \Phi[k] \rceil^k$. Let l_k be such that $\lceil \Phi[k] \rceil^k \trianglelefteq_L \lceil P \rceil^{l_k}$. Then $(\sqcup_L \lceil \Phi[k] \rceil^k)/\lceil P \rceil^{l_k} \approx_L (\sqcup \lceil \Phi[k] \rceil^k)/\lceil P \rceil^{l_k} \approx_L \sqcup (\lceil \Phi[k] \rceil^k / \lceil P \rceil^{l_k}) = \emptyset$, and we are done.

Theorem 3.9 Let $\mathcal{S}$ be a regular stable semantics of an SDRS $\mathcal{R}$, and let Φ be a set of co-initial reductions in $\mathcal{R}$. Then:

(1) $\sqcap_{\mathcal{S}} \Phi$ is a (unique up to $\approx_{\mathcal{S}}$) $\trianglelefteq_{\mathcal{S}}$-glb of Φ.

(2) $\sqcup_{\mathcal{S}} \Phi$ is a (unique up to $\approx_{\mathcal{S}}$) $\trianglelefteq_{\mathcal{S}}$-lub of Φ.

Proof (1) Let $\sqcap_{\mathcal{S}} \Phi = Q : t_0 \xrightarrow{U_0} t_1 \xrightarrow{U_1} t_2 \twoheadrightarrow \dots$. It is immediate from Definition 3.4 that $Q \trianglelefteq_{\mathcal{S}} \Phi$. Thus we need to show that for any P, $P \trianglelefteq_{\mathcal{S}} \Phi \Rightarrow P \trianglelefteq_{\mathcal{S}} Q$, that is, for any $n \leq |P|$, $\lceil P \rceil^n \trianglelefteq_{\mathcal{S}} Q$. We show this by induction on n. The case $n = 0$ (i.e., $P = \emptyset$) is clear. So let $n = k + 1$, and let $\lceil P \rceil^k \trianglelefteq_{\mathcal{S}} Q$. Then $\lceil P \rceil^k \trianglelefteq_{\mathcal{S}} \lceil Q \rceil^{l_k}$ for some l_k. We can assume that $\lceil Q \rceil^{l_k}$ ends at t_m for some m. Now assume that the $(k+1)th$ step v of P has an $\mathcal{S}$-needed residual v' under $\lceil Q \rceil^{l_k}/\lceil P \rceil^k$ (otherwise, there is nothing to prove). Since $\lceil P \rceil^k/\lceil Q \rceil^{l_k}$ is $\mathcal{S}$-unneeded, by Lemma 2.4.(2) there must be an $\mathcal{S}$-needed redex v'' in the final term t_m of $\lceil Q \rceil^{l_k}$ such that v' is its $(\lceil P \rceil^k/\lceil Q \rceil^{l_k})$-residual. Furthermore, v' is the only $(\lceil P \rceil^k/\lceil Q \rceil^{l_k})$-residual of v'' by regularity of $\mathcal{S}$, thus $v'' \trianglelefteq_{\mathcal{S}} P/\lceil Q \rceil^{l_k}$. But $P \trianglelefteq_{\mathcal{S}} \Phi$, hence $P/\lceil Q \rceil^{l_k} \trianglelefteq_{\mathcal{S}} \Phi/\lceil Q \rceil^{l_k}$ by Lemma 3.6. Thus, $v'' \trianglelefteq_{\mathcal{S}} \Phi/\lceil Q \rceil^{l_k}$, and v'' must be contracted in U_m (by Definition 3.4). Hence $v'/(U_m/(\lceil P \rceil^k/\lceil Q \rceil^{l_k})) = \emptyset$, and we are done.

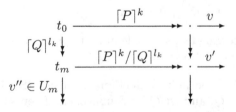

(2) By Definition 3.4.(2), $\Phi \trianglelefteq_L \sqcup_{\mathcal{S}} \Phi$, implying $\Phi \trianglelefteq_{\mathcal{S}} \sqcup_{\mathcal{S}} \Phi$. Now let $\Phi \trianglelefteq_{\mathcal{S}} P$ and let us show $\sqcup_{\mathcal{S}} \Phi \trianglelefteq_{\mathcal{S}} P$, i.e., that $\lceil \sqcup_{\mathcal{S}} \Phi \rceil^k \trianglelefteq_{\mathcal{S}} \lceil P \rceil^{l_k}$ for any k and some

l_k. By Lemma 3.7, $\lceil\sqcup_S\Phi\rceil^k = \sqcup_S\lceil\Phi[k]\rceil^k \approx_L \sqcup\lceil\Phi[k]\rceil^k$, and $\Phi \trianglelefteq_S P$ implies $\lceil\Phi[k]\rceil^k \trianglelefteq_S P$. Let l_k be such that $\lceil\Phi[k]\rceil^k \trianglelefteq_S \lceil P\rceil^{l_k}$. Then $(\sqcup_S\lceil\Phi[k]\rceil^k)/\lceil P\rceil^{l_k} \approx_L (\sqcup\lceil\Phi[k]\rceil^k)/\lceil P\rceil^{l_k} \approx_L \sqcup(\lceil\Phi[k]\rceil^k/\lceil P\rceil^{l_k})$, and $\sqcup(\lceil\Phi[k]\rceil^k/\lceil P\rceil^{l_k})$ is S-unneeded by Lemma 2.4.(1). Thus $(\sqcup_S\lceil\Phi[k]\rceil^k)/\lceil P\rceil^{l_k}$ is S-unneeded by Lemma 3.5, i.e., $\sqcup_S\lceil\Phi\rceil^k \trianglelefteq_S \lceil P\rceil^{l_k}$, implying $\sqcup_S\Phi \trianglelefteq_S P$.

Corollary 3.10 Let S be a regular stable semantics of an SDRS $\mathcal{R}$. Then $\mathcal{L}^{\trianglelefteq_S}(\mathcal{R})$ is a complete lattice with meet and join operations $\sqcup_S$ and $\sqcap_S$ defined by: $\sqcup_S\langle\Phi\rangle_S = \langle\sqcup_S\Phi\rangle_S$ and $\sqcap_S\langle\Phi\rangle_S = \langle\sqcap_S\Phi\rangle_S$.

Now we can soundly define the *relativized stable computational semantics* for an SDRS $\mathcal{R}$, as follows: Let S be a regular stable semantics of $\mathcal{R}$, and let t be an S-normalizable term in $\mathcal{R}$. Then the *value* of t in $\mathcal{R}$ w.r.t. S is the $\trianglelefteq_S$-maximal $\approx_S$-equivalence class of reductions starting from t, in $\mathcal{L}^{\trianglelefteq_S}(\mathcal{R})$. Thus for example in the case of Böhm-semantics, the Böhm-tree $BT(t)$ of t is represented by the set of all reductions computing $BT(t)$, which form the $\trianglelefteq_{S_B}$-maximal $\approx_{S_B}$-class of reductions starting from t (where S_B is the set of all reductions computing Böhm-trees, see [GK02] for details).

Lemma 3.11 Let S be a regular stable semantics of an SDRS $\mathcal{R}$, let $U \in t$ be a set of S-needed redexes in t, let $N : t \twoheadrightarrow$ be S-needed, and let $N \trianglelefteq_S U$. Then N is a development of U, thus is finite.

This lemma is used in the proof of the following crucial lemma for establishing finiteness of $\mathcal{L}^{\trianglelefteq_S}(\mathcal{R})$.

Lemma 3.12 Let S be a regular stable semantics of an SDRS $\mathcal{R}$, let $P \trianglelefteq_S Q$, and let $[Q]_S$ be finite. Then so is $[P]_S$.

Hence, by Lemma 2.4.(4), we can soundly define $\langle P\rangle_S$ to be *finite* iff P contracts only a finite number of S-needed redexes, or equivalently if $[P]_S$ is finite. The following lemma justifies our definition:

Lemma 3.13 Let S be regular stable semantics for an SDRS $\mathcal{R}$. Then $\langle P\rangle_S$ is finite iff it is a finite element of $\mathcal{L}^{\trianglelefteq_S}(\mathcal{R})$.

Now, using Lemmas 3.13 and 2.4.(4) and Theorem 3.9, we can prove finiteness and algebraicity of $\mathcal{L}^{\trianglelefteq_S}(\mathcal{R})$:

Theorem 3.14 Let S be a regular stable semantics for an SDRS $\mathcal{R}$. Then $\mathcal{L}^{\trianglelefteq_S}(\mathcal{R})$ is a finitary ω-algebraic complete lattice.

Proof (Algebraicity) Let Q be a reduction in $\mathcal{R}$ and let $\Phi = \{N|\langle N\rangle_S$ finite, $N \trianglelefteq_S Q\}$. Then $\langle\Phi\rangle_S$ consists of all finite elements of $\mathcal{L}^{\trianglelefteq_S}(\mathcal{R})$ dominated by $\langle Q\rangle_S$. It follows from Lemma 3.1 and Lemma 2.4.(1) that for any finite subset $\Phi' \subseteq \Phi$, $\sqcup_S\Phi' \in \Phi$ (since we can assume that all reductions in Φ are finite), thus $\langle\Phi\rangle_S$ is directed. Thus we want to prove that $\langle\sqcup_S\Phi\rangle_S = \langle Q\rangle_S$. It is immediate from Definition 3.4 that $Q = \sqcup_S\{\lceil Q\rceil^n|n \leq |Q|\}$. But $\{\lceil Q\rceil^n|n \leq |Q|\} \subseteq \Phi$, thus $Q = \sqcup_S \lceil Q \rceil^n \trianglelefteq_S \sqcup_S \Phi$. On the other hand, $\sqcup_S \Phi$ is the $\trianglelefteq_S$-lub of Φ by Theorem 3.9, thus $\sqcup_S \Phi \trianglelefteq_S Q$. Hence $\langle \sqcup_S \Phi \rangle_S = \langle Q \rangle_S$.

(Finiteness) Let $\langle P \rangle_S$ be finite in $\mathcal{L}^{\trianglelefteq_S}(\mathcal{R})$. By Lemmas 3.13 and 2.4.(4), we can assume P to be S-needed and finite. Suppose on the contrary that $\langle P \rangle_S$ dominates an infinite number of elements of $\mathcal{L}^{\trianglelefteq_S}(\mathcal{R})$. Then by Lemma 2.4.(4) there is an infinite set Φ of S-needed reductions such that $\Phi \trianglelefteq_S P$. Since the reduction tree corresponding to Φ is finitely-branching (because a term may contain only a finite number of redexes), Φ must contain an infinite S-needed reduction $Q \trianglelefteq_S P$ (by König's Lemma), contradicting Lemma 3.12.

The above theorem fails for (irregular) stable semantics S in general [KG03].

4   A Representation Theorem for the Reduction Orderings

In a previous section, we defined reduction orderings $\trianglelefteq_S$ as orderings generated by pairs $(\mathcal{R}, S)$, where S is a regular stable semantics for an SDRS $\mathcal{R}$. Now we wish to give an equivalent definition in domain-theoretic terms. Such results in the literature are called *representation theorems*: for example, concrete domains (defined by restricting partial orders with a number of axioms) are exactly the domains generated by *Information Matrices* [KP93] (often called *Concrete Data Structures* [Cur86]), *dI*-domains are domains generated by *Prime* (or equivalently, *Stable*) *Event Structures* [Win89], and Scott domains are domains generated by *Information Systems* [Sco82,LW93].

To define (i.e., to fully characterize) orderings $\trianglelefteq_S$ domain-theoretically, we note that $\trianglelefteq_S$ is built from a pair $(\mathcal{R}, S)$, and in the transition from $(\mathcal{R}, S)$ to $\trianglelefteq_S$ some information, namely the *residual information*, gets ignored. This suggests that, up to some isomorphism, $(\mathcal{R}, S)$ is nothing but $\trianglelefteq_S$ equipped with appropriate residual information. The idea of partial orders with residuals is not precisely new: all the above mentioned representation results implicitly use a *linear* residual concept. In the case of reduction orderings, the crucial step enabling us to define the correct residual relation is the observation that all reduction orderings can actually be generated as permutation orderings $\trianglelefteq_L$ on some *non-erasing* SDRSs $\mathcal{R}_S$ that are *(syntactic) accident-free* (defined shortly).

The next definition shows how to define such 'projections' of $\trianglelefteq_S$ onto $\trianglelefteq_L$. There, it is enough (and convenient) to consider only *comma-SDRSs* $\mathcal{R}$, whose underlying ARSs are reduction graphs of a fixed *initial term*. The S-projection of an SDRS consists of (isomorphic copies of) projections of its comma-(sub)SDRSs.

Definition 4.1 (S-projection) Let $\mathcal{R}$ be a comma-SDRS with a regular stable semantics S. Then the *S-projection* of $\mathcal{R}$ is an SDRS $\mathcal{R}_S$ defined as follows:

• Terms in $\mathcal{R}_S$ are $\approx_S$-classes $\langle P \rangle_S$ of finite *initial* reductions P in $\mathcal{R}$ (that is, P starts with the initial term);

• Arrows in $\mathcal{R}_S$ are pairs $\langle P \rangle_S \rightarrow_S \langle P + u \rangle_S$, where u is an S-needed redex in the final term of P. (The empty redex in $\langle P \rangle_S$ can be defined as the pair $\langle P \rangle_S \xrightarrow{\emptyset}_S \langle P \rangle_S$.)

- The residual relation $/_S$ in $\mathcal{R}_S$ is defined as follows: Let $\langle P\rangle_S \overset{u^*}{\twoheadrightarrow}_S \langle P+u\rangle_S$ and $\langle P\rangle_S \overset{v^*}{\twoheadrightarrow}_S \langle P+v\rangle_S$ in $\mathcal{R}_S$. Then for any S-needed $v' \in v/u$, $\langle P+u\rangle_S \overset{v'^*}{\twoheadrightarrow}_S$ $\langle P+u+v'\rangle_S$ is a u^*-residual of v, written $v'^* \in v^*/_S u^*$.

Thus any redex Pu in $\mathcal{R}$ (whose *history* P is an initial reduction) is assigned a unique redex $\langle P\rangle_S \to_S \langle P+u\rangle_S$ in $\mathcal{R}_S$, although different redexes (with histories) in $\mathcal{R}$ may have the same corresponding redex in $\mathcal{R}_S$. This assignment induces a function h from (parts of) initial reductions in $\mathcal{R}$ to initial reductions in $\mathcal{R}_S$ with the following properties:

- If $P = P_1 + P_2$ is an initial reduction in $\mathcal{R}$, then $h(P_1+P_2) = h(P_1)+h(P_2)$;
- If N is an initial reduction in $\mathcal{R}$, then $h(N) = \emptyset$ iff N is S-unneeded.

Although the converse of h is not a function, for any initial reduction P' in $\mathcal{R}_S$ there is a unique S-needed initial reduction in $\mathcal{R}$, noted $h'(P')$, that contracts the 'same' redexes as P', i.e., $h(h'(P')) = P'$, and therefore $h'(h(P)) = P$ for any S-needed initial reduction P in $\mathcal{R}$. Thus (h, h') gives an isomorphism between S-needed initial reductions in $\mathcal{R}$ and initial reductions in $\mathcal{R}_S$. Using these properties of h, we can quite easily prove the correctness of Definition 4.1. First a definition:

Definition 4.2 Let $\mathcal{R}$ be a comma-SDRS. We call $\mathcal{R}$ *good* if it is *non-erasing* and *accident-free*:

- [NE]: for any co-initial distinct redexes $t \overset{u}{\to} s$ and $t \overset{v}{\to} e$ in $\mathcal{R}$, $v/u \neq \emptyset$.
- [AF]: for any initial reductions P and Q in $\mathcal{R}$ that end at the same term t, $P \approx_L Q$.[1] Note that $P \sqcup Q$ ends at t, too.

Lemma 4.3 Let $\mathcal{R}$ be a comma-SDRS with a regular stable semantics S. Then $\mathcal{R}_S$ is a good SDRS. (Hence in particular Definition 4.1 is sound.)

For a comma-SDRS $\mathcal{R}$, assume that $\mathcal{L}^{\trianglelefteq_L}(\mathcal{R})$ and $\mathcal{L}^{\trianglelefteq_S}(\mathcal{R})$ denote the corresponding orderings w.r.t. the initial term. Proof of the desired result is easy:

Theorem 4.4 Let S be a regular stable semantics of a comma-SDRS $\mathcal{R}$. Then $\mathcal{L}^{\trianglelefteq_L}(\mathcal{R}_S)$ and $\mathcal{L}^{\trianglelefteq_S}(\mathcal{R})$ are isomorphic.
Proof Since initial reductions in $\mathcal{R}_S$ are exactly reductions $h(P)$ for initial (S-needed) reductions P in $\mathcal{R}$, the theorem follows immediately from the fact that $P \trianglelefteq_S Q$ in $\mathcal{R}$ iff $h(P) \trianglelefteq_L h(Q)$ in $\mathcal{R}_S$.

In non-erasing SDRSs, $\trianglelefteq_L$ coincides with the *fair* ordering $\trianglelefteq_{fair}$, i.e., the ordering $\trianglelefteq_{fair}$ where S_{fair} is the set of all fair [Ter03] reductions; this follows immediately from the fact that at least one residual of any redex $u \in t$ in a non-erasing SDRS must be contracted in every fair reduction starting from t (and from the fact that a reduction is fair iff so is any of its tails).

---

[1] A simple pair of co-initial reductions, namely $P : I(Ix) \overset{Ix}{\to} Ix$ and $Q : I(Ix) \overset{I(Ix)}{\to} Ix$, that end at the same term but are not Lévy-equivalent was given by Lévy [Lév78], where this phenomenon is called a *syntactic accident*.

Furthermore, because of accident-freeness, in good SDRSs (differently from SDRSs in general) there is at most one step between any pair of terms (t, s), thus the reduction relation can be given as sets of pairs. That is, a good SDRS is a triple $\mathcal{R} = (Ter, \rightarrow, /)$, where Ter is a set of objects (called terms) containing an initial term $t_\emptyset$, $\rightarrow$ is a set of pairs, and $/$ is a residual relation (satisfying SDRS-axioms). Furthermore, in good SDRSs $\mathcal{R}$, $\trianglelefteq_L$ on finite elements is isomorphic to $\twoheadrightarrow$, the reduction relation on $\mathcal{R}$:

Theorem 4.5 Let $\mathcal{R} = (Ter, \rightarrow, /)$ be a good SDRS and $\mathcal{L}_{fin}(\mathcal{R})$ be the set of all finite initial reductions in $\mathcal{R}$. Then $\mathcal{L}^{\trianglelefteq_L}_{fin}(\mathcal{R}) = (\mathcal{L}^{\approx_L}_{fin}(\mathcal{R}), \trianglelefteq_L)$ is isomorphic to $(Ter, \twoheadrightarrow)$, and $\mathcal{L}^{\trianglelefteq_L}(\mathcal{R}) = (\mathcal{L}^{\approx_L}(\mathcal{R}), \trianglelefteq_L)$ is isomorphic to $\leq_\mathcal{R} = IC(Ter, \twoheadrightarrow)$, the ideal completion of $(Ter, \twoheadrightarrow)$ (infinite ideals of $\leq_\mathcal{R}$ correspond to $\approx_L$-classes of infinite reductions in $\mathcal{R}$).

Proof By [AF], every term $t \in Ter$ uniquely determines exactly one element $\langle P_t \rangle_L$ of $\mathcal{L}^{\approx_L}_{fin}(\mathcal{R})$, where P_t is any initial reduction ending with t. Furthermore, $t \twoheadrightarrow s$ iff $\langle P_t \rangle_L \trianglelefteq_L \langle P_s \rangle_L$: Indeed, if $N : t \twoheadrightarrow s$, then by [AF] $P_s \approx_L P_t + N$, implying $P_t \trianglelefteq_L P_s$; and conversely, $P_t \trianglelefteq_L P_s$ implies $P_s \approx_L P_t + P_s/P_t$ and clearly $P_s/P_t : t \twoheadrightarrow s$. By Lemma 3.13, $\mathcal{L}^{\approx_L}_{fin}(\mathcal{R})$ coincides with the set of finite elements of $\mathcal{L}^{\trianglelefteq_L}(\mathcal{R})$, hence $\mathcal{L}^{\trianglelefteq_L}(\mathcal{R})$ is isomorphic to $\leq_\mathcal{R}$ (see [DP90], pp82-83).

Thus, we need to provide a domain-theoretic characterization of (ideal completions of) orderings $(Ter, \twoheadrightarrow)$ for good SDRSs $\mathcal{R} = (Ter, \rightarrow, /)$, which are finitary w-algebraic complete lattices of a special form. It is standard (after [KP93]) to associate with a partial order $\leq = (D, \leq_D)$ an ARS (or a transition system) $A_\leq = (Ter_\leq, \rightarrow_\leq)$ such that $Ter_\leq = D$ and $t \rightarrow_\leq s$ iff $t \prec_D s$ (in D), where $t \prec_D s$ iff $t <_D s \land \forall o \in D : (t \leq_D o \leq_D s \Rightarrow t = o \lor s = o)\}$. The relation $\prec_D$ is called *covering*. A sequence of the form $t \prec_D t_1 \prec_D \ldots$ is called a *covering chain, or a covering (t, s)-chain* when $t_i \leq_D s$. We call a covering (t, s)-chain *maximal* if it is infinite or cannot be extended.

Since any algebraic cpo $\mathcal{L}$ is obtained as the ideal completion of its subset of finite elements (noted $F(\mathcal{L})$), it is enough to axiomatize properties of finite elements only. Therefore, following [Cur86], if in a pair $t \prec_D s$ in an algebraic cpo both t and s are finite, we write it as $[t, s]_D$ (or simply as $[t, s]$) and call it a *prime interval*, although the definition of (prime) intervals $[t, s]$ say in [KP93,Win80] does not require t and s to be finite. Similarly, if all t_i in a covering chain $t \prec_D t_1 \prec_D \ldots$ are finite, we write it also as $[t \prec_D t_1 \prec_D \ldots]$.

Note that in non-erasing SDRSs, the residual relation is defined uniquely by the corresponding lub operation: If $t \xrightarrow{u} s$ and $v \in t$, exactly the redexes $v' \in s$ such that $u + v' \trianglelefteq_L u \sqcup v$ are u-residuals of v. This is of course not true in erasing SDRSs. This observation allows us to define a residual relation in complete lattices:

Definition 4.6 Let $\leq = (D, \leq_D, \sqcup_D, \sqcap_D)$, be a complete lattice.

(1) We define the *residual* relation $/_D$ as the reflexive and transitive closure of the following relation:

- For any pair of co-initial prime intervals $u = [t, o], v = [t, s]$ in D, $u/_D v = \{[s, e] \mid e \leq s \sqcup o\}$.

(2) We write $t \prec_D s \overset{c}{\prec}_D s^*$ if, for any $o \in D$ such that $t \prec_D o$, $s^* \not\leq_D s \sqcup_D o$, and say that $t \prec_D s$ *creates* $s \overset{c}{\prec}_D s^*$. We write $[t \prec_D s \overset{c}{\prec}_D s^*]$ to indicate that t, s and s^* are finite.

We now reformulate the axioms of good SDRSs in domain-theoretic terms.

Definition 4.7 Let $\leq = (D, \leq_D, \sqcup_D, \sqcap_D)$ be a (finitary ω-algebraic) complete lattice such that:

• [FB] (finite branching) For any $t \in F(D)$, there are only a finite number of $s \in D$ such that $t \prec_D s$ (such an s must be finite).

• [NT] (no triangles) For any pair of different co-initial prime intervals $[t, s]$ and $[t, o]$ in D, $s, o <_D s \sqcup o$.

• [SD] (semi-distributivity) For any triple of co-initial prime intervals $[t, s]$, $[t, e]$, and $[t, o]$ in D, $s \sqcup_D (o \sqcup_D e) = (s \sqcup_D o) \sqcap_D (s \sqcup_D e)$. (Note here that, by [NT], $s \sqcup_D (o \sqcap_D e) = s$.)

• [FC] (finite chains) For any set of co-initial prime intervals $[t, s_i]$, any maximal covering $(t, \sqcup_D s_i)$-chain is finite and ends with $\sqcup_D s_i$.

• [S] (stability) For any $t, s, s^*, e, e^* \in F(D)$ such that $[t \prec_D s \overset{c}{\prec}_D s^*]$ and $[t \prec_D e \overset{c}{\prec}_D e^*]$, $(s \sqcup_D e^*) \sqcap_D (e \sqcup_D s^*) = e \sqcup_D s$.

Then we call $\leq$ a *complete regular domain* (CRD).

By Definition 4.6, we may as well refer to a CRD as a triple $\leq - (D, \leq_D, /_D)$. Using this definition, we can show that good SDRSs and CRDs are equivalent models. We need two simple lemmas first:

Lemma 4.8 Let $(D, \leq, \sqcup, \sqcap)$ be a CRD, and let $[t, s]$, $[t, s_i]$ $(0 \leq i \leq m)$ be prime intervals such that $s \neq s_i$. Then $s < s \sqcup (\sqcup s_i)$ and $\sqcup s_i < s \sqcup (\sqcup s_i)$.

Lemma 4.9 Let $\leq = (D, \leq_D, \sqcup_D, \sqcap_D)$ be a CRD, let $[e_0 \prec_D e_1 \prec_D \dots \prec_D e_m]$, and let $[e_0 \prec e_0^*]$. Then $[e_m, e_m^*]$ is a residual, w.r.t. $/_D$, of $[e_0, e_0^*]$ iff $e_m^* \leq_D e_0^* \sqcup_D e_m$, and the lub of all such e_m^* is $e_0^* \sqcup_D e_m$.

The above lemma says that the residual relation is independent of a covering sequence between e_0 and e_m.

Theorem 4.10 Good SDRSs and complete regular domains are equivalent models. More precisely:

(1) For any good SDRS $\mathcal{R} = (Ter, \rightarrow, /)$, $\leq = IC(Ter, \twoheadrightarrow)$ is a CRD (where $\twoheadrightarrow$ is the transitive reflexive closure of $\rightarrow$).

(2) If $\leq = (D, \leq_D, /_D)$ is a CRD, then $\mathcal{R}_\leq = (F(D), \prec_D, /_D)$ is a good SDRS and $\leq$ is isomorphic to $IC(F(D), \prec_D)$ (where $\prec_D, /_D$ in $\mathcal{R}_\leq$ are restrictions, to $F(D)$, of these relations in $\leq$).

Proof

(1) By Theorems 3.14, 4.4 and 4.5, $\leq = IC(Ter, \twoheadrightarrow)$ is a finitary ω-algebraic complete lattice (we denote by $\sqcup_\leq$ and $\sqcap_\leq$ the corresponding lub and glb operations). Then [FB] is immediate. [NT] is immediate from [NE]. To show

[SD] (in its simplified form), let $[t, s]$, $[t, e]$, and $[t, o]$ be prime intervals in $\leq$. Then $s \twoheadrightarrow s\sqcup_{\leq} e$ and $s \twoheadrightarrow s\sqcup_{\leq} o$, hence $s \twoheadrightarrow (s\sqcup_{\leq} e) \sqcap_{\leq} (s\sqcup_{\leq} o) = s^*$. If on the contrary $s \xrightarrow{+} s^*$, then for any s' such that $s \to s' \twoheadrightarrow s^*$, we would have that the redex $[s, s']$ is a $[t, s]$-residual of both redexes $[t, o]$ and $[t, e]$ in $\mathcal{R}$ – contradiction. To prove [FC], let $[t_0, s_i]$ be prime intervals in $\leq$, and let $P : t_0 \to t_1 \to \ldots$ be a $(t_0, \sqcup_{\leq} s_i)$-chain. Then P is a development of the set of redexes $[t_0, s_i]$ in $\mathcal{R}$ by Lemma 4.9 (since the residual relation generated by $(Ter, \twoheadrightarrow)$ coincides with $/$), and [FC] follows from [FD] (finiteness of developments) for $\mathcal{R}$. Finally, [S] follows immediately from [NT] and stability of $\mathcal{R}$.

(2) We need to prove that the residual relation in $\mathcal{R}_{\leq}$ satisfies the axioms of good SDRSs. The fact that every term contains a finite number of redexes is immediate from [FB], and the fact that every redex is a residual of at most one redex follows from [SD]. The axiom [AF] follows from the fact in a complete lattice, the lub of two elements a and b does not depend on covering chains leading from the bottom element to a and b. By Lemma 4.9, [FD] implies [FC], and stability of $\mathcal{R}_{\leq}$ follows from [S].

Remark 4.11 (Imposing more structure on $\trianglelefteq_S$) The projection of pairs $(\mathcal{R}, \mathcal{S})$ onto SDRSs $\mathcal{R}_S$ induces a projection of pairs $(\mathcal{F}, \mathcal{S})$ onto $\mathcal{F}_S = (\mathcal{R}_S, \simeq_S)$, where $\mathcal{F} = (\mathcal{R}, \simeq)$ is a DFS with family relation $\simeq$. It is easy to show that for any DFS $\mathcal{F}$ with a regular stable semantics $\mathcal{S}$, $\mathcal{F}_S$ is a DFS (see [KG03]). Thus orderings $\trianglelefteq_S$ generated by pairs $(\mathcal{F}, \mathcal{S})$ are generated by *good* DFSs, i.e., DFSs $\mathcal{F} = (\mathcal{R}, \simeq)$ such that $\mathcal{R}$ is good. And furthermore the family relation $\simeq$ induces an equivalence relation on prime intervals in $\leq_{\mathcal{R}}$ that is a family relation (when considering $\leq_{\mathcal{R}}$ as an SDRS). There may be more than one way to define a family relation on a (good) SDRS,[2] so in general the family axioms do add strength to complete regular domains. Furthermore, we can impose the *minimality* property (the counterpart of superstability of reduction sets) on regular stable domains to obtain an even better behaved ordering.

5   Conclusions and Future Work

We have defined *stable computational semantics* for deterministic reduction systems based on very natural orderings $\trianglelefteq_S$ reflecting the growth of information towards the value of an expression w.r.t. a semantics $\mathcal{S}$ specified by a set of computations. We showed that $\trianglelefteq_S$ are finitary ω-algebraic complete lattices of a special form (containing dI-domains as substructures), and gave their equivalent domain-theoretic characterization. The proposed semantics unifies Boudol's computational approach to semantics [Bou85] with Winskel's stable Event Structure Semantics [Win89] (in the conflict-free case). We have learned that the 'finest' good domains to model functional calculi are actually the domains generated by the calculi themselves.

---

[2] This is related to the *separability* problem: a redex may create a number of redexes that may be put in different families, as well as in the same family, without violating the family axioms [KG97].

The importance of the concepts of stability and dI-domains for construction of models of functional calculi (based on the λ-calculus) and for the full abstraction problem [BCL85,Ong95], as well as for modelling polymorphism [Gir86,CGW89], is well understood, and we hope that our results will contribute to progress in these areas. The interpretation of DFSs into non-duplicating ones proposed in [KG97] maps good DFSs into linear DFSs which generate dI-domains, and we can readily get denotational models for lambda-calculi with different stable semantics using Berry's construction [Ber79]. However, more direct ways of using the orderings $\trianglelefteq_S$ in the study of denotational models of λ- and related calculi deserve further investigation. The precise relevance of family axioms and the minimality for regular stable domains is presently unknown.

References

[AGM] Abramsky S., Gabbay D., and Maibaum T., eds. Handbook of Logic in Computer Science, vol. 1-4, Oxford University Press, 1992-1995.

[Bar84] Barendregt H. P. The Lambda Calculus, its Syntax and Semantics. North-Holland, 1984.

[Ber96] Berarducci A. Infinite lambda-calculus and non-sensible models. Logic and Algebra, Lecture Notes in Pure and Applied Mathematics 180, Marcel Dekker Inc., 1996, p. 339-378.

[Ber79] Berry G. Modéles complétement adéquats et stables des λ-calculs typés. Thèse de l'Université de Paris VII, 1979.

[BL79] Berry G., Lévy J.-J. Minimal and optimal computations of recursive programs. JACM 26, 1979, p. 148-175.

[BCL85] Berry G., Curien P.-L., Lévy J.-J. Full abstraction for sequential languages: the state of the art. In [NR85], p. 89-132.

[Bou85] Boudol G. Computational semantics of term rewriting systems. In [NR85], p. 169-236.

[CGW89] Coquand T., Gunter C.A., Winskel G. dI-domains as a model of polymorphism. In Proc. of MFPLS'87, Springer LNCS, vol. 298, 1987, p. 344-363.

[CGM95] Corradini A., Gadduchi F., Montanari U. Relating two categorical models of term rewriting. In: Proc. of RTA'95, springer LNCS, Vol. 914, 1995, p. 25-240.

[Cur86] Curien P.-L. Categorical combinators, Sequential algorithms and functional programming. John Wiley & Sons, 1986.

[DP90] Davey, B.A., Priestley H.A., Introduction to Lattices and Order Cambridge University Press, 1990.

[Gir86] Girard J.Y. The system F of variable types: fifteen years later. TCS 45:159-192, 1986.

[Gir87] Girard J.Y. Linear logic. TCS 50:1-101, 1987.

[GKK00] Glauert J. R. W., Kennaway J. R., Khasidashvili Z. Stable results and relative normalization. J. Log. and Comp., vol. 10(3), OUP, 2000, p. 1-26.

[GK96] Glauert J.R.W., Khasidashvili Z. Relative normalization in deterministic residual structures. In: Proc. of CAAP'96, Springer LNCS, vol. 1059, 1996, p. 180-195.

[GK02] Glauert J. R. W, Khasidashvili Z. An abstract Böhm-normalization. in: Proc. WRS'02, Electronic Notes in Computer Science, Elsevier Science B.V., 2002.

[GLM92] Gonthier G., Lévy J.-J., Melliès P.-A. An abstract Standardisation theorem. In: Proc. of LICS'92, 1992, p. 72-81.

[Gun93] Gunter C.A. Semantics of programming languages: structures and techniques. MIT Press, 1993.

[HL91] Huet G., Lévy J.-J. Computations in Orthogonal Rewriting Systems. In: Computational Logic, Essays in Honor of Alan Robinson, MIT Press, 1991.

[KP93] Kahn G., Plotkin G.D. Concrete domains. TCS 121:186-277, 1993.

[KKSV93] Kennaway J. R., Klop J. W., Sleep M. R, de Vries F.-J. Event structures and orthogonal term graph rewriting. In: Term Graph Rewriting: Theory and Practice. John Wiley, 1993, p. 141-156.

[KG97] Khasidashvili Z., Glauert J.R.W. Zig-zag, extraction and separable families in non-duplicating stable deterministic residual structures. Report IR-420, Free University, February 1997.

[KG02] Khasidashvili Z., Glauert J.R.W. Relating conflict-free stable transition and event models. Theoretical Computer Science, vol. 286, 2002, p. 65-95.

[KG03] Khasidashvili Z., Glauert J.R.W. Stable Computational Semantics of Conflict-free Rewrite Systems,
available from http://www.cmp.uea.ac.uk/~jrwg/papers/KhaGlaRTARep.pdf.

[Lan94] Laneve C. Distributive evaluations of λ-calculus, Fundamenta Informaticae, 20(4):333 – 352, 1994.

[LW93] Larsen K., Winskel G. Using information systems to solve recursive domain equations effectively. In: Proc. of Int. Symposium on the Semantics of Data Types, Springer LNCS, vol. 173, 1984.

[Lév76] Lévy J.-J. An algebraic interpretation of the $\lambda\beta K$-calculus; and an application of a labelled λ-calculus. TCS 2(1):97-114, 1976.

[Lév78] Lévy J.-J. Réductions correctes et optimales dans le lambda-calcul, Thèse de l'Université de Paris VII, 1978.

[Lév80] Lévy J.-J. Optimal reductions in the Lambda-calculus. In: To H. B. Curry: Essays on Combinatory Logic, Lambda-calculus and Formalism, Hindley J. R., Seldin J. P. eds, Academic Press, 1980, p. 159-192.

[Lon83] Longo G. Set theoretic models of lambda calculus: theories, expansions and isomorphisms. Annals of Pure and Applied Logic, 24:153-188, 1983.

[Mel96] Melliès P.-A. Description Abstraite des Systèmes de Réécriture. Thèse de l'Université Paris 7, 1996.

[Mel97] Melliès P.-A. A factorization theorem in rewriting theory. In; Proc. of CTCS'97, Springer LNCS vol. 1290.

[Mel98] Melliès P.-A. A stability theorem in rewriting theory. In: Proc. LICS'98, 1998.

[Mid97] Middeldorp A. Call by need computations to root-stable form, in: POPL'97, 1997, 94-105.

[NPW81] Nielsen M., Plotkin G., Winskel G. Petri nets, event structures and domains. Part 1. TCS 13:85-108, 1981.

[NR85] Nivat M., Reynolds J.C., eds. Algebraic methods in semantics. CUP, 1985.

[Ong95] Ong C.-H. Correspondence between operational and denotational semantics: the full abstraction problem for PCF. In: [AGM], vol. 4, 1995, p. 269-356.

[Plo83] Plotkin G. Domains. University of Edinburgh, 1983 (Manuscript).

[Sco82] Scott D. Domains for denotational semantics. In Proc. ICALP'82, Springer LNCS, vol. 140, pp. 577-613, 1982.

[Sta89] Stark E. W. Concurrent transition systems. TCS 64(3):221-270, 1989.

[Ter03] Terese. Term Rewriting Systems. Cambridge Tracts in Theoretical Computer Science, Volume 55, Cambridge University Press, 2003.

[Win80] Winskel G. Events in Computation. Ph.D. Thesis, Univ. Edinburgh, 1980.

[Win89] Winskel G. An introduction to Event Structures. Springer LNCS, vol. 354, 1989, p. 364-397. Extended version in Cam. Univ. Comp. Lab. Report 95, 1986.

Recognizing Boolean Closed A-Tree Languages with Membership Conditional Rewriting Mechanism

Hitoshi Ohsaki[1,2], Hiroyuki Seki[3], and Toshinori Takai[2]

[1] PRESTO "Information and Systems"
Japan Science and Technology Corporation
[2] National Institute of Advanced Industrial Science and Technology
Nakoji 3–11–46, Amagasaki 661–0974, Japan
{ohsaki,takai}@ni.aist.go.jp
[3] Nara Institute of Science and Technology
Takayama 8916–5, Ikoma 630–0192, Japan
seki@is.aist-nara.ac.jp

Abstract. This paper provides an algorithm to compute the complement of tree languages recognizable with A-TA (tree automata with associativity axioms [16]). Due to this closure property together with the previously obtained results, we know that the class is boolean closed, while keeping recognizability of A-closures of regular tree languages. In the proof of the main result, a new framework of tree automata, called *sequence-tree automata*, is introduced as a generalization of Lugiez and Dal Zilio's multi-tree automata [14] of an associativity case. It is also shown that recognizable A-tree languages are closed under a one-step rewrite relation in case of ground A-term rewriting. This result allows us to compute an under-approximation of A-rewrite descendants of recognizable A-tree languages with arbitrary accuracy.

1   Introduction

In the tree automata theory, the following question has been asked frequently: What are natural definitions of *equationally* and *boolean* closed tree languages? The class of *regular* tree languages, which is the counterpart of regular word languages, is known to be well-behaved, such as to be closed under boolean operations together with many positive decidability properties [4,8]. However, under consideration of several equational axioms, the equational closures of regular tree languages are no longer regular [6]. Due to this problem, recently there have been several attempts in which the tree automata framework is extended. Alternating two-way AC-tree automata of Goubault-Larrecq and Verma [9] succeeded in the sense that AC-closed tree languages can be recognized, while keeping decidability of the intersection-emptiness problem. Lugiez and Dal Zilio coped with the same question by inventing multi-tree automata [14]. Their extended framework is useful for manipulating *flattened*-tree languages. Actually, the framework provides the starting basis of this research, because the authors have shown that there

R. Nieuwenhuis (Ed.): RTA 2003, LNCS 2706, pp. 483–498, 2003.
© Springer-Verlag Berlin Heidelberg 2003

exists *some* subclass of regular tree languages closed under the AC-congruence relation and under boolean operations. However, multi-tree automata for associativity axioms are not powerful in practice. For instance, the multi-trees like $f(a, \ldots, a, b, \ldots, b)$, assuming the numbers of a and b are the same and f has a flexible arity, are not recognizable with multi-tree automata. In the usual term model the previous example can be represented as the A-closure of the language recognized by a regular tree automaton with the following transition rules $f(q_a, q_b) \rightarrow q_f$, $f(q_a, q_f) \rightarrow q$, $f(q, q_b) \rightarrow q_f$.

The past couple of years we have investigated in [16,17] the recognizability and closure properties of associative and/or commutative tree languages by introducing a new framework, called *equational tree automata*. This framework allows us to handle equational tree languages, such as recognizable A-tree languages, which are effectively closed under union and intersection. The same closure property also holds in the AC-case. Our extension is useful for infinite-state model checking based on algebraic description languages of concurrent systems [18]. For instance, in protocol verification, network messages consisting of sequential data components are modeled with multiple lists, which are represented as terms with A-symbols. Besides, it is known that the emptiness problem for A-regular tree languages (i.e, tree languages recognizable with regular A-tree automata) is decidable. Unfortunately, there is also a negative result on A-tree languages: A-regular tree languages are *not* boolean closed. However, in the equational tree automata setting, the class of recognizable A-tree languages is properly wider than that of A-regular tree languages. So the remaining question arises again, as to whether or not recognizable A-tree languages are closed under complementation.

In the paper we obtain the solution to the unsolved question, in the way that A-tree languages are translated into sequence-tree languages. The translation is performed by a *flattening* operation, which is the standard technique in term rewriting, e.g. found in [2]. Intuitively, every non-empty and maximal context consisting of an A-symbol is replaced by a special function symbol $\langle \, \rangle$ which has a flexible arity. For instance, the term $f(a, f(f(b, c), d))$ is interpreted as $\langle a, b, c, d \rangle$. The resulting term is called a *sequence-term* (or sequence-tree). We thus need a new mechanism that manipulates sequence-terms. In Section 2 we introduce *sequence-tree automata* that allow a Galois connection to A-tree automata, even that have a bijective correspondence in recognizability. The new tree automata definition is inspired from Toyama's membership conditional term rewriting systems [20]. Furthermore, our formalization of sequence-tree automata generalizes Lugiez and Dal Zilio's multi-tree automata of the associativity case. In Section 3 we discuss the determinization of sequence-tree automata, which leads to the desired answer, that is, the complement closedness of recognizable A-tree languages. In Section 4 we demonstrate the usefulness of A-tree languages by showing that recognizable A-tree languages are closed under one-step ground A-rewriting. More precisely, since the tree language $\{ s \mid t \rightarrow^*_{\mathcal{R}/A} s \}$ can not be handled with a decidable tree automata theory [6], we show in the paper that $\{ s \mid \exists t \in L$ such that $t \rightarrow_{\mathcal{R}/A} s \}$ is recognizable with A-tree automata, provided

L is recognizable with A-tree automata and $\mathcal{R}/A$ is a ground A-rewrite system (i.e. rewrite rules in $\mathcal{R}$ are ground and equations in A are associativity axioms for some binary symbols). This result is helpful in figuring out decidable subclasses for the first-order theories of one-step rewriting [5].

In the paper we assume the readers are familiar with the basics of term rewriting (explained, e.g., in [1,3]). A subset $\mathcal{F}_A$ of the signature $\mathcal{F}$ consists of some binary function symbols. An equational system (ES for short) denoted by A is a set of associativity axioms $f(f(x,y),z) \approx f(x,f(y,z))$ for all f in $\mathcal{F}_A$. An *associative term rewriting system* (A-TRS for short) $\mathcal{R}/A$ over $\mathcal{F}$ is the combination of a TRS $\mathcal{R}$ and an ES A. We write $s \to_{\mathcal{R}/A} t$ if there exist terms s' and t' such that $s \sim_A s' \to_{\mathcal{R}} t' \sim_A t$. The binary relation $\sim_A$ is the equivalence relation induced by A. The reflexive-transitive closure and the transitive closure of $\to_{\mathcal{R}/A}$ are denoted by $\to_{\mathcal{R}/A}^*$ and $\to_{\mathcal{R}/A}^+$, respectively. A term t reachable from a term s with respect to $\mathcal{R}/A$, i.e. $s \to_{\mathcal{R}/A}^* t$, is called an $\mathcal{R}/A$-*descendant* of s. A term t with $s \to_{\mathcal{R}/A} t$ is called a *one-step* $\mathcal{R}/A$-*descendant* of s. The sets $\{ t \mid \exists s \in L.\ s \to_{\mathcal{R}/A}^* t \}$ and $\{ t \mid \exists s \in L.\ s \to_{\mathcal{R}/A} t \}$ for some set L of terms are denoted by $(\to_{\mathcal{R}/A}^*)[L]$ and $(\to_{\mathcal{R}/A})[L]$, respectively.

Next we fix our terminologies on tree automata. A *tree automaton* (TA for short) $\mathcal{A}$ is the 4-tuple $(\mathcal{F}, \mathcal{Q}, \mathcal{Q}_{fin}, \Delta)$ consisting of the signature $\mathcal{F}$, a finite set $\mathcal{Q}$ of state symbols (special constants with $\mathcal{F} \cap \mathcal{Q} = \varnothing$), a set $\mathcal{Q}_{fin}$ ($\subseteq \mathcal{Q}$) of final state symbols, and a finite set Δ of transition rules in one of the following forms:

$$f(p_1,\ldots,p_n) \to q \qquad \text{or} \qquad f(p_1,\ldots,p_n) \to f(q_1,\ldots,q_n)$$

for some $f \in \mathcal{F}$ with arity$(f) = n$ and $p_1,\ldots,p_n,q,q_1,\ldots,q_n \in \mathcal{Q}$. In the latter form, the root function symbols of the left- and right-hand sides must be the same. An *associative tree automaton* (A-TA for short) $\mathcal{A}/A$ is the combination of a TA $\mathcal{A}$ and an ES A over the same signature $\mathcal{F}$ with $\mathcal{F}_A$. An A-TA $\mathcal{A}/A$ is called *regular* if Δ consists only of rules in the former shape $f(p_1,\ldots,p_n) \to q$.

An A-TA $\mathcal{A}/A$ is a special A-TRS. In fact, Δ/A defines an A-TRS over the signature $\mathcal{F} \cup \mathcal{Q}$. We write $s \to_{\mathcal{A}/A} t$ if $s \to_{\Delta/A} t$. The binary relation $\to_{\mathcal{A}/A}$ over $\mathcal{T}(\mathcal{F} \cup \mathcal{Q})$ is called the *move relation* of $\mathcal{A}/A$. A term t in $\mathcal{T}(\mathcal{F})$ is *accepted* by $\mathcal{A}/A$ if $t \to_{\mathcal{A}/A}^* q$ for some $q \in \mathcal{Q}_{fin}$. The set of terms accepted by $\mathcal{A}/A$ is denoted by $\mathcal{L}(\mathcal{A}/A)$. A *tree language* L over $\mathcal{F}$ is some subset of $\mathcal{T}(\mathcal{F})$. A tree language L is *recognizable* with A-TA if there exists $\mathcal{A}/A$ such that $L = \mathcal{L}(\mathcal{A}/A)$. If L is recognizable with regular A-TA, it is called A-*regular*. A tree language closed under A-congruence relation is called an A-closed tree language, or simply called an A-tree language.

2 Sequence-Tree Automata

We begin this section by introducing a new concept of tree automata, which is called *sequence-tree automata*. The new framework enables us to accept (ground) *sequence-terms*: Given the signature $\mathcal{F}$, we say t is a sequence-term (or sequence-tree) in s-$\mathcal{T}(\mathcal{F})$

if $t = f(t_1, \ldots, t_n)$ such that $f \in \mathcal{F}_n$ and $t_i \in$ s-$\mathcal{T}(\mathcal{F})$ for all $1 \leqslant i \leqslant n$, or

if $t = \langle t_1, \ldots, t_m \rangle$ such that $m \geqslant 2$ and $t_i \in$ s-$\mathcal{T}(\mathcal{F})$ and root(t_i) $\in \mathcal{F}$ for all $1 \leqslant i \leqslant m$.

We assume $\langle \, \rangle$ to be a special symbol with a flexible arity. Each function symbol f in $\mathcal{F}$ has a fixed arity, which is represented by the mapping arity : $\mathcal{F} \to \mathbb{N}$. A subset $\mathcal{F}_n$ of $\mathcal{F}$ consists of function symbols f with arity$(f) = n$.

A sequence-tree automaton (s-TA for short) $\mathcal{M} = (\mathcal{F}, \mathcal{Q}, \mathcal{Q}_{fin}, \Delta)$ is defined as an easy extension of the standard TA, by allowing transition rules for the special symbol $\langle \, \rangle$ with the following shape:

$$\langle X \rangle \to q \Leftarrow \mathsf{concat}(X) \text{ in } \mathcal{L}(\mathcal{G})$$

Here the capital letter X is called a *sequence-variable* [10,13]. In the above transition rule, X is expected to be instantiated to some sequence $q_1, \ldots, q_n$ $(n \geqslant 2)$ of states. So in the *conditional part* of the rule, the concatenation $q_1 \cdots q_n$ of state symbols, denoted by $\mathsf{concat}(X)$, is examined whether it is accepted by a *word grammar* $\mathcal{G}$ over $\mathcal{Q}$. Each grammar in conditional rules is not necessarily the same as each other grammar in different rules. If the membership condition $\mathsf{concat}(X)$ in $\mathcal{L}(\mathcal{G})$ is satisfied for some instance of X, the left pattern can be replaced by a single state q.

A word grammar $\mathcal{G} = (\Sigma, \mathcal{S}, \mathsf{s}_0, \Lambda)$ over the alphabet Σ with $\mathcal{S}$ nonterminal symbols and s_0 the starting symbol is called (1) *context-sensitive* (CSG for short) if $|l| \leqslant |r|$, (2) *context-free* if $l \in \mathcal{S}$, (3) *regular* if $l \in \mathcal{S}$ and $r \in \{ a \, s \mid a \in \Sigma \text{ and } s \in \mathcal{S} \} \cup \{ a \mid a \in \Sigma \}$ for all production rules $l \to r$ in Λ. We say $\mathcal{G}$ is a *monotone* grammar if every rule in Λ has one of the following forms:

$$p \to a \qquad \text{or} \qquad p \to q_1 \, q_2 \qquad \text{or} \qquad p_1 \, p_2 \to q_1 \, q_2$$

with $p, p_1, p_2, q_1, q_2 \in \mathcal{S}$ and $a \in \Sigma$.

An s-TA is called a monotone (resp. context-sensitive, context-free, regular) s-TA if word grammars in the conditional part are monotone (resp. context-sensitive, context-free, regular). In the paper we say an s-TA instead of a monotone s-TA. A sequence-tree language recognizable with a monotone (resp. context-sensitive, context-free, regular) s-TA is called monotone (resp. context-sensitive, context-free, regular). In the literature, e.g. in [15], monotone grammars are called *Kuroda normal forms* of CSG. Moreover, it is known that for every CSG, we can compute an equivalent grammar in Kuroda normal form [12]. The expressive power of sequence-tree automata is determined by the generative power of $\mathcal{G}$. In fact, we have the strict language hierarchy between the classes of monotone, context-free, and regular sequence-tree languages.

Next we discuss the relationship between A-TA and s-TA. Hereafter we assume $\mathcal{F}_A = \{ \mathsf{f} \}$. Moreover, we say a context of a term is an f-*block* if it is a non-empty maximal context consisting of f only. For notational convenience, we write $C'[C_\mathsf{f}[\![t_1, \ldots, t_n]\!]]$ for $C'[C[t_1, \ldots, t_n]]$ if C is an f-block. For instance, $\mathsf{g}(C_\mathsf{f}[\![\mathsf{a}, \mathsf{b}, \mathsf{c}]\!])$ represents the terms $\mathsf{g}(\mathsf{f}(\mathsf{a}, \mathsf{f}(\mathsf{b}, \mathsf{c})))$ and $\mathsf{g}(\mathsf{f}(\mathsf{f}(\mathsf{a}, \mathsf{b}), \mathsf{c}))$.

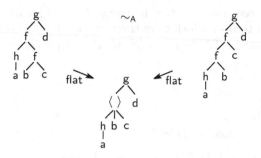

Fig. 1. Flattening by flat

We define the two mappings flat and unflat as follows: Let t be a term in $T(\mathcal{F})$,

$$\mathsf{flat}(t) = \begin{cases} \langle \mathsf{flat}(t_1), \ldots, \mathsf{flat}(t_m) \rangle & \text{if } t = C_{\mathsf{f}}[\![t_1, \ldots, t_m]\!], \\ f(\mathsf{flat}(t_1), \ldots, \mathsf{flat}(t_n)) & \text{if } t = f(t_1, \ldots, t_n) \text{ and } f \neq \mathsf{f}. \end{cases}$$

Let $\mathcal{F}' = \mathcal{F} - \{\mathsf{f}\}$ and let t be a sequence-term in s-$T(\mathcal{F}')$,

$$\mathsf{unflat}(t) = \begin{cases} \mathsf{f}(\ldots \mathsf{f}(\mathsf{unflat}(t_1), \mathsf{unflat}(t_2)) \ldots, \mathsf{unflat}(t_m)) \\ \qquad \text{if } t = \langle t_1, t_2, \ldots, t_m \rangle, \\ f(\mathsf{unflat}(t_1), \ldots, \mathsf{unflat}(t_n)) & \text{if } t = f(t_1, \ldots, t_n) \text{ and } f \neq \mathsf{f}. \end{cases}$$

An example of a flat-transformation is illustrated in Fig. 1. One should notice that $\mathsf{flat}(\mathsf{unflat}(t)) = t$ for any sequence-term t in s-$T(\mathcal{F}', \mathcal{V})$. However, $\mathsf{unflat}(\mathsf{flat}(t))$ and t are not always the same, but $\mathsf{unflat}(\mathsf{flat}(t)) \sim_A t$. For instance,

$$\mathsf{unflat}(\mathsf{flat}(\ g(f(h(a), f(b, c)), d)\ )) = g(f(f(h(a), b), c), d) \neq g(f(h(a), f(b, c)), d)$$

although $g(f(f(h(a), b), c), d) \sim_A g(f(h(a), f(b, c)), d)$.

Using the mappings flat and unflat, we show that the classes of A-TA and s-TA have a bijective correspondence in recognizability. More precisely, in the remaining part of this section, we prove the next statement.

Theorem 1. *Given an A-tree language L over the signature $\mathcal{F}$ with $\mathcal{F}_A = \{\mathsf{f}\}$, there exists an A-TA $\mathcal{A}/A$ such that $\mathcal{L}(\mathcal{A}/A) = L$ if and only if there exists an s-TA $\mathcal{M}$ such that $\mathcal{L}(\mathcal{M}) = \mathsf{flat}(L)$.* □

In the above theorem A-closedness of L is essential. For instance, the tree language $\{\ f(f(a, a), a)\ \}$ is not recognizable with A-TA, because an A-TA which accepts $f(f(a, a), a)$ also accepts $f(a, f(a, a))$. On the other hand, we can easily define an s-TA that accepts $\langle a, a, a \rangle$ only.

Let us explain the idea for the "only if" proof of the above theorem. We consider the A-TA $\mathcal{A}/A$ with $\mathcal{A} = (\{\mathsf{f}, a, b\}, \{\mathsf{p}, q_1, q_2\}, \{\mathsf{p}\}, \Delta)$ where Δ:

$$
\begin{array}{lll}
a \to q_1 & f(q_1, q_2) \to p & f(q_1, q_2) \to f(q_2, q_1) \\
b \to q_2 & f(p, p) \to p & f(q_2, q_1) \to f(q_1, q_2)
\end{array}
$$

The A-TA $\mathcal{A}/A$ recognizes the tree language $\{\, t \in \mathcal{T}(\{\,f, a, b\,\}) \mid |t|_a = |t|_b \,\}$, i.e. the set of ground terms t which have the same numbers of a and b in t. Now we define the associated s-TA $\mathcal{M}_{\mathcal{A}/A} = (\mathcal{F}, \mathcal{Q}, \mathcal{Q}_{fin}, \Delta_1 \cup \Delta_2)$ as follows:

$$\mathcal{F} : \ a, b$$
$$\mathcal{Q} : \ p, q_1, q_2$$
$$\mathcal{Q}_{fin} : \ p$$
$$\Delta_1 : \ a \to q_1, \ b \to q_2$$
$$\Delta_2 : \ \langle X \rangle \to p \Leftarrow \mathsf{concat}(X) \text{ in } \mathcal{L}(\mathcal{G}_p)$$

where $\mathcal{G}_p = (\{\, p, q_1, q_2 \,\}, \{\, \alpha_p, \alpha_{q1}, \alpha_{q2} \,\}, \alpha_p, \Lambda)$ and

$$\Lambda = \{\, \alpha_p \to \alpha_{q1}\,\alpha_{q2}, \ \alpha_p \to \alpha_p\,\alpha_p, \ \alpha_{q2}\,\alpha_{q1} \to \alpha_{q1}\,\alpha_{q2}, \ \alpha_{q1}\,\alpha_{q2} \to \alpha_{q2}\,\alpha_{q1} \,\}$$
$$\cup \{\, \alpha_p \to p, \ \alpha_{q1} \to q_1, \ \alpha_{q2} \to q_2 \,\}.$$

In the construction, a monotone grammar $\mathcal{G}_p$ has a production rule of the form $\alpha_p \to \alpha_q\,\alpha_r$ if Δ contains a transition rule $f(q, r) \to p \in \Delta$. Likewise, $\mathcal{G}_p$ has a rule $\alpha_p\,\alpha_q \to \alpha_r\,\alpha_s$ if $f(r, s) \to f(p, q)$ in Δ. As a consequence, we obtain the s-TA $\mathcal{M}_{\mathcal{A}/A}$ satisfying that: $\mathcal{M}_{\mathcal{A}/A}$ allows a one-step move $\langle p_1, \ldots, p_n \rangle \to_{\mathcal{M}_{\mathcal{A}/A}} p$ if and only if $\alpha_p \to^*_{\mathcal{G}_p} \alpha_{p_1} \cdots \alpha_{p_n}$. In fact, the above s-TA construction satisfies the following property.

Lemma 1. *Given an A-TA $\mathcal{A}/A$ with $\mathcal{A} = (\mathcal{F}, \mathcal{Q}, \mathcal{Q}_{fin}, \Delta)$. Suppose $\mathcal{M}_{\mathcal{A}/A} = (\mathcal{F}', \mathcal{Q}', \mathcal{Q}'_{fin}, \Delta')$ is the s-TA obtained by the above construction. Then, for all $p_1, \ldots, p_n, q \in \mathcal{Q}$, $C_f[p_1, \ldots, p_n] \to^*_{\mathcal{A}/A} q$ if and only if $\alpha_q \to^*_{\mathcal{G}_q} \alpha_{p_1} \cdots \alpha_{p_n}$.* □

Using this lemma, we can prove the "only if" direction of Theorem 1.

Lemma 2. *Given an A-TA $\mathcal{A}/A$ with $\mathcal{A} = (\mathcal{F}, \mathcal{Q}, \mathcal{Q}_{fin}, \Delta)$. Suppose $\mathcal{M}_{\mathcal{A}/A} = (\mathcal{F}', \mathcal{Q}', \mathcal{Q}'_{fin}, \Delta')$ is the s-TA obtained as in the previous lemma. Then, $t \in \mathcal{L}(\mathcal{A}/A)$ if and only if $\mathsf{flat}(t) \in \mathcal{L}(\mathcal{M}_{\mathcal{A}/A})$.*

Proof. We show the "only if" part. The reverse can be proved in a similar way. We assume $t \to^*_{\mathcal{A}/A} q$ for some $q \in \mathcal{Q}$. Then we show by the structural induction that $\mathsf{flat}(t) \to^*_{\mathcal{M}_{\mathcal{A}/A}} q$. If t is a constant c, there exists a transition rule $c \to q \in \Delta$. Then, by construction, $c \to q \in \Delta'$. If $t = f(t_1, \ldots, t_n)$ with $f \neq \mathsf{f}$, then $t_i \to^*_{\mathcal{A}/A} p_i$ for some $p_i \in \mathcal{Q}$ $(1 \leqslant i \leqslant n)$ such that $f(p_1, \ldots, p_n) \to q \in \Delta$. By induction hypothesis, $\mathsf{flat}(t_i) \to^*_{\mathcal{M}_{\mathcal{A}/A}} p_i$ $(1 \leqslant i \leqslant n)$. Moreover, $f(p_1, \ldots, p_n) \to q \in \Delta'$. Thus, $\mathsf{flat}(t) \to^*_{\mathcal{M}_{\mathcal{A}/A}} f(p_1, \ldots, p_n) \to_{\mathcal{M}_{\mathcal{A}/A}} q$. If $t = C_f[t_1, \cdots, t_m]$, then $t_i \to^*_{\mathcal{A}/A} p_i$ for all $1 \leqslant i \leqslant m$ and $C_f[p_1, \ldots, p_m] \to^*_{\mathcal{A}/A} q$. By induction hypothesis, $\mathsf{flat}(t_i) \to^*_{\mathcal{M}_{\mathcal{A}/A}} p_i$ $(1 \leqslant i \leqslant n)$. Thus, $\mathsf{flat}(t) = \langle \mathsf{flat}(t_1), \ldots, \mathsf{flat}(t_m) \rangle \to^*_{\mathcal{M}_{\mathcal{A}/A}} \langle p_1, \ldots, p_m \rangle \to_{\mathcal{M}_{\mathcal{A}/A}} q$, because there exists a transition rule $\langle X \rangle \to q \Leftarrow \mathsf{concat}(X)$ in $\mathcal{L}(\mathcal{G}_q)$. By Lemma 1, $p_1 \cdots p_m \in \mathcal{L}(\mathcal{G}_q)$ is guaranteed.   □

Next we show the reverse (the "if" part of Theorem 1). The proof is achieved as in the previous lemma. Suppose $\mathcal{M} = (\mathcal{F}, \mathcal{Q}, \mathcal{Q}_{fin}, \Delta)$. Without loss of generality, we assume that for every rule of the form $\langle X \rangle \to q \Leftarrow \mathsf{concat}(X)$ in $\mathcal{L}(\mathcal{G})$, nonterminal symbols of $\mathcal{G}$ are pairwise distinct from the other word grammars.

We define the associated A-TA $\mathcal{A}_\mathcal{M}/\mathsf{A}$ as follows: $\mathcal{A}_\mathcal{M} = (\mathcal{F} \cup \{\,\mathsf{f}\,\}, \mathcal{Q}', \mathcal{Q}_{fin}, \Delta')$ and $\mathcal{F}_\mathsf{A} = \{\,\mathsf{f}\,\}$ where

$$
\begin{aligned}
\Delta' = \{\, l \to r \in \Delta \mid \mathsf{root}(l) \in \mathcal{F}\,\} \\
\cup\; \{\,\mathsf{f}(\alpha, \beta) \to \mathsf{f}(\gamma, \delta) \mid \langle X \rangle \to q \Leftarrow \mathsf{concat}(X) \text{ in } \mathcal{L}(\mathcal{G}) \in \Delta,\; \gamma\delta \to \alpha\beta \in \mathcal{G}\,\} \\
\cup\; \{\,\mathsf{f}(\alpha, \beta) \to \gamma \quad\; \mid \langle X \rangle \to q \Leftarrow \mathsf{concat}(X) \text{ in } \mathcal{L}(\mathcal{G}) \in \Delta,\;\; \gamma \to \alpha\beta \in \mathcal{G}\,\} \\
\cup\; \{\,\mathsf{f}(\alpha, \beta) \to q \quad\; \mid \langle X \rangle \to q \Leftarrow \mathsf{concat}(X) \text{ in } \mathcal{L}(\mathcal{G}) \in \Delta,\;\; \gamma \to \alpha\beta \in \mathcal{G}, \\
\text{and } \gamma \text{ is a starting symbol of } \mathcal{G}\,\} \\
\cup\; \{\, f(p_1, \ldots, p_n) \to \alpha \mid f(p_1, \ldots, p_n) \to p \in \Delta \text{ with } f \neq \mathsf{f}, \\
\langle X \rangle \to q \Leftarrow \mathsf{concat}(X) \text{ in } \mathcal{L}(\mathcal{G}) \in \Delta,\;\; \alpha \to p \in \mathcal{G} \quad\}
\end{aligned}
$$

The set $\mathcal{Q}'$ of new nonterminal symbols is $\mathcal{Q}$ together with nonterminal symbols of all word grammars of conditional rules in Δ. Then we can prove the next lemma.

Lemma 3. *Given an s-TA $\mathcal{M}$ over the signature $\mathcal{F}$ such that $\mathsf{f} \notin \mathcal{F}$. Suppose $\mathcal{F}' = \mathcal{F} \cup \mathcal{F}_\mathsf{A}$ with $\mathcal{F}_\mathsf{A} = \{\,\mathsf{f}\,\}$ and $\mathcal{A}_\mathcal{M}/\mathsf{A}$ is the A-TA over $\mathcal{F}'$ obtained from $\mathcal{M}$ by the above construction. Then, $t \in \mathcal{L}(\mathcal{M})$ if and only if $\mathsf{unflat}(t) \in \mathcal{L}(\mathcal{A}_\mathcal{M}/\mathsf{A})$.* ☐

Bijective correspondence between s-TA and A-TA is beneficial: For instance, the proof of the emptiness problem for A-TA (Corollary 1 in [16]) can be simplified. We prove the same undecidability for s-TA below: Given a monotone grammar $\mathcal{G} = (\Sigma, \mathcal{S}, \mathsf{s}_0, \Lambda)$, we define the s-TA $\mathcal{M}_\mathcal{G} = (\mathcal{F}, \mathcal{Q}, \mathcal{Q}_{fin}, \Delta)$ associated with $\mathcal{G}$ as follows. $\mathcal{F} = \{\, \mathsf{c}_a \mid a \in \Sigma \,\}$, $\mathcal{Q} = \Sigma \cup \{\mathsf{q}\}$ with $\mathsf{q} \notin \Sigma$, $\mathcal{Q}_{fin} = \{\,\mathsf{q}\,\}$, $\Delta = \{\, \mathsf{c}_a \to a \mid a \in \Sigma \,\} \cup \{\, \langle X \rangle \to \mathsf{q} \Leftarrow \mathsf{concat}(X) \text{ in } \mathcal{L}(\mathcal{G}_\mathsf{q}) \,\}$. Then $\mathcal{L}(\mathcal{M}_\mathcal{G}) - \varnothing$ if and only if $\mathcal{L}(\mathcal{G}_\mathsf{q}) = \varnothing$. It is known that the emptiness problem for monotone grammars is undecidable, and thus, the problem is also undecidable for s-TA.

Using our transformation (from s-TA to A-TA, and the reverse), it can also be proved that the class of monotone sequence-tree languages is effectively closed under union and intersection, because the class of A-tree languages is also effectively closed under union and intersection (Theorems 2,3 in [16]). The additional benefit from using Theorem 1 is that a complexity result in one framework yields the same result in the other framework.

Theorem 2. *The membership problem for s-TA is PSPACE-complete.* ☐

Proof (Outline). The nontrivial part, showing the PSPACE-hardness, of this theorem can be achieved by reducing from the membership problem for CSG, which is known to be PSPACE-complete. ☐

As an immediate consequence, we obtain the complexity result for A-TA.

Corollary 1. *The membership problem for A-TA is PSPACE-complete.* ☐

3   Determinization of Sequence-Tree Automata

We show in this section that context-sensitive sequence-tree automata can be determinized using the algorithm in Fig. 2. The algorithm is obtained by generalizing the standard *subset construction* technique. This implies that recognizable sequence-tree languages and hence A-tree languages are closed under

Let $\mathcal{M} = (\mathcal{F}, \mathcal{Q}, \mathcal{Q}_{fin}, \Delta)$ be an s-TA. We assume without loss of generality that Δ does not contain different conditional rules for the same right-hand side q. In case Δ contains $\langle X \rangle \to q \Leftarrow \mathsf{concat}(X)$ in $\mathcal{L}(\mathcal{G}_1)$ and $\langle X \rangle \to q \Leftarrow \mathsf{concat}(X)$ in $\mathcal{L}(\mathcal{G}_2)$ with $\mathcal{G}_1 \neq \mathcal{G}_2$, they can be merged to a single rule $\langle X \rangle \to q \Leftarrow \mathsf{concat}(X)$ in $\mathcal{L}(\mathcal{G}_3)$ such that $\mathcal{L}(\mathcal{G}_3) = \mathcal{L}(\mathcal{G}_1) \cup \mathcal{L}(\mathcal{G}_2)$.

Next, for every conditional rule $\langle X \rangle \to q \Leftarrow \mathsf{concat}(X)$ in $\mathcal{L}(\mathcal{G}_q)$ in Δ, we define a monotone (but not necessarily deterministic) grammar $\mathcal{G}_q^d$ as follows: Let $\mathcal{G}_q = (\Sigma, \mathcal{S}, \mathsf{s}_0, \Lambda)$, then $\mathcal{G}_q^d = (2^\Sigma, \mathcal{S}, \mathsf{s}_0, \Lambda')$ where

$$\Lambda' = (\Lambda - \{\alpha \to a \mid a \in \Sigma\}) \cup \{\alpha \to A \mid \alpha \to a \in \Lambda,\ A \in 2^\Sigma,\ a \in A\}.$$

Finally, we define an s-TA $\mathcal{M}_d = (\mathcal{F}, \mathcal{Q}_d, \mathcal{Q}_{dfin}, \Delta_d)$ as follows:

$$\mathcal{Q}_d = 2^{\mathcal{Q}}$$
$$\mathcal{Q}_{dfin} = \{A \in \mathcal{Q}_d \mid A \cap \mathcal{Q}_{fin} \neq \varnothing\}$$
$$\Delta_d = \Delta_{d1} \cup \Delta_{d2} \cup \Delta_{d3} \text{ where}$$

Δ_{d1} : $f(A_1, \ldots, A_n) \to A$
  for $A_i \in \mathcal{Q}_d$ $(1 \leqslant i \leqslant n)$ and
  $A = \{q \mid f(q_1, \ldots, q_n) \to q \in \Delta \text{ such that } q_i \in A_i\ (1 \leqslant i \leqslant n)\}$,

Δ_{d2} : $\langle X \rangle \to A \Leftarrow \mathsf{concat}(X)$ in $\mathcal{L}(\mathcal{G}_A)$
  for $A \in (\mathcal{Q}_d - \{\varnothing\})$ and
  $\mathcal{L}(\mathcal{G}_A) = \bigcap_{q \in A} \mathcal{L}(\mathcal{G}_q^d) - \bigcup_{q \in \mathcal{Q}-A} \mathcal{L}(\mathcal{G}_q^d)$,

Δ_{d3} : $\langle X \rangle \to \varnothing \Leftarrow \mathsf{concat}(X)$ in $\mathcal{L}(\mathcal{G}_0)$,
  where $\mathcal{L}(\mathcal{G}_0) = \{w \in \mathcal{Q}_d^* \mid |w| \geqslant 2\} - \bigcup_{q \in \mathcal{Q}} \mathcal{L}(\mathcal{G}_q^d)$.

Fig. 2. Determinization of sequence-tree automata

complementation, which provides a positive answer to an important remaining question in [16,17].

Lemma 4. *Given some subsets* A_i $(1 \leqslant i \leqslant n)$ *of a set* S, *for every subset* I *of indices* $\{1, \ldots, n\}$, *we define* $C_I = \bigcap_{i \in I} A_i - \bigcup_{i \in (\{1,\ldots,n\}-I)} A_i$. *Then* $C_I \cap C_J = \varnothing$ *if* $I \neq J$. $\qquad\square$

Lemma 5. $\mathcal{M}_d$ *is a complete and deterministic s-TA.*

Proof. First we show that $\mathcal{M}_d$ is a deterministic s-TA. By Kuroda's Lemma ([12]), given a context-sensitive grammar, there effectively exists a monotone grammar with the same generative power. Moreover, monotone languages are effectively closed under boolean operations [11,12]. Thus a language $\mathcal{L}(\mathcal{G}_A)$ of a conditional rule in Δ_{d2} can be defined by a monotone grammar. The same holds for $\mathcal{L}(\mathcal{G}_0)$ of Δ_{d3}. So we can compute an s-TA $\mathcal{M}_d$. Next we show the determinism of Δ_d. By definition, there is no overlapping at the root position in the left-hand sides of two different rules in Δ_{d1}. For transition rules in Δ_{d2}, we take two rules $\langle X \rangle \to A_1 \Leftarrow \mathsf{concat}(X)$ in $\mathcal{L}(\mathcal{G}_{A1})$ and $\langle X \rangle \to A_2 \Leftarrow \mathsf{concat}(X)$ in $\mathcal{L}(\mathcal{G}_{A2})$ in

Δ_{d2}. By Lemma 4, we obtain $\mathcal{L}(\mathcal{G}_{A1}) \cap \mathcal{L}(\mathcal{G}_{A2}) = \varnothing$. Then there is no instance t of $\langle X \rangle$ such that $t \in \mathcal{L}(\mathcal{G}_{A1}) \cap \mathcal{L}(\mathcal{G}_{A2})$. For Δ_{d3}, the intersection of $\{w \in \mathcal{Q}_d^* \mid |w| \geqslant 2\} - \bigcup_{q \in \mathcal{Q}} \mathcal{L}(\mathcal{G}_q^d)$ and $\bigcap_{q \in \mathcal{Q}} \mathcal{L}(\mathcal{G}_q^d)$ is empty. Hence, there is no overlapping between Δ_{d3} and Δ_{d2}.

Next we show that $\mathcal{M}_d$ is complete. By definition, for every $f \in \mathcal{F}$ and $A_1, \ldots, A_n \in \mathcal{Q}_d$, there exists a transition rule of the form $f(A_1, \ldots, A_n) \to A$ in Δ_{d1}. For another pattern $\langle A_1, \ldots, A_m \rangle$ with $A_1, \ldots, A_m \in \mathcal{Q}_d$ and $m \geqslant 2$, we take $L = \bigcup_{A \in (\mathcal{Q}_d - \{\varnothing\})} \mathcal{L}(\mathcal{G}_A)$. Then we can show that $\bigcup_{q \in \mathcal{Q}} \mathcal{L}(\mathcal{G}_q^d)$ is the same as L. This implies $L \cup \mathcal{L}(\mathcal{G}_0) = \{w \in \mathcal{Q}_d^* \mid |w| \geqslant 2\}$. Hence, if $A_1 \cdots A_m \in L$, there exists a transition rule $\langle X \rangle \to A \Leftarrow \mathrm{concat}X$ in $\mathcal{L}(\mathcal{G}_A)$ in Δ_{d2} that is applicable to $\langle A_1, \ldots, A_m \rangle$; otherwise, Δ_{d3} is applicable.   □

Lemma 6. *Suppose* $\langle X \rangle \to A \Leftarrow \mathrm{concat}(X)$ *in* $\mathcal{L}(\mathcal{G}_A)$ *is a transition rule in* Δ_{d2}. *Let* $L_A - \{A_1 \cdots A_k \in \mathcal{Q}_d^* \mid q \in A$ *if and only if* $\exists q_i \in A_i (1 \leqslant i \leqslant k)$ *and* $q_1 \cdots q_k \in \mathcal{L}(\mathcal{G}_q)\}$. *Then* $\mathcal{L}(\mathcal{G}_A) = L_A$.   □

Lemma 7. $\mathcal{L}(\mathcal{M}) = \mathcal{L}(\mathcal{M}_d)$.

Proof. We show that for every sequence-term $t \in \text{s-}\mathcal{T}(\mathcal{F})$ and state symbol $A \in \mathcal{Q}_d$, if $t \to_{\mathcal{M}_d}^* A$ then A is the same as the set $\{q \in \mathcal{Q} \mid t \to_{\mathcal{M}}^* q\}$. We use the structural induction on t. If t is a constant, $\mathcal{M}_d$ has a transition rule $t \to \{q \in \mathcal{Q} \mid t \to q \in \Delta\}$, and $\mathcal{M}_d$ has no other rule for t. We suppose $t = f(t_1, \ldots, t_n)$ with $f \in \mathcal{F}$. Then, $t_i \to_{\mathcal{M}_d}^* A_i$ $(1 \leqslant i \leqslant n)$ and $f(A_1, \ldots, A_n) \to A \in \Delta_d$. By Lemma 5, $\mathcal{M}_d$ does not allow the move relation for t except $t \to_{\mathcal{M}_d}^* f(A_1, \ldots, A_n) \to_{\mathcal{M}_d} A$. By definition, $A = \{q \in \mathcal{Q} \mid \exists f(q_1, \ldots, q_n) \to q \in \Delta$ such that $q_i \in A_i$ $(1 \leqslant i \leqslant n)\}$. On the other hand, by induction hypothesis, we obtain $A_i = \{q_i \in \mathcal{Q} \mid t_i \to_{\mathcal{M}}^* q_i\}$. Then, $A = \{q \in \mathcal{Q} \mid \exists f(q_1, \ldots, q_n) \to q \in \Delta$ such that $t_i \to_{\mathcal{M}}^* q_i$ $(1 \leqslant i \leqslant n)\} = \{q \in \mathcal{Q} \mid f(t_1, \ldots, t_n) \to_{\mathcal{M}}^* q\}$. Next we suppose $t = \langle t_1, \ldots, t_m \rangle$ such that $m \geqslant 2$ and $t_i \to_{\mathcal{M}_d}^* A_i$ $(1 \leqslant i \leqslant m)$. By Lemma 5, $\mathcal{M}_d$ does not allow the move relation for t except $t \to_{\mathcal{M}_d}^* \langle A_1, \ldots, A_m \rangle \to_{\mathcal{M}_d} A$. By construction, the last move relation $\langle A_1, \ldots, A_m \rangle \to_{\mathcal{M}_d} A$ is made by the rule $\langle X \rangle \to A \Leftarrow \mathrm{concat}(X)$ in $\mathcal{L}(\mathcal{G}_A)$ in Δ_d. By Lemma 6, $q \in A$ if and only if $\exists q_i \in A_i (1 \leqslant i \leqslant m)$ and $q_1 \cdots q_m \in \mathcal{L}(\mathcal{G}_q)$. Hence, by induction hypothesis, A is the same as the set $\{q \in \mathcal{Q} \mid \exists q_i \in \mathcal{Q}$ such that $t_i \to_{\mathcal{M}}^* q_i$ $(1 \leqslant i \leqslant m)$ and $\langle q_1, \ldots, q_m \rangle \to_{\mathcal{M}} q\}$.

The rest of the proof is easy. By Lemma 5 for every $t \in \text{s-}\mathcal{T}(\mathcal{F})$ there exists a (and only one) state $A \in \mathcal{Q}_d$ such that $t \to_{\mathcal{M}_d}^* A$. From the above property, $A \in \mathcal{Q}_{d fin}$ if and only if $t \to_{\mathcal{M}}^* q \in \mathcal{Q}_{fin}$ for some $q \in A$.   □

Theorem 3. *Given an s-TA* $\mathcal{M}$, *we can compute a complete and deterministic s-TA* $\mathcal{M}_d$ *such that* $\mathcal{L}(\mathcal{M}_d) = \mathcal{L}(\mathcal{M})$. *Thus monotone sequence-tree languages are effectively closed under complementation.*   □

Corollary 2. *Tree languages recognizable with A-TA are effectively closed under complementation.*

Proof. Given an A-TA $\mathcal{A}/A$ over the signature $\mathcal{F}$ with $\mathcal{F}_A = \{f\}$, by Lemmata 2 and 3 and Theorem 3, we can compute $\mathcal{B}/A$ such that $t \in \text{flat}(\mathcal{T}(\mathcal{F}) - \mathcal{L}(\mathcal{A}/A))$ if and only if unflat(t) $\in \mathcal{L}(\mathcal{B}/A)$. Note that s-$\mathcal{T}(\mathcal{F} - \mathcal{F}_A) - \text{flat}(\mathcal{L}(\mathcal{A}/A)) = \text{flat}(\mathcal{T}(\mathcal{F}) - \mathcal{L}(\mathcal{A}/A))$. Thus, by showing that $\mathcal{B}/A$ recognizes the A-closure of unflat(flat($\mathcal{T}(\mathcal{F}) - \mathcal{L}(\mathcal{A}/A))$)), we know that the complement of $\mathcal{A}/A$ is recognizable with $\mathcal{B}/A$. $\qquad\square$

4   Recognizing One-Step A-Rewrite Descendants

In order to validate a safety property with model checking approach, *reachability* is a fundamental problem to be handled. Nevertheless, it is proved in equational term rewriting that, there is no algorithm capable of deciding $s \to^*_{\mathcal{R}/A} t$ even if $\mathcal{R}$ is ground. Due to this fact, we know that the tree language $(\to^*_{\mathcal{R}/A})[\{s\}]$ is no longer *effectively* recognizable. However, these negative results do not imply incomputability of $(\to^n_{\mathcal{R}/A})[\{s\}]$ for an arbitrary but fixed n. In fact, we show in this section that, given a ground A-TRS $\mathcal{R}/A$ and an A-TA $\mathcal{A}/A$, the tree language $(\to_{\mathcal{R}/A})[\mathcal{L}(\mathcal{A}/A)]$ is effectively recognizable with A-TA.

In case that $\mathcal{R}$ is ground, every rule $l \to r$ in $\mathcal{R}$ can be simulated by decomposed rules $f(c_1, \ldots, c_m) \to c_0$ and $d_0 \to g(d_1, \ldots, d_n)$, where c_i ($0 \leq i \leq m$) and d_j ($0 \leq j \leq n$) are fresh constants. The nontrivial case to be considered in the proofs occurs in the rewrite relation made by a rule $f(c_1, c_2) \to c_0$ with f an associativity symbol. First we consider in the following the string rewriting case. We then generalize this result to the A-term rewriting case.

Lemma 8. *Given a monotone grammar* $\mathcal{G} = (\Sigma, \mathcal{S}, s_0, \Lambda)$ *and a string rewrite system* $\mathcal{R} = \{ab \to c\}$ *with* $a, b, c \in \Sigma$, *we can compute a monotone grammar that recognizes* $(\to_{\mathcal{R}})[\mathcal{L}(\mathcal{G})]$.

Proof. We assume without loss of generality that in Λ, (1) there is only one transition rule whose left-hand side is s_0 and (2) s_0 does not appear in the right-hand sides. We define a monotone grammar $\mathcal{G}' = (\Sigma, \mathcal{S}', s_0, \Lambda')$ as follows: $\mathcal{S}' = \mathcal{S} \cup \{ [pq] \mid p, q \in \mathcal{S} \}$ and

$$
\begin{array}{llll}
\Lambda' = \{ & s_0 \to c & \mid s_0 \to^*_{\mathcal{G}} ab & \} \quad \cdots (1) \\
\cup \{ & s_0 \to [pq]r & \mid p, q, r \in \mathcal{S} \text{ such that } s_0 \to^*_{\mathcal{G}} pqr & \} \quad \cdots (2) \\
\cup \{ & [pq] \to c & \mid p \to a, q \to b \in \Lambda & \} \quad \cdots (3) \\
\cup \{ & p \to a & \mid p \to a \in \Lambda, p \neq s_0, a \in \Sigma & \} \quad \cdots (4) \\
\cup \left\{ \begin{array}{rl}
[pq] &\to [p_1 p_2]q \\
[qp] &\to [qp_1]p_2 \\
p &\to p_1 p_2
\end{array} \middle| \begin{array}{l} p \to p_1 p_2 \in \Lambda, p \neq s_0, q \in \mathcal{S} \end{array} \right\} \quad \cdots (5) \\
\cup \left\{ \begin{array}{rl}
[p_1 p_2]q &\to [q_1 q_2]q \\
q[p_1 p_2] &\to q[q_1 q_2] \\
p_1 p_2 &\to q_1 q_2
\end{array} \middle| \begin{array}{l} p_1 p_2 \to q_1 q_2 \in \Lambda, q \in \mathcal{S} \end{array} \right\} \quad \cdots (6) \\
\cup \left\{ \begin{array}{rl}
[pq]r &\to p[qr] \\
p[qr] &\to [pq]r
\end{array} \middle| \begin{array}{l} p, q, r \in \mathcal{S} \end{array} \right\} \quad \cdots (7)
\end{array}
$$

Rules in (1) and (2) are computable, because the membership problem is decidable for monotone grammar. The rest of the proof is done by case analysis. ☐

In Lemma 8, each of the letters a, b, c is not necessarily different from each other. Moreover, we can take a string rewrite rule, such that the length of the left-hand side is more than 2. In fact, if $\mathcal{R} = \{w \to c\}$ such that $w \in \Sigma^+$ and $|w| = n$ ($\geqslant 2$), we define Λ' as follows: (1)–(3) are replaced by

$$\{ \qquad s_0 \to c \quad | \quad s_0 \to_{\mathcal{G}}^* w \qquad\qquad\qquad \} \quad \cdots (1')$$
$$\{ \qquad s_0 \to [p_1 \cdots p_n]\, q \mid s_0 \to_{\mathcal{G}}^* p_1 \cdots p_n\, q \in \mathcal{S}^+ \quad \} \quad \cdots (2')$$
$$\{ [p_1 \cdots p_n] \to c \quad | \quad p_i \to a_i \in \Lambda,\ w = a_1 \cdots a_n \quad \} \quad \cdots (3')$$

Rules in (5) are replaced by, e.g.

$$[p_1 \cdots p_i \cdots p_{n-1}\, p_n] \to [p_1 \cdots q_1\, q_2 \cdots p_{n-1}]\, p_n$$

if $1 \leqslant i \leqslant n - 1$ and $p_i \to q_1\, q_2$ in Λ. For $p_n \to q_1\, q_2$ in Λ,

$$[p_1 \cdots p_{n-1}\, p_n] \to [p_1 \cdots p_{n-1}\, q_1]\, q_2.$$

Likewise, rules in (6) and (7) are modified. Using the general version of $\mathcal{G}'$, we can show that $(\to_{\mathcal{R}})[\, \mathcal{L}(\mathcal{G})\,]$ is a monotone language for $\mathcal{R} = \{\, w \to c \,\}$.

Lemma 9. *Given an A-TA $\mathcal{A}/A$ and a ground TRS $\mathcal{R} = \{f(a, b) \to c\}$ over the same signature $\mathcal{F}$ with $\mathcal{F}_A = \{f\}$, we can compute an Λ-TA that recognizes $(\to_{\mathcal{R}/A})[\, \mathcal{L}(\mathcal{A}/A)\,]$.*

Proof. Suppose $\mathcal{M}_A = (\mathcal{F} - \{f\}, \mathcal{Q}, \mathcal{Q}_{fin}, \Delta)$ is an s-TA associated with $\mathcal{A}/A$. Without loss of generality, we assume that for all $a \to p,\, b \to q \in \Delta$ with $a, b \in \mathcal{F}_0,\, a \neq b$ implies $p \neq q$. Let $\diamond$ be a fresh symbol with $\diamond \notin \mathcal{F} \cup \mathcal{Q}$ and $W = \{\, pq \mid a \to p,\, b \to q \in \Delta \,\}$. We write $\to_c$ for the binary relation induced by the string rewrite system (SRS for short) $\{w \to \diamond \mid w \in W\}$ over the language $(\mathcal{Q} \cup \{\diamond\})^+$. Similarly, $\to_\diamond$ for the induced binary relation of the SRS $\{p \to p_\diamond \mid p \in \mathcal{Q}\}$. Define $\mathcal{M}'_A = (\mathcal{F} - \{f\}, \mathcal{Q}', \mathcal{Q}'_{fin}, \Delta')$ as follows: $\mathcal{Q}' = \mathcal{Q} \cup \{\diamond\} \cup \{q_\diamond \mid q \in \mathcal{Q}\}$, $\mathcal{Q}'_{fin} = \{q_\diamond \mid q \in \mathcal{Q}_{fin}\}$ and

$$\Delta' = \Delta \cup \{\, c \to \diamond \,\}$$
$$\cup\, \{\, c \to q_\diamond \mid \langle X \rangle \to q \Leftarrow \mathsf{concat}(X) \text{ in } L \in \Delta,\ L \cap W \neq \varnothing \,\}$$
$$\cup\, \{\, f(p_1, \ldots, p_{i\diamond}, \ldots, p_n) \to q_\diamond \mid f(p_1, \ldots, p_i, \ldots, p_n) \to q \in \Delta \,\}$$
$$\cup\, \{\, \langle X \rangle \to q_\diamond \Leftarrow \mathsf{concat}(X) \text{ in } (\to_\diamond)[L] \mid \langle X \rangle \to q \Leftarrow \mathsf{concat}(X) \text{ in } L \in \Delta \,\}$$
$$\cup\, \left\{ \langle X \rangle \to q_\diamond \Leftarrow \mathsf{concat}(X) \text{ in } (\to_c)[L'] \,\middle|\, \begin{array}{l} \langle X \rangle \to q \Leftarrow \mathsf{concat}(X) \text{ in } L \in \Delta \\ L' = L - W \end{array} \right\}$$

By Lemma 8, a monotone grammar generating $(\to_c)[L']$ is computable. Furthermore, for every $\langle X \rangle \to q \Leftarrow \mathsf{concat}(X)$ in L in Δ, a monotone grammar generating $(\to_\diamond)[L]$ is computable. So it can be proved by the structural induction that the s-TA $\mathcal{M}'_A$ recognizes the sequence-term representation of $(\to_{\mathcal{R}/A})[\, \mathcal{L}(\mathcal{A}/A)\,]$. ☐

$\mathcal{A}_0 := \mathcal{A}; \; i := 0; \; j := 0;$
$S \; := \mathsf{pos}(l);$
$T \; := \mathsf{pos}(r);$

while $S \neq \varnothing$ do
$\quad$ select $p \in S$ such that $\nexists p' \in S. \; p' \succ p$
$\quad$ let $l_{|p} = f(t_1, \ldots, t_n)$ and
$\quad$ compute $\mathcal{A}_{i+1}/\mathsf{A}$ such that
$\qquad \mathcal{L}(\mathcal{A}_{i+1}/\mathsf{A}) = (\rightarrow_{\{f(c_{t_1}^{p\cdot 1}, \ldots, c_{t_n}^{p\cdot n}) \rightarrow c_{l_{|p}}^{p}\}/\mathsf{A}})[\,\mathcal{L}(\mathcal{A}_i/\mathsf{A})\,]$
$\quad i := i + 1;$
$\quad S := S - \{p\};$
od

compute $\mathcal{B}_0/\mathsf{A}$ such that
$\qquad \mathcal{L}(\mathcal{B}_0/\mathsf{A}) = (\rightarrow_{\{c_l^{\epsilon} \rightarrow d_r^{\epsilon}\}/\mathsf{A}})[\,\mathcal{L}(\mathcal{A}_i/\mathsf{A})\,]$

while $T \neq \varnothing$ do
$\quad$ select $q \in T$ such that $\nexists q' \in T. \; q \succ q'$
$\quad$ let $r_{|q} = f(t_1, \ldots, t_n)$ and
$\quad$ compute $\mathcal{B}_{j+1}/\mathsf{A}$ such that
$\qquad \mathcal{L}(\mathcal{B}_{j+1}/\mathsf{A}) = (\rightarrow_{\{d_{r_{|q}}^{q} \rightarrow f(d_{t_1}^{q\cdot 1}, \ldots, d_{t_n}^{q\cdot n})\}/\mathsf{A}})[\,\mathcal{L}(\mathcal{B}_j/\mathsf{A})\,]$
$\quad j := j + 1;$
$\quad T := T - \{q\};$
od

$\mathcal{B}_{l \rightarrow r} := \mathcal{B}_j;$
return $\mathcal{B}_{l \rightarrow r}/\mathsf{A}$

Fig. 3. One-Step A-Rewrite Descendants for One-Rule Case

Theorem 4. *Given a ground A-TRS $\mathcal{R}/\mathsf{A}$ over the signature $\mathcal{F}$ with $\mathcal{F}_\mathsf{A} = \{f\}$:
(1) For every A-TA $\mathcal{A}/\mathsf{A}$ over the same signature $\mathcal{F}$, we can compute an A-TA
that recognizes $(\rightarrow_{\mathcal{R}/\mathsf{A}})[\,\mathcal{L}(\mathcal{A}/\mathsf{A})\,]$. (2) In case that $\mathcal{A}$ is regular, we can compute
a regular A-TA that recognizes $(\rightarrow_{\mathcal{R}/\mathsf{A}})[\,\mathcal{L}(\mathcal{A}/\mathsf{A})\,]$.*

Proof. For (1), let $l \rightarrow r$ be a rewrite rule in $\mathcal{R}$. We define the ground TRS

$$\mathcal{R}_{l \rightarrow r} = \{\, f(c_{t_1}^{p\cdot 1}, \ldots, c_{t_n}^{p\cdot n}) \rightarrow c_{f(t_1, \ldots, t_n)}^{p} \mid p \in \mathsf{pos}(l), \; l_{|p} = f(t_1, \ldots, t_n) \,\}$$
$$\cup \{\, d_{f(t_1, \ldots, t_n)}^{p} \rightarrow f(d_{t_1}^{p\cdot 1}, \ldots, d_{t_n}^{p\cdot n}) \mid p \in \mathsf{pos}(r), \; r_{|p} = f(t_1, \ldots, t_n) \,\}$$

It can be proved that for every s, t in $\mathcal{T}(\mathcal{F})$, $s = C[l]$ and $t = C[r]$ if and
only if $s \rightarrow^{+}_{\mathcal{R}_{l \rightarrow r}} C[c_l^{\epsilon}]$ and $C[d_r^{\epsilon}] \rightarrow^{+}_{\mathcal{R}_{l \rightarrow r}} t$. Moreover, this statement is generalized as follows: $s \sim_\mathsf{A} C[l]$ and $t \sim_\mathsf{A} C[r]$ if and only if $s \rightarrow^{+}_{\mathcal{R}_{l \rightarrow r}/\mathsf{A}} C[c_l^{\epsilon}]$
and $C[d_r^{\epsilon}] \rightarrow^{+}_{\mathcal{R}_{l \rightarrow r}/\mathsf{A}} t$. Using this fact, we define the procedure in Fig. 3. If
the root symbol f of a decomposed rule $f(c_1, \ldots, c_n) \rightarrow c$ is an A-symbol, we
know that the one-step A-rewrite descendants are effectively recognizable by
Lemma 9; otherwise, the one-step A-rewrite descendants $(\rightarrow_{\mathcal{R}_{l \rightarrow r}/\mathsf{A}})[L]$ are the

same as $A((\to_{\mathcal{R}_{l\to r}})[L])$, which has been noted by Dauchet and Tison [5]. Then the procedure is capable of computing an A-TA $\mathcal{B}_{l\to r}/A$ that recognizes the tree language

$$L_{l\to r} = \left\{ t \in \mathcal{T}(\mathcal{F}) \mid s \in \mathcal{L}(\mathcal{A}/A),\ s \to^{+}_{\mathcal{R}_{l\to r}/A} C[c_i^{\epsilon}]\ \text{and}\ C[d_r^{\epsilon}] \to^{+}_{\mathcal{R}_{l\to r}/A} t \right\}.$$

Since $(\to_{\mathcal{R}/A})[\mathcal{L}(\mathcal{A}/A)] = \bigcup_{l\to r \in \mathcal{R}} L_{l\to r}$ and tree languages recognizable with A-TA are effectively closed under union, we can compute an A-TA that recognizes $(\to_{\mathcal{R}/A})[\mathcal{L}(\mathcal{A}/A)]$.

The second statement can be shown in a similar way. First we prove that context-free languages are closed under one-step string rewriting of $\{a\,b \to c\}$, that corresponds to Lemma 8. Then we apply the result to the A-tree case. In the construction of context-free grammars, we use different transition rules. The set of transition rules Λ' of $\mathcal{G}'$ consists of (1), (3), (4) and the following rules:

$$\left\{ \begin{array}{ll} s_0 & \to\ \lfloor p\,q\rfloor\,r \\ s_0 & \to\ p\,\lceil q\,r\rceil \end{array} \ \middle|\ p,q,r \in \mathcal{S}\ \text{such that}\ s_0 \to^{*}_{\mathcal{G}} p\,q\,r \right\} \quad \cdots\ (2')$$

$$\left\{ \begin{array}{ll} \lfloor p\,q\rfloor & \to\ \lfloor p_1\,p_2\rfloor\,q \\ \lfloor p\,q\rfloor & \to\ p_1\,\lfloor p_2\,q\rfloor \\ \lceil q\,p\rceil & \to\ \lceil q\,p_1\rceil\,p_2 \\ \lceil q\,p\rceil & \to\ q\,\lceil p_1\,p_2\rceil \\ p & \to\ p_1\,p_2 \end{array} \ \middle|\ p \to p_1\,p_2 \in \Lambda,\ p \neq s_0,\ q \in \mathcal{S} \right\} \quad \cdots\ (5')$$

In this case, transition rules (6) and (7) in Lemma 8 are unnecessary.   □

5   Concluding Remarks

We have shown in this paper that A-tree languages recognizable with A-tree automata are closed under boolean operations. The newly obtained closure property is a direct consequence of (1) complement closedness of monotone sequence-tree languages (Theorem 3), and (2) bijective correspondence between A-tree automata and sequence-tree automata (Theorem 1). The theorem is also helpful for simplifying the proof of undecidability of the emptiness problem for A-tree automata. The new framework introduced in Section 2, called sequence-tree automata, enables us to have an easy proof of the complexity of the membership problem for A-tree languages (Corollary 1).

In the previous section, we also showed that recognizable A-tree languages are closed under one-step ground A-rewrite descendants (Theorem 4). This allows us to provide an *under-approximation* algorithm for computing A-rewrite descendants of A-tree languages with arbitrary accuracy, which is useful in practice, e.g. for infinite-state model checking [7].

In this paper, we introduced a special symbol $\langle\,\rangle$ for translating A-tree languages of a singleton $\mathcal{F}_A$ case. But, for many arbitrary associative symbols, the sequence-term model has to be allowed to contain more special symbols, e.g. $\langle\,\rangle_1, \ldots, \langle\,\rangle_n$. More precisely, by modifying the definition of sequence-terms and

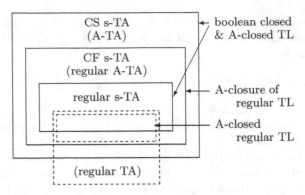

Fig. 4. Relationships in sequence-tree automata

indexing the special symbol $\langle\ \rangle$ as above, Theorems 1–4 and Corollaries 1–2 can be extended to the general case.

By restricting grammars in the conditional part of transition rules, as mentioned already, we obtain the language hierarchy, which is illustrated in Fig. 4. The outermost square represents the class of sequence-tree languages recognizable with the context-sensitive s-TA. The second largest square is the class of context-free s-TA. Since it has the bijective correspondence to regular A-TA, the class in the usual term model is the same as the A-congruence closure of regular tree languages. The third largest square, i.e. the class of regular s-TA, is identical to multi-tree automata for associativity axioms only [14]. This class and the class of CS s-TA are closed under boolean operations and the A-congruence relation. Furthermore, the third class is important in the following sense:

Theorem 5. *Given a ground A-TRS $\mathcal{R}/A$ over the signature $\mathcal{F}$ with $\mathcal{F}_A = \{f\}$, the set of normal forms with respect to $\mathcal{R}/A$ is effectively recognizable with regular A-TA. In the sequence-term model, the language is effectively recognizable with regular s-TA.*

Proof. Let $l \to r$ be a rewrite rule in $\mathcal{R}$. We define an s-TA $\mathcal{M}_{l \to r}$ that recognizes the sequence-term representation of the A-closure of terms $C[l]$, where C is an arbitrary ground context: $\mathcal{M}_{l \to r} = (\mathcal{F} - \{f\}, \mathcal{Q}, \mathcal{Q}_{fin}, \Delta)$ such that $\mathcal{Q} = \{q\} \cup \{q_t \mid p \in \mathsf{pos}(l),\ t = l|_p\}$, $\mathcal{Q}_{fin} = \{q_l\}$ and Δ consists of the transition rules

$$\langle X \rangle \to q_t \Leftarrow \mathsf{concat}(X) \text{ in } \{q_{t_1} \cdots q_{t_n}\} \quad \text{if } t = C_f[\![t_1, \ldots, t_n]\!] \text{ is an f-block of } l,$$

$$f(q_{t_1}, \ldots, q_{t_m}) \to q_t \qquad\qquad \text{if } t = f(t_1, \ldots, t_m) \trianglelefteq l \text{ and } f \neq \mathsf{f}$$

together with $\langle X \rangle \to q_l \Leftarrow \mathsf{concat}(X)$ in $\{w \mid w = q^* q_l q^* \text{ and } |w| \geqslant 2\}$, $\langle X \rangle \to q \Leftarrow \mathsf{concat}(X)$ in $\{w \mid w = q^* \text{ and } |w| \geqslant 2\}$, $f(q, \ldots, q_l, \ldots, q) \to q_l$ and $f(q, \ldots, q) \to q$ for all $f \in \mathcal{F} - \{f\}$. Observe that the membership test in each conditional rule can be represented by a regular grammar. Let $\mathcal{M}_{\mathcal{R}}$ be an s-TA that recognizes $\bigcup_{l \to r \in \mathcal{R}} \mathcal{L}(\mathcal{M}_{l \to r})$. The (sequence-term representation of) set of normal forms of $\mathcal{R}/A$ is the complement of $\mathcal{L}(\mathcal{M}_{\mathcal{R}})$. Determinizing $\mathcal{M}_{\mathcal{R}}$

with subset construction results in a regular s-TA $\mathcal{M}'_{\mathcal{R}}$, and it is computable, because the conditional part of a transition rule of $\mathcal{M}'_{\mathcal{R}}$ is represented as follows: $\mathsf{concat}(X)$ in $\bigcap_{i \in I} \mathcal{L}(\mathcal{G}_i) - \bigcup_{i \in (K-I)} \mathcal{L}(\mathcal{G}_i)$, where $\mathcal{G}_i$ is a regular grammar for every $i \in (K \cup I)$. Therefore, the set of normal forms of $\mathcal{R}/\mathsf{A}$ is effectively recognizable with regular A-TA. $\qquad\square$

The larger dotted square in Fig. 4 denotes the class of regular tree languages. This square contains the subclass allowed to be A-closed (and thus, it is both regular and A-closed). Since it can be shown that every regular and A-closed tree language is recognizable with regular A-TA, the innermost dotted square has no overlapping with the class of CS s-TA, i.e., there is no example that is regular, A-closed, and recognizable with A-TA, but not recognizable with regular A-TA.

Acknowledgments

The authors are grateful to Aart Middeldorp for his comments on the early draft. We also thank anonymous referees for their detailed comments.

References

1. F. Baader and T. Nipkow: *Term Rewriting and All That*, Cambridge University Press, 1998.
2. L. Bachmair and D.A. Plaisted: *Associative Path Orderings*, Proc. of 1st RTA, Dijon (France), LNCS 202, pp. 241–254, 1985.
3. M. Bezem, R. de Vrijer, and J.W. Klop (eds.): *Term Rewriting Systems*, Cambridge Tracts in Theoretical Computer Science 55, Cambridge University Press, 2003.
4. H. Comon, M. Dauchet, R. Gilleron, F. Jacquemard, D. Lugiez, S. Tison, and M. Tommasi: *Tree Automata Techniques and Applications*, 2002. Draft available on http://www.grappa.univ-lille3.fr/tata/
5. M. Dauchet and S. Tison: *The Theory of Ground Rewrite Systems is Decidable*, Proc. of 5th LICS, Philadelphia (Pennsylvania), pp. 242–248, 1990.
6. A. Deruyver and R. Gilleron: *The Reachability Problem for Ground TRS and Some Extensions*, Proc. of 14th CAAP, Barcelona (Spain), LNCS 351, pp. 227–243, 1989.
7. A. Finkel and Ph. Schnoebelen: *Well-Structured Transition Systems Everywhere!*, Theoretical Computer Science 256, pp. 63–92, 2001.
8. F. Gécseg and M. Steinby: *Tree Languages*, Handbook of Formal Languages 3, pp. 1–68 (Chapter 1), Springer-Verlag, 1996.
9. J. Goubault-Larrecq and K.N. Verma: *Alternating Two-Way AC-Tree Automata*, Research Report LSV-02-11, ENS de Cachan (France), 2002.
10. M. Hamana: *Term Rewriting with Sequences*, Proc. of 1st Theorema Workshop, Hagenberg (Austria), 1997. Draft included in technical report 97–20, RISC - Linz.
11. N. Immerman: *Nondeterministic Space is Closed Under Complementation*, SIAM Journal on Computing 17(5), pp. 935–938, 1988.
12. S.Y. Kuroda: *Classes of Languages and Linear Bounded Automata*, Information and Control 7, pp. 207–223, 1964.
13. T. Kutsia: *Unification in the Empty and Flat Theories with Sequence Variables and Flexible Arity Symbols*, technical report 01–13, RISC - Linz, 2001. Available on http://www.sfb013.uni-linz.ac.at/~sfb/reports/2001/ps-files/

14. D. Lugiez and S. Dal Zilio: *Multitrees Automata, Presburger's Constraints and Tree Logics*, technical report 08–2002, LIF - CNRS - Université Provence, 2002. Available on `http://www.lim.univ-mrs.fr/Rapports/`
15. A. Mateescu and A. Salomaa: *Aspects of Classical Language Theory*, Handbook of Formal Languages 1, pp. 175–251 (Chapter 4), Springer-Verlag, 1996.
16. H. Ohsaki: *Beyond Regularity: Equational Tree Automata for Associative and Commutative Theories*, Proc. of 15th CSL, Paris (France), LNCS 2142, pp. 539–553, 2001.
17. H. Ohsaki and T. Takai: *Decidability and Closure Properties of Equational Tree Languages*, Proc. of 13th RTA, Copenhagen (Denmark), LNCS 2378, pp. 114–128, 2002.
18. H. Ohsaki and T. Takai: *A Tree Automata Theory for Unification Modulo Equational Rewriting*, 16th UNIF, Copenhagen (Denmark), 2002. Draft available from `http://staff.aist.go.jp/hitoshi.ohsaki/unif2002.ps.gz`
19. H. Ohsaki, H. Seki, and T. Takai: *Recognizable A-Tree Languages are Boolean Closed*, technical report AIST–PS–2003–001, Programming Science Group, AIST, 2003. The revised version with the new title (*Recognizing Boolean Closed A-Tree Languages with Membership Conditional Rewriting Mechanism*) is available from `http://staff.aist.go.jp/hitoshi.ohsaki/rta2003.ps.gz`
20. Y. Toyama: *Membership Conditional Term Rewriting Systems*, Trans. of IEICE E72(11), pp. 1224–1229, 1989.

Testing Extended Regular Language Membership Incrementally by Rewriting

Grigore Roşu and Mahesh Viswanathan

Department of Computer Science
University of Illinois at Urbana-Champaign, USA

Abstract. In this paper we present lower bounds and rewriting algorithms for testing membership of a word in a regular language described by an extended regular expression. Motivated by intuitions from monitoring and testing, where the words to be tested (execution traces) are typically much longer than the size of the regular expressions (patterns or requirements), and by the fact that in many applications the traces are only available incrementally, on an event by event basis, our algorithms are based on an event-consumption idea: a just arrived event is "consumed" by the regular expression, i.e., the regular expression modifies itself into another expression discarding the event. We present an exponential space lower bound for monitoring extended regular expressions and argue that the presented rewriting-based algorithms, besides their simplicity and elegance, are practical and almost as good as one can hope. We experimented with and evaluated our algorithms in Maude.

1 Introduction

Regular expressions represent a compact and useful technique to specify patterns in strings. There are programming and/or scripting languages, such as Perl, which are mostly based on efficient implementations of pattern matching via regular expressions. Extended regular expressions (ERA), which add complementation ($\neg R$) to the usual union ($R_1 + R_2$), concatenation ($R_1 \cdot R_2$), and repetition (R^*) operators, make the description of regular languages more convenient and more succinct. The membership problem for an extended regular expression R and a word $w = a_1 a_2 \ldots a_n$ is to decide whether w is in the regular language generated by R. The size of w is typically much larger than that of R.

Due to their convenience in specifying patterns, regular expressions, and implicitly the membership problem, have many applications and not only in computer science. For example, [14] suggests interesting applications in molecular biology. Monitoring and testing are other interesting application areas for regular expressions, because the execution of physical processes or computer programs can usually be abstracted by an external observer, or monitor, as a linear sequence of events. Since monitoring or testing of a process or program typically terminates after a period of time and a result of the monitoring/testing session is desired quickly, efficient implementations of the membership problem are of critical importance to these areas. Moreover, since monitoring sessions can be

R. Nieuwenhuis (Ed.): RTA 2003, LNCS 2706, pp. 499–514, 2003.

quite long, sometimes days or weeks, algorithms which do not need to store the execution trace or equivalent size information are typically preferred.

There has been some interest manifested recently in the software analysis community in using temporal logics in testing [9,10]. The Temporal Rover tool (TR) and its follower DB Rover [5] are already commercial; they are based on the idea of extending or instrumenting Java programs to enforce checking their execution trace against formulae expressed in temporal logics. The MaC tool [18] has developed its own language to express monitoring safety requirements, using an interval past time temporal logic at its core. In [21,20] various algorithms to generate testing automata from temporal logic formulae are described. Java PathExplorer [7] is a runtime verification environment under current development at NASA Ames, whose logical monitoring part consists of checking execution traces against formulae expressed in both future time and past time temporal logics. [6,8] present efficient algorithms for monitoring future time linear temporal logic formulae, while [11] gives a method to synthesize efficient monitors from past time temporal formulae. An interesting aspect of linear temporal logics in the context of monitoring/testing, is that they specify *patterns* for the execution traces of the monitored processes, which can also be specified by extended regular expressions of comparable or sometimes smaller size.

In this paper we focus on the membership problem for EREs. Previous work on the membership problem for regular expressions and their extensions [12,19,22,17], have focussed on developing dynamic programming or automata based algorithms that run in time that is polynomial in both the size of the regular expression and the trace. These algorithms, however, suffer from a couple of drawbacks that make them unamenable as monitoring or testing algorithms. First, they are not incremental. They assume that the entire word is available when the algorithm is run. Second, the running time of these algorithms is at least quadratic in the size of the word. This is an unacceptably high overhead in monitoring and testing, because the word is usually enormous.

We, instead, investigate the membership problem in a model that is more appropriate for the context of monitoring and testing. More precisely, we assume that the ERE R to monitor is given apriori, but the letters $a_1, a_2, ..., a_n$ forming the word w are received one by one, from the first (1) to the last (n). We often call the expression R a "requirement formula" and the letters in w "events". We also assume that w is large enough that one does not want to store it for future processing; therefore, each event has to be processed as it arrives. For that reason, we interchangeably call this problem the "monitoring" or the "incremental membership" problem. We give an exponential space lower bound by showing that any monitoring algorithm for EREs uses space that is $\Omega(2^{c\sqrt{m}})$ in the size m of the ERE, for some fixed constant c. Then, inspired by a related technique in [8] for future time linear temporal logic, we give a simple exponential space rewriting algorithm which solves the incremental membership problem in space $O(2^{m^2})$, thus giving an upper bound for the membership problem. In the end we give an improved version of the algorithm which we implemented and evaluated using Maude, which performs much better than the proved upper bound, thus opening the door for further interesting research in this direction.

Note that the simple-minded technique to first generate a nondeterministic (NFA) or a deterministic finite automaton (DFA) from the ERE and then to monitor against that NFA or DFA is not practical. This is because the size of the NFA or DFA can be non-elementarily larger than the initial regular ERE, because negation involves an NFA-to-DFA translation, which implies an exponential blow-up; since negations can be nested, the size of such NFAs or DFAs could be highly exponential. Even if one would succeed in storing such an immense automaton, say a DFA, monitoring against it would still be highly exponential because a transition in a DFA requires time logarithmic in the total number of states (the next state needs to be at least read and each state label/name needs at least a logarithmic number of bits). ERE to (perhaps alternating) automata effective translations may well be possible, and we believe they are, but the simplistic ones are clearly too inconvenient to be considered.

2   Monitoring Extended Regular Expressions

In this section we define extended regular expressions (ERE) and languages formally, and give an exponential space lower bound for monitoring ERE.

2.1   Definitions

Extended regular expressions (ERE) define languages by inductively applying union ($+$), concatenation ($\cdot$), Kleene Closure ($\star$), intersection ($\cap$), and complementation ($\neg$). More precisely, for an alphabet Σ, an ERE over Σ is defined as follows, where $A \in \Sigma$: $R ::= \emptyset \mid \epsilon \mid A \mid R + R \mid R \cdot R \mid R^{\star} \mid R \cap R \mid \neg R$.

The language defined by an expression R, denoted by $\mathcal{L}(R)$, is defined inductively as $\mathcal{L}(\emptyset) = \emptyset$, $\mathcal{L}(\epsilon) = \{\epsilon\}$, $\mathcal{L}(A) = \{A\}$, $\mathcal{L}(R_1 + R_2) = \mathcal{L}(R_1) \cup \mathcal{L}(R_2)$, $\mathcal{L}(R_1 \cdot R_2) = \{w_1 \cdot w_2 \mid w_1 \in \mathcal{L}(R_1) \text{ and } w_2 \in \mathcal{L}(R_2)\}$, $\mathcal{L}(R^{\star}) = (\mathcal{L}(R))^{\star}$, $\mathcal{L}(R_1 \cap R_2) = \mathcal{L}(R_1) \cap \mathcal{L}(R_2)$, $\mathcal{L}(\neg R) = \Sigma^{\star} \setminus \mathcal{L}(R)$. Given an ERE, as defined above using union, concatenation, Kleene Closure, intersection and complementation, one can translate it into an equivalent expression that does not have any intersection operation, by applying De Morgan's Laws. The translation only results in a linear blowup in size. Therefore, in the rest of the paper we do not consider expressions containing intersection. More precisely, we only consider EREs of the form $R ::= R + R \mid R \cdot R \mid R^{\star} \mid \neg R \mid A \mid \epsilon \mid \emptyset$.

2.2   Monitoring

In this subsection we will show that any monitoring algorithm for extended regular expressions must use space that is exponential in the size of the regular expression describing the correctness property. We will give an example of a language for which a lot of information needs to be remembered in order for it to determine if a trace satisfies the property.

The language that will be used in proving the lower bound was first present in [3] to show the power of alternation. Since then this example also has been used to prove lower bounds on LTL model checking [15,16]. Consider the language

$$L_k = \{\sigma \# w \# \sigma' \$ w \mid w \in \{0,1\}^k \text{ and } \sigma, \sigma' \in \{0,1,\#\}^*\}.$$

We will first show that the above language can be described using an ERE of size $\Theta(k^2)$. We will then show that any monitoring algorithm must keep track of all strings over $\{0,1\}$ of length k that appear between $\#$ symbols before the $\$$ in the trace, in order for it to decide membership in L_k. This will give us a space lower bound of 2^k for monitoring algorithms.

Proposition 1. *There is an ERE R_k such that $L(R_k) = L_k$ and $|R_k| = \Theta(k^2)$.*

Proof. The ERE will be a conjunction of the following two facts.

(a) There is exactly one $\$$ symbol in the trace, and
(b) There is a $\#$ symbols after which there is a string of length k over $\{0,1\}$ before the next $\#$, such that for every i, the ith symbol after the $\#$ is exactly the same as the ith symbol after the $\$$.

In other words, R_k is the following extended regular expression.

$$R_k = (\neg \$)^* \$ (\neg \$)^* \bigcap$$

$$(0+1+\#)^* \# [\bigcap_{i=0}^{k} [((0+1)^i 0 (0+1)^{k-i-1} \# (0+1+\#)^* \$ (0+1)^i 0 (0+1)^{k-i-1})$$

$$+ ((0+1)^i 1 (0+1)^{k-i-1} \# (0+1+\#)^* \$ (0+1)^i 1 (0+1)^{k-i-1})]]$$

Observe that $|R_k| = \Theta(k^2)$.

In order to prove the space lower bound, the following equivalence relation on strings over $(0+1+\#)^*$ is useful. For a string $\sigma \in (0+1+\#)^*$, define $S(\sigma) = \{w \in (0+1)^k \mid \exists \lambda_1, \lambda_2. \ \lambda_1 \# w \# \lambda_2 = \sigma\}$. We will say that $\sigma_1 \equiv_k \sigma_2$ iff $S(\sigma_1) = S(\sigma_2)$. Now observe that the number of equivalence classes of $\equiv_k$ is 2^{2^k}; this is because for any $S \subseteq (0+1)^k$, there is a σ such that $S(\sigma) = S$. We are now ready to prove the space lower bound.

Theorem 1. *Any ERE monitoring algorithm requires space $\Omega(2^{c\sqrt{m}})$, where m is the size of the input ERE and c is some fixed constant.*

Proof. Since $|R_k| = \theta(k^2)$ by Proposition 1, it follows that there is some constant c' such that $|R_k| \le c'k^2$ for all large enough k. Let c be the constant $1/\sqrt{c'}$. We will prove this lower bound result by contradiction. Suppose A is an ERE monitoring algorithm that uses less that $2^{c\sqrt{m}}$ space for any EREs of large enough size m. We will look at the behavior of the algorithm A on inputs of the form R_k. So $m = |R_k| \le c'k^2$, and A uses less than 2^k space. Since the number of equivalence classes of $\equiv_k$ is 2^{2^k}, by pigeon hole principle, there must be two strings $\sigma_1 \ne_k \sigma_2$ such that the memory of $A(R_k)$ after reading $\sigma_1 \$$ is the same as the memory after reading $\sigma_2\$$. In other words, $A(R_k)$ will give the same answer on all inputs of the form $\sigma_1\$w$ and $\sigma_2\$w$. Now since $\sigma_1 \neq_k \sigma_2$, it follows that $(S(\sigma_1) \setminus S(\sigma_2) \cup (S(\sigma_2) \setminus S(\sigma_1)) \neq \emptyset$. Take $w \in (S(\sigma_1) \setminus S(\sigma_2) \cup (S(\sigma_2) \setminus S(\sigma_1))$. Then clearly, exactly one out of $\sigma_1\$w$ and $\sigma_2\$w$ is in L_k, and so $A(R_k)$ gives the wrong answer on one of these inputs. Therefore, A is not a correct.

3   An Event Consuming Rewriting Algorithm

In this section we introduce a rewriting-based monitoring procedure. It is based on an event consumption idea, in the sense that an extended regular expression R and an event a produce another extended regular expression, denoted $R\{a\}$, with the property that for any trace w, $aw \in R$ if and only if $w \in R\{a\}$. The ERE $R\{a\}$ is also known as a "derivative" of "residual" in the literature (see [2,1], where several interesting properties of derivatives are also presented). The intuition here is that in order to incrementally test for membership of an incoming sequence of events to a given ERE, one can "process" the events as they are available, by modifying accordingly the monitoring requirement expression.

The rewriting systems in this paper are all considering that the operator $\_ + \_$ is associative and commutative and that the operator $\_ \cdot \_$ is associative. In other words, rewriting is performed modulo the equations:

$$(R_1 + R_2) + R_3 \equiv R_1 + (R_2 + R_3),$$
$$R_1 + R_2 \equiv R_2 + R_1,$$
$$(R_1 \cdot R_2) \cdot R_3 \equiv R_1 \cdot (R_2 \cdot R_3).$$

3.1   Rewriting Rules

We next consider an operation $\_\{\_\}$ which takes an extended regular expression and an event, and give seven rewriting rules which define its operational semantics recursively, on the structure of the regular expression:

$$(R_1 + R_2)\{a\} \rightarrow R_1\{a\} + R_2\{a\} \tag{1}$$
$$(R_1 \cdot R_2)\{a\} \rightarrow (R_1\{a\}) \cdot R_2 + \text{if } (\epsilon \in R_1) \text{ then } R_2\{a\} \text{ else } \emptyset \text{ fi} \tag{2}$$
$$(R^\star)\{a\} \rightarrow (R\{a\}) \cdot R^\star \tag{3}$$
$$(\neg R)\{a\} \rightarrow \neg(R\{a\}) \tag{4}$$
$$b\{a\} \rightarrow \text{if } (b = a) \text{ then } \epsilon \text{ else } \emptyset \text{ fi} \tag{5}$$
$$\epsilon\{a\} \rightarrow \emptyset \tag{6}$$
$$\emptyset\{a\} \rightarrow \emptyset \tag{7}$$

The right-hand sides of these rules use operations which we describe next. "if $(\_)$ then $\_$ else $\_$ fi" takes a boolean term and two EREs as arguments and has the expected meaning defined by two rewriting rules:

$$\text{if } (true) \text{ then } R_1 \text{ else } R_2 \text{ fi} \rightarrow R_1 \tag{8}$$
$$\text{if } (false) \text{ then } R_1 \text{ else } R_2 \text{ fi} \rightarrow R_2 \tag{9}$$

We assume a set of rewriting rules that properly evaluate boolean expressions. Boolean expressions include the constants *true* and *false*, as well as the usual connectors $\_ \wedge \_$, $\_ \vee \_$, and *not*. Testing for empty trace membership (which is used by (2)) can be efficiently implemented via the following rewriting rules:

$$\epsilon \in (R_1 + R_2) \rightarrow (\epsilon \in R_1) \vee (\epsilon \in R_2) \tag{10}$$
$$\epsilon \in (R_1 \cdot R_2) \rightarrow (\epsilon \in R_1) \wedge (\epsilon \in R_2) \tag{11}$$
$$\epsilon \in (R^\star) \rightarrow true \tag{12}$$
$$\epsilon \in (\neg R) \rightarrow not(\epsilon \in R) \tag{13}$$
$$\epsilon \in b \rightarrow false \tag{14}$$
$$\epsilon \in \epsilon \rightarrow true \tag{15}$$
$$\epsilon \in \emptyset \rightarrow false \tag{16}$$

The 16 rules defined above are natural and intuitive. Since the memory of our monitoring algorithm will consist of an ERE and since our main consideration here is memory, we pay special attention to the *size* of an ERE. The following three rules keep the size of the ERE generated by the other rules small. For that reason, we call them "simplifying rules". The latter may seem backwards at first sight. Its crucial role in maintaining EREs small will become clearer later:

$$R + \emptyset \rightarrow R \tag{17}$$
$$R + R \rightarrow R \tag{18}$$
$$R_1 \cdot R + R_2 \cdot R \rightarrow (R_1 + R_2) \cdot R \tag{19}$$

The sizes of the right-hand sides of these three rules are smaller (by at least 2) than their corresponding left-hand sides.

Let $\mathcal{R}$ denote the rewriting system defined above. Some notions and notations are needed before we can state the important results. Let $\equiv_{\mathcal{C}}$ denote the congruence relation generated by the set $\mathcal{C}$ containing the three equations just before Subsection 3.1 (associativity of $\_ + \_$ and $\_ \cdot \_$ and commutativity of $\_ + \_$). Then the rewriting relation *modulo* $\mathcal{C}$ generated by the rules above, written $\rightarrow_{\mathcal{R}/\mathcal{C}}$, is the relation $\equiv_{\mathcal{C}}; \rightarrow_{\mathcal{R}}; \equiv_{\mathcal{C}}$, where semicolon denotes composition of binary relations and $\rightarrow_{\mathcal{R}}$ is the ordinary (non-AC) relation generated by $\mathcal{R}$. We say that $\mathcal{R}$ is *terminating modulo* $\mathcal{C}$ if and only if $\rightarrow_{\mathcal{R}/\mathcal{C}}$ is terminating, and that it is *ground Church-Rosser modulo* $\mathcal{C}$ if and only if $\leftrightarrow^*_{\mathcal{R}\cup\mathcal{C}}$ is contained in $\rightarrow^*_{\mathcal{R}/\mathcal{C}}; \equiv_{\mathcal{C}}; \leftrightarrow^*_{\mathcal{R}/\mathcal{C}}$ on all ground terms (concrete EREs in our case). The typical technique to show termination modulo some equations is to define a weight function of terms, assigning a natural number to each term, and then show that this map is invariant with respect to equations and decreasing with respect to the rewriting rules.

Theorem 2. $\mathcal{R}$ *is terminating and ground Church-Rosser modulo* $\mathcal{C}$; *let* $nf_{\mathcal{R}/\mathcal{C}}(R)$ *be the normal form of* R *in* $\mathcal{R}$ *modulo* $\mathcal{C}$. *Furthermore, for a given extended regular expression* R *and a given event* a, $\mathcal{L}(nf_{\mathcal{R}/\mathcal{C}}(R\{a\})) = \{w \mid aw \in R\}$.

Proof. Let γ be a function to natural numbers defined inductively as follows on terms of sort extended regular expression:

$$\gamma(R\{a\}) = (\gamma(R) + 1)^2,$$
$$\gamma(R_1 + R_2) = \gamma(R_1 \cdot R_2) = \gamma(R_1) + \gamma(R_2) + 1,$$
$$\gamma(R^*) = \gamma(\neg R) = \gamma(R) + 1,$$
$$\gamma(b) = \gamma(\epsilon) = \gamma(\emptyset) = 1,$$

and on terms of sort bool:

$$\gamma(\epsilon \in R) = 2 \cdot \gamma(R),$$
$$\gamma(B_1 \wedge B_2) = \gamma(B_1 \vee B_2) = \gamma(B_1) + \gamma(B_2) + 1,$$
$$\gamma(not(B)) = \gamma(B) + 1,$$
$$\gamma(true) = \gamma(false) = 1.$$

Let us now define a binary relation $\succ$ on extended regular expression terms as $R \succ R'$ if and only if $\gamma(R) > \gamma(R')$. It can easily be seen that $\succ$ is well-founded and that $\gamma(R) = \gamma(R')$ for each associativity or commutativity equation $R = R'$ in $\mathcal{C}$. We claim that $\succ$ includes the rewriting relation $\rightarrow_{\mathcal{R}/\mathcal{C}}$. It suffices to show that $\succ$ includes the relation $\rightarrow_{\mathcal{R}}$, which can be simply tested on each of the rewriting rules in $\mathcal{R}$ above. For example, rule (2) can be tested as follows:

$$\gamma((R_1 \cdot R_2)\{a\}) > \gamma((R_1\{a\}) \cdot R_2 + \texttt{if } (\epsilon \in R_1) \texttt{ then } R_2\{a\} \texttt{ else } \emptyset \texttt{ fi}), \qquad \text{iff}$$
$$(\gamma(R_1 \cdot R_2) + 1)^2 > \gamma((R_1\{a\}) \cdot R_2) + \gamma(\texttt{if } (\epsilon \in R_1) \texttt{ then } R_2\{a\} \texttt{ else } \emptyset \texttt{ fi}) + 1, \text{ iff}$$
$$(\gamma(R_1) + \gamma(R_2) + 2)^2 > (\gamma(R_1) + 1)^2 + \gamma(R_2) + 2 \cdot \gamma(R_1) + (\gamma(R_2) + 1)^2 + 3, \qquad \text{iff}$$
$$2 \cdot \gamma(R_1) \cdot \gamma(R_2) + \gamma(R_2) > 1.$$

For simplicity, assume that rule (5) is replaced by a finite set of rules $b\{a\} \rightarrow \emptyset$ for each different a, b in the alphabet and $a\{a\} \rightarrow \epsilon$ for each a. We therefore can conclude that $\mathcal{R}$ is terminating modulo $\mathcal{C}$. Due to space limitations, the Church-Rosser property of $\mathcal{R}$ modulo $\mathcal{C}$ will be shown elsewhere. However, since $\mathcal{R}$ is *not* left-linear (see rules (18) and (19)), one *cannot* apply the classical critical pair completion procedure by Huet in [13].

We next show that for any extended regular expression R and any event a, $\mathcal{L}(nf_{\mathcal{R}/\mathcal{C}}(R\{a\})) = \{w \mid aw \in R\}$. First notice that for any two extended regular expressions (without containing the operation $\_\{\_\}$) R and R', it is the case that $\mathcal{L}(R) = \mathcal{L}(R')$ whenever $R \rightarrow_{\mathcal{R}/\mathcal{C}} R'$; this is because the rules (17), (18) and (19) in R and all the equations in $\mathcal{C}$, the only which can be applied, are all valid properties of regular languages. In particular, $\mathcal{L}(R) = \mathcal{L}(nf_{\mathcal{R}/\mathcal{C}}(R))$ for any extended regular expression R. We can now start showing our main result inductively, on the structure of the extended regular expression:

$$\begin{aligned}
\mathcal{L}(nf_{\mathcal{R}/\mathcal{C}}((R_1 + R_2)\{a\})) &= \mathcal{L}(nf_{\mathcal{R}/\mathcal{C}}(R_1\{a\} + R_2\{a\})) \\
&= \mathcal{L}(nf_{\mathcal{R}/\mathcal{C}}(R_1\{a\}) + nf_{\mathcal{R}/\mathcal{C}}(R_2\{a\})) \\
&= \mathcal{L}(nf_{\mathcal{R}/\mathcal{C}}(R_1\{a\})) \cup \mathcal{L}(nf_{\mathcal{R}/\mathcal{C}}(R_2\{a\})) \\
&= \{w \mid aw \in \mathcal{L}(R_1)\} \cup \{w \mid aw \in \mathcal{L}(R_2)\} \\
&= \{w \mid aw \in \mathcal{L}(R_1 + R_2)\}.
\end{aligned}$$

Before we continue, note that for any ground or concrete ERE R, the normal form of $\epsilon \in R$ in $\mathcal{R}$ modulo $\mathcal{C}$ is either *true* or *false*. Moreover, it follows that $nf_{\mathcal{R}/\mathcal{C}}(\epsilon \in R) = true$ if and only if $\epsilon \in \mathcal{L}(R)$, which implies that

$nf_{\mathcal{R}/\mathcal{C}}(\text{if } (\epsilon \in R_1) \text{ then } R_2\{a\} \text{ else } \emptyset \text{ fi})$ is either $nf_{\mathcal{R}/\mathcal{C}}(R_2\{a\})$ when $\epsilon \in \mathcal{L}(R_1)$ or $\emptyset$ when $\epsilon \notin \mathcal{L}(R_1)$. Then

$$
\begin{aligned}
\mathcal{L}(nf_{\mathcal{R}/\mathcal{C}}((R_1 \cdot R_2)\{a\})) &= \mathcal{L}(nf_{\mathcal{R}/\mathcal{C}}((R_1\{a\}) \cdot R_2 + \\
&\quad \text{if } (\epsilon \in R_1) \text{ then } R_2\{a\} \text{ else } \emptyset \text{ fi})) \\
&= \mathcal{L}(nf_{\mathcal{R}/\mathcal{C}}(nf_{\mathcal{R}/\mathcal{C}}(R_1\{a\}) \cdot R_2 + \\
&\quad nf_{\mathcal{R}/\mathcal{C}}(\text{if } (\epsilon \in R_1) \text{ then } R_2\{a\} \text{ else } \emptyset \text{ fi}))) \\
&= \mathcal{L}(nf_{\mathcal{R}/\mathcal{C}}(nf_{\mathcal{R}/\mathcal{C}}(R_1\{a\}) \cdot R_2 + \\
&\quad nf_{\mathcal{R}/\mathcal{C}}(R_2\{a\}))) \text{ when } \epsilon \in \mathcal{L}(R_1), \text{ or} \\
&\quad \mathcal{L}(nf_{\mathcal{R}/\mathcal{C}}(nf_{\mathcal{R}/\mathcal{C}}(R_1\{a\}) \cdot R_2 + \emptyset)) \text{ when } \epsilon \notin \mathcal{L}(R_1) \\
&= \mathcal{L}(nf_{\mathcal{R}/\mathcal{C}}(R_1\{a\})) \cdot \mathcal{L}(R_2) \cup \mathcal{L}(nf_{\mathcal{R}/\mathcal{C}}(R_2\{a\})) \\
&\quad \text{when } \epsilon \in \mathcal{L}(R_1), \text{ or} \\
&\quad \mathcal{L}(nf_{\mathcal{R}/\mathcal{C}}(R_1\{a\})) \cdot \mathcal{L}(R_2) \text{ when } \epsilon \notin \mathcal{L}(R_1) \\
&= \{w \mid aw \in \mathcal{L}(R_1)\} \cdot \mathcal{L}(R_2) \cup \{w \mid aw \in \mathcal{L}(R_2) \\
&\quad \text{when } \epsilon \in \mathcal{L}(R_1), \text{ or} \\
&\quad \{w \mid aw \in \mathcal{L}(R_1) \cdot \mathcal{L}(R_2) \text{ when } \epsilon \notin \mathcal{L}(R_1) \\
&= \{w \mid aw \in \mathcal{L}(R_1 \cdot R_2)\}.
\end{aligned}
$$

Similarly, the inductive property follows for repetition and complement:

$$
\begin{aligned}
\mathcal{L}(nf_{\mathcal{R}/\mathcal{C}}(R^\star\{a\})) &= \mathcal{L}(nf_{\mathcal{R}/\mathcal{C}}(R\{a\} \cdot R^\star)) \\
&= \mathcal{L}(nf_{\mathcal{R}/\mathcal{C}}(R\{a\}) \cdot R^\star) \\
&= \mathcal{L}(nf_{\mathcal{R}/\mathcal{C}}(R\{a\})) \cdot \mathcal{L}(R^\star) \\
&= \{w \mid aw \in R\} \cdot \mathcal{L}(R^\star) \\
&= \{w \mid aw \in R^\star\},
\end{aligned}
$$

and

$$
\begin{aligned}
\mathcal{L}(nf_{\mathcal{R}/\mathcal{C}}((\neg R)\{a\})) &= \mathcal{L}(nf_{\mathcal{R}/\mathcal{C}}(\neg(R\{a\}))) \\
&= \mathcal{L}(\neg nf_{\mathcal{R}/\mathcal{C}}(R\{a\})) \\
&= \Sigma^\star \setminus \mathcal{L}(nf_{\mathcal{R}/\mathcal{C}}(R\{a\})) \\
&= \Sigma^\star \setminus \{w \mid aw \in R\} \\
&= \{w \mid aw \notin R\} \\
&= \{w \mid aw \in \neg R\}.
\end{aligned}
$$

The remaining proofs, when R is a singleton, ϵ or $\emptyset$, are trivial. Thus we conclude that $\mathcal{L}(nf_{\mathcal{R}/\mathcal{C}}(R\{a\})) = \{w \mid aw \in R\}$ for any extended regular expression R and any event a.

From now on in the paper, we let $R\{a\}$ also (ambiguously) denote the term $nf_{\mathcal{R}/\mathcal{C}}(R\{a\})$, and consider that the rewrites in $\mathcal{R}$ modulo $\mathcal{C}$ are always applied automatically.

3.2   The Algorithm

We can now introduce our rewriting based algorithm for incrementally testing membership of words or traces to extended regular languages:

Algorithm $\mathcal{A}(R, a_1, a_2, ..., a_n)$
INPUT: An ERE R and events a_1, a_2, ..., a_n received incrementally
OUTPUT: *true* if and only if $a_1 a_2 ... a_n \in \mathcal{L}(R)$; `false` otherwise
1. **let** R' **be** R
2. **let** i **be** 1
3. **while** $i \leq n$ **do**
4.   **wait** until a_i is available
5.   **let** R' **be** $nf_{\mathcal{R}/\mathcal{C}}(R'\{a_i\})$
6.   **if** $R' = \emptyset$ **then return** *false*
7.   **if** $R' = \neg(\emptyset)$ **then return** *true*
8.   **let** i **be** $i + 1$
9. **return** $(\epsilon \in R')$; calculated using $\mathcal{R}$ (modulo $\mathcal{C}$ or not)

Therefore, a local ERE R' is updated after receiving each of the events a_i. If R' ever becomes empty (step 6) then, by Theorem 2, there is no way for the remaining events to make the whole trace into an accepting one, so the algorithm returns *fail* and the remaining events are not processed anymore. Similarly, if R' becomes the total language (step 7), then also by Theorem 2 it follows that any continuation will be accepted so the algorithm safely returns *true*. Step 8 finally tests whether the empty word is in R' after all the events have been processed, which, by Theorem 2 again, tells whether the sequence $a_1 a_2 ... a_n$ is in the language of R.

3.3   Analysis

We will now show that the space and time requirements of our rewriting algorithm are not much worse than the lower bounds proved in the previous section. Our rewriting algorithm keeps track of one extended regular expression which it modifies every time it receives a new event from the trace. We will prove that the size of this regular expression is bounded, no matter how many events are processed, and this will give us the desired bounds.

For an extended regular expression R, define the function size as follows:

$$\text{size}(R) = \max_{n, a_1, a_2, ... a_n} |R\{a_1\}\{a_2\} \cdots \{a_n\}|$$

So size(R) is the maximum size that R can grow to for any sequence of events.

Proposition 2. $\max_{|R|=m} \text{size}(R) \leq 2^{m^2}$.

Proof. Before presenting a proof of the bounds, we introduce some notation that will be useful in the proof. For a regular expression R, we will denote by $\overline{R\{a_1\}\{a_2\} \cdots \{a_n\}}$ the regular expression (actually its normal form in $\mathcal{R}$):

$$R\{a_1\}\{a_2\} \cdots \{a_n\} + R\{a_2\}\{a_3\} \cdots \{a_n\} + \cdots R\{a_n\}.$$

In addition, we define the following functions:

$$\overline{\text{size}}(R) = \max_{n, a_1, a_2, ... a_n} |\overline{R\{a_1\}\{a_2\} \cdots \{a_n\}}|,$$
$$\text{diff}(R) = \max_{n, a_1, a_2, ... a_n} |\{R\{a_i\}\{a_{i+1}\} \cdots \{a_n\} \mid 1 \leq i \leq n\}|,$$
$$\overline{\text{diff}}(R) = \max_{n, a_1, a_2 ... a_n} |\{\overline{R\{a_i\}\{a_{i+1}\} \cdots \{a_n\}} \mid 1 \leq i \leq n\}|.$$

So $\overline{\text{size}}(R)$ measures the maximum size the expression $\overline{R}$ can grow to, $\text{diff}(R)$ measures the number of syntactically different terms in $\overline{R}$, and finally $\overline{\text{diff}}(R)$ is similar to $\text{diff}(R)$ but defined for $\overline{R}$

Using the above functions, we will be able to give bounds on the size of size, inductively. We first make some important observations regarding the expression $|R\{a_1\}\{a_2\}\cdots\{a_n\}|$ based on its form:

$$|(R_1 + R_2)\{a_1\}\cdots\{a_n\}| = |R_1\{a_1\}\cdots\{a_n\} + R_2\{a_1\}\cdots\{a_n\}|$$
$$\leq |R_1\{a_1\}\cdots\{a_n\}| + |R_2\{a_1\}\cdots\{a_n\}| + 1$$
$$|(R_1 \cdot R_2)\{a_1\}\cdots\{a_n\}| \leq |(R_1\{a_1\}\cdots\{a_n\}) \cdot R_2 + R_2\{a_n\} + \cdots + R_2\{a_1\}\cdots\{a_n\}|$$
$$\leq |(R_1\{a_1\}\cdots\{a_n\})| + 1 + |R_2| + |\overline{R\{a_1\}}\cdots\{a_n\}| + 1$$
$$|(R_1^\star)\{a_1\}\cdots\{a_n\}| \leq |(\overline{R_1\{a_1\}}\cdots\{a_n\}) \cdot R_1^\star|$$
$$= |\overline{R_1\{a_1\}}\cdots\{a_n\}| + |R_1^\star| + 1$$
$$|(\neg R_1)\{a_1\}\cdots\{a_n\}| = |\neg(R_1\{a_1\}\cdots\{a_n\})|$$
$$= |R_1\{a_1\}\cdots\{a_n\}| + 1$$

The only observation that needs some explanation is the one corresponding to $R_1^\star$. Observe that, $R_1^\star\{a_1\}\cdots\{a_n\}$ will get rewritten, in the worst case, as

$$(R_1\{a_1\}\cdots\{a_n\}) \cdot R_1^\star + (R_1\{a_2\}\cdots\{a_n\}) \cdot R_1^\star + \cdots (R_1\{a_n\}) \cdot R_1^\star$$

which after simplification using the rule (19) will be $(\overline{R_1\{a_1\}}\cdots\{a_n\}) \cdot R_1^\star$. Note that, in making the above observations, we make use of the fact that $\mathcal{R}$ is ground Church-Rosser modulo $\mathcal{C}$ (see Theorem 2).

Based on these observations, we can give an inductive bound on size:

$$\text{size}(R_1 + R_2) \leq \text{size}(R_1) + \text{size}(R_2) + 1,$$
$$\text{size}(R_1 \cdot R_2) \leq \text{size}(R_1) + |R_2| + \overline{\text{size}}(R_2) + 2,$$
$$\text{size}(R_1^\star) \leq \overline{\text{size}}(R_1) + |R_1^\star| + 1,$$
$$\text{size}(\neg R_1) \leq \text{size}(R_1) + 1.$$

We are now ready to give bounds on $\overline{\text{size}}$. Observe that:

$$\overline{\text{size}}(R_1 + R_2) \leq \overline{\text{size}}(R_1) + \overline{\text{size}}(R_2) + 1,$$
$$\overline{\text{size}}(R_1 \cdot R_2) \leq \overline{\text{size}}(R_1) + |R_2| + \overline{\text{size}}(R_2) + 2,$$
$$\overline{\text{size}}(R_1^\star) \leq \overline{\text{size}}(R_1) + |R_1^\star| + 1,$$
$$\overline{\text{size}}(\neg R_1) \leq \text{diff}(R_1) \cdot \text{size}(R_1) + 2\text{diff}(R_1).$$

The reasons for the above inequalities is similar to those for size. The only case that needs explanation is the one for $\neg R_1$. Observe that $(\neg R_1)\{a_1\}\cdots\{a_n\} + (\neg R_1)\{a_2\}\cdots\{a_n\} + \cdots + (\neg R_1)\{a_n\}$ is the same as $\neg(R_1\{a_1\}\cdots\{a_n\}) + \cdots + \neg(R_1\{a_n\})$. So based on how many of the terms $R_1\{a_i\}\cdots\{a_n\}$ are different, we can bound $\overline{\text{size}}(\neg R_1)$.

Finally, we give the bounds on the function diff and $\overline{\text{diff}}$ based on a similar reasoning:

$$\text{diff}(R_1 + R_2) \leq \text{diff}(R_1) \cdot \text{diff}(R_2),$$
$$\text{diff}(R_1 \cdot R_2) \leq \text{diff}(R_1) \cdot \overline{\text{diff}}(R_2),$$
$$\text{diff}(R_1^\star) \leq \overline{\text{diff}}(R_1),$$
$$\text{diff}(\neg R_1) \leq \text{diff}(R_1).$$

To complete the analysis, observe that $\overline{\text{diff}}(R) \leq \text{diff}(R)$.

If we take $(\max_{|R|=m} \overline{\text{diff}}(R))$ and $(\max_{|R|=m} \text{diff}(R))$ to be bounded by 2^m, and $(\max_{|R|=m} \overline{\text{size}}(R))$ and $(\max_{|R|=m} \text{size}(R))$ to be bounded by 2^{m^2}, then we see that all of the inequalities are satisfied. Hence the proposition follows.

Theorem 3. *The monitoring algorithm based on rewriting uses space $O(2^{2m^2})$ and time $O(n \cdot 2^{2m^2})$; time is measured in number or rewriting steps.*

Proof. The space needed by the algorithm consists of the space needed to store the evolving ERE. By the proposition above, we know that, after simplification, such an ERE will never be larger than $O(2^{m^2})$, where m is the size of the initial ERE. However, before simplification, the stored ERE first suffers an increase in size. We claim that, regardless of the order in which rewrite rules are applied, the size of the intermediate term obtained by deriving a given ERE of size M will never grow larger than M^2. This is indeed true, because if one analyzes the rewriting rules which can increase the size of the term, namely rules (1)–(7) and (10)–(11), then one can see that the worst case scenario is given by a recurrence $S(M_1 + M_2 + 1) \leq S(M_1) + S(M_2) + M_1 + M_2 + c$, where c is some (small) constant; this recurrence implies $S(M) = O(M^2)$. Therefore, the space needed by our rewriting algorithm is $O(2^{2m^2})$.

The number of rewrites needed to process one event is also $O(2^{2m^2})$. Note first that the number of rewrites for a test $\epsilon \in R$ is $|R|$. Then one can easily give a recurrence for the number of rewrites to push an event to leaves; for example, in the case of concatenation this is $N((R_1 R_2)\{a\}) \leq N(R_1) + |R_1| + N(R_2) + 1$. Therefore, there are $O(2^{2m^2})$ applications of rules (1)–(16). Since each of the remaining rules, the simplifying ones, decrease the size of the term by 2 and the maximum size of the term is $O(2^{2m^2})$, it follows that the total number of rewrites needed to process an event is indeed $O(2^{2m^2})$.

The above results can be improved if one considers only regular expressions, instead of extended regular expressions. Applying the same rewrite algorithm to expressions that do not have negations, we can use the very same analysis to observe that the rewrite algorithm uses space $O(m^2)$ and running time $O(n \cdot m^2)$

Theorem 4. *The monitoring algorithm based on rewriting, when applied to expressions not containing any negation, use space $O(m^2)$ and time $O(n \cdot m^2)$.*

4   Implementation, Evaluation and Conclusion

We have implemented in Maude [4] several improved versions of the rewriting-based algorithm in Section 3. In this section we present an implementation which worked best on our test suits. Space/time analysis seems hard to do rigorously and is not given for this implementation, but the given experimental data suggest that the $O(2^{m^2})$ space upper bound proved in Subsection 3.3 is more of a theoretical importance than practical. We hope to calculate the exact worst-case complexity of the next rewriting procedure soon, but for now are happy to present it as a procedure for monitoring extended regular expressions which performs very well in practice. The usual operations on extended regular expressions can be defined in a functional module (`fmod ... endfm`) as follows:

```
fmod ERE is
   sorts Event Ere .
   subsort Event < Ere .
   op _+_ : Ere Ere -> Ere [assoc comm prec 60] .
   op __  : Ere Ere -> Ere [assoc prec 50] .
   ops (_*) (~_)  : Ere -> Ere .
   ops epsilon empty : -> Ere .
endfm
```

Precedences were given to some operators to avoid writing parentheses: the lower the precedence the tighter the binding.

10 rules for ϵ-membership and for simplifying extended regular expressions were given in Section 3 (rules (10)-(19)). These rules were shown to keep the size of any evolving extended regular expression lower than $O(2^{m^2})$, where m is its initial size. Driven by practical experiments, we have decided to define a partial ERE inclusion operator, called _in_, using 22 rewriting rules (some of them conditional) which correctly extends the needed (total) ϵ-membership in Section 3. Together with other 10 simplifying rules, ERE inclusion is defined in the following module:

```
fmod SYMPLIFY-ERE is including ERE .
   vars R R' R1 R2 R1' R2' : Ere .  vars A B : Event .
   eq empty R = empty .              eq R empty = empty .
   eq epsilon R = R .                eq R epsilon = R .
   eq ~ ~ R = R .                    eq R * * = R * .
   eq epsilon * = epsilon .          eq empty * = empty .
   ceq R1 + R2 = R2 if R1 in R2 .    eq R1 R + R2 R = (R1 + R2) R .

   op _in_ : Ere Ere -> Bool .
   eq empty in R = true .            eq epsilon in A = false .
   eq A in B = (A == B) .            eq R in R = true .
   eq epsilon in (R1 + R2) = epsilon in R1 or epsilon in R2 .
   eq A in (R1 + R2) = A in R1 or A in R2 .
   ceq R in (R1 + R2) = true if R in R1 .
   eq (R1 + R2) in R = R1 in R and R2 in R .
   eq epsilon in (R1 R2) = epsilon in R1 and epsilon in R2 .
   eq A in (R1 R2) =
         A in R1 and epsilon in R2 or A in R2 and epsilon in R1 .
   ceq (R1 R2) in (R1' R2') = true if (R1 in R1') /\ (R2 in R2') .
   eq epsilon in (R *) = true .
   ceq R1 in (R *) = true if R1 in R .
   ceq (R1 R2) in (R *) = true if (R1 in (R *)) /\ (R2 in (R *)) .
   eq R in (~ empty) = true .
```

```
    eq R in (~ epsilon) = not (epsilon in R) .
    eq R in (~ A) = not (A in R) .
    eq epsilon in (~ R) = not (epsilon in R) .
    eq A in (~ R) = not(A in R) .
    eq (~ R) in (~ R') = R' in R .
    eq R in empty = R == empty .
    eq R in epsilon = R == empty or R == epsilon .
  endfm
```

The module above therefore adds 32 equational constraints to the EREs defined
syntactically in the module ERE (included with the Maude keyword including).
Maude executes these equations as (conditional) rewrite rules. The major simplifying rule in SIMPLIFY-ERE is the 5th on the left column, which properly generalizes rule (18) in Section 3; this was the rule motivating the definition of the
ERE partial inclusion.

We can now define the event consuming operator, _{_}, together with its
associated seven rules (1)-(7) from Section 3:

```
  fmod CONSUME-EVENT is protecting SIMPLIFY-ERE .
    vars R1 R2 R : Ere .  vars A B C : Event .
    op _{_} : Ere Event -> Ere [prec 45] .
    eq (R1 + R2){A} = R1{A} + R2{A} .
    eq (R1 R2){A} =
        R1{A} R2 + if (epsilon in R1) then R2{A} else empty fi .
    eq (R *){A} = R{A} (R *) .
    eq (~ R){A} = ~ (R{A}) .
    eq B{A} = if B == A then epsilon else empty fi .
    eq epsilon{A} = empty .
    eq empty{A} = empty .
  endfm
```

The conditional operator if_then_else_fi, whose semantics was given by the
rules (8)-(9) in Section 3, is part of the builtin BOOL module in Maude.

One can now use the rewriting procedure above by either launching Maude
reduce commands directly, such as:

```
  red (A(A + B)*)* {A} .
  red ((A + B)((C + A)* (A B *)*)*)* {A} .
  red ((A + B)((C + A)* (A B *)*)*)* {B} .
  red ((A + B)((C + A)* (A B *)*)*)* {C} .
```

which give the following expected answers,

```
============================================
reduce in CONSUME-EVENT : (A (A + B) *) *{A} .
rewrites: 14 in 0ms cpu (0ms real) (~ rewrites/second)
result Ere: (A + B) * (A (A + B) *) *
============================================
reduce in CONSUME-EVENT : ((A + B) ((A + C) * (A B *) *) *) *{A} .
rewrites: 32 in 0ms cpu (0ms real) (~ rewrites/second)
```

```
result Ere: ((A + C) * (A B *) *) * ((A + B) ((A + C) * (A B *)*)*)*
============================================
reduce in CONSUME-EVENT : ((A + B) ((A + C) * (A B *) *) *) *{B} .
rewrites: 32 in 0ms cpu (0ms real) (~ rewrites/second)
result Ere: ((A + C) * (A B *) *) * ((A + B) ((A + C) * (A B *)*)*)*
============================================
reduce in CONSUME-EVENT : ((A + B) ((A + C) * (A B *) *) *) *{C} .
rewrites: 31 in 0ms cpu (0ms real) (~ rewrites/second)
result Ere: empty
```

or by calling it from a different place (procedure, thread, process) where the
algorithm in Subsection 3.2 is implemented – it is worth mentioning that this
algorithm can also be implemented directly in Maude, using its *loop mode* feature
[4] which is specially designed to process events interactively.

We have tested the event consuming procedure above on several extended
regular expressions and several sequences of events, and the results were quite
encouraging. We were not able to notice any measurable running time on meaningful formulae that one would want to enforce in real software monitoring applications. In order to do proper worst-case measurements, we have implemented
(also by rewriting in Maude) another procedure which takes as input a natural
number m and does the following:

1. Generates all extended regular expressions of size m over 0 and 1;
2. For each such expression R, it calculates the number $size(R)$ (see Subsection
   3.3) by exhaustively generating the *set* of all the extended regular expressions
   $R\{a_1\}\{a_2\}\cdots\{a_n\}$ for all n and $a_1, a_2, ..., a_n \in \{0, 1\}$; by Proposition 2, this
   set is finite;
3. It returns the largest of $size(R)$ for all R above.

This algorithm is obviously very inefficient[1]. We were only able to run it for all
$m \leq 12$ in less than 24 hours, generating the following table:

m	1	2	3	4	5	6	7	8	9	10	11	12
$\max_{|R|=m}(size(R))$	1	2	6	8	18	24	39	51	57	77	92	108

Since the space requirements of our rewriting monitoring procedure is given
by the size of the current formula, the table above gives us a measure of the
space needed in the worst case by our rewriting algorithm. It shows for example that an extended regular expression of size 12, in the worst possible
case grows to size 108, which is of course infinitely better than the upper
bound that we were able to prove for the simplified algorithm, namely $2^{12^2} =$
$22, 300, 745, 198, 530, 623, 141, 535, 718, 272, 648, 361, 505, 980, 416$. This tells us
that there is plenty of room for further research in finding better rewriting based
algorithms and better upper bounds for space requirements than the ones we
were able to find in Section 3. The improved rewriting procedure presented in
this section can be such a significantly better membership algorithm, but proving
it seems to be hard.

---

[1] We are, however, happy to provide it on request.

It is worth mentioning that, even if one removes the auxiliary rewriting rules from the module above and keeps only the 19 rules presented in the previous section, the size of the evolving ERE still stays smaller that 2^m. This stimulates us to conclude with the following:

Conjecture. *The rewriting-based algorithm presented in Section 3 runs in space $O(2^m)$ and time $O(n2^m)$, where m is the size of the ERE and n is the size of the event trace. Moreover, these are the lower bounds for the membership problem.*

References

1. V.M. Antimirov. Partial derivatives of regular expressions and finite automaton constructions. *Journal of Theoretical Computer Science*, 155(2):291–319, 1996.
2. V.M. Antimirov and P.D. Mosses. Rewriting extended regular expressions. *Journal of Theoretical Computer Science*, 143(1):51–72, 1995.
3. A. K. Chandra, D. C. Kozen, and L. J. Stockmeyer. Alternation. *Journal of the ACM*, 28(1):114–133, 1981.
4. M. Clavel, F. Durán, S. Eker, P. Lincoln, N. Martí-Oliet, J. Meseguer, and J. Quesada. Maude: specification and programming in rewriting logic. SRI International, January 1999, http://maude.csl.sri.com.
5. D. Drusinsky. The Temporal Rover and the ATG Rover. In *SPIN Model Checking and Software Verification*, volume 1885 of *Lecture Notes in Computer Science*, pages 323–330. Springer, 2000.
6. D. Giannakopoulou and K. Havelund. Automata-Based Verification of Temporal Properties on Running Programs. In *Proceedings, International Conference on Automated Software Engineering (ASE'01)*, pages 412–416. Institute of Electrical and Electronics Engineers, 2001. Coronado Island, California.
7. K. Havelund and G. Roşu. Monitoring Java Programs with Java PathExplorer. In *Proceedings of Runtime Verification (RV'01)*, volume 55 of *Electronic Notes in Theoretical Computer Science*. Elsevier Science, 2001.
8. K. Havelund and G. Roşu. Monitoring Programs using Rewriting. In *Proceedings, International Conference on Automated Software Engineering (ASE'01)*, pages 135–143. Institute of Electrical and Electronics Engineers, 2001. Coronado Island, California.
9. K. Havelund and G. Roşu. *Runtime Verification 2001*, volume 55 of *Electronic Notes in Theoretical Computer Science*. Elsevier Science, 2001. Proceedings of a *Computer Aided Verification (CAV'01)* satellite workshop.
10. K. Havelund and G. Roşu. *Runtime Verification 2002*, volume 70(4) of *Electronic Notes in Theoretical Computer Science*. Elsevier Science, 2002. Proceedings of a *Computer Aided Verification (CAV'02)* satellite workshop.
11. K. Havelund and G. Roşu. Synthesizing monitors for safety properties. In *Tools and Algorithms for Construction and Analysis of Systems (TACAS'02)*, volume 2280 of *Lecture Notes in Computer Science*, pages 342–356. Springer, 2002.
12. S. Hirst. A new algorithm solving membership of extended regular expressions. Technical report, The University of Sydney, 1989.
13. G. Huet. Confluent reductions: Abstract properties and applications to term rewriting systems. *Journal of the ACM*, 27(4):797–821, 1980.
14. J.R. Knight and E.W. Myers. Super-pattern matching. *Algorithmica*, 13(1/2):211–243, 1995.

15. O. Kupferman and M. Y. Vardi. Freedom, Weakness, and Determinism: From linear-time to branching-time. In *Proceedings of the IEEE Symposium on Logic in Computer Science*, pages 81–92, 1998.
16. O. Kupferman and M. Y. Vardi. Model Checking of Safety Properties. In *Proceedings of the Conference on Computer-Aided Verification*, 1999.
17. O. Kupferman and S. Zuhovitzky. An Improved Algorithm for the Membership Problem for Extended Regular Expressions. In *Proceedings of the International Symposium on Mathematical Foundations of Computer Science*, 2002.
18. I. Lee, S. Kannan, M. Kim, O. Sokolsky, and M. Viswanathan. Runtime Assurance Based on Formal Specifications. In *Proceedings of the International Conference on Parallel and Distributed Processing Techniques and Applications*, 1999.
19. G. Myers. A four russians algorithm for regular expression pattern matching. *Journal of the ACM*, 39(4):430–448, 1992.
20. T. O'Malley, D. Richardson, and L. Dillon. Efficient Specification-Based Oracles for Critical Systems. In *In Proceedings of the California Software Symposium*, 1996.
21. D. J. Richardson, S. L. Aha, and T. O. O'Malley. Specification-Based Test Oracles for Reactive Systems. In *Proceedings of the Fourteenth International Conference on Software Engineering, Melbourne, Australia*, pages 105–118, 1992.
22. H. Yamamoto. An automata-based recognition algorithm for semi-extended regular expressions. In *Proceedings of the International Symposium on Mathematical Foundations of Computer Science*, pages 699–708, 2000.

Author Index

Lecture Notes in Computer Science

For information about Vols. 1–2592

please contact your bookseller or Springer-Verlag

Vol. 2634: F. Zhao, L. Guibas (Eds.), Information Processing in Sensor Networks. Proceedings, 2003. XII, 692 pages. 2003.

Vol. 2636: E. Alonso, D, Kudenko, D. Kazakov (Eds.), Adaptive Agents and Multi-Agent Systems. XIV, 323 pages. 2003. (Subseries LNAI).

Vol. 2637: K.-Y. Whang, J. Jeon, K. Shim, J. Srivastava (Eds.), Advances in Knowledge Discovery and Data Mining. Proceedings, 2003. XVIII, 610 pages. 2003. (Subseries LNAI).

Vol. 2638: J. Jeuring, S. Peyton Jones (Eds.), Advanced Functional Programming. Proceedings, 2002. VII, 213 pages. 2003.

Vol. 2639: G. Wang, Q. Liu, Y. Yao, A. Skowron (Eds.), Rough Sets, Fuzzy Sets, Data Mining, and Granular Computing. Proceedings, 2003. XVII, 741 pages. 2003. (Subseries LNAI).

Vol. 2641: P.J. Nürnberg (Ed.), Metainformatics. Proceedings, 2002. VIII, 187 pages. 2003.

Vol. 2642: X. Zhou, Y. Zhang, M.E. Orlowska (Eds.), Web Technologies and Applications. Proceedings, 2003. XIII, 608 pages. 2003.

Vol. 2643: M. Fossorier, T. Høholdt, A. Poli (Eds.), Applied Algebra, Algebraic Algorithms and Error-Correcting Codes. Proceedings, 2003. X, 256 pages. 2003.

Vol. 2644: D. Hogrefe, A. Wiles (Eds.), Testing of Communicating Systems. Proceedings, 2003. XII, 311 pages. 2003.

Vol. 2645: M.A. Wimmer (Ed.), Knowledge Management in Electronic Government. Proceedings, 2003. XI, 320 pages. 2003. (Subseries LNAI).

Vol. 2646: H. Geuvers, F, Wiedijk (Eds.), Types for Proofs and Programs. Proceedings, 2002. VIII, 331 pages. 2003.

Vol. 2647: K.Jansen, M. Margraf, M. Mastrolli, J.D.P. Rolim (Eds.), Experimental and Efficient Algorithms. Proceedings, 2003. VIII, 267 pages. 2003.

Vol. 2648: T. Ball, S.K. Rajamani (Eds.), Model Checking Software. Proceedings, 2003. VIII, 241 pages. 2003.

Vol. 2649: B. Westfechtel, A. van der Hoek (Eds.), Software Configuration Management. Proceedings, 2003. VIII, 241 pages. 2003.

Vol. 2651: D. Bert, J.P. Bowen, S. King, M, Waldén (Eds.), ZB 2003: Formal Specification and Development in Z and B. Proceedings, 2003. XIII, 547 pages. 2003.

Vol. 2652: F.J. Perales, A.J.C. Campilho, N. Pérez de la Blanca, A. Sanfeliu (Eds.), Pattern Recognition and Image Analysis. Proceedings, 2003. XIX, 1142 pages. 2003.

Vol. 2653: R. Petreschi, Giuseppe Persiano, R. Silvestri (Eds.), Algorithms and Complexity. Proceedings, 2003. XI, 289 pages. 2003.

Vol. 2656: E. Biham (Ed.), Advances in Cryptology – EUROCRPYT 2003. Proceedings, 2003. XIV, 649 pages. 2003.

Vol. 2657: P.M.A. Sloot, D. Abramson, A.V. Bogdanov, J.J. Dongarra, A.Y. Zomaya, Y.E. Gorbachev (Eds.), Computational Science – ICCS 2003. Proceedings, Part I. 2003. LV, 1095 pages. 2003.

Vol. 2658: P.M.A. Sloot, D. Abramson, A.V. Bogdanov, J.J. Dongarra, A.Y. Zomaya, Y.E. Gorbachev (Eds.), Computational Science – ICCS 2003. Proceedings, Part II. 2003. LV, 1129 pages. 2003.

Vol. 2659: P.M.A. Sloot, D. Abramson, A.V. Bogdanov, J.J. Dongarra, A.Y. Zomaya, Y.E. Gorbachev (Eds.), Computational Science – ICCS 2003. Proceedings, Part III. 2003. LV, 1165 pages. 2003.

Vol. 2660: P.M.A. Sloot, D. Abramson, A.V. Bogdanov, J.J. Dongarra, A.Y. Zomaya, Y.E. Gorbachev (Eds.), Computational Science – ICCS 2003. Proceedings, Part IV. 2003. LVI, 1161 pages. 2003.

Vol. 2663: E. Menasalvas, J. Segovia, P.S. Szczepaniak (Eds.), Advances in Web Intelligence. Proceedings, 2003. XII, 350 pages. 2003. (Subseries LNAI).

Vol. 2665: H. Chen, R. Miranda, D.D. Zeng, C. Demchak, J. Schroeder, T. Madhusudan (Eds.), Intelligence and Security Informatics. Proceedings, 2003. XIV, 392 pages. 2003.

Vol. 2667: V. Kumar, M.L. Gavrilova, C.J.K. Tan, P. L'Ecuyer (Eds.), Computational Science and Its Applications – ICCSA 2003. Proceedings, Part I. 2003. XXXIV, 1060 pages. 2003.

Vol. 2668: V. Kumar, M.L. Gavrilova, C.J.K. Tan, P. L'Ecuyer (Eds.), Computational Science and Its Applications – ICCSA 2003. Proceedings, Part II. 2003. XXXIV, 942 pages. 2003.

Vol. 2669: V. Kumar, M.L. Gavrilova, C.J.K. Tan, P. L'Ecuyer (Eds.), Computational Science and Its Applications – ICCSA 2003. Proceedings, Part III. 2003. XXXIV, 948 pages. 2003.

Vol. 2670: R. Peña, T. Arts (Eds.), Implementation of Functional Languages. Proceedings, 2002. X, 249 pages. 2003.

Vol. 2674: I.E. Magnin, J. Montagnat, P. Clarysse, J. Nenonen, T. Katila (Eds.), Functional Imaging and Modeling of the Heart. Proceedings, 2003. XI, 308 pages. 2003.

Vol. 2675: M. Marchesi, G. Succi (Eds.), Extreme Programming and Agile Processes in Software Engineering. Proceedings, 2003. XV, 464 pages. 2003.

Vol. 2676: R. Baeza-Yates, E. Chávez, M. Crochemore (Eds.), Combinatorial Pattern Matching. Proceedings, 2003. XI, 403 pages. 2003.

Vol. 2678: W. van der Aalst, A. ter Hofstede, M. Weske (Eds.), Business Process Management. Proceedings, 2003. XI, 391 pages. 2003.

Vol. 2679: W. van der Aalst, E. Best (Eds.), Applications and Theory of Petri Nets 2003. Proceedings, 2003. XI, 508 pages. 2003.

Vol. 2686: J. Mira, J.R. Álvarez (Eds.), Computational Methods in Neural Modeling. Proceedings, Part I. 2003. XXVII, 764 pages. 2003.

Vol. 2687: J. Mira, J.R. Álvarez (Eds.), Artificial Neural Nets Problem Solving Methods. Proceedings, Part II. 2003. XXVII, 820 pages. 2003.

Vol. 2692: P. Nixon, S. Terzis (Eds.), Trust Management. Proceedings, 2003. X, 349 pages. 2003.

Vol. 2694: R. Cousot (Ed.), Static Analysis. Proceedings, 2003. XIV, 505 pages. 2003.

Vol. 2701: M. Hofmann (Ed.), Typed Lambda Calculi and Applications. Proceedings, 2003. VIII, 317 pages. 2003.

Vol. 2706: R. Nieuwenhuis (Ed.), Rewriting Techniques and Applications. Proceedings, 2003. XI, 515 pages. 2003.

Vol. 2707: K. Jeffay, I. Stoica, K. Wehrle (Eds.), Quality of Service – IWQoS 2003. Proceedings, 2003. XI, 517 pages. 2003.